COLLINS POCKET SPANISH DICTIONARY

SPANISH·ENGLISH   ENGLISH·SPANISH

HarperCollins*Publishers*

First published in this edition 1990

© William Collins Sons & Co. Ltd. 1990

Latest reprint 1993

ISBN 0 00 433250 4 (vinyl)
ISBN 0 00 470310 3 (hardback)

Mike Gonzalez, Alicia de Benito de Harland
Soledad Pérez-López, José Ramón Parrondo

assistant editor/redacción
Claire Evans

supplement/suplemento
Roy Simon
*reproduced by kind permission of
Tayside Region Education Department*

*Printed in Great Britain by
HarperCollins Manufacturing, Glasgow*

INTRODUCTION

Produced for today's learner and user of Spanish, this is a dictionary adapted to the requirements of the 1990's.

The new colour format introduces a more user-friendly approach to word search, and a wealth of modern and idiomatic phrases not normally found in a volume this size.

In addition, the supplement contains a variety of entertaining ways to improve your dictionary skills, and to help you to get the most out of the bilingual dictionary.

We hope you will enjoy using it and that it will significantly enhance your language studies.

ABREVIATURAS

ABBREVIATIONS

adjetivo, locución adjetiva	adj	adjective, adjectival phrase
abreviatura	ab(b)r	abbreviation
adverbio, locución adverbial	adv	adverb, adverbial phrase
administración, lengua administrativa	ADMIN	administration
agricultura	AGR	agriculture
América Latina	AM	Latin America
anatomía	ANAT	anatomy
arquitectura	ARQ, ARCH	architecture
el automóvil	AUT(O)	the motor car and motoring
aviación, viajes aéreos	AVIAT	flying, air travel
biología	BIO(L)	biology
botánica, flores	BOT	botany
inglés británico	BRIT	British English
química	CHEM	chemistry
comercio, finanzas, banca	COM(M)	commerce, finance, banking
informática	COMPUT	computers
conjunción	conj	conjunction
construcción	CONSTR	building
compuesto	cpd	compound element
cocina	CULIN	cookery
economía	ECON	economics
electricidad, electrónica	ELEC	electricity, electronics
enseñanza, sistema escolar y universitario	ESCOL	schooling, schools and universities
España	ESP	Spain
especialmente	esp	especially
exclamación, interjección	excl	exclamation, interjection
femenino	f	feminine
lengua familiar (! vulgar)	fam(!)	colloquial usage (! particularly offensive)
ferrocarril	FERRO	railways
uso figurado	fig	figurative use
fotografía	FOTO	photography
(verbo inglés) del cual la partícula es inseparable	fus	(phrasal verb) where the particle is inseparable
generalmente	gen	generally
geografía, geología	GEO	geography, geology
geometría	GEOM	geometry
uso familiar (! vulgar)	inf(!)	colloquial usage (! particularly offensive)
infinitivo	infin	infinitive
informática	INFORM	computers
invariable	inv	invariable
irregular	irreg	irregular
lo jurídico	JUR	law
América Latina	LAM	Latin America
gramática, lingüística	LING	grammar, linguistics
masculino	m	masculine
matemáticas	MAT(H)	mathematics

iv

ABREVIATURAS

ABBREVIATIONS

medicina	MED	medical term, medicine
masculino/femenino	m/f	masculine/feminine
lo militar, ejército	MIL	military matters
música	MUS	music
sustantivo, nombre	n	noun
navegación, náutica	NAUT	sailing, navigation
sustantivo numérico	num	numeral noun
complemento	obj	(grammatical) object
	o.s.	oneself
peyorativo	pey, pej	derogatory, pejorative
fotografía	PHOT	photography
fisiología	PHYSIOL	physiology
plural	pl	plural
política	POL	politics
participio de pasado	pp	past participle
preposición	prep	preposition
pronombre	prón	pronoun
psicología, psiquiatría	PSICO, PSYCH	psychology, psychiatry
tiempo pasado	pt	past tense
química	QUIM	chemistry
ferrocarril	RAIL	railways
religión, lo eclesiástico	REL	religion, church service
	sb	somebody
enseñanza, sistema escolar y universitario	SCH	schooling, schools and universities
singular	sg	singular
España	SP	Spain
	sth	something
sujeto	su(b)j	(grammatical) subject
subjuntivo	subjun	subjunctive
tauromaquia	TAUR	bullfighting
también	tb	also
técnica, tecnología	TEC(H)	technical term, technology
telecomunicaciones	TELEC, TEL	telecommunications
televisión	TV	television
imprenta, tipografía	TIP, TYP	typography, printing
inglés norteamericano	US	American English
verbo	vb	verb
verbo intransitivo	vi	intransitive verb
verbo pronominal	vr	reflexive verb
verbo transitivo	vt	transitive verb
zoología, animales	ZOOL	zoology
marca registrada	®	registered trademark
indica un equivalente cultural	≈	introduces a cultural equivalent

SPANISH PRONUNCIATION

Consonants

b	[b, ß]	*b*oda *b*om*b*a la*b*or	see notes on *v* below
c	[k]	*c*aja	*c* before *a*, *o* or *u* is pronounced as in *c*at
ce, ci	[θe, θi]	*c*ero *c*ielo	*c* before *e* or *i* is pronounced as in *th*in
ch	[tʃ]	*ch*iste	*ch* is pronounced as *ch* in *ch*air
d	[d, ð]	*d*anés ciu*d*a*d*	at the beginning of a phrase or after *l* or *n*, *d* is pronounced as in English. In any other position it is pronounced like *th* in *th*e
g	[g, ɣ]	*g*afas pa*g*a	*g* before *a*, *o* or *u* is pronounced as in *g*ap, if at the beginning of a phrase or after *n*. In other positions the sound is softened
ge, gi	[xe, xi]	*g*ente *g*irar	*g* before *e* or *i* is pronounced similar to *ch* in Scottish lo*ch*
h		*h*aber	*h* is always silent in Spanish
j	[x]	*j*ugar	*j* is pronounced similar to *ch* in Scottish lo*ch*
ll	[ʎ]	ta*ll*e	*ll* is pronounced like the *lli* in mi*lli*on
ñ	[ɲ]	ni*ñ*o	*ñ* is pronounced like the *ni* in o*ni*on
q	[k]	*q*ue	*q* is pronounced as *k* in *k*ing
r, rr	[r, rr]	quita*r* ga*rr*a	*r* is always pronounced in Spanish, unlike the silent *r* in dance*r*. *rr* is trilled, like a Scottish *r*
s	[s]	qui*z*ás i*s*la	*s* is usually pronounced as in pa*ss*, but before *b*, *d*, *g*, *l*, *m* or *n* it is pronounced as in ro*s*e
v	[b, ß]	*v*ía di*v*idir	*v* is pronounced something like *b*. At the beginning of a phrse or after *m* or *n* it is pronounced as *b* in *b*oy. In any other position the sound is softened
z	[θ]	tena*z*	*z* is pronounced as *th* in *th*in

f, k, l, m, n, p, t and x are pronounced as in English.

Vowels

a	[a]	p*a*ta	not as long as *a* in f*a*r. When followed by a consonant in the same syllable (i.e. in a closed syllable), as in am*a*nte, the *a* is short, as in b*a*t
e	[e]	m*e*	like *e* in th*e*y. In a closed syllable, as in g*e*nte, the *e* is short as in p*e*t
i	[i]	p*i*no	as in m*ea*n or mach*i*ne
o	[o]	l*o*	as in l*o*cal. In a closed syllable, as in con- tr*o*l, the *o* is short as in c*o*t
u	[u]	l*u*nes	as in r*u*le. It is silent after *q*, and in *gue, gui*, unless marked *güe, güi* e.g. antig*ü*edad, when it is pronounced like *w* in *w*olf

Semivowels

i, y	[j]	b*i*en	pronounced like *y* in *y*es
		h*i*elo	
		*y*unta	
u	[w]	h*u*evo	unstressed *u* between consonant and vowel
		f*u*ente	is pronounced like *w* in *w*ell. See also notes
		antig*ü*edad	on *u* above

Diphthongs

ai, ay	[ai]	b*ai*le	as *i* in r*i*de
au	[au]	*au*to	as *ou* in sh*ou*t
ei, ey	[ei]	bu*ey*	as *ey* in gr*ey*
eu	[eu]	d*eu*da	both elements pronounced independently [e]+[u]
oi, oy	[oi]	h*oy*	as *oy* in t*oy*

Stress

The rules of stress in Spanish are as follows:

(a) when a word ends in a vowel or in *n* or *s*, the second last syllable is stressed: pat*a*ta, pat*a*tas, c*o*me, c*o*men
(b) when a word ends in a consonant other than *n* or *s*, the stress falls on the last syllable: par*e*d, habl*a*r
(c) when the rules set out in a and b are not applied, an acute accent appears over the stressed vowel: com*ú*n, geograf*í*a, ingl*é*s

In the phonetic transcription, the symbol ['] precedes the syllable on which the stress falls.

PRONUNCIACIÓN INGLESA

Vocales y diptongos

	Ejemplo inglés	*Ejemplo español/explicación*
ɑ:	f*a*ther	Entre *a* de p*a*dre y *o* de n*o*che
ʌ	b*u*t, c*o*me	*a* muy breve
æ	m*a*n, c*a*t	Con los labios en la posición de *e* en p*e*na se pronuncia el sonido *a* parecido a la *a* de c*a*rro
ə	f*a*the*r*, *a*go	Vocal neutra parecida a una *e* u *o* casi mudas
ə:	b*i*rd, h*ea*rd	Entre *e* abierta, y *o* cerrada, sonido alargado
ɛ	g*e*t, b*e*d	Como en p*e*rro
ɪ	*i*t, b*i*g	Más breve que en s*i*
i:	t*ea*, s*ee*	Como en f*i*no
ɔ	h*o*t, w*a*sh	Como en t*o*rre
ɔ:	s*aw*, *a*ll	Como en p*o*r
u	p*u*t, b*oo*k	Sonido breve, más cerrado que b*u*rro
u:	t*oo*, y*ou*	Sonido largo, como en *u*no
aɪ	fl*y*, h*i*gh	Como en fr*ai*le
au	h*ow*, h*ou*se	Como en p*au*sa
ɛə	th*ere*, b*ear*	Casi como en v*ea*, pero el segundo elemento es la vocal neutra [ə]
eɪ	d*ay*, ob*ey*	*e* cerrada seguida por una *i* débil
ɪə	h*ere*, h*ear*	Como en man*ía*, mezclándose el sonido *a* con la vocal neutra [ə]
əu	g*o*, n*o*te	[ə] seguido por una breve *u*
ɔɪ	b*oy*, *oi*l	Como en v*oy*
uə	p*oor*, s*ure*	*u* bastante larga más la vocal neutra [ə]

Consonantes

	Ejemplo inglés	*Ejemplo español/explicación*
b	*b*ig, lo*bb*y	Como en tum*b*a
d	men*ded*	Como en con*d*e, an*d*ar
g	*g*o, *g*et, bi*g*	Como en *g*rande, *g*ol
dʒ	*g*in, *j*u*dg*e	Como en la *ll* andaluza y en *G*eneralitat (catalán)
ŋ	si*ng*	Como en ví*n*culo
h	*h*ouse, *h*e	Como la jota hispanoamericana
j	*y*oung, *y*es	Como en *y*a
k	*c*ome, mo*ck*	Como en *c*aña, Es*c*ocia
r	*r*ed, t*r*ead	Se pronuncia con la punta de la lengua hacia atrás y sin hacerla vibrar
s	*s*and, ye*s*	Como en ca*s*a, *sc*sión
z	ro*s*e, *z*ebra	Como en de*s*de, mi*s*mo
ʃ	*sh*e, ma*ch*ine	Como en *ch*ambre (francés), ro*x*o (portugués)
tʃ	*ch*in, ri*ch*	Como en *ch*ocolate
v	*v*alley	Como en f, pero se retiran los dientes superiores vibrándolos contra el labio inferior
w	*w*ater, *wh*ich	Como en la *u* de h*u*evo, p*u*ede
ʒ	vi*si*on	Como en *j*ournal (francés)
θ	*th*ink, my*th*	Como en re*c*eta, *z*apato
ð	*th*is, *th*c	Como en la *d* de habla*d*o, verda*d*

p, f, m, n, l, t iguales que en español
El signo * indica que la r final escrita apenas se pronuncia en inglés británico cuando la palabra siguiente empieza con vocal. El signo ['] indica la sílaba acentuada.

SPANISH VERB TABLES

1 Gerund *2* Imperative *3* Present *4* Preterite *5* Future *6* Present subjunctive *7* Imperfect subjunctive *8* Past participle *9* Imperfect. *Etc* indicates that the irregular root is used for all persons of the tense, e.g. **oír** *6* oiga *etc* = oigas, oigamos, oigáis, oigan. Forms which consist of the unmodified verb root + verb ending are not shown, e.g. acertamos, acertáis.

acertar *2* acierta *3* acierto, aciertas, acierta, aciertan *6* acierte, aciertes, acierte, acierten

acordar *2* acuerda *3* acuerdo, acuerdas, acuerda, acuerdan *6* acuerde, acuerdes, acuerde, acuerden

advertir *1* advirtiendo *2* advierte *3* advierto, adviertes, advierte, advierten *4* advirtió, advirtieron *6* advierta, adviertas, advierta, advirtamos, advirtáis, adviertan *7* advirtiera *etc*

agradecer *3* agradezco *6* agradezca *etc*

aparecer *3* aparezco *6* aparezca *etc*

aprobar *2* aprueba *3* apruebo, apruebas, aprueba, aprueban *6* apruebe, apruebes, apruebe, aprueben

atravesar *2* atraviesa *3* atravieso, atraviesas, atraviesan *6* atraviese, atravieses, atraviese, atraviesen

caber *3* quepo *4* cupe, cupiste, cupo, cupimos, cupisteis, cupieron *5* cabré *etc* *6* quepa *etc* *7* cupiera *etc*

caer *1* cayendo *3* caigo *4* cayó, cayeron *6* caiga *etc* *7* cayera *etc*

calentar *2* calienta *3* caliento, calientas, calienta, calientan *6* caliente, calientes, caliente, calienten

cerrar *2* cierra *3* cierro, cierras, cierra, cierran *6* cierre, cierres, cierre, cierren

COMER *1* comiendo *2* come, comed *3* como, comes, come, comemos, coméis, comen *4* comí, comiste, comió, comimos, comisteis, comieron *5* comeré, comerás, comerá, comeremos, comeréis, comerán *6* coma, comas, coma, comamos, comáis, coman *7* comiera, comieras, comiera, comiéramos, comierais, comieran *8* comido *9* comía, comías, comía, comíamos, comíais, comían

conocer *3* conozco *6* conozca *etc*

contar *2* cuenta *3* cuento, cuentas, cuenta, cuentan *6* cuente, cuentes, cuente, cuenten

costar *2* cuesta *3* cuesto, cuestas, cuesta, cuestan *6* cueste, cuestes, cueste, cuesten

dar *3* doy *4* di, diste, dio, dimos, disteis, dieron *7* diera *etc*

decir *2* di *3* digo *4* dije, dijiste, dijo, dijimos, dijisteis, dijeron *5* diré *etc* *6* diga *etc* *7* dijera *etc* *8* dicho

despertar *2* despierta *3* despierto, despiertas, despierta, despiertan *6* despierte, despiertes, despierte, despierten

divertir *1* divirtiendo *2* divierte *3* divierto, diviertes, divierten *4* divirtió, divirtieron *6* divierta, diviertas, divierta, divirtamos, divirtáis, diviertan *7* divirtiera *etc*

dormir *1* durmiendo *2* duerme *3* duermo, duermes, duerme, duermen *4* durmió, durmieron *6* duerma, duermas, duerma, durmamos, durmáis, duerman *7* durmiera *etc*

empezar *2* empieza *3* empiezo, empiezas, empieza, empiezan *4* empecé *6* empiece, empieces, empiece, empecemos, empecéis, empiecen

entender *2* entiende *3* entiendo, entiendes, entiende, entienden *6* entienda, entiendas, entienda, entiendan

ESTAR *2* está *3* estoy, estás, está, están *4* estuve, estuviste, estuvo, estuvimos, estuvisteis, estuvieron *6* esté, estés, esté, estén *7* estuviera *etc*

HABER *3* he, has, ha, hemos, han *4* hube, hubiste, hubo, hubimos, hubisteis, hubieron *5* habré *etc* *6* haya *etc* *7* hubiera *etc*

HABLAR *1* hablando *2* habla, hablad *3* hablo, hablas, habla, hablamos, habláis, hablan *4* hablé, hablaste, habló, hablamos, hablasteis, hablaron *5* hablaré, hablarás, hablará, hablaremos, hablaréis, hablarán *6* hable, hables, hable, hablemos, habléis, hablen *7* hablara, hablaras, hablara, habláramos, hablarais, hablaran *8* hablado *9* hablaba, hablabas, hablaba, hablábamos, hablabais, hablaban

hacer *2* haz *3* hago *4* hice, hiciste, hizo, hicimos, hicisteis, hicieron *5* haré *etc* *6* haga *etc* *7* hiciera *etc* *8* hecho

instruir *1* instruyendo *2* instruye *3* instruyo, instruyes, instruye, instruyen *4* instruyó, instruyeron *6* instruya *etc* *7* instruyera *etc*

ir *1* yendo *2* ve *3* voy, vas, va, vamos, vais, van *4* fui, fuiste, fue, fuimos, fuisteis, fueron *6* vaya, vayas, vaya, vayamos, vayáis, vayan *7* fuera *etc* *8* iba, ibas, iba, íbamos, ibais, iban

jugar *2* juega *3* juego, juegas, juega, juegan *4* jugué *6* juegue *etc*

leer *1* leyendo *4* leyó, leyeron *7* leyera *etc*

morir *1* muriendo *2* muere *3* muero, mueres, muere, mueren *4* murió, murieron *6* muera, mueras, muera, muramos, muráis, mueran *7* muriera *etc* *8* muerto

mostrar *2* muestra *3* muestro, muestras, muestra, muestran *6* muestre, muestres, muestre, muestren

mover *2* mueve *3* muevo, mueves, mueve, mueven *6* mueva, muevas, mueva, muevan

negar *2* niega *3* niego, niegas, niega, niegan *4* negué *6* niegue, niegues, niegue, neguemos, neguéis, nieguen

ofrecer *3* ofrezco *6* ofrezca *etc*

oír *1* oyendo *2* oye *3* oigo, oyes, oye, oyen *4* oyó, oyeron *6* oiga *etc* *7* oyera *etc*

oler *2* huele *3* huelo, hueles, huele, huelen *6* huela, huelas, huela, huelan

parecer *3* parezco *6* parezca *etc*

pedir *1* pidiendo *2* pide *3* pido, pides, pide, piden *4* pidió, pidieron *6* pida *etc* *7* pidiera *etc*

pensar *2* piensa *3* pienso, piensas, piensa, piensan *6* piense, pienses, piense, piensen

perder *2* pierde *3* pierdo, pierdes, pierde, pierden *6* pierda, pierdas, pierda, pierdan

poder *1* pudiendo *2* puede *3* puedo, puedes, puede, pueden *4* pude, pudo, pudimos, pudisteis, pudieron *5* podré *etc* *6* pueda, puedas, pueda, puedan *7* pudiera *etc*

poner *2* pon *3* pongo *4* puse, pusiste, puso, pusimos, pusisteis, pusieron *5* pondré *etc* *6* ponga *etc* *7* pusiera *etc* *8* puesto

preferir *1* prefiriendo *2* prefiere *3* prefiero, prefieres, prefiere, prefieren *4* prefirió, prefirieron *6* prefiera, prefieras, prefiera, prefiramos, prefiráis, prefieran *7* prefiriera *etc*

querer *2* quiere *3* quiero, quieres, quiere, quieren *4* quise, quisiste, quiso, quisimos, quisisteis, quisieron *5* querré *etc* *6* quiera, quieras, quiera, quieran *7* quisiera *etc*

reír *2* ríe *3* río, ríes, ríe, ríen *4* rio, rieron *6* ría, rías, ría, riamos, riáis, rían *7* riera *etc*

repetir *1* repitiendo *2* repite *3* repito, repites, repite, repiten *4* repitió, repitieron *6* repita *etc* *7* repitiera *etc*

rogar *2* ruega *3* ruego, ruegas, ruega, ruegan *4* rogué *6* ruegue, ruegues, ruegue, roguemos, roguéis, rueguen

saber *3* sé *4* supe, supiste, supo, supimos, supisteis, supieron *5* sabré *etc*

salir *2* sal *3* salgo *5* saldré *etc* *6* salga *etc*

seguir *1* siguiendo *2* sigue *3* sigo, sigues, sigue, siguen *4* siguió, siguieron *6* siga *etc* *7* siguiera *etc*

sentar *2* sienta *3* siento, sientas, sienta, sientan *6* siente, sientes, siente, sienten

sentir *1* sintiendo *2* siente *3* siento, sientes, siente, sienten *4* sintió, sintieron *6* sienta, sientas, sienta, sintamos, sintáis, sientan *7* sintiera *etc*

SER *2* sé *3* soy, eres, es, somos, sois, son *4* fui, fuiste, fue, fuimos, fuisteis, fueron *6* sea *etc* *7* fuera *etc* *9* era, eras, era, éramos, erais, eran

servir *1* sirviendo *2* sirve *3* sirvo, sirves, sirve, sirven *4* sirvió, sirvieron *6* sirva *etc* *7* sirviera *etc*

soñar *2* sueña *3* sueño, sueñas, sueña, sueñan *6* sueñe, sueñes, sueñe, sueñen

tener *2* ten *3* tengo, tienes, tiene, tienen *4* tuve, tuviste, tuvo, tuvimos, tuvisteis, tuvieron *5* tendré *etc* *6* tenga *etc* *7* tuviera *etc*

traer *1* trayendo *3* traigo *4* traje, trajiste, trajo, trajimos, trajisteis, trajeron *6* traiga *etc* *7* trajera *etc*

valer *2* val *3* valgo *5* valdré *etc* *6* valga *etc*

venir *2* ven *3* vengo, vienes, viene, vienen *4* vine, viniste, vino, vinimos, vinisteis, vinieron *5* vendré *etc* *6* venga *etc* *7* viniera *etc*

ver *3* veo *6* vea *etc* *8* visto *9* veía *etc*

vestir *1* vistiendo *2* viste *3* visto, vistes, viste, visten *4* vistió, vistieron *6* vista *etc* *7* vistiera *etc*

VIVIR *1* viviendo *2* vive, vivid *3* vivo, vives, vive, vivimos, vivís, viven *4* viví, viviste, vivió, vivimos, vivisteis, vivieron *5* viviré, vivirás, vivirá, viviremos, viviréis, vivirán *6* viva, vivas, viva, vivamos, viváis, vivan *7* viviera, vivieras, viviera, viviéramos, vivierais, vivieran *8* vivido *9* vivía, vivías, vivía, vivíamos, vivíais, vivían

volver *2* vuelve *3* vuelvo, vuelves, vuelve, vuelven *6* vuelva, vuelvas, vuelva, vuelvan *8* vuelto

LOS NÚMEROS

NUMBERS

un, uno(a)	1	one
dos	2	two
tres	3	three
cuatro	4	four
cinco	5	five
seis	6	six
siete	7	seven
ocho	8	eight
nueve	9	nine
diez	10	ten
once	11	eleven
doce	12	twelve
trece	13	thirteen
catorce	14	fourteen
quince	15	fifteen
dieciséis	16	sixteen
diecisiete	17	seventeen
dieciocho	18	eighteen
diecinueve	19	nineteen
veinte	20	twenty
veintiuno	21	twenty-one
veintidós	22	twenty-two
treinta	30	thirty
treinta y uno(a)	31	thirty-one
treinta y dos	32	thirty-two
cuarenta	40	forty
cuarenta y uno(a)	41	forty-one
cincuenta	50	fifty
sesenta	60	sixty
setenta	70	seventy
ochenta	80	eighty
noventa	90	ninety
cien, ciento	100	a hundred, one hundred
ciento uno(a)	101	a hundred and one
doscientos(as)	200	two hundred
doscientos(as) uno(a)	201	two hundred and one
trescientos(as)	300	three hundred
trescientos(as) uno(a)	301	three hundred and one
cuatrocientos(as)	400	four hundred
quinientos(as)	500	five hundred
seiscientos(as)	600	six hundred
setecientos(as)	700	seven hundred
ochocientos(as)	800	eight hundred
novecientos(as)	900	nine hundred
mil	1 000	a thousand
mil dos	1 002	a thousand and two
cinco mil	5 000	five thousand
un millón	1 000 000	a million

LOS NÚMEROS

NUMBERS

primer, primero(a), 1º, 1er (1ª, 1era) — first, 1st
segundo(a) 2º (2ª) — second, 2nd
tercer, tercero(a), 3º (3ª) — third, 3rd
cuarto(a), 4º (4ª) — fourth, 4th
quinto(a), 5º (5ª) — fifth, 5th
sexto(a), 6º (6ª) — sixth, 6th
séptimo(a) — seventh
octavo(a) — eighth
noveno(a) — ninth
décimo(a) — tenth
undécimo(a) — eleventh
duodécimo(a) — twelfth
decimotercio(a) — thirteenth
decimocuarto(a) — fourteenth
decimoquinto(a) — fifteenth
decimosexto(a) — sixteenth
decimoséptimo(a) — seventeenth
decimoctavo(a) — eighteenth
decimonoveno(a) — nineteenth
vigésimo(a) — twentieth
vigésimo(a) primero(a) — twenty-first
vigésimo(a) segundo(a) — twenty-second
trigésimo(a) — thirtieth
centésimo(a) — hundredth
centésimo(a) primero(a) — hundred-and-first
milésimo(a) — thousandth

Números Quebrados etc

Fractions etc

un medio — a half
un tercio — a third
dos tercios — two thirds
un cuarto — a quarter
un quinto — a fifth
cero coma cinco, 0,5 — (nought) point five, 0.5
tres coma cuatro, 3,4 — three point four, 3.4
diez por cien(to) — ten per cent
cien por cien — a hundred per cent

Ejemplos

Examples

va a llegar el 7 (de mayo) — he's arriving on the 7th (of May)
vive en el número 7 — he lives at number 7
el capítulo/la página 7 — chapter/page 7
llegó séptimo — he came in 7th

N.B. In Spanish the ordinal numbers from 1 to 10 are commonly used; from 11 to 20 rather less; above 21 they are rarely written and almost never heard in speech. The custom is to replace the forms for 21 and above by the cardinal number.

LA HORA

THE TIME

¿qué hora es?

what time is it?

es/son

it's o it is

medianoche, las doce (de la noche)	midnight, twelve p.m.
la una (de la madrugada)	one o'clock (in the morning), one (a.m.)
la una y cinco	five past one
la una y diez	ten past one
la una y cuarto *or* quince	a quarter past one, one fifteen
la una y veinticinco	twenty-five past one, one twenty-five
la una y media *or* treinta	half-past one, one thirty
las dos menos veinticinco, la una treinta y cinco	twenty-five to two, one thirty-five
las dos menos veinte, la una cuarenta	twenty to two, one forty
las dos menos cuarto, la una cuarenta y cinco	a quarter to two, one forty-five
las dos menos diez, la una cincuenta	ten to two, one fifty
mediodía, las doce (de la tarde)	twelve o'clock, midday, noon
la una (de la tarde)	one o'clock (in the afternoon), one (p.m.)
las siete (de la tarde)	seven o'clock (in the evening), seven (p.m.)

¿a qué hora?

(at) what time?

a medianoche	at midnight
a las siete	at seven o'clock
en veinte minutos	in twenty minutes
hace quince minutos	fifteen minutes ago

ESPAÑOL - INGLÉS
SPANISH - ENGLISH

A

a [a] (*a+el = al*) *prep* **1** (*dirección*) to;
fueron ~ Madrid/Grecia they went to
Madrid/Greece; **me voy ~ casa** I'm
going home
2 (*distancia*): **está ~ 15 km de aquí** it's
15 kms from here
3 (*posición*): **estar ~ la mesa** to be at
table; **al lado de** next to, beside; *ver tb*
puerta
4 (*tiempo*): **~ las 10/~ medianoche** at
10/midnight; **~ la mañana siguiente** the
following morning; **~ los pocos días**
after a few days; **estamos ~ 9 de julio**
it's the ninth of July; **~ los 24 años** at
the age of 24; **al año/~ la semana** (*AM*)
a year/week later
5 (*manera*): **~ la francesa** the French
way; **~ caballo** on horseback; **~
oscuras** in the dark
6 (*medio, instrumento*): **~ lápiz** in
pencil; **~ mano** by hand; **cocina ~ gas**
gas stove
7 (*razón*): **00 ptas el kilo al 30**
pesetas a kilo; ~ más de 50 km/h at
more than 50 kms per hour
8 (*dativo*): **se lo di ~ él** I gave it to
him; **vi al policía** I saw the policeman;
se lo compré ~ él I bought it from him
9 (*tras ciertos verbos*): **voy ~ verle**
I'm going to see him; **empezó ~
trabajar** he started working *o* to work
10 (+*infin*): **al verle, le reconocí
inmediatamente** when I saw him I recognized him at once; **el camino ~ recorrer** the distance we (*etc*) have to
travel; **¡~ callar!** keep quiet!; **¡~
comer!** let's eat!

abad, esa [a'βað, 'ðesa] *nm/f* abbot/
abbess; **~ía** *nf* abbey.

abajo [a'βaxo] *adv* (*situación*) (down)
below, underneath; (*en edificio*) downstairs; (*dirección*) down, downwards; **el
piso de ~** the downstairs flat; **la parte
de ~** the lower part; **¡~ el gobierno!**
down with the government!; **cuesta/río
~** downhill/downstream; **de arriba ~**
from top to bottom; **el ~ firmante** the
undersigned; **más ~** lower *o* further
down.

abalanzarse [aβalan'θarse] *vr*: **~ sobre** *o*
contra to throw o.s. at.

abalorios [aβa'lorjos] *nmpl* (*chucherías*)
trinkets.

abanderado [aβande'raðo] *nm* standard
bearer.

abandonado, a [aβando'naðo, a] *adj*
derelict; (*desatendido*) abandoned;
(*desierto*) deserted; (*descuidado*)
neglected.

abandonar [aβando'nar] *vt* to leave;
(*persona*) to abandon, desert; (*cosa*) to
abandon, leave behind; (*descuidar*) to
neglect; (*renunciar a*) to give up; (*IN-
FORM*) to quit; **~se** *vr*: **~se a** to
abandon o.s. to; **abandono** *nm* (*acto*)
desertion, abandonment; (*estado*)
abandon, neglect; (*renuncia*) withdrawal, retirement; **ganar por abandono** to win by default.

abanicar [aβani'kar] *vt* to fan; **abanico**
nm fan; (*NAUT*) derrick.

abaratar [aβara'tar] *vt* to lower the price
of ♦ *vi* to go *o* come down in price; **~se**
vr to go *o* come down in price.

abarcar [aβar'kar] *vt* to include, embrace; (*AM*) to monopolize.

abarrotado, a [aβarro'taðo, a] *adj*
packed.

abarrote [aβa'rrote] *nm* packing; **~s**
nmpl (*AM*) groceries, provisions; **~ro,** a
(*AM*) *nm/f* grocer.

abastecer [aβaste'θer] *vt*: ~ **(de)** to supply (with); **abastecimiento** *nm* supply.

abasto [a'βasto] *nm* supply; (*abundancia*) abundance; **no dar ~ a** to be unable to cope with.

abatido, a [aβa'tiðo, a] *adj* dejected, downcast.

abatimiento [aβati'mjento] *nm* (*depresión*) dejection, depression.

abatir [aβa'tir] *vt* (*muro*) to demolish; (*pájaro*) to shoot *o* bring down; (*fig*) to depress; ~**se** *vr* to get depressed; ~**se sobre** to swoop *o* pounce on.

abdicación [aβðika'θjon] *nf* abdication.

abdicar [aβði'kar] *vi* to abdicate.

abdomen [aβ'ðomen] *nm* abdomen.

abecedario [aβeθe'ðarjo] *nm* alphabet.

abedul [aβe'ðul] *nm* birch.

abeja [a'βexa] *nf* bee.

abejorro [aβe'xorro] *nm* bumblebee.

aberración [aβerra'θjon] *nf* aberration.

abertura [aβer'tura] *nf* = **apertura**.

abeto [a'βeto] *nm* fir.

abierto, a [a'βjerto, a] *pp de* **abrir** ♦ *adj* open; (*AM*) generous.

abigarrado, a [aβiɣa'rraðo, a] *adj* multi-coloured.

abismal [aβis'mal] *adj* (*fig*) vast, enormous.

abismar [aβis'mar] *vt* to humble, cast down; ~**se** *vr* to sink; ~**se en** (*fig*) to be plunged into.

abismo [a'βismo] *nm* abyss.

abjurar [aβxu'rar] *vi*: ~ **de** to abjure, forswear.

ablandar [aβlan'dar] *vt* to soften ♦ *vi* to get softer; ~**se** *vr* to get softer.

abnegación [aβneɣa'θjon] *nf* self-denial.

abnegado, a [aβne'ɣaðo, a] *adj* self-sacrificing.

abocado, a [aβo'kaðo, a] *adj*: **verse ~ al desastre** to be heading for disaster.

abochornar [aβotʃor'nar] *vt* to embarrass; ~**se** *vr* to get flustered; (*BOT*) to wilt.

abofetear [aβofete'ar] *vt* to slap (in the face).

abogacía [aβoɣa'θia] *nf* legal profession; (*ejercicio*) practice of the law.

abogado, a [aβo'ɣaðo, a] *nm/f* lawyer; (*notario*) solicitor; (*en tribunal*) barrister (*BRIT*), attorney (*US*); ~ **defensor** defence lawyer *o* attorney (*US*).

abogar [aβo'ɣar] *vi*: ~ **por** to plead for; (*fig*) to advocate.

abolengo [aβo'lengo] *nm* ancestry, lineage.

abolición [aβoli'θjon] *nf* abolition.

abolir [aβo'lir] *vt* to abolish; (*cancelar*) to cancel.

abolladura [aβoʎa'ðura] *nf* dent.

abollar [aβo'ʎar] *vt* to dent.

abominable [aβomi'naβle] *adj* abominable.

abominación [aβomina'θjon] *nf* abomination.

abonado, a [aβo'naðo, a] *adj* (*deuda*) paid(-up) ♦ *nm/f* subscriber.

abonar [aβo'nar] *vt* (*deuda*) to settle; (*terreno*) to fertilize; (*idea*) to endorse; ~**se** *vr* to subscribe; **abono** *nm* payment; fertilizer; subscription.

abordar [aβor'ðar] *vt* (*barco*) to board; (*asunto*) to broach.

aborigen [aβo'rixen] *nm/f* aborigine.

aborrecer [aβorre'θer] *vt* to hate, loathe.

abortar [aβor'tar] *vi* (*malparir*) to have a miscarriage; (*deliberadamente*) to have an abortion; **aborto** *nm* miscarriage; abortion.

abotagado, a [aβota'ɣaðo, a] *adj* swollen.

abotonar [aβoto'nar] *vt* to button (up), do up.

abovedado, a [aβoβe'ðaðo, a] *adj* vaulted, domed.

abrasar [aβra'sar] *vt* to burn (up); (*AGR*) to dry up, parch.

abrazadera [aβraθa'ðera] *nf* bracket.

abrazar [aβra'θar] *vt* to embrace, hug.

abrazo [a'βraθo] *nm* embrace, hug; **un ~** (*en carta*) with best wishes.

abrebotellas [aβreβo'teʎas] *nm inv* bottle opener.

abrecartas [aβre'kartas] *nm inv* letter opener.

abrelatas [aβre'latas] *nm inv* tin (*BRIT*) *o* can opener.

abreviar [aβre'βjar] *vt* to abbreviate; (*texto*) to abridge; (*plazo*) to reduce; **abreviatura** *nf* abbreviation.

abridor [aβri'ðor] *nm* bottle opener; (*de latas*) tin (*BRIT*) o can opener.

abrigar [aβri'ɣar] *vt* (*proteger*) to shelter; (*suj: ropa*) to keep warm; (*fig*) to cherish.

abrigo [a'βriɣo] *nm* (*prenda*) coat, overcoat; (*lugar protegido*) shelter.

abril [a'βril] *nm* April.

abrillantar [aβriʎan'tar] *vt* to polish.

abrir [a'βrir] *vt* to open (up) ♦ *vi* to open; **~se** *vr* to open (up); (*extenderse*) to open out; (*cielo*) to clear; **~se paso** to find o force a way through.

abrochar [aβro'tʃar] *vt* (*con botones*) to button (up); (*zapato, con broche*) to do up.

abrumar [aβru'mar] *vt* to overwhelm; (*sobrecargar*) to weigh down.

abrupto, a [a'βrupto, a] *adj* abrupt; (*empinado*) steep.

absceso [aßs'θeso] *nm* abscess.

absentismo [aßsen'tismo] *nm* absenteeism.

absolución [aßsolu'θjon] *nf* (*REL*) absolution; (*JUR*) acquittal.

absoluto, a [aßso'luto, a] *adj* absolute; **en ~** *adv* not at all.

absolver [aßsol'ßer] *vt* to absolve; (*JUR*) to pardon; (: *acusado*) to acquit.

absorbente [aßsor'ßente] *adj* absorbent; (*interesante*) absorbing.

absorber [aßsor'ßer] *vt* to absorb; (*embeber*) to soak up.

absorción [aßsor'θjon] *nf* absorption; (*COM*) takeover.

absorto, a [aß'sorto, a] *pp de* **absorber** ♦ *adj* absorbed, engrossed.

abstemio, a [aßs'temjo, a] *adj* teetotal.

abstención [aßsten'θjon] *nf* abstention.

abstenerse [aßste'nerse] *vr*: **~ (de)** to abstain o refrain (from).

abstinencia [aßsti'nenθja] *nf* abstinence; (*ayuno*) fasting.

abstracción [aßstrak'θjon] *nf* abstraction.

abstracto, a [aß'strakto, a] *adj* abstract.

abstraer [aßstra'er] *vt* to abstract; **~se** *vr* to be o become absorbed.

abstraído, a [aßstra'iðo, a] *adj* absent-minded.

absuelto [aß'swelto] *pp de* **absolver**.

absurdo, a [aß'surðo, a] *adj* absurd.

abuelo, a [a'βwelo, a] *nm/f* grandfather/mother; **~s** *nmpl* grandparents.

abulia [a'βulja] *nf* apathy.

abultado, a [aßul'taðo, a] *adj* bulky.

abultar [aßul'tar] *vt* to enlarge; (*aumentar*) to increase; (*fig*) to exaggerate ♦ *vi* to be bulky.

abundancia [aßun'danθja] *nf*: **una ~ de** plenty of; **abundante** *adj* abundant, plentiful.

abundar [aßun'dar] *vi* to abound, be plentiful.

aburguesarse [aßurɣe'sarse] *vr* to become middle-class.

aburrido, a [aßu'rriðo, a] *adj* (*hastiado*) bored; (*que aburre*) boring; **aburrimiento** *nm* boredom, tedium.

aburrir [aßu'rrir] *vt* to bore; **~se** *vr* to be bored, get bored.

abusar [aßu'sar] *vi* to go too far; **~ de** to abuse.

abusivo, a [aßu'sißo, a] *adj* (*precio*) exorbitant.

abuso [a'ßuso] *nm* abuse.

abyecto, a [aß'jekto, a] *adj* wretched, abject.

A.C. *abr* (= *Año de Cristo*) A.D.

a/c *abr* (= *al cuidado de*) c/o.

acá [a'ka] *adv* (*lugar*) here; **¿de cuándo ~?** since when?

acabado, a [aka'ßaðo, a] *adj* finished, complete; (*perfecto*) perfect; (*agotado*) worn out; (*fig*) masterly ♦ *nm* finish.

acabar [aka'ßar] *vt* (*llevar a su fin*) to finish, complete; (*consumir*) to use up; (*rematar*) to finish off ♦ *vi* to finish, end; **~se** *vr* to finish, stop; (*terminarse*) to be over; (*agotarse*) to run out; **~ con** to put an end to; **~ de llegar** to have just arrived; **~ por hacer** to end (up) by doing; **¡se acabó!** it's all over!; (*¡basta!*) that's enough!

acabóse [aka'ßose] *nm*: **esto es el ~** this is the last straw.

academia [aka'ðemja] *nf* academy; **académico, a** *adj* academic.
acaecer [akae'θer] *vi* to happen, occur.
acalorado, a [akalo'raðo, a] *adj* (*discusión*) heated.
acalorarse [akalo'rarse] *vr* (*fig*) to get heated.
acampar [akam'par] *vi* to camp.
acanalar [akana'lar] *vt* to groove; (*ondular*) to corrugate.
acantilado [akanti'laðo] *nm* cliff.
acaparar [akapa'rar] *vt* to monopolize; (*acumular*) to hoard.
acariciar [akari'θjar] *vt* to caress; (*esperanza*) to cherish.
acarrear [akarre'ar] *vt* to transport; (*fig*) to cause, result in.
acaso [a'kaso] *adv* perhaps, maybe ♦ *nm* chance; (**por**) **si** ~ (just) in case.
acatamiento [akata'mjento] *nm* respect; (*ley*) observance.
acatar [aka'tar] *vt* to respect; (*ley*) obey.
acatarrarse [akata'rrarse] *vr* to catch a cold.
acaudalado, a [akauða'laðo, a] *adj* well-off.
acaudillar [akauði'ʎar] *vt* to lead, command.
acceder [akθe'ðer] *vi*: ~ **a** (*petición etc*) to agree to; (*tener acceso a*) to have access to; (*INFORM*) to access.
accesible [akθe'siβle] *adj* accessible.
acceso [ak'θeso] *nm* access, entry; (*camino*) access, approach; (*MED*) attack, fit.
accesorio, a [akθe'sorjo, a] *adj, nm* accessory.
accidentado, a [akθiðen'taðo, a] *adj* uneven; (*montañoso*) hilly; (*azaroso*) eventful ♦ *nm/f* accident victim.
accidental [akθiðen'tal] *adj* accidental; **accidentarse** *vr* to have an accident.
accidente [akθi'ðente] *nm* accident; ~**s** *nmpl* (*de terreno*) unevenness *sg*.
acción [ak'θjon] *nf* action, act; (*acto*) action, act; (*COM*) share; (*JUR*) action, lawsuit; ~ **ordinaria/preferente** ordinary/preference share; **accionar** *vt* to work, operate; (*INFORM*) to drive.

accionista [akθjo'nista] *nm/f* shareholder, stockholder.
acebo [a'θeβo] *nm* holly; (*árbol*) holly tree.
acechanza [aθe'tʃanθa] *nf* = **acecho**.
acechar [aθe'tʃar] *vt* to spy on; (*aguardar*) to lie in wait for; **acecho** *nm*: **estar al acecho (de)** to lie in wait (for).
aceitar [aθei'tar] *vt* to oil, lubricate.
aceite [a'θeite] *nm* oil; (*de oliva*) olive oil; ~**ra** *nf* oilcan; **aceitoso, a** *adj* oily.
aceituna [aθei'tuna] *nf* olive.
acelerador [aθelera'ðor] *nm* accelerator.
acelerar [aθele'rar] *vt* to accelerate.
acelga [a'θelɣa] *nf* chard, beet.
acento [a'θento] *nm* accent; (*acentuación*) stress.
acentuar [aθen'twar] *vt* to accent; to stress; (*fig*) to accentuate.
acepción [aθep'θjon] *nf* meaning.
aceptable [aθep'taβle] *adj* acceptable.
aceptación [aθepta'θjon] *nf* acceptance; (*aprobación*) approval.
aceptar [aθep'tar] *vt* to accept; (*aprobar*) to approve.
acequia [a'θekja] *nf* irrigation ditch.
acera [a'θera] *nf* pavement (*BRIT*), sidewalk (*US*).
acerado, a [aθe'raðo, a] *adj* steel; (*afilado*) sharp; (*fig: duro*) (: *mordaz*) biting.
acerbo, a [a'θerβo, a] *adj* bitter; (*fig*) harsh.
acerca [a'θerka]: ~ **de** *prep* about, concerning.
acercar [aθer'kar] *vt* to bring o move nearer; ~**se** *vr* to approach, come near.
acerico [aθe'riko] *nm* pincushion.
acero [a'θero] *nm* steel.
acérrimo, a [a'θerrimo, a] *adj* (*partidario*) staunch; (*enemigo*) bitter.
acertado, a [aθer'taðo, a] *adj* correct; (*apropiado*) apt; (*sensato*) sensible.
acertar [aθer'tar] *vt* (*blanco*) to hit; (*solución*) to get right; (*adivinar*) to guess ♦ *vi* to get it right, be right; ~ **a** to manage to; ~ **con** to happen o hit on.
acertijo [aθer'tixo] *nm* riddle, puzzle.
acervo [a'θerβo] *nm* heap; ~ **común** un-

divided estate.

aciago, a [a'θjaɣo, a] *adj* ill-fated, fateful.

acicalar [aθika'lar] *vt* to polish; (*persona*) to dress up; ~**se** *vr* to get dressed up.

acicate [aθi'kate] *nm* spur.

acidez [aθi'ðeθ] *nf* acidity.

ácido, a ['aθiðo, a] *adj* sour, acid ♦ *nm* acid.

acierto *etc* [a'θjerto] *vb ver* **acertar** ♦ *nm* success; (*buen paso*) wise move; (*solución*) solution; (*habilidad*) skill, ability.

aclamación [aklama'θjon] *nf* acclamation; (*aplausos*) applause.

aclamar [akla'mar] *vt* to acclaim; (*aplaudir*) to applaud.

aclaración [aklara'θjon] *nf* clarification, explanation.

aclarar [akla'rar] *vt* to clarify, explain; (*ropa*) to rinse ♦ *vi* to clear up; ~**se** *vr* (*explicarse*) to understand; ~**se la garganta** to clear one's throat.

aclaratorio, a [aklara'torjo, a] *adj* explanatory.

aclimatación [aklimata'θjon] *nf* acclimatization.

aclimatar [aklima'tar] *vt* to acclimatize; ~**se** *vr* to become acclimatized.

acné [ak'ne] *nm* acne.

acobardar [akoβar'ðar] *vt* to intimidate.

acodarse [ako'ðarse] *vr*: ~ **en** to lean on.

acogedor, a [akoxe'ðor, a] *adj* welcoming; (*hospitalario*) hospitable.

acoger [ako'xer] *vt* to welcome; (*abrigar*) to shelter; ~**se** *vr* to take refuge.

acogida [ako'xiða] *nf* reception; refuge.

acolchar [akol'tʃar] *vt* to pad; (*fig*) to cushion.

acometer [akome'ter] *vt* to attack; (*emprender*) to undertake; **acometida** *nf* attack, assault.

acomodado, a [akomo'ðaðo, a] *adj* (*persona*) well-to-do.

acomodador, a [akomoða'ðor, a] *nm/f* usher(ette).

acomodar [akomo'ðar] *vt* to adjust; (*alojar*) to accommodate; ~**se** *vr* to conform; (*instalarse*) to install o.s.; (*adaptarse*): ~**se (a)** to adapt (to).

acomodaticio, a [akomoða'tiθjo, a] *adj* (*pey*) accommodating, obliging; (*manejable*) pliable.

acompañar [akompa'ɲar] *vt* to accompany; (*documentos*) to enclose.

acondicionar [akondiθjo'nar] *vt* to arrange, prepare; (*pelo*) to condition.

acongojar [akoŋgo'xar] *vt* to distress, grieve.

aconsejar [akonse'xar] *vt* to advise, counsel; ~**se** *vr*: ~**se con** to consult.

acontecer [akonte'θer] *vi* to happen, occur; **acontecimiento** *nm* event.

acopio [a'kopjo] *nm* store, stock.

acoplamiento [akopla'mjento] *nm* coupling, joint; **acoplar** *vt* to fit; (*ELEC*) to connect; (*vagones*) to couple.

acorazado, a [akora'θaðo, a] *adj* armour-plated, armoured ♦ *nm* battleship.

acordar [akor'ðar] *vt* (*resolver*) to agree, resolve; (*recordar*) to remind; ~**se** *vr* to agree; ~**se (de algo)** to remember (sth); **acorde** *adj* (*MUS*) harmonious; **acorde con** (*medidas etc*) in keeping with ♦ *nm* chord.

acordeón [akorðe'on] *nm* accordion.

acordonado, a [akorðo'naðo, a] *adj* (*calle*) cordoned-off.

acorralar [akorra'lar] *vt* to round up, corral.

acortar [akor'tar] *vt* to shorten; (*duración*) to cut short; (*cantidad*) to reduce; ~**se** *vr* to become shorter.

acosar [ako'sar] *vt* to pursue relentlessly; (*fig*) to hound, pester.

acostar [akos'tar] *vt* (*en cama*) to put to bed; (*en suelo*) to lay down; (*barco*) to bring alongside; ~**se** *vr* to go to bed; to lie down; ~**se con uno** to sleep with sb.

acostumbrado, a [akostum'braðo, a] *adj* usual; ~ **a** used to.

acostumbrar [akostum'brar] *vt*: ~ **a uno a algo** to get sb used to sth ♦ *vi*: ~ **(a) hacer** to be in the habit of doing; ~**se** *vr*: ~**se a** to get used to.

acotación [akota'θjon] *nf* marginal note;

(*GEO*) elevation mark; (*de límite*) boundary mark; (*TEATRO*) stage direction.

ácrata ['akrata] *adj, nm/f* anarchist.

acre ['akre] *adj* (*sabor*) sharp, bitter; (*olor*) acrid; (*fig*) biting ♦ *nm* acre.

acrecentar [akreθen'tar] *vt* to increase, augment.

acreditar [akreði'tar] *vt* (*garantizar*) to vouch for, guarantee; (*autorizar*) to authorize; (*dar prueba de*) to prove; (*COM: abonar*) to credit; (*embajador*) to accredit; ~**se** *vr* to become famous.

acreedor, a [akree'ðor, a] *adj*: ~ **de** ♦ worthy of ♦ *nm/f* creditor.

acribillar [akriβi'ʎar] *vt*: ~ **a balazos** to riddle with bullets.

acrimonia [akri'monja] *nf* acrimony.

acritud [akri'tuð] *nf* = **acrimonia**.

acróbata [a'kroβata] *nm/f* acrobat.

acta ['akta] *nf* certificate; (*de comisión*) minutes *pl*, record; ~ **de nacimiento/de matrimonio** birth/marriage certificate; ~ **notarial** affidavit.

actitud [akti'tuð] *nf* attitude; (*postura*) posture.

activar [akti'ßar] *vt* to activate; (*acelerar*) to speed up.

actividad [aktißi'ðað] *nf* activity.

activo, a [ak'tißo, a] *adj* active; (*vivo*) lively ♦ *nm* (*COM*) assets *pl*.

acto ['akto] *nm* act, action; (*ceremonia*) ceremony; (*TEATRO*) act; **en el** ~ immediately.

actor [ak'tor] *nm* actor; (*JUR*) plaintiff ♦ *adj*: **parte** ~**a** prosecution.

actriz [ak'triθ] *nf* actress.

actuación [aktwa'θjon] *nf* action; (*comportamiento*) conduct, behaviour; (*JUR*) proceedings *pl*; (*desempeño*) performance.

actual [ak'twal] *adj* present(-day), current; ~**idad** *nf* present; ~**idades** *nfpl* (*noticias*) news *sg*; **en la** ~**idad** at present; (*hoy día*) nowadays.

actualizar [aktwali'θar] *vt* to update, modernize.

actualmente [aktwal'mente] *adv* at present; (*hoy día*) nowadays.

actuar [ak'twar] *vi* (*obrar*) to work,

operate; (*actor*) to act, perform ♦ *vt* to work, operate; ~ **de** to act as.

actuario, a [ak'twarjo, a] *nm/f* clerk; (*COM*) actuary.

acuarela [akwa'rela] *nf* watercolour.

acuario [a'kwarjo] *nm* aquarium; (*ASTROLOGÍA*): **A**~ Aquarius.

acuartelar [akwarte'lar] *vt* (*MIL: disciplinar*) to confine to barracks.

acuático, a [a'kwatiko, a] *adj* aquatic.

acuciar [aku'θjar] *vt* to urge on.

acuclillarse [akukli'ʎarse] *vr* to crouch down.

acuchillar [akutʃi'ʎar] *vt* (*TEC*) to plane (down), smooth.

acudir [aku'ðir] *vi* (*asistir*) to attend; (*ir*) to go; ~ **a** (*fig*) to turn to; ~ **en ayuda de** to go to the aid of.

acuerdo *etc* [a'kwerðo] *vb ver* **acordar** ♦ *nm* agreement; **¡de** ~**!** agreed!; **de** ~ **con** (*persona*) in agreement with; (*acción, documento*) in accordance with; **estar de** ~ to be agreed, agree.

acumular [akumu'lar] *vt* to accumulate, collect.

acuñar [aku'ɲar] *vt* (*moneda*) to mint; (*frase*) to coin.

acuoso, a [a'kwoso, a] *adj* watery.

acurrucarse [akurru'karse] *vr* to crouch; (*ovillarse*) to curl up.

acusación [akusa'θjon] *nf* accusation.

acusar [aku'sar] *vt* to accuse; (*revelar*) to reveal; (*denunciar*) to denounce.

acuse [a'kuse] *nm*: ~ **de recibo** acknowledgement of receipt.

acústica [a'kustika] *nf* acoustics *pl*.

acústico, a [a'kustiko, a] *adj* acoustic.

achacar [atʃa'kar] *vt* to attribute.

achacoso, a [atʃa'koso, a] *adj* sickly.

achantar [atʃan'tar] (*fam*) *vt* to scare, frighten; ~**se** *vr* to back down.

achaque *etc* [a'tʃake] *vb ver* **achacar** ♦ *nm* ailment.

achicar [atʃi'kar] *vt* to reduce; (*humillar*) to humiliate; (*NAUT*) to bale out.

achicoria [atʃi'korja] *nf* chicory.

achicharrar [atʃitʃa'rrar] *vt* to scorch, burn.

adagio [a'ðaxjo] *nm* adage; (*MUS*)

adagio.

adaptación [aðapta'θjon] *nf* adaptation.

adaptador [aðapta'ðor] *nm* (*ELEC*) adapter.

adaptar [aðap'tar] *vt* to adapt; (*acomodar*) to fit.

adecuado, a [aðe'kwaðo, a] *adj* (*apto*) suitable; (*oportuno*) appropriate.

adecuar [aðe'kwar] *vt* to adapt; to make suitable.

a. de J.C. *abr* (= *antes de Jesucristo*) B.C.

adelantado, a [aðelan'taðo, a] *adj* advanced; (*reloj*) fast; **pagar por ~** to pay in advance.

adelantamiento [aðelanta'mjento] *nm* advance, advancement; (*AUTO*) overtaking.

adelantar [aðelan'tar] *vt* to move forward; (*avanzar*) to advance; (*acelerar*) to speed up; (*AUTO*) to overtake ♦ *vi* to go forward, advance; **~se** *vr* to go forward, advance.

adelante [aðe'lante] *adv* forward(s), ahead ♦ *excl* come in!; **de hoy en ~** from now on; **más ~** later on; (*más allá*) further on.

adelanto [aðe'lanto] *nm* advance; (*mejora*) improvement; (*progreso*) progress.

adelgazar [aðelɣa'θar] *vt* to thin (down) ♦ *vi* to get thin; (*con régimen*) to slim down, lose weight.

ademán [aðe'man] *nm* gesture; **ademanes** *nmpl* manners; **en ~ de** as if to.

además [aðe'mas] *adv* besides; (*por otra parte*) moreover; (*también*) also; **~ de** besides, in addition to.

adentrarse [aðen'trarse] *vr*: **~ en** to go into, get inside; (*penetrar*) to penetrate (into).

adentro [a'ðentro] *adv* inside, in; **mar ~** out at sea; **tierra ~** inland.

adepto, a [a'ðepto, a] *nm/f* supporter.

aderezar [aðere'θar] *vt* (*ensalada*) to dress; (*comida*) to season; **aderezo** *nm* dressing; seasoning.

adeudar [aðeu'ðar] *vt* to owe; **~se** *vr* to run into debt.

adherirse [aðe'rirse] *vr*: **~ a** to adhere to; (*partido*) to join.

adhesión [aðe'sjon] *nf* adhesion; (*fig*) adherence.

adición [aði'θjon] *nf* addition.

adicionar [aðiθjo'nar] *vt* to add.

adicto, a [a'ðikto, a] *adj*: **~ a** addicted to; (*dedicado*) devoted to ♦ *nm/f* supporter, follower; (*toxicómano etc*) addict.

adiestrar [aðjes'trar] *vt* to train, teach; (*conducir*) to guide, lead; **~se** *vr* to practise; (*enseñarse*) to train o.s.

adinerado, a [aðine'raðo, a] *adj* wealthy.

adiós [a'ðjos] *excl* (*para despedirse*) goodbye!, cheerio!; (*al pasar*) hello!

aditivo [aði'tiβo] *nm* additive.

adivinanza [aðiβi'nanθa] *nf* riddle.

adivinar [aðiβi'nar] *vt* to prophesy; (*conjeturar*) to guess; **adivino, a** *nm/f* fortune-teller.

adj *abr* (= *adjunto*) encl.

adjetivo [aðxe'tiβo] *nm* adjective.

adjudicación [aðxuðika'θjon] *nf* award; adjudication.

adjudicar [aðxuði'kar] *vt* to award; **~se** *vr*: **~se algo** to appropriate sth.

adjuntar [aðxun'tar] *vt* to attach, enclose; **adjunto, a** *adj* attached, enclosed ♦ *nm/f* assistant.

administración [aðministra'θjon] *nf* administration; (*dirección*) management; **administrador, a** *nm/f* administrator; manager(ess).

administrar [aðminis'trar] *vt* to administer; **administrativo, a** *adj* administrative.

admirable [aðmi'raβle] *adj* admirable.

admiración [aðmira'θjon] *nf* admiration; (*asombro*) wonder; (*LING*) exclamation mark.

admirar [aðmi'rar] *vt* to admire; (*extrañar*) to surprise; **~se** *vr* to be surprised.

admisible [aðmi'siβle] *adj* admissible.

admisión [aðmi'sjon] *nf* admission; (*reconocimiento*) acceptance.

admitir [aðmi'tir] *vt* to admit; (*aceptar*) to accept.

admonición [aðmoni'θjon] *nf* warning.

adobar [aðo'ßar] vt (CULIN) to season.
adobe [a'ðoße] nm adobe, sun-dried brick.
adoctrinar [aðoktri'nar] vt: ~ en to indoctrinate with.
adolecer [aðole'θer] vi: ~ de to suffer from.
adolescente [aðoles'θente] nm/f adolescent, teenager.
adonde [a'ðonðe] conj (to) where.
adónde [a'ðonðe] adv = dónde.
adopción [aðop'θjon] nf adoption.
adoptar [aðop'tar] vt to adopt.
adoptivo, a [aðop'tißo, a] adj (padres) adoptive; (hijo) adopted.
adoquín [aðo'kin] nm paving stone.
adorar [aðo'rar] vt to adore.
adormecer [aðorme'θer] vt to put to sleep; ~se vr to become sleepy; (dormirse) to fall asleep.
adornar [aðor'nar] vt to adorn.
adorno [a'ðorno] nm adornment; (decoración) decoration.
adosado, a [aðo'saðo, a] adj: **casa adosada** semi-detached house.
adquiero etc vb ver **adquirir**.
adquirir [aðki'rir] vt to acquire, obtain.
adquisición [aðkisi'θjon] nf acquisition.
adrede [a'ðreðe] adv on purpose.
adscribir [aðskri'ßir] vt to appoint.
adscrito pp de **adscribir**.
aduana [a'ðwana] nf customs pl.
aduanero, a [aðwa'nero, a] adj customs cpd ♦ nm/f customs officer.
aducir [aðu'θir] vt to adduce; (dar como prueba) to offer as proof.
adueñarse [aðwe'narse] vr: ~ de to take possession of.
adulación [aðula'θjon] nf flattery.
adular [aðu'lar] vt to flatter.
adulterar [aðulte'rar] vt to adulterate ♦ vi to commit adultery.
adulterio [aðul'terjo] nm adultery.
adúltero, a [a'ðultero, a] adj adulterous ♦ nm/f adulterer/adulteress.
adulto, a [a'ðulto, a] adj, nm/f adult.
adusto, a [a'ðusto, a] adj stern; (austero) austere.
advenedizo, a [aðßene'ðiθo, a] nm/f upstart.

advenimiento [aðßeni'mjento] nm arrival; (al trono) accession.
adverbio [að'ßerßjo] nm adverb.
adversario, a [aðßer'sarjo, a] nm/f adversary.
adversidad [aðßersi'ðað] nf adversity; (contratiempo) setback.
adverso, a [að'ßerso, a] adj adverse.
advertencia [aðßer'tenθja] nf warning; (prefacio) preface, foreword.
advertir [aðßer'tir] vt to notice; (avisar): ~ a uno de to warn sb about o of.
Adviento [að'ßjento] nm Advent.
advierto etc vb ver **advertir**.
adyacente [aðja'θente] adj adjacent.
aéreo, a [a'ereo, a] adj aerial.
aerobic [ae'roßik] nm aerobics sg.
aerodeslizador [aeroðesliθa'ðor] nm hovercraft.
aerodeslizante [aeroðesli'θante] nm = aerodeslizador.
aeromozo, a [aero'moθo, a] (AM) nm/f air steward(ess).
aeronáutica [aero'nautika] nf aeronautics sg.
aeronave [aero'naße] nm spaceship.
aeroplano [aero'plano] nm aeroplane.
aeropuerto [aero'pwerto] nm airport.
aerosol [aero'sol] nm aerosol.
afabilidad [afaßili'ðað] nf friendliness; **afable** adj affable.
afamado, a [afa'maðo, a] adj famous.
afán [a'fan] nm hard work; (deseo) desire.
afanar [afa'nar] vt to harass; (fam) to pinch; ~se vr: ~se por hacer to strive to do; **afanoso, a** adj (trabajo) hard; (trabajador) industrious.
afear [afe'ar] vt to disfigure.
afección [afek'θjon] nf (MED) disease.
afectación [afekta'θjon] nf affectation; **afectado, a** adj affected.
afectar [afek'tar] vt to affect.
afectísimo, a [afek'tisimo, a] adj affectionate; ~ **suyo** yours truly.
afectivo, a [afek'tißo, a] adj (problema etc) emotional.
afecto [a'fekto] nm affection; **tenerle ~ a uno** to be fond of sb.

afectuoso, a [afek'twoso, a] *adj* affectionate.

afeitar [afei'tar] *vt* to shave; ~**se** *vr* to shave.

afeminado, a [afemi'naðo, a] *adj* effeminate.

aferrado, a [afe'rraðo, a] *adj* stubborn.

aferrar [afe'rrar] *vt* to grasp; (*barco*) to moor ♦ *vi* to moor.

Afganistán [afvanis'tan] *nm* Afghanistan.

afianzamiento [afjanθa'mjento] *nm* strengthening; security.

afianzar [afjan'θar] *vt* to strengthen; to secure; ~**se** *vr* to become established.

afición [afi'θjon] *nf* fondness, liking; **la** ~ **the fans** *pl*; **pinto por** ~ I paint as a hobby; **aficionado, a** *adj* keen, enthusiastic; (*no profesional*) amateur ♦ *nm/f* enthusiast, fan; amateur; **ser aficionado a algo** to be very keen on *o* fond of sth.

aficionar [afiθjo'nar] *vt*: ~ **a uno a algo** to make sb like sth; ~**se** *vr*: ~**se a algo** to grow fond of sth.

afiche [a'fitʃe] (*AM*) *nm* poster.

afilado, a [afi'laðo, a] *adj* sharp.

afilar [afi'lar] *vt* to sharpen.

afiliarse [afi'ljarse] *vr* to affiliate.

afín [a'fin] *adj* (*parecido*) similar; (*conexo*) related.

afinar [afi'nar] *vt* (*TEC*) to refine; (*MUS*) to tune ♦ *vi* to play (*or* sing) in tune.

afincarse [afin'karse] *vr* to settle.

afinidad [afini'ðað] *nf* affinity; (*parentesco*) relationship; **por** ~ by marriage.

afirmación [afirma'θjon] *nf* affirmation.

afirmar [afir'mar] *vt* to affirm, state; (*reforzar*) to strengthen; **afirmativo, a** *adj* affirmative.

aflicción [aflik'θjon] *nf* affliction; (*dolor*) grief.

afligir [afli'xir] *vt* to afflict; (*apenar*) to distress; ~**se** *vr* to grieve.

aflojar [aflo'xar] *vt* to slacken; (*desatar*) to loosen, undo; (*relajar*) to relax ♦ *vi* to drop; (*bajar*) to go down; ~**se** *vr* to relax.

aflorar [aflo'rar] *vi* to come to the surface, emerge.

afluente [aflu'ente] *adj* flowing ♦ *nm* tributary.

afluir [aflu'ir] *vi* to flow.

afmo, a *abr* (= *afectísimo(a) suyo(a)*) Yours.

afónico, a [a'foniko, a] *adj*: **estar** ~ to have a sore throat; to have lost one's voice.

aforo [a'foro] *nm* (*de teatro etc*) capacity.

afortunado, a [afortu'naðo, a] *adj* fortunate, lucky.

afrancesado, a [afranθe'saðo, a] *adj* francophile; (*pey*) Frenchified.

afrenta [a'frenta] *nf* affront, insult; (*deshonra*) dishonour, shame.

África ['afrika] *nf* Africa; ~ **del Sur** South Africa; **africano, a** *adj, nm/f* African.

afrontar [afron'tar] *vt* to confront; (*poner cara a cara*) to bring face to face.

afuera [a'fwera] *adv* out, outside; ~**s** *nfpl* outskirts.

agachar [aɣa'tʃar] *vt* to bend, bow; ~**se** *vr* to stoop, bend.

agalla [a'ɣaʎa] *nf* (*ZOOL*) gill; ~**s** *nfpl* (*MED*) tonsillitis *sg*; (*ANAT*) tonsils; **tener** ~**s** (*fam*) to have guts.

agarradera [aɣarra'ðera] (*AM*) *nf* = **agarradero**.

agarradero [aɣarra'ðero] *nm* handle; ~**s** *nmpl* (*fig*) pull *sg*, influence *sg*.

agarrado, a [aɣa'rraðo, a] *adj* mean, stingy.

agarrar [aɣa'rrar] *vt* to grasp, grab; (*AM*) to take, catch; (*recoger*) to pick up ♦ *vi* (*planta*) to take root; ~**se** *vr* to hold on (tightly).

agarrotar [aɣarro'tar] *vt* (*lío*) to tie tightly; (*persona*) to squeeze tightly; (*reo*) to garrotte; ~**se** *vr* (*motor*) to seize up; (*MED*) to stiffen.

agasajar [aɣasa'xar] *vt* to treat well, fête.

agencia [a'xenθja] *nf* agency; ~ **inmobiliaria** estate (*BRIT*) *o* real estate (*US*) agent's (office); ~ **matrimonial** marriage bureau; ~ **de viajes** travel agency.

agenciarse [axen'θjarse] *vr* to obtain, procure.

agenda [a'xenda] *nf* diary.

agente [a'xente] *nm* agent; (*de policía*) policeman; ~ **femenino** policewoman; ~ **inmobiliario** estate agent (*BRIT*), realtor (*US*); ~ **de bolsa** stockbroker; ~ **de seguros** insurance agent.

ágil ['axil] *adj* agile, nimble; **agilidad** *nf* agility, nimbleness.

agitación [axita'θjon] *nf* (*de mano etc*) shaking, waving; (*de líquido etc*) stirring; (*fig*) agitation.

agitar [axi'tar] *vt* to wave, shake; (*líquido*) to stir; (*fig*) to stir up, excite; ~**se** *vr* to get excited; (*inquietarse*) to get worried *o* upset.

aglomeración [axlomera'θjon] *nf*: ~ **de tráfico/gente** traffic jam/mass of people.

aglomerar [axlome'rar] *vt* to crowd together; ~**se** *vr* to crowd together.

agnóstico, a [ax'nostiko, a] *adj, nm/f* agnostic.

agobiar [axo'βjar] *vt* to weigh down; (*oprimir*) to oppress; (*cargar*) to burden.

agolparse [axol'parse] *vr* to crowd together.

agonía [axo'nia] *nf* death throes *pl*; (*fig*) agony, anguish.

agonizante [axoni'θante] *adj* dying.

agonizar [axoni'θar] *vi* (*tb: estar agonizando*) to be dying.

agosto [a'xosto] *nm* August.

agotado, a [axo'taðo, a] *adj* (*persona*) exhausted; (*libros*) out of print; (*acabado*) finished; (*COM*) sold out.

agotador, a [axota'ðor, a] *adj* exhausting.

agotamiento [axota'mjento] *nm* exhaustion.

agotar [axo'tar] *vt* to exhaust; (*consumir*) to drain; (*recursos*) to use up, deplete; ~**se** *vr* to be exhausted; (*acabarse*) to run out; (*libro*) to go out of print.

agraciado, a [axra'θjaðo, a] *adj* (*atractivo*) attractive; (*en sorteo etc*) lucky.

agraciar [axra'θjar] *vt* (*con premio*) to reward.

agradable [axra'ðaβle] *adj* pleasant, nice.

agradar [axra'ðar] *vt*: **él me agrada** I like him.

agradecer [axraðe'θer] *vt* to thank; (*favor etc*) to be grateful for; **agradecido, a** *adj* grateful; ¡**muy** ~! thanks a lot!; **agradecimiento** *nm* thanks *pl*; gratitude.

agradezco *etc vb ver* **agradecer**.

agrado [a'xraðo] *nm*: **ser de tu** *etc* ~ to be to your *etc* liking.

agrandar [axran'dar] *vt* to enlarge; (*fig*) to exaggerate; ~**se** *vr* to get bigger.

agrario, a [a'xrarjo, a] *adj* agrarian, land *cpd*; (*política*) agricultural, farming.

agravante [axra'βante] *adj* aggravating ♦ *nf*: **con la** ~ **de que ...** with the further difficulty that ....

agravar [axra'βar] *vt* (*pesar sobre*) to make heavier; (*irritar*) to aggravate; ~**se** *vr* to worsen, get worse.

agraviar [axra'βjar] *vt* to offend; (*ser injusto con*) to wrong; ~**se** *vr* to take offence; **agravio** *nm* offence; wrong; (*JUR*) grievance.

agredir [axre'ðir] *vt* to attack.

agregado, a [axre'xaðo, a] *nm/f*: **A**~ ≈ teacher (*who is not head of department*) ♦ *nm* aggregate; (*persona*) attaché.

agregar [axre'xar] *vt* to gather; (*añadir*) to add; (*persona*) to appoint.

agresión [axre'sjon] *nf* aggression.

agresivo, a [axre'siβo, a] *adj* aggressive.

agriar [a'xrjar] *vt* to (turn) sour; ~**se** *vr* to turn sour.

agrícola [a'xrikola] *adj* farming *cpd*, agricultural.

agricultor, a [axrikul'tor, a] *nm/f* farmer.

agricultura [axrikul'tura] *nf* agriculture, farming.

agridulce [axri'ðulθe] *adj* bittersweet; (*CULIN*) sweet and sour.

agrietarse [axrje'tarse] *vr* to crack;

(*piel*) to chap.

agrimensor, a [aɣrimen'sor, a] *nm/f* surveyor.

agrio, a ['aɣrjo, a] *adj* bitter.

agronomía [aɣrono'mia] *nf* agronomy, agriculture.

agropecuario, a [aɣrope'kwarjo, a] *adj* farming *cpd*, agricultural.

agrupación [aɣrupa'θjon] *nf* group; (*acto*) grouping.

agrupar [aɣru'par] *vt* to group.

agua ['aɣwa] *nf* water; (*NAUT*) wake; (*ARQ*) slope of a roof; ~s *nfpl* (*de piedra*) water *sg*, sparkle *sg*; (*MED*) water *sg*, urine *sg*; (*NAUT*) waters; ~s **abajo/arriba** downstream/upstream; ~ **bendita/destilada/potable** holy/distilled/ drinking water; ~ **caliente** hot water; ~ **corriente** running water; ~ **de colonia** eau de cologne; ~ **mineral (con/sin gas)** (carbonated/uncarbonated) mineral water; ~s **jurisdiccionales** territorial waters; ~s **mayores** excrement *sg*.

aguacate [aɣwa'kate] *nm* avocado (pear).

aguacero [aɣwa'θero] *nm* (heavy) shower, downpour.

aguada [a'ɣwaða] *nf* (*AGR*) watering place; (*NAUT*) water supply; (*ARTE*) watercolour.

aguado, a [a'ɣwaðo, a] *adj* watery, watered down.

aguafiestas [aɣwa'fjestas] *nm/f inv* spoilsport, killjoy.

aguafuerte [aɣwa'fwerte] *nm o f* etching.

aguamanil [aɣwama'nil] *nm* (*jofaina*) washbasin.

aguanieve [aɣwa'njeβe] *nf* sleet.

aguantar [aɣwan'tar] *vt* to bear, put up with; (*sostener*) to hold up ♦ *vi* to last; ~se *vr* to restrain o.s.; **aguante** *nm* (*paciencia*) patience; (*resistencia*) endurance.

aguar [a'ɣwar] *vt* to water down.

aguardar [aɣwar'ðar] *vt* to wait for.

aguardiente [aɣwar'ðjente] *nm* brandy, liquor.

aguarrás [aɣwa'rras] *nm* turpentine.

agudeza [aɣu'ðeθa] *nf* sharpness; (*in-genio*) wit.

agudizar [aɣuði'θar] *vt* (*crisis*) to make worse; ~se *vr* to get worse.

agudo, a [a'ɣuðo, a] *adj* sharp; (*voz*) high-pitched, piercing; (*dolor, enfermedad*) acute.

agüero [a'ɣwero] *nm*: **buen/mal** ~ good/ bad omen.

aguijar [aɣi'xar] *vt* to goad; (*incitar*) to urge on ♦ *vi* to hurry along.

aguijón [aɣi'xon] *nm* sting; (*fig*) spur; **aguijonear** *vt* = **aguijar.**

águila ['aɣila] *nf* eagle; (*fig*) genius.

aguileño, a [aɣi'leɲo, a] *adj* (*nariz*) aquiline; (*rostro*) sharp-featured.

aguinaldo [aɣi'naldo] *nm* Christmas box.

aguja [a'ɣuxa] *nf* needle; (*de reloj*) hand; (*ARQ*) spire; (*TEC*) firing-pin; ~s *nfpl* (*ZOOL*) ribs; (*FERRO*) points.

agujerear [aɣuxere'ar] *vt* to make holes in.

agujero [aɣu'xero] *nm* hole.

agujetas [aɣu'xetas] *nfpl* stitch *sg*; (*rigidez*) stiffness *sg*.

aguzar [aɣu'θar] *vt* to sharpen; (*fig*) to incite.

ahí [a'i] *adv* there; **de** ~ **que** so that, with the result that; ~ **llega** here he comes; **por** ~ that way; (*allá*) over there; **200 o por** ~ 200 or so.

ahijado, a [ai'xaðo, a] *nm/f* godson/ daughter.

ahínco [a'inko] *nm* earnestness.

ahíto, a [a'ito, a] *adj*: **estoy** ~ I'm full up.

ahogar [ao'ɣar] *vt* to drown; (*asfixiar*) to suffocate, smother; (*fuego*) to put out; ~se *vr* (*en el agua*) to drown; (*por asfixia*) to suffocate.

ahogo [a'oɣo] *nm* breathlessness; (*fig*) financial difficulty.

ahondar [aon'dar] *vt* to deepen, make deeper; (*fig*) to study thoroughly ♦ *vi*: ~ **en** to study thoroughly.

ahora [a'ora] *adv* now; (*hace poco*) a moment ago, just now; (*dentro de poco*) in a moment; ~ **voy** I'm coming; ~ **mismo** right now; ~ **bien** now then; **por** ~ for the present.

ahorcar [aor'kar] *vt* to hang; ~**se** *vr* to hang o.s.

ahorita [ao'rita] (*fam: esp AM*) *adv* right now.

ahorrar [ao'rrar] *vt* (*dinero*) to save; (*esfuerzos*) to save, avoid; **ahorro** *nm* (*acto*) saving; (*frugalidad*) thrift; **ahorros** *nmpl* (*dinero*) savings.

ahuecar [awe'kar] *vt* to hollow (out); (*voz*) to deepen; ~**se** *vr* to give o.s. airs.

ahumar [au'mar] *vt* to smoke, cure; (*llenar de humo*) to fill with smoke ♦ *vi* to smoke; ~**se** *vr* to fill with smoke.

ahuyentar [aujen'tar] *vt* to drive off, frighten off; (*fig*) to dispel.

airado, a [ai'raðo, a] *adj* angry.

airar [ai'rar] *vt* to anger; ~**se** *vr* to get angry.

aire ['aire] *nm* air; (*viento*) wind; (*corriente*) draught; (*MUS*) tune; ~**s** *nmpl*: **darse** ~**s** to give o.s. airs; **al** ~ **libre** in the open air; ~ **acondicionado** air conditioning; **airoso, a** *adj* windy; draughty; (*fig*) graceful.

aislado, a [ais'laðo, a] *adj* isolated; (*incomunicado*) cut-off; (*ELEC*) insulated.

aislar [ais'lar] *vt* to isolate; (*ELEC*) to insulate.

ajar [a'xar] *vt* to spoil; (*fig*) to abuse.

ajardinado, a [axarði'naðo, a] *adj* landscaped.

ajedrez [axe'ðreθ] *nm* chess.

ajeno, a [a'xeno, a] *adj* (*que pertenece a otro*) somebody else's; ~ **a** foreign to; ~ **de** free from, devoid of.

ajetreado, a [axetre'aðo, a] *adj* busy.

ajetreo [axe'treo] *nm* bustle.

ají [a'xi] *nm* chilli, red pepper; (*salsa*) chilli sauce.

ajo ['axo] *nm* garlic.

ajuar [a'xwar] *nm* household furnishings *pl*; (*de novia*) trousseau; (*de niño*) layette.

ajustado, a [axus'taðo, a] *adj* (*tornillo*) tight; (*cálculo*) right; (*ropa*) tight(- fitting); (*DEPORTE: resultado*) close.

ajustar [axus'tar] *vt* (*adaptar*) to adjust; (*encajar*) to fit; (*TEC*) to engage; (*IMPRENTA*) to make up; (*apretar*) to tighten; (*concertar*) to agree (on); (*reconciliar*) to reconcile; (*cuentas, deudas*) to settle ♦ *vi* to fit; ~**se** *vr*: ~**se a** (*precio etc*) to be in keeping with, fit in with; ~ **las cuentas a uno** to get even with sb.

ajuste [a'xuste] *nm* adjustment; (*COSTURA*) fitting; (*acuerdo*) compromise; (*de cuenta*) settlement.

al [al] (= **a** +**el**) *ver* **a**.

ala ['ala] *nf* wing; (*de sombrero*) brim; (*futbolista*) winger.

alabanza [ala'βanθa] *nf* praise.

alabar [ala'βar] *vt* to praise.

alacena [ala'θena] *nf* kitchen cupboard (*BRIT*), kitchen closet (*US*).

alacrán [ala'kran] *nm* scorpion.

alado, a [a'laðo, a] *adj* winged.

alambique [alam'bike] *nm* still.

alambrada [alam'braða] *nf* wire fence; (*red*) wire netting.

alambrado [alam'braðo] *nm* = **alambrada**.

alambre [a'lambre] *nm* wire; ~ **de púas** barbed wire; **alambrista** *nm/f* tightrope walker.

alameda [ala'meða] *nf* (*plantío*) poplar grove; (*lugar de paseo*) avenue, boulevard.

álamo ['alamo] *nm* poplar; ~ **temblón** aspen.

alano [a'lano] *nm* mastiff.

alarde [a'larðe] *nm* show, display; **hacer** ~ **de** to boast of.

alargador [alarγa'ðor] *nm* (*ELEC*) extension lead.

alargar [alar'γar] *vt* to lengthen, extend; (*paso*) to hasten; (*brazo*) to stretch out; (*cuerda*) to pay out; (*conversación*) to spin out; ~**se** *vr* to get longer.

alarido [ala'riðo] *nm* shriek.

alarma [a'larma] *nf* alarm.

alarmante [alar'mante] *adj* alarming.

alazán [ala'θan] *nm* sorrel.

alba ['alβa] *nf* dawn.

albacea [alβa'θea] *nm/f* executor/ executrix.

albahaca [al'βaka] *nf* basil.

Albania [al'βanja] *nf* Albania.

albañal [alβa'ɲal] *nm* drain, sewer.

albañil [alβa'ɲil] *nm* bricklayer; (*cantero*) mason.

albarán [alβa'ran] *nm* (*COM*) delivery note, invoice.

albaricoque [alβari'koke] *nm* apricot.

albedrío [alβe'ðrio] *nm*: **libre ~** free will.

alberca [al'βerka] *nf* reservoir; (*AM*) swimming pool.

albergar [alβer'xar] *vt* to shelter.

albergue *etc* [al'βerxe] *vb ver* **albergar** ♦ *nm* shelter, refuge; **~ de juventud** youth hostel.

albóndiga [al'βondixa] *nf* meatball.

albor [al'βor] *nm* whiteness; (*amanecer*) dawn; **~ear** *vi* to dawn.

albornoz [alβor'noθ] *nm* (*de los árabes*) burnous; (*para el baño*) bathrobe.

alborotar [alβoro'tar] *vi* to make a row ♦ *vt* to agitate, stir up; **~se** *vr* to get excited; (*mar*) to get rough; **alboroto** *nm* row, uproar.

alborozar [alβoro'θar] *vt* to gladden; **~se** *vr* to rejoice.

alborozo [alβo'roθo] *nm* joy.

albricias [al'βriθjas] *nfpl*: **~!** good news!

álbum ['alβum] (*pl* **~s**, **~es**) *nm* album; **~ de recortes** scrapbook.

albumen [al'βumen] *nm* egg white, albumen.

alcachofa [alka'tʃofa] *nf* artichoke.

alcalde, **esa** [al'kalde, esal] *nm/f* mayor(ess).

alcaldía [alkal'dia] *nf* mayoralty; (*lugar*) mayor's office.

alcance *etc* [al'kanθe] *vb ver* **alcanzar** ♦ *nm* reach; (*COM*) adverse balance.

alcancía [alkan'θia] *nf* money box.

alcantarilla [alkanta'riʎa] *nf* (*de aguas cloacales*) sewer; (*en la calle*) gutter.

alcanzar [alkan'θar] *vt* (*algo: con la mano, el pie*) to reach; (*alguien: en el camino etc*) to catch up (with); (*autobús*) to catch; (*suj: bala*) to hit, strike ♦ *vi* (*ser suficiente*) to be enough; **~ a hacer** to manage to do.

alcaparra [alka'parra] *nf* caper.

alcatraz [alka'traθ] *nm* gannet.

alcayata [alka'jata] *nf* hook.

alcázar [al'kaθar] *nm* fortress; (*NAUT*) quarter-deck.

alcoba [al'koβa] *nf* bedroom.

alcohol [al'kol] *nm* alcohol; **~ metílico** methylated spirits *pl* (*BRIT*), wood alcohol (*US*); **alcohólico**, **a** *adj*, *nm/f* alcoholic.

alcoholímetro [alko'limetro] *nm* Breathalyser ® (*BRIT*), drunkometer (*US*).

alcoholismo [alko'lismo] *nm* alcoholism.

alcornoque [alkor'noke] *nm* cork tree; (*fam*) idiot.

aldaba [al'daβa] *nf* (door) knocker.

aldea [al'dea] *nf* village; **~no, a** *adj* village *cpd* ♦ *nm/f* villager.

ale ['ale] *excl* come on!, let's go!

aleación [alea'θjon] *nf* alloy.

aleatorio, a [alea'torjo, a] *adj* random.

aleccionar [alekθjo'nar] *vt* to instruct; (*adiestrar*) to train.

alegación [alexa'θjon] *nf* allegation.

alegar [ale'xar] *vt* to allege; (*JUR*) to plead ♦ *vi* (*AM*) to argue.

alegato [ale'xato] *nm* (*JUR*) allegation; (*AM*) argument.

alegoría [alexo'ria] *nf* allegory.

alegrar [ale'xrar] *vt* (*causar alegría*) to cheer (up); (*fuego*) to poke; (*fiesta*) to liven up; **~se** *vr* (*fam*) to get merry *o* tight; **~se de** to be glad about.

alegre [a'lexre] *adj* happy, cheerful; (*fam*) merry, tight; (*chiste*) risqué. blue; **alegría** *nf* happiness; merriment.

alejamiento [alexa'θjento] *nm* removal; (*distancia*) remoteness.

alejar [ale'xar] *vt* to remove; (*fig*) to estrange; **~se** *vr* to move away.

alemán, ana [ale'man, ana] *adj*, *nm/f* German ♦ *nm* (*LING*) German.

Alemania [ale'manja] *nf*: **~ Occidental/Oriental** West/East Germany.

alentador, a [alenta'ðor, a] *adj* encouraging.

alentar [alen'tar] *vt* to encourage.

alergia [a'lerxja] *nf* allergy.

alero [a'lero] *nm* (*de tejado*) eaves *pl*; (*de carruaje*) mudguard.

alerta [a'lerta] *adj*, *nm* alert.

aleta [a'leta] *nf* (*de pez*) fin; (*de ave*) wing; (*de foca*, *DEPORTE*) flipper;

(*AUTO*) mudguard.

aletargar [aletar'γar] *vt* to make drowsy; (*entumecer*) to make numb; ~se *vr* to grow drowsy; to become numb.

aletear [alete'ar] *vi* to flutter.

alevín [ale'βin] *nm* fry, young fish.

alevino [ale'βino] *nm* = alevín.

alevosía [aleβo'sia] *nf* treachery.

alfabeto [alfa'βeto] *nm* alphabet.

alfalfa [al'falfa] *nf* alfalfa, lucerne.

alfarería [alfare'ria] *nf* pottery; (*tienda*) pottery shop; **alfarero, a** *nm/f* potter.

alféizar [al'feiðar] *nm* window-sill.

alférez [al'fereθ] *nm* (*MIL*) second lieutenant; (*NAUT*) ensign.

alfil [al'fil] *nm* (*AJEDREZ*) bishop.

alfiler [alfi'ler] *nm* pin; (*broche*) clip; (*pinza*) clothes peg.

alfiletero [alfile'tero] *nm* needlecase.

alfombra [al'fombra] *nf* carpet; (*más pequeña*) rug; **alfombrar** *vt* to carpet; **alfombrilla** *nf* rug, mat.

alforja [al'forxa] *nf* saddlebag.

alforza [al'forθa] *nf* pleat.

algarabía [alγara'βia] (*fam*) *nf* gibberish.

algarrobo [alγa'rroβo] *nm* carob tree.

algas ['alγas] *nfpl* seaweed.

algazara [alγa'θara] *nf* din, uproar.

álgebra ['alxeβra] *nf* algebra.

álgido, a ['alxiðo] *adj* icy, chilly; (*momento etc*) crucial, decisive.

algo ['alγo] *pron* something; anything ♦ *adv* somewhat, rather; ¿~ más? anything else?; (*en tienda*) is that all?; por ~ será there must be some reason for it.

algodón [alγo'ðon] *nm* cotton; (*planta*) cotton plant; ~ de azúcar candy floss (*BRIT*), cotton candy (*US*); ~ hidrófilo cotton wool (*BRIT*), absorbent cotton (*US*).

algodonero, a [alγoðo'nero, a] *adj* cotton *cpd* ♦ *nm/f* cotton grower ♦ *nm* cotton plant.

alguacil [alγwa'θil] *nm* bailiff; (*TAUR*) mounted official.

alguien ['alγjen] *pron* someone, somebody; (*en frases interrogativas*) anyone, anybody.

alguno, a [al'γuno, a] *adj* (*delante de nm*: **algún**) some; (*después de n*): no tiene talento alguno he has no talent, he doesn't have any talent ♦ *pron* (*alguien*) someone, somebody; algún que otro libro some book or other; algún día iré I'll go one o some day; sin interés ~ without the slightest interest; ~ que otro an occasional one; ~s piensan some (people) think.

alhaja [a'laxa] *nf* jewel; (*tesoro*) precious object, treasure.

alhelí [ale'li] *nm* wallflower, stock.

aliado, a [a'ljaðo, a] *adj* allied.

alianza [a'ljanθa] *nf* alliance; (*anillo*) wedding ring.

aliar [a'ljar] *vt* to ally; ~se *vr* to form an alliance.

alias ['aljas] *adv* alias.

alicates [ali'kates] *nmpl* pliers; ~ de uñas nail clippers.

aliciente [ali'θjente] *nm* incentive; (*atracción*) attraction.

alienación [aljena'θjon] *nf* alienation.

aliento [a'ljento] *nm* breath; (*respiración*) breathing; sin ~ breathless.

aligerar [alixe'rar] *vt* to lighten; (*reducir*) to shorten; (*aliviar*) to alleviate; (*mitigar*) to ease; (*paso*) to quicken.

alimaña [ali'maɲa] *nf* pest.

alimentación [alimenta'θjon] *nf* (*comida*) food; (*acción*) feeding; (*tienda*) grocer's (shop); **alimentador** *nm*: **alimentador de papel** sheet-feeder.

alimentar [alimen'tar] *vt* to feed; (*nutrir*) to nourish; ~se *vr* to feed.

alimenticio, a [alimen'tiθjo, a] *adj* food *cpd*; (*nutritivo*) nourishing, nutritious.

alimento [ali'mento] *nm* food; (*nutrición*) nourishment; ~s *nmpl* (*JUR*) alimony *sg*.

alineación [alinea'θjon] *nf* alignment; (*DEPORTE*) line-up.

alinear [aline'ar] *vt* to align; ~se *vr* (*DEPORTE*) to line up; ~se en to fall in with.

aliñar [ali'ɲar] *vt* (*CULIN*) to season; **aliño** *nm* (*CULIN*) dressing.

alioli [ali'oli] *nm* garlic mayonnaise.

alisar [ali'sar] *vt* to smooth.

aliso [a'liso] *nm* alder.

alistarse [alis'tarse] *vr* to enlist;' (*inscribirse*) to enrol.

aliviar [ali'βjar] *vt* (*carga*) to lighten; (*persona*) to relieve; (*dolor*) to relieve, alleviate.

alivio [a'liβjo] *nm* alleviation, relief.

aljibe [al'xiβe] *nm* cistern.

alma ['alma] *nf* soul; (*persona*) person; (*TEC*) core.

almacén [alma'θen] *nm* (*depósito*) warehouse, store; (*MIL*) magazine; (*AM*) shop; (**grandes**) **almacenes** *nmpl* department store *sg*; **almacenaje** *nm* storage; **almacenaje secundaria** (*INFORM*) backing storage.

almacenar [almaθe'nar] *vt* to store, put in storage; (*proveerse*) to stock up with; **almacenero** *nm* warehouseman; (*AM*) shopkeeper.

almanaque [alma'nake] *nm* almanac.

almeja [al'mexa] *nf* clam.

almendra [al'mendra] *nf* almond; **almendro** *nm* almond tree.

almiar [al'mjar] *nm* haystack.

almíbar [al'miβar] *nm* syrup.

almidón [almi'ðon] *nm* starch; **almidonar** *vt* to starch.

almirantazgo [almiran'taθɣo] *nm* admiralty.

almirante [almi'rante] *nm* admiral.

almirez [almi'reθ] *nm* mortar.

almizcle [al'miθkle] *nm* musk.

almohada [almo'aða] *nf* pillow; (*funda*) pillowcase; **almohadilla** *nf* cushion; (*TEC*) pad; (*AM*) pincushion.

almohadón [almoa'ðon] *nm* large pillow; bolster.

almorranas [almo'rranas] *nfpl* piles, haemorrhoids.

almorzar [almor'θar] *vt*: ~ **una tortilla** to have an omelette for lunch ♦ *vi* to (have) lunch.

almuerzo *etc* [al'mwerθo] *vb ver* **almorzar** ♦ *nm* lunch.

alocado, a [alo'kaðo, a] *adj* crazy.

alojamiento [aloxa'mjento] *nm* lodging(s) (*pl*); (*viviendas*) housing.

alojar [alo'xar] *vt* to lodge; ~**se** *vr* to lodge, stay.

alondra [a'londra] *nf* lark, skylark.

alpargata [alpar'ɣata] *nf* rope-soled sandal, espadrille.

Alpes ['alpes] *nmpl*: **los** ~ the Alps.

alpinismo [alpi'nismo] *nm* mountaineering, climbing; **alpinista** *nm/f* mountaineer, climber.

alpiste [al'piste] *nm* birdseed.

alquería [alke'ria] *nf* farmhouse.

alquilar [alki'lar] *vt* (*suj: propietario*: *inmuebles*) to let, rent (out); (*: coche*) to hire out; (*: TV*) to rent (out); (*suj: alquilador*: *inmuebles, TV*) to rent; (*: coche*) to hire; **"se alquila casa"** "house to let (*BRIT*) o to rent (*US*)".

alquiler [alki'ler] *nm* renting; letting; hiring; (*arriendo*) rent; hire charge; ~ **de automóviles** car hire; **de** ~ for hire.

alquimia [al'kimja] *nf* alchemy.

alquitrán [alki'tran] *nm* tar.

alrededor [alreðe'ðor] *adv* around, about; ~ **de** around, about; **mirar a su** ~ to look (round) about one; ~**es** *nmpl* surroundings.

alta ['alta] *nf* (certificate of) discharge; **dar de** ~ to discharge.

altanería [altane'ria] *nf* haughtiness, arrogance; **altanero, a** *adj* arrogant, haughty.

altar [al'tar] *nm* altar.

altavoz [alta'βoθ] *nm* loudspeaker; (*amplificador*) amplifier.

alteración [altera'θjon] *nf* alteration; (*alboroto*) disturbance.

alterar [alte'rar] *vt* to alter; to disturb; ~**se** *vr* (*persona*) to get upset.

altercado [alter'kaðo] *nm* argument.

alternar [alter'nar] *vt* to alternate ♦ *vi* to alternate; (*turnar*) to take turns; ~**se** *vr* to alternate; to take turns; ~ **con** to mix with; **alternativa** *nf* alternative; (*elección*) choice; **alternativo, a** *adj* alternative; (*alterno*) alternating; **alterno, a** *adj* alternate; (*ELEC*) alternating.

Alteza [al'teθa] *nf* (*tratamiento*) Highness.

altibajos [alti'βaxos] *nmpl* ups and downs.

altiplanicie [altipla'niθje] *nf* high plateau.
altiplano [alti'plano] *nm* = **altiplanicie**.
altisonante [altiso'nante] *adj* high-flown, high-sounding.
altitud [alti'tuð] *nf* height; (*AVIAT, GEO*) altitude.
altivez [alti'ßeθ] *nf* haughtiness, arrogance; **altivo, a** *adj* haughty, arrogant.
alto, a ['alto, a] *adj* high; (*persona*) tall; (*sonido*) high, sharp; (*noble*) high, lofty ♦ *nm* halt; (*MUS*) alto; (*GEO*) hill; (*AM*) pile ♦ *adv* (*de sitio*) high; (*de sonido*) loud, loudly ♦ *excl* halt!; **la pared tiene 2 metros de ~** the wall is 2 metres high; **en alta mar** on the high seas; **en voz alta** in a loud voice; **las altas horas de la noche** the small o wee hours; **en lo ~ de** at the top of; **pasar por ~** to overlook.
altoparlante [altopar'lante] (*AM*) *nm* loudspeaker.
altura [al'tura] *nf* height; (*NAUT*) depth; (*GEO*) latitude; **la pared tiene 1.80 de ~** the wall is 1 metre 80cm high; **a estas ~s** at this stage; **a estas ~s del año** at this time of the year.
alubia [a'lußja] *nf* French bean, kidney bean.
alucinación [aluθina'θjon] *nf* hallucination.
alucinar [aluθi'nar] *vi* to hallucinate ♦ *vt* to deceive; (*fascinar*) to fascinate.
alud [a'luð] *nm* avalanche; (*fig*) flood.
aludir [alu'ðir] *vi*: **~ a** to allude to; **darse por aludido** to take the hint.
alumbrado [alum'braðo] *nm* lighting; **alumbramiento** *nm* lighting; (*MED*) childbirth, delivery.
alumbrar [alum'brar] *vt* to light (up) ♦ *vi* (*MED*) to give birth.
aluminio [alu'minjo] *nm* aluminium (*BRIT*), aluminum (*US*).
alumno, a [a'lumno, a] *nm/f* pupil, student.
alunizar [aluni'θar] *vi* to land on the moon.
alusión [alu'sjon] *nf* allusion.
alusivo, a [alu'sißo, a] *adj* allusive.

aluvión [alu'ßjon] *nm* alluvium; (*fig*) flood.
alverja [al'ßerxa] (*AM*) *nf* pea.
alza ['alθa] *nf* rise; (*MIL*) sight.
alzada [al'θaða] *nf* (*de caballos*) height; (*JUR*) appeal.
alzamiento [alθa'mjento] *nm* (*aumento*) rise, increase; (*acción*) lifting, raising; (*mejor postura*) higher bid; (*rebelión*) rising; (*COM*) fraudulent bankruptcy.
alzar [al'θar] *vt* to lift (up); (*precio, muro*) to raise; (*cuello de abrigo*) to turn up; (*AGR*) to gather in; (*IMPRENTA*) to gather; **~se** *vr* to get up, rise; (*rebelarse*) to revolt; (*COM*) to go fraudulently bankrupt; (*JUR*) to appeal.
allá [a'ʎa] *adv* (*lugar*) there; (*por ahí*) over there; (*tiempo*) then; **~ abajo** down there; **más ~** further on; **más ~ de** beyond; **¡~ tú!** that's your problem!
allanamiento [aʎana'mjento] *nm*: **~ de morada** burglary.
allanar [aʎa'nar] *vt* to flatten, level (out); (*igualar*) to smooth (out); (*fig*) to subdue; (*JUR*) to burgle, break into; **~se** *vr* to fall down; **~se a** to submit to, accept.
allegado, a [aʎe'ɣaðo, a] *adj* near, close ♦ *nm/f* relation.
allí [a'ʎi] *adv* there; **~ mismo** right there; **por ~** over there; (*por ese camino*) that way.
ama ['ama] *nf* lady of the house; (*dueña*) owner; (*institutriz*) governess; (*madre adoptiva*) foster mother; **~ de casa** housewife; **~ de cría** o **de leche** wet-nurse; **~ de llaves** housekeeper.
amabilidad [amaßili'ðað] *nf* kindness; (*simpatía*) niceness; **amable** *adj* kind; nice; **es usted muy amable** that's very kind of you.
amaestrado, a [amaes'traðo, a] *adj* (*animal: en circo etc*) performing.
amaestrar [amaes'trar] *vt* to train.
amagar [ama'ɣar] *vt, vi* to threaten; (*DEPORTE, MIL*) to feint; **amago** *nm* threat; (*gesto*) threatening gesture; (*MED*) symptom.
amalgama [amal'ɣama] *nf* amalgam; **amalgamar** *vt* to amalgamate;

(*combinar*) to combine, mix.

amamantar [amaman'tar] *vt* to suckle, nurse.

amanecer [amane'θer] *vi* to dawn ♦ *nm* dawn; ~ **afiebrado** to wake up with a fever.

amanerado, a [amane'raðo, a] *adj* affected.

amansar [aman'sar] *vt* to tame; (*persona*) to subdue; ~**se** *vr* (*persona*) to calm down.

amante [a'mante] *adj*: ~ **de** fond of ♦ *nm/f* lover.

amapola [ama'pola] *nf* poppy.

amar [a'mar] *vt* to love.

amarar [ama'rar] *vi* (*avión*) to land (on the sea).

amargado, a [amar'ɣaðo, a] *adj* bitter.

amargar [amar'ɣar] *vt* to make bitter; (*fig*) to embitter; ~**se** *vr* to become embittered.

amargo, a [a'marɣo, a] *adj* bitter; **amargura** *nf* bitterness.

amarillento, a [amari'ʎento, a] *adj* yellowish; (*tez*) sallow; **amarillo, a** *adj*, *nm* yellow.

amarrar [ama'rrar] *vt* to moor; (*sujetar*) to tie up.

amarras [a'marras] *nfpl*: **soltar** ~ to set sail.

amartillar [amarti'ʎar] *vt* (*fusil*) to cock.

amasar [ama'sar] *vt* (*masa*) to knead; (*mezclar*) to mix, prepare; (*confeccionar*) to concoct; **amasijo** *nm* kneading; mixing; (*fig*) hotchpotch.

amateur ['amatur] *nm/f* amateur.

amatista [ama'tista] *nf* amethyst.

amazona [ama'θona] *nf* horsewoman; **A~s** *nm*: **el A~s** the Amazon.

ambages [am'baxes] *nmpl*: **sin** ~ in plain language.

ámbar ['ambar] *nm* amber.

ambición [ambi'θjon] *nf* ambition; **ambicionar** *vt* to aspire to; **ambicioso, a** *adj* ambitious.

ambidextro, a [ambi'ðekstro, a] *adj* ambidextrous.

ambientación [ambjenta'θjon] *nf* (*CINE, TEATRO etc*) setting; (*RADIO*) sound effects.

ambiente [am'bjente] *nm* (*tb fig*) atmosphere; (*medio*) environment.

ambigüedad [ambiɣwe'ðað] *nf* ambiguity; **ambigüo, a** *adj* ambiguous.

ámbito ['ambito] *nm* (*campo*) field; (*fig*) scope.

ambos, as ['ambos, as] *adj pl, pron pl* both.

ambulancia [ambu'lanθja] *nf* ambulance.

ambulante [ambu'lante] *adj* travelling *cpd*, itinerant.

ambulatorio [ambula'torjo] *nm* state health-service clinic.

ameba [a'meßa] *nf* amoeba.

amedrentar [ameðren'tar] *vt* to scare.

amén [a'men] *excl* amen; ~ **de** besides.

amenaza [ame'naθa] *nf* threat.

amenazar [amena'θar] *vt* to threaten ♦ *vi*: ~ **con hacer** to threaten to do.

amenguar [amen'ɣwar] *vt* to diminish; (*fig*) to dishonour.

amenidad [ameni'ðað] *nf* pleasantness.

ameno, a [a'meno, a] *adj* pleasant.

América [a'merika] *nf* America; ~ **del Norte/del Sur** North/South America; ~ **Central/Latina** Central/Latin America; **americana** *nf* coat, jacket; *ver tb* **americano**; **americano, a** *adj*, *nm/f* American.

amerizar [ameri'θar] *vi* (*avión*) to land (on the sea).

ametralladora [ametraʎa'ðora] *nf* machine gun.

amianto [a'mjanto] *nm* asbestos.

amigable [ami'xaßle] *adj* friendly.

amígdala [a'miɣðala] *nf* tonsil; **amigdalitis** *nf* tonsillitis.

amigo, a [a'miɣo, a] *adj* friendly ♦ *nm/f* friend; (*amante*) lover; **ser** ~ **de algo** to be fond of sth; **ser muy** ~**s** to be close friends.

amilanar [amila'nar] *vt* to scare; ~**se** *vr* to get scared.

aminorar [amino'rar] *vt* to diminish; (*reducir*) to reduce; ~ **la marcha** to slow down.

amistad [amis'tað] *nf* friendship; ~**es** *nfpl* (*amigos*) friends; **amistoso, a** *adj* friendly.

amnesia [am'nesja] *nf* amnesia.

amnistía [amnis'tia] *nf* amnesty.

amo ['amo] *nm* owner; *(jefe)* boss.

amodorrarse [amoðo'rrarse] *vr* to get sleepy.

amolar [amo'lar] *vt* *(perseguir)* to annoy.

amoldar [amol'dar] *vt* to mould; *(adaptar)* to adapt.

amonestación [amonesta'θjon] *nf* warning; **amonestaciones** *nfpl* (REL) marriage banns.

amonestar [amones'tar] *vt* to warn; (REL) to publish the banns of.

amontonar [amonto'nar] *vt* to collect, pile up; ~**se** *vr* to crowd together; *(acumularse)* to pile up.

amor [a'mor] *nm* love; *(amante)* lover; **hacer el** ~ to make love.

amoratado, a [amora'taðo, a] *adj* purple.

amordazar [amorða'θar] *vt* to muzzle; *(fig)* to gag.

amorfo, a [a'morfo, a] *adj* amorphous, shapeless.

amorío [amo'rio] *(fam) nm* love affair.

amoroso, a [amo'roso, a] *adj* affectionate, loving.

amortajar [amorta'xar] *vt* to shroud.

amortiguador [amortigwa'ðor] *nm* shock absorber; *(parachoques)* bumper; ~**es** *nmpl* (AUTO) suspension *sg*.

amortiguar [amorti'ɣwar] *vt* to deaden; *(ruido)* to muffle; *(color)* to soften.

amortización [amortiθa'θjon] *nf* *(de deuda)* repayment; *(de bono)* redemption.

amotinar [amoti'nar] *vt* to stir up, incite (to riot); ~**se** *vr* to mutiny.

amparar [ampa'rar] *vt* to protect; ~**se.** *vr* to seek protection; *(de la lluvia etc)* to shelter; **amparo** *nm* help, protection; **al** ~ **de** under the protection of.

amperio [am'perjo] *nm* ampère, amp.

ampliación [amplja'θjon] *nf* enlargement; *(extensión)* extension.

ampliar [am'pljar] *vt* to enlarge; to extend.

amplificación [amplifika'θjon] *nf* enlargement; **amplificador** *nm* amplifier.

amplificar [amplifi'kar] *vt* to amplify.

amplio, a ['ampljo, a] *adj* spacious; *(de falda etc)* full; *(extenso)* extensive; *(ancho)* wide; **amplitud** *nf* spaciousness; extent; *(fig)* amplitude.

ampolla [am'poʎa] *nf* blister; (MED) ampoule.

ampuloso, a [ampu'loso, a] *adj* bombastic, pompous.

amputar [ampu'tar] *vt* to cut off, amputate.

amueblar [amwe'ßlar] *vt* to furnish.

amurallar [amura'ʎar] *vt* to wall up *o* in.

anacronismo [anakro'nismo] *nm* anachronism.

ánade ['anaðe] *nm* duck.

anadear [anaðe'ar] *vi* to waddle.

anales [a'nales] *nmpl* annals.

analfabetismo [analfaße'tismo] *nm* illiteracy; **analfabeto, a** *adj, nm/f* illiterate.

analgésico [anal'xesiko] *nm* painkiller, analgesic.

análisis [a'nalisis] *nm inv* analysis.

analista [ana'lista] *nm/f* *(gen)* analyst.

analizar [anali'θar] *vt* to analyse.

analogía [analo'xia] *nf* analogy.

analógico, a [ana'loxiko, a] *adj* (INFORM) analog; *(reloj)* analogue (BRIT), analog (US).

análogo, a [a'naloɣo, a] *adj* analogous, similar.

ananá(s) [ana'na(s)] *nm* pineapple.

anaquel [ana'kel] *nm* shelf.

anarquía [anar'kia] *nf* anarchy; **anarquismo** *nm* anarchism; **anarquista** *nm/f* anarchist.

anatomía [anato'mia] *nf* anatomy.

anca ['anka] *nf* rump, haunch; ~**s** *nfpl* *(fam)* behind *sg*.

anciano, a [an'θjano, a] *adj* old, aged ♦ *nm/f* old man/woman; elder.

ancla ['ankla] *nf* anchor; ~**dero** *nm* anchorage; **anclar** *vi* to (drop) anchor.

ancho, a ['antʃo, a] *adj* wide; *(falda)* full; *(fig)* liberal ♦ *nm* width; (FERRO) gauge; **ponerse** ~ to get conceited; **estar a sus anchas** to be at one's ease.

anchoa [an'tʃoa] *nf* anchovy.

anchura [an'tʃura] *nf* width; *(extensión)* wideness.

andaderas [anda'ðeras] *nfpl* baby walker *sg*.

andadura [anda'ðura] *nf* gait; (*de caballo*) pace.

Andalucía [andalu'θia] *nf* Andalusia; **andaluz, a** *adj, nm/f* Andalusian.

andamiaje [anda'mjaxe] *nm* = **andamio**.

andamio [an'damjo] *nm* scaffold(ing).

andar [an'dar] *vt* to go, cover, travel ♦ *vi* to go, walk, travel; (*funcionar*) to go, work; (*estar*) to be ♦ *nm* walk, gait, pace; ~**se** *vr* to go away; ~ **a pie/a caballo/en bicicleta** to go on foot/on horseback/by bicycle; ~ **haciendo algo** to be doing sth; **¡anda!** (*sorpresa*) go on!; **anda por** *o* **en los 40** he's about 40.

andariego, a [anda'rjeɣo, a] *adj* (*itinerante*) wandering.

andén [an'den] *nm* (*FERRO*) platform; (*NAUT*) quayside; (*AM: de la calle*) pavement (*BRIT*), sidewalk (*US*).

Andes ['andes] *nmpl*: **los** ~ the Andes.

Andorra [an'dorra] *nf* Andorra.

andrajo [an'draxo] *nm* rag; ~**so, a** *adj* ragged.

andurriales [andu'rrjales] *nmpl* wilds.

anduve *etc* [an'duße] *vb ver* **andar**.

anécdota [a'nekðota] *nf* anecdote, story.

anegar [ane'ɣar] *vt* to flood; (*ahogar*) to drown; ~**se** *vr* to drown; (*hundirse*) to sink.

anejo, a [a'nexo, a] *adj, nm* = **anexo**.

anemia [a'nemja] *nf* anaemia.

anestésico [anes'tesiko] *nm* anaesthetic.

anexar [anek'sar] *vt* to annex; (*documento*) to attach; **anexión** *nf* annexation; **anexionamiento** *nm* annexation; **anexo, a** *adj* attached ♦ *nm* annexe.

anfibio, a [an'fißjo, a] *adj* amphibious ♦ *nm* amphibian.

anfiteatro [anfite'atro] *nm* amphitheatre; (*TEATRO*) dress circle.

anfitrión, ona [anfi'trjon, ona] *nm/f* host(ess).

ángel ['anxel] *nm* angel; ~ **de la guarda** guardian angel; **tener** ~ to be charming; **angélico, a** *adj* angelic(al); **angelical** *adj* angelic(al).

angina [an'xina] *nf* (*MED*) inflammation

of the throat; ~ **de pecho** angina; **tener** ~**s** to have tonsillitis.

anglicano, a [angli'kano, a] *adj, nm/f* Anglican.

angosto, a [an'gosto, a] *adj* narrow.

anguila [an'gila] *nf* eel; ~**s** *nfpl* (*NAUT*) slipway *sg*.

angula [an'gula] *nf* elver, baby eel.

ángulo ['angulo] *nm* angle; (*esquina*) corner; (*curva*) bend.

angustia [an'gustja] *nf* anguish; **angustiar** *vt* to distress, grieve.

anhelante [ane'lante] *adj* eager; (*deseoso*) longing.

anhelar [ane'lar] *vt* to be eager for; (*desear*) to long for, desire ♦ *vi* to pant, gasp; **anhelo** *nm* eagerness; desire.

anidar [ani'ðar] *vi* to nest.

anillo [a'niʎo] *nm* ring; ~ **de boda** wedding ring.

ánima ['anima] *nf* soul; **las** ~**s** the Angelus (bell) *sg*.

animación [anima'θjon] *nf* liveliness; (*vitalidad*) life; (*actividad*) activity; bustle.

animado, a [ani'maðo, a] *adj* lively; (*vivaz*) animated; **animador, a** *nm/f* (*TV*) host(ess), compère; (*DEPORTE*) cheerleader.

animadversión [animaðßer'sjon] *nf* illwill, antagonism.

animal [ani'mal] *adj* animal; (*fig*) stupid ♦ *nm* animal; (*fig*) fool; (*bestia*) brute.

animar [ani'mar] *vt* (*BIO*) to animate, give life to; (*fig*) to liven up, brighten up, cheer up; (*estimular*) to stimulate; ~**se** *vr* to cheer up; to feel encouraged; (*decidirse*) to make up one's mind.

ánimo ['animo] *nm* (*alma*) soul; (*mente*) mind; (*valentía*) courage ♦ *excl* cheer up!

animoso, a [ani'moso, a] *adj* brave; (*vivo*) lively.

aniquilar [aniki'lar] *vt* to annihilate, destroy.

anís [a'nis] *nm* aniseed; (*licor*) anisette.

aniversario [anißer'sarjo] *nm* anniversary.

anoche [a'notʃe] *adv* last night; **antes de** ~ the night before last.

anochecer [anotʃe'θer] *vi* to get dark ♦ *nm* nightfall, dark; **al** ~ at nightfall.
anodino, a [ano'ðino, a] *adj* dull, anodyne.
anomalía [anoma'lia] *nf* anomaly.
anonimato [anoni'mato] *nm* anonymity.
anónimo, a [a'nonimo, a] *adj* anonymous; (COM) limited ♦ *nm* (carta) anonymous letter; (: maliciosa) poison-pen letter.
anormal [anor'mal] *adj* abnormal.
anotación [anota'θjon] *nf* note; annotation.
anotar [ano'tar] *vt* to note down; (comentar) to annotate.
anquilosamiento [ankilosa'mjento] *nm* (fig) paralysis; stagnation.
ansia ['ansja] *nf* anxiety; (añoranza) yearning; **ansiar** *vt* to long for.
ansiedad [ansje'ðað] *nf* anxiety.
ansioso, a [an'sjoso, a] *adj* anxious; (anhelante) eager; ~ **de** *o* **por algo** greedy for sth.
antagónico, a [anta'ɣoniko, a] *adj* antagonistic; (opuesto) contrasting; **antagonista** *nm/f* antagonist.
antaño [an'taɲo] *adv* long ago, formerly.
Antártico [an'tartiko] *nm*: **el** ~ the Antarctic.
ante ['ante] *prep* before, in the presence of; (problema etc) faced with ♦ *nm* (piel) suede; ~ **todo** above all.
anteanoche [antea'notʃe] *adv* the night before last.
anteayer [antea'jer] *adv* the day before yesterday.
antebrazo [ante'ßraðo] *nm* forearm.
antecedente [anteθe'ðente] *adj* previous ♦ *nm* antecedent; ~**s** *nmpl* (JUR): ~**s penales** criminal record; (procedencia) background.
anteceder [anteθe'ðer] *vt* to precede, go before.
antecesor, a [anteθe'sor, a] *nm/f* predecessor.
antedicho, a [ante'ðitʃo, a] *adj* aforementioned.
antelación [antela'θjon] *nf*: **con** ~ in advance.

antemano [ante'mano]: **de** ~ *adv* beforehand, in advance.
antena [an'tena] *nf* antenna; (de televisión etc) aerial.
anteojo [ante'oxo] *nm* eyeglass; ~**s** *nmpl* (AM) glasses, spectacles.
antepasados [antepa'saðos] *nmpl* ancestors.
antepecho [ante'petʃo] *nm* guardrail, parapet; (repisa) ledge, sill.
anteponer [antepo'ner] *vt* to place in front; (fig) to prefer.
anteproyecto [antepro'jekto] *nm* preliminary sketch; (fig) blueprint.
anterior [ante'rjor] *adj* preceding, previous; ~**idad** *nf*: **con** ~**idad a** prior to, before.
antes ['antes] *adv* (con prioridad) before ♦ *prep*: ~ **de** before ♦ *conj*: ~ **de** **ir/de que te vayas** before going/before you go; ~ **bien** (but) rather; **dos días** ~ two days before *o* previously; **no quiso venir** ~ she didn't want to come any earlier; **tomo el avión** ~ **que el barco** I take the plane rather than the boat; ~ **que yo** before me; **lo** ~ **posible** as soon as possible; **cuanto** ~ **mejor** the sooner the better.
antesala [ante'sala] *nf* anteroom.
antiaéreo, a [antia'ereo, a] *adj* antiaircraft.
antibalas [anti'ßalas] *adj inv*: **chaleco** ~ bullet-proof jacket.
antibiótico [anti'ßjotiko] *nm* antibiotic.
anticiclón [antiθi'klon] *nm* anticyclone.
anticipación [antiθipa'θjon] *nf* anticipation; **con 10 minutos de** ~ 10 minutes early.
anticipado, a [antiθi'paðo, a] *adj* (pago) advance; **por** ~ in advance.
anticipar [antiθi'par] *vt* to anticipate; (adelantar) to bring forward; (COM) to advance; ~**se** *vr*: ~**se a su época** to be ahead of one's time.
anticipo [anti'θipo] *nm* (COM) advance.
anticonceptivo, a [antikonθep'tißo, a] *adj, nm* contraceptive.
anticongelante [antikonxe'lante] *nm* antifreeze.
anticuado, a [anti'kwaðo, a] *adj* out-of-

date, old-fashioned; (*desusado*) obsolete.

anticuario [anti'kwarjo] *nm* antique dealer.

anticuerpo [anti'kwerpo] *nm* (*MED*) antibody.

antídoto [an'tiðoto] *nm* antidote.

antiestético, a [anties'tetiko, a] *adj* unsightly.

antifaz [anti'faθ] *nm* mask; (*velo*) veil.

antigualla [anti'ɣwaʎa] *nf* antique; (*reliquia*) relic.

antiguamente [antiɣwa'mente] *adv* formerly; (*hace mucho tiempo*) long ago.

antigüedad [antiɣwe'ðað] *nf* antiquity; (*artículo*) antique; (*rango*) seniority.

antiguo, a [an'tiɣwo, a] *adj* old, ancient; (*que fue*) former.

antílope [an'tilope] *nm* antelope.

antillano, a [anti'ʎano, a] *adj, nm/f* West Indian.

Antillas [an'tiʎas] *nfpl*: **las ~** the West Indies.

antinatural [antinatu'ral] *adj* unnatural.

antipatía [antipa'tia] *nf* antipathy, dislike; **antipático, a** *adj* disagreeable, unpleasant.

antirrobo [anti'rroβo] *adj inv* (*alarma etc*) anti-theft.

antisemita [antise'mita] *adj* anti-Semitic ♦ *nm/f* anti-Semite.

antiséptico, a [anti'septiko, a] *adj* antiseptic ♦ *nm* antiseptic.

antítesis [an'titesis] *nf inv* antithesis.

antojadizo, a [antoxa'ðiθo, a] *adj* capricious.

antojarse [anto'xarse] *vr* (*desear*): **se me antoja comprarlo** I have a mind to buy it; (*pensar*): **se me antoja que** I have a feeling that.

antojo [an'toxo] *nm* caprice, whim; (*rosa*) birthmark; (*lunar*) mole.

antología [antolo'xia] *nf* anthology.

antorcha [an'tortʃa] *nf* torch.

antro ['antro] *nm* cavern.

antropófago, a [antro'pofaɣo, a] *adj, nm/f* cannibal.

antropología [antropolo'xia] *nf* anthropology.

anual [a'nwal] *adj* annual; **~idad** *nf* annuity.

anuario [a'nwarjo] *nm* yearbook.

anudar [anu'ðar] *vt* to knot, tie; (*unir*) to join; **~se** *vr* to get tied up.

anulación [anula'θjon] *nf* annulment; (*cancelación*) cancellation.

anular [anu'lar] *vt* (*contrato*) to annul, cancel; (*ley*) to revoke, repeal; (*suscripción*) to cancel ♦ *nm* ring finger.

anunciación [anunθja'θjon] *nf* announcement; (*REL*): **A~** Annunciation.

anunciante [anun'θjante] *nm/f* (*COM*) advertiser.

anunciar [anun'θjar] *vt* to announce; (*proclamar*) to proclaim; (*COM*) to advertise.

anuncio [a'nunθjo] *nm* announcement; (*señal*) sign; (*COM*) advertisement; (*cartel*) poster.

anzuelo [an'θwelo] *nm* hook; (*para pescar*) fish hook.

añadidura [aɲaði'ðura] *nf* addition, extra; **por ~** besides, in addition.

añadir [aɲa'ðir] *vt* to add.

añejo, a [a'ɲexo, a] *adj* old; (*vino*) mellow.

añicos [a'ɲikos] *nmpl*: **hacer ~** to smash, shatter.

añil [a'ɲil] *nm* (*BOT, color*) indigo.

año ['aɲo] *nm* year; **¡Feliz A~ Nuevo!** Happy New Year!; **tener 15 ~s** to be 15 (years old); **los ~s 90** the nineties; **~ bisiesto/escolar** leap/school year; **el ~ que viene** next year.

añoranza [aɲo'ranθa] *nf* nostalgia; (*anhelo*) longing.

apabullar [apaβu'ʎar] *vt* (*tb fig*) to crush, squash.

apacentar [apaθen'tar] *vt* to pasture, graze.

apacible [apa'θiβle] *adj* gentle, mild.

apaciguar [apaθi'ɣwar] *vt* to pacify, calm (down).

apadrinar [apaðri'nar] *vt* to sponsor, support; (*REL*) to be godfather to.

apagado, a [apa'ɣaðo, a] *adj* (*volcán*) extinct; (*color*) dull; (*voz*) quiet; (*sonido*) muted, muffled; (*persona: apático*) listless; **estar ~** (*fuego, luz*) to be out; (*RADIO*, *TV etc*) to be off.

apagar [apa'ɣar] *vt* to put out; (*ELEC*, *RADIO*, *TV*) to turn off; (*sonido*) to silence, muffle; (*sed*) to quench.

apagón [apa'ɣon] *nm* blackout; power cut.

apalabrar [apala'βrar] *vt* to agree to; (*contratar*) to engage.

apalear [apale'ar] *vt* to beat, thrash; (*AGR*) to winnow.

apañar [apa'ɲar] *vt* to pick up; (*asir*) to take hold of, grasp; (*reparar*) to mend, patch up; ~**se** *vr* to manage, get along.

aparador [apara'ðor] *nm* sideboard; (*escaparate*) shop window.

aparato [apa'rato] *nm* apparatus; (*máquina*) machine; (*doméstico*) appliance; (*boato*) ostentation; ~ **de facsímil** facsimile (machine), fax; ~**so, a** *adj* showy, ostentatious.

aparcamiento [aparka'mjento] *nm* car park (*BRIT*), parking lot (*US*).

aparcar [apar'kar] *vt*, *vi* to park.

aparear [apare'ar] *vt* (*objetos*) to pair, match; (*animales*) to mate; ~**se** *vr* to make a pair; to mate.

aparecer [apare'θer] *vi* to appear; ~**se** *vr* to appear.

aparejado, a [apare'xaðo, a] *adj* fit, suitable; **llevar** *o* **traer** ~ to involve.

aparejo [apa'rexo] *nm* preparation; harness; rigging; (*de poleas*) block and tackle.

aparentar [aparen'tar] *vt* (*edad*) to look; (*fingir*): ~ **tristeza** to pretend to be sad.

aparente [apa'rente] *adj* apparent; (*adecuado*) suitable.

aparezco *etc vb ver* **aparecer**.

aparición [apari'θjon] *nf* appearance; (*de libro*) publication; (*espectro*) apparition.

apariencia [apa'rjenθja] *nf* (outward) appearance; **en** ~ outwardly, seemingly.

apartado, a [apar'taðo, a] *adj* separate; (*lejano*) remote ♦ *nm* (*tipográfico*) paragraph; ~ **(de correos)** post office box.

apartamento [aparta'mento] *nm* apartment, flat (*BRIT*).

apartamiento [aparta'mjento] *nm* separation; (*aislamiento*) remoteness, isolation; (*AM*) apartment, flat (*BRIT*).

apartar [apar'tar] *vt* to separate; (*quitar*) to remove; (*MINEROLOGÍA*) to extract; ~**se** *vr* to separate, part; (*irse*) to move away; to keep away.

aparte [a'parte] *adv* (*separadamente*) separately; (*además*) besides ♦ *nm* aside; (*tipográfico*) new paragraph.

apasionado, a [apasjo'naðo, a] *adj* passionate; biassed, prejudiced.

apasionar [apasjo'nar] *vt* to excite; **le apasiona el fútbol** she's crazy about football; ~**se** *vr* to get excited.

apatía [apa'tia] *nf* apathy.

apático, a [a'patiko, a] *adj* apathetic.

apátrida [a'patrida] *adj* stateless.

Apdo *abr* (= *Apartado (de Correos)*) PO Box.

apeadero [apea'ðero] *nm* halt, stop, stopping place.

apearse [ape'arse] *vr* (*jinete*) to dismount; (*bajarse*) to get down *o* out; (*AUTO*, *FERRO*) to get off *o* out.

apechugar [apetʃu'ɣar] *vr*: ~ **con algo** to face up to sth.

apedrear [apeðre'ar] *vt* to stone.

apegarse [ape'ɣarse] *vr*: ~ **a** to become attached to; **apego** *nm* attachment, devotion.

apelación [apela'θjon] *nf* appeal.

apelar [ape'lar] *vi* to appeal; ~ **a** (*fig*) to resort to.

apellidar [apeʎi'ðar] *vt* to call, name; ~**se** *vr*: **se apellida Pérez** her (sur)name's Pérez.

apellido [ape'ʎiðo] *nm* surname.

apenar [ape'nar] *vt* to grieve, trouble; (*AM*: *avergonzar*) to embarrass; ~**se** *vr* to grieve; (*AM*) to be embarrassed.

apenas [a'penas] *adv* scarcely, hardly ♦ *conj* as soon as, no sooner.

apéndice [a'pendiθe] *nm* appendix; **apendicitis** *nf* appendicitis.

apercibirse [aperθi'βirse] *vr*: ~ **de** to notice.

aperitivo [aperi'tiβo] *nm* (*bebida*) aperitif; (*comida*) appetizer.

apero [a'pero] *nm* (*AGR*) implement; ~**s**

nmpl farm equipment *sg*.

apertura [aper'tura] *nf* opening; (*POL*) liberalization.

apesadumbrar [apesaðum'brar] *vt* to grieve, sadden; ~**se** *vr* to distress o.s.

apestar [apes'tar] *vt* to infect ♦ *vi*: ~ (a) to stink (of).

apetecer [apete'θer] *vt*: ¿te apetece un café? do you fancy a (cup of) coffee?; **apetecible** *adj* desirable; (*comida*) appetizing.

apetito [ape'tito] *nm* appetite; ~**so, a** *adj* appetizing; (*fig*) tempting.

apiadarse [apja'ðarse] *vr*: ~ de to take pity on.

ápice ['apiθe] *nm* apex; (*fig*) whit, iota.

apilar [api'lar] *vt* to pile *o* heap up; ~**se** *vr* to pile up.

apiñarse [api'narse] *vr* to crowd *o* press together.

apio ['apjo] *nm* celery.

apisonadora [apisona'ðora] *nf* (*máquina*) steamroller.

aplacar [apla'kar] *vt* to placate; ~**se** *vr* to calm down.

aplanar [apla'nar] *vt* to smooth, level; (*allanar*) to roll flat, flatten.

aplastar [aplas'tar] *vt* to squash (flat); (*fig*) to crush.

aplatanarse [aplata'narse] *vr* to get lethargic.

aplaudir [aplau'ðir] *vt* to applaud.

aplauso [a'plauso] *nm* applause; (*fig*) approval, acclaim.

aplazamiento [aplaθa'mjento] *nm* postponement.

aplazar [apla'θar] *vt* to postpone, defer.

aplicación [aplika'θjon] *nf* application; (*esfuerzo*) effort.

aplicado, a [apli'kaðo, a] *adj* diligent, hard-working.

aplicar [apli'kar] *vt* (*ejecutar*) to apply; ~**se** *vr* to apply o.s.

aplique *etc* [a'plike] *vb ver* **aplicar** ♦ *nm* wall light.

aplomo [a'plomo] *nm* aplomb, self-assurance.

apocado, a [apo'kaðo, a] *adj* timid.

apocamiento [apoka'mjento] *nm* timidity; (*depresión*) depression.

apocarse [apo'karse] *vr* to feel small *o* humiliated.

apodar [apo'ðar] *vt* to nickname.

apoderado [apoðe'raðo] *nm* agent, representative.

apoderar [apoðe'rar] *vt* to authorize, empower; (*JUR*) to grant (a) power of attorney to; ~**se** *vr*: ~**se de** to take possession of.

apodo [a'poðo] *nm* nickname.

apogeo [apo'xeo] *nm* peak, summit.

apolillarse [apoli'Aarse] *vr* to get moth-eaten.

apología [apolo'xia] *nf* eulogy; (*defensa*) defence.

apoltronarse [apoltro'narse] *vr* to get lazy.

apoplejía [aople'xia] *nf* apoplexy, stroke.

apoquinar [apoki'nar] (*fam*) *vt* to fork out, cough up.

aporrear [aporre'ar] *vt* to beat (up).

aportar [apor'tar] *vt* to contribute ♦ *vi* to reach port; ~**se** *vr* (*AM: llegar*) to arrive, come.

aposentar [aposen'tar] *vt* to lodge, put up; **aposento** *nm* lodging; (*habitación*) room.

apósito [a'posito] *nm* (*MED*) dressing.

apostar [apos'tar] *vt* to bet, stake; (*tropas etc*) to station, post ♦ *vi* to bet.

apostilla [apos'tiΛa] *nf* note, comment.

apóstol [a'postol] *nm* apostle.

apóstrofo [a'postrofo] *nm* apostrophe.

apostura [apos'tura] *nf* neatness; (*elegancia*) elegance.

apoyar [apo'jar] *vt* to lean, rest; (*fig*) to support, back; ~**se** *vr*: ~**se en** to lean on; **apoyo** *nm* (*gen*) support; backing, help.

apreciable [apre'θjaβle] *adj* considerable; (*fig*) esteemed.

apreciación [apreθja'θjon] *nf* appreciation; (*COM*) valuation.

apreciar [apre'θjar] *vt* to evaluate, assess; (*COM*) to appreciate, value.

aprecio [a'preθjo] *nm* valuation, estimate; (*fig*) appreciation.

aprehender [apreen'der] *vt* to apprehend, detain; **aprehensión** *nf* detention, capture.

apremiante [apre'mjante] *adj* urgent, pressing.

apremiar [apre'mjar] *vt* to compel, force ♦ *vi* to be urgent, press; **apremio** *nm* urgency.

aprender [apren'der] *vt, vi* to learn.

aprendiz, a [apren'diθ, a] *nm/f* apprentice; (*principiante*) learner; ~ **de conductor** learner driver; ~**aje** *nm* apprenticeship.

aprensión [apren'sjon] *nm* apprehension, fear; **aprensivo, a** *adj* apprehensive.

apresar [apre'sar] *vt* to seize; (*capturar*) to capture.

aprestar [apres'tar] *vt* to prepare, get ready; (*TEC*) to prime, size; ~**se** *vr* to get ready.

apresurado, a [apresu'raðo, a] *adj* hurried, hasty; **apresuramiento** *nm* hurry, haste.

apresurar [apresu'rar] *vt* to hurry, accelerate; ~**se** *vr* to hurry, make haste.

apretado, a [apre'taðo, a] *adj* tight; (*escritura*) cramped.

apretar [apre'tar] *vt* to squeeze; (*TEC*) to tighten; (*presionar*) to press together, pack ♦ *vi* to be too tight.

apretón [apre'ton] *nm* squeeze; ~ **de manos** handshake.

aprieto [a'prjeto] *nm* squeeze; (*dificultad*) difficulty; **estar en un** ~ **to** be in a fix.

aprisa [a'prisa] *adv* quickly, hurriedly.

aprisionar [aprisjo'nar] *vt* to imprison.

aprobación [aproßa'θjon] *nf* approval.

aprobar [apro'ßar] *vt* to approve (of); (*examen, materia*) to pass ♦ *vi* to pass.

apropiación [apropja'θjon] *nf* appropriation.

apropiado, a [apro'pjaðo, a] *adj* appropriate.

apropiarse [apro'pjarse] *vr*: ~ **de** to appropriate.

aprovechado, a [aproße'tʃaðo, a] *adj* industrious, hard-working; (*económico*) thrifty; (*pey*) unscrupulous; **aprovechamiento** *nm* use; exploitation.

aprovechar [aproße'tʃar] *vt* to use;

(*explotar*) to exploit; (*experiencia*) to profit from; (*oferta, oportunidad*) to take advantage of ♦ *vi* to progress, improve; ~**se** *vr*: ~**se de** to make use of; to take advantage of; ¡**que aproveche!** enjoy your meal!

aproximación [aproksima'θjon] *nf* approximation; (*de lotería*) consolation prize; **aproximado, a** *adj* approximate.

aproximar [aproksi'mar] *vt* to bring nearer; ~**se** *vr* to come near, approach.

apruebo *etc vb ver* **aprobar**.

aptitud [apti'tuð] *nf* aptitude.

apto, a ['apto, a] *adj* suitable.

apuesta [a'pwesta] *nf* bet, wager.

apuesto, a [a'pwesto, a] *adj* neat, elegant.

apuntador [apunta'ðor] *nm* prompter.

apuntalar [apunta'lar] *vt* to prop up.

apuntar [apun'tar] *vt* (*con arma*) to aim at; (*con dedo*) to point at o to; (*anotar*) to note (down); (*TEATRO*) to prompt; ~**se** *vr* (*DEPORTE*: *tanto, victoria*) to score; (*ESCOL*) to enrol.

apunte [a'punte] *nm* note.

apuñalar [apuɲa'lar] *vt* to stab.

apurado, a [apu'raðo, a] *adj* needy; (*difícil*) difficult; (*peligroso*) dangerous; (*AM*) hurried, rushed.

apurar [apu'rar] *vt* (*agotar*) to drain; (*recursos*) to use up; (*molestar*) to annoy; ~**se** *vr* (*preocuparse*) to worry; (*darse prisa*) to hurry.

apuro [a'puro] *nm* (*aprieto*) fix, jam; (*escasez*) want, hardship; (*vergüenza*) embarrassment; (*AM*) haste, urgency.

aquejado, a [ake'xaðo, a] *adj*: ~ **de** (*MED*) afflicted by.

aquel, aquella [a'kel, a'keʎa] (*pl* **aquellos, as**) *adj* that; (*pl*) those.

aquél, aquélla [a'kel, a'keʎa] (*pl* **aquéllos, as**) *pron* that (one); (*pl*) those (ones).

aquello [a'keʎo] *pron* that, that business.

aquí [a'ki] *adv* (*lugar*) here; (*tiempo*) now; ~ **arriba** up here; ~ **mismo** right here; ~ **yace** here lies; **de** ~ **a siete días** a week from now.

aquietar [akje'tar] *vt* to quieten (down),

calm (down).

ara ['ara] *nf:* **en ~s de** for the sake of.

árabe ['araβe] *adj, nm/f* Arab ♦ *nm* (*LING*) Arabic.

Arabia [a'raβja] *nf:* ~ **Saudí** o **Saudita** Saudi Arabia.

arado [a'raðo] *nm* plough.

Aragón [ara'von] *nm* Aragon; **aragonés, esa** *adj, nm/f* Aragonese.

arancel [aran'θel] *nm* tariff, duty; ~ **de aduanas** customs (duty).

arandela [aran'dela] *nf* (*TEC*) washer.

araña [a'raɲa] *nf* (*ZOOL*) spider; (*lámpara*) chandelier.

arañar [ara'ɲar] *vt* to scratch.

arañazo [ara'ɲaθo] *nm* scratch.

arar [a'rar] *vt* to plough, till.

arbitraje [arβi'traxe] *nm* arbitration.

arbitrar [arβi'trar] *vt* to arbitrate in; (*DEPORTE*) to referee ♦ *vi* to arbitrate.

arbitrariedad [arβitrarje'ðað] *nf* arbitrariness; (*acto*) arbitrary act; **arbitrario, a** *adj* arbitrary.

arbitrio [ar'βitrjo] *nm* free will; (*JUR*) adjudication, decision.

árbitro ['arβitro] *nm* arbitrator; (*DEPORTE*) referee; (*TENIS*) umpire.

árbol ['arβol] *nm* (*BOT*) tree; (*NAUT*) mast; (*TEC*) axle, shaft; **arbolado, a** *adj* wooded; (*camino etc*) tree-lined ♦ *nm* woodland.

arboladura [arβola'ðura] *nf* rigging.

arbolar [arβo'lar] *vt* to hoist, raise.

arboleda [arβo'leða] *nf* grove, plantation.

arbusto [ar'βusto] *nm* bush, shrub.

arca ['arka] *nf* chest, box.

arcada [ar'kaða] *nf* arcade; (*de puente*) arch, span; ~**s** *nfpl* (*náuseas*) retching *sg*.

arcaico, a [ar'kaiko, a] *adj* archaic.

arce ['arθe] *nm* maple tree.

arcén [ar'θen] *nm* (*de autopista*) hard shoulder; (*de carretera*) verge.

arcilla [ar'θiʎa] *nf* clay.

arco ['arko] *nm* arch; (*MAT*) arc; (*MIL, MUS*) bow; ~ **iris** rainbow.

archipiélago [artʃi'pjelaxo] *nm* archipelago.

archivador [artʃiβa'ðor] *nm* filing

cabinet.

archivar [artʃi'βar] *vt* to file (away); **archivo** *nm* file, archive(s) (*pl*).

arder [ar'ðer] *vi* to burn; **estar que arde** (*persona*) to fume.

ardid [ar'ðið] *nm* ploy, trick.

ardiente [ar'ðjente] *adj* burning, ardent.

ardilla [ar'ðiʎa] *nf* squirrel.

ardor [ar'ðor] *nm* (*calor*) heat; (*fig*) ardour; ~ **de estómago** heartburn.

arduo, a ['arðwo, a] *adj* arduous.

área ['area] *nf* area; (*DEPORTE*) penalty area.

arena [a'rena] *nf* sand; (*de una lucha*) arena.

arenal [are'nal] *nm* (*arena movediza*) quicksand.

arengar [aren'gar] *vt* to harangue.

arenisca [are'niska] *nf* sandstone; (*cascajo*) grit.

arenoso, a [are'noso, a] *adj* sandy.

arenque [a'renke] *nm* herring.

arete [a'rete] *nm* earring.

argamasa [arva'masa] *nf* mortar, plaster.

Argel [ar'xel] *n* Algiers; ~**ia** *nf* Algeria; **argelino, a** *adj, nm/f* Algerian.

Argentina [arxen'tina] *nf:* **(la) A~** Argentina.

argentino, a [arxen'tino, a] *adj* Argentinian; (*de plata*) silvery ♦ *nm/f* Argentinian.

argolla [ar'voʎa] *nf* (large) ring.

argot [ar'vo] (*pl* ~**s**) *nm* slang.

argucia [ar'vuθja] *nf* subtlety, sophistry.

argüir [ar'vwir] *vt* to deduce; (*discutir*) to argue; (*indicar*) to indicate, imply; (*censurar*) to reproach ♦ *vi* to argue.

argumentación [arvumenta'θjon] *nf* (line of) argument.

argumentar [arvumen'tar] *vt, vi* to argue.

argumento [arvu'mento] *nm* argument; (*razonamiento*) reasoning; (*de novela etc*) plot; (*CINE, TV*) storyline.

aria ['arja] *nf* aria.

aridez [ari'ðeθ] *nf* aridity, dryness.

árido, a ['ariðo, a] *adj* arid, dry; ~**s** *nmpl* (*COM*) dry goods.

Aries ['arjes] *nm* Aries.

ariete [a'rjete] *nm* battering ram.

ario, a ['arjo, a] *adj* Aryan.

arisco, a [a'risko, a] *adj* surly; *(insocia-• ble)* unsociable.

aristócrata [aris'tokrata] *nm/f* aristocrat.

aritmética [arit'metika] *nf* arithmetic.

arma ['arma] *nf* arm; ~**s** *nfpl* arms; ~ **blanca** blade, knife; *(espada)* sword; ~ **de fuego** firearm; ~**s cortas** small arms.

armada [ar'maða] *nf* armada; *(flota)* fleet.

armadillo [arma'ðiʎo] *nm* armadillo.

armado, a [ar'maðo, a] *adj* armed; *(TEC)* reinforced.

armadura [arma'ðura] *nf* (*MIL*) armour; *(TEC)* framework; (*ZOOL*) skeleton; *(FÍSICA)* armature.

armamento [arma'mento] *nm* armament; *(NAUT)* fitting-out.

armar [ar'mar] *vt* (*soldado*) to arm; (*máquina*) to assemble; *(navío)* to fit out; ~**la, ~ un lío** to start a row, kick up a fuss.

armario [ar'marjo] *nm* wardrobe.

armatoste [arma'toste] *nm* (*mueble*) monstrosity; *(máquina)* contraption.

armazón [arma'θon] *nf o m* body, chassis; *(de mueble etc)* frame; *(ARQ)* skeleton.

armería [arme'ria] *nf* (*museo*) military museum; *(tienda)* gunsmith's.

armiño [ar'miɲo] *nm* stoat; *(piel)* ermine.

armisticio [armis'tiθjo] *nm* armistice.

armonía [armo'nia] *nf* harmony.

armónica [ar'monika] *nf* harmonica.

armonioso, a [armo'njoso, a] *adj* harmonious.

armonizar [armoni'θar] *vt* to harmonize; *(diferencias)* to reconcile ♦ *vi*: ~ **con** *(fig)* to be in keeping with; *(colores)* to tone in with, blend.

arnés [ar'nes] *nm* armour; **arneses** *nmpl* *(de caballo etc)* harness *sg*.

aro ['aro] *nm* ring; *(tejo)* quoit; *(AM: pendiente)* earring.

aroma [a'roma] *nm* aroma, scent.

aromático, a [aro'matiko, a] *adj* aromatic.

arpa ['arpa] *nf* harp.

arpía [ar'pia] *nf* shrew.

arpillera [arpi'ʎera] *nf* sacking, sackcloth.

arpón [ar'pon] *nm* harpoon.

arquear [arke'ar] *vt* to arch, bend; ~**se** *vr* to arch, bend; **arqueo** *nm* (*gen*) arching; *(NAUT)* tonnage.

arqueología [arkeolo'xia] *nf* archaeology; **arqueólogo, a** *nm/f* archaeologist.

arquero [ar'kero] *nm* archer, bowman.

arquetipo [arke'tipo] *nm* archetype.

arquitecto [arki'tekto] *nm* architect; **arquitectura** *nf* architecture.

arrabal [arra'ßal] *nm* suburb; *(AM)* slum; ~**es** *nmpl* *(afueras)* outskirts.

arraigado, a [arrai'yaðo, a] *adj* deeprooted; *(fig)* established.

arraigar [arrai'var] *vt* to establish ♦ *vi* to take root; ~**se** *vr* to take root; *(persona)* to settle.

arrancar [arran'kar] *vt* (*sacar*) to extract, pull out; *(arrebatar)* to snatch (away); *(INFORM)* to boot; *(fig)* to extract ♦ *vi* (*AUTO, máquina*) to start; *(ponerse en marcha)* to get going; ~ **de** to stem from.

arranque *etc* [a'rranke] *vb ver* **arrancar** ♦ *nm* sudden start; *(AUTO)* start; *(fig)* fit, outburst.

arras ['arras] *nfpl* pledge *sg*, security *sg*.

arrasar [arra'sar] *vt* (*aplanar*) to level, flatten; *(destruir)* to demolish.

arrastrado, a [arras'traðo, a] *adj* poor, wretched; *(AM)* servile.

arrastrar [arras'trar] *vt* to drag (along); *(fig)* to drag down, degrade; *(suj: agua, viento)* to carry away ♦ *vi* to drag, trail on the ground; ~**se** *vr* to crawl; *(fig)* to grovel; **llevar algo arrastrado** to drag sth along.

arrastre [a'rrastre] *nm* drag, dragging.

arrayán [arra'jan] *nm* myrtle.

arre ['arre] *excl* gee up!

arrear [arre'ar] *vt* to drive on, urge on ♦ *vi* to hurry along.

arrebatado, a [arreßa'taðo, a] *adj* rash, impetuous; *(repentino)* sudden, hasty.

arrebatar [arreßa'tar] *vt* to snatch (away), seize; *(fig)* to captivate; ~**se**

vr to get carried away, get excited.
arrebato [arre'βato] *nm* fit of rage, fury; (*éxtasis*) rapture.
arreglado, a [arre'ɣlaðo, a] *adj* (*ordenado*) neat, orderly; (*moderado*) moderate, reasonable.
arreglar [arre'ɣlar] *vt* (*poner orden*) to tidy up; (*algo roto*) to fix, repair; (*problema*) to solve; ~**se** *vr* to reach an understanding; **arreglárselas** (*fam*) to get by, manage.
arreglo [a'rreɣlo] *nm* settlement; (*orden*) order; (*acuerdo*) agreement; (*MUS*) arrangement, setting.
arremangar [arreman'gar] *vt* to roll up, turn up; ~**se** *vr* to roll up one's sleeves.
arremeter [arreme'ter] *vt* to attack, assault.
arrendador, a [arrenda'ðor, a] *nm/f* landlord/lady.
arrendamiento [arrenda'mjento] *nm* letting; (*alquilar*) hiring; (*contrato*) lease; (*alquiler*) rent; **arrendar** *vt* to let, lease; to rent; **arrendatario, a** *nm/f* tenant.
arreo [a'rreo] *nm* adornment; ~**s** *nmpl* (*de caballo*) harness *sg*, trappings.
arrepentimiento [arrepenti'mjento] *nm* regret, repentance.
arrepentirse [arrepen'tirse] *vr* to repent; ~ **de** to regret.
arrestar [arres'tar] *vt* to arrest; (*encarcelar*) to imprison; **arresto** *nm* arrest; (*MIL*) detention; (*audacia*) boldness, daring; **arresto domiciliario** house arrest.
arriar [a'rrjar] *vt* (*velas*) to haul down; (*bandera*) to lower, strike; (*cable*) to pay out.

arriba [a'rriβa] *adv* **1** (*posición*) above; desde ~ from above; ~ **de todo** at the very top, right on top; **Juan está** ~ Juan is upstairs; **lo** ~ **mencionado** the aforementioned
2 (*dirección*): **calle** ~ up the street
3: **de** ~ **abajo** from top to bottom; **mirar a uno de** ~ **abajo** to look sb up and down

4: **para** ~: **de 5000 pesetas para** ~ from 5000 pesetas up(wards)
♦ *adj*: **de** ~: **el piso de** ~ the upstairs flat (*BRIT*) *o* apartment; **la parte de** ~ the top *o* upper part
♦ *prep*: ~ **de** (*AM*) above; ~ **de 200 dólares** more than 200 dollars
♦ *excl*: ¡~! up!; ¡**manos** ~! hands up!; ¡~ **España!** long live Spain!

arribar [arri'βar] *vi* to put into port; (*llegar*) to arrive.
arribista [arri'βista] *nm/f* parvenu(e), upstart.
arriendo *etc* [a'rrjendo] *vb ver* **arrendar**
♦ *nm* = **arrendamiento**.
arriero [a'rrjero] *nm* muleteer.
arriesgado, a [arrjes'ɣaðo, a] *adj* (*peligroso*) risky; (*audaz*) bold, daring.
arriesgar [arrjes'xar] *vt* to risk; (*poner en peligro*) to endanger; ~**se** *vr* to take a risk.
arrimar [arri'mar] *vt* (*acercar*) to bring close; (*poner de lado*) to set aside; ~**se** *vr* to come close *o* closer; ~**se a** to lean on.
arrinconar [arrinko'nar] *vt* (*colocar*) to put in a corner; (*enemigo*) to corner; (*fig*) to put on one side; (*abandonar*) to push aside.
arrobado, a [arro'βaðo, a] *adj* entranced, enchanted.
arrodillarse [arroði'ʎarse] *vr* to kneel (down).
arrogancia [arro'ɣanθja] *nf* arrogance; **arrogante** *adj* arrogant.
arrojar [arro'xar] *vt* to throw, hurl; (*humo*) to emit, give out; (*COM*) to yield, produce; ~**se** *vr* to throw *o* hurl o.s.
arrojo [a'rroxo] *nm* daring.
arrollador, a [arroʎa'ðor, a] *adj* crushing, overwhelming.
arrollar [arro'ʎar] *vt* (*AUTO etc*) to run over, knock down; (*DEPORTE*) to crush.
arropar [arro'par] *vt* to cover, wrap up; ~**se** *vr* to wrap o.s. up.
arrostrar [arros'trar] *vt* to face (up to); ~**se** *vr*: ~**se con uno** to face up to sb.
arroyo [a'rrojo] *nm* stream; (*de la*

calle) gutter.

arroz [a'rroθ] *nm* rice; **~ con leche** rice pudding.

arruga [a'rruɣa] *nf* fold; (*de cara*) wrinkle; (*de vestido*) crease.

arrugar [arru'ɣar] *vt* to fold; to wrinkle; to crease; **~se** *vr* to get creased.

arruinar [arrwi'nar] *vt* to ruin, wreck; **~se** *vr* to be ruined, go bankrupt.

arrullar [arru'ʎar] *vi* to coo ♦ *vt* to lull to sleep.

arrumaco [arru'mako] *nm* (*caricia*) caress; (*halago*) piece of flattery.

arsenal [arse'nal] *nm* naval dockyard; (*MIL*) arsenal.

arsénico [ar'seniko] *nm* arsenic.

arte ['arte] (*gen m en sg y siempre f en pl*) *nm* art; (*maña*) skill, guile; **~s** *nfpl* (*bellas ~s*) arts.

artefacto [arte'fakto] *nm* appliance; (*ARQUEOLOGÍA*) artefact.

arteria [ar'terja] *nf* artery.

artesanía [artesa'nia] *nf* craftsmanship; (*artículos*) handicrafts *pl*; **artesano, a** *nm/f* artisan, craftsman/woman.

ártico, a ['artiko, a] *adj* Arctic ♦ *nm*: **el Á~** the Arctic.

articulación [artikula'θjon] *nf* articulation; (*MED, TEC*) joint; **articulado, a** *adj* articulated; jointed.

articular [artiku'lar] *vt* to articulate; to join together.

artículo [ar'tikulo] *nm* article; (*cosa*) thing, article; **~s** *nmpl* (*COM*) goods.

artífice [ar'tifiθe] *nm/f* artist, craftsman/woman; (*fig*) architect.

artificial [artifi'θjal] *adj* artificial.

artificio [arti'fiθjo] *nm* art, skill; (*artesanía*) craftsmanship; (*astucia*) cunning.

artillería [artiʎe'ria] *nf* artillery.

artillero [arti'ʎero] *nm* artilleryman, gunner.

artimaña [arti'maɲa] *nf* trap, snare; (*astucia*) cunning.

artista [ar'tista] *nm/f* (*pintor*) artist, painter; (*TEATRO*) artist, artiste; **artístico, a** *adj* artistic.

artritis [ar'tritis] *nf* arthritis.

arveja [ar'ßexa] (*AM*) *nf* pea.

arzobispo [arθo'ßispo] *nm* archbishop.

as [as] *nm* ace.

asa ['asa] *nf* handle; (*fig*) lever.

asado [a'saðo] *nm* roast (meat); (*AM*: *barbacoa*) barbecue.

asador [asa'ðor] *nm* spit.

asadura [asa'ðura] *nf* entrails *pl*, offal.

asalariado, a [asala'rjaðo, a] *adj* paid, salaried ♦ *nm/f* wage earner.

asaltador, a [asalta'ðor, a] *nm/f* assailant.

asaltante [asal'tante] *nm/f* = **asaltador, a**.

asaltar [asal'tar] *vt* to attack, assault; (*fig*) to assail; **asalto** *nm* attack, assault; (*DEPORTE*) round.

asamblea [asam'blea] *nf* assembly; (*reunión*) meeting.

asar [a'sar] *vt* to roast.

asbesto [as'ßesto] *nm* asbestos.

ascendencia [asθen'denθja] *nf* ancestry; (*AM*) ascendancy; **de ~ francesa** of French origin.

ascender [asθen'der] *vi* (*subir*) to ascend, rise; (*ser promovido*) to gain promotion ♦ *vt* to promote; **~ a** to amount to; **ascendiente** *nm* influence ♦ *nm/f* ancestor.

ascensión [asθen'sjon] *nf* ascent; (*REL*): **la A~** the Ascension.

ascenso [as'θenso] *nm* ascent; (*promoción*) promotion.

ascensor [asθen'sor] *nm* lift (*BRIT*), elevator (*US*).

ascético, a [as'θetiko, a] *adj* ascetic.

asco ['asko] *nm*: **¡qué ~!** how revolting o disgusting; **el ajo me da ~** I hate o loathe garlic; **estar hecho un ~** to be filthy.

ascua ['askwa] *nf* ember; **estar en ~s** to be on tenterhooks.

aseado, a [ase'aðo, a] *adj* clean; (*arreglado*) tidy; (*pulcro*) smart.

asear [ase'ar] *vt* to clean, wash; to tidy (up).

asediar [ase'ðjar] *vt* (*MIL*) to besiege, lay siege to; (*fig*) to chase, pester; **asedio** *nm* siege; (*COM*) run.

asegurado, a [aseɣu'raðo, a] *adj* insured; **asegurador, a** *nm/f* insurer.

asegurar [aseɣu'rar] vt (consolidar) to secure, fasten; (dar garantía de) to guarantee; (preservar) to safeguard; (afirmar, dar por cierto) to assure, affirm; (tranquilizar) to reassure; (tomar un seguro) to insure; ~se vr to assure o.s., make sure.

asemejarse [aseme'xarse] vr to be alike; ~ a to be like, resemble.

asentado, a [asen'taðo, a] adj established, settled.

asentar [asen'tar] vt (sentar) to seat, sit down; (poner) to place, establish; (alisar) to level, smooth down o out; (anotar) to note down ♦ vi to be suitable, suit.

asentir [asen'tir] vi to assent, agree; ~ con la cabeza to nod (one's head).

aseo [a'seo] nm cleanliness; ~s nmpl (servicios) toilet sg (BRIT), cloakroom sg (BRIT), restroom sg (US).

aséptico, a [a'septiko, a] adj germ-free, free from infection.

asequible [ase'kiβle] adj (precio) reasonable; (meta) attainable; (persona) approachable.

aserradero [aserra'ðero] nm sawmill; **aserrar** vt to saw.

aserrín [ase'rrin] nm sawdust.

asesinar [asesi'nar] vt to murder; (POL) to assassinate; **asesinato** nm murder; assassination.

asesino, a [ase'sino, a] nm/f murderer, killer; (POL) assassin.

asesor, a [ase'sor, a] nm/f adviser, consultant.

asesorar [aseso'rar] vt (JUR) to advise, give legal advice to; (COM) to act as consultant to; ~se vr: ~se con o de to take advice from, consult; ~ía nf (cargo) consultancy; (oficina) consultant's office.

asestar [ases'tar] vt (golpe) to deal, strike; (arma) to aim; (tiro) to fire.

asfalto [as'falto] nm asphalt.

asfixia [as'fiksja] nf asphyxia, suffocation.

asfixiar [asfik'sjar] vt to asphyxiate, suffocate; ~se vr to be asphyxiated, suffocate.

asgo etc vb ver **asir**.

así [a'si] adv (de esta manera) in this way, like this, thus; (aunque) although; (tan pronto como) as soon as; ~ que so; ~ como as well as; ~ y todo even so; ¿no es ~? isn't it?, didn't you? etc; ~ de grande this big.

Asia ['asja] nf Asia; **asiático, a** adj, nm/f Asian, Asiatic.

asidero [asi'ðero] nm handle.

asiduidad [asiðwi'ðað] nf assiduousness; **asiduo, a** adj assiduous; (frecuente) frequent ♦ nm/f regular (customer).

asiento [a'sjento] nm (mueble) seat, chair; (de coche, en tribunal etc) seat; (localidad) seat, place; (fundamento) site; ~ delantero/trasero front/back seat.

asignación [asiɣna'θjon] nf (atribución) assignment; (reparto) allocation; (sueldo) salary; ~ (semanal) pocket money.

asignar [asiɣ'nar] vt to assign, allocate.

asignatura [asiɣna'tura] nf subject; course.

asilado, a [asi'laðo, a] nm/f inmate; (POL) refugee.

asilo [a'silo] nm (refugio) asylum, refuge; (establecimiento) home, institution; ~ político political asylum.

asimilación [asimila'θjon] nf assimilation.

asimilar [asimi'lar] vt to assimilate.

asimismo [asi'mismo] adv in the same way, likewise.

asir [a'sir] vt to seize, grasp.

asistencia [asis'tenθja] nf audience; (MED) attendance; (ayuda) assistance; **asistente** nm/f assistant; los asistentes those present.

asistido, a [asis'tiðo, a] adj: ~ por ordenador computer-assisted.

asistir [asis'tir] vt to assist, help ♦ vi: ~ a to attend, be present at.

asma ['asma] nf asthma.

asno ['asno] nm donkey; (fig) ass.

asociación [asoθja'θjon] nf association; (COM) partnership; **asociado, a** adj associate ♦ nm/f associate; (COM) partner.

asociar [aso'θjar] *vt* to associate.

asolar [aso'lar] *vt* to destroy.

asolear [asole'ar] *vt* to put in the sun; ~se *vr* to sunbathe.

asomar [aso'mar] *vt* to show, stick out ♦ *vi* to appear; ~se *vr* to appear, show up; ~ **la cabeza por la ventana** to put one's head out of the window.

asombrar [asom'brar] *vt* to amaze, astonish; ~se *vr* (*sorprenderse*) to be amazed; (*asustarse*) to get a fright; **asombro** *nm* amazement, astonishment; (*susto*) fright; **asombroso, a** *adj* astonishing, amazing.

asomo [a'somo] *nm* hint, sign.

aspa ['aspa] *nf* (*cruz*) cross; (*de molino*) sail; **en ~ X-shaped**.

aspaviento [aspa'βjento] *nm* exaggerated display of feeling; (*fam*) fuss.

aspecto [as'pekto] *nm* (*apariencia*) look, appearance; (*fig*) aspect.

aspereza [aspe'reθa] *nf* roughness; (*agrura*) sourness; (*de carácter*) surliness; **áspero, a** *adj* rough; bitter, sour; harsh.

aspersión [asper'sjon] *nf* sprinkling.

aspiración [aspira'θjon] *nf* breath, inhalation; (*MUS*) short pause; **aspiraciones** *nfpl* (*ambiciones*) aspirations.

aspirador [aspira'ðor] *nm* = **aspiradora**.

aspiradora [aspira'ðora] *nf* vacuum cleaner, Hoover ®.

aspirante [aspi'rante] *nm/f* (*candidato*) candidate; (*DEPORTE*) contender.

aspirar [aspi'rar] *vt* to breathe in ♦ *vi*: ~ a to aspire to.

aspirina [aspi'rina] *nf* aspirin.

asquear [aske'ar] *vt* to sicken ♦ *vi* to sickening; ~se *vr* to feel disgusted; **asqueroso, a** *adj* disgusting, sickening.

asta ['asta] *nf* lance; (*arpón*) spear; (*mango*) shaft, handle; (*ZOOL*) horn; **a media ~** at half mast.

astado, a [as'taðo, a] *adj* horned ♦ *nm* bull.

asterisco [aste'risko] *nm* asterisk.

astilla [as'tiʎa] *nf* splinter; (*pedacito*) chip; ~s *nfpl* (*leña*) firewood *sg*.

astillero [asti'ʎero] *nm* shipyard.

astringente [astrin'xente] *adj*, *nm* astringent.

astro ['astro] *nm* star.

astrología [astrolo'xia] *nf* astrology; **astrólogo, a** *nm/f* astrologer.

astronauta [astro'nauta] *nm/f* astronaut.

astronave [astro'naße] *nm* spaceship.

astronomía [astrono'mia] *nf* astronomy; **astrónomo, a** *nm/f* astronomer.

astucia [as'tuθja] *nf* astuteness; (*ardid*) clever trick; **astuto, a** *adj* astute; (*taimado*) cunning.

asueto [a'sweto] *nm* holiday; (*tiempo libre*) time off *no pl*.

asumir [asu'mir] *vt* to assume.

asunción [asun'θjon] *nf* assumption; (*REL*): **A~** Assumption.

asunto [a'sunto] *nm* (*tema*) matter, subject; (*negocio*) business.

asustar [asus'tar] *vt* to frighten; ~se *vr* to be (o become) frightened.

atacar [ata'kar] *vt* to attack.

atadura [ata'ðura] *nf* bond, tie.

atajo [a'taxo] *nm* short cut; (*DEPORTE*) tackle.

atañer [ata'ɲer] *vi*: ~ a to concern.

ataque *etc* [a'take] *vb ver* **atacar** ♦ *nm* attack; ~ **cardíaco** heart attack.

atar [a'tar] *vt* to tie, tie up.

atardecer [atarðe'θer] *vi* to get dark ♦ *nm* evening; (*crepúsculo*) dusk.

atareado, a [atare'aðo, a] *adj* busy.

atascar [atas'kar] *vt* to clog up; (*obstruir*) to jam; (*fig*) to hinder; ~se *vr* to stall; (*cañería*) to get blocked up; **atasco** *nm* obstruction; (*AUTO*) traffic jam.

ataúd [ata'uð] *nm* coffin.

ataviar [ata'βjar] *vt* to deck, array; ~se *vr* to dress up.

atavío [ata'βio] *nm* attire, dress; ~s *nmpl* finery *sg*.

atemorizar [atemori'θar] *vt* to frighten, scare; ~se *vr* to get scared.

Atenas [a'tenas] *n* Athens.

atención [aten'θjon] *nf* attention; (*bondad*) kindness ♦ *excl* (be) careful!, look out!

atender [aten'der] *vt* to attend to, look

after ♦ *vi* to pay attention.

atenerse [ate'nerse] *vr*: ~ **a** to abide by, adhere to.

atentado [aten'taðo] *nm* crime, illegal act; (*asalto*) assault; ~ **contra la vida de uno** attempt on sb's life.

atentamente [atenta'mente] *adv*: **Le saluda** ~ Yours faithfully.

atentar [aten'tar] *vi*: ~ **a** *o* **contra** to commit an outrage against.

atento, a [a'tento, a] *adj* attentive, observant; (*cortés*) polite, thoughtful.

atenuante [ate'nwante] *adj* extenuating.

atenuar [ate'nwar] *vt* (*disminuir*) to lessen, minimize.

ateo, a [a'teo, a] *adj* atheistic ♦ *nm/f* atheist.

aterciopelado, a [aterθjope'laðo, a] *adj* velvety.

aterido, a [ate'riðo, a] *adj*: ~ **de frío** frozen stiff.

aterrador, a [aterra'ðor, a] *adj* frightening.

aterrar [ate'rrar] *vt* to frighten; to terrify; ~**se** *vr* to be frightened; to be terrified.

aterrizaje [aterri'θaxe] *nm* (*AVIAT*) landing.

aterrizar [aterri'θar] *vi* to land.

aterrorizar [aterrori'θar] *vt* to terrify.

atesorar [ateso'rar] *vt* to hoard, store up.

atestado, a [ates'taðo, a] *adj* packed ♦ *nm* (*JUR*) affidavit.

atestar [ates'tar] *vt* to pack, stuff; (*JUR*) to attest, testify to.

atestiguar [atesti'ɣwar] *vt* to testify to, bear witness to.

atiborrar [atiβo'rrar] *vt* to fill, stuff; ~**se** *vr* to stuff o.s.

ático ['atiko] *nm* attic; ~ **de lujo** penthouse (flat (*BRIT*) *o* apartment).

atildar [atil'dar] *vt* to criticize; ~**se** *vr* to spruce o.s. up.

atinado, a [ati'naðo, a] *adj* (*sensato*) wise; (*correcto*) right, correct.

atisbar [atis'βar] *vt* to spy on; (*echar una ojeada*) to peep at.

atizar [ati'θar] *vt* to poke; (*horno etc*) to stoke; (*fig*) to stir up, rouse.

atlántico, a [at'lantiko, a] *adj* Atlantic ♦ *nm*: **el** (**océano**) **A**~ the Atlantic (Ocean).

atlas ['atlas] *nm* atlas.

atleta [at'leta] *nm* athlete; **atlético, a** *adj* athletic; **atletismo** *nm* athletics *sg*.

atmósfera [at'mosfera] *nf* atmosphere.

atolondramiento [atolondra'mjento] *nm* bewilderment; (*insensatez*) silliness.

atollar [ato'ʎar] *vi* to get stuck; (*fig*) to get into a jam; ~**se** *vr* to get stuck; to get into a jam.

atómico, a [a'tomiko, a] *adj* atomic.

atomizador [atomiθa'ðor] *nm* atomizer; (*de perfume*) spray.

átomo ['atomo] *nm* atom.

atónito, a [a'tonito, a] *adj* astonished, amazed.

atontado, a [aton'taðo, a] *adj* stunned; (*bobo*) silly, daft.

atontar [aton'tar] *vt* to stun; ~**se** *vr* to become confused.

atormentar [atormen'tar] *vt* to torture; (*molestar*) to torment; (*acosar*) to plague, harass.

atornillar [atorni'ʎar] *vt* to screw on *o* down.

atracador, a [atraka'ðor, a] *nm/f* robber.

atracar [atra'kar] *vt* (*NAUT*) to moor; (*robar*) to hold up, rob ♦ *vi* to moor; ~**se** *vr*: ~**se** (**de**) to stuff o.s. (with).

atracción [atrak'θjon] *nf* attraction.

atraco [a'trako] *nm* holdup, robbery.

atractivo, a [atrak'tiβo, a] *adj* attractive ♦ *nm* appeal.

atraer [atra'er] *vt* to attract.

atragantarse [atraɣan'tarse] *vr*: ~ (**con**) to choke (on); **se me ha atragantado el chico** I can't stand the boy.

atrancar [atran'kar] *vt* (*puerta*) to bar, bolt.

atrapar [atra'par] *vt* to trap; (*resfriado etc*) to catch.

atrás [a'tras] *adv* (*movimiento*) back(wards); (*lugar*) behind; (*tiempo*) previously; **ir hacia** ~ to go back(wards); **ir a la rear**; **estar** ~ to be behind *o* at the back.

atrasado, a [atra'saðo, a] *adj* slow; (*pago*) overdue, late; (*país*) backward.

atrasar [atra'sar] *vi* to be slow; ~se *vr* to remain behind; (*tren*) to be *o* run late; **atraso** *nm* slowness; lateness; delay; (*de país*) backwardness; **atrasos** *nmpl* (*COM*) arrears.

atravesar [atraβe'sar] *vt* (*cruzar*) to cross (over); (*traspasar*) to pierce; to go through; (*poner al través*) to lay *o* put across; ~se *vr* to come in between; (*intervenir*) to interfere.

atravieso *etc vb ver* **atravesar**.

atrayente [atra'jente] *adj* attractive.

atreverse [atre'βerse] *vr* to dare; (*insolentarse*) to be insolent; **atrevido, a** *adj* daring; insolent; **atrevimiento** *nm* daring; insolence.

atribución [atriβu'θjon] *nf*: **atribuciones** (*POL*) powers; (*ADMIN*) responsibilities.

atribuir [atriβu'ir] *vt* to attribute; (*funciones*) to confer.

atribular [atriβu'lar] *vt* to afflict, distress.

atributo [atri'βuto] *nm* attribute.

atrocidad [atroθi'ðað] *nf* atrocity, outrage.

atropellar [atrope'ʎar] *vt* (*derribar*) to knock over *o* down; (*empujar*) to push (aside); (*AUTO*) to run over, run down; (*agraviar*) to insult; ~se *vr* to act hastily; **atropello** *nm* (*AUTO*) accident; (*empujón*) push; (*agravio*) wrong; (*atrocidad*) outrage.

atroz [a'troθ] *adj* atrocious, awful.

atto, a *abr* = **atento**.

atuendo [a'twendo] *nm* attire.

atún [a'tun] *nm* tuna.

aturdir [atur'ðir] *vt* to stun; (*de ruido*) to deafen; (*fig*) to dumbfound, bewilder.

atusar [atu'sar] *vt* to smooth (down).

audacia [au'ðaθja] *nf* boldness, audacity; **audaz** *adj* bold, audacious.

audible [au'ðiβle] *adj* audible.

audición [auði'θjon] *nf* hearing; (*TEATRO*) audition.

audiencia [au'ðjenθja] *nf* audience; **A~** (*JUR*) High Court.

auditor [auði'tor] *nm* (*JUR*) judge advocate; (*COM*) auditor.

auditorio [auði'torjo] *nm* audience; (*sala*) auditorium.

auge ['auxe] *nm* boom; (*clímax*) climax.

augurar [auɣu'rar] *vt* to predict; (*presagiar*) to portend.

augurio [au'vurjo] *nm* omen.

aula ['aula] *nf* classroom; (*en universidad etc*) lecture room.

aullar [au'ʎar] *vi* to howl, yell.

aullido [au'ʎiðo] *nm* howl, yell.

aumentar [aumen'tar] *vt* to increase; (*precios*) to put up; (*producción*) to step up; (*con microscopio, anteojos*) to magnify ♦ *vi* to increase, be on the increase; ~se *vr* to increase, be on the increase; **aumento** *nm* increase; rise.

aun [a'un] *adv* even; ~ **así** even so; ~ **más** even *o* yet more.

aún [a'un] *adv*: ~ **está aquí** he's still here; ~ **no lo sabemos** we don't know yet; ¿**no ha venido** ~? hasn't she come yet?

aunque [a'unke] *conj* though, although, even though.

aúpa [a'upa] *excl* come on!

aureola [aure'ola] *nf* halo.

auricular [auriku'lar] *nm* (*TEL*) earpiece, receiver; ~**es** *nmpl* (*para escuchar música etc*) headphones.

aurora [au'rora] *nf* dawn.

auscultar [auskul'tar] *vt* (*MED: pecho*) to listen to, sound.

ausencia [au'senθja] *nf* absence.

ausentarse [ausen'tarse] *vr* to go away; (*por poco tiempo*) to go out.

ausente [au'sente] *adj* absent.

auspicios [aus'piθjos] *nmpl* auspices; (*protección*) protection *sg*.

austeridad [austeri'ðað] *nf* austerity; **austero, a** *adj* austere.

austral [aus'tral] *adj* southern ♦ *nm monetary unit of Argentina*.

Australia [aus'tralja] *nf* Australia; **australiano, a** *adj*, *nm/f* Australian.

Austria [aus'trja] *nf* Austria; **austríaco, a** *adj*, *nm/f* Austrian.

autenticar [autenti'kar] *vt* to authenticate; **auténtico, a** *adj* authentic.

auto ['auto] *nm* (*JUR*) edict, decree; (: *orden*) writ; (*AUTO*) car; ~**s** *nmpl* (*JUR*) proceedings; (: *acta*) court record *sg.*

autoadhesivo [autoaðe'siβo] *adj* self-adhesive; (*sobre*) self-sealing.

autobiografía [autoβjovra'fia] *nf* autobiography.

autobús [auto'βus] *nm* bus.

autocar [auto'kar] *nm* coach (*BRIT*), (passenger) bus (*US*).

autóctono, a [au'toktono, a] *adj* native, indigenous.

autodefensa [autoðe'fensa] *nf* self-defence.

autodeterminación [autoðetermina-'θjon] *nf* self-determination.

autoescuela [autoes'kwela] *nf* driving school.

autógrafo [au'toɣrafo] *nm* autograph.

automación [automa'θjon] *nf* = **automatización**.

autómata [au'tomata] *nm* automaton.

automático, a [auto'matiko, a] *adj* automatic ♦ *nm* press stud.

automatización [automatiθa'θjon] *nf* automation.

automotor, triz [automo'tor, 'triθ] *adj* self-propelled ♦ *nm* diesel train.

automóvil [auto'moβil] *nm* (motor) car (*BRIT*), automobile (*US*); **automovilismo** *nm* (*actividad*) motoring; (*DEPORTE*) motor racing; **automovilista** *nm/f* motorist, driver; **automovilístico, a** *adj* (*industria*) motor *cpd*.

autonomía [autono'mia] *nf* autonomy; **autónomo, a** (*ESP*) *adj* (*POL*) autonomous; **autonómico, a** (*ESP*) *adj* (*POL*) autonomous.

autopista [auto'pista] *nf* motorway (*BRIT*), freeway (*US*); ~ **de peaje** toll road (*BRIT*), turnpike road (*US*).

autopsia [au'topsja] *nf* autopsy, post-mortem.

autor, a [au'tor, a] *nm/f* author.

autoridad [autori'ðað] *nf* authority; **autoritario, a** *adj* authoritarian.

autorización [autoriθa'θjon] *nf* authorization; **autorizado, a** *adj* authorized; (*aprobado*) approved.

autorizar [autori'θar] *vt* to authorize; (*aprobar*) to approve.

autorretrato [autorre'trato] *nm* self-portrait.

autoservicio [autoser'βiθjo] *nm* (*tienda*) self-service shop (*BRIT*) o store (*US*); (*restaurante*) self-service restaurant.

autostop [auto'stop] *nm* hitch-hiking; **hacer** ~ to hitch-hike; ~**ista** *nm/f* hitch-hiker.

autosuficiencia [autosufi'θjenθja] *nf* self-sufficiency.

autovía [auto'βia] *nf* ≈ A-road (*BRIT*), dual carriageway (*BRIT*), ≈ state highway (*US*).

auxiliar [auksi'ljar] *vt* to help ♦ *nm/f* assistant; **auxilio** *nm* assistance, help; **primeros auxilios** first aid *sg.*

Av *abr* (= *Avenida*) Av(e).

aval [a'βal] *nm* guarantee; (*persona*) guarantor.

avalancha [aβa'lantʃa] *nf* avalanche.

avance [a'βanθe] *nm* advance; (*pago*) advance payment; (*CINE*) trailer.

avanzar [aβan'θar] *vt, vi* to advance.

avaricia [aβa'riθja] *nf* avarice, greed; **avaricioso, a** *adj* avaricious, greedy.

avaro, a [a'βaro, a] *adj* miserly, mean ♦ *nm/f* miser.

avasallar [aβasa'ʎar] *vt* to subdue, subjugate.

Avda *abr* (= *Avenida*) Av(e).

ave ['aβe] *nf* bird; ~ **de rapiña** bird of prey.

avecinarse [aβeθi'narse] *vr* (*tormenta, fig*) to be on the way.

avellana [aβe'ʎana] *nf* hazelnut; **avellano** *nm* hazel tree.

avemaría [aβema'ria] *nm* Hail Mary, Ave Maria.

avena [a'βena] *nf* oats *pl.*

avenida [aβe'niða] *nf* (*calle*) avenue.

avenir [aβe'nir] *vt* to reconcile; ~**se** *vr* to come to an agreement, reach a compromise.

aventajado, a [aβenta'xaðo, a] *adj* outstanding.

aventajar [aβenta'xar] *vt* (*sobrepasar*) to surpass, outstrip.

aventar [aβen'tar] *vt* to fan, blow; (*grano*) to winnow.

aventura [aβen'tura] *nf* adventure; **aventurado, a** *adj* risky; **aventurero, a**

adj adventurous.
avergonzar [aβerɣon'θar] *vt* to shame; (*desconcertar*) to embarrass; ~se *vr* to be ashamed; to be embarrassed.
avería [aβe'ria] *nf* (*TEC*) breakdown, fault.
averiado, a [aβe'rjaðo, a] *adj* broken down; "~" "out of order".
averiguación [aβeriɣwa'θjon] *nf* investigation; (*descubrimiento*) ascertainment.
averiguar [aβeri'ɣwar] *vt* to investigate; (*descubrir*) to find out, ascertain.
aversión [aβer'sjon] *nf* aversion, dislike.
avestruz [aβes'truθ] *nm* ostrich.
aviación [aβja'θjon] *nf* aviation; (*fuerzas aéreas*) air force.
aviador, a [aβja'ðor, a] *nm/f* aviator, airman/woman.
aviar [a'βjar] *vt* to prepare; **estar aviado** (*fig*) to be in a mess.
avicultura [aβikul'tura] *nf* poultry farming.
avidez [aβi'ðeθ] *nf* avidity, eagerness; **ávido, a** *adj* avid, eager.
avinagrado, a [aβina'ɣraðo, a] *adj* sour, acid.
avinagrarse [aβina'ɣrarse] *vr* to go o turn sour.
avío [a'βio] *nm* preparation; ~s *nmpl* (*equipamiento*) gear *sg*, kit *sg*.
avión [a'βjon] *nm* aeroplane; (*ave*) martin; ~ **de reacción** jet (plane).
avioneta [aβjo'neta] *nf* light aircraft.
avisar [aβi'sar] *vt* (*advertir*) to warn, notify; (*informar*) to tell; (*aconsejar*) to advise, counsel; **aviso** *nm* warning; (*noticia*) notice.
avispa [a'βispa] *nf* wasp.
avispado, a [aβis'paðo, a] *adj* sharp, clever.
avispero [aβis'pero] *nm* wasp's nest.
avispón [aβis'pon] *nm* hornet.
avistar [aβis'tar] *vt* to sight, spot.
avituallar [aβitwa'ʎar] *vt* to supply with food.
avivar [aβi'βar] *vt* to strengthen, intensify; ~se *vr* to revive, acquire new life.
axila [ak'sila] *nf* armpit.

axioma [ak'sjoma] *nm* axiom.
ay [ai] *excl* (*dolor*) ow!, ouch!; (*aflicción*) oh!, oh dear!; ¡~ **de mi!** poor me!
aya ['aja] *nf* governess; (*niñera*) nanny.
ayer [a'jer] *adv, nm* yesterday; **antes de** ~ the day before yesterday.
ayo ['ajo] *nm* tutor.
ayote [a'jote] (*AM*) *nm* pumpkin.
ayuda [a'juða] *nf* help, assistance ♦ *nm* page; **ayudante, a** *nm/f* assistant, helper; (*ESCOL*) assistant; (*MIL*) adjutant.
ayudar [aju'ðar] *vt* to help, assist.
ayunar [aju'nar] *vi* to fast; **ayunas** *nfpl*: **estar en ayunas** (*no haber comido*) to be fasting; (*ignorar*) to be in the dark; **ayuno** *nm* fast; fasting.
ayuntamiento [ajunta'mjento] *nm* (*consejo*) town (o city) council; (*edificio*) town (o city) hall.
azabache [aθa'βatʃe] *nm* jet.
azada [a'θaða] *nf* hoe.
azafata [aθa'fata] *nf* air stewardess.
azafrán [aθa'fran] *nm* saffron.
azahar [aθa'ar] *nm* orange/lemon blossom.
azar [a'θar] *nm* (*casualidad*) chance, fate; (*desgracia*) misfortune, accident; **por** ~ by chance; **al** ~ at random.
azogue [a'θoɣe] *nm* mercury.
azoramiento [aθora'mjento] *nm* alarm; (*confusión*) confusion.
azorar [aθo'rar] *vt* to alarm; ~se *vr* to get alarmed.
Azores [a'θores] *nfpl*: **las** ~ the Azores.
azotar [aθo'tar] *vt* to whip, beat; (*pegar*) to spank; **azote** *nm* (*látigo*) whip; (*latigazo*) lash, stroke; (*en las nalgas*) spank; (*calamidad*) calamity.
azotea [aθo'tea] *nf* (flat) roof.
azteca [aθ'teka] *adj, nm/f* Aztec.
azúcar [a'θukar] *nm* sugar; **azucarado, a** *adj* sugary, sweet.
azucarero, a [aθuka'rero, a] *adj* sugar *cpd* ♦ *nm* sugar bowl.
azucena [aθu'θena] *nf* white lily.
azufre [a'θufre] *nm* sulphur.
azul [a'θul] *adj, nm* blue.
azulejo [aθu'lexo] *nm* tile.

azuzar [aθu'θar] *vt* to incite, egg on.

B

B.A. *abr* (= *Buenos Aires*) B.A.
baba ['baβa] *nf* spittle, saliva; **babear** *vi* to drool, slaver.
babel [ba'βel] *nm o f* bedlam.
babero [ba'βero] *nm* bib.
babor [ba'βor] *nm* port (side).
baboso, a [ba'βoso, a] (*AM: fam*) *adj* silly.
babucha [ba'βutʃa] *nf* slipper.
baca ['baka] *nf* (*AUTO*) luggage *o* roof rack.
bacalao [baka'lao] *nm* cod(fish).
bacinica [baθi'nika] *nf* = **bacinilla**.
bacinilla [baθi'niʎa] *nf* chamber pot.
bacteria [bak'terja] *nf* bacterium, germ.
báculo ['bakulo] *nm* stick, staff.
bache ['batʃe] *nm* pothole, rut; (*fig*) bad patch.
bagaje [ba'xaxe] *nm* baggage, luggage.
bagatela [baɣa'tela] *nf* trinket, trifle.
Bahama [ba'ama]: **las (Islas) ~** *nfpl* the Bahamas.
bahía [ba'ia] *nf* bay.
bailar [bai'lar] *vt, vi* to dance; **~ín, ina** *nm/f* (*ballet*) dancer; **baile** *nm* dance; (*formal*) ball.
baja ['baxa] *nf* drop, fall; (*MIL*) casualty; **dar de ~** (*soldado*) to discharge; (*empleado*) to dismiss.
bajada [ba'xaða] *nf* descent; (*camino*) slope; (*de aguas*) ebb.
bajamar [baxa'mar] *nf* low tide.
bajar [ba'xar] *vi* to go down, come down; (*temperatura, precios*) to drop, fall ♦ *vt* (*cabeza*) to bow; (*escalera*) to go down, come down; (*precio, voz*) to lower; (*llevar abajo*) to take down; **~se** *vr* (*de coche*) to get out; (*de autobús, tren*) to get off; **~ de** (*coche*) to get out of; (*autobús, tren*) to get off.
bajeza [ba'xeθa] *nf* baseness *no pl*; (*una ~*) vile deed.
bajío [ba'xio] *nm* shoal, sandbank; (*AM*) lowlands *pl*.
bajo, a ['baxo, a] *adj* (*mueble, número,*

precio) low; (*piso*) ground; (*de estatura*) small, short; (*color*) pale; (*sonido*) faint, soft, low; (*voz: en tono*) deep; (*metal*) base; (*humilde*) low, humble ♦ *adv* (*hablar*) softly, quietly; (*volar*) low ♦ *prep* under, below, underneath ♦ *nm* (*MUS*) bass; **~ la lluvia** in the rain.
bajón [ba'xon] *nm* fall, drop.
bala ['bala] *nf* bullet.
baladí [bala'ði] *adj* trivial.
baladronada [balaðro'naða] *nf* (*dicho*) boast, brag; (*hecho*) piece of bravado.
balance [ba'lanθe] *nm* (*COM*) balance; (: *libro*) balance sheet; (: *cuenta general*) stocktaking.
balancear [balanθe'ar] *vt* to balance ♦ *vi* to swing (to and fro); (*vacilar*) to hesitate; **~se** *vr* to swing (to and fro); to hesitate; **balanceo** *nm* swinging.
balanza [ba'lanθa] *nf* scales *pl*, balance; (*ASTROLOGÍA*): **B~** Libra; **~ comercial** balance of trade; **~ de pagos** balance of payments.
balar [ba'lar] *vi* to bleat.
balaustrada [balaus'traða] *nf* balustrade; (*pasamanos*) banisters *pl*.
balazo [ba'laθo] *nm* (*golpe*) shot; (*herida*) bullet wound.
balbucear [balβuθe'ar] *vi, vt* to stammer, stutter; **balbuceo** *nm* stammering, stuttering.
balbucir [balβu'θir] *vi, vt* to stammer, stutter.
balcón [bal'kon] *nm* balcony.
baldar [bal'dar] *vt* to cripple.
balde ['balde] *nm* bucket, pail; **de ~** (for) free, for nothing; **en ~** in vain.
baldío, a [bal'dio, a] *adj* uncultivated; (*terreno*) waste ♦ *nm* waste land.
baldosa [bal'dosa] *nf* (*azulejo*) floor tile; (*grande*) flagstone.
Baleares [bale'ares] *nfpl*: **las (Islas) ~** the Balearic Islands.
balido [ba'liðo] *nm* bleat, bleating.
balín [ba'lin] *nm* pellet; **balines** *nmpl* buckshot *sg*.
balística [ba'listika] *nf* ballistics *sg*.
baliza [ba'liθa] *nf* (*AVIAT*) beacon; (*NAUT*) buoy.

balneario, a [balne'arjo, a] *adj*: **estación balnearia** (bathing) resort ♦ *nm* spa, health resort.

balón [ba'lon] *nm* ball.

baloncesto [balon'θesto] *nm* basketball.

balonmano [balom'mano] *nm* handball.

balonvolea [balombo'lea] *nm* volleyball.

balsa ['balsa] *nf* raft; (*BOT*) balsa wood.

bálsamo ['balsamo] *nm* balsam, balm.

baluarte [ba'lwarte] *nm* bastion, bulwark.

ballena [ba'ʎena] *nf* whale.

ballesta [ba'ʎesta] *nf* crossbow; (*AUTO*) spring.

ballet [ba'le] (*pl* ~s) *nm* ballet.

bambolear [bambole'ar] *vi* to swing, sway; (*silla*) to wobble; ~**se** *vr* to swing, sway; to wobble; **bamboleo** *nm* swinging, swaying; wobbling.

bambú [bam'bu] *nm* bamboo.

banana [ba'nana] (*AM*) *nf* banana; **banano** (*AM*) *nm* banana tree.

banca ['banka] *nf* (*asiento*) bench; (*COM*) banking.

bancario, a [ban'karjo, a] *adj* banking *cpd*, bank *cpd*.

bancarrota [banka'rrota] *nf* bankruptcy; **hacer** ~ to go bankrupt.

banco ['banko] *nm* bench; (*ESCOL*) desk; (*COM*) bank; (*GEO*) stratum; ~ **de crédito/de ahorros** credit/savings bank; ~ **de arena** sandbank; ~ **de hielo** iceberg.

banda ['banda] *nf* band; (*pandilla*) gang; (*NAUT*) side, edge; **la B~ Oriental** Uruguay; ~ **sonora** sound-track.

bandada [ban'daða] *nf* (*de pájaros*) flock; (*de peces*) shoal.

bandeja [ban'dexa] *nf* tray.

bandera [ban'dera] *nf* (*de tela*) flag; (*estandarte*) banner.

banderilla [bande'riʎa] *nf* banderilla.

banderín [bande'rin] *nm* pennant, small flag.

banderola [bande'rola] *nf* banderole; (*MIL*) pennant.

bandido [ban'diðo] *nm* bandit.

bando ['bando] *nm* (*edicto*) edict, proclamation; (*facción*) faction; **los** ~**s** (*REL*) the banns.

bandolero [bando'lero] *nm* bandit, brigand.

banquero [ban'kero] *nm* banker.

banqueta [ban'keta] *nf* stool; (*AM*: *en la calle*) pavement (*BRIT*), sidewalk (*US*).

banquete [ban'kete] *nm* banquet; (*para convidados*) formal dinner.

banquillo [ban'kiʎo] *nm* (*JUR*) dock, prisoner's bench; (*banco*) bench; (*para los pies*) footstool.

bañador [baɲa'ðor] *nm* swimming costume (*BRIT*), bathing suit (*US*).

bañar [ba'ɲar] *vt* to bath, bathe; (*objeto*) to dip; (*de barniz*) to coat; ~**se** *vr* (*en el mar*) to bathe, swim; (*en la bañera*) to have a bath.

bañera [ba'ɲera] *nf* bath(tub).

bañero, a [ba'ɲero, a] *nm/f* lifeguard.

bañista [ba'ɲista] *nm/f* bather.

baño ['baɲo] *nm* (*en bañera*) bath; (*en río*) dip, swim; (*cuarto*) bathroom; (*bañera*) bath(tub); (*capa*) coating.

baptista [bap'tista] *nm/f* Baptist.

baqueta [ba'keta] *nf* (*MUS*) drumstick.

bar [bar] *nm* bar.

barahúnda [bara'unda] *nf* uproar, hubbub.

baraja [ba'raxa] *nf* pack (of cards); **barajar** *vt* (*naipes*) to shuffle; (*fig*) to jumble up.

baranda [ba'randa] *nf* = **barandilla**.

barandilla [baran'diʎa] *nf* rail, railing.

baratija [bara'tixa] *nf* trinket.

baratillo [bara'tiʎo] *nm* (*tienda*) junk-shop; (*subasta*) bargain sale; (*conjunto de cosas*) secondhand goods *pl*.

barato, a [ba'rato, a] *adj* cheap ♦ *adv* cheap, cheaply.

baraúnda [bara'unda] *nf* = **barahúnda**.

barba ['barβa] *nf* (*mentón*) chin; (*pelo*) beard.

barbacoa [barβa'koa] *nf* (*parrilla*) barbecue; (*carne*) barbecued meat.

barbaridad [barβari'ðað] *nf* barbarity; (*acto*) barbarism; (*atrocidad*) outrage; **una** ~ (*fam*) loads; **¡qué** ~! (*fam*) how awful!

barbarie [bar'βarje] *nf* barbarism, savagery; (*crueldad*) barbarity.

barbarismo [barβa'rismo] *nm* = **barbarie**.

bárbaro, a ['barβaro, a] *adj* barbarous, cruel; (*grosero*) rough, uncouth ♦ *nm/f* barbarian ♦ *adv*: **lo pasamos ~** (*fam*) we had a great time; **¡qué ~!** (*fam*) how marvellous!; **un éxito ~** (*fam*) a terrific success; **es un tipo ~** (*fam*) he's a great bloke.

barbecho [bar'βetʃo] *nm* fallow land.

barbero [bar'βero] *nm* barber, hairdresser.

barbilampiño [barβilam'piɲo] *adj* clean-shaven, smooth-faced; (*fig*) inexperienced.

barbilla [bar'βiʎa] *nf* chin, tip of the chin.

barbo ['barβo] *nm*: **~ de mar** red mullet.

barbotar [barβo'tar] *vt, vi* to mutter, mumble.

barbotear [barβote'ar] *vt, vi* = **barbotar**.

barbudo, a [bar'βuðo, a] *adj* bearded.

barca ['barka] *nf* (small) boat; **~ pesquera** fishing boat; **~ de pasaje** ferry; **~za** *nf* barge; **~za de desembarco** landing craft.

Barcelona [barθe'lona] *n* Barcelona.

barcelonés, esa [barθelo'nes, esa] *adj* of *o* from Barcelona.

barco ['barko] *nm* boat; (*buque*) ship; **~ de carga** cargo boat.

barítono [ba'ritono] *nm* baritone.

barman ['barman] *nm* barman.

Barna. *abr* = **Barcelona**.

barniz [bar'niθ] *nm* varnish; (*en la loza*) glaze; (*fig*) veneer; **~ar** *vt* to varnish; (*loza*) to glaze.

barómetro [ba'rometro] *nm* barometer.

barquero [bar'kero] *nm* boatman.

barquillo [bar'kiʎo] *nm* cone, cornet.

barra ['barra] *nf* bar, rod; (*de un bar, café*) bar; (*de pan*) French stick; (*palanca*) lever; **~ de carmín** *o* **de labios** lipstick.

barraca [ba'rraka] *nf* hut, cabin.

barranca [ba'rranka] *nf* ravine, gully; **barranco** *nm* ravine; (*fig*) difficulty.

barrena [ba'rrena] *nf* drill; **barrenar** *vt* to drill (through), bore; **barreno** *nm*

large drill.

barrer [ba'rrer] *vt* to sweep; (*quitar*) to sweep away.

barrera [ba'rrera] *nf* barrier.

barriada [ba'rrjaða] *nf* quarter, district.

barricada [barri'kaða] *nf* barricade.

barrida [ba'rriða] *nf* sweep, sweeping.

barrido [ba'rriðo] *nm* = **barrida**.

barriga [ba'rriɣa] *nf* belly; (*panza*) paunch; **barrigón, ona** *adj* potbellied; **barrigudo, a** *adj* potbellied.

barril [ba'rril] *nm* barrel, cask.

barrio ['barrjo] *nm* (*vecindad*) area, neighborhood (*US*); (*en las afueras*) suburb; **~ chino** red-light district.

barro ['barro] *nm* (*lodo*) mud; (*objetos*) earthenware; (*MED*) pimple.

barroco, a [ba'rroko, a] *adj, nm* baroque.

barrote [ba'rrote] *nm* (*de ventana*) bar.

barruntar [barrun'tar] *vt* (*conjeturar*) to guess; (*presentir*) to suspect; **barrunto** *nm* guess; suspicion.

bartola [bar'tola]: **a la ~** *adv*: **tirarse la ~** to take it easy, be lazy.

bártulos ['bartulos] *nmpl* things, belongings.

barullo [ba'ruʎo] *nm* row, uproar.

basamento [basa'mento] *nm* base, plinth.

basar [ba'sar] *vt* to base; **~se** *vr*: **~se en** to be based on.

basca ['baska] *nf* nausea.

báscula ['baskula] *nf* (*platform*) scales.

base ['base] *nf* base; **a ~ de** on the basis of; (*mediante*) by means of; **~ de datos** (*INFORM*) database.

básico, a ['basiko, a] *adj* basic.

basílica [ba'silika] *nf* basilica.

PALABRA CLAVE

bastante [bas'tante] *adj* **1** (*suficiente*) enough; **~ dinero** enough *o* sufficient money; **~s libros** enough books
2 (*valor intensivo*): **~ gente** quite a lot of people; **tener ~ calor** to be rather hot
♦ *adv*: **~ bueno/malo** quite good/rather bad; **~ rico** pretty rich; **(lo) ~ inteligente (como) para hacer algo**

clever enough *o* sufficiently clever to do sth.

bastar [bas'tar] *vi* to be enough *o* sufficient; **~se** *vr* to be self-sufficient; **~ para** to be enough to; **¡basta!** (that's) enough!

bastardilla [bastar'ðiʎa] *nf* italics.

bastardo, a [bas'tarðo, a] *adj, nm/f* bastard.

bastidor [basti'ðor] *nm* frame; (*de coche*) chassis; (*TEATRO*) wing; **entre ~es** (*fig*) behind the scenes.

basto, a ['basto, a] *adj* coarse, rough; **~s** *nmpl* (*NAIPES*) ≈ clubs.

bastón [bas'ton] *nm* stick, staff; (*para pasear*) walking stick.

basura [ba'sura] *nf* rubbish (*BRIT*), garbage (*US*).

basurero [basu'rero] *nm* (*hombre*) dustman (*BRIT*), garbage man (*US*); (*lugar*) dump; (*cubo*) (rubbish) bin (*BRIT*), trash can (*US*).

bata ['bata] *nf* (*gen*) dressing gown; (*cubretodo*) smock, overall; (*MED, TEC etc*) lab(oratory) coat.

batalla [ba'taʎa] *nf* battle; **de ~** (*fig*) for everyday use.

batallar [bata'ʎar] *vi* to fight.

batallón [bata'ʎon] *nm* battalion.

batata [ba'tata] (*AM*) *nf* sweet potato.

bate ['bate] *nm* bat; **~ador** (*AM*) *nm* batter, batsman.

batería [bate'ria] *nf* battery; (*MUS*) drums; **~ de cocina** kitchen utensils.

batido, a [ba'tiðo, a] *adj* (*camino*) beaten, well-trodden ♦ *nm* (*CULIN*): **~ (de leche)** milk shake.

batidora [bati'ðora] *nf* beater, mixer; **~ eléctrica** food mixer, blender.

batir [ba'tir] *vt* to beat, strike; (*vencer*) to beat, defeat; (*revolver*) to beat, mix; **~se** *vr* to fight; **~ palmas** to clap, applaud.

batuta [ba'tuta] *nf* baton; **llevar la ~** (*fig*) to be the boss, be in charge.

baúl [ba'ul] *nm* trunk; (*AUTO*) boot (*BRIT*), trunk (*US*).

bautismo [bau'tismo] *nm* baptism, christening.

bautizar [bauti'θar] *vt* to baptize, christen; (*fam: diluir*) to water down; **bautizo** *nm* baptism, christening.

baya ['baja] *nf* berry.

bayeta [ba'jeta] *nf* floorcloth.

bayo, a ['bajo, a] *adj* bay.

bayoneta [bajo'neta] *nf* bayonet.

baza ['baθa] *nf* trick; **meter ~** to butt in.

bazar [ba'θar] *nm* bazaar.

bazofia [ba'θofja] *nf* pigswill (*BRIT*), hogwash (*US*); (*libro etc*) trash.

beato, a [be'ato, a] *adj* blessed; (*piadoso*) pious.

bebé [be'βe] (*pl* ~s) *nm* baby.

bebedero [beβe'ðero] *nm* (*para animales*) drinking trough.

bebedizo, a [beβe'ðiθo, a] *adj* drinkable ♦ *nm* potion.

bebedor, a [beβe'ðor, a] *adj* hard-drinking.

beber [be'βer] *vt, vi* to drink.

bebida [be'βiða] *nf* drink.

beca ['beka] *nf* grant, scholarship.

befarse [be'farse] *vr*: **~ de algo** to scoff at sth.

beldad [bel'dað] *nf* beauty.

belén [be'len] *nm* (*de navidad*) nativity scene, crib; **B~** Bethlehem.

belga ['belɣa] *adj, nm/f* Belgian.

Bélgica ['belxika] *nf* Belgium.

Belice [be'liθe] *nf* Belize.

bélico, a ['beliko, a] *adj* (*actitud*) warlike; **belicoso, a** *adj* (*guerrero*) warlike; (*agresivo*) aggressive, bellicose.

beligerante [belixe'rante] *adj* belligerent.

bellaco, a [be'ʎako, a] *adj* sly, cunning ♦ *nm* villain, rogue; **bellaquería** *nf* (*acción*) dirty trick; (*calidad*) wickedness.

belleza [be'ʎeθa] *nf* beauty.

bello, a ['beʎo, a] *adj* beautiful, lovely; **Bellas Artes** Fine Art.

bellota [be'ʎota] *nf* acorn.

bemol [be'mol] *nm* (*MUS*) flat; **esto tiene ~es** (*fam*) this is a tough one.

bencina [ben'θina] (*AM*) *nf* (*gasolina*) petrol (*BRIT*), gasoline (*US*).

bendecir [bende'θir] *vt* to bless.

bendición [bendi'θjon] *nf* blessing.

bendito, a [ben'dito, a] pp de **bendecir** ♦ adj holy; (afortunado) lucky; (feliz) happy; (sencillo) simple ♦ nm/f simple soul.

benedictino, a [beneðik'tino, a] adj, nm Benedictine.

beneficencia [benefi'θenθja] nf charity.

beneficiar [benefi'θjar] vt to benefit, be of benefit to; ~**se** vr to benefit, profit; ~**io, a** nm/f beneficiary.

beneficio [bene'fiθjo] nm (bien) benefit, advantage; (ganancia) profit, gain; ~**so, a** adj beneficial.

benéfico, a [be'nefiko, a] adj charitable.

beneplácito [bene'plaθito] nm approval, consent.

benevolencia [beneβo'lenθja] nf benevolence, kindness; **benévolo, a** adj benevolent, kind.

benigno, a [be'niɣno, a] adj kind; (suave) mild; (MED: tumor) benign, non-malignant.

beodo, a [be'oðo, a] adj drunk.

berenjena [beren'xena] nf aubergine (BRIT), eggplant (US).

Berlín [ber'lin] n Berlin; **berlinés, esa** adj of o from Berlin ♦ nm/f Berliner.

bermejo, a [ber'mexo, a] adj red.

berrear [berre'ar] vi to bellow, low.

berrido [be'rriðo] nm bellow(ing).

berrinche [be'rrintʃe] (fam) nm temper, tantrum.

berro ['berro] nm watercress.

berza ['berθa] nf cabbage.

besamel [besa'mel] nf (CULIN) white sauce, bechamel sauce.

besar [be'sar] vt to kiss; (fig: tocar) to graze; ~**se** vr to kiss (one another); **beso** nm kiss.

bestia ['bestja] nf beast, animal; (fig) idiot; ~ **de carga** beast of burden.

bestial [bes'tjal] adj bestial; (fam) terrific; ~**idad** nf bestiality; (fam) stupidity.

besugo [be'suɣo] nm sea bream; (fam) idiot.

besuquear [besuke'ar] vt to cover with kisses; ~**se** vr to kiss and cuddle.

betún [be'tun] nm shoe polish; (QUIMICA) bitumen.

biberón [biße'ron] nm feeding bottle.

Biblia ['bißlja] nf Bible.

bibliografía [bißljoxra'fia] nf bibliography.

biblioteca [bißljo'teka] nf library; (mueble) bookshelves; ~ **de consulta** reference library; ~**rio, a** nm/f librarian.

B.I.C. nf abr (= Brigada de Investigación Criminal) ≈ CID (BRIT), ≈ FBI (US).

bicarbonato [bikarßo'nato] nm bicarbonate.

bici ['biθi] (fam) nf bike.

bicicleta [biθi'kleta] nf bicycle, cycle; **ir en** ~ to cycle.

bicho ['bitʃo] nm (animal) small animal; (sabandija) bug, insect; (TAUR) bull.

bidé [bi'ðe] (pl ~s) nm bidet.

┌─────────────────┐
│ **PALABRA CLAVE** │
└─────────────────┘

bien [bjen] nm **1** (bienestar) good; **te lo digo por tu** ~ I'm telling you for your own good; **el** ~ **y el mal** good and evil **2** (posesión): ~**es** goods; ~**es de consumo** consumer goods; ~**es inmuebles** o **raíces**/~**es muebles** real estate sg/personal property sg

♦ adv **1** (de manera satisfactoria, correcta etc) well; **trabaja/come** ~ she works/eats well; **contestó** ~ he answered correctly; **me siento** ~ I feel fine; **no me siento** ~ I don't feel very well; **se está** ~ **aquí** it's nice here

2 (frases): **hiciste** ~ **en llamarme** you were right to call me

3 (valor intensivo) very; **un cuarto** ~ **caliente** a nice warm room; ~ **se ve que ...** it's quite clear that ...

4: **estar** ~: **estoy muy bien aquí** I feel very happy here; **está bien que vengan** it's alright for them to come; **¡está bien! lo haré** oh alright, I'll do it

5 (de buena gana): **yo** ~ **que iría pero ...** I'd gladly go but ...

♦ excl: **¡~!** (aprobación) O.K!; **¡muy ~!** well done!

♦ adj inv (matiz despectivo): **niño** ~ rich kid; **gente** ~ posh people

♦ *conj* **1**: ~ ... ~: ~ **en coche** ~ **en tren** either by car or by train
2: **no** ~ (*esp AM*): **no** ~ **llegue te llamaré** as soon as I arrive I'll call you
3: **si** ~ even though; *ver tb* **más**.

bienal [bje'nal] *adj* biennial.

bienaventurado, a [bjenaßentu'raðo, a] *adj* (*feliz*) happy, fortunate.

bienestar [bjenes'tar] *nm* well-being, welfare.

bienhechor, a [bjene'tʃor, a] *adj* beneficent ♦ *nm/f* benefactor/benefactress.

bienvenida [bjembe'niða] *nf* welcome; **dar la** ~ **a uno** to welcome sb.

bienvenido [bjembe'niðo] *excl* welcome!

bife ['bife] (*AM*) *nm* steak.

bifurcación [bifurka'θjon] *nf* fork.

bigamia [bi'ɣamja] *nf* bigamy; **bígamo, a** *adj* bigamous ♦ *nm/f* bigamist.

bigote [bi'ɣote] *nm* moustache; **bigotudo, a** *adj* with a big moustache.

bikini [bi'kini] *nm* bikini; (*CULIN*) toasted ham and cheese sandwich.

bilingüe [bi'lingwe] *adj* bilingual.

billar [bi'ʎar] *nm* billiards *sg*; (*lugar*) billiard hall; (*mini-casino*) amusement arcade.

billete [bi'ʎete] *nm* ticket; (*de banco*) (bank)note (*BRIT*), bill (*US*); (*carta*) note; ~ **sencillo**, ~ **de ida solamente** single (*BRIT*) *o* one-way (*US*) ticket; ~ **de ida y vuelta** return (*BRIT*) *o* round-trip (*US*) ticket; ~ **de 20 libras** £20 note.

billetera [biʎe'tera] *nf* wallet.

billetero [biʎe'tero] *nm* = **billetera**.

billón [bi'ʎon] *nm* billion.

bimensual [bimen'swal] *adj* twice monthly.

bimotor [bimo'tor] *adj* twin-engined ♦ *nm* twin-engined plane.

binóculo [bi'nokulo] *nm* pince-nez.

biografía [bjoɣra'fia] *nf* biography; **biógrafo, a** *nm/f* biographer.

biología [bjolo'xia] *nf* biology; **biológico, a** *adj* biological; **biólogo, a** *nm/f* biologist.

biombo ['bjombo] *nm* (folding) screen.

biopsia [bi'opsja] *nf* biopsy.

birlar [bir'lar] (*fam*) *vt* to pinch.

Birmania [bir'manja] *nf* Burma.

bis [bis] *excl* encore! ♦ *adv*: **viven en el 27** ~ they live at 27a.

bisabuelo, a [bisa'ßwelo, a] *nm/f* great-grandfather/mother.

bisagra [bi'saɣra] *nf* hinge.

bisbisar [bisßi'sar] *vt* to mutter, mumble.

bisbisear [bisßise'ar] *vt* = **bisbisar**.

bisiesto [bi'sjesto] *adj*: **año** ~ leap year.

bisnieto, a [bis'njeto, a] *nm/f* great-grandson/daughter.

bisonte [bi'sonte] *nm* bison.

bisté [bis'te] *nm* = **bistec**.

bistec [bis'tek] *nm* steak.

bisturí [bistu'ri] *nm* scalpel.

bisutería [bisute'ria] *nf* imitation *o* costume jewellery.

bit [bit] *nm* (*INFORM*) bit.

bizcar [biθ'kar] *vi* to squint.

bizco, a ['biθko, a] *adj* cross-eyed.

bizcocho [biθ'kotʃo] *nm* (*CULIN*) sponge cake.

bizquear [biθke'ar] *vi* to squint.

blanca ['blanka] *nf* (*MUS*) minim; **estar sin** ~ to be broke; *ver tb* **blanco**.

blanco, a ['blanko, a] *adj* white ♦ *nm/f* white man/woman, white ♦ *nm* (*color*) white; (*en texto*) blank; (*MIL, fig*) target; **en** ~ blank; **noche en** ~ sleepless night.

blancura [blan'kura] *nf* whiteness.

blandir [blan'dir] *vt* to brandish.

blando, a ['blando, a] *adj* soft; (*tierno*) tender, gentle; (*carácter*) mild; (*fam*) cowardly; **blandura** *nf* softness; tenderness; mildness.

blanquear [blanke'ar] *vt* to whiten; (*fachada*) to whitewash; (*paño*) to bleach ♦ *vi* to turn white; **blanquecino, a** *adj* whitish.

blasfemar [blasfe'mar] *vi* to blaspheme, curse; **blasfemia** *nf* blasphemy.

blasón [bla'son] *nm* coat of arms; (*fig*) honour; **blasonar** *vt* to emblazon ♦ *vi* to boast, brag.

bledo ['bleðo] *nm*: **me importa un** ~ I couldn't care less.

blindado, a [blin'daðo, a] *adj* (*MIL*) armour-plated; (*antibala*) bullet-proof;

coche (*ESP*) *o* **carro** (*AM*) ~ armoured car.

blindaje [blin'daxe] *nm* armour, armour-plating.

bloc [blok] (*pl* ~s) *nm* writing pad.

bloque ['bloke] *nm* block; (*POL*) bloc; ~ **de cilindros** cylinder block.

bloquear [bloke'ar] *vt* to blockade; **bloqueo** *nm* blockade; (*COM*) freezing, blocking.

blusa ['blusa] *nf* blouse.

boato [bo'ato] *nm* show, ostentation.

bobada [bo'βaða] *nf* foolish action; foolish statement; **decir** ~s to talk nonsense.

bobería [boβe'ria] *nf* = **bobada**.

bobina [bo'βina] *nf* (*TEC*) bobbin; (*FOTO*) spool; (*ELEC*) coil.

bobo, a ['boβo, a] *adj* (*tonto*) daft, silly; (*cándido*) naïve ♦ *nm/f* fool, idiot ♦ *nm* (*TEATRO*) clown, funny man.

boca ['boka] *nf* mouth; (*de crustáceo*) pincer; (*de cañón*) muzzle; (*entrada*) mouth, entrance; ~s *nfpl* (*de río*) mouth *sg*; ~ **abajo/arriba** face down/up; **a** ~**jarro** point-blank; **se me hace agua la** ~ my mouth is watering.

bocacalle [boka'kaʎe] *nf* (entrance to a) street; **la primera** ~ the first turning *o* street.

bocadillo [boka'ðiʎo] *nm* sandwich.

bocado [bo'kaðo] *nm* mouthful, bite; (*de caballo*) bridle; ~ **de Adán** Adam's apple.

bocanada [boka'naða] *nf* (*de vino*) mouthful, swallow; (*de aire*) gust, puff.

bocazas [bo'kaθas] (*fam*) *nm inv* big-mouth.

boceto [bo'θeto] *nm* sketch, outline.

bocina [bo'θina] *nf* (*MUS*) trumpet; (*AUTO*) horn; (*para hablar*) megaphone.

bocha ['botʃa] *nf* bowl; ~s *nfpl* bowls *sg*.

bochinche [bo'tʃintʃe] (*fam*) *nm* uproar.

bochorno [bo'tʃorno] *nm* (*vergüenza*) embarrassment; (*calor*): **hace** ~ it's very muggy; ~**so, a** *adj* muggy; embarrassing.

boda ['boða] *nf* (*tb*: ~s) wedding, marriage; (*fiesta*) wedding reception; ~s **de plata/de oro** silver/golden wedding.

bodega [bo'ðeɣa] *nf* (*de vino*) (wine) cellar; (*depósito*) storeroom; (*de barco*) hold.

bodegón [boðe'ɣon] *nm* (*ARTE*) still life.

bofe ['bofe] *nm* (*tb*: ~s: **de res**) lights.

bofetada [bofe'taða] *nf* slap (in the face).

bofetón [bofe'ton] *nm* = **bofetada**.

boga ['boɣa] *nf*: **en** ~ (*fig*) in vogue.

bogar [bo'ɣar] *vi* (*remar*) to row; (*navegar*) to sail.

Bogotá [boɣo'ta] *n* Bogotá; **bogotano, a** *adj* of *o* from Bogotá.

bohemio, a [bo'emjo, a] *adj*, *nm/f* Bohemian.

boicot [boi'kot] (*pl* ~s) *nm* boycott; ~**ear** *vt* to boycott; ~**eo** *nm* boycott.

boina ['boina] *nf* beret.

bola ['bola] *nf* ball; (*canica*) marble; (*NAIPES*) (grand) slam; (*betún*) shoe polish; (*mentira*) tale, story; ~s (*AM*) *nfpl* bolas *sg*; ~ **de billar** billiard ball; ~ **de nieve** snowball.

bolchevique [boltʃe'βike] *adj*, *nm/f* Bolshevik.

boleadoras [bolea'ðoras] (*AM*) *nfpl* bolas *sg*.

bolera [bo'lera] *nf* skittle *o* bowling alley.

boleta [bo'leta] (*AM*) *nf* (*billete*) ticket; (*permiso*) pass, permit.

boletería [bolete'ria] (*AM*) *nf* ticket office.

boletín [bole'tin] *nm* bulletin; (*periódico*) journal, review; ~ **escolar** (*ESP*) school report; ~ **de noticias** news bulletin; ~ **de pedido** application form; ~ **de precios** price list; ~ **de prensa** press release.

boleto [bo'leto] *nm* ticket.

boli ['boli] (*fam*) *nm* Biro ®, pen.

boliche [bo'litʃe] *nm* (*bola*) jack; (*juego*) bowls *sg*; (*lugar*) bowling alley.

bolígrafo [bo'liɣrafo] *nm* ball-point pen, Biro ®.

bolívar [bo'liβar] *nm* *monetary unit of*

Venezuela.

Bolivia [bo'lißja] *nf* Bolivia; **boliviano, a** *adj, nm/f* Bolivian.

bolo ['bolo] *nm* skittle; (*píldora*) (large) pill; (*juego de*) ~s *nmpl* skittles *sg*.

bolsa ['bolsa] *nf* (*cartera*) purse; (*saco*) bag; (*AM*) pocket; (*ANAT*) cavity, sac; (*COM*) stock exchange; (*MINERÍA*) pocket; **de ~** pocket *cpd*; **~ de agua caliente** hot water bottle; **~ de aire** air pocket; **~ de papel** paper bag; **~ de plástico** plastic bag.

bolsillo [bol'siʎo] *nm* pocket; (*cartera*) purse; **de ~** pocket(-size).

bolsista [bol'sista] *nm/f* stockbroker.

bolso ['bolso] *nm* (*bolsa*) bag; (*de mujer*) handbag.

bollo ['boʎo] *nm* (*pan*) roll; (*bulto*) bump, lump; (*abolladura*) dent.

bomba ['bomba] *nf* (*MIL*) bomb; (*TEC*) pump ♦ (*fam*) *adj*: **noticia ~** bombshell ♦ (*fam*) *adv*: **pasarlo ~** to have a great time; **~ atómica/de humo/de retardo** atomic/smoke/time bomb; **~ de gasolina** petrol pump.

bombardear [bombarðe'ar] *vt* to bombard; (*MIL*) to bomb; **bombardeo** *nm* bombardment; bombing.

bombardero [bombar'ðero] *nm* bomber.

bombear [bombe'ar] *vt* (*agua*) to pump (out *o* up); (*MIL*) to bomb; **~se** *vr* to warp.

bombero [bom'bero] *nm* fireman.

bombilla [bom'biʎa] (*ESP*) *nf* (light) bulb.

bombín [bom'bin] *nm* bowler hat.

bombo ['bombo] *nm* (*MUS*) bass drum; (*TEC*) drum.

bombón [bom'bon] *nm* chocolate.

bonachón, ona [bona'tʃon, ona] *adj* good-natured, easy-going.

bonaerense [bonae'rense] *adj* of *o* from Buenos Aires.

bonanza [bo'nanθa] *nf* (*NAUT*) fair weather; (*fig*) bonanza; (*MINERÍA*) rich pocket *o* vein.

bondad [bon'dað] *nf* goodness, kindness; **tenga la ~ de** (please) be good enough to; **~oso, a** *adj* good, kind.

bonificación [bonifika'θjon] *nf* bonus.

bonito, a [bo'nito, a] *adj* pretty; (*agradable*) nice ♦ *nm* (*atún*) tuna (fish).

bono ['bono] *nm* voucher; (*FINANZAS*) bond.

bonobús [bono'ßus] (*ESP*) *nm* bus pass.

boquear [boke'ar] *vi* to gasp.

boquerón [boke'ron] *nm* (*pez*) (kind of) anchovy; (*agujero*) large hole.

boquete [bo'kete] *nm* gap, hole.

boquiabierto, a [bokja'ßjerto, a] *adj*: **quedar ~** to be amazed *o* flabbergasted.

boquilla [bo'kiʎa] *nf* (*para riego*) nozzle; (*para cigarro*) cigarette holder; (*MUS*) mouthpiece.

borbollar [borßo'ʎar] *vi* to bubble.

borbollear [borßoʎe'ar] *vi* = **borbollar**.

borbotar [borßo'tar] *vi* = **borbollar**.

borbotón [borßo'ton] *nm*: **salir a borbotones** to gush out.

bordado [bor'ðaðo] *nm* embroidery.

bordar [bor'ðar] *vt* to embroider.

borde ['borðe] *nm* edge, border; (*de camino etc*) side; (*en la costura*) hem; **al ~ de** (*fig*) on the verge *o* brink of; **ser ~** (*ESP: fam*) to be a pain (in the neck); **~ar** *vt* to border.

bordillo [bor'ðiʎo] *nm* kerb (*BRIT*), curb (*US*).

bordo ['borðo] *nm* (*NAUT*) side; **a ~ on** board.

borinqueño, a [borin'keɲo, a] *adj, nm/f* Puerto Rican.

borra ['borra] *nf* (*pelusa*) fluff; (*sedimento*) sediment.

borrachera [borra'tʃera] *nf* (*ebriedad*) drunkenness; (*orgía*) spree, binge.

borracho, a [bo'rratʃo, a] *adj* drunk ♦ *nm/f* (*que bebe mucho*) drunkard, drunk; (*temporalmente*) drunk, drunk man/woman.

borrador [borra'ðor] *nm* (*escritura*) first draft, rough sketch; (*cuaderno*) scribbling pad; (*goma*) rubber (*BRIT*), eraser.

borrajear [borraxe'ar] *vt, vi* to scribble.

borrar [bo'rrar] *vt* to erase, rub out.

borrasca [bo'rraska] *nf* storm.

borrico, a [bo'rriko, a] *nm/f* donkey/she-donkey; (*fig*) stupid man/woman.

borrón [bo'rron] *nm* (*mancha*) stain.

borroso, a [bo'rroso, a] *adj* vague, unclear; *(escritura)* illegible.

bosque ['boske] *nm* wood; *(grande)* forest.

bosquejar [boske'xar] *vt* to sketch; **bosquejo** *nm* sketch.

bosta ['bosta] *nf* dung; *(abono)* manure.

bostezar [boste'θar] *vi* to yawn; **bostezo** *nm* yawn.

bota ['bota] *nf* (*calzado*) boot; *(saco)* leather wine bottle.

botánica [bo'tanika] *nf* (*ciencia*) botany; *ver tb* **botánico**.

botánico, a [bo'taniko, a] *adj* botanical ♦ *nm/f* botanist.

botar [bo'tar] *vt* to throw, hurl; *(NAUT)* to launch; *(fam)* to throw out ♦ *vi* to bounce.

bote ['bote] *nm* (*salto*) bounce; *(golpe)* thrust; *(vasija)* tin, can; *(embarcación)* boat; **de ~ en ~** packed, jammed full; **~ de la basura** (*AM*) dustbin (*BRIT*), trashcan (*US*); **~ salvavidas** lifeboat.

botella [bo'teʎa] *nf* bottle.

botica [bo'tika] *nf* chemist's (shop) (*BRIT*), pharmacy; **~rio, a** *nm/f* chemist (*BRIT*), pharmacist.

botijo [bo'tixo] *nm* (earthenware) jug.

botín [bo'tin] *nm* (*calzado*) half boot; *(polaina)* spat; *(MIL)* booty.

botiquín [boti'kin] *nm* (*armario*) medicine cabinet; *(portátil)* first-aid kit.

botón [bo'ton] *nm* button; *(BOT)* bud; *(de florete)* tip; **~ de oro** buttercup.

botones [bo'tones] *nm inv* bellboy (*BRIT*), bellhop (*US*).

bóveda ['boßeða] *nf* (*ARQ*) vault.

boxeador [boksea'ðor] *nm* boxer.

boxeo [bok'seo] *nm* boxing.

boya ['boja] *nf* (*NAUT*) buoy; *(flotador)* float.

bozal [bo'θal] *nm* (*de caballo*) halter; *(de perro)* muzzle.

bracear [braθe'ar] *vi* (*agitar los brazos*) to wave one's arms.

bracero [bra'θero] *nm* labourer; *(en el campo)* farmhand.

bracete [bra'θete]: **de ~** *adv* arm in arm.

braga ['braɣa] *nf* (*cuerda*) sling, rope; *(de bebé)* nappy (*BRIT*), diaper (*US*); **~s** *nfpl* (*de mujer*) panties, knickers (*BRIT*).

bragueta [bra'ɣeta] *nf* fly, flies *pl*.

braille [breil] *nm* braille.

bramar [bra'mar] *vi* to bellow, roar; **bramido** *nm* bellow, roar.

brasa ['brasa] *nf* live o hot coal.

brasero [bra'sero] *nm* brazier.

Brasil [bra'sil] *nm*: **(el) ~** Brazil; **brasileño, a** *adj, nm/f* Brazilian.

bravata [bra'ßata] *nf* boast.

braveza [bra'ßeθa] *nf* (*valor*) bravery; *(ferocidad)* ferocity.

bravío, a [bra'ßio, a] *adj* wild; *(feroz)* fierce.

bravo, a ['braßo, a] *adj* (*valiente*) brave; *(bueno)* fine, splendid; *(feroz)* ferocious; *(salvaje)* wild; *(mar etc)* rough, stormy ♦ *excl* bravo!; **bravura** *nf* bravery; ferocity; *(pey)* boast.

braza ['braθa] *nf* fathom; **nadar a la ~** to swim (the) breast-stroke.

brazada [bra'θaða] *nf* stroke.

brazado [bra'θaðo] *nm* armful.

brazalete [braθa'lete] *nm* (*pulsera*) bracelet; *(banda)* armband.

brazo ['braθo] *nm* arm; *(ZOOL)* foreleg; *(BOT)* limb, branch; **luchar a ~ partido** to fight hand-to-hand; **ir cogidos del ~** to walk arm in arm.

brea ['brea] *nf* pitch, tar.

brebaje [bre'ßaxe] *nm* potion.

brecha ['bretʃa] *nf* (*hoyo, vacío*) gap, opening; *(MIL, fig)* breach.

brega ['breɣa] *nf* (*lucha*) struggle; *(trabajo)* hard work. ·

breve ['breße] *adj* short, brief ♦ *nf* (*MUS*) breve; **~dad** *nf* brevity, shortness.

brezal [bre'θal] *nm* moor(land), heath; **brezo** *nm* heather.

bribón, ona [bri'ßon, ona] *adj* idle, lazy ♦ *nm/f* (*vagabundo*) vagabond; *(pícaro)* rascal, rogue.

bricolaje [briko'laxe] *nm* do-it-yourself, DIY.

brida ['briða] *nf* bridle, rein; *(TEC)* clamp; **a toda ~** at top speed.

bridge [brit∫] *nm* bridge.
brigada [bri'ɣaða] *nf* (*unidad*) brigade; (*trabajadores*) squad, gang ♦ *nm* ≈ staff-sergeant, sergeant-major.
brillante [bri'ʎante] *adj* brilliant ♦ *nm* diamond.
brillar [bri'ʎar] *vi* (*tb fig*) to shine; (*joyas*) to sparkle.
brillo [bri'ʎo] *nm* shine; (*brillantez*) brilliance; (*fig*) splendour; **sacar** ~ **a** to polish.
brincar [brin'kar] *vi* to skip about, hop about, jump about; **está que brinca** he's hopping mad.
brinco [brinko] *nm* jump, leap.
brindar [brin'dar] *vi*: ~ **a** *o* **por** to drink (a toast) to ♦ *vt* to offer, present.
brindis [brindis] *nm inv* toast; (*TAUR*) (ceremony of) dedication.
brío [brio] *nm* spirit, dash; **brioso, a** *adj* spirited, dashing.
brisa [brisa] *nf* breeze.
británico, a [bri'taniko, a] *adj* British ♦ *nm/f* Briton, British person.
brocal [bro'kal] *nm* rim.
brocha [brot∫a] *nf* (large) paintbrush; ~ **de afeitar** shaving brush.
broche [brot∫e] *nm* brooch.
broma [broma] *nf* joke; **en** ~ in fun, as a joke; **bromear** *vi* to joke.
bromista [bro'mista] *adj* fond of joking ♦ *nm/f* joker, wag.
bronca [bronka] *nf* row; **echar una** ~ **a uno** to tick sb off.
bronce [bronθe] *nm* bronze; ~**ado, a** *adj* bronze; (*por el sol*) tanned ♦ *nm* (sun)tan; (*TEC*) bronzing.
broncearse [bronθe'arse] *vr* to get a suntan.
bronco, a [bronko, a] *adj* (*manera*) rude, surly; (*voz*) harsh.
bronquitis [bron'kitis] *nf inv* bronchitis.
brotar [bro'tar] *vi* (*BOT*) to sprout; (*aguas*) to gush (forth); (*MED*) to break out.
brote [brote] *nm* (*BOT*) shoot; (*MED, fig*) outbreak.
bruces [bruθes]: **de** ~ *adv*: **caer** *o* **dar de** ~ to fall headlong, fall flat.
bruja [bruxa] *nf* witch; **brujería** *nf* witchcraft.
brujo [bruxo] *nm* wizard, magician.
brújula [bruxula] *nf* compass.
bruma [bruma] *nf* mist; **brumoso, a** *adj* misty.
bruñido [bru'ɲiðo] *nm* polish.
bruñir [bru'ɲir] *vt* to polish.
brusco, a [brusko, a] *adj* (*súbito*) sudden; (*áspero*) brusque.
Bruselas [bru'selas] *n* Brussels.
brutal [bru'tal] *adj* brutal.
brutalidad [brutali'ðað] *nf* brutality.
bruto, a [bruto, a] *adj* (*idiota*) stupid; (*bestial*) brutish; (*peso*) gross; **en** ~ raw, unworked.
Bs.As. *abr* (= *Buenos Aires*) B.A.
bucal [bu'kal] *adj* oral; **por vía** ~ orally.
bucear [buθe'ar] *vi* to dive ♦ *vt* to explore; **buceo** *nm* diving; (*fig*) investigation.
bucle [bukle] *nm* curl.
budismo [bu'ðismo] *nm* Buddhism.
buen [bwen] *adj m ver* **bueno**.
buenamente [bwena'mente] *adv* (*fácilmente*) easily; (*voluntariamente*) willingly.
buenaventura [bwenaßen'tura] *nf* (*suerte*) good luck; (*adivinación*) fortune.

╔══════════════════════════════╗
║ *PALABRA CLAVE* ║
╚══════════════════════════════╝

bueno, a [bweno, a] (*antes de nmsg*: **buen**) *adj* **1** (*excelente etc*) good; **es un libro** ~ *o* **es un buen libro** it's a good book; **hace** ~, **hace buen tiempo** the weather is fine, it is fine; **el** ~ **de Paco** good old Paco; **fue muy** ~ **conmigo** he was very nice *o* kind to me
2 (*apropiado*): **ser** ~ **para** to be good for; **creo que vamos por buen camino** I think we're on the right track
3 (*irónico*): **le di un buen rapapolvo** I gave him a good *o* real ticking off; **¡buen conductor estás hecho!** some *o* a fine driver you are!; **¡estaría** ~ **que ...!** a fine thing it would be if ...!
4 (*atractivo, sabroso*): **está** ~ **este bizcocho** this sponge is delicious; **Carmen está muy buena** Carmen is looking good

5 (*saludos*): ¡buen día!, ¡~s días! (good) morning!; ¡buenas (tardes)! (good) afternoon!; (*más tarde*) (good) evening!; ¡buenas noches! good night! **6** (*otras locuciones*): estar de buenas to be in a good mood; por las buenas o por las malas by hook or by crook; de buenas a primeras all of a sudden ♦ *excl*: ¡~! all right!; ~, ¿y qué? well, so what?

Buenos Aires *nm* Buenos Aires.
buey [bwei] *nm* ox.
búfalo ['bufalo] *nm* buffalo.
bufanda [bu'fanda] *nf* scarf.
bufar [bu'far] *vi* to snort.
bufete [bu'fete] *nm* (*despacho de abogado*) lawyer's office.
buffer ['bufer] *nm* (*INFORM*) buffer.
bufón [bu'fon, ona] *nm* clown.
buhardilla [bμar'ðiʎa] *nf* (*desván*) attic.
búho ['buo] *nm* owl; (*fig*) hermit, recluse.
buhonero [buo'nero] *nm* pedlar.
buitre ['bwitre] *nm* vulture.
bujía [bu'xia] *nf* (*vela*) candle; (*ELEC*) candle (power); (*AUTO*) spark plug.
bula ['bula] *nf* (*papal*) bull.
bulbo ['bulβo] *nm* bulb.
bulevar [bule'βar] *nm* boulevard.
Bulgaria [bul'varja] *nf* Bulgaria; **búlgaro, a** *adj, nm/f* Bulgarian.
bulto ['bulto] *nm* (*paquete*) package; (*fardo*) bundle; (*tamaño*) size, bulkiness; (*MED*) swelling, lump; (*silueta*) vague shape; (*estatua*) bust, statue.
bulla ['buʎa] *nf* (*ruido*) uproar; (*de gente*) crowd.
bullicio [bu'ʎiθjo] *nm* (*ruido*) uproar; (*movimiento*) bustle.
bullir [bu'ʎir] *vi* (*hervir*) to boil; (*burbujear*) to bubble; (*mover*) to move, stir.
buñuelo [bu'ɲwelo] *nm* ≈ doughnut (*BRIT*), ≈ donut (*US*); (*fruta de sartén*) fritter.
BUP [bup] *nm abr* (*ESP*: = *Bachillerato Unificado Polivalente*) *secondary education and leaving certificate for 14–17 age group.*

buque ['buke] *nm* ship, vessel.
burbuja [bur'βuxa] *nf* bubble; **burbujear** *vi* to bubble.
burdel [bur'ðel] *nm* brothel.
burdo, a ['burðo, a] *adj* coarse, rough.
burgués, esa [bur'ves, esa] *adj* middle-class, bourgeois; **burguesía** *nf* middle class, bourgeoisie.
burla ['burla] *nf* (*mofa*) gibe; (*broma*) joke; (*engaño*) trick.
burladero [burla'ðero] *nm* (bullfighter's) refuge.
burlador, a [burla'ðor, a] *adj* mocking ♦ *nm/f* (*bromista*) joker ♦ *nm* (*libertino*) seducer.
burlar [bur'lar] *vt* (*engañar*) to deceive; (*seducir*) to seduce ♦ *vi* to joke; ~se *vr* to joke; ~se de to make fun of.
burlesco, a [bur'lesko, a] *adj* burlesque.
burlón, ona [bur'lon, ona] *adj* mocking.
burocracia [buro'kraθja] *nf* civil service; (*pey*) bureaucracy.
burócrata [bu'rokrata] *nm/f* civil servant; (*pey*) bureaucrat.
buromática [buro'matika] *nf* office automation.
burro, a ['burro] *nm/f* donkey/she-donkey; (*fig*) ass, idiot.
bursátil [bur'satil] *adj* stock-exchange *cpd*.
bus [bus] *nm* bus.
busca ['buska] *nf* search, hunt ♦ *nm* (*TEL*) bleeper; en ~ de in search of.
buscapleitos [buska'pleitos] *nm/f inv* troublemaker.
buscar [bus'kar] *vt* to look for, search for, seek ♦ *vi* to look, search, seek; se busca secretaria secretary wanted.
buscón, ona [bus'kon, ona] *adj* thieving ♦ *nm* petty thief; **buscona** *nf* whore.
busilis [bu'silis] (*fam*) *nm inv* snag.
busque *etc vb ver* **buscar**.
búsqueda ['buskeða] *nf* = **busca** *nf*.
busto ['busto] *nm* (*ANAT, ARTE*) bust.
butaca [bu'taka] *nf* armchair; (*de cine, teatro*) stall, seat.
butano [bu'tano] *nm* butane (gas).
buzo ['buθo] *nm* diver.
buzón [bu'θon] *nm* (*en puerta*) letter box; (*en la calle*) pillar box.

C

C. *abr* (= *centígrado*) C; (= *compañía*) Co.

c. *abr* (= *capítulo*) ch.

C/ *abr* (= *calle*) St.

c.a. *abr* (= *corriente alterna*) AC.

cabal [ka'βal] *adj* (*exacto*) exact; (*correcto*) right, proper; (*acabado*) finished, complete; **~es** *nmpl*: **estar en sus ~es** to be in one's right mind.

cabalgadura [kaβalɣa'ðura] *nf* mount, horse.

cabalgar [kaβal'ɣar] *vt, vi* to ride.

cabalgata [kaβal'ɣata] *nf* procession.

caballa [ka'βaʎa] *nf* mackerel.

caballeresco, a [kaβaʎe'resko, a] *adj* noble, chivalrous.

caballería [kaβaʎe'ria] *nf* mount; (*MIL*) cavalry.

caballeriza [kaβaʎe'riθa] *nf* stable; **caballerizo** *nm* groom, stableman.

caballero [kaβa'ʎero] *nm* (*hombre galante*) gentleman; (*de la orden de caballería*) knight; (*trato directo*) sir.

caballerosidad [kaβaʎerosi'ðað] *nf* chivalry.

caballete [kaβa'ʎete] *nm* (*ARTE*) easel; (*TEC*) trestle.

caballito [kaβa'ʎito] *nm* (*caballo pequeño*) small horse, pony; **~s** *nmpl* (*en verbena*) roundabout, merry-go-round.

caballo [ka'βaʎo] *nm* horse; (*AJEDREZ*) knight; (*NAIPES*) queen; **ir en ~** to ride; **~ de vapor** *o* **de fuerza** horsepower.

cabaña [ka'βaɲa] *nf* (*casita*) hut, cabin.

cabaré [kaβa're] (*pl* **~s**) *nm* cabaret.

cabaret [kaβa're] (*pl* **~s**) *nm* cabaret.

cabecear [kaβeθe'ar] *vt, vi* to nod.

cabecera [kaβe'θera] *nf* head; (*de distrito*) chief town; (*IMPRENTA*) headline.

cabecilla [kaβe'θiʎa] *nm* ringleader.

cabellera [kaβe'ʎera] *nf* (head of) hair; (*de cometa*) tail.

cabello [ka'βeʎo] *nm* (*tb*: **~s**) hair.

caber [ka'βer] *vi* (*entrar*) to fit, go; **caben 3 más** there's room for 3 more.

cabestrillo [kaβes'triʎo] *nm* sling.

cabestro [ka'βestro] *nm* halter.

cabeza [ka'βeθa] *nf* head; (*POL*) chief, leader; **~da** *nf* (*golpe*) butt; **dar ~das** to nod off.

cabida [ka'βiða] *nf* space.

cabildo [ka'βildo] *nm* (*de iglesia*) chapter; (*POL*) town council.

cabina [ka'βina] *nf* cabin; (*de camión*) cab; **~ telefónica** telephone box (*BRIT*) *o* booth.

cabizbajo, a [kaβiθ'βaxo, a] *adj* crestfallen, dejected.

cable [ka'βle] *nm* cable.

cabo ['kaβo] *nm* (*de objeto*) end, extremity; (*MIL*) corporal; (*NAUT*) rope, cable; (*GEO*) cape; **al ~ de 3 días** after 3 days.

cabra ['kaβra] *nf* goat.

cabré *etc vb ver* **caber**.

cabrío, a [ka'βrio, a] *adj* goatish; **macho ~** (he-) goat, billy goat.

cabriola [ka'βrjola] *nf* caper.

cabritilla [kaβri'tiʎa] *nf* kid, kidskin.

cabrito [ka'βrito] *nm* kid.

cabrón [ka'βron] *nm* cuckold; (*fam!*) bastard (!).

cacahuete [kaka'wete] (*ESP*) *nm* peanut.

cacao [ka'kao] *nm* cocoa; (*BOT*) cacao.

cacarear [kakare'ar] *vi* (*persona*) to boast; (*gallina*) to crow.

cacería [kaθe'ria] *nf* hunt.

cacerola [kaθe'rola] *nf* pan, saucepan.

cacique [ka'θike] *nm* chief, local ruler; (*POL*) local party boss; **caciquismo** *nm* system of control by the local boss.

caco ['kako] *nm* pickpocket.

cacto ['kakto] *nm* cactus.

cactus ['kaktus] *nm inv* cactus.

cacharro [ka'tʃarro] *nm* earthenware pot; **~s** *nmpl* pots and pans.

cachear [katʃe'ar] *vt* to search, frisk.

cachemir [katʃe'mir] *nm* cashmere.

cacheo [ka'tʃeo] *nm* searching, frisking.

cachete [ka'tʃete] *nm* (*ANAT*) cheek; (*bofetada*) slap (in the face).

cachimba [ka'tʃimba] *nf* pipe.

cachiporra [katʃi'porra] *nf* truncheon.

cachivache [katʃi'βatʃe] *nm* (*trasto*) piece of junk; **~s** *nmpl* junk *sg*.

cacho [ˈkatʃo, a] *nm* (small) bit; (*AM:* *cuerno*) horn.
cachondeo [katʃonˈdeo] (*fam*) *nm* farce, joke.
cachondo, a [kaˈtʃondo, a] *adj* (*ZOOL*) on heat; (*fam*) sexy; (*gracioso*) funny.
cachorro, a [kaˈtʃorro, a] *nm/f* (*perro*) pup, puppy; (*león*) cub.
cada [ˈkaða] *adj inv* each; (*antes de número*) every; ~ **día** each day, every day; ~ **dos días** every other day; ~ **uno/a** each one, every one; ~ **vez más/ menos** more and more/less and less; **uno** ~ **diez** one out of every ten.
cadalso [kaˈðalso] *nm* scaffold.
cadáver [kaˈðaβer] *nm* (dead) body, corpse.
cadena [kaˈðena] *nf* chain; (*TV*) channel; **trabajo en** ~ assembly line work.
cadencia [kaˈðenθja] *nf* cadence, rhythm.
cadera [kaˈðera] *nf* hip.
cadete [kaˈðete] *nm* cadet.
caducar [kaðuˈkar] *vi* to expire; **caduco, a** *adj* expired; (*persona*) very old.
C.A.E. *abr* (= *cóbrese al entregar*) COD.
caer [kaˈer] *vi* to fall (down); ~**se** *vr* to fall (down); **me cae bien/mal** I get on well with him/I can't stand him; ~ **en la cuenta** to catch on; **su cumpleaños cae en viernes** her birthday falls on a Friday.
café [kaˈfe] (*pl* ~**s**) *nm* (*bebida, planta*) coffee; (*lugar*) café ♦ *adj* (*color*) brown; ~ **con leche** white coffee; ~ **solo** black coffee; **cafetal** *nm* coffee plantation.
cafetera [kafeˈtera] *nf* coffee pot.
cafetería [kafeteˈria] *nf* (*gen*) café.
cafetero, a [kafeˈtero, a] *adj* coffee *cpd*; **ser muy** ~ to be a coffee addict.
cagar [kaˈxar] (*fam!*) *vt* to shit (!); to bungle, mess up ♦ *vi* to have a shit (!).
caída [kaˈiða] *nf* fall; (*declive*) slope; (*disminución*) fall, drop.
caiga *etc vb ver* **caer.**
caimán [kaiˈman] *nm* alligator.
caja [ˈkaxa] *nf* box; (*para reloj*) case;

(*de ascensor*) shaft; (*COM*) cashbox; (*donde se hacen los pagos*) cashdesk; (: *en supermercado*) checkout, till; ~ **de ahorros** savings bank; ~ **de cambios** gearbox; ~ **fuerte**, ~ **de caudales** safe, strongbox.
cajero, a [kaˈxero, a] *nm/f* cashier.
cajetilla [kaxeˈtiʎa] *nf* (*de cigarrillos*) packet.
cajón [kaˈxon] *nm* big box; (*de mueble*) drawer.
cal [kal] *nf* lime.
cala [ˈkala] *nf* (*GEO*) cove, inlet; (*de barco*) hold.
calabacín [kalaβaˈθin] *nm* (*BOT*) baby marrow; (: *más pequeño*) courgette (*BRIT*), zucchini (*US*).
calabacita [kalaβaˈθita] (*AM*) *nf* courgette (*BRIT*), zucchini (*US*).
calabaza [kalaˈβaθa] *nf* (*BOT*) pumpkin.
calabozo [kalaˈβoθo] *nm* (*cárcel*) prison; (*celda*) cell.
calada [kaˈlaða] *nf* (*de cigarrillo*) puff.
calado, a [kaˈlaðo, a] *adj* (*prenda*) lace *cpd* ♦ *nm* (*NAUT*) draught.
calamar [kalaˈmar] *nm* squid *no pl.*
calambre [kaˈlambre] *nm* (*tb:* ~**s**) cramp.
calamidad [kalamiˈðað] *nf* calamity, disaster.
calamina [kalaˈmina] *nf* calamine.
calaña [kaˈlaɲa] *nf* model, pattern.
calar [kaˈlar] *vt* to soak, drench; (*penetrar*) to pierce, penetrate; (*comprender*) to see through; (*vela, red*) to lower; ~**se** *vr* (*AUTO*) to stall; ~**se las gafas** to stick one's glasses on.
calavera [kalaˈβera] *nf* skull.
calcañal [kalkaˈɲal] *nm* = **calcañar.**
calcañar [kalkaˈɲar] *nm* heel.
calcaño [kalˈkaɲo] *nm* = **calcañar.**
calcar [kalˈkar] *vt* (*reproducir*) to trace; (*imitar*) to copy.
calceta [kalˈθeta] *nf* (knee-length) stocking; **hacer** ~ to knit.
calcetín [kalθeˈtin] *nm* sock.
calcinar [kalθiˈnar] *vt* to burn, blacken.
calcio [ˈkalθjo] *nm* calcium.
calco [ˈkalko] *nm* tracing.
calcomanía [kalkomaˈnia] *nf* transfer.

calculadora [kalkula'ðora] *nf* calculator.
calcular [kalku'lar] *vt* (*MAT*) to calculate, compute; ~ **que** ... to reckon that ...; **cálculo** *nm* calculation.
caldear [kalde'ar] *vt* to warm (up), heat (up).
caldera [kal'dera] *nf* boiler.
calderilla [kalde'riʎa] *nf* (*moneda*) small change.
caldero [kal'dero] *nm* small boiler.
caldo ['kaldo] *nm* stock; (*consomé*) consommé.
calefacción [kalefak'θjon] *nf* heating; ~ **central** central heating.
calendario [kalen'darjo] *nm* calendar.
calentador [kalenta'ðor] *nm* heater.
calentar [kalen'tar] *vt* to heat (up); ~**se** *vr* to heat up, warm up; (*fig: discusión etc*) to get heated.
calentura [kalen'tura] *nf* (*MED*) fever, (high) temperature.
calibrar [kali'ßrar] *vt* to gauge, measure; **calibre** *nm* (*de cañón*) calibre, bore; (*diámetro*) diameter; (*fig*) calibre.
calidad [kali'ðað] *nf* quality; **de** ~ quality *cpd*; **en** ~ **de** in the capacity of, as.
cálido, a ['kaliðo, a] *adj* hot; (*fig*) warm.
caliente *etc* [ka'ljente] *vb ver* **calentar** ♦ *adj* hot; (*fig*) fiery; (*disputa*) heated; (*fam: cachondo*) randy.
calificación [kalifika'θjon] *nf* qualification; (*de alumno*) grade, mark.
calificar [kalifi'kar] *vt* to qualify; (*alumno*) to grade, mark; ~ **de** to describe as.
caliza [ka'liθa] *nf* limestone.
calizo, a [ka'liθo, a] *adj* lime *cpd*.
calma ['kalma] *nf* calm; (*pachorra*) slowness.
calmante [kal'mante] *nm* sedative, tranquillizer.
calmar [kal'mar] *vt* to calm, calm down ♦ *vi* (*tempestad*) to abate; (*mente etc*) to become calm.
calmoso, a [kal'moso, a] *adj* calm, quiet.
calor [ka'lor] *nm* heat; (~ *agradable*) warmth; **hace** ~ it's hot; **tener** ~ to be

hot.
caloría [kalo'ria] *nf* calorie.
calorífero, a [kalo'rifero, a] *adj* heat-producing, heat-giving ♦ *nm* heating system.
calumnia [ka'lumnja] *nf* calumny, slander; **calumnioso, a** *adj* slanderous.
caluroso, a [kalu'roso, a] *adj* hot; (*sin exceso*) warm; (*fig*) enthusiastic.
calva ['kalßa] *nf* bald patch; (*en bosque*) clearing.
calvario [kal'ßarjo] *nm* stations *pl* of the cross.
calvicie [kal'ßiθje] *nf* baldness.
calvo, a ['kalßo, a] *adj* bald; (*terreno*) bare, barren; (*tejido*) threadbare.
calza ['kalθa] *nf* wedge, chock.
calzada [kal'θaða] *nf* roadway, highway.
calzado, a [kal'θaðo, a] *adj* shod ♦ *nm* footwear.
calzador [kalθa'ðor] *nm* shoehorn.
calzar [kal'θar] *vt* (*zapatos etc*) to wear; (*un mueble*) to put a wedge under; ~**se** *vr*: ~**se los zapatos** to put on one's shoes; ¿**qué (número) calza?** what size do you take?
calzón [kal'θon] *nm* (*tb: calzones nmpl*) shorts; (*AM: de hombre*) pants; (*: de mujer*) panties.
calzoncillos [kalθon'θiʎos] *nmpl* underpants.
callado, a [ka'ʎaðo, a] *adj* quiet.
callar [ka'ʎar] *vt* (*asunto delicado*) to keep quiet about, say nothing about; (*persona, opinión*) to silence ♦ *vi* to keep quiet, be silent; ~**se** *vr* to keep quiet, be silent; ¡**cállate!** be quiet!, shut up!
calle ['kaʎe] *nf* street; (*DEPORTE*) lane; ~ **arriba/abajo** up/down the street; ~ **de un solo sentido** one-way street.
calleja [ka'ʎexa] *nf* alley, narrow street; **callejear** *vi* to wander (about) the streets; **callejero, a** *adj* street *cpd* ♦ *nm* street map; **callejón** *nm* alley, passage; **callejón sin salida** cul-de-sac; **callejuela** *nf* side-street, alley.
callista [ka'ʎista] *nm/f* chiropodist.
callo ['kaʎo] *nm* callus; (*en el pie*) corn; ~**s** *nmpl* (*CULIN*) tripe *sg*; ~**so, a**

adj horny, rough.

cama ['kama] *nf* bed; (*GEO*) stratum; ~ **individual/de matrimonio** single/double bed.

camada [ka'maða] *nf* litter; (*de personas*) gang, band.

camafeo [kama'feo] *nm* cameo.

cámara ['kamara] *nf* chamber; (*habitación*) room; (*sala*) hall; (*CINE*) cine camera; (*fotográfica*) camera; ~ **de aire** inner tube.

camarada [kama'raða] *nm* comrade, companion.

camarera [kama'rera] *nf* (*en restaurante*) waitress; (*en casa, hotel*) maid.

camarero [kama'rero] *nm* waiter.

camarilla [kama'riʎa] *nf* (*clan*) clique; (*POL*) lobby.

camarín [kama'rin] *nm* dressing room.

camarón [kama'ron] *nm* shrimp.

camarote [kama'rote] *nm* cabin.

cambiable [kam'bjaßle] *adj* (*variable*) changeable, variable; (*intercambiable*) interchangeable.

cambiante [kam'bjante] *adj* variable.

cambiar [kam'bjar] *vt* to change; (*dinero*) to exchange ♦ *vi* to change; ~**se** *vr* (*mudarse*) to move; (*de ropa*) to change; ~ **de idea** to change one's mind; ~ **de ropa** to change (one's clothes).

cambiazo [kam'bjaθo] *nm*: **dar el** ~ **a uno** to swindle sb.

cambio ['kambjo] *nm* change; (*trueque*) exchange; (*COM*) rate of exchange; (*oficina*) bureau de change; (*dinero menudo*) small change; **en** ~ on the other hand; (*en lugar de*) instead; ~ **de divisas** foreign exchange; ~ **de velocidades** gear lever; ~ **de vía** points *pl.*

cambista [kam'bista] *nm* (*COM*) exchange broker.

camelar [kame'lar] *vt* (*con mujer*) to flirt with; (*persuadir*) to cajole.

camello [ka'meʎo] *nm* camel; (*fam: traficante*) pusher.

camilla [ka'miʎa] *nf* (*MED*) stretcher.

caminante [kami'nante] *nm/f* traveller.

caminar [kami'nar] *vi* (*marchar*) to

walk, go; (*viajar*) to travel, journey ♦ *vt* (*recorrer*) to cover, travel.

caminata [kami'nata] *nf* long walk; (*por el campo*) hike.

camino [ka'mino] *nm* way, road; (*sendero*) track; **a medio** ~ halfway (there); **en el** ~ on the way, en route; ~ **de** on the way to; ~ **particular** private road.

camión [ka'mjon] *nm* lorry (*BRIT*), truck (*US*); **camionero, a** *nm/f* lorry o truck driver.

camioneta [kamjo'neta] *nf* van, light truck.

camisa [ka'misa] *nf* shirt; (*BOT*) skin; ~ **de dormir** nightdress; ~ **de fuerza** straitjacket; **camisería** *nf* outfitter's (shop).

camiseta [kami'seta] *nf* (*prenda*) tee-shirt; (: *ropa interior*) vest; (*de deportista*) top.

camisón [kami'son] *nm* nightdress, nightgown.

camorra [ka'morra] *nf*: **armar** o **buscar** ~ to look for trouble, kick up a fuss.

campamento [kampa'mento] *nm* camp.

campana [kam'pana] *nf* bell; ~**da** *nf* peal; ~**rio** *nm* belfry.

campanilla [kampa'niʎa] *nf* small bell.

campaña [kam'paɲa] *nf* (*MIL, POL*) campaign.

campechano, a [kampe'tʃano, a] *adj* (*franco*) open.

campeón, ona [kampe'on, ona] *nm/f* champion; **campeonato** *nm* championship.

campesino, a [kampe'sino, a] *adj* country *cpd*, rural; (*gente*) peasant *cpd* ♦ *nm/f* countryman/woman; (*agricultor*) farmer.

campestre [kam'pestre] *adj* country *cpd*, rural.

camping ['kampin] (*pl* ~s) *nm* camping; (*lugar*) campsite; **ir de** o **hacer** ~ to go camping.

campiña [kam'piɲa] *nf* countryside.

campo ['kampo] *nm* (*fuera de la ciudad*) country, countryside; (*AGR, ELEC*) field; (*de fútbol*) pitch; (*de golf*) course; (*MIL*) camp.

camposanto [kampo'santo] *nm* cemetery.

camuflaje [kamu'flaxe] *nm* camouflage.

cana ['kana] *nf* white *o* grey hair; **tener ~s** to be going grey.

Canadá [kana'ða] *nm* Canada; **canadiense** *adj, nm/f* Canadian ♦ *nf* fur-lined jacket.

canal [ka'nal] *nm* canal; (*GEO*) channel, strait; (*de televisión*) channel; (*de tejado*) gutter; **~ de Panamá** Panama Canal; **~izar** *vt* to channel.

canalón [kana'lon] *nm* (*conducto vertical*) drainpipe; (*del tejado*) gutter.

canalla [ka'naʎa] *nf* rabble, mob ♦ *nm* swine.

canapé [kana'pe] (*pl* **~s**) *nm* sofa, settee; (*CULIN*) canapé.

Canarias [ka'narjas] *nfpl*: (**las Islas**) **~** the Canary Islands, the Canaries.

canario, a [ka'narjo, a] *adj, nm/f* (native) of the Canary Isles ♦ *nm* (*ZOOL*) canary.

canasta [ka'nasta] *nf* (round) basket; **canastilla** *nf* small basket; (*de niño*) layette.

canasto [ka'nasto] *nm* large basket.

cancela [kan'θela] *nf* gate.

cancelación [kanθela'θjon] *nf* cancellation.

cancelar [kanθe'lar] *vt* to cancel; (*una deuda*) to write off.

cáncer ['kanθer] *nm* (*MED*) cancer; (*ASTROLOGÍA*): **C~** Cancer.

canciller [kanθi'ʎer] *nm* chancellor.

canción [kan'θjon] *nf* song; **~ de cuna** lullaby; **cancionero** *nm* song book.

cancha ['kantʃa] *nf* (*de baloncesto, tenis etc*) court; (*AM: de fútbol*) pitch.

candado [kan'daðo] *nm* padlock.

candela [kan'dela] *nf* candle.

candelero [kande'lero] *nm* (*para vela*) candlestick; (*de aceite*) oil lamp.

candente [kan'dente] *adj* red-hot; (*fig: tema*) burning.

candidato, a [kandi'ðato, a] *nm/f* candidate.

candidez [kandi'ðeθ] *nf* (*sencillez*) simplicity; (*simpleza*) naiveté; **cándido, a** *adj* simple; naive.

candil [kan'dil] *nm* oil lamp; **~ejas** *nfpl* (*TEATRO*) footlights.

candor [kan'dor] *nm* (*sinceridad*) frankness; (*inocencia*) innocence.

canela [ka'nela] *nf* cinnamon.

cangrejo [kan'grexo] *nm* crab.

canguro [kan'guro] *nm* kangaroo; **hacer de ~** to babysit.

caníbal [ka'niβal] *adj, nm/f* cannibal.

canica [ka'nika] *nf* marble.

canijo, a [ka'nixo, a] *adj* frail, sickly.

canino, a [ka'nino, a] *adj* canine ♦ *nm* canine (tooth).

canjear [kanxe'ar] *vt* to exchange.

cano, a ['kano, a] *adj* grey-haired, white-haired.

canoa [ka'noa] *nf* canoe.

canon ['kanon] *nm* canon; (*pensión*) rent; (*COM*) tax.

canónigo [ka'noniʝo] *nm* canon.

canonizar [kanoni'θar] *vt* to canonize.

cansado, a [kan'saðo, a] *adj* tired, weary; (*tedioso*) tedious, boring.

cansancio [kan'sanθjo] *nm* tiredness, fatigue.

cansar [kan'sar] *vt* (*fatigar*) to tire, tire out; (*aburrir*) to bore; (*fastidiar*) to bother; **~se** *vr* to tire, get tired; (*aburrirse*) to get bored.

cantábrico, a [kan'taβriko, a] *adj* Cantabrian; **mar C~** Bay of Biscay.

cantante [kan'tante] *adj* singing ♦ *nm/f* singer.

cantar [kan'tar] *vt* to sing ♦ *vi* to sing; (*insecto*) to chirp; (*rechinar*) to squeak ♦ *nm* (*acción*) singing; (*canción*) song; (*poema*) poem.

cántara ['kantara] *nf* large pitcher.

cántaro ['kantaro] *nm* pitcher, jug; **llover a ~s** to rain cats and dogs.

cante ['kante] *nm*: **~ jondo** flamenco singing.

cantera [kan'tera] *nf* quarry.

cantidad [kanti'ðað] *nf* quantity, amount.

cantilena [kanti'lena] *nf* = **cantinela**.

cantimplora [kantim'plora] *nf* (*frasco*) water bottle, canteen.

cantina [kan'tina] *nf* canteen; (*de estación*) buffet.

cantinela [kanti'nela] *nf* ballad, song.

canto ['kanto] *nm* singing; (*canción*) song; (*borde*) edge, rim; (*de un cuchillo*) back; ~ **rodado** boulder.

cantor, a [kan'tor, a] *nm/f* singer.

canturrear [kanturre'ar] *vi* to sing softly.

canuto [ka'nuto] *nm* (*tubo*) small tube; (*fam: droga*) joint.

caña ['kaɲa] *nf* (*BOT: tallo*) stem, stalk; (*carrizo*) reed; (*vaso*) tumbler; (*de cerveza*) glass of beer; (*ANAT*) shin-bone; ~ **de azúcar** sugar cane; ~ **de pescar** fishing rod.

cañada [ka'naða] *nf* (*entre dos mon-tañas*) gully, ravine; (*camino*) cattle track.

cáñamo ['kaɲamo] *nm* hemp.

caño ['kaɲo] *nm* (*tubo*) tube, pipe; (*de albañal*) sewer; (*MUS*) pipe; (*de fuente*) jet.

cañón [ka'ɲon] *nm* (*MIL*) cannon; (*de fusil*) barrel; (*GEO*) canyon, gorge.

cañonera [kaɲo'nera] *nf* (*tb: lancha* ~) gunboat.

caoba [ka'oßa] *nf* mahogany.

caos ['kaos] *nm* chaos.

cap. *abr* (= *capítulo*) ch.

capa ['kapa] *nf* cloak, cape; (*GEO*) layer, stratum; **so** ~ **de** under the pretext of.

capacidad [kapaθi'ðað] *nf* (*medida*) capacity; (*aptitud*) capacity, ability.

capacitación [kapaθita'θjon] *nf* training.

capar [ka'par] *vt* to castrate, geld.

caparazón [kapara'θon] *nm* shell.

capataz [kapa'taθ] *nm* foreman.

capaz [ka'paθ] *adj* able, capable; (*amplio*) capacious, roomy.

capcioso, a [kap'θjoso, a] *adj* wily, deceitful.

capellán [kape'ʎan] *nm* chaplain; (*sacerdote*) priest.

caperuza [kape'ruθa] *nf* hood.

capilla [ka'piʎa] *nf* chapel.

capital [kapi'tal] *adj* capital ♦ *nm* (*COM*) capital ♦ *nf* (*ciudad*) capital; ~ **social** share capital.

capitalismo [kapita'lismo] *nm* capital-ism; **capitalista** *adj, nm/f* capitalist.

capitalizar [kapitali'θar] *vt* to capitalize.

capitán [kapi'tan] *nm* captain.

capitanear [kapitane'ar] *vt* to captain.

capitolio [kapi'toljo] *nm* capitol.

capitulación [kapitula'θjon] *nf* (*rendi-ción*) capitulation, surrender; (*acuerdo*) agreement, pact; **capitulaciones** (*ma-trimoniales*) *nfpl* marriage contract *sg*.

capitular [kapitu'lar] *vi* to come to terms, make an agreement.

capítulo [ka'pitulo] *nm* chapter.

capó [ka'po] *nm* (*AUTO*) bonnet.

capón [ka'pon] *nm* (*gallo*) capon.

caporal [kapo'ral] *nm* chief, leader.

capota [ka'pota] *nf* (*de mujer*) bonnet; (*AUTO*) hood (*BRIT*), top (*US*).

capote [ka'pote] *nm* (*abrigo: de militar*) greatcoat; (: *de torero*) cloak.

Capricornio [kapri'kornjo] *nm* Capri-corn.

capricho [ka'pritʃo] *nm* whim, caprice; ~**so, a** *adj* capricious.

cápsula ['kapsula] *nf* capsule.

captar [kap'tar] *vt* (*comprender*) to understand; (*RADIO*) to pick up; (*aten-ción, apoyo*) to attract.

captura [kap'tura] *nf* capture; (*JUR*) arrest; **capturar** *vt* to capture; to arrest.

capucha [ka'putʃa] *nf* hood, cowl.

capullo [ka'puʎo] *nm* (*BOT*) bud; (*ZOOL*) cocoon; (*fam*) idiot.

caqui ['kaki] *nm* khaki.

cara ['kara] *nf* (*ANAT, de moneda*) face; (*aspecto*) appearance; (*de disco*) side; (*fig*) boldness; ~ **a** facing; **de** ~ opposite, facing; **dar la** ~ to face the consequences; ¿~ **o cruz?** heads or tails?; ¡**qué** ~ (**más dura**)! what a nerve!

carabina [kara'ßina] *nf* carbine, rifle; (*persona*) chaperone.

Caracas [ka'rakas] *n* Caracas.

caracol [kara'kol] *nm* (*ZOOL*) snail; (*concha*) (sea) shell.

caracolear [karakole'ar] *vi* (*caballo*) to prance about.

carácter [ka'rakter] (*pl* **caracteres**) *nm* character; **tener buen/mal** ~ to be good natured/bad tempered.

característica [karakte'ristika] *nf* char-acteristic.

característico, a [karakte'ristiko, a] *adj* characteristic.

caracterizar [karakteri'θar] *vt* (*distinguir*) to characterize, typify; (*honrar*) to confer (a) distinction on.

caradura [kara'ðura] *nm/f*: **es un ~** he's got a nerve.

carajo [ka'raxo] (*fam!*) *nm*: **¡~!** shit! (*!*).

caramba [ka'ramba] *excl* good gracious!

carámbano [ka'rambano] *nm* icicle.

caramelo [kara'melo] *nm* (*dulce*) sweet; (*azúcar fundida*) caramel.

carapacho [kara'patʃo] *nm* shell, carapace.

caraqueño, a [kara'keɲo, a] *adj* of o from Caracas.

carátula [ka'ratula] *nf* (*careta, máscara*) mask; (*TEATRO*): **la ~** the stage.

caravana [kara'ßana] *nf* caravan; (*fig*) group; (*AUTO*) tailback.

carbón [kar'ßon] *nm* coal; **papel ~** carbon paper; **carboncillo** *nm* (*ARTE*) charcoal; **carbonero, a** *nm/f* coal merchant; **carbonilla** [-'niʎa] *nf* coal dust.

carbonizar [karßoni'θar] *vt* to carbonize; (*quemar*) to char.

carbono [kar'ßono] *nm* carbon.

carburador [karßura'ðor] *nm* carburettor.

carcajada [karka'xaða] *nf* (loud) laugh, guffaw.

cárcel ['karθel] *nf* prison, jail; (*TEC*) clamp; **carcelero, a** *adj* prison *cpd* ♦ *nm/f* warder.

carcomer [karko'mer] *vt* to bore into, eat into; (*fig*) to undermine; **~se** *vr* to become worm-eaten; (*fig*) to decay; **carcomido, a** *adj* worm-eaten; (*fig*) rotten.

cardenal [karðe'nal] *nm* (*REL*) cardinal; (*MED*) bruise.

cárdeno, a ['karðeno, a] *adj* purple; (*lívido*) livid.

cardíaco, a [kar'ðiako, a] *adj* cardiac, heart *cpd*.

cardinal [karði'nal] *adj* cardinal.

cardo ['karðo] *nm* thistle.

carear [kare'ar] *vt* to bring face to face;

(*comparar*) to compare; **~se** *vr* to come face to face, meet.

carecer [kare'θer] *vi*: **~ de** to lack, be in need of.

carencia [ka'renθja] *nf* lack; (*escasez*) shortage; (*MED*) deficiency.

carente [ka'rente] *adj*: **~ de** lacking in, devoid of.

carestía [kares'tia] *nf* (*escasez*) scarcity, shortage; (*COM*) high cost.

careta [ka'reta] *nf* mask.

carga ['karya] *nf* (*peso, ELEC*) load; (*de barco*) cargo, freight; (*MIL*) charge; (*obligación, responsabilidad*) duty, obligation.

cargado, a [kar'yaðo, a] *adj* loaded; (*ELEC*) live; (*café, té*) strong; (*cielo*) overcast.

cargamento [karya'mento] *nm* (*acción*) loading; (*mercancías*) load, cargo.

cargar [kar'yar] *vt* (*barco, arma*) to load; (*ELEC*) to charge; (*COM: algo en cuenta*) to charge; (*INFORM*) to load ♦ *vi* (*MIL: enemigo*) to charge; (*AUTO*) to load (up); (*inclinarse*) to lean; **~ con** to pick up, carry away; (*peso, fig*) to shoulder, bear; **~se** (*fam*) *vr* (*estropear*) to break; (*matar*) to bump off.

cargo ['karyo] *nm* (*puesto*) post, office; (*responsabilidad*) duty, obligation; (*fig*) weight, burden; (*JUR*) charge; **hacerse ~ de** to take charge of o responsibility for.

carguero [kar'yero] *nm* freighter, cargo boat; (*avión*) freight plane.

Caribe [ka'rißе] *nm*: **el ~** the Caribbean; **del ~** Caribbean.

caribeño, a [kari'ßeɲo, a] *adj* Caribbean.

caricatura [karika'tura] *nf* caricature.

caricia [ka'riθja] *nf* caress.

caridad [kari'ðað] *nf* charity.

caries ['karjes] *nf inv* (*MED*) tooth decay.

cariño [ka'riɲo] *nm* affection, love; (*caricia*) caress; (*en carta*) love ...; **tener ~ a** to be fond of; **~so, a** *adj* affectionate.

caritativo, a [karita'tißo, a] *adj* charitable.

cariz [ka'riθ] *nm*: **tener** *o* **tomar buen/mal** ~ to look good/bad.

carmesí [karme'si] *adj, nm* crimson.

carmín [kar'min] *nm* lipstick.

carnal [kar'nal] *adj* carnal; **primo** ~ first cousin.

carnaval [karna'βal] *nm* carnival.

carne ['karne] *nf* flesh; (*CULIN*) meat; ~ **de cerdo/cordero/ternera/vaca** pork/lamb/veal/beef.

carné [kar'ne] (*pl* ~s) *nm*: ~ **de conducir** driving licence (*BRIT*), driver's license (*US*); ~ **de identidad** identity card.

carnero [kar'nero] *nm* sheep, ram; (*carne*) mutton.

carnet [kar'ne] (*pl* ~s) *nm* = **carné**.

carnicería [karniθe'ria] *nf* butcher's (shop); (*fig*: *matanza*) carnage, slaughter.

carnicero, a [karni'θero, a] *adj* carnivorous ♦ *nm/f* (*tb fig*) butcher; (*carnívoro*) carnivore.

carnívoro, a [kar'niβoro, a] *adj* carnivorous.

carnoso, a [kar'noso, a] *adj* beefy, fat.

caro, a ['karo, a] *adj* dear; (*COM*) dear, expensive ♦ *adv* dear, dearly.

carpa ['karpa] *nf* (*pez*) carp; (*de circo*) big top; (*AM*: *de camping*) tent.

carpeta [kar'peta] *nf* folder, file.

carpintería [karpinte'ria] *nf* carpentry, joinery; **carpintero** *nm* carpenter.

carraspera [karras'pera] *nf* hoarseness.

carrera [ka'rrera] *nf* (*acción*) run(ning); (*espacio recorrido*) run; (*certamen*) race; (*trayecto*) course; (*profesión*) career; (*ESCOL*) course.

carreta [ka'rreta] *nf* wagon, cart.

carrete [ka'rrete] *nm* reel, spool; (*TEC*) coil.

carretera [karre'tera] *nf* (main) road, highway; ~ **de circunvalación** ring road; ~ **nacional** ≈ A road (*BRIT*), ≈ state highway (*US*).

carretilla [karre'tiʎa] *nf* trolley; (*AGR*) (wheel)barrow.

carril [ka'rril] *nm* furrow; (*de autopista*) lane; (*FERRO*) rail.

carrillo [ka'rriʎo] *nm* (*ANAT*) cheek; (*TEC*) pulley.

carrizo [ka'rriθo] *nm* reed.

carro ['karro] *nm* cart, wagon; (*MIL*) tank; (*AM*: *coche*) car.

carrocería [karroθe'ria] *nf* bodywork, coachwork.

carroña [ka'rroɲa] *nf* carrion *no pl*.

carrusel [karru'sel] *nm* merry-go-round, roundabout.

carta ['karta] *nf* letter; (*CULIN*) menu; (*naipe*) card; (*mapa*) map; (*JUR*) document; ~ **de crédito** credit card; ~ **certificada** registered letter; ~ **marítima** chart; ~ **verde** (*AUTO*) green card.

cartel [kar'tel] *nm* (*anuncio*) poster, placard; (*ESCOL*) wall chart; (*COM*) cartel; ~**era** *nf* hoarding, billboard; (*en periódico etc*) entertainments guide; **"en ~era"** "showing".

cartera [kar'tera] *nf* (*de bolsillo*) wallet; (*de colegial, cobrador*) satchel; (*de señora*) handbag; (*para documentos*) briefcase; (*COM*) portfolio; **ocupa la ~ de Agricultura** she is Minister of Agriculture.

carterista [karte'rista] *nm/f* pickpocket.

cartero [kar'tero] *nm* postman.

cartilla [kar'tiʎa] *nf* primer, first reading book; ~ **de ahorros** savings book.

cartón [kar'ton] *nm* cardboard.

cartucho [kar'tutʃo] *nm* (*MIL*) cartridge.

casa ['kasa] *nf* house; (*hogar*) home; (*edificio*) building; (*COM*) firm, company; **en** ~ at home; ~ **consistorial** town hall; ~ **de huéspedes** boarding house; ~ **de socorro** first aid post.

casadero, a [kasa'ðero, a] *adj* of marrying age.

casado, a [ka'saðo, a] *adj* married ♦ *nm/f* married man/woman.

casamiento [kasa'mjento] *nm* marriage, wedding.

casar [ka'sar] *vt* to marry; (*JUR*) to quash, annul; ~**se** *vr* to marry, get married.

cascabel [kaska'βel] *nm* (small) bell.

cascada [kas'kaða] *nf* waterfall.

cascanueces [kaska'nweθes] *nm inv* nutcrackers *pl*.

cascar [kas'kar] *vt* to crack, split, break (open); **~se** *vr* to crack, split, break (open).

cáscara ['kaskara] *nf* (*de huevo, fruta seca*) shell; (*de fruta*) skin; (*de limón*) peel.

casco ['kasko] *nm* (*de bombero, soldado*) helmet; (*NAUT: de barco*) hull; (*ZOOL: de caballo*) hoof; (*botella*) empty bottle; (*de ciudad*): **el ~ antiguo** the old part; **el ~ urbano** the town centre.

cascote [kas'kote] *nm* rubble.

caserío [kase'rio] *nm* hamlet; (*casa*) country house.

casero, a [ka'sero, a] *adj* (*pan etc*) home-made ♦ *nm/f* (*propietario*) landlord/lady; (*COM*) house agent; **ser muy ~** to be home-loving; **"comida casera"** "home cooking".

caseta [ka'seta] *nf* hut; (*para bañista*) cubicle; (*de feria*) stall.

casete [ka'sete] *nm o f* cassette.

casi ['kasi] *adv* almost, nearly; **~ nada** hardly anything; **~ nunca** hardly ever, almost never; **~ te caes** you almost fell.

casilla [ka'siʎa] *nf* (*casita*) hut, cabin; (*TEATRO*) box office; (*AJEDREZ*) square; (*para cartas*) pigeonhole.

casino [ka'sino] *nm* club; (*de juego*) casino.

caso ['kaso] *nm* case; **en ~ de ...** in case of ...; **en ~ de que ...** in case ...; **el ~ es que** the fact is that; **en ese ~** in that case; **hacer ~ a** to pay attention to; **hacer o venir al ~** to be relevant.

caspa ['kaspa] *nf* dandruff.

cassette [ka'sete] *nm o f* = **casete**.

casta ['kasta] *nf* caste; (*raza*) breed; (*linaje*) lineage.

castaña [kas'taɲa] *nf* chestnut.

castañetear [kastaɲete'ar] *vi* (*dientes*) to chatter.

castaño, a [kas'taɲo, a] *adj* chestnut(-coloured), brown ♦ *nm* chestnut tree.

castañuelas [kasta'ɲwelas] *nfpl* castanets.

castellano, a [kaste'ʎano, a] *adj, nm/f* Castilian ♦ *nm* (*LING*) Castilian, Span-ish.

castidad [kasti'ðað] *nf* chastity, purity.

castigar [kasti'ɣar] *vt* to punish; (*DEPORTE*) to penalize; (*afligir*) to afflict; **castigo** *nm* punishment; (*DEPORTE*) penalty.

Castilla [kas'tiʎa] *nf* Castille.

castillo [kas'tiʎo] *nm* castle.

castizo, a [kas'tiθo, a] *adj* (*LING*) pure; (*de buena casta*) purebred, pedigree.

casto, a ['kasto, a] *adj* chaste, pure.

castor [kas'tor] *nm* beaver.

castrar [kas'trar] *vt* to castrate.

casual [ka'swal] *adj* chance, accidental; **~idad** *nf* chance, accident; (*combinación de circunstancias*) coincidence; **¡qué ~idad!** what a coincidence!

cataclismo [kata'klismo] *nm* cataclysm.

catador, a [kata'ðor, a] *nm/f* wine taster.

catalán, ana [kata'lan, ana] *adj, nm/f* Catalan ♦ *nm* (*LING*) Catalan.

catalizador [kataliθa'ðor] *nm* catalyst.

catálogo [ka'taloɣo] *nm* catalogue.

Cataluña [kata'luɲa] *nf* Catalonia.

catar [ka'tar] *vt* to taste, sample.

catarata [kata'rata] *nf* (*GEO*) waterfall; (*MED*) cataract.

catarro [ka'tarro] *nm* catarrh; (*constipado*) cold.

catástrofe [ka'tastrofe] *nf* catastrophe.

catedral [kate'ðral] *nf* cathedral.

catedrático, a [kate'ðratiko, a] *nm/f* professor.

categoría [kateɣo'ria] *nf* category; (*rango*) rank, standing; (*calidad*) quality; **de ~** (*hotel*) top-class.

categórico, a [kate'ɣoriko, a] *adj* categorical.

catolicismo [katoli'θismo] *nm* Catholi-cism.

católico, a [ka'toliko, a] *adj, nm/f* Catholic.

catorce [ka'torθe] *num* fourteen.

cauce ['kauθe] *nm* (*de río*) riverbed; (*fig*) channel.

caución [kau'θjon] *nf* bail; **caucionar** *vt* (*JUR*) to bail, go bail for.

caucho ['kautʃo] *nm* rubber; (*AM*) llanta* tyre.

caudal [kau'ðal] *nm* (*de río*) volume, flow; (*fortuna*) wealth; (*abundancia*) abundance; **~oso, a** *adj* (*río*) large; (*persona*) wealthy, rich.

caudillo [kau'ðiʎo] *nm* leader, chief.

causa [kau'sa] *nf* cause; (*razón*) reason; (*JUR*) lawsuit, case; **a ~ de** because of.

causar [kau'sar] *vt* to cause.

cautela [kau'tela] *nf* caution, cautiousness; **cauteloso, a** *adj* cautious, wary.

cautivar [kauti'βar] *vt* to capture; (*fig*) to captivate.

cautiverio [kauti'βerjo] *nm* captivity.

cautividad [kautiβi'ðað] *nf* = **cautiverio.**

cautivo, a [kau'tiβo, a] *adj, nm/f* captive.

cauto, a ['kauto, a] *adj* cautious, careful.

cava ['kaβa] *nm champagne-type wine.*

cavar [ka'βar] *vt* to dig.

caverna [ka'βerna] *nf* cave, cavern.

cavidad [kaβi'ðað] *nf* cavity.

cavilar [kaβi'lar] *vt* to ponder.

cayado [ka'jaðo] *nm* (*de pastor*) crook; (*de obispo*) crozier.

cayendo *etc vb ver* **caer.**

caza ['kaθa] *nf* (*acción: gen*) hunting; (: *con fusil*) shooting; (*una ~*) hunt, chase; (*animales*) game ♦ *nm* (*AVIAT*) fighter.

cazador, a [kaθa'ðor, a] *nm/f* hunter; **cazadora** *nf* jacket.

cazar [ka'θar] *vt* to hunt; (*perseguir*) to chase; (*prender*) to catch.

cazo ['kaθo] *nm* saucepan.

cazuela [ka'θwela] *nf* (*vasija*) pan; (*guisado*) casserole.

cebada [θe'βaða] *nf* barley.

cebar [θe'βar] *vt* (*animal*) to fatten (up); (*anzuelo*) to bait; (*MIL, TEC*) to prime.

cebo ['θeβo] *nm* (*para animales*) feed, food; (*para peces, fig*) bait; (*de arma*) charge.

cebolla [θe'βoʎa] *nf* onion; **cebollín** *nm* spring onion.

cebra ['θeβra] *nf* zebra.

cecear [θeθe'ar] *vi* to lisp; **ceceo** *nm* lisp.

cedazo [θe'ðaθo] *nm* sieve.

ceder [θe'ðer] *vt* to hand over, give up, part with ♦ *vi* (*renunciar*) to give in, yield; (*disminuir*) to diminish, decline; (*romperse*) to give way.

cedro ['θeðro] *nm* cedar.

cédula ['θeðula] *nf* certificate, document.

CEE *nf abr* (= *Comunidad Económica Europea*) EEC.

cegar [θe'xar] *vt* to blind; (*tubería etc*) to block up, stop up ♦ *vi* to go blind; **~se** *vr*: **~se (de)** to be blinded (by).

ceguera [θe'ɣera] *nf* blindness.

ceja ['θexa] *nf* eyebrow.

cejar [θe'xar] *vi* (*fig*) to back down.

celada [θe'laða] *nf* ambush, trap.

celador, a [θela'ðor, a] *nm/f* (*de edificio*) watchman; (*de museo etc*) attendant.

celda ['θelda] *nf* cell.

celebración [θeleβra'θjon] *nf* celebration.

celebrar [θele'βrar] *vt* to celebrate; (*alabar*) to praise ♦ *vi* to be glad; **~se** *vr* to occur, take place.

célebre ['θelebre] *adj* famous.

celebridad [θeleβri'ðað] *nf* fame; (*persona*) celebrity.

celeste [θe'leste] *adj* sky-blue; celestial, heavenly.

celestial [θeles'tjal] *adj* celestial, heavenly.

celibato [θeli'βato] *nm* celibacy.

célibe ['θeliβe] *adj, nm/f* celibate.

celo ['θelo] *nm* zeal; (*REL*) fervour; (*ZOOL*): **en ~** on heat; **~s** *nmpl* (*envidia*) jealousy *sg*; **tener ~s** to be jealous.

celofán [θelo'fan] *nm* cellophane.

celoso, a [θe'loso, a] *adj* (*envidioso*) jealous; (*trabajador*) zealous; (*desconfiado*) suspicious.

celta ['θelta] *adj* Celtic ♦ *nm/f* Celt.

célula ['θelula] *nf* cell.

celuloide [θelu'loiðe] *nm* celluloid.

cementerio [θemen'terjo] *nm* cemetery, graveyard.

cemento [θe'mento] *nm* cement; (*hormigón*) concrete; (*AM: cola*) glue.

cena ['θena] *nf* evening meal, dinner.

cenagal [θena'val] *nm* bog, quagmire.

cenar [θe'nar] *vt* to have for dinner ♦ *vi*

to have dinner.

cenicero [θeni'θero] *nm* ashtray.

cenit [θe'nit] *nm* zenith.

ceniza [θe'niθa] *nf* ash, ashes *pl*.

censo ['θenso] *nm* census; ~ **electoral** electoral roll.

censura [θen'sura] *nf* (*POL*) censorship; (*moral*) censure, criticism.

censurar [θensu'rar] *vt* (*idea*) to censure; (*cortar: película*) to censor.

centella [θen'teʎa] *nf* spark.

centellear [θenteʎe'ar] *vi* (*metal*) to gleam; (*estrella*) to twinkle; (*fig*) to sparkle; **centelleo** *nm* gleam(ing); twinkling; sparkling.

centenar [θente'nar] *nm* hundred.

centenario, a [θente'narjo, a] *adj* centenary; hundred-year-old ♦ *nm* centenary.

centésimo, a [θen'tesimo, a] *adj* hundredth.

centígrado [θen'tiɣraðo] *adj* centigrade.

centímetro [θen'timetro] *nm* centimetre (*BRIT*), centimeter (*US*).

céntimo [θentimo] *nm* cent.

centinela [θenti'nela] *nm* sentry, guard.

centolla [θen'toʎa] *nf* = **centollo**.

centollo [θen'toʎo] *nm* spider crab.

central [θen'tral] *adj* central ♦ *nf* head office; (*TEC*) plant; (*TEL*) exchange; ~ **nuclear** nuclear power station.

centralización [θentraliθa'θjon] *nf* centralization.

centralizar [θentrali'θar] *vt* to centralize.

centrar [θen'trar] *vt* to centre.

céntrico, a [θentriko, a] *adj* central.

centrista [θen'trista] *adj* centre *cpd*.

centro ['θentro] *nm* centre; ~ **comercial** shopping centre; ~ **juvenil** youth club.

centroamericano, a [θentroameri'kano, a] *adj*, *nm/f* Central American.

ceñir [θe'ɲir] *vt* (*rodear*) to encircle, surround; (*ajustar*) to fit (tightly); (*apretar*) to tighten.

ceño ['θeɲo] *nm* frown, scowl; **fruncir el ~** to frown, knit one's brow.

CEOE *nf abr* (*ESP*: = *Confederación Española de Organizaciones Empresariales*) ≈ CBI (*BRIT*), employers' organization.

cepillar [θepi'ʎar] *vt* to brush; (*madera*) to plane (down).

cepillo [θe'piʎo] *nm* brush; (*para madera*) plane.

cera ['θera] *nf* wax.

cerámica [θe'ramika] *nf* pottery; (*arte*) ceramics.

cerca ['θerka] *nf* fence ♦ *adv* near, nearby, close ♦ *nmpl*: ~s foreground *sg*; ~ **de** near, close to.

cercanía [θerka'nia] *nf* nearness, closeness; ~s *nfpl* (*afueras*) outskirts, suburbs.

cercano, a [θer'kano, a] *adj* close, near.

cercar [θer'kar] *vt* to fence in; (*rodear*) to surround.

cerciorar [θerθjo'rar] *vt* (*asegurar*) to assure; ~se *vr* (*descubrir*) to find out; (*asegurarse*) to make sure.

cerco ['θerko] *nm* (*AGR*) enclosure; (*AM*) fence; (*MIL*) siege.

cerdo, a ['θerðo, a] *nm/f* pig/sow.

cereal [θere'al] *nm* cereal; ~es *nmpl* cereals, grain *sg*.

cerebro [θe'reβro] *nm* brain; (*fig*) brains *pl*.

ceremonia [θere'monja] *nf* ceremony; **ceremonial** *adj*, *nm* ceremonial; **ceremonioso, a** *adj* ceremonious; (*cumplido*) formal.

cereza [θe'reθa] *nf* cherry.

cerilla [θe'riʎa] *nf* (*fósforo*) match.

cernerse [θer'nerse] *vr* to hover.

cernidor [θerni'ðor] *nm* sieve.

cero ['θero] *nm* nothing, zero.

cerrado, a [θe'rraðo, a] *adj* closed, shut; (*con llave*) locked; (*tiempo*) cloudy, overcast; (*curva*) sharp; (*acento*) thick, broad.

cerradura [θerra'ðura] *nf* (*acción*) closing; (*mecanismo*) lock.

cerrajero [θerra'xero] *nm* locksmith.

cerrar [θe'rrar] *vt* to close, shut; (*paso, carretera*) to close; (*grifo*) to turn off; (*cuenta, negocio*) to close ♦ *vi* to close, shut; (*la noche*) to come down; ~se *vr* to close, shut; ~ **con llave** to lock; ~ **un trato** to strike a bargain.

cerro ['θerro] *nm* hill.

cerrojo [θe'rroxo] *nm* (*herramienta*)

bolt; (*de puerta*) latch.

certamen [θer'tamen] *nm* competition, contest.

certero, a [θer'tero, a] *adj* (*gen*) accurate.

certeza [θer'teθa] *nf* certainty.

certidumbre [θerti'ðumßre] *nf* = **certeza**.

certificado [θertifi'kaðo] *nm* certificate.

certificar [θertifi'kar] *vt* (*asegurar*, *atestar*) to certify.

cervatillo [θerßa'tiʎo] *nm* fawn.

cervecería [θerßeθe'ria] *nf* (*fábrica*) brewery; (*bar*) public house, pub.

cerveza [θer'ßeθa] *nf* beer.

cesación [θesa'θjon] *nf* cessation, suspension.

cesante [θe'sante] *adj* redundant.

cesantía [θesan'tia] *nf* unemployment.

cesar [θe'sar] *vi* to cease, stop ♦ *vt* (*funcionario*) to remove from office.

cese ['θese] *nm* (*de trabajo*) dismissal; (*de pago*) suspension.

césped ['θespeð] *nm* grass, lawn.

cesta ['θesta] *nf* basket.

cesto ['θesto] *nm* (large) basket, hamper.

cetro ['θetro] *nm* sceptre.

cfr *abr* (= *confróntese*) cf.

ch... *see under letter* CH, *after* C.

Cía *abr* (= *compañía*) Co.

cianuro [θja'nuro] *nm* cyanide.

cicatriz [θika'triθ] *nf* scar; **~ar** *vt* to heal; **~arse** *vr* to heal (up), form a scar.

ciclismo [θi'klismo] *nm* cycling.

ciclo ['θiklo] *nm* cycle.

ciclón [θi'klon] *nm* cyclone.

ciego, a ['θjeɣo, a] *adj* blind ♦ *nm/f* blind man/woman.

cielo ['θjelo] *nm* sky; (*REL*) heaven; **¡~s!** good heavens!

ciempiés [θjem'pjes] *nm inv* centipede.

cien [θjen] *num ver* **ciento**.

ciénaga ['θjenaɣa] *nf* marsh, swamp.

ciencia ['θjenθja] *nf* science; **~s** *nfpl* (*ESCOL*) science *sg*; **~-ficción** *nf* science fiction.

cieno ['θjeno] *nm* mud, mire.

científico, a [θjen'tifiko, a] *adj* scientific

♦ *nm/f* scientist.

ciento ['θjento] (*tb:* **cien**) *num* hundred; **pagar al 10 por** **~** to pay at 10 per cent.

cierne ['θjerne] *nm*: **en ~** in blossom.

cierre *etc* ['θjerre] *vb ver* **cerrar** ♦ *nm* closing, shutting; (*con llave*) locking; **~ de cremallera** zip (fastener).

cierro *etc vb ver* **cerrar**.

cierto, a ['θjerto, a] *adj* sure, certain; (*un tal*) a certain; (*correcto*) right, correct; **~ hombre** a certain man; **ciertas personas** certain *o* some people; **sí, es ~** yes, that's correct.

ciervo ['θjerßo] *nm* (*ZOOL*) deer; (: *macho*) stag.

cierzo ['θjerθo] *nm* north wind.

cifra ['θifra] *nf* number, numeral; (*cantidad*) number, quantity; (*secreta*) code.

cifrar [θi'frar] *vt* to code, write in code; (*resumir*) to abridge.

cigala [θi'ɣala] *nf* Norway lobster.

cigarra [θi'ɣarra] *nf* cicada.

cigarrera [θiɣa'rrera] *nf* cigar case.

cigarrillo [θiɣa'rriʎo] *nm* cigarette.

cigarro [θi'ɣarro] *nm* cigarette; (*puro*) cigar.

cigüeña [θi'ɣweɲa] *nf* stork.

cilíndrico, a [θi'lindriko, a] *adj* cylindrical.

cilindro [θi'lindro] *nm* cylinder.

cima ['θima] *nf* (*de montaña*) top, peak; (*de árbol*) top; (*fig*) height.

címbalo ['θimbalo] *nm* cymbal.

cimbrar [θim'brar] *vt* to brandish; **~se** *vr* to sway.

cimbrear [θimbre'ar] *vt* = **cimbrar**.

cimentar [θimen'tar] *vt* to lay the foundations of; (*fig: fundar*) to found.

cimiento [θi'mjento] *nm* foundation.

cinc [θink] *nm* zinc.

cincel [θin'θel] *nm* chisel; **~ar** *vt* to chisel.

cinco ['θinko] *num* five.

cincuenta [θin'kwenta] *num* fifty.

cine ['θine] *nm* cinema.

cineasta [θine'asta] *nm/f* (*director de cine*) film director.

cinematográfico, a [θinemato'ɣrafiko, a] *adj* cine-, film *cpd*.

cínico, a ['θiniko, a] *adj* cynical ♦ *nm/f* cynic.

cinismo [θi'nismo] *nm* cynicism.

cinta ['θinta] *nf* band, strip; *(de tela)* ribbon; *(película)* reel; *(de máquina de escribir)* ribbon; ~ **adhesiva** sticky tape; ~ **magnetofónica** tape; ~ **métrica** tape measure.

cinto ['θinto] *nm* belt.

cintura [θin'tura] *nf* waist.

cinturón [θintu'ron] *nm* belt; ~ **de seguridad** safety belt.

ciprés [θi'pres] *nm* cypress (tree).

circo ['θirko] *nm* circus.

circuito [θir'kwito] *nm* circuit.

circulación [θirkula'θjon] *nf* circulation; *(AUTO)* traffic.

circular [θirku'lar] *adj*, *nf* circular ♦ *vi*, *vt* to circulate ♦ *vi* *(AUTO)* to drive; **"circule por la derecha"** "keep (to the) right".

círculo ['θirkulo] *nm* circle.

circuncidar [θirkunθi'dar] *vt* to circumcise.

circundar [θirkun'dar] *vt* to surround.

circunferencia [θirkunfe'renθja] *nf* circumference.

circunscribir [θirkunskri'βir] *vt* to circumscribe; ~**se** *vr* to be limited.

circunscripción [θirkunskrip'θjon] *nf* division; *(POL)* constituency.

circunspecto, a [θirkuns'pekto, a] *adj* circumspect, cautious.

circunstancia [θirkuns'tanθja] *nf* circumstance.

circunstante [θirkuns'tante] *nm/f* onlooker, bystander.

cirio ['θirjo] *nm* (wax) candle.

ciruela [θi'rwela] *nf* plum; ~ **pasa** prune.

cirugía [θiru'xia] *nf* surgery; ~ **estética** *o* **plástica** plastic surgery.

cirujano [θiru'xano] *nm* surgeon.

cisne ['θisne] *nm* swan.

cisterna [θis'terna] *nf* cistern, tank.

cita ['θita] *nf* appointment, meeting; *(de novios)* date; *(referencia)* quotation.

citación [θita'θjon] *nf* *(JUR)* summons *sg*.

citar [θi'tar] *vt* *(gen)* to make an appointment with; *(JUR)* to summons; *(un autor, texto)* to quote; ~**se** *vr*: se

citaron en el cine they arranged to meet at the cinema.

cítricos ['θitrikos] *nmpl* citrus fruit(s).

ciudad [θju'ðað] *nf* town; *(más grande)* city; ~**anía** *nf* citizenship; ~**ano, a** *nm/f* citizen.

cívico, a ['θiβiko, a] *adj* civic.

civil [θi'βil] *adj* civil ♦ *nm* *(guardia)* policeman.

civilización [θiβiliθa'θjon] *nf* civilization.

civilizar [θiβili'θar] *vt* to civilize.

civismo [θi'βismo] *nm* public spirit.

cizaña [θi'θaɲa] *nf* *(fig)* discord.

cl. *abr* (= *centilitro*) cl.

clamar [kla'mar] *vt* to clamour for, cry out for ♦ *vi* to cry out, clamour.

clamor [kla'mor] *nm* *(grito)* cry, shout; *(fig)* clamour, protest.

clandestino, a [klandes'tino, a] *adj* clandestine; *(POL)* underground.

clara ['klara] *nf* *(de huevo)* egg white.

claraboya [klara'βoja] *nf* skylight.

clarear [klare'ar] *vi* *(el día)* to dawn; *(el cielo)* to clear up, brighten up; ~**se** *vr* to be transparent.

clarete [kla'rete] *nm* rosé (wine).

claridad [klari'ðað] *nf* *(del día)* brightness; *(de estilo)* clarity.

clarificar [klarifi'kar] *vt* to clarify.

clarín [kla'rin] *nm* bugle.

clarinete [klari'nete] *nm* clarinet.

clarividencia [klariβi'ðenθja] *nf* clairvoyance; *(fig)* far-sightedness.

claro, a ['klaro, a] *adj* clear; *(luminoso)* bright; *(color)* light; *(evidente)* clear, evident; *(poco espeso)* thin ♦ *nm* *(en bosque)* clearing ♦ *adv* clearly ♦ *excl* *(tb:* ~ *que sí)* of course!

clase ['klase] *nf* class; ~ **alta/media/obrera** upper/middle/working class.

clásico, a ['klasiko, a] *adj* classical; *(fig)* classic.

clasificación [klasifika'θjon] *nf* classification; *(DEPORTE)* league (table).

clasificar [klasifi'kar] *vt* to classify.

claudia ['klauðja] *nf* greengage.

claudicar [klauði'kar] *vi* *(fig)* to back down.

claustro ['klaustro] *nm* cloister.

cláusula ['klausula] *nf* clause.

clausura [klau'sura] *nf* closing, closure; **clausurar** *vt* (*congreso etc*) to bring to a close.

clavar [kla'ßar] *vt* (*clavo*) to hammer in; (*cuchillo*) to stick, thrust; (*tablas etc*) to nail (together).

clave ['klaße] *nf* key; (*MUS*) clef.

clavel [kla'ßel] *nm* carnation.

clavícula [kla'ßikula] *nf* collar bone.

clavija [kla'ßixa] *nf* peg, dowel, pin; (*ELEC*) plug.

clavo ['klaßo] *nm* (*de metal*) nail; (*BOT*) clove.

claxon ['klakson] (*pl* ~s) *nm* horn.

clemencia [kle'menθja] *nf* mercy, clemency.

cleptómano, a [klep'tomano, a] *nm/f* kleptomaniac.

clerical [kleri'kal] *adj* clerical.

clérigo ['klerivo] *nm* priest.

clero ['klero] *nm* clergy.

cliché [kli'tʃe] *nm* cliché; (*FOTO*) negative.

cliente, a ['kljente, a] *nm/f* client, customer.

clientela [kljen'tela] *nf* clientele, customers *pl*.

clima ['klima] *nm* climate.

climatizado, a [klimati'θaðo, a] *adj* air-conditioned.

clínica ['klinika] *nf* clinic; (*particular*) private hospital.

clip [klip] (*pl* ~s) *nm* paper clip.

clorhídrico, a [klo'ridriko, a] *adj* hydrochloric.

club [klub] (*pl* ~s *o* ~es) *nm* club; ~ **de jóvenes** youth club.

cm *abr* (= *centímetro, centímetros*) cm.

C.N.T. (*ESP*) *abr* = *Confederación Nacional de Trabajo*.

coacción [koak'θjon] *nf* coercion, compulsion.

coagular [koavu'lar] *vt* (*leche, sangre*) to clot; ~**se** *vr* to clot; **coágulo** *nm* clot.

coalición [koali'θjon] *nf* coalition.

coartada [koar'taða] *nf* alibi.

coartar [koar'tar] *vt* to limit, restrict.

coba ['koßa] *nf*: **dar** ~ **a uno** to soft-soap sb.

cobarde [ko'ßarðe] *adj* cowardly ♦ *nm* coward; **cobardía** *nf* cowardice.

cobaya [ko'ßaja] *nf* guinea pig.

cobayo [ko'ßajo] *nm* = **cobaya**.

cobertizo [koßer'tiθo] *nm* shelter.

cobertor [koßer'tor] *nm* bedspread.

cobertura [koßer'tura] *nf* cover.

cobija [ko'ßixa] (*AM*) *nf* blanket.

cobijar [koßi'xar] *vt* (*cubrir*) to cover; (*abrigar*) to shelter; **cobijo** *nm* shelter.

cobra ['koßra] *nf* cobra.

cobrador, a [koßra'ðor, a] *nm/f* (*de autobús*) conductor/conductress; (*de impuestos, gas*) collector.

cobrar [ko'ßrar] *vt* (*cheque*) to cash; (*sueldo*) to collect, draw; (*objeto*) to recover; (*precio*) to charge; (*deuda*) to collect ♦ *vi* to draw one's pay; ~**se** *vr* to recover, get well; **cóbrese al entregar** cash on delivery.

cobre ['koßre] *nm* copper; ~s *nmpl* (*MUS*) brass instruments.

cobro ['koßro] *nm* (*de cheque*) cashing; (*pago*) payment; **presentar al** ~ to cash.

Coca-Cola ['koka'kola] ® *nf* Coca-Cola ®.

cocaína [koka'ina] *nf* cocaine.

cocción [kok'θjon] *nf* (*CULIN*) cooking; (: *el hervir*) boiling.

cocear [koθe'ar] *vi* to kick.

cocer [ko'θer] *vt, vi* to cook; (*en agua*) to boil; (*en horno*) to bake.

cocido [ko'θiðo] *nm* stew.

cocina [ko'θina] *nf* kitchen; (*aparato*) cooker, stove; (*acto*) cookery; ~ **eléctrica/de gas** electric/gas cooker; ~ **francesa** French cuisine; **cocinar** *vt, vi* to cook.

cocinero, a [koθi'nero, a] *nm/f* cook.

coco ['koko] *nm* coconut; ~**tero** *nm* coconut palm.

cocodrilo [koko'ðrilo] *nm* crocodile.

coche ['kotʃe] *nm* (*AUTO*) car (*BRIT*), automobile (*US*); (*de tren, de caballos*) coach, carriage; (*para niños*) pram (*BRIT*), baby carriage (*US*); **ir en** ~ to drive; ~ **celular** Black Maria, prison van; ~ **fúnebre** hearse; **coche-cama** (*pl*

coches-cama) *nm* (*FERRO*) sleeping car, sleeper.

cochera [ko'tʃera] *nf* garage; (*de autobuses, trenes*) depot.

coche restaurante (*pl* **coches restaurante**) *nm* (*FERRO*) dining car, diner.

cochino, a [ko'tʃino, a] *adj* filthy, dirty ♦ *nm/f* pig.

codazo [ko'ðaθo] *nm*: **dar un ~ a uno** to nudge sb.

codear [koðe'ar] *vi* to elbow, nudge; **~se** *vr*: **~se con** to rub shoulders with.

codicia [ko'ðiθja] *nf* greed; (*fig*) lust; **codiciar** *vt* to covet; **codicioso, a** *adj* covetous.

código ['koðiɣo] *nm* code; **~ de barras** bar code; **~ civil** common law.

codillo [ko'ðiʎo] *nm* (*ZOOL*) knee; (*TEC*) elbow (joint).

codo ['koðo] *nm* (*ANAT, de tubo*) elbow; (*ZOOL*) knee.

codorniz [koðor'niθ] *nf* quail.

coerción [koer'θjon] *nf* coercion.

coetáneo, a [koe'taneo, a] *adj*, *nm/f* contemporary.

coexistir [koe(k)sis'tir] *vi* to coexist.

cofradía [kofra'ðia] *nf* brotherhood, fraternity.

coger [ko'xer] (*ESP*) *vt* to take (hold of); (*objeto caído*) to pick up; (*frutas*) to pick, harvest; (*resfriado, ladrón, pelota*) to catch ♦ *vi*: **~ por el buen camino** to take the right road; **~se** *vr* (*el dedo*) to catch; **~se a algo** to get hold of sth.

cogollo [ko'ɣoʎo] *nm* (*de lechuga*) heart.

cogote [ko'ɣote] *nm* back *o* nape of the neck.

cohabitar [koaβi'tar] *vi* to live together, cohabit.

cohecho [ko'etʃo] *nm* (*acción*) bribery; (*soborno*) bribe.

coherente [koe'rente] *adj* coherent.

cohesión [koe'sjon] *nm* cohesion.

cohete [ko'ete] *nm* rocket.

cohibido, a [koi'βiðo, a] *adj* (*PSICO*) inhibited; (*tímido*) shy.

cohibir [koi'βir] *vt* to restrain, restrict.

coima [ko'ima] (*AM*) *nf* bribe.

coincidencia [koinθi'ðenθja] *nf* coincidence.

coincidir [koinθi'ðir] *vi* (*en idea*) to coincide, agree; (*en lugar*) to coincide.

coito ['koito] *nm* intercourse, coitus.

coja *etc vb ver* **coger**.

cojear [koxe'ar] *vi* (*persona*) to limp, hobble; (*mueble*) to wobble, rock.

cojera [ko'xera] *nf* lameness; (*andar cojo*) limp.

cojín [ko'xin] *nm* cushion; **cojinete** *nm* small cushion, pad; (*TEC*) ball bearing.

cojo, a *etc* ['koxo, a] *vb ver* **coger** ♦ *adj* (*que no puede andar*) lame, crippled; (*mueble*) wobbly ♦ *nm/f* lame person, cripple.

cojón [ko'xon] (*fam*) *nm*: **¡cojones!** shit! (*!*); **cojonudo, a** (*fam*) *adj* great, fantastic.

col [kol] *nf* cabbage; **~es de Bruselas** Brussels sprouts.

cola ['kola] *nf* tail; (*de gente*) queue; (*lugar*) end, last place; (*para pegar*) glue, gum; **hacer ~** to queue (up).

colaborador, a [kolaβora'ðor, a] *nm/f* collaborator.

colaborar [kolaβo'rar] *vi* to collaborate.

colada [ko'laða] *nf*: **hacer la ~** to do the washing.

colador [kola'ðor] *nm* (*de té*) strainer; (*para verduras etc*) colander.

colapso [ko'lapso] *nm* collapse; **~ nervioso** nervous breakdown.

colar [ko'lar] *vt* (*líquido*) to strain off; (*metal*) to cast ♦ *vi* to ooze, seep (through); **~se** *vr* to jump the queue; **~se en** to get into without paying; (*fiesta*) to gatecrash.

colateral [kolate'ral] *nm* collateral.

colcha ['koltʃa] *nf* bedspread.

colchón [kol'tʃon] *nm* mattress.

colchoneta [koltʃo'neta] *nf* (*en gimnasio*) mattress.

colear [kole'ar] *vi* (*perro*) to wag its tail.

colección [kolek'θjon] *nf* collection; **coleccionar** *vt* to collect; **coleccionista** *nm/f* collector.

colecta [ko'lekta] *nf* collection.

colectivo, a [kolek'tiβo, a] *adj* collective, joint ♦ nm (AM) (small) bus.

colector [kolek'tor] nm collector; (sumidero) sewer.

colega [ko'leɣa] nm/f colleague.

colegial, a [kole'xjal, a] nm/f schoolboy/girl.

colegio [ko'lexjo] nm college; (escuela) school; (de abogados etc) association.

colegir [kole'xir] vt (juntar) to collect, gather; (deducir) to infer, conclude.

cólera ['kolera] nf (ira) anger; (MED) cholera; **colérico, a** [ko'leriko, a] adj irascible, bad-tempered.

colesterol [koleste'rol] nm cholesterol.

coleta [ko'leta] nf pigtail.

colgante [kol'ɣante] adj hanging ♦ nm (joya) pendant.

colgar [kol'ɣar] vt to hang (up); (ropa) to hang out ♦ vi to hang; (teléfono) to hang up.

coliflor [koli'flor] nf cauliflower.

colilla [ko'liʎa] nf cigarette end, butt.

colina [ko'lina] nf hill.

colindante [kolin'dante] adj adjacent, neighbouring.

colindar [kolin'dar] vi to adjoin, be adjacent.

colisión [koli'sjon] nf collision; ~ de frente head-on crash.

colmado, a [kol'maðo, a] adj full.

colmar [kol'mar] vt to fill to the brim; (fig) to fulfil, realize.

colmena [kol'mena] nf beehive.

colmillo [kol'miʎo] nm (diente) eye tooth; (de elefante) tusk; (de perro) fang.

colmo ['kolmo] nm height, summit; ¡es el ~! it's the limit!

colocación [koloka'θjon] nf (acto) placing; (empleo) job, position; (situación) place, position.

colocar [kolo'kar] vt to place, put, position; (dinero) to invest; (poner en empleo) to find a job for; ~se vr to get a job.

Colombia [ko'lombja] nf Colombia; **colombiano, a** adj, nm/f Colombian.

colonia [ko'lonja] nf colony; (de casas) housing estate; (agua de ~) cologne.

colonización [koloniθa'θjon] nf coloniza-

tion; **colonizador, a** [koloniθa'ðor, a] adj colonizing ♦ nm/f colonist, settler.

colonizar [koloni'θar] vt to colonize.

coloquio [ko'lokjo] nm conversation; (congreso) conference.

color [ko'lor] nm colour.

colorado, a [kolo'raðo, a] adj (rojo) red; (chiste) rude.

colorante [kolo'rante] nm colouring.

colorar [kolo'rar] vt to colour; (teñir) to dye.

colorear [kolore'ar] vt to colour.

colorete [kolo'rete] nm blusher.

colorido [kolo'riðo] nm colouring.

columna [ko'lumna] nf column; (pilar) pillar; (apoyo) support.

columpiar [kolum'pjar] vt to swing; ~se vr to swing; **columpio** nm swing.

collar [ko'ʎar] nm necklace; (de perro) collar.

coma ['koma] nf comma ♦ nm (MED) coma.

comadre [ko'maðre] nf (madrina) godmother; (vecina) neighbour; (chismosa) gossip; ~ar vi to gossip.

comandancia [koman'danθja] nf command.

comandante [koman'dante] nm commandant.

comandar [koman'dar] vt to command.

comarca [ko'marka] nf region.

comba ['komba] nf (curva) curve; (cuerda) skipping rope; saltar a la ~ to skip.

combar [kom'bar] vt to bend, curve.

combate [kom'bate] nm fight; (fig) battle; **combatiente** nm combatant.

combatir [komba'tir] vt to fight, combat.

combinación [kombina'θjon] nf combination; (QUÍMICA) compound; (bebida) cocktail; (plan) scheme, setup; (prenda) slip.

combinar [kombi'nar] vt to combine.

combustible [kombus'tiβle] nm fuel.

combustión [kombus'tjon] nf combustion.

comedia [ko'meðja] nf comedy; (TEATRO) play, drama.

comediante [kome'ðjante] nm/f (comic) actor/actress.

comedido, a [kome'ðiðo, a] *adj* moderate.

comedor, a [kome'ðor, a] *nm/f* (*persona*) glutton ♦ *nm* (*habitación*) dining room; (*restaurante*) restaurant; (*cantina*) canteen.

comensal [komen'sal] *nm/f* fellow guest (*o diner*).

comentar [komen'tar] *vt* to comment on; (*fam*) to discuss.

comentario [komen'tarjo] *nm* comment, remark; (*literario*) commentary; ~s *nmpl* (*chismes*) gossip *sg*.

comentarista [komenta'rista] *nm/f* commentator.

comenzar [komen'θar] *vt*, *vi* to begin, start, commence; ~ **a hacer algo** to begin *o* start doing sth. •

comer [ko'mer] *vt* to eat; (*DAMAS, AJEDREZ*) to take, capture ♦ *vi* to eat; (*almorzar*) to have lunch; ~se *vr* to eat up.

comercial [komer'θjal] *adj* commercial; (*relativo al negocio*) business *cpd*.

comerciante [komer'θjante] *nm/f* trader, merchant.

comerciar [komer'θjar] *vi* to trade, do business.

comercio [ko'merθjo] *nm* commerce, trade; (*negocio*) business; (*fig*) dealings *pl*.

comestible [komes'tiβle] *adj* eatable, edible; ~s *nmpl* food *sg*, foodstuffs.

cometa [ko'meta] *nm* comet ♦ *nf* kite.

cometer [kome'ter] *vt* to commit.

cometido [kome'tiðo] *nm* (*misión*) task, assignment; (*deber*) commitment.

comezón [kome'θon] *nf* itch, itching.

comicios [ko'miθjos] *nmpl* elections.

cómico, a ['komiko, a] *adj* comic(al) ♦ *nm/f* comedian; (*de teatro*) (comic) actor/actress.

comida [ko'miða] *nf* (*alimento*) food; (*almuerzo, cena*) meal; (*de mediodía*) lunch.

comidilla [komi'ðiʎa] *nf*: **ser la ~ de la ciudad** to be the talk of the town.

comienzo *etc* [ko'mjenθo] *vb ver* **comenzar** ♦ *nm* beginning, start.

comilona [komi'lona] (*fam*) *nf* blow-out.

comillas [ko'miʎas] *nfpl* quotation marks.

comino [ko'mino] *nm*: **(no) me importa un ~** I don't give a damn.

comisaría [komisa'ria] *nf* (*de policía*) police station; (*MIL*) commissariat.

comisario [komi'sarjo] *nm* (*MIL etc*) commissary; (*POL*) commissar.

comisión [komi'sjon] *nf* commission.

comité [komi'te] (*pl* ~s) *nm* committee.

como ['komo] *adv* as; (*tal* ~) like; (*aproximadamente*) about, approximately ♦ *conj* (*ya que, puesto que*) as, since; (*en cuanto*) as soon as; ¡~ no! of course!; ~ **no lo haga hoy** unless he does it today; ~ **si** as if; **es tan alto ~ ancho** it is as high as it is wide.

cómo ['komo] *adv* how?, why? ♦ *excl* what?, I beg your pardon? ♦ *nm*: **el ~ y el porqué** the whys and wherefores.

cómoda ['komoða] *nf* chest of drawers.

comodidad [komoði'ðað] *nf* comfort; **venga a su** ~ come at your convenience.

comodín [komo'ðin] *nm* joker.

cómodo, a ['komoðo, a] *adj* comfortable; (*práctico, de fácil uso*) convenient.

compacto, a [kom'pakto, a] *adj* compact.

compadecer [kompaðe'θer] *vt* to pity, be sorry for; ~se *vr*: ~se **de** to pity, be *o* feel sorry for.

compadre [kom'paðre] *nm* (*padrino*) godfather; (*amigo*) friend, pal.

compañero, a [kompa'ɲero, a] *nm/f* companion; (*novio*) boy/girlfriend; ~ **de clase** classmate.

compañía [kompa'ɲia] *nf* company.

comparación [kompara'θjon] *nf* comparison; **en** ~ **con** in comparison with.

comparar [kompa'rar] *vt* to compare.

comparativo, a [kompara'tiβo, a] *adj* comparative.

comparecer [kompare'θer] *vi* to appear (in court).

comparsa [kom'parsa] *nm/f* (*TEATRO*) extra.

compartimiento [komparti'mjento] *nm* (*FERRO*) compartment.

compartir [kompar'tir] *vt* to share; (*dinero, comida etc*) to divide (up), share (out).

compás [kom'pas] *nm* (*MUS*) beat, rhythm; (*MAT*) compasses *pl*; (*NAUT etc*) compass.

compasión [kompa'sjon] *nf* compassion, pity.

compasivo, a [kompa'siβo, a] *adj* compassionate.

compatibilidad [kompatiβili'ðað] *nf* compatibility.

compatible [kompa'tiβle] *adj* compatible.

compatriota [kompa'trjota] *nm/f* compatriot, fellow countryman/woman.

compendiar [kompen'djar] *vt* to summarize; (*libro*) to abridge; **compendio** *nm* summary; abridgement.

compensación [kompensa'θjon] *nf* compensation.

compensar [kompen'sar] *vt* to compensate.

competencia [kompe'tenθja] *nf* (*incumbencia*) domain, field; (*JUR, habilidad*) competence; (*rivalidad*) competition.

competente [kompe'tente] *adj* (*JUR, persona*) competent; (*conveniente*) suitable.

competición [kompeti'θjon] *nf* competition.

competir [kompe'tir] *vi* to compete.

compilar [kompi'lar] *vt* to compile.

complacencia [kompla'θenθja] *nf* (*placer*) pleasure; (*tolerancia excesiva*) complacency.

complacer [kompla'θer] *vt* to please; **~se** *vr* to be pleased.

complaciente [kompla'θjente] *adj* kind, obliging, helpful.

complejo, a [kom'plexo, a] *adj, nm* complex.

complementario, a [komplemen'tarjo, a] *adj* complementary.

completar [komple'tar] *vt* to complete.

completo, a [kom'pleto, a] *adj* complete; (*perfecto*) perfect; (*lleno*) full ♦ *nm* full complement.

complicado, a [kompli'kaðo, a] *adj* complicated; **estar ~ en** to be mixed up in.

complicar [kompli'kar] *vt* to complicate.

cómplice ['kompliθe] *nm/f* accomplice.

complot [kom'plo(t)] (*pl* ~s) *nm* plot; (*conspiración*) conspiracy.

componer [kompo'ner] *vt* to make up, put together; (*MUS, LITERATURA, IMPRENTA*) to compose; (*algo roto*) to mend, repair; (*arreglar*) to arrange; **~se** *vr*: **~se de** to consist of; **componérselas para hacer algo** to manage to do sth.

comportamiento [komporta'mjento] *nm* behaviour, conduct.

comportarse [kompor'tarse] *vr* to behave.

composición [komposi'θjon] *nf* composition.

compositor, a [komposi'tor, a] *nm/f* composer.

compostura [kompos'tura] *nf* (*composición*) composition; (*reparación*) mending, repair; (*acuerdo*) agreement; (*actitud*) composure.

compra ['kompra] *nf* purchase; **~s** *nfpl* purchases, shopping *sg*; **ir de ~s** to go shopping; **comprador, a** *nm/f* buyer, purchaser.

comprar [kom'prar] *vt* to buy, purchase.

comprender [kompren'der] *vt* to understand; (*incluir*) to comprise, include.

comprensión [kompren'sjon] *nf* understanding; (*totalidad*) comprehensiveness; **comprensivo, a** *adj* comprehensive; (*actitud*) understanding.

compresa [kom'presa] *nf*: **~ higiénica** sanitary towel (*BRIT*) o napkin (*US*).

comprimido, a [kompri'miðo, a] *adj* compressed ♦ *nm* (*MED*) pill, tablet.

comprimir [kompri'mir] *vt* to compress; (*fig*) to control.

comprobante [kompro'βante] *nm* proof; (*COM*) voucher; **~ de recibo** receipt.

comprobar [kompro'βar] *vt* to check; (*probar*) to prove; (*TEC*) to check, test.

comprometer [komprome'ter] *vt* to compromise; (*exponer*) to endanger; **~se** *vr* to compromise o.s.; (*in-*

volucrarse) to get involved.

compromiso [kompro'miso] *nm* (*obligación*) obligation; (*cometido*) commitment; (*convenio*) agreement; (*dificultad*) awkward situation.

compuesto, a [kom'pwesto, a] *adj*: ~ **de** composed of, made up of ♦ *nm* compound.

computador [komputa'ðor] *nm* computer; ~ **central** mainframe computer; ~ **personal** personal computer.

computadora [komputa'ðora] *nf* = **computador**.

cómputo ['komputo] *nm* calculation.

comulgar [komul'ɣar] *vi* to receive communion.

común [ko'mun] *adj* common ♦ *nm*: **el** ~ the community.

comunicación [komunika'θjon] *nf* communication; (*informe*) report.

comunicado [komuni'kado] *nm* announcement; ~ **de prensa** press release.

comunicar [komuni'kar] *vt, vi* to communicate; ~**se** *vr* to communicate; **está comunicando** (*TEL*) the line's engaged (*BRIT*) o busy (*US*); **comunicativo, a** *adj* communicative.

comunidad [komuni'ðað] *nf* community.

comunión [komu'njon] *nf* communion.

comunismo [komu'nismo] *nm* communism; **comunista** *adj, nm/f* communist.

con [kon] *prep* **1** (*medio, compañía*) with; **comer** ~ **cuchara** to eat with a spoon; **pasear** ~ **uno** to go for a walk with sb

2 (*a pesar de*): ~ **todo, merece nuestros respetos** all the same, he deserves our respect

3 (*para* ~): **es muy bueno para** ~ **los niños** he's very good with (the) children

4 (+*infin*): ~ **llegar tan tarde se quedó sin comer** by arriving so late he missed out on eating

♦ *conj*: ~ **que: será suficiente** ~ **que le escribas** it will be sufficient if you write to her.

conato [ko'nato] *nm* attempt; ~ **de robo** attempted robbery.

concebir [konθe'βir] *vt, vi* to conceive.

conceder [konθe'ðer] *vt* to concede.

concejal, a [konθe'xal, a] *nm/f* town councillor.

concejo [kon'θexo] *nm* council.

concentración [konθentra'θjon] *nf* concentration.

concentrar [konθen'trar] *vt* to concentrate; ~**se** *vr* to concentrate.

concepción [konθep'θjon] *nf* conception.

concepto [kon'θepto] *nm* concept.

concertar [konθer'tar] *vt* (*MUS*) to harmonize; (*acordar: precio*) to agree; (: *tratado*) to conclude; (*trato*) to arrange, fix up; (*combinar: esfuerzos*) to coordinate; (*reconciliar: personas*) to reconcile ♦ *vi* to harmonize, be in tune.

concesión [konθe'sjon] *nf* concession.

concesionario [konθesjo'narjo] *nm* (licensed) dealer, agent.

conciencia [kon'θjenθja] *nf* conscience; **tener/tomar** ~ **de** to be/become aware of; **tener la** ~ **limpia/tranquila** to have a clear conscience.

concienciar [konθjen'θjar] *vt* to make aware; ~**se** *vr* to become aware.

concienzudo, a [konθjen'θuðo, a] *adj* conscientious.

concierto *etc* [kon'θjerto] *vb ver* **concertar** ♦ *nm* concert; (*obra*) concerto.

conciliar [konθi'ljar] *vt* to reconcile.

concilio [kon'θiljo] *nm* council.

conciso, a [kon'θiso, a] *adj* concise.

conciudadano, a [konθjuða'ðano, a] *nm/f* fellow citizen.

concluir [konklu'ir] *vt, vi* to conclude; ~**se** *vr* to conclude.

conclusión [konklu'sjon] *nf* conclusion.

concluyente [konklu'jente] *adj* (*prueba, información*) conclusive.

concordar [konkor'ðar] *vt* to reconcile ♦ *vi* to agree, tally.

concordia [kon'korðja] *nf* harmony.

concretar [konkre'tar] *vt* to make concrete, make more specific; ~**se** *vr* to become more definite.

concreto, a [kon'kreto, a] *adj, nm* (*AM*) concrete; **en ~** (*en resumen*) to sum up; (*específicamente*) specifically; **no hay nada en ~** there's nothing definite.

concurrencia [konku'rrenθja] *nf* turnout.

concurrido, a [konku'rriðo, a] *adj* (*calle*) busy; (*local, reunión*) crowded.

concurrir [konku'rrir] *vi* (*juntarse: ríos*) to meet, come together; (: *personas*) to gather, meet.

concursante [konkur'sante] *nm/f* competitor.

concurso [kon'kurso] *nm* (*de público*) crowd; (*ESCOL, DEPORTE, competencia*) competition; (*ayuda*) help, cooperation.

concha ['kontʃa] *nf* shell.

condal [kon'dal] *adj*: **la ciudad ~** Barcelona.

conde ['konde] *nm* count.

condecoración [kondekora'θjon] *nf* (*MIL*) medal.

condecorar [kondeko'rar] *vt* (*MIL*) to decorate.

condena [kon'dena] *nf* sentence.

condenación [kondena'θjon] *nf* condemnation; (*REL*) damnation.

condenar [konde'nar] *vt* to condemn; (*JUR*) to convict; **~se** *vr* (*JUR*) to confess (one's guilt); (*REL*) to be damned.

condensar [konden'sar] *vt* to condense.

condesa [kon'desa] *nf* countess.

condescender [kondesθen'der] *vi* to acquiesce, comply.

condición [kondi'θjon] *nf* condition; **condicional** *adj* conditional.

condicionar [kondiθjo'nar] *vt* (*acondicionar*) to condition; **~ algo a** to make sth conditional on.

condimento [kondi'mento] *nm* seasoning.

condolerse [kondo'lerse] *vr* to sympathize.

condón [kon'don] *nm* condom.

conducir [kondu'θir] *vt* to take, convey; (*AUTO*) to drive ♦ *vi* to drive; (*fig*) to lead; **~se** *vr* to behave.

conducta [kon'dukta] *nf* conduct, behaviour.

conducto [kon'dukto] *nm* pipe, tube;

(*fig*) channel.

conductor, a [konduk'tor, a] *adj* leading, guiding ♦ *nm* (*FÍSICA*) conductor; (*de vehículo*) driver.

conduje *etc vb ver* **conducir**.

conduzco *etc vb ver* **conducir**.

conectado, a [konek'taðo, a] *adj* (*INFORM*) on-line.

conectar [konek'tar] *vt* to connect (up); (*enchufar*) plug in.

conejo [ko'nexo] *nm* rabbit.

conexión [konek'sjon] *nf* connection.

confección [confe(k)'θjon] *nf* preparation; (*industria*) clothing industry.

confeccionar [konfekθjo'nar] *vt* to make (up).

confederación [konfeðera'θjon] *nf* confederation.

conferencia [konfe'renθja] *nf* conference; (*lección*) lecture; (*TEL*) call.

conferir [konfe'rir] *vt* to award.

confesar [konfe'sar] *vt* to confess, admit.

confesión [konfe'sjon] *nf* confession.

confesionario [konfesjo'narjo] *nm* confessional.

confeti [kon'feti] *nm* confetti.

confiado, a [kon'fjaðo, a] *adj* (*crédulo*) trusting; (*seguro*) confident; (*presumido*) conceited, vain.

confianza [kon'fjanθa] *nf* trust; (*aliento, confidencia*) confidence; (*familiaridad*) intimacy, familiarity; (*pey*) vanity, conceit.

confiar [kon'fjar] *vt* to entrust ♦ *vi* to trust.

confidencia [konfi'ðenθja] *nf* confidence.

confidencial [konfiðen'θjal] *adj* confidential.

confidente [konfi'ðente] *nm/f* confidant/e; (*policial*) informer.

configurar [konfiɣu'rar] *vt* to shape, form.

confín [kon'fin] *nm* limit; **confines** *nmpl* confines, limits.

confinar [konfi'nar] *vi* to confine; (*desterrar*) to banish.

confirmar [konfir'mar] *vt* to confirm.

confiscar [konfis'kar] *vt* to confiscate.

confite [kon'fite] *nm* sweet (*BRIT*),

candy (US).

confitería [konfite'ria] nf confectionery; (tienda) confectioner's (shop).

confitura [konfi'tura] nf jam.

conflictivo, a [konflik'tißo, a] adj (asunto, propuesta) controversial; (país, situación) troubled.

conflicto [kon'flikto] nm conflict; (fig) clash.

confluir [kon'flwir] vi (ríos) to meet; (gente) to gather.

conformar [konfor'mar] vt to shape, fashion ♦ vi to agree; ~se vr to conform; (resignarse) to resign o.s.

conforme [kon'forme] adj (correspondiente): ~ con in line with; (de acuerdo): estar ~s (con algo) to be in agreement (with sth) ♦ adv as ♦ excl agreed! ♦ prep: ~ a in accordance with; quedarse ~ (con algo) to be satisfied (with sth).

conformidad [konformi'ðað] nf (semejanza) similarity; (acuerdo) agreement; (resignación) resignation; **conformista** adj, nm/f conformist.

confortable [konfor'taßle] adj comfortable.

confortar [konfor'tar] vt to comfort.

confrontar [konfron'tar] vt to confront; (dos personas) to bring face to face; (cotejar) to compare ♦ vi to border.

confundir [konfun'dir] vt (borrar) to blur; (equivocar) to mistake, confuse; (mezclar) to mix; (turbar) to confuse; ~se vr (hacerse borroso) to become blurred; (turbarse) to get confused; (equivocarse) to make a mistake; (mezclarse) to mix.

confusión [konfu'sjon] nf confusion.

confuso, a [kon'fuso, a] adj confused.

congelado, a [konxe'laðo, a] adj frozen; ~s nmpl frozen food(s); **congelador** nm (aparato) freezer, deep freeze; **congeladora** nf freezer, deep freeze.

congelar [konxe'lar] vt to freeze; ~se vr (sangre, grasa) to congeal.

congeniar [konxe'njar] vi to get on (BRIT) o along (US) well.

congestionar [konxestjo'nar] vt to congest; ~se vr: se le congestionó la cara

his face became flushed.

congoja [kon'goxa] nf distress, grief.

congraciarse [kongra'θjarse] vr to ingratiate o.s.

congratular [kongratu'lar] vt to congratulate.

congregación [kongreya'θjon] nf congregation.

congregar [kongre'var] vt to gather together; ~se vr to gather together.

congresista [kongre'sista] nm/f delegate, congressman/woman.

congreso [kon'greso] nm congress.

conjetura [konxe'tura] nf guess; **conjeturar** vt to guess.

conjugar [konxu'var] vt to combine, fit together; (LING) to conjugate.

conjunción [konxun'θjon] nf conjunction.

conjunto, a [kon'xunto, a] adj joint, united ♦ nm whole; (MUS) band; en ~ as a whole.

conjurar [konxu'rar] vt (REL) to exorcise; (fig) to ward off ♦ vi to plot.

conmemoración [konmemora'θjon] nf commemoration.

conmemorar [konmemo'rar] vt to commemorate.

conmigo [kon'miyo] pron with me.

conminar [konmi'nar] vt to threaten.

conmoción [konmo'θjon] nf shock; (fig) upheaval; ~ cerebral (MED) concussion.

conmovedor, a [konmoße'ðor, a] adj touching, moving; (emocionante) exciting.

conmover [konmo'ßer] vt to shake, disturb; (fig) to move.

conmutador [konmuta'ðor] nm switch; (AM: TEL: centralita) switchboard; (: central) telephone exchange.

cono ['kono] nm cone.

conocedor, a [konoθe'ðor, a] adj expert, knowledgeable ♦ nm/f expert.

conocer [kono'θer] vt to know; (por primera vez) to meet, get to know; (entender) to know about; (reconocer) to recognize; ~se vr (una persona) to know o.s.; (dos personas) to (get to) know each other.

conocido, a [kono'θiðo, a] adj (well-)

known ♦ *nm/f* acquaintance.
conocimiento [konoθi'mjento] *nm* knowledge; (*MED*) consciousness; ~s *nmpl* (*personas*) acquaintances; (*saber*) knowledge *sg*.
conozco *etc vb ver* **conocer**.
conque ['konke] *conj* and so, so then.
conquista [kon'kista] *nf* conquest; **conquistador, a** *adj* conquering ♦ *nm* conqueror.
conquistar [konkis'tar] *vt* to conquer.
consagrar [konsa'γrar] *vt* (*REL*) to consecrate; (*fig*) to devote.
consciente [kons'θjente] *adj* conscious.
consecución [konseku'θjon] *nf* acquisition; (*de fin*) attainment.
consecuencia [konse'kwenθja] *nf* consequence, outcome; (*firmeza*) consistency.
consecuente [konse'kwente] *adj* consistent.
consecutivo, a [konseku'tiβo, a] *adj* consecutive.
conseguir [konse'γir] *vt* to get, obtain; (*sus fines*) to attain.
consejero, a [konse'xero, a] *nm/f* adviser, consultant; (*POL*) councillor.
consejo [kon'sexo] *nm* advice; (*POL*) council.
consenso [kon'senso] *nm* consensus.
consentimiento [konsenti'mjento] *nm* consent.
consentir [konsen'tir] *vt* (*permitir, tolerar*) to consent to; (*mimar*) to pamper, spoil; (*aguantar*) to put up with ♦ *vi* to agree, consent; ~ **que uno haga algo** to allow sb to do sth.
conserje [kon'serxe] *nm* caretaker; (*portero*) porter.
conservación [konserβa'θjon] *nf* conservation; (*de alimentos, vida*) preservation.
conservador, a [konserβa'ðor, a] *adj* (*POL*) conservative ♦ *nm/f* conservative.
conservante [konser'βante] *nm* preservative.
conservar [konser'βar] *vt* to conserve, keep; (*alimentos, vida*) to preserve; ~**se** *vr* to survive.
conservas [kon'serβas] *nfpl* canned

food(s) (*pl*).
conservatorio [konserβa'torjo] *nm* (*MUS*) conservatoire, conservatory.
considerable [konsiðe'raβle] *adj* considerable.
consideración [konsiðera'θjon] *nf* consideration; (*estimación*) respect.
considerado, a [konsiðe'raðo, a] *adj* (*atento*) considerate; (*respetado*) respected.
considerar [konsiðe'rar] *vt* to consider.
consigna [kon'siγna] *nf* (*orden*) order, instruction; (*para equipajes*) left-luggage office.
consigo *etc* [kon'sivo] *vb ver* **conseguir** ♦ *pron* (*m*) with him; (*f*) with her; (*Vd*) with you; (*reflexivo*) with o.s.
consiguiendo *etc vb ver* **conseguir**.
consiguiente [konsi'γjente] *adj* consequent; **por** ~ and so, therefore, consequently.
consistente [konsis'tente] *adj* consistent; (*sólido*) solid, firm; (*válido*) sound.
consistir [konsis'tir] *vi*: ~ **en** (*componerse de*) to consist of; (*ser resultado de*) to be due to.
consola [kon'sola] *nf* control panel.
consolación [konsola'θjon] *nf* consolation.
consolar [konso'lar] *vt* to console.
consolidar [konsoli'ðar] *vt* to consolidate.
consomé [konso'me] (*pl* ~**s**) *nm* consommé, clear soup.
consonante [konso'nante] *adj* consonant, harmonious ♦ *nf* consonant.
consorcio [kon'sorθjo] *nm* consortium.
conspiración [konspira'θjon] *nf* conspiracy.
conspirador, a [konspira'ðor, a] *nm/f* conspirator.
conspirar [konspi'rar] *vi* to conspire.
constancia [kon'stanθja] *nf* constancy; **dejar** ~ **de** to put on record.
constante [kons'tante] *adj, nf* constant.
constar [kons'tar] *vi* (*evidenciarse*) to be clear *o* evident; ~ **de** to consist of.
constatar [konsta'tar] *vt* (*controlar*) to check; (*observar*) to note.

consternación [konsterna'θjon] *nf* consternation.

constipado, a [konsti'paðo, a] *adj*: **estar ~** to have a cold ♦ *nm* cold.

constitución [konstitu'θjon] *nf* constitution; **constitucional** *adj* constitutional.

constituir [konstitu'ir] *vt* (*formar, componer*) to constitute, make up; (*fundar, erigir, ordenar*) to constitute, establish.

constitutivo, a [konstitu'tißo, a] *adj* constitutive, constituent.

constituyente [konstitu'jente] *adj* constituent.

constreñir [konstre'ɲir] *vt* (*restringir*) to restrict.

construcción [konstruk'θjon] *nf* construction, building.

constructor, a [konstruk'tor, a] *nm/f* builder.

construir [konstru'ir] *vt* to build, construct.

construyendo *etc vb ver* **construir**.

consuelo [kon'swelo] *nm* consolation, solace.

cónsul ['konsul] *nm* consul; **consulado** *nm* consulate.

consulta [kon'sulta] *nf* consultation; (*MED*): **horas de ~** surgery hours.

consultar [konsul'tar] *vt* to consult.

consultorio [konsul'torjo] *nm* (*MED*) surgery.

consumar [konsu'mar] *vt* to complete, carry out; (*crimen*) to commit; (*sentencia*) to carry out.

consumición [konsumi'θjon] *nf* consumption; (*bebida*) drink; (*comida*) food; **~ mínima** cover charge.

consumidor, a [konsumi'ðor, a] *nm/f* consumer.

consumir [konsu'mir] *vt* to consume; **~se** *vr* to be consumed; (*persona*) to waste away.

consumismo [konsu'mismo] *nm* consumerism.

consumo [kon'sumo] *nm* consumption.

contabilidad [kontaßili'ðað] *nf* accounting, book-keeping; (*profesión*) accountancy; **contable** *nm/f* accountant.

contacto [kon'takto] *nm* contact;

(*AUTO*) ignition.

contado, a [kon'taðo, a] *adj*: **~s** (*escasos*) numbered, scarce, few ♦ *nm*: **pagar al ~** to pay (in) cash.

contador [konta'ðor] *nm* (*aparato*) meter; (*AM*: *contante*) accountant.

contagiar [konta'xjar] *vt* (*enfermedad*) to pass on, transmit; (*persona*) to infect; **~se** *vr* to become infected.

contagio [kon'taxjo] *nm* infection; **contagioso, a** *adj* infectious; (*fig*) catching.

contaminación [kontamina'θjon] *nf* contamination; (*polución*) pollution.

contaminar [kontami'nar] *vt* to contaminate; (*aire, agua*) to pollute.

contante [kon'tante] *adj*: **dinero ~ (y sonante)** cash.

contar [kon'tar] *vt* (*páginas, dinero*) to count; (*anécdota, chiste etc*) to tell ♦ *vi* to count; **~ con** to rely on, count on.

contemplación [kontempla'θjon] *nf* contemplation.

contemplar [kontem'plar] *vt* to contemplate; (*mirar*) to look at.

contemporáneo, a [kontempo'raneo, a] *adj, nm/f* contemporary.

contendiente [konten'djente] *nm/f* contestant.

contenedor [kontene'ðor] *nm* container.

contener [konte'ner] *vt* to contain, hold; (*retener*) to hold back, contain; **~se** *vr* to control *o* restrain o.s.

contenido, a [konte'niðo, a] *adj* (*moderado*) restrained; (*risa etc*) suppressed ♦ *nm* contents *pl*, content.

contentar [konten'tar] *vt* (*satisfacer*) to satisfy; (*complacer*) to please; **~se** *vr* to be satisfied.

contento, a [kon'tento, a] *adj* contented, content; (*alegre*) pleased; (*feliz*) happy.

contestación [kontesta'θjon] *nf* answer, reply.

contestador [kontesta'ðor] *nm*: **~ automático** answering machine.

contestar [kontes'tar] *vt* to answer, reply; (*JUR*) to corroborate, confirm.

contexto [kon'te(k)sto] *nm* context.

contienda [kon'tjenda] *nf* contest.

contigo [kon'tiɣo] *pron* with you.

contiguo, a [kon'tiɣwo, a] *adj* (*de al lado*) next; (*vecino*) adjacent, adjoining.

continente [konti'nente] *adj, nm* continent.

contingencia [kontin'xenθja] *nf* contingency; (*riesgo*) risk; **contingente** *adj, nm* contingent.

continuación [kontinwa'θjon] *nf* continuation; **a ~** then, next.

continuar [konti'nwar] *vt* to continue, go on with ♦ *vi* to continue, go on; **~ hablando** to continue talking *o* to talk.

continuidad [kontinwi'ðað] *nf* continuity.

continuo, a [kon'tinwo, a] *adj* (*sin interrupción*) continuous; (*acción perseverante*) continual.

contorno [kon'torno] *nm* outline; (*GEO*) contour; **~s** *nmpl* neighbourhood *sg*, surrounding area *sg*.

contorsión [kontor'sjon] *nf* contortion.

contra ['kontra] *prep, ad* against ♦ *nm inv* con ♦ *nf:* **la C~** (*de Nicaragua*) the Contras *pl*.

contraataque [kontraa'take] *nm* counter-attack.

contrabajo [kontra'ßaxo] *nm* double bass.

contrabandista [kontraßan'dista] *nm/f* smuggler.

contrabando [kontra'ßando] *nm* (*acción*) smuggling; (*mercancías*) contraband.

contracción [kontrak'θjon] *nf* contraction.

contrachapado [kontratʃa'paðo] *nm* plywood.

contradecir [kontraðe'θir] *vt* to contradict.

contradicción [kontraðik'θjon] *nf* contradiction.

contradictorio, a [kontraðik'torjo, a] *adj* contradictory.

contraer [kontra'er] *vt* to contract; (*limitar*) to restrict; **~se** *vr* to contract; (*limitarse*) to limit o.s.

contragolpe [kontra'ɣolpe] *nm* backlash.

contraluz [kontra'luθ] *nf:* **a ~** against the light.

contramaestre [kontrama'estre] *nm* foreman.

contrapartida [kontrapar'tiða] *nf:* **como ~ (de)** in return (for).

contrapelo [kontra'pelo] **a ~** *adv* the wrong way.

contrapesar [kontrape'sar] *vt* to counterbalance; (*fig*) to offset; **contrapeso** *nm* counterweight.

contraproducente [kontraproðu'θente] *adj* counterproductive.

contrariar [kontra'rjar] *vt* (*oponerse*) to oppose; (*poner obstáculo*) to impede; (*enfadar*) to vex.

contrariedad [kontrarje'ðað] *nf* (*oposición*) opposition; (*obstáculo*) obstacle, setback; (*disgusto*) vexation, annoyance.

contrario, a [kon'trarjo, a] *adj* contrary; (*persona*) opposed; (*sentido, lado*) opposite ♦ *nm/f* enemy, adversary; (*DEPORTE*) opponent; **al/por el ~** on the contrary; **de lo ~** otherwise.

contrarrestar [kontrarres'tar] *vt* to counteract.

contrasentido [kontrasen'tiðo] *nm:* **es un ~ que él ...** it doesn't make sense for him to ....

contraseña [kontra'seɲa] *nf* (*INFORM*) password.

contrastar [kontras'tar] *vt* to resist ♦ *vi* to contrast.

contraste [kon'traste] *nm* contrast.

contratar [kontra'tar] *vt* (*firmar un acuerdo para*) to contract for; (*empleados, obreros*) to hire, engage; **~se** *vr* to sign on.

contratiempo [kontra'tjempo] *nm* setback.

contratista [kontra'tista] *nm/f* contractor.

contrato [kon'trato] *nm* contract.

contravenir [kontraße'nir] *vi:* **~ a** to contravene, violate.

contraventana [kontraßen'tana] *nf* shutter.

contribución [kontrißu'θjon] *nf* (*municipal etc*) tax; (*ayuda*) contribution.

contribuir [kontriβu'ir] *vt, vi* to contribute; (*COM*) to pay (in taxes).

contribuyente [kontriβu'jente] *nm/f* (*COM*) taxpayer; (*que ayuda*) contributor.

control [kon'trol] *nm* control; (*inspección*) inspection, check; ~**ador, a** *nm/f* controller; ~**ador aéreo** air-traffic controller.

controlar [kontro'lar] *vt* to control; (*inspeccionar*) to inspect, check.

controversia [kontro'βersja] *nf* controversy.

contundente [kontun'dente] *adj* (*instrumento*) blunt; (*argumento, derrota*) overwhelming.

contusión [kontu'sjon] *nf* bruise.

convalecencia [kombale'θenθja] *nf* convalescence.

convalecer [kombale'θer] *vi* to convalesce, get better.

convaleciente [kombale'θjente] *adj, nm/f* convalescent.

convalidar [kombali'ðar] *vt* (*título*) to recognize.

convencer [komben'θer] *vt* to convince; (*persuadir*) to persuade.

convencimiento [kombenθi'mjento] *nm* (*acción*) convincing; (*persuasión*) persuasion; (*certidumbre*) conviction.

convención [komben'θjon] *nf* convention.

conveniencia [kombe'njenθja] *nf* suitability; (*conformidad*) agreement; (*utilidad, provecho*) usefulness; ~**s** *nfpl* (*convenciones*) conventions; (*COM*) property *sg.*

conveniente [kombe'njente] *adj* suitable; (*útil*) useful.

convenio [kom'benjo] *nm* agreement, treaty.

convenir [kombe'nir] *vi* (*estar de acuerdo*) to agree; (*ser conveniente*) to suit, be suitable.

convento [kom'bento] *nm* convent.

convenza *etc vb ver* **convencer.**

converger [komber'xer] *vi* to converge.

convergir [komber'xir] *vi* = **converger.**

conversación [kombersa'θjon] *nf* conversation.

conversar [komber'sar] *vi* to talk, converse.

conversión [komber'sjon] *nf* conversion.

convertir [komber'tir] *vt* to convert.

convicción [kombik'θjon] *nf* conviction.

convicto, a [kom'bikto, a] *adj* convicted, found guilty; (*condenado*) condemned.

convidado, a [kombi'ðaðo, a] *nm/f* guest.

convidar [kombi'ðar] *vt* to invite.

convincente [kombin'θente] *adj* convincing.

convite [kom'bite] *nm* invitation; (*banquete*) banquet.

convivencia [kombi'βenθja] *nf* coexistence, living together.

convocar [kombo'kar] *vt* to summon, call (together).

convulsión [kombul'sjon] *nf* convulsion.

conyugal [konju'xal] *adj* conjugal; **cónyuge** ['konjuxe] *nm/f* spouse.

coñac [ko'ɲa(k)] (*pl* ~**s**) *nm* cognac, brandy.

coño ['koɲo] (*fam!*) *excl* (*enfado*) shit! (!); (*sorpresa*) bloody hell! (!).

cooperación [koopera'θjon] *nf* cooperation.

cooperar [koope'rar] *vi* to cooperate.

cooperativa [koopera'tiβa] *nf* cooperative.

coordinadora [koorðina'ðora] *nf* (*comité*) coordinating committee.

coordinar [koorði'nar] *vt* to coordinate.

copa ['kopa] *nf* cup; (*vaso*) glass; (*bebida*): (**tomar una**) ~ (to have a) drink; (*de árbol*) top; (*de sombrero*) crown; ~**s** *nfpl* (*NAIPES*) ≈ hearts.

copia ['kopja] *nf* copy; ~ **de respaldo** *o* **seguridad** (*INFORM*) back-up copy; **copiar** *vt* to copy.

copioso, a [ko'pjoso, a] *adj* copious, plentiful.

copla ['kopla] *nf* verse; (*canción*) (popular) song.

copo ['kopo] *nm*: ~ **de nieve** snowflake; ~**s de maíz** cornflakes.

copropietarios [kopropje'tarjos] *nmpl* joint owners.

coqueta [ko'keta] *adj* flirtatious,

coquettish; **coquetear** vi to flirt.

coraje [ko'raxe] nm courage; (ánimo) spirit; (ira) anger.

coral [ko'ral] adj choral ♦ nf (MUS) choir ♦ nm (ZOOL) coral.

coraza [ko'raθa] nf (armadura) armour; (blindaje) armour-plating.

corazón [kora'θon] nm heart.

corazonada [koraθo'naða] nf impulse; (presentimiento) hunch.

corbata [kor'ßata] nf tie.

corchete [kor'tʃete] nm catch, clasp.

corcho ['kortʃo] nm cork; (PESCA) float.

cordel [kor'ðel] nm cord, line.

cordero [kor'ðero] nm lamb.

cordial [kor'ðjal] adj cordial; ~**idad** nf warmth, cordiality.

cordillera [korði'ʎera] nf range (of mountains).

Córdoba ['korðoßa] n Cordova.

cordón [kor'ðon] nm (cuerda) cord, string; (de zapatos) lace; (MIL etc) cordon.

corneta [kor'neta] nf bugle.

coro ['koro] nm chorus; (conjunto de cantores) choir.

corona [ko'rona] nf crown; (de flores) garland; ~**ción** nf coronation; **coronar** vt to crown.

coronel [koro'nel] nm colonel.

coronilla [koro'niʎa] nf (ANAT) crown (of the head).

corporación [korpora'θjon] nf corporation.

corporal [korpo'ral] adj corporal, bodily.

corpulento, a [korpu'lento a] adj (persona) heavily-built.

corral [ko'rral] nm farmyard.

correa [ko'rrea] nf strap; (cinturón) belt; (de perro) lead, leash.

corrección [korrek'θjon] nf correction; (represión) rebuke; **correccional** nm reformatory.

correcto, a [ko'rrekto, a] adj correct; (persona) well-mannered.

corredizo, a [korre'ðiθo, a] adj (puerta etc) sliding.

corredor, a [korre'ðor, a] adj running ♦ nm (pasillo) corridor; (balcón corrido) gallery; (COM) agent, broker ♦ nm/f

(DEPORTE) runner.

corregir [korre'xir] vt (error) to correct; (amonestar, reprender) to rebuke, reprimand; ~**se** vr to reform.

correo [ko'rreo] nm post, mail; (persona) courier; C~**s** nmpl Post Office sg; ~ **aéreo** airmail.

correr [ko'rrer] vt to run; (viajar) to cover, travel; (cortinas) to draw; (cerrojo) to shoot ♦ vi to run; (líquido) to run, flow; ~**se** vr to slide, move; (colores) to run.

correspondencia [korrespon'denθja] nf correspondence; (FERRO) connection.

corresponder [korrespon'der] vi to correspond; (convenir) to be suitable; (pertenecer) to belong; (tocar) to concern; ~**se** vr (por escrito) to correspond; (amarse) to love one another.

correspondiente [korrespon'djente] adj corresponding.

corresponsal [korrespon'sal] nm/f correspondent.

corrida [ko'rriða] nf (de toros) bullfight.

corrido, a [ko'rriðo, a] adj (avergonzado) abashed; **3 noches corridas** 3 nights running; **un kilo ~** a good kilo.

corriente [ko'rrjente] adj (agua) running; (fig) flowing; (dinero etc) current; (común) ordinary, normal ♦ nf current ♦ nm current month; ~ **eléctrica** electric current.

corrija etc vb ver **corregir**.

corrillo [ko'rriʎo] nm ring, circle (of people); (fig) clique.

corro ['korro] nm ring, circle (of people).

corroborar [korroßo'rar] vt to corroborate.

corroer [korro'er] vt to corrode; (GEO) to erode.

corromper [korrom'per] vt (madera) to rot; (fig) to corrupt.

corrosivo, a [korro'sißo, a] adj corrosive.

corrupción [korrup'θjon] nf rot, decay; (fig) corruption.

corsé [kor'se] nm corset.

cortacésped [korta'θespeð] *nm* lawn mower.

cortado, a [kor'taðo, a] *adj* (*gen*) cut; (*leche*) sour; (*confuso*) confused; (*desconcertado*) embarrassed ♦ *nm* coffee (with a little milk).

cortar [kor'tar] *vt* to cut; (*suministro*) to cut off; (*un pasaje*) to cut out ♦ *vi* to cut; **~se** *vr* (*turbarse*) to become embarrassed; (*leche*) to turn, curdle; **~se el pelo** to have one's hair cut.

cortauñas [korta'uɲas] *nm inv* nail clippers *pl*.

corte ['korte] *nm* cut, cutting; (*de tela*) piece, length ♦ *nf*: **las C~s** the Spanish Parliament; **~ y confección** dressmaking; **~ de luz** power cut.

cortedad [korte'ðað] *nf* shortness; (*fig*) bashfulness, timidity.

cortejar [korte'xar] *vt* to court.

cortejo [kor'texo] *nm* entourage; **~ fúnebre** funeral procession.

cortés [kor'tes] *adj* courteous, polite.

cortesía [korte'sia] *nf* courtesy.

corteza [kor'teθa] *nf* (*de árbol*) bark; (*de pan*) crust.

cortina [kor'tina] *nf* curtain.

corto, a ['korto, a] *adj* (*breve*) short; (*tímido*) bashful; **~ de luces** not very bright; **~ de vista** short-sighted; **estar ~ de fondos** to be short of funds; **~circuito** *nm* short circuit.

corvo, a ['korßo, a] *adj* curved.

cosa ['kosa] *nf* thing; (*asunto*) affair; **~ de** about; **eso es ~ mía** that's my business.

cosecha [ko'setʃa] *nf* (*AGR*) harvest; (*de vino*) vintage.

cosechar [kose'tʃar] *vt* to harvest, gather (in).

coser [ko'ser] *vt* to sew.

cosmético, a [kos'metiko, a] *adj*, *nm* cosmetic.

cosquillas [kos'kiʎas] *nfpl*: **hacer ~** to tickle; **tener ~** to be ticklish.

costa ['kosta] *nf* (*GEO*) coast; **C~ Brava** Costa Brava; **C~ Cantábrica** Cantabrian Coast; **C~ del Sol** Costa del Sol; **a toda ~** at any price.

costado [kos'taðo] *nm* side.

costal [kos'tal] *nm* sack.

costar [kos'tar] *vt* (*valer*) to cost; (*necesitar*) to require, need; **me cuesta hablarle** I find it hard to talk to him.

Costa Rica *nf* Costa Rica; **costarricense** *adj*, *nm/f* Costa Rican; **costarriqueño, a** *adj*, *nm/f* Costa Rican.

coste ['koste] *nm* = **costo**.

costear [koste'ar] *vt* to pay for.

costilla [kos'tiʎa] *nf* rib; (*CULIN*) cutlet.

costo ['kosto] *nm* cost, price; **~ de la vida** cost of living; **~so, a** *adj* costly, expensive.

costra ['kostra] *nf* (*corteza*) crust; (*MED*) scab.

costumbre [kos'tumbre] *nf* custom, habit.

costura [kos'tura] *nf* sewing, needlework; (*zurcido*) seam.

costurera [kostu'rera] *nf* dressmaker.

costurero [kostu'rero] *nm* sewing box *o* case.

cotejar [kote'xar] *vt* to compare.

cotidiano, a [koti'ðjano, a] *adj* daily, day to day.

cotización [kotiθa'θjon] *nf* (*COM*) quotation, price; (*de club*) dues *pl*.

cotizar [koti'θar] *vt* (*COM*) to quote, price; **~se** *vr*: **~se a** to sell at, fetch; (*BOLSA*) to stand at, be quoted at.

coto ['koto] *nm* (*terreno cercado*) enclosure; (*de caza*) reserve.

cotorra [ko'torra] *nf* parrot.

COU [kou] (*ESP*) *nm abr* (= *Curso de Orientación Universitaria*) *1 year course leading to final school leaving certificate and university entrance examinations*.

coyote [ko'jote] *nm* coyote, prairie wolf.

coyuntura [kojun'tura] *nf* (*ANAT*) joint; (*fig*) juncture, occasion.

coz [koθ] *nf* kick.

cráneo ['kraneo] *nm* skull, cranium.

cráter ['krater] *nm* crater.

creación [krea'θjon] *nf* creation.

creador, a [krea'ðor, a] *adj* creative ♦ *nm/f* creator.

crear [kre'ar] *vt* to create, make.

crecer [kre'θer] *vi* to grow; (*precio*) to rise.

creces ['kreθes]: **con ~** *adv* amply, fully.
crecido, a [kre'θiðo, a] *adj* (*persona*, *planta*) full-grown; (*cantidad*) large.
creciente [kre'θjente] *adj* growing; (*cantidad*) increasing; (*luna*) crescent ♦ *nm* crescent.
crecimiento [kreθi'mjento] *nm* growth; (*aumento*) increase.
credenciales [kreðen'θjales] *nfpl* credentials.
crédito ['kreðito] *nm* credit.
credo ['kreðo] *nm* creed.
crédulo, a ['kreðulo, a] *adj* credulous.
creencia [kre'enθja] *nf* belief.
creer [kre'er] *vt*, *vi* to think, believe; **~se** *vr* to believe o.s. (to be); **~ en** to believe in; **¡ya lo creo!** I should think so!
creíble [kre'ißle] *adj* credible, believable.
creído, a [kre'iðo, a] *adj* (*engreído*) conceited.
crema ['krema] *nf* cream; (*natillas*) custard; **~ pastelera** (confectioner's) custard.
cremallera [krema'ʎera] *nf* zip (fastener).
crepitar [krepi'tar] *vi* to crackle.
crepúsculo [kre'puskulo] *nm* twilight, dusk.
crespo, a ['krespo, a] *adj* (*pelo*) curly.
crespón [kres'pon] *nm* crêpe.
cresta ['kresta] *nf* (GEO, ZOOL) crest.
creyendo *vb ver* creer.
creyente [kre'jente] *nm/f* believer.
creyó *etc vb ver* creer.
crezco *etc vb ver* crecer.
cría *etc* ['kria] *vb ver* **criar** ♦ *nf* (de *animales*) rearing, breeding; (*animal*) young; *ver tb* crio.
criadero [kria'ðero] *nm* nursery; (ZOOL) breeding place.
criado, a [kri'aðo, a] *nm* servant ♦ *nf* servant, maid.
criador [kria'ðor] *nm* breeder.
crianza [kri'anθa] *nf* rearing, breeding; (*fig*) breeding.
criar [kri'ar] *vt* (*amamantar*) to suckle, feed; (*educar*) to bring up; (*producir*) to grow, produce; (*animales*) to breed.

criatura [kria'tura] *nf* creature; (*niño*) baby, (small) child.
criba ['krißa] *nf* sieve; **cribar** *vt* to sieve.
crimen ['krimen] *nm* crime.
criminal [krimi'nal] *adj*, *nm/f* criminal.
crin [krin] *nf* (*tb*: **~es** *nfpl*) mane.
crio, a ['krio, a] (*fam*) *nm/f* (*niño*) kid.
crisis ['krisis] *nf inv* crisis; **~ nerviosa** nervous breakdown.
crispar [kris'par] *vt* (*músculo*) to tense (up); (*nervios*) to set on edge.
cristal [kris'tal] *nm* crystal; (de *ventana*) glass, pane; (*lente*) lens; **~ino, a** *adj* crystalline; (*fig*) clear ♦ *nm* lens (of the eye); **~izar** *vt*, *vi* to crystallize.
cristiandad [kristjan'daδ] *nf* Christendom.
cristianismo [kristja'nismo] *nm* Christianity.
cristiano, a [kris'tjano, a] *adj*, *nm/f* Christian.
Cristo ['kristo] *nm* Christ; (*crucifijo*) crucifix.
criterio [kri'terjo] *nm* criterion; (*juicio*) judgement.
crítica ['kritika] *nf* criticism; *ver tb* crítico.
criticar [kriti'kar] *vt* to criticize.
crítico, a ['kritiko, a] *adj* critical ♦ *nm/f* critic.
croar [kro'ar] *vi* to croak.
cromo ['kromo] *nm* chrome.
crónica ['kronika] *nf* chronicle, account.
crónico, a ['kroniko, a] *adj* chronic.
cronómetro [kro'nometro] *nm* (DEPORTE) stopwatch.
cruce *etc* ['kruθe] *vb ver* **cruzar** ♦ *nm* crossing; (de *carreteras*) crossroads.
crucificar [kruθifi'kar] *vt* to crucify.
crucifijo [kruθi'fixo] *nm* crucifix.
crucigrama [kruθi'ɣrama] *nm* crossword (puzzle).
crudo, a ['kruðo, a] *adj* raw; (*no maduro*) unripe; (*petróleo*) crude; (*rudo, cruel*) cruel ♦ *nm* crude (oil).
cruel [krwel] *adj* cruel; **~dad** *nf* cruelty.
crujido [kru'xiðo] *nm* (de *madera etc*) creak.
crujiente [kru'xjente] *adj* (*galleta etc*)

crunchy.

crujir [kru'xir] *vi (madera etc)* to creak; *(dedos)* to crack; *(dientes)* to grind; *(nieve, arena)* to crunch.

cruz [kruθ] *nf* cross; *(de moneda)* tails *sg*.

cruzada [kru'θaða] *nf* crusade.

cruzado, a [kru'θaðo, a] *adj* crossed ♦ *nm* crusader.

cruzar [kru'θar] *vt* to cross; **~se** *vr (líneas etc)* to cross; *(personas)* to pass each other.

Cruz Roja *nf* Red Cross.

cuaderno [kwa'ðerno] *nm* notebook; *(de escuela)* exercise book; *(NAUT)* logbook.

cuadra ['kwaðra] *nf (caballeriza)* stable; *(AM)* block.

cuadrado, a [kwa'ðraðo, a] *adj* square ♦ *nm (MAT)* square.

cuadrar [kwa'ðrar] *vt* to square ♦ *vi:* ~ **con** to square with, tally with; **~se** *vr (soldado)* to stand to attention.

cuadrilátero [kwaðri'latero] *nm (DEPORTE)* boxing ring; *(GEOM)* quadrilateral.

cuadrilla [kwa'ðriʎa] *nf* party, group.

cuadro ['kwaðro] *nm* square; *(ARTE)* painting; *(TEATRO)* scene; *(diagrama)* chart; *(DEPORTE, MED)* team; *(POL)* executive; **tela a ~s** checked *(BRIT)* o chequered *(US)* material.

cuádruple ['kwaðruple] *adj* quadruple.

cuádruplo, a ['kwaðruplo, a] *adj* quadruple.

cuajar [kwa'xar] *vt* to thicken; *(leche)* to curdle; *(sangre)* to congeal; *(adornar)* to adorn; *(CULIN)* to set; **~se** *vr* to curdle; to congeal; to set; *(llenarse)* to fill up.

cual [kwal] *adv* like, as ♦ *pron:* **el ~** *etc* which; *(persona: sujeto)* who; *(: objeto)* whom ♦ *adj* such as; **cada ~** each one; **tal ~** just as it is.

cuál [kwal] *pron interr* which (one).

cualesquier(a) [kwales'kjer(a)] *pl de* **cualquier(a)**.

cualidad [kwali'ðað] *nf* quality.

cualquier [kwal'kjer] *adj ver* **cualquiera**.

cualquiera [kwal'kjera] *(pl* **cualesquiera)** *adj (delante de nm y f:* **cualquier)** any

♦ *pron* anybody; **un coche ~ servirá** any car will do; **no es un hombre ~** he isn't just anybody; **cualquier día/libro** any day/book; **eso ~ lo sabe hacer** anybody can do that; **es un ~** he's a nobody.

cuán [kwan] *ad* how.

cuando ['kwando] *adv* when; *(aún si)* if, even if ♦ *conj (puesto que)* since ♦ *prep:* **yo, ~ niño ...** when I was a child ...; **~ no sea así** even if it is not so; **~ más** at (the) most; **~ menos** at least; **~ no** if not, otherwise; **de ~ en ~** from time to time.

cuándo ['kwando] *adv* when; **¿desde ~?**, **¿de ~ acá?** since when?

cuantioso, a [kwan'tjoso, a] *adj* substantial.

PALABRA CLAVE
---

cuanto, a ['kwanto, a] *adj* **1** *(todo):* **tiene todo ~ desea** he's got everything he wants; **le daremos ~s ejemplares necesite** we'll give him as many copies as o all the copies he needs; **~s hombres la ven** all the men who see her

2: **unos ~s: había unos ~s periodistas** there were (quite) a few journalists

3 *(+más):* ~ **más vino bebes peor te sentirás** the more wine you drink the worse you'll feel

♦ *pron:* **tiene ~ desea** he has everything he wants; **tome ~/~s quiera** take as much/many as you want

♦ *adv:* **en ~: en ~ profesor** as a teacher; **en ~ a mí** as for me; *ver tb* **antes**

♦ *conj* **1:** ~ **más gana menos gasta** the more he earns the less he spends; ~ **más joven se es más se es confiado** the younger you are the more trusting you are

2: en ~: **en ~ llegue/llegué** as soon as I arrive/arrived

---

cuánto, a ['kwanto, a] *adj (exclamación)* what a lot of; *(interr: sg)* how much?; *(: pl)* how many? ♦ *pron, adv* how; *(interr: sg)* how much?; *(: pl)* how many?; **¡cuánta gente!** what a lot of people!; ¿~ **cuesta**? how much does it cost?; ¿a ~s estamos? what's the date?; Señor no sé ~s Mr. So-and-So.

cuarenta [kwaˈrenta] *num* forty.

cuarentena [kwarenˈtena] *nf* quarantine.

cuaresma [kwaˈresma] *nf* Lent.

cuarta [ˈkwarta] *nf* (*MAT*) quarter, fourth; (*palmo*) span.

cuartear [kwarteˈar] *vt* to quarter; (*dividir*) to divide up; ~se *vr* to crack, split.

cuartel [kwarˈtel] *nm* (*de ciudad*) quarter, district; (*MIL*) barracks *pl*; ~ general headquarters *pl*.

cuarteto [kwarˈteto] *nm* quartet.

cuarto, a [ˈkwarto, a] *adj* fourth ♦ *nm* (*MAT*) quarter, fourth; (*habitación*) room; ~ de baño bathroom; ~ de estar living room; ~ de hora quarter (of an) hour; ~ de kilo quarter kilo.

cuatro [ˈkwatro] *num* four.

cuba [ˈkuβa] *nf* cask, barrel.

Cuba [ˈkuβa] *nf* Cuba; **cubano, a** *adj, nm/f* Cuban.

cúbico, a [ˈkuβiko, a] *adj* cubic.

cubierta [kuˈβjerta] *nf* cover, covering; (*neumático*) tyre; (*NAUT*) deck.

cubierto, a [kuˈβjerto, a] *pp de* **cubrir** ♦ *adj* covered ♦ *nm* cover; (*en la mesa*) place; ~s *nmpl* cutlery *sg*; a ~ de covered with o in.

cubil [kuˈβil] *nm* den; ~**ete** *nm* (*en juegos*) cup.

cubo [ˈkuβo] *nm* cube; (*balde*) bucket, tub; (*TEC*) drum.

cubrecama [kuβreˈkama] *nm* bedspread.

cubrir [kuˈβrir] *vt* to cover; ~se *vr* (*cielo*) to become overcast.

cucaracha [kukaˈratʃa] *nf* cockroach.

cuco, a [ˈkuko, a] *adj* pretty; (*astuto*) sharp ♦ *nm* cuckoo.

cucurucho [kukuˈrutʃo] *nm* cornet.

cuchara [kuˈtʃara] *nf* spoon; (*TEC*) scoop; ~**da** *nf* spoonful; ~**dita** *nf* teaspoonful.

cucharita [kutʃaˈrita] *nf* teaspoon.

cucharón [kutʃaˈron] *nm* ladle.

cuchichear [kutʃitʃeˈar] *vi* to whisper.

cuchilla [kuˈtʃiʎa] *nf* (large) knife; (*de arma blanca*) blade; ~ de afeitar razor blade.

cuchillo [kuˈtʃiʎo] *nm* knife.

cuchitril [kutʃiˈtril] *nm* hovel; (*habitación etc*) pigsty.

cuello [ˈkweʎo] *nm* (*ANAT*) neck; (*de vestido, camisa*) collar.

cuenca [ˈkwenka] *nf* (*ANAT*) eye socket; (*GEO*) bowl, deep valley.

cuenta *etc* [ˈkwenta] *vb ver* **contar** ♦ *nf* (*cálculo*) count, counting; (*en café, restaurante*) bill; (*COM*) account; (*de collar*) bead; (*fig*) account; a fin de ~s in the end; caer en la ~ to catch on; darse ~ de to realize; tener en ~ to bear in mind; echar ~s to take stock; ~ corriente/de ahorros current/savings account; ~-kilómetros *nm inv* ≈ milometer; (*de velocidad*) speedometer.

cuento *etc* [ˈkwento] *vb ver* **contar** ♦ *nm* story.

cuerda [ˈkwerða] *nf* rope; (*hilo*) string; (*de reloj*) spring; dar ~ a un reloj to wind up a clock.

cuerdo, a [ˈkwerðo, a] *adj* sane; (*prudente*) wise, sensible.

cuerno [ˈkwerno] *nm* horn.

cuero [ˈkwero] *nm* (*ZOOL*) skin, hide; (*TEC*) leather; en ~s stark naked; ~ cabelludo scalp.

cuerpo [ˈkwerpo] *nm* body.

cuervo [ˈkwerβo] *nm* crow.

cuesta *etc* [ˈkwesta] *vb ver* **costar** ♦ *nf* slope; (*en camino etc*) hill; ~ arriba/ abajo uphill/downhill; a ~s on one's back.

cueste *etc vb ver* **costar**.

cuestión [kwesˈtjon] *nf* matter, question, issue; (*riña*) quarrel, dispute.

cueva [ˈkweβa] *nf* cave.

cuidado [kwiˈðaðo] *nm* care, carefulness; (*preocupación*) care, worry ♦ *excl* careful!, look out!

cuidadoso, a [kwiða'ðoso, a] *adj* careful; (*preocupado*) anxious.

cuidar [kwiˈðar] *vt* (*MED*) to care for; (*ocuparse de*) to take care of, look after ♦ *vi*: ~ de to take care of, look after; ~se *vr* to look after o.s.; ~se de hacer algo to take care to do sth.

culata [kuˈlata] *nf* (*de fusil*) butt.

culebra [ku'leβra] *nf* snake.
culinario, a [kuli'narjo, a] *adj* culinary, cooking *cpd*.
culminación [kulmina'θjon] *nf* culmination.
culo ['kulo] *nm* bottom, backside; *(de vaso, botella)* bottom.
culpa ['kulpa] *nf* fault; *(JUR)* guilt; **por ~ de** because of, through; **tener la ~ (de)** to be to blame (for); **~bilidad** *nf* guilt; **~ble** *adj* guilty ♦ *nm/f* culprit.
culpar [kul'par] *vt* to blame; *(acusar)* to accuse.
cultivar [kulti'βar] *vt* to cultivate.
cultivo [kul'tiβo] *nm* *(acto)* cultivation; *(plantas)* crop.
culto, a ['kulto, a] *adj* *(cultivado)* cultivated; *(que tiene cultura)* cultured, educated ♦ *nm* *(homenaje)* worship; *(religión)* cult.
cultura [kul'tura] *nf* culture.
cumbre ['kumbre] *nf* summit, top.
cumpleaños [kumple'aɲos] *nm inv* birthday.
cumplido, a [kum'pliðo, a] *adj* complete, perfect; *(abundante)* plentiful; *(cortés)* courteous ♦ *nm* compliment; **visita de ~** courtesy call.
cumplidor, a [kumpli'ðor, a] *adj* reliable.
cumplimentar [kumplimen'tar] *vt* to congratulate.
cumplimiento [kumpli'mjento] *nm* *(de un deber)* fulfilment; *(acabamiento)* completion.
cumplir [kum'plir] *vt* *(orden)* to carry out, obey; *(promesa)* to carry out, fulfil; *(condena)* to serve; *(años)* to reach, attain ♦ *vi*: **~ con** *(deberes)* to carry out, fulfil; **~se** *vr* *(plazo)* to expire; **hoy cumple dieciocho años** he is eighteen today.
cúmulo ['kumulo] *nm* heap.
cuna ['kuna] *nf* cradle, cot.
cundir [kun'dir] *vi* *(noticia, rumor, pánico)* to spread; *(rendir)* to go a long way.
cuneta [ku'neta] *nf* ditch.
cuña ['kuɲa] *nf* wedge.
cuñado, a [ku'ɲaðo, a] *nm/f* brother/ sister-in-law.
cuota ['kwota] *nf* *(parte proporcional)* share; *(cotización)* fee, dues *pl*.
cupe *etc vb ver* **caber**.
cupiera *etc vb ver* **caber**.
cupo ['kupo] *vb ver* **caber** ♦ *nm* quota.
cupón [ku'pon] *nm* coupon.
cúpula ['kupula] *nf* dome.
cura ['kura] *nf* *(curación)* cure; *(método curativo)* treatment ♦ *nm* priest.
curación [kura'θjon] *nf* cure; *(acción)* curing.
curar [ku'rar] *vt* *(MED: herida)* to treat, dress; *(: enfermo)* to cure; *(CULIN)* to cure, salt; *(cuero)* to tan ♦ *vi* to get well, recover; **~se** *vr* to get well, recover.
curiosear [kurjose'ar] *vt* to glance at, look over ♦ *vi* to look round, wander round; *(explorar)* to poke about.
curiosidad [kurjosi'ðað] *nf* curiosity.
curioso, a [ku'rjoso, a] *adj* curious ♦ *nm/f* bystander, onlooker.
curita [ku'rita] *nf* *(sticking)* plaster *(BRIT)*, bandaid ® *(US)*.
currante [ku'rrante] *(fam)* *nm/f* worker.
currar [ku'rrar] *(fam)* *vi* to work.
currelar [kurre'lar] *(fam)* *vi* to work.
currículo [ku'rrikolo] = **curriculum**.
curriculum [ku'rrikulum] *nm* curriculum vitae.
curro ['kurro] *(fam)* *nm* work, job.
cursi ['kursi] *(fam)* *adj* pretentious; *(amanerado)* affected.
cursiva [kur'siβa] *nf* italics *pl*.
curso ['kurso] *nm* course; **en ~** *(año)* current; *(proceso)* going on, under way.
cursor [kur'sor] *nm* *(INFORM)* cursor.
curtido, a [kur'tiðo, a] *adj* *(cara etc)* weather-beaten; *(fig: persona)* experienced.
curtir [kur'tir] *vt* *(cuero etc)* to tan.
curva ['kurβa] *nf* curve, bend.
curvo, a ['kurβo, a] *adj* *(gen)* curved; *(torcido)* bent.
cúspide ['kuspiðe] *nf* *(GEO)* peak; *(fig)* top.
custodia [kus'toðja] *nf* safekeeping; custody; **custodiar** *vt* *(conservar)* to take care of; *(vigilar)* to guard.

custodio [kus'toðjo] *nm* guardian, keeper.

cutícula [ku'tikula] *nf* cuticle.

cutis ['kutis] *nm inv* skin, complexion.

cutre ['kutre] *(fam) adj (lugar)* grotty; *(persona)* naff.

cuyo, a ['kujo, a] *pron (de quien)* whose; *(de que)* whose, of which; **en ~ caso** in which case.

C.V. *abr (= caballos de vapor)* H.P.

CH

chabacano, a [tʃaßa'kano, a] *adj* vulgar, coarse.

chabola [tʃa'βola] *nf* shack; **·-s** *nfpl* shanty town *sg*.

chacal [tʃa'kal] *nm* jackal.

chacra ['tʃakra] *(AM) nf* smallholding.

chacha ['tʃatʃa] *(fam) nf* maid.

cháchara ['tʃatʃara] *nf* chatter; **estar de ~** to chatter away.

chafar [tʃa'far] *vt (aplastar)* to crush; *(arruinar)* to ruin.

chal [tʃal] *nm* shawl.

chalado, a [tʃa'lado, a] *(fam) adj* crazy.

chalé [tʃa'le] *(pl ~s) nm* villa; ≈ detached house.

chaleco [tʃa'leko] *nm* waistcoat, vest *(US)*; **~ salvavidas** life jacket.

chalet [tʃa'le] *(pl ~s) nm* = **chalé.**

chalupa [tʃa'lupa] *nf* launch, boat.

champán [tʃam'pan] *nm* champagne.

champaña [tʃam'paɲa] *nm* = **champán.**

champiñón [tʃampi'ɲon] *nm* mushroom.

champú [tʃam'pu] *(pl* **champúes, champús)** *nm* shampoo.

chamuscar [tʃamus'kar] *vt* to scorch, sear, singe.

chance ['tʃanθe] *(AM) nm* chance.

chancho, a ['tʃantʃo, a] *(AM) nm/f* pig.

chanchullo [tʃan'tʃuʎo] *(fam) nm* fiddle.

chantaje [tʃan'taxe] *nm* blackmail.

chapa ['tʃapa] *nf (de metal)* plate, sheet; *(de madera)* board, panel; *(AM: AUTO)* number *(BRIT)* o license *(US)* plate.

chaparrón [tʃapa'rron] *nm* downpour, cloudburst.

chapotear [tʃapote'ar] *vi* to splash about.

chapucero, a [tʃapu'θero, a] *adj* rough, crude ♦ *nm/f* bungler.

chapurrear [tʃapurre'ar] *vt (idioma)* to speak badly.

chapuza [tʃa'puθa] *nf* botched job.

chaqueta [tʃa'keta] *nf* jacket.

charca ['tʃarka] *nf* pond, pool.

charco ['tʃarko] *nm* pool, puddle.

charcutería [tʃarkute'ria] *nf (tienda)* shop selling chiefly pork meat products; *(productos)* cooked pork meats *pl*.

charla ['tʃarla] *nf* talk, chat; *(conferencia)* lecture.

charlar [tʃar'lar] *vi* to talk, chat.

charlatán, ana [tʃarla'tan, ana] *nm/f* chatterbox; *(estafador)* trickster.

charol [tʃa'rol] *nm* varnish; *(cuero)* patent leather.

chascarrillo [tʃaska'rriʎo] *(fam) nm* funny story.

chasco ['tʃasko] *nm (broma)* trick, joke; *(desengaño)* disappointment.

chasis ['tʃasis] *nm inv* chassis.

chasquear [tʃaske'ar] *vt (látigo)* to crack; *(lengua)* to click; **chasquido** *nm* crack; click.

chatarra [tʃa'tarra] *nf* scrap (metal).

chato, a ['tʃato, a] *adj* flat; *(nariz)* snub.

chaval, a [tʃa'ßal, a] *nm/f* kid, lad/lass.

checo(e)slovaco, a [tʃeko(e)slo'ßako, a] *adj, nm/f* Czech, Czechoslovak.

Checo(e)slovaquia [tʃeko(e)slo'ßakja] *nf* Czechoslovakia.

cheque ['tʃeke] *nm* cheque *(BRIT)*, check *(US)*; **~ de viajero** traveller's cheque *(BRIT)*, traveler's check *(US)*.

chequeo [tʃe'keo] *nm (MED)* check-up; *(AUTO)* service.

chequera [tʃe'kera] *(AM) nf* chequebook *(BRIT)*, checkbook *(US)*.

chicano, a [tʃi'kano, a] *adj, nm/f* chicano.

chicle ['tʃikle] *nm* chewing gum.

chico, a ['tʃiko, a] *adj* small, little ♦ *nm/f (niño)* child; *(muchacho)* boy/girl.

chícharo ['tʃitʃaro] *(AM) nm* pea.

chicharrón [tʃitʃa'rron] *nm* (pork)

crackling.

chichón [tʃi'tʃon] nm bump, lump.

chiflado, a [tʃi'flaðo, a] adj crazy.

chiflar [tʃi'flar] vt to hiss, boo.

chile ['tʃile] nm chilli pepper.

Chile ['tʃile] nm Chile; **chileno, a** adj, nm/f Chilean.

chillar [tʃi'ʎar] vi (persona) to yell, scream; (animal salvaje) to howl; (cerdo) to squeal; (puerta) to creak.

chillido [tʃi'ʎiðo] nm (de persona) yell, scream; (de animal) howl; (de frenos) screech(ing).

chillón, ona [tʃi'ʎon, ona] adj (niño) noisy; (color) loud, gaudy.

chimenea [tʃime'nea] nf chimney; (hogar) fireplace.

China ['tʃina] nf: (la) ~ China.

chinche ['tʃintʃe] nf (insecto) (bed)bug; (TEC) drawing pin (BRIT), thumbtack (US) ♦ nm/f nuisance, pest.

chincheta [tʃin'tʃeta] nf drawing pin (BRIT), thumbtack (US).

chino, a ['tʃino, a] adj, nm/f Chinese ♦ nm (LING) Chinese.

Chipre ['tʃipre] nf Cyprus; **chipriota** adj, nm/f Cypriot.

chiquito, a [tʃi'kito, a] adj very small, tiny ♦ nm/f kid.

chiripa [tʃi'ripa] nf fluke.

chirriar [tʃi'rrjar] vi (goznes etc) to creak, squeak; (pájaros) to chirp, sing.

chirrido [tʃi'rriðo] nm creak(ing), squeak(ing); (de pájaro) chirp(ing).

chis [tʃis] excl sh!

chisme ['tʃisme] nm (habladurías) piece of gossip; (fam: objeto) thingummyjig.

chismoso, a [tʃis'moso, a] adj gossiping ♦ nm/f gossip.

chispa ['tʃispa] nf spark; (fig) sparkle; (ingenio) wit; (fam) drunkenness.

chispeante [tʃispe'ante] adj sparkling.

chispear [tʃispe'ar] vi to spark; (lloviznar) to drizzle.

chisporrotear [tʃisporrote'ar] vi (fuego) to throw out sparks; (leña) to crackle; (aceite) to hiss, splutter.

chiste ['tʃiste] nm joke, funny story.

chistoso, a [tʃis'toso, a] adj (gracioso) funny, amusing; (bromista) witty.

chivo, a ['tʃiβo, a] nm/f (billy-/nanny-) goat; ~ expiatorio scapegoat.

chocante [tʃo'kante] adj startling; (extraño) odd; (ofensivo) shocking.

chocar [tʃo'kar] vi (coches etc) to collide, crash ♦ vt to shock; (sorprender) to startle; ~ con to collide with; (fig) to run into, run up against; ¡chócala! (fam) put it there!

chocolate [tʃoko'late] adj, nm chocolate.

chochear [tʃotʃe'ar] vi to dodder, be senile.

chocho, a ['tʃotʃo, a] adj doddering, senile; (fig) soft, doting.

chofer [tʃo'fer] nm = **chófer.**

chófer ['tʃofer] nm driver.

chollo ['tʃoʎo] (fam) nm bargain, snip.

choque etc ['tʃoke] vb ver **chocar** ♦ nm (impacto) impact; (golpe) jolt; (AUTO) crash; (fig) conflict; ~ frontal head-on collision.

chorizo [tʃo'riθo] nm hard pork sausage, (type of) salami.

chorrear [tʃorre'ar] vi to gush (out), spout (out); (gotear) to drip, trickle.

chorro ['tʃorro] nm jet; (fig) stream.

choza ['tʃoθa] nf hut, shack.

chubasco [tʃu'βasko] nm squall.

chuleta [tʃu'leta] nf chop, cutlet.

chulo ['tʃulo] nm (pícaro) rascal; (rufián) pimp.

chupado, a [tʃu'paðo, a] adj (delgado) skinny, gaunt.

chupar [tʃu'par] vt to suck; (absorber) to absorb; ~se vr to grow thin.

chupete [tʃu'pete] nm dummy (BRIT), pacifier (US).

churro, a ['tʃurro, a] adj coarse ♦ nm (type of) fritter.

chusco, a ['tʃusko, a] adj funny.

chusma ['tʃusma] nf rabble, mob.

chutar [tʃu'tar] vi (DEPORTE) to shoot (at goal).

D

D. abr (= Don) Esq.

Da. abr = Doña.

dactilógrafo, a [dakti'loɣrafo, a] *nm/f* typist.

dádiva ['daðiβa] *nf* (*donación*) donation; (*regalo*) gift; **dadivoso, a** *adj* generous.

dado, a ['daðo, a] *pp de* **dar** ♦ *nm* die; ~s *nmpl* dice; ~ **que** given that.

daltónico, a [dal'toniko, a] *adj* colour-blind.

dama ['dama] *nf* (*gen*) lady; (*AJEDREZ*) queen; ~s *nfpl* (*juego*) draughts *sg*.

damasco [da'masko] *nm* damask.

damnificar [damnifi'kar] *vt* to harm; (*persona*) to injure.

danés, esa [da'nes, esa] *adj* Danish ♦ *nm/f* Dane.

danzar [dan'θar] *vt, vi* to dance.

dañar [da'ɲar] *vt* (*objeto*) to damage; (*persona*) to hurt; ~**se** *vr* (*objeto*) to get damaged.

dañino, a [da'ɲino, a] *adj* harmful.

daño ['daɲo] *nm* (*a un objeto*) damage; (*a una persona*) harm, injury; ~**s y perjuicios** (*JUR*) damages; **hacer** ~ **a** to damage; (*persona*) to hurt, injure; **hacerse** ~ to hurt o.s.

---

dar [dar] *vt* **1** (*gen*) to give; (*obra de teatro*) to put on; (*film*) to show; (*fiesta*) to hold; ~ **algo a uno** to give sb sth *o* sth to sb; ~ **de beber a uno** to give sb a drink

2 (*producir: intereses*) to yield; (*fruta*) to produce

3 (*locuciones +n*): **da gusto escucharle** it's a pleasure to listen to him; *ver tb* **paseo** *y otros sustantivos*

4 (*+n*: = *perífrasis de verbo*): **me da pena/asco** it frightens/sickens me

5 (*considerar*): ~ **algo por descontado/entendido** to take sth for granted/as read; ~ **algo por concluido** to consider sth finished

6 (*hora*): **el reloj dio las 6** the clock struck 6 (o'clock)

7. **me da lo mismo** it's all the same to me; *ver tb* **igual, más**

♦ *vi* **1** ~ **con**: **dimos con él dos horas más tarde** we came across him two hours later; **al final di con la solución** I

eventually came up with the answer

2: ~ **en**: ~ **en** (*blanco, suelo*) to hit; **el sol me da en la cara** the sun is shining (right) on my face

3: ~ **de sí** (*zapatos etc*) to stretch, give

♦ ~**se** *vr* **1**: ~**se por vencido** to give up

2 (*ocurrir*): **se han dado muchos casos** there have been a lot of cases

3: ~**se a**: **se ha dado a la bebida** he's taken to drinking

4: **se me dan bien/mal las ciencias** I'm good/bad at science

5: **dárselas de**: **se las da de experto** he fancies himself *o* poses as an expert.

---

dardo ['darðo] *nm* dart.

dársena ['darsena] *nf* dock.

datar [da'tar] *vi*: ~ **de** to date from.

dátil ['datil] *nm* date.

dato ['dato] *nm* fact, piece of information.

dcha. *abr* (= *derecha*) r.h.

d. de J.C. *abr* (= *después de Jesucristo*) A.D.

---

de [de] *prep* (*de+el* = *del*) **1** (*posesión*) of; **la casa** ~ **Isabel/mis padres** Isabel's/my parents' house; **es** ~ **ellos** it's theirs

2 (*origen, distancia, con números*) from; **soy** ~ **Gijón** I'm from Gijón; ~ **8 a 20** from 8 to 20; **salir del cine** to go out *o* leave the cinema; ~ ... **en** ... from ... to ...; ~ **2 en 2** 2 by 2, 2 at a time

3 (*valor descriptivo*): **una copa** ~ **vino** a glass of wine; **la mesa** ~ **la cocina** the kitchen table; **un billete** ~ **1000 pesetas** a 1000 peseta note; **un niño** ~ **tres años** a three-year-old (child); **una máquina** ~ **coser** a sewing machine; **ir vestido** ~ **gris** to be dressed in grey; **la niña del vestido azul** the girl in the blue dress; **trabaja** ~ **profesora** she works as a teacher; ~ **lado** sideways; ~ **atrás/delante** rear/front

4 (*hora, tiempo*): **a las 8** ~ **la mañana** at 8 o'clock in the morning; ~ **día/noche** by day/night; ~ **hoy en ocho días** a

week from now; ~ **niño era gordo** as a
child he was fat
5 (*comparaciones*): **más/menos ~ cien
personas** more/less than a hundred
people; **el más caro ~ la tienda** the
most expensive in the shop; **menos/más
~ lo pensado** less/more than expected
6 (*causa*): **del calor** from the heat; ~
puro tonto out of sheer stupidity
7 (*tema*) about; **clases ~ inglés**
English classes; **¿sabes algo ~ él?** do
you know anything about him?; **un libro
~ física** a physics book
8 (*adj +de +infin*): **fácil ~ entender**
easy to understand
9 (*oraciones pasivas*): **fue respetado ~
todos** he was loved by all
10 (*condicional +infin*) if; ~ **ser posible**
if possible; ~ **no terminarlo hoy** if I *etc*
don't finish it today.

dé *vb ver* **dar.**
deambular [deambu'lar] *vi* to stroll,
wander.
debajo [de'βaxo] *adv* underneath; ~ **de**
below, under; **por ~ de** beneath.
debate [de'βate] *nm* debate; **debatir** *vt*
to debate.
deber [de'βer] *nm* duty ♦ *vt* to owe ♦ *vi*:
debe (de) it must, it should; ~**es** *nmpl*
(*ESCOL*) homework; **debo hacerlo** I
must do it; **debe de ir** he should go;
~**se** *vr*: ~**se a** to be owing *o* due to.
debido, a [de'βiðo, a] *adj* proper, just;
~ **a** due to, because of.
débil ['deβil] *adj* (*persona, carácter*)
weak; (*luz*) dim; **debilidad** *nf* weakness; dimness.
debilitar [deβili'tar] *vt* to weaken; ~**se**
vr to grow weak.
debutar [deβu'tar] *vi* to make one's
debut.
década ['dekaða] *nf* decade.
decadencia [deka'ðenθja] *nf* (*estado*)
decadence; (*proceso*) decline, decay.
decaer [deka'er] *vi* (*declinar*) to decline;
(*debilitarse*) to weaken.
decaído, a [deka'iðo, a] *adj*: **estar ~**
(*abatido*) to be down.
decaimiento [dekai'mjento] *nm* (*decli-*

nación) decline; (*desaliento*) discouragement; (*MED: estado débil*) weakness.
decano, a [de'kano, a] *nm/f* (*de universidad etc*) dean.
decapitar [dekapi'tar] *vt* to behead.
decena [de'θena] *nf*: **una ~** ten (or so).
decencia [de'θenθja] *nf* (*modestia*)
modesty; (*honestidad*) respectability.
decente [de'θente] *adj* (*correcto*)
seemly, proper; (*honesto*) respectable.
decepción [deθep'θjon] *nf* disappointment.
decepcionar [deθepθjo'nar] *vt* to disappoint.
decidir [deθi'ðir] *vt* (*persuadir*) to convince, persuade; (*resolver*) to decide ♦
vi to decide; ~**se** *vr*: ~**se a** to make up
one's mind to.
décimo, a ['deθimo, a] *adj* tenth ♦ *nm*
tenth.
decir [de'θir] *vt* (*expresar*) to say; (*contar*) to tell; (*hablar*) to speak ♦ *nm*
saying; ~**se** *vr*: **se dice que** it is said
that; ~ **para** *o* **entre sí** to say to o.s.;
querer ~ to mean; **¡dígame!** (*TEL*)
hello!; (*en tienda*) can I help you?
decisión [deθi'sjon] *nf* (*resolución*) decision; (*firmeza*) decisiveness.
decisivo, a [deθi'siβo, a] *adj* decisive.
declamar [dekla'mar] *vt, vi* to declaim.
declaración [deklara'θjon] *nf* (*manifestación*) statement; (*explicación*) explanation.
declarar [dekla'rar] *vt* to declare ♦ *vi* to
declare; (*JUR*) to testify; ~**se** *vr* to
propose.
declinar [dekli'nar] *vt* (*gen*) to decline;
(*JUR*) to reject ♦ *vi* (*el día*) to draw to a
close.
declive [de'kliβe] *nm* (*cuesta*) slope;
(*fig*) decline.
decolorarse [dekolo'rarse] *vr* to become
discoloured.
decoración [dekora'θjon] *nf* decoration.
decorado [deko'raðo] *nm* (*CINE, TEA-
TRO*) scenery, set.
decorar [deko'rar] *vt* to decorate;
decorativo, a *adj* ornamental, decorative.

decoro [de'koro] *nm* (*respeto*) respect; (*dignidad*) decency; (*recato*) propriety; ~**so, a** *adj* (*decente*) decent; (*modesto*) modest; (*digno*) proper.

decrecer [dekre'θer] *vi* to decrease, diminish.

decrépito, a [de'krepito, a] *adj* decrepit.

decretar [dekre'tar] *vt* to decree; **decreto** *nm* decree.

dedal [de'ðal] *nm* thimble.

dedicación [deðika'θjon] *nf* dedication.

dedicar [deðɪ'kar] *vt* (*libro*) to dedicate; (*tiempo, dinero*) to devote; (*palabras: decir, consagrar*) to dedicate, devote; **dedicatoria** *nf* (*de libro*) dedication.

dedo ['deðo] *nm* finger; ~ (**del pie**) toe; ~ **pulgar** thumb; ~ **índice** index finger; ~ **mayor** o **cordial** middle finger; ~ **anular** ring finger; ~ **meñique** little finger; **hacer** ~ (*fam*) to hitch (a lift).

deducción [deðuk'θjon] *nf* deduction.

deducir [deðu'θir] *vt* (*concluir*) to deduce, infer; (*COM*) to deduct.

defecto [de'fekto] *nm* defect, flaw; **defectuoso, a** *adj* defective, faulty.

defender [defen'der] *vt* to defend.

defensa [de'fensa] *nf* defence ♦ *nm* (*DEPORTE*) defender, back; **defensiva** *nf*: **a la** ~ on the defensive; **defensivo, a** *adj* defensive.

defensor, a [defen'sor, a] *adj* defending ♦ *nm/f* (*abogado* ~) defending counsel; (*protector*) protector.

deficiencia [defi'θjenθja] *nf* deficiency.

deficiente [defi'θjente] *adj* (*defectuoso*) defective; ~ **en** lacking o deficient in; **ser un** ~ **mental** to be mentally handicapped.

déficit ['defiθit] (*pl* ~**s**) *nm* deficit.

definición [defini'θjon] *nf* definition.

definir [defi'nir] *vt* (*determinar*) to determine, establish; (*decidir*) to define; (*aclarar*) to clarify; **definitivo, a** *adj* definitive; **en definitiva** definitively; (*en resumen*) in short.

deformación [deforma'θjon] *nf* (*alteración*) deformation; (*RADIO etc*) distortion.

deformar [defor'mar] *vt* (*gen*) to deform; ~**se** *vr* to become deformed;

deforme *adj* (*informe*) deformed; (*feo*) ugly; (*malhecho*) misshapen.

defraudar [defrau'ðar] *vt* (*decepcionar*) to disappoint; (*estafar*) to cheat; to defraud.

defunción [defun'θjon] *nf* death, demise.

degeneración [dexenera'θjon] *nf* (*de las células*) degeneration; (*moral*) degeneracy.

degenerar [dexene'rar] *vi* to degenerate.

degollar [devo'ʎar] *vt* to behead; (*fig*) to slaughter.

degradar [devra'ðar] *vt* to debase, degrade; ~**se** *vr* to demean o.s.

degustación [devusta'θjon] *nf* sampling, tasting.

deificar [deifi'kar] *vt* (*persona*) to deify.

dejadez [dexa'ðeθ] *nf* (*negligencia*) neglect; (*descuido*) untidiness, carelessness; **dejado, a** *adj* (*negligente*) careless; (*indolente*) lazy.

dejar [de'xar] *vt* to leave; (*permitir*) to allow, let; (*abandonar*) to abandon, forsake; (*beneficios*) to produce, yield ♦ *vi*: ~ **de** (*parar*) to stop; (*no hacer*) to fail to; **no dejes de comprar un billete** make sure you buy a ticket; ~ **a un lado** to leave o set aside.

dejo ['dexo] *nm* (*LING*) accent.

del [del] (= **de**+ **el**) *ver* **de**.

delantal [delan'tal] *nm* apron.

delante [de'lante] *adv* in front, (*enfrente*) opposite; (*adelante*) ahead; ~ **de** in front of, before.

delantera [delan'tera] *nf* (*de vestido, casa etc*) front part; (*DEPORTE*) forward line; **llevar la** ~ (**a uno**) to be ahead (of sb).

delantero, a [delan'tero, a] *adj* front ♦ *nm* (*DEPORTE*) forward, striker.

delatar [dela'tar] *vt* to inform on o against, betray; **delator, a** *nm/f* informer.

delegación [deleva'θjon] *nf* (*acción, delegados*) delegation; (*COM: oficina*) office, branch; ~ **de policía** police station.

delegado, a [dele'vaðo, a] *nm/f* delegate; (*COM*) agent.

delegar [dele'var] *vt* to delegate.

deletrear [deletre'ar] *vt* to spell (out).

deleznable [dele0'naßle] *adj* brittle; (*excusa, idea*) feeble.

delfín [del'fin] *nm* dolphin.

delgadez [delɣa'ðeθ] *nf* thinness, slimness.

delgado, a [del'ɣaðo, a] *adj* thin; (*persona*) slim, thin; (*tierra*) poor; (*tela etc*) light, delicate.

deliberación [delißera'θjon] *nf* deliberation.

deliberar [deliße'rar] *vt* to debate, discuss.

delicadeza [delika'ðeθa] *nf* (*gen*) delicacy; (*refinamiento, sutileza*) refinement.

delicado, a [deli'kaðo, a] *adj* (*gen*) delicate; (*sensible*) sensitive; (*quisquilloso*) touchy.

delicia [de'liθja] *nf* delight.

delicioso, a [deli'θjoso, a] *adj* (*gracioso*) delightful; (*exquisito*) delicious.

delincuencia [delin'kwenθja] *nf* delinquency; **delincuente** *nm/f* delinquent; (*criminal*) criminal.

delineante [deline'ante] *nm/f* draughtsman/woman.

delinear [deline'ar] *vt* (*dibujo*) to draw; (*fig, contornos*) to outline.

delinquir [delin'kir] *vi* to commit an offence.

delirante [deli'rante] *adj* delirious.

delirar [deli'rar] *vi* to be delirious, rave.

delirio [de'lirjo] *nm* (*MED*) delirium; (*palabras insensatas*) ravings *pl*.

delito [de'lito] *nm* (*gen*) crime; (*infracción*) offence.

demacrado, a [dema'krado, a] *adj*: **estar** ~ to look pale and drawn, be wasted away.

demagogo, a [dema'ɣoɣo, a] *nm/f* demagogue.

demanda [de'manda] *nf* (*pedido, COM*) demand; (*petición*) request; (*JUR*) action, lawsuit.

demandante [deman'dante] *nm/f* claimant.

demandar [deman'dar] *vt* (*gen*) to demand; (*JUR*) to sue, file a lawsuit against.

demarcación [demarka'θjon] *nf* (*de terreno*) demarcation.

demás [de'mas] *adj*: **los** ~ **niños** the other children, the remaining children ♦ *pron*: **los/las** ~ the others, the rest (of them); **lo** ~ the rest (of it).

demasía [dema'sia] *nf* (*exceso*) excess, surplus; **comer en** ~ to eat to excess.

demasiado, a [dema'sjaðo, a] *adj*: ~ **vino** too much wine; ~**s libros** too many books ♦ *adv* (*antes de adj, adv*) too; **¡esto es** ~! that's the limit!; **hace** ~ **calor** it's too hot; ~ **despacio** too slowly; ~**s** too many.

demencia [de'menθja] *nf* (*locura*) madness; **demente** *nm/f* lunatic ♦ *adj* mad, insane.

democracia [demo'kraθja] *nf* democracy.

demócrata [de'mokrata] *nm/f* democrat; **democrático, a** *adj* democratic.

demoler [demo'ler] *vt* to demolish; **demolición** *nf* demolition.

demonio [de'monjo] *nm* devil, demon; **¡**~**s!** hell!, damn!; **¿cómo** ~**s?** how the hell?

demora [de'mora] *nf* delay; **demorar** *vt* (*retardar*) to delay, hold back; (*detener*) to hold up ♦ *vi* to linger, stay on; ~**se** *vr* to be delayed.

demos *vb ver* **dar**.

demostración [demostra'θjon] *nf* (*MAT*) proof; (*de afecto*) show, display.

demostrar [demos'trar] *vt* (*probar*) to prove; (*mostrar*) to show; (*manifestar*) to demonstrate; **demostrativo, a** *adj* demonstrative.

demudado, a [demu'ðaðo, a] *adj* (*rostro*) pale.

den *vb ver* **dar**.

denegar [dene'ɣar] *vt* (*rechazar*) to refuse; (*JUR*) to reject.

denigrar [deni'ɣrar] *vt* (*desacreditar, infamar*) to denigrate; (*injuriar*) to insult.

denominación [denomina'θjon] *nf* (*clase*) denomination.

denotar [deno'tar] *vt* (*indicar*) to indicate; (*significar*) to denote.

densidad [densi'ðað] *nf* (*FÍSICA*) density;

(*fig*) thickness.

denso, a ['denso, a] *adj* (*apretado*) solid; (*espeso, pastoso*) thick; (*fig*) heavy.

dentadura [denta'ðura] *nf* (set of) teeth *pl*; ~ **postiza** false teeth *pl*.

dentera [den'tera] *nf* (*sensación desagradable*) the shivers *pl*.

dentífrico, a [den'tifriko, a] *adj* dental ♦ *nm* toothpaste.

dentista [den'tista] *nm/f* dentist.

dentro ['dentro] *adv* inside ♦ *prep*: ~ **de** in, inside, within; **por** ~ (on the) inside; **mirar por** ~ to look inside; ~ **de tres meses** within three months.

denuncia [de'nunθja] *nf* (*delación*) denunciation; (*acusación*) accusation; (*de accidente*) report; **denunciar** *vt* to report; (*delatar*) to inform on *o* against.

departamento [departa'mento] *nm* (*sección administrativa*) department, section; (*AM: apartamento*) flat (*BRIT*), apartment.

departir [depar'tir] *vi* to converse.

dependencia [depen'denθja] *nf* dependence; (*POL*) dependency; (*COM*) office, section.

depender [depen'der] *vi*: ~ **de** to depend on.

dependienta [depen'djenta] *nf* saleswoman, shop assistant.

dependiente [depen'djente] *adj* dependent ♦ *nm* salesman, shop assistant.

depilar [depi'lar] *vt* (*con cera*) to wax; (*cejas*) to pluck; **depilatorio** *nm* hair remover.

deplorable [deplo'raβle] *adj* deplorable.

deplorar [deplo'rar] *vt* to deplore.

deponer [depo'ner] *vt* to lay down ♦ *vi* (*JUR*) to give evidence; (*declarar*) to make a statement.

deportar [depor'tar] *vt* to deport.

deporte [de'porte] *nm* sport; **hacer** ~ to play sports; **deportista** *adj* sports *cpd* ♦ *nm/f* sportsman/woman; **deportivo, a** *adj* (*club, periódico*) sports *cpd* ♦ *nm* sports car.

depositador, a [deposita'ðor, a] *nm/f* =

depositante.

depositante [deposi'tante] *nm/f* depositor.

depositar [deposi'tar] *vt* (*dinero*) to deposit; (*mercancías*) to put away, store; (*persona*) to confide; ~**se** *vr* to settle; ~**io, a** *nm/f* trustee.

depósito [de'posito] *nm* (*gen*) deposit; (*almacén*) warehouse, store; (*de agua, gasolina etc*) tank.

depravar [depra'βar] *vt* to deprave, corrupt; ~**se** *vr* to become depraved.

depreciar [depre'θjar] *vt* to depreciate, reduce the value of; ~**se** *vr* to depreciate, lose value.

depredador, a [depreða'ðor, a] *adj* predatory ♦ *nm* predator.

depresión [depre'sjon] *nf* depression.

deprimido, a [depri'miðo, a] *adj* depressed.

deprimir [depri'mir] *vt* to depress; ~**se** *vr* (*persona*) to become depressed.

deprisa [de'prisa] *adv* quickly, hurriedly.

depuración [depura'θjon] *nf* purification; (*POL*) purge.

depurar [depu'rar] *vt* to purify; (*purgar*) to purge.

derecha [de'retʃa] *nf* right(-hand) side; (*POL*) right; **a la** ~ (*estar*) on the right; (*torcer etc*) (to the) right.

derecho, a [de'retʃo, a] *adj* right, right-hand ♦ *nm* (*privilegio*) right; (*lado*) right(-hand) side; (*leyes*) law ♦ *adv* straight, directly; ~**s** *nmpl* (*de aduana*) duty *sg*; (*de autor*) royalties; **tener** ~ **a** to have a right to.

deriva [de'riβa] *nf*: **ir** *o* **estar a la** ~ to drift, be adrift.

derivado [deri'βaðo] *nm* (*COM*) by-product.

derivar [deri'βar] *vt* to derive; (*desviar*) to direct ♦ *vi* to derive, be derived; (*NAUT*) to drift; ~**se** *vr* to derive, be derived; to drift.

derramamiento [derrama'mjento] *nm* (*dispersión*) spilling; ~ **de sangre** bloodshed.

derramar [derra'mar] *vt* to spill; (*verter*) to pour out; (*esparcir*) to scatter; ~**se** *vr* to pour out; ~ **lágrimas**

to weep.

derrame [de'rrame] *nm* (*de líquido*) spilling; (*de sangre*) shedding; (*de tubo etc*) overflow; (*pérdida*) leakage; (*MED*) discharge; (*declive*) slope.

derredor [derre'ðor] *adv*: al *o* en ~ de around, about.

derretido, a [derre'tiðo, a] *adj* melted; (*metal*) molten.

derretir [derre'tir] *vt* (*gen*) to melt; (*nieve*) to thaw; (*fig*) to squander; ~se *vr* to melt.

derribar [derri'ßar] *vt* to knock down; (*construcción*) to demolish; (*persona, gobierno, político*) to bring down.

derrocar [derro'kar] *vt* (*gobierno*) to bring down, overthrow.

derrochar [derro'tʃar] *vt* to squander; **derroche** *nm* (*despilfarro*) waste, squandering.

derrota [de'rrota] *nf* (*NAUT*) course; (*MIL, DEPORTE etc*) defeat, rout; **derrotar** *vt* (*gen*) to defeat; **derrotero** *nm* (*rumbo*) course.

derrumbar [derrum'bar] *vt* (*edificio*) to knock down; ~se *vr* to collapse.

des *vb ver* **dar**.

desabotonar [desaßoto'nar] *vt* to unbutton, undo ♦ *vi* (*flores*) to bloom; ~se *vr* to come undone.

desabrido, a [desa'ßriðo, a] *adj* (*comida*) insipid, tasteless; (*persona*) rude, surly; (*respuesta*) sharp; (*tiempo*) unpleasant.

desabrochar [desaßro'tʃar] *vt* (*botones, broches*) to undo, unfasten; ~se *vr* (*ropa etc*) to come undone.

desacato [desa'kato] *nm* (*falta de respeto*) disrespect; (*JUR*) contempt.

desacertado, a [desaθer'taðo, a] *adj* (*equivocado*) mistaken; (*inoportuno*) unwise.

desacierto [desa'θjerto] *nm* mistake, error.

desaconsejado, a [desakonse'xaðo, a] *adj* ill-advised.

desaconsejar [desakonse'xar] *vt* to advise against.

desacorde [desa'korðe] *adj* discordant; **estar** ~ **con algo** to disagree with sth.

desacreditar [desakreði'tar] *vt* (*desprestigiar*) to discredit, bring into disrepute; (*denigrar*) to run down.

desacuerdo [desa'kwerðo] *nm* (*conflicto*) disagreement, discord; (*error*) error, blunder.

desafiar [desa'fjar] *vt* (*retar*) to challenge; (*enfrentarse a*) to defy.

desafilado, a [desafi'laðo, a] *adj* blunt.

desafinado, a [desafi'naðo, a] *adj*: **estar** ~ to be out of tune.

desafinarse [desafi'narse] *vr* to go out of tune.

desafío *etc* [desa'fio] *vb ver* **desafiar** ♦ *nm* (*reto*) challenge; (*combate*) duel; (*resistencia*) defiance.

desaforado, a [desafo'raðo, a] *adj* (*grito*) ear-splitting; (*comportamiento*) outrageous.

desafortunadamente [desafortunaða-'mente] *adv* unfortunately.

desafortunado, a [desafortu'naðo, a] *adj* (*desgraciado*) unfortunate, unlucky.

desagradable [desaɣra'ðaßle] *adj* (*fastidioso, enojoso*) unpleasant; (*irritante*) disagreeable.

desagradar [desaɣra'ðar] *vi* (*disgustar*) to displease; (*molestar*) to bother.

desagradecido, a [desaɣraðe'θiðo, a] *adj* ungrateful.

desagrado [desa'ɣraðo] *nm* (*disgusto*) displeasure; (*contrariedad*) dissatisfaction.

desagraviar [desaɣra'ßjar] *vt* to make amends to; **desagravio** *nm* (*satisfacción*) amends; (*compensación*) compensation.

desagüe [des'aɣwe] *nm* (*de un líquido*) drainage; (*cañería*) drainpipe; (*salida*) outlet, drain.

desaguisado, a [desaɣi'saðo, a] *adj* illegal ♦ *nm* outrage.

desahogado, a [desao'xaðo, a] *adj* (*holgado*) comfortable; (*espacioso*) roomy, large.

desahogar [desao'ɣar] *vt* (*aliviar*) to ease, relieve; (*ira*) to vent; ~se *vr* (*relajarse*) to relax; (*desfogarse*) to let off steam.

desahogo [desa'oxo] *nm* (*alivio*) relief;

(*comodidad*) comfort, ease.

desahuciar [desau'θjar] *vt* (*enfermo*) to give up hope for; (*inquilino*) to evict; **desahucio** *nm* eviction.

desairar [desai'rar] *vt* (*menospreciar*) to slight, snub; (*cosa*) to disregard.

desaire [des'aire] *nm* (*menosprecio*) slight; (*falta de garbo*) unattractiveness.

desajustar [desaxus'tar] *vt* (*desarreglar*) to disarrange; (*desconcertar*) to throw off balance; ~**se** *vr* to get out of order; (*aflojarse*) to loosen.

desajuste [desa'xuste] *nm* (*de máquina*) disorder; (*situación*) imbalance.

desalentador, a [desalenta'ðor, a] *adj* discouraging.

desalentar [desalen'tar] *vt* (*desanimar*) to discourage.

desaliento *etc* [desa'ljento] *vb ver* **desalentar** ♦ *nm* discouragement.

desaliño [desa'liɲo] *nm* (*negligencia*) slovenliness.

desalmado, a [desal'maðo, a] *adj* (*cruel*) cruel, heartless.

desalojar [desalo'xar] *vt* (*expulsar*, *echar*) to eject; (*abandonar*) to move out of ♦ *vi* to move out.

desamarrar [desama'rrar] *vt* to untie; (*NAUT*) to cast off.

desamor [desa'mor] *nm* (*frialdad*) indifference; (*odio*) dislike.

desamparado, a [desampa'raðo, a] *adj* (*persona*) helpless; (*lugar: expuesto*) exposed; (*desierto*) deserted.

desamparar [desampa'rar] *vt* (*abandonar*) to desert, abandon; (*JUR*) to leave defenceless; (*barco*) to abandon.

desandar [desan'dar] *vt*: ~ **lo andado** *o* **el camino** to retrace one's steps.

desangrar [desan'grar] *vt* to bleed; (*fig: persona*) to bleed dry; ~**se** *vr* to lose a lot of blood.

desanimado, a [desani'maðo, a] *adj* (*persona*) downhearted; (*espectáculo*, *fiesta*) dull.

desanimar [desani'mar] *vt* (*desalentar*) to discourage; (*deprimir*) to depress; ~**se** *vr* to lose heart.

desapacible [desapa'θiβle] *adj* (*gen*) unpleasant.

desaparecer [desapare'θer] *vi* (*gen*) to disappear; (*el sol, la luz*) to vanish; **desaparecido, a** *adj* missing; **desaparecidos** *nmpl* (*en accidente*) people missing; **desaparición** *nf* disappearance.

desapasionado, a [desapasjo'naðo, a] *adj* dispassionate, impartial.

desapego [desa'peɣo] *nm* (*frialdad*) coolness; (*distancia*) detachment.

desapercibido, a [desaperθi'βiðo, a] *adj* (*desprevenido*) unprepared; **pasar** ~ to go unnoticed.

desaplicado, a [desapli'kaðo, a] *adj* slack, lazy.

desaprensivo, a [desapren'siβo, a] *adj* unscrupulous.

desaprobar [desapro'βar] *vt* (*reprobar*) to disapprove of; (*condenar*) to condemn; (*no consentir*) to reject.

desaprovechado, a [desaproβe'tʃaðo, a] *adj* (*oportunidad*, *tiempo*) wasted; (*estudiante*) slack.

desaprovechar [desaproβe'tʃar] *vt* to waste.

desarmar [desar'mar] *vt* (*MIL*, *fig*) to disarm; (*TEC*) to take apart, dismantle; **desarme** *nm* disarmament.

desarraigar [desarrai'ɣar] *vt* to uproot; **desarraigo** *nm* uprooting.

desarreglado, a [desarre'ɣlaðo, a] *adj* (*desordenado*) disorderly, untidy.

desarreglar [desarre'ɣlar] *vt* (*desordenar*) to disarrange; (*trastocar*) to upset, disturb.

desarreglo [desa'rreɣlo] *nm* (*de casa*, *persona*) untidiness; (*desorden*) disorder.

desarrollar [desarro'ʎar] *vt* (*gen*) to develop; (*extender*) to unfold; ~**se** *vr* to develop; (*extenderse*) to open (out); (*FOTO*) to develop; **desarrollo** *nm* development.

desarticular [desartiku'lar] *vt* (*hueso*) to dislocate; (*objeto*) to take apart; (*fig*) to break up.

desaseo [desa'seo] *nm* (*suciedad*) slovenliness; (*desarreglo*) untidiness.

desasir [desa'sir] *vt* to loosen; ~se *vr* to extricate o.s.; ~se **de** to let go, give up.

desasosegar [desasose'ɣar] *vt* (*inquietar*) to disturb, make uneasy; ~se *vr* to become uneasy.

desasosiego *etc* [desaso'sjeɣo] *vb ver* **desasosegar** ♦ *nm* (*intranquilidad*) uneasiness, restlessness; (*ansiedad*) anxiety.

desastrado, a [desas'traðo, a] *adj* (*desaliñado*) shabby; (*sucio*) dirty.

desastre [de'sastre] *nm* disaster; **desastroso, a** *adj* disastrous.

desatado, a [desa'taðo, a] *adj* (*desligado*) untied; (*violento*) violent, wild.

desatar [desa'tar] *vt* (*nudo*) to untie; (*paquete*) to undo; (*separar*) to detach; ~se *vr* (*zapatos*) to come untied; (*tormenta*) to break.

desatascar [desatas'kar] *vt* (*cañería*) to unblock, clear.

desatender [desaten'der] *vt* (*no prestar atención a*) to disregard; (*abandonar*) to neglect.

desatento, a [desa'tento, a] *adj* (*distraído*) inattentive; (*descortés*) discourteous.

desatinado, a [desati'naðo, a] *adj* foolish, silly; **desatino** *nm* (*idiotez*) foolishness, folly; (*error*) blunder.

desatornillar [desatorni'ʎar] *vt* to unscrew.

desautorizado, a [desautori'θaðo, a] *adj* unauthorized.

desautorizar [desautori'θar] *vt* (*oficial*) to deprive of authority; (*informe*) to deny.

desavenencia [desaβe'nenθja] *nf* (*desacuerdo*) disagreement; (*discrepancia*) quarrel.

desaventajado, a [desaβenta'xaðo, a] *adj* (*inferior*) inferior; (*poco ventajoso*) disadvantageous.

desayunar [desaju'nar] *vi* to have breakfast ♦ *vt* to have for breakfast; **desayuno** *nm* breakfast.

desazón [desa'θon] *nf* (*angustia*) anxiety; (*fig*) annoyance.

desazonar [desaθo'nar] *vt* (*fig*) to

annoy, upset; ~se *vr* (*enojarse*) to be annoyed; (*preocuparse*) to worry, be anxious.

desbandarse [desβan'darse] *vr* (*MIL*) to disband; (*fig*) to flee in disorder.

desbarajuste [desβara'xuste] *nm* confusion, disorder.

desbaratar [desβara'tar] *vt* (*deshacer, destruir*) to ruin.

desbloquear [desβloke'ar] *vt* (*negociaciones, tráfico*) to get going again; (*COM: cuenta*) to unfreeze.

desbocado, a [desβo'kaðo, a] *adj* (*caballo*) runaway.

desbordar [desβor'ðar] *vt* (*sobrepasar*) to go beyond; (*exceder*) to exceed ♦ *vi* (*río*) to overflow; (*entusiasmo*) to erupt; ~se *vr* to overflow; to erupt.

descabalgar [deskaβal'ɣar] *vi* to dismount.

descabellado, a [deskaβe'ʎaðo, a] *adj* (*disparatado*) wild, crazy.

descabellar [deskaβe'ʎar] *vt* to ruffle; (*TAUR: toro*) to give the coup de grace to.

descafeinado, a [deskafei'naðo, a] *adj* decaffeinated ♦ *nm* decaffeinated coffee.

descalabro [deska'laβro] *nm* blow; (*desgracia*) misfortune.

descalificar [deskalifi'kar] *vt* to disqualify; (*desacreditar*) to discredit.

descalzar [deskal'θar] *vt* (*zapato*) to take off; **descalzo, a** *adj* barefoot(ed); (*fig*) destitute.

descambiar [deskam'bjar] *vt* to exchange.

descaminado, a [deskami'naðo, a] *adj* (*equivocado*) on the wrong road; (*fig*) misguided.

descampado [deskam'paðo] *nm* open space.

descansado, a [deskan'saðo, a] *adj* (*gen*) rested; (*que tranquiliza*) restful.

descansar [deskan'sar] *vt* (*gen*) to rest ♦ *vi* to rest, have a rest; (*echarse*) to lie down.

descansillo [deskan'siʎo] *nm* (*de escalera*) landing.

descanso [des'kanso] *nm* (*reposo*) rest;

(*alivio*) relief; (*pausa*) break; (*DEPORTE*) interval, half time.

descapotable [deskapo'taβle] *nm* (*tb: coche* ~) convertible.

descarado, a [deska'raðo, a] *adj* shameless; (*insolente*) cheeky.

descarga [des'karγa] *nf* (*ARQ, ELEC, MIL*) discharge; (*NAUT*) unloading.

descargar [deskar'γar] *vt* to unload; (*golpe*) to let fly; ~se *vr* to unburden o.s.; **descargo** *nm* (*COM*) receipt; (*JUR*) evidence.

descarnado, a [deskar'naðo, a] *adj* scrawny; (*fig*) bare.

descaro [des'karo] *nm* nerve.

descarriar [deska'rrjar] *vt* (*descaminar*) to misdirect; (*fig*) to lead astray; ~se *vr* (*perderse*) to lose one's way; (*separarse*) to stray; (*pervertirse*) to err, go astray.

descarrilamiento [deskarrila'mjento] *nm* (*de tren*) derailment.

descarrilar [deskarri'lar] *vi* to be derailed.

descartar [deskar'tar] *vt* (*rechazar*) to reject; (*eliminar*) to rule out; ~se *vr* (*NAIPES*) to discard; ~se de to shirk.

descascarillado, a [deskaskari'ʎaðo, a] *adj* (*paredes*) peeling.

descendencia [desθen'denθja] *nf* (*origen*) origin, descent; (*hijos*) offspring.

descender [desθen'der] *vt* (*bajar: escalera*) to go down ♦ *vi* to descend; (*temperatura, nivel*) to fall, drop; ~ de to be descended from.

descendiente [desθen'djente] *nm/f* descendant.

descenso [des'θenso] *nm* descent; (*de temperatura*) drop.

descifrar [desθi'frar] *vt* to decipher; (*mensaje*) to decode.

descolgar [deskol'γar] *vt* (*bajar*) to take down; (*teléfono*) to pick up; ~se *vr* to let o.s. down.

descolorido, a [deskolo'riðo, a] *adj* faded; (*pálido*) pale.

descompaginar [deskompaxi'nar] *vt* (*desordenar*) to disarrange, mess up.

descompasado, a [deskompa'saðo, a] *adj* (*sin proporción*) out of all proportion; (*excesivo*) excessive.

descomponer [deskompo'ner] *vt* (*desordenar*) to disarrange, disturb; (*TEC*) to put out of order; (*dividir*) to break down (into parts); (*fig*) to provoke; ~se *vr* (*corromperse*) to rot, decompose; (*el tiempo*) to change (for the worse); (*TEC*) to break down.

descomposición [deskomposi'θjon] *nf* (*gen*) breakdown; (*de fruta etc*) decomposition.

descompostura [deskompos'tura] *nf* (*TEC*) breakdown; (*desorganización*) disorganization; (*desorden*) untidiness.

descompuesto, a [deskom'pwesto, a] *adj* (*corrompido*) decomposed; (*roto*) broken.

descomunal [deskomu'nal] *adj* (*enorme*) huge.

desconcertado, a [deskonθer'taðo, a] *adj* disconcerted, bewildered.

desconcertar [deskonθer'tar] *vt* (*confundir*) to baffle; (*incomodar*) to upset, put out; ~se *vr* (*turbarse*) to be upset.

desconcierto *etc* [deskon'θjerto] *vb ver* **desconcertar** ♦ *nm* (*gen*) disorder; (*desorientación*) uncertainty; (*inquietud*) uneasiness.

desconchado, a [deskon'tʃaðo, a] *adj* (*pintura*) peeling.

desconectar [deskonek'tar] *vt* to disconnect.

desconfianza [deskon'fjanθa] *nf* distrust.

desconfiar [deskon'fjar] *vi* to be distrustful; ~ de to distrust, suspect.

descongelar [deskonxe'lar] *vt* to defrost; (*COM, POL*) to unfreeze.

descongestionar [deskonxestjo'nar] *vt* (*cabeza, tráfico*) to clear.

desconocer [deskono'θer] *vt* (*ignorar*) not to know, be ignorant of; (*no aceptar*) to deny; (*repudiar*) to disown.

desconocido, a [deskono'θiðo, a] *adj* unknown ♦ *nm/f* stranger.

desconocimiento [deskonoθi'mjento] *nm* (*falta de conocimientos*) ignorance; (*repudio*) disregard.

desconsiderado, a [deskonsiðe'raðo, a] *adj* inconsiderate; (*insensible*) thoughtless.

desconsolar [deskonso'lar] *vt* to distress; ~**se** *vr* to despair.
desconsuelo *etc* [deskon'swelo] *vb ver* **desconsolar** ♦ *nm* (*tristeza*) distress; (*desesperación*) despair.
descontado, a [deskon'taðo, a] *adj*: **dar por** ~ (**que**) to take (it) for granted (that).
descontar [deskon'tar] *vt* (*deducir*) to take away, deduct; (*rebajar*) to discount.
descontento, a [deskon'tento, a] *adj* dissatisfied ♦ *nm* dissatisfaction, discontent.
descorazonar [deskoraθo'nar] *vt* to discourage, dishearten.
descorchar [deskor'tʃar] *vt* to uncork.
descorrer [desko'rrer] *vt* (*cortinas, cerrojo*) to draw back.
descortés [deskor'tes] *adj* (*mal educado*) discourteous; (*grosero*) rude.
descoser [desko'ser] *vt* to unstitch; ~**se** *vr* to come apart (at the seams).
descosido, a [desko'siðo, a] *adj* (*COSTURA*) unstitched; (*desordenado*) disjointed.
descrédito [des'kreðito] *nm* discredit.
descreído, a [deskre'iðo, a] *adj* (*incrédulo*) incredulous; (*falto de fe*) unbelieving.
descremado, a [deskre'maðo, a] *adj* skimmed.
describir [deskri'βir] *vt* to describe; **descripción** [deskrip'θjon] *nf* description.
descrito [des'krito] *pp de* **describir**.
descuartizar [deskwarti'θar] *vt* (*animal*) to cut up.
descubierto, a [desku'βjerto, a] *pp de* **descubrir** ♦ *adj* uncovered, bare; (*persona*) bareheaded ♦ *nm* (*bancario*) overdraft; **al** ~ in the open.
descubrimiento [deskuβri'mjento] *nm* (*hallazgo*) discovery; (*revelación*) revelation.
descubrir [desku'βrir] *vt* to discover, find; (*inaugurar*) to unveil; (*vislumbrar*) to detect; (*revelar*) to reveal, show; (*destapar*) to uncover; ~**se** *vr* to reveal o.s.; (*quitarse sombrero*) to take off one's hat; (*confesar*) to confess.

descuento *etc* [des'kwento] *vb ver* **descontar** ♦ *nm* discount.
descuidado, a [deskwi'ðaðo, a] *adj* (*sin cuidado*) careless; (*desordenado*) untidy; (*olvidadizo*) forgetful; (*dejado*) neglected; (*desprevenido*) unprepared.
descuidar [deskwi'ðar] *vt* (*dejar*) to neglect; (*olvidar*) to overlook ♦ *vi* (*distraerse*) to be careless; (*estar desaliñado*) to let o.s. go; (*desprevenirse*) to drop one's guard; ~**se** *vr* to be careless; to let o.s. go; to drop one's guard; ¡**descuida**! don't worry!; **descuido** *nm* (*dejadez*) carelessness; (*olvido*) negligence.

<hr>
PALABRA CLAVE
<hr>

desde ['desðe] *prep* **1** (*lugar*) from; ~ **Burgos hasta mi casa hay 30 km** it's 30 kms from Burgos to my house
2 (*posición*): **hablaba** ~ **el balcón** she was speaking from the balcony
3 (*tiempo*: +*ad, n*): ~ **ahora** from now on; ~ **la boda** since the wedding; ~ **niño** since I *etc* was a child; ~ **3 años atrás** since 3 years ago
4 (*tiempo*: +*vb*) since; for; **nos conocemos** ~ **1978/hace 20 años** we've known each other since 1978/for 20 years; **no le veo** ~ **1983/hace 5 años** I haven't seen him since 1983/for 5 years
5 (*gama*): ~ **los más lujosos hasta los más económicos** from the most luxurious to the most reasonably priced
6 ~ **luego** (**que**) of course (not)
♦ *conj*: ~ **que**: ~ **que recuerdo** for as long as I can remember; ~ **que llegó no ha salido** he hasn't been out since he arrived.

<hr>

desdecirse [desðe'θirse] *vr* to retract; ~ **de** to go back on.
desdén [des'ðen] *nm* scorn.
desdeñar [desðe'nar] *vt* (*despreciar*) to scorn.
desdicha [des'ðitʃa] *nf* (*desgracia*) misfortune; (*infelicidad*) unhappiness; **desdichado, a** *adj* (*sin suerte*) unlucky; (*infeliz*) unhappy.
desdoblar [desðo'βlar] *vt* (*extender*) to

spread out; (*desplegar*) to unfold.

desear [dese'ar] *vt* to want, desire, wish for.

desecar [dese'kar] *vt* to dry up; ~**se** *vr* to dry up.

desechar [dese't∫ar] *vt* (*basura*) to throw out *o* away; (*ideas*) to reject, discard; **desechos** *nmpl* rubbish *sg*, waste *sg*.

desembalar [desemba'lar] *vt* to unpack.

desembarazado, a [desembara'θaðo, a] *adj* (*libre*) clear, free; (*desenvuelto*) free and easy.

desembarazar [desembara'θar] *vt* (*desocupar*) to clear; (*desenredar*) to free; ~**se** *vr*: ~**se de** to free o.s. of, get rid of.

desembarcar [desembar'kar] *vt* (*mercancías etc*) to unload ♦ *vi* to disembark; ~**se** *vr* to disembark.

desembocadura [desemboka'ðura] *nf* (*de río*) mouth; (*de calle*) opening.

desembocar [desembo'kar] *vi* to flow into; (*fig*) to result in.

desembolso [desem'bolso] *nm* payment.

desembragar [desembra'xar] *vi* to declutch.

desemejanza [deseme'xanθa] *nf* dissimilarity.

desempatar [desempa'tar] *vi* to replay, hold a play-off; **desempate** *nm* (*FÚTBOL*) replay, play-off; (*TENIS*) tie-break(er).

desempeñar [desempe'ɲar] *vt* (*cargo*) to hold; (*papel*) to perform; (*lo empeñado*) to redeem; ~**se** *vr* to get out of debt; ~ **un papel** (*fig*) to play a role).

desempeño [desem'peɲo] *nm* redeeming; (*de cargo*) occupation.

desempleado, a [desemple'aðo, a] *nm/f* unemployed person; **desempleo** *nm* unemployment.

desempolvar [desempol'ßar] *vt* (*muebles etc*) to dust; (*lo olvidado*) to revive.

desencadenar [desenkaðe'nar] *vt* to unchain; (*ira*) to unleash; ~**se** *vr* to break loose; (*tormenta*) to burst; (*guerra*) to break out.

desencajar [desenka'xar] *vt* (*hueso*) to dislocate; (*mecanismo, pieza*) to disconnect, disengage.

desencanto [desen'kanto] *nm* disillusionment.

desenchufar [desent∫u'far] *vt* to unplug.

desenfadado, a [desenfa'ðaðo, a] *adj* (*desenvuelto*) uninhibited; (*descarado*) forward; **desenfado** *nm* (*libertad*) freedom; (*comportamiento*) free and easy manner; (*descaro*) forwardness.

desenfocado, a [desenfo'kaðo, a] *adj* (*FOTO*) out of focus.

desenfrenado, a [desenfre'naðo, a] *adj* (*descontrolado*) uncontrolled; (*inmoderado*) unbridled; **desenfreno** *nm* (*vicio*) wildness; (*de las pasiones*) lack of self-control.

desenganchar [desengan't∫ar] *vt* (*gen*) to unhook; (*FERRO*) to uncouple.

desengañar [desenga'ɲar] *vt* to disillusion; ~**se** *vr* to become disillusioned; **desengaño** *nm* disillusionment; (*decepción*) disappointment.

desenlace [desen'laθe] *nm* outcome.

desenmarañar [desenmara'ɲar] *vt* (*fig*) to unravel.

desenmascarar [desenmaska'rar] *vt* to unmask.

desenredar [desenre'ðar] *vt* (*pelo*) to untangle; (*problema*) to sort out.

desentenderse [desenten'derse] *vr*: ~ **de** to pretend not to know about; (*apartarse*) to have nothing to do with.

desenterrar [desente'rrar] *vt* to exhume; (*tesoro, fig*) to unearth, dig up.

desentonar [desento'nar] *vi* (*MUS*) to sing (*o* play) out of tune; (*color*) to clash.

desentrañar [desentra'ɲar] *vt* (*misterio*) to unravel.

desentumecer [desentume'θer] *vt* (*pierna etc*) to stretch; (*DEPORTE*) to loosen up.

desenvoltura [desenßol'tura] *nf* (*libertad, gracia*) ease; (*descaro*) free and easy manner.

desenvolver [desenßol'ßer] *vt* (*paquete*) to unwrap; (*fig*) to develop; ~**se** *vr* (*desarrollarse*) to unfold, develop;

(*arreglárselas*) to cope.

deseo [de'seo] *nm* desire, wish; ~**so, a** *adj*: estar ~**so de** to be anxious to.

desequilibrado, a [desekili'βraðo, a] *adj* unbalanced.

desertar [deser'tar] *vi* to desert.

desértico, a [de'sertiko, a] *adj* desert *cpd*.

desesperación [desespera'θjon] *nf* (*impaciencia*) desperation, despair; (*irritación*) fury.

desesperar [desespe'rar] *vt* to drive to despair; (*exasperar*) to drive to distraction ♦ *vi*: ~ **de** to despair of; ~**se** *vr* to despair, lose hope.

desestabilizar [desestaβili'θar] *vt* to destabilize.

desestimar [desesti'mar] *vt* (*menospreciar*) to have a low opinion of; (*rechazar*) to reject.

desfachatez [desfatʃa'teθ] *nf* (*insolencia*) impudence; (*descaro*) rudeness.

desfalco [des'falko] *nm* embezzlement.

desfallecer [desfaʎe'θer] *vi* (*perder las fuerzas*) to become weak; (*desvanecerse*) to faint.

desfasado, a [desfa'saðo, a] *adj* (*anticuado*) old-fashioned; **desfase** *nm* (*diferencia*) gap.

desfavorable [desfaβo'raβle] *adj* unfavourable.

desfigurar [desfiɣu'rar] *vt* (*cara*) to disfigure; (*cuerpo*) to deform.

desfiladero [desfila'ðero] *nm* gorge.

desfilar [desfi'lar] *vi* to parade; **desfile** *nm* procession.

desfogarse [desfo'ɣarse] *vr* (*fig*) to let off steam.

desgajar [desɣa'xar] *vt* (*arrancar*) to tear off; (*romper*) to break off; ~**se** *vr* to come off.

desgana [des'ɣana] *nf* (*falta de apetito*) loss of appetite; (*renuncia*) unwillingness; ~**do, a** *adj*: estar ~**do** (*sin apetito*) to have no appetite; (*sin entusiasmo*) to have lost interest.

desgarrador, a [desɣarra'ðor, a] *adj* (*fig*) heartrending.

desgarrar [desɣa'rrar] *vt* to tear (up);

(*fig*) to shatter; **desgarro** *nm* (*en tela*) tear; (*aflicción*) grief; (*descaro*) impudence.

desgastar [desɣas'tar] *vt* (*deteriorar*) to wear away *o* down; (*estropear*) to spoil; ~**se** *vr* to get worn out; **desgaste** *nm* wear (and tear).

desgracia [des'ɣraθja] *nf* misfortune; (*accidente*) accident; (*vergüenza*) disgrace; (*contratiempo*) setback; **por** ~ unfortunately.

desgraciado, a [desɣra'θjaðo, a] *adj* (*sin suerte*) unlucky, unfortunate; (*miserable*) wretched; (*infeliz*) miserable.

desgreñado, a [desɣre'ɲaðo, a] *adj* dishevelled.

deshabitado, a [desaβi'taðo, a] *adj* uninhabited.

deshacer [desa'θer] *vt* (*casa*) to break up; (*TEC*) to take apart; (*enemigo*) to defeat; (*diluir*) to melt; (*contrato*) to break; (*intriga*) to solve; ~**se** *vr* (*disolverse*) to melt; (*despedazarse*) to come apart *o* undone; ~**se de** to get rid of; ~**se en lágrimas** to burst into tears.

deshecho, a [des'etʃo, a] *adj* undone; (*roto*) smashed; (*persona*): estar ~ to be shattered.

desheredar [desere'ðar] *vt* to disinherit.

deshidratar [desiðra'tar] *vt* to dehydrate.

deshielo [des'jelo] *nm* thaw.

deshonesto, a [deso'nesto, a] *adj* indecent.

deshonra [des'onra] *nf* (*deshonor*) dishonour; (*vergüenza*) shame; **deshonrar** *vt* to dishonour.

deshora [des'ora] : **a** ~ *adv* at the wrong time.

deshuesar [deswe'sar] *vt* (*carne*) to bone; (*fruta*) to stone.

desierto, a [de'sjerto, a] *adj* (*casa, calle, negocio*) deserted ♦ *nm* desert.

designar [desiɣ'nar] *vt* (*nombrar*) to designate; (*indicar*) to fix.

designio [de'siɣnjo] *nm* plan.

desigual [desi'ɣwal] *adj* (*terreno*) uneven; (*lucha etc*) unequal.

desilusión [desilu'sjon] *nf* disillusionment; (*decepción*) disappointment;

desilusionar *vt* to disillusion; to disappoint; **desilusionarse** *vr* to become disillusioned.

desinfectar [desinfek'tar] *vt* to disinfect.

desinflar [desin'flar] *vt* to deflate.

desintegración [desinteɣra'θjon] *nf* disintegration.

desinterés [desinte'res] *nm* (*objetividad*) disinterestedness; (*altruismo*) unselfishness.

desistir [desis'tir] *vi* (*renunciar*) to stop, desist.

desleal [desle'al] *adj* (*infiel*) disloyal; (*COM*: *competencia*) unfair; ~**tad** *nf* disloyalty.

desleír [desle'ir] *vt* (*líquido*) to dilute; (*sólido*) to dissolve.

deslenguado, a [deslen'gwaðo, a] *adj* (*grosero*) foul-mouthed.

desligar [desli'ɣar] *vt* (*desatar*) to untie, undo; (*separar*) to separate; ~**se** *vr* (*de un compromiso*) to extricate o.s.

desliz [des'liθ] *nm* (*fig*) lapse; ~**ar** *vt* to slip, slide; ~**arse** *vr* (*escurrirse*: *persona*) to slip, slide; (*coche*) to skid; (*aguas mansas*) to flow gently; (*error*) to creep in.

deslucido, a [deslu'θiðo, a] *adj* dull; (*torpe*) awkward, graceless; (*deslustrado*) tarnished.

deslumbrar [deslum'brar] *vt* to dazzle.

desmán [des'man] *nm* (*exceso*) outrage; (*abuso de poder*) abuse.

desmandarse [desman'darse] *vr* (*portarse mal*) to behave badly; (*excederse*) to get out of hand; (*caballo*) to bolt.

desmantelar [desmante'lar] *vt* (*deshacer*) to dismantle; (*casa*) to strip.

desmaquillador [desmakiʎa'ðor] *nm* make-up remover.

desmayado, a [desma'jaðo, a] *adj* (*sin sentido*) unconscious; (*carácter*) dull; (*débil*) faint, weak.

desmayar [desma'jar] *vi* to lose heart; ~**se** *vr* (*MED*) to faint; **desmayo** *nm* (*MED*: *acto*) faint; (: *estado*) unconsciousness; (*depresión*) dejection.

desmedido, a [desme'ðiðo, a] *adj* excessive.

desmejorar [desmexo'rar] *vt* (*dañar*) to impair, spoil; (*MED*) to weaken.

desmembrar [desmem'brar] *vt* (*MED*) to dismember; (*fig*) to separate.

desmemoriado, a [desmemo'rjaðo, a] *adj* forgetful.

desmentir [desmen'tir] *vt* (*contradecir*) to contradict; (*refutar*) to deny ♦ *vi*: ~ **de** to refute; ~**se** *vr* to contradict o.s.

desmenuzar [desmenu'θar] *vt* (*deshacer*) to crumble; (*carne*) to chop; (*examinar*) to examine closely.

desmerecer [desmere'θer] *vt* to be unworthy of ♦ *vi* (*deteriorarse*) to deteriorate.

desmesurado, a [desmesu'raðo, a] *adj* disproportionate.

desmontar [desmon'tar] *vt* (*deshacer*) to dismantle; (*tierra*) to level ♦ *vi* to dismount.

desmoralizar [desmorali'θar] *vt* to demoralize.

desmoronar [desmoro'nar] *vt* to wear away, erode; ~**se** *vr* (*edificio, dique*) to fall into disrepair; (*economía*) to decline.

desnatado, a [desna'taðo, a] *adj* skimmed.

desnivel [desni'ßel] *nm* (*de terreno*) unevenness.

desnudar [desnu'ðar] *vt* (*desvestir*) to undress; (*despojar*) to strip; ~**se** *vr* (*desvestirse*) to get undressed; **desnudo, a** *adj* naked ♦ *nm/f* nude; **desnudo de** devoid o bereft of.

desnutrición [desnutri'θjon] *nf* malnutrition; **desnutrido, a** *adj* undernourished.

desobedecer [desoßeðe'θer] *vt*, *vi* to disobey; **desobediencia** *nf* disobedience.

desocupado, a [desoku'paðo, a] *adj* at leisure; (*desempleado*) unemployed; (*deshabitado*) empty, vacant.

desocupar [desoku'par] *vt* to vacate.

desodorante [desoðo'rante] *nm* deodorant.

desolación [desola'θjon] *nf* (*lugar*) desolation; (*fig*) grief.

desolar [deso'lar] *vt* to ruin, lay waste.

desorden [des'orðen] *nm* confusion; (*político*) disorder, unrest.

desorganizar [desorɣani'θar] *vt* (*desordenar*) to disorganize.

desorientar [desorjen'tar] *vt* (*extraviar*) to mislead; (*confundir, desconcertar*) to confuse; **~se** *vr* (*perderse*) to lose one's way.

desovar [deso'ßar] *vi* (*peces*) to spawn; (*insectos*) to lay eggs.

despabilado, a [despaßi'laðo, a] *adj* (*despierto*) wide-awake; (*fig*) alert, sharp.

despabilar [despaßi'lar] *vt* (*el ingenio*) to sharpen ♦ *vi* to wake up; (*fig*) to get a move on; **~se** *vr* to wake up; to get a move on.

despacio [des'paθjo] *adv* slowly.

despachar [despa'tʃar] *vt* (*negocio*) to do, complete; (*enviar*) to send, dispatch; (*vender*) to sell, deal in; (*billete*) to issue; (*mandar ir*) to send away.

despacho [des'patʃo] *nm* (*oficina*) office; (*de paquetes*) dispatch; (*venta*) sale; (*comunicación*) message.

desparpajo [despar'paxo] *nm* self-confidence; (*pey*) nerve.

desparramar [desparra'mar] *vt* (*esparcir*) to scatter; (*líquido*) to spill.

despavorido, a [despaßo'riðo, a] *adj* terrified.

despectivo, a [despek'tißo, a] *adj* (*despreciativo*) derogatory; (*LING*) pejorative.

despecho [des'petʃo] *nm* spite; **a ~ de** in spite of.

despedazar [despeða'θar] *vt* to tear to pieces.

despedida [despe'ðiða] *nf* (*adiós*) farewell; (*de obrero*) sacking.

despedir [despe'ðir] *vt* (*visita*) to see off, show out; (*empleado*) to dismiss; (*inquilino*) to evict; (*objeto*) to hurl; (*olor etc*) to give out *o* off; **~se** *vr*: **~se de** to say goodbye to.

despegar [despe'ɣar] *vt* to unstick ♦ *vi* (*avión*) to take off; **~se** *vr* to come loose, come unstuck; **despego** *nm* detachment.

despegue *etc* [des'peɣe] *vb ver* **despegar** ♦ *nm* takeoff.

despeinado, a [despei'naðo, a] *adj* dishevelled, unkempt.

despejado, a [despe'xaðo, a] *adj* (*lugar*) clear, free; (*cielo*) clear; (*persona*) wide-awake, bright.

despejar [despe'xar] *vt* (*gen*) to clear; (*misterio*) to clear up ♦ *vi* (*el tiempo*) to clear; **~se** *vr* (*tiempo, cielo*) to clear (up); (*misterio*) to become clearer; (*cabeza*) to clear.

despellejar [despeʎe'xar] *vt* (*animal*) to skin.

despensa [des'pensa] *nf* larder.

despeñadero [despeɲa'ðero] *nm* (*GEO*) cliff, precipice.

desperdicio [desper'ðiθjo] *nm* (*despilfarro*) squandering; **~s** *nmpl* (*basura*) rubbish *sg* (*BRIT*), garbage *sg* (*US*); (*residuos*) waste *sg*.

desperezarse [despere'θarse] *vr* to stretch.

desperfecto [desper'fekto] *nm* (*deterioro*) slight damage; (*defecto*) flaw, imperfection.

despertador [desperta'ðor] *nm* alarm clock.

despertar [desper'tar] *nm* awakening ♦ *vt* (*persona*) to wake up; (*recuerdos*) to revive; (*sentimiento*) to arouse ♦ *vi* to awaken, wake up; **~se** *vr* to awaken, wake up.

despiadado, a [despja'ðaðo, a] *adj* (*ataque*) merciless; (*persona*) heartless.

despido *etc* [des'piðo] *vb ver* **despedir** ♦ *nm* dismissal, sacking.

despierto, a *etc* [des'pjerto, a] *vb ver* **despertar** ♦ *adj* awake; (*fig*) sharp, alert.

despilfarro [despil'farro] *nm* (*derroche*) squandering; (*lujo desmedido*) extravagance.

despistar [despis'tar] *vt* to throw off the track *o* scent; (*fig*) to mislead, confuse; **~se** *vr* to take the wrong road; (*fig*) to become confused.

desplazamiento [desplaθa'mjento] *nm* displacement.

desplazar [despla'θar] *vt* to move; (*NAUT*) to displace; (*INFORM*) to scroll; (*fig*) to oust; ~**se** *vr* (*persona*) to travel.

desplegar [desple'ɣar] *vt* (*tela, papel*) to unfold, open out; (*bandera*) to unfurl; **despliegue** *etc* [des'pleɣe] *vb ver* **desplegar ♦** *nm* display.

desplomarse [desplo'marse] *vr* (*edificio, gobierno, persona*) to collapse.

desplumar [desplu'mar] *vt* (*ave*) to pluck; (*fam: estafar*) to fleece.

despoblado, a [despo'βlaðo, a] *adj* (*sin habitantes*) uninhabited.

despojar [despo'xar] *vt* (*alguien: de sus bienes*) to divest of, deprive of; (*casa*) to strip, leave bare; (*alguien: de su cargo*) to strip of.

despojo [des'poxo] *nm* (*acto*) plundering; (*objetos*) plunder, loot; ~**s** *nmpl* (*de ave, res*) offal *sg*.

desposado, a [despo'saðo, a] *adj, nm/f* newly-wed.

desposeer [despose'er] *vt*: ~ **a uno de** (*puesto, autoridad*) to strip sb of.

déspota ['despota] *nm/f* despot.

despreciar [despre'θjar] *vt* (*desdeñar*) to despise, scorn; (*afrentar*) to slight; **desprecio** *nm* scorn, contempt; slight.

desprender [despren'der] *vt* (*broche*) to unfasten; (*olor*) to give off; ~**se** *vr* (*botón: caerse*) to fall off; (*broche*) to come unfastened; (*olor, perfume*) to be given off; ~**se de algo que** ... to draw from sth that ....

desprendimiento [desprendi'mjento] *nm* (*gen*) loosening; (*generosidad*) disinterestedness; (*indiferencia*) detachment; (*de gas*) leak; (*de tierra, rocas*) landslide.

despreocupado, a [despreoku'paðo, a] *adj* (*sin preocupación*) unworried, nonchalant; (*negligente*) careless.

despreocuparse [despreoku'parse] *vr* not to worry; ~ **de** to have no interest in.

desprestigiar [despresti'xjar] *vt* (*criticar*) to run down; (*desacreditar*) to discredit.

desprevenido, a [despreβe'niðo, a] *adj* (*no preparado*) unprepared, unready.

desproporcionado, a [desproporθjo-'naðo, a] *adj* disproportionate, out of proportion.

después [des'pwes] *adv* afterwards, later; (*próximo paso*) next; ~ **de comer** after lunch; **un año** ~ a year later; ~ **se debatió el tema** next the matter was discussed; ~ **de corregido el texto** after the text had been corrected; ~ **de todo** after all.

desquite [des'kite] *nm* (*satisfacción*) satisfaction; (*venganza*) revenge.

destacar [desta'kar] *vt* to emphasize, point up; (*MIL*) to detach, detail **♦** *vi* (*resaltarse*) to stand out; (*persona*) to be outstanding *o* exceptional; ~**se** *vr* to stand out; to be outstanding *o* exceptional.

destajo [des'taxo] *nm*: **trabajar a** ~ to do piecework.

destapar [desta'par] *vt* (*botella*) to open; (*cacerola*) to take the lid off; (*descubrir*) to uncover; ~**se** *vr* (*revelarse*) to reveal one's true character.

destartalado, a [destarta'laðo, a] *adj* (*desordenado*) untidy; (*ruinoso*) tumbledown.

destello [des'teʎo] *nm* (*de estrella*) twinkle; (*de faro*) signal light.

destemplado, a [destem'plaðo, a] *adj* (*MUS*) out of tune; (*voz*) harsh; (*MED*) out of sorts; (*tiempo*) unpleasant, nasty.

desteñir [deste'ɲir] *vt* to fade **♦** *vi* to fade; ~**se** *vr* to fade; **esta tela no destiñe** this fabric will not run.

desternillarse [desterni'ʎarse] *vr*: ~ **de risa** to split one's sides laughing.

desterrar [deste'rrar] *vt* (*exilar*) to exile; (*fig*) to banish, dismiss.

destetar [deste'tar] *vt* to wean.

destierro *etc* [des'tjerro] *vb ver* **desterrar ♦** *nm* exile.

destilar [desti'lar] *vt* to distil; **destilería** *nf* distillery.

destinar [desti'nar] *vt* (*funcionario*) to appoint, assign; (*fondos*): ~ **(a)** to set aside (for).

destinatario, a [destina'tarjo, a] *nm/f*

addressee.

destino [des'tino] *nm* (*suerte*) destiny; (*de avión, viajero*) destination.

destituir [destitu'ir] *vt* to dismiss.

destornillador [destorniʎa'ðor] *nm* screwdriver.

destornillar [destorni'ʎar] *vt* (*tornillo*) to unscrew; ~**se** *vr* to unscrew.

destreza [des'treθa] *nf* (*habilidad*) skill; (*maña*) dexterity.

destrozar [destro'θar] *vt* (*romper*) to smash, break (up); (*estropear*) to ruin; (*nervios*) to shatter.

destrozo [des'troθo] *nm* (*acción*) destruction; (*desastre*) smashing; ~**s** *nmpl* (*pedazos*) pieces; (*daños*) havoc *sg*.

destrucción [destruk'θjon] *nf* destruction.

destruir [destru'ir] *vt* to destroy.

desuso [des'uso] *nm* disuse; **caer en ~** to become obsolete.

desvalido, a [desβa'liðo, a] *adj* (*desprotegido*) destitute; (*sin fuerzas*) helpless.

desvalijar [desvali'xar] *vt* (*persona*) to rob; (*casa, tienda*) to burgle; (*coche*) to break into.

desván [des'βan] *nm* attic.

desvanecer [desβane'θer] *vt* (*disipar*) to dispel; (*borrar*) to blur; ~**se** *vr* (*humo etc*) to vanish, disappear; (*color*) to fade; (*recuerdo, sonido*) to fade away; (*MED*) to pass out; (*duda*) to be dispelled.

desvanecimiento [desβaneθi'mjento] *nm* (*desaparición*) disappearance; (*de colores*) fading; (*evaporación*) evaporation; (*MED*) fainting fit.

desvariar [desβa'rjar] *vi* (*enfermo*) to be delirious; **desvarío** *nm* delirium.

desvelar [desβe'lar] *vt* to keep awake; ~**se** *vr* (*no poder dormir*) to stay awake; (*vigilar*) to be vigilant *o* watchful.

desvencijado, a [desβenθi'xaðo, a] *adj* (*silla*) rickety; (*máquina*) broken-down.

desventaja [desβen'taxa] *nf* disadvantage.

desventura [desβen'tura] *nf* misfortune.

desvergonzado, a [desβerɣon'θaðo, a] *adj* shameless.

desvergüenza [desβer'ɣwenθa] *nf* (*descaro*) shamelessness; (*insolencia*) impudence; (*mala conducta*) effrontery.

desvestir [desβes'tir] *vt* to undress; ~**se** *vr* to undress.

desviación [desβja'θjon] *nf* deviation; (*AUTO*) diversion, detour.

desviar [des'βjar] *vt* to turn aside; (*río*) to alter the course of; (*navío*) to divert, re-route; (*conversación*) to sidetrack; ~**se** *vr* (*apartarse del camino*) to turn aside; (: *barco*) to go off course.

desvío *etc* [des'βio] *vb ver* **desviar** ♦ *nm* (*desviación*) detour, diversion; (*fig*) indifference.

desvirtuar [desβir'twar] *vt* to spoil; ~**se** *vr* to spoil.

desvivirse [desβi'βirse] *vr*: ~ **por** (*anhelar*) to long for, crave for; (*hacer lo posible por*) to do one's utmost for.

detallar [deta'ʎar] *vt* to detail.

detalle [de'taʎe] *nm* detail; (*fig*) gesture, token; **al ~** in detail; (*COM*) retail.

detallista [deta'ʎista] *nm/f* retailer.

detener [dete'ner] *vt* (*gen*) to stop; (*JUR*) to arrest; (*objeto*) to keep; ~**se** *vr* to stop; (*demorarse*): ~**se en** to delay over, linger over.

detenidamente [deteniða'mente] *adv* (*minuciosamente*) carefully; (*extensamente*) at great length.

detenido, a [dete'niðo, a] *adj* (*arrestado*) under arrest; (*minucioso*) detailed ♦ *nm/f* person under arrest, prisoner.

detergente [deter'xente] *nm* detergent.

deteriorar [deterjo'rar] *vt* to spoil, damage; ~**se** *vr* to deteriorate; **deterioro** *nm* deterioration.

determinación [determina'θjon] *nf* (*empeño*) determination; (*decisión*) decision.

determinar [determi'nar] *vt* (*plazo*) to fix; (*precio*) to settle; ~**se** *vr* to decide.

detestar [detes'tar] *vt* to detest.

detonar [deto'nar] *vi* to detonate.

detrás [de'tras] *adv* behind; (*atrás*) at the back; ~ **de** behind.

detrimento [detri'mento] *nm*: **en** ~ **de** to the detriment of.

deuda ['deuða] *nf* (*condición*) indebtedness, debt; (*cantidad*) debt.

deudor, a [deu'ðor, a] *nm/f* debtor.

devaluación [deßalwa'θjon] *nf* devaluation.

devastar [deßas'tar] *vt* (*destruir*) to devastate.

devengar [deßen'gar] *vt* (*COM*) to accrue, earn.

devoción [deßo'θjon] *nf* devotion.

devolución [deßolu'θjon] *nf* (*reenvío*) return, sending back; (*reembolso*) repayment; (*JUR*) devolution.

devolver [deßol'ßer] *vt* to return; (*lo extraviado, lo prestado*) to give back; (*carta al correo*) to send back; (*COM*) to repay, refund; (*lo prestado*) to give back ♦ *vi* (*vomitar*) to be sick.

devorar [deßo'rar] *vt* to devour.

devoto, a [de'ßoto, a] *adj* devout ♦ *nm/f* admirer.

devuelto *pp de* **devolver.**

devuelva *etc vb ver* **devolver.**

di *vb ver* **dar; decir.**

día ['dia] *nm* day; ¿**qué** ~ **es?** what's the date?; **estar/poner al** ~ to be/keep up to date; **el** ~ **de hoy/de mañana** today/tomorrow; **al** ~ **siguiente** (on) the following day; **vivir al** ~ to live from hand to mouth; **de** ~ by day, in daylight; **en pleno** ~ in full daylight; ~ **festivo** (*ESP*) *o* **feriado** (*AM*) holiday; ~ **libre** day off.

diablo ['djaßlo] *nm* devil; **diablura** *nf* prank.

diafragma [dja'fraɣma] *nm* diaphragm.

diagnosis [djaɣ'nosis] *nf inv* diagnosis.

diagnóstico [djaɣ'nostiko] *nm* = **diagnosis.**

diagrama [dja'ɣrama] *nm* diagram; ~ **de flujo** flowchart.

dialecto [dja'lekto] *nm* dialect.

dialogar [djalo'xar] *vi*: ~ **con** (*POL*) to hold talks with.

diálogo ['djaloɣo] *nm* dialogue.

diamante [dja'mante] *nm* diamond.

diana ['djana] *nf* (*MIL*) reveille; (*de blanco*) centre, bull's-eye.

diapositiva [djaposi'tißa] *nf* (*FOTO*) slide, transparency.

diario, a ['djarjo, a] *adj* daily ♦ *nm* newspaper; **a** ~ daily; **de** ~ everyday.

diarrea [dja'rrea] *nf* diarrhoea.

dibujar [dißu'xar] *vt* to draw, sketch; **dibujo** *nm* drawing; **dibujos animados** cartoons.

diccionario [dikθjo'narjo] *nm* dictionary.

dice *etc vb ver* **decir.**

diciembre [di'θjembre] *nm* December.

dictado [dik'taðo] *nm* dictation.

dictador [dikta'ðor] *nm* dictator; **dictadura** *nf* dictatorship.

dictamen [dik'tamen] *nm* (*opinión*) opinion; (*juicio*) judgment; (*informe*) report.

dictar [dik'tar] *vt* (*carta*) to dictate; (*JUR: sentencia*) to pronounce; (*decreto*) to issue; (*AM: clase*) to give.

dicho, a ['ditʃo, a] *pp de* **decir** ♦ *adj*: **en** ~**s países** in the aforementioned countries ♦ *nm* saying.

diecinueve [djeθi'nweße] *num* nineteen.

dieciocho [djeθi'otʃo] *num* eighteen.

dieciséis [djeθi'seis] *num* sixteen.

diecisiete [djeθi'sjete] *num* seventeen.

diente ['djente] *nm* (*ANAT, TEC*) tooth; (*ZOOL*) fang; (: *de elefante*) tusk; (*de ajo*) clove; **hablar entre** ~**s** to mutter, mumble.

diera *etc vb ver* **dar.**

diesel ['disel] *adj*: **motor** ~ diesel engine.

dieta ['djeta] *nf* diet.

diez [djeθ] *num* ten.

difamar [difa'mar] *vt* (*JUR: hablando*) to slander; (: *por escrito*) to libel.

diferencia [dife'renθja] *nf* difference; **diferenciar** *vt* to differentiate between ♦ *vi* to differ; **diferenciarse** *vr* to differ, be different; (*distinguirse*) to distinguish o.s.

diferente [dife'rente] *adj* different.

diferido [dife'riðo] *nm*: **en** ~ (*TV etc*) recorded.

difícil [di'fiθil] *adj* difficult.

dificultad [difikul'tað] *nf* difficulty;

(*problema*) trouble; (*objeción*) objection.

dificultar [difikul'tar] *vt* (*complicar*) to complicate, make difficult; (*estorbar*) to obstruct.

difundir [difun'dir] *vt* (*calor*, *luz*) to diffuse; (*RADIO*, *TV*) to broadcast; ~ **una noticia** to spread a piece of news; ~**se** *vr* to spread (out).

difunto, a [di'funto, a] *adj* dead, deceased ♦ *nm/f* deceased (person).

diga *etc vb ver* **decir**.

digerir [dixe'rir] *vt* to digest; (*fig*) to absorb.

digital [dixi'tal] *adj* (*INFORM*) digital.

dignarse [dix'narse] *vr* to deign to.

dignidad [dixni'ðað] *nf* dignity.

digno, a ['dixno, a] *adj* worthy.

digo *etc vb ver* **decir**.

dije *etc vb ver* **decir**.

dilatado, a [dila'taðo, a] *adj* dilated; (*período*) long drawn-out; (*extenso*) extensive.

dilatar [dila'tar] *vt* (*cuerpo*) to dilate; (*prolongar*) to prolong; (*aplazar*) to delay.

dilema [di'lema] *nm* dilemma.

diligencia [dili'xenθja] *nf* diligence; (*ocupación*) errand, job; ~**s** *nfpl* (*JUR*) formalities; **diligente** *adj* diligent.

diluir [dilu'ir] *vt* to dilute.

diluvio [di'lußjo] *nm* deluge, flood.

dimensión [dimen'sjon] *nf* dimension.

diminuto, a [dimi'nuto, a] *adj* tiny, diminutive.

dimitir [dimi'tir] *vi* to resign.

dimos *vb ver* **dar**.

Dinamarca [dina'marka] *nf* Denmark; **dinamarqués, esa** *adj* Danish ♦ *nm/f* Dane.

dinámico, a [di'namiko, a] *adj* dynamic.

dinamita [dina'mita] *nf* dynamite.

dínamo ['dinamo] *nf* dynamo.

dineral [dine'ral] *nm* large sum of money, fortune.

dinero [di'nero] *nm* money; ~ **contante**, ~ **efectivo** (ready) cash.

dio *vb ver* **dar**.

dios [djos] *nm* god; ¡**D**~ **mío!** (oh,) my God!

diosa ['djosa] *nf* goddess.

diploma [di'ploma] *nm* diploma.

diplomacia [diplo'maθja] *nf* diplomacy; (*fig*) tact.

diplomado, a [diplo'maðo, a] *adj* qualified.

diplomático, a [diplo'matiko, a] *adj* diplomatic ♦ *nm/f* diplomat.

diputado, a [dipu'taðo, a] *nm/f* delegate; (*POL*) ≈ member of parliament (*BRIT*), ≈ representative (*US*).

dique ['dike] *nm* dyke.

diré *etc vb ver* **decir**.

dirección [direk'θjon] *nf* direction; (*señas*) address; (*AUTO*) steering; (*gerencia*) management; (*POL*) leadership; ~ **única/prohibida** one-way street/no entry.

directo, a [di'rekto, a] *adj* direct; (*RADIO*, *TV*) live; **transmitir en** ~ to broadcast live.

director, a [direk'tor, a] *adj* leading ♦ *nm/f* director; (*ESCOL*) head(teacher) (*BRIT*), principal (*US*); (*gerente*) manager(ess); (*PRENSA*) editor; ~ **de cine** film director; ~ **general** managing director.

dirigir [diri'xir] *vt* to direct; (*carta*) to address; (*obra de teatro*, *film*) to direct; (*MUS*) to conduct; (*comercio*) to manage; ~**se** *vr*: ~**se a** to go towards, make one's way towards; (*hablar con*) to speak to.

dirija *etc vb ver* **dirigir**.

discernir [disθer'nir] *vt* (*distinguir*, *discriminar*) to discern.

disciplina [disθi'plina] *nf* discipline.

discípulo, a [dis'θipulo, a] *nm/f* disciple.

disco ['disko] *nm* disc; (*DEPORTE*) discus; (*TEL*) dial; (*AUTO*: *semáforo*) light; (*MUS*) record; (*INFORM*): ~ **flexible/rígido** floppy/hard disk; ~ **compacto/de larga duración** compact disc/long-playing record; ~ **de freno** brake disc.

disconforme [diskon'forme] *adj* differing; **estar** ~ (**con**) to be in disagreement (with).

discordia [dis'korðja] *nf* discord.

discoteca [disko'teka] *nf* disco(theque).

discreción [diskre'θjon] *nf* discretion; (*reserva*) prudence; **comer a ~** to eat as much as one wishes; **discrecional** *adj* (*facultativo*) discretionary.

discrepancia [diskre'panθja] *nf* (*diferencia*) discrepancy; (*desacuerdo*) disagreement.

discreto, a [dis'kreto, a] *adj* (*diplomático*) discreet; (*sensato*) sensible; (*reservado*) quiet; (*sobrio*) sober.

discriminación [diskrimina'θjon] *nf* discrimination.

disculpa [dis'kulpa] *nf* excuse; (*pedir perdón*) apology; **pedir ~s a/por** to apologize to/for; **disculpar** *vt* to excuse, pardon; **disculparse** *vr* to excuse o.s.; to apologize.

discurrir [disku'rrir] *vi* (*pensar, reflexionar*) to think, meditate; (*recorrer*) to roam, wander; (*el tiempo*) to pass, go by.

discurso [dis'kurso] *nm* speech.

discutir [disku'tir] *vt* (*debatir*) to discuss; (*pelear*) to argue about; (*contradecir*) to argue against ♦ *vi* to discuss; (*disputar*) to argue.

disecar [dise'kar] *vt* (*conservar: animal*) to stuff; (: *planta*) to dry.

diseminar [disemi'nar] *vt* to disseminate, spread.

diseño [di'seɲo] *nm* design; (*ARTE*) drawing.

disfraz [dis'fraθ] *nm* (*máscara*) disguise; (*excusa*) pretext; **~ar** *vt* to disguise; **~arse** *vr*: **~arse de** to disguise o.s. as.

disfrutar [disfru'tar] *vt* to enjoy ♦ *vi* to enjoy o.s.; **~ de** to enjoy, possess.

disgustar [disɣus'tar] *vt* (*no gustar*) to displease; (*contrariar, enojar*) to annoy, upset; **~se** *vr* to be annoyed; (*dos personas*) to fall out.

disgusto [dis'ɣusto] *nm* (*repugnancia*) disgust; (*contrariedad*) annoyance; (*tristeza*) grief; (*riña*) quarrel; (*avería*) misfortune.

disidente [disi'ðente] *nm* dissident.

disimular [disimu'lar] *vt* (*ocultar*) to hide, conceal ♦ *vi* to dissemble.

disipar [disi'par] *vt* to dispel; (*fortuna*)

to squander; **~se** *vr* (*nubes*) to vanish; (*indisciplinarse*) to dissipate.

disminución [disminu'θjon] *nf* decrease, reduction.

disminuir [disminu'ir] *vt* to decrease, diminish.

disolver [disol'ßer] *vt* (*gen*) to dissolve; **~se** *vr* to dissolve; (*COM*) to go into liquidation.

disparar [dispa'rar] *vt, vi* to shoot, fire.

disparate [dispa'rate] *nm* (*tontería*) foolish remark; (*error*) blunder; **decir ~s** to talk nonsense.

disparo [dis'paro] *nm* shot.

dispensar [dispen'sar] *vt* to dispense; (*disculpar*) to excuse.

dispersar [disper'sar] *vt* to disperse; **~se** *vr* to scatter.

disponer [dispo'ner] *vt* (*arreglar*) to arrange; (*ordenar*) to put in order; (*preparar*) to prepare, get ready ♦ *vi*: **~ de** to have, own; **~se** *vr*: **~se a** o **para hacer** to prepare to do.

disponible [dispo'nißle] *adj* available.

disposición [disposi'θjon] *nf* arrangement, disposition; (*aptitud*) aptitude; (*INFORM*) layout; **a la ~ de** at the disposal of.

dispositivo [disposi'tißo] *nm* device, mechanism.

dispuesto, a [dis'pwesto, a] *pp de* **disponer** ♦ *adj* (*arreglado*) arranged; (*preparado*) disposed.

disputar [dispu'tar] *vt* (*discutir*) to dispute, question; (*contender*) to contend for ♦ *vi* to argue.

disquete [dis'kete] *nm* floppy disk, diskette.

distancia [dis'tanθja] *nf* distance.

distanciar [distan'θjar] *vt* to space out; **~se** *vr* to become estranged.

distante [dis'tante] *adj* distant.

diste *vb ver* **dar**.

distinción [distin'θjon] *nf* distinction; (*elegancia*) elegance; (*honor*) honour.

distinguido, a [distin'ɣiðo, a] *adj* distinguished.

distinguir [distin'gir] *vt* to distinguish; (*escoger*) to single out; **~se** *vr* to be distinguished.

distinto, a [dis'tinto, a] *adj* different; (*claro*) clear.

distracción [distrak'θjon] *nf* distraction; (*pasatiempo*) hobby, pastime; (*olvido*) absent-mindedness, distraction.

distraer [distra'er] *vt* (*atención*) to distract; (*divertir*) to amuse; (*fondos*) to embezzle; ~**se** *vr* (*entretenerse*) to amuse o.s.; (*perder la concentración*) to allow one's attention to wander.

distraído, a [distra'iðo, a] *adj* (*gen*) absent-minded; (*entretenido*) amusing.

distribuir [distriβu'ir] *vt* to distribute.

distrito [dis'trito] *nm* (*sector, territorio*) region; (*barrio*) district.

disturbio [dis'turβjo] *nm* disturbance; (*desorden*) riot.

disuadir [diswa'ðir] *vt* to dissuade.

disuelto [di'swelto] *pp de* **disolver.**

DIU *nm abr* (= *dispositivo intrauterino*) IUD.

diurno, a ['djurno, a] *adj* day *cpd*.

divagar [diβa'var] *vi* (*desviarse*) to digress.

diván [di'βan] *nm* divan.

divergencia [diβer'xenθja] *nf* divergence.

diversidad [diβersi'ðað] *nf* diversity, variety.

diversificar [diβersifi'kar] *vt* to diversify.

diversión [diβer'sjon] *nf* (*gen*) entertainment; (*actividad*) hobby, pastime.

diverso, a [di'βerso, a] *adj* diverse; ~**s** *nmpl* sundries; ~**s libros** several books.

divertido, a [diβer'tiðo, a] *adj* (*chiste*) amusing; (*fiesta etc*) enjoyable.

divertir [diβer'tir] *vt* (*entretener, recrear*) to amuse; ~**se** *vr* (*pasarlo bien*) to have a good time; (*distraerse*) to amuse o.s.

dividir [diβi'ðir] *vt* (*gen*) to divide; (*separar*) to separate; (*distribuir*) to distribute, share out.

divierta *etc vb ver* **divertir.**

divino, a [di'βino, a] *adj* divine.

divirtiendo *etc vb ver* **divertir.**

divisa [di'βisa] *nf* (*emblema, moneda*) emblem, badge; ~**s** *nfpl* foreign exchange *sg*.

divisar [diβi'sar] *vt* to make out, distinguish.

división [diβi'sjon] *nf* (*gen*) division; (*de partido*) split; (*de país*) partition.

divorciar [diβor'θjar] *vt* to divorce; ~**se** *vr* to get divorced; **divorcio** *nm* divorce.

divulgar [diβul'var] *vt* (*desparramar*) to spread; (*hacer circular*) to divulge, circulate; ~**se** *vr* to leak out.

DNI (*ESP*) *nm abr* (= *Documento Nacional de Identidad*) *national identity card*.

dobladillo [doβla'ðiʎo] *nm* (*de vestido*) hem; (*de pantalón: vuelta*) turn-up (*BRIT*), cuff (*US*).

doblar [do'βlar] *vt* to double; (*papel*) to fold; (*caño*) to bend; (*la esquina*) to turn, go round; (*film*) to dub ♦ *vi* to turn; (*campana*) to toll; ~**se** *vr* (*plegarse*) to fold (up), crease; (*encorvarse*) to bend.

doble ['doβle] *adj* double; (*fig*) double; (*de dos aspectos*) dual; (*fig*) two-faced ♦ *nm* double ♦ *nm/f* (*TEATRO*) double, standing; ~**s** *nmpl* (*DEPORTE*) doubles *sg*; **con sentido** ~ with a double meaning.

doblegar [doβle'var] *vt* to fold, crease; ~**se** *vr* to yield.

doce ['doθe] *num* twelve; ~**na** *nf* dozen.

docente [do'θente] *adj*: **centro/personal** ~ teaching establishment/staff.

dócil ['doθil] *adj* (*pasivo*) docile; (*obediente*) obedient.

doctor, a [dok'tor, a] *nm/f* doctor.

doctrina [dok'trina] *nf* doctrine, teaching.

documentación [dokumenta'θjon] *nf* documentation, papers *pl*.

documental [dokumen'tal] *adj, nm* documentary.

documento [doku'mento] *nm* (*certificado*) document.

dólar ['dolar] *nm* dollar.

doler [do'ler] *vt, vi* to hurt; (*fig*) to grieve; ~**se** *vr* (*de su situación*) to grieve, feel sorry; (*de las desgracias ajenas*) to sympathize; **me duele el brazo** my arm hurts.

dolor [do'lor] *nm* pain; (*fig*) grief, sorrow; ~ **de cabeza** headache; ~ **de**

estómago stomachache.

domar [do'mar] *vt* to tame.

domesticar [domesti'kar] *vt* = **domar**.

domiciliación [domiθilia'θjon] *nf*: ~ de pagos (*COM*) standing order.

domicilio [domi'θiljo] *nm* home; ~ particular private residence; ~ social (*COM*) head office; sin ~ fijo of no fixed abode.

dominante [domi'nante] *adj* dominant; (*persona*) domineering.

dominar [domi'nar] *vt* (*gen*) to dominate; (*idiomas*) to be fluent in ♦ *vi* to dominate, prevail; ~se *vr* to control o.s.

domingo [do'mingo] *nm* Sunday.

dominio [do'minjo] *nm* (*tierras*) domain; (*autoridad*) power, authority; (*de las pasiones*) grip, hold; (*de idiomas*) command.

don [don] *nm* (*talento*) gift; ~ Juan Gómez Mr Juan Gomez o Juan Gomez Esq.

donaire [do'naire] *nm* charm.

donar [do'nar] *vt* to donate.

doncella [don'θeʎa] *nf* (*criada*) maid.

donde ['donde] *adv* where ♦ *prep*: el coche está allí ~ el farol the car is over there by the lamppost o where the lamppost is; por ~ through which; en ~ where, in which.

dónde ['donde] *adv interrogativo* where?; ¿a ~ vas? where are you going (to)?; ¿de ~ vienes? where have you come from?; ¿por ~? where?, whereabouts?

dondequiera [donde'kjera] *adv* anywhere; por ~ everywhere, all over the place ♦ *conj*: ~ que wherever.

doña ['doɲa] *nf*: ~ Alicia Alicia; ~ Victoria Benito Mrs Victoria Benito.

dorado, a [do'raðo, a] *adj* (*color*) golden; (*TEC*) gilt.

dormir [dor'mir] *vt*: ~ la siesta por la tarde to have an afternoon nap ♦ *vi* to sleep; ~se *vr* to fall asleep.

dormitar [dormi'tar] *vi* to doze.

dormitorio [dormi'torjo] *nm* bedroom; ~ común dormitory.

dorsal [dor'sal] *nm* (*DEPORTE*) number.

dos [dos] *num* two.

dosis ['dosis] *nf inv* dose, dosage.

dotado, a [do'taðo, a] *adj* gifted; ~ de endowed with.

dotar [do'tar] *vt* to endow; **dote** *nf* dowry; **dotes** *nfpl* (*talentos*) gifts.

doy *vb ver* dar.

drama ['drama] *nm* drama.

dramaturgo [drama'turɣo] *nm* dramatist, playwright.

droga ['droɣa] *nf* drug.

drogadicto, a [droɣa'ðikto, a] *nm/f* drug addict.

droguería [droɣe'ria] *nf* hardware shop (*BRIT*) o store (*US*).

ducha ['dutʃa] *nf* (*baño*) shower; (*MED*) douche; **ducharse** *vr* to take a shower.

duda ['duða] *nf* doubt; **dudar** *vt*, *vi* to doubt; **dudoso, a** [du'ðoso, a] *adj* (*incierto*) hesitant; (*sospechoso*) doubtful.

duela *etc vb ver* **doler**.

duelo ['dwelo] *vb ver* **doler** ♦ *nm* (*combate*) duel; (*luto*) mourning.

duende ['dwende] *nm* imp, goblin.

dueño, a ['dweɲo, a] *nm/f* (*propietario*) owner; (*de pensión, taberna*) landlord/lady; (*empresario*) employer.

duermo *etc vb ver* **dormir**.

dulce ['dulθe] *adj* sweet ♦ *adv* gently, softly ♦ *nm* sweet; ~ría (*AM*) *nf* confectioner's.

dulzura [dul'θura] *nf* sweetness; (*ternura*) gentleness.

duplicar [dupli'kar] *vt* (*hacer el doble de*) to duplicate; ~se *vr* to double.

duque ['duke] *nm* duke; ~sa *nf* duchess.

duración [dura'θjon] *nf* (*de película, disco etc*) length; (*de pila etc*) life; (*curso: de acontecimientos etc*) duration.

duradero, a [dura'ðero, a] *adj* (*tela etc*) hard-wearing; (*fe, paz*) lasting.

durante [du'rante] *prep* during.

durar [du'rar] *vi* (*permanecer*) to last; (*recuerdo*) to remain.

durazno [du'raθno] (*AM*) *nm* (*fruta*) peach; (*árbol*) peach tree.

durex ['dureks] (*AM*) *nm* (*tira adhesiva*) Sellotape ® (*BRIT*), Scotch tape ® (*US*).

dureza [du'reθa] *nf* (*calidad*) hardness.
durmiente [dur'mjente] *nm/f* sleeper.
duro, a ['duro, a] *adj* hard; (*carácter*) tough ♦ *adv* hard ♦ *nm* (*moneda*) five peseta coin *o* piece.

E

e [e] *conj* and.
E *abr* (= *este*) E.
ebanista [eβa'nista] *nm/f* cabinetmaker.
ébano ['eβano] *nm* ebony.
ebrio, a ['eβrjo, a] *adj* drunk.
ebullición [eβuʎi'θjon] *nf* boiling.
eccema [ek'θema] *nf* (*MED*) eczema.
eclesiástico, a [ekle'sjastiko, a] *adj* ecclesiastical.
eclipse [e'klipse] *nm* eclipse.
eco ['eko] *nm* echo; **tener ~** to catch on.
ecología [ekolo'ɣia] *nf* ecology.
economato [ekono'mato] *nm* cooperative store.
economía [ekono'mia] *nf* (*sistema*) economy; (*cualidad*) thrift.
económico, a [eko'nomiko, a] *adj* (*barato*) cheap, economical; (*persona*) thrifty; (*COM*: *año etc*) financial; (: *situación*) economic.
economista [ekono'mista] *nm/f* economist.
ecuador [ekwa'ðor] *nm* equator; **(el) E~** Ecuador.
ecuánime [e'kwanime] *adj* (*carácter*) level-headed; (*estado*) calm.
ecuatoriano, a [ekwato'rjano, a] *adj, nm/f* Ecuadorian.
ecuestre [e'kwestre] *adj* equestrian.
echar [e'tʃar] *vt* to throw; (*agua, vino*) to pour (out); (*empleado: despedir*) to fire, sack; (*hojas*) to sprout; (*cartas*) to post; (*humo*) to emit, give out ♦ *vi*: **~ a correr/llorar** to run off/burst into tears; **~se** *vr* to lie down; **~ llave a** to lock (up); **~ abajo** (*gobierno*) to overthrow; (*edificio*) to demolish; **~ mano a** to lay hands on; **~ una mano a uno** (*ayudar*) to give sb a hand; **~ de menos** to miss.
edad [e'ðað] *nf* age; ¿**qué ~ tienes?** how

old are you?; **tiene ocho años de ~** he is eight (years old); **de ~ mediana/ avanzada** middle-aged/advanced in years; **la E~ Media** the Middle Ages.
edición [eði'θjon] *nf* (*acto*) publication; (*ejemplar*) edition.
edicto [e'ðikto] *nm* edict, proclamation.
edificio [eði'fiθjo] *nm* building; (*fig*) edifice, structure.
Edimburgo [eðim'burɣo] *nm* Edinburgh.
editar [eði'tar] *vt* (*publicar*) to publish; (*preparar textos*) to edit.
editor, a [eði'tor, a] *nm/f* (*que publica*) publisher; (*redactor*) editor ♦ *adj*: **casa ~a** publishing house, publisher; **~ial** *adj* editorial ♦ *nm* leading article, editorial; **casa ~ial** publishing house, publisher.
educación [eðuka'θjon] *nf* education; (*crianza*) upbringing; (*modales*) (good) manners *pl*.
educar [eðu'kar] *vt* to educate; (*criar*) to bring up; (*voz*) to train.
EE. UU. *nmpl abr* (= *Estados Unidos*) US(A).
efectista [efek'tista] *adj* sensationalist.
efectivamente [efectiβa'mente] *adv* (*como respuesta*) exactly, precisely; (*verdaderamente*) really; (*de hecho*) in fact.
efectivo, a [efek'tiβo, a] *adj* effective; (*real*) actual, real ♦ *nm*: **pagar en ~** to pay (in) cash; **hacer ~ un cheque** to cash a cheque.
efecto [e'fekto] *nm* effect, result; **~s** *nmpl* (**~s personales**) effects; (*bienes*) goods; (*COM*) assets; **en ~** in fact; (*respuesta*) exactly, indeed.
efectuar [efek'twar] *vt* to carry out; (*viaje*) to make.
eficacia [efi'kaθja] *nf* (*de persona*) efficiency; (*de medicamento etc*) effectiveness.
eficaz [efi'kaθ] *adj* (*persona*) efficient; (*acción*) effective.
efusivo, a [efu'siβo, a] *adj* effusive; **mis más efusivas gracias** my warmest thanks.
EGB (*ESP*) *nf abr* (*ESCOL*) = *Educación General Básica*.

egipcio, a [e'xipθjo, a] *adj, nm/f* Egyptian.

Egipto [e'xipto] *nm* Egypt.

egoísmo [eɣo'ismo] *nm* egoism.

egoísta [eɣo'ista] *adj* egoistical, selfish ♦ *nm/f* egoist.

egregio, a [e'ɣrexjo, a] *adj* eminent, distinguished.

Eire ['eire] *nm* Eire.

ej. *abr* (= *ejemplo*) eg.

eje ['exe] *nm* (*GEO, MAT*) axis; (*de rueda*) axle; (*de máquina*) shaft, spindle.

ejecución [exeku'θjon] *nf* execution; (*cumplimiento*) fulfilment; (*actuación*) performance; (*JUR: embargo de deudor*) attachment.

ejecutar [exeku'tar] *vt* to execute, carry out; (*matar*) to execute; (*cumplir*) to fulfil; (*MUS*) to perform; (*JUR: embargar*) to attach, distrain (on).

ejecutivo, a [exeku'tiβo, a] *adj* executive; **el (poder)** ~ the executive (power).

ejemplar [exem'plar] *adj* exemplary ♦ *nm* example; (*ZOOL*) specimen; (*de libro*) copy; (*de periódico*) number, issue.

ejemplo [e'xemplo] *nm* example; **por** ~ for example.

ejercer [exer'θer] *vt* to exercise; (*influencia*) to exert; (*un oficio*) to practise ♦ *vi* (*practicar*): ~ **(de)** to practise (as); (*tener oficio*) to hold office.

ejercicio [exer'θiθjo] *nm* exercise; (*período*) tenure; ~ **comercial** financial year.

ejército [e'xerθito] *nm* army; **entrar en el** ~ to join the army, join up.

ejote [e'xote] *nm* (*AM*) green bean.

PALABRA CLAVE

el [el] (*f* **la**, *pl* **los, las,** *neutro* **lo**) *art def*
1 the; **el libro/la mesa/los estudiantes** the book/table/students

2 (*con n abstracto: no se traduce*): **el amor/la juventud** love/youth

3 (*posesión: se traduce a menudo por adj posesivo*): **romperse el brazo** to break one's arm; **levantó la mano** he put his hand up; **se puso el sombrero** she put her hat on

4 (*valor descriptivo*): **tener la boca grande/los ojos azules** to have a big mouth/blue eyes

5 (*con días*) on; **me iré el viernes** I'll leave on Friday; **los domingos suelo ir a nadar** on Sundays I generally go swimming

6 (*lo +adj*): **lo difícil/caro** what is difficult/expensive; (= *cuán*): **no se da cuenta de lo pesado que es** he doesn't realise how boring he is

♦ *pron demos* **1**: **mi libro y el de usted** my book and yours; **las de Pepe son mejores** Pepe's are better; **no la(s) blanca(s) sino la(s) gris(es)** not the white one(s) but the grey one(s)

2: **lo de: lo de ayer** what happened yesterday; **lo de las facturas** that business about the invoices

♦ *pron relativo*: **el que** *etc* **1** (*indef*): **el (los) que quiera(n) que se vaya(n)** anyone who wants to can leave; **llévese el que más le guste** take the one you like best

2 (*def*): **el que compré ayer** the one I bought yesterday; **los que se van** those who leave

3: **lo que: lo que pienso yo/más me gusta** what I think/like most

♦ *conj*: **el que: el que lo diga** the fact that he says so; **el que sea tan vago me molesta** his being so lazy bothers me

♦ *excl*: **¡el susto que me diste!** what a fright you gave me!

♦ *pron personal* **1** (*persona: m*) him; (: *f*) her; (: *pl*) them; **lo/las veo** I can see him/them

2 (*animal, cosa: sg*) it; (: *pl*) them; **lo (o la) veo** I can see it; **los (o las) veo** I can see them

3: **lo** (*como sustituto de frase*): **no lo sabía** I didn't know; **ya lo entiendo** I understand now.

él [el] *pron* (*persona*) he; (*cosa*) it; (*después de prep: persona*) him; (: *cosa*) it; **de** ~ his.

elaborar [elaβo'rar] *vt* (*producto*) to make, manufacture; (*preparar*) to prepare; (*madera, metal etc*) to work; (*proyecto etc*) to work on o out.
elasticidad [elastiθi'ðað] *nf* elasticity.
elástico, a [e'lastiko, a] *adj* elastic; (*flexible*) flexible ♦ *nm* elastic; (*un ~*) elastic band.
elección [elek'θjon] *nf* election; (*selección*) choice, selection.
electorado [elekto'raðo] *nm* electorate, voters *pl*.
electricidad [elektriθi'ðað] *nf* electricity.
electricista [elektri'θista] *nm/f* electrician.
eléctrico, a [e'lektriko, a] *adj* electric.
electrizar [elektri'θar] *vt* to electrify.
electro... [elektro] *prefijo* electro...; **~cución** *nf* electrocution; **~cutar** *vt* to electrocute; **~do** *nm* electrode; **~domésticos** *nmpl* (electrical) household appliances; **~imán** *nm* electromagnet; **~magnético, a** *adj* electromagnetic.
electrónica [elek'tronika] *nf* electronics *sg*.
electrónico, a [elek'troniko, a] *adj* electronic.
electrotecnia [elektro'teknja] *nf* electrical engineering; **electrotécnico, a** *nm/f* electrical engineer.
electrotermo [elektro'termo] *nm* immersion heater.
elefante [ele'fante] *nm* elephant.
elegancia [ele'ɣanθja] *nf* elegance, grace; (*estilo*) stylishness.
elegante [ele'ɣante] *adj* elegant, graceful; (*estiloso*) stylish, fashionable.
elegía [ele'xia] *nf* elegy.
elegir [ele'xir] *vt* (*escoger*) to choose, select; (*optar*) to opt for; (*presidente*) to elect.
elemental [elemen'tal] *adj* (*claro, obvio*) elementary; (*fundamental*) elemental, fundamental.
elemento [ele'mento] *nm* element; (*fig*) ingredient; **~s** *nmpl* elements, rudiments.
elenco [e'lenko] *nm* (*TEATRO, CINE*) cast.
elevación [eleβa'θjon] *nf* elevation;

(*acto*) raising, lifting; (*de precios*) rise; (*GEO etc*) height, altitude; (*de persona*) nobleness.
elevar [ele'βar] *vt* to raise, lift (up); (*precio*) to put up; **~se** *vr* (*edificio*) to rise; (*precios*) to go up; (*transportarse, enajenarse*) to get carried away.
eligiendo *etc vb ver* **elegir**.
elija *etc vb ver* **elegir**.
eliminar [elimi'nar] *vt* to eliminate, remove.
eliminatoria [elimina'torja] *nf* heat, preliminary (round).
elite [e'lite] *nf* elite.
elocuencia [elo'kwenθja] *nf* eloquence.
elogiar [elo'xjar] *vt* to praise, eulogize; **elogio** *nm* praise.
elote [e'lote] (*AM*) *nm* corn on the cob.
eludir [elu'ðir] *vt* (*evitar*) to avoid, evade; (*escapar*) to escape, elude.
ella ['eʎa] *pron* (*persona*) she; (*cosa*) it; (*después de prep: persona*) her; (: *cosa*) it; **de ~** hers.
ellas ['eʎas] *pron* (*personas y cosas*) they; (*después de prep*) them; **de ~** theirs.
ello ['eʎo] *pron* it.
ellos ['eʎos] *pron* they; (*después de prep*) them; **de ~** theirs.
emanar [ema'nar] *vi*: **~ de** to emanate from, come from; (*derivar de*) to originate in.
emancipar [emanθi'par] *vt* to emancipate; **~se** *vr* to become emancipated, free o.s.
embadurnar [embaður'nar] *vt* to smear.
embajada [emba'xaða] *nf* embassy.
embajador, a [embaxa'ðor, a] *nm/f* ambassador/ambassadress.
embalar [emba'lar] *vt* (*envolver*) to parcel, wrap (up); (*envasar*) to package; **~se** *vr* to go fast.
embalsamar [embalsa'mar] *vt* to embalm.
embalse [em'balse] *nm* (*presa*) dam; (*lago*) reservoir.
embarazada [embara'θaða] *adj* pregnant ♦ *nf* pregnant woman.
embarazar [embara'θar] *vt* to obstruct, hamper; **~se** *vr* (*aturdirse*) to become

embarrassed; (*confundirse*) to get into a mess.

embarazo [embaˈraθo] *nm* (*de mujer*) pregnancy; (*impedimento*) obstacle, obstruction; (*timidez*) embarrassment.

embarcación [embarkaˈθjon] *nf* (*barco*) boat, craft; (*acto*) embarkation, boarding.

embarcadero [embarkaˈðero] *nm* pier, landing stage.

embarcar [embarˈkar] *vt* (*cargamento*) to ship, stow; (*persona*) to embark, put on board; ~**se** *vr* to embark, go on board.

embargar [embarˈɣar] *vt* (*JUR*) to seize, impound.

embarque *etc* [emˈbarke] *vb* **ver embarcar** ♦ *nm* shipment, loading.

embaucar [embauˈkar] *vt* to trick, fool.

embeber [embeˈβer] *vt* (*absorber*) to absorb, soak up; (*empapar*) to saturate ♦ *vi* to shrink; ~**se** *vr*: ~**se en un libro** to be engrossed *o* absorbed in a book.

embellecer [embeʎeˈθer] *vt* to embellish, beautify.

embestida [embesˈtiða] *nf* attack, onslaught; (*carga*) charge.

embestir [embesˈtir] *vt* to attack, assault; to charge, attack ♦ *vi* to attack.

emblema [emˈblema] *nm* emblem.

embobado, a [emboˈβaðo, a] *adj* (*atontado*) stunned, bewildered.

émbolo [ˈembolo] *nm* (*AUTO*) piston.

embolsar [embolˈsar] *vt* to pocket, put in one's pocket.

emborrachar [emborraˈtʃar] *vt* to make drunk, intoxicate; ~**se** *vr* to get drunk.

emboscada [embosˈkaða] *nf* (*celada*) ambush.

embotar [emboˈtar] *vt* to blunt, dull; ~**se** *vr* (*adormecerse*) to go numb.

embotellamiento [emboteʎaˈmjento] *nm* (*AUTO*) traffic jam.

embotellar [emboteˈʎar] *vt* to bottle; ~**se** *vr* (*circulación*) to get into a jam.

embrague [emˈbraɣe] *nm* (*tb: pedal de* ~) clutch.

embriagar [embrjaˈɣar] *vt* (*emborrachar*) to make drunk; (*ale-*

grar) to delight; ~**se** *vr* (*emborracharse*) to get drunk.

embriaguez [embrjaˈɣeθ] *nf* (*borrachera*) drunkenness.

embrión [emˈbrjon] *nm* embryo.

embrollar [embroˈʎar] *vt* (*el asunto*) to confuse, complicate; (*persona*) to involve, embroil; ~**se** *vr* (*confundirse*) to get into a muddle *o* mess.

embrollo [emˈbroʎo] *nm* (*enredo*) muddle, confusion; (*aprieto*) fix, jam.

embromar [embroˈmar] *vt* (*burlarse de*) to tease, make fun of.

embrujado, a [embruˈxado, a] *adj* bewitched; **casa embrujada** haunted house.

embrutecer [embruteˈθer] *vt* (*atontar*) to stupefy; ~**se** *vr* to be stupefied.

embudo [emˈbuðo] *nm* funnel.

embuste [emˈbuste] *nm* trick; (*mentira*) lie; (*hum*) fib; ~**ro, a** *adj* lying, deceitful ♦ *nm/f* (*tramposo*) cheat; (*mentiroso*) liar; (*humorístico*) fibber.

embutido [embuˈtiðo] *nm* (*CULIN*) sausage; (*TEC*) inlay.

embutir [embuˈtir] *vt* (*TEC*) to inlay; (*llenar*) to pack tight, cram.

emergencia [emerˈxenθja] *nf* emergency; (*surgimiento*) emergence.

emerger [emerˈxer] *vi* to emerge, appear.

emigración [emiɣraˈθjon] *nf* emigration; (*de pájaros*) migration.

emigrar [emiˈɣrar] *vi* (*personas*) to emigrate; (*pájaros*) to migrate.

eminencia [emiˈnenθja] *nf* eminence; **eminente** *adj* eminent, distinguished; (*elevado*) high.

emisario [emiˈsarjo] *nm* emissary.

emisión [emiˈsjon] *nf* (*acto*) emission; (*COM etc*) issue; (*RADIO, TV: acto*) broadcasting; (: *programa*) broadcast, programme (*BRIT*), program (*US*).

emisora [emiˈsora] *nf* radio *o* broadcasting station.

emitir [emiˈtir] *vt* (*olor etc*) to emit, give off; (*moneda etc*) to issue; (*opinión*) to express; (*RADIO*) to broadcast.

emoción [emoˈθjon] *nf* emotion; (*excita-*

ción) excitement; (*sentimiento*) feeling.

emocionante [emoθjo'nante] *adj* (*excitante*) exciting, thrilling.

emocionar [emoθjo'nar] *vt* (*excitar*) to excite, thrill; (*conmover*) to move, touch; (*impresionar*) to impress.

emotivo, a [emo'tiβo, a] *adj* emotional.

empacar [empa'kar] *vt* (*gen*) to pack; (*en caja*) to bale, crate.

empacho [em'patʃo] *nm* (MED) indigestion; (*fig*) embarrassment.

empadronarse [empaðro'narse] *vr* (POL: *como elector*) to register.

empalagoso, a [empala'voso, a] *adj* cloying; (*fig*) tiresome.

empalmar [empal'mar] *vt* to join, connect ♦ *vi* (*dos caminos*) to meet, join; **empalme** *nm* joint, connection; junction; (*de trenes*) connection.

empanada [empa'naða] *nf* pie, pasty.

empantanarse [empanta'narse] *vr* to get swamped; (*fig*) to get bogged down.

empañarse [empa'narse] *vr* (*cristales etc*) to steam up.

empapar [empa'par] *vt* (*mojar*) to soak, saturate; (*absorber*) to soak up, absorb; ~se *vr*: ~**se de** to soak up.

empapelar [empape'lar] *vt* (*paredes*) to paper.

empaquetar [empake'tar] *vt* to pack, parcel up.

emparedado [empare'ðaðo] *nm* sandwich.

empastar [empas'tar] *vt* (*embadurnar*) to paste; (*diente*) to fill.

empaste [em'paste] *nm* (*de diente*) filling.

empatar [empa'tar] *vi* to draw, tie; **empate** *nm* draw, tie.

empecé *etc vb ver* **empezar**.

empedernido, a [empeðer'niðo, a] *adj* hard, heartless; (*fijado*) hardened, inveterate.

empedrado, a [empe'ðraðo, a] *adj* paved ♦ *nm* paving.

empedrar [empe'ðrar] *vt* to pave.

empeine [em'peine] *nm* (*de pie, zapato*) instep.

empeñado, a [empe'ɲaðo, a] *adj* (*persona*) determined; (*objeto*) pawned.

empeñar [empe'ɲar] *vt* (*objeto*) to pawn, pledge; (*persona*) to compel; ~se *vr* (*obligarse*) to bind o.s., pledge o.s.; (*endeudarse*) to get into debt; ~se **en** to be set on, be determined to.

empeño [em'peɲo] *nm* (*determinación, insistencia*) determination, insistence; (*cosa prendada*) pledge; **casa de** ~s pawnshop.

empeorar [empeo'rar] *vt* to make worse, worsen ♦ *vi* to get worse, deteriorate.

empequeñecer [empekeɲe'θer] *vt* to dwarf; (*fig*) to belittle.

emperador [empera'ðor] *nm* emperor; **emperatriz** *nf* empress.

empezar [empe'θar] *vt, vi* to begin, start.

empiece *etc vb ver* **empezar**.

empiezo *etc vb ver* **empezar**.

empinar [empi'nar] *vt* to raise; ~se *vr* (*persona*) to stand on tiptoe; (*animal*) to rear up; (*camino*) to climb steeply.

empírico, a [em'piriko, a] *adj* empirical.

emplaste [em'plaste] *nm* (MED) = **emplasto**.

emplasto [em'plasto] *nm* (MED) plaster.

emplazamiento [emplaθa'mjento] *nm* site, location; (JUR) summons *sg*.

emplazar [empla'θar] *vt* (*ubicar*) to site, place, locate; (JUR) to summons; (*convocar*) to summon.

empleado, a [emple'aðo, a] *nm/f* (*gen*) clerk; (*de banco etc*) employee; (*dar trabajo a*) to employ; ~se *vr* (*conseguir trabajo*) to be employed; (*ocuparse*) to occupy o.s.

emplear [emple'ar] *vt* (*usar*) to use, employ; (*dar trabajo a*) to employ; ~se *vr* (*conseguir trabajo*) to be employed; (*ocuparse*) to occupy o.s.

empleo [em'pleo] *nm* (*puesto*) job; (*puestos: colectivamente*) employment; (*uso*) use, employment.

empobrecer [empoβre'θer] *vt* to impoverish; ~se *vr* to become poor *o* impoverished.

empollar [empo'ʎar] (*fam*) *vt, vi* to swot (up); **empollón, ona** (*fam*) *nm/f* swot.

emporio [em'porjo] *nm* emporium, trading centre; (AM: *gran almacén*) department store.

empotrado, a [empoˈtraðo, a] *adj* (*armario etc*) built-in.

emprender [emprenˈder] *vt* (*empezar*) to begin, embark on; (*acometer*) to tackle, take on.

empresa [emˈpresa] *nf* (*de espíritu etc*) enterprise; (*COM*) company, firm; ~**rio**, **a** *nm/f* (*COM*) manager.

empréstito [emˈprestito] *nm* (public) loan.

empujar [empuˈxar] *vt* to push, shove; **empuje** *nm* thrust; (*presión*) pressure; (*fig*) vigour, drive.

empujón [empuˈxon] *nm* push, shove.

empuñar [empuˈɲar] *vt* (*asir*) to grasp, take (firm) hold of.

emular [emuˈlar] *vt* to emulate; (*rivalizar*) to rival.

PALABRA CLAVE
---

en [en] *prep* **1** (*posición*) in; (: *sobre*) on; **está ~ el cajón** it's in the drawer; **~ Argentina/La Paz** in Argentina/La Paz; **~ la oficina/el colegio** at the office/school; **está ~ el suelo/quinto piso** it's on the floor/the fifth floor

2 (*dirección*) into; **entró ~ el aula** she went into the classroom; **meter algo ~ el bolso** to put sth into one's bag

3 (*tiempo*) in; on; **~ 1605/3 semanas/invierno** in 1605/3 weeks/winter; **~ (el mes de) enero** in (the month of) January; **~ aquella ocasión/época** on that occasion/at that time

4 (*precio*) for; **lo vendió ~ 20 dólares** he sold it for 20 dollars

5 (*diferencia*) by; **reducir/aumentar ~ una tercera parte/un 20 por ciento** to reduce/increase by a third/20 per cent

6 (*manera*): **~ avión/autobús** by plane/bus; **escrito ~ inglés** written in English

7 (*después de vb que indica gastar etc*) on; **han cobrado demasiado ~ dietas** they've charged too much to expenses; **se le va la mitad del sueldo ~ comida** he spends half his salary on food

8 (*tema, ocupación*): **experto ~ la materia** expert on the subject; **trabaja ~ la construcción** he works in the building industry

9 (*adj + ~ + infin*): **lento ~ reaccionar** slow to react.

---

enajenación [enaxenaˈθjon] *nf* (*fig: distracción*) absent-mindedness; (: *embelesamiento*) rapture, trance.

enajenamiento [enaxenaˈmjento] *nm* = **enajenación.**

enajenar [enaxeˈnar] *vt* to alienate; (*fig*) to carry away.

enamorado, a [enamoˈraðo, a] *adj* in love ♦ *nm/f* lover.

enamorar [enamoˈrar] *vt* to win the love of; ~**se** *vr*: ~**se de alguien** to fall in love with sb.

enano, a [eˈnano, a] *adj* tiny ♦ *nm/f* dwarf.

enardecer [enarðeˈθer] *vt* (*pasiones*) to fire, inflame; (*persona*) to fill with enthusiasm; ~**se** *vr*: ~**se por** to get excited about; (*entusiasmarse*) to get enthusiastic about.

encabezamiento [enkaβeθaˈmjento] *nm* (*de carta*) heading; (*de periódico*) headline; (*preámbulo*) foreword, preface.

encabezar [enkaβeˈθar] *vt* (*movimiento, revolución*) to lead, head; (*lista*) to head, be at the top of; (*carta*) to put a heading to; (*libro*) to entitle.

encadenar [enkaðeˈnar] *vt* to chain (together); (*poner grilletes a*) to shackle.

encajar [enkaˈxar] *vt* (*ajustar*): ~ **(en)** to fit (into); (*fam: golpe*) to give, deal; (*entrometer*) to insert ♦ *vi* to fit (well); (*fig: corresponder a*) to match; ~**se** *vr*: ~**se en un sillón** to squeeze into a chair.

encaje [enˈkaxe] *nm* (*labor*) lace.

encalar [enkaˈlar] *vt* (*pared*) to whitewash.

encallar [enkaˈʎar] *vi* (*NAUT*) to run aground.

encaminar [enkamiˈnar] *vt* to direct, send; ~**se** *vr*: ~**se a** to set out for.

encandilar [enkandiˈlar] *vt* to dazzle.

encantado, a [enkanˈtaðo, a] *adj* (*hechizado*) bewitched; (*muy contento*) delighted; ¡~! how do you do, pleased to meet you.

encantador, a [enkanta'ðor, a] *adj* charming, lovely ♦ *nm/f* magician, enchanter/enchantress.

encantar [enkan'tar] *vt* to charm, delight; (*hechizar*) to bewitch, cast a spell on; **encanto** *nm* (*magia*) spell, charm; (*fig*) charm, delight.

encarcelar [enkarθe'lar] *vt* to imprison, jail.

encarecer [enkare'θer] *vt* to put up the price of ♦ *vi* to get dearer; ~**se** *vr* to get dearer.

encarecimiento [enkareθi'mjento] *nm* price increase.

encargado, a [enkar'ɣaðo, a] *adj* in charge ♦ *nm/f* agent, representative; (*responsable*) person in charge.

encargar [enkar'ɣar] *vt* to entrust; (*recomendar*) to urge, recommend; ~**se** *vr*: ~**se de** to look after, take charge of.

encargo [en'karɣo] *nm* (*pedido*) assignment, job; (*responsabilidad*) responsibility; (*recomendación*) recommendation; (*COM*) order.

encariñarse [enkari'ɲarse] *vr*: ~ **con** to grow fond of, get attached to.

encarnación [enkarna'θjon] *nf* incarnation, embodiment.

encarnizado, a [enkarni'θaðo, a] *adj* (*lucha*) bloody, fierce.

encarrilar [enkarri'lar] *vt* (*tren*) to put back on the rails; (*fig*) to correct, put on the right track.

encasillar [enkasi'ʎar] *vt* (*tb fig*) to pigeonhole; (*actor*) to typecast.

encauzar [enkau'θar] *vt* to channel.

encendedor [enθende'ðor] *nm* lighter.

encender [enθen'der] *vt* (*con fuego*) to light; (*incendiar*) to set fire to; (*luz, radio*) to put on, switch on; (*avivar: pasiones*) to inflame; ~**se** *vr* to catch fire; (*excitarse*) to get excited; (*de cólera*) to flare up; (*el rostro*) to blush.

encendido [enθen'diðo] *nm* (*AUTO*) ignition.

encerado [enθe'raðo] *nm* (*ESCOL*) blackboard.

encerar [enθe'rar] *vt* (*suelo*) to wax, polish.

encerrar [enθe'rrar] *vt* (*confinar*) to shut in, shut up; (*comprender, incluir*) to include, contain.

encía [en'θia] *nf* gum.

encienda *etc vb ver* **encender**.

encierro *etc* [en'θjerro] *vb ver* **encerrar** ♦ *nm* shutting in, shutting up; (*calabozo*) prison.

encima [en'θima] *adv* (*sobre*) above, over; (*además*) besides; ~ **de** (*en*) on, on top of; (*sobre*) above, over; (*además de*) besides, on top of; **por** ~ **de** over; **¿llevas dinero** ~? have you (got) any money on you?; **se me vino** ~ it took me by surprise.

encinta [en'θinta] *adj* pregnant.

enclenque [en'klenke] *adj* weak, sickly.

encoger [enko'xer] *vt* to shrink, contract; (*fig: asustar*) to scare; ~**se** *vr* to shrink, contract; (*fig*) to cringe; ~**se de hombros** to shrug one's shoulders.

encolar [enko'lar] *vt* (*engomar*) to glue, paste; (*pegar*) to stick down.

encolerizar [enkoleri'θar] *vt* to anger, provoke; ~**se** *vr* to get angry.

encomendar [enkomen'dar] *vt* to entrust, commend; ~**se** *vr*: ~**se a** to put one's trust in.

encomiar [enko'mjar] *vt* to praise, pay tribute to.

encomienda *etc* [enko'mjenda] *vb ver* **encomendar** ♦ *nf* (*encargo*) charge, commission; (*elogio*) tribute; ~ **postal** (*AM*) parcel post.

encono [en'kono] *nm* (*rencor*) rancour, spite.

encontrado, a [enkon'traðo, a] *adj* (*contrario*) contrary, conflicting; (*hostil*) hostile.

encontrar [enkon'trar] *vt* (*hallar*) to find; (*inesperadamente*) to meet, run into; ~**se** *vr* to meet (each other); (*situarse*) to be (situated); (*entrar en conflicto*) to crash, collide; ~**se con** to meet; ~**se bien (de salud)** to feel well.

encorvar [enkor'ßar] *vt* to curve; (*inclinar*) to bend (down); ~**se** *vr* to bend down, bend over.

encrespar [enkres'par] *vt* (*cabellos*) to curl; (*fig*) to anger, irritate; ~**se** *vr* (*el mar*) to get rough; (*fig*) to get cross, get irritated.

encrucijada [enkruθi'xaða] *nf* crossroads *sg*; (*empalme*) junction.

encuadernación [enkwaðerna'θjon] *nf* binding.

encuadernador, a [enkwaðerna'ðor, a] *nm/f* bookbinder.

encuadrar [enkwa'ðrar] *vt* (*retrato*) to frame; (*ajustar*) to fit, insert; (*encerrar*) to contain.

encubrir [enku'ßrir] *vt* (*ocultar*) to hide, conceal; (*criminal*) to harbour, shelter.

encuentro *etc* [en'kwentro] *vb ver* **encontrar ♦** *nm* (*de personas*) meeting; (*AUTO etc*) collision, crash; (*DEPORTE*) match, game; (*MIL*) encounter.

encuesta [en'kwesta] *nf* inquiry, investigation; (*sondeo*) (public) opinion poll; ~ **judicial** post mortem.

encumbrado, a [enkum'braðo, a] *adj* eminent, distinguished.

encumbrar [enkum'brar] *vt* (*persona*) to exalt; ~**se** *vr* (*fig*) to become conceited.

encharcado, a [entʃar'kaðo, a] *adj* (*terreno*) flooded.

enchufar [entʃu'far] *vt* (*ELEC*) to plug in; (*TEC*) to connect, fit together; **enchufe** *nm* (*ELEC*: *clavija*) plug; (: *toma*) socket; (*de dos tubos*) joint, connection; (*fam*: *influencia*) contact, connection; (: *puesto*) cushy job.

endeble [en'deßle] *adj* (*argumento*, *excusa*, *persona*) weak.

endemoniado, a [endemo'njaðo, a] *adj* possessed (of the devil); (*travieso*) devilish.

enderezar [endere'θar] *vt* (*poner derecho*) to straighten (out); (: *verticalmente*) to set upright; (*fig*) to straighten *o* sort out; (*dirigir*) to direct; ~**se** *vr* (*persona sentada*) to straighten up.

endeudarse [endeu'ðarse] *vr* to get into debt.

endiablado, a [endja'ßlaðo, a] *adj* devilish, diabolical; (*travieso*) mischievous.

endilgar [endil'ɣar] (*fam*) *vt*: ~**le algo a uno** to lumber sb with sth; ~**le un sermón a uno** to lecture sb.

endomingarse [endomin'garse] *vr* to

dress up, put on one's Sunday best.

endosar [endo'sar] *vt* (*cheque etc*) to endorse.

endulzar [endul'θar] *vt* to sweeten; (*suavizar*) to soften.

endurecer [endure'θer] *vt* to harden; ~**se** *vr* to harden, grow hard.

endurecido, a [endure'θiðo, a] *adj* (*duro*) hard; (*fig*) hardy, tough; **estar** ~ **a algo** to be hardened *o* used to sth.

enemigo, a [ene'mixo, a] *adj* enemy, hostile ♦ *nm/f* enemy.

enemistad [enemis'tað] *nf* enmity.

enemistar [enemis'tar] *vt* to make enemies of, cause a rift between; ~**se** *vr* to become enemies; (*amigos*) to fall out.

energía [ener'xia] *nf* (*vigor*) energy, drive; (*empuje*) push; (*TEC*, *ELEC*) energy, power.

enérgico, a [e'nerxiko, a] *adj* (*gen*) energetic; (*voz*, *modales*) forceful.

energúmeno, a [ener'xumeno, a] (*fam*) *nm/f* (*fig*) madman/woman.

enero [e'nero] *nm* January.

enfadado, a [enfa'ðaðo, a] *adj* angry, annoyed.

enfadar [enfa'ðar] *vt* to anger, annoy; ~**se** *vr* to get angry *o* annoyed.

enfado [en'faðo] *nm* (*enojo*) anger, annoyance; (*disgusto*) trouble, bother.

énfasis ['enfasis] *nm* emphasis, stress.

enfático, a [en'fatiko, a] *adj* emphatic.

enfermar [enfer'mar] *vt* to make ill ♦ *vi* to fall ill, be taken ill.

enfermedad [enferme'ðað] *nf* illness; ~ **venérea** venereal disease.

enfermera [enfer'mera] *nf* nurse.

enfermería [enferme'ria] *nf* infirmary; (*de colegio etc*) sick bay.

enfermero [enfer'mero] *nm* (male) nurse.

enfermizo, a [enfer'miθo, a] *adj* (*persona*) sickly, unhealthy; (*fig*) unhealthy.

enfermo, a [en'fermo, a] *adj* ill, sick ♦ *nm/f* invalid, sick person; (*en hospital*) patient.

enflaquecer [enflake'θer] *vt* (*adelgazar*) to make thin; (*debilitar*) to weaken.

enfocar [enfo'kar] vt (foto etc) to focus; (problema etc) to consider, look at.

enfoque etc [en'foke] vb ver **enfocar** ♦ nm focus.

enfrentar [enfren'tar] vt (peligro) to face (up to), confront; (oponer) to bring face to face; ~se vr (dos personas) to face o confront each other; (DEPORTE: dos equipos) to meet; ~se a o con to face up to, confront.

enfrente [en'frente] adv opposite; **la casa de** ~ the house opposite, the house across the street; ~ **de** opposite, facing.

enfriamiento [enfria'mjento] nm chilling, refrigeration; (MED) cold, chill.

enfriar [enfri'ar] vt (alimentos) to cool, chill; (algo caliente) to cool down; (habitación) to air, freshen; ~se vr to cool down; (MED) to catch a chill; (amistad) to cool.

enfurecer [enfure'θer] vt to enrage, madden; ~se vr to become furious, fly into a rage; (mar) to get rough.

engalanar [engala'nar] vt (adornar) to adorn; (ciudad) to decorate; ~se vr to get dressed up.

enganchar [engan'tʃar] vt to hook; (ropa) to hang up; (dos vagones) to hitch up; (TEC) to couple, connect; (MIL) to recruit; (fam: persona) to rope in; ~se vr (MIL) to enlist, join up.

enganche [en'gantʃe] nm hook; (TEC) coupling, connection; (acto) hooking (up); (MIL) recruitment, enlistment; (AM: depósito) deposit.

engañar [enga'ɲar] vt to deceive; (estafar) to cheat, swindle; ~se vr (equivocarse) to be wrong; (disimular la verdad) to deceive o.s.

engaño [en'gaɲo] nm deceit; (estafa) trick, swindle; (error) mistake, misunderstanding; (ilusión) delusion; ~**so, a** adj (tramposo) crooked; (mentiroso) dishonest, deceitful; (aspecto) deceptive; (consejo) misleading.

engarzar [engar'θar] vt (joya) to set, mount; (fig) to link, connect.

engatusar [engatu'sar] (fam) vt to coax.

engendrar [enxen'drar] vt to breed; (procrear) to beget; (fig) to cause,

produce; **engendro** nm (BIO) foetus; (fig) monstrosity; (idea) brainchild.

englobar [englo'βar] vt (incluir) to include, comprise.

engomar [engo'mar] vt to glue, stick.

engordar [engor'ðar] vt to fatten ♦ vi to get fat, put on weight.

engorroso, a [engo'rroso, a] adj bothersome, trying.

engranaje [engra'naxe] nm (AUTO) gear.

engrandecer [engrande'θer] vt to enlarge, magnify; (alabar) to praise, speak highly of; (exagerar) to exaggerate.

engrasar [engra'sar] vt (TEC: poner grasa) to grease; (: lubricar) to lubricate, oil; (manchar) to make greasy.

engreído, a [engre'iðo, a] adj vain, conceited.

engrosar [engro'sar] vt (ensanchar) to enlarge; (aumentar) to increase; (hinchar) to swell.

enhebrar [ene'βrar] vt to thread.

enhorabuena [enora'βwena] excl: ¡~! congratulations! ♦ nf: **dar la** ~ **a** to congratulate.

enigma [e'niɣma] nm enigma; (problema) puzzle; (misterio) mystery.

enjabonar [enxaβo'nar] vt to soap; (fam: adular) to soft-soap; (: regañar) to tick off.

enjambre [en'xambre] nm swarm.

enjaular [enxau'lar] vt to (put in a) cage; (fam) to jail, lock up.

enjuagar [enxwa'ɣar] vt (ropa) to rinse (out).

enjuague etc [en'xwaɣe] vb ver **enjuagar** ♦ nm (MED) mouthwash; (de ropa) rinse, rinsing.

enjugar [enxu'ɣar] vt to wipe (off); (lágrimas) to dry; (déficit) to wipe out.

enjuiciar [enxwi'θjar] vt (JUR: procesar) to prosecute, try; (fig) to judge.

enjuto, a [en'xuto, a] adj dry, dried up; (fig) lean, skinny.

enlace [en'laθe] nm link, connection; (relación) relationship; (tb: ~ matrimonial) marriage; (de carretera, trenes) connection; ~ **sindical** shop steward.

enlazar [enla'θar] *vt* (*unir con lazos*) to bind together; (*atar*) to tie; (*conectar*) to link, connect; (*AM*) to lasso.

enlodar [enlo'ðar] *vt* to cover in mud; (*fig: manchar*) to stain; (: *rebajar*) to debase.

enloquecer [enloke'θer] *vt* to drive mad ♦ *vi* to go mad; ~**se** *vr* to go mad.

enlutado, a [enlu'taðo, a] *adj* (*persona*) in mourning.

enmarañar [enmara'ɲar] *vt* (*enredar*) to tangle (up), entangle; (*complicar*) to complicate; (*confundir*) to confuse; ~**se** *vr* (*enredarse*) to become entangled; (*confundirse*) to get confused.

enmarcar [enmar'kar] *vt* (*cuadro*) to frame.

enmascarar [enmaska'rar] *vt* to mask; ~**se** *vr* to put on a mask.

enmendar [enmen'dar] *vt* to emend, correct; (*constitución etc*) to amend; (*comportamiento*) to reform; ~**se** *vr* to reform, mend one's ways; **enmienda** *nf* correction; amendment; reform.

enmohecerse [enmoe'θerse] *vr* (*metal*) to rust, go rusty; (*muro, plantas*) to get mouldy.

enmudecer [enmuðe'θer] *vi* (*perder el habla*) to fall silent; (*guardar silencio*) to remain silent; ~**se** *vr* to fall silent; to remain silent.

ennegrecer [enneɣre'θer] *vt* (*poner negro*) to blacken; (*oscurecer*) to darken; ~**se** *vr* to turn black; (*oscurecerse*) to get dark, darken.

ennoblecer [ennoβle'θer] *vt* to ennoble.

enojadizo, a [enoxa'ðiθo, a] *adj* irritable, short-tempered.

enojar [eno'xar] *vt* (*encolerizar*) to anger; (*disgustar*) to annoy, upset; ~**se** *vr* to get angry; to get annoyed.

enojo [e'noxo] *nm* (*cólera*) anger; (*irritación*) annoyance; ~**so, a** *adj* annoying.

enorgullecerse [enorɣuʎe'θerse] *vr* to be proud; ~ **de** to pride o.s. on, be proud of.

enorme [e'norme] *adj* enormous, huge; (*fig*) monstrous; **enormidad** *nf* hugeness, immensity.

enraizar [enrai'θar] *vi* to take root.

enredadera [enreða'ðera] *nf* (*BOT*) creeper, climbing plant.

enredar [enre'ðar] *vt* (*cables, hilos etc*) to tangle (up), entangle; (*situación*) to complicate, confuse; (*meter cizaña*) to sow discord among *o* between; (*implicar*) to embroil, implicate; ~**se** *vr* to get entangled, get tangled (up); (*situación*) to get complicated; (*persona*) to get embroiled; (*AM: fam*) to meddle.

enredo [en'reðo] *nm* (*maraña*) tangle; (*confusión*) mix-up, confusion; (*intriga*) intrigue.

enrevesado, a [enreβe'saðo, a] *adj* (*asunto*) complicated, involved.

enriquecer [enrike'θer] *vt* to make rich, enrich; ~**se** *vr* to get rich.

enrojecer [enroxe'θer] *vt* to redden ♦ *vi* (*persona*) to blush; ~**se** *vr* to blush.

enrolar [enro'lar] *vt* (*MIL*) to enlist; (*reclutar*) to recruit; ~**se** *vr* (*MIL*) to join up; (*afiliarse*) to enrol.

enrollar [enro'ʎar] *vt* to roll (up), wind (up).

enroscar [enros'kar] *vt* (*torcer, doblar*) to coil (round), wind; (*tornillo, rosca*) to screw in; ~**se** *vr* to coil, wind.

ensalada [ensa'laða] *nf* salad; **ensaladilla (rusa)** *nf* Russian salad.

ensalzar [ensal'θar] *vt* (*alabar*) to praise, extol; (*exaltar*) to exalt.

ensambladura [ensambla'ðura] *nf* assembly; (*TEC*) joint.

ensamblaje [ensam'blaxe] *nm* = **ensambladura**.

ensamblar [ensam'blar] *vt* to assemble.

ensanchar [ensan'tʃar] *vt* (*hacer más ancho*) to widen; (*agrandar*) to enlarge, expand; (*COSTURA*) to let out; ~**se** *vr* to get wider, expand; (*pey*) to give o.s. airs; **ensanche** *nm* (*de calle*) widening; (*de negocio*) expansion.

ensangrentar [ensangren'tar] *vt* to stain with blood.

ensañar [ensa'ɲar] *vt* to enrage; ~**se con** to treat brutally.

ensartar [ensar'tar] *vt* (*cuentas, perlas etc*) to string (together).

ensayar [ensa'jar] *vt* to test, try (out);
(*TEATRO*) to rehearse.
ensayista [ensa'jista] *nm/f* essayist.
ensayo [en'sajo] *nm* test, trial;
(*QUÍMICA*) experiment; (*TEATRO*) rehearsal; (*DEPORTE*) try; (*ESCOL, LITE-
RATURA*) essay.
ensenada [ense'naða] *nf* inlet, cove.
enseñanza [ense'panθa] *nf* (*educación*)
education; (*acción*) teaching; (*doctrina*) teaching, doctrine.
enseñar [ense'par] *vt* (*educar*) to teach;
(*instruir*) to teach, instruct; (*mostrar,
señalar*) to show.
enseres [en'seres] *nmpl* belongings.
ensillar [ensi'ʎar] *vt* to saddle (up).
ensimismarse [ensimis'marse] *vr*
(*abstraerse*) to become lost in thought;
(*estar absorto*) to be lost in thought;
(*AM*) to become conceited.
ensordecer [ensorðe'θer] *vt* to deafen ♦
vi to go deaf.
ensortijado, a [ensorti'xaðo, a] *adj*
(*pelo*) curly.
ensuciar [ensu'θjar] *vt* (*manchar*) to
dirty, soil; (*fig*) to defile; ~**se** *vr* to get
dirty; (*niño*) to wet o.s.
ensueño [en'sweɲo] *nm* (*sueño*) dream,
fantasy; (*ilusión*) illusion; (*soñando
despierto*) daydream.
entablado [enta'ßlaðo] *nm* (*piso*) floor-
boards *pl*; (*armazón*) boarding.
entablar [enta'ßlar] *vt* (*recubrir*) to
board (up); (*AJEDREZ, DAMAS*) to set
up; (*conversación*) to strike up; (*JUR*)
to file ♦ *vi* to draw.
entablillar [entaßli'ʎar] *vt* (*MED*) to (put
in a) splint.
entallar [enta'ʎar] *vt* (*traje*) to tailor ♦
vi: **el traje entalla bien** the suit fits
well.
ente ['ente] *nm* (*organización*) body,
organization; (*fam: persona*) odd character.
entender [enten'der] *vt* (*comprender*) to
understand; (*darse cuenta*) to realize;
(*querer decir*) to mean ♦ *vi* to understand; (*creer*) to think, believe; ~**se** *vr*
(*comprenderse*) to be understood; (*2
personas*) to get on together; (*ponerse*

de acuerdo) to agree, reach an agreement; ~ **de** to know all about; ~ **algo
de** to know a little about; ~ **en** to deal
with, have to do with; ~**se mal** (*2
personas*) to get on badly.
entendido, a [enten'diðo, a] *adj*
(*comprendido*) understood; (*hábil*)
skilled; (*inteligente*) knowledgeable ♦
nm/f (*experto*) expert ♦ *excl* agreed!;
entendimiento *nm* (*comprensión*)
understanding; (*inteligencia*) mind, intellect; (*juicio*) judgement.
enterado, a [ente'raðo, a] *adj* well-
informed; **estar** ~ **de** to know about, be
aware of.
enteramente [entera'mente] *adv* entirely, completely.
enterar [ente'rar] *vt* (*informar*) to inform, tell; ~**se** *vr* to find out, get to
know.
entereza [ente'reθa] *nf* (*totalidad*) en-
tirety; (*fig: carácter*) strength of
mind; (*: honradez*) integrity.
enternecer [enterne'θer] *vt* (*ablandar*)
to soften; (*apiadar*) to touch, move;
~**se** *vr* to be touched, be moved.
entero, a [en'tero, a] *adj* (*total*) whole,
entire; (*fig: recto*) honest; (*: firme*)
firm, resolute ♦ *nm* (*COM: punto*) point;
(*AM: pago*) payment.
enterrador [enterra'ðor] *nm*
gravedigger.
enterrar [ente'rrar] *vt* to bury.
entibiar [enti'ßjar] *vt* (*enfriar*) to cool;
(*calentar*) to warm; ~**se** *vr* (*fig*) to
cool.
entidad [enti'ðað] *nf* (*empresa*) firm,
company; (*organismo*) body;
(*sociedad*) society; (*FILOSOFÍA*) entity.
entiendo *etc vb ver* entender.
entierro [en'tjerro] *nm* (*acción*) burial;
(*funeral*) funeral.
entomología [entomolo'xia] *nf* entomol-
ogy.
entonación [entona'θjon] *nf* (*LING*) intonation; (*fig*) conceit.
entonar [ento'nar] *vt* (*canción*) to in-
tone; (*colores*) to tone; (*MED*) to tone
up ♦ *vi* to be in tune; ~**se** *vr* (*en-
greírse*) to give o.s. airs.

entonces [en'tonθes] *adv* then, at that time; **desde** ~ since then; **en aquel** ~ at that time; **(pues)** ~ and so.

entornar [entor'nar] *vt* (*puerta*, *ventana*) to half close, leave ajar; (*los ojos*) to screw up.

entorpecer [entorpe'θer] *vt* (*entendimiento*) to dull; (*impedir*) to obstruct, hinder; (: *tránsito*) to slow down, delay.

entrada [en'traða] *nf* (*acción*) entry, access; (*sitio*) entrance, way in; (*INFORM*) input; (*COM*) receipts *pl*, takings *pl*; (*CULIN*) starter; (*DEPORTE*) innings *sg*; (*TEATRO*) house, audience; (*para el cine etc*) ticket; (*COM*): ~s y salidas income and expenditure; (*TEC*): ~ de aire air intake *o* inlet; de ~ from the outset.

entrado, a [en'traðo, a] *adj*: ~ en años elderly; **una vez** ~ **el verano** in the summer(time), when summer comes.

entrante [en'trante] *adj* next, coming; **mes/año** ~ next month/year.

entraña [en'traɲa] *nf* (*fig: centro*) heart, core; (*raíz*) root; ~s *nfpl* (*ANAT*) entrails; (*fig*) heart *sg*; **entrañable** *adj* close, intimate.

entrar [en'trar] *vt* (*introducir*) to bring in; (*INFORM*) to input ♦ *vi* (*meterse*) to go in, come in, enter; (*comenzar*): ~ **diciendo** to begin by saying; **hacer** ~ to show in; **no me entra** I can't get the hang of it.

entre ['entre] *prep* (*dos*) between; (*más de dos*) among(st).

entreabrir [entrea'ßrir] *vt* to half-open, open halfway.

entrecejo [entre'θexo] *nm*: **fruncir el** ~ to frown.

entrecortado, a [entrekor'taðo, a] *adj* (*respiración*) difficult; (*habla*) faltering.

entredicho [entre'ðitʃo] *nm* (*JUR*) injunction; **poner en** ~ to cast doubt on; **estar en** ~ to be banned.

entrega [en'treɣa] *nf* (*de mercancías*) delivery; (*de novela etc*) instalment.

entregar [entre'ɣar] *vt* (*dar*) to hand (over), deliver; ~**se** *vr* (*rendirse*) to

surrender, give in, submit; (*dedicarse*) to devote o.s.

entrelazar [entrela'θar] *vt* to entwine.

entremeses [entre'meses] *nmpl* hors d'œuvres.

entremeter [entreme'ter] *vt* to insert, put in; ~**se** *vr* to meddle, interfere; **entremetido, a** *adj* meddling, interfering.

entremezclar [entremeθ'klar] *vt* to intermingle; ~**se** *vr* to intermingle.

entrenador, a [entrena'ðor, a] *nm/f* trainer, coach.

entrenarse [entre'narse] *vr* to train.

entrepierna [entre'pjerna] *nf* crotch.

entresacar [entresa'kar] *vt* to pick out, select.

entresuelo [entre'swelo] *nm* mezzanine.

entretanto [entre'tanto] *adv* meanwhile, meantime.

entretejer [entrete'xer] *vt* to interweave.

entretener [entrete'ner] *vt* (*divertir*) to entertain, amuse; (*detener*) to hold up, delay; (*mantener*) to maintain; ~**se** *vr* (*divertirse*) to amuse o.s.; (*retrasarse*) to delay, linger; **entretenido, a** *adj* entertaining, amusing; **entretenimiento** *nm* entertainment, amusement; (*mantenimiento*) upkeep, maintenance.

entrever [entre'ßer] *vt* to glimpse, catch a glimpse of.

entrevista [entre'ßista] *nf* interview; **entrevistar** *vt* to interview; **entrevistarse** *vr* to have an interview.

entristecer [entriste'θer] *vt* to sadden, grieve; ~**se** *vr* to grow sad.

entrometer [entrome'ter] *vt etc* = **entremeter** *etc*.

entroncar [entron'kar] *vi* to be connected *o* related.

entumecer [entume'θer] *vt* to numb, benumb; ~**se** *vr* (*por el frío*) to go *o* become numb; **entumecido, a** *adj* numb, stiff.

enturbiar [entur'ßjar] *vt* (*el agua*) to make cloudy; (*fig*) to confuse; ~**se** *vr* (*oscurecerse*) to become cloudy; (*fig*) to get confused, become obscure.

entusiasmar [entusjas'mar] *vt* to excite, fill with enthusiasm; (*gustar mucho*) to delight; ~**se** *vr*: ~**se con** *o* **por** to get enthusiastic *o* excited about.

entusiasmo [entu'sjasmo] *nm* enthusiasm; (*excitación*) excitement.

entusiasta [entu'sjasta] *adj* enthusiastic ♦ *nm/f* enthusiast.

enumerar [enume'rar] *vt* to enumerate.

enunciación [enunθja'θjon] *nf* enunciation.

enunciado [enun'θjaðo] *nm* enunciation; (*declaración*) declaration, statement.

envainar [embai'nar] *vt* to sheathe.

envalentonar [embalento'nar] *vt* to give courage to; ~se *vr* (*pey*: *jactarse*) to boast, brag.

envanecer [embane'θer] *vt* to make conceited; ~se *vr* to grow conceited.

envasar [emba'sar] *vt* (*empaquetar*) to pack, wrap; (*enfrascar*) to bottle; (*enlatar*) to can; (*embolsar*) to pocket.

envase [em'base] *nm* (*en paquete*) packing, wrapping; (*en botella*) bottling; (*en lata*) canning; (*recipiente*) container; (*paquete*) package; (*botella*) bottle; (*lata*) tin (*BRIT*), can.

envejecer [embexe'θer] *vt* to make old, age ♦ *vi* (*volverse viejo*) to grow old; (*parecer viejo*) to age; ~se *vr* to grow old; to age.

envenenar [embene'nar] *vt* to poison; (*fig*) to embitter.

envergadura [emberɣa'ðura] *nf* (*fig*) scope, compass.

envés [em'bes] *nm* (*de tela*) back, wrong side.

enviar [em'bjar] *vt* to send.

envidia [em'biðja] *nf* envy; **tener ~ a** to envy, be jealous of; **envidiar** *vt* (*desear*) to envy; (*tener celos de*) to be jealous of.

envío [em'bio] *nm* (*acción*) sending; (*de mercancías*) consignment; (*de dinero*) remittance.

enviudar [embju'ðar] *vi* to be widowed.

envoltura [embol'tura] *nf* (*cobertura*) cover; (*embalaje*) wrapper, wrapping.

envolver [embol'ßer] *vt* to wrap (up); (*cubrir*) to cover; (*enemigo*) to surround; (*implicar*) to involve, implicate.

envuelto [em'bwelto] *pp de* **envolver**.

enyesar [enje'sar] *vt* (*pared*) to plaster; (*MED*) to put in plaster.

épica ['epika] *nf* epic.

épico, a ['epiko, a] *adj* epic.

epidemia [epi'ðemja] *nf* epidemic.

epilepsia [epi'lepsja] *nf* epilepsy.

epílogo [e'piloɣo] *nm* epilogue.

episodio [epi'soðjo] *nm* episode.

epístola [e'pistola] *nf* epistle.

época ['epoka] *nf* period, time; (*HISTORIA*) age, epoch; **hacer ~** to be epoch-making.

equidad [eki'ðað] *nf* equity.

equilibrar [ekili'ßrar] *vt* to balance; **equilibrio** *nm* balance, equilibrium; **equilibrista** *nm/f* (*funámbulo*) tightrope walker; (*acróbata*) acrobat.

equipaje [eki'paxe] *nm* luggage; (*avíos*) equipment, kit; **~ de mano** hand luggage.

equipar [eki'par] *vt* (*proveer*) to equip.

equipararse [ekipa'rarse] *vr*: **~ con** to be on a level with.

equipo [e'kipo] *nm* (*conjunto de cosas*) equipment; (*DEPORTE*) team; (*de obreros*) shift.

equis ['ekis] *nf inv* (the letter) X.

equitación [ekita'θjon] *nf* (*acto*) riding; (*arte*) horsemanship.

equitativo, a [ekita'tißo, a] *adj* equitable, fair.

equivalente [ekißa'lente] *adj*, *nm* equivalent.

equivaler [ekißa'ler] *vi* to be equivalent *o* equal.

equivocación [ekißoka'θjon] *nf* mistake, error.

equivocado, a [ekißo'kaðo, a] *adj* wrong, mistaken.

equivocarse [ekißo'karse] *vr* to be wrong, make a mistake; **~ de camino** to take the wrong road.

equívoco, a [e'kißoko, a] *adj* (*dudoso*) suspect; (*ambiguo*) ambiguous ♦ *nm* ambiguity; (*malentendido*) misunderstanding.

era ['era] *vb ver* **ser** ♦ *nf* era, age.

erais *vb ver* **ser.**

éramos *vb ver* **ser.**

eran *vb ver* **ser.**

erario [e'rarjo] *nm* exchequer (*BRIT*), treasury.

eras *vb ver* **ser**.

eres *vb ver* **ser**.

erguir [er'xir] *vt* to raise, lift; (*poner derecho*) to straighten; ~**se** *vr* to straighten up.

erigir [eri'xir] *vt* to erect, build; ~**se** *vr*: ~**se en** to set o.s. up as.

erizado, a [eri'θaðo, a] *adj* bristly.

erizarse [eri'θarse] *vr* (*pelo: de perro*) to bristle; (: *de persona*) to stand on end.

erizo [e'riθo] *nm* (*ZOOL*) hedgehog; ~ **de mar** sea-urchin.

ermitaño, a [ermi'taɲo, a] *nm/f* hermit.

erosionar [erosjo'nar] *vt* to erode.

erótico, a [e'rotiko, a] *adj* erotic; **erotismo** *nm* eroticism.

erradicar [erraði'kar] *vt* to eradicate.

errante [e'rrante] *adj* wandering, errant.

errar [e'rrar] *vi* (*vagar*) to wander, roam; (*equivocarse*) to be mistaken ♦ *vt*: ~ **el camino** to take the wrong road; ~ **el tiro** to miss.

erróneo, a [e'rroneo, a] *adj* (*equivocado*) wrong, mistaken; (*falso*) false, untrue.

error [e'rror] *nm* error, mistake; (*INFORM*) bug; ~ **de imprenta** misprint.

eructar [eruk'tar] *vt* to belch, burp.

erudito, a [eru'ðito, a] *adj* erudite, learned.

erupción [erup'θjon] *nf* eruption; (*MED*) rash.

es *vb ver* **ser**.

esa ['esa] (*pl* **esas**) *adj demos ver* **ese**.

ésa ['esa] (*pl* **ésas**) *pron ver* **ése**.

esbelto, a [es'βelto, a] *adj* slim, slender.

esbozo [es'βoθo] *nm* sketch, outline.

escabeche [eska'βetʃe] *nm* brine; (*de aceitunas etc*) pickle; **en** ~ pickled.

escabroso, a [eska'βroso, a] *adj* (*accidentado*) rough, uneven; (*fig*) tough, difficult; (: *atrevido*) risqué.

escabullirse [eskaβu'ʎirse] *vr* to slip away, to clear out.

escafandra [eska'fandra] *nf* (*buzo*) diving suit; (~ *espacial*) space suit.

escala [es'kala] *nf* (*proporción, MUS*) scale; (*de mano*) ladder; (*AVIAT*) stop-

over; **hacer** ~ **en** to stop *o* call in at.

escalafón [eskala'fon] *nm* (*escala de salarios*) salary scale, wage scale.

escalar [eska'lar] *vt* to climb, scale.

escalera [eska'lera] *nf* stairs *pl*, staircase; (*escala*) ladder; (*NAIPES*) run; ~ **mecánica** escalator; ~ **de caracol** spiral staircase.

escalfar [eskal'far] *vt* (*huevos*) to poach.

escalinata [eskali'nata] *nf* staircase.

escalofriante [eskalo'frjante] *adj* chilling.

escalofrío [eskalo'frio] *nm* (*MED*) chill; ~**s** *nmpl* (*fig*) shivers.

escalón [eska'lon] *nm* step, stair; (*de escalera*) rung.

escalope [eska'lope] *nm* (*CULIN*) escalope.

escama [es'kama] *nf* (*de pez, serpiente*) scale; (*de jabón*) flake; (*fig*) resentment.

escamotear [eskamote'ar] *vt* (*robar*) to lift, swipe; (*hacer desaparecer*) to make disappear.

escampar [eskam'par] *vb impers* to stop raining.

escandalizar [eskandali'θar] *vt* to scandalize, shock; ~**se** *vr* to be shocked; (*ofenderse*) to be offended.

escándalo [es'kandalo] *nm* scandal; (*alboroto, tumulto*) row, uproar; **escandaloso, a** *adj* scandalous, shocking.

escandinavo, a [eskandi'naβo, a] *adj*, *nm/f* Scandinavian.

escaño [es'kaɲo] *nm* bench; (*POL*) seat.

escapar [eska'par] *vi* (*gen*) to escape, run away; (*DEPORTE*) to break away; ~**se** *vr* to escape, get away; (*agua, gas*) to leak (out).

escaparate [eskapa'rate] *nm* shop window.

escape [es'kape] *nm* (*de agua, gas*) leak; (*de motor*) exhaust; (*de persona*) escape.

escarabajo [eskara'βaxo] *nm* beetle.

escaramuza [eskara'muθa] *nf* skirmish; (*fig*) brush.

escarbar [eskar'βar] *vt* (*gallina*) to scratch; (*fig*) to inquire into, investigate.

escarcha [es'kartʃa] *nf* frost.

escarlata [eskar'lata] *adj inv* scarlet; **escarlatina** *nf* scarlet fever.

escarmentar [eskarmen'tar] *vt* to punish severely ♦ *vi* to learn one's lesson.

escarmiento *etc* [eskar'mjento] *vb ver* **escarmentar** ♦ *nm* (*ejemplo*) lesson; (*castigo*) punishment.

escarnio [es'karnjo] *nm* mockery; (*injuria*) insult.

escarola [eska'rola] *nf* endive.

escarpado, a [eskar'paðo, a] *adj* (*pendiente*) sheer, steep; (*rocas*) craggy.

escasear [eskase'ar] *vi* to be scarce.

escasez [eska'seθ] *nf* (*falta*) shortage, scarcity; (*pobreza*) poverty.

escaso, a [es'kaso, a] *adj* (*poco*) scarce; (*raro*) rare; (*ralo*) thin, sparse; (*limitado*) limited.

escatimar [eskati'mar] *vt* (*limitar*) to skimp (on), be sparing with.

escena [es'θena] *nf* scene.

escenario [esθe'narjo] *nm* (*TEATRO*) stage; (*CINE*) set; (*fig*) scene; **escenografía** *nf* set design.

escepticismo [esθepti'θismo] *nm* scepticism; **escéptico, a** *adj* sceptical ♦ *nm/f* sceptic.

esclarecer [esklare'θer] *vt* (*iluminar*) to light up, illuminate; (*misterio*, *problema*) to shed light on.

esclavitud [esklaβi'tuð] *nf* slavery.

esclavizar [esklaβi'θar] *vt* to enslave.

esclavo, a [es'klaβo, a] *nm/f* slave.

esclusa [es'klusa] *nf* (*de canal*) lock; (*compuerta*) floodgate.

escoba [es'koβa] *nf* broom.

escocer [esko'θer] *vi* to burn, sting; ~se *vr* to chafe, get chafed.

escocés, esa [esko'θes, esa] *adj* Scottish ♦ *nm/f* Scotsman/woman, Scot.

Escocia [es'koθja] *nf* Scotland.

escoger [esko'xer] *vt* to choose, pick, select; **escogido, a** *adj* chosen, selected; (*calidad*) choice, select.

escolar [esko'lar] *adj* school *cpd* ♦ *nm/f* schoolboy/girl, pupil.

escolta [es'kolta] *nf* escort; **escoltar** *vt* to escort.

escombros [es'kombros] *nmpl* (*basura*) rubbish *sg*; (*restos*) debris *sg*.

esconder [eskon'der] *vt* to hide, conceal; ~se *vr* to hide; **escondite** *nm* hiding place; (*juego*) hide-and-seek; **escondrijo** *nm* hiding place, hideout.

escopeta [esko'peta] *nf* shotgun.

escoria [es'korja] *nf* (*de alto horno*) slag; (*fig*) scum, dregs *pl*.

Escorpio [es'korpjo] *nm* Scorpio.

escorpión [eskor'pjon] *nm* scorpion.

escotado, a [esko'taðo, a] *adj* low-cut.

escote [es'kote] *nm* (*de vestido*) low neck; **pagar a ~** to share the expenses.

escotilla [esko'tiʎa] *nf* (*NAUT*) hatch(way).

escozor [esko'θor] *nm* (*dolor*) sting(ing).

escribano, a [eskri'βano, a] *nm/f* clerk.

escribir [eskri'βir] *vt*, *vi* to write; ~ **a máquina** to type; ¿cómo se escribe? how do you spell it?

escrito, a [es'krito, a] *pp de* **escribir** ♦ *nm* (*documento*) document; (*manuscrito*) text, manuscript; **por** ~ in writing.

escritor, a [eskri'tor, a] *nm/f* writer.

escritorio [eskri'torjo] *nm* desk; (*oficina*) office.

escritura [eskri'tura] *nf* (*acción*) writing; (*caligrafía*) (hand)writing; (*JUR*: *documento*) deed.

escrúpulo [es'krupulo] *nm* scruple; (*minuciosidad*) scrupulousness; **escrupuloso, a** *adj* scrupulous.

escrutar [eskru'tar] *vt* to scrutinize, examine; (*votos*) to count.

escrutinio [eskru'tinjo] *nm* (*examen atento*) scrutiny; (*POL: recuento de votos*) count(ing).

escuadra [es'kwaðra] *nf* (*MIL etc*) squad; (*NAUT*) squadron; (*de coches etc*) fleet; **escuadrilla** *nf* (*de aviones*) squadron; (*AM: de obreros*) gang.

escuadrón [eskwa'ðron] *nm* squadron.

escuálido, a [es'kwaliðo, a] *adj* skinny, scraggy; (*sucio*) squalid.

escuchar [esku'tʃar] *vt* to listen to ♦ *vi* to listen.

escudilla [esku'ðiʎa] nf bowl, basin.

escudo [es'kuðo] nm shield.

escudriñar [eskuðri'ɲar] vt (examinar) to investigate, scrutinize; (mirar de lejos) to scan.

escuela [es'kwela] nf school; ~ de artes y oficios (ESP) ≈ technical college; ~ normal teacher training college.

escueto, a [es'kweto, a] adj plain; (estilo) simple.

escuincle [es'kwinkle] (AM: fam) nm/f kid.

esculpir [eskul'pir] vt to sculpt; (grabar) to engrave; (tallar) to carve; **escultor, a** nm/f sculptor/tress; **escultura** nf sculpture.

escupidera [eskupi'ðera] nf spittoon.

escupir [esku'pir] vt, vi to spit (out).

escurreplatos [eskurre'platos] nm inv plate rack.

escurridizo, a [eskurri'ðiθo, a] adj slippery.

escurrir [esku'rrir] vt (ropa) to wring out; (verduras, platos) to drain ♦ vi (líquidos) to drip; ~se vr (secarse) to drain; (resbalarse) to slip, slide; (escaparse) to slip away.

ese ['ese] (f esa, pl esos, esas) adj demos (sg) that; (pl) those.

ése ['ese] (f ésa, pl ésos, ésas) pron (sg) that (one); (pl) those (ones); ~ ... éste ... the former ... the latter ...; **no me vengas con ésas** don't give me any more of that nonsense.

esencia [e'senθja] nf essence; **esencial** adj essential.

esfera [es'fera] nf sphere; (de reloj) face; **esférico, a** adj spherical.

esforzado, a [esfor'θaðo, a] adj (enérgico) energetic, vigorous.

esforzarse [esfor'θarse] vr to exert o.s., make an effort.

esfuerzo etc [es'fwerθo] vb ver **esforzar** ♦ nm effort.

esfumarse [esfu'marse] vr (apoyo, esperanzas) to fade away.

esgrima [es'xrima] nf fencing.

esguince [es'xinθe] nm (MED) sprain.

eslabón [esla'ßon] nm link.

esmaltar [esmal'tar] vt to enamel;

esmalte nm enamel; **esmalte de uñas** nail varnish o polish.

esmerado, a [esme'raðo, a] adj careful, neat.

esmeralda [esme'ralda] nf emerald.

esmerarse [esme'rarse] vr (aplicarse) to take great pains, exercise great care; (afanarse) to work hard.

esmero [es'mero] nm (great) care.

esnob [es'nob] (pl ~s) adj (persona) snobbish; (coche etc) posh ♦ nm/f snob; **~ismo** nm snobbery.

eso ['eso] pron that, that thing o matter; ~ de su coche that business about his car; ~ de ir al cine all that about going to the cinema; **a ~ de las cinco** at about five o'clock; **en ~** thereupon, at that point; ~ **es** that's it; **¡~ sí que es vida!** now that is really living!; **por ~ te lo dije** that's why I told you; **y ~ que llovía** in spite of the fact it was raining.

esos ['esos] adj demos ver **ese**.

ésos ['esos] pron ver **ése**.

espabilar etc [espaßi'lar] = **despabilar** etc.

espacial [espa'θjal] adj (del espacio) space cpd.

espaciar [espa'θjar] vt to space (out).

espacio [es'paθjo] nm space; (MUS) interval; (RADIO, TV) programme (BRIT), program (US); **el ~** space; **~so, a** adj spacious, roomy.

espada [es'paða] nf sword; **~s** nfpl (NAIPES) spades.

espaguetis [espa'xetis] nmpl spaghetti sg.

espalda [es'palda] nf (gen) back; **~s** nfpl (hombros) shoulders; **a ~s de uno** behind sb's back; **tenderse de ~s** to lie (down) on one's back; **volver la ~ a alguien** to cold-shoulder sb.

espaldilla [espal'ðiʎa] nf shoulder blade.

espantadizo, a [espanta'ðiθo, a] adj timid, easily frightened.

espantajo [espan'taxo] nm = **espantapájaros**.

espantapájaros [espanta'paxaros] nm inv scarecrow.

espantar [espan'tar] vt (asustar) to frighten, scare; (ahuyentar) to frighten off; (*asombrar*) to horrify, appal; ~**se** *vr* to get frightened *o* scared; to be appalled.

espanto [es'panto] *nm* (*susto*) fright; (*terror*) terror; (*asombro*) astonishment; ~**so, a** *adj* frightening; terrifying; astonishing.

España [es'paɲa] *nf* Spain; **español, a** *adj* Spanish ♦ *nm/f* Spaniard ♦ *nm* (*LING*) Spanish.

esparadrapo [espara'ðrapo] *nm* (sticking) plaster (*BRIT*), adhesive tape (*US*).

esparcimiento [esparθi'mjento] *nm* (*dispersión*) spreading; (*derramamiento*) scattering; (*fig*) cheerfulness.

esparcir [espar'θir] *vt* to spread; (*derramar*) to scatter; ~**se** *vr* to spread (out); to scatter; (*divertirse*) to enjoy o.s.

espárrago [es'parraɣo] *nm* asparagus.

espasmo [es'pasmo] *nm* spasm.

espátula [es'patula] *nf* spatula.

especia [es'peθja] *nf* spice.

especial [espe'θjal] *adj* special; ~**idad** *nf* speciality (*BRIT*), specialty (*US*).

especie [es'peθje] *nf* (*BIO*) species; (*clase*) kind, sort; **en ~** in kind.

especificar [espeθifi'kar] *vt* to specify; **específico, a** *adj* specific.

espécimen [es'peθimen] (*pl* **especímenes**) *nm* specimen.

espectáculo [espek'takulo] *nm* (*gen*) spectacle; (*TEATRO etc*) show.

espectador, a [espekta'ðor, a] *nm/f* spectator.

espectro [es'pektro] *nm* ghost; (*fig*) spectre.

especular [espeku'lar] *vt*, *vi* to speculate.

espejismo [espe'xismo] *nm* mirage.

espejo [es'pexo] *nm* mirror; (*fig*) model; ~ **retrovisor** rear-view mirror.

espeluznante [espeluθ'nante] *adj* horrifying, hair-raising.

espera [es'pera] *nf* (*pausa, intervalo*) wait; (*JUR: plazo*) respite; **en ~ de** waiting for; (*con expectativa*) expecting.

esperanza [espe'ranθa] *nf* (*confianza*) hope; (*expectativa*) expectation; **hay**

pocas ~s de que venga there is little prospect of his coming; **esperanzar** *vt* to give hope to.

esperar [espe'rar] *vt* (*aguardar*) to wait for; (*tener expectativa de*) to expect; (*desear*) to hope for ♦ *vi* to wait; to expect; to hope.

esperma [es'perma] *nf* sperm.

espesar [espe'sar] *vt* to thicken; ~**se** *vr* to thicken, get thicker.

espeso, a [es'peso, a] *adj* thick; **espesor** *nm* thickness.

espía [es'pia] *nm/f* spy; **espiar** *vt* (*observar*) to spy on ♦ *vi*: ~ **para** to spy for.

espiga [es'piɣa] *nf* (*BOT: de trigo etc*) ear.

espina [es'pina] *nf* thorn; (*de pez*) bone; ~ **dorsal** (*ANAT*) spine.

espinaca [espi'naka] *nf* spinach.

espinazo [espi'naθo] *nm* spine, backbone.

espinilla [espi'niʎa] *nf* (*ANAT: tibia*) shin(bone); (*grano*) blackhead.

espino [es'pino] *nm* hawthorn.

espinoso, a [espi'noso, a] *adj* (*planta*) thorny, prickly; (*fig*) difficult.

espionaje [espjo'naxe] *nm* spying, espionage.

espiral [espi'ral] *adj*, *nf* spiral.

espirar [espi'rar] *vt* to breathe out, exhale.

espiritista [espiri'tista] *adj*, *nm/f* spiritualist.

espíritu [es'piritu] *nm* spirit; **espiritual** *adj* spiritual.

espita [es'pita] *nf* tap.

espléndido, a [es'plendiðo, a] *adj* (*magnífico*) magnificent, splendid; (*generoso*) generous.

esplendor [esplen'dor] *nm* splendour.

espolear [espole'ar] *vt* to spur on.

espoleta [espo'leta] *nf* (*de bomba*) fuse.

espolvorear [espolβore'ar] *vt* to dust, sprinkle.

esponja [es'ponxa] *nf* sponge; (*fig*) sponger; **esponjoso, a** *adj* spongy.

espontaneidad [espontanei'ðað] *nf* spontaneity; **espontáneo, a** *adj* spontaneous.

esposa [es'posa] *nf* wife; ~**s** *nfpl* handcuffs; **esposar** *vt* to handcuff.

esposo [es'poso] *nm* husband.

espuela [es'pwela] *nf* spur.

espuma [es'puma] *nf* foam; (*de cerveza*) froth, head; (*de jabón*) lather; **espumoso, a** *adj* frothy, foamy; (*vino*) sparkling.

esqueje [es'kexe] *nm* (*de planta*) cutting.

esqueleto [eske'leto] *nm* skeleton.

esquema [es'kema] *nm* (*diagrama*) diagram; (*dibujo*) plan; (*plan*) scheme; (*FILOSOFÍA*) schema.

esquí [es'ki] (*pl* ~**s**) *nm* (*objeto*) ski; (*DEPORTE*) skiing; ~ **acuático** waterskiing; **esquiar** *vi* to ski.

esquilar [eski'lar] *vt* to shear.

esquimal [eski'mal] *adj, nm/f* Eskimo.

esquina [es'kina] *nf* corner.

esquirol [eski'rol] *nm* blackleg.

esquivar [eski'ßar] *vt* to avoid; (*evadir*) to dodge, elude.

esquivo, a [es'kißo, a] *adj* evasive; (*tímido*) reserved; (*huraño*) unsociable.

esta ['esta] *adj demos ver* **este**.

ésta ['esta] *pron ver* **éste**.

está *vb ver* **estar**.

estabilidad [estaßili'ðað] *nf* stability; **estable** *adj* stable.

establecer [estaßle'θer] *vt* to establish; ~**se** *vr* to establish o.s.; (*echar raíces*) to settle (down); **establecimiento** *nm* establishment.

estaca [es'taka] *nf* stake, post; (*de tienda de campaña*) peg.

estacada [esta'kaða] *nf* (*cerca*) fence, fencing; (*palenque*) stockade.

estación [esta'θjon] *nf* station; (*del año*) season; ~ **de autobuses** bus station; ~ **balnearia** seaside resort; ~ **de servicio** service station.

estacionamiento [estaθjona'mjento] *nm* (*AUTO*) parking; (*MIL*) stationing.

estacionar [estaθjo'nar] *vt* (*AUTO*) to park; (*MIL*) to station; ~**io, a** *adj* stationary; (*COM: mercado*) slack.

estadio [es'taðjo] *nm* (*fase*) stage, phase; (*DEPORTE*) stadium.

estadista [esta'ðista] *nm* (*POL*) states-

man; (*ESTADÍSTICA*) statistician.

estadística [esta'ðistika] *nf* (*una* ~) figure, statistic; (*ciencia*) statistics *sg*.

estado [es'taðo] *nm* (*POL: condición*) state; ~ **de cuenta** bank statement; ~ **civil** marital status; ~ **mayor** staff; **estar en** ~ to be pregnant; (**los**) **E~s Unidos** *nmpl* the United States (of America) *sg*.

estadounidense [estaðouni'ðense] *adj* United States *cpd*, American ♦ *nm/f* American.

estafa [es'tafa] *nf* swindle, trick; **estafar** *vt* to swindle, defraud.

estafeta [esta'feta] *nf* (*oficina de correos*) post office; ~ **diplomática** diplomatic bag.

estáis *vb ver* **estar**.

estallar [esta'ʎar] *vi* to burst; (*bomba*) to explode, go off; (*epidemia, guerra, rebelión*) to break out; ~ **en llanto** to burst into tears; **estallido** *nm* explosion; (*fig*) outbreak.

estampa [es'tampa] *nf* (*impresión, imprenta*) print, engraving; (*imagen, figura: de persona*) appearance.

estampado, a [estam'paðo, a] *adj* printed ♦ *nm* (*impresión: acción*) printing; (: *efecto*) print; (*marca*) stamping.

estampar [estam'par] *vt* (*imprimir*) to print; (*marcar*) to stamp; (*metal*) to engrave; (*poner sello en*) to stamp; (*fig*) to stamp, imprint.

estampida [estam'piða] *nf* stampede.

estampido [estam'piðo] *nm* bang, report.

estampilla [estam'piʎa] *nf* stamp.

están *vb ver* **estar**.

estancado, a [estan'kaðo, a] *adj* stagnant.

estancar [estan'kar] *vt* (*aguas*) to hold up, hold back; (*COM*) to monopolize; (*fig*) to block, hold up; ~**se** *vr* to stagnate.

estancia [es'tanθja] *nf* (*permanencia*) stay; (*sala*) room; (*AM*) farm, ranch; **estanciero** (*AM*) *nm* farmer, rancher.

estanco, a [es'tanko, a] *adj* watertight ♦ *nm* tobacconist's (shop), cigar store

(*US*).

estándar [es'tandar] *adj*, *nm* standard;
estandarizar *vt* to standardize.

estandarte [estan'darte] *nm* banner,
standard.

estanque [es'tanke] *nm* (*lago*) pool,
pond; (*AGR*) reservoir.

estanquero, a [estan'kero, a] *nm/f*
tobacconist.

estante [es'tante] *nm* (*armario*) rack,
stand; (*biblioteca*) bookcase; (*anaquel*)
shelf; (*AM*) prop; **estantería** *nf* shelv-
ing, shelves *pl*.

estaño [es'taɲo] *nm* tin.

PALABRA CLAVE

estar [es'tar] *vi* **1** (*posición*) to be; **está
en la plaza** it's in the square; **¿está
Juan?** is Juan in?; **estamos a 30 km de
Junín** we're 30 kms from Junín

2 (+ *adj*: *estado*) to be; ~ **enfermo** to
be ill; **está muy elegante** he's looking
very smart; **¿cómo estás?** how are you
keeping?

3 (+ *gerundio*) to be; **estoy leyendo** I'm
reading

4 (*uso pasivo*): **está condenado a
muerte** he's been condemned to death;
está envasado en ... it's packed in ...

5 (*con fechas*): **¿a cuántos estamos?**
what's the date today?; **estamos a 5 de
mayo** it's the 5th of May

6 (*locuciones*): **¿estamos?** (*¿de
acuerdo?*) okay?; (*¿listo?*) ready?; **¡ya
está bien!** that's enough!

7. ~ **de**: ~ **de vacaciones/viaje** to be on
holiday/away *o* on a trip; **está de
camarero** he's working as a waiter

8 ~ **para**: **está para salir** he's about to
leave; **no estoy para bromas** I'm not in
the mood for jokes

9 ~ **por** (*propuesta etc*) to be in
favour of; (*persona etc*) to support,
side with; **está por limpiar** it still has to
be cleaned

10 ~ **sin**: ~ **sin dinero** to have no
money; **está sin terminar** it isn't
finished yet

♦ ~**se** *vr*: **se estuvo en la cama toda
la tarde** he stayed in bed all after-

noon.

estas ['estas] *adj demos ver* este.

éstas ['estas] *pron ver* éste.

estatal [esta'tal] *adj* state *cpd*.

estático, a [es'tatiko, a] *adj* static.

estatua [es'tatwa] *nf* statue.

estatura [esta'tura] *nf* stature, height.

estatuto [esta'tuto] *nm* (*JUR*) statute;
(*de ciudad*) bye-law; (*de comité*) rule.

este¹ ['este] *nm* east.

este² ['este] (*f* esta, *pl* estos, estas) *adj
demos* (*sg*) this; (*pl*) these.

éste ['este] (*f* ésta, *pl* éstos, éstas) *pron*
(*sg*) this (one); (*pl*) these (ones); **ése
... ~ ...** the former ... the latter ....

esté *etc vb ver* estar.

estela [es'tela] *nf* wash; (*fig*) trail.

estén *etc vb ver* estar.

estenografía [estenoɣra'fia] *nf* shorthand
(*BRIT*), stenography (*US*).

estera [es'tera] *nf* mat(ting).

estéreo [es'tereo] *adj inv*, *nm* stereo;
estereotipo *nm* stereotype.

estéril [es'teril] *adj* sterile, barren; (*fig*)
vain, futile.

esterlina [ester'lina] *adj*: **libra ~** pound
sterling.

estés *etc vb ver* estar.

estética [es'tetika] *nf* aesthetics *sg*.

estético, a [es'tetiko, a] *adj* aesthetic.

estiércol [es'tjerkol] *nm* dung, manure.

estigma [es'tiɣma] *nm* stigma.

estilar [esti'lar] *vi* (*estar de moda*) to be
in fashion; ~**se** *vr* to be in fashion.

estilo [es'tilo] *nm* style; (*TEC*) stylus;
(*NATACIÓN*) stroke; **algo por el ~** something along those lines.

estima [es'tima] *nf* esteem, respect.

estimación [estima'θjon] *nf* (*evaluación*)
estimation; (*aprecio, afecto*) esteem,
regard.

estimar [esti'mar] *vt* (*evaluar*) to estimate; (*valorar*) to value; (*apreciar*) to
esteem, respect; (*pensar, considerar*)
to think, reckon.

estimulante [estimu'lante] *adj* stimulating ♦ *nm* stimulant.

estimular [estimu'lar] *vt* to stimulate;
(*excitar*) to excite.

estímulo [es'timulo] *nm* stimulus; (*ánimo*) encouragement.

estío [es'tio] *nm* summer.

estipulación [estipula'θjon] *nf* stipulation, condition.

estipular [estipu'lar] *vt* to stipulate.

estirado, a [esti'raðo, a] *adj* (*tenso*) (stretched *o* drawn) tight; (*fig: persona*) stiff, pompous.

estirar [esti'rar] *vt* to stretch; (*dinero, suma etc*) to stretch out; ~se *vr* to stretch.

estirón [esti'ron] *nm* pull, tug; (*crecimiento*) spurt, sudden growth; **dar un ~** (*niño*) to shoot up.

estirpe [es'tirpe] *nf* stock, lineage.

estival [esti'βal] *adj* summer *cpd*.

esto ['esto] *pron* this, this thing *o* matter; ~ **de la boda** this business about the wedding.

Estocolmo [esto'kolmo] *nm* Stockholm.

estofa [es'tofa] *nf*: **de baja ~** poor-quality.

estofado [esto'faðo] *nm* (*CULIN*) stew.

estofar [esto'far] *vt* (*CULIN*) to stew.

estómago [es'tomaɣo] *nm* stomach; **tener ~** to be thick-skinned.

estorbar [estor'βar] *vt* to hinder, obstruct; (*fig*) to bother, disturb ♦ *vi* to be in the way; **estorbo** *nm* (*molestia*) bother, nuisance; (*obstáculo*) hindrance, obstacle.

estornudar [estornu'ðar] *vi* to sneeze.

estos ['estos] *adj demos ver* **este**.

éstos ['estos] *pron ver* **éste**.

estoy *vb ver* **estar**.

estrafalario, a [estrafa'larjo, a] *adj* odd, eccentric; (*desarreglado*) slovenly, sloppy.

estrago [es'traɣo] *nm* ruin, destruction; **hacer ~s en** to wreak havoc among.

estragón [estra'ɣon] *nm* tarragon.

estrangulador, a [estrangula'ðor, a] *nm/f* strangler ♦ *nm* (*TEC*) throttle; (*AUTO*) choke.

estrangulamiento [estrangula'mjento] *nm* (*AUTO*) bottleneck.

estrangular [estrangu'lar] *vt* (*persona*) to strangle; (*MED*) to strangulate.

estraperlo [estra'perlo] *nm* black market.

estratagema [estrata'xema] *nf* (*MIL*) stratagem; (*astucia*) cunning.

estrategia [estra'texja] *nf* strategy; **estratégico, a** *adj* strategic.

estratificar [estratifi'kar] *vt* to stratify.

estrato [es'trato] *nm* stratum, layer.

estrechar [estre'tʃar] *vt* (*reducir*) to narrow; (*COSTURA*) to take in; (*persona*) to hug, embrace; ~se *vr* (*reducirse*) to narrow, grow narrow; (*2 personas*) to embrace; ~ **la mano** to shake hands.

estrechez [estre'tʃeθ] *nf* narrowness; (*de ropa*) tightness; (*intimidad*) intimacy; (*COM*) want *o* shortage of money; **estrecheces** *nfpl* (*dificultades económicas*) financial difficulties.

estrecho, a [es'tretʃo, a] *adj* narrow; (*apretado*) tight; (*íntimo*) close, intimate; (*miserable*) mean ♦ *nm* strait; ~ **de miras** narrow-minded.

estrella [es'treʎa] *nf* star.

estrellar [estre'ʎar] *vt* (*hacer añicos*) to smash (to pieces); (*huevos*) to fry; ~se *vr* to smash; (*chocarse*) to crash; (*fracasar*) to fail.

estremecer [estreme'θer] *vt* to shake; ~se *vr* to shake, tremble; **estremecimiento** *nm* (*temblor*) trembling, shaking.

estrenar [estre'nar] *vt* (*vestido*) to wear for the first time; (*casa*) to move into; (*película, obra de teatro*) to première; ~se *vr* (*persona*) to make one's début; **estreno** *nm* (*primer uso*) first use; (*CINE etc*) première.

estreñido, a [estre'ɲiðo, a] *adj* constipated.

estreñimiento [estreɲi'mjento] *nm* constipation.

estrépito [es'trepito] *nm* noise, racket; (*fig*) fuss; **estrepitoso, a** *adj* noisy; (*fiesta*) rowdy.

estría [es'tria] *nf* groove.

estribar [estri'βar] *vi*: ~ **en** to rest on, be supported by.

estribillo [estri'βiʎo] *nm* (*LITERATURA*) refrain; (*MUS*) chorus.

estribo [es'triβo] *nm* (*de jinete*) stirrup;

(de coche, tren) step; (de puente) support; (GEO) spur; **perder los** ~s to fly off the handle.

estribor [estri'βor] nm (NAUT) starboard.

estricnina [estrik'nina] nf strychnine.

estricto, a [es'trikto, a] adj (riguroso) strict; (severo) severe.

estropajo [estro'paxo] nm scourer.

estropear [estrope'ar] vt (arruinar) to spoil; (dañar) to damage; ~se vr (objeto) to get damaged; (persona: la piel etc) to be ruined.

estructura [estruk'tura] nf structure.

estruendo [es'trwendo] nm (ruido) racket, din; (fig: alboroto) uproar, turmoil.

estrujar [estru'xar] vt (apretar) to squeeze; (aplastar) to crush; (fig) to drain, bleed.

estuario [es'twarjo] nm estuary.

estuche [es'tutʃe] nm box, case.

estudiante [estu'ðjante] nm/f student; **estudiantil** adj student cpd.

estudiar [estu'ðjar] vt to study.

estudio [es'tuðjo] nm study; (CINE, ARTE, RADIO) studio; ~s nmpl studies; (erudición) learning sg; ~so, a adj studious.

estufa [es'tufa] nf heater, fire.

estupefaciente [estupefa'θjente] nm drug, narcotic.

estupefacto, a [estupe'fakto, a] adj speechless, thunderstruck.

estupendo, a [estu'pendo, a] adj wonderful, terrific; (fam) great; ¡~! that's great!, fantastic!

estupidez [estupi'ðeθ] nf (torpeza) stupidity; (acto) stupid thing (to do).

estúpido, a [es'tupiðo, a] adj stupid, silly.

estupor [estu'por] nm stupor; (fig) astonishment, amazement.

estupro [es'tupro] nm rape.

estuve etc vb ver **estar**.

esvástica [es'βastika] nf swastika.

ETA ['eta] (ESP) nf abr (= Euskadi ta Askatasuna) ETA.

etapa [e'tapa] nf (de viaje) stage; (DEPORTE) leg; (parada) stopping place; (fig) stage, phase.

etarra [e'tarra] nm/f member of ETA.

etc. abr (= etcétera) etc.

etcétera [et'θetera] adv etcetera.

eternidad [eterni'ðað] nf eternity; **eterno, a** adj eternal, everlasting.

ética ['etika] nf ethics pl.

ético, a ['etiko, a] adj ethical.

etiqueta [eti'keta] nf (modales) etiquette; (rótulo) label, tag.

Eucaristía [eukaris'tia] nf Eucharist.

eufemismo [eufe'mismo] nm euphemism.

euforia [eu'forja] nf euphoria.

eunuco [eu'nuko] nm eunuch.

Europa [eu'ropa] nf Europe; **europeo, a** adj, nm/f European.

éuscaro, a ['euskaro, a] adj Basque ♦ nm (LING) Basque.

Euskadi [eus'kaði] nm the Basque Country o Provinces pl.

euskera [eus'kera] nm (LING) Basque.

evacuación [eβakwa'θjon] nf evacuation.

evacuar [eβa'kwar] vt to evacuate.

evadir [eβa'ðir] vt to evade, avoid; ~se vr to escape.

evaluar [eβa'lwar] vt to evaluate.

evangélico, a [eβan'xeliko, a] adj evangelic(al).

evangelio [eβan'xeljo] nm gospel.

evaporar [eβapo'rar] vt to evaporate; ~se vr to vanish.

evasión [eβa'sjon] nf escape, flight; (fig) evasion.

evasiva [eβa'siβa] nf (pretexto) excuse.

evasivo, a [eβa'siβo, a] adj evasive, non-committal.

evento [e'βento] nm event.

eventual [eβen'twal] adj possible, conditional (upon circumstances); (trabajador) casual, temporary.

evidencia [eβi'ðenθja] nf evidence, proof; **evidenciar** vt (hacer patente) to make evident; (probar) to prove, show; **evidenciarse** vr to be evident.

evidente [eβi'ðente] adj obvious, clear, evident.

evitar [eβi'tar] vt (evadir) to avoid; (impedir) to prevent.

evocar [eβo'kar] vt to evoke, call forth.

evolución [eβolu'θjon] nf (desarrollo) evolution, development; (cambio)

change; (*MIL*) manoeuvre; **evolucionar**
vi to evolve; to manoeuvre.
ex [eks] *adj* ex-; **el ~ ministro** the former minister, the ex-minister.
exacerbar [eksaθer'ßar] *vt* to irritate,
annoy.
exactamente [eksakta'mente] *adv*
exactly.
exactitud [eksakti'tuð] *nf* exactness;
(*precisión*) accuracy; (*puntualidad*)
punctuality; **exacto, a** *adj* exact; accurate; punctual; ¡**exacto!** exactly!
exageración [eksaxera'θjon] *nf*
exaggeration.
exagerar [eksaxe'rar] *vt, vi* to exaggerate.
exaltado, a [eksal'taðo, a] *adj*
(*apasionado*) over-excited, worked-up;
(*exagerado*) extreme.
exaltar [eksal'tar] *vt* to exalt, glorify;
~se *vr* (*excitarse*) to get excited *o*
worked-up.
examen [ek'samen] *nm* examination.
examinar [eksami'nar] *vt* to examine;
~se *vr* to be examined, take an
examination.
exasperar [eksaspe'rar] *vt* to exasperate; **~se** *vr* to get exasperated, lose
patience.
Exca. *abr* = **Excelencia.**
excavadora [ekskaßa'ðora] *nf* excavator.
excavar [ekska'ßar] *vt* to excavate.
excedente [eksθe'ðente] *adj, nm* excess,
surplus.
exceder [eksθe'ðer] *vt* to exceed,
surpass; **~se** *vr* (*extralimitarse*) to go
too far; (*sobrepasarse*) to excel o.s.
excelencia [eksθe'lenθja] *nf* excellence;
E~ Excellency; **excelente** *adj*
excellent.
excelso, a [eks'θelso, a] *adj* lofty, sublime.
excentricidad [eksθentriθi'ðað] *nf* eccentricity; **excéntrico, a** *adj, nm/f* eccentric.
excepción [eksθep'θjon] *nf* exception;
excepcional *adj* exceptional.
excepto [eks'θepto] *adv* excepting,
except (for).
exceptuar [eksθep'twar] *vt* to except,

exclude.
excesivo, a [eksθe'sißo, a] *adj*
excessive.
exceso [eks'θeso] *nm* (*gen*) excess;
(*COM*) surplus; **~ de equipaje/peso**
excess luggage/weight.
excitación [eksθita'θjon] *nf* (*sensación*)
excitement; (*acción*) excitation.
excitado, a [eksθi'taðo, a] *adj* excited;
(*emociones*) aroused.
excitar [eksθi'tar] *vt* to excite; (*incitar*)
to urge; **~se** *vr* to get excited.
exclamación [eksklama'θjon] *nf* exclamation.
exclamar [ekskla'mar] *vi* to exclaim.
excluir [eksklu'ir] *vt* to exclude; (*dejar
fuera*) to shut out; (*descartar*) to reject; **exclusión** *nf* exclusion.
exclusiva [eksklu'sißa] *nf* (*PRENSA*)
exclusive, scoop; (*COM*) sole right.
exclusivo, a [eksklu'sißo, a] *adj*
exclusive; **derecho ~** sole *o* exclusive
right.
Excmo. *abr* = **excelentísimo.**
excomulgar [ekskomul'xar] *vt* (*REL*) to
excommunicate.
excomunión [ekskomu'njon] *nf*
excommunication.
excursión [ekskur'sjon] *nf* excursion,
outing; **excursionista** *nm/f* (*turista*)
sightseer.
excusa [eks'kusa] *nf* excuse; (*disculpa*)
apology.
excusar [eksku'sar] *vt* to excuse;
(*evitar*) to avoid, prevent; **~se** *vr* (*disculparse*) to apologize.
exento, a [ek'sento, a] *adj* exempt.
exequias [ek'sekjas] *nfpl* funeral rites.
exhalar [eksa'lar] *vt* to exhale, breathe
out; (*olor etc*) to give off; (*suspiro*) to
breathe, heave.
exhausto, a [ek'sausto, a] *adj*
exhausted.
exhibición [eksißi'θjon] *nf* exhibition,
display, show.
exhibir [eksi'ßir] *vt* to exhibit, display,
show.
exhortación [eksorta'θjon] *nf* exhorta-
tion.
exhortar [eksor'tar] *vt:* **~ a** to exhort to.

exigencia [eksi'xenθja] *nf* demand, requirement; **exigente** *adj* demanding.
exigir [eksi'xir] *vt* (*gen*) to demand, require; ~ **el pago** to demand payment.
exiliado, a [eksi'ljaðo, a] *adj* exiled ♦ *nm/f* exile.
exilio [ek'siljo] *nm* exile.
eximio, a [ek'simjo, a] *adj* (*eminente*) distinguished, eminent.
eximir [eksi'mir] *vt* to exempt.
existencia [eksis'tenθja] *nf* existence; ~**s** *nfpl* stock(s) (*pl*).
existir [eksis'tir] *vi* to exist, be.
éxito ['eksito] *nm* (*resultado*) result, outcome; (*triunfo*) success; (*MUS etc*) hit; **tener** ~ to be successful.
exonerar [eksone'rar] *vt* to exonerate; ~ **de una obligación** to free from an obligation.
exorcizar [eksorθi'θar] *vt* to exorcize.
exótico, a [ek'sotiko, a] *adj* exotic.
expandir [ekspan'dir] *vt* to expand.
expansión [ekspan'sjon] *nf* expansion.
expatriarse [ekspa'trjarse] *vr* to emigrate; (*POL*) to go into exile.
expectativa [ekspekta'tißa] *nf* (*espera*) expectation; (*perspectiva*) prospect.
expedición [ekspeði'θjon] *nf* (*excursión*) expedition.
expediente [ekspe'ðjente] *nm* expedient; (*JUR: procedimento*) action, proceedings *pl*; (*: papeles*) dossier, file, record.
expedir [ekspe'ðir] *vt* (*despachar*) to send, forward; (*pasaporte*) to issue.
expedito, a [ekspe'ðito, a] *adj* (*libre*) clear, free.
expendedor, a [ekspende'ðor, a] *nm/f* (*vendedor*) dealer.
expendedora [ekspende'ora] *nf* (*aparato*) (vending) machine; ~ **de cigarrillos** cigarette machine; *ver tb* **expendedor**.
expendeduría [ekspendedu'ria] *nf* (*estanco*) tobacconist's (shop).
expensas [eks'pensas] *nfpl*: **a** ~ **de** at the expense of.
experiencia [ekspe'rjenθja] *nf* experience.
experimentado, a [eksperimen'taðo, a] *adj* experienced.

experimentar [eksperimen'tar] *vt* (*en laboratorio*) to experiment with; (*probar*) to test, try out; (*notar, observar*) to experience; (*deterioro, pérdida*) to suffer; **experimento** *nm* experiment.
experto, a [eks'perto, a] *adj* expert, skilled ♦ *nm/f* expert.
expiar [ekspi'ar] *vt* to atone for.
expirar [ekspi'rar] *vi* to expire.
explayarse [ekspla'jarse] *vr* (*en discurso*) to speak at length; ~ **con uno** to confide in sb.
explicación [eksplika'θjon] *nf* explanation.
explicar [ekspli'kar] *vt* to explain; ~**se** *vr* to explain (o.s.).
explícito, a [eks'pliθito, a] *adj* explicit.
explique *etc vb ver* **explicar**.
explorador, a [eksplora'ðor, a] *nm/f* (*pionero*) explorer; (*MIL*) scout ♦ *nm* (*MED*) probe; (*TEC*) (radar) scanner.
explorar [eksplo'rar] *vt* to explore; (*MED*) to probe; (*radar*) to scan.
explosión [eksplo'sjon] *nf* explosion; **explosivo, a** *adj* explosive.
explotación [eksplota'θjon] *nf* exploitation; (*de planta etc*) running.
explotar [eksplo'tar] *vt* to exploit; to run, operate ♦ *vi* to explode.
exponer [ekspo'ner] *vt* to expose; (*cuadro*) to display; (*vida*) to risk; (*idea*) to explain; ~**se** *vr*: ~**se a (hacer) algo** to run the risk of (doing) sth.
exportación [eksporta'θjon] *nf* (*acción*) export; (*mercancías*) exports *pl*.
exportar [ekspor'tar] *vt* to export.
exposición [eksposi'θjon] *nf* (*gen*) exposure; (*de arte*) show, exhibition; (*explicación*) explanation; (*narración*) account, statement.
exposímetro [ekspo'simetro] *nm* exposure meter.
expresar [ekspre'sar] *vt* to express; **expresión** *nf* expression.
expreso, a [eks'preso, a] *pp de* **expresar** ♦ *adj* (*explícito*) express; (*claro*) specific, clear; (*tren*) fast ♦ *adv*: **mandar** ~ to send by express

(delivery).

express [eks'pres] *(AM)* *adv*: **enviar algo ~ to** send sth special delivery.

exprimidor [eksprimi'ðor] *nm* squeezer.

exprimir [ekspri'mir] *vt (fruta)* to squeeze; *(zumo)* to squeeze out.

expropiar [ekspro'pjar] *vt* to expropriate.

expuesto, a [eks'pwesto, a] *pp de* **exponer** ♦ *adj* exposed; *(cuadro etc)* on show, on display.

expulsar [ekspul'sar] *vt (echar)* to eject, throw out; *(alumno)* to expel; *(despedir)* to sack, fire; *(DEPORTE)* to send off; **expulsión** *nf* expulsion; sending-off.

exquisito, a [ekski'sito, a] *adj* exquisite; *(comida)* delicious.

éxtasis ['ekstasis] *nm* ecstasy.

extender [eksten'der] *vt* to extend; *(los brazos)* to stretch out, hold out; *(mapa, tela)* to spread (out), open (out); *(mantequilla)* to spread; *(certificado)* to issue; *(cheque, recibo)* to make out; *(documento)* to draw up; **~se** *vr (gen)* to extend; *(persona: en el suelo)* to stretch out; *(epidemia)* to spread; **extendido, a** *adj (abierto)* spread out, open; *(brazos)* outstretched; *(costumbre)* widespread; *(pey)* rife.

extensión [eksten'sjon] *nf (de terreno, mar)* expanse, stretch; *(de tiempo)* length, duration; *(TEL)* extension; **en toda la ~ de la palabra** in every sense of the word.

extenso, a [eks'tenso, a] *adj* extensive.

extenuar [ekste'nwar] *vt (debilitar)* to weaken.

exterior [ekste'rjor] *adj (de fuera)* external; *(afuera)* outside, exterior; *(apariencia)* outward; *(deuda, relaciones)* foreign ♦ *nm (gen)* exterior, outside; *(aspecto)* outward appearance; *(DEPORTE)* wing(er); *(países extranjeros)* abroad; **en el ~** abroad; **al ~** outwardly, on the surface.

exterminar [ekstermi'nar] *vt* to exterminate; **exterminio** *nm* extermination.

externo, a [eks'terno, a] *adj (exterior)*

external, outside; *(superficial)* outward ♦ *nm/f* day pupil.

extinguir [ekstin'gir] *vt (fuego)* to extinguish, put out; *(raza, población)* to wipe out; **~se** *vr (fuego)* to go out; *(BIO)* to die out, become extinct.

extinto, a [eks'tinto, a] *adj* extinct.

extintor [ekstin'tor] *nm (fire)* extinguisher.

extra ['ekstra] *adj inv (tiempo)* extra; *(chocolate, vino)* good-quality ♦ *nm/f* extra ♦ *nm* extra; *(bono)* bonus.

extracción [ekstrak'θjon] *nf* extraction; *(en lotería)* draw.

extracto [eks'trakto] *nm* extract.

extraer [ekstra'er] *vt* to extract, take out.

extralimitarse [ekstralimi'tarse] *vr* to go too far.

extranjero, a [ekstran'xero, a] *adj* foreign ♦ *nm/f* foreigner ♦ *nm* foreign countries *pl*; **en el ~** abroad.

extrañar [ekstra'nar] *vt (sorprender)* to find strange *o* odd; *(echar de menos)* to miss; **~se** *vr (sorprenderse)* to be amazed, be surprised; *(distanciarse)* to become estranged, grow apart.

extrañeza [ekstra'neθa] *nf (rareza)* strangeness, oddness; *(asombro)* amazement, surprise.

extraño, a [eks'trano, a] *adj (extranjero)* foreign; *(raro, sorprendente)* strange, odd.

extraordinario, a [ekstraorði'narjo, a] *adj* extraordinary; *(edición, número)* special ♦ *nm (de periódico)* special edition; **horas extraordinarias** overtime *sg*.

extrarradio [ekstra'rraðjo] *nm* poor suburban area.

extravagancia [ekstraβa'xanθja] *nf* oddness; outlandishness; **extravagante** *adj (excéntrico)* eccentric; *(estrafalario)* outlandish.

extraviado, a [ekstra'βjaðo, a] *adj* lost, missing.

extraviar [ekstra'βjar] *vt (persona: desorientar)* to mislead, misdirect; *(perder)* to lose, misplace; **~se** *vr* to lose one's way, get lost; **extravío** *nm* loss; *(fig)* deviation.

extremar [ekstre'mar] *vt* to carry to extremes; **~se** *vr* to do one's utmost, make every effort.

extremaunción [ekstremaun'θjon] *nf* extreme unction.

extremidad [ekstremi'ðað] *nf* (*punta*) extremity; (*fila*) edge; **~es** *nfpl* (*ANAT*) extremities.

extremo, a [eks'tremo, a] *adj* extreme; (*último*) last ♦ *nm* end; (*límite, grado sumo*) extreme; **en último ~** as a last resort.

extrovertido, a [ekstroßer'tiðo, a] *adj, nm/f* extrovert.

exuberancia [eksuße'ranθja] *nf* exuberance; **exuberante** *adj* exuberant; (*fig*) luxuriant, lush.

eyacular [ejaku'lar] *vt, vi* to ejaculate.

F

f.a.b. *abr* (= *franco a bordo*) f.o.b.

fábrica ['faßrika] *nf* factory; **marca de ~** trademark; **precio de ~** factory price.

fabricación [faßrika'θjon] *nf* (*manufactura*) manufacture; (*producción*) production; **de ~ casera** homemade; **~ en serie** mass production.

fabricante [faßri'kante] *nm/f* manufacturer.

fabricar [faßri'kar] *vt* (*manufacturar*) to manufacture, make; (*construir*) to build; (*cuento*) to fabricate, devise.

fábula ['faßula] *nf* (*cuento*) fable; (*chisme*) rumour; (*mentira*) fib.

facción [fak'θjon] *nf* (*POL*) faction; **facciones** *nfpl* (*del rostro*) features.

fácil ['faθil] *adj* (*simple*) easy; (*probable*) likely.

facilidad [faθili'ðað] *nf* (*capacidad*) ease; (*sencillez*) simplicity; (*de palabra*) fluency; **~es** *nfpl* facilities.

facilitar [faθili'tar] *vt* (*hacer fácil*) to make easy; (*proporcionar*) to provide.

fácilmente ['faθilmente] *adv* easily.

facsímil [fak'simil] *nm* facsimile, fax.

factible [fak'tißle] *adj* feasible.

factor [fak'tor] *nm* factor.

factura [fak'tura] *nf* (*cuenta*) bill; (*hechura*) manufacture; **facturar** *vt* (*COM*) to invoice, charge for; (*equipaje*) to register (*BRIT*), check (*US*).

facultad [fakul'tað] *nf* (*aptitud, ESCOL etc*) faculty; (*poder*) power.

facha ['fatʃa] (*fam*) *nf* (*aspecto*) look; (*cara*) face.

fachada [fa'tʃaða] *nf* (*ARQ*) façade, front.

faena [fa'ena] *nf* (*trabajo*) work; (*quehacer*) task, job.

fagot [fa'ɣot] (*pl* **~es**) *nm* (*MUS*) bassoon.

faisán [fai'san] *nm* pheasant.

faja ['faxa] *nf* (*para la cintura*) sash; (*de mujer*) corset; (*de tierra*) strip.

fajo ['faxo] *nm* (*de papeles*) bundle; (*de billetes*) wad.

Falange [fa'lanxe] *nf* (*POL*) Falange.

falda ['falda] *nf* (*prenda de vestir*) skirt.

falo ['falo] *nm* phallus.

falsedad [false'ðað] *nf* falseness; (*hipocresía*) hypocrisy; (*mentira*) falsehood.

falsificar [falsifi'kar] *vt* (*firma etc*) to forge; (*voto etc*) to rig; (*moneda*) to counterfeit.

falso, a ['falso, a] *adj* false; (*erróneo*) mistaken; (*documento, moneda etc*) fake; **en ~** falsely.

falta ['falta] *nf* (*defecto*) fault, flaw; (*privación*) lack, want; (*ausencia*) absence; (*carencia*) shortage; (*equivocación*) mistake; (*DEPORTE*) foul; **echar en ~** to miss; **hacer ~ hacer algo** to be necessary to do sth; **me hace ~ una pluma** I need a pen.

faltar [fal'tar] *vi* (*escasear*) to be lacking, be wanting; (*ausentarse*) to be absent, be missing; **faltan 2 horas para llegar** there are 2 hours to go till arrival; **~ al respeto a uno** to be disrespectful to sb; **¡no faltaba más!** that's the last straw!

falto, a ['falto, a] *adj* (*desposeído*) deficient, lacking; (*necesitado*) poor, wretched.

falla ['faʎa] *nf* (*defecto*) fault, flaw.

fallar [fa'ʎar] *vt* (*JUR*) to pronounce sentence on ♦ *vi* (*memoria*) to fail;

(*motor*) to miss.

fallecer [faʎe'θer] *vi* to pass away, die; **fallecimiento** *nm* decease, demise.

fallido, a [fa'ʎiðo, a] *adj* (*gen*) frustrated, unsuccessful.

fallo ['faʎo] *nm* (*JUR*) verdict, ruling; (*fracaso*) failure.

fama ['fama] *nf* (*renombre*) fame; (*reputación*) reputation.

famélico, a [fa'meliko, a] *adj* starving.

familia [fa'milja] *nf* family.

familiar [fami'ljar] *adj* (*relativo a la familia*) family *cpd*; (*conocido, informal*) familiar ♦ *nm* relative, relation; ~**idad** *nf* (*gen*) familiarity; (*informalidad*) homeliness; ~**izarse** *vr*: ~**izarse con** to familiarize o.s. with.

famoso, a [fa'moso, a] *adj* (*renombrado*) famous.

fanático, a [fa'natiko, a] *adj* fanatical ♦ *nm/f* fanatic; (*CINE, DEPORTE*) fan; **fanatismo** *nm* fanaticism.

fanfarrón, ona [fanfa'rron, ona] *adj* boastful; (*pey*) showy.

fango ['fango] *nm* mud; ~**so, a** *adj* muddy.

fantasía [fanta'sia] *nf* fantasy, imagination; **joyas de** ~ imitation jewellery *sg*.

fantasma [fan'tasma] *nm* (*espectro*) ghost, apparition; (*presumido*) show-off.

fantástico, a [fan'tastiko, a] *adj* fantastic.

farmacéutico, a [farma'θeutiko, a] *adj* pharmaceutical ♦ *nm/f* chemist (*BRIT*), pharmacist.

farmacia [far'maθja] *nf* chemist's (shop) (*BRIT*), pharmacy; ~ **de turno** duty chemist.

fármaco ['farmako] *nm* drug.

faro ['faro] *nm* (*NAUT: torre*) lighthouse; (*AUTO*) headlamp; (*foco*) floodlight; ~**s antiniebla** fog lamps; ~**s delanteros/ traseros** headlights/rear lights.

farol [fa'rol] *nm* lantern, lamp.

farola [fa'rola] *nf* street lamp (*BRIT*) o light (*US*).

farsa ['farsa] *nf* (*gen*) farce.

farsante [far'sante] *nm/f* fraud, fake.

fascículo [fas'θikulo] *nm* (*de revista*)

part, instalment.

fascinar [fasθi'nar] *vt* (*gen*) to fascinate.

fascismo [fas'θismo] *nm* fascism; **fascista** *adj, nm/f* fascist.

fase ['fase] *nf* phase.

fastidiar [fasti'ðjar] *vt* (*disgustar*) to annoy, bother; (*estropear*) to spoil; ~**se** *vr* (*disgustarse*) to get annoyed o cross; **¡que se fastidie!** (*fam*) he'll just have to put up with it!

fastidio [fas'tiðjo] *nm* (*disgusto*) annoyance; ~**so, a** *adj* (*molesto*) annoying.

fatal [fa'tal] *adj* (*gen*) fatal; (*desgraciado*) ill-fated; (*fam: malo, pésimo*) awful; ~**idad** *nf* (*destino*) fate; (*mala suerte*) misfortune.

fatiga [fa'tiɣa] *nf* (*cansancio*) fatigue, weariness.

fatigar [fati'ɣar] *vt* to tire, weary; ~**se** *vr* to get tired.

fatigoso, a [fati'ɣoso, a] *adj* (*cansador*) tiring.

fatuo, a ['fatwo, a] *adj* (*vano*) fatuous; (*presuntuoso*) conceited.

fauces ['fauθes] *nfpl* jaws, mouth *sg*.

favor [fa'βor] *nm* favour; **estar a** ~ **de** to be in favour of; **haga el** ~ **de...** would you be so good as to..., kindly...; **por** ~ please; ~**able** *adj* favourable.

favorecer [faβore'θer] *vt* to favour; (*vestido etc*) to become, flatter; **este peinado le favorece** this hairstyle suits him.

favorito, a [faβo'rito, a] *adj, nm/f* favourite.

faz [faθ] *nf* face; **la** ~ **de la tierra** the face of the earth.

fe [fe] *nf* (*REL*) faith; (*confianza*) belief; (*documento*) certificate; **prestar** ~ **a** to believe, credit; **actuar con buena/mala** ~ to act in good/bad faith; **dar** ~ **de** to bear witness to.

fealdad [feal'dað] *nf* ugliness.

febrero [fe'βrero] *nm* February.

fecundar [fekun'dar] *vt* (*generar*) to fertilize, make fertile; **fecundo, a** *adj* (*fértil*) fertile; (*fig*) prolific; (*productivo*) productive.

fecha ['fetʃa] *nf* date; ~ **de caducidad**

(*de producto alimenticio*) sell-by date; (*de contrato etc*) expiry date; **con ~ adelantada** postdated; **en ~ próxima** soon; **hasta la ~** to date, so far; **poner ~ to date; fechar** *vt* to date.

federación [feðera'θjon] *nf* federation.

federal [feðe'ral] *adj* federal.

felicidad [feliθi'ðað] *nf* (*satisfacción, contento*) happiness; **~es** *nfpl* (*felicitaciones*) best wishes, congratulations.

felicitación [feliθita'θjon] *nf*: **¡felicitaciones!** congratulations!

felicitar [feliθi'tar] *vt* to congratulate.

feligrés, esa [feli'xres, esa] *nm/f* parishioner.

feliz [fe'liθ] *adj* (*contento*) happy; (*afortunado*) lucky.

felpudo [fel'puðo] *nm* doormat.

femenino, a [feme'nino, a] *adj, nm* feminine.

feminista [femi'nista] *adj, nm/f* feminist.

fenómeno [fe'nomeno] *nm* phenomenon; (*fig*) freak, accident ♦ *adj* great ♦ *excl* great!, marvellous!

feo, a ['feo, a] *adj* (*gen*) ugly; (*desagradable*) bad, nasty.

féretro ['feretro] *nm* (*ataúd*) coffin; (*sarcófago*) bier.

feria ['ferja] *nf* (*gen*) fair; (*descanso*) holiday, rest day; (*AM*: *mercado*) village market; (:*cambio*) loose *o* small change.

fermentar [fermen'tar] *vi* to ferment.

ferocidad [feroθi'ðað] *nf* fierceness, ferocity.

feroz [fe'roθ] *adj* (*cruel*) cruel; (*salvaje*) fierce.

férreo, a ['ferreo, a] *adj* iron.

ferretería [ferrete'ria] *nf* (*tienda*) ironmonger's (*shop*) (*BRIT*), hardware store.

ferrocarril [ferroka'rril] *nm* railway.

ferroviario, a [ferro'βjarjo, a] *adj* rail *cpd*.

fértil ['fertil] *adj* (*productivo*) fertile; (*rico*) rich; **fertilidad** *nf* (*gen*) fertility; (*productividad*) fruitfulness.

fertilizar [fertili'θar] *vt* to fertilize.

fervor [fer'βor] *nm* fervour; **~oso, a** *adj* fervent.

festejar [feste'xar] *vt* (*celebrar*) to celebrate; **festejo** *nm* celebration; **festejos** *nmpl* (*fiestas*) festivals.

festividad [festiβi'ðað] *nf* festivity.

festivo, a [fes'tiβo, a] *adj* (*de fiesta*) festive; (*fig*) witty; (*CINE, LITERATURA*) humorous; **día ~** holiday.

fétido, a ['fetiðo, a] *adj* (*hediondo*) foul-smelling.

feto ['feto] *nm* foetus.

fiable ['fjaßle] *adj* (*persona*) trustworthy; (*máquina*) reliable.

fiador, a [fia'ðor, a] *nm/f* (*JUR*) surety, guarantor; (*COM*) backer; **salir ~ por uno** to stand bail for sb.

fiambre ['fjambre] *nm* cold meat.

fianza ['fjanθa] *nf* surety; (*JUR*): **libertad bajo ~** release on bail.

fiar [fi'ar] *vt* (*salir garante de*) to guarantee; (*vender a crédito*) to sell on credit; (*secreto*): **~ a** to confide (to) ♦ *vi* to trust; **~se** *vr* to trust (in), rely on; **~se de uno** to rely on sb.

fibra ['fiβra] *nf* fibre; **~ óptica** optical fibre.

ficción [fik'θjon] *nf* fiction.

ficticio, a [fik'tiθjo, a] *adj* (*imaginario*) fictitious; (*falso*) fabricated.

ficha ['fitʃa] *nf* (*TEL*) token; (*en juegos*) counter, marker; (*tarjeta*) (index) card; **fichar** *vt* (*archivar*) to file, index; (*DEPORTE*) to sign; **estar fichado** to have a record; **fichero** *nm* box file; (*INFORM*) file.

fidelidad [fiðeli'ðað] *nf* (*lealtad*) fidelity, loyalty; **alta ~** high fidelity, hi-fi.

fideos [fi'ðeos] *nmpl* noodles.

fiebre ['fjeβre] *nf* (*MED*) fever; (*fig*) fever, excitement; **~ amarilla/del heno** yellow/hay fever; **~ palúdica** malaria; **tener ~** to have a temperature.

fiel [fjel] *adj* (*leal*) faithful, loyal; (*fiable*) reliable; (*exacto*) accurate, faithful ♦ *nm*: **los ~es** the faithful.

fieltro ['fjeltro] *nm* felt.

fiera ['fjera] *nf* (*animal feroz*) wild animal *o* beast; (*fig*) dragon; *ver tb* **fiero**.

fiero, a ['fjero, a] *adj* (*cruel*) cruel; (*feroz*) fierce; (*duro*) harsh ♦ *nm/f* (*fig*) fiend.

fiesta ['fjesta] *nf* party; (*de pueblo*) festival; (*vacaciones, tb*: ~s) holiday *sg*; (*REL*): ~ **de guardar** day of obligation.

figura [fi'ɣura] *nf* (*gen*) figure; (*forma, imagen*) shape, form; (*NAIPES*) face card.

figurar [fiɣu'rar] *vt* (*representar*) to represent; (*fingir*) to figure ♦ *vi* to figure; ~**se** *vr* (*imaginarse*) to imagine; (*suponer*) to suppose.

fijador [fixa'ðor] *nm* (*FOTO etc*) fixative; (*de pelo*) gel.

fijar [fi'xar] *vt* (*gen*) to fix; (*estampilla*) to affix, stick (on); (*fig*) to settle (on), decide; ~**se** *vr*: ~**se en** to notice.

fijo, a ['fixo, a] *adj* (*gen*) fixed; (*firme*) firm; (*permanente*) permanent ♦ *adv*: **mirar** ~ to stare.

fila ['fila] *nf* row; (*MIL.*) rank; (*cadena*) line; **ponerse en** ~ to line up, get into line.

filántropo, a [fi'lantropo, a] *nm/f* philanthropist.

filatelia [fila'telja] *nf* philately, stamp collecting.

filete [fi'lete] *nm* (*carne*) fillet steak; (*pescado*) fillet.

filial [fi'ljal] *adj* filial ♦ *nf* subsidiary.

Filipinas [fili'pinas] *nfpl*: **las** ~ the Philippines; **filipino, a** *adj, nm/f* Philippine.

filmar [fil'mar] *vt* to film, shoot.

filo ['filo] *nm* (*gen*) edge; **sacar** ~ **a** to sharpen; **al** ~ **del mediodía** at about midday; **de doble** ~ double-edged.

filón [fi'lon] *nm* (*MINERÍA*) vein, lode; (*fig*) goldmine.

filosofía [filoso'fia] *nf* philosophy; **filósofo, a** *nm/f* philosopher.

filtrar [fil'trar] *vt, vi* to filter, strain; ~**se** *vr* to filter; (*fig: dinero*) to dwindle; **filtro** *nm* (*TEC, utensilio*) filter.

fin [fin] *nm* end; (*objetivo*) aim, purpose; **al** ~ **y al cabo** when all's said and done; **a** ~ **de** in order to; **por** ~ finally; **en** ~ in short; ~ **de semana** weekend.

final [fi'nal] *adj* final ♦ *nm* end, conclu-

sion ♦ *nf* final; ~**idad** *nf* (*propósito*) purpose, intention; ~**ista** *nm/f* finalist; ~**izar** *vt* to end, finish; (*INFORM*) to log out o off ♦ *vi* to end, come to an end.

financiar [finan'θjar] *vt* to finance; **financiero, a** *adj* financial ♦ *nm/f* financier.

finca ['finka] *nf* (*bien inmueble*) property, land; (*casa de campo*) country house; (*AM*) farm.

fingir [fin'xir] *vt* (*simular*) to simulate, feign; (*pretextar*) to sham, fake ♦ *vi* (*aparentar*) to pretend; ~**se** *vr* to pretend to be.

finlandés, esa [finlan'des, esa] *adj* Finnish ♦ *nm/f* Finn ♦ *nm* (*LING*) Finnish.

Finlandia [fin'landja] *nf* Finland.

fino, a ['fino, a] *adj* fine; (*delgado*) slender; (*de buenas maneras*) polite, refined; (*jerez*) fino, dry.

firma ['firma] *nf* signature; (*COM*) firm, company; **firmar** *vt* to sign.

firme ['firme] *adj* firm; (*estable*) stable; (*sólido*) solid; (*constante*) steady; (*decidido*) resolute ♦ *nm* road (surface); ~**mente** *adv* firmly; ~**za** *nf* firmness; (*constancia*) steadiness; (*solidez*) solidity.

fiscal [fis'kal] *adj* fiscal ♦ *nm/f* public prosecutor; **año** ~ tax o fiscal year.

fisco ['fisko] *nm* (*hacienda*) treasury, exchequer (*BRIT*).

fisgar [fis'ɣar] *vt* to pry into.

física ['fisika] *nf* physics *sg*; *ver tb* **físico**.

físico, a ['fisiko, a] *adj* physical ♦ *nm* physique ♦ *nm/f* physicist.

flaco, a ['flako, a] *adj* (*muy delgado*) skinny, thin; (*débil*) weak, feeble.

flagrante [fla'ɣrante] *adj* flagrant.

flamante [fla'mante] (*fam*) *adj* brilliant; (*nuevo*) brand-new.

flamenco, a [fla'menko, a] *adj* (*de Flandes*) Flemish; (*baile, música*) flamenco ♦ *nm* (*baile, música*) flamenco.

flan [flan] *nm* creme caramel.

flaqueza [fla'keθa] *nf* (*delgadez*) thinness, leanness; (*fig*) weakness.

flash [flaʃ] (pl ~s o ~es) nm (FOTO) flash.

flauta ['flauta] nf (MUS) flute.

fleco ['fleko] nm fringe.

flecha ['fletʃa] nf arrow.

flema ['flema] nm phlegm.

flequillo [fle'kiʎo] nm (pelo) fringe.

flete ['flete] nm (carga) freight; (alquiler) charter; (precio) freightage.

flexible [flek'siβle] adj flexible.

flipper ['fliper] nm pinball (machine).

flojera [flo'xera] (AM: fam) nf: me da ~ I can't be bothered.

flojo, a ['floxo, a] adj (gen) loose; (sin fuerzas) limp; (débil) weak.

flor [flor] nf flower; (piropo) compliment; **a ~ de** on the surface of; **~ecer** vi (BOT) to flower, bloom; (fig) to flourish; **~eciente** adj (BOT) in flower, flowering; (fig) thriving; **~ero** nm vase; **~ista** nm/f florist.

flota ['flota] nf fleet.

flotador [flota'ðor] nm (gen) float; (para nadar) rubber ring.

flotar [flo'tar] vi (gen) to float; **flote** nm: **a flote** afloat; **salir a flote** (fig) to get back on one's feet.

fluctuar [fluk'twar] vi (oscilar) to fluctuate.

fluidez [flui'ðeθ] nf fluidity; (fig) fluency.

flúido, a ['fluiðo, a] adj, nm fluid.

fluir [flu'ir] vi to flow.

flujo ['fluxo] nm flow; **~ y reflujo** ebb and flow; **~ de sangre** (MED) loss of blood; **~grama** nm flowchart.

foca ['foka] nf seal.

foco ['foko] nm focus; (ELEC) floodlight; (AM) (light) bulb.

fogón [fo'ɣon] nm (de cocina) ring, burner.

fogoso, a [fo'ɣoso, a] adj spirited.

follaje [fo'ʎaxe] nm foliage.

folleto [fo'ʎeto] nm (POL) pamphlet.

follón [fo'ʎon] (fam) nm (lío) mess; (conmoción) fuss; **armar un ~** to kick up a row.

fomentar [fomen'tar] vt (MED) to foment; **fomento** nm (promoción) promotion.

fonda ['fonda] nf inn.

fondo ['fondo] nm (de mar) bottom; (de coche, sala) back; (ARTE etc) background; (reserva) fund; **~s** nmpl (COM) funds, resources; **una investigación a ~** a thorough investigation; **en el ~** at bottom, deep down.

fono ['fono] (AM) nm telephone number.

fontanería [fontane'ria] nf plumbing; **fontanero, a** nm/f plumber.

footing ['futιn] nm jogging; **hacer ~** to jog, go jogging.

forastero, a [foras'tero, a] nm/f stranger.

forcejear [forθexe'ar] vi (luchar) to struggle.

forjar [for'xar] vt to forge.

forma ['forma] nf (figura) form, shape; (molde) mould, pattern; (MED) fitness; (método) way, means; **las ~s** the conventions; **estar en ~** to be fit.

formación [forma'θjon] nf (gen) formation; (educación) education; **~ profesional** vocational training.

formal [for'mal] adj (gen) formal; (fig: persona) serious; (: de fiar) reliable; **~idad** nf formality; seriousness; **~izar** vt (JUR) to formalize; (situación) to put in order, regularize; **~izarse** vr (situación) to be put in order, be regularized.

formar [for'mar] vt (componer) to form, shape; (constituir) to make up, constitute; (ESCOL) to train, educate; **~se** vr (ESCOL) to be trained, educated; (cobrar forma) to form, take form; (desarrollarse) to develop.

formatear [formate'ar] vt to format.

formidable [formi'ðaβle] adj (temible) formidable; (asombroso) tremendous.

formulario [formu'larjo] nm form.

fornido, a [for'niðo, a] adj well-built.

foro ['foro] nm (gen) forum; (JUR) court.

forrar [fo'rrar] vt (abrigo) to line; (libro) to cover; **forro** nm (de cuaderno) cover; (COSTURA) lining; (de sillón) upholstery.

fortalecer [fortale'θer] vt to strengthen.

fortaleza [forta'leθa] nf (MIL) fortress, stronghold; (fuerza) strength; (determinación) resolution.

fortuito, a [for'twito, a] *adj* accidental.

fortuna [for'tuna] *nf* (*suerte*) fortune, (good) luck; (*riqueza*) fortune, wealth.

forzar [for'θar] *vt* (*puerta*) to force (open); (*compeler*) to compel.

forzoso, a [for'θoso, a] *adj* necessary.

fosa ['fosa] *nf* (*sepultura*) grave; (*en tierra*) pit; (MED) cavity.

fósforo ['fosforo] *nm* (QUÍMICA) phosphorus; (AM) match.

foso ['foso] *nm* ditch; (TEATRO) pit; (AUTO): ~ **de reconocimiento** inspection pit.

foto ['foto] *nf* photo, snap(shot); **sacar una** ~ to take a photo *o* picture.

fotocopia [foto'kopja] *nf* photocopy; **fotocopiadora** *nf* photocopier; **fotocopiar** *vt* to photocopy.

fotografía [fotoɣra'fia] *nf* (ARTE) photography; (*una* ~) photograph; **fotografiar** *vt* to photograph.

fotógrafo, a [fo'toɣrafo, a] *nm/f* photographer.

fracasar [fraka'sar] *vi* (*gen*) to fail.

fracaso [fra'kaso] *nm* (*desgracia, revés*) failure.

fracción [frak'θjon] *nf* fraction; (POL) faction; **fraccionamiento** (AM) *nm* housing estate.

fractura [frak'tura] *nf* fracture, break.

fragancia [fra'ɣanθja] *nf* (*olor*) fragrance, perfume.

frágil ['fraxil] *adj* (*débil*) fragile; (COM) breakable.

fragmento [fraɣ'mento] *nm* (*pedazo*) fragment.

fragua ['fraɣwa] *nf* forge; **fraguar** *vt* to forge; (*fig*) to concoct ♦ *vi* to harden.

fraile ['fraile] *nm* (REL) friar; (: *monje*) monk.

frambuesa [fram'bwesa] *nf* raspberry.

francés, esa [fran'θes, esa] *adj* French ♦ *nm/f* Frenchman/woman ♦ *nm* (LING) French.

Francia ['franθja] *nf* France.

franco, a ['franko, a] *adj* (*cándido*) frank, open; (COM: *exento*) free ♦ *nm* (*moneda*) franc.

francotirador, a [frankotira'ðor, a] *nm/f* sniper.

franela [fra'nela] *nf* flannel.

franja ['franxa] *nf* fringe.

franquear [franke'ar] *vt* (*camino*) to clear; (*carta, paquete postal*) to frank, stamp; (*obstáculo*) to overcome.

franqueo [fran'keo] *nm* postage.

franqueza [fran'keθa] *nf* (*candor*) frankness.

frasco ['frasko] *nm* bottle, flask; ~ **al vacío** (vacuum) flask.

frase ['frase] *nf* sentence; ~ **hecha** set phrase; (*pey*) stock phrase.

fraude ['frauðe] *nm* (*cualidad*) dishonesty; (*acto*) fraud; **fraudulento, a** *adj* fraudulent.

frazada [fra'saða] (AM) *nf* blanket.

frecuencia [fre'kwenθja] *nf* frequency; **con** ~ frequently, often.

fregadero [freɣa'ðero] *nm* (kitchen) sink.

fregar [fre'ɣar] *vt* (*frotar*) to scrub; (*platos*) to wash (up); (AM) to annoy.

fregona [fre'ɣona] *nf* (*utensilio*) mop; (*pey*: *sirvienta*) skivvy.

freir [fre'ir] *vt* to fry.

frenar [fre'nar] *vt* to brake; (*fig*) to check.

frenesí [frene'si] *nm* frenzy; **frenético, a** *adj* frantic.

freno ['freno] *nm* (TEC, AUTO) brake; (*de cabalgadura*) bit; (*fig*) check.

frente ['frente] *nm* (ARQ, POL) front; (*de objeto*) front part ♦ *nf* forehead, brow; ~ **a** in front of; (*en situación opuesta de*) opposite; **al** ~ **de** (*fig*) at the head of, **chocar de** ~ to crash head-on; **hacer** ~ **a** to face up to.

fresa ['fresa] (ESP) *nf* strawberry.

fresco, a ['fresko, a] *adj* (*nuevo*) fresh; (*frío*) cool; (*descarado*) cheeky ♦ *nm* (*aire*) fresh air; (ARTE) fresco; (AM: *jugo*) fruit drink ♦ *nm/f* (*fam*): **ser un(a)** ~ to have a nerve; **tomar el** ~ to get some fresh air; **frescura** *nf* freshness; (*descaro*) cheek, nerve; (*calma*) calmness.

frialdad [frial'daθ] *nf* (*gen*) coldness; (*indiferencia*) indifference.

fricción [frik'θjon] *nf* (*gen*) friction; (*acto*) rub(bing); (MED) massage.

frigidez [frixi'ðeθ] *nf* frigidity.

frigorífico [frixo'rifiko] *nm* refrigerator.

frijol [fri'xol] *nm* kidney bean.

frío, a *etc* ['frio, a] *vb ver* **freír** ♦ *adj* cold; (*indiferente*) indifferent ♦ *nm* cold; indifference; **hace** ~ it's cold; **tener** ~ to be cold.

frito, a ['frito, a] *adj* fried; **me trae** ~ **ese hombre** I'm sick and tired of that man.

frívolo, a ['friβolo, a] *adj* frivolous.

frontal [fron'tal] *adj* frontal; **choque** ~ head-on collision.

frontera [fron'tera] *nf* frontier; **fronterizo, a** *adj* frontier *cpd*; (*contiguo*) bordering.

frontón [fron'ton] *nm* (*DEPORTE*: *cancha*) pelota court; (: *juego*) pelota.

frotar [fro'tar] *vt* to rub; ~**se** *vr*: ~**se las manos** to rub one's hands.

fructífero, a [fruk'tifero, a] *adj* fruitful.

frugal [fru'val] *adj* frugal.

fruncir [frun'θir] *vt* to pucker; (*COSTURA*) to pleat; ~ **el ceño** to knit one's brow.

frustrar [frus'trar] *vt* to frustrate.

fruta ['fruta] *nf* fruit; **frutería** *nf* fruit shop; **frutero, a** *adj* fruit *cpd* ♦ *nm/f* fruiterer ♦ *nm* fruit bowl.

frutilla [fru'tiʎa] (*AM*) *nf* strawberry.

fruto ['fruto] *nm* fruit; (*fig*: *resultado*) result; (: *utilidad*) benefit; ~**s secos** nuts; (*pasas etc*) dried fruit *sg*.

fue *vb ver* **ser**; **ir**.

fuego ['fwexo] *nm* (*gen*) fire; **a** ~ **lento** on a low flame *o* gas; **¿tienes** ~? have you (got) a light?

fuente ['fwente] *nf* fountain; (*manantial*, *fig*) spring; (*origen*) source; (*plato*) large dish.

fuera *etc* ['fwera] *vb ver* **ser, ir** ♦ *adv* out(side); (*en otra parte*) away; (*excepto, salvo*) except, save ♦ *prep*: ~ **de** outside; (*fig*) besides; ~ **de sí** beside o.s.; **por** ~ (on the) outside.

fuerte ['fwerte] *adj* strong; (*golpe*) hard; (*ruido*) loud; (*comida*) rich; (*lluvia*) heavy; (*dolor*) intense ♦ *adv* strongly; hard; loud(ly).

fuerza *etc* ['fwerθa] *vb ver* **forzar** ♦ *nf* (*fortaleza*) strength; (*TEC, ELEC*)

power; (*coacción*) force; (*MIL*: *tb*: ~**s**) forces *pl*; **a** ~ **de** by dint of; **cobrar** ~**s** to recover one's strength; **tener** ~**s para** to have the strength to; **a la** ~ forcibly, by force; **por** ~ of necessity.

fuga ['fuxa] *nf* (*huida*) flight, escape; (*de gas etc*) leak.

fugarse [fu'xarse] *vr* to flee, escape.

fugaz [fu'xaθ] *adj* fleeting.

fugitivo, a [fuxi'tiβo, a] *adj, nm/f* fugitive.

fui *vb ver* **ser**; **ir**.

fulano, a [fu'lano, a] *nm/f* so-and-so, what's-his-name/what's-her-name.

fulgor [ful'xor] *nm* brilliance.

fumador, a [fuma'ðor, a] *nm/f* smoker.

fumar [fu'mar] *vt, vi* to smoke; ~**se** *vr* (*disipar*) to squander; ~ **en pipa** to smoke a pipe.

funambulista [funambu'lista] *nm/f* tightrope walker.

función [fun'θjon] *nf* function; (*de puesto*) duties *pl*; (*espectáculo*) show; **entrar en funciones** to take up one's duties.

funcionar [funθjo'nar] *vi* (*gen*) to function; (*máquina*) to work; **"no funciona"** "out of order".

funcionario, a [funθjo'narjo, a] *nm/f* official; (*público*) civil servant.

funda ['funda] *nf* (*gen*) cover; (*de almohada*) pillowcase.

fundación [funda'θjon] *nf* foundation.

fundamental [fundamen'tal] *adj* fundamental, basic.

fundamentar [fundamen'tar] *vt* (*poner base*) to lay the foundations of; (*establecer*) to found; (*fig*) to base; **fundamento** *nm* (*base*) foundation.

fundar [fun'dar] *vt* to found; ~**se** *vr*: ~**se en** to be founded on.

fundición [fundi'θjon] *nf* fusing; (*fábrica*) foundry.

fundir [fun'dir] *vt* (*gen*) to fuse; (*metal*) to smelt, melt down; (*nieve etc*) to melt; (*COM*) to merge; (*estatua*) to cast; ~**se** *vr* (*colores etc*) to merge, blend; (*unirse*) to fuse together; (*ELEC*: *fusible, lámpara etc*) to fuse, blow; (*nieve etc*) to melt.

fúnebre ['funeßre] *adj* funeral *cpd*, funereal.

funeral [fune'ral] *nm* funeral.

furgón [fur'ɣon] *nm* wagon; **furgoneta** *nf* (*AUTO*, *COM*) (transit) van (*BRIT*), pick-up (truck) (*US*).

furia ['furja] *nf* (*ira*) fury; (*violencia*) violence; **furibundo, a** *adj* furious; **furioso, a** *adj* (*iracundo*) furious; (*violento*) violent; **furor** *nm* (*cólera*) rage.

furúnculo [fu'runkulo] *nm* boil.

fusible [fu'sißle] *nm* fuse.

fusil [fu'sil] *nm* rifle; **~ar** *vt* to shoot.

fusión [fu'sjon] *nf* (*gen*) melting; (*unión*) fusion; (*COM*) merger.

fusta ['fusta] *nf* (*látigo*) riding crop.

fútbol ['futßol] *nm* football; **futbolista** *nm* footballer.

fútil ['futil] *adj* trifling; **futilidad** *nf* triviality.

futuro, a [fu'turo, a] *adj, nm* future.

G

gabán [ga'ßan] *nm* overcoat.

gabardina [gaßar'ðina] *nf* raincoat, gabardine.

gabinete [gaßi'nete] *nm* (*POL*) cabinet; (*estudio*) study; (*de abogados etc*) office.

gaceta [ga'θeta] *nf* gazette.

gachas ['gatʃas] *nfpl* porridge *sg*.

gafar [ga'far] *vt* to jinx.

gafas ['gafas] *nfpl* glasses; **~ de sol** sunglasses.

gafe ['gafe] *nm* jinx.

gaita ['gaita] *nf* bagpipes *pl*.

gajes ['gaxes] *nmpl*: **los ~ del oficio** occupational hazards.

gajo ['gaxo] *nm* (*de naranja*) segment.

gala ['gala] *nf* (*traje de etiqueta*) full dress; (*fig: lo mejor*) cream, flower; **~s** *nfpl* (*ropa*) finery *sg*; **estar de ~** to be in one's best clothes; **hacer ~ de** to display, show off.

galán [ga'lan] *nm* lover; (*Don Juan*) ladies' man; (*TEATRO*): **primer ~** leading man.

galante [ga'lante] *adj* gallant; **galantear** *vt* (*hacer la corte a*) to court, woo; **galantería** *nf* (*caballerosidad*) gallantry; (*cumplido*) politeness; (*comentario*) compliment.

galápago [ga'lapaɣo] *nm* (*ZOOL*) turtle.

galaxia [ga'laksja] *nf* galaxy.

galera [ga'lera] *nf* (*nave*) galley; (*carro*) wagon; (*IMPRENTA*) galley.

galería [gale'ria] *nf* (*gen*) gallery; (*balcón*) veranda(h); (*pasillo*) corridor.

Gales ['gales] *nm* (*tb: País de ~*) Wales; **galés, esa** *adj* Welsh ♦ *nm/f* Welshman/woman ♦ *nm* (*LING*) Welsh.

galgo, a ['galɣo, a] *nm/f* greyhound.

galimatías [galima'tias] *nmpl* (*lenguaje*) gibberish *sg*, nonsense *sg*.

galón [ga'lon] *nm* (*MIL*) stripe; (*COSTURA*) braid; (*medida*) gallon.

galopar [galo'par] *vi* to gallop.

gallardía [gaʎar'ðia] *nf* (*galantería*) dash; (*valor*) bravery; (*elegancia*) elegance.

gallego, a [ga'ʎeɣo, a] *adj, nm/f* Galician.

galleta [ga'ʎeta] *nf* biscuit (*BRIT*), cookie (*US*).

gallina [ga'ʎina] *nf* hen ♦ *nm/f* (*fam*: *cobarde*) chicken.

gallo ['gaʎo] *nm* cock, rooster.

gama ['gama] *nf* (*fig*) range.

gamba ['gamba] *nf* prawn (*BRIT*), shrimp (*US*).

gamberro, a [gam'berro, a] *nm/f* hooligan, lout.

gamuza [ga'muθa] *nf* chamois.

gana ['gana] *nf* (*deseo*) desire, wish; (*apetito*) appetite; (*voluntad*) will; (*añoranza*) longing; **de buena ~** willingly; **de mala ~** reluctantly; **me da ~s de I'd feel like it, I want to; **no me da la ~** I don't feel like it; **tener ~s de** to feel like.

ganadería [ganaðe'ria] *nf* (*ganado*) livestock; (*ganado vacuno*) cattle *pl*; (*cría, comercio*) cattle raising.

ganado [ga'naðo] *nm* livestock; **~ lanar** sheep *pl*; **~ mayor** cattle *pl*; **~ porcino** pigs *pl*.

ganador, a [gana'ðor, a] *adj* winning ♦

nm/f winner.

ganancia [ga'nanθja] *nf* (*lo ganado*) gain; (*aumento*) increase; (*beneficio*) profit; ~s *nfpl* (*ingresos*) earnings; (*beneficios*) profit *sg*, winnings.

ganar [ga'nar] *vt* (*obtener*) to get, obtain; (*sacar ventaja*) to gain; (*salario etc*) to earn; (*DEPORTE, premio*) to win; (*derrotar a*) to beat; (*alcanzar*) to reach ♦ *vi* (*DEPORTE*) to win; ~se *vr*: ~se la vida to earn one's living.

gancho ['gantʃo] *nm* (*gen*) hook; (*colgador*) hanger.

gandul, a [gan'dul, a] *adj, nm/f* good-for-nothing, layabout.

ganga ['ganga] *nf* (*cosa buena y barata*) bargain; (*buena situación*) cushy job.

gangrena [gan'grena] *nf* gangrene.

gansada [gan'saða] (*fam*) *nf* stupid thing to do.

ganso, a ['ganso, a] *nm/f* (*ZOOL*) goose; (*fam*) idiot.

ganzúa [gan'θua] *nf* skeleton key.

garabatear [garaßate'ar] *vi, vt* (*al escribir*) to scribble, scrawl.

garabato [gara'ßato] *nm* (*escritura*) scrawl, scribble.

garaje [ga'raxe] *nm* garage.

garante [ga'rante] *adj* responsible ♦ *nm/f* guarantor.

garantía [garan'tia] *nf* guarantee.

garantizar [garanti'θar] *vt* (*hacerse responsable de*) to vouch for; (*asegurar*) to guarantee.

garbanzo [gar'ßanθo] *nm* chickpea (*BRIT*), garbanzo (*US*).

garbo ['garßo] *nm* grace, elegance.

garfio ['garfjo] *nm* grappling iron.

garganta [gar'xanta] *nf* (*ANAT*) throat; (*de botella*) neck; **gargantilla** *nf* necklace.

gárgaras ['garɣaras] *nfpl*: hacer ~ to gargle.

garita [ga'rita] *nf* cabin, hut; (*MIL*) sentry box.

garito [ga'rito] *nm* (*lugar*) gambling house o den.

garra ['garra] *nf* (*de gato, TEC*) claw; (*de ave*) talon; (*fam*) hand, paw.

garrafa [ga'rrafa] *nf* carafe, decanter.

garrapata [garra'pata] *nf* tick.

garrapatear [garrapate'ar] *vi, vt* = garabatear.

garrote [ga'rrote] *nm* (*palo*) stick; (*porra*) cudgel; (*suplicio*) garrotte.

garúa [ga'rua] (*AM*) *nf* drizzle.

garza ['garθa] *nf* heron.

gas [gas] *nm* gas.

gasa ['gasa] *nf* gauze.

gaseosa [gase'osa] *nf* lemonade.

gaseoso, a [gase'oso, a] *adj* gassy, fizzy.

gasfitero [gasfi'tero] *nm* (*AM*) plumber.

gasoil [ga'soil] *nm* diesel (oil).

gasóleo [ga'soleo] *nm* = gasoil.

gasolina [gaso'lina] *nf* petrol, gas(oline) (*US*); **gasolinera** *nf* petrol (*BRIT*) o gas (*US*) station.

gastado, a [gas'taðo, a] *adj* (*rendido*) spent; (*raído*) worn out; (*usado: frase etc*) trite.

gastar [gas'tar] *vt* (*dinero, tiempo*) to spend; (*fuerzas*) to use up; (*desperdiciar*) to waste; (*llevar*) to wear; ~se *vr* to wear out; (*estropearse*) to waste; ~ en to spend on; ~ bromas to crack jokes; ¿qué número gastas? what size (shoe) do you take?

gasto ['gasto] *nm* (*desembolso*) expenditure, spending; (*consumo, uso*) use; ~s *nmpl* (*desembolsos*) expenses; (*cargos*) charges, costs.

gatear [gate'ar] *vi* (*andar a gatas*) to go on all fours.

gatillo [ga'tiʎo] *nm* (*de arma de fuego*) trigger; (*de dentista*) forceps.

gato, a ['gato, a] *nm/f* cat ♦ *nm* (*TEC*) jack; andar a gatas to go on all fours.

gaveta [ga'ßeta] *nf* drawer.

gaviota [ga'ßjota] *nf* seagull.

gay [ge] *adj inv, nm* gay, homosexual.

gazapo [ga'θapo] *nm* young rabbit.

gazpacho [gaθ'patʃo] *nm* gazpacho.

gelatina [xela'tina] *nf* jelly; (*polvos etc*) gelatine.

gema ['xema] *nf* gem.

gemelo, a [xe'melo, a] *adj, nm/f* twin; ~s *nmpl* (*de camisa*) cufflinks; ~s de campo field glasses, binoculars.

gemido [xe'miðo] *nm* (*quejido*) moan,

groan; (*aullido*) howl.

Géminis ['xeminis] *nm* Gemini.

gemir [xe'mir] *vi* (*quejarse*) to moan, groan; (*aullar*) to howl.

generación [xenera'θjon] *nf* generation.

general [xene'ral] *adj* general ♦ *nm* general; **por lo o en ~** in general; **G~itat** *nf Catalan parliament*; **~izar** *vt* to generalize; **~izarse** *vr* to become generalized, spread; **~mente** *adv* generally.

generar [xene'rar] *vt* to generate.

género ['xenero] *nm* (*clase*) kind, sort; (*tipo*) type; (*BIO*) genus; (*LING*) gender; (*COM*) material; **~ humano** human race.

generosidad [xenerosi'ðað] *nf* generosity; **generoso, a** *adj* generous.

genial [xe'njal] *adj* inspired; (*idea*) brilliant; (*afable*) gènial.

genio ['xenjo] *nm* (*carácter*) nature, disposition; (*humor*) temper; (*facultad creadora*) genius; **de mal ~** badtempered.

genitales [xeni'tales] *nmpl* genitals.

gente ['xente] *nf* (*personas*) people *pl*; (*raza*) race; (*nación*) nation; (*parientes*) relatives *pl*.

gentil [xen'til] *adj* (*elegante*) graceful; (*encantador*) charming; **~eza** *nf* grace; charm; (*cortesía*) courtesy.

gentío [xen'tio] *nm* crowd, throng.

genuino, a [xe'nwino, a] *adj* genuine.

geografía [xeoɣra'fia] *nf* geography.

geología [xeolo'xia] *nf* geology.

geometría [xeome'tria] *nf* geometry.

gerencia [xe'renθja] *nf* management; **gerente** *nm/f* (*supervisor*) manager; (*jefe*) director.

geriatría [xeria'tria] *nf* (*MED*) geriatrics *sg*.

germen ['xermen] *nm* germ.

germinar [xermi'nar] *vi* to germinate.

gesticulación [xestikula'θjon] *nf* gesticulation; (*mueca*) grimace.

gestión [xes'tjon] *nf* management; (*diligencia, acción*) negotiation; **gestionar** *vt* (*lograr*) to try to arrange; (*llevar*) to manage.

gesto ['xesto] *nm* (*mueca*) grimace;

(*ademán*) gesture.

Gibraltar [xiβral'tar] *nm* Gibraltar; **gibraltareño, a** *adj, nm/f* Gibraltarian.

gigante [xi'ɣante] *adj, nm/f* giant.

gilipollas [xili'poʎas] (*fam*) *adj inv* daft ♦ *nm/f inv* wally.

gimnasia [xim'nasja] *nf* gymnastics *pl*; **gimnasio** *nm* gymnasium; **gimnasta** *nm/f* gymnast.

gimotear [ximote'ar] *vi* to whine, whimper.

ginebra [xi'neβra] *nf* gin.

ginecólogo, a [xine'koloɣo, a] *nm/f* gynaecologist.

gira ['xira] *nf* tour, trip.

girar [xi'rar] *vt* (*dar la vuelta*) to turn (around); (: *rápidamente*) to spin; (*COM*: *giro postal*) to draw; (*comerciar: letra de cambio*) to issue ♦ *vi* to turn (round); (*rápido*) to spin; (*COM*) to draw.

girasol [xira'sol] *nm* sunflower.

giratorio, a [xira'torjo, a] *adj* (*gen*) revolving; (*puente*) swing.

giro ['xiro] *nm* (*movimiento*) turn, revolution; (*LING*) expression; (*COM*) draft; **~ bancario/postal** bank giro/postal order.

gis [xis] (*AM*) *nm* chalk.

gitano, a [xi'tano, a] *adj, nm/f* gypsy.

glacial [gla'θjal] *adj* icy, freezing.

glaciar [gla'θjar] *nm* glacier.

glándula ['glandula] *nf* gland.

global [glo'ßal] *adj* global.

globo ['gloßo] *nm* (*esfera*) globe, sphere; (*aerostato, juguete*) balloon.

glóbulo ['gloßulo] *nm* globule; (*ANAT*) corpuscle.

gloria ['glorja] *nf* glory.

glorieta [glo'rjeta] *nf* (*de jardín*) bower, arbour; (*plazoleta*) roundabout (*BRIT*), traffic circle (*US*).

glorificar [glorifi'kar] *vt* (*enaltecer*) to glorify, praise.

glorioso, a [glo'rjoso, a] *adj* glorious.

glosa ['glosa] *nf* comment; **glosar** *vt* (*comentar*) to comment on.

glosario [glo'sarjo] *nm* glossary.

glotón, ona [glo'ton, ona] *adj* gluttonous, greedy ♦ *nm/f* glutton.

gobernación [goßerna'θjon] *nf* government, governing; G~ (*AM: ADMIN*) Ministry of the Interior; **gobernador, a** *adj* governing ♦ *nm/f* governor; **gobernante** *adj* governing.

gobernar [goßer'nar] *vt* (*dirigir*) to guide, direct; (*POL*) to rule, govern ♦ *vi* to govern; (*NAUT*) to steer.

gobierno *etc* [go'ßjerno] *vb ver* **gobernar** ♦ *nm* (*POL*) government; (*dirección*) guidance, direction; (*NAUT*) steering.

goce *etc* ['goθe] *vb ver* **gozar** ♦ *nm* enjoyment.

gol [gol] *nm* goal.

golf [golf] *nm* golf.

golfa ['golfa] (*fam*) *nf* (*mujer*) slut, whore.

golfo, a ['golfo, a] *nm* (*GEO*) gulf ♦ *nm/f* (*fam: niño*) urchin; (*gamberro*) lout.

golondrina [golon'drina] *nf* swallow.

golosina [golo'sina] *nf* titbit; (*dulce*) sweet; **goloso, a** *adj* sweet-toothed.

golpe ['golpe] *nm* blow; (*de puño*) punch; (*de mano*) smack; (*de remo*) stroke; (*fig: choque*) clash; **no dar ~** to be bone idle; **de un ~** with one blow; **de ~** suddenly; (**de estado**) coup (d'état); **golpear** *vt, vi* to strike, knock; (*asestar*) to beat; (*de puño*) to punch; (*golpetear*) to tap.

goma ['goma] *nf* (*caucho*) rubber; (*elástico*) elastic; (*una ~*) elastic band; **~ espuma** foam rubber; **~ de pegar** gum, glue.

gordo, a ['gorðo, a] *adj* (*gen*) fat; (*persona*) plump; (*fam*) enormous; **el** (**premio**) **~** (*en lotería*) first prize; **gordura** *nf* fat; (*corpulencia*) fatness, stoutness.

gorila [go'rila] *nm* gorilla.

gorjear [gorxe'ar] *vi* to twitter, chirp.

gorra ['gorra] *nf* cap; (*de niño*) bonnet; (*militar*) bearskin; **entrar de ~** (*fam*) to gatecrash; **ir de ~** to sponge.

gorrión [go'rrjon] *nm* sparrow.

gorro ['gorro] *nm* (*gen*) cap; (*de niño, mujer*) bonnet.

gorrón, ona [go'rron, ona] *nm/f* scrounger.

gota ['gota] *nf* (*gen*) drop; (*de sudor*) bead; (*MED*) gout; **gotear** *vi* to drip; (*lloviznar*) to drizzle; **gotera** *nf* leak.

gozar [go'θar] *vi* to enjoy o.s.; **~ de** (*disfrutar*) to enjoy; (*poseer*) to possess.

gozne ['goθne] *nm* hinge.

gozo ['goθo] *nm* (*alegría*) joy; (*placer*) pleasure.

gr. *abr* (= *gramo, gramos*) g.

grabación [graßa'θjon] *nf* recording.

grabado [gra'ßaðo] *nm* print, engraving.

grabadora [graßa'ðora] *nf* tape-recorder.

grabar [gra'ßar] *vt* to engrave; (*discos, cintas*) to record.

gracia ['graθja] *nf* (*encanto*) grace, gracefulness; (*humor*) humour, wit; ¡(**muchas**) **~s!** thanks (very much)!; **~s a** thanks to; **tener ~** (*chiste etc*) to be funny; **no me hace ~** I am not keen; **gracioso, a** *adj* (*divertido*) funny, amusing; (*cómico*) comical ♦ *nm/f* (*TEATRO*) comic character.

grada ['graða] *nf* (*de escalera*) step; (*de anfiteatro*) tier, row; **~s** *nfpl* (*DEPORTE*: *de estadio*) terraces.

gradación [graða'θjon] *nf* gradation.

gradería [graðe'ria] *nf* (*gradas*) (flight of) steps *pl*; (*de anfiteatro*) tiers *pl*, rows *pl*; (*DEPORTE*: *de estadio*) terraces *pl*; **~ cubierta** covered stand.

grado ['graðo] *nm* degree; (*de aceite, vino*) grade; (*grada*) step; (*MIL*) rank; **de buen ~** willingly.

graduación [graðwa'θjon] *nf* (*del alcohol*) proof, strength; (*ESCOL*) graduation; (*MIL*) rank.

gradual [gra'ðwal] *adj* gradual.

graduar [gra'ðwar] *vt* (*gen*) to graduate; (*MIL*) to commission; **~se** *vr* to graduate; **~se la vista** to have one's eyes tested.

gráfica ['grafika] *nf* graph.

gráfico, a ['grafiko, a] *adj* graphic ♦ *nm* diagram; **~s** *nmpl* (*INFORM*) graphics.

grajo ['graxo] *nm* rook.

Gral *abr* (= *General*) Gen.

gramática [gra'matika] *nf* grammar.

gramo ['gramo] *nm* gramme (*BRIT*), gram (*US*).

gran [gran] *adj ver* **grande**.

grana ['grana] *nf* (*BOT*) seedling; (*color, tela*) scarlet.

granada [gra'naða] *nf* pomegranate; (*MIL*) grenade.

Gran Bretaña [-bre'taŋa] *nf* Great Britain.

grande ['grande] (*antes de nmsg*: **gran**) *adj* (*de tamaño*) big, large; (*alto*) tall; (*distinguido*) great; (*impresionante*) grand ♦ *nm* grandee; **grandeza** *nf* greatness.

grandioso, a [gran'djoso, a] *adj* magnificent, grand.

granel [gra'nel]: **a ~** *adv* (*COM*) in bulk.

granero [gra'nero] *nm* granary, barn.

granito [gra'nito] *nm* (*AGR*) small grain; (*roca*) granite.

granizado [grani'θaðo] *nm* iced drink.

granizar [grani'θar] *vi* to hail; **granizo** *nm* hail.

granja ['granxa] *nf* (*gen*) farm; **granjero, a** *nm/f* farmer.

grano ['grano] *nm* grain; (*semilla*) seed; (*baya*) berry; (*MED*) pimple, spot; **~s** *nmpl* (*cereales*) cereals.

granuja [gra'nuxa] *nm/f* rogue; (*golfillo*) urchin.

grapa ['grapa] *nf* staple; (*TEC*) clamp.

grasa ['grasa] *nf* (*gen*) grease; (*de cocina*) fat, lard; (*sebo*) suet; (*mugre*) filth; **grasiento, a** *adj* greasy; (*de aceite*) oily.

gratificación [gratifika'θjon] *nf* (*propina*) tip; (*bono*) bonus; (*recompensa*) reward.

gratificar [gratifi'kar] *vt* to tip; to reward.

gratis ['gratis] *adv* free.

gratitud [grati'tuð] *nf* gratitude.

grato, a ['grato, a] *adj* (*agradable*) pleasant, agreeable; (*bienvenido*) welcome.

gratuito, a [gra'twito, a] *adj* (*gratis*) free; (*sin razón*) gratuitous.

gravamen [gra'ßamen] *nm* (*carga*) burden; (*impuesto*) tax.

gravar [gra'ßar] *vt* to burden; (*COM*) to tax.

grave ['graße] *adj* heavy; (*serio*) grave,

serious; **~dad** *nf* gravity.

gravilla [gra'ßiʎa] *nf* gravel.

gravitar [graßi'tar] *vi* to gravitate; **~ sobre** to rest on.

gravoso, a [gra'ßoso, a] *adj* (*pesado*) burdensome; (*costoso*) costly.

graznar [graθ'nar] *vi* (*cuervo*) to squawk; (*pato*) to quack; (*hablar ronco*) to croak.

Grecia ['greθja] *nf* Greece.

gremio ['gremjo] *nm* (*asociación*) trade, industry.

greña ['greŋa] *nf* (*cabellos*) shock of hair; (*maraña*) tangle.

gresca ['greska] *nf* uproar.

griego, a ['grjexo, a] *adj, nm/f* Greek.

grieta ['grjeta] *nf* crack.

grifo ['grifo] *nm* tap; (*AM: AUTO*) petrol (*BRIT*) o gas (*US*) station.

grilletes [gri'ʎetes] *nmpl* fetters.

grillo ['griʎo] *nm* (*ZOOL*) cricket; (*BOT*) shoot.

gripe ['gripe] *nf* flu, influenza.

gris [gris] *adj* (*color*) grey.

gritar [gri'tar] *vt, vi* to shout, yell; **grito** *nm* shout, yell; (*de horror*) scream.

grosella [gro'seʎa] *nf* (red)currant; **~ negra** blackcurrant.

grosería [grose'ria] *nf* (*actitud*) rudeness; (*comentario*) vulgar comment; **grosero, a** *adj* (*poco cortés*) rude, bad-mannered; (*ordinario*) vulgar, crude.

grosor [gro'sor] *nm* thickness.

grúa ['grua] *nf* (*TEC*) crane; (*de petróleo*) derrick.

grueso, a ['grweso, a] *adj* thick; (*persona*) stout ♦ *nm* bulk; **el ~ de** the bulk of.

grulla ['gruʎa] *nf* crane.

grumo ['grumo] *nm* clot, lump.

gruñido [gru'ɲiðo] *nm* grunt; (*fig*) grumble.

gruñir [gru'ɲir] *vi* (*animal*) to growl; (*fam*) to grumble.

grupa ['grupa] *nf* (*ZOOL*) rump.

grupo ['grupo] *nm* group; (*TEC*) unit, set.

gruta ['gruta] *nf* grotto.

guadaña [gwa'ðaŋa] *nf* scythe.

guagua [gwa'ɣwa] (*AM*) *nf* (*niño*) baby;

(bus) bus.
guante ['gwante] *nm* glove.
guapo, a ['gwapo, a] *adj* good-looking, attractive; *(elegante)* smart.
guarda ['gwarða] *nm/f (persona)* guard, keeper ♦ *nf (acto)* guarding; *(custodia)* custody; ~**bosques** *nm inv* game-keeper; ~**costas** *nm inv* coastguard vessel; ~**dor, a** *adj* protective ♦ *nm/f* guardian, protector; ~**espaldas** *nm/f inv* bodyguard; ~**meta** *nm/f* goal-keeper; ~**polvo** *nm* dust cover; *(prenda de vestir)* overalls *pl*; **guardar** *vt (gen)* to keep; *(vigilar)* to guard, watch over; *(dinero: ahorrar)* to save; **guardarse** *vr (preservarse)* to protect o.s.; *(evitar)* to avoid; **guardar cama** to stay in bed; ~**rropa** *nm (armario)* wardrobe; *(en establecimiento público)* cloakroom.
guardería [gwarðe'ria] *nf* nursery.
guardia ['gwarðja] *nf (MIL)* guard; *(cuidado)* care, custody ♦ *nm/f* guard; *(policía)* policeman/woman; **estar de** ~ to be on guard; **montar** ~ to mount guard; **G~ Civil** Civil Guard; **G~ Nacional** National Guard.
guardián, ana [gwar'ðjan, ana] *nm/f (gen)* guardian, keeper.
guardilla [gwar'ðiʎa] *nf* attic.
guarecer [gware'θer] *vt (proteger)* to protect; *(abrigar)* to shelter; ~**se** *vr* to take refuge.
guarida [gwa'riða] *nf (de animal)* den, lair; *(refugio)* refuge.
guarnecer [gwarne'θer] *vt (equipar)* to provide; *(adornar)* to adorn; *(TEC)* to reinforce; **guarnición** *nf (de vestimenta)* trimming; *(de piedra)* mount; *(CULIN)* garnish; *(arneses)* harness; *(MIL)* garrison.
guarro, a ['gwarro, a] *nm/f* pig.
guasa ['gwasa] *nf* joke; **guasón, ona** *adj* witty; *(bromista)* joking ♦ *nm/f* wit; joker.
Guatemala [gwate'mala] *nf* Guatemala.
gubernativo, a [guβerna'tiβo, a] *adj* governmental.
guerra ['gerra] *nf* war; *(pelea)* struggle; ~ **civil** civil war; ~ **fría** cold war; **dar**

~ to annoy; **guerrear** *vi* to wage war; **guerrero, a** *adj* fighting; *(carácter)* warlike ♦ *nm/f* warrior.
guerrilla [ge'rriʎa] *nf* guerrilla warfare; *(tropas)* guerrilla band *o* group.
guía *etc* ['gia] *vb ver* **guiar** ♦ *nm/f (persona)* guide ♦ *nf (libro)* guidebook; **G~** Girl Guide; ~ **de ferrocarriles** railway timetable; ~ **telefónica** telephone directory.
guiar [gi'ar] *vt* to guide, direct; *(AUTO)* to steer; ~**se** *vr*: ~**se por** to be guided by.
guijarro [gi'xarro] *nm* pebble.
guinda ['ginda] *nf* morello cherry.
guindilla [gin'diʎa] *nf* chilli pepper.
guiñapo [gi'ɲapo] *nm (harapo)* rag; *(persona)* reprobate, rogue.
guiñar [gi'ɲar] *vt* to wink.
guión [gi'on] *nm (LING)* hyphen, dash; *(CINE)* script; **guionista** *nm/f* script-writer.
guirnalda [gir'nalda] *nf* garland.
guisa ['gisa] *nf*: **a** ~ **de** as, like.
guisado [gi'saðo] *nm* stew.
guisante [gi'sante] *nm* pea.
guisar [gi'sar] *vt, vi* to cook; **guiso** *nm* cooked dish.
guitarra [gi'tarra] *nf* guitar.
gula ['gula] *nf* gluttony, greed.
gusano [gu'sano] *nm* maggot; *(lombriz)* earthworm.
gustar [gus'tar] *vt* to taste, sample ♦ *vi* to please, be pleasing; ~ **de algo** to like *o* enjoy sth; **me gustan las uvas** I like grapes; **le gusta nadar** she likes *o* enjoys swimming.
gusto ['gusto] *nm (sentido, sabor)* taste; *(placer)* pleasure; **tiene** ~ **a menta** it tastes of mint; **tener buen** ~ to have good taste; **sentirse a** ~ to feel at ease; **mucho** ~ **(en conocerle)** pleased to meet you; **el** ~ **es mío** the pleasure is mine; **con** ~ willingly, gladly; ~**so, a** *adj (sabroso)* tasty; *(agradable)* pleasant.
gutural [gutu'ral] *adj* guttural.

H

ha *vb ver* **haber**.
haba ['aßa] *nf* bean.
Habana [a'ßana] *nf*: la ~ Havana.
habano [a'ßano] *nm* Havana cigar.
habéis *vb ver* **haber**.

PALABRA CLAVE
---

haber [a'ßer] *vb aux* **1** (*tiempos compuestos*) to have; **había comido I have/had eaten**; **antes/después de ~lo visto** before seeing/after seeing *o* having seen it
2: ¡~lo dicho antes! you should have said so before!
3: ~ **de**: **he de hacerlo** I have to do it; **ha de llegar mañana** it should arrive tomorrow
♦ *vb impers* **1** (*existencia: sg*) there is; (*: pl*) there are; **hay un hermano/dos hermanos** there is one brother/there are two brothers; ¿**cuánto hay de aquí a Sucre?** how far is it from here to Sucre?
2 (*obligación*): **hay que hacer algo** something must be done; **hay que apuntarlo para acordarse** you have to write it down to remember
3: ¡hay que ver! well I never!
4: ¡no hay de *o* por (*AM*) qué! don't mention it!, not at all!
5: ¿qué hay? (¿*qué pasa?*) what's up?, what's the matter?; (¿*qué tal?*) how's it going?
♦ ~se *vr*: **habérselas con uno** to have it out with sb
♦ *vt*: **he aquí unas sugerencias** here are some suggestions; **no hay cintas blancas pero sí las hay rojas** there aren't any white ribbons but there are some red ones
♦ *nm* (*en cuenta*) credit side; ~**es** *nmpl* assets; ¿**cuánto tengo en el** ~? how much do I have in my account?; **tiene varias novelas en su** ~ he has several novels to his credit.

---

habichuela [aßi'tʃwela] *nf* kidney bean.

hábil ['aßil] *adj* (*listo*) clever, smart; (*capaz*) fit, capable; (*experto*) expert; **día** ~ working day; **habilidad** *nf* (*gen*) skill, ability; (*inteligencia*) cleverness.
habilitar [aßili'tar] *vt* (*capacitar*) to enable; (*dar instrumentos*) to equip; (*financiar*) to finance.
hábilmente [aßil'mente] *adv* skilfully, expertly.
habitación [aßita'θjon] *nf* (*cuarto*) room; (*casa*) dwelling, abode; (*BIO: morada*) habitat; ~ **sencilla** *o* individual single room; ~ **doble** *o* **de matrimonio** double room.
habitante [aßi'tante] *nm/f* inhabitant.
habitar [aßi'tar] *vt* (*residir en*) to inhabit; (*ocupar*) to occupy ♦ *vi* to live.
hábito ['aßito] *nm* habit.
habituar [aßi'twar] *vt* to accustom; ~**se** *vr*: ~**se a** to get used to.
habla ['aßla] *nf* (*capacidad de hablar*) speech; (*idioma*) language; (*dialecto*) dialect; **perder el** ~ to become speechless; **de** ~ **francesa** French-speaking; **estar al** ~ to be in contact; (*TEL*) to be on the line; ¡**González al** ~! (*TEL*) González speaking!
hablador, a [aßla'ðor, a] *adj* talkative ♦ *nm/f* chatterbox.
habladuría [aßlaðu'ria] *nf* rumour; ~**s** *nfpl* gossip *sg*.
hablante [a'ßlante] *adj* speaking ♦ *nm/f* speaker.
hablar [a'ßlar] *vt* to speak, talk ♦ *vi* to speak; ~**se** *vr* to speak to each other; ~ **con** to speak to; ~ **de** to speak of *o* about; "**se habla inglés**" "English spoken here"; ¡**ni** ~! it's out of the question!
habré *etc vb ver* **haber**.
hacedor, a [aθe'ðor, a] *nm/f* maker.
hacendado [asen'daðo] (*AM*) *nm* large landowner.
hacendoso, a [aθen'doso, a] *adj* industrious.

PALABRA CLAVE
---

hacer [a'θer] *vt* **1** (*fabricar, producir*) to make; (*construir*) to build; ~ **una película/un ruido** to make a film/noise;

el guisado lo hice yo I made o cooked the stew
2 (*ejecutar: trabajo etc*) to do; ~ **la colada** to do the washing; ~ **la comida** to do the cooking; **¿qué haces?** what are you doing?; ~ **el malo** o **el papel del malo** (*TEATRO*) to play the villain
3 (*estudios, algunos deportes*) to do; ~ **español/económicas** to do o study Spanish/economics; ~ **yoga/gimnasia** to do yoga/go to gym
4 (*transformar, incidir en*): **esto lo hará más difícil** this will make it more difficult; **salir te hará sentir mejor** going out will make you feel better
5 (*cálculo*): **2 y 2 hacen** 4 2 and 2 make 4; **éste hace 100** this one makes 100
6 (+ *sub*): **esto hará que ganemos** this will make us win; **harás que no quiera venir** you'll stop him wanting to come
7 (*como sustituto de vb*) to do; **él bebió y yo hice lo mismo** he drank and I did likewise
8: no hace más que criticar all he does is criticize
♦ *vb semi-aux*: ~ + *infin* **1** (*directo*): **les hice venir** I made o had them come; ~ **trabajar a los demás** to get others to work
2 (*por intermedio de otros*): ~ **reparar algo** to get sth repaired
♦ *vi* **1: haz como que no lo sabes** act as if you don't know
2 (*ser apropiado*): **si os hace** if it's alright with you
3: ~ **de:** ~ **de madre para uno** to be like a mother to sb; (*TEATRO*): ~ **de Otelo** to play Othello
♦ *vb impers* **1: hace calor/frío** it's hot/cold; *ver tb* **bueno; sol; tiempo**
2 (*tiempo*): **hace 3 años** 3 years ago; **hace un mes que voy/no voy** I've been going/I haven't been for a month
3: ¿cómo has hecho para llegar tan rápido? how did you manage to get here so quickly?
♦ ~**se** *vr* **1** (*volverse*) to become; **se hicieron amigos** they became friends
2 (*acostumbrarse*): ~**se a** to get used to

3: se hace con huevos y leche it's made out of eggs and milk; **eso no se hace** that's not done
4 (*obtener*): ~**se de** o **con algo** to get hold of sth
5 (*fingirse*): ~**se el sueco** to turn a deaf ear.

hacia ['aθja] *prep* (*en dirección de*) towards; (*cerca de*) near; (*actitud*) towards; ~ **arriba/abajo** up(wards)/down(wards); ~ **mediodía** about noon.
hacienda [a'θjenda] *nf* (*propiedad*) property; (*finca*) farm; (*AM*) ranch; ~ **pública** public finance; (**Ministerio de**) **H~** Exchequer (*BRIT*), Treasury Department (*US*).
hacha ['atʃa] *nf* axe; (*antorcha*) torch.
hada ['aða] *nf* fairy.
hago *etc vb ver* **hacer**.
Haití [ai'ti] *nm* Haiti.
halagar [ala'ɣar] *vt* (*lisonjear*) to flatter.
halago [a'laɣo] *nm* (*adulación*) flattery; **halagüeño, a** *adj* flattering.
halcón [al'kon] *nm* falcon, hawk.
hálito ['alito] *nm* breath.
halterofilia [altero'filja] *nf* weightlifting.
hallar [a'ʎar] *vt* (*gen*) to find; (*descubrir*) to discover; (*toparse con*) to run into; ~**se** *vr* to be (situated); **hallazgo** *nm* discovery; (*cosa*) find.
hamaca [a'maka] *nf* hammock.
hambre ['ambre] *nf* hunger; (*carencia*) famine; (*fig*) longing; **tener** ~ to be hungry; **hambriento, a** *adj* hungry, starving.
hamburguesa [ambur'ɣesa] *nf* hamburger.
hampón [am'pon] *nm* thug.
han *vb ver* **haber**.
haragán, ana [ara'ɣan, ana] *adj, nm/f* good-for-nothing.
harapiento, a [ara'pjento, a] *adj* tattered, in rags.
harapo [a'rapo] *nm* rag.
haré *etc vb ver* **hacer**.
harina [a'rina] *nf* flour.
hartar [ar'tar] *vt* to satiate, glut; (*fig*) to tire, sicken; ~**se** *vr* (*de comida*) to fill o.s., gorge o.s.; (*cansarse*) to get fed

up (de with); **hartazgo** nm surfeit, glut; **harto, a** adj (lleno) full; (cansado) fed up ♦ adv (bastante) enough; (muy) very; **estar harto de** to be fed up with; **hartura** nf (exceso) surfeit; (abundancia) abundance; (satisfacción) satisfaction.

has vb ver **haber**.

hasta ['asta] adv even ♦ prep (alcanzando a) as far as; up to; down to; (de tiempo: a tal hora) till, until; (antes de) before ♦ conj: ~ **que** until; ~ **luego/el sábado** see you soon/on Saturday.

hastiar [as'tjar] vt (gen) to weary; (aburrir) to bore; ~**se** vr: ~**se de** to get fed up with; **hastío** nm weariness; boredom.

hatillo [a'tiʎo] nm belongings pl, kit; (montón) bundle, heap.

hay vb ver **haber**.

Haya ['aja] nf: **la** ~ The Hague.

haya etc ['aja] vb ver **haber** ♦ nf beech tree.

haz [aθ] vb ver **hacer** ♦ nm bundle, bunch; (rayo: de luz) beam.

hazaña [a'θaɲa] nf feat, exploit.

hazmerreír [aθmerre'ir] nm inv laughing stock.

he vb ver **haber**.

hebilla [e'βiʎa] nf buckle, clasp.

hebra ['eβra] nf thread; (BOT: fibra) fibre, grain.

hebreo, a [e'βreo, a] adj, nm/f Hebrew ♦ nm (LING) Hebrew.

hectárea [ek'tarea] nf hectare.

hechizar [etʃi'θar] vt to cast a spell on, bewitch.

hechizo [e'tʃiθo] nm witchcraft, magic; (acto de magia) spell, charm.

hecho, a ['etʃo, a] pp de **hacer** ♦ adj complete; (maduro) mature; (COSTURA) ready-to-wear ♦ nm deed, act; (dato) fact; (cuestión) matter; (suceso) event ♦ excl agreed!, done!; **¡bien ~!** well done!; **de** ~ in fact, as a matter of fact.

hechura [e'tʃura] nf making, creation; (producto) product; (forma) form, shape; (de persona) build; (TEC) craftsmanship.

heder [e'ðer] vi to stink, smell; (fig) to be unbearable.

hediondo, a [e'ðjondo, a] adj stinking.

hedor [e'ðor] nm stench.

helada [e'laða] nf frost.

heladera [ela'ðera] (AM) nf (refrigerador) refrigerator.

helado, a [e'laðo, a] adj frozen; (glacial) icy; (fig) chilly, cold ♦ nm ice cream.

helar [e'lar] vt to freeze, ice (up); (dejar atónito) to amaze; (desalentar) to discourage ♦ vi to freeze; ~**se** vr to freeze.

helecho [e'letʃo] nm fern.

hélice ['eliθe] nf spiral; (TEC) propeller.

helicóptero [eli'koptero] nm helicopter.

hembra ['embra] nf (BOT, ZOOL) female; (mujer) woman; (TEC) nut.

hemorroides [emo'rroiðes] nfpl haemorrhoids, piles.

hemos vb ver **haber**.

hendidura [endi'ðura] nf crack, split; (GEO) fissure.

heno ['eno] nm hay.

herbicida [erβi'θiða] nm weedkiller.

heredad [ere'ðað] nf landed property; (granja) farm.

heredar [ere'ðar] vt to inherit; **heredero, a** nm/f heir(ess).

hereje [e'rexe] nm/f heretic.

herencia [e'renθja] nf inheritance.

herida [e'riða] nf wound, injury; ver tb **herido**.

herido, a [e'riðo, a] adj injured, wounded ♦ nm/f casualty.

herir [e'rir] vt to wound, injure; (fig) to offend.

hermanastro, a [erma'nastro, a] nm/f stepbrother/sister.

hermandad [erman'dað] nf brotherhood.

hermano, a [er'mano, a] nm/f brother/ sister; ~ **gemelo** twin brother; ~ **político** brother-in-law; **hermana política** sister-in-law.

hermético, a [er'metiko, a] adj hermetic; (fig) watertight.

hermoso, a [er'moso, a] adj beautiful, lovely; (estupendo) splendid; (guapo) handsome; **hermosura** nf beauty.

héroe ['eroe] *nm* hero.
heroína [ero'ina] *nf* (*mujer*) heroine; (*droga*) heroin.
heroísmo [ero'ismo] *nm* heroism.
herradura [erra'ðura] *nf* horseshoe.
herramienta [erra'mjenta] *nf* tool.
herrería [erre'ria] *nf* smithy; (*TEC*) forge; **herrero** *nm* blacksmith.
herrumbre [e'rrumbre] *nf* rust.
hervidero [erßi'ðero] *nm* (*fig*) swarm; (*POL etc*) hotbed.
hervir [er'ßir] *vi* to boil; (*burbujear*) to bubble; (*fig*): ~ **de** to teem with; ~ **a fuego lento** to simmer; **hervor** *nm* boiling; (*fig*) ardour, fervour.
heterosexual [eterosek'swal] *adj* heterosexual.
hice *etc vb ver* **hacer**.
hidratante [iðra'tante] *adj*: **crema** ~ moisturizing cream, moisturizer.
hidráulica [i'ðraulika] *nf* hydraulics *sg*.
hidráulico, a [i'ðrauliko, a] *adj* hydraulic.
hidro... [iðro] *prefijo* hydro..., water-...; ~**eléctrico, a** *adj* hydroelectric; ~**fobia** *nf* hydrophobia, rabies; **hidrógeno** *nm* hydrogen.
hiedra ['jeðra] *nf* ivy.
hiel [jel] *nf* gall, bile; (*fig*) bitterness.
hiela *etc vb ver* **helar**.
hielo ['jelo] *nm* (*gen*) ice; (*escarcha*) frost; (*fig*) coldness, reserve.
hiena ['jena] *nf* hyena.
hierba ['jerßa] *nf* (*pasto*) grass; (*CULIN, MED*: *planta*) herb; **mala** ~ weed; (*fig*) evil influence; ~**buena** *nf* mint.
hierro ['jerro] *nm* (*metal*) iron; (*objeto*) iron object.
hígado ['ixaðo] *nm* liver.
higiene [i'xjene] *nf* hygiene; **higiénico, a** *adj* hygienic.
higo ['ixo] *nm* fig; **higuera** *nf* fig tree.
hijastro, a [i'xastro, a] *nm/f* stepson/daughter.
hijo, a ['ixo, a] *nm/f* son/daughter, child; ~**s** *nmpl* children, sons and daughters; ~ **de papá/mamá** daddy's/mummy's boy; ~ **de puta** (*fam!*) bastard (!), son of a bitch (!).
hilar [i'lar] *vt* to spin; ~ **fino** to split

hairs.
hilera [i'lera] *nf* row, file.
hilo ['ilo] *nm* thread; (*BOT*) fibre; (*metal*) wire; (*de agua*) trickle, thin stream; (*de luz*) beam, ray.
hilvanar [ilßa'nar] *vt* (*COSTURA*) to tack (*BRIT*), baste (*US*); (*fig*) to do hurriedly.
himno ['imno] *nm* hymn; ~ **nacional** national anthem.
hincapié [inka'pje] *nm*: **hacer** ~ **en** to emphasize.
hincar [in'kar] *vt* to drive (in), thrust (in); ~**se** *vr*: ~**se de rodillas** to kneel down.
hincha ['intʃa] (*fam*) *nm/f* fan.
hinchado, a [in'tʃaðo, a] *adj* (*gen*) swollen; (*persona*) pompous.
hinchar [in'tʃar] *vt* (*gen*) to swell; (*inflar*) to blow up, inflate; (*fig*) to exaggerate; ~**se** *vr* (*inflarse*) to swell up; (*fam*: *llenarse*) to stuff o.s.; **hinchazón** *nf* (*MED*) swelling; (*altivez*) arrogance.
hinojo [i'noxo] *nm* fennel.
hipermercado [ipermer'kado] *nm* hypermarket, superstore.
hipnotismo [ipno'tismo] *nm* hypnotism; **hipnotizar** *vt* to hypnotize.
hipo ['ipo] *nm* hiccups *pl*.
hipocresía [ipokre'sia] *nf* hypocrisy; **hipócrita** *adj* hypocritical ♦ *nm/f* hypocrite.
hipódromo [i'poðromo] *nm* racetrack.
hipopótamo [ipo'potamo] *nm* hippopotamus.
hipoteca [ipo'teka] *nf* mortgage.
hipótesis [i'potesis] *nf inv* hypothesis.
hiriente [i'rjente] *adj* offensive, wounding.
hispánico, a [is'paniko, a] *adj* Hispanic.
hispano, a [is'pano, a] *adj* Hispanic, Spanish, Hispano- ♦ *nm/f* Spaniard; **H**~**américa** *nf* Latin America; ~**americano, a** *adj, nm/f* Latin American.
histeria [is'terja] *nf* hysteria.
historia [is'torja] *nf* history; (*cuento*) story, tale; ~**s** *nfpl* (*chismes*) gossip *sg*; **dejarse de** ~**s** to come to the point; **pasar a la** ~ to go down in history;

~**dor, a** *nm/f* historian; **historiar** *vt* to chronicle, write the history of; **histórico, a** *adj* historical; (*fig*) historic.

historieta [isto'rjeta] *nf* tale, anecdote; (*dibujos*) comic strip.

hito ['ito] *nm* (*fig*) landmark; (*objetivo*) goal, target.

hizo *vb ver* **hacer.**

Hnos *abr* (= *Hermanos*) Bros.

hocico [o'θiko] *nm* snout; (*fig*) grimace.

hockey ['xoki] *nm* hockey; ~ **sobre hielo** ice hockey.

hogar [o'ɣar] *nm* fireplace, hearth; (*casa*) home; (*vida familiar*) home life; ~**eño, a** *adj* home *cpd*; (*persona*) home-loving.

hoguera [o'ɣera] *nf* (*gen*) bonfire.

hoja ['oxa] *nf* (*gen*) leaf; (*de flor*) petal; (*de papel*) sheet; (*página*) page; ~ **de afeitar** razor blade.

hojalata [oxa'lata] *nf* tin(plate).

hojaldre [o'xaldre] *nm* (*CULIN*) puff pastry.

hojear [oxe'ar] *vt* to leaf through, turn the pages of.

hola ['ola] *excl* hello!

Holanda [o'landa] *nf* Holland; **holandés, esa** *adj* Dutch ♦ *nm/f* Dutchman/woman ♦ *nm* (*LING*) Dutch.

holgado, a [ol'ɣaðo, a] *adj* loose, baggy; (*rico*) well-to-do.

holgar [ol'ɣar] *vi* (*descansar*) to rest; (*sobrar*) to be superfluous; **huelga decir que** it goes without saying that.

holgazán, ana [olɣa'θan, ana] *adj* idle, lazy ♦ *nm/f* loafer.

holgura [ol'ɣura] *nf* looseness, bagginess; (*TEC*) play, free movement; (*vida*) comfortable living, luxury.

hollín [o'ʎin] *nm* soot.

hombre ['ombre] *nm* (*gen*) man; (*raza humana*): **el** ~ man(kind); (*uno*) man ♦ *excl* ¡**sí** ~! (*claro*) of course!; (*para énfasis*) man, old boy! ~ **de negocios** businessman; ~ **de pro** honest man; ~**rana** frogman.

hombrera [om'brera] *nf* shoulder strap.

hombro ['ombro] *nm* shoulder.

hombruno, a [om'bruno, a] *adj* mannish.

homenaje [ome'naxe] *nm* (*gen*) homage; (*tributo*) tribute.

homicida [omi'θiða] *adj* homicidal ♦ *nm/f* murderer; **homicidio** *nm* murder, homicide.

homosexual [omosek'swal] *adj, nm/f* homosexual.

hondo, a ['ondo, a] *adj* deep; **lo** ~ the depth(s) (*pl*), the bottom; ~**nada** *nf* hollow, depression; (*cañón*) ravine; (*GEO*) lowland; **hondura** *nf* depth, profundity.

Honduras [on'duras] *nf* Honduras.

hondureño, a [ondu'reɲo, a] *adj, nm/f* Honduran.

honestidad [onesti'ðað] *nf* purity, chastity; (*decencia*) decency; **honesto, a** *adj* chaste; decent, honest; (*justo*) just.

hongo ['ongo] *nm* (*BOT: gen*) fungus; (: *comestible*) mushroom; (: *venenoso*) toadstool.

honor [o'nor] *nm* (*gen*) honour; (*gloria*) glory; **en** ~ **a la verdad** to be fair; ~**able** *adj* honourable.

honorario, a [ono'rarjo, a] *adj* honorary; ~**s** *nmpl* fees.

honra ['onra] *nf* (*gen*) honour; (*renombre*) good name; ~**dez** *nf* honesty; (*de persona*) integrity; ~**do, a** *adj* honest, upright.

honrar [on'rar] *vt* to honour; ~**se** *vr*: ~**se con algo/de hacer algo** to be honoured by sth/to do sth.

honroso, a [on'roso, a] *adj* (*honrado*) honourable; (*respetado*) respectable.

hora ['ora] *nf* (*una* ~) hour; (*tiempo*) time; ¿**qué** ~ **es?** what time is it?; ¿**a qué** ~? at what time?; **media** ~ half an hour; **a la** ~ **de recreo** at playtime; **a primera** ~ first thing (in the morning); **a última** ~ at the last moment; **a altas** ~**s** in the small hours; ¡**a buena** ~! about time, too!; **dar la** ~ to strike the hour; ~**s de oficina/de trabajo** office/working hours; ~**s de visita** visiting times; ~**s extras** *o* **extraordinarias** overtime *sg*; ~**s punta** rush hours.

horadar [ora'ðar] *vt* to drill, bore.

horario, a [o'rarjo, a] *adj* hourly, hour *cpd* ♦ *nm* timetable; **~ comercial** business hours *pl*.

horca ['orka] *nf* gallows *sg*.

horcajadas [orka'xaðas]: **a ~** *adv* astride.

horchata [or'tʃata] *nf* cold drink made from tiger nuts and water, tiger nut milk.

horda ['orða] *nf* horde.

horizontal [oriθon'tal] *adj* horizontal.

horizonte [ori'θonte] *nm* horizon.

horma ['orma] *nf* mould.

hormiga [or'miɣa] *nf* ant; **~s** *nfpl* (*MED*) pins and needles.

hormigón [ormi'ɣon] *nm* concrete; **~ armado/pretensado** reinforced/prestressed concrete.

hormigueo [ormi'ɣeo] *nm* (*comezón*) itch; (*fig*) uneasiness.

hormona [or'mona] *nf* hormone.

hornada [or'naða] *nf* batch (of loaves etc).

hornillo [or'niʎo] *nm* (*cocina*) portable stove.

horno ['orno] *nm* (*CULIN*) oven; (*TEC*) furnace; **alto ~** blast furnace.

horóscopo [o'roskopo] *nm* horoscope.

horquilla [or'kiʎa] *nf* hairpin; (*AGR*) pitchfork.

horrendo, a [o'rrendo, a] *adj* horrendous, frightful.

horrible [o'rriβle] *adj* horrible, dreadful.

horripilante [orripi'lante] *adj* hair-raising, horrifying.

horror [o'rror] *nm* horror, dread; (*atrocidad*) atrocity; **¡qué ~!** (*fam*) how awful!; **~izar** *vt* to horrify, frighten; **~izarse** *vr* to be horrified; **~oso, a** *adj* horrifying, ghastly.

hortaliza [orta'liθa] *nf* vegetable.

hortelano, a [orte'lano, a] *nm/f* (market) gardener.

hosco, a ['osko, a] *adj* dark; (*persona*) sullen, gloomy.

hospedar [ospe'ðar] *vt* to put up; **~se** *vr* to stay, lodge.

hospital [ospi'tal] *nm* hospital.

hospitalario, a [ospita'larjo, a] *adj* (*acogedor*) hospitable; **hospitalidad** *nf* hospitality.

hostal [os'tal] *nm* small hotel.

hostelería [ostele'ria] *nf* hotel business *o* trade.

hostelero, a [oste'lero, a] *nm/f* innkeeper, landlord/lady.

hostia ['ostja] *nf* (*REL*) host, consecrated wafer; (*fam: golpe*) whack, punch ♦ *excl* (*fam!*): **¡~(s)!** damn!

hostigar [osti'ɣar] *vt* to whip; (*fig*) to harass, pester.

hostil [os'til] *adj* hostile; **~idad** *nf* hostility.

hotel [o'tel] *nm* hotel; **~ero, a** *adj* hotel *cpd* ♦ *nm/f* hotelier.

hoy [oi] *adv* (*este día*) today; (*la actualidad*) now(adays) ♦ *nm* present time; **~ (en) día** now(adays).

hoyo ['ojo] *nm* hole, pit; **hoyuelo** *nm* dimple.

hoz [oθ] *nf* sickle.

hube *etc vb ver* **haber**.

hucha ['utʃa] *nf* money box.

hueco, a ['weko, a] *adj* (*vacío*) hollow, empty; (*resonante*) booming ♦ *nm* hollow, cavity.

huelga *etc* ['welɣa] *vb ver* **holgar** ♦ *nf* strike; **declararse en ~** to go on strike, come out on strike; **~ de hambre** hunger strike.

huelguista [wel'ɣista] *nm/f* striker.

huelo *etc vb ver* **oler**.

huella ['weʎa] *nf* (*acto de pisar, pisada*) tread(ing); (*marca del paso*) footprint, footstep; (: *de animal, máquina*) track; **~ digital** fingerprint.

huérfano, a ['werfano, a] *adj* orphan(ed) ♦ *nm/f* orphan.

huerta ['werta] *nf* market garden; (*en Murcia y Valencia*) irrigated region.

huerto ['werto] *nm* kitchen garden; (*de árboles frutales*) orchard.

hueso ['weso] *nm* (*ANAT*) bone; (*de fruta*) stone.

huésped, a ['wespeð, a] *nm/f* (*invitado*) guest; (*habitante*) resident; (*anfitrión*) host(ess).

huesudo, a [we'suðo, a] *adj* bony, big-boned.

huevera [we'βera] *nf* eggcup.

huevo ['weßo] *nm* egg; ~ **duro/
escalfado/frito** (*ESP*) *o* **estrellado** (*AM*)/
pasado por agua hard-boiled/poached/
fried/soft-boiled egg; ~**s revueltos**
scrambled eggs.

huida [u'iða] *nf* escape, flight.

huidizo, a [ui'ðiθo, a] *adj* (*tímido*) shy;
(*pasajero*) fleeting.

huir [u'ir] *vi* (*escapar*) to flee, escape;
(*evadir*) to avoid; ~**se** *vr* (*escaparse*)
to escape.

hule ['ule] *nm* (*encerado*) oilskin.

humanidad [umani'ðað] *nf* (*género
humano*) man(kind); (*cualidad*)
humanity.

humano, a [u'mano, a] *adj* (*gen*)
human; (*humanitario*) humane ♦ *nm*
human; **ser** ~ human being.

humareda [uma'reða] *nf* cloud of
smoke.

humedad [ume'ðað] *nf* (*del clima*)
humidity; (*de pared etc*) dampness; a
prueba de ~ damp-proof; **humedecer**
vt to moisten, wet; **humedecerse** *vr* to
get wet.

húmedo, a ['umeðo, a] *adj* (*mojado*)
damp, wet; (*tiempo etc*) humid.

humildad [umil'dað] *nf* humility,
humbleness; **humilde** *adj* humble,
modest.

humillación [umiʎa'θjon] *nf* humiliation;
humillante *adj* humiliating.

humillar [umi'ʎar] *vt* to humiliate; ~**se**
vr to humble o.s., grovel.

humo ['umo] *nm* (*de fuego*) smoke;
(*gas nocivo*) fumes *pl*; (*vapor*) steam,
vapour; ~**s** *nmpl* (*fig*) conceit *sg*.

humor [u'mor] *nm* (*disposición*) mood,
temper; (*lo que divierte*) humour; **de
buen/mal** ~ in a good/bad mood; ~**ismo**
nm humour; ~**ista** *nm/f* comic; ~**ístico,
a** *adj* funny, humorous.

hundimiento [undi'mjento] *nm* (*gen*)
sinking; (*colapso*) collapse.

hundir [un'dir] *vt* to sink; (*edificio,
plan*) to ruin, destroy; ~**se** *vr* to sink,
collapse.

húngaro, a ['ungaro, a] *adj*, *nm/f*
Hungarian.

Hungría [un'gria] *nf* Hungary.

huracán [ura'kan] *nm* hurricane.

huraño, a [u'raɲo, a] *adj* shy; (*anti-
social*) unsociable.

hurgar [ur'ɣar] *vt* to poke, jab; (*remover*) to stir (up); ~**se** *vr*: ~**se (las
narices)** to pick one's nose.

hurón, ona [u'ron, ona] *nm* (*ZOOL*)
ferret.

hurtadillas [urta'ðiʎas]: **a** ~ *adv*
·stealthily, on the sly.

hurtar [ur'tar] *vt* to steal; **hurto** *nm*
theft, stealing.

husmear [usme'ar] *vt* (*oler*) to sniff out,
scent; (*fam*) to pry into ♦ *vi* to smell
bad.

huyo *etc vb ver* **huir.**

I

iba *etc vb ver* **ir.**

ibérico, a [i'ßeriko, a] *adj* Iberian.

iberoamericano, a [ißeroameri'kano, a]
adj, *nm/f* Latin American.

íbice ['ißiθe] *nm* ibex.

Ibiza [i'ßiθa] *nf* Ibiza.

iceberg [iθe'ßer] *nm* iceberg.

ícono ['ikono] *nm* icon, icon.

iconoclasta [ikono'klasta] *adj* iconoclas-
tic ♦ *nm/f* iconoclast.

ictericia [ikte'riθja] *nf* jaundice.

ida ['iða] *nf* going, departure; ~ **y vuelta**
round trip, return.

idea [i'ðea] *nf* idea; **no tengo la menor** ~
I haven't a clue.

ideal [iðe'al] *adj*, *nm* ideal; ~**ista** *nm/f*
idealist; ~**izar** *vt* to idealize.

idear [iðe'ar] *vt* to think up; (*aparato*)
to invent; (*viaje*) to plan.

ídem ['iðem] *pron* ditto.

idéntico, a [i'ðentiko, a] *adj* identical.

identidad [iðenti'ðað] *nf* identity.

identificación [iðentifika'θjon] *nf*
identification.

identificar [iðentifi'kar] *vt* to identify;
~**se** *vr*: ~**se con** to identify with.

ideología [iðeolo'xia] *nf* ideology.

idioma [i'ðjoma] *nm* (*gen*) language.

idiota [i'ðjota] *adj* idiotic ♦ *nm/f* idiot;
idiotez *nf* idiocy.

ídolo ['iðolo] *nm* (*tb: fig*) idol.
idóneo, a [i'ðoneo, a] *adj* suitable.
iglesia [i'ɣlesja] *nf* church.
ignominia [iɣno'minja] *nf* ignominy.
ignorancia [iɣno'ranθja] *nf* ignorance;
ignorante *adj* ignorant, uninformed ♦
nm/f ignoramus.
ignorar [iɣno'rar] *vt* not to know, be
ignorant of; (*no hacer caso a*) to
ignore.
igual [i'ɣwal] *adj* (*gen*) equal; (*similar*)
like, similar; (*mismo*) (the) same;
(*constante*) constant; (*temperatura*)
even ♦ *nm/f* equal; ~ *que* like, the
same as; **me da** *o* **es** ~ I don't care;
son ~**es** they're the same; **al** ~ **que**
prep, conj like, just like.
igualada [iɣwa'laða] *nf* equaliser.
igualar [iɣwa'lar] *vt* (*gen*) to equalize,
make equal; (*allanar, nivelar*) to level
(off), even (out); ~**se** *vr* (*platos de
balanza*) to balance out.
igualdad [iɣwal'dað] *nf* equality;
(*similaridad*) sameness; (*uniformidad*)
uniformity.
igualmente [iɣwal'mente] *adv* equally;
(*también*) also, likewise ♦ *excl* the
same to you!
ikurriña [iku'rriɲa] *nf* Basque flag.
ilegal [ile'ɣal] *adj* illegal.
ilegítimo, a [ile'xitimo, a] *adj* illegitimate.
ileso, a [i'leso, a] *adj* unhurt.
ilícito, a [i'liθito, a] *adj* illicit.
ilimitado, a [ilimi'taðo, a] *adj* unlimited.
ilógico, a [i'loxiko, a] *adj* illogical.
iluminación [ilumina'θjon] *nf* illumination; (*alumbrado*) lighting.
iluminar [ilumi'nar] *vt* to illuminate,
light (up); (*fig*) to enlighten.
ilusión [ilu'sjon] *nf* illusion; (*quimera*)
delusion; (*esperanza*) hope; **hacerse
ilusiones** to build up one's hopes;
ilusionado, a *adj* excited.
ilusionista [ilusjo'nista] *nm/f* conjurer.
iluso, a [i'luso, a] *adj* easily deceived ♦
nm/f dreamer.
ilusorio, a [ilu'sorjo, a] *adj* (*de ilusión*)
illusory, deceptive; (*esperanza*) vain.
ilustración [ilustra'θjon] *nf* illustration;

(*saber*) learning, erudition; **la I~** the
Enlightenment; **ilustrado, a** *adj*
illustrated; learned.
ilustrar [ilus'trar] *vt* to illustrate; (*instruir*) to instruct; (*explicar*) to explain,
make clear; ~**se** *vr* to acquire knowledge.
ilustre [i'lustre] *adj* famous, illustrious.
imagen [i'maxen] *nf* (*gen*) image;
(*dibujo*) picture.
imaginación [imaxina'θjon] *nf* imagination.
imaginar [imaxi'nar] *vt* (*gen*) to
imagine; (*idear*) to think up; (*suponer*)
to suppose; ~**se** *vr* to imagine; ~**io, a**
adj imaginary; **imaginativo, a** *adj*
imaginative.
imán [i'man] *nm* magnet.
imbécil [im'beθil] *nm/f* imbecile, idiot.
imbuir [imbu'ir] *vt* to imbue.
imitación [imita'θjon] *nf* imitation.
imitar [imi'tar] *vt* to imitate; (*parodiar,
remedar*) to mimic, ape.
impaciencia [impa'θjenθja] *nf*
impatience; **impaciente** *adj* impatient;
(*nervioso*) anxious.
impacto [im'pakto] *nm* impact.
impar [im'par] *adj* odd.
imparcial [impar'θjal] *adj* impartial,
fair; ~**idad** *nf* impartiality, fairness.
impartir [impar'tir] *vt* to impart, give.
impasible [impa'sißle] *adj* impassive.
impávido, a [im'paßiðo, a] *adj* fearless,
intrepid.
impecable [impe'kaßle] *adj* impeccable.
impedimento [impeði'mento] *nm*
impediment, obstacle.
impedir [impe'ðir] *vt* (*obstruir*) to
impede, obstruct; (*estorbar*) to prevent.
impeler [impe'ler] *vt* to drive, propel;
(*fig*) to impel.
impenetrable [impene'traßle] *adj*
impenetrable; (*fig*) incomprehensible.
imperar [impe'rar] *vi* (*reinar*) to rule,
reign; (*fig*) to prevail, reign; (*precio*)
to be current.
imperativo, a [impera'tißo, a] *adj*
(*persona*) imperious; (*urgente, LING*)
imperative.
imperceptible [imperθep'tißle] *adj*

imperceptible.

imperdible [imper'ðißle] *nm* safety pin.

imperdonable [imperðo'naßle] *adj* unforgivable, inexcusable.

imperfección [imperfek'θjon] *nf* imperfection.

imperfecto, a [imper'fekto, a] *adj* imperfect.

imperial [impe'rjal] *adj* imperial; ~**ismo** *nm* imperialism.

imperio [im'perjo] *nm* empire; (*autoridad*) rule, authority; (*fig*) pride, haughtiness; ~**so, a** *adj* imperious; (*urgente*) urgent; (*imperativo*) imperative.

impermeable [imperme'aßle] *adj* (*a prueba de agua*) waterproof ♦ *nm* raincoat, mac (*BRIT*).

impersonal [imperso'nal] *adj* impersonal.

impertérrito, a [imper'territo, a] *adj* undaunted.

impertinencia [imperti'nenθja] *nf* impertinence; **impertinente** *adj* impertinent.

imperturbable [impertur'ßaßle] *adj* imperturbable.

ímpetu ['impetu] *nm* (*impulso*) impetus, impulse; (*impetuosidad*) impetuosity; (*violencia*) violence.

impetuoso, a [impe'twoso, a] *adj* impetuous; (*río*) rushing; (*acto*) hasty.

impío, a [im'pio, a] *adj* impious, ungodly.

implacable [impla'kaßle] *adj* implacable.

implicar [impli'kar] *vt* to involve; (*entrañar*) to imply.

implícito, a [im'pliθito, a] *adj* (*tácito*) implicit; (*sobreentendido*) implied.

implorar [implo'rar] *vt* to beg, implore.

imponente [impo'nente] *adj* (*impresionante*) impressive, imposing; (*solemne*) grand.

imponer [impo'ner] *vt* (*gen*) to impose; (*exigir*) to exact; ~**se** *vr* to assert o.s.; (*prevalecer*) to prevail; **imponible** *adj* (*COM*) taxable.

impopular [impopu'lar] *adj* unpopular.

importación [importa'θjon] *nf* (*acto*) importing; (*mercancías*) imports *pl*.

importancia [impor'tanθja] *nf* importance; (*valor*) value, significance; (*extensión*) size, magnitude; **importante** *adj* important; valuable, significant.

importar [impor'tar] *vt* (*del extranjero*) to import; (*costar*) to amount to ♦ *vi* to be important, matter; **me importa un rábano** I couldn't care less; **no importa** it doesn't matter; **¿le importa que fume?** do you mind if I smoke?

importe [im'porte] *nm* (*total*) amount; (*valor*) value.

importunar [importu'nar] *vt* to bother, pester.

imposibilidad [imposißili'ðað] *nf* impossibility; **imposibilitar** *vt* to make impossible, prevent.

imposible [impo'sißle] *adj* (*gen*) impossible; (*insoportable*) unbearable, intolerable.

imposición [imposi'θjon] *nf* imposition; (*COM: impuesto*) tax; (: *inversión*) deposit.

impostor, a [impos'tor, a] *nm/f* impostor.

impotencia [impo'tenθja] *nf* impotence; **impotente** *adj* impotent.

impracticable [imprakti'kaßle] *adj* (*irrealizable*) impracticable; (*intransitable*) impassable.

imprecar [impre'kar] *vi* to curse.

impreciso, a [impre'θiso, a] *adj* imprecise, vague.

impregnar [impreʁ'nar] *vt* to impregnate; ~**se** *vr* to become impregnated.

imprenta [im'prenta] *nf* (*acto*) printing; (*aparato*) press; (*casa*) printer's; (*letra*) print.

imprescindible [impresθin'dißle] *adj* essential, vital.

impresión [impre'sjon] *nf* (*gen*) impression; (*IMPRENTA*) printing; (*edición*) edition; (*FOTO*) print; (*marca*) imprint; ~ **digital** fingerprint.

impresionable [impresjo'naßle] *adj* (*sensible*) impressionable.

impresionante [impresjo'nante] *adj* impressive; (*tremendo*) tremendous;

(*maravilloso*) great, marvellous.
impresionar [impresjo'nar] *vt* (*conmover*) to move; (*afectar*) to impress, strike; (*película fotográfica*) to expose; ~**se** *vr* to be impressed; (*conmoverse*) to be moved.
impreso, a [im'preso, a] *pp de* **imprimir** ♦ *adj* printed; ~**s** *nmpl* printed matter; **impresora** *nf* printer.
imprevisto, a [impre'βisto, a] *adj* (*gen*) unforeseen; (*inesperado*) unexpected ~**s** *nmpl* (*gastos*) unforeseen expenses.
imprimir [impri'mir] *vt* to imprint, impress, stamp; (*textos*) to print; (*INFORM*) to output, print out.
improbable [impro'βaβle] *adj* improbable; (*inverosímil*) unlikely.
improcedente [improθe'ðente] *adj* inappropriate.
improductivo, a [improðuk'tiβo, a] *adj* unproductive.
improperio [impro'perjo] *nm* insult.
impropiedad [impropje'ðað] *nf* impropriety (of language).
impropio, a [im'propjo, a] *adj* improper.
improvisación [improβisa'θjon] *nf* improvisation; **improvisado, a** *adj* improvised.
improvisar [improβi'sar] *vt* to improvise.
improviso, a [impro'βiso, a] *adj*: **de** ~ unexpectedly, suddenly.
imprudencia [impru'ðenθja] *nf* imprudence; (*indiscreción*) indiscretion; (*descuido*) carelessness; **imprudente** *adj* unwise, imprudent; (*indiscreto*) indiscreet.
impúdico, a [im'puðiko, a] *adj* shameless; (*lujurioso*) lecherous.
impudor [impu'ðor] *nm* shamelessness; (*lujuria*) lechery.
impuesto, a [im'pwesto, a] *adj* imposed ♦ *nm* tax; ~ **sobre el valor añadido** value added tax.
impugnar [impuɣ'nar] *vt* to oppose, contest; (*refutar*) to refute, impugn.
impulsar [impul'sar] *vt* = **impeler**.
impulso [im'pulso] *nm* impulse; (*fuerza, empuje*) thrust, drive; (*fig: sentimiento*) urge, impulse.
impune [im'pune] *adj* unpunished;

impunidad *nf* impunity.
impureza [impu'reθa] *nf* impurity; (*fig*) lewdness; **impuro, a** *adj* impure; lewd.
imputar [impu'tar] *vt*: ~ **a** to attribute to.
inacabable [inaka'βaβle] *adj* (*infinito*) endless; (*interminable*) interminable.
inaccesible [inakθe'siβle] *adj* inaccessible.
inacción [inak'θjon] *nf* inactivity.
inaceptable [inaθep'taβle] *adj* unacceptable.
inactividad [inaktiβi'ðað] *nf* inactivity; (*COM*) dullness; **inactivo, a** *adj* inactive.
inadaptación [inaðapta'θjon] *nf* maladjustment.
inadecuado, a [inaðe'kwaðo, a] *adj* (*insuficiente*) inadequate; (*inapto*) unsuitable.
inadmisible [inaðmi'siβle] *adj* inadmissible.
inadvertido, a [inaðβer'tiðo, a] *adj* (*no visto*) unnoticed.
inagotable [inaɣo'taβle] *adj* inexhaustible.
inaguantable [inaɣwan'taβle] *adj* unbearable.
inalterable [inalte'raβle] *adj* immutable, unchangeable.
inanición [inani'θjon] *nf* starvation.
inanimado, a [inani'maðo, a] *adj* inanimate.
inapto, a [in'apto] *adj* unsuited.
inaudito, a [inau'ðito, a] *adj* unheard-of.
inauguración [inauɣura'θjon] *nf* inauguration; opening.
inaugurar [inauɣu'rar] *vt* to inaugurate; (*exposición*) to open.
I.N.B. (*ESP*) *abr* (= *Instituto Nacional de Bachillerato*) ≈ comprehensive school (*BRIT*), ≈ high school (*US*).
inca ['inka] *nm/f* Inca; ~**ico, a** *adj* Inca *cpd*.
incalculable [inkalku'laβle] *adj* incalculable.
incandescente [inkandes'θente] *adj* incandescent.
incansable [inkan'saβle] *adj* tireless, untiring.

incapacidad [inkapaθi'ðað] *nf* in-capacity; (*incompetencia*) in-competence; ~ **física/mental** physical/mental disability.

incapacitar [inkapaθi'tar] *vt* (*inhabilitar*) to incapacitate, render unfit; (*descalificar*) to disqualify.

incapaz [inka'paθ] *adj* incapable.

incautación [inkauta'θjon] *nf* confiscation.

incautarse [inkau'tarse] *vr*: ~ **de** to seize, confiscate.

incauto, a [in'kauto, a] *adj* (*imprudente*) incautious, unwary.

incendiar [inθen'djar] *vt* to set fire to; (*fig*) to inflame; ~**se** *vr* to catch fire; ~**io, a** *adj* incendiary.

incendio [in'θendjo] *nm* fire.

incentivo [inθen'tiβo] *nm* incentive.

incertidumbre [inθerti'ðumbre] *nf* (*inseguridad*) uncertainty; (*duda*) doubt.

incesante [inθe'sante] *adj* incessant.

incesto [in'θesto] *nm* incest.

incidencia [inθi'ðenθja] *nf* (*MAT*) incidence.

incidente [inθi'ðente] *nm* incident.

incidir [inθi'ðir] *vi* (*influir*) to influence; (*afectar*) to affect; ~ **en un error** to fall into error.

incienso [in'θjenso] *nm* incense.

incierto, a [in'θjerto, a] *adj* uncertain.

incineración [inθinera'θjon] *nf* incineration; (*de cadáveres*) cremation.

incinerar [inθine'rar] *vt* to burn; (*cadáveres*) to cremate.

incipiente [inθi'pjente] *adj* incipient.

incisión [inθi'sjon] *nf* incision.

incisivo, a [inθi'siβo, a] *adj* sharp, cutting; (*fig*) incisive.

incitar [inθi'tar] *vt* to incite, rouse.

incivil [inθi'βil] *adj* rude, uncivil.

inclemencia [inkle'menθja] *nf* (*severidad*) harshness, severity; (*del tiempo*) inclemency.

inclinación [inklina'θjon] *nf* (*gen*) inclination; (*de tierras*) slope, incline; (*de cabeza*) nod, bow; (*fig*) leaning, bent.

inclinar [inkli'nar] *vt* to incline; (*cabeza*) to nod, bow ♦ *vi* to lean, slope; ~**se** *vr*

to bow; (*encorvarse*) to stoop; ~**se a** (*parecerse a*) to take after, resemble; ~**se ante** to bow down to; **me inclino a pensar que** I'm inclined to think that.

incluir [inklu'ir] *vt* to include; (*incorporar*) to incorporate; (*meter*) to enclose.

inclusive [inklu'siβe] *adv* inclusive ♦ *prep* including.

incluso, a [in'kluso, a] *adj* included ♦ *adv* inclusively; (*hasta*) even.

incógnito [in'koɣnito] *nm*: **de** ~ incognito.

incoherente [inkoe'rente] *adj* incoherent.

incoloro, a [inko'loro, a] *adj* colourless.

incólume [in'kolume] *adj* (*gen*) safe; (*indemne*) unhurt, unharmed.

incomodar [inkomo'ðar] *vt* to inconvenience; (*molestar*) to bother, trouble; (*fastidiar*) to annoy; ~**se** *vr* to put o.s. out; (*fastidiarse*) to get annoyed.

incomodidad [inkomoði'ðað] *nf* inconvenience; (*fastidio*, *enojo*) annoyance; (*de vivienda*) discomfort.

incómodo, a [in'komoðo, a] *adj* (*inconfortable*) uncomfortable; (*molesto*) annoying; (*inconveniente*) inconvenient.

incomparable [inkompa'raβle] *adj* incomparable.

incompatible [inkompa'tiβle] *adj* incompatible.

incompetencia [inkompe'tenθja] *nf* incompetence; **incompetente** *adj* incompetent.

incompleto, a [inkom'pleto, a] *adj* incomplete, unfinished.

incomprensible [inkompren'siβle] *adj* incomprehensible.

incomunicado, a [inkomuni'kaðo, a] *adj* (*aislado*) cut off, isolated; (*confinado*) in solitary confinement.

inconcebible [inkonθe'βiβle] *adj* inconceivable.

inconcluso, a [inkon'kluso, a] *adj* (*inacabado*) unfinished.

incondicional [inkondiθjo'nal] *adj* unconditional; (*apoyo*) wholehearted; (*partidario*) staunch.

inconexo, a [inko'nekso, a] *adj* (*gen*)

unconnected; (*desunido*) disconnected.

inconfundible [inkonfun'diβle] *adj* unmistakable.

incongruente [inkon'grwente] *adj* incongruous.

inconmensurable [inkonmensu'raβle] *adj* immeasurable, vast.

inconsciencia [inkons'θjenθja] *nf* unconsciousness; (*fig*) thoughtlessness; **inconsciente** *adj* unconscious; thoughtless.

inconsecuente [inkonse'kwente] *adj* inconsistent.

inconsiderado, a [inkonsiðe'raðo, a] *adj* inconsiderate.

inconsistente [inkonsis'tente] *adj* weak; (*tela*) flimsy.

inconstancia [inkon'stanθja] *nf* inconstancy; (*inestabilidad*) unsteadiness; **inconstante** *adj* inconstant.

incontable [inkon'taβle] *adj* countless, innumerable.

incontestable [inkontes'taβle] *adj* unanswerable; (*innegable*) undeniable.

incontinencia [inkonti'nenθja] *nf* incontinence.

inconveniencia [inkombe'njenθja] *nf* unsuitability, inappropriateness; (*descortesía*) impoliteness; **inconveniente** *adj* unsuitable; impolite ♦ *nm* obstacle; (*desventaja*) disadvantage; **el inconveniente es que ...** the trouble is that ....

incorporación [inkorpora'θjon] *nf* incorporation.

incorporar [inkorpo'rar] *vt* to incorporate; ~**se** *vr* to sit up.

incorrección [inkorrek'θjon] *nf* (*gen*) incorrectness, inaccuracy; (*descortesía*) bad-mannered behaviour; **incorrecto, a** *adj* (*gen*) incorrect, wrong; (*comportamiento*) bad-mannered.

incorregible [inkorre'xiβle] *adj* incorrigible.

incredulidad [inkreðuli'ðað] *nf* incredulity; (*escepticismo*) scepticism; **incrédulo, a** *adj* incredulous, unbelieving; sceptical.

increíble [inkre'iβle] *adj* incredible.

incremento [inkre'mento] *nm* increment; (*aumento*) rise, increase.

increpar [inkre'par] *vt* to reprimand.

incruento, a [in'krwento, a] *adj* bloodless.

incrustar [inkrus'tar] *vt* to incrust; (*piedras: en joya*) to inlay.

incubar [inku'βar] *vt* to incubate; (*fig*) to hatch.

inculcar [inkul'kar] *vt* to inculcate.

inculpar [inkul'par] *vt* (*acusar*) to accuse; (*achacar, atribuir*) to charge, blame.

inculto, a [in'kulto, a] *adj* (*persona*) uneducated; (*grosero*) uncouth ♦ *nm/f* ignoramus.

incumplimiento [inkumpli'mjento] *nm* non-fulfilment; ~ **de contrato** breach of contract.

incurrir [inku'rrir] *vi*: ~ **en** to incur; (*crimen*) to commit; ~ **en un error** to make a mistake.

indagación [indaɣa'θjon] *nf* investigation; (*búsqueda*) search; (*JUR*) inquest.

indagar [inda'ɣar] *vt* to investigate; to search; (*averiguar*) to ascertain.

indecente [inde'θente] *adj* indecent, improper; (*lascivo*) obscene.

indecible [inde'θiβle] *adj* unspeakable; (*indescriptible*) indescribable.

indeciso, a [inde'θiso, a] *adj* (*por decidir*) undecided; (*vacilante*) hesitant.

indefenso, a [inde'fenso, a] *adj* defenceless.

indefinido, a [indefi'niðo, a] *adj* indefinite; (*vago*) vague, undefined.

indeleble [inde'leβle] *adj* indelible.

indemne [in'demne] *adj* (*objeto*) undamaged; (*persona*) unharmed, unhurt.

indemnizar [indemni'θar] *vt* to indemnify; (*compensar*) to compensate.

independencia [indepen'denθja] *nf* independence.

independiente [indepen'djente] *adj* (*libre*) independent; (*autónomo*) self-sufficient.

indeterminado, a [indetermi'naðo, a] *adj* indefinite; (*desconocido*) indeterminate.

India ['indja] *nf*: **la** ~ India.

indicación [indika'θjon] *nf* indication; (*señal*) sign; (*sugerencia*) suggestion, hint.

indicador [indika'ðor] *nm* indicator; (*TEC*) gauge, meter.

indicar [indi'kar] *vt* (*mostrar*) to indicate, show; (*termómetro etc*) to read, register; (*señalar*) to point to.

índice ['indiθe] *nm* index; (*catálogo*) catalogue; (*ANAT*) index finger, forefinger.

indicio [in'diθjo] *nm* indication, sign; (*en pesquisa etc*) clue.

indiferencia [indife'renθja] *nf* indifference; (*apatía*) apathy; **indiferente** *adj* indifferent.

indígena [in'dixena] *adj* indigenous, native ♦ *nm/f* native.

indigencia [indi'xenθja] *nf* poverty, need.

indigestión [indixes'tjon] *nf* indigestion.

indigesto, a [indi'xesto, a] *adj* undigested; (*indigestible*) indigestible; (*fig*) turgid.

indignación [indiɣna'θjon] *nf* indignation.

indignar [indiɣ'nar] *vt* to anger, make indignant; ~**se** *vr*: ~**se por** to get indignant about.

indigno, a [in'diɣno, a] *adj* (*despreciable*) low, contemptible; (*inmerecido*) unworthy.

indio, a ['indjo, a] *adj, nm/f* Indian.

indirecta [indi'rekta] *nf* insinuation, innuendo; (*sugerencia*) hint.

indirecto, a [indi'rekto, a] *adj* indirect.

indiscreción [indiskre'θjon] *nf* (*imprudencia*) indiscretion; (*irreflexión*) tactlessness; (*acto*) gaffe, faux pas.

indiscreto, a [indis'kreto, a] *adj* indiscreet.

indiscutible [indisku'tiβle] *adj* indisputable, unquestionable.

indispensable [indispen'saβle] *adj* indispensable, essential.

indisponer [indispo'ner] *vt* to spoil, upset; (*salud*) to make ill; ~**se** *vr* to fall ill; ~**se con uno** to fall out with sb.

indisposición [indisposi'θjon] *nf* indisposition.

indispuesto, a [indis'pwesto, a] *adj* (*enfermo*) unwell, indisposed.

indistinto, a [indis'tinto, a] *adj* indistinct; (*vago*) vague.

individual [indiβi'ðwal] *adj* individual; (*habitación*) single ♦ *nm* (*DEPORTE*) singles *sg*.

individuo, a [indi'βiðwo, a] *adj, nm* individual.

índole ['indole] *nf* (*naturaleza*) nature; (*clase*) sort, kind.

indolencia [indo'lenθja] *nf* indolence, laziness.

indómito, a [in'domito, a] *adj* indomitable.

inducir [indu'θir] *vt* to induce; (*inferir*) to infer; (*persuadir*) to persuade.

indudable [indu'ðaβle] *adj* undoubted; (*incuestionable*) unquestionable.

indulgencia [indul'xenθja] *nf* indulgence.

indultar [indul'tar] *vt* (*perdonar*) to pardon, reprieve; (*librar de pago*) to exempt; **indulto** *nm* pardon; exemption.

industria [in'dustrja] *nf* industry; (*habilidad*) skill; **industrial** *adj* industrial ♦ *nm* industrialist.

inédito, a [in'eðito, a] *adj* (*texto*) unpublished; (*nuevo*) new.

inefable [ine'faβle] *adj* ineffable, indescribable.

ineficaz [inefi'kaθ] *adj* (*inútil*) ineffective; (*ineficiente*) inefficient.

ineludible [inelu'ðiβle] *adj* inescapable, unavoidable.

ineptitud [inepti'tuð] *nf* ineptitude, incompetence; **inepto, a** *adj* inept, incompetent.

inequívoco, a [ine'kiβoko, a] *adj* unequivocal; (*inconfundible*) unmistakable.

inercia [in'erθja] *nf* inertia; (*pasividad*) passivity.

inerme [in'erme] *adj* (*sin armas*) unarmed; (*indefenso*) defenceless.

inerte [in'erte] *adj* inert; (*inmóvil*) motionless.

inesperado, a [inespe'raðo, a] *adj* unexpected, unforeseen.

inestable [ines'taβle] *adj* unstable.

inevitable [ineßi'taßle] *adj* inevitable.
inexactitud [ineksakti'tuð] *nf* inaccuracy; **inexacto, a** *adj* inaccurate; (*falso*) untrue.
inexperto, a [inek'sperto, a] *adj* (*novato*) inexperienced.
infalible [infa'lißle] *adj* infallible; (*plan*) foolproof.
infame [in'fame] *adj* infamous; (*horrible*) dreadful; **infamia** *nf* infamy; (*deshonra*) disgrace.
infancia [in'fanθja] *nf* infancy, childhood.
infante [in'fante] *nm* (*hijo del rey*) infante, prince; (MIL) infantryman.
infantería [infante'ria] *nf* infantry.
infantil [infan'til] *adj* (*pueril, aniñado*) infantile; (*cándido*) childlike; (*literatura, ropa etc*) children's.
infarto [in'farto] *nm* (*tb: ~ de miocardio*) heart attack.
infatigable [infati'ɣaßle] *adj* tireless, untiring.
infección [infek'θjon] *nf* infection; **infeccioso, a** *adj* infectious.
infectar [infek'tar] *vt* to infect; ~**se** *vr* to become infected.
infeliz [infe'liθ] *adj* unhappy, wretched ♦ *nm/f* wretch.
inferior [infe'rjor] *adj* inferior; (*situación*) lower ♦ *nm/f* inferior, subordinate.
inferir [infe'rir] *vt* (*deducir*) to infer, deduce; (*causar*) to cause.
infestar [infes'tar] *vt* to infest.
infidelidad [infiðeli'ðað] *nf* (*gen*) infidelity, unfaithfulness.
infiel [in'fjel] *adj* unfaithful, disloyal; (*erróneo*) inaccurate ♦ *nm/f* infidel, unbeliever.
infierno [in'fjerno] *nm* hell.
ínfimo, a ['infimo, a] *adj* (*más bajo*) lowest; (*despreciable*) vile, mean.
infinidad [infini'ðað] *nf* infinity; (*abundancia*) great quantity.
infinito, a [infi'nito, a] *adj, nm* infinite.
inflación [infla'θjon] *nf* (*hinchazón*) swelling; (*monetaria*) inflation; (*fig*) conceit; **inflacionario, a** *adj* inflationary.
inflamar [infla'mar] *vt* (MED, *fig*) to inflame; ~**se** *vr* to catch fire; to become inflamed.

inflar [in'flar] *vt* (*hinchar*) to inflate, blow up; (*fig*) to exaggerate; ~**se** *vr* to swell (up); (*fig*) to get conceited.
inflexible [inflek'sißle] *adj* inflexible; (*fig*) unbending.
infligir [infli'xir] *vt* to inflict.
influencia [influ'enθja] *nf* influence; **influenciar** *vt* to influence.
influir [influ'ir] *vt* to influence.
influjo [in'fluxo] *nm* influence.
influya *etc vb ver* **influir**.
influyente [influ'jente] *adj* influential.
información [informa'θjon] *nf* information; (*noticias*) news *sg*; (JUR) inquiry; **I~** (*oficina*) Information Office; (*mostrador*) Information Desk; (TEL) Directory Enquiries.
informal [infor'mal] *adj* (*gen*) informal.
informante [infor'mante] *nm/f* informant.
informar [infor'mar] *vt* (*gen*) to inform; (*revelar*) to reveal, make known ♦ *vi* (JUR) to plead; (*denunciar*) to inform; (*dar cuenta de*) to report on; ~**se** *vr* to find out; ~**se de** to inquire into.
informática [infor'matika] *nf* computer science, information technology.
informe [in'forme] *adj* shapeless ♦ *nm* report.
infortunio [infor'tunjo] *nm* misfortune.
infracción [infrak'θjon] *nf* infraction, infringement.
infranqueable [infranke'aßle] *adj* impassable; (*fig*) insurmountable.
infringir [infrin'xir] *vt* to infringe, contravene.
infructuoso, a [infruk'twoso, a] *adj* fruitless, unsuccessful.
infundado, a [infun'daðo, a] *adj* groundless, unfounded.
infundir [infun'dir] *vt* to infuse, instil.
infusión [infu'sjon] *nf* infusion; ~ **de manzanilla** camomile tea.
ingeniar [inxe'njar] *vt* to think up, devise; ~**se** *vr*: ~**se para** to manage to.
ingeniería [inxenje'ria] *nf* engineering; **ingeniero, a** *nm/f* engineer; **ingeniero de caminos/de sonido** civil engineer/ sound engineer.

ingenio [in'xenjo] *nm* (*talento*) talent; (*agudeza*) wit; (*habilidad*) ingenuity, inventiveness; (*TEC*): ~ **azucarero** sugar refinery.

ingenioso, a [inxe'njoso, a] *adj* ingenious, clever; (*divertido*) witty.

ingenuidad [inxenwi'ðað] *nf* ingenuousness; (*sencillez*) simplicity; **ingenuo, a** *adj* ingenuous.

ingerir [inxe'rir] *vt* to ingest; (*tragar*) to swallow; (*consumir*) to consume.

Inglaterra [ingla'terra] *nf* England.

ingle ['ingle] *nf* groin.

inglés, esa [in'gles, esa] *adj* English ♦ *nm/f* Englishman/woman ♦ *nm* (*LING*) English.

ingratitud [ingrati'tuð] *nf* ingratitude; **ingrato, a** *adj* (*gen*) ungrateful.

ingrediente [ingre'ðjente] *nm* ingredient.

ingresar [ingre'sar] *vt* (*dinero*) to deposit ♦ *vi* to come in; ~ **en un club** to join a club; ~ **en el hospital** to go into hospital.

ingreso [in'greso] *nm* (*entrada*) entry; (: *en hospital etc*) admission; ~s *nmpl* (*dinero*) income *sg*; (: *COM*) takings *pl*.

inhabitable [inaßi'taßle] *adj* uninhabitable.

inhalar [ina'lar] *vt* to inhale.

inherente [ine'rente] *adj* inherent.

inhibir [ini'ßir] *vt* to inhibit; (*REL*) to restrain.

inhumano, a [inu'mano, a] *adj* inhuman.

INI ['ini] (*ESP*) *nm abr* (= *Instituto Nacional de Industria*) ≈ NEB (*BRIT*).

inicial [ini'θjal] *adj, nf* initial.

iniciar [ini'θjar] *vt* (*persona*) to initiate; (*empezar*) to begin, commence; (*conversación*) to start up.

iniciativa [iniθja'tißa] *nf* initiative; **la** ~ **privada** private enterprise.

inicuo, a [in'ikwo, a] *adj* iniquitous.

ininterrumpido, a [ininterrum'piðo, a] *adj* uninterrupted.

injerencia [inxe'renθja] *nf* interference.

injertar [inxer'tar] *vt* to graft; **injerto** *nm* graft.

injuria [in'xurja] *nf* (*agravio, ofensa*)

offence; (*insulto*) insult; **injuriar** *vt* to insult; **injurioso, a** *adj* offensive; insulting.

injusticia [inxus'tiθja] *nf* injustice.

injusto, a [in'xusto, a] *adj* unjust, unfair.

inmadurez [inmaðu're θ] *nf* immaturity.

inmediaciones [inmeðja'θjones] *nfpl* neighbourhood *sg*, environs.

inmediato, a [inme'ðjato, a] *adj* immediate; (*contiguo*) adjoining; (*rápido*) prompt; (*próximo*) neighbouring, next; **de** ~ immediately.

inmejorable [inmexo'raßle] *adj* unsurpassable; (*precio*) unbeatable.

inmenso, a [in'menso, a] *adj* immense, huge.

inmerecido, a [inmere'θiðo, a] *adj* undeserved.

inmigración [inmiɣra'θjon] *nf* immigration.

inmiscuirse [inmisku'irse] *vr* to interfere, meddle.

inmobiliaria [inmoßi'ljarja] *nf* - estate agency.

inmobiliario, a [inmoßi'ljarjo, a] *adj* real-estate *cpd*, property *cpd*.

inmolar [inmo'lar] *vt* to immolate, sacrifice.

inmoral [inmo'ral] *adj* immoral.

inmortal [inmor'tal] *adj* immortal; ~**izar** *vt* to immortalize.

inmóvil [in'moßil] *adj* immobile.

inmueble [in'mweßle] *adj*: **bienes** ~s real estate, landed property ♦ *nm* property.

inmundicia [inmun'diθja] *nf* filth; **inmundo, a** *adj* filthy.

inmunidad [inmuni'ðað] *nf* immunity.

inmutarse [inmu'tarse] *vr* to turn pale; **no se inmutó** he didn't turn a hair.

innato, a [in'nato, a] *adj* innate.

innecesario, a [inneθe'sarjo, a] *adj* unnecessary.

innoble [in'noßle] *adj* ignoble.

innovación [innoßa'θjon] *nf* innovation.

innovar [inno'ßar] *vt* to introduce.

inocencia [ino'θenθja] *nf* innocence.

inocentada [inoθen'taða] *nf* practical joke.

inocente [ino'θente] *adj* (*ingenuo*) naive, innocent; (*inculpable*) innocent; (*sin malicia*) harmless ♦ *nm/f* simpleton.

inodoro [ino'ðoro] *nm* toilet, lavatory (*BRIT*).

inofensivo, a [inofen'sißo, a] *adj* inoffensive, harmless.

inolvidable [inolßi'ðaßle] *adj* unforgettable.

inoperante [inope'rante] *adj* ineffective.

inopinado, a [inopi'naðo, a] *adj* unexpected.

inoportuno, a [inopor'tuno, a] *adj* untimely; (*molesto*) inconvenient.

inoxidable [inoksi'ðaßle] *adj*: **acero** ~ stainless steel.

inquebrantable [inkeßran'taßle] *adj* unbreakable.

inquietar [inkje'tar] *vt* to worry, trouble; ~**se** *vr* to worry, get upset; **inquieto, a** *adj* anxious, worried; **inquietud** *nf* anxiety, worry.

inquilino, a [inki'lino, a] *nm/f* tenant.

inquirir [inki'rir] *vt* to enquire into, investigate.

insaciable [insa'θjaßle] *adj* insatiable.

insalubre [insa'lußre] *adj* unhealthy.

inscribir [inskri'ßir] *vt* to inscribe; ~ **a uno en** (*lista*) to put sb on; (*censo*) to register sb on.

inscripción [inskrip'θjon] *nf* inscription; (*ESCOL etc*) enrolment; (*censo*) registration.

insecticida [insekti'θiða] *nm* insecticide.

insecto [in'sekto] *nm* insect.

inseguridad [inseɣuri'ðað] *nf* insecurity.

inseguro, a [inse'ɣuro, a] *adj* insecure; (*inconstante*) unsteady; (*incierto*) uncertain.

insensato, a [insen'sato, a] *adj* foolish, stupid.

insensibilidad [insensißili'ðað] *nf* (*gen*) insensitivity; (*dureza de corazón*) callousness.

insensible [insen'sißle] *adj* (*gen*) insensitive; (*movimiento*) imperceptible; (*sin sentido*) numb.

insertar [inser'tar] *vt* to insert.

inservible [inser'ßißle] *adj* useless.

insidioso, a [insi'ðjoso, a] *adj* insidious.

insignia [in'siɣnja] *nf* (*señal distintiva*) badge; (*estandarte*) flag.

insignificante [insiɣnifi'kante] *adj* insignificant.

insinuar [insi'nwar] *vt* to insinuate, imply; ~**se** *vr*: ~**se con uno** to ingratiate o.s. with sb.

insípido, a [in'sipiðo, a] *adj* insipid.

insistencia [insis'tenθja] *nf* insistence.

insistir [insis'tir] *vi* to insist; ~ **en algo** to insist on sth; (*enfatizar*) to stress sth.

insolación [insola'θjon] *nf* (*MED*) sunstroke.

insolencia [inso'lenθja] *nf* insolence; **insolente** *adj* insolent.

insólito, a [in'solito, a] *adj* unusual.

insoluble [inso'lußle] *adj* insoluble.

insolvencia [insol'ßenθja] *nf* insolvency.

insomnio [in'somnjo] *nm* insomnia.

insondable [inson'daßle] *adj* bottomless; (*fig*) impenetrable.

insonorizado, a [insonori'θaðo, a] *adj* (*cuarto etc*) soundproof.

insoportable [insopor'taßle] *adj* unbearable.

insospechado, a [insospe'tʃaðo, a] *adj* (*inesperado*) unexpected.

inspección [inspek'θjon] *nf* inspection, check; **inspeccionar** *vt* (*examinar*) to inspect, examine; (*controlar*) to check.

inspector, a [inspek'tor, a] *nm/f* inspector.

inspiración [inspira'θjon] *nf* inspiration.

inspirar [inspi'rar] *vt* to inspire; (*MED*) to inhale; ~**se** *vr*: ~**se en** to be inspired by.

instalación [instala'θjon] *nf* (*equipo*) fittings *pl*, equipment; ~ **eléctrica** wiring.

instalar [insta'lar] *vt* (*establecer*) to instal; (*erguir*) to set up, erect; ~**se** *vr* to establish o.s.; (*en una vivienda*) to move into.

instancia [ins'tanθja] *nf* (*JUR*) petition; (*ruego*) request; **en última** ~ as a last resort.

instantánea [instan'tanea] *nf* snap(shot).

instantáneo, a [instan'taneo, a] *adj* in-

stantaneous; **café** ~ instant coffee.
instante [ins'tante] *nm* instant, moment.
instar [ins'tar] *vt* to press, urge.
instigar [insti'var] *vt* to instigate.
instinto [ins'tinto] *nm* instinct; **por** ~ instinctively.
institución [institu'θjon] *nf* institution, establishment.
instituir [institu'ir] *vt* to establish; (*fundar*) to found; **instituto** *nm* (*gen*) institute; **Instituto Nacional de Enseñanza** (*ESP*) ≈ comprehensive (*BRIT*) *o* high (*US*) school.
institutriz [institu'triθ] *nf* governess.
instrucción [instruk'θjon] *nf* instruction.
instructivo, a [instruk'tiβo, a] *adj* instructive.
instruir [instru'ir] *vt* (*gen*) to instruct; (*enseñar*) to teach, educate.
instrumento [instru'mento] *nm* (*gen*) instrument; (*herramienta*) tool, implement.
insubordinarse [insuβorði'narse] *vr* to rebel.
insuficiencia [insufi'θjenθja] *nf* (*carencia*) lack; (*inadecuación*) inadequacy; **insuficiente** (*gen*) insufficient; (*ESCOL: calificación*) unsatisfactory.
insufrible [insu'friβle] *adj* insufferable.
insular [insu'lar] *adj* insular.
insultar [insul'tar] *vt* to insult; **insulto** *nm* insult.
insuperable [insupe'raβle] *adj* (*excelente*) unsurpassable; (*problema etc*) insurmountable.
insurgente [insur'xente] *adj, nm/f* insurgent.
insurrección [insurrek'θjon] *nf* insurrection, rebellion.
intacto, a [in'takto, a] *adj* intact.
intachable [inta'tʃaβle] *adj* irreproachable.
integral [inte'vral] *adj* integral; (*completo*) complete; **pan** ~ wholemeal (*BRIT*) *o* wholewheat (*US*) bread.
integrar [inte'vrar] *vt* to make up, compose; (*MAT, fig*) to integrate.
integridad [intevri'ðað] *nf* wholeness; (*carácter*) integrity; **íntegro, a** *adj*

whole, entire; (*honrado*) honest.
intelectual [intelek'twal] *adj, nm/f* intellectual.
inteligencia [inteli'xenθja] *nf* intelligence; (*ingenio*) ability; **inteligente** *adj* intelligent.
inteligible [inteli'xiβle] *adj* intelligible.
intemperie [intem'perje] *nf*: **a la** ~ out in the open, exposed to the elements.
intempestivo, a [intempes'tiβo, a] *adj* untimely.
intención [inten'θjon] *nf* (*gen*) intention, purpose; **con segundas intenciones** maliciously; **con** ~ deliberately.
intencionado, a [intenθjo'naðo, a] *adj* deliberate; **bien/mal** ~ well-meaning/ill-disposed, hostile.
intensidad [intensi'ðað] *nf* (*gen*) intensity; (*ELEC, TEC*) strength; **llover con** ~ to rain hard.
intenso, a [in'tenso, a] *adj* intense; (*sentimiento*) profound, deep.
intentar [inten'tar] *vt* (*tratar*) to try, attempt; **intento** *nm* (*intención*) intention, purpose; (*tentativa*) attempt.
intercalar [interka'lar] *vt* to insert.
intercambio [inter'kambjo] *nm* exchange, swap.
interceder [interθe'ðer] *vi* to intercede.
interceptar [interθep'tar] *vt* to intercept.
intercesión [interθe'sjon] *nf* intercession.
interés [inte'res] *nm* (*gen*) interest; (*parte*) share, part; (*pey*) self-interest; **intereses creados** vested interests.
interesado, a [intere'saðo, a] *adj* interested; (*prejuiciado*) prejudiced; (*pey*) mercenary, self-seeking.
interesante [intere'sante] *adj* interesting.
interesar [intere'sar] *vt, vi* to interest, be of interest to; ~**se** *vr*: ~**se en** *o* **por** to take an interest in.
interface [inter'faθe] *nm* (*INFORM*) interface.
interfase [inter'fase] *nm* = **interface**.
interferir [interfe'rir] *vt* to interfere with; (*TEL*) to jam ♦ *vi* to interfere.
interfono [inter'fono] *nm* intercom.
interino, a [inte'rino, a] *adj* temporary ♦ *nm/f* temporary holder of a post; (*MED*)

locum; (*ESCOL*) supply teacher.

interior [inte'rjor] *adj* inner, inside;
(*COM*) domestic, internal ♦ *nm* interior,
inside; (*fig*) soul, mind; **Ministerio del
I~** ≈ Home Office (*BRIT*), ≈ Department of the Interior (*US*).

interjección [interxek'θjon] *nf* interjection.

interlocutor, a [interloku'tor, a] *nm/f*
speaker.

intermediario, a [interme'ðjarjo, a] *nm/f*
intermediary.

intermedio, a [inter'meðjo, a] *adj* intermediate ♦ *nm* interval.

interminable [intermi'naβle] *adj* endless.

intermitente [intermi'tente] *adj* intermittent ♦ *nm* (*AUTO*) indicator.

internacional [internaθjo'nal] *adj* international.

internado [inter'naðo] *nm* boarding
school.

internar [inter'nar] *vt* to intern; (*en un
manicomio*) to commit; ~**se** *vr* (*penetrar*) to penetrate.

interno, a [in'terno, a] *adj* internal,
interior; (*POL etc*) domestic ♦ *nm/f*
(*alumno*) boarder.

interponer [interpo'ner] *vt* to interpose,
put in; ~**se** *vr* to intervene.

interpretación [interpreta'θjon] *nf* inter-
pretation.

interpretar [interpre'tar] *vt* to interpret;
(*TEATRO, MUS*) to perform, play; **intérprete** *nm/f* (*LING*) interpreter,
translator; (*MUS, TEATRO*) performer,
artist(e).

interrogación [interroɣa'θjon] *nf* interrogation; (*LING: tb: signo de ~*) question mark.

interrogar [interro'ɣar] *vt* to interrogate,
question.

interrumpir [interrum'pir] *vt* to interrupt.

interrupción [interrup'θjon] *nf* interruption.

interruptor [interrup'tor] *nm* (*ELEC*)
switch.

intersección [intersek'θjon] *nf* intersec-
tion.

interurbano, a [interur'βano, a] *adj*:

llamada **interurbana** long-distance call.

intervalo [inter'βalo] *nm* interval;
(*descanso*) break; **a ~s** at intervals,
every now and then.

intervenir [interβe'nir] *vt* (*controlar*) to
control, supervise; (*MED*) to operate on
♦ *vi* (*participar*) to take part,
participate; (*mediar*) to intervene.

interventor, a [interβen'tor, a] *nm/f* inspector; (*COM*) auditor.

interviú [inter'βju] *nf* interview.

intestino [intes'tino] *nm* intestine.

intimar [inti'mar] *vi* to become friendly.

intimidad [intimi'ðað] *nf* intimacy;
(*familiaridad*) familiarity; (*vida
privada*) private life; (*JUR*) privacy.

íntimo, a ['intimo, a] *adj* intimate.

intolerable [intole'raβle] *adj* intolerable,
unbearable.

intranquilizarse [intrankili'θarse] *vr* to
get worried *o* anxious; **intranquilo, a**
adj worried.

intransigente [intransi'xente] *adj* in-
transigent.

intransitable [intransi'taβle] *adj* impassable.

intrepidez [intrepi'ðeθ] *nf* courage,
bravery; **intrépido, a** *adj* intrepid.

intriga [in'triɣa] *nf* intrigue; (*plan*) plot;
intrigar *vt, vi* to intrigue.

intrincado, a [intrin'kaðo, a] *adj* intricate.

intrínseco, a [in'trinseko, a] *adj* intrinsic.

introducción [introðuk'θjon] *nf* introduction.

introducir [introðu'θir] *vt* (*gen*) to introduce; (*moneda etc*) to insert; (*IN-
FORM*) to input, enter.

intromisión [intromi'sjon] *nf* interference, meddling.

introvertido, a [introβer'tiðo, a] *adj,
nm/f* introvert.

intruso, a [in'truso, a] *adj* intrusive ♦
nm/f intruder.

intuición [intwi'θjon] *nf* intuition.

inundación [inunda'θjon] *nf* flood(ing);
inundar *vt* to flood; (*fig*) to swamp, inundate.

inusitado, a [inusi'taðo, a] *adj* unusual,

rare.

inútil [in'util] *adj* useless; *(esfuerzo)* vain, fruitless; **inutilidad** *nf* uselessness.

inutilizar [inutili'θar] *vt* to make *o* render useless; **~se** *vr* to become useless.

invadir [imba'ðir] *vt* to invade.

inválido, a [im'baliðo, a] *adj* invalid ♦ *nm/f* invalid.

invariable [imba'rjaßle] *adj* invariable.

invasión [imba'sjon] *nf* invasion.

invasor, a [imba'sor, a] *adj* invading ♦ *nm/f* invader.

invención [imben'θjon] *nf* invention.

inventar [imben'tar] *vt* to invent.

inventario [imben'tarjo] *nm* inventory.

inventiva [imben'tißa] *nf* inventiveness.

inventor, a [imben'tor, a] *nm/f* inventor.

invernadero [imberna'ðero] *nm* greenhouse.

inverosímil [imbero'simil] *adj* implausible.

inversión [imber'sjon] *nf* (COM) investment.

inverso, a [im'berso, a] *adj* inverse, opposite; **en el orden ~** in reverse order; **a la inversa** inversely, the other way round.

inversor, a [imber'sor, a] *nm/f* (COM) investor.

invertir [imber'tir] *vt* (COM) to invest; *(volcar)* to turn upside down; *(tiempo etc)* to spend.

investigación [imbestiɣa'θjon] *nf* investigation; *(ESCOL)* research; **~ de mercado** market research.

investigar [imbesti'ɣar] *vt* to investigate; *(ESCOL)* to do research into.

invicto, a [im'bikto, a] *adj* unconquered.

invierno [im'bjerno] *nm* winter.

invisible [imbi'sißle] *adj* invisible.

invitado, a [imbi'taðo, a] *nm/f* guest.

invitar [imbi'tar] *vt* to invite; *(incitar)* to entice; *(pagar)* to buy, pay for.

invocar [imbo'kar] *vt* to invoke, call on.

inyección [injek'θjon] *nf* injection.

inyectar [injek'tar] *vt* to inject.

PALABRA CLAVE

ir [ir] *vi* **1** to go; *(a pie)* to walk; *(viajar)* to travel; **~ caminando** to walk; **fui en tren** I went *o* travelled by train; **¡(ahora) voy!** (I'm just) coming!

2: **~ (a) por**: **~ (a) por el médico** to fetch the doctor

3 *(progresar: persona, cosa)* to go; **el trabajo va muy bien** work is going very well; **¿cómo te va?** how are things going?; **me va muy bien** I'm getting on very well; **le fue fatal** it went awfully badly for him

4 *(funcionar)*: **el coche no va muy bien** the car isn't running very well

5: **te va estupendamente ese color** that colour suits you fantastically well

6 *(locuciones)*: **¿vino? – ¡que va!** did he come? – of course not!; **vamos, no llores** come on, don't cry; **¡vaya coche!** what a car!, that's some car!

7: **no vaya a ser**: **tienes que correr, no vaya a ser que pierdas el tren** you'll have to run so as not to miss the train

8 (+*pp*): **iba vestido muy bien** he was very well dressed

9: **no me** *etc* **va ni me viene** I *etc* don't care

♦ *vb aux* **1**: **~ a**: **voy/iba a hacerlo hoy** I am/was going to do it today

2 (+*gerundio*): **iba anocheciendo** it was getting dark; **todo se me iba aclarando** everything was gradually becoming clearer to me

3 (+*pp* = *pasivo*): **van vendidos 300 ejemplares** 300 copies have been sold so far

♦ **~se** *vr* **1**: **¿por dónde se va al zoológico?** which is the way to the zoo?

2 *(marcharse)* to leave; **ya se habrán ido** they must already have left *o* gone.

---

ira ['ira] *nf* anger, rage.

iracundo, a [ira'kundo, a] *adj* irascible.

Irak [i'rak] *nm* = Iraq.

Irán [i'ran] *nm* Iran; **iraní** *adj*, *nm/f* Iranian.

Iraq [i'rak] *nm* Iraq; **iraquí** *adj*, *nm/f* Iraqui.

iris ['iris] *nm inv* (*tb: arco* ~) rainbow; (*ANAT*) iris.

Irlanda [ir'landa] *nf* Ireland; **irlandés, esa** *adj* Irish ♦ *nm/f* Irishman/woman; **los irlandeses** the Irish.

ironía [iro'nia] *nf* irony; **irónico, a** *adj* ironic(al).

irreal [irre'al] *adj* unreal.

irrecuperable *adj* [irrekupe'raßle] irrecoverable, irretrievable.

irreflexión [irreflek'sjon] *nf* thoughtlessness.

irregular [irreɣu'lar] *adj* (*gen*) irregular; (*situación*) abnormal.

irremediable [irreme'ðjaßle] *adj* irremediable; (*vicio*) incurable.

irresoluto, a [irreso'luto, a] *adj* irresolute, hesitant.

irrespetuoso, a [irrespe'twoso, a] *adj* disrespectful.

irresponsable [irrespon'saßle] *adj* irresponsible.

irrigar [irri'ɣar] *vt* to irrigate.

irrisorio, a [irri'sorjo, a] *adj* derisory, ridiculous.

irritar [irri'tar] *vt* to irritate, annoy.

irrupción [irrup'θjon] *nf* irruption; (*invasión*) invasion.

isla ['isla] *nf* island.

islandés, esa [islan'des, esa] *adj* Icelandic ♦ *nm/f* Icelander.

Islandia [is'landja] *nf* Iceland.

isleño, a [is'leɲo, a] *adj* island *cpd* ♦ *nm/f* islander.

Israel [isra'el] *nm* Israel; **israelí** *adj*, *nm/f* Israeli.

istmo ['istmo] *nm* isthmus.

Italia [i'talja] *nf* Italy; **italiano, a** *adj*, *nm/f* Italian.

itinerario [itine'rarjo] *nm* itinerary, route.

IVA ['ißa] *nm abr* (= *impuesto sobre el valor añadido*) VAT.

izar [i'θar] *vt* to hoist.

izdo, a *abr* (= *izquierdo, a*) l.

izquierda [iθ'kjerda] *nf* left; (*POL*) left (wing); **a la** ~ (*estar*) on the left; (*torcer etc*) (to the) left.

izquierdista [iθkjer'ðista] *nm/f* leftwinger, leftist.

izquierdo, a [iθ'kjerðo, a] *adj* left.

J

jabalí [xaßa'li] *nm* wild boar.

jabalina [xaßa'lina] *nf* javelin.

jabón [xa'ßon] *nm* soap; **jabonar** *vt* to soap.

jaca ['xaka] *nf* pony.

jacinto [xa'θinto] *nm* hyacinth.

jactarse [xak'tarse] *vr* to boast, brag.

jadear [xaðe'ar] *vi* to pant, gasp for breath; **jadeo** *nm* panting, gasping.

jaguar [xa'ɣwar] *nm* jaguar.

jalar [xa'lar] (*AM*) *vt* to pull; (*arrastrar*) to haul ♦ *vi* to go off.

jalbegue [xal'ßeɣe] *nm* (*pintura*) whitewash.

jalea [xa'lea] *nf* jelly.

jaleo [xa'leo] *nm* racket, uproar; **armar un** ~ to kick up a racket.

jalón [xa'lon] (*AM*) *nm* tug.

Jamaica [xa'maika] *nf* Jamaica.

jamás [xa'mas] *adv* never; (*interrogación*) ever.

jamón [xa'mon] *nm* ham; ~ **dulce**, ~ **de York** cooked ham; ~ **serrano** cured ham.

Japón [xa'pon] *nm*: **el** ~ Japan; **japonés, esa** *adj*, *nm/f* Japanese ♦ *nm* (*LING*) Japanese.

jaque ['xake] *nm*: ~ **mate** checkmate.

jaqueca [xa'keka] *nf* (very bad) headache, migraine.

jarabe [xa'raße] *nm* syrup.

jarcia ['xarθja] *nf* (*NAUT*) ropes *pl*, rigging.

jardín [xar'ðin] *nm* garden; ~ **de (la) infancia** (*ESP*) o **de niños** (*AM*) nursery (school); **jardinería** *nf* gardening; **jardinero, a** *nm/f* gardener.

jarra ['xarra] *nf* jar; (*jarro*) jug.

jarro ['xarro] *nm* jug.

jaula ['xaula] *nf* cage.

jauría [xau'ria] *nf* pack of hounds.

J. C. *abr* (= *Jesucristo*) J.C.

jefa ['xefa] *nf ver* **jefe**.

jefatura [xefa'tura] *nf*: ~ **de policía** police headquarters *sg*.

jefe, a ['xefe, a] *nm/f* (*gen*) chief, head; (*patrón*) boss; ~ **de camareros** head waiter; ~ **de cocina** chef; ~ **de estación** stationmaster; ~ **de estado** head of state; ~ **supremo** commander-in-chief; **ser el** ~ (*fig*) to be the boss.

jengibre [xen'xiβre] *nm* ginger.

jeque ['xeke] *nm* sheik.

jerarquía [xerar'kia] *nf* (*orden*) hierarchy; (*rango*) rank; **jerárquico, a** *adj* hierarchic(al).

jerez [xe'reθ] *nm* sherry.

jerga ['xerɣa] *nf* (*tela*) coarse cloth; (*lenguaje*) jargon.

jerigonza [xeri'ɣonθa] *nf* (*jerga*) jargon, slang; (*galimatías*) nonsense, gibberish.

jeringa [xe'ringa] *nf* syringe; (*AM*) annoyance, bother; ~ **de engrase** grease gun; **jeringar** (*AM*) *vt* to annoy, bother.

jeroglífico [xero'ɣlifiko] *nm* hieroglyphic.

jersé [xer'se] *nm* = **jersey**.

jersey [xer'sei] (*pl* ~**s**) *nm* jersey, pullover, jumper.

Jerusalén [xerusa'len] *n* Jerusalem.

Jesucristo [xesu'kristo] *nm* Jesus Christ.

jesuita [xe'swita] *adj, nm* Jesuit.

Jesús [xe'sus] *nm* Jesus; ¡~! good heavens!; (*al estornudar*) bless you!

jet ['jet] (*pl* ~**s**) *nm* jet (plane).

jícara ['xikara] *nf* small cup.

jinete, a [xi'nete, a] *nm/f* horseman/woman, rider.

jipijapa [xipi'xapa] (*AM*) *nm* straw hat.

jirafa [xi'rafa] *nf* giraffe.

jirón [xi'ron] *nm* rag, shred.

jocoso, a [xo'koso, a] *adj* humorous, jocular.

jofaina [xo'faina] *nf* washbasin.

jornada [xor'naða] *nf* (*viaje de un día*) day's journey; (*camino o viaje entero*) journey; (*día de trabajo*) working day.

jornal [xor'nal] *nm* (day's) wage; ~**ero** *nm* (day) labourer.

joroba [xo'roβa] *nf* hump, hunched back; ~**do, a** *adj* hunchbacked ♦ *nm/f* hunchback.

jota ['xota] *nf* (the letter) J; (*danza*) Aragonese dance; (*fam*) jot, iota; **no saber ni** ~ to have no idea.

joven ['xoβen] (*pl* **jóvenes**) *adj* young ♦ *nm* young man, youth ♦ *nf* young woman, girl.

jovial [xo'βjal] *adj* cheerful, jolly; ~**idad** *nf* cheerfulness, jolliness.

joya ['xoja] *nf* jewel, gem; (*fig: persona*) gem; **joyería** *nf* (*joyas*) jewellery; (*tienda*) jeweller's (shop); **joyero** *nm* (*persona*) jeweller; (*caja*) jewel case.

juanete [xwa'nete] *nm* (*del pie*) bunion.

jubilación [xuβila'θjon] *nf* (*retiro*) retirement.

jubilado, a [xuβi'laðo, a] *adj* retired ♦ *nm/f* pensioner (*BRIT*), senior citizen.

jubilar [xuβi'lar] *vt* to pension off, retire; (*fam*) to discard; ~**se** *vr* to retire.

jubileo [xuβi'leo] *nm* jubilee.

júbilo ['xuβilo] *nm* joy, rejoicing; **jubiloso, a** *adj* jubilant.

judía [xu'ðia] *nf* (*CULIN*) bean; ~ **verde** French bean; *ver tb* **judío**.

judicial [xuði'θjal] *adj* judicial.

judío, a [xu'ðio, a] *adj* Jewish ♦ *nm/f* Jew(ess).

judo ['juðo] *nm* judo.

juego *etc* ['xweɣo] *vb ver* **jugar** ♦ *nm* (*gen*) play; (*pasatiempo, partido*) game; (*en casino*) gambling; (*conjunto*) set; **fuera de** ~ (*DEPORTE: persona*) offside; (: *pelota*) out of play; **J**~**s Olímpicos** Olympic Games.

juerga ['xwerɣa] *nf* binge; (*fiesta*) party; **ir de** ~ to go out on a binge.

jueves ['xweβes] *nm inv* Thursday.

juez [xweθ] *nm/f* judge; ~ **de línea** linesman; ~ **de salida** starter.

jugada [xu'ɣaða] *nf* play; **buena** ~ good move/shot/stroke *etc*.

jugador, a [xuɣa'ðor, a] *nm/f* player; (*en casino*) gambler.

jugar [xu'ɣar] *vt, vi* to play; (*en casino*) to gamble; (*apostar*) to bet; ~**se** *vr* to gamble (away); ~ **al fútbol** to play football.

juglar [xu'ɣlar] *nm* minstrel.

jugo ['xuɣo] *nm* (*BOT*) juice; (*fig*) essence, substance; ~ **de fruta** (*AM*) fruit juice; ~**so, a** *adj* juicy; (*fig*) substantial, important.

juguete [xu'ɣete] *nm* toy; ~**ar** *vi* to play; ~**ría** *nf* toyshop.
juguetón, ona [xuɣe'ton, ona] *adj* playful.
juicio ['xwiθjo] *nm* judgement; (*razón*) sanity, reason; (*opinión*) opinion; **estar fuera de** ~ to be out of one's mind; ~**so, a** *adj* wise, sensible.
julio ['xuljo] *nm* July.
junco ['xunko] *nm* rush, reed.
jungla ['xungla] *nf* jungle.
junio ['xunjo] *nm* June.
junta ['xunta] *nf* (*asamblea*) meeting, assembly; (*comité, consejo*) board, council, committee; (*articulación*) joint.
juntar [xun'tar] *vt* to join, unite; (*maquinaria*) to assemble, put together; (*dinero*) to collect; ~**se** *vr* to join, meet; (*reunirse: personas*) to meet, assemble; (*arrimarse*) to approach, draw closer; ~**se con uno** to join sb.
junto, a ['xunto, a] *adj* joined; (*unido*) united; (*anexo*) near, close; (*contiguo, próximo*) next, adjacent ♦ *adv*: **todo** ~ all at once; ~**s** together; ~ **a** near (to), next to.
jurado [xu'raðo] *nm* (*JUR: individuo*) juror; (: *grupo*) jury; (*de concurso: grupo*) panel (of judges); (: *individuo*) member of a panel.
juramento [xura'mento] *nm* oath; (*maldición*) oath, curse; **prestar** ~ to take the oath; **tomar** ~ **a** to swear in, administer the oath to.
jurar [xu'rar] *vt, vi* to swear; ~ **en falso** to commit perjury; **jurárselas a uno** to have it in for sb.
jurídico, a [xu'riðiko, a] *adj* legal.
jurisdicción [xurisðik'θjon] *nf* (*poder, autoridad*) jurisdiction; (*territorio*) district.
jurisprudencia [xurispru'ðenθja] *nf* jurisprudence.
jurista [xu'rista] *nm/f* jurist.
justamente [xusta'mente] *adv* justly, fairly; (*precisamente*) just, exactly.
justicia [xus'tiθja] *nf* justice; (*equidad*) fairness, justice; **justiciero, a** *adj* just, righteous.

justificación [xustifika'θjon] *nf* justification; **justificar** *vt* to justify.
justo, a ['xusto, a] *adj* (*equitativo*) just, fair, right; (*preciso*) exact, correct; (*ajustado*) tight ♦ *adv* (*precisamente*) exactly, precisely; (*AM: apenas a tiempo*) just in time.
juvenil [xuβe'nil] *adj* youthful.
juventud [xuβen'tuð] *nf* (*adolescencia*) youth; (*jóvenes*) young people *pl*.
juzgado [xuθ'ɣaðo] *nm* tribunal; (*JUR*) court.
juzgar [xuθ'ɣar] *vt* to judge; **a** ~ **por ...** to judge by ..., judging by ... .

K

kg *abr* (= *kilogramo*) kg.
kilo ['kilo] *nm* kilo ♦ *pref*: ~**gramo** *nm* kilogramme; ~**metraje** *nm* distance in kilometres, ≈ mileage; **kilómetro** *nm* kilometre; ~**vatio** *nm* kilowatt.
kiosco ['kjosko] *nm* = **quiosco.**
km *abr* (= *kilómetro*) km.
kv *abr* (= *kilovatio*) kw.

L

l *abr* (= *litro*) l.
la [la] *art def* the ♦ *pron* her; (*Ud.*) you; (*cosa*) it ♦ *nm* (*MUS*) la; ~ **del sombrero rojo** the girl in the red hat; *tb ver* **el.**
laberinto [laβe'rinto] *nm* labyrinth.
labia ['laβja] *nf* fluency; (*pey*) glib tongue.
labial [la'βjal] *adj* labial.
labio ['laβjo] *nm* lip.
labor [la'βor] *nf* labour; (*AGR*) farm work; (*tarea*) job, task; (*COSTURA*) needlework; ~**able** *adj* (*AGR*) workable; **día** ~**able** working day; ~**ar** *vi* to work.
laboratorio [laβora'torjo] *nm* laboratory.
laborioso, a [laβo'rjoso, a] *adj* (*persona*) hard-working; (*trabajo*) tough.
laborista [laβo'rista] *adj*: **Partido L**~ Labour Party.

labrado, a [la'βraðo, a] *adj* worked; (*madera*) carved; (*metal*) wrought ♦ *nm* (*AGR*) cultivated field.

labrador, a [laβra'ðor, a] *adj* farming *cpd* ♦ *nm/f* farmer.

labranza [la'βranθa] *nf* (*AGR*) cultivation.

labrar [la'βrar] *vt* (*gen*) to work; (*madera etc*) to carve; (*fig*) to cause, bring about.

labriego, a [la'βrjeɣo, a] *nm/f* peasant.

laca ['laka] *nf* lacquer.

lacayo [la'kajo] *nm* lackey.

lacerar [laθe'rar] *vt* to lacerate.

lacio, a ['laθjo, a] *adj* (*pelo*) lank, straight.

lacónico, a [la'koniko, a] *adj* laconic.

lacrar [la'krar] *vt* (*cerrar*) to seal (with sealing wax); **lacre** *nm* sealing wax.

lacrimoso, a [lakri'moso, a] *adj* tearful.

lactar [lak'tar] *vt*, *vi* to suckle.

lácteo, a ['lakteo, a] *adj*: **productos ~s** dairy products.

ladear [laðe'ar] *vt* to tip, tilt ♦ *vi* to tilt; **~se** *vr* to lean.

ladera [la'ðera] *nf* slope.

ladino, a [la'ðino, a] *adj* cunning.

lado ['laðo] *nm* (*gen*) side; (*fig*) protection; (*MIL*) flank; **al ~ de** beside; **poner de ~** to put on its side; **poner a un ~** to put aside; **por todos ~s** on all sides, all round (*BRIT*).

ladrar [la'ðrar] *vi* to bark; **ladrido** *nm* bark, barking.

ladrillo [la'ðriʎo] *nm* (*gen*) brick; (*azulejo*) tile.

ladrón, ona [la'ðron, ona] *nm/f* thief.

lagar [la'ɣar] *nm* (wine/oil) press.

lagartija [laɣar'tixa] *nf* (*ZOOL*) (small) lizard.

lagarto [la'ɣarto] *nm* (*ZOOL*) lizard.

lago ['laɣo] *nm* lake.

lágrima ['laɣrima] *nf* tear.

laguna [la'ɣuna] *nf* (*lago*) lagoon; (*hueco*) gap.

laico, a ['laiko, a] *adj* lay.

lamentable [lamen'taβle] *adj* lamentable, regrettable; (*miserable*) pitiful.

lamentar [lamen'tar] *vt* (*sentir*) to regret; (*deplorar*) to lament; **lo lamento**

mucho I'm very sorry; **~se** *vr* to lament; **lamento** *nm* lament.

lamer [la'mer] *vt* to lick.

lámina ['lamina] *nf* (*plancha delgada*) sheet; (*para estampar, estampa*) plate; **laminar** *vt* to laminate.

lámpara ['lampara] *nf* lamp; **~ de alcohol/gas** spirit/gas lamp; **~ de pie** standard lamp.

lamparón [lampa'ron] *nm* grease spot.

lampiño [lam'piɲo] *adj* clean-shaven.

lana ['lana] *nf* wool.

lance *etc* ['lanθe] *vb ver* **lanzar** ♦ *nm* (*golpe*) stroke; (*suceso*) event, incident.

lancha ['lantʃa] *nf* launch; **~ de pesca** fishing boat; **~ salvavidas/torpedera** lifeboat/torpedo boat.

lanero, a [la'nero, a] *adj* woollen.

langosta [lan'gosta] *nf* (*crustáceo*) lobster; (: *de río*) crayfish; **langostino** *nm* Dublin Bay prawn; (: *de río*) crayfish.

languidecer [langiðe'θer] *vi* to languish; **languidez** *nf* langour; **lánguido, a** *adj* (*gen*) languid; (*sin energía*) listless.

lanilla [la'niʎa] *nf* nap.

lanudo, a [la'nuðo, a] *adj* woolly.

lanza ['lanθa] *nf* (*arma*) lance, spear.

lanzadera [lanθa'ðera] *nf* shuttle.

lanzamiento [lanθa'mjento] *nm* (*gen*) throwing; (*NAUT, COM*) launch, launching; **~ de peso** putting the shot.

lanzar [lan'θar] *vt* (*gen*) to throw; (*DEPORTE: pelota*) to bowl; (*NAUT, COM*) to launch; (*JUR*) to evict; **~se** *vr* to throw o.s.

lapa ['lapa] *nf* limpet.

lapicero [lapi'θero] *nm* propelling (*BRIT*) *o* mechanical (*US*) pencil; (*AM: bolígrafo*) Biro ®.

lápida ['lapiða] *nf* stone; **~ mortuoria** headstone; **~ conmemorativa** memorial stone; **lapidar** *vt* to stone; **lapidario, a** *adj*, *nm* lapidary.

lápiz ['lapiθ] *nm* pencil; **~ de color** coloured pencil; **~ de labios** lipstick.

lapón, ona [la'pon, ona] *nm/f* Laplander, Lapp.

Laponia [la'ponja] *nf* Lapland.

lapso ['lapso] *nm* (*de tiempo*) interval;

(error) error.

lapsus ['lapsus] *nm inv* error, mistake.

largar [lar'ɣar] *vt (soltar)* to release; *(aflojar)* to loosen; *(lanzar)* to launch; *(fam)* to let fly; *(velas)* to unfurl; *(AM)* to throw; **~se** *vr (fam)* to beat it; **~se a** *(AM)* to start to.

largo, a ['larɣo, a] *adj (longitud)* long; *(tiempo)* lengthy; *(fig)* generous ♦ *nm* length; *(MUS)* largo; **dos años ~s** two long years; **tiene 9 metros de ~** it is 9 metres long; **a lo ~ de** along; *(tiempo)* all through, throughout.

laringe [la'rinxe] *nf* larynx; **laringitis** *nf* laryngitis.

larva ['larβa] *nf* larva.

las [las] *art def* the ♦ *pron* them; **~ que cantan** the ones/women/girls who sing; *tb ver* **el**.

lascivo, a [las'θiβo, a] *adj* lewd.

láser ['laser] *nm* laser.

lástima ['lastima] *nf (pena)* pity; **dar ~** to be pitiful; **es una ~ que** it's a pity that; **¡qué ~!** what a pity!; **ella está hecha una ~** she looks pitiful.

lastimar [lasti'mar] *vt (herir)* to wound; *(ofender)* to offend; **~se** *vr* to hurt o.s.; **lastimero, a** *adj* pitiful, pathetic.

lastre ['lastre] *nm (TEC, NAUT)* ballast; *(fig)* dead weight.

lata ['lata] *nf (metal)* tin; *(caja)* tin *(BRIT)*, can; *(fam)* nuisance; **en ~** tinned *(BRIT)*, canned; **dar (la) ~** to be a nuisance.

latente [la'tente] *adj* latent.

lateral [late'ral] *adj* side *cpd*, lateral ♦ *nm (TEATRO)* wings.

latido [la'tiðo] *nm (del corazón)* beat.

latifundio [lati'fundjo] *nm* large estate; **latifundista** *nm/f* owner of a large estate.

latigazo [lati'ɣaθo] *nm (golpe)* lash; *(sonido)* crack.

látigo ['latiɣo] *nm* whip.

latín [la'tin] *nm* Latin.

latino, a [la'tino, a] *adj* Latin; **~americano, a** *adj, nm/f* Latin-American.

latir [la'tir] *vi (corazón, pulso)* to beat.

latitud [lati'tuð] *nf (GEO)* latitude.

latón [la'ton] *nm* brass.

latoso, a [la'toso, a] *adj (molesto)* annoying; *(aburrido)* boring.

laúd [la'uð] *nm* lute.

laureado, a [laure'aðo, a] *adj* honoured ♦ *nm* laureate.

laurel [lau'rel] *nm (BOT)* laurel; *(CULIN)* bay.

lava ['laβa] *nf* lava.

lavabo [la'βaβo] *nm (jofaina)* washbasin; *(tb: ~s)* toilet.

lavadero [laβa'ðero] *nm* laundry.

lavado [la'βaðo] *nm* washing; *(de ropa)* laundry; *(ARTE)* wash; **~ de cerebro** brainwashing; **~ en seco** dry-cleaning.

lavadora [laβa'ðora] *nf* washing machine.

lavanda [la'βanda] *nf* lavender.

lavandería [laβande'ria] *nf* laundry; **~ automática** launderette.

lavaplatos [laβa'platos] *nm inv* dish-washer.

lavar [la'βar] *vt* to wash; *(borrar)* to wipe away; **~se** *vr* to wash o.s.; **~se las manos** to wash one's hands; **~ y marcar** *(pelo)* to shampoo and set; **~ en seco** to dry-clean.

lavavajillas [laβaβa'xiʎas] *nm inv* dish-washer.

laxante [lak'sante] *nm* laxative.

lazada [la'θaða] *nf* bow.

lazarillo [laθa'riʎo] *nm*: **perro ~** guide dog.

lazo ['laθo] *nm* knot; *(lazada)* bow; *(para animales)* lasso; *(trampa)* snare; *(vínculo)* tie.

le [le] *pron (directo)* him *(o her)*; *(: usted)* you; *(indirecto)* to him *(o her o it)*; *(: usted)* to you.

leal [le'al] *adj* loyal; **~tad** *nf* loyalty.

lebrel [le'βrel] *nm* greyhound.

lección [lek'θjon] *nf* lesson.

lector, a [lek'tor, a] *nm/f* reader.

lectura [lek'tura] *nf* reading.

leche ['letʃe] *nf* milk; **tiene mala ~** *(fam!)* he's a swine *(!)*; **~ condensada/en polvo** condensed/powdered milk; **~ desnatada** skimmed milk; **~ra** *nf (vendedora)* milkmaid; *(recipiente)* (milk) churn; *(AM)* cow;

~**ría** nf dairy; ~**ro, a** adj dairy.
lecho ['letʃo] nm (cama, de río) bed; (GEO) layer.
lechón [le'tʃon] nm sucking (BRIT) o suckling (US) pig.
lechoso, a [le'tʃoso, a] adj milky.
lechuga [le'tʃuɣa] nf lettuce.
lechuza [le'tʃuθa] nf owl.
leer [le'er] vt to read.
legado [le'ɣaðo] nm (don) bequest; (herencia) legacy; (enviado) legate.
legajo [le'ɣaxo] nm file.
legal [le'ɣal] adj (gen) legal; (persona) trustworthy; ~**idad** nf legality; ~**izar** vt to legalize; (documento) to authenticate.
legaña [le'ɣaɲa] nf sleep (in eyes).
legar [le'ɣar] vt to bequeath, leave.
legendario, a [lexen'darjo, a] adj legendary.
legión [le'xjon] nf legion; **legionario, a** adj legionary ♦ nm legionnaire.
legislación [lexisla'θjon] nf legislation.
legislar [lexis'lar] vi to legislate.
legitimar [lexiti'mar] vt to legitimize; **legítimo, a** adj (genuino) authentic; (legal) legitimate.
lego, a ['lexo, a] adj (REL) secular; (ignorante) ignorant ♦ nm layman.
legua ['lewa] nf league.
legumbres [le'ɣumbres] nfpl pulses.
leído, a [le'iðo, a] adj well read.
lejanía [lexa'nia] nf distance; **lejano, a** adj far-off; (en el tiempo) distant; (fig) remote.
lejía [le'xia] nf bleach.
lejos ['lexos] adv far, far away; **a lo** ~ in the distance; **de** o **desde** ~ from afar; ~ **de** far from.
lelo, a ['lelo, a] adj silly ♦ nm/f idiot.
lema ['lema] nm motto; (POL) slogan.
lencería [lenθe'ria] nf linen, drapery.
lengua ['lenwa] nf tongue; (LING) language; **morderse la** ~ to hold one's tongue.
lenguado [len'gwaðo] nm sole.
lenguaje [len'gwaxe] nm language.
lengüeta [len'gweta] nf (ANAT) epiglottis; (zapatos, MUS) tongue.
lente ['lente] nf lens; (lupa) magnifying

glass; ~**s** nfpl (gafas) glasses; ~**s de contacto** contact lenses.
lenteja [len'texa] nf lentil; **lentejuela** nf sequin.
lentilla [len'tiʎa] nf contact lens.
lentitud [lenti'tuð] nf slowness; **con** ~ slowly.
lento, a ['lento, a] adj slow.
leña ['leɲa] nf firewood; ~**dor, a** nm/f woodcutter.
leño ['leɲo] nm (trozo de árbol) log; (madera) timber; (fig) blockhead.
Leo ['leo] nm Leo.
león [le'on] nm lion; ~ **marino** sea lion; **leonino, a** adj leonine.
leopardo [leo'parðo] nm leopard.
leotardos [leo'tarðos] nmpl tights.
lepra ['lepra] nf leprosy; **leproso, a** nm/f leper.
lerdo, a ['lerðo, a] adj (lento) slow; (patoso) clumsy.
les [les] pron (directo) them; (: ustedes) you; (indirecto) to them; (: ustedes) to you.
lesbiana [les'βjana] adj, nf lesbian.
lesión [le'sjon] nf wound, lesion; (DEPORTE) injury; **lesionado, a** adj injured ♦ nm/f injured person.
letal [le'tal] adj lethal.
letanía [leta'nia] nf litany.
letargo [le'tarɣo] nm lethargy.
letra ['letra] nf letter; (escritura) handwriting; · (MUS) lyrics pl; ~ **de cambio** bill of exchange; ~ **de imprenta** print; ~**do, a** adj learned; (fam) pedantic ♦ nm lawyer; **letrero** nm (cartel) sign; (etiqueta) label.
letrina [le'trina] nf latrine.
leucemia [leu'θemja] nf leukaemia.
levadizo [leβa'ðiθo] adj: **puente** ~ drawbridge.
levadura [leβa'ðura] nf (para el pan) yeast; (de la cerveza) brewer's yeast.
levantamiento [leβanta'mjento] nm raising, lifting; (rebelión) revolt, rising; ~ **de pesos** weight-lifting.
levantar [leβan'tar] vt (gen) to raise; (del suelo) to pick up; (hacia arriba) to lift (up); (plan) to make, draw up; (mesa) to clear; (campamento) to

strike; *(fig)* to cheer up, hearten; ~se
vr to get up; *(enderezarse)* to straight-
en up; *(rebelarse)* to rebel; ~ **el ánimo**
to cheer up.

levante [le'βante] *nm* east coast; **el L~**
*region of Spain extending from
Castellón to Murcia.*

levar [le'βar] *vt* to weigh anchor.

leve ['leβe] *adj* light; *(fig)* trivial; ~**dad**
nf lightness.

levita [le'βita] *nf* frock coat.

léxico ['leksiko] *nm (vocabulario)*
vocabulary.

ley [lei] *nf (gen)* law; *(metal)* standard.

leyenda [le'jenda] *nf* legend.

leyó *etc vb ver* **leer.**

liar [li'ar] *vt* to tie (up); *(unir)* to bind;
(envolver) to wrap (up); *(enredar)* to
confuse; *(cigarrillo)* to roll; ~**se** *vr
(fam)* to get involved; ~**se a palos** to
get involved in a fight.

Líbano ['liβano] *nm*: **el** ~ (the)
Lebanon.

libar [li'βar] *vt* to suck.

libelo [li'βelo] *nm* satire, lampoon; *(JUR)*
petition.

libélula [li'βelula] *nf* dragonfly.

liberación [liβera'θjon] *nf* liberation; *(de
la cárcel)* release.

liberal [liβe'ral] *adj, nm/f* liberal; ~**idad**
nf liberality, generosity.

liberar [liβe'rar] *vt* to liberate.

libertad [liβer'tað] *nf* liberty, freedom;
~ **de culto/de prensa/de comercio** freedom of worship/of the press/of trade; ~
condicional probation; ~ **bajo palabra**
parole; ~ **bajo fianza** bail.

libertar [liβer'tar] *vt (preso)* to set free;
(de una obligación) to release; *(eximir)*
to exempt.

libertino, a [liβer'tino, a] *adj* permissive
♦ *nm/f* permissive person.

libra ['liβra] *nf* pound; *(ASTROLOGÍA)*:
L~ Libra; ~ **esterlina** pound sterling.

librador [liβra'ðor] *nm* drawer.

libradora [liβra'ðora] *nf* = **librador.**

libramiento [liβra'mjento] *nm* rescue;
(COM) delivery.

libranza [li'βranθa] *nf (COM)* draft; *(letra de cambio)* bill of exchange.

librar [li'βrar] *vt (de peligro)* to save;
(batalla) to wage, fight; *(de impuestos)*
to exempt; *(cheque)* to make out; *(JUR)*
to exempt; ~**se** *vr*: ~**se de** to escape
from, free o.s. from.

libre ['liβre] *adj* free; *(lugar)* unoccupied; *(asiento)* vacant; *(de
deudas)* free of debts; ~ **de impuestos**
free of tax; **tiro** ~ free kick; **los 100
metros** ~ the 100 metres free-style
(race); **al aire** ~ in the open air.

librería [liβre'ria] *nf (tienda)* bookshop;
librero, a *nm/f* bookseller.

libreta [li'βreta] *nf* notebook; ~ **de ahorros** savings book.

libro ['liβro] *nm* book; ~ **de bolsillo**
paperback; ~ **de caja** cashbook; ~ **de
cheques** chequebook *(BRIT)*, checkbook
(US); ~ **de texto** textbook.

Lic. *abr* = **licenciado, a.**

licencia [li'θenθja] *nf (gen)* licence;
(permiso) permission; ~ **por
enfermedad/con goce de sueldo** sick
leave/paid leave; ~ **de caza** game
licence; ~**do, a** *adj* licensed ♦ *nm/f*,
graduate; **licenciar** *vt (empleado)* to
dismiss; *(permitir)* to permit, allow;
(soldado) to discharge; *(estudiante)* to
confer a degree upon; **licenciarse** *vr*:
licenciarse en letras to graduate in
arts.

licencioso, a [liθen'θjoso, a] *adj*
licentious.

liceo [li'θeo] *nm* (high) school.

licitar [liθi'tar] *vt* to bid for; *(AM)* to sell
by auction.

lícito, a ['liθito, a] *adj (legal)* lawful;
(justo) fair, just; *(permisible)* permissible.

licor [li'kor] *nm* spirits *pl (BRIT)*, liquor
(US); *(de frutas etc)* liqueur.

licuadora [likwa'ðora] *nf* blender.

licuar [li'kwar] *vt* to liquidize.

lid [lið] *nf* combat; *(fig)* controversy.

líder ['liðer] *nm/f* leader; **liderato** *nm*
leadership; **liderazgo** *nm* leadership.

lidia ['liðja] *nf* bullfighting; *(una ~)*
bullfight; **toros de** ~ fighting bulls;
lidiar *vt, vi* to fight.

liebre ['ljeβre] *nf* hare.

lienzo ['ljenθo] *nm* linen; (*ARTE*) canvas; (*ARQ*) wall.

liga ['liɣa] *nf* (*de medias*) garter, suspender; (*AM: gomita*) rubber band; (*confederación*) league.

ligadura [liɣa'ðura] *nf* bond, tie; (*MED, MUS*) ligature.

ligamento [liɣa'mento] *nm* (*ANAT*) ligament; (*atadura*) tie; (*unión*) bond.

ligar [li'ɣar] *vt* (*atar*) to tie; (*unir*) to join; (*MED*) to bind up; (*MUS*) to slur ♦ *vi* to mix, blend; (*fam*): (**él**) **liga mucho** he pulls a lot of women; **~se** *vr* to commit o.s.

ligereza [lixe'reθa] *nf* lightness; (*rapidez*) swiftness; (*agilidad*) agility; (*superficialidad*) flippancy.

ligero, a [li'xero, a] *adj* (*de peso*) light; (*tela*) thin; (*rápido*) swift, quick; (*ágil*) agile, nimble; (*de importancia*) slight; (*de carácter*) flippant, superficial ♦ *adv*: **a la ligera** superficially.

liguero [li'ɣero] *nm* suspender (*BRIT*) o garter (*US*) belt.

lija ['lixa] *nf* (*ZOOL*) dogfish; (*tb: papel de ~*) sandpaper.

lila ['lila] *nf* lilac.

lima ['lima] *nf* file; (*BOT*) lime; **~ de uñas** nailfile; **L~** *n* (*GEO*) Lima; **limar** *vt* to file.

limitación [limita'θjon] *nf* limitation, limit; **~ de velocidad** speed limit.

limitar [limi'tar] *vt* to limit; (*reducir*) to reduce, cut down ♦ *vi*: **~ con** to border on; **~se** *vr*: **~se a** to limit o.s. to.

límite ['limite] *nm* (*gen*) limit; (*fin*) end; (*frontera*) border; **~ de velocidad** speed limit.

limítrofe [li'mitrofe] *adj* bordering, neighbouring.

limón [li'mon] *nm* lemon ♦ *adj*: **amarillo ~** lemon-yellow; **limonada** *nf* lemonade; **limonero** *nm* lemon tree.

limosna [li'mosna] *nf* alms *pl*; **vivir de ~** to live on charity.

limpiabotas [limpja'ßotas] *nm/f inv* bootblack (*BRIT*), shoeshine boy/girl.

limpiaparabrisas [limpjapara'ßrisas] *nm inv* windscreen (*BRIT*) o windshield (*US*) wiper.

limpiar [lim'pjar] *vt* to clean; (*con trapo*) to wipe; (*quitar*) to wipe away; (*zapatos*) to shine, polish; (*fig*) to clean up.

limpieza [lim'pjeθa] *nf* (*estado*) cleanliness; (*acto*) cleaning; (: *de las calles*) cleansing; (: *de zapatos*) polishing; (*habilidad*) skill; (*fig: POLICÍA*) clean-up; (*pureza*) purity; (*MIL*): **operación de ~** mopping-up operation; **~ en seco** dry cleaning.

limpio, a ['limpjo, a] *adj* clean; (*moralmente*) pure; (*COM*) clear, net; (*fam*) honest ♦ *adv*: **jugar ~** to play fair; **pasar a** (*ESP*) o **en** (*AM*) **~** to make a clean copy.

linaje [li'naxe] *nm* lineage, family.

linaza [li'naθa] *nf* linseed.

lince ['linθe] *nm* lynx.

linchar [lin'tʃar] *vt* to lynch.

lindar [lin'dar] *vi* to adjoin; **~ con** to border on; **linde** *nm* o *f* boundary; **lindero, a** *adj* adjoining ♦ *nm* boundary.

lindo, a ['lindo, a] *adj* pretty, lovely ♦ *adv*: **nos divertimos de lo ~** we had a marvellous time; **canta muy ~** (*AM*) he sings beautifully.

línea ['linea] *nf* (*gen*) line; **en ~** (*INFORM*) on line; **~ aérea** airline; **~ de meta** goal line; (*de carrera*) finishing line; **~ recta** straight line.

lingote [lin'gote] *nm* ingot.

lingüista [lin'gwista] *nm/f* linguist; **lingüística** *nf* linguistics *sg*.

linimento [lini'mento] *nm* liniment.

lino ['lino] *nm* linen; (*BOT*) flax.

linóleo [li'noleo] *nm* lino, linoleum.

linterna [lin'terna] *nf* lantern, lamp; **~ eléctrica** o **a pilas** torch (*BRIT*), flashlight (*US*).

lío ['lio] *nm* bundle; (*fam*) fuss; (*desorden*) muddle, mess; **armar un ~** to make a fuss.

liquen ['liken] *nm* lichen.

liquidación [likiða'θjon] *nf* liquidation; **venta de ~** clearance sale.

liquidar [liki'ðar] *vt* (*mercancías*) to liquidate; (*deudas*) to pay off; (*empresa*) to wind up.

líquido, a ['likiðo, a] *adj* liquid;

(*ganancia*) net ♦ *nm* liquid; ~ **imponible** net taxable income.

lira ['lira] *nf* (*MUS*) lyre; (*moneda*) lira.

lírico, a ['liriko, a] *adj* lyrical.

lirio ['lirjo] *nm* (*BOT*) iris.

lirón [li'ron] *nm* (*ZOOL*) dormouse; (*fig*) sleepyhead.

Lisboa [lis'βoa] *n* Lisbon.

lisiado, a [li'sjaðo, a] *adj* injured ♦ *nm/f* cripple.

lisiar [li'sjar] *vt* to maim; ~**se** *vr* to injure o.s.

liso, a ['liso, a] *adj* (*terreno*) flat; (*cabello*) straight; (*superficie*) even; (*tela*) plain.

lisonja [li'sonxa] *nf* flattery; **lisonjear** *vt* to flatter; (*fig*) to please; **lisonjero, a** *adj* flattering; (*agradable*) gratifying, pleasing ♦ *nm/f* flatterer.

lista ['lista] *nf* list; (*de alumnos*) school register; (*de libros*) catalogue; (*de platos*) menu; (*de precios*) price list; **pasar** ~ to call the roll; ~ **de correos** poste restante; ~ **de espera** waiting list; **tela a** ~**s** striped material.

listado, a [lis'taðo, a] *adj* striped.

listo, a ['listo, a] *adj* (*perspicaz*) smart, clever; (*preparado*) ready.

listón [lis'ton] *nm* (*tela*) ribbon; (*de madera, metal*) strip.

litera [li'tera] *nf* (*en barco, tren*) berth; (*en dormitorio*) bunk, bunk bed.

literal [lite'ral] *adj* literal.

literario, a [lite'rarjo, a] *adj* literary.

literato, a [lite'rato, a] *adj* literary ♦ *nm/f* writer.

literatura [litera'tura] *nf* literature.

litigar [liti'var] *vt* to fight ♦ *vi* (*JUR*) to go to law; (*fig*) to dispute, argue.

litigio [li'tixjo] *nm* (*JUR*) lawsuit; (*fig*): **en** ~ **con** in dispute with.

litografía [litovra'fia] *nf* lithography; (*una* ~) lithograph.

litoral [lito'ral] *adj* coastal ♦ *nm* coast, seaboard.

litro ['litro] *nm* litre.

liviano, a [li'βjano, a] *adj* (*persona*) fickle; (*cosa, objeto*) trivial.

lívido, a ['liβiðo, a] *adj* livid.

ll... *see under letter LL, after L.*

lo [lo] *art def*: ~ **bello** the beautiful, what is beautiful, that which is beautiful ♦ *pron* (*persona*) him; (*cosa*) it; *tb ver* **el**.

loa ['loa] *nf* praise; **loable** *adj* praiseworthy; **loar** *vt* to praise.

lobato [lo'βato] *nm* (*ZOOL*) wolf cub; **L**~ Cub Scout.

lobo ['loβo] *nm* wolf; ~ **de mar** (*fig*) sea dog; ~ **marino** seal.

lóbrego, a ['loβrevo, a] *adj* dark; (*fig*) gloomy.

lóbulo ['loβulo] *nm* lobe.

local [lo'kal] *adj* local ♦ *nm* place, site; (*oficinas*) premises *pl*; ~**idad** *nf* (*barrio*) locality; (*lugar*) location; (*TEATRO*) seat, ticket; ~**izar** *vt* (*ubicar*) to locate, find; (*restringir*) to localize; (*situar*) to place.

loción [lo'θjon] *nf* lotion.

loco, a ['loko, a] *adj* mad ♦ *nm/f* lunatic, mad person.

locomoción [lokomo'θjon] *nf* locomotion.

locomotora [lokomo'tora] *nf* engine, locomotive.

locuaz [lo'kwaθ] *adj* loquacious.

locución [loku'θjon] *nf* expression.

locura [lo'kura] *nf* madness; (*acto*) crazy act.

locutor, a [loku'tor, a] *nm/f* (*RADIO*) announcer; (*comentarista*) commentator; (*TV*) newsreader.

locutorio [loku'torjo] *nm* (*en telefónica*) telephone booth.

lodo ['loðo] *nm* mud.

lógica ['loxika] *nf* logic.

lógico, a ['loxiko, a] *adj* logical.

logística [lo'xistika] *nf* logistics *sg*.

lograr [lo'vrar] *vt* to achieve; (*obtener*) to get, obtain; ~ **hacer** to manage to do; ~ **que uno venga** to manage to get sb to come.

logro ['lovro] *nm* achievement, success.

loma ['loma] *nf* hillock (*BRIT*), small hill.

lombriz [lom'briθ] *nf* worm.

lomo ['lomo] *nm* (*de animal*) back; (*CULIN: de cerdo*) pork loin; (*: de vaca*) rib steak; (*de libro*) spine.

lona ['lona] *nf* canvas.

loncha ['lontʃa] *nf* = **lonja**.

lonche ['lontʃe] (*AM*) *nm* lunch; ~**ría** (*AM*) *nf* snack bar, diner (*US*).

Londres ['londres] *n* London.

longaniza [longa'niθa] *nf* pork sausage.

longitud [lonxi'tuð] *nf* length; (*GEO*) longitude; **tener 3 metros de** ~ to be 3 metres long; ~ **de onda** wavelength.

lonja ['lonxa] *nf* slice; (*de tocino*) rasher; ~ **de pescado** fish market.

loro ['loro] *nm* parrot.

los [los] *art def-* the ♦ *pron* them; (*ustedes*) you; **mis libros y** ~ **de Ud** my books and yours; *tb ver* **el**.

losa ['losa] *nf* stone; ~ **sepulcral** gravestone.

lote ['lote] *nm* portion; (*COM*) lot.

lotería [lote'ria] *nf* lottery; (*juego*) lotto.

loza ['loθa] *nf* crockery.

lozanía [loθa'nia] *nf* (*lujo*) luxuriance; **lozano, a** *adj* luxuriant; (*animado*) lively.

lubricante [luβri'kante] *nm* lubricant.

lubricar [luβri'kar] *vt* to lubricate.

lucero [lu'θero] *nm* bright star; (*fig*) brilliance.

lucidez [luθi'ðeθ] *nf* lucidity; **lúcido, a** *adj* lucid.

luciérnaga [lu'θjernaxa] *nf* glow-worm.

lucimiento [luθi'mjento] *nm* (*brillo*) brilliance; (*éxito*) success.

lucir [lu'θir] *vt* to illuminate, light (up); (*ostentar*) to show off ♦ *vi* (*brillar*) to shine; ~**se** *vr* (*irónico*) to make a fool of o.s.

lucro ['lukro] *nm* profit, gain.

lucha ['lutʃa] *nf* fight, struggle; ~ **de clases** class struggle; ~ **libre** wrestling; **luchar** *vi* to fight.

luego ['lweɣo] *adv* (*después*) next; (*más tarde*) later, afterwards.

lugar [lu'ɣar] *nm* place; (*sitio*) spot; **en** ~ **de** instead of; **hacer** ~ to make room; **fuera de** ~ out of place; **tener** ~ to take place; ~ **común** commonplace.

lugareño, a [luɣa'reɲo, a] *adj* village *cpd* ♦ *nm/f* villager.

lugarteniente [luɣarte'njente] *nm* deputy.

lúgubre ['luɣuβre] *adj* mournful.

lujo ['luxo] *nm* luxury; (*fig*) profusion, abundance; ~**so, a** *adj* luxurious.

lujuria [lu'xurja] *nf* lust.

lumbre ['lumbre] *nf* (*gen*) light.

lumbrera [lum'brera] *nf* luminary.

luminoso, a [lumi'noso, a] *adj* luminous, shining.

luna ['luna] *nf* moon; (*de un espejo*) glass; (*de gafas*) lens; (*fig*) crescent; ~ **llena/nueva** full/new moon; **estar en la** ~ to have one's head in the clouds; ~ **de miel** honeymoon.

lunar [lu'nar] *adj* lunar ♦ *nm* (*ANAT*) mole; **tela a** ~**es** spotted material.

lunes ['lunes] *nm inv* Monday.

lupa ['lupa] *nf* magnifying glass.

lustrar [lus'trar] *vt* (*mueble*) to polish; (*zapatos*) to shine; **lustre** *nm* polish; (*fig*) lustre; **dar lustre a** to polish; **lustroso, a** *adj* shining.

luterano, a [lute'rano, a] *adj* Lutheran.

luto ['luto] *nm* mourning; (*congoja*) grief, sorrow; **llevar el** *o* **vestirse de** ~ to be in mourning.

Luxemburgo [luksem'burɣo] *nm* Luxembourg.

luz [luθ] (*pl* **luces**) *nf* light; **dar a** ~ **un niño** to give birth to a child; **sacar a la** ~ to bring to light; **dar** *o* **encender** (*ESP*) *o* **prender** (*AM*)/**apagar la** ~ to switch the light on/off; **a todas luces** by any reckoning; **hacer la** ~ **sobre** to shed light on; **tener pocas luces** to be dim *o* stupid; ~ **roja/verde** red/green light; ~ **de freno** brake light; **luces de tráfico** traffic lights; **traje de luces** bullfighter's costume.

LL

llaga ['ʎaɣa] *nf* wound.

llama ['ʎama] *nf* flame; (*ZOOL*) llama.

llamada [ʎa'maða] *nf* call; ~ **al orden** call to order; ~ **a pie de página** reference note.

llamamiento [ʎama'mjento] *nm* call.

llamar [ʎa'mar] *vt* to call; (*atención*) to attract ♦ *vi* (*por teléfono*) to telephone;

(*a la puerta*) to knock (*o ring*); (*por señas*) to beckon; (*MIL*) to call up; ~**se** *vr* to be called, be named; ¿cómo se **llama usted?** what's your name?

llamarada [ʎamaˈraða] *nf* (*llamas*) blaze; (*rubor*) flush; (*fig*) flare-up.

llamativo, a [ʎamaˈtiβo, a] *adj* showy; (*color*) loud.

llamear [ʎameˈar] *vi* to blaze.

llano, a [ˈʎano, a] *adj* (*superficie*) flat; (*persona*) straightforward; (*estilo*) clear ♦ *nm* plain, flat ground.

llanta [ˈʎanta] *nf* (wheel) rim; (*AM*): ~ (**de goma**) tyre; (: *cámara*) inner (tube).

llanto [ˈʎanto] *nm* weeping.

llanura [ʎaˈnura] *nf* plain.

llave [ˈʎaβe] *nf* key; (*del agua*) tap; (*MECÁNICA*) spanner; (*de la luz*) switch; (*MUS*) key; ~ **inglesa** monkey wrench; ~ **maestra** master key; ~ **de contacto** (*AUTO*) ignition key; ~ **de paso** stopcock; **echar** ~ **a** to lock up; ~**ro** *nm* keyring; **llavín** *nm* latchkey.

llegada [ʎeˈɣaða] *nf* arrival.

llegar [ʎeˈɣar] *vi* to arrive; (*alcanzar*) to reach; (*bastar*) to be enough; ~**se** *vr*: ~**se a** to approach; ~ **a** to manage to, succeed in; ~ **a saber** to find out; ~ **a ser** to become; ~ **a las manos de** to come into the hands of.

llenar [ʎeˈnar] *vt* to fill; (*espacio*) to cover; (*formulario*) to fill in *o* up; (*fig*) to heap.

lleno, a [ˈʎeno, a] *adj* full, filled; (*repleto*) full up ♦ *nm* (*abundancia*) abundance; (*TEATRO*) full house; **dar de** ~ **contra un muro** to hit a wall head-on.

llevadero, a [ʎeβaˈðero, a] *adj* bearable, tolerable.

llevar [ʎeˈβar] *vt* to take; (*ropa*) to wear; (*cargar*) to carry; (*quitar*) to take away; (*en coche*) to drive; (*transportar*) to transport; (*traer: dinero*) to carry; (*conducir*) to lead; (*MAT*) to carry ♦ *vi* (*suj: camino etc*): ~ **a** to lead to; ~**se** *vr* to carry off, take away; **llevamos dos días aquí** we have been here for two days; **él me lleva 2 años** he's 2 years older than me;

(*COM*): ~ **los libros** to keep the books; ~**se bien** to get on well (together).

llorar [ʎoˈrar] *vt, vi* to cry, weep; ~ **de risa** to cry with laughter.

lloriquear [ʎorikeˈar] *vi* to snivel, whimper.

lloro [ˈʎoro] *nm* crying, weeping; **llorón, ona** *adj* tearful ♦ *nm/f* cry-baby; ~**so, a** *adj* (*gen*) weeping, tearful; (*triste*) sad, sorrowful.

llover [ʎoˈβer] *vi* to rain.

llovizna [ʎoˈβiθna] *nf* drizzle; **llovizmar** *vi* to drizzle.

llueve *etc vb ver* **llover**.

lluvia [ˈʎuβja] *nf* rain; ~ **radioactiva** (radioactive) fallout; **lluvioso, a** *adj* rainy.

M

m *abr* (= *metro*) m; (= *minuto*) m.

macarrones [makaˈrrones] *nmpl* macaroni *sg*.

macedonia [maθeˈðonja] *nf*: ~ **de frutas** fruit salad.

macerar [maθeˈrar] *vt* to macerate.

maceta [maˈθeta] *nf* (*de flores*) pot of flowers; (*para plantas*) flowerpot.

macizo, a [maˈθiθo, a] *adj* (*grande*) massive; (*fuerte, sólido*) solid ♦ *nm* mass, chunk.

mácula [ˈmakula] *nf* stain, blemish.

machacar [matʃaˈkar] *vt* to crush, pound ♦ *vi* (*insistir*) to go on, keep on.

machete [maˈtʃete] (*AM*) *nm* machete, (large) knife.

machista [maˈtʃista] *adj, nm* sexist.

macho [ˈmatʃo] *adj* male; (*fig*) virile ♦ *nm* male; (*fig*) he-man.

machucar [matʃuˈkar] *vt* to pound.

madeja [maˈðexa] *nf* (*de lana*) skein, hank; (*de pelo*) mass, mop.

madera [maˈðera] *nf* wood; (*fig*) nature, character; **una** ~ a piece of wood.

madero [maˈðero] *nm* beam; (*fig*) ship.

madrastra [maˈðrastra] *nf* stepmother.

madre [ˈmaðre] *adj* mother *cpd*; (*AM*) tremendous ♦ *nf* mother; (*de vino etc*) dregs *pl*; ~ **política/soltera** mother-in-law/unmarried mother.

madreperla [maðre'perla] *nf* mother-of-pearl.

madreselva [maðre'selßa] *nf* honeysuckle.

Madrid [ma'ðrið] *n* Madrid.

madriguera [maðri'vera] *nf* burrow.

madrileño, a [maðri'leɲo, a] *adj* of *o* from Madrid ♦ *nm/f* native of Madrid.

madrina [ma'ðrina] *nf* godmother; (*ARQ*) prop, shore; (*TEC*) brace; ~ **de boda** bridesmaid.

madrugada [maðru'vaða] *nf* early morning; (*alba*) dawn, daybreak.

madrugador, a [maðruva'ðor, a] *adj* early-rising.

madrugar [maðru'var] *vi* to get up early; (*fig*) to get ahead.

madurar [maðu'rar] *vt, vi* (*fruta*) to ripen; (*fig*) to mature; **madurez** *nf* ripeness; maturity; **maduro, a** *adj* ripe; mature.

maestra [ma'estra] *nf ver* **maestro**.

maestría [maes'tria] *nf* mastery; (*habilidad*) skill, expertise.

maestro, a [ma'estro, a] *adj* masterly; (*perito*) skilled, expert; (*principal*) main; (*educado*) trained ♦ *nm/f* master/mistress; (*profesor*) teacher ♦ *nm* (*autoridad*) authority; (*MUS*) maestro; (*AM*) skilled workman; ~ **albañil** master mason.

magia ['maxja] *nf* magic; **mágico, a** *adj* magic(al) ♦ *nm/f* magician.

magisterio [maxis'terjo] *nm* (*enseñanza*) teaching; (*profesión*) teaching profession; (*maestros*) teachers *pl*.

magistrado [maxis'traðo] *nm* magistrate.

magistral [maxis'tral] *adj* magisterial; (*fig*) masterly.

magnánimo, a [mav'nanimo, a] *adj* magnanimous.

magnate [mav'nate] *nm* magnate, tycoon.

magnético, a [mav'netiko, a] *adj* magnetic; **magnetizar** *vt* to magnetize.

magnetófon [mavneto'fon] *nm* tape recorder; **magnetofónico, a** *adj*: **cinta magnetofónica** recording tape.

magnetófono [mavne'tofono] *nm* = **magnetofón**.

magnífico, a [mav'nifiko, a] *adj* splendid, magnificent.

magnitud [mavni'tuð] *nf* magnitude.

mago, a ['mavo, a] *nm/f* magician; **los Reyes M~s** the Magi, the Three Wise Men.

magro, a ['mavro, a] *adj* (*persona*) thin, lean; (*carne*) lean.

maguey [ma'vei] *nm* agave.

magullar [mavu'ʎar] *vt* (*amoratar*) to bruise; (*dañar*) to damage; (*fam: golpear*) to bash, beat.

mahometano, a [maome'tano, a] *adj* Mohammedan.

mahonesa [mao'nesa] *nf* = **mayonesa**.

maíz [ma'iθ] *nm* maize (*BRIT*), corn (*US*); sweet corn.

majadero, a [maxa'ðero, a] *adj* silly, stupid.

majestad [maxes'tað] *nf* majesty; **majestuoso, a** *adj* majestic.

majo, a ['maxo, a] *adj* nice; (*guapo*) attractive, good-looking; (*elegante*) smart.

mal [mal] *adv* badly; (*equivocadamente*) wrongly; (*con dificultad*) with difficulty ♦ *adj* = **malo** ♦ *nm* evil; (*desgracia*) misfortune; (*daño*) harm, damage; (*MED*) illness; ~ **que bien** rightly or wrongly; **ir de ~ en peor** to get worse and worse.

mala ['mala] *nf* spell of bad luck; **estar de ~s** to be in a bad mood; *ver tb* **malo.**

malabarismo [malaßa'rismo] *nm* juggling; **malabarista** *nm/f* juggler.

malaconsejado, a [malakonse'xaðo, a] *adj* ill-advised.

malaria [ma'larja] *nf* malaria.

malcriado, a [mal'krjaðo, a] *adj* (*consentido*) spoiled.

maldad [mal'dað] *nf* evil, wickedness.

maldecir [malde'θir] *vt* to curse ♦ *vi*: ~ **de** to speak ill of.

maldición [maldi'θjon] *nf* curse.

maldito, a [mal'dito, a] *adj* (*condenado*) damned; (*perverso*) wicked; ¡~ **sea!** damn it!

maleante [male'ante] *adj* wicked ♦ *nm/f* criminal, crook.
malecón [male'kon] *nm* pier, jetty.
maledicencia [maleði'θenθja] *nf* slander, scandal.
maleducado, a [maleðu'kaðo, a] *adj* bad-mannered, rude.
maleficio [male'fiθjo] *nm* curse, spell.
malestar [males'tar] *nm* (*gen*) discomfort; (*fig: inquietud*) uneasiness; (*POL*) unrest.
maleta [ma'leta] *nf* case, suitcase; (*AUTO*) boot (*BRIT*), trunk (*US*); **hacer las ~s** to pack; **maletera** (*AM*) *nf* = **maletero**; **maletero** *nm* (*AUTO*) boot (*BRIT*), trunk (*US*); **maletín** *nm* small case, bag.
malévolo, a [ma'leßolo, a] *adj* malicious, spiteful.
maleza [ma'leθa] *nf* (*hierbas malas*) weeds *pl*; (*arbustos*) thicket.
malgastar [malvas'tar] *vt* (*tiempo, dinero*) to waste; (*salud*) to ruin.
malhechor, a [male'tʃor, a] *nm/f* delinquent.
malhumorado, a [malumo'raðo, a] *adj* bad-tempered.
malicia [ma'liθja] *nf* (*maldad*) wickedness; (*astucia*) slyness, guile; (*mala intención*) malice, spite; (*carácter travieso*) mischievousness; **malicioso, a** *adj* wicked, evil; sly, crafty; malicious, spiteful; mischievous.
maligno, a [ma'liɣno, a] *adj* evil; (*malévolo*) malicious; (*MED*) malignant.
malo, a ['malo, a] *adj* bad; (*falso*) false ♦ *nm/f* villain; **estar ~** to be ill.
malograr [malo'ɣrar] *vt* to spoil; (*plan*) to upset; (*ocasión*) to waste; **~se** *vr* (*plan etc*) to fail, come to grief; (*persona*) to die before one's time.
malparado, a [malpa'raðo, a] *adj*: **salir ~** to come off badly.
malparir [malpa'rir] *vi* to have a miscarriage.
malsano, a [mal'sano, a] *adj* unhealthy.
Malta ['malta] *nf* Malta.
malteada [malte'aða] (*AM*) *nf* milk shake.
maltratar [maltra'tar] *vt* to ill-treat, mis-

treat.
maltrecho, a [mal'tretʃo, a] *adj* battered, damaged.
malvado, a [mal'ßaðo, a] *adj* evil, villainous.
malvavisco [malßa'ßisko] *nm* marshmallow.
malversar [malßer'sar] *vt* to embezzle, misappropriate.
Malvinas [mal'ßinas]: **Islas ~** *nfpl* Falkland Islands.
malla ['maʎa] *nf* mesh; (*de baño*) swimsuit; (*de ballet, gimnasia*) leotard; **~s** *nfpl* tights; **~ de alambre** wire mesh.
Mallorca [ma'ʎorka] *nf* Majorca.
mama ['mama] *nf* (*de animal*) teat; (*de mujer*) breast.
mamá [ma'ma] (*pl* ~s) (*fam*) *nf* mum, mummy.
mamar [ma'mar] *vt* (*pecho*) to suck; (*fig*) to absorb, assimilate ♦ *vi* to suck.
mamarracho [mama'rratʃo] *nm* sight, mess.
mamífero [ma'mifero] *nm* mammal.
mampara [mam'para] *nf* (*entre habitaciones*) partition; (*biombo*) screen.
mampostería [mamposte'ria] *nf* masonry.
mamut [ma'mut] (*pl* ~s) *nm* mammoth.
manada [ma'naða] *nf* (*ZOOL*) herd; (: *de leones*) pride; (: *de lobos*) pack.
Managua [ma'naɣwa] *n* Managua.
manantial [manan'tjal] *nm* spring; (*fuente*) fountain; (*fig*) source.
manar [ma'nar] *vt* to run with, flow with ♦ *vi* to run, flow; (*abundar*) to abound.
mancilla [man'θiʎa] *nf* stain, blemish.
manco, a ['manko, a] *adj* (*de un brazo*) one-armed; (*de una mano*) one-handed; (*fig*) defective, faulty.
mancomunar [mankomu'nar] *vt* to unite, bring together; (*recursos*) to pool; (*JUR*) to make jointly responsible; **mancomunidad** *nf* union, association; (*comunidad*) community; (*JUR*) joint responsibility.
mancha ['mantʃa] *nf* stain, mark; (*ZOOL*) patch; (*boceto*) sketch, outline; **manchar** *vt* (*gen*) to stain, mark; (*en-*

suciar) to soil, dirty.

manchego, a [man'tʃeɣo, a] *adj* of o from La Mancha.

mandado [man'daðo] *nm* (*orden*) order; (*comisión*) commission, errand.

mandamiento [manda'mjento] *nm* (*orden*) order, command; (*REL*) commandment; ~ **judicial** warrant.

mandar [man'dar] *vt* (*ordenar*) to order; (*dirigir*) to lead, command; (*enviar*) to send; (*pedir*) to order, ask for ♦ *vi* to be in charge; (*pey*) to be bossy; ¿**mande?** pardon?, excuse me?; ~ **hacer un traje** to have a suit made.

mandarín [manda'rin] *nm* (*persona*) mandarin.

mandarina [manda'rina] *nf* (*fruta*) tangerine, mandarin (orange).

mandatario, a [manda'tarjo, a] *nm/f* (*representante*) agent; **primer** ~ head of state.

mandato [man'dato] *nm* (*orden*) order; (*INFORM*) command; (*POL: período*) term of office; (*t: territorio*) mandate; ~ **judicial** (search) warrant.

mandíbula [man'diβula] *nf* jaw.

mandil [man'dil] *nm* (*delantal*) apron.

mando ['mando] *nm* (*MIL*) command; (*de país*) rule; (*el primer lugar*) lead; (*POL*) term of office; (*TEC*) control; ~ **a la izquierda** left-hand drive.

mandolina [mando'lina] *nf* mandolin(e).

mandón, ona [man'don, ona] *adj* bossy, domineering.

manejable [mane'xaβle] *adj* manageable.

manejar [mane'xar] *vt* to manage; (*máquina*) to work, operate; (*caballo etc*) to handle; (*casa*) to run, manage; (*AM: AUTO*) to drive; ~**se** *vr* (*comportarse*) to act, behave; (*arreglárselas*) to manage; **manejo** *nm* management; handling; running; driving; (*facilidad de trato*) ease, confidence; **manejos** *nmpl* (*intrigas*) intrigues.

manera [ma'nera] *nf* way, manner, fashion; ~**s** *nfpl* (*modales*) manners; **su** ~ **de ser** the way he is; (*aire*) his manner; **de ninguna** ~ no way, by no

means; **de otra** ~ otherwise; **de todas** ~**s** at any rate; **no hay** ~ **de persuadirle** there's no way of convincing him.

manga ['manga] *nf* (*de camisa*) sleeve; (*de riego*) hose.

mangana [man'gana] *nf* lasso.

mango ['mango] *nm* handle; (*BOT*) mango.

mangonear [mangone'ar] *vi* (*meterse*) to meddle, interfere; (*ser mandón*) to boss people about.

manguera [man'gera] *nf* (*de riego*) hose; (*tubo*) pipe.

maní [ma'ni] (*AM*) *nm* peanut.

manía [ma'nia] *nf* (*MED*) mania; (*fig: moda*) rage, craze; (*disgusto*) dislike; (*malicia*) spite; **maníaco, a** *adj* maniac(al) ♦ *nm/f* maniac.

maniatar [manja'tar] *vt* to tie the hands of.

maniático, a [ma'njatiko, a] *adj* maniac(al) ♦ *nm/f* maniac.

manicomio [mani'komjo] *nm* mental hospital (*BRIT*), insane asylum (*US*).

manicura [mani'kura] *nf* manicure.

manifestación [manifesta'θjon] *nf* (*declaración*) statement, declaration; (*de emoción*) show, display; (*POL: desfile*) demonstration; (*t: concentración*) mass meeting.

manifestar [manifes'tar] *vt* to show, manifest; (*declarar*) to state, declare; **manifiesto, a** *adj* clear, manifest ♦ *nm* manifesto.

manija [ma'nixa] *nf* handle.

maniobra [ma'njoβra] *nf* manœuvring; (*manejo*) handling; (*fig*) manœuvre; (*estratagema*) stratagem; ~**s** *nfpl* (*MIL*) manœuvres; **maniobrar** *vt* to manœuvre; (*manejar*) to handle.

manipulación [manipula'θjon] *nf* manipulation.

manipular [manipu'lar] *vt* to manipulate; (*manejar*) to handle.

maniquí [mani'ki] *nm* dummy ♦ *nm/f* model.

manirroto, a [mani'rroto, a] *adj* lavish, extravagant ♦ *nm/f* spendthrift.

manivela [mani'βela] *nf* crank.

manjar [man'xar] *nm* (tasty) dish.
mano ['mano] *nf* hand; (*ZOOL*) foot,
paw; (*de pintura*) coat; (*serie*) lot, series; **a ~ by** hand; **a ~ derecha/
izquierda** on the right(-hand side)/left(-
hand side); **de primera ~** (at) first
hand; **de segunda ~** (at) second hand;
robo a ~ armada armed robbery; **~ de
obra** labour, manpower; **estrechar la ~
a uno** to shake sb's hand.
manojo [ma'noxo] *nm* handful, bunch;
~ de llaves bunch of keys.
manopla [ma'nopla] *nf* (*guante*) glove;
(*paño*) face cloth.
manoseado, a [manose'aðo, a] *adj*
well-worn.
manosear [manose'ar] *vt* (*tocar*) to
handle, touch; (*desordenar*) to mess up,
rumple; (*insistir en*) to overwork; (*AM*)
to caress, fondle.
manotazo [mano'taθo] *nm* slap, smack.
mansalva [man'salβa]: **a ~** *adv* in-
discriminately.
mansedumbre [manse'ðumbre] *nf*
gentleness, meekness.
mansión [man'sjon] *nf* mansion.
manso, a ['manso, a] *adj* gentle, mild;
(*animal*) tame.
manta ['manta] *nf* blanket; (*AM:
poncho*) poncho.
manteca [man'teka] *nf* fat; (*AM*) butter;
~ de cacahuete/cacao peanut/cocoa
butter; **~ de cerdo** lard.
mantecado [mante'kaðo] (*AM*) *nm* ice
cream.
mantel [man'tel] *nm* tablecloth.
mantendré *etc vb ver* **mantener**.
mantener [mante'ner] *vt* to support,
maintain; (*alimentar*) to sustain; (*conservar*) to keep; (*TEC*) to maintain,
service; **~se** *vr* (*seguir de pie*) to be
still standing; (*no ceder*) to hold one's
ground; (*subsistir*) to sustain o.s., keep
going; **mantenimiento** *nm* maintenance; sustenance; (*sustento*) support.
mantequilla [mante'kiʎa] *nf* butter.
mantilla [man'tiʎa] *nf* mantilla; **~s** *nfpl*
(*de bebé*) baby clothes.
manto ['manto] *nm* (*capa*) cloak; (*de

ceremonia*) robe, gown.
mantón [man'ton] *nm* shawl.
mantuve *etc vb ver* **mantener**.
manual [ma'nwal] *adj* manual ♦ *nm*
manual, handbook.
manufactura [manufak'tura] *nf*
manufacture; (*fábrica*) factory.
manuscrito, a [manus'krito, a] *adj*
handwritten ♦ *nm* manuscript.
manutención [manuten'θjon] *nf* maintenance; (*sustento*) support.
manzana [man'θana] *nf* apple; (*ARQ*)
block (of houses).
manzanilla [manθa'niʎa] *nf* (*planta*)
camomile; (*infusión*) camomile tea.
manzano [man'θano] *nm* apple tree.
maña ['maɲa] *nf* (*gen*) skill, dexterity;
(*pey*) guile; (*costumbre*) habit;
(*destreza*) trick, knack.
mañana [ma'ɲana] *adv* tomorrow ♦ *nm*
future ♦ *nf* morning; **de** *o* **por la ~** in
the morning; **¡hasta ~!** see you
tomorrow!; **~ por la ~** tomorrow morning; **mañanero, a** *adj* early-rising.
mañoso, a [ma'ɲoso, a] *adj* (*hábil*) skilful; (*astuto*) smart, clever.
mapa ['mapa] *nm* map.
maqueta [ma'keta] *nf* (scale) model.
maquillaje [maki'ʎaxe] *nm* make-up;
(*acto*) making up.
maquillar [maki'ʎar] *vt* to make up; **~se**
vr to put on (some) make-up.
máquina ['makina] *nf* machine; (*de
tren*) locomotive, engine; (*FOTO*)
camera; (*AM: coche*) car; (*fig*)
machinery; (: *proyecto*) plan, project;
escrito a ~ typewritten; **~ de escribir**
typewriter; **~ de coser/lavar** sewing/
washing machine.
maquinación [makina'θjon] *nf* machina-
tion, plot.
maquinal [maki'nal] *adj* (*fig*) mechanical, automatic.
maquinaria [maki'narja] *nf* (*máquinas*)
machinery; (*mecanismo*) mechanism,
works *pl*.
maquinilla [maki'niʎa] *nf*: **~ de afeitar**
razor.
maquinista [maki'nista] *nm/f* (*de tren*)
engine driver; (*TEC*) operator; (*NAUT*)

engineer.

mar [mar] *nm o f* sea; ~ **adentro** *o* **afuera** out at sea; **en alta** ~ on the high seas; **la** ~ **de** *(fam)* lots of; **el M~ Negro/Báltico** the Black/Baltic Sea.

maraña [maˈraɲa] *nf (maleza)* thicket; *(confusión)* tangle.

maravilla [maraˈβiʎa] *nf* marvel, wonder; *(BOT)* marigold; **maravillar** *vt* to astonish, amaze; **maravillarse** *vr* to be astonished, be amazed; **maravilloso, a** *adj* wonderful, marvellous.

marca [ˈmarka] *nf (gen)* mark; *(sello)* stamp; *(COM)* make, brand; **de** ~ excellent, outstanding; ~ **de fábrica** trademark; ~ **registrada** registered trademark.

marcado, a [marˈkaðo, a] *adj* marked, strong.

marcador [markaˈðor] *nm (DEPORTE)* scoreboard; (: *persona*) scorer.

marcar [marˈkar] *vt (gen)* to mark; *(número de teléfono)* to dial; *(gol)* to score; *(números)* to record, keep a tally of; *(pelo)* to set ♦ *vi (DEPORTE)* to score; *(TEL)* to dial.

marcial [marˈθjal] *adj* martial, military.

marciano, a [marˈθjano, a] *adj, nm/f* Martian.

marco [ˈmarko] *nm* frame; *(DEPORTE)* goal posts *pl*; *(moneda)* mark; *(fig)* framework; ~ **de chimenea** mantelpiece.

marcha [ˈmartʃa] *nf* march; *(TEC)* running, working; *(AUTO)* gear; *(velocidad)* speed; *(fig)* progress; *(dirección)* course; **poner en** ~ to put into gear; *(fig)* to set in motion, get going; **dar** ~ **atrás** to reverse, put into reverse; **estar en** ~ to be under way, be in motion.

marchar [marˈtʃar] *vi (ir)* to go; *(funcionar)* to work, go; ~**se** *vr* to go (away), leave.

marchitar [martʃiˈtar] *vt* to wither, dry up; ~**se** *vr (BOT)* to wither; *(fig)* to fade away; **marchito, a** *adj* withered, faded; *(fig)* in decline.

marea [maˈrea] *nf* tide; *(llovizna)* drizzle.

marear [mareˈar] *vt (fig)* to annoy, upset; *(MED)*: ~ **a uno** to make sb feel sick; ~**se** *vr (tener náuseas)* to feel sick; *(desvanecerse)* to feel faint; *(aturdirse)* to feel dizzy; *(fam: emborracharse)* to get tipsy.

maremoto [mareˈmoto] *nm* tidal wave.

mareo [maˈreo] *nm (náusea)* sick feeling; *(en viaje)* travel sickness; *(aturdimiento)* dizziness; *(fam: lata)* nuisance.

marfil [marˈfil] *nm* ivory.

margarina [marɣaˈrina] *nf* margarine.

margarita [marɣaˈrita] *nf (BOT)* daisy; *(rueda)* ~ daisywheel.

margen [ˈmarxen] *nm (borde)* edge, border; *(fig)* margin, space ♦ *nf (de río etc)* bank; **dar** ~ **para** to give an opportunity for; **mantenerse al** ~ to keep out (of things).

marica [maˈrika] *(fam) nm* sissy.

maricón [mariˈkon] *(fam) nm* queer.

marido [maˈriðo] *nm* husband.

mariguana [mariˈɣwana] *nf* marijuana, cannabis.

marimacho [mariˈmatʃo] *(fam) nm* mannish woman.

marina [maˈrina] *nf* navy; ~ **mercante** merchant navy.

marinero, a [mariˈnero, a] *adj* sea *cpd*; *(barco)* seaworthy ♦ *nm* sailor, seaman.

marino, a [maˈrino, a] *adj* sea *cpd*, marine ♦ *nm* sailor.

marioneta [marjoˈneta] *nf* puppet.

mariposa [mariˈposa] *nf* butterfly.

mariquita [mariˈkita] *nf* ladybird *(BRIT)*, ladybug *(US)*.

mariscos [maˈriskos] *nmpl* shellfish *inv*, seafood(s).

marisma [maˈrisma] *nf* marsh, swamp.

marítimo, a [maˈritimo, a] *adj* sea *cpd*, maritime.

mariuana [mariˈwana] *nf* = **mariguana**.

marmita [marˈmita] *nf* pot.

mármol [ˈmarmol] *nm* marble.

marqués, esa [marˈkes, esa] *nm/f* marquis/marchioness.

marrón [maˈrron] *adj* brown.

marroquí [marroˈki] *adj, nm/f* Moroccan

♦ *nm* Morocco (leather).
Marruecos [ma'rrwekos] *nm* Morocco.
martes ['martes] *nm inv* Tuesday.
martillar [marti'ʎar] *vt* to hammer.
martillo [mar'tiʎo] *nm* hammer; ~ **neumático** pneumatic drill (*BRIT*), jackhammer.
mártir ['martir] *nm/f* martyr; **martirio** *nm* martyrdom; (*fig*) torture, torment.
Marxismo [mark'sismo] *nm* Marxism; **marxista** *adj*, *nm/f* Marxist.
marzo ['marθo] *nm* March.
mas [mas] *conj* but.

PALABRA CLAVE
---

más [mas] *adj*, *adv* **1**: ~ **(que, de)** (*compar*) more (than), ...+ er (than); ~ **grande/inteligente** bigger/more intelligent; **trabaja ~ (que yo)** he works more (than me); *ver tb* **cada**
2 (*superl*): **el ~** the most, ...+ est; **el ~ grande/inteligente (de)** the biggest/most intelligent (in)
3 (*negativo*): **no tengo ~ dinero** I haven't got any more money; **no viene ~ por aquí** he doesn't come round here any more
4 (*adicional*): **no le veo ~ solución que** ... I see no other solution than to ...; **¿quién ~?** anybody else?
5 (+*adj*: *valor intensivo*): **¡qué perro ~ sucio!** what a filthy dog!; **¡es ~ tonto!** he's so stupid!
6 (*locuciones*): **~ o menos** more or less; **los ~** most people; **es ~** furthermore; **~ bien** rather; **¡qué ~ da!** what does it matter!; *ver tb* **no**
7: **por ~: por ~ que te esfuerces** no matter how hard you try; **por ~ que quisiera** ... much as I should like to ...
8: **de ~: veo que aquí estoy de ~** I can see I'm not needed here; **tenemos uno de ~** we've got one extra
♦ *prep*: **2 ~ 2 son 4** 2 and *o* plus 2 are 4
♦ *nm inv*: **este trabajo tiene sus ~ y sus menos** this job's got its good points and its bad points.

---

masa ['masa] *nf* (*mezcla*) dough; (*volumen*) volume, mass; (*FÍSICA*) mass; **en**

~ **en masse**; **las ~s** (*POL*) the masses.
masacre [ma'sakre] *nf* massacre.
masaje [ma'saxe] *nm* massage.
mascar [mas'kar] *vt* to chew; (*fig*) to mumble, mutter.
máscara ['maskara] *nf* (*gen*) mask ♦ *nm/f* masked person; **mascarada** *nf* masquerade; **mascarilla** *nf* (*de belleza*, *MED*) mask.
masculino, a [masku'lino, a] *adj* masculine; (*BIO*) male.
mascullar [masku'ʎar] *vt* to mumble, mutter.
masilla [ma'siʎa] *nf* putty.
masivo, a [ma'siβo, a] *adj* (*en masa*) mass.
masón [ma'son] *nm* (*free*)mason.
masoquista [maso'kista] *nm/f* masochist.
masticar [masti'kar] *vt* to chew; (*fig*) to ponder.
mástil ['mastil] *nm* (*de navío*) mast; (*de guitarra*) neck.
mastín [mas'tin] *nm* mastiff.
masturbación [masturβa'θjon] *nf* masturbation.
masturbarse [mastur'βarse] *vr* to masturbate.
mata ['mata] *nf* (*arbusto*) bush, shrub; (*de hierba*) tuft.
matadero [mata'ðero] *nm* slaughter-house, abattoir.
matador, a [mata'ðor, a] *adj* killing ♦ *nm/f* killer ♦ *nm* (*TAUR*) matador, bullfighter.
matamoscas [mata'moskas] *nm inv* (*palo*) fly swat.
matanza [ma'tanθa] *nf* slaughter.
matar [ma'tar] *vt*, *vi* to kill; ~**se** *vr* (*suicidarse*) to kill o.s., commit suicide; (*morir*) to be *o* get killed; ~ **el hambre** to stave off hunger.
matasellos [mata'seʎos] *nm inv* post-mark.
mate ['mate] *adj* (*sin brillo: color*) dull, matt ♦ *nm* (*en ajedrez*) (check)mate; (*AM: hierba*) maté; (: *vasija*) gourd.
matemáticas [mate'matikas] *nfpl* mathematics; **matemático, a** *adj* mathematical ♦ *nm/f* mathematician.

materia [ma'terja] *nf* (*gen*) matter; (*TEC*) material; (*ESCOL*) subject; **en ~ de** on the subject of; **~ prima** raw material; **material** *adj* material; (*dolor*) physical ♦ *nm* material; (*TEC*) equipment; **materialismo** *nm* materialism; **materialista** *adj* materialist(ic); **materialmente** *adv* materially; (*fig*) absolutely.

maternal [mater'nal] *adj* motherly, maternal.

maternidad [materni'ðað] *nf* motherhood, maternity; **materno, a** *adj* maternal; (*lengua*) mother *cpd*.

matinal [mati'nal] *adj* morning *cpd*.

matiz [ma'tiθ] *nm* shade; **~ar** *vt* (*variar*) to vary; (*ARTE*) to blend; **~ar de** to tinge with.

matón [ma'ton] *nm* bully.

matorral [mato'rral] *nm* thicket.

matraca [ma'traka] *nf* rattle.

matrícula [ma'trikula] *nf* (*registro*) register; (*AUTO*) registration number; (: *placa*) number plate; **matricular** *vt* to register, enrol.

matrimonial [matrimo'njal] *adj* matrimonial.

matrimonio [matri'monjo] *nm* (*pareja*) (married) couple; (*unión*) marriage.

matriz [ma'triθ] *nf* (*ANAT*) womb; (*TEC*) mould; **casa ~** (*COM*) head office.

matrona [ma'trona] *nf* (*persona de edad*) matron.

maullar [mau'ʎar] *vi* to mew, miaow.

mausoleo [mauso'leo] *nm* mausoleum.

maxilar [maksi'lar] *nm* jaw(bone).

máxima ['maksima] *nf* maxim.

máxime ['maksime] *adv* especially.

máximo, a ['maksimo, a] *adj* maximum; (*más alto*) highest; (*más grande*) greatest ♦ *nm* maximum.

mayo ['majo] *nm* May.

mayonesa [majo'nesa] *nf* mayonnaise.

mayor [ma'jor] *adj* main, chief; (*adulto*) adult; (*de edad avanzada*) elderly; (*MUS*) major; (*compar: de tamaño*) bigger; (: *de edad*) older; (*superl: de tamaño*) biggest; (: *de edad*) oldest ♦ *nm* chief, boss; (*adulto*) adult; **al por ~** wholesale; **~ de edad** adult; **~es** *nmpl*

(*antepasados*) ancestors.

mayoral [majo'ral] *nm* foreman.

mayordomo [major'ðomo] *nm* butler.

mayoría [majo'ria] *nf* majority, greater part.

mayorista [majo'rista] *nm/f* wholesaler.

mayúscula [ma'juskula] *nf* capital letter.

mayúsculo, a [ma'juskulo, a] *adj* (*fig*) big, tremendous.

mazapán [maθa'pan] *nm* marzipan.

mazo ['maθo] *nm* (*martillo*) mallet; (*de flores*) bunch; (*DEPORTE*) bat.

me [me] *pron* (*directo*) me; (*indirecto*) (to) me; (*reflexivo*) (to) myself; ¡**dámelo**! give it to me!

mear [me'ar] (*fam*) *vi* to pee, piss.

mecánica [me'kanika] *nf* (*ESCOL*) mechanics *sg*; (*mecanismo*) mechanism; *ver tb* **mecánico**.

mecánico, a [me'kaniko, a] *adj* mechanical ♦ *nm/f* mechanic.

mecanismo [meka'nismo] *nm* mechanism; (*marcha*) gear.

mecanografía [mekanovra'fia] *nf* typewriting; **mecanógrafo, a** *nm/f* typist.

mecate [me'kate] (*AM*) *nm* rope.

mecedora [meθe'ðora] *nf* rocking chair.

mecer [me'θer] *vt* (*cuna*) to rock; **~se** *vr* to rock; (*ramo*) to sway.

mecha ['metʃa] *nf* (*de vela*) wick; (*de bomba*) fuse.

mechero [me'tʃero] *nm* (cigarette) lighter.

mechón [me'tʃon] *nm* (*gen*) tuft; (*manojo*) bundle; (*de pelo*) lock.

medalla [me'ðaʎa] *nf* medal.

media ['meðja] *nf* (*ESP*) stocking; (*AM*) sock; (*promedio*) average.

mediado, a [me'ðjaðo, a] *adj* half-full; (*trabajo*) half-completed; **a ~s de** in the middle of, halfway through.

mediano, a [me'ðjano, a] *adj* (*regular*) medium, average; (*mediocre*) mediocre.

medianoche [meðja'notʃe] *nf* midnight.

mediante [me'ðjante] *adv* by (means of), through.

mediar [me'ðjar] *vi* (*interceder*) to mediate, intervene.

medicación [meðika'θjon] *nf* medication, treatment.

medicamento [meðika'mento] *nm* medicine, drug.

medicina [meði'θina] *nf* medicine.

medición [meði'θjon] *nf* measurement.

médico, a ['meðiko, a] *adj* medical ♦ *nm/f* doctor.

medida [me'ðiða] *nf* measure; *(medición)* measurement; *(prudencia)* moderation, prudence; **en cierta/gran ~** up to a point/to a great extent; **un traje a la ~** made-to-measure suit; **~ de cuello** collar size; **a ~ de** in proportion to; *(de acuerdo con)* in keeping with; **a ~ que** *(conforme)* as.

medio, a ['meðjo, a] *adj* half (a); *(punto)* mid, middle; *(promedio)* average ♦ *adv* half ♦ *nm (centro)* middle, centre; *(promedio)* average; *(método)* means, way; *(ambiente)* environment; **~s** *nmpl* means, resources; **~ litro** half a litre; **las tres y media** half past three; **M~ Oriente** Middle East; **a ~ terminar** half finished; **pagar a medias** to share the cost.

mediocre [me'ðjokre] *adj* middling, average; *(pey)* mediocre.

mediodía [meðjo'ðia] *nm* midday, noon.

medir [me'ðir] *vt, vi (gen)* to measure.

meditar [meði'tar] *vt* to ponder, think over, meditate on; *(planear)* to think out.

mediterráneo, a [meðite'rraneo, a] *adj* Mediterranean ♦ *nm*: **el M~** the Mediterranean (Sea).

médula ['meðula] *nf (ANAT)* marrow; **~ espinal** spinal cord.

medusa [me'ðusa] *(ESP) nf* jellyfish.

megáfono [me'ɣafono] *nm* megaphone.

megalómano, a [meɣa'lomano, a] *nm/f* megalomaniac.

mejicano, a [mexi'kano, a] *adj, nm/f* Mexican.

Méjico ['mexiko] *nm* Mexico.

mejilla [me'xiʎa] *nf* cheek.

mejillón [mexi'ʎon] *nm* mussel.

mejor [me'xor] *adj, adv (compar)* better; *(superl)* best; **a lo ~** probably; *(quizá)* maybe; **~ dicho** rather; **tanto ~** so much the better.

mejora [me'xora] *nf* improvement;

mejorar *vt* to improve, make better ♦ *vi* to improve, get better; **mejorarse** *vr* to improve, get better.

melancólico, a [melan'koliko, a] *adj (triste)* sad, melancholy; *(soñador)* dreamy.

melena [me'lena] *nf (de persona)* long hair; *(ZOOL)* mane.

melocotón [meloko'ton] *(ESP) nm* peach.

melodía [melo'ðia] *nf* melody, tune.

melodrama [melo'ðrama] *nm* melodrama; **melodramático, a** *adj* melodramatic.

melón [me'lon] *nm* melon.

meloso, a [me'loso, a] *adj* honeyed, sweet.

mellizo, a [me'ʎiθo, a] *adj, nm/f* twin; **~s** *nmpl (AM)* cufflinks.

membrete [mem'brete] *nm* letterhead.

membrillo [mem'briʎo] *nm* quince; **carne de ~** quince jelly.

memorable [memo'raßle] *adj* memorable.

memorándum [memo'randum] *(pl ~s) nm (libro)* notebook; *(comunicación)* memorandum.

memoria [me'morja] *nf (gen)* memory; **~s** *nfpl (de autor)* memoirs; **~ intermedia** *(INFORM)* buffer; **memorizar** *vt* to memorize.

menaje [me'naxe] *nm*: **~ de cocina** kitchenware.

mencionar [menθjo'nar] *vt* to mention.

mendigar [mendi'ɣar] *vt* to beg (for).

mendigo, a [men'diɣo, a] *nm/f* beggar.

mendrugo [men'druɣo] *nm* crust.

menear [mene'ar] *vt* to move; *(fig)* to handle; **~se** *vr* to shake; *(balancearse)* to sway; *(moverse)* to move; *(fig)* to get a move on.

menester [menes'ter] *nm (necesidad)* necessity; **~es** *nmpl (deberes)* duties; **es ~** it is necessary.

menestra [me'nestra] *nf*: **~ de verduras** vegetable stew.

menguante [men'gwante] *adj* decreasing, diminishing.

menguar [men'gwar] *vt* to lessen, diminish; (*fig*) to discredit ♦ *vi* to diminish, decrease; (*fig*) to decline.

menopausia [meno'pausja] *nf* menopause.

menor [me'nor] *adj* (*más pequeño*: *compar*) smaller; (: *superl*) smallest; (*más joven*: *compar*) younger; (: *superl*) youngest; (*MUS*) minor ♦ *nm/f* (*joven*) young person, juvenile; **no tengo la ~ idea** I haven't the faintest idea; **al por ~** retail; **~ de edad** person under age.

Menorca [me'norka] *nf* Minorca.

PALABRA CLAVE

menos [menos] *adj* **1**: **~ (que, de)** (*compar*: *cantidad*) less (than); (: *número*) fewer (than); **con ~ entusiasmo** with less enthusiasm; **~ gente** fewer people; *ver tb* **cada**

2 (*superl*): **es el que ~ culpa tiene** he is the least to blame

♦ *adv* **1** (*compar*): **~ (que, de)** less (than); **me gusta ~ que el otro** I like it less than the other one

2 (*superl*): **es el ~ listo (de su clase)** he's the least bright in his class; **de todas ellas es la que ~ me agrada** out of all of them she's the one I like least; **(por) lo ~** at (the very) least

3 (*locuciones*): **no quiero verle y ~ visitarle** I don't want to see him let alone visit him; **tenemos 7 de ~** we're seven short

♦ *prep* except; (*cifras*) minus; **todos ~ él** everyone except (for) him; **5 ~ 2** 5 minus 2

♦ *conj*: **a ~ que: a ~ que venga mañana** unless he comes tomorrow.

---

menoscabar [menoska'ßar] *vt* (*estropear*) to damage, harm; (*fig*) to discredit.

menospreciar [menospre'θjar] *vt* to underrate, undervalue; (*despreciar*) to scorn, despise.

mensaje [men'saxe] *nm* message; **~ro, a** *nm/f* messenger.

menstruación [menstrua'θjon] *nf* menstruation.

menstruar [mens'trwar] *vi* to menstruate.

mensual [men'swal] *adj* monthly; **1000 ptas ~es** 1000 ptas a month; **~idad** *nf* (*salario*) monthly salary; (*COM*) monthly payment, monthly instalment.

menta ['menta] *nf* mint.

mental [men'tal] *adj* mental; **~idad** *nf* mentality.

mentar [men'tar] *vt* to mention, name.

mente ['mente] *nf* mind.

mentecato, a [mente'kato, a] *adj* silly, stupid ♦ *nm/f* fool, idiot.

mentir [men'tir] *vi* to lie.

mentira [men'tira] *nf* (*una ~*) lie; (*acto*) lying; (*invención*) fiction; **parece ~ que ...** it seems incredible that ..., I can't believe that ....

mentiroso, a [menti'roso, a] *adj* lying ♦ *nm/f* liar.

menú [me'nu] (*pl ~s*) *nm* menu; (*AM*) set meal.

menudo, a [me'nuðo, a] *adj* (*pequeño*) small, tiny; (*sin importancia*) petty, insignificant; **¡~ negocio!** (*fam*) some deal!; **a ~** often, frequently.

meñique [me'ɲike] *nm* little finger.

meollo [me'oʎo] *nm* (*fig*) core.

mercadería [merkaðe'ria] *nf* commodity; **~s** *nfpl* goods, merchandise *sg*.

mercado [mer'kaðo] *nm* market; **M~ Común** Common Market.

mercancía [merkan'θia] *nf* commodity; **~s** *nfpl* goods, merchandise *sg*.

mercantil [merkan'til] *adj* mercantile, commercial.

mercenario, a [merθe'narjo, a] *adj, nm* mercenary.

mercería [merθe'ria] *nf* haberdashery (*BRIT*), notions (*US*); (*tienda*) haberdasher's (*BRIT*), notions store (*US*); (*AM*) drapery.

mercurio [mer'kurjo] *nm* mercury.

merecer [mere'θer] *vt* to deserve, merit ♦ *vi* to be deserving, be worthy; **merece la pena** it's worthwhile; **merecido, a** *adj* (well) deserved; **llevar su merecido** to get one's deserts.

merendar [meren'dar] *vt* to have for tea ♦ *vi* to have tea; (*en el campo*) to have a picnic.

merengue [me'renge] *nm* meringue.

meridiano [meri'ðjano] *nm* (*GEO*) meridian.

merienda [me'rjenda] *nf* (light) tea, afternoon snack; (*de campo*) picnic.

mérito ['merito] *nm* merit; (*valor*) worth, value.

merluza [mer'luθa] *nf* hake.

merma ['merma] *nf* decrease; (*pérdida*) wastage; **mermar** *vt* to reduce, lessen ♦ *vi* to decrease, dwindle.

mermelada [merme'laða] *nf* jam.

mero, a ['mero, a] *adj* mere; (*AM: fam*) very.

mes [mes] *nm* month; (*salario*) month's pay.

mesa ['mesa] *nf* table; (*de trabajo*) desk; (*GEO*) plateau; (*ARQ*) landing; ~ **directiva** board; ~ **redonda** (*reunión*) round table; **poner/quitar la** ~ to lay/clear the table; **mesero, a** (*AM*) *nm/f* waiter/waitress.

meseta [me'seta] *nf* (*GEO*) meseta, tableland; (*ARQ*) landing.

mesilla [me'siʎa] *nf*: ~ **(de noche)** bedside table.

mesita [me'sita] *nf* = **mesilla**.

mesón [me'son] *nm* inn.

mestizo, a [mes'tiθo, a] *adj* half-caste, of mixed race; (*ZOOL*) crossbred ♦ *nm/f* half-caste.

mesura [me'sura] *nf* (*moderación*) moderation, restraint; (*cortesía*) courtesy.

meta ['meta] *nf* goal; (*de carrera*) finish.

metáfora [me'tafora] *nf* metaphor.

metal [me'tal] *nm* (*materia*) metal; (*MUS*) brass; **metálico, a** *adj* metallic; (*de metal*) metal ♦ *nm* (*dinero contante*) cash.

metalurgia [meta'lurxja] *nf* metallurgy.

meteoro [mete'oro] *nm* meteor.

meter [me'ter] *vt* (*colocar*) to put, place; (*introducir*) to put in, insert; (*involucrar*) to involve; (*causar*) to make, cause; ~**se** *vr*: ~**se en** to go into, enter; (*fig*) to interfere in, meddle in; ~**se a** to start; ~**se a escritor** to become a writer; ~**se con uno** to provoke sb, pick a quarrel with sb.

meticuloso, a [metiku'loso, a] *adj* meticulous, thorough.

metódico, a [me'toðiko, a] *adj* methodical.

metodismo [meto'ðismo] *nm* Methodism.

método ['metoðo] *nm* method.

metralleta [metra'ʎeta] *nf* sub-machine-gun.

métrico, a ['metriko, a] *adj* metric.

metro ['metro] *nm* metre; (*tren*) underground (*BRIT*), subway (*US*).

México ['mexiko] *nm* Mexico; **Ciudad de** ~ Mexico City.

mezcla [me'θkla] *nf* mixture; **mezclar** *vt* to mix (up); **mezclarse** *vr* to mix, mingle; **mezclarse en** to get mixed up in, get involved in.

mezquino, a [meθ'kino, a] *adj* (*cicatero*) mean.

mezquita [meθ'kita] *nf* mosque.

mg. *abr* (= *miligramo*) mg.

mi [mi] *adj pos* my ♦ *nm* (*MUS*) E.

mí [mi] *pron* me; myself.

mía ['mia] *pron ver* **mío**.

miaja ['mjaxa] *nf* crumb.

micro ['mikro] (*AM*) *nm* minibus.

microbio [mi'kroβjo] *nm* microbe.

microbús [mikro'βus] *nm* minibus.

micrófono [mi'krofono] *nm* microphone.

microordenador [mikro(o)rðena'ðor] *nm* microcomputer.

microscopio [mikro'skopjo] *nm* microscope.

miedo ['mjeðo] *nm* fear; (*nerviosismo*) apprehension, nervousness; **tener** ~ to be afraid; **de** ~ wonderful, marvellous; **hace un frío de** ~ (*fam*) it's terribly cold; ~**so, a** *adj* fearful, timid.

miel [mjel] *nf* honey.

miembro ['mjembro] *nm* limb; (*socio*) member; ~ **viril** penis.

mientras ['mjentras] *conj* while; (*duración*) as long as ♦ *adv* meanwhile; ~ **tanto** meanwhile; ~ **más tiene, más quiere** the more he has, the more he wants.

miércoles ['mjerkoles] *nm inv* Wednesday.

mierda ['mjerða] (*fam!*) *nf* shit (*!*).

miga ['miɣa] *nf* crumb; (*fig: meollo*) essence; **hacer buenas ~s** (*fam*) to get on well.

migración [miɣra'θjon] *nf* migration.

mil [mil] *num* thousand; **dos ~ libras** two thousand pounds.

milagro [mi'laɣro] *nm* miracle; **~so, a** *adj* miraculous.

mili ['mili] (*fam*) *nf*: **hacer la ~** to do one's military service.

milicia [mi'liθja] *nf* militia; (*servicio militar*) military service.

milímetro [mi'limetro] *nm* millimetre.

militante [mili'tante] *adj* militant.

militar [mili'tar] *adj* military ♦ *nm/f* soldier ♦ *vi* to serve in the army; (*fig*) to be a member of a party.

milla ['miʎa] *nf* mile.

millar [mi'ʎar] *nm* thousand.

millón [mi'ʎon] *num* million; **millonario, a** *nm/f* millionaire.

mimar [mi'mar] *vt* (*gen*) to spoil, pamper.

mimbre ['mimbre] *nm* wicker.

mímica ['mimika] *nf* (*para comunicarse*) sign language; (*imitación*) mimicry.

mimo ['mimo] *nm* (*caricia*) caress; (*de niño*) spoiling; (*TEATRO*) mime; (: *actor*) mime artist.

mina ['mina] *nf* mine; **minar** *vt* to mine; (*fig*) to undermine.

mineral [mine'ral] *adj* mineral ♦ *nm* (*GEO*) mineral; (*mena*) ore.

minero, a [mi'nero, a] *adj* mining *cpd* ♦ *nm/f* miner.

miniatura [minja'tura] *adj inv*, *nf* miniature.

minifalda [mini'falda] *nf* miniskirt.

mínimo, a ['minimo, a] *adj*, *nm* minimum.

minino, a [mi'nino, a] (*fam*) *nm/f* puss, pussy.

ministerio [minis'terjo] *nm* Ministry; **M~ de Hacienda/del Exterior** Treasury (*BRIT*), Treasury Department (*US*)/Foreign Office (*BRIT*), State Department (*US*).

ministro, a [mi'nistro, a] *nm/f* minister.

minoría [mino'ria] *nf* minority.

minucioso, a [minu'θjoso, a] *adj* thorough, meticulous; (*prolijo*) very detailed.

minúscula [mi'nuskula] *nf* small letter.

minúsculo, a [mi'nuskulo, a] *adj* tiny, minute.

minusválido, a [minus'βaliðo, a] *adj* (physically) handicapped ♦ *nm/f* (physically) handicapped person.

minuta [mi'nuta] *nf* (*de comida*) menu.

minutero [minu'tero] *nm* minute hand.

minuto [mi'nuto] *nm* minute.

mío, a ['mio, a] *pron*: **el ~/la mía** mine; **un amigo ~** a friend of mine; **lo ~** what is mine.

miope [mi'ope] *adj* short-sighted.

mira ['mira] *nf* (*de arma*) sight(s) (*pl*); (*fig*) aim, intention.

mirada [mi'raða] *nf* look, glance; (*expresión*) look, expression; **clavar la ~ en** to stare at; **echar una ~ a** to glance at.

mirado, a [mi'raðo, a] *adj* (*sensato*) sensible; (*considerado*) considerate; **bien/mal ~** well/not well thought of; **bien ~** all things considered.

mirador [mira'ðor] *nm* viewpoint, vantage point.

mirar [mi'rar] *vt* to look at; (*observar*) to watch; (*considerar*) to consider, think over; (*vigilar, cuidar*) to watch, look after ♦ *vi* to look; (*ARQ*) to face; **~se** *vr* (*dos personas*) to look at each other; **~ bien/mal** to think highly of/have a poor opinion of; **~se al espejo** to look at o.s. in the mirror.

mirilla [mi'riʎa] *nf* (*agujero*) spyhole, peephole.

mirlo ['mirlo] *nm* blackbird.

misa ['misa] *nf* (*REL*) mass.

miserable [mise'raßle] *adj* (*avaro*) mean, stingy; (*nimio*) miserable, paltry; (*lugar*) squalid; (*fam*) vile, despicable ♦ *nm/f* (*malvado*) rogue.

miseria [mi'serja] *nf* misery; (*pobreza*) poverty; (*tacañería*) meanness, stinginess; (*condiciones*) squalor; **una ~** a pittance.

misericordia [miseri'korðja] *nf* (*compa-*

sión) compassion, pity; (*piedad*) mercy.

misil [mi'sil] *nm* missile.

misión [mi'sjon] *nf* mission; **misionero, a** *nm/f* missionary.

mismo, a ['mismo, a] *adj* (*semejante*) same; (*después de pron*) -self; (*para enfásis*) very ♦ *adv*: **aquí/hoy** ~ right here/this very day; **ahora** ~ right now ♦ *conj*: **lo** ~ **que** just like, just as; **el** ~ **traje** the same suit; **en ese** ~ **momento** at that very moment; **vino el** ~ **Ministro** the minister himself came; **yo** ~ **lo vi** I saw it myself; **lo** ~ the same (thing); **da lo** ~ it's all the same; **quedamos en las mismas** we're no further forward; **por lo** ~ for the same reason.

misterio [mis'terjo] *nm* (*gen*) mystery; (*lo secreto*) secrecy; ~**so, a** *adj* mysterious.

mitad [mi'tað] *nf* (*medio*) half; (*centro*) middle; **a** ~ **de precio** (at) half-price; **en** *o* **a** ~ **del camino** halfway along the road; **cortar por la** ~ to cut through the middle.

mitigar [miti'ɣar] *vt* to mitigate; (*dolor*) to ease; (*sed*) to quench.

mitin ['mitin] (*pl* **mítines**) *nm* meeting.

mito ['mito] *nm* myth.

mixto, a ['miksto, a] *adj* mixed.

ml. *abr* (= *mililitro*) ml.

mm. *abr* (= *milímetro*) mm.

mobiliario [moßi'ljarjo] *nm* furniture.

moción [mo'θjon] *nf* motion.

moco ['moko] *nm* mucus; ~**s** *nmpl* (*fam*) snot; **quitarse los** ~**s de la nariz** (*fam*) to wipe one's nose.

mochila [mo'tʃila] *nf* rucksack (*BRIT*), back-pack.

moda ['moða] *nf* fashion; (*estilo*) style; **de** *o* **a la** ~ in fashion, fashionable; **pasado de** ~ out of fashion.

modales [mo'ðales] *nmpl* manners.

modalidad [moðali'ðað] *nf* kind, variety.

modelar [moðe'lar] *vt* to model.

modelo [mo'ðelo] *adj inv, nm/f* model.

moderado, a [moðe'raðo, a] *adj* moderate.

moderar [moðe'rar] *vt* to moderate;

(*violencia*) to restrain, control; (*velocidad*) to reduce; ~**se** *vr* to restrain o.s., control o.s.

modernizar [moðerni'θar] *vt* to modernize.

moderno, a [mo'ðerno, a] *adj* modern; (*actual*) present-day.

modestia [mo'ðestja] *nf* modesty; **modesto, a** *adj* modest.

módico, a ['moðiko, a] *adj* moderate, reasonable.

modificar [moðifi'kar] *vt* to modify.

modista [mo'ðista] *nm/f* dressmaker.

modo ['moðo] *nm* (*manera, forma*) way, manner; (*MUS*) mode; ~**s** *nmpl* manners; **de ningún** ~ in no way; **de todos** ~**s** at any rate; ~ **de empleo** directions *pl* (for use).

modorra [mo'ðorra] *nf* drowsiness.

modular [moðu'lar] *vt* to modulate.

mofa ['mofa] *nf*: **hacer** ~ **de** to mock; **mofarse** *vr*: **mofarse de** to mock, scoff at.

moho ['moo] *nm* (*BOT*) mould, mildew; (*en metal*) rust; ~**so, a** *adj* mouldy; rusty.

mojar [mo'xar] *vt* to wet; (*humedecer*) to damp(en), moisten; (*calar*) to soak; ~**se** *vr* to get wet.

mojón [mo'xon] *nm* boundary stone.

molde ['molde] *nm* mould; (*COSTURA*) pattern; (*fig*) model; ~**ar** *vt* to mould.

mole ['mole] *nf* mass, bulk; (*edificio*) pile.

moler [mo'ler] *vt* to grind, crush; (*cansar*) to tire out, exhaust.

molestar [moles'tar] *vt* to bother; (*fastidiar*) to annoy; (*incomodar*) to inconvenience, put out ♦ *vi* to be a nuisance; ~**se** *vr* to bother; (*incomodarse*) to go to trouble; (*ofenderse*) to take offence.

molestia [mo'lestja] *nf* bother, trouble; (*incomodidad*) inconvenience; (*MED*) discomfort; **es una** ~ it's a nuisance; **molesto, a** *adj* (*que fastidia*) annoying; (*incómodo*) inconvenient; (*inquieto*) uncomfortable, ill at ease; (*enfadado*) annoyed.

molinillo [moli'niʎo] *nm*: ~ **de carne/**

café mincer/coffee grinder.

molino [mo'lino] *nm* (*edificio*) mill; (*máquina*) grinder.

momentáneo, a [momen'taneo, a] *adj* momentary.

momento [mo'mento] *nm* (*gen*) moment; (*TEC*) momentum; **de ~** at the moment, for the moment.

momia ['momja] *nf* mummy.

monarca [mo'narka] *nm/f* monarch, ruler; **monarquía** *nf* monarchy; **monárquico, a** *nm/f* royalist, monarchist.

monasterio [monas'terjo] *nm* monastery.

mondadientes [monda'ðjentes] *nm inv* toothpick.

mondar [mon'dar] *vt* (*limpiar*) to clean; (*pelar*) to peel; **~se** *vr*: **~se de risa** (*fam*) to split one's sides laughing.

moneda [mo'neða] *nf* (*tipo de dinero*) currency, money; (*pieza*) coin; **una ~ de 5 pesetas** a 5 peseta piece; **monedero** *nm* purse; **monetario, a** *adj* monetary, financial.

monja ['monxa] *nf* nun.

monje ['monxe] *nm* monk.

mono, a ['mono, a] *adj* (*bonito*) lovely, pretty; (*gracioso*) nice, charming ♦ *nm/f* monkey, ape ♦ *nm* dungarees *pl*; (*overoles*) overalls *pl*.

monopatín [monopa'tin] *nm* skateboard.

monopolio [mono'poljo] *nm* monopoly; **monopolizar** *vt* to monopolize.

monotonía [monoto'nia] *nf* (*sonido*) monotone; (*fig*) monotony.

monótono, a [mo'notono, a] *adj* monotonous.

monstruo ['monstrwo] *nm* monster ♦ *adj inv* fantastic; **~so, a** *adj* monstrous.

monta ['monta] *nf* total, sum; **de poca ~** unimportant, of little account.

montaje [mon'taxe] *nm* assembly; (*TEATRO*) décor; (*CINE*) montage.

montaña [mon'tana] *nf* (*monte*) mountain; (*sierra*) mountains *pl*, mountainous area; (*AM: selva*) forest; **~ rusa** roller coaster; **montañero, a**

nm/f mountaineer; **montañés, esa** *adj* mountain *cpd* ♦ *nm/f* highlander; **montañismo** *nm* mountaineering.

montar [mon'tar] *vt* (*subir a*) to mount, get on; (*TEC*) to assemble, put together; (*negocio*) to set up; (*arma*) to cock; (*colocar*) to lift on to; (*CULIN*) to beat ♦ *vi* to mount, get on; (*sobresalir*) to overlap; **~ en cólera** to get angry; **~ a caballo** to ride, go horseriding.

montaraz [monta'raθ] *adj* mountain *cpd*, highland *cpd*; (*salvaje*) wild, untamed; (*pey*) uncivilized.

monte ['monte] *nm* (*montaña*) mountain; (*bosque*) woodland; (*área sin cultivar*) wild area, wild country; **M~ de Piedad** pawnshop.

Montevideo [monteßi'ðeo] *n* Montevideo.

monto ['monto] *nm* total, amount.

montón [mon'ton] *nm* heap, pile; (*fig*): **un ~ de** heaps of, lots of.

monumento [monu'mento] *nm* monument.

monzón [mon'θon] *nm* monsoon.

moño ['mono] *nm* bun.

mora ['mora] *nf* blackberry; *ver tb* **moro**.

morada [mo'raða] *nf* (*casa*) dwelling, abode.

morado, a [mo'raðo, a] *adj* purple, violet ♦ *nm* bruise.

moral [mo'ral] *adj* moral ♦ *nf* (*ética*) ethics *pl*; (*moralidad*) morals *pl*, morality; (*ánimo*) morale.

moraleja [mora'lexa] *nf* moral.

moralizar [morali'θar] *vt* to moralize.

morboso, a [mor'ßoso, a] *adj* morbid.

morcilla [mor'θiʎa] *nf* blood sausage, ≈ black pudding (*BRIT*).

mordaz [mor'ðaθ] *adj* (*crítica*) biting, scathing.

mordaza [mor'ðaθa] *nf* (*para la boca*) gag; (*TEC*) clamp.

morder [mor'ðer] *vt* to bite; (*mordisquear*) to nibble; (*fig: consumir*) to eat away, eat into; **mordisco** *nm* bite.

moreno, a [mo'reno, a] *adj* (*color*)

(dark) brown; (*de tez*) dark; (*de pelo*
~) dark-haired; (*negro*) black.
moretón [more'ton] (*fam*) *nm* bruise.
morfina [mor'fina] *nf* morphine.
moribundo, a [mori'ßundo, a] *adj*
dying.
morir [mo'rir] *vi* to die; (*fuego*) to die
down; (*luz*) to go out; ~**se** *vr* to die;
(*fig*) to be dying; **fue muerto en un
accidente** he was killed in an accident;
~**se por algo** to be dying for sth.
moro, a ['moro, a] *adj* Moorish ♦ *nm/f*
Moor.
moroso, a [mo'roso, a] *nm/f* (*COM*) bad
debtor, defaulter.
morral [mo'rral] *nm* haversack.
morro ['morro] *nm* (*ZOOL*) snout, nose;
(*AUTO, AVIAT*) nose.
morsa ['morsa] *nf* walrus.
mortaja [mor'taxa] *nf* shroud.
mortal [mor'tal] *adj* mortal; (*golpe*)
deadly; ~**idad** *nf* mortality; **mortandad**
nf mortality.
mortero [mor'tero] *nm* mortar.
mortífero, a [mor'tifero, a] *adj* deadly,
lethal.
mortificar [mortifi'kar] *vt* to mortify.
mosca ['moska] *nf* fly.
Moscú [mos'ku] *n* Moscow.
mosquearse [moske'arse] (*fam*) *vr*
(*enojarse*) to get cross; (*ofenderse*) to
take offence.
mosquitero [moski'tero] *nm* mosquito
net.
mosquito [mos'kito] *nm* mosquito.
mostaza [mos'taθa] *nf* mustard.
mostrador [mostra'ðor] *nm* (*de tienda*)
counter; (*de café*) bar.
mostrar [mos'trar] *vt* to show; (*exhibir*)
to display, exhibit; (*explicar*) to
explain; ~**se** *vr*: ~**se amable** to be
kind; to prove to be kind; **no se muestra muy inteligente** he doesn't seem (to
be) very intelligent.
mota ['mota] *nf* speck, tiny piece; (*en
diseño*) dot.
mote ['mote] *nm* (*apodo*) nickname.
motín [mo'tin] *nm* (*del pueblo*) revolt,
rising; (*del ejército*) mutiny.
motivar [moti'ßar] *vt* (*causar*) to cause,

motivate; (*explicar*) to explain, justify;
motivo *nm* motive, reason.
moto ['moto] (*fam*) *nf* = motocicleta.
motocicleta [motoθi'kleta] *nf* motorbike
(*BRIT*), motorcycle.
motor [mo'tor] *nm* motor, engine; ~ **a
chorro** *o* **de reacción/de explosión** jet
engine/internal combustion engine.
motora [mo'tora] *nf* motorboat.
motorbote [motor'ßote] *nm* = motora.
motosierra [moto'sjerra] *nf* mechanical
saw.
movedizo, a [moße'ðiθo, a] *adj* (*inseguro*) unsteady; (*fig*) unsettled,
changeable; (*persona*) fickle.
mover [mo'ßer] *vt* to move; (*cabeza*) to
shake; (*accionar*) to drive; (*fig*) to
cause, provoke; ~**se** *vr* to move; (*fig*)
to get a move on.
móvil ['moßil] *adj* mobile; (*pieza de
máquina*) moving; (*mueble*) movable ♦
nm motive; **movilidad** *nf* mobility;
movilizar *vt* to mobilize.
movimiento [moßi'mjento] *nm* movement; (*TEC*) motion; (*actividad*)
activity.
mozo, a ['moθo, a] *adj* (*joven*) young ♦
nm/f (*joven*) youth, young man/girl;
(*camarero*) waiter; (*camarera*) waitress.
muchacho, a [mu'tʃatʃo, a] *nm/f* (*niño*)
boy/girl; (*criado*) servant; (*criada*)
maid.
muchedumbre [mutʃe'ðumbre] *nf*
crowd.

PALABRA CLAVE

---

mucho, a ['mutʃo, a] *adj* **1** (*cantidad*) a
lot of, much; (*número*) lots of, a lot of,
many; ~ **dinero** a lot of money; **hace** ~
calor it's very hot; **muchas amigas** lots
o a lot of friends
2 (*sg*: *grande*): **ésta es mucha casa
para él** this house is much too big for
him
♦ *pron*: **tengo** ~ **que hacer** I've got a
lot to do; ~**s dicen que** ... a lot of
people say that ...; *ver tb* **tener**
♦ *adv* **1**: **me gusta** ~ I like it a lot; **lo
siento** ~ I'm very sorry; **come** ~ he

eats a lot; ¿**te vas a quedar** ~? are you going to be staying long?
2 (*respuesta*) very; ¿**estás cansado?** – ¡~! are you tired? – very!
3 (*locuciones*): **como** ~ at (the) most; **con** ~: **el mejor con** ~ by far the best; **ni** ~ **menos: no es rico ni** ~ **menos** he's far from being rich
4: **por** ~ **que: por** ~ **que le creas** no matter how *o* however much you believe her.

muda ['muða] *nf* change of clothes.
mudanza [mu'ðanθa] *nf* (*cambio*) change; (*de casa*) move.
mudar [mu'ðar] *vt* to change; (*ZOOL*) to shed ♦ *vi* to change; ~**se** *vr* (*la ropa*) to change; ~**se de casa** to move house.
mudo, a ['muðo, a] *adj* dumb; (*callado, CINE*) silent.
mueble ['mweßle] *nm* piece of furniture; ~**s** *nmpl* furniture *sg*.
mueca ['mweka] *nf* face, grimace; **hacer** ~**s a** to make faces at.
muela ['mwela] *nf* (*diente*) tooth; (: *de atrás*) molar.
muelle ['mweʎe] *nm* spring; (*NAUT*) wharf; (*malecón*) pier.
muero *etc vb ver* **morir**.
muerte ['mwerte] *nf* death; (*homicidio*) murder; **dar** ~ **a** to kill.
muerto, a ['mwerto, a] *pp de* **morir** ♦ *adj* dead; (*color*) dull ♦ *nm/f* dead man/woman; (*difunto*) deceased; (*cadáver*) corpse; **estar** ~ **de cansancio** to be dead tired.
muestra ['mwestra] *nf* (*señal*) indication, sign; (*demostración*) demonstration; (*prueba*) proof; (*estadística*) sample; (*modelo*) model, pattern; (*testimonio*) token.
muestreo [mwes'treo] *nm* sample, sampling.
muestro *etc vb ver* **mostrar**.
muevo *etc vb ver* **mover**.
mugir [mu'xir] *vi* (*vaca*) to moo.
mugre ['muxre] *nf* dirt, filth; **mugriento, a** *adj* dirty, filthy.
mujer [mu'xer] *nf* woman; (*esposa*) wife; ~**iego** *nm* womanizer.

mula ['mula] *nf* mule.
mulato, a [mu'lato, a] *adj*, *nm/f* mulatto.
muleta [mu'leta] *nf* (*para andar*) crutch; (*TAUROMAQUIA*) *stick with red cape attached*.
multa ['multa] *nf* fine; **poner una** ~ **a** to fine; **multar** *vt* to fine.
multicopista [multiko'pista] *nm* duplicator.
múltiple ['multiple] *adj* multiple; (*pl*) many, numerous.
multiplicar [multipli'kar] *vt* (*MAT*) to multiply; (*fig*) to increase; ~**se** *vr* (*BIO*) to multiply; (*fig*) to be everywhere at once.
multitud [multi'tuð] *nf* (*muchedumbre*) crowd; ~ **de** lots of.
mullido, a [mu'ʎiðo, a] *adj* (*cama*) soft; (*hierba*) soft, springy.
mundano, a [mun'dano, a] *adj* worldly; (*de moda*) fashionable.
mundial [mun'djal] *adj* world-wide, universal; (*guerra, récord*) world *cpd*.
mundo ['mundo] *nm* world; **todo el** ~ everybody; **tener** ~ to be experienced, know one's way around.
munición [muni'θjon] *nf* (*MIL*: *provisiones*) stores *pl*, supplies *pl*; (: *balas*) ammunition.
municipio [muni'θipjo] *nm* (*ayuntamiento*) town council, corporation; (*territorio administrativo*) town, municipality.
muñeca [mu'ɲeka] *nf* (*ANAT*) wrist; (*juguete*) doll.
muñeco [mu'ɲeko] *nm* (*figura*) figure; (*marioneta*) puppet; (*fig*) puppet, pawn.
mural [mu'ral] *adj* mural, wall *cpd* ♦ *nm* mural.
muralla [mu'raʎa] *nf* (city) wall(s) (*pl*).
murciélago [mur'θjelaxo] *nm* bat.
murmullo [mur'muʎo] *nm* murmur(ing); (*cuchicheo*) whispering; (*de arroyo*) murmur, rippling.
murmuración [murmura'θjon] *nf* gossip; **murmurar** *vi* to murmur, whisper; (*criticar*) to criticize; (*cotillear*) to gossip.
muro ['muro] *nm* wall.

muscular [musku'lar] *adj* muscular.
músculo ['muskulo] *nm* muscle.
museo [mu'seo] *nm* museum.
musgo ['musyo] *nm* moss.
música ['musika] *nf* music; *ver tb* **músico**.
músico, a ['musiko, a] *adj* musical ♦ *nm/f* musician.
musitar [musi'tar] *vt, vi* to mutter, mumble.
muslo ['muslo] *nm* thigh.
mustio, a ['mustjo, a] *adj* (*persona*) depressed, gloomy; (*planta*) faded, withered.
musulmán, ana [musul'man, ana] *nm/f* Moslem.
mutación [muta'θjon] *nf* (*BIO*) mutation; (: *cambio*) (sudden) change.
mutilar [muti'lar] *vt* to mutilate; (*a una persona*) to maim.
mutuamente [mutwa'mente] *adv* mutually.
mutuo, a ['mutwo, a] *adj* mutual.
muy [mwi] *adv* very; (*demasiado*) too; M~ Señor mío Dear Sir; ~ de noche very late at night; eso es ~ de él that's just like him.

N

N *abr* (= *norte*) N.
n/ *abr* = **nuestro, a**.
nabo ['naßo] *nm* turnip.
nácar ['nakar] *nm* mother-of-pearl.
nacer [na'θer] *vi* to be born; (*de huevo*) to hatch; (*vegetal*) to sprout; (*río*) to rise; **nací en Barcelona** I was born in Barcelona; **nació una sospecha en su mente** a suspicion formed in her mind; **nacido, a** *adj* born; **recién nacido** newborn; **naciente** *adj* new, emerging; (*sol*) rising; **nacimiento** *nm* birth; (*fig*) birth, origin; (*de Navidad*) Nativity; (*linaje*) descent, family; (*de río*) source.
nación [na'θjon] *nf* nation; **nacional** *adj* national; **nacionalismo** *nm* nationalism; **nacionalista** *nm/f* nationalist; **nacionalizar** *vt* to nationalize; **naciona-**lizarse *vr* (*persona*) to become naturalized.
nada ['naða] *pron* nothing ♦ *adv* not at all, in no way; **no decir** ~ to say nothing, not to say anything; ~ **más** nothing else; **de** ~ don't mention it.
nadador, a [naða'ðor, a] *nm/f* swimmer.
nadar [na'ðar] *vi* to swim.
nadie ['naðje] *pron* nobody, no-one; ~ **habló** nobody spoke; **no había** ~ there was nobody there, there wasn't anybody there.
nado ['naðo]: **a** ~ *adv*: **pasar a** ~ to swim across.
nafta ['nafta] (*AM*) *nf* petrol (*BRIT*), gas (*US*).
naipe ['naipe] *nm* (playing) card; ~**s** *nmpl* cards.
nalgas ['nalyas] *nfpl* buttocks.
nana ['nana] *nf* lullaby.
naranja [na'ranxa] *adj inv, nf* orange; **media** ~ (*fam*) better half; **naranjada** *nf* orangeade; **naranjo** *nm* orange tree.
narciso [nar'θiso] *nm* narcissus.
narcótico, a [nar'kotiko, a] *adj, nm* narcotic; **narcotizar** *vt* to drug.
nardo ['narðo] *nm* lily.
narigón, ona, [nari'ɣon, ona] *adj* big-nosed.
narigudo, a [nari'ɣuðo, a] *adj* = **narigón**.
nariz [na'riθ] *nf* nose; **narices** *nfpl* nostrils; **delante de las narices de uno** under one's (very) nose.
narración [narra'θjon] *nf* narration; **narrador, a** *nm/f* narrator.
narrar [na'rrar] *vt* to narrate, recount; **narrativa** *nf* narrative, story.
nata ['nata] *nf* cream.
natación [nata'θjon] *nf* swimming.
natal [na'tal] *adj*: **ciudad** ~ home town; ~**icio** *nm* birthday; ~**idad** *nf* birth rate.
natillas [na'tiʎas] *nfpl* custard *sg*.
natividad [natißi'ðað] *nf* nativity.
nativo, a [na'tiβo, a] *adj, nm/f* native.
nato, a ['nato, a] *adj* born; **un músico** ~ a born musician.
natural [natu'ral] *adj* natural; (*fruta etc*) fresh ♦ *nm/f* native ♦ *nm* (*disposición*) nature.

naturaleza [natura'leθa] *nf* nature; *(género)* nature, kind; ~ **muerta** still life.

naturalidad [naturali'ðað] *nf* naturalness.

naturalización [naturaliθa'θjon] *nf* naturalization.

naturalizarse [naturali'θarse] *vr* to become naturalized; *(aclimatarse)* to become acclimatized.

naturalmente [natural'mente] *adv (de modo natural)* in a natural way; ¡~! of course!

naufragar [naufra'ɣar] *vi* to sink; **naufragio** *nm* shipwreck; **náufrago, a** *nm/f* castaway, shipwrecked person.

nauseabundo, a [nausea'ßundo, a] *adj* nauseating, sickening.

náuseas ['nauseas] *nfpl* nausea; **me da** ~ it makes me feel sick.

náutico, a ['nautiko, a] *adj* nautical.

navaja [na'ßaxa] *nf (cortaplumas)* clasp knife *(BRIT)*, penknife; *(de barbero, peluquero)* razor.

Navarra [na'ßarra] *n* Navarre.

nave ['naße] *nf (barco)* ship, vessel; *(ARQ)* nave; ~ **espacial** spaceship.

navegación [naßeɣa'θjon] *nf* navigation; *(viaje)* sea journey; ~ **aérea** air traffic; ~ **costera** coastal shipping; **navegante** *nm/f* navigator; **navegar** *vi (barco)* to sail; *(avión)* to fly ♦ *vt* to sail; to fly; *(dirigir el rumbo)* to navigate.

navidad [naßi'ðað] *nf* Christmas; ~**es** *nfpl* Christmas time; **navideño, a** *adj* Christmas *cpd*.

navío [na'ßio] *nm* ship.

nazca *etc vb ver* **nacer**.

nazi ['naθi] *adj, nm/f* Nazi.

NE *abr (= nor(d)este)* NE.

neblina [ne'ßlina] *nf* mist.

nebuloso, a [neßu'loso, a] *adj* foggy; *(calinoso)* misty; *(indefinido)* nebulous, vague ♦ *nf* nebula.

necedad [neθe'ðað] *nf* foolishness; *(una ~)* foolish act.

necesario, a [neθe'sarjo, a] *adj* necessary.

neceser [neθe'ser] *nm* toilet bag; *(bolsa grande)* holdall.

necesidad [neθesi'ðað] *nf* need; *(lo in-*

evitable) necessity; *(miseria)* poverty, need; **en caso de** ~ in case of need *o* emergency; **hacer sus** ~**es** to relieve o.s.

necesitado, a [neθesi'taðo, a] *adj* needy, poor; ~ **de** in need of.

necesitar [neθesi'tar] *vt* to need, require ♦ *vi:* ~ **de** to have need of.

necio, a ['neθjo, a] *adj* foolish.

necrología [nekrolo'xia] *nf* obituary.

necrópolis [ne'kropolis] *nf inv* cemetery.

nectarina [nekta'rina] *nf* nectarine.

nefasto, a [ne'fasto, a] *adj* ill-fated, unlucky.

negación [neɣa'θjon] *nf* negation; *(rechazo)* refusal, denial.

negar [ne'ɣar] *vt (renegar, rechazar)* to refuse; *(prohibir)* to refuse, deny; *(desmentir)* to deny; ~**se** *vr:* ~**se a** to refuse to.

negativa [neɣa'tißa] *nf* negative; *(rechazo)* refusal, denial.

negativo, a [neɣa'tißo, a] *adj, nm* negative.

negligencia [neɣli'xenθja] *nf* negligence; **negligente** *adj* negligent.

negociable [neɣo'θjaßle] *adj (COM)* negotiable.

negociado [neɣo'θjaðo] *nm* department, section.

negociante [neɣo'θjante] *nm/f* businessman/woman.

negociar [neɣo'θjar] *vt, vi* to negotiate; ~ **en** to deal in, trade in.

negocio [ne'ɣoθjo] *nm (COM)* business; *(asunto)* affair, business; *(operación comercial)* deal, transaction; *(AM)* firm; *(lugar)* place of business; **los** ~**s** business *sg*; **hacer** ~ to do business.

negra ['neɣra] *nf (MUS)* crotchet; *ver tb* **negro**.

negro, a ['neɣro, a] *adj* black; *(suerte)* awful ♦ *nm* black ♦ *nm/f* Negro/ Negress, Black; **negrura** *nf* blackness.

nene, a ['nene, a] *nm/f* baby, small child.

nenúfar [ne'nufar] *nm* water lily.

neologismo [neolo'xismo] *nm* neologism.

neoyorquino, a [neojor'kino, a] *adj (of)*

New York.

nepotismo [nepo'tismo] *nm* nepotism.

nervio ['nerβjo] *nm* (*ANAT*) nerve; (: *tendón*) tendon; (*fig*) vigour; **nerviosismo** *nm* nervousness, nerves *pl*; ~**so, a** *adj* nervous; **nervudo, a** *adj* (*persona*) wiry; (*brazo, mano*) veiny.

neto, a ['neto, a] *adj* clear; (*limpio*) clean; (*COM*) net.

neumático, a [neu'matiko, a] *adj* pneumatic ♦ *nm* (*ESP*) tyre (*BRIT*), tire (*US*); ~ **de recambio** spare tyre.

neurasténico, a [neuras'teniko, a] *adj* (*fig*) hysterical.

neurólogo, a [neu'roloγo, a] *nm/f* neurologist.

neutral [neu'tral] *adj* neutral; ~**izar** *vt* to neutralize; (*contrarrestar*) to counteract.

neutro, a ['neutro, a] *adj* (*BIO, LING*) neuter.

neutrón [neu'tron] *nm* neutron.

nevada [ne'βaða] *nf* snowstorm; (*caída de nieve*) snowfall.

nevar [ne'βar] *vi* to snow.

nevera [ne'βera] (*ESP*) *nf* refrigerator (*BRIT*), icebox (*US*).

nevería [neβe'ria] (*AM*) *nf* ice-cream parlour.

nevisca [ne'βiska] *nf* flurry of snow.

nexo ['nekso] *nm* link, connection.

ni [ni] *conj* nor, neither; (*tb*: ~ **siquiera**) not ... even; ~ **que** not even if; ~ **blanco** ~ **negro** neither white nor black.

Nicaragua [nika'rawwa] *nf* Nicaragua; **nicaragüense** *adj, nm/f* Nicaraguan.

nicotina [niko'tina] *nf* nicotine.

nicho ['nitʃo] *nm* niche.

nido ['niðo] *nm* nest; (*fig*) hiding place.

niebla ['njeβla] *nf* fog; (*neblina*) mist.

niego *etc vb ver* **negar**.

nieto, a ['njeto, a] *nm/f* grandson/daughter; ~**s** *nmpl* grandchildren.

nieve *etc* ['njeβe] *vb ver* **nevar** ♦ *nf* snow; (*AM*) icecream.

nigromancia [niγro'manθja] *nf* black magic.

Nilo ['nilo] *nm*: **el** ~ **the** Nile.

nimiedad [nimje'ðað] *nf* smallmindedness; (*trivialidad*) triviality.

nimio, a ['nimjo, a] *adj* trivial, insignificant.

ninfa ['ninfa] *nf* nymph.

ninfómana [nin'fomana] *nf* nymphomaniac.

ningún [nin'gun] *adj ver* **ninguno**.

ninguno, a [nin'guno, a] (*delante de nm*: **ningún**) *adj* no ♦ *pron* (*nadie*) nobody; (*ni uno*) none, not one; (*ni uno ni otro*) neither; **de ninguna manera** by no means, not at all.

niña ['nina] *nf* (*ANAT*) pupil; *ver tb* **niño**.

niñera [ni'nera] *nf* nursemaid, nanny; **niñería** *nf* childish act.

niñez [ni'neθ] *nf* childhood; (*infancia*) infancy.

niño, a ['nino, a] *adj* (*joven*) young; (*inmaduro*) immature ♦ *nm/f* child, boy/girl.

nipón, ona [ni'pon, ona] *adj, nm/f* Japanese.

níquel ['nikel] *nm* nickel; **niquelar** *vt* (*TEC*) to nickel-plate.

níspero ['nispero] *nm* medlar.

nitidez [niti'ðeθ] *nf* (*claridad*) clarity; (: *de atmósfera*) brightness; (: *de imagen*) sharpness; **nítido, a** *adj* clear; sharp.

nitrato [ni'trato] *nm* nitrate.

nitrógeno [ni'troxeno] *nm* nitrogen.

nitroglicerina [nitroγliθe'rina] *nf* nitroglycerine.

nivel [ni'βel] *nm* (*GEO*) level; (*norma*) level, standard; (*altura*) height; ~ **de aceite** oil level; ~ **de aire** spirit level; ~ **de vida** standard of living; ~**ar** *vt* to level out; (*fig*) to even up; (*COM*) to balance.

NN. UU. *nfpl abr* (= *Naciones Unidas*) UN *sg*.

no [no] *adv* no; not; (*con verbo*) not ♦ *excl* no!; ~ **tengo nada** I don't have anything, I have nothing; ~ **es el mío** it's not mine; **ahora** ~ not now; ¿~ **lo sabes?** don't you know?; ~ **mucho** not much; ~ **bien termine, lo entregaré** as soon as I finish I'll hand it over; ~ **más: ayer** ~ **más** just yesterday; ¡**pase** ~ **más!** come in!; ¡**a que** ~ **lo sabes!** I bet you don't know!; ¡**cómo** ~! of course!; **los países ~ alineados** the non-aligned countries; **la ~ intervención** non-intervention.

noble ['noβle] *adj, nm/f* noble; **~za** *nf* nobility.

noción [no'θjon] *nf* notion.

nocivo, a [no'θiβo, a] *adj* harmful.

noctámbulo, a [nok'tambulo, a] *nm/f* sleepwalker.

nocturno, a [nok'turno, a] *adj (de la noche)* nocturnal, night *cpd; (de la tarde)* evening *cpd ♦ nm* nocturne.

noche ['notʃe] *nf* night, night-time; *(la tarde)* evening; *(fig)* darkness; **de ~, por la ~** at night.

nochebuena [notʃe'βwena] *nf* Christmas Eve.

nochevieja [notʃe'βjexa] *nf* New Year's Eve.

nodriza [no'ðriθa] *nf* wet nurse; **buque o nave ~** supply ship.

nogal [no'val] *nm* walnut tree.

nómada ['nomaða] *adj* nomadic ♦ *nm/f* nomad.

nombramiento [nombra'mjento] *nm* naming; *(a un empleo)* appointment.

nombrar [nom'brar] *vt (designar)* to name; *(mencionar)* to mention; *(dar puesto a)* to appoint.

nombre ['nombre] *nm* name; *(sustantivo)* noun; *(fama)* renown; **~ y apellidos** name in full; **~ común/propio** common/proper noun; **~ de pila/de soltera** Christian/maiden name; **poner ~ a** to call, name.

nomenclatura [nomenkla'tura] *nf* nomenclature.

nomeolvides [nomeol'βiðes] *nm inv* forget-me-not.

nómina ['nomina] *nf (lista)* list; *(COM)* payroll.

nominal [nomi'nal] *adj* nominal.

nominar [nomi'nar] *vt* to nominate.

nominativo, a [nomina'tiβo, a] *adj (COM)*: **cheque ~ a X** cheque made out to X.

non [non] *adj* odd, uneven ♦ *nm* odd number.

nono, a ['nono, a] *adj* ninth.

nordeste [nor'ðeste] *adj* north-east,

north-eastern, north-easterly ♦ *nm* north-east.

nórdico, a ['norðiko, a] *adj (del norte)* northern, northerly; *(escandinavo)* Nordic.

noreste [no'reste] *adj, nm* = **nordeste**.

noria ['norja] *nf (AGR)* waterwheel; *(de carnaval)* big *(BRIT)* o Ferris *(US)* wheel.

normal [nor'mal] *adj (corriente)* normal; *(habitual)* usual, natural; **(gasolina) ~** two-star petrol; **~idad** *nf* normality; **restablecer la ~idad** to restore order; **~izar** *vt (reglamentar)* to normalize; *(TEC)* to standardize; **~izarse** *vr* to return to normal.

normando, a [nor'mando, a] *adj, nm/f* Norman.

noroeste [noro'este] *adj* north-west, north-western, north-westerly ♦ *nm* north-west.

norte ['norte] *adj* north, northern, northerly ♦ *nm* north; *(fig)* guide.

norteamericano, a [norteameri'kano, a] *adj, nm/f* (North) American.

Noruega [no'rweɣa] *nf* Norway.

noruego, a [no'rweɣo, a] *adj, nm/f* Norwegian.

nos [nos] *pron (directo)* us; *(indirecto)* us; to us; for us; from us; *(reflexivo)* (to) ourselves; *(recíproco)* (to) each other; **~ levantamos a las 7** we get up at 7.

nosotros, as [no'sotros, as] *pron (sujeto)* we; *(después de prep)* us.

nostalgia [nos'talxja] *nf* nostalgia.

nota ['nota] *nf* note; *(ESCOL)* mark.

notable [no'taβle] *adj* notable; *(ESCOL)* outstanding ♦ *nm/f* notable.

notar [no'tar] *vt* to notice, note; **~se** *vr* to be obvious; **se nota que ...** one observes that ....

notarial [nota'rjal] *adj*: **acta ~** affidavit.

notario [no'tarjo] *nm* notary.

noticia [no'tiθja] *nf (información)* piece of news; **las ~s** the news *sg*; **tener ~s de alguien** to hear from sb.

noticiario [noti'θjarjo] *nm (CINE)* newsreel; *(TV)* news bulletin.

noticiero [noti'θjero] *(AM) nm* news

bulletin.

notificación [notifika'θjon] *nf* notification; **notificar** *vt* to notify, inform.

notoriedad [notorje'ðað] *nf* fame, renown; **notorio, a** *adj* (*público*) well-known; (*evidente*) obvious.

novato, a [no'ßato, a] *adj* inexperienced ♦ *nm/f* beginner, novice.

novecientos, as [noße'θjentos, as] *num* nine hundred.

novedad [noße'ðað] *nf* (*calidad de nuevo*) newness; (*noticia*) piece of news; (*cambio*) change, (new) development.

novedoso, a [noße'ðoso, a] *adj* novel.

novel [no'ßel] *adj* new; (*inexperto*) inexperienced ♦ *nm/f* beginner.

novela [no'ßela] *nf* novel.

novelero, a [noße'lero, a] *adj* highly imaginative.

novelesco, a [noße'lesko, . a] *adj* fictional; (*romántico*) romantic; (*fantástico*) fantastic.

noveno, a [no'ßeno, a] *adj* ninth.

noventa [no'ßenta] *num* ninety.

novia ['noßja] *nf ver* **novio**.

noviazgo [no'ßjaθvo] *nm* engagement.

novicio, a [no'ßiθjo, a] *nm/f* novice.

noviembre [no'ßjembre] *nm* November.

novilla [no'ßiʎa] *nf* heifer; **~da** *nf* (*TAUROMAQUIA*) bullfight with young bulls; **novillero** *nm* novice bullfighter; **novillo** *nm* young bull, bullock; **hacer novillos** (*fam*) to play truant.

novio, a ['noßjo, a] *nm/f* boyfriend/girlfriend; (*prometido*) fiancé/fiancée; (*recién casado*) bridegroom/bride; **los ~s** the newly-weds.

N. S. *abr* = *Nuestro Señor*.

nubarrón [nußa'rron] *nm* storm cloud.

nube ['nuße] *nf* cloud.

nublado, a [nu'ßlaðo, a] *adj* cloudy ♦ *nm* storm cloud; **nublar** *vt* (*oscurecer*) to darken; (*confundir*) to cloud; **nublarse** *vr* to grow dark.

nubosidad [nußosi'ðað] *nf* cloudiness; **había mucha ~** it was very cloudy.

nuca ['nuka] *nf* nape of the neck.

nuclear [nukle'ar] *adj* nuclear.

núcleo ['nukleo] *nm* (*centro*) core; (*FÍSICA*) nucleus.

nudillo [nu'ðiʎo] *nm* knuckle.

nudo ['nuðo] *nm* knot; (*unión*) bond; (*de problema*) crux; **~so, a** *adj* knotty.

nuera ['nwera] *nf* daughter-in-law.

nuestro, a ['nwestro, a] *adj pos* our ♦ *pron* ours; **~ padre** our father; **un amigo ~** a friend of ours; **es el ~** it's ours.

nueva ['nweßa] *nf* piece of news.

nuevamente [nweßa'mente] *adv* (*otra vez*) again; (*de nuevo*) anew.

Nueva York [-'jork] *n* New York.

Nueva Zelandia [-θe'landja] *nf* New Zealand.

nueve ['nweße] *num* nine.

nuevo, a ['nweßo, a] *adj* (*gen*) new; **de ~** again.

nuez [nweθ] *nf* (*fruto*) nut; (*del nogal*) walnut; **~ de Adán** Adam's apple; **~ moscada** nutmeg.

nulidad [nuli'ðað] *nf* (*incapacidad*) incompetence; (*abolición*) nullity.

nulo, a ['nulo, a] *adj* (*inepto, torpe*) useless; (*inválido*) (null and) void; (*DEPORTE*) drawn, tied.

núm. *abr* (= *número*) no.

numeración [numera'θjon] *nf* (*cifras*) numbers *pl*; (*arábiga, romana etc*) numerals *pl*.

numeral [nume'ral] *nm* numeral.

numerar [nume'rar] *vt* to number.

numérico, a [nu'meriko, a] *adj* numerical.

número ['numero] *nm* (*gen*) number; (*tamaño: de zapato*) size; (*ejemplar: de diario*) number, issue; **sin ~** numberless, unnumbered; **~ de matrícula/de teléfono** registration/telephone number; **~ atrasado** back number.

numeroso, a [nume'roso, a] *adj* numerous.

nunca ['nunka] *adv* (*jamás*) never; **~ lo pensé** I never thought it; **no viene ~** he never comes; **~ más** never again; **más que ~** more than ever.

nuncio ['nunθjo] *nm* (*REL*) nuncio.

nupcias ['nupθjas] *nfpl* wedding *sg*, nuptials.

nutria ['nutrja] *nf* otter.
nutrición [nutri'θjon] *nf* nutrition.
nutrido, a [nu'triðo, a] *adj* (*alimentado*) nourished; (*fig: grande*) large; (*abundante*) abundant.
nutrir [nu'trir] *vt* (*alimentar*) to nourish; (*dar de comer*) to feed; (*fig*) to strengthen; **nutritivo, a** *adj* nourishing, nutritious.
nylon [ni'lon] *nm* nylon.

Ñ

ñato, a ['ɲato, a] (*AM*) *adj* snub-nosed.
ñoñería [ɲoɲe'ria] *nf* insipidness.
ñoñez [ɲo'ɲeθ] *nf* = ñoñería.
ñoño, a ['ɲoɲo, a] *adj* (*AM: tonto*) silly, stupid; (*soso*) insipid; (*persona*) spineless.

O

o [o] *conj* or.
O *abr* (= *oeste*) W.
o/ *abr* (= *orden*) o.
oasis [o'asis] *nm inv* oasis.
obcecar [oββe'kar] *vt* to blind.
obedecer [oββeðe'θer] *vt* to obey; **obediencia** *nf* obedience; **obediente** *adj* obedient.
obertura [oββer'tura] *nf* overture.
obesidad [oββesi'ðað] *nf* obesity; **obeso, a** *adj* obese.
obispo [o'βispo] *nm* bishop.
objeción [oββxe'θjon] *nf* objection; **poner objeciones** to raise objections.
objetar [oββxe'tar] *vt, vi* to object.
objetivo, a [oββxe'tiββo, a] *adj, nm* objective.
objeto [oββ'xeto] *nm* (*cosa*) object; (*fin*) aim.
objetor, a [oββxe'tor, a] *nm/f* objector.
oblicuo, a [o'βlikwo, a] *adj* oblique; (*mirada*) sidelong.
obligación [oββliɣa'θjon] *nf* obligation; (*COM*) bond.
obligar [oββli'ɣar] *vt* to force; ~**se** *vr* to bind o.s.; **obligatorio, a** *adj* compulsory, obligatory.

oboe [o'βoe] *nm* oboe.
obra ['oββra] *nf* work; (*hechura*) piece of work; (*ARQ*) construction, building; (*TEATRO*) play; ~ **maestra** masterpiece; ~**s públicas** public works; **por** ~ **de** thanks to (the efforts of); **obrar** *vt* to work; (*tener efecto*) to have an effect on ♦ *vi* to act, behave; (*tener efecto*) to have an effect; **la carta obra en su poder** the letter is in his/her possession.
obrero, a [o'βrero, a] *adj* (*clase*) working; (*movimiento*) labour *cpd*; **clase obrera** working class ♦ *nm/f* (*gen*) worker; (*sin oficio*) labourer.
obscenidad [oββsθeni'ðað] *nf* obscenity; **obsceno, a** *adj* obscene.
obscu... = **oscu....**
obsequiar [oββse'kjar] *vt* (*ofrecer*) to present with; (*agasajar*) to make a fuss of, lavish attention on; **obsequio** *nm* (*regalo*) gift; (*cortesía*) courtesy, attention; **obsequioso, a** *adj* attentive.
observación [oββserβa'θjon] *nf* observation; (*reflexión*) remark.
observador, a [oββserβa'ðor, a] *nm/f* observer.
observancia [oββser'βanθja] *nf* observance.
observar [oββser'βar] *vt* to observe; (*anotar*) to notice; ~**se** *vr* to keep to, observe.
obsesión [oββse'sjon] *nf* obsession; **obsesionar** *vt* to obsess.
obstaculizar [oββstakuli'θar] *vt* (*dificultar*) to hinder, hamper.
obstáculo [oββs'takulo] *nm* (*gen*) obstacle; (*impedimento*) hindrance, drawback.
obstante [oββs'tante]: **no** ~ *adv* nevertheless ♦ *prep* in spite of.
obstetricia [oββste'triθja] *nf* obstetrics *sg*; **obstétrico, a** *adj* obstetric ♦ *nm/f* obstetrician.
obstinado, a [oββsti'naðo, a] *adj* (*gen*) obstinate, stubborn.
obstinarse [oββsti'narse] *vr* to be obstinate; ~ **en** to persist in.

obstrucción [oβstruk'θjon] *nf* obstruction; **obstruir** *vt* to obstruct.

obtener [oβte'ner] *vt* (*conseguir*) to obtain; (*ganar*) to gain.

obturador [oβtura'ðor] *nm* (*FOTO*) shutter.

obtuso, a [oβ'tuso, a] *adj* (*filo*) blunt; (*MAT, fig*) obtuse.

obviar [oβ'βjar] *vt* to obviate, remove.

obvio, a ['oβßjo, a] *adj* obvious.

ocasión [oka'sjon] *nf* (*oportunidad*) opportunity, chance; (*momento*) occasion, time; (*causa*) cause; **de ~** secondhand; **ocasionar** *vt* to cause.

ocaso [o'kaso] *nm* (*fig*) decline.

occidente [okθi'ðente] *nm* west.

océano [o'θeano] *nm* ocean; **el ~ Índico** the Indian Ocean.

OCDE *nf abr* (= *Organización de Cooperación y Desarrollo Económico*) OECD.

ocio ['oθjo] *nm* (*tiempo*) leisure; (*pey*) idleness; **~sidad** *nf* idleness; **~so, a** *adj* (*inactivo*) idle; (*inútil*) useless.

octanaje [okta'naxe] *nm*: **de alto ~** high octane; **octano** *nm* octane.

octavilla [okta'viʎa] *nf* leaflet, pamphlet.

octavo, a [ok'taßo, a] *adj* eighth.

octogenario, a [oktoxe'narjo, a] *adj* octogenarian.

octubre [ok'tuβre] *nm* October.

ocular [oku'lar] *adj* ocular, eye *cpd*; **testigo ~** eyewitness.

oculista [oku'lista] *nm/f* oculist.

ocultar [okul'tar] *vt* (*esconder*) to hide; (*callar*) to conceal; **oculto, a** *adj* hidden; (*fig*) secret.

ocupación [okupa'θjon] *nf* occupation.

ocupado, a [oku'paðo, a] *adj* (*persona*) busy; (*plaza*) occupied, taken; (*teléfono*) engaged; **ocupar** *vt* (*gen*) to occupy; **ocuparse** *vr*: **ocuparse de** *o* **en** (*gen*) to concern o.s. with; (*cuidar*) to look after.

ocurrencia [oku'rrenθja] *nf* (*suceso*) incident, event; (*idea*) bright idea.

ocurrir [oku'rrir] *vi* to happen; **~se** *vr*: **se me ocurrió que ...** it occurred to me that ....

ochenta [o'tʃenta] *num* eighty.

ocho ['otʃo] *num* eight; **~ días** a week.

odiar [o'ðjar] *vt* to hate; **odio** *nm* (*gen*) hate, hatred; (*disgusto*) dislike; **odioso, a** *adj* (*gen*) hateful; (*malo*) nasty.

odontólogo, a [oðon'toloxo, a] *nm/f* dentist, dental surgeon.

OEA *nf abr* (= *Organización de Estados Americanos*) OAS.

oeste [o'este] *nm* west; **una película del ~** a western.

ofender [ofen'der] *vt* (*agraviar*) to offend; (*insultar*) to insult; **~se** *vr* to take offence; **ofensa** *nf* offence; **ofensiva** *nf* offensive; **ofensivo, a** *adj* (*insultante*) insulting; (*MIL*) offensive.

oferta [o'ferta] *nf* offer; (*propuesta*) proposal; **la ~ y la demanda** supply and demand; **artículos en ~** goods on offer.

oficial [ofi'θjal] *adj* official ♦ *nm* official; (*MIL*) officer.

oficina [ofi'θina] *nf* office; **~ de correos** post office; **~ de turismo** tourist office; **oficinista** *nm/f* clerk.

oficio [o'fiθjo] *nm* (*profesión*) profession; (*puesto*) post; (*REL*) service; **ser del ~** to be an old hand; **tener mucho ~** to have a lot of experience; **~ de difuntos** funeral service; **de ~** officially.

oficioso, a [ofi'θjoso, a] *adj* (*pey*) officious; (*no oficial*) unofficial, informal.

ofimática [ofi'matika] *nf* office automation.

ofrecer [ofre'θer] *vt* (*dar*) to offer; (*proponer*) to propose; **~se** *vr* (*persona*) to offer o.s., volunteer; (*situación*) to present itself; **¿qué se le ofrece?**, **¿se le ofrece algo?** what can I do for you?, can I get you anything?

ofrecimiento [ofreθi'mjento] *nm* offer, offering.

ofrendar [ofren'dar] *vt* to offer, contribute.

oftalmólogo, a [oftal'moloxo, a] *nm/f* ophthalmologist.

ofuscación [ofuska'θjon] *nf* (*fig*) bewilderment.

ofuscamiento [ofuska'mjento] *nm* = **ofuscación**.

ofuscar [ofus'kar] *vt* (*confundir*) to

bewilder; (*enceguecer*) to dazzle, blind.

oída [o'iða] *nf*: **de ~s** by hearsay.

oído [o'iðo] *nm* (*ANAT*) ear; (*sentido*) hearing.

oigo *etc vb ver* **oír**.

oír [o'ir] *vt* (*gen*) to hear; (*atender a*) to listen to; **¡oiga!** listen!; **~ misa** to attend mass.

OIT *nf abr* (= *Organización Internacional del Trabajo*) ILO.

ojal [o'xal] *nm* buttonhole.

ojalá [oxa'la] *excl* if only (it were so)!, some hope! ♦ *conj* if only ...!, would that ...!; **~ que venga hoy** I hope he comes today.

ojeada [oxe'aða] *nf* glance.

ojera [o'xera] *nf*: **tener ~s** to have bags under one's eyes.

ojeriza [oxe'riθa] *nf* ill-will.

ojeroso, a [oxe'roso, a] *adj* haggard.

ojete [o'xete] *nm* eye(let).

ojo ['oxo] *nm* eye; (*de puente*) span; (*de cerradura*) keyhole ♦ *excl* careful!; **tener ~ para** to have an eye for; **~ de buey** porthole.

ola ['ola] *nf* wave.

olé [o'le] *excl* bravo!, olé!

oleada [ole'aða] *nf* big wave, swell; (*fig*) wave.

oleaje [ole'axe] *nm* swell.

óleo ['oleo] *nm* oil; **oleoducto** *nm* (oil) pipeline.

oler [o'ler] *vt* (*gen*) to smell; (*inquirir*) to pry into; (*fig: sospechar*) to sniff out ♦ *vi* to smell; **~ a** to smell of.

olfatear [olfate'ar] *vt* to smell; (*fig: sospechar*) to sniff out; (*inquirir*) to pry into; **olfato** *nm* sense of smell.

oligarquía [olivar'kia] *nf* oligarchy.

olimpíada, a [olim'piaða] *nf*: **las O~s** the Olympics.

oliva [o'lißa] *nf* (*aceituna*) olive; **aceite de ~** olive oil; **olivo** *nm* olive tree.

olmo ['olmo] *nm* elm (tree).

olor [o'lor] *nm* smell; **~oso, a** *adj* scented.

olvidadizo, a [olßiða'ðiθo, a] *adj* (*desmemoriado*) forgetful; (*distraído*) absent-minded.

olvidar [olßi'ðar] *vt* to forget; (*omitir*)

to omit; **~se** *vr* (*fig*) to forget o.s.; **se me olvidó** I forgot.

olvido [ol'ßiðo] *nm* oblivion; (*despiste*) forgetfulness.

olla ['oʎa] *nf* pan; (*comida*) stew; **~ a presión** *o* **exprés** pressure cooker; **~ podrida** *type of Spanish stew*.

ombligo [om'blivo] *nm* navel.

ominoso, a [omi'noso, a] *adj* ominous.

omisión [omi'sjon] *nf* (*abstención*) omission; (*descuido*) neglect.

omiso, a [o'miso, a] *adj*: **hacer caso ~ de** to ignore, pass over.

omitir [omi'tir] *vt* to omit.

omnipotente [omnipo'tente] *adj* omnipotent.

omnívoro, a [om'nißoro, a] *adj* omnivorous.

omóplato [o'moplato] *nm* shoulder blade.

OMS *nf abr* (= *Organización Mundial de la Salud*) WHO.

once ['onθe] *num* eleven; **~s** (*AM*) *nmpl* tea break.

onda ['onda] *nf* wave; **~ corta/larga/ media** short/long/medium wave; **ondear** *vt, vi* to wave; (*tener ondas*) to be wavy; (*agua*) to ripple; **ondearse** *vr* to swing, sway.

ondulación [ondula'θjon] *nf* undulation; **ondulado, a** *adj* wavy ♦ *nm* wave; **ondulante** *adj* undulating.

ondular [ondu'lar] *vt* (*el pelo*) to wave ♦ *vi* to undulate; **~se** *vr* to undulate.

oneroso, a [one'roso, a] *adj* onerous.

ONU ['onu] *nf abr* (= *Organización de las Naciones Unidas*) UNO.

opaco, a [o'pako, a] *adj* opaque; (*fig*) dull.

ópalo ['opalo] *nm* opal.

opción [op'θjon] *nf* (*gen*) option; (*derecho*) right, option.

OPEP ['opep] *nf abr* (= *Organización de Países Exportadores de Petróleo*) OPEC.

ópera ['opera] *nf* opera; **~ bufa** *o* **cómica** comic opera.

operación [opera'θjon] *nf* (*gen*) operation; (*COM*) transaction, deal.

operador, a [opera'ðor, a] *nm/f* opera-

tor; (*CINE: proyección*) projectionist; (:
rodaje) cameraman.

operante [ope'rante] *adj* operating.

operar [ope'rar] *vt* (*producir*) to
produce, bring about; (*MED*) to operate
on ♦ *vi* (*COM*) to operate, deal; ~**se** *vr*
to occur; (*MED*) to have an operation.

opereta [ope'reta] *nf* operetta.

opinar [opi'nar] *vt* (*estimar*) to think ♦
vi (*enjuiciar*) to give one's opinion;
opinión *nf* (*creencia*) belief; (*criterio*)
opinion.

opio ['opjo] *nm* opium.

oponente [opo'nente] *nm/f* opponent.

oponer [opo'ner] *vt* (*resistencia*) to put
up, offer; (*negativa*) to raise; ~**se** *vr*
(*objetar*) to object; (*estar frente a
frente*) to be opposed; (*dos personas*) to
oppose each other; ~ **A a B** to set A
against B; **me opongo a pensar que ...** I
refuse to believe *o* think that ....

oportunidad [oportuni'ðað] *nf* (*ocasión*)
opportunity; (*posibilidad*) chance.

oportunismo [oportu'nismo] *nm* oppor-
tunism; **oportunista** *nm/f* opportunist.

oportuno, a [opor'tuno, a] *adj* (*en su
tiempo*) opportune, timely; (*respuesta*)
suitable; **en el momento** ~ at the right
moment.

oposición [oposi'θjon] *nf* opposition;
oposiciones *nfpl* (*ESCOL*) public
examinations.

opositor, a [oposi'tor, a] *nm/f*
(*adversario*) opponent; (*candidato*): ~
(**a**) candidate (for).

opresión [opre'sjon] *nf* oppression;
opresivo, a *adj* oppressive; **opresor, a**
nm/f oppressor.

oprimir [opri'mir] *vt* to squeeze; (*fig*) to
oppress.

oprobio [o'proβjo] *nm* (*infamia*)
ignominy; (*descrédito*) shame.

optar [op'tar] *vi* (*elegir*) to choose; ~ **a
o por** to opt for; **optativo, a** *adj*
optional.

óptico, a ['optiko, a] *adj* optic(al) ♦
nm/f optician.

optimismo [opti'mismo] *nm* optimism;
optimista *nm/f* optimist.

óptimo, a ['optimo, a] *adj* (*el mejor*)

very best.

opuesto, a [o'pwesto, a] *adj* (*contrario*)
opposite; (*antagónico*) opposing.

opulencia [opu'lenθja] *nf* opulence;
opulento, a *adj* opulent.

oración [ora'θjon] *nf* (*discurso*) speech;
(*REL*) prayer; (*LING*) sentence.

oráculo [o'rakulo] *nm* oracle.

orador, a [ora'ðor, a] *nm/f* (*conferenciante*) speaker, orator.

oral [o'ral] *adj* oral.

orangután [orangu'tan] *nm* orang-utan.

orar [o'rar] *vi* (*REL*) to pray.

oratoria [ora'torja] *nf* oratory.

órbita ['orβita] *nf* orbit.

orden ['orðen] *nm* (*gen*) order ♦ *nf*
(*gen*) order; (*INFORM*) command; ~ **del
día** agenda; **de primer** ~ first-rate; **en**
~ **de prioridad** in order of priority.

ordenado, a [orðe'naðo, a] *adj*
(*metódico*) methodical; (*arreglado*)
orderly.

ordenador [orðena'ðor] *nm* computer;
~ **central** mainframe computer.

ordenanza [orðe'nanθa] *nf* ordinance.

ordenar [orðe'nar] *vt* (*mandar*) to
order; (*poner orden*) to put in order,
arrange; ~**se** *vr* (*REL*) to be ordained.

ordeñar [orðe'ɲar] *vt* to milk.

ordinario, a [orði'narjo, a] *adj* (*común*)
ordinary, usual; (*vulgar*) vulgar,
common.

orégano [o'reɣano] *nm* oregano.

oreja [o'rexa] *nf* ear; (*MECÁNICA*) lug,
flange.

orfanato [orfa'nato] *nm* orphanage.

orfandad [orfan'dað] *nf* orphanhood.

orfebrería [orfeβre'ria] *nf* gold/silver
work.

orgánico, a [or'ɣaniko, a] *adj* organic.

organigrama [orɣani'ɣrama] *nm* flow
chart.

organismo [orɣa'nismo] *nm* (*BIO*)
organism; (*POL*) organization.

organista [orɣa'nista] *nm/f* organist.

organización [orɣaniθa'θjon] *nf*
organization; **organizar** *vt* to organize.

órgano ['orɣano] *nm* organ.

orgasmo [or'ɣasmo] *nm* orgasm.

orgía [or'xia] *nf* orgy.

orgullo [or'ɣuʎo] nm (altanería) pride; (autorespeto) self-respect; **orgulloso, a** adj (gen) proud; (altanero) haughty.

orientación [orjenta'θjon] nf (posición) position; (dirección) direction.

orientar [orjen'tar] vt (situar) to orientate; (señalar) to point; (dirigir) to direct; (guiar) to guide; ~se vr to get one's bearings; (decidirse) to decide on a course of action.

oriente [o'rjente] nm east; **Cercano/Medio/Lejano O~** Near/Middle/Far East.

origen [o'rixen] nm origin; (nacimiento) lineage, birth.

original [orixi'nal] adj (nuevo) original; (extraño) odd, strange; ~**idad** nf originality.

originar [orixi'nar] vt to start, cause; ~se vr to originate; ~**io, a** adj (nativo) native; (primordial) original.

orilla [o'riʎa] nf (borde) border; (de río) bank; (de bosque, tela) edge; (de mar) shore.

orín [o'rin] nm rust.

orina [o'rina] nf urine; **orinal** nm (chamber) pot; **orinar** vi to urinate; **orinarse** vr to wet o.s.; **orines** nmpl urine.

oriundo, a [o'rjundo, a] adj: ~ **de** native of.

ornamento [orna'mento] nm ornament.

ornar [or'nar] vt to adorn.

ornitología [ornitolo'xia] nf ornithology, bird-watching.

oro ['oro] nm gold; ~**s** nmpl (NAIPES) hearts.

oropel [oro'pel] nm tinsel.

orquesta [or'kesta] nf orchestra; ~ **de cámara/sinfónica** chamber/symphony orchestra.

orquídea [or'kiðea] nf orchid.

ortiga [or'tiɣa] nf nettle.

ortodoxo, a [orto'ðokso, a] adj orthodox.

ortografía [ortoɣra'fia] nf spelling.

ortopedia [orto'peðja] nf orthopaedics sg.

oruga [o'ruɣa] nf caterpillar.

orzuelo [or'θwelo] nm (MED) stye.

os [os] pron (gen) you; (a vosotros) to you.

osa ['osa] nf (she-)bear; **O~ Mayor/Menor** Great/Little Bear.

osadía [osa'ðia] nf daring.

osar [o'sar] vi to dare.

oscilación [osθila'θjon] nf (movimiento) oscillation; (fluctuación) fluctuation; (vacilación) hesitation; (columpio) swinging, movement to and fro.

oscilar [osθi'lar] vi to oscillate; to fluctuate; to hesitate.

oscurecer [oskure'θer] vt to darken ♦ vi to grow dark; ~se vr to grow o get dark.

oscuridad [oskuri'ðað] nf obscurity; (tinieblas) darkness.

oscuro, a [os'kuro, a] adj dark; (fig) obscure; **a oscuras** in the dark.

óseo, a ['oseo, a] adj bony.

oso ['oso] nm bear; ~ **de peluche** teddy bear; ~ **hormiguero** anteater.

ostensible [osten'siβle] adj obvious.

ostentación [ostenta'θjon] nf (gen) ostentation; (acto) display.

ostentar [osten'tar] vt (gen) to show; (pey) to flaunt, show off; (poseer) to have, possess; **ostentoso, a** adj ostentatious, showy.

ostra ['ostra] nf oyster.

OTAN ['otan] nf abr (= Organización del Tratado del Atlántico Norte) NATO.

otear [ote'ar] vt to observe; (fig) to look into.

otitis [o'titis] nf earache.

otoñal [oto'ɲal] adj autumnal.

otoño [o'toɲo] nm autumn.

otorgamiento [otorɣa'mjento] nm conferring, granting; (JUR) execution.

otorgar [otor'ɣar] vt (conceder) to concede; (dar) to grant.

otorrino, a [oto'rrino, a] nm/f ear, nose and throat specialist.

otorrinolaringólogo, a [otorrinolarin'goloɣo, a] nm/f = **otorrino**.

PALABRA CLAVE
---

otro, a ['otro, a] adj **1** (distinto: sg) another; (: pl) other; **con ~s amigos** with other o different friends

2 (*adicional*): **tráigame ~ café** (**más**), **por favor** can I have another coffee please; **~s 10 días más** another ten days
♦ *pron* **1**: **el ~** the other one; (**los**) **~s** (the) others; **de ~** somebody else's; **que lo haga ~** let somebody else do it **2** (*recíproco*): **se odian** (**la**) **una a** (**la**) **otra** they hate one another *o* each other **3**: **~ tanto**: **comer ~ tanto** to eat the same *o* as much again; **recibió una decena de telegramas y otras tantas llamadas** he got about ten telegrams and as many calls.

ovación [oβa'θjon] *nf* ovation.
oval [o'βal] *adj* oval; **~ado, a** *adj* oval; **óvalo** *nm* oval.
oveja [o'βexa] *nf* sheep.
overol [oβe'rol] (*AM*) *nm* overalls *pl*.
ovillo [o'βiʎo] *nm* (*de lana*) ball of wool; **hacerse un ~** to curl up.
OVNI ['oβni] *nm abr* (= *objeto volante no identificado*) UFO.
ovulación [oβula'θjon] *nf* ovulation; **óvulo** *nm* ovum.
oxidación [oksiða'θjon] *nf* rusting.
oxidar [oksi'ðar] *vt* to rust; **~se** *vr* to go rusty.
óxido ['oksiðo] *nm* oxide.
oxigenado, a [oksixe'naðo, a] *adj* (*QUÍMICA*) oxygenated; (*pelo*) bleached.
oxígeno [ok'sixeno] *nm* oxygen.
oyente [o'jente] *nm/f* listener, hearer.
oyes *etc vb ver* **oír**.

P

P *abr* (= *padre*) Fr.
pabellón [paβe'ʎon] *nm* bell tent; (*ARQ*) pavilion; (*de hospital etc*) block, section; (*bandera*) flag.
pábilo ['paβilo] *nm* wick.
pacer [pa'θer] *vi* to graze.
paciencia [pa'θjenθja] *nf* patience.
paciente [pa'θjente] *adj, nm/f* patient.
pacificación [paθifika'θjon] *nf* pacification.
pacificar [paθifi'kar] *vt* to pacify;

(*tranquilizar*) to calm.
pacífico, a [pa'θifiko, a] *adj* (*persona*) peaceable; (*existencia*) peaceful; **el** (*océano*) **P~** the Pacific (Ocean).
pacifismo [paθi'fismo] *nm* pacifism; **pacifista** *nm/f* pacifist.
pacotilla [pako'tiʎa] *nf*: **de ~** (*actor, escritor*) third-rate; (*mueble etc*) cheap.
pactar [pak'tar] *vt* to agree to *o* on ♦ *vi* to come to an agreement.
pacto ['pakto] *nm* (*tratado*) pact; (*acuerdo*) agreement.
padecer [paðe'θer] *vt* (*sufrir*) to suffer; (*soportar*) to endure, put up with; (*engaño, error*) to be a victim of; **padecimiento** *nm* suffering.
padrastro [pa'ðrastro] *nm* stepfather.
padre ['paðre] *nm* father ♦ *adj* (*fam*): **un éxito ~** a tremendous success; **~s** *nmpl* parents.
padrino [pa'ðrino] *nm* (*REL*) godfather; (*tb*: **~ de boda**) best man; (*fig*) sponsor, patron; **~s** *nmpl* godparents.
padrón [pa'ðron] *nm* (*censo*) census, roll; (*de socios*) register.
paella [pa'eʎa] *nf* paella, *dish of rice with meat, shellfish etc*.
paga ['paxa] *nf* (*pago*) payment; (*sueldo*) pay, wages *pl*.
pagadero, a [paxa'ðero, a] *adj* payable; **~ a plazos** payable in instalments.
pagano, a [pa'xano, a] *adj, nm/f* pagan, heathen.
pagar [pa'xar] *vt* to pay; (*las compras, crimen*) to pay for; (*fig: favor*) to repay ♦ *vi* to pay; **~ al contado/a plazos** to pay (in) cash/in instalments.
pagaré [paxa're] *nm* I.O.U.
página ['paxina] *nf* page.
pago ['paxo] *nm* (*dinero*) payment; (*fig*) return; **estar ~** to be even *o* quits; **~ anticipado/a cuenta/contra reembolso/en especie** advance payment/payment on account/cash on delivery/payment in kind.
pág(s). *abr* (= *página(s)*) p(p).
pague *etc vb ver* **pagar**.
país [pa'is] *nm* (*gen*) country; (*región*) land; **los P~es Bajos** the Low Coun-

tries; **el P~ Vasco** the Basque Country.
paisaje [pai'saxe] *nm* countryside, scenery.
paisano, a [pai'sano, a] *adj* of the same country ♦ *nm/f* (*compatriota*) fellow countryman/woman; **vestir de ~** (*soldado*) to be in civvies; (*guardia*) to be in plain clothes.
paja ['paxa] *nf* straw; (*fig*) rubbish (*BRIT*), trash (*US*).
pájara ['paxara] *nf* hen (bird).
pajarita [paxa'rita] *nf* (*corbata*) bow tie.
pájaro ['paxaro] *nm* bird; **~ carpintero** woodpecker.
pajita [pa'xita] *nf* (drinking) straw.
pala ['pala] *nf* spade, shovel; (*raqueta etc*) bat; (: *de tenis*) racquet; (*CULIN*) slice; **~ matamoscas** fly swat.
palabra [pa'laβra] *nf* word; (*facultad*) (power of) speech; (*derecho de hablar*) right to speak; **tomar la ~** (*en mitin*) to take the floor.
palabrota [pala'brota] *nf* swearword.
palacio [pa'laθjo] *nm* palace; (*mansión*) mansion, large house; **~ de justicia** courthouse; **~ municipal** town/city hall.
paladar [pala'ðar] *nm* palate; **paladear** *vt* to taste.
palanca [pa'lanka] *nf* lever; (*fig*) pull, influence.
palangana [palan'gana] *nf* washbasin.
palco ['palko] *nm* box.
Palestina [pales'tina] *nf* Palestine; **palestino, a** *nm/f* Palestinian.
paleta [pa'leta] *nf* (*de pintor*) palette; (*de albañil*) trowel; (*de ping-pong*) bat; (*AM*) ice lolly.
paliar [pa'ljar] *vt* (*mitigar*) to mitigate, alleviate; **paliativo** *nm* palliative.
palidecer [paliðe'θer] *vi* to turn pale; **palidez** *nf* paleness; **pálido, a** *adj* pale.
palillo [pa'liʎo] *nm* small stick; (*mondadientes*) toothpick; (*para comer*) chopstick.
paliza [pa'liθa] *nf* beating, thrashing.
palma ['palma] *nf* (*ANAT*) palm; (*árbol*) palm tree; **batir** *o* **dar ~s** to clap, applaud; **~da** *nf* slap; **~das** *nfpl* clapping *sg*, applause *sg*.
palmear [palme'ar] *vi* to clap.

palmo ['palmo] *nm* (*medida*) span; (*fig*) small amount; **~ a ~** inch by inch.
palmotear [palmote'ar] *vi* to clap, applaud; **palmoteo** *nm* clapping, applause.
palo ['palo] *nm* stick; (*poste*) post; (*de tienda de campaña*) pole; (*mango*) handle, shaft; (*golpe*) blow, hit; (*de golf*) club; (*de béisbol*) bat; (*NAUT*) mast; (*NAIPES*) suit.
paloma [pa'loma] *nf* dove, pigeon.
palomilla [palo'miʎa] *nf* moth; (*TEC*: *tuerca*) wing nut; (: *hierro*) angle iron.
palomitas [palo'mitas] *nfpl* popcorn *sg*.
palpar [pal'par] *vt* to touch, feel.
palpitación [palpita'θjon] *nf* palpitation.
palpitante [palpi'tante] *adj* palpitating; (*fig*) burning.
palpitar [palpi'tar] *vi* to palpitate; (*latir*) to beat.
palta ['palta] (*AM*) *nf* avocado (pear).
palúdico, a [pa'luðiko, a] *adj* marshy.
paludismo [palu'ðismo] *nm* malaria.
pampa ['pampa] (*AM*) *nf* pampas, prairie.
pan [pan] *nm* bread; (*una barra*) loaf; **~ integral** wholemeal (*BRIT*) *o* wholewheat (*US*) bread; **~ rallado** breadcrumbs *pl*.
pana ['pana] *nf* corduroy.
panadería [panaðe'ria] *nf* baker's (shop); **panadero, a** *nm/f* baker.
Panamá [pana'ma] *nm* Panama; **panameño, a** *adj* Panamanian.
pancarta [pan'karta] *nf* placard, banner.
panda ['panda] *nm* (*ZOOL*) panda.
pandereta [pande'reta] *nf* tambourine.
pandilla [pan'diʎa] *nf* set, group; (*de criminales*) gang; (*pey*: *camarilla*) clique.
panecillo [pane'θiʎo] *nm* (bread) roll.
panel [pa'nel] *nm* panel.
panfleto [pan'fleto] *nm* pamphlet.
pánico [ˈpaniko] *nm* panic.
panorama [pano'rama] *nm* panorama; (*vista*) view.
pantalón [panta'lon] *nm* trousers; **pantalones** *nmpl* trousers.
pantalla [pan'taʎa] *nf* (*de cine*) screen; (*de lámpara*) lampshade.

pantano [pan'tano] *nm* (*ciénaga*) marsh, swamp; (*depósito: de agua*) reservoir; (*fig*) jam, difficulty.
panteón [pante'on] *nm*: ~ **familiar** family tomb.
pantera [pan'tera] *nf* panther.
pantomima [panto'mima] *nf* pantomime.
pantorrilla [panto'rriʎa] *nf* calf (of the leg).
pantufla [pan'tufla] *nf* slipper.
panza ['panθa] *nf* belly, paunch; **panzón, ona** *adj* fat, potbellied; **panzudo, a** *adj* = **panzón.**
pañal [pa'ɲal] *nm* nappy (*BRIT*), diaper (*US*); ~**s** *nmpl* (*fig*) early stages, infancy *sg*.
pañería [paɲe'ria] *nf* drapery.
paño ['paɲo] *nm* (*tela*) cloth; (*pedazo de tela*) (piece of) cloth; (*trapo*) duster, rag; ~ **higiénico** sanitary towel; ~**s menores** underclothes.
pañuelo [pa'ɲwelo] *nm* handkerchief, hanky (*fam*); (*para la cabeza*) (head)scarf.
papa ['papa] *nm*: **el P**~ the Pope ♦ (*AM*) *nf* potato.
papá [pa'pa] (*pl* ~**s**) (*fam*) *nm* dad(dy), pa (*US*).
papagayo [papa'ɣajo] *nm* parrot.
papanatas [papa'natas] (*fam*) *nm inv* simpleton.
paparrucha [papa'rrutʃa] *nf* piece of nonsense.
papaya [pa'paja] *nf* papaya.
papel [pa'pel] *nm* paper; (*hoja de* ~) sheet of paper; (*TEATRO, fig*) role; ~ **de calco/carbón/de cartas** tracing paper/ carbon paper/stationery; ~ **de envolver/pintado** wrapping paper/wallpaper; ~ **de aluminio/higiénico** aluminium (*BRIT*) o aluminum (*US*) foil/toilet paper; ~ **de lija** sandpaper; ~ **moneda** paper money; ~ **secante** blotting paper.
papeleo [pape'leo] *nm* red tape.
papelera [pape'lera] *nf* wastepaper basket; (*escritorio*) desk.
papelería [papele'ria] *nf* stationer's (shop).
papeleta [pape'leta] *nf* (*pedazo de*

papel) slip of paper; (*POL*) ballot paper; (*ESCOL*) report.
paperas [pa'peras] *nfpl* mumps *sg*.
papilla [pa'piʎa] *nf* (*para niños*) baby food.
paquete [pa'kete] *nm* (*de cigarrillos etc*) packet; (*CORREOS etc*) parcel; (*AM*) package tour; (: *fam*) nuisance, bore.
par [par] *adj* (*igual*) like, equal; (*MAT*) even ♦ *nm* equal; (*de guantes*) pair; (*de veces*) couple; (*POL*) peer; (*GOLF, COM*) par; **abrir de** ~ **en** ~ to open wide.
para ['para] *prep* for; **no es** ~ **comer** it's not for eating; **decir** ~ **sí** to say to o.s.; **¿**~ **qué lo quieres?** what do you want it for?; **se casaron** ~ **separarse otra vez** they married only to separate again; **lo tendré** ~ **mañana** I'll have it (for) tomorrow; **ir** ~ **casa** to go home, head for home; ~ **profesor es muy estúpido** he's very stupid for a teacher; **¿quién es usted** ~ **gritar así?** who are you to shout like that?; **tengo bastante** ~ **vivir** I have enough to live on; *ver tb* **con.**
parabién [para'βjen] *nm* congratulations *pl*.
parábola [pa'raβola] *nf* parable; (*MAT*) parabola.
parabrisas [para'βrisas] *nm inv* windscreen (*BRIT*), windshield (*US*).
paracaídas [paraka'iðas] *nm inv* parachute; **paracaidista** *nm/f* parachutist; (*MIL*) paratrooper.
parachoques [para'tʃokes] *nm inv* (*AUTO*) bumper; (*MECÁNICA etc*) shock absorber.
parada [pa'raða] *nf* stop; (*acto*) stopping; (*de industria*) shutdown, stoppage; (*lugar*) stopping place; ~ **de autobús** bus stop.
paradero [para'ðero] *nm* stopping-place; (*situación*) whereabouts.
parado, a [pa'raðo, a] *adj* (*persona*) motionless, standing still; (*fábrica*) closed, at a standstill; (*coche*) stopped; (*AM*) standing (up); (*sin empleo*) unemployed, idle.
paradoja [para'ðoxa] *nf* paradox.

parador [para'ðor] *nm* parador, state-run hotel.

paráfrasis [pa'rafrasis] *nf inv* paraphrase.

paraguas [pa'raɣwas] *nm inv* umbrella.

Paraguay [para'ɣwai] *nm*: el ~ Paraguay; **paraguayo, a** *adj, nm/f* Paraguayan.

paraíso [para'iso] *nm* paradise, heaven.

paraje [pa'raxe] *nm* place, spot.

paralelo, a [para'lelo, a] *adj* parallel.

parálisis [pa'ralisis] *nf inv* paralysis; **paralítico, a** *adj, nm/f* paralytic.

paralizar [parali'θar] *vt* to paralyse; ~se *vr* to become paralysed; (*fig*) to come to a standstill.

paramilitar [paramili'tar] *adj* paramilitary.

páramo ['paramo] *nm* bleak plateau.

parangón [paran'gon] *nm*: sin ~ incomparable.

paranoico, a [para'noiko, a] *nm/f* paranoiac.

parapléjico, a [para'plexiko, a] *adj, nm/f* paraplegic.

parar [pa'rar] *vt* to stop; (*golpe*) to ward off ♦ *vi* to stop; ~se *vr* to stop; (*AM*) to .stand up; **ha parado de llover** it has stopped raining; **van a ~ en la comisaria** they're going to end up in the police station; ~se en to pay attention to.

parásito, a [pa'rasito, a] *nm/f* parasite.

parasol [para'sol] *nm* parasol, sunshade.

parcela [par'θela] *nf* plot, piece of ground.

parcial [par'θjal] *adj* (*pago*) part-; (*eclipse*) partial; (*JUR*) prejudiced, biased; (*POL*) partisan; ~idad *nf* (*prejuicio*) prejudice, bias.

parco, a ['parko, a] *adj* (*moderado*) moderate.

parche ['partʃe] *nm* (*gen*) patch.

parear [pare'ar] *vt* (*juntar, hacer par*) to match, put together; (*BIO*) to mate, pair.

parecer [pare'θer] *nm* (*opinión*) opinion, view; (*aspecto*) looks *pl* ♦ *vi* (*tener apariencia*) to seem, look; (*asemejarse*) to look *o* seem like; (*aparecer, llegar*) to appear; ~se *vr* to look alike, resemble each other; ~se a to look like, resemble; **según** *o* **a lo que parece** evidently, apparently; **me parece que** I think (that), it seems to me that.

parecido, a [pare'θiðo, a] *adj* similar ♦ *nm* similarity, likeness, resemblance; **bien** ~ good-looking, nice-looking.

pared [pa'reð] *nf* wall.

pareja [pa'rexa] *nf* (*par*) pair; (*dos personas*) couple; (*otro: de un par*) other one (of a pair); (*persona*) partner.

parejo, a [pa'rexo, a] *adj* (*igual*) equal; (*liso*) smooth, even.

parentela [paren'tela] *nf* relations *pl*.

parentesco [paren'tesko] *nm* relationship.

paréntesis [pa'rentesis] *nm inv* parenthesis; (*digresión*) digression; (*en escrito*) bracket.

parezco *etc vb ver* **parecer**.

pariente, a [pa'rjente, a] *nm/f* relative, relation.

parir [pa'rir] *vt* to give birth to ♦ *vi* (*mujer*) to give birth, have a baby.

París [pa'ris] *n* Paris.

parking ['parkin] *nm* car park (*BRIT*), parking lot (*US*).

parlamentar [parlamen'tar] *vi* (*negociar*) to parley.

parlamentario, a [parlamen'tarjo, a] *adj* parliamentary ♦ *nm/f* member of parliament.

parlamento [parla'mento] *nm* (*POL*) parliament.

parlanchín, ina [parlan'tʃin, ina] *adj* indiscreet ♦ *nm/f* chatterbox.

paro ['paro] *nm* (*huelga*) stoppage (of work), strike; (*desempleo*) unemployment; **subsidio de** ~ unemployment benefit; **hay** ~ **en la industria** work in the industry is at a standstill.

parodia [pa'roðja] *nf* parody; **parodiar** *vt* to parody.

parpadear [parpaðe'ar] *vi* (*ojos*) to blink; (*luz*) to flicker.

párpado ['parpaðo] *nm* eyelid.

parque ['parke] *nm* (*lugar verde*) park;

~ de atracciones/infantil/zoológico fairground/playground/zoo.

parquímetro [par'kimetro] *nm* parking meter.

parra ['parra] *nf* (*grape*)vine.

párrafo ['parrafo] *nm* paragraph; **echar un ~** (*fam*) to have a chat.

parranda [pa'rranda] (*fam*) *nf* spree, binge.

parrilla [pa'rriʎa] *nf* (*CULIN*) grill; (*de coche*) grille; (**carne a la**) ~ barbecue; **~da** *nf* barbecue.

párroco ['parroko] *nm* parish priest.

parroquia [pa'rrokja] *nf* parish; (*iglesia*) parish church; (*COM*) clientele, customers *pl*; **~no, a** *nm/f* parishioner; client, customer.

parte ['parte] *nm* message; (*informe*) report ♦ *nf* part; (*lado, cara*) side; (*de reparto*) share; (*JUR*) party; **en alguna ~ de Europa** somewhere in Europe; **en/por todas ~s** everywhere; **en gran ~** to a large extent; **la mayor ~ de los españoles** most Spaniards; **de un tiempo a esta ~** for some time past; **de ~ de alguien** on sb's behalf; **¿de ~ de quién?** (*TEL*) who is speaking?; **por ~ de** on the part of; **yo por mi ~** I for my part; **por otra ~** on the other hand; **dar ~** to inform; **tomar ~** to take part.

partera [par'tera] *nf* midwife.

partición [parti'θjon] *nf* division, sharing-out; (*POL*) partition.

participación [partiθipa'θjon] *nf* (*acto*) participation, taking part; (*parte, COM*) share; (*de lotería*) shared prize; (*aviso*) notice, notification.

participante [partiθi'pante] *nm/f* participant.

participar [partiθi'par] *vt* to notify, inform ♦ *vi* to take part, participate.

partícipe [par'tiθipe] *nm/f* participant.

particular [partiku'lar] *adj* (*especial*) particular, special; (*individual, personal*) private, personal ♦ *nm* (*punto, asunto*) particular, point; (*individuo*) individual; **tiene coche ~** he has a car of his own; **~izar** *vt* to distinguish; (*especificar*) to specify; (*detallar*) to give details about.

partida [par'tiða] *nf* (*salida*) departure; (*COM*) entry, item; (*juego*) game; (*grupo de personas*) band, group; **mala ~** dirty trick; **~ de nacimiento/matrimonio/defunción** birth/marriage/death certificate.

partidario, a [parti'ðarjo, a] *adj* partisan ♦ *nm/f* supporter, follower.

partido [par'tiðo] *nm* (*POL*) party; (*DEPORTE: encuentro*) game, match; (: *equipo*) team; (*apoyo*) support; **sacar ~ de** to profit o benefit from; **tomar ~** to take sides.

partir [par'tir] *vt* (*dividir*) to split, divide; (*compartir, distribuir*) to share (out), distribute; (*romper*) to break open, split open; (*rebanada*) to cut (off) ♦ *vi* (*ponerse en camino*) to set off o out; (*comenzar*) to start (off o out); **~se** *vr* to crack o split o break (in two *etc*); **a ~ de** (starting) from.

parto ['parto] *nm* birth; (*fig*) product, creation; **estar de ~** to be in labour.

parvulario [parβu'larjo] *nm* nursery school, kindergarten.

pasa ['pasa] *nf* raisin; **~ de Corinto/de Esmirna** currant/sultana.

pasada [pa'saða] *nf* passing, passage; **de ~** in passing, incidentally; **una mala ~** a dirty trick.

pasadizo [pasa'ðiθo] *nm* (*pasillo*) passage, corridor; (*callejuela*) alley.

pasado, a [pa'saðo, a] *adj* past; (*malo: comida, fruta*) bad; (*muy cocido*) overdone; (*anticuado*) out of date ♦ *nm* past; **~ mañana** the day after tomorrow; **el mes ~** last month.

pasador [pasa'ðor] *nm* (*gen*) bolt; (*de pelo*) hair slide; (*horquilla*) grip.

pasaje [pa'saxe] *nm* passage; (*pago de viaje*) fare; (*los pasajeros*) passengers *pl*; (*pasillo*) passageway.

pasajero, a [pasa'xero, a] *adj* passing; (*situación, estado*) temporary; (*amor, enfermedad*) brief ♦ *nm/f* passenger.

pasamanos [pasa'manos] *nm inv* (hand)rail; (*de escalera*) banisters *pl*.

pasamontañas [pasamon'taɲas] *nm inv* balaclava helmet.

pasaporte [pasa'porte] *nm* passport.

pasar [pa'sar] *vt* to pass; (*tiempo*) to spend; (*desgracias*) to suffer, endure; (*noticia*) to give, pass on; (*río*) to cross; (*barrera*) to pass through; (*falta*) to overlook, tolerate; (*contrincante*) to surpass, do better than; (*coche*) to overtake; (*CINE*) to show; (*enfermedad*) to give, infect with ♦ *vi* (*gen*) to pass; (*terminarse*) to be over; (*ocurrir*) to happen; ~**se** *vr* (*flores*) to fade; (*comida*) to go bad *o* off; (*fig*) to overdo it, go too far; ~ **de** *o* go beyond, exceed; ~ **por** (*AM*) to fetch; ~**lo bien/mal** to have a good/bad time; **¡pase!** come in!; **hacer** ~ to show in; ~**se al enemigo** to go over to the enemy; **se me pasó** I forgot; **no se le pasa nada** he misses nothing; **pase lo que pase** come what may.

pasarela [pasa'rela] *nf* footbridge; (*en barco*) gangway.

pasatiempo [pasa'tjempo] *nm* pastime, hobby.

Pascua ['paskwa] *nf*: ~ (**de Resurrección**) Easter; ~ **de Navidad** Christmas; ~**s** *nfpl* Christmas (time); **¡felices** ~**s!** Merry Christmas!

pase ['pase] *nm* pass; (*CINE*) performance, showing.

pasear [pase'ar] *vt* to take for a walk; (*exhibir*) to parade, show off ♦ *vi* to walk, go for a walk; ~**se** *vr* to walk, go for a walk; ~ **en coche** to go for a drive; **paseo** *nm* (*avenida*) avenue; (*distancia corta*) walk, stroll; **dar un** *o* **ir de paseo** to go for a walk.

pasillo [pa'siʎo] *nm* passage, corridor.

pasión [pa'sjon] *nf* passion.

pasivo, a [pa'siβo, a] *adj* passive; (*inactivo*) inactive ♦ *nm* (*COM*) liabilities *pl*, debts *pl*; (*LING*) passive.

pasmar [pas'mar] *vt* (*asombrar*) to amaze, astonish; **pasmo** *nm* amazement, astonishment; (*resfriado*) chill; (*fig*) wonder, marvel; **pasmoso, a** *adj* amazing, astonishing.

paso, a ['paso, a] *adj* dried ♦ *nm* step; (*modo de andar*) walk; (*huella*) footprint; (*rapidez*) speed, pace, rate; (*camino accesible*) way through,

passage; (*cruce*) crossing; (*pasaje*) passing, passage; (*GEO*) pass; (*estrecho*) strait; ~ **de peatones** pedestrian crossing; **a ese** ~ (*fig*) at that rate; **salir al** ~ **de** *o* **a** to waylay; **estar de** ~ to be passing through; ~ **elevado** flyover; **prohibido el** ~ no entry; **ceda el** ~ give way.

pasota [pa'sota] (*fam*) *adj*, *nm/f* ≈ dropout; **ser un (tipo)** ~ to be a bit of a dropout; (*ser indiferente*) not to care about anything.

pasta ['pasta] *nf* paste; (*CULIN: masa*) dough; (: *de bizcochos etc*) pastry; (*fam*) dough; ~**s** *nfpl* (*bizcochos*) pastries, small cakes; (*fideos, espaguetis etc*) pasta; ~ **de dientes** *o* **dentífrica** toothpaste.

pastar [pas'tar] *vt*, *vi* to graze.

pastel [pas'tel] *nm* (*dulce*) cake; ~ **de carne** meat pie; (*ARTE*) pastel; ~**ería** *nf* cake shop.

pasteurizado, a [pasteuri'θaðo, a] *adj* pasteurized.

pastilla [pas'tiʎa] *nf* (*de jabón, chocolate*) bar; (*píldora*) tablet, pill.

pasto ['pasto] *nm* (*hierba*) grass; (*lugar*) pasture, field.

pastor, a [pas'tor, a] *nm/f* shepherd/ess ♦ *nm* (*REL*) clergyman, pastor.

pata ['pata] *nf* (*pierna*) leg; (*pie*) foot; (*de muebles*) leg; ~**s arriba** upside down; **meterura de** ~ (*fam*) gaffe; **meter la** ~ (*fam*) to put one's foot in it; (*TEC*): ~ **de cabra** crowbar; **tener buena/mala** ~ to be lucky/unlucky; ~**da** *nf* kick; (*en el suelo*) stamp.

patalear [patale'ar] *vi* (*en el suelo*) to stamp one's feet.

patata [pa'tata] *nf* potato; ~**s fritas** *o* **a la española** chips, French fries; ~**s fritas** (*de bolsa*) crisps.

paté [pa'te] *nm* pâté.

patear [pate'ar] *vt* (*pisar*) to stamp on, trample (on); (*pegar con el pie*) to kick ♦ *vi* to stamp (with rage), stamp one's feet.

patente [pa'tente] *adj* obvious, evident; (*COM*) patent ♦ *nf* patent.

paternal [pater'nal] *adj* fatherly,

paternal; **paterno, a** *adj* paternal.

patético, a [pa'tetiko, a] *adj* pathetic, moving.

patillas [pa'tiʎas] *nfpl* sideburns.

patín [pa'tin] *nm* skate; (*de trineo*) runner; **patinaje** *nm* skating; **patinar** *vi* to skate; (*resbalarse*) to skid, slip; (*fam*) to slip up, blunder.

patio ['patjo] *nm* (*de casa*) patio, courtyard; ~ **de recreo** playground.

pato ['pato] *nm* duck; **pagar el** ~ (*fam*) to take the blame, carry the can.

patológico, a [pato'loxiko, a] *adj* pathological.

patoso, a [pa'toso, a] (*fam*) *adj* clumsy.

patraña [pa'traɲa] *nf* story, fib.

patria ['patrja] *nf* native land, mother country.

patrimonio [patri'monjo] *nm* inheritance; (*fig*) heritage.

patriota [pa'trjota] *nm/f* patriot; **patriotismo** *nm* patriotism.

patrocinar [patroθi'nar] *vt* to sponsor; (*apoyar*) to back, support; **patrocinio** *nm* sponsorship; backing, support.

patrón, ona [pa'tron, ona] *nm/f* (*jefe*) boss, chief, master/mistress; (*propietario*) landlord/lady; (*REL*) patron saint ♦ *nm* (*TEC, COSTURA*) pattern.

patronal [patro'nal] *adj*: **la clase** ~ management.

patronato [patro'nato] *nm* sponsorship; (*acto*) patronage; (*fundación benéfica*) trust, foundation.

patrulla [pa'truʎa] *nf* patrol.

pausa ['pausa] *nf* pause, break.

pausado, a [pau'saðo, a] *adj* slow, deliberate.

pauta ['pauta] *nf* line, guide line.

pavimento [paβi'mento] *nm* (*con losas*) pavement, paving.

pavo ['paβo] *nm* turkey; ~ **real** peacock.

pavor [pa'βor] *nm* dread, terror.

payaso, a [pa'jaso, a] *nm/f* clown.

payo, a ['pajo] *nm/f* (*para gitanos*) nongipsy.

paz [paθ] *nf* peace; (*tranquilidad*) peacefulness, tranquillity; **hacer las paces** to make peace; (*fig*) to make up;

La P~ *n* (*GEO*) La Paz.

PC *abr* = **Partido Comunista**.

P.D. *abr* (= *posdata*) PS, ps.

peaje [pe'axe] *nm* toll.

peatón [pea'ton] *nm* pedestrian.

peca ['peka] *nf* freckle.

pecado [pe'kaðo] *nm* sin; **pecador, a** *adj* sinful ♦ *nm/f* sinner.

pecaminoso, a [pekami'noso, a] *adj* sinful.

pecar [pe'kar] *vi* (*REL*) to sin; (*fig*): **peca de generoso** he is generous to a fault.

peculiar [peku'ljar] *adj* special, peculiar; (*característico*) typical, characteristic; ~**idad** *nf* peculiarity; special feature, characteristic.

pecho ['petʃo] *nm* (*ANAT*) chest; (*de mujer*) breast(s) (*pl*), bosom; (*fig: corazón*) heart, breast; (: *valor*) courage, spirit; **dar el** ~ **a** to breast-feed; **tomar algo a** ~ to take sth to heart.

pechuga [pe'tʃuxa] *nf* breast.

pedal [pe'ðal] *nm* pedal; ~**ear** *vi* to pedal.

pédalo ['peðalo] *nm* pedal boat.

pedante [pe'ðante] *adj* pedantic ♦ *nm/f* pedant; ~**ría** *nf* pedantry.

pedazo [pe'ðaθo] *nm* piece, bit; **hacerse** ~**s** (*romperse*) to smash, shatter.

pedernal [peðer'nal] *nm* flint.

pediatra [pe'ðjatra] *nm/f* paediatrician.

pedicuro, a [peði'kuro, a] *nm/f* chiropodist (*BRIT*), podiatrist (*US*).

pedido [pe'ðiðo] *nm* (*COM: mandado*) order; (*petición*) request.

pedir [pe'ðir] *vt* to ask for, request; (*comida, COM: mandar*) to order; (*exigir: precio*) to ask; (*necesitar*) to need, demand, require ♦ *vi* to ask; **me pidió que cerrara la puerta** he asked me to shut the door; **¿cuánto piden por el coche?** how much are they asking for the car?

pegadizo, a [peɣa'ðiθo, a] *adj* (*MUS*) catchy.

pegajoso, a [peɣa'xoso, a] *adj* sticky, adhesive.

pegamento [peɣa'mento] *nm* gum, glue.

pegar [pe'ɣar] *vt* (*papel, sellos*) to stick

(on); (*cartel*) to stick up; (*coser*) to sew (on); (*unir: partes*) to join, fix together; (*MED*) to give, infect with; (*dar: golpe*) to give, deal ♦ *vi* (*adherirse*) to stick, adhere; (*ir juntos: colores*) to match, go together; (*golpear*) to hit; (*quemar: el sol*) to strike hot, burn (*fig*); (*pegar*) to stick; (*dos personas*) to hit each other, fight; (*fam*): ~ **un grito** to let out a yell; ~ **un salto** to jump (with fright); ~ **en** to touch; ~**se un tiro** to shoot o.s.

pegatina [peɣa'tina] *nf* sticker.

peinado [pei'naðo] *nm* (*en peluquería*) hairdo; (*estilo*) hair style.

peinar [pei'nar] *vt* to comb; (*hacer estilo*) to style; ~**se** *vr* to comb one's hair.

peine ['peine] *nm* comb; ~**ta** *nf* ornamental comb.

p.ej. *abr* (= *por ejemplo*) eg.

Pekín [pe'kin] *n* Pekin(g).

pelado, a [pe'laðo, a] *adj* (*fruta, patata etc*) peeled; (*cabeza*) shorn; (*campo, fig*) bare; (*fam: sin dinero*) broke.

pelaje [pe'laxe] *nm* (*ZOOL*) fur, coat; (*fig*) appearance.

pelambre [pe'lambre] *nm* (*pelo largo*) long hair, mop.

pelar [pe'lar] *vt* (*fruta, patatas etc*) to peel; (*cortar el pelo a*) to cut the hair of; (*quitar la piel: animal*) to skin; ~**se** *vr* (*la piel*) to peel off; **voy a** ~**me** I'm going to get my hair cut.

peldaño [pel'daɲo] *nm* step.

pelea [pe'lea] *nf* (*lucha*) fight; (*discusión*) quarrel, row.

peleado, a [pele'aðo, a] *adj*: **estar** ~ (**con uno**) to have fallen out (with sb).

pelear [pele'ar] *vi* to fight; ~**se** *vr* to fight; (*reñirse*) to fall out, quarrel.

peletería [pelete'ria] *nf* furrier's, fur shop.

pelícano [pe'likano] *nm* pelican.

película [pe'likula] *nf* film; (*cobertura ligera*) thin covering; (*FOTO: rollo*) roll o reel of film.

peligro [pe'liɣro] *nm* danger; (*riesgo*) risk; **correr** ~ **de** to run the risk of; ~**so, a** *adj* dangerous; risky.

pelirrojo, a [peli'rroxo, a] *adj* red-haired, red-headed ♦ *nm/f* redhead.

pelma ['pelma] (*fam*) *nm/f* pain (in the neck).

pelmazo [pel'maθo] (*fam*) *nm* = **pelma**.

pelo ['pelo] *nm* (*cabellos*) hair; (*de barba, bigote*) whisker; (*de animal: pellejo*) hair, fur, coat; **al** ~ just right; **venir al** ~ to be exactly what one needs; **un hombre de** ~ **en pecho** a brave man; **por los** ~**s** by the skin of one's teeth; **no tener** ~**s en la lengua** to be outspoken, not mince words; **tomar el** ~ **a uno** to pull sb's leg.

pelón, ona [pe'lon, ona] *adj* hairless, bald.

pelota [pe'lota] *nf* ball; (*fam: cabeza*) nut; **en** ~ stark naked; **hacer la** ~ (**a uno**) (*fam*) to creep (to sb); ~ **vasca** pelota.

pelotari [pelo'tari] *nm* pelota player.

pelotón [pelo'ton] *nm* (*MIL*) squad, detachment.

peluca [pe'luka] *nf* wig.

peluche [pe'lutʃe] *nm*: **oso/muñeco de** ~ teddy bear/soft toy.

peludo, a [pe'luðo, a] *adj* hairy, shaggy.

peluquería [peluke'ria] *nf* hairdresser's; (*para hombres*) barber's (shop); **peluquero, a** *nm/f* hairdresser; barber.

pelusa [pe'lusa] *nf* (*BOT*) down; (*COSTURA*) fluff.

pellejo [pe'ʎexo] *nm* (*de animal*) skin, hide.

pellizcar [peʎiθ'kar] *vt* to pinch, nip.

pena ['pena] *nf* (*congoja*) grief, sadness; (*remordimiento*) regret; (*dificultad*) trouble; (*dolor*) pain; (*JUR*) sentence; **merecer** *o* **valer la** ~ to be worthwhile; **a duras** ~**s** with great difficulty; ~ **de muerte** death penalty; ~ **pecuniaria** fine; **¡qué** ~! what a shame!

penal [pe'nal] *adj* penal ♦ *nm* (*cárcel*) prison.

penalidad [penali'ðað] *nf* (*problema, dificultad*) trouble, hardship; (*JUR*) penalty, punishment.

penalti [pe'nalti] (*pl* ~**s** *o* ~**es**) *nm* penalty (kick).

penalty [pe'naltı] (*pl* ~s *o* ~es) *nm* = penalti.

penar [pe'nar] *vt* to penalize; (*castigar*) to punish ♦ *vi* to suffer.

pendiente [pen'djente] *adj* pending, unsettled ♦ *nm* earring ♦ *nf* hill, slope.

pene ['pene] *nm* penis.

penetración [penetra'θjon] *nf* (*acto*) penetration; (*agudeza*) sharpness, insight.

penetrante [pene'trante] *adj* (*herida*) deep; (*persona, arma*) sharp; (*sonido*) penetrating, piercing; (*mirada*) searching; (*viento, ironía*) biting.

penetrar [pene'trar] *vt* to penetrate, pierce; (*entender*) to grasp ♦ *vi* to penetrate, go in; (*entrar*) to enter, go in; (*líquido*) to soak in; (*fig*) to pierce.

penicilina [peniθi'lina] *nf* penicillin.

península [pe'ninsula] *nf* peninsula; **peninsular** *adj* peninsular.

penique [pe'nike] *nm* penny.

penitencia [peni'tenθja] *nf* (*remordimiento*) penitence; (*castigo*) penance; ~**ría** *nf* prison, penitentiary.

penoso, a [pe'noso, a] *adj* (*difícil*) arduous, difficult.

pensador, a [pensa'ðor, a] *nm/f* thinker.

pensamiento [pensa'mjento] *nm* thought; (*mente*) mind; (*idea*) idea.

pensar [pen'sar] *vt* to think; (*considerar*) to think over, think out; (*proponerse*) to intend, plan; (*imaginarse*) to think up, invent ♦ *vi* to think; ~ **en** to aim at, aspire to; **pensativo, a** *adj* thoughtful, pensive.

pensión [pen'sjon] *nf* (*casa*) boarding *o* guest house; (*dinero*) pension; (*cama y comida*) board and lodging; ~ **completa** full board; **pensionista** *nm/f* (*jubilado*) (old-age) pensioner; (*huésped*) lodger.

penúltimo, a [pe'nultimo, a] *adj* penultimate, last but one.

penumbra [pe'numbra] *nf* half-light.

penuria [pe'nurja] *nf* shortage, want.

peña ['pena] *nf* (*roca*) rock; (*cuesta*) cliff, crag; (*grupo*) group, circle; (*AM: club*) folk club.

peñasco [pe'nasko] *nm* large rock, boulder.

peñón [pe'non] *nm* wall of rock; **el P~** the Rock (of Gibraltar).

peón [pe'on] *nm* labourer; (*AM*) farm labourer, farmhand; (*AJEDREZ*) pawn.

peonza [pe'onθa] *nf* spinning top.

peor [pe'or] *adj* (*comparativo*) worse; (*superlativo*) worst ♦ *adv* worse; worst; **de mal en** ~ from bad to worse.

pepinillo [pepi'niʎo] *nm* gherkin.

pepino [pe'pino] *nm* cucumber; (**no**) **me importa un** ~ I don't care one bit.

pepita [pe'pita] *nf* (*BOT*) pip; (*MINERÍA*) nugget.

pequeñez [peke'neθ] *nf* smallness, littleness; (*trivialidad*) trifle, triviality.

pequeño, a [pe'keno, a] *adj* small, little.

pera ['pera] *nf* pear; **peral** *nm* pear tree.

percance [per'kanθe] *nm* setback, misfortune.

percatarse [perka'tarse] *vr*: ~ **de** to notice, take note of.

percepción [perθep'θjon] *nf* (*vista*) perception; (*idea*) notion, idea.

perceptible [perθep'tiβle] *adj* perceptible, noticeable; (*COM*) payable, receivable.

percibir [perθi'βir] *vt* to perceive, notice; (*COM*) to earn, get.

percusión [perku'sjon] *nf* percussion.

percha ['pertʃa] *nf* (*ganchos*) coat hooks *pl*; (*colgador*) coat hanger; (*de ave*) perch.

perdedor, a [perðe'ðor, a] *adj* losing ♦ *nm/f* loser.

perder [per'ðer] *vt* to lose; (*tiempo, palabras*) to waste; (*oportunidad*) to lose, miss; (*tren*) to miss ♦ *vi* to lose; ~**se** *vr* (*extraviarse*) to get lost; (*desaparecer*) to disappear, be lost to view; (*arruinarse*) to be ruined; **echar a** ~ (*comida*) to spoil, ruin; (*oportunidad*) to waste.

perdición [perði'θjon] *nf* perdition, ruin.

pérdida ['perðiða] *nf* loss; (*de tiempo*) waste; ~**s** *nfpl* (*COM*) losses.

perdido, a [per'ðiðo, a] *adj* lost.

perdiz [per'ðiθ] *nf* partridge.

perdón [per'ðon] *nm* (*disculpa*) pardon, forgiveness; (*clemencia*) mercy; ¡~!

sorry!, I beg your pardon!; **perdonar** vt to pardon, forgive; (la vida) to spare; (excusar) to exempt, excuse; ¡**perdone** (usted)! sorry!, I beg your pardon!

perdurable [perðu'raßle] adj lasting; (eterno) everlasting.

perdurar [perdu'rar] vi (resistir) to last, endure; (seguir existiendo) to stand, still exist.

perecedero, a [pereθe'ðero, a] adj (COM etc) perishable.

perecer [pere'θer] vi (morir) to perish, die; (objeto) to shatter.

peregrinación [pereɣrina'θjon] nf (REL) pilgrimage.

peregrino, a [pere'ɣrino, a] adj (idea) strange, absurd ♦ nm/f pilgrim.

perejil [pere'xil] nm parsley.

perenne [pe'renne] adj everlasting, perennial.

perentorio, a [peren'torjo, a] adj (urgente) urgent, peremptory; (fijo) set, fixed.

pereza [pe'reθa] nf laziness, idleness; **perezoso, a** adj lazy, idle.

perfección [perfek'θjon] nf perfection; **perfeccionar** vt to perfect; (mejorar) to improve; (acabar) to complete, finish.

perfectamente [perfecta'mente] adv perfectly.

perfecto, a [per'fekto, a] adj perfect; (terminado) complete, finished.

perfidia [per'fiðja] nf perfidy, treachery.

perfil [per'fil] nm profile; (contorno) silhouette, outline; (ARQ) (cross) section; ~es nmpl features; (fig) social graces; ~**ado, a** adj (bien formado) well-shaped; (largo: cara) long; ~**ar** vt (trazar) to outline; (fig) to shape, give character to.

perforación [perfora'θjon] nf perforation; (con taladro) drilling; **perforadora** nf punch.

perforar [perfo'rar] vt to perforate; (agujero) to drill, bore; (papel) to punch a hole in ♦ vi to drill, bore.

perfume [per'fume] nm perfume, scent.

pericia [pe'riθja] nf skill, expertise.

periferia [peri'ferja] nf periphery; (de ciudad) outskirts pl.

periférico [peri'feriko] (AM) nm ring road (BRIT), beltway (US).

perímetro [pe'rimetro] nm perimeter.

periódico, a [pe'rjoðiko, a] adj periodic(al) ♦ nm newspaper.

periodismo [perjo'ðismo] nm journalism; **periodista** nm/f journalist.

periodo [pe'rjoðo] nm period.

período [pe'rioðo] nm = **periodo**.

periquito [peri'kito] nm budgerigar, budgie.

perito, a [pe'rito, a] adj (experto) expert; (diestro) skilled, skilful ♦ nm/f expert; skilled worker; (técnico) technician.

perjudicar [perxuði'kar] vt (gen) to damage, harm; **perjudicial** adj damaging, harmful; (en detrimento) detrimental; **perjuicio** nm damage, harm.

perjurar [perxu'rar] vi to commit perjury.

perla ['perla] nf pearl; **me viene de ~** it suits me fine.

permanecer [permane'θer] vi (quedarse) to stay, remain; (seguir) to continue to be.

permanencia [perma'nenθja] nf permanence; (estancia) stay.

permanente [perma'nente] adj permanent, constant ♦ nf perm.

permisible [permi'sißle] adj permissible, allowable.

permiso [per'miso] nm permission; (licencia) permit, licence; **con ~** excuse me; **estar de ~** (MIL) to be on leave; **~ de conducir** driving licence (BRIT), driver's license (US).

permitir [permi'tir] vt to permit, allow.

pernera [per'nera] nf trouser leg.

pernicioso, a [perni'θjoso, a] adj (maligno, MED) pernicious; (persona) wicked.

pernio ['pernjo] nm hinge.

perno ['perno] nm bolt.

pero ['pero] conj but; (aún) yet ♦ nm (defecto) flaw, defect; (reparo) objection.

perol [pe'rol] nm (large metal) pan.

perola [pe'rola] nf = **perol**.

perpendicular [perpendiku'lar] *adj* perpendicular.

perpetrar [perpe'trar] *vt* to perpetrate.

perpetuar [perpe'twar] *vt* to perpetuate; **perpetuo, a** *adj* perpetual.

perplejo, a [per'plexo, a] *adj* perplexed, bewildered.

perra ['perra] *nf* (*ZOOL*) bitch; (*fam: dinero*) money; **estar sin una ~** to be flat broke.

perrera [pe'rrera] *nf* kennel.

perro ['perro] *nm* dog.

persa ['persa] *adj, nm/f* Persian.

persecución [perseku'θjon] *nf* pursuit, chase; (*REL, POL*) persecution.

perseguir [perse'vir] *vt* to pursue, hunt; (*cortejar*) to chase after; (*molestar*) to pester, annoy; (*REL, POL*) to persecute.

perseverante [perseβe'rante] *adj* persevering, persistent.

perseverar [perseβe'rar] *vi* to persevere, persist; **~ en** to persevere in, persist with.

persiana [per'sjana] *nf* (Venetian) blind.

persignarse [persiɣ'narse] *vr* to cross o.s.

persistente [persis'tente] *adj* persistent.

persistir [persis'tir] *vi* to persist.

persona [per'sona] *nf* person; **~ mayor** elderly person; **10 ~s** 10 people.

personaje [perso'naxe] *nm* important person, celebrity; (*TEATRO etc*) character.

personal [perso'nal] *adj* (*particular*) personal; (*para una persona*) single, for one person ♦ *nm* personnel, staff; **~idad** *nf* personality.

personarse [perso'narse] *vr* to appear in person.

personificar [personifi'kar] *vt* to personify.

perspectiva [perspek'tiβa] *nf* perspective; (*vista, panorama*) view, panorama; (*posibilidad futura*) outlook, prospect.

perspicacia [perspi'kaθja] *nf* (*fig*) discernment, perspicacity.

perspicaz [perspi'kaθ] *adj* shrewd.

persuadir [perswa'ðir] *vt* (*gen*) to persuade; (*convencer*) to convince; **~se** *vr* to become convinced; **persuasión** *nf* persuasion; **persuasivo, a** *adj* persuasive; convincing.

pertenecer [pertene'θer] *vi* to belong; (*fig*) to concern; **perteneciente** *adj*: **perteneciente a** belonging to; **pertenencia** *nf* ownership; **pertenencias** *nfpl* (*bienes*) possessions, property *sg*.

pertenezca *etc vb ver* pertenecer.

pértiga ['pertiɣa] *nf*: **salto de ~** pole vault.

pertinaz [perti'naθ] *adj* (*persistente*) persistent; (*terco*) obstinate.

pertinente [perti'nente] *adj* relevant, pertinent; (*apropiado*) appropriate; **~ a** concerning, relevant to.

perturbación [perturβa'θjon] *nf* (*POL*) disturbance; (*MED*) upset, disturbance.

perturbado, a [pertur'βaðo, a] *adj* mentally unbalanced.

perturbador, a [perturβa'ðor, a] *adj* perturbing, disturbing; (*subversivo*) subversive.

perturbar [pertur'βar] *vt* (*el orden*) to disturb; (*MED*) to upset, disturb; (*mentalmente*) to perturb.

Perú [pe'ru] *nm*: **el ~** Peru; **peruano, a** *adj, nm/f* Peruvian.

perversión [perβer'sjon] *nf* perversion; **perverso, a** *adj* perverse; (*depravado*) depraved.

pervertido, a [perβer'tiðo, a] *adj* perverted ♦ *nm/f* pervert.

pervertir [perβer'tir] *vt* to pervert, corrupt.

pesa ['pesa] *nf* weight; (*DEPORTE*) shot.

pesadez [pesa'ðeθ] *nf* (*peso*) heaviness; (*lentitud*) slowness; (*aburrimiento*) tediousness.

pesadilla [pesa'ðiʎa] *nf* nightmare, bad dream.

pesado, a [pe'saðo, a] *adj* heavy; (*lento*) slow; (*difícil, duro*) tough, hard; (*aburrido*) boring, tedious; (*tiempo*) sultry.

pesadumbre [pesa'ðumbre] *nf* grief, sorrow.

pésame ['pesame] *nm* expression of condolence, message of sympathy; **dar el ~** to express one's condolences.

pesar [pe'sar] *vt* to weigh ♦ *vi* to weigh; (*ser pesado*) to weigh a lot, be heavy; (*fig: opinión*) to carry weight; **no pesa mucho** it doesn't weigh much ♦ *nm* (*arrepentimiento*) regret; (*pena*) grief, sorrow; **a ~ de** *o* **pese a** (**que**) in spite of, despite.

pesario [pe'sarjo] *nm* pessary.

pesca ['peska] *nf* (*acto*) fishing; (*lo pescado*) catch; **ir de ~** to go fishing.

pescadería [peskaðe'ria] *nf* fish shop, fishmonger's (*BRIT*).

pescado [pes'kaðo] *nm* fish.

pescador, a [peska'ðor, a] *nm/f* fisherman/woman.

pescar [pes'kar] *vt* (*tomar*) to catch; (*intentar tomar*) to fish for; (*conseguir: trabajo*) to manage to get ♦ *vi* to fish, go fishing.

pescuezo [pes'kweθo] *nm* (*ZOOL*) neck.

pesebre [pe'seβre] *nm* manger.

peseta [pe'seta] *nf* peseta.

pesimista [pesi'mista] *adj* pessimistic ♦ *nm/f* pessimist.

pésimo, a ['pesimo, a] *adj* awful, dreadful.

peso ['peso] *nm* weight; (*balanza*) scales *pl*; (*moneda*) peso; **~ bruto/neto** gross/net weight; **vender a ~** to sell by weight.

pesquero, a [pes'kero, a] *adj* fishing *cpd*.

pesquisa [pes'kisa] *nf* inquiry, investigation.

pestaña [pes'taɲa] *nf* (*ANAT*) eyelash; (*borde*) rim; **pestañear** *vi* to blink.

peste ['peste] *nf* plague; (*mal olor*) stink, stench.

pesticida [pesti'θiða] *nm* pesticide.

pestilencia [pesti'lenθja] *nf* (*mal olor*) stink, stench.

pestillo [pes'tiʎo] *nm* (*cerrojo*) bolt; (*picaporte*) doorhandle.

petaca [pe'taka] *nf* (*de cigarros*) cigarette case; (*de pipa*) tobacco pouch; (*AM: maleta*) suitcase.

pétalo ['petalo] *nm* petal.

petardo [pe'tardo] *nm* firework, firecracker.

petición [peti'θjon] *nf* (*pedido*) request,

plea; (*memorial*) petition; (*JUR*) plea.

petrificar [petrifi'kar] *vt* to petrify.

petróleo [pe'troleo] *nm* oil, petroleum; **petrolero, a** *adj* petroleum *cpd* ♦ *nm* (*COM: persona*) oil man; (*buque*) (oil) tanker.

peyorativo, a [pejora'tiβo, a] *adj* pejorative.

pez [peθ] *nm* fish.

pezón [pe'θon] *nm* teat, nipple.

pezuña [pe'θuɲa] *nf* hoof.

piadoso, a [pja'ðoso, a] *adj* (*devoto*) pious, devout; (*misericordioso*) kind, merciful.

pianista [pja'nista] *nm/f* pianist.

piano ['pjano] *nm* piano.

piar [pjar] *vi* to cheep.

pibe, a ['piβe, a] (*AM*) *nm/f* boy/girl.

picadero [pika'ðero] *nm* riding school.

picadillo [pika'ðiʎo] *nm* mince, minced meat.

picado, a [pi'kaðo, a] *adj* pricked, punctured; (*CULIN*) minced, chopped; (*mar*) choppy; (*diente*) bad; (*tabaco*) cut; (*enfadado*) cross.

picador [pika'ðor] *nm* (*TAUR*) picador; (*minero*) faceworker.

picadura [pika'ðura] *nf* (*pinchazo*) puncture; (*de abeja*) sting; (*de mosquito*) bite; (*tabaco picado*) cut tobacco.

picante [pi'kante] *adj* hot; (*comentario*) racy, spicy.

picaporte [pika'porte] *nm* (*manija*) doorhandle; (*pestillo*) latch.

picar [pi'kar] *vt* (*agujerear, perforar*) to prick, puncture; (*abeja*) to sting; (*mosquito, serpiente*) to bite; (*CULIN*) to mince, chop; (*incitar*) to incite, goad; (*dañar, irritar*) to annoy, bother; (*quemar: lengua*) to burn, sting ♦ *vi* (*pez*) to bite, take the bait; (*sol*) to burn, scorch; (*abeja, MED*) to sting; (*mosquito*) to bite; **~se** *vr* (*agriarse*) to turn sour, go off; (*ofenderse*) to take offence.

picardía [pikar'ðia] *nf* villainy; (*astucia*) slyness, craftiness; (*una ~*) dirty trick; (*palabra*) rude/bad word *o* expression.

pícaro, a ['pikaro, a] *adj* (*malicioso*)

villainous; (*travieso*) mischievous ♦ *nm*
(*astuto*) crafty sort; (*sinvergüenza*)
rascal, scoundrel.
pico ['piko] *nm* (*de ave*) beak; (*punta*)
sharp point; (*TEC*) pick, pickaxe; (*GEO*)
peak, summit; **y ~** and a bit.
picotear [pikote'ar] *vt* to peck ♦ *vi* to
nibble, pick.
picudo, a [pi'kuðo, a] *adj* pointed, with
a point.
pichón [pi'tʃon] *nm* young pigeon.
pidió *etc vb ver* **pedir**.
pido *etc vb ver* **pedir**.
pie [pje] (*pl* ~**s**) *nm* foot; (*fig: motivo*)
motive, basis; (: *fundamento*) foothold;
ir a ~ to go on foot, walk; **estar de ~** to
be standing (up); **ponerse de ~** to stand
up; **de ~s a cabeza** from top to bottom;
al ~ de la letra (*citar*) literally,
verbatim; (*copiar*) exactly, word for
word; **en ~ de guerra** on a war footing;
dar ~ a to give cause for; **hacer ~** (*en
el agua*) to touch (the) bottom.
piedad [pje'ðað] *nf* (*lástima*) pity,
compassion; (*clemencia*) mercy; (*devoción*) piety, devotion.
piedra ['pjeðra] *nf* stone; (*roca*) rock;
(*de mechero*) flint; (*METEOROLOGÍA*)
hailstone.
piel [pjel] *nf* (*ANAT*) skin; (*ZOOL*) skin,
hide, fur; (*cuero*) leather; (*BOT*) skin,
peel.
pienso *etc vb ver* **pensar**.
pierdo *etc vb ver* **perder**.
pierna ['pjerna] *nf* leg.
pieza ['pjeθa] *nf* piece; (*habitación*)
room; **~ de recambio** *o* **repuesto** spare
(part).
pigmeo, a [piɣ'meo, a] *adj, nm/f* pigmy.
pijama [pi'xama] *nm* pyjamas *pl*.
pila ['pila] *nf* (*ELEC*) battery; (*montón*)
heap, pile; (*lavabo*) sink.
píldora ['pildora] *nf* pill; **la ~** (*anti-
conceptiva*) the (contraceptive) pill.
pileta [pi'leta] *nf* basin, bowl; (*AM*)
swimming pool.
piloto [pi'loto] *nm* pilot; (*de aparato*)
(pilot) light; (*AUTO: luz*) tail *o* rear
light; (: *conductor*) driver.
pillaje [pi'ʎaxe] *nm* pillage, plunder.

pillar [pi'ʎar] *vt* (*saquear*) to pillage,
plunder; (*fam: coger*) to catch;
(: *agarrar*) to grasp, seize; (: *entender*) to grasp, catch on to; **~se** *vr*:
~se un dedo con la puerta to catch
one's finger in the door.
pillo, a ['piʎo, a] *adj* villainous; (*astuto*)
sly, crafty ♦ *nm/f* rascal, rogue,
scoundrel.
pimentón [pimen'ton] *nm* paprika.
pimienta [pi'mjenta] *nf* pepper.
pimiento [pi'mjento] *nm* pepper,
pimiento.
pinacoteca [pinako'teka] *nf* art gallery.
pinar [pi'nar] *nm* pine forest (*BRIT*), pine
grove (*US*).
pincel [pin'θel] *nm* paintbrush.
pinchar [pin'tʃar] *vt* (*perforar*) to prick,
pierce; (*neumático*) to puncture; (*fig*)
to prod.
pinchazo [pin'tʃaθo] *nm* (*perforación*)
prick; (*de neumático*) puncture; (*fig*)
prod.
pinchito [pin'tʃito] *nm* shish kebab.
pincho ['pintʃo] *nm* savoury (snack); **~
moruno** shish kebab; **~ de tortilla** small
slice of omelette.
ping-pong ['pin'pon] *nm* table tennis.
pingüino [pin'gwino] *nm* penguin.
pino ['pino] *nm* pine (tree).
pinta ['pinta] *nf* spot; (*de líquidos*) spot,
drop; (*aspecto*) appearance, look(s)
(*pl*); **~do, a** *adj* spotted; (*de muchos
colores*) colourful; **~das** *nfpl* graffiti *sg*.
pintar [pin'tar] *vt* to paint ♦ *vi* to paint;
(*fam*) to count, be important; **~se** *vr* to
put on make-up.
pintor, a [pin'tor, a] *nm/f* painter.
pintoresco, a [pinto'resko, a] *adj* picturesque.
pintura [pin'tura] *nf* painting; **~ a la
acuarela** watercolour; **~ al óleo** oil
painting.
pinza ['pinθa] *nf* (*ZOOL*) claw; (*para
colgar ropa*) clothes peg; (*TEC*) pincers
pl; **~s** *nfpl* (*para depilar etc*) tweezers
pl.
piña ['piɲa] *nf* (*fruto del pino*) pine
cone; (*fruta*) pineapple; (*fig*) group.
piñon [pi'ɲon] *nm* (*fruto*) pine nut;

(TEC) pinion.

pío, a ['pio, a] adj (devoto) pious, devout; (misericordioso) merciful.

piojo ['pjoxo] nm louse.

pionero, a [pjo'nero, a] adj pioneering ♦ nm/f pioneer.

pipa ['pipa] nf pipe; ~s nfpl (BOT) (edible) sunflower seeds.

pipí [pi'pi] (fam) nm: **hacer ~** to have a wee(-wee) (BRIT), have to go (wee-wee) (US).

pique ['pike] nm (resentimiento) pique, resentment; (rivalidad) rivalry, competition; **irse a ~** to sink; (esperanza, familia) to be ruined.

piqueta [pi'keta] nf pick(axe).

piquete [pi'kete] nm (agujerito) small hole; (MIL) squad, party; (de obreros) picket.

piragua [pi'raɣwa] nf canoe; **piragüismo** nm canoeing.

pirámide [pi'ramiðe] nf pyramid.

pirata [pi'rata] adj, nm pirate.

Pirineo(s) [piri'neo(s)] nm(pl) Pyrenees pl.

piropo [pi'ropo] nm compliment, (piece of) flattery.

pirueta [pi'rweta] nf pirouette.

pisada [pi'saða] nf (paso) footstep; (huella) footprint.

pisar [pi'sar] vt (caminar sobre) to walk on, tread on; (apretar con el pie) to press; (fig) to trample on, walk all over ♦ vi to tread, step, walk.

piscina [pis'θina] nf swimming pool.

Piscis ['pisθis] nm Pisces.

piso ['piso] nm (suelo, planta) floor; (apartamento) flat (BRIT), apartment; **primer ~** (ESP) first floor; (AM) ground floor.

pisotear [pisote'ar] vt to trample (on o underfoot).

pista ['pista] nf track, trail; (indicio) clue; ~ **de aterrizaje** runway; ~ **de baile** dance floor; ~ **de hielo** ice rink; ~ **de tenis** tennis court.

pistola [pis'tola] nf pistol; (TEC) spray-gun; **pistolera** nf holster; ver tb **pistolero**; **pistolero, a** nm/f gunman/woman, gangster.

pistón [pis'ton] nm (TEC) piston; (MUS) key.

pitar [pi'tar] vt (silbato) to blow; (rechiflar) to whistle at, boo ♦ vi to whistle; (AUTO) to sound o toot one's horn; (AM) to smoke.

pitillo [pi'tiʎo] nm cigarette.

pito ['pito] nm whistle; (de coche) horn.

pitón [pi'ton] nm (ZOOL) python.

pitonisa [pito'nisa] nf fortune-teller.

pitorreo [pito'rreo] nm joke; **estar de ~** to be joking.

pizarra [pi'θarra] nf (piedra) slate; (encerado) blackboard.

pizca ['piθka] nf pinch, spot; (fig) spot, speck; **ni ~** not a bit.

placa ['plaka] nf plate; (distintivo) badge, insignia; ~ **de matrícula** number plate.

placentero, a [plaθen'tero, a] adj pleasant, agreeable.

placer [pla'θer] nm pleasure ♦ vt to please.

plácido, a ['plaθiðo, a] adj placid.

plaga ['plaɣa] nf pest; (MED) plague; (abundancia) abundance; **plagar** vt to infest, plague; (llenar) to fill.

plagio ['plaxjo] nm plagiarism.

plan [plan] nm (esquema, proyecto) plan; (idea, intento) idea, intention; **tener ~** (fam) to have a date; **tener un ~** (fam) to have an affair; **en ~ económico** (fam) on the cheap; **vamos en ~ de turismo** we're going as tourists; **si te pones en ese ~ ...** if that's your attitude ....

plana ['plana] nf sheet (of paper), page; (TEC) trowel; **en primera ~** on the front page; ~ **mayor** staff.

plancha ['plantʃa] nf (para planchar) iron; (rótulo) plate, sheet; (NAUT) gangway; **a la ~** (CULIN) grilled; ~**do** nm ironing; **planchar** vt to iron ♦ vi to do the ironing.

planeador [planea'ðor] nm glider.

planear [plane'ar] vt to plan ♦ vi to glide.

planeta [pla'neta] nm planet.

planicie [pla'niθje] nf plain.

planificación [planifika'θjon] nf planning; ~ **familiar** family planning.

plano, a ['plano, a] *adj* flat, level, even ♦ *nm* (*MAT, TEC, AVIAT*) plane; (*FOTO*) shot; (*ARQ*) plan; (*GEO*) map; (*de ciudad*) map, street plan; **primer** ~ close-up; **caer de** ~ to fall flat.

planta ['planta] *nf* (*BOT, TEC*) plant; (*ANAT*) sole of the foot, foot; (*piso*) floor; (*AM: personal*) staff; ~ **baja** ground floor.

plantación [planta'θjon] *nf* (*AGR*) plantation; (*acto*) planting.

plantar [plan'tar] *vt* (*BOT*) to plant; (*levantar*) to erect, set up; ~**se** *vr* to stand firm; ~ **a uno en la calle** to throw sb out; **dejar plantado a uno** (*fam*) to stand sb up.

plantear [plante'ar] *vt* (*problema*) to pose; (*dificultad*) to raise.

plantilla [plan'tiʎa] *nf* (*de zapato*) insole; (*personal*) personnel; **ser de** ~ to be on the staff.

plantón [plan'ton] *nm* (*MIL*) guard, sentry; (*fam*) long wait; **dar (un)** ~ **a uno** to stand sb up.

plañir [pla'ɲir] *vi* to mourn.

plasmar [plas'mar] *vt* (*dar forma*) to mould, shape; (*representar*) to represent ♦ *vi*: ~ **en** to take the form of.

Plasticina [plasti'θina] ® *nf* Plasticine ®.

plástica ['plastika] *nf* (art of) sculpture, modelling.

plástico, a ['plastiko, a] *adj* plastic ♦ *nm* plastic.

Plastilina [plasti'lina] ® (*AM*) *nf* Plasticine ®.

plata ['plata] *nf* (*metal*) silver; (*cosas hechas de* ~) silverware; (*AM*) cash, dough; **hablar en** ~ to speak bluntly *o* frankly.

plataforma [plata'forma] *nf* platform; ~ **de lanzamiento/perforación** launch(ing) pad/drilling rig.

plátano ['platano] *nm* (*fruta*) banana; (*árbol*) banana tree.

platea [pla'tea] *nf* (*TEATRO*) pit.

plateado, a [plate'aðo, a] *adj* silver; (*TEC*) silver-plated.

plática ['platika] *nf* talk, chat; **platicar**

platillo [pla'tiʎo] *nm* saucer; ~**s** *nmpl* (*MUS*) cymbals; ~ **volador** *o* **volante** flying saucer.

platino [pla'tino] *nm* platinum; ~**s** *nmpl* (*AUTO*) contact points.

plato ['plato] *nm* plate, dish; (*parte de comida*) course; (*comida*) dish; ~ **combinado** set main course (*served on one plate*); ~ **fuerte** main course; **primer** ~ first course.

playa ['plaja] *nf* beach; (*costa*) seaside; ~ **de estacionamiento** (*AM*) car park.

playera [pla'jera] *nf* (*AM: camiseta*) T-shirt; ~**s** *nfpl* (*zapatos*) (slip-on) canvas shoes.

plaza ['plaθa] *nf* square; (*mercado*) market(place); (*sitio*) room, space; (*en vehículo*) seat, place; (*colocación*) post, job; ~ **de toros** bullring.

plazo ['plaθo] *nm* (*lapso de tiempo*) time, period; (*fecha de vencimiento*) expiry date; (*pago parcial*) instalment; **a corto/largo** ~ short-/long-term; **comprar algo a** ~**s** to buy sth on hire purchase (*Brit*) *o* on time (*US*).

plazoleta [plaθo'leta] *nf* small square.

plazuela [pla'θwela] *nf* = **plazoleta**.

pleamar [plea'mar] *nf* high tide.

plebe ['pleβe] *nf*: **la** ~ the common people *pl*, the masses *pl*; (*pey*) the plebs *pl*; ~**yo, a** *adj* plebeian; (*pey*) coarse, common.

plebiscito [pleβis'θito] *nm* plebiscite.

plegable [ple'ɣaβle] *adj* pliable; (*silla*) folding.

plegar [ple'ɣar] *vt* (*doblar*) to fold, bend; (*COSTURA*) to pleat; ~**se** *vr* to yield, submit.

pleito ['pleito] *nm* (*JUR*) lawsuit, case; (*fig*) dispute, feud.

plenilunio [pleni'lunjo] *nm* full moon.

plenitud [pleni'tuð] *nf* plenitude, fullness; (*abundancia*) abundance.

pleno, a ['pleno, a] *adj* full; (*completo*) complete ♦ *nm* plenum; **en** ~ **día** in broad daylight; **en** ~ **verano** at the height of summer; **en plena cara** full in the face.

pleuresía [pleure'sia] *nf* pleurisy.

Plexiglás [pleksi'ɣlas] ® *nm* acrylic glass, Plexiglas ® (*US*).

pliego *etc* ['pljeɣo] *vb ver* **plegar** ♦ *nm* (*hoja*) sheet (of paper); (*carta*) sealed letter/document; ~ **de condiciones** details *pl*, specifications *pl*.

pliegue *etc* ['pljeɣe] *vb ver* **plegar** ♦ *nm* fold, crease; (*de vestido*) pleat.

plisado [pli'saðo] *nm* pleating.

plomero [plo'mero] *nm* (*AM*) plumber.

plomo ['plomo] *nm* (*metal*) lead; (*ELEC*) fuse.

pluma ['pluma] *nf* feather; (*para escribir*): ~ (**estilográfica**) ink pen; ~ **fuente** (*AM*) fountain pen.

plumero [plu'mero] *nm* (*quitapolvos*) feather duster.

plumón [plu'mon] *nm* (*AM: fino*) felt-tip pen; (: *ancho*) marker.

plural [plu'ral] *adj* plural; ~**idad** *nf* plurality; **una ~idad de votos** a majority of votes.

plus [plus] *nm* bonus; ~**valía** *nf* (*COM*) appreciation.

plutocracia [pluto'kraθja] *nf* plutocracy.

población [poβla'θjon] *nf* population; (*pueblo, ciudad*) town, city.

poblado, a [po'βlaðo, a] *adj* inhabited ♦ *nm* (*aldea*) village; (*pueblo*) (small) town; **densamente** ~ densely populated.

poblador, a [poβla'ðor, a] *nm/f* settler, colonist.

poblar [po'βlar] *vt* (*colonizar*) to colonize; (*fundar*) to found; (*habitar*) to inhabit.

pobre ['poβre] *adj* poor ♦ *nm/f* poor person; ¡~! poor thing!; ~**za** *nf* poverty.

pocilga [po'θilɣa] *nf* pigsty.

pocillo [po'siʎo] (*AM*) *nm* coffee cup.

pócima ['poθima] *nf* = **poción**.

poción [po'θjon] *nf* potion.

poco, a ['poko, a] *adj* **1** (*sg*) little, not much; ~ **tiempo** little *o* not much time; **de** ~ **interés** of little interest, not very interesting; **poca cosa** not much

2 (*pl*) few, not many; **unos** ~s a few, some; ~s **niños comen lo que les** **conviene** few children eat what they should

♦ *adv* **1** little, not much; **cuesta** ~ it doesn't cost much

2 (+ *adj*: = *negativo, antónimo*): ~ **amable/inteligente** not very nice/intelligent

3: **por** ~ **me caigo** I almost fell

4: **a** ~: **a** ~ **de haberse casado** shortly after getting married

5: ~ **a** ~ little by little

♦ *nm* a little, a bit; **un** ~ **triste/de dinero** a little sad/money.

podar [po'ðar] *vt* to prune.

poder [po'ðer] *vi* **1** (*capacidad*) can, be able to; **no puedo hacerlo** I can't do it, I'm unable to do it

2 (*permiso*) can, may, be allowed to; **¿se puede?** may I (*o* we)?; **puedes irte ahora** you may go now; **no se puede fumar en este hospital** smoking is not allowed in this hospital

3 (*posibilidad*) may, might, could; **puede llegar mañana** he may *o* might arrive tomorrow; **pudiste haberte hecho daño** you might *o* could have hurt yourself; **¡podías habérmelo dicho antes!** you might have told me before!

4: **puede ser: puede ser** perhaps; **puede ser que lo sepa Tomás** Tomás may *o* might know

5: **¡no puedo más!** I've had enough!; **no pude menos que dejarlo** I couldn't help but leave it; **es tonto a más no** ~ he's as stupid as they come

6: ~ **con: no puedo con este crío** this kid's too much for me

♦ *nm* power; ~ **adquisitivo** purchasing power; **detentar** *o* **ocupar** *o* **estar en el** ~ to be in power.

podrido, a [po'ðriðo, a] *adj* rotten, bad; (*fig*) rotten, corrupt.

podrir [po'ðrir] = **pudrir**.

poema [po'ema] *nm* poem.

poesía [poe'sia] *nf* poetry.

poeta [po'eta] *nm* poet; **poético, a** *adj*

poetic (al).

poetisa [poe'tisa] *nf* (woman) poet.

póker ['poker] *nm* poker.

polaco, a [po'lako, a] *adj* Polish ♦ *nm/f* Pole.

polar [po'lar] *adj* polar; **~idad** *nf* polarity; **~izarse** *vr* to polarize.

polea [po'lea] *nf* pulley.

polémica [po'lemika] *nf* polemics *sg*; (*una ~*) controversy, polemic.

polen ['polen] *nm* pollen.

policía [poli'θia] *nm/f* policeman/woman ♦ *nf* police; **~co, a** *adj* police *cpd*; **novela policíaca** detective story; **policial** *adj* police *cpd*.

polideportivo [poliðepor'tiβo] *nm* sports centre *o* complex.

polietileno [polieti'leno] *nm* polythene (*BRIT*), polyethylene (*US*).

poligamia [poli'ɣamja] *nf* polygamy.

polilla [po'liʎa] *nf* moth.

polio ['poljo] *nf* polio.

politécnico [poli'tekniko] *nm* polytechnic.

política [po'litika] *nf* politics *sg*; (*económica, agraria etc*) policy; *ver tb* **político; politicastro** (*pey*) *nm* politician, politico.

político, a [po'litiko, a] *adj* political; (*discreto*) tactful; (*de familia*) -in-law ♦ *nm/f* politician; **padre ~** father-in-law.

póliza ['poliθa] *nf* certificate, voucher; (*impuesto*) tax stamp; **~ de seguros** insurance policy.

polizón [poli'θon] *nm* (*en barco etc*) stowaway.

polo ['polo] *nm* (*GEO, ELEC*) pole; (*helado*) ice lolly; (*DEPORTE*) polo; (*suéter*) polo-neck; **~ Norte/Sur** North/South Pole.

Polonia [po'lonja] *nf* Poland.

poltrona [pol'trona] *nf* easy chair.

polución [polu'θjon] *nf* pollution.

polvera [pol'ßera] *nf* powder compact.

polvo ['polßo] *nm* dust; (*QUÍMICA, CULIN, MED*) powder; **~s** *nmpl* (*maquillage*) powder *sg*; **~ de talco** talcum powder; **estar hecho ~** (*fam*) to be worn out *o* exhausted.

pólvora ['polßora] *nf* gunpowder;

(*fuegos artificiales*) fireworks *pl*.

polvoriento, a [polßo'rjento, a] *adj* (*superficie*) dusty; (*sustancia*) powdery.

pollera [po'ʎera] (*AM*) *nf* skirt.

pollería [poʎe'ria] *nf* poulterer's (shop).

pollo ['poʎo] *nm* chicken.

pomada [po'maða] *nf* (*MED*) cream, ointment.

pomelo [po'melo] *nm* grapefruit.

pómez ['pomeθ] *nf*: **piedra ~** pumice stone.

pompa ['pompa] *nf* (*burbuja*) bubble; (*bomba*) pump; (*esplendor*) pomp, splendour; **pomposo, a** *adj* splendid, magnificent; (*pey*) pompous.

pómulo ['pomulo] *nm* cheekbone.

pon [pon] *vb ver* **poner**.

ponche ['pontʃe] *nm* punch.

poncho ['pontʃo] (*AM*) *nm* poncho.

ponderar [ponde'rar] *vt* (*considerar*) to weigh up, consider; (*elogiar*) to praise highly, speak in praise of.

pondré *etc vb ver* **poner**.

┌─────────────────┐
│ *PALABRA CLAVE* │
└─────────────────┘

poner [po'ner] *vt* **1** (*colocar*) to put; (*telegrama*) to send; (*obra de teatro*) to put on; (*película*) to show; **ponlo más fuerte** turn it up; **¿qué ponen en el Excelsior?** what's on at the Excelsior?

2 (*tienda*) to open; (*instalar: gas etc*) to put in; (*radio, TV*) to switch *o* turn on

3 (*suponer*): **pongamos que ...** let's suppose that ...

4 (*contribuir*): **el gobierno ha puesto otro millón** the government has contributed another million

5 (*TELEC*): **póngame con el Sr. López** can you put me through to Mr. López

6: **~ de**: **le han puesto de director general** they've appointed him general manager

7 (+ *adj*) to make; **me estás poniendo nerviosa** you're making me nervous

8 (*dar nombre*): **al hijo le pusieron Diego** they called their son Diego

♦ *vi* (*gallina*) to lay

♦ **~se** *vr* **1** (*colocarse*): **se puso a mi**

lado he came and stood beside me; **tú pónte en esa silla** you go and sit on that chair
2 (*vestido, cosméticos*) to put on; **¿por qué no te pones el vestido nuevo?** why don't you put on o wear your new dress?
3 (+ *adj*) to turn; to get, become; **se puso muy serio** he got very serious; **después de lavarla la tela se puso azul** after washing it the material turned blue
4: ~**se a: se puso a llorar** he started to cry; **tienes que** ~**te a estudiar** you must get down to studying
5: ~**se a bien con uno** to make it up with sb; **-se a mal con uno** to get on the wrong side of sb.

pongo *etc vb ver* **poner.**
poniente [po'njente] *nm* (*occidente*) west; (*viento*) west wind.
pontificado [pontifi'kaðo] *nm* papacy, pontificate; **pontífice** *nm* pope, pontiff.
pontón [pon'ton] *nm* pontoon.
ponzoña [pon'θoɲa] *nf* poison, venom.
popa ['popa] *nf* stern.
popular [popu'lar] *adj* popular; (*cultura*) of the people, folk *cpd*; ~**idad** *nf* popularity; ~**izarse** *vr* to become popular.

por [por] *prep* **1** (*objetivo*) for; **luchar** ~ **la patria** to fight for one's country
2 (+ *infin*): ~ **no llegar tarde** so as not to arrive late; ~ **citar unos ejemplos** to give a few examples
3 (*causa*) out of, because of; ~ **escasez de fondos** for lack of funds
4 (*tiempo*): ~ **la mañana/noche** in the morning/at night; **se queda** ~ **una semana** she's staying (for) a week
5 (*lugar*): **pasar** ~ **Madrid** to pass through Madrid; **ir a Guayaquil** ~ **Quito** to go to Guayaquil via Quito; **caminar** ~ **la calle** to walk along the street; *ver tb* **todo**
6 (*cambio, precio*): **te doy uno nuevo** ~ **el que tienes** I'll give you a new one (in

return) for the one you've got
7 (*valor distributivo*): **550 pesetas** ~ **hora/cabeza** 550 pesetas an o per hour/a o per head
8 (*modo, medio*) by; ~ **correo/avión** by post/air; **día** ~ **día** day by day; **entrar** ~ **la entrada principal** to go in through the main entrance
9: 10 ~ **10 son 100** 10 by 10 is 100
10 (*en lugar de*): **vino él** ~ **su jefe** he came instead of his boss
11: ~ **mí que revienten** as far as I'm concerned they can drop dead.

porcelana [porθe'lana] *nf* porcelain; (*china*) china.
porcentaje [porθen'taxe] *nm* percentage.
porción [por'θjon] *nf* (*parte*) portion, share; (*cantidad*) quantity, amount.
pordiosero, a [porðjo'sero, a] *nm/f* beggar.
porfía [por'fia] *nf* persistence; (*terquedad*) obstinacy.
porfiado, a [por'fjaðo, a] *adj* persistent; obstinate.
porfiar [por'fjar] *vi* to persist, insist; (*disputar*) to argue stubbornly.
pormenor [porme'nor] *nm* detail, particular.
pornografía [pornovra'fia] *nf* pornography.
poro ['poro] *nm* pore; ~**so, a** *adj* porous.
porque ['porke] *conj* (*a causa de*) because; (*ya que*) since; (*con el fin de*) so that, in order that.
porqué [por'ke] *nm* reason, cause.
porquería [porke'ria] *nf* (*suciedad*) filth, dirt; (*acción*) dirty trick; (*objeto*) small thing, trifle; (*fig*) rubbish.
porra ['porra] *nf* (*arma*) stick, club.
porrón [po'rron] *nm* glass wine jar with a long spout.
portaaviones [porta'(a)ßjones] *nm inv* aircraft carrier.
portada [por'taða] *nf* (*de revista*) cover.
portador, a [por'ðor, a] *nm/f* carrier, bearer; (*COM*) bearer, payee.
portaequipajes [portaeki'paxes] *nm inv* (*AUTO: maletero*) boot; (: *baca*)

luggage rack.

portal [por'tal] *nm* (*entrada*) vestibule, hall; (*portada*) porch, doorway; (*puerta de entrada*) main door; (*DEPORTE*) goal.

portaligas [porta'liɣas] *nm inv* suspender belt.

portamaletas [portama'letas] *nm inv* (*AUTO: maletero*) boot; (: *baca*) roof rack.

portamonedas [portamo'neðas] *nm inv* purse.

portarse [por'tarse] *vr* to behave, conduct o.s.

portátil [por'tatil] *adj* portable.

portavoz [porta'ßoθ] *nm/f* (*persona*) spokesman/woman.

portazo [por'taθo] *nm*: **dar un ~** to slam the door.

porte ['porte] *nm* (*COM*) transport; (*precio*) transport charges *pl*.

portento [por'tento] *nm* marvel, wonder; **~so, a** *adj* marvellous, extraordinary.

porteño, a [por'teɲo, a] *adj* of o from Buenos Aires.

portería [porte'ria] *nf* (*oficina*) porter's office; (*gol*) goal.

portero, a [por'tero, a] *nm/f* porter; (*conserje*) caretaker; (*ujier*) doorman; (*DEPORTE*) goalkeeper.

pórtico ['portiko] *nm* (*patio*) portico, porch; (*fig*) gateway; (*arcada*) arcade.

portilla [por'tiʎa] *nf* (*cancela*) gate.

portillo [por'tiʎo] *nm* = **portilla**.

portorriqueño, a [portorri'keɲo, a] *adj* Puerto Rican.

Portugal [portu'ɣal] *nm* Portugal; **portugués, esa** *adj*, *nm/f* Portuguese ♦ *nm* (*LING*) Portuguese.

porvenir [porße'nir] *nm* future.

pos [pos] *prep*: **en ~ de** after, in pursuit of.

posada [po'saða] *nf* (*refugio*) shelter, lodging; (*mesón*) guest house; **dar ~ a** to give shelter to, take in.

posaderas [posa'ðeras] *nfpl* backside *sg*, buttocks.

posar [po'sar] *vt* (*en el suelo*) to lay down, put down; (*la mano*) to place, put gently ♦ *vi* to sit, pose; **~se** *vr* to settle; (*pájaro*) to perch; (*avión*) to land, come down.

posdata [pos'ðata] *nf* postscript.

pose ['pose] *nf* pose.

poseedor, a [posee'ðor, a] *nm/f* owner, possessor; (*de récord, puesto*) holder.

poseer [pose'er] *vt* to possess, own; (*ventaja*) to enjoy; (*récord, puesto*) to hold; **poseído, a** *adj* possessed.

posesión [pose'sjon] *nf* possession; **posesionarse** *vr*: **posesionarse de** to take possession of, take over.

posesivo, a [pose'sißo, a] *adj* possessive.

posibilidad [posißili'ðað] *nf* possibility; (*oportunidad*) chance; **posibilitar** *vt* to make possible; (*hacer realizable*) to make feasible.

posible [po'sißle] *adj* possible; (*realizable*) feasible; **de ser ~** if possible; **en lo ~** as far as possible.

posición [posi'θjon] *nf* position; (*rango social*) status.

positiva [posi'tißa] *nf* (*FOTO*) print.

positivo, a [posi'tißo, a] *adj* positive.

poso ['poso] *nm* sediment; (*heces*) dregs *pl*.

posponer [pospo'ner] *vt* to put behind/below; (*aplazar*) to postpone.

posta ['posta] *nf*: **a ~** deliberately, on purpose.

postal [pos'tal] *adj* postal ♦ *nf* postcard.

poste ['poste] *nm* (*de telégrafos etc*) post, pole; (*columna*) pillar.

póster ['poster] (*pl* **pósteres, pósters**) *nm* poster.

postergar [poster'ɣar] *vt* to postpone, delay.

posteridad [posteri'ðað] *nf* posterity.

posterior [poste'rjor] *adj* back, rear; (*siguiente*) following, subsequent; (*más tarde*) later; **~idad** *nf*: **con ~idad** later, subsequently.

postizo, a [pos'tiθo, a] *adj* false, artificial ♦ *nm* hairpiece.

postor, a [pos'tor, a] *nm/f* bidder.

postrado, a [pos'traðo, a] *adj* prostrate.

postre ['postre] *nm* sweet, dessert.

postrero, a [pos'trero, a] (*delante de*

nmsg: **postrer**) *adj* (*último*) last; (*que viene detrás*) rear.
postulado [postu'laðo] *nm* postulate.
póstumo, a ['postumo, a] *adj* posthumous.
postura [pos'tura] *nf* (*del cuerpo*) posture, position; (*fig*) attitude, position.
potable [po'taßle] *adj* drinkable; **agua** ~ drinking water.
potaje [po'taxe] *nm* thick vegetable soup.
pote ['pote] *nm* pot, jar.
potencia [po'tenθja] *nf* power.
potencial [poten'θjal] *adj*, *nm* potential.
potenciar [poten'θjar] *vt* to boost.
potente [po'tente] *adj* powerful.
potro, a ['potro, a] *nm/f* (*ZOOL*) colt/filly ♦ *nm* (*de gimnasia*) vaulting horse.
pozo ['poθo] *nm* well; (*de río*) deep pool; (*de mina*) shaft.
P.P. *abr* (= *porte pagado*) CP.
p.p. *abr* (= *por poder*) p.p.
práctica ['praktika] *nf* practice; (*método*) method; (*arte, capacidad*) skill; **en la** ~ in practice.
practicable [prakti'kaßle] *adj* practicable; (*camino*) passable.
practicante [prakti'kante] *nm/f* (*MED*: *ayudante de doctor*) medical assistant; (: *enfermero*) male nurse; (*quien practica algo*) practitioner ♦ *adj* practising.
practicar [prakti'kar] *vt* to practise; (*DEPORTE*) to go in for (*BRIT*) *o* out for (*US*), play; (*realizar*) to carry out, perform.
práctico, a ['praktiko, a] *adj* practical; (*instruído*: *persona*) skilled, expert.
practique *etc vb ver* **practicar**.
pradera [pra'ðera] *nf* meadow; (*US* etc) prairie.
prado ['praðo] *nm* (*campo*) meadow, field; (*pastizal*) pasture.
Praga ['praɣa] *n* Prague.
pragmático, a [praɣ'matiko, a] *adj* pragmatic.
preámbulo [pre'ambulo] *nm* preamble, introduction.
precario, a [pre'karjo, a] *adj* precarious.
precaución [prekau'θjon] *nf* (*medida*

preventiva) preventive measure, precaution; (*prudencia*) caution, wariness.
precaver [preka'ßer] *vt* to guard against; (*impedir*) to forestall; ~**se** *vr*: ~**se de** *o* **contra algo** to (be on one's) guard against sth; **precavido, a** *adj* cautious, wary.
precedencia [preθe'ðenθja] *nf* precedence; (*prioridad*) priority; (*preeminencia*) greater importance, superiority; **precedente** *adj* preceding; (*anterior*) former ♦ *nm* precedent.
preceder [preθe'ðer] *vt*, *vi* to precede, go before, come before.
precepto [pre'θepto] *nm* precept.
preciado, a [pre'θjaðo, a] *adj* (*estimado*) esteemed, valuable.
preciar [pre'θjar] *vt* to esteem, value; ~**se** *vr* to boast; ~**se de** to pride o.s. on, boast of being.
precinto [pre'θinto] *nm* (*tb*: ~ **de garantía**) seal.
precio ['preθjo] *nm* price; (*costo*) cost; (*valor*) value, worth; (*de viaje*) fare; ~ **al contado/de coste/de oportunidad** cash/cost/bargain price; ~ **al detalle** *o* **al por menor** retail price; ~ **tope** top price.
preciosidad [preθjosi'ðað] *nf* (*valor*) (high) value, (great) worth; (*encanto*) charm; (*cosa bonita*) beautiful thing; **es una** ~ it's lovely, it's really beautiful.
precioso, a [pre'θjoso, a] *adj* precious; (*de mucho valor*) valuable; (*fam*) lovely, beautiful.
precipicio [preθi'piθjo] *nm* cliff, precipice; (*fig*) abyss.
precipitación [preθipita'θjon] *nf* haste; (*lluvia*) rainfall.
precipitado, a [preθipi'taðo, a] *adj* (*conducta*) hasty, rash; (*salida*) hasty, sudden.
precipitar [preθipi'tar] *vt* (*arrojar*) to hurl down, throw; (*apresurar*) to hasten; (*acelerar*) to speed up, accelerate; ~**se** *vr* to throw o.s.; (*apresurarse*) to rush; (*actuar sin pensar*) to act rashly.
precisamente [preθisa'mente] *adv* pre-

cisely; (*exactamente*) precisely, exactly.

precisar [preθi'sar] *vt* (*necesitar*) to need, require; (*fijar*) to determine exactly, fix; (*especificar*) to specify.

precisión [preθi'sjon] *nf* (*exactitud*) precision.

preciso, a [pre'θiso, a] *adj* (*exacto*) precise; (*necesario*) necessary, essential.

preconcebido, a [prekonθe'βiðo, a] *adj* preconceived.

precoz [pre'koθ] *adj* (*persona*) precocious; (*calvicie etc*) premature.

precursor, a [prekur'sor, a] *nm/f* predecessor, forerunner.

predecir [preðe'θir] *vt* to predict, forecast.

predestinado, a [preðesti'naðo, a] *adj* predestined.

predeterminar [preðetermi'nar] *vt* to predetermine.

prédica ['preðika] *nf* sermon.

predicador, a [preðika'ðor, a] *nm/f* preacher.

predicar [preði'kar] *vt, vi* to preach.

predicción [preðik'θjon] *nf* prediction.

predilecto, a [preði'lekto, a] *adj* favourite.

predisponer [preðispo'ner] *vt* to predispose; (*pey*) to prejudice; **predisposición** *nf* inclination; prejudice, bias.

predominante [preðomi'nante] *adj* predominant.

predominar [preðomi'nar] *vt* to dominate ♦ *vi* to predominate; (*prevalecer*) to prevail; **predominio** *nm* predominance; prevalence.

preescolar [pre(e)sko'lar] *adj* preschool.

prefabricado, a [prefaβri'kaðo, a] *adj* prefabricated.

prefacio [pre'faθjo] *nm* preface.

preferencia [prefe'renθja] *nf* preference; **de ~** preferably, for preference.

preferible [prefe'riβle] *adj* preferable.

preferir [prefe'rir] *vt* to prefer.

prefiero *etc vb ver* **preferir**.

prefigurar [prefiɣu'rar] *vt* to foreshadow, prefigure.

pregonar [preɣo'nar] *vt* to proclaim,

announce.

pregunta [pre'ɣunta] *nf* question; **hacer una ~** to ask o put (forth (*US*)) a question.

preguntar [preɣun'tar] *vt* to ask; (*cuestionar*) to question ♦ *vi* to ask; **~se** *vr* to wonder; **~ por alguien** to ask for sb.

preguntón, ona [preɣun'ton, ona] *adj* inquisitive.

prehistórico, a [preis'toriko, a] *adj* prehistoric.

prejuicio [pre'xwiθjo] *nm* (*acto*) prejudgement; (*idea preconcebida*) preconception; (*parcialidad*) prejudice, bias.

preliminar [prelimi'nar] *adj* preliminary.

preludio [pre'luðjo] *nm* prelude.

prematuro, a [prema'turo, a] *adj* premature.

premeditación [premeðita'θjon] *nf* premeditation.

premeditar [premeði'tar] *vt* to premeditate.

premiar [pre'mjar] *vt* to reward; (*en un concurso*) to give a prize to.

premio ['premjo] *nm* reward; prize; (*COM*) premium.

premonición [premoni'θjon] *nf* premonition.

premura [pre'mura] *nf* (*aprieto*) pressure; (*prisa*) haste, urgency.

prenatal [prena'tal] *adj* antenatal, prenatal.

prenda ['prenda] *nf* (*ropa*) garment, article of clothing; (*garantía*) pledge; **~s** *nfpl* (*talentos*) talents, gifts.

prendar [pren'dar] *vt* to captivate, enchant; **~se de uno** to fall in love with sb.

prendedor [prende'ðor] *nm* brooch.

prender [pren'der] *vt* (*captar*) to catch, capture; (*detener*) to arrest; (*COSTURA*) to pin, attach; (*sujetar*) to fasten ♦ *vi* to catch; (*arraigar*) to take root; **~se** *vr* (*encenderse*) to catch fire.

prendido, a [pren'diðo, a] (*AM*) *adj* (*luz etc*) on.

prensa ['prensa] *nf* press; **la P~** the press; **prensar** *vt* to press.

preñado, a [pre'ɲaðo, a] *adj* (*ZOOL*) pregnant; ~ **de** pregnant with, full of; **preñez** *nf* pregnancy.

preocupación [preokupa'θjon] *nf* worry, concern; (*ansiedad*) anxiety.

preocupado, a [preoku'paðo, a] *adj* worried, concerned; (*ansioso*) anxious.

preocupar [preoku'par] *vt* to worry; ~**se** *vr* to worry; ~**se de algo** (*hacerse cargo*) to take care of sth.

preparación [prepara'θjon] *nf* (*acto*) preparation; (*estado*) readiness; (*entrenamiento*) training.

preparado, a [prepa'raðo, a] *adj* (*dispuesto*) prepared; (*CULIN*) ready (to serve) ♦ *nm* preparation.

preparador, a [prepara'ðor, a] *nm/f* trainer.

preparar [prepa'rar] *vt* (*disponer*) to prepare, get ready; (*TEC: tratar*) to prepare, process; (*entrenar*) to teach, train; ~**se** *vr*: ~**se a** *o* **para** to prepare to *o* for, get ready to *o* for; **preparativo, a** *adj* preparatory, preliminary; **preparativos** *nmpl* preparations; **preparatoria** (*AM*) *nf* sixth-form college (*BRIT*), senior high school (*US*); **preparatorio, a** *adj* preparatory.

prerrogativa [prerroɣa'tiβa] *nf* prerogative, privilege.

presa ['presa] *nf* (*cosa apresada*) catch; (*víctima*) victim; (*de animal*) prey; (*de agua*) dam.

presagiar [presa'xjar] *vt* to presage, forebode.

presbítero [pres'βitero] *nm* priest.

prescindir [presθin'dir] *vi*: ~ **de** (*privarse de*) to do without, go without; (*descartar*) to dispense with.

prescribir [preskri'βir] *vt* to prescribe; **prescripción** *nf* prescription.

presencia [pre'senθja] *nf* presence; **presencial** *adj*: **testigo presencial** eyewitness; **presenciar** *vt* to be present at; (*asistir a*) to attend; (*ver*) to see, witness.

presentación [presenta'θjon] *nf* presentation; (*introducción*) introduction. ⁓

presentador, a [presenta'ðor, a] *nm/f* presenter, compère.

presentar [presen'tar] *vt* to present; (*ofrecer*) to offer; (*mostrar*) to show, display; (*a una persona*) to introduce; ~**se** *vr* (*llegar inesperadamente*) to appear, turn up; (*ofrecerse como candidato*) to run, stand; (*aparecer*) to show, appear; (*solicitar empleo*) to apply.

presente [pre'sente] *adj* present ♦ *nm* present; **hacer** ~ to state, declare; **tener** ~ to remember, bear in mind.

presentimiento [presenti'mjento] *nm* premonition, presentiment.

presentir [presen'tir] *vt* to have a premonition of.

preservación [preserβa'θjon] *nf* protection, preservation.

preservar [preser'βar] *vt* to protect, preserve; **preservativo** *nm* sheath, condom.

presidencia [presi'ðenθja] *nf* presidency; (*de comité*) chairmanship.

presidente [presi'ðente] *nm/f* president; (*de comité*) chairman/woman.

presidiario [presi'ðjarjo] *nm* convict.

presidio [pre'sidjo] *nm* prison, penitentiary.

presidir [presi'ðir] *vt* (*dirigir*) to preside at, preside over; (: *comité*) to take the chair at; (*dominar*) to dominate, rule ♦ *vi* to preside; to take the chair.

presión [pre'sjon] *nf* pressure; **presionar** *vt* to press; (*fig*) to press, put pressure on ♦ *vi*: **presionar para** to press for.

preso, a ['preso, a] *nm/f* prisoner; **tomar** *o* **llevar** ~ **a uno** to arrest sb, take sb prisoner.

prestado, a [pres'taðo, a] *adj* on loan; **pedir** ~ to borrow.

prestamista [presta'mista] *nm/f* moneylender.

préstamo ['prestamo] *nm* loan; ~ **hipotecario** mortgage.

prestar [pres'tar] *vt* to lend, loan; (*atención*) to pay; (*ayuda*) to give.

presteza [pres'teθa] *nf* speed, promptness.

prestigio [pres'tixjo] *nm* prestige; ~**so, a** *adj* (*honorable*) prestigious; (*famoso, renombrado*) renowned, famous.

presto, a ['presto, a] *adj* (*rápido*) quick, prompt; (*dispuesto*) ready ♦ *adv* at once, right away.

presumir [presu'mir] *vt* to presume ♦ *vi* (*tener aires*) to be conceited; **según cabe** ~ as may be presumed, presumably; **presunción** *nf* presumption; **presunto, a** *adj* (*supuesto*) supposed, presumed; (*así llamado*) so-called; **presuntuoso, a** *adj* conceited, presumptuous.

presuponer [presupo'ner] *vt* to presuppose.

presupuesto [presu'pwesto] *pp de* **presuponer** ♦ *nm* (*FINANZAS*) budget; (*estimación: de costo*) estimate.

presuroso, a [presu'roso, a] *adj* (*rápido*) quick, speedy; (*que tiene prisa*) hasty.

pretencioso, a [preten'θjoso, a] *adj* pretentious.

pretender [preten'der] *vt* (*intentar*) to try to, seek to; (*reivindicar*) to claim; (*buscar*) to seek, try for; (*cortejar*) to woo, court; ~ **que** to expect that; **pretendiente** *nm/f* (*candidato*) candidate, applicant; (*amante*) suitor; **pretensión** *nf* (*aspiración*) aspiration; (*reivindicación*) claim; (*orgullo*) pretension.

pretexto [pre'teksto] *nm* pretext; (*excusa*) excuse.

prevalecer [preβale'θer] *vi* to prevail.

prevención [preβen'θjon] *nf* (*preparación*) preparation; (*estado*) preparedness, readiness; (*el evitar*) prevention; (*previsión*) foresight, forethought; (*precaución*) precaution.

prevenido, a [preβe'niðo, a] *adj* prepared, ready; (*cauteloso*) cautious.

prevenir [preβe'nir] *vt* (*impedir*) to prevent; (*prever*) to foresee, anticipate; (*predisponer*) to prejudice, bias; (*avisar*) to warn; (*preparar*) to prepare, get ready; ~**se** *vr* to get ready, prepare; ~**se contra** to take precautions against; **preventivo, a** *adj* preventive, precautionary.

prever [pre'βer] *vt* to foresee.

previo, a ['preβjo, a] *adj* (*anterior*) previous; (*preliminar*) preliminary ♦ *prep*:

~ **acuerdo de los otros** subject to the agreement of the others.

previsión [preβi'sjon] *nf* (*perspicacia*) foresight; (*predicción*) forecast.

prima ['prima] *nf* (*COM*) bonus; ~ **de seguro** insurance premium; *ver tb* **primo**.

primacía [prima'θia] *nf* primacy.

primario, a [pri'marjo, a] *adj* primary.

primavera [prima'βera] *nf* spring(time).

primera [pri'mera] *nf* (*AUTO*) first gear; (*FERRO: tb*: ~ **clase**) first class; **de** ~ (*fam*) first-class, first-rate.

primero, a [pri'mero, a] (*delante de nmsg*: **primer**) *adj* first; (*principal*) prime ♦ *adv* first; (*más bien*) sooner, rather; **primera plana** front page.

primitivo, a [primi'tiβo, a] *adj* primitive; (*original*) original.

primo, a ['primo, a] *adj* prime ♦ *nm/f* cousin; (*fam*) fool, idiot; ~ **hermano** first cousin; **materias primas** raw materials.

primogénito, a [primo'xenito, a] *adj* first-born.

primordial [primor'ðjal] *adj* basic, fundamental.

primoroso, a [primo'roso, a] *adj* exquisite, delicate.

princesa [prin'θesa] *nf* princess.

principal [prinθi'pal] *adj* principal, main ♦ *nm* (*jefe*) chief, principal.

príncipe ['prinθipe] *nm* prince.

principiante [prinθi'pjante] *nm/f* beginner.

principiar [prinθi'pjar] *vt* to begin.

principio [prin'θipjo] *nm* (*comienzo*) beginning, start; (*origen*) origin; (*primera etapa*) rudiment, basic idea; (*moral*) principle; **a** ~**s de** at the beginning of.

pringoso, a [prin'γoso, a] *adj* (*grasiento*) greasy; (*pegajoso*) sticky.

pringue ['pringe] *nm* (*grasa*) grease, fat, dripping.

prioridad [priori'ðað] *nf* priority.

prisa ['prisa] *nf* (*apresuramiento*) hurry, haste; (*rapidez*) speed; (*urgencia*) (sense of) urgency; **a** *o* **de** ~ quickly; **correr** ~ to be urgent; **darse** ~ to hurry

up; **estar de** o **tener** ~ to be in a hurry.
prisión [pri'sjon] *nf* (*cárcel*) prison;
(*período de cárcel*) imprisonment;
prisionero, a *nm/f* prisoner.
prismáticos [pris'matikos] *nmpl* binoculars.
privación [priβa'θjon] *nf* deprivation;
(*falta*) want, privation.
privado, a [pri'βaðo, a] *adj* private.
privar [pri'βar] *vt* to deprive; **privativo,
a** *adj* exclusive.
privilegiado, a [priβile'xjaðo, a] *adj*
privileged; (*memoria*) very good.
privilegiar [priβile'xjar] *vt* to grant a
privilege to; (*favorecer*) to favour.
privilegio [priβi'lexjo] *nm* privilege;
(*concesión*) concession.
pro [pro] *nm* o *f* profit, advantage ♦
prep: **asociación ~ ciegos** association
for the blind ♦ *prefijo*: ~ **soviético/
americano** pro-Soviet/American; **en ~
de** on behalf of, for; **los ~s y los contras** the pros and cons.
proa ['proa] *nf* bow, prow; **de ~** bow
cpd, fore.
probabilidad [proβaβili'ðað] *nf* probability, likelihood; (*oportunidad,
posibilidad*) chance, prospect; **probable**
adj probable, likely.
probador [proβa'ðor] *nm* (*en tienda*)
fitting room.
probar [pro'βar] *vt* (*demostrar*) to
prove; (*someter a prueba*) to test, try
out; (*ropa*) to try on; (*comida*) to taste
♦ *vi* to try; **~se un traje** to try on a
suit.
probeta [pro'βeta] *nf* test tube.
problema [pro'βlema] *nm* problem.
procedente [proθe'ðente] *adj* (*razonable*) reasonable; (*conforme a derecho*) proper, fitting; **~ de** coming from,
originating in.
proceder [proθe'ðer] *vi* (*avanzar*) to
proceed; (*actuar*) to act; (*ser correcto*)
to be right (and proper), be fitting ♦ *nm*
(*comportamiento*) behaviour, conduct;
~ de to come from, originate in;
procedimiento *nm* procedure;
(*proceso*) process; (*método*) means *pl*,
method.

procesado, a [proθe'saðo, a] *nm/f*
accused.
procesador [proθesa'ðor] *nm*: ~ **de
textos** word processor.
procesar [proθe'sar] *vt* to try, put on
trial.
procesión [proθe'sjon] *nf* procession.
proceso [pro'θeso] *nm* process; (*JUR*)
trial; (*lapso*) course (of time).
proclamar [prokla'mar] *vt* to proclaim.
procreación [prokrea'θjon] *nf* procrea-
tion.
procrear [prokre'ar] *vt, vi* to procreate.
procurador, a [prokura'ðor, a] *nm/f*
attorney.
procurar [proku'rar] *vt* (*intentar*) to try,
endeavour; (*conseguir*) to get, obtain;
(*asegurar*) to secure; (*producir*) to
produce.
prodigio [pro'ðixjo] *nm* prodigy; (*milagro*) wonder, marvel; **~so, a** *adj*
prodigious, marvellous.
pródigo, a ['proðiyo, a] *adj*: **hijo ~**
prodigal son.
producción [proðuk'θjon] *nf* (*gen*)
production; (*producto*) product; ~ **en
serie** mass production.
producir [proðu'θir] *vt* to produce;
(*causar*) to cause, bring about; **~se** *vr*
(*cambio*) to come about; (*accidente*) to
take place; (*problema etc*) to arise;
(*hacerse*) to be produced, be made;
(*estallar*) to break out.
productividad [proðuktiβi'ðað] *nf*
productivity; **productivo, a** *adj* productive; (*provechoso*) profitable.
producto [pro'ðukto] *nm* product;
(*producción*) production.
productor, a [proðuk'tor, a] *adj* productive, producing ♦ *nm/f* producer.
proeza [pro'eθa] *nf* exploit, feat.
profanar [profa'nar] *vt* to desecrate,
profane; **profano, a** *adj* profane ♦ *nm/f*
layman/woman.
profecía [profe'θia] *nf* prophecy.
proferir [profe'rir] *vt* (*palabra, sonido*)
to utter; (*injuria*) to hurl, let fly.
profesar [profe'sar] *vt* (*practicar*) to
practise.
profesión [profe'sjon] *nf* profession;

profesional *adj* professional.
profesor, a [profe'sor, a] *nm/f* teacher;
~**ado** *nm* teaching profession.
profeta [pro'feta] *nm/f* prophet;
profetizar *vt, vi* to prophesy.
prófugo, a ['profuɣo, a] *nm/f* fugitive;
(*MIL: desertor*) deserter.
profundidad [profundi'ðað] *nf* depth;
profundizar *vt* (*fig*): **profundizar en** to
go deeply into; **profundo, a** *adj* deep;
(*misterio, pensador*) profound.
profusión [profu'sjon] *nf* (*abundancia*)
profusion; (*prodigalidad*) extravagance.
progenitor [proxeni'tor] *nm* ancestor;
~**es** *nmpl* (*padres*) parents.
programa [pro'ɣrama] *nm* programme
(*BRIT*), program (*US*); ~**ción** *nf* programming; ~**dor, a** *nm/f* programmer;
programar *vt* to program.
progresar [proɣre'sar] *vi* to progress,
make progress; **progresista** *adj, nm/f*
progressive; **progresivo, a** *adj* progressive; (*gradual*) gradual; (*continuo*)
continuous; **progreso** *nm* progress.
prohibición [proiβi'θjon] *nf* prohibition,
ban.
prohibir [proi'βir] *vt* to prohibit, ban,
forbid; **se prohíbe fumar, prohibido
fumar** no smoking.
prójimo, a ['proximo, a] *nm/f* fellow
man; (*vecino*) neighbour.
proletariado [proleta'rjaðo] *nm* proletariat.
proletario, a [prole'tarjo, a] *adj, nm/f*
proletarian.
proliferación [prolifera'θjon] *nf*
proliferation.
proliferar [prolife'rar] *vi* to proliferate;
prolífico, a *adj* prolific.
prolijo, a [pro'lixo, a] *adj* long-winded,
tedious.
prólogo ['proloɣo] *nm* prologue.
prolongación [prolonga'θjon] *nf* extension; **prolongado, a** *adj* (*largo*) long;
(*alargado*) lengthy.
prolongar [prolon'ɣar] *vt* to extend; (*reunión etc*) to prolong; (*calle, tubo*) to
extend.
promedio [pro'meðjo] *nm* average; (*de
distancia*) middle, mid-point.

promesa [pro'mesa] *nf* promise.
prometer [prome'ter] *vt* to promise ♦ *vi*
to show promise; ~**se** *vr* (*novios*) to get
engaged; **prometido, a** *adj* promised;
engaged ♦ *nm/f* fiancé/fiancée.
prominente [promi'nente] *adj*
prominent.
promiscuo, a [pro'miskwo, a] *adj*
promiscuous.
promoción [promo'θjon] *nf* promotion.
promotor [promo'tor] *nm* promoter;
(*instigador*) instigator.
promover [promo'βer] *vt* to promote;
(*causar*) to cause; (*instigar*) to instigate, stir up.
promulgar [promul'ɣar] *vt* to
promulgate; (*fig*) to proclaim.
pronombre [pro'nombre] *nm* pronoun.
pronosticar [pronosti'kar] *vt* to predict,
foretell, forecast; **pronóstico** *nm* prediction, forecast; **pronóstico del tiempo**
weather forecast.
pronto, a ['pronto, a] *adj* (*rápido*)
prompt, quick; (*preparado*) ready ♦
adv quickly, promptly; (*en seguida*) at
once, right away; (*dentro de poco*)
soon; (*temprano*) early ♦ *nm*: **tener ~s
de enojo** to be quick-tempered; **al ~** at
first; **de ~** suddenly; **por lo ~** meanwhile, for the present.
pronunciación [pronunθja'θjon] *nf*
pronunciation.
pronunciar [pronun'θjar] *vt* to
pronounce; (*discurso*) to make, deliver;
~**se** *vr* to revolt, rebel; (*declararse*) to
declare o.s.
propagación [propaɣa'θjon] *nf* propaga-
tion.
propaganda [propa'ɣanda] *nf* (*política*)
propaganda; (*comercial*) advertising.
propagar [propa'ɣar] *vt* to propagate.
propensión [propen'sjon] *nf* inclination,
propensity; **propenso, a** *adj* inclined
to; **ser propenso a** to be inclined to,
have a tendency to.
propiamente [propja'mente] *adv*
properly; (*realmente*) really, exactly.
propicio, a [pro'piθjo, a] *adj* favourable,
propitious.
propiedad [propje'ðað] *nf* property;

(*posesión*) possession, ownership; ~ **particular** private property.

propietario, a [propje'tarjo, a] *nm/f* owner, proprietor.

propina [pro'pina] *nf* tip.

propio, a ['propjo, a] *adj* own, of one's own; (*característico*) characteristic, typical; (*debido*) proper; (*mismo*) self-same, very; **el ~ ministro** the minister himself; **¿tienes casa propia?** have you a house of your own?

proponer [propo'ner] *vt* to propose, put forward; (*problema*) to pose; **~se** *vr* to propose, intend.

proporción [propor'θjon] *nf* proportion; (*MAT*) ratio; **proporciones** *nfpl* (*dimensiones*) dimensions; (*fig*) size *sg*; **proporcionado, a** *adj* proportionate; (*regular*) medium, middling; (*justo*) just right; **proporcionar** *vt* (*dar*) to give, supply, provide.

proposición [proposi'θjon] *nf* proposition; (*propuesta*) proposal.

propósito [pro'posito] *nm* purpose; (*intento*) aim, intention ♦ *adv*: **a ~** by the way, incidentally; (*a posta*) on purpose, deliberately; **a ~ de** about, with regard to.

propuesta [pro'pwesta] *vb ver* **proponer** ♦ *nf* proposal.

propulsar [propul'sar] *vt* to drive, propel; (*fig*) to promote, encourage; **propulsión** *nf* propulsion; **propulsión a chorro** *o* **por reacción** jet propulsion.

prórroga ['prorroxa] *nf* extension; (*JUR*) stay; (*COM*) deferment; (*DEPORTE*) extra time; **prorrogar** *vt* (*período*) to extend; (*decisión*) to defer, postpone.

prorrumpir [prorrum'pir] *vi* to burst forth, break out.

prosa ['prosa] *nf* prose.

proscripción [proscrip'θjon] *nf* prohibition, ban; (*destierro*) banishment; (*de un partido*) proscription.

proscrito, a [pro'skrito, a] *adj* (*prohibido, desterrado*) banned.

prosecución [proseku'θjon] *nf* continuation.

proseguir [prose'xir] *vt* to continue, carry on ♦ *vi* to continue, go on.

prospección [prospek'θjon] *nf* exploration; (*del oro*) prospecting.

prospecto [pros'pekto] *nm* prospectus.

prosperar [prospe'rar] *vi* to prosper, thrive, flourish; **prosperidad** *nf* prosperity; (*éxito*) success; **próspero, a** *adj* prosperous, flourishing; (*que tiene éxito*) successful.

prostíbulo [pros'tiβulo] *nm* brothel (*BRIT*), house of prostitution (*US*).

prostitución [prostitu'θjon] *nf* prostitution.

prostituir [prosti'twir] *vt* to prostitute; **~se** *vr* to prostitute o.s., become a prostitute.

prostituta [prosti'tuta] *nf* prostitute.

protagonista [protaɣo'nista] *nm/f* protagonist.

protagonizar [protaɣoni'θar] *vt* to take the chief rôle in.

protección [protek'θjon] *nf* protection.

protector, a [protek'tor, a] *adj* protective, protecting ♦ *nm/f* protector.

proteger [prote'xer] *vt* to protect; **protegido, a** *nm/f* protégé/protégée.

proteína [prote'ina] *nf* protein.

protesta [pro'testa] *nf* protest; (*declaración*) protestation.

protestante [protes'tante] *adj* Protestant.

protestar [protes'tar] *vt* to protest, declare; (*fe*) to protest ♦ *vi* to protest.

protocolo [proto'kolo] *nm* protocol.

prototipo [proto'tipo] *nm* prototype.

prov. *abr* (= *provincia*) prov.

provecho [pro'βetʃo] *nm* advantage, benefit; (*FINANZAS*) profit; **¡buen ~!** bon appétit!; **en ~ de** to the benefit of; **sacar ~ de** to benefit from, profit by.

proveer [proβe'er] *vt* to provide, supply ♦ *vi*: **~ a** to provide for.

provenir [proβe'nir] *vi*: **~ de** to come from, stem from.

proverbio [pro'βerβjo] *nm* proverb.

providencia [proβi'ðenθja] *nf* providence; (*previsión*) foresight.

provincia [pro'βinθja] *nf* province; **~no, a** *adj* provincial; (*del campo*) country *cpd*.

provisión [proβi'sjon] *nf* provision;

(*abastecimiento*) provision, supply; (*medida*) measure, step.

provisional [proβisjo'nal] *adj* provisional.

provocación [proβoka'θjon] *nf* provocation.

provocar [proβo'kar] *vt* to provoke; (*alentar*) to tempt, invite; (*causar*) to bring about, lead to; (*promover*) to promote; (*estimular*) to rouse, stimulate; ¿**te provoca un café?** (*AM*) would you like a coffee?; **provocativo, a** *adj* provocative.

próximamente [proksima'mente] *adv* shortly, soon.

proximidad [proksimi'ðað] *nf* closeness, proximity; **próximo, a** *adj* near, close; (*vecino*) neighbouring; (*siguiente*) next.

proyectar [projek'tar] *vt* (*objeto*) to hurl, throw; (*luz*) to cast, shed; (*CINE*) to screen, show; (*planear*) to plan.

proyectil [projek'til] *nm* projectile, missile.

proyecto [pro'jekto] *nm* plan; (*estimación de costo*) detailed estimate.

proyector [projek'tor] *nm* (*CINE*) projector.

prudencia [pru'ðenθja] *nf* (*sabiduría*) wisdom; (*cuidado*) care; **prudente** *adj* sensible, wise; (*conductor*) careful.

prueba *etc* ['prweβa] *vb ver* **probar** ♦ *nf* proof; (*ensayo*) test, trial; (*degustación*) tasting, sampling; (*de ropa*) fitting; **a ~** on trial; **a ~ de** proof against; **a ~ de agua/fuego** waterproof/fireproof; **someter a ~** to put to the test.

prurito [pru'rito] *nm* itch; (*de bebé*) nappy (*BRIT*) o diaper (*US*) rash.

psico... [siko] *prefijo* psycho...; **~análisis** *nm inv* psychoanalysis; **~logía** *nf* psychology; **~lógico, a** *adj* psychological; **psicólogo, a** *nm/f* psychologist; **psicópata** *nm/f* psychopath; **~sis** *nf inv* psychosis.

psiquiatra [si'kjatra] *nm/f* psychiatrist; **psiquiátrico, a** *adj* psychiatric.

psíquico, a ['sikiko, a] *adj* psychic(al).

PSOE [pe'soe] *nm abr* = **Partido Socialista Obrero Español.**

pta(s) *abr* = **peseta**(s).

pts *abr* = **pesetas.**

púa ['pua] *nf* sharp point; (*BOT, ZOOL*) prickle, spine; (*para guitarra*) plectrum (*BRIT*), pick (*US*); **alambre de ~** barbed wire.

pubertad [puβer'tað] *nf* puberty.

publicación [puβlika'θjon] *nf* publication.

publicar [puβli'kar] *vt* (*editar*) to publish; (*hacer público*) to publicize; (*divulgar*) to make public, divulge.

publicidad [puβliθi'ðað] *nf* publicity; (*COM: propaganda*) advertising; **publicitario, a** *adj* publicity *cpd*; advertising *cpd*.

público, a ['puβliko, a] *adj* public ♦ *nm* public; (*TEATRO etc*) audience.

puchero [pu'tʃero] *nm* (*CULIN: guiso*) stew; (: *olla*) cooking pot; **hacer ~s** to pout.

pude *etc vb ver* **poder.**

púdico, a ['puðiko, a] *adj* modest.

pudiente [pu'ðjente] *adj* (*rico*) wealthy, well-to-do.

pudiera *etc vb ver* **poder.**

pudor [pu'ðor] *nm* modesty.

pudrir [pu'ðrir] *vt* to rot; (*fam*) to upset, annoy; **~se** *vr* to rot, decay.

pueblo ['pweβlo] *nm* people; (*nación*) nation; (*aldea*) village.

puedo *etc vb ver* **poder.**

puente ['pwente] *nm* bridge; **hacer ~** (*inf*) to take an extra day off work between 2 public holidays; to take a long weekend; **~ aéreo** shuttle service; **~ colgante** suspension bridge.

puerco, a ['pwerko, a] *nm/f* pig/sow ♦ *adj* (*sucio*) dirty, filthy; (*obsceno*) disgusting; **~ de mar** porpoise; **~ marino** dolphin.

pueril [pwe'ril] *adj* childish.

puerro ['pwerro] *nm* leek.

puerta ['pwerta] *nf* door; (*de jardín*) gate; (*portal*) doorway; (*fig*) gateway; (*portería*) goal; **a la ~** at the door; **a ~ cerrada** behind closed doors; **~ giratoria** revolving door.

puertaventana [pwertaβen'tana] *nf* shutter.

puerto ['pwerto] *nm* port; (*paso*) pass; (*fig*) haven, refuge.

Puerto Rico [pwerto'riko] *nm* Puerto Rico; **puertorriqueño, a** *adj*, *nm/f* Puerto Rican.

pues [pwes] *adv* (*entonces*) then; (*bueno*) well, well then; (*así que*) so ♦ *conj* (*ya que*) since; ¡~! (*sí*) yes!, certainly!

puesta ['pwesta] *nf* (*apuesta*) bet, stake; ~ **en marcha** starting; ~ **del sol** sunset.

puesto, a ['pwesto, a] *pp de* **poner** ♦ *adj*: **tener algo** ~ to have sth on, be wearing sth ♦ *nm* (*lugar, posición*) place; (*trabajo*) post, job; (*COM*) stall ♦ *conj*: ~ **que** since, as.

púgil ['puxil] *nm* boxer.

pugna ['puxna] *nf* battle, conflict; ~**cidad** *nf* pugnacity, aggressiveness; **pugnar** *vi* (*luchar*) to struggle, fight; (*pelear*) to fight.

pujar [pu'xar] *vi* (*en subasta*) to bid; (*esforzarse*) to struggle, strain.

pulcro, a ['pulkro, a] *adj* neat, tidy; (*bello*) exquisite.

pulga ['pulxa] *nf* flea.

pulgada [pul'xaða] *nf* inch.

pulgar [pul'xar] *nm* thumb.

pulimentar [pulimen'tar] *vt* = **pulir**.

pulir [pu'lir] *vt* to polish; (*alisar*) to smooth; (*fig*) to polish up, touch up.

pulmón [pul'mon] *nm* lung; **pulmonía** *nf* pneumonia.

pulpa ['pulpa] *nf* pulp; (*de fruta*) flesh, soft part.

pulpería [pulpe'ria] (*AM*) *nf* (*tienda*) small grocery store.

púlpito ['pulpito] *nm* pulpit.

pulpo ['pulpo] *nm* octopus.

pulsación [pulsa'θjon] *nf* beat, pulsation; (*ANAT*) throb(bing).

pulsador [pulsa'ðor] *nm* button, push button.

pulsar [pul'sar] *vt* (*tecla*) to touch, tap; (*MUS*) to play; (*botón*) to press, push ♦ *vi* to pulsate; (*latir*) to beat, throb; (*MED*): ~ **a uno** to take sb's pulse.

pulsera [pul'sera] *nf* bracelet.

pulso ['pulso] *nm* (*ANAT*) pulse; (: *muñeca*) wrist; (*fuerza*) strength;

(*firmeza*) steadiness, steady hand; (*tacto*) tact, good sense.

pulverizador [pulβeriθa'ðor] *nm* spray, spray gun.

pulverizar [pulβeri'θar] *vt* to pulverize; (*líquido*) to spray.

pulla ['puʎa] *nf* cutting remark; (*expresión grosera*) obscene remark.

puna ['puna] (*AM*) *nf* mountain sickness.

pungir [pun'xir] *vt* to puncture, pierce; (*fig*) to cause suffering to.

punición [puni'θjon] *nf* punishment; **punitivo, a** *adj* punitive.

punta ['punta] *nf* point, tip; (*extremidad*) end; (*fig*) touch, trace; **horas** ~**s** peak hours, rush hours; **sacar** ~ **a** to sharpen; **estar de** ~ to be edgy.

puntada [pun'taða] *nf* (*COSTURA*) stitch.

puntal [pun'tal] *nm* prop, support.

puntapié [punta'pje] *nm* kick.

puntear [punte'ar] *vt* to tick, mark.

puntería [punte'ria] *nf* (*de arma*) aim, aiming; (*destreza*) marksmanship.

puntero, a [pun'tero, a] *adj* leading ♦ *nm* (*palo*) pointer.

puntiagudo, a [puntja'xuðo, a] *adj* sharp, pointed.

puntilla [pun'tiʎa] *nf* (*encaje*) lace edging *o* trim; (**andar) de** ~**s** (to walk) on tiptoe.

punto ['punto] *nm* (*gen*) point; (*señal diminuta*) spot, dot; (*COSTURA, MED*) stitch; (*lugar*) spot, place; (*momento*) point, moment; **a** ~ ready; **estar a** ~ **de** to be on the point of *o* about to; **en** ~ on the dot; ~ **muerto** dead centre; (*AUTO*) neutral (gear); ~ **final** full stop (*BRIT*), period (*US*); ~ **y coma** semicolon; ~ **de interrogación** question mark; **hacer** ~ (*tejer*) to knit.

puntuación [puntwa'θjon] *nf* punctuation; (*puntos: en examen*) mark(s) (*pl*); (: *DEPORTE*) score.

puntual [pun'twal] *adj* (*a tiempo*) punctual; (*exacto*) exact, accurate; (*seguro*) reliable; ~**idad** *nf* punctuality; exactness, accuracy; reliability; ~**izar** *vt* to fix, specify.

punzante [pun'θante] *adj* (*dolor*) shooting, sharp; (*herramienta*) sharp;

punzar vt to prick, pierce ♦ vi to shoot, stab.

puñado [pu'ɲaðo] nm handful.

puñal [pu'ɲal] nm dagger; **~ada** nf stab.

puñetazo [puɲe'taθo] nm punch.

puño ['puɲo] nm (ANAT) fist; (cantidad) fistful, handful; (COSTURA) cuff; (de herramienta) handle.

pupila [pu'pila] nf pupil.

pupitre [pu'pitre] nm desk.

puré [pu're] nm puree; (sopa) (thick) soup; **~ de patatas** mashed potatoes.

pureza [pu'reθa] nf purity.

purga ['purɣa] nf purge; **purgante** adj, nm purgative; **purgar** vt to purge.

purgatorio [purɣa'torjo] nm purgatory.

purificar [purifi'kar] vt to purify; (refinar) to refine.

puritano, a [puri'tano, a] adj (actitud) puritanical; (iglesia, tradición) puritan ♦ nm/f puritan.

puro, a ['puro, a] adj pure; (cielo) clear; (verdad) simple, plain ♦ adv: de ~ **cansado** out of sheer tiredness ♦ nm cigar.

púrpura ['purpura] nf purple; **purpúreo, a** adj purple.

pus [pus] nm pus.

puse etc vb ver **poner**.

pusiera etc vb ver **poner**.

pústula ['pustula] nf pimple, sore.

puta ['puta] nf whore, prostitute.

putrefacción [putrefak'θjon] nf rotting, putrefaction.

pútrido, a ['putriðo, a] adj rotten.

PVP abr (ESP: = precio venta al público) RRP.

Q

q.e.p.d. abr (= que en paz descanse) R.I.P.

que [ke] conj 1 (con oración subordinada: muchas veces no se traduce) that; **dijo ~ vendría** he said (that) he would come; **espero ~ lo encuentres** I

hope (that) you find it; ver tb **el**
2 (en oración independiente): **¡~ entre!** send him in; **¡que se mejore tu padre!** I hope your father gets better
3 (enfático): **¿me quieres? - ¡~ sí!** do you love me? – of course!
4 (consecutivo: muchas veces no se traduce) that; **es tan grande ~ no lo puedo levantar** it's so big (that) I can't lift it
5 (comparaciones) than; **yo ~ tú/él** if I were you/him; ver tb **más; menos; mismo**
6 (valor disyuntivo): **~ le guste o no** whether he likes it or not; **~ venga o ~ no venga** whether he comes or not
7 (porque): **no puedo, ~ tengo ~ quedarme en casa** I can't, I've got to stay in
♦ pron 1 (cosa) that, which; (+prep) which; **el sombrero ~ te compraste** the hat (that o which) you bought; **la cama en ~ dormí** the bed (that o which) I slept in
2 (persona: suj) that, who; (: objeto) that, whom; **el amigo ~ me acompañó al museo** the friend that o who went to the museum with me: **la chica que invité** the girl (that o whom) I invited

qué [ke] adj what?, which? ♦ pron what?; **¡~ divertido!** how funny!; **¿~ edad tienes?** how old are you?; **¿de ~ me hablas?** what are you saying to me?; **¿~ tal?** how are you?, how are things?; **¿~ hay (de nuevo)?** what's new?

quebrada [ke'βraða] nf ravine; ver tb **quebrado**.

quebradizo, a [keβra'ðiθo, a] adj fragile; (persona) frail.

quebrado, a [ke'βraðo, a] adj (roto) broken ♦ nm/f bankrupt ♦ nm (MAT) fraction.

quebradura [keβra'ðura] nf (fisura) fissure; (GEO) gorge; (MED) rupture.

quebrantar [keβran'tar] vt (infringir) to violate, transgress; **~se** vr (persona) to fail in health.

quebranto [ke'βranto] nm damage,

harm; (*decaimiento*) exhaustion; (*dolor*) grief, pain.

quebrar [ke'ßrar] *vt* to break, smash ♦ *vi* to go bankrupt; ~se *vr* to break, get broken; (*MED*) to be ruptured.

quedar [ke'ðar] *vi* to stay, remain; (*encontrarse: sitio*) to be; (*restar*) to remain, be left; ~se *vr* to remain, stay (behind); ~se (con) algo to keep sth; ~ en (*acordar*) to agree on/to; ~ en nada to come to nothing; ~ por hacer to be still to be done; ~ ciego/mudo to be left blind/dumb; no te queda bien ese vestido that dress doesn't suit you; eso queda muy lejos that's a long way (away); quedamos a las seis we agreed to meet at six.

quedo, a ['keðo, a] *adj* still ♦ *adv* softly, gently.

quehacer [kea'θer] *nm* task, job; ~es (*domésticos*) *nmpl* household chores.

queja ['kexa] *nf* complaint; **quejarse** *vr* (*enfermo*) to moan, groan; (*protestar*) to complain; **quejarse de que** to complain (about the fact) that; **quejido** *nm* moan; **quejoso, a** *adj* complaining.

quemado, a [ke'maðo, a] *adj* burnt.

quemadura [kema'ðura] *nf* burn, scald.

quemar [ke'mar] *vt* to burn; (*fig: malgastar*) to burn up, squander ♦ *vi* to be burning hot; ~se *vr* (*consumirse*) to burn (up); (*del sol*) to get sunburnt.

quemarropa [kema'rropa]: **a ~** *adv* point-blank.

quemazón [kema'θon] *nf* burn; (*calor*) intense heat; (*sensación*) itch.

quepo *etc vb ver* **caber.**

querella [ke'reʎa] *nf* (*JUR*) charge; (*disputa*) dispute.

PALABRA CLAVE

querer [ke'rer] *vt* **1** (*desear*) to want; quiero más dinero I want more money; quisiera *o* querría un té I'd like a tea; sin ~ unintentionally; quiero ayudar/que vayas I want to help/you to go
2 (*preguntas: para pedir algo*): ¿quiere abrir la ventana? could you open the window?; ¿quieres echarme una mano? can you give me a hand?

3 (*amar*) to love; (*tener cariño a*) to be fond of; quiere mucho a sus hijos he's very fond of his children
4 (*requerir*): esta planta quiere más luz this plant needs more light
5: le pedí que me dejara ir pero no quiso I asked him to let me go but he refused.

---

querido, a [ke'riðo, a] *adj* dear ♦ *nm/f* darling; (*amante*) lover.

quesería [kese'ria] *nf* dairy; (*fábrica*) cheese factory.

queso ['keso] *nm* cheese; ~ crema cream cheese.

quicio ['kiθjo] *nm* hinge; sacar a uno de ~ to get on sb's nerves.

quiebra ['kjeßra] *nf* break, split; (*COM*) bankruptcy; (*ECON*) slump.

quiebro ['kjeßro] *nm* (*del cuerpo*) swerve.

quien [kjen] *pron* who; hay ~ piensa que there are those who think that; no hay ~ lo haga no-one will do it.

quién [kjen] *pron* who, whom; ¿~ es? who's there?

quienquiera [kjen'kjera] (*pl* quienesquiera) *pron* whoever.

quiero *etc vb ver* **querer.**

quieto, a ['kjeto, a] *adj* still; (*carácter*) placid; **quietud** *nf* stillness.

quijada [ki'xaða] *nf* jaw, jawbone.

quilate [ki'late] *nm* carat.

quilla ['kiʎa] *nf* keel.

quimera [ki'mera] *nf* chimera; **quimérico, a** *adj* fantastic.

químico, a ['kimiko, a] *adj* chemical ♦ *nm/f* chemist ♦ *nf* chemistry.

quincalla [kin'kaʎa] *nf* hardware, ironmongery (*BRIT*).

quince ['kinθe] *num* fifteen; ~ días a fortnight; ~añero, a *nm/f* teenager; ~na *nf* fortnight; (*pago*) fortnightly pay; ~nal *adj* fortnightly.

quiniela [ki'njela] *nf* football pools *pl*; ~s *nfpl* (*impreso*) pools coupon *sg*.

quinientos, as [ki'njentos, as] *adj, num* five hundred.

quinina [ki'nina] *nf* quinine.

quinqui ['kinki] *nm* delinquent.

quinto, a ['kinto, a] *adj* fifth ♦ *nf* country house; (*MIL*) call-up, draft.
quiosco ['kjosko] *nm* (*de música*) bandstand; (*de periódicos*) news stand.
quirúrgico, a [ki'rurxiko, a] *adj* surgical.
quise *etc vb ver* **querer**.
quisiera *etc vb ver* **querer**.
quisquilloso, a [kiski'ʎoso, a] *adj* (*susceptible*) touchy; (*meticuloso*) pernickety.
quiste ['kiste] *nm* cyst.
quitaesmalte [kitaes'malte] *nm* nailpolish remover.
quitamanchas [kita'mantʃas] *nm inv* stain remover.
quitanieves [kita'njeβes] *nm inv* snowplough (*BRIT*), snowplow (*US*).
quitar [ki'tar] *vt* to remove, take away; (*ropa*) to take off; (*dolor*) to relieve; ¡quita de ahí! get away!; ~se *vr* to withdraw; (*ropa*) to take off; **se quitó el sombrero** he took off his hat.
quitasol [kita'sol] *nm* sunshade (*BRIT*), parasol.
quite ['kite] *nm* (*esgrima*) parry; (*evasión*) dodge.
Quito ['kito] *n* Quito.
quizá(s) [ki'θa(s)] *adv* perhaps, maybe.

R

rábano ['raβano] *nm* radish; **me importa un ~** I don't give a damn.
rabia ['raβja] *nf* (*MED*) rabies *sg*; (*fig: ira*) fury, rage; **rabiar** *vi* to have rabies; to rage, be furious; **rabiar por algo** to long for sth.
rabieta [ra'βjeta] *nf* tantrum, fit of temper.
rabino [ra'βino] *nm* rabbi.
rabioso, a [ra'βjoso, a] *adj* rabid; (*fig*) furious.
rabo ['raβo] *nm* tail.
racial [ra'θjal] *adj* racial, race *cpd*.
racimo [ra'θimo] *nm* bunch.
raciocinio [raθjo'θinjo] *nm* reason.
ración [ra'θjon] *nf* portion; **raciones** *nfpl* rations.

racional [raθjo'nal] *adj* (*razonable*) reasonable; (*lógico*) rational; ~**izar** *vt* to rationalize.
racionar [raθjo'nar] *vt* to ration (out).
racismo [ra'θismo] *nm* racialism, racism; **racista** *adj, nm/f* racist.
racha ['ratʃa] *nf* gust of wind: **buena/ mala ~** (*fig*) spell of good/bad luck.
radar [ra'ðar] *nm* radar.
radiactivo, a [raðiak'tiβo, a] *adj* = **radioactivo**.
radiador [raðja'ðor] *nm* radiator.
radiante [ra'ðjante] *adj* radiant.
radical [raði'kal] *adj, nm/f* radical.
radicar [raði'kar] *vi* to take root; ~ **en** to lie *o* consist in; ~**se** *vr* to establish o.s., put down (one's) roots.
radio ['raðjo] *nf* radio; (*aparato*) radio (set) ♦ *nm* (*MAT*) radius; (*QUÍMICA*) radium; ~**activo, a** *adj* radioactive; ~**difusión** *nf* broadcasting; ~**emisora** *nf* transmitter, radio station; ~**escucha** *nm/f* listener; ~**grafía** *nf* X-ray; ~**grafiar** *vt* to X-ray; ~**terapia** *nf* radiotherapy; ~**yente** *nm/f* listener.
ráfaga ['rafaxa] *nf* gust; (*de luz*) flash; (*de tiros*) burst.
raído, a [ra'iðo, a] *adj* (*ropa*) threadbare.
raigambre [rai'ɣambre] *nf* (*BOT*) roots *pl*; (*fig*) tradition.
raíz [ra'iθ] *nf* root; ~ **cuadrada** square root; **a ~ de** as a result of.
raja ['raxa] *nf* (*de melón etc*) slice; (*grieta*) crack; **rajar** *vt* to split; (*fam*) to slash; **rajarse** *vr* to split, crack; **rajarse de** to back out of.
rajatabla [raxa'taβla]: **a ~** *adv* (*estrictamente*) strictly, to the letter.
ralo, a ['ralo, a] *adj* thin, sparse.
rallado, a [ra'ʎaðo, a] *adj* grated; **rallador** *nm* grater.
rallar [ra'ʎar] *vt* to grate.
RAM [ram] *nf abr* (= *memoria de acceso aleatorio*) RAM.
rama ['rama] *nf* branch; ~**je** *nm* branches *pl*, foliage; **ramal** *nm* (*de cuerda*) strand; (*FERRO*) branch line (*BRIT*); (*AUTO*) branch (road) (*BRIT*).
rambla ['rambla] *nf* (*avenida*) avenue.

ramera [ra'mera] nf whore.
ramificación [ramifika'θjon] nf ramification.
ramificarse [ramifi'karse] vr to branch out.
ramillete [rami'ʎete] nm bouquet.
ramo ['ramo] nm branch; (sección) department, section.
rampa ['rampa] nf ramp.
ramplón, ona [ram'plon, ona] adj uncouth, coarse.
rana ['rana] nf frog; **salto de ~** leapfrog.
rancio, a ['ranθjo, a] adj (comestibles) rancid; (vino) aged, mellow; (fig) ancient.
ranchero [ran'tʃero] nm (AM) rancher; smallholder.
rancho ['rantʃo] nm grub (fam); (AM: grande) ranch; (: pequeño) small farm.
rango ['rango] nm rank, standing.
ranura [ra'nura] nf groove; (de teléfono etc) slot.
rapar [ra'par] vt to shave; (los cabellos) to crop.
rapaz [ra'paθ] (nf: **rapaza**) nm/f young boy/girl ♦ adj (ZOOL) predatory.
rape ['rape] nm quick shave; (pez) angler fish; **al ~** cropped.
rapé [ra'pe] nm snuff.
rapidez [rapi'ðeθ] nf speed, rapidity; **rápido, a** adj fast, quick ♦ adv quickly ♦ nm (FERRO) express; **rápidos** nmpl rapids.
rapiña [ra'pina] nm robbery; **ave de ~** bird of prey.
raptar [rap'tar] vt to kidnap; **rapto** nm kidnapping; (impulso) sudden impulse; (éxtasis) ecstasy, rapture.
raqueta [ra'keta] nf racquet.
raquítico, a [ra'kitiko, a] adj stunted; (fig) poor, inadequate; **raquitismo** nm rickets sg.
rareza [ra'reθa] nf rarity; (fig) eccentricity.
raro, a ['raro, a] adj (poco común) rare; (extraño) odd, strange; (excepcional) remarkable.
ras [ras] nm: **a ~ de** level with; **a ~ de tierra** at ground level.

rasar [ra'sar] vt (igualar) to level.
rascacielos [raska'θjelos] nm inv skyscraper.
rascar [ras'kar] vt (con las uñas etc) to scratch; (raspar) to scrape; **~se** vr to scratch (o.s.).
rasgar [ras'ɣar] vt to tear, rip (up).
rasgo ['rasɣo] nm (con pluma) stroke; **~s** nmpl (facciones) features, characteristics; **a grandes ~s** in outline, broadly.
rasguñar [rasɣu'nar] vt to scratch; **rasguño** nm scratch.
raso, a ['raso, a] adj (liso) flat, level; (a baja altura) very low ♦ nm satin; **cielo ~** clear sky.
raspadura [raspa'ðura] nf (acto) scrape, scraping; (marca) scratch; **~s** nfpl (de papel etc) scrapings.
raspar [ras'par] vt to scrape; (arañar) to scratch; (limar) to file.
rastra ['rastra] nf (AGR) rake; **a ~s** by dragging; (fig) unwillingly.
rastreador [rastrea'ðor] nm tracker; **~ de minas** minesweeper.
rastrear [rastre'ar] vt (seguir) to track.
rastrero, a [ras'trero, a] adj (BOT, ZOOL) creeping; (fig) despicable, mean.
rastrillar [rastri'ʎar] vt to rake; **rastrillo** nm rake.
rastro ['rastro] nm (AGR) rake; (pista) track, trail; (vestigio) trace; **el R~** the Madrid fleamarket.
rastrojo [ras'troxo] nm stubble.
rasurador [rasura'ðor] (AM) nm electric shaver.
rasuradora [rasura'ðora] (AM) nf = **rasurador**.
rasurarse [rasu'rarse] vr to shave.
rata ['rata] nf rat.
ratear [rate'ar] vt (robar) to steal.
ratería [rate'ria] nf petty theft.
ratero, a [ra'tero, a] adj light-fingered ♦ nm/f (carterista) pickpocket; (AM: de casas) burglar.
ratificar [ratifi'kar] vt to ratify.
rato ['rato] nm while, short time; **a ~s** from time to time; **hay para ~** there's still a long way to go; **al poco ~** soon afterwards; **pasar el ~** to kill time;

pasar un buen/mal ~ to have a good/ rough time.
ratón [ra'ton] *nm* mouse; **ratonera** *nf* mousetrap.
raudal [rau'ðal] *nm* torrent; **a ~es** in abundance.
raya ['raja] *nf* line; (*marca*) scratch; (*en tela*) stripe; (*de pelo*) parting; (*límite*) boundary; (*pez*) ray; (*puntuación*) dash; **a ~s** striped; **pasarse de la ~** to go too far: **tener a ~** to keep in check; **rayar** *vt* to line; to scratch; (*subrayar*) to underline ♦ *vi*: **rayar en** *o* **con** to border on.
rayo ['rajo] *nm* (*del sol*) ray, beam; (*de luz*) shaft; (*en una tormenta*) (flash of) lightning; **~s X** X-rays.
rayón [ra'jon] *nm* rayon.
raza ['raθa] *nf* race; **~ humana** human race.
razón [ra'θon] *nf* reason; (*justicia*) right, justice; (*razonamiento*) reasoning; (*motivo*) reason, motive; (*MAT*) ratio; **a ~ de 10 cada día** at the rate of 10 a day; **"~: ..."** "inquiries to ..."; **en ~ de** with regard to; **dar ~ a uno** to agree that sb is right; **tener ~** to be right; **~ directa/inversa** direct/inverse proportion; **~ de ser** raison d'être; **razonable** *adj* reasonable; (*justo, moderado*) fair; **razonamiento** *nm* (*juicio*) judgement; (*argumento*) reasoning; **razonar** *vt, vi* to reason, argue.
reacción [reak'θjon] *nf* reaction; **avión a ~** jet plane; **~ en cadena** chain reaction; **reaccionar** *vi* to react; **reaccionario, a** *adj* reactionary.
reacio, a [re'aθjo, a] *adj* stubborn.
reactivar [reakti'βar] *vt* to revitalize.
reactor [reak'tor] *nm* reactor.
readaptación [reaðapta'θjon] *nf*: **~ profesional** industrial retraining.
reajuste [rea'xuste] *nm* readjustment.
real [re'al] *adj* real; (*del rey, fig*) royal.
realce [re'alθe] *nm* (*TEC*) embossing; (*lustre, fig*) splendour; (*ARTE*) highlight; **poner de ~** to emphasize.
realidad [reali'ðað] *nf* reality, fact; (*verdad*) truth.

realista [rea'lista] *nm/f* realist.
realización [realiθa'θjon] *nf* fulfilment; (*COM*) selling up (*BRIT*), conversion into money (*US*).
realizador, a [realiθa'ðor, a] *nm/f* (*TV etc*) producer.
realizar [reali'θar] *vt* (*objetivo*) to achieve; (*plan*) to carry out; (*viaje*) to make, undertake; (*COM*) to sell up (*BRIT*), convert into money (*US*); **~se** *vr* to come about, come true.
realmente [real'mente] *adv* really, actually.
realquilar [realki'lar] *vt* (*subarrendar*) to sublet.
realzar [real'θar] *vt* (*TEC*) to raise; (*embellecer*) to enhance; (*acentuar*) to highlight.
reanimar [reani'mar] *vt* to revive; (*alentar*) to encourage; **~se** *vr* to revive.
reanudar [reanu'ðar] *vt* (*renovar*) to renew; (*historia, viaje*) to resume.
reaparición [reapari'θjon] *nf* reappearance.
rearme [re'arme] *nm* rearmament.
rebaja [re'βaxa] *nf* (*COM*) reduction; (: *descuento*) discount; **~s** *nfpl* (*COM*) sale; **rebajar** *vt* (*bajar*) to lower; (*reducir*) to reduce; (*disminuir*) to lessen; (*humillar*) to humble.
rebanada [reβa'naða] *nf* slice.
rebaño [re'βaɲo] *nm* herd; (*de ovejas*) flock.
rebasar [reβa'sar] *vt* (*tb*: **~ de**) to exceed.
rebatir [reβa'tir] *vt* to refute.
rebeca [re'βeka] *nf* cardigan.
rebelarse [reβe'larse] *vr* to rebel, revolt.
rebelde [re'βelde] *adj* rebellious; (*niño*) unruly ♦ *nm/f* rebel; **rebeldía** *nf* rebelliousness; (*desobediencia*) disobedience.
rebelión [reβe'ljon] *nf* rebellion.
reblandecer [reβlande'θer] *vt* to soften.
rebosante [reβo'sante] *adj* overflowing.
rebosar [reβo'sar] *vi* (*líquido, recipiente*) to overflow; (*abundar*) to abound, be plentiful.
rebotar [reβo'tar] *vt* to bounce; (*re-*

chazar) to repel ♦ *vi* (*pelota*) to bounce; (*bala*) to ricochet; **rebote** *nm* rebound; **de rebote** on the rebound.

rebozado, a [reβo'θaðo, a] *adj* fried in batter *o* breadcrumbs.

rebozar [reβo'θar] *vt* to wrap up; (*CULIN*) to fry in batter *o* breadcrumbs.

rebuscado, a [reβus'kaðo, a] *adj* (*amanerado*) affected; (*palabra*) recherché; (*idea*) far-fetched.

rebuznar [reβuθ'nar] *vi* to bray.

recabar [reka'βar] *vt* (*obtener*) to manage to get.

recado [re'kaðo] *nm* message; **tomar un** ~ (*TEL*) to take a message.

recaer [reka'er] *vi* to relapse; ~ **en** to fall to *o* on; (*criminal etc*) to fall back into, relapse into; **recaída** *nf* relapse.

recalcar [rekal'kar] *vt* (*fig*) to stress, emphasize.

recalcitrante [rekalθi'trante] *adj* recalcitrant.

recalentar [rekalen'tar] *vt* (*volver a calentar*) to reheat; (*calentar demasiado*) to overheat.

recámara [re'kamara] (*AM*) *nf* bedroom.

recambio [re'kambjo] *nm* spare; (*de pluma*) refill.

recapacitar [rekapaθi'tar] *vi* to reflect.

recargado, a [rekar'xaðo, a] *adj* overloaded.

recargar [rekar'xar] *vt* to overload; (*batería*) to recharge; **recargo** *nm* surcharge; (*aumento*) increase.

recatado, a [reka'taðo, a] *adj* (*modesto*) modest, demure; (*prudente*) cautious.

recato [re'kato] *nm* (*modestia*) modesty, demureness; (*cautela*) caution.

recaudación [rekauða'θjon] *nf* (*acción*) collection; (*cantidad*) takings *pl*; (*en deporte*) gate; **recaudador, a** *nm/f* tax collector.

recelar [reθe'lar] *vt*: ~ **que** (*sospechar*) to suspect that; (*temer*) to fear that ♦ *vi*: ~ **de** to distrust; **recelo** *nm* distrust, suspicion; **receloso, a** *adj* distrustful, suspicious.

recepción [reθep'θjon] *nf* reception; **recepcionista** *nm/f* receptionist.

receptáculo [reθep'takulo] *nm* receptacle.

receptivo, a [reθep'tiβo, a] *adj* receptive.

receptor, a [reθep'tor, a] *nm/f* recipient ♦ *nm* (*TEL*) receiver.

recesión [reθe'sjon] *nf* (*COM*) recession.

receta [re'θeta] *nf* (*CULIN*) recipe; (*MED*) prescription.

recibidor, a [reθiβi'ðor, a] *nm* entrance hall.

recibimiento [reθiβi'mjento] *nm* reception, welcome.

recibir [reθi'βir] *vt* to receive; (*dar la bienvenida*) to welcome ♦ *vi* to entertain; ~**se** *vr*: ~**se de** to qualify as; **recibo** *nm* receipt.

recién [re'θjen] *adv* recently, newly; **los** ~ **casados** the newly-weds; **el** ~ **llegado** the newcomer; **el** ~ **nacido** the newborn child.

reciente [re'θjente] *adj* recent; (*fresco*) fresh; ~**mente** *adv* recently.

recinto [re'θinto] *nm* enclosure; (*área*) area, place.

recio, a ['reθjo, a] *adj* strong, tough; (*voz*) loud ♦ *adv* hard; loud(ly).

recipiente [reθi'pjente] *nm* receptacle.

reciprocidad [reθiproθi'ðað] *nf* reciprocity; **recíproco, a** *adj* reciprocal.

recital [reθi'tal] *nm* (*MUS*) recital; (*LITERATURA*) reading.

recitar [reθi'tar] *vt* to recite.

reclamación [reklama'θjon] *nf* claim, demand; (*queja*) complaint.

reclamar [rekla'mar] *vt* to claim, demand ♦ *vi*: ~ **contra** to complain about; ~ **a uno en justicia** to take sb to court; **reclamo** *nm* (*anuncio*) advertisement; (*tentación*) attraction.

reclinar [rekli'nar] *vt* to recline, lean; ~**se** *vr* to lean back.

recluir [reklu'ir] *vt* to intern, confine.

reclusión [reklu'sjon] *nf* (*prisión*) prison; (*refugio*) seclusion; ~ **perpetua** life imprisonment.

recluta [re'kluta] *nm/f* recruit ♦ *nf* recruitment.

reclutamiento [rekluta'mjento] *nm* recruitment.

recobrar [reko'βrar] *vt* (*salud*) to recover; (*rescatar*) to get back; ~se *vr* to recover.

recodo [re'koðo] *nm* (*de río, camino*) bend.

recoger [reko'xer] *vt* to collect; (*AGR*) to harvest; (*levantar*) to pick up; (*juntar*) to gather; (*pasar a buscar*) to come for, get; (*dar asilo*) to give shelter to; (*faldas*) to gather up; (*pelo*) to put up; ~se *vr* (*retirarse*) to retire; **recogido, a** *adj* (*lugar*) quiet, secluded; (*pequeño*) small ♦ *nf* (*CORREOS*) collection; (*AGR*) harvest.

recolección [rekolek'θjon] *nf* (*AGR*) harvesting; (*colecta*) collection.

recomendación [rekomenda'θjon] *nf* (*sugerencia*) suggestion, recommendation; (*referencia*) reference.

recomendar [rekomen'dar] *vt* to suggest, recommend; (*confiar*) to entrust.

recompensa [rekom'pensa] *nf* reward, recompense; **recompensar** *vt* to reward, recompense.

recomponer [rekompo'ner] *vt* to mend.

reconciliación [rekonθilja'θjon] *nf* reconciliation.

reconciliar [rekonθi'ljar] *vt* to reconcile; ~se *vr* to become reconciled.

recóndito, a [re'kondito, a] *adj* (*lugar*) hidden, secret.

reconfortar [rekonfor'tar] *vt* to comfort.

reconocer [rekono'θer] *vt* to recognize; (*registrar*) to search; (*MED*) to examine; **reconocido, a** *adj* recognized; (*agradecido*) grateful; **reconocimiento** *nm* recognition; search; examination; gratitude; (*confesión*) admission.

reconquista [rekon'kista] *nf* reconquest; **la R~** the Reconquest (of Spain).

reconstituyente [rekonstitu'jente] *nm* tonic.

reconstruir [rekonstru'ir] *vt* to reconstruct.

reconversión [rekonßer'sjon] *nf*: ~ **industrial** industrial rationalization.

recopilación [rekopila'θjon] *nf* (*resumen*) summary; (*compilación*) compilation; **recopilar** *vt* to compile.

récord ['rekorð] (*pl* ~s) *adj inv*, *nm* record.

recordar [rekor'ðar] *vt* (*acordarse de*) to remember; (*acordar a otro*) to remind ♦ *vi* to remember.

recorrer [reko'rrer] *vt* (*país*) to cross, travel through; (*distancia*) to cover; (*registrar*) to search; (*repasar*) to look over; **recorrido** *nm* run, journey; **tren de largo recorrido** main-line train.

recortado, a [rekor'taðo, a] *adj* uneven, irregular.

recortar [rekor'tar] *vt* to cut out; **recorte** *nm* (*acción, de prensa*) cutting; (*de telas, chapas*) trimming.

recostado, a [rekos'taðo, a] *adj* leaning; **estar ~** to be lying down.

recostar [rekos'tar] *vt* to lean; ~se *vr* to lie down.

recoveco [reko'ßeko] *nm* (*de camino, río etc*) bend; (*en casa*) cubby hole.

recreación [rekrea'θjon] *nf* recreation.

recrear [rekre'ar] *vt* (*entretener*) to entertain; (*volver a crear*) to recreate; **recreativo, a** *adj* recreational; **recreo** *nm* recreation; (*ESCOL*) break, playtime.

recriminar [rekrimi'nar] *vt* to reproach ♦ *vi* to recriminate; ~se *vr* to reproach each other.

recrudecer [rekruðe'θer] *vt*, *vi* to worsen; ~se *vr* to worsen.

recrudecimiento [rekruðeθi'mjento] *nm* upsurge.

recta ['rekta] *nf* straight line.

rectángulo, a [rek'tangulo, a] *adj* rectangular ♦ *nm* rectangle.

rectificar [rektifi'kar] *vt* to rectify; (*volverse recto*) to straighten ♦ *vi* to correct o.s.

rectitud [rekti'tuð] *nf* straightness; (*fig*) rectitude.

recto, a ['rekto, a] *adj* straight; (*persona*) honest, upright ♦ *nm* rectum.

rector, a [rek'tor, a] *adj* governing.

recua ['rekwa] *nf* mule train.

recuadro [re'kwaðro] *nm* box; (*TIPOGRAFÍA*) inset.

recuento [re'kwento] *nm* inventory; **hacer el ~ de** to count o reckon up.

recuerdo [re'kwerðo] *nm* souvenir; **~s** *nmpl* (*memorias*) memories; **¡~s a tu madre!** give my regards to your mother!

recular [reku'lar] *vi* to back down.

recuperable [rekupe'raßle] *adj* recoverable.

recuperación [rekupera'θjon] *nf* recovery.

recuperar [rekupe'rar] *vt* to recover; (*tiempo*) to make up; **~se** *vr* to recuperate.

recurrir [reku'rrir] *vi* (*JUR*) to appeal; **~ a** to resort to; (*persona*) to turn to; **recurso** *nm* resort; (*medios*) means *pl*, resources *pl*; (*JUR*) appeal.

recusar [reku'sar] *vt* to reject, refuse.

rechazar [retʃa'θar] *vt* to repel, drive back; (*idea*) to reject; (*oferta*) to turn down.

rechazo [re'tʃaθo] *nm* (*de fusil*) recoil; (*rebote*) rebound; (*negación*) rebuff.

rechifla [re'tʃifla] *nf* hissing, booing; (*fig*) derision.

rechiflar [retʃi'flar] *vt* to hiss, boo.

rechinar [retʃi'nar] *vi* to creak; (*dientes*) to grind.

rechistar [retʃis'tar] *vi*: **sin ~** without a murmur.

rechoncho, a [re'tʃontʃo, a] (*fam*) *adj* thickset (*BRIT*), heavy-set (*US*).

red [reð] *nf* net, mesh; (*FERRO etc*) network; (*trampa*) trap.

redacción [reðak'θjon] *nf* (*acción*) editing; (*personal*) editorial staff; (*ESCOL*) essay, composition.

redactar [reðak'tar] *vt* to draw up, draft; (*periódico*) to edit.

redactor, a [reðak'tor, a] *nm/f* editor.

redada [re'ðaða] *nf*: **~ policial** police raid, round-up.

rededor [reðe'ðor] *nm*: **al o en ~** around, round about.

redención [reðen'θjon] *nf* redemption; **redentor, a** *adj* redeeming.

redescubrir [reðesku'ßrir] *vt* to rediscover.

redicho, a [re'ðitʃo, a] *adj* affected.

redil [re'ðil] *nm* sheepfold.

redimir [reði'mir] *vt* to redeem.

rédito ['reðito] *nm* interest, yield.

redoblar [reðo'ßlar] *vt* to redouble ♦ *vi* (*tambor*) to play a roll on the drums.

redomado, a [reðo'maðo, a] *adj* (*astuto*) sly, crafty; (*perfecto*) utter.

redonda [re'ðonda] *nf*: **a la ~** around, round about.

redondear [reðonde'ar] *vt* to round, round off.

redondel [reðon'del] *nm* (*círculo*) circle; (*TAUR*) bullring, arena; (*AUTO*) roundabout.

redondo, a [re'ðondo, a] *adj* (*circular*) round; (*completo*) complete.

reducción [reðuk'θjon] *nf* reduction.

reducido, a [reðu'θiðo, a] *adj* reduced; (*limitado*) limited; (*pequeño*) small.

reducir [reðu'θir] *vt* to reduce; to limit; **~se** *vr* to diminish.

redundancia [reðun'danθja] *nf* redundancy.

reembolsar [re(e)mbol'sar] *vt* (*persona*) to reimburse; (*dinero*) to repay, pay back; (*depósito*) to refund; **reembolso** *nm* reimbursement; refund.

reemplazar [re(e)mpla'θar] *vt* to replace; **reemplazo** *nm* replacement; **de reemplazo** (*MIL*) reserve.

referencia [refe'renθja] *nf* reference; **con ~ a** with reference to.

referéndum [refe'rendum] (*pl* **~s**) *nm* referendum.

referente [refe'rente] *adj*: **~ a** concerning, relating to.

referir [refe'rir] *vt* (*contar*) to tell, recount; (*relacionar*) to refer, relate; **~se** *vr*: **~se a** to refer to.

refilón [refi'lon]: **de ~** *adv* obliquely.

refinado, a [refi'naðo, a] *adj* refined.

refinamiento [refina'mjento] *nm* refinement.

refinar [refi'nar] *vt* to refine; **refinería** *nf* refinery.

reflejar [refle'xar] *vt* to reflect; **reflejo, a** *adj* reflected; (*movimiento*) reflex ♦ *nm* reflection; (*ANAT*) reflex.

reflexión [reflek'sjon] *nf* reflection; **reflexionar** *vt* to reflect on ♦ *vi* to reflect; (*detenerse*) to pause (to think).

reflexivo, a [reflek'sißo, a] *adj* thought-

ful; (*LING*) reflexive.
reflujo [re'fluxo] *nm* ebb.
reforma [re'forma] *nf* reform; (*ARQ etc*) repair; ~ **agraria** agrarian reform.
reformar [refor'mar] *vt* to reform; (*modificar*) to change, alter; (*ARQ*) to repair; ~**se** *vr* to mend one's ways.
reformatorio [reforma'torjo] *nm* reformatory.
reforzar [refor'θar] *vt* to strengthen; (*ARQ*) to reinforce; (*fig*) to encourage.
refractario, a [refrak'tarjo, a] *adj* (*TEC*) heat-resistant.
refrán [re'fran] *nm* proverb, saying.
refregar [refre'ɣar] *vt* to scrub.
refrenar [refre'nar] *vt* to check, restrain.
refrendar [refren'dar] *vt* (*firma*) to endorse, countersign; (*ley*) to approve.
refrescante [refres'kante] *adj* refreshing, cooling.
refrescar [refres'kar] *vt* to refresh ♦ *vi* to cool down; ~**se** *vr* to get cooler; (*tomar aire fresco*) to go out for a breath of fresh air; (*beber*) to have a drink.
refresco [re'fresko] *nm* soft drink, cool drink; "~**s**" "refreshments".
refriega [re'frjeɣa] *nf* scuffle, brawl.
refrigeración [refrixera'θjon] *nf* refrigeration; (*de sala*) air-conditioning.
refrigerador [refrixera'ðor] *nm* refrigerator (*BRIT*), icebox (*US*).
refrigeradora [refrixera'ðora] *nf* = **refrigerador**.
refrigerar [refrixe'rar] *vt* to refrigerate; (*sala*) to air-condition.
refuerzo [re'fwerθo] *nm* reinforcement; (*TEC*) support.
refugiado, a [refu'xjaðo, a] *nm/f* refugee.
refugiarse [refu'xjarse] *vr* to take refuge, shelter.
refugio [re'fuxjo] *nm* refuge; (*protección*) shelter.
refulgir [reful'xir] *vi* to shine, be dazzling.
refunfuñar [refunfu'ɲar] *vi* to grunt, growl; (*quejarse*) to grumble.
refutar [refu'tar] *vt* to refute.
regadera [reɣa'ðera] *nf* watering can.
regadío [reɣa'ðio] *nm* irrigated land.

regalado, a [reɣa'laðo, a] *adj* comfortable, luxurious; (*gratis*) free, for nothing.
regalar [reɣa'lar] *vt* (*dar*) to give (as a present); (*entregar*) to give away; (*mimar*) to pamper, make a fuss of.
regalía [reɣa'lia] *nf* privilege, prerogative; (*COM*) bonus; (*de autor*) royalty.
regaliz [reɣa'liθ] *nm* liquorice.
regalo [re'ɣalo] *nm* (*obsequio*) gift, present; (*gusto*) pleasure; (*comodidad*) comfort.
regalón, ona [reɣa'lon, ona] *adj* spoiled, pampered.
regañadientes [reɣaɲa'ðjentes]: **a** ~ *adv* reluctantly.
regañar [reɣa'ɲar] *vt* to scold ♦ *vi* to grumble; **regaño** *nm* scolding, telling-off; (*queja*) grumble; **regañón, ona** *adj* nagging.
regar [re'ɣar] *vt* to water, irrigate; (*fig*) to scatter, sprinkle.
regatear [reɣate'ar] *vt* (*COM*) to bargain over; (*escatimar*) to be mean with ♦ *vi* to bargain, haggle; (*DEPORTE*) to dribble; **regateo** *nm* bargaining; dribbling; (*del cuerpo*) swerve, dodge.
regazo [re'ɣaθo] *nm* lap.
regeneración [rexenera'θjon] *nf* regeneration.
regenerar [rexene'rar] *vt* to regenerate.
regentar [rexen'tar] *vt* to direct, manage; **regente** *nm* (*COM*) manager; (*POL*) regent.
régimen ['reximen] (*pl* **regímenes**) *nm* regime; (*MED*) diet.
regimiento [rexi'mjento] *nm* regiment.
regio, a ['rexjo, a] *adj* royal, regal; (*fig: suntuoso*) splendid; (*AM: fam*) great, terrific.
región [re'xjon] *nf* region; **regionalista** *nm/f* regionalist.
regir [re'xir] *vt* to govern, rule; (*dirigir*) to manage, run ♦ *vi* to apply, be in force.
registrador [rexistra'ðor] *nm* registrar, recorder.
registrar [rexis'trar] *vt* (*buscar*) to search; (: *en cajón*) to look through; (*inspeccionar*) to inspect; (*anotar*) to

register, record; (*INFORM*) to log; ~se
vr to register; (*ocurrir*) to happen.

registro [re'xistro] *nm* (*acto*) registration; (*MUS*, *libro*) register; (*inspección*) inspection, search; ~ **civil** registry office.

regla ['rexla] *nf* (*ley*) rule, regulation;
(*de medir*) ruler, rule; (*MED*: *período*)
period.

reglamentación [rexlamenta'θjon] *nf*
(*acto*) regulation; (*lista*) rules *pl*.

reglamentar [rexlamen'tar] *vt* to regulate; **reglamentario, a** *adj* statutory;
reglamento *nm* rules *pl*, regulations *pl*.

reglar [re'xlar] *vt* (*acciones*) to regulate.

regocijarse [rexoθi'xarse] *vr*: ~ **de** to rejoice at, be happy about; **regocijo** *nm*
joy, happiness.

regodearse [rexoðe'arse] *vr* to be glad,
be delighted; **regodeo** *nm* delight.

regresar [rexre'sar] *vi* to come back, go
back, return; **regresivo, a** *adj* backward; (*fig*) regressive; **regreso** *nm* return.

reguero [re'xero] *nm* (*de sangre etc*)
trickle; (*de humo*) trail.

regulador [rexula'ðor] *nm* regulator;
(*de radio etc*) knob, control.

regular [rexu'lar] *adj* regular; (*normal*)
normal, usual; (*común*) ordinary;
(*organizado*) regular, orderly;
(*mediano*) average; (*fam*) not bad, soso ♦ *adv* so-so, alright ♦ *vt* (*controlar*)
to control, regulate; (*TEC*) to adjust;
por lo ~ as a rule; ~**idad** *nf* regularity;
~**izar** *vt* to regularize.

regusto [re'xusto] *nm* aftertaste.

rehabilitación [reaβilita'θjon] *nf* re-
habilitation; (*ARQ*) restoration.

rehabilitar [reaβili'tar] *vt* to rehabilitate;
(*ARQ*) to restore; (*reintegrar*) to reinstate.

rehacer [rea'θer] *vt* (*reparar*) to mend,
repair; (*volver a hacer*) to redo, repeat; ~se *vr* (*MED*) to recover.

rehén [re'en] *nm* hostage.

rehuir [reu'ir] *vt* to avoid, shun.

rehusar [reu'sar] *vt*, *vi* to refuse.

reina ['reina] *nf* queen; ~**do** *nm* reign.

reinante [rei'nante] *adj* (*fig*) prevailing.

reinar [rei'nar] *vi* to reign.

reincidir [reinθi'ðir] *vi* to relapse.

reincorporarse [reinkorpo'rarse] *vr*: ~ **a**
to rejoin.

reino ['reino] *nm* kingdom; **el R~ Unido**
the United Kingdom.

reintegrar [reinte'xrar] *vt* (*reconstituir*)
to reconstruct; (*persona*) to reinstate;
(*dinero*) to refund, pay back; ~se *vr*:
~se **a** to return to.

reír [re'ir] *vi* to laugh; ~se *vr* to laugh;
~se **de** to laugh at.

reiterar [reite'rar] *vt* to reiterate.

reivindicación [reiβindika'θjon] *nf*
(*demanda*) claim, demand; (*justificación*) vindication.

reivindicar [reiβindi'kar] *vt* to claim.

reja ['rexa] *nf* (*de ventana*) grille, bars
pl; (*en la calle*) grating.

rejilla [re'xiʎa] *nf* grating, grille;
(*muebles*) wickerwork; (*de ventilación*)
vent; (*de coche etc*) luggage rack.

rejoneador [rexonea'ðor] *nm* mounted
bullfighter.

rejuvenecer [rexuβene'θer] *vt*, *vi* to rejuvenate.

relación [rela'θjon] *nf* relation, relationship; (*MAT*) ratio; (*narración*) report;
relaciones públicas public relations; **con
~ a, en ~ con** in relation to; **relacionar**
vt to relate, connect; **relacionarse** *vr* to
be connected, be linked.

relajación [relaxa'θjon] *nf* relaxation.

relajado, a [rela'xaðo, a] *adj* (*disoluto*)
loose; (*cómodo*) relaxed; (*MED*)
ruptured.

relajar [rela'xar] *vt* to relax; ~se *vr* to
relax.

relamerse [rela'merse] *vr* to lick one's
lips.

relamido, a [rela'miðo, a] *adj* (*pulcro*)
overdressed; (*afectado*) affected.

relámpago [re'lampaxo] *nm* flash of
lightning; **visita/huelga** ~ lightning
visit/strike; **relampaguear** *vi* to flash.

relatar [rela'tar] *vt* to tell, relate.

relativo, a [rela'tiβo, a] *adj* relative; **en
lo** ~ **a** concerning.

relato [re'lato] *nm* (*narración*) story,
tale.

relax [re'la(k)s] *nm*: **hacer** ~ to relax.
relegar [rele'ɣar] *vt* to relegate.
relevante [rele'ßante] *adj* eminent, outstanding.
relevar [rele'ßar] *vt* (*sustituir*) to relieve; ~**se** *vr* to relay; ~ **a uno de un cargo** to relieve sb of his post.
relevo [re'leßo] *nm* relief; **carrera de** ~**s** relay race.
relieve [re'ljeße] *nm* (*ARTE, TEC*) relief; (*fig*) prominence, importance; **bajo** ~ bas-relief.
religión [reli'xjon] *nf* religion; **religioso, a** *adj* religious ♦ *nm/f* monk/nun.
relinchar [relin'tʃar] *vi* to neigh; **relincho** *nm* neigh; (*acto*) neighing.
reliquia [re'likja] *nf* relic; ~ **de familia** heirloom.
reloj [re'lo(x)] *nm* clock; ~ (**de pulsera**) wristwatch; ~ **despertador** alarm (clock); **poner el** ~ to set one's watch (*o* the clock); ~**ero, a** *nm/f* clockmaker; watchmaker.
reluciente [relu'θjente] *adj* brilliant, shining.
relucir [relu'θir] *vi* to shine; (*fig*) to excel.
relumbrar [relum'brar] *vi* to dazzle, shine brilliantly.
rellano [re'ʎano] *nm* (*ARQ*) landing.
rellenar [reʎe'nar] *vt* (*llenar*) to fill up; (*CULIN*) to stuff; (*COSTURA*) to pad; **relleno, a** *adj* full up; stuffed ♦ *nm* stuffing; (*de tapicería*) padding.
remachar [rema'tʃar] *vt* to rivet; (*fig*) to hammer home, drive home; **remache** *nm* rivet.
remanente [rema'nente] *nm* remainder; (*COM*) balance; (*de producto*) surplus.
remangar [reman'gar] *vt* to roll up.
remanso [re'manso] *nm* pool.
remar [re'mar] *vi* to row.
rematado, a [rema'taðo, a] *adj* complete, utter.
rematar [rema'tar] *vt* to finish off; (*COM*) to sell off cheap ♦ *vi* to end, finish off; (*DEPORTE*) to shoot.
remate [re'mate] *nm* end, finish; (*punta*) tip; (*DEPORTE*) shot; (*ARQ*) top; (*COM*) auction sale; **de** *o* **para** ~ to crown it

all (*BRIT*), to top it off.
remedar [reme'ðar] *vt* to imitate.
remediar [reme'ðjar] *vt* to remedy; (*subsanar*) to make good, repair; (*evitar*) to avoid.
remedio [re'meðjo] *nm* remedy; (*alivio*) relief, help; (*JUR*) recourse, remedy; **poner** ~ **a** to correct, stop; **no tener más** ~ to have no alternative; ¡**qué** ~! there's no choice!; **sin** ~ hopeless.
remedo [re'meðo] *nm* imitation; (*pey*) parody.
remendar [remen'dar] *vt* to repair; (*con parche*) to patch.
remesa [re'mesa] *nf* remittance; (*COM*) shipment.
remiendo [re'mjendo] *nm* mend; (*con parche*) patch; (*cosido*) darn.
remilgado, a [remil'ɣaðo, a] *adj* prim; (*afectado*) affected.
remilgo [re'milɣo] *nm* primness; (*afectación*) affectation.
reminiscencia [reminis'θenθja] *nf* reminiscence.
remiso, a [re'miso, a] *adj* slack, slow.
remitir [remi'tir] *vt* to remit, send ♦ *vi* to slacken; (*en carta*): **remite: X** sender: X; **remitente** *nm/f* sender.
remo ['remo] *nm* (*de barco*) oar; (*DEPORTE*) rowing.
remojar [remo'xar] *vt* to steep, soak; (*galleta etc*) to dip, dunk.
remojo [re'moxo] *nm*: **dejar la ropa en** ~ to leave clothes to soak.
remolacha [remo'latʃa] *nf* beet, beetroot.
remolcador [remolka'ðor] *nm* (*NAUT*) tug; (*AUTO*) breakdown lorry.
remolcar [remol'kar] *vt* to tow.
remolino [remo'lino] *nm* eddy; (*de agua*) whirlpool; (*de viento*) whirlwind; (*de gente*) crowd.
remolque [re'molke] *nm* tow, towing; (*cuerda*) towrope; **llevar a** ~ to tow.
remontar [remon'tar] *vt* to mend; ~**se** *vr* to soar; ~**se a** (*COM*) to amount to; ~ **el vuelo** to soar.
remorder [remor'ðer] *vt* to distress, disturb; ~**le la conciencia a uno** to have a guilty conscience; **remordimiento** *nm*

remorse.
remoto, a [re'moto, a] *adj* remote.
remover [remo'ßer] *vt* to stir; *(tierra)* to turn over; *(objetos)* to move round.
remozar [remo'θar] *vt (ARQ)* to refurbish.
remuneración [remunera'θjon] *nf* remuneration.
remunerar [remune'rar] *vt* to remunerate; *(premiar)* to reward.
renacer [rena'θer] *vi* to be reborn; *(fig)* to revive; **renacimiento** *nm* rebirth; el **Renacimiento** the Renaissance.
renacuajo [rena'kwaxo] *nm (ZOOL)* tadpole.
renal [re'nal] *adj* renal, kidney *cpd.*
rencilla [ren'θiʎa] *nf* quarrel.
rencor [ren'kor] *nm* rancour, bitterness; **~oso, a** *adj* spiteful.
rendición [rendi'θjon] *nf* surrender.
rendido, a [ren'diðo, a] *adj (sumiso)* submissive; *(cansado)* worn-out, exhausted.
rendija [ren'dixa] *nf (hendedura)* crack, cleft.
rendimiento [rendi'mjento] *nm (producción)* output; *(TEC, COM)* efficiency.
rendir [ren'dir] *vt (vencer)* to defeat; *(producir)* to produce; *(dar beneficio)* to yield; *(agotar)* to exhaust ♦ *vi* to pay; **~se** *vr (someterse)* to surrender; *(cansarse)* to wear o.s. out; **~ homenaje** *o* **culto a** to pay homage to.
renegado, a [rene'xaðo, a] *adj, nm/f* renegade.
renegar [rene'xar] *vi (renunciar)* to renounce; *(blasfemar)* to blaspheme; *(quejarse)* to complain.
RENFE ['renfe] *nf abr* (= *Red Nacional de los Ferrocarriles Españoles*) ≈ BR *(BRIT).*
renglón [ren'glon] *nm (línea)* line; *(COM)* item, article; **a ~ seguido** immediately after.
renombrado, a [renom'braðo, a] *adj* renowned.
renombre [re'nombre] *nm* renown.
renovación [renoßa'θjon] *nf (de contrato)* renewal; *(ARQ)* renovation.
renovar [reno'ßar] *vt* to renew; *(ARQ)* to

renovate.
renta ['renta] *nf (ingresos)* income; *(beneficio)* profit; *(alquiler)* rent; **~ vitalicia** annuity; **rentable** *adj* profitable; **rentar** *vt* to produce, yield.
rentista [ren'tista] *nm/f (accionista)* stockholder.
renuencia [re'nwenθja] *nf* reluctance.
renuncia [re̩'nunθja] *nf* resignation.
renunciar [renun'θjar] *vt* to renounce; *(tabaco, alcohol etc)*: **~ a** to give up; *(oferta, oportunidad)* to turn down; *(puesto)* to resign ♦ *vi* to resign.
reñido, a [re'ɲiðo, a] *adj (batalla)* bitter, hard-fought; **estar ~ con uno** to be on bad terms with sb.
reñir [re'ɲir] *vt (regañar)* to scold ♦ *vi (estar peleado)* to quarrel, fall out; *(combatir)* to fight.
reo ['reo] *nm/f* culprit, offender; **~ de muerte** prisoner condemned to death.
reojo [re'oxo] **: de ~** *adv* out of the corner of one's eye.
reparación [repara'θjon] *nf (acto)* mending, repairing; *(TEC)* repair; *(fig)* amends, reparation.
reparar [repa'rar] *vt* to repair; *(fig)* to make amends for; *(observar)* to observe ♦ *vi*: **~ en** *(darse cuenta de)* to notice; *(prestar atención a)* to pay attention to.
reparo [re'paro] *nm (advertencia)* observation; *(duda)* doubt; *(dificultad)* difficulty; **poner ~s (a)** to raise objections (to).
repartición [reparti'θjon] *nf* distribution; *(división)* division; **repartidor, a** *nm/f* distributor.
repartir [repar'tir] *vt* to distribute, share out; *(CORREOS)* to deliver; **reparto** *nm* distribution; delivery; *(TEATRO, CINE)* cast; *(AM: urbanización)* housing estate *(BRIT)*, real estate development *(US).*
repasar [repa'sar] *vt (ESCOL)* to revise; *(MECÁNICA)* to check, overhaul; *(COSTURA)* to mend; **repaso** *nm* revision; overhaul, checkup; mending.
repatriar [repa'trjar] *vt* to repatriate.
repecho [re'petʃo] *nm* steep incline.
repelente [repe'lente] *adj* repellent, re-

pulsive.

repeler [repe'ler] *vt* to repel.

repensar [repen'sar] *vt* to reconsider.

repente [re'pente] *nm*: **de ~** suddenly; **~ de ira** fit of anger.

repentino, a [repen'tino, a] *adj* sudden.

repercusión [reperku'sjon] *nf* repercussion.

repercutir [reperku'tir] *vi* (*objeto*) to rebound; (*sonido*) to echo; **~ en** (*fig*) to have repercussions on.

repertorio [reper'torjo] *nm* list; (*TEATRO*) repertoire.

repetición [repeti'θjon] *nf* repetition.

repetir [repe'tir] *vt* to repeat; (*plato*) to have a second helping of ♦ *vi* to repeat; (*sabor*) to come back; **~se** *vr* (*volver sobre un tema*) to repeat o.s.

repetitivo, a [repeti'tiβo, a] *adj* repetitive, repetitious.

repicar [repi'kar] *vt* (*campanas*) to ring.

repique [re'pike] *nm* pealing, ringing; **~teo** *nm* pealing; (*de tambor*) drumming.

repisa [re'pisa] *nf* ledge, shelf; (*de ventana*) windowsill; **~ de chimenea** mantelpiece.

repito *etc vb ver* **repetir.**

replegarse [reple'ɣarse] *vr* to fall back, retreat.

repleto, a [re'pleto, a] *adj* replete, full up.

réplica ['replika] *nf* answer; (*ARTE*) replica.

replicar [repli'kar] *vi* to answer; (*objetar*) to argue, answer back.

repliegue [re'pljeɣe] *nm* (*MIL*) withdrawal.

repoblación [repoβla'θjon] *nf* repopulation; (*de río*) restocking; **~ forestal** reafforestation.

repoblar [repo'βlar] *vt* to repopulate; (*con árboles*) to reafforest.

repollo [re'poʎo] *nm* cabbage.

reponer [repo'ner] *vt* to replace, put back; (*TEATRO*) to revive; **~se** *vr* to recover; **~ que** to reply that.

reportaje [repor'taxe] *nm* report, article.

reportero, a [repor'tero, a] *nm/f* reporter.

reposacabezas [reposaka'βeθas] *nm inv* headrest.

reposado, a [repo'saðo, a] *adj* (*descansado*) restful; (*tranquilo*) calm.

reposar [repo'sar] *vi* to rest, repose.

reposición [reposi'θjon] *nf* replacement; (*CINE*) remake.

reposo [re'poso] *nm* rest.

repostar [repos'tar] *vt* to replenish; (*AUTO*) to fill up (with petrol (*BRIT*) o gasoline (*US*)).

repostería [reposte'ria] *nf* confectioner's (shop); **repostero, a** *nm/f* confectioner.

reprender [repren'der] *vt* to reprimand.

represa [re'presa] *nf* dam; (*lago artificial*) lake, pool.

represalia [repre'salja] *nf* reprisal.

representación [representa'θjon] *nf* representation; (*TEATRO*) performance; **representante** *nm/f* representative; performer.

representar [represen'tar] *vt* to represent; (*TEATRO*) to perform; (*edad*) to look; **~se** *vr* to imagine; **representativo, a** *adj* representative.

represión [repre'sjon] *nf* repression.

reprimenda [repri'menda] *nf* reprimand, rebuke.

reprimir [repri'mir] *vt* to repress.

reprobar [repro'βar] *vt* to censure, reprove.

réprobo, a ['reproβo, a] *nm/f* reprobate.

reprochar [repro'tʃar] *vt* to reproach; **reproche** *nm* reproach.

reproducción [reproðuk'θjon] *nf* reproduction.

reproducir [reproðu'θir] *vt* to reproduce; **~se** *vr* to breed; (*situación*) to recur.

reproductor, a [reproðuc'tor, a] *adj* reproductive.

reptil [rep'til] *nm* reptile.

república [re'puβlika] *nf* republic; **republicano, a** *adj, nm/f* republican.

repudiar [repu'ðjar] *vt* to repudiate; (*fe*) to renounce; **repudio** *nm* repudiation.

repuesto [re'pwesto] *nm* (*pieza de recambio*) spare (part); (*abastecimiento*) supply; **rueda de ~** spare wheel.

repugnancia [repuɣ'nanθja] *nf* repugnance; **repugnante** *adj* repugnant, repulsive.

repugnar [repux'nar] *vt* to disgust.

repujar [repu'xar] *vt* to emboss.

repulsa [re'pulsa] *nf* rebuff.

repulsión [repul'sjon] *nf* repulsion, aversion; **repulsivo, a** *adj* repulsive.

reputación [reputa'θjon] *nf* reputation.

reputar [repu'tar] *vt* to consider, deem.

requemado, a [reke'maðo, a] *adj* (*quemado*) scorched; (*bronceado*) tanned.

requerimiento [rekeri'mjento] *nm* request; (*JUR*) summons.

requerir [reke'rir] *vt* (*pedir*) to ask, request; (*exigir*) to require; (*llamar*) to send for, summon.

requesón [reke'son] *nm* cottage cheese.

requete... [re'kete] *prefijo* extremely.

réquiem ['rekjem] (*pl* ~s) *nm* requiem.

requisa [re'kisa] *nf* (*inspección*) survey, inspection; (*MIL*) requisition.

requisito [reki'sito] *nm* requirement, requisite.

res [res] *nf* beast, animal.

resabido, a [resa'βiðo, a] *adj*: **tener algo sabido y ~** to know sth perfectly well.

resabio [re'saβjo] *nm* (*maña*) vice, bad habit; (*dejo*) (unpleasant) aftertaste.

resaca [re'saka] *nf* (*en el mar*) undertow, undercurrent; (*fig*) backlash; (*fam*) hangover.

resalado, a [resa'laðo, a] (*fam*) *adj* lively.

resaltar [resal'tar] *vi* to project, stick out; (*fig*) to stand out.

resarcir [resar'θir] *vt* to compensate; **~se** *vr* to make up for.

resbaladizo, a [resβala'ðiθo, a] *adj* slippery.

resbalar [resβa'lar] *vi* to slip, slide; (*fig*) to slip (up); **~se** *vr* to slip, slide; to slip (up); **resbalón** *nm* (*acción*) slip.

rescatar [reska'tar] *vt* (*salvar*) to save, rescue; (*objeto*) to get back, recover; (*cautivos*) to ransom.

rescate [res'kate] *nm* rescue; (*de objeto*) recovery; **pagar un ~** to pay a ransom.

rescindir [resθin'dir] *vt* to rescind.

rescisión [resθi'sjon] *nf* cancellation.

rescoldo [res'koldo] *nm* embers *pl*.

resecar [rese'kar] *vt* to dry thoroughly; (*MED*) to cut out, remove; **~se** *vr* to dry up.

reseco, a [re'seko, a] *adj* very dry; (*fig*) skinny.

resentido, a [resen'tiðo, a] *adj* resentful.

resentimiento [resenti'mjento] *nm* resentment, bitterness.

resentirse [resen'tirse] *vr* (*debilitarse*: *persona*) to suffer; **~ de** (*consecuencias*) to feel the effects of; **~ de** (*o por*) **algo** to resent sth, be bitter about sth.

reseña [re'seɲa] *nf* (*cuenta*) account; (*informe*) report; (*LITERATURA*) review.

reseñar [rese'ɲar] *vt* to describe; (*LITERATURA*) to review.

reserva [re'serβa] *nf* reserve; (*reservación*) reservation; **a ~ de que ...** unless ...; **con toda ~** in strictest confidence.

reservado, a [reser'βaðo, a] *adj* reserved; (*retraído*) cold, distant ♦ *nm* private room.

reservar [reser'βar] *vt* (*guardar*) to keep; (*habitación, entrada*) to reserve; **~se** *vr* to save o.s.; (*callar*) to keep to o.s.

resfriado [resfri'aðo] *nm* cold; **resfriarse** *vr* to cool; (*MED*) to catch (a) cold.

resguardar [resɣwar'ðar] *vt* to protect, shield; **~se** *vr*: **~se de** to guard against; **resguardo** *nm* defence (*vale*) voucher; (*recibo*) receipt, slip.

residencia [resi'ðenθja] *nf* residence; **~l** *nf* (*urbanización*) housing estate.

residente [resi'ðente] *adj*, *nm/f* resident.

residir [resi'ðir] *vi* to reside, live; **~ en** to reside in, lie in.

residuo [re'siðwo] *nm* residue.

resignación [resixna'θjon] *nf* resignation; **resignarse** *vr*: **resignarse a** *o* **con** to resign o.s. to, be resigned to.

resina [re'sina] *nf* resin.

resistencia [resis'tenθja] *nf* (*dureza*) endurance, strength; (*oposición, ELEC*) resistance; **resistente** *adj* strong, hardy; resistant;

resistir [resis'tir] *vt* (*soportar*) to bear; (*oponerse a*) to resist, oppose; (*aguantar*) to put up with ♦ *vi* to resist; (*aguantar*) to last, endure; ~se *vr*: ~se a to refuse to, resist.

resma ['resma] *nf* ream.

resol [re'sol] *nm* glare of the sun.

resolución [resolu'θjon] *nf* resolution; (*decisión*) decision; **resoluto, a** *adj* resolute.

resolver [resol'βer] *vt* to resolve; (*solucionar*) to solve, resolve; (*decidir*) to decide, settle; ~se *vr* to make up one's mind.

resollar [reso'λar] *vi* to breathe noisily, wheeze.

resonancia [reso'nanθja] *nf* (*del sonido*) resonance; (*repercusión*) repercussion; **resonante** *adj* resonant, resounding; (*fig*) tremendous.

resonar [reso'nar] *vi* to ring, echo.

resoplar [reso'plar] *vi* to snort; **resoplido** *nm* heavy breathing.

resorte [re'sorte] *nm* spring; (*fig*) lever.

respaldar [respal'dar] *vt* to back (up), support; ~se *vr* to lean back; ~se con *o* en (*fig*) to take one's stand on; **respaldo** *nm* (*de sillón*) back; (*fig*) support, backing.

respectivo, a [respek'tiβo, a] *adj* respective; **en lo** ~ **a** with regard to.

respecto [res'pekto] *nm*: **al** ~ on this matter; **con** ~ **a**, ~ **de** with regard to, in relation to.

respetable [respe'taβle] *adj* respectable.

respetar [respe'tar] *vt* to respect; **respeto** *nm* respect; (*acatamiento*) deference; **respetos** *nmpl* respects; **respetuoso, a** *adj* respectful.

respingar [respin'gar] *vi* to shy; **respingo** *nm* start, jump.

respiración [respira'θjon] *nf* breathing; (*MED*) respiration; (*ventilación*) ventilation.

respirar [respi'rar] *vi* to breathe; **respiratorio, a** *adj* respiratory; **respiro** *nm* breathing; (*fig*: *descanso*) respite.

resplandecer [resplande'θer] *vi* to shine; **resplandeciente** *adj* resplendent, shining; **resplandor** *nm* brilliance, bright-

ness; (*de luz, fuego*) blaze.

responder [respon'der] *vt* to answer ♦ *vi* to answer; (*fig*) to respond; (*pey*) to answer back; ~ **de** *o* **por** to answer for; **respondón, ona** *adj* cheeky.

responsabilidad [responsaβili'ðað] *nf* responsibility.

responsabilizarse [responsaβili'θarse] *vr* to make o.s. responsible, take charge.

responsable [respon'saβle] *adj* responsible.

respuesta [res'pwesta] *nf* answer, reply.

resquebrajar [reskeβra'xar] *vt* to crack, split; ~se *vr* to crack, split.

resquemor [reske'mor] *nm* resentment.

resquicio [res'kiθjo] *nm* chink; (*hendedura*) crack.

restablecer [restaβle'θer] *vt* to re-establish, restore; ~se *vr* to recover.

restallar [resta'λar] *vi* to crack.

restante [res'tante] *adj* remaining; **lo** ~ the remainder.

restar [res'tar] *vt* (*MAT*) to subtract; (*fig*) to take away ♦ *vi* to remain, be left.

restauración [restaura'θjon] *nf* restoration.

restaurante [restau'rante] *nm* restaurant.

restaurar [restau'rar] *vt* to restore.

restitución [restitu'θjon] *nf* return, restitution.

restituir [restitu'ir] *vt* (*devolver*) to return, give back; (*rehabilitar*) to restore.

resto ['resto] *nm* (*residuo*) rest, remainder; (*apuesta*) stake; ~s *nmpl* remains.

restregar [restre'var] *vt* to scrub, rub.

restricción [restrik'θjon] *nf* restriction.

restrictivo, a [restrik'tiβo, a] *adj* restrictive.

restringir [restrin'xir] *vt* to restrict, limit.

resucitar [resuθi'tar] *vt*, *vi* to resuscitate, revive.

resuelto, a [re'swelto, a] *pp de* **resolver** ♦ *adj* resolute, determined.

resuello [re'sweλo] *nm* (*aliento*) breath; **estar sin** ~ to be breathless.

resultado [resul'taðo] *nm* result; (*conclusión*) outcome; **resultante** *adj* resulting, resultant.

resultar [resul'tar] *vi* (*ser*) to be; (*llegar a ser*) to turn out to be; (*salir bien*) to turn out well; (*COM*) to amount to; ~ **de** to stem from; **me resulta difícil hacerlo** it's difficult for me to do it.

resumen [re'sumen] (*pl* **resúmenes**) *nm* summary, résumé; **en** ~ in short.

resumir [resu'mir] *vt* to sum up; (*cortar*) to abridge, cut down; (*condensar*) to summarize.

resurgir [resur'xir] *vi* (*reaparecer*) to reappear.

resurrección [resurre(k)'θjon] *nf* resurrection.

retablo [re'taβlo] *nm* altarpiece.

retaguardia [reta'ɣwarðja] *nf* rearguard.

retahíla [reta'ila] *nf* series, string.

retal [re'tal] *nm* remnant.

retar [re'tar] *vt* to challenge; (*desafiar*) to defy, dare.

retardar [retar'ðar] *vt* (*demorar*) to delay; (*hacer más lento*) to slow down; (*retener*) to hold back; **retardo** *nm* delay.

retazo [re'taθo] *nm* snippet (*BRIT*), fragment.

rete... ['rete] *prefijo* very, extremely.

retener [rete'ner] *vt* (*intereses*) to withhold.

retina [re'tina] *nf* retina.

retintín [retin'tin] *nm* jangle, jingle.

retirada [reti'raða] *nf* (*MIL*, *refugio*) retreat; (*de dinero*) withdrawal; (*de embajador*) recall; **retirado, a** *adj* (*lugar*) remote; (*vida*) quiet; (*jubilado*) retired.

retirar [reti'rar] *vt* to withdraw; (*quitar*) to remove; (*jubilar*) to retire, pension off; ~**se** *vr* to retreat, withdraw; to retire; (*acostarse*) to retire, go to bed; **retiro** *nm* retreat; retirement; (*pago*) pension.

reto ['reto] *nm* dare, challenge.

retocar [reto'kar] *vt* (*fotografía*) to touch up, retouch.

retoño [re'toɲo] *nm* sprout, shoot; (*fig*) offspring, child.

retoque [re'toke] *nm* retouching.

retorcer [retor'θer] *vt* to twist; (*manos, lavado*) to wring; ~**se** *vr* to become twisted; (*mover el cuerpo*) to writhe.

retorcimiento [retorθi'mjento] *nm* twist, twisting.

retórica [re'torika] *nf* rhetoric; (*pey*) affectedness.

retornar [retor'nar] *vt* to return, give back ♦ *vi* to return, go/come back; **retorno** *nm* return.

retortijón [retorti'xon] *nm* twist, twisting.

retozar [reto'θar] *vi* (*juguetear*) to frolic, romp; (*saltar*) to gambol; **retozón, ona** *adj* playful.

retracción [retrak'θjon] *nf* retraction.

retractarse [retrak'tarse] *vr* to retract; **me retracto** I take that back.

retraerse [retra'erse] *vr* to retreat, withdraw; **retraído, a** *adj* shy, retiring; **retraimiento** *nm* retirement; (*timidez*) shyness.

retransmisión [retransmi'sjon] *nf* repeat (broadcast).

retransmitir [retransmi'tir] *vt* (*mensaje*) to relay; (*TV etc*) to repeat, retransmit; (: *en vivo*) to broadcast live.

retrasado, a [retra'saðo, a] *adj* late; (*MED*) mentally retarded; (*país etc*) backward, underdeveloped.

retrasar [retra'sar] *vt* (*demorar*) to postpone, put off; (*retardar*) to slow down ♦ *vi* (*atrasarse*) to be late; (*reloj*) to be slow; (*producción*) to fall (away); (*quedarse atrás*) to lag behind; ~**se** *vr* to be late; to be slow; to fall away; to lag behind.

retraso [re'traso] *nm* (*demora*) delay; (*lentitud*) slowness; (*tardanza*) lateness; (*atraso*) backwardness; ~**s** (*FINANZAS*) *nmpl* arrears; **llegar con** ~ to arrive late; ~ **mental** mental deficiency.

retratar [retra'tar] *vt* (*ARTE*) to paint the portrait of; (*fotografiar*) to photograph; (*fig*) to depict, describe; ~**se** *vr* to have one's portrait painted; to have one's photograph taken; **retrato** *nm* portrait; (*fig*) likeness; **retrato-robot** *nm* identikit picture.

retreta [re'treta] *nf* retreat.

retrete [re'trete] *nm* toilet.

retribución [retriβu'θjon] *nf* (*recompensa*) reward; (*pago*) pay, payment.

retribuir [retri'βwir] *vt* (*recompensar*) to reward; (*pagar*) to pay.

retro... ['retro] *prefijo* retro....

retroactivo, a [retroak'tiβo, a] *adj* retroactive, retrospective.

retroceder [retroθe'ðer] *vi* (*echarse atrás*) to move back(wards); (*fig*) to back down.

retroceso [retro'θeso] *nm* backward movement; (*MED*) relapse; (*fig*) backing down.

retrógrado, a [re'troɣraðo, a] *adj* retrograde, retrogressive; (*POL*) reactionary.

retropropulsión [retropropul'sjon] *nf* jet propulsion.

retrospectivo, a [retrospek'tiβo, a] *adj* retrospective.

retrovisor [retroβi'sor] *nm* (*tb: espejo* ~) rear-view mirror.

retumbar [retum'bar] *vi* to echo, resound.

reuma ['reuma] *nm* rheumatism.

reumatismo [reuma'tismo] *nm* = **reuma**.

reunificar [reunifi'kar] *vt* to reunify.

reunión [reu'njon] *nf* (*asamblea*) meeting; (*fiesta*) party.

reunir [reu'nir] *vt* (*juntar*) to reunite, join (together); (*recoger*) to gather (together); (*personas*) to get together; (*cualidades*) to combine; ~**se** *vr* (*personas: en asamblea*) to meet, gather.

revalidar [reβali'ðar] *vt* (*ratificar*) to confirm, ratify.

revalorar [reβalo'rar] *vt* = **revalorizar**.

revalorizar [reβalori'θar] *vt* to revalue, reassess.

revancha [re'βantʃa] *nf* revenge.

revelación [reβela'θjon] *nf* revelation.

revelado [reβe'laðo] *nm* developing.

revelar [reβe'lar] *vt* to reveal; (*FOTO*) to develop.

reventar [reβen'tar] *vt* to burst, explode.

reventón [reβen'ton] *nm* (*AUTO*) blowout (*BRIT*), flat (*US*).

reverberación [reβerβera'θjon] *nf* reverberation.

reverberar [reβerβe'rar] *vi* to reverberate.

reverencia [reβe'renθja] *nf* reverence; **reverenciar** *vt* to revere.

reverendo, a [reβe'rendo, a] *adj* reverend.

reverente [reβe'rente] *adj* reverent.

reverso [re'βerso] *nm* back, other side; (*de moneda*) reverse.

revertir [reβer'tir] *vi* to revert.

revés [re'βes] *nm* back, wrong side; (*fig*) reverse, setback; (*DEPORTE*) backhand; **al** ~ the wrong way round; (*de arriba abajo*) upside down; (*ropa*) inside out; **volver algo al** ~ to turn sth round; (*ropa*) to turn sth inside out.

revestir [reβes'tir] *vt* (*poner*) to put on; (*cubrir*) to cover, coat; ~ **con** *o* **de** to invest with.

revisar [reβi'sar] *vt* (*examinar*) to check; (*texto etc*) to revise; **revisión** *nf* revision.

revisor, a [reβi'sor, a] *nm/f* inspector; (*FERRO*) ticket collector.

revista [re'βista] *nf* magazine, review; (*TEATRO*) revue; (*inspección*) inspection; **pasar** ~ **a** to review, inspect.

revivir [reβi'βir] *vi* to revive.

revocación [reβoka'θjon] *nf* repeal.

revocar [reβo'kar] *vt* to revoke.

revolcarse [reβol'karse] *vr* to roll about.

revolotear [reβolote'ar] *vi* to flutter.

revoltijo [reβol'tixo] *nm* mess, jumble.

revoltoso, a [reβol'toso, a] *adj* (*travieso*) naughty, unruly.

revolución [reβolu'θjon] *nf* revolution; **revolucionar** *vt* to revolutionize; **revolucionario, a** *adj, nm/f* revolutionary.

revolver [reβol'βer] *vt* (*desordenar*) to disturb, mess up; (*mover*) to move about; (*POL*) to stir up ♦ *vi*: ~ **en** to go through, rummage (about) in; ~**se** *vr* (*volver contra*) to turn on *o* against.

revólver [re'βolβer] *nm* revolver.

revuelo [re'βwelo] *nm* fluttering; (*fig*)

commotion.

revuelta [re'ßwelta] *nf* (*motín*) revolt; (*agitación*) commotion.

revuelto, a [re'ßwelto, a] *pp de* **revolver** ♦ *adj* (*mezclado*) mixed-up, in disorder.

revulsivo [reßul'sißo] *nm* enema.

rey [rei] *nm* king; **Día de R~es** Twelfth Night.

reyerta [re'jerta] *nf* quarrel, brawl.

rezagado, a [reθa'xaðo, a] *nm/f* straggler.

rezagar [reθa'xar] *vt* (*dejar atrás*) to leave behind; (*retrasar*) to delay, postpone.

rezar [re'θar] *vi* to pray; **~ con** (*fam*) to concern, have to do with; **rezo** *nm* prayer.

rezongar [reθon'gar] *vi* to grumble.

rezumar [reθu'mar] *vt* to ooze.

ría ['ria] *nf* estuary.

riada [ri'aða] *nf* flood.

ribera [ri'ßera] *nf* (*de río*) bank; (: *área*) riverside.

ribete [ri'ßete] *nm* (*de vestido*) border; (*fig*) addition; **~ar** *vt* to edge, border.

ricino [ri'θino] *nm*: **aceite de ~** castor oil.

rico, a ['riko, a] *adj* rich; (*adinerado*) wealthy, rich; (*lujoso*) luxurious; (*comida*) delicious; (*niño*) lovely, cute ♦ *nm/f* rich person.

rictus ['riktus] *nm* (*mueca*) sneer, grin.

ridiculez [riðiku'leθ] *nf* absurdity.

ridiculizar [riðikuli'θar] *vt* to ridicule.

ridículo, a [ri'ðikulo, a] *adj* ridiculous; **hacer el ~** to make a fool of o.s.; **poner a uno en ~** to make a fool of sb.

riego ['rjexo] *nm* (*aspersión*) watering; (*irrigación*) irrigation.

riel [rjel] *nm* rail.

rienda ['rjenda] *nf* rein; **dar ~ suelta a** to give free rein to.

riesgo ['rjesxo] *nm* risk; **correr el ~ de** to run the risk of.

rifa ['rifa] *nf* (*lotería*) raffle; **rifar** *vt* to raffle.

rifle ['rifle] *nm* rifle.

rigidez [rixi'ðeθ] *nf* rigidity, stiffness; (*fig*) strictness; **rígido, a** *adj* rigid, stiff; strict, inflexible.

rigor [ri'xor] *nm* strictness, rigour; (*inclemencia*) harshness; **de ~** de rigueur, essential; **riguroso, a** *adj* rigorous; harsh; (*severo*) severe.

rimar [ri'mar] *vi* to rhyme.

rimbombante [rimbom'bante] *adj* (*fig*) pompous.

rimel ['rimel] *nm* mascara.

rímmel ['rimel] *nm* = **rímel**.

rincón [rin'kon] *nm* corner (*inside*).

rinoceronte [rinoθe'ronte] *nm* rhinoceros.

riña ['riɲa] *nf* (*disputa*) argument; (*pelea*) brawl.

riñón [ri'ɲon] *nm* kidney; **tener riñones** to have guts.

río *etc* ['rio] *vb ver* **reír** ♦ *nm* river; (*fig*) torrent, stream; **~ abajo/arriba** downstream/upstream; **~ de la Plata** River Plate.

rioja [ri'oxa] *nm* (*vino*) rioja (wine).

rioplatense [riopla'tense] *adj* of o from the River Plate region.

riqueza [ri'keθa] *nf* wealth, riches *pl*; (*cualidad*) richness.

risa ['risa] *nf* laughter; (*una ~*) laugh; ¡**qué ~!** what a laugh!

risco ['risko] *nm* crag, cliff.

risible [ri'sißle] *adj* ludicrous, laughable.

risotada [riso'taða] *nf* guffaw, loud laugh.

ristra ['ristra] *nf* string.

risueño, a [ri'sweɲo, a] *adj* (*sonriente*) smiling; (*contento*) cheerful.

ritmo ['ritmo] *nm* rhythm; **a ~ lento** slowly; **trabajar a ~ lento** to go slow.

rito ['rito] *nm* rite.

ritual [ri'twal] *adj, nm* ritual.

rival [ri'ßal] *adj, nm/f* rival; **~idad** *nf* rivalry; **~izar** *vi*: **~izar con** to rival, vie with.

rizado, a [ri'θaðo, a] *adj* curly ♦ *nm* curls *pl*.

rizar [ri'θar] *vt* to curl; **~se** *vr* (*pelo*) to curl; (*agua*) to ripple; **rizo** *nm* curl; ripple.

RNE *nf abr* = **Radio Nacional de España**.

robar [ro'ßar] *vt* to rob; (*objeto*) to steal; (*casa etc*) to break into; (*NAIPES*)

to draw.
roble ['roßle] *nm* oak; ~**dal** *nm* =
robledo; ~**do** *nm* oakwood.
robo ['roßo] *nm* robbery, theft.
robot [ro'ßot] *nm* robot; ~ (**de cocina**)
food processor.
robustecer [roßuste'θer] *vt* to strength-
en.
robusto, a [ro'ßusto, a] *adj* robust,
strong.
roca ['roka] *nf* rock.
rocalla [ro'kaλa] *nf* pebbles *pl*.
roce ['roθe] *nm* (*caricia*) brush; (*TEC*)
friction; (*en la piel*) graze; **tener** ~ **con**
to be in close contact with.
rociar [ro'θjar] *vt* to spray.
rocín [ro'θin] *nm* nag, hack.
rocío [ro'θio] *nm* dew.
rocoso, a [ro'koso, a] *adj* rocky.
rodada [ro'ðaða] *nf* rut.
rodado, a [ro'ðaðo, a] *adj* (*con ruedas*)
wheeled.
rodaja [ro'ðaxa] *nf* (*raja*) slice.
rodaje [ro'ðaxe] *nm* (*CINE*) shooting,
filming; (*AUTO*): **en** ~ running in.
rodar [ro'ðar] *vt* (*vehículo*) to wheel
(along); (*escalera*) to roll down;
(*viajar por*) to travel (over) ♦ *vi* to
roll; (*coche*) to go, run; (*CINE*) to
shoot, film.
rodear [roðe'ar] *vt* to surround ♦ *vi* to
go round; ~**se** *vr*: ~**se de amigos** to
surround o.s. with friends.
rodeo [ro'ðeo] *nm* (*ruta indirecta*)
detour; (*evasión*) evasion; (*AM*) rodeo;
hablar sin ~**s** to come to the point,
speak plainly.
rodilla [ro'ðiλa] *nf* knee; **de** ~**s** kneel-
ing; **ponerse de** ~**s** to kneel (down).
rodillo [ro'ðiλo] *nm* roller; (*CULIN*)
rolling-pin.
rododendro [roðo'ðendro] *nm*
rhododendron.
roedor, a [roe'ðor, a] *adj* gnawing ♦ *nm*
rodent.
roer [ro'er] *vt* (*masticar*) to gnaw;
(*corroer, fig*) to corrode.
rogar [ro'xar] *vt, vi* (*pedir*) to ask for;
(*suplicar*) to beg, plead; **se ruega no
fumar** please do not smoke.

rojizo, a [ro'xiθo, a] *adj* reddish.
rojo, a ['roxo, a] *adj, nm* red; **al** ~ **vivo**
red-hot.
rol [rol] *nm* list, roll; (*AM: papel*) role.
rollizo, a [ro'λiθo, a] *adj* (*objeto*)
cylindrical; (*persona*) plump.
rollo ['roλo] *nm* roll; (*de cuerda*) coil;
(*madera*) log; (*fam*) bore; ¡**qué** ~!
what a carry-on!
ROM [rom] *nf abr* (= *memoria de sólo
lectura*) ROM.
Roma ['roma] *n* Rome.
romance [ro'manθe] *nm* (*idioma
castellano*) Romance language; (*LITE-
RATURA*) ballad; **hablar en** ~ to speak
plainly.
romanticismo [romanti'θismo] *nm*
romanticism.
romántico, a [ro'mantiko, a] *adj* romantic.
romería [rome'ria] *nf* (*REL*) pilgrimage;
(*excursión*) trip, outing.
romero, a [ro'mero, a] *nm/f* pilgrim ♦
nm rosemary.
romo, a ['romo, a] *adj* blunt; (*fig*) dull.
rompecabezas [rompeka'ßeθas] *nm inv*
riddle, puzzle; (*juego*) jigsaw (puzzle).
rompehuelgas [rompe'welɣas] *nm inv*
strikebreaker, blackleg.
rompeolas [rompe'olas] *nm inv* break-
water.
romper [rom'per] *vt* to break; (*hacer
pedazos*) to smash; (*papel, tela etc*) to
tear, rip ♦ *vi* (*olas*) to break; (*sol,
diente*) to break through; ~ **un contrato**
to break a contract; ~ **a** (*empezar a*)
to start (suddenly) to; ~ **a llorar** to
burst into tears; ~ **con uno** to fall out
with sb.
rompimiento [rompi'mjento] *nm* (*acto*)
breaking; (*fig*) break; (*quiebra*) crack.
ron [ron] *nm* rum.
roncar [ron'kar] *vi* to snore.
ronco, a ['ronko, a] *adj* (*afónico*)
hoarse; (*áspero*) raucous.
roncha ['rontʃa] *nf* weal; (*contusión*)
bruise.
ronda ['ronda] *nf* (*gen*) round; (*patrulla*) patrol; **rondar** *vt* to patrol ♦ *vi*
to patrol; (*fig*) to prowl round.

ronquido [ron'kiðo] *nm* snore, snoring.

ronronear [ronrone'ar] *vi* to purr; **ronroneo** *nm* purr.

roña ['roɲa] *nf* (*VETERINARIA*) mange; (*mugre*) dirt, grime; (*óxido*) rust.

roñoso, a [ro'ɲoso, a] *adj* (*mugriento*) filthy; (*tacaño*) mean.

ropa ['ropa] *nf* clothes *pl*, clothing; ~ **blanca** linen; ~ **de cama** bed linen; ~ **interior** underwear; ~ **para lavar** washing; ~**je** *nm* gown, robes *pl*; ~**vejero, a** *nm/f* second-hand clothes dealer.

ropero [ro'pero] *nm* linen cupboard; (*guardarropa*) wardrobe.

rosa ['rosa] *adj* pink ♦ *nf* rose; (*ANAT*) red birthmark; ~ **de los vientos** the compass.

rosado, a [ro'saðo, a] *adj* pink ♦ *nm* rosé.

rosal [ro'sal] *nm* rosebush.

rosario [ro'sarjo] *nm* (*REL*) rosary; **rezar el** ~ to say the rosary.

rosca ['roska] *nf* (*de tornillo*) thread; (*de humo*) coil, spiral; (*pan, postre*) ring-shaped roll/pastry.

rosetón [rose'ton] *nm* rosette; (*ARQ*) rose window.

rosquilla [ros'kiʎa] *nf* doughnut-shaped fritter.

rostro ['rostro] *nm* (*cara*) face.

rotación [rota'θjon] *nf* rotation; ~ **de cultivos** crop rotation.

rotativo, a [rota'tiβo, a] *adj* rotary.

roto, a ['roto, a] *pp de* **romper** ♦ *adj* broken.

rótula ['rotula] *nf* kneecap; (*TEC*) ball-and-socket joint.

rotulador [rotula'ðor] *nm* felt-tip pen.

rotular [rotu'lar] *vt* (*carta, documento*) to head, entitle; (*objeto*) to label; **rótulo** *nm* heading, title; label; (*letrero*) sign.

rotundo, a [ro'tundo, a] *adj* round; (*enfático*) emphatic.

rotura [ro'tura] *nf* (*rompimiento*) breaking; (*MED*) fracture.

roturar [rotu'rar] *vt* to plough.

rozadura [roθa'ðura] *nf* abrasion, graze.

rozar [ro'θar] *vt* (*frotar*) to rub; (*arañar*) to scratch; (*tocar ligeramente*) to shave, touch lightly; ~**se** *vr* to rub (together); ~**se con** (*fam*) to rub shoulders with.

r.p.m. *abr* (= *revoluciones por minuto*) rpm.

rte. *abr* (= *remite, remitente*) sender.

RTVE *nf abr* = **Radiotelevisión Española**.

rubí [ru'βi] *nm* ruby; (*de reloj*) jewel.

rubicundo, a [ruβi'kundo, a] *adj* ruddy.

rubio, a ['ruβjo, a] *adj* fair-haired, blond(e) ♦ *nm/f* blond/blonde; **tabaco** ~ Virginia tobacco.

rubor [ru'βor] *nm* (*sonrojo*) blush; (*timidez*) bashfulness; ~**izarse** *vr* to blush; ~**oso, a** *adj* blushing.

rúbrica [ru'βrika] *nf* (*título*) title, heading; (*de la firma*) flourish; **rubricar** *vt* (*firmar*) to sign with a flourish; (*concluir*) to sign and seal.

rudeza [ru'ðeθa] *nf* (*tosquedad*) coarseness; (*sencillez*) simplicity.

rudimento [ruði'mento] *nm* rudiment.

rudo, a ['ruðo, a] *adj* (*sin pulir*) unpolished; (*grosero*) coarse; (*violento*) violent; (*sencillo*) simple.

rueda ['rweða] *nf* wheel; (*círculo*) ring, circle; (*rodaja*) slice, round; ~ **delantera/trasera/de repuesto** front/back/spare wheel; ~ **de prensa** press conference.

ruedo ['rweðo] *nm* (*contorno*) edge, border; (*de vestido*) hem; (*círculo*) circle; (*TAUR*) arena, bullring.

ruego *etc* ['rweɣo] *vb ver* **rogar** ♦ *nm* request.

rufián [ru'fjan] *nm* scoundrel.

rugby ['ruɣβi] *nm* rugby.

rugido [ru'xiðo] *nm* roar.

rugir [ru'xir] *vi* to roar.

rugoso, a [ru'ɣoso, a] *adj* (*arrugado*) wrinkled; (*áspero*) rough; (*desigual*) ridged.

ruibarbo [rui'βarβo] *nm* rhubarb.

ruido ['rwiðo] *nm* noise; (*sonido*) sound; (*alboroto*) racket, row; (*escándalo*) commotion, rumpus; ~**so, a** *adj* noisy, loud; (*fig*) sensational.

ruin [rwin] *adj* contemptible, mean.

ruina ['rwina] *nf* ruin; (*colapso*)

collapse; (de persona) ruin, downfall.
ruindad [rwin'dað] nf lowness, meanness; (acto) low o mean act.
ruinoso, a [rwi'noso, a] adj ruinous; (destartalado) dilapidated, tumbledown; (COM) disastrous.
ruiseñor [rwise'ɲor] nm nightingale.
ruleta [ru'leta] nf roulette.
rulo ['rulo] nm (para el pelo) curler.
rulota [ru'lota] nf caravan (BRIT), trailer (US).
Rumania [ru'manja] nf Rumania.
rumba ['rumba] nf rumba.
rumbo ['rumbo] nm (ruta) route, direction; (ángulo de dirección) course, bearing; (fig) course of events: **ir con ~ a** to be heading for.
rumboso, a [rum'boso, a] adj (generoso) generous.
rumiante [ru'mjante] nm ruminant.
rumiar [ru'mjar] vt to chew; (fig) to chew over ♦ vi to chew the cud.
rumor [ru'mor] nm (ruido sordo) low sound; (murmuración) murmur, buzz.
rumorearse vr: **se rumorea que** it is rumoured that.
runrún [run'run] nm (voces) murmur, sound of voices; (fig) rumour.
rupestre [ru'pestre] adj rock cpd.
ruptura [rup'tura] nf rupture.
rural [ru'ral] adj rural.
Rusia ['rusja] nf Russia; **ruso, a** adj, nm/f Russian.
rústica ['rustika] nf: **libro en ~** paperback (book); ver tb **rústico**.
rústico, a ['rustiko, a] adj rustic; (ordinario) coarse, uncouth ♦ nm/f yokel.
ruta ['ruta] nf route.
rutina [ru'tina] nf routine; **~rio, a** adj routine.

S

S abr (= santo, a) St; (= sur) S.
s. abr (= siglo) C.; (= siguiente) foll.
S.A. abr (= Sociedad Anónima) Ltd (BRIT), Inc (US).
sábado ['saβaðo] nm Saturday.

sábana ['saβana] nf sheet.
sabandija [saβan'dixa] nf bug, insect.
sabañón [saβa'ɲon] nm chilblain.
sabelotodo [saβelo'toðo] nm/f know-all.
saber [sa'βer] vt to know; (llegar a conocer) to find out, learn; (tener capacidad de) to know how to ♦ vi: **~ a** to taste of, taste like ♦ nm knowledge, learning; **a ~** namely; **¿sabes conducir/nadar?** can you drive/swim?; **¿sabes francés?** do you speak French?; **~ de memoria** to know by heart; **hacer ~ algo a uno** to inform sb of sth, let sb know sth.
sabiduría [saβiðu'ria] nf (conocimientos) wisdom; (instrucción) learning.
sabiendas [sa'βjendas]: **a ~** adv knowingly.
sabio, a ['saβjo,a] adj (docto) learned; (prudente) wise, sensible.
sabor [sa'βor] nm taste, flavour; **~ear** vt to taste, savour; (fig) to relish.
sabotaje [saβo'taxe] nm sabotage.
saboteador, a [saβotea'ðor, a] nm/f saboteur.
sabotear [saβote'ar] vt to sabotage.
sabré etc vb ver **saber**.
sabroso, a [sa'βroso, a] adj tasty; (fig: fam) racy, salty.
sacacorchos [saka'kortʃos] nm inv corkscrew.
sacapuntas [saka'puntas] nm inv pencil sharpener.
sacar [sa'kar] vt to take out; (fig: extraer) to get (out); (quitar) to remove, get out; (hacer salir) to bring out; (conclusión) to draw; (novela etc) to publish, bring out; (ropa) to take off; (obra) to make; (premio) to receive; (entradas) to get; (TENIS) to serve; **~ adelante** (niño) to bring up; (negocio) to carry on, go on with; **~ a uno a bailar** to get sb up to dance; **~ una foto** to take a photo; **~ la lengua** to stick out one's tongue; **~ buenas/malas notas** to get good/bad marks.
sacarina [saka'rina] nf saccharin(e).
sacerdote [saθer'ðote] nm priest.
saco ['sako] nm bag; (grande) sack; (su contenido) bagful; (AM) jacket; **~ de**

dormir sleeping bag.
sacramento [sakra'mento] *nm* sacramento.
sacrificar [sakrifi'kar] *vt* to sacrifice; **sacrificio** *nm* sacrifice.
sacrilegio [sakri'lexjo] *nm* sacrilege; **sacrílego, a** *adj* sacrilegious.
sacristía [sakris'tia] *nf* sacristy.
sacro, a ['sakro, a] *adj* sacred.
sacudida [saku'ðiða] *nf* (*agitación*) shake, shaking; (*sacudimiento*) jolt, bump; ~ **eléctrica** electric shock.
sacudir [saku'ðir] *vt* to shake; (*golpear*) to hit.
sádico, a ['saðiko, a] *adj* sadistic ♦ *nm/f* sadist; **sadismo** *nm* sadism.
saeta [sa'eta] *nf* (*flecha*) arrow.
sagacidad [saxaθi'ðað] *nf* shrewdness, cleverness; **sagaz** *adj* shrewd, clever.
sagitario [saxi'tarjo] *nm* Sagittarius.
sagrado, a [sa'xraðo, a] *adj* sacred, holy.
Sáhara ['saara] *nm*: **el** ~ **the** Sahara (desert).
sal [sal] *vb ver* **salir** ♦ *nf* salt.
sala ['sala] *nf* (*cuarto grande*) large room; (~ *de estar*) living room; (*TEATRO*) house, auditorium; (*de hospital*) ward; ~ **de apelación** court; ~ **de espera** waiting room; ~ **de estar** living room; ~ **de fiestas** dance hall.
salado, a [sa'laðo, a] *adj* salty; (*fig*) witty, amusing; **agua salada** salt water.
salar [sa'lar] *vt* to salt, add salt to.
salarial [sala'rjal] *adj* (*aumento, revisión*) wage *cpd*, salary *cpd*.
salario [sa'larjo] *nm* wage, pay.
salchicha [sal'tʃitʃa] *nf* (*pork*) sausage; **salchichón** *nm* (salami-type) sausage.
saldar [sal'dar] *vt* to pay; (*vender*) to sell off; (*fig*) to settle, resolve; **saldo** *nm* (*pago*) settlement; (*de una cuenta*) balance; (*lo restante*) remnant(s) (*pl*), remainder; ~**s** *nmpl* (*en tienda*) sale.
saldré *etc vb ver* **salir**.
salero [sa'lero] *nm* salt cellar.
salgo *etc vb ver* **salir**.
salida [sa'liða] *nf* (*puerta etc*) exit, way out; (*acto*) leaving, going out; (*de tren, AVIAT*) departure; (*TEC*) output, produc-

tion; (*fig*) way out; (*COM*) opening; (*GEO, válvula*) outlet; (*de gas*) leak; **calle sin** ~ cul-de-sac; ~ **de incendios** fire escape.
saliente [sa'ljente] *adj* (*ARQ*) projecting; (*sol*) rising; (*fig*) outstanding.

PALABRA CLAVE

salir [sa'lir] *vi* **1** (*partir: tb*: ~ **de**) to leave; **Juan ha salido** Juan is out; **salió de la cocina** he came out of the kitchen
2 (*aparecer*) to appear; (*disco, libro*) to come out; **anoche salió en la tele** she appeared o was on TV last night; **salió en todos los periódicos** it was in all the papers
3 (*resultar*): **la muchacha nos salió muy trabajadora** the girl turned out to be a very hard worker; **la comida te ha salido exquisita** the food was delicious; **sale muy caro** it's very expensive
4: ~**le a uno algo: la entrevista que hice me salió bien/mal** the interview I did went o turned out well/badly
5: ~ **adelante: no sé como haré para** ~ **adelante** I don't know how I'll get by
♦ ~**se** *vr* (*líquido*) to spill; (*animal*) to escape.

saliva [sa'liβa] *nf* saliva.
salmo ['salmo] *nm* psalm.
salmón [sal'mon] *nm* salmon.
salmuera [sal'mwera] *nf* pickle, brine.
salón [sa'lon] *nm* (*de casa*) living room, lounge; (*muebles*) lounge suite; ~ **de belleza** beauty parlour; ~ **de baile** dance hall.
salpicadero [salpika'ðero] *nm* (*AUTO*) dashboard.
salpicar [salpi'kar] *vt* (*rociar*) to sprinkle, spatter; (*esparcir*) to scatter.
salsa ['salsa] *nf* sauce; (*con carne asada*) gravy; (*fig*) spice.
saltado, a [sal'taðo, a] *adj* (*botón etc*) missing; (*ojos*) bulging.
saltamontes [salta'montes] *nm inv* grasshopper.
saltar [sal'tar] *vt* to jump (over), leap (over); (*dejar de lado*) to skip, miss out ♦ *vi* to jump, leap; (*pelota*) to

bounce; (al aire) to fly up; (quebrarse) to break; (al agua) to dive; (fig) to explode, blow up.

saltear [salte'ar] vt (robar) to rob (in a holdup); (asaltar) to assault, attack; (CULIN) to sauté.

saltimbanqui [saltim'banki] nm/f acrobat.

salto ['salto] nm jump, leap; (al agua) dive; ~ **de agua** waterfall; ~ **de altura** high jump.

saltón, ona [sal'ton, ona] adj (ojos) bulging, popping; (dientes) protruding.

salubre [sa'luβre] adj healthy, salubrious.

salud [sa'luð] nf health; ¡(a su) ~! cheers!, good health!; ~able adj (de buena ~) healthy; (provechoso) good, beneficial.

saludar [salu'ðar] vt to greet; (MIL) to salute; **saludo** nm greeting; "saludos" (en carta) "best wishes", "regards".

salva ['salβa] nf: ~ **de aplausos** ovation.

salvación [salβa'θjon] nf salvation; (rescate) rescue.

salvado [sal'βaðo] nm bran.

Salvador [salβa'ðor]: **El ~** El Salvador; **San ~** San Salvador; **s~eño, a** adj, nm/f Salvadorian.

salvaguardar [salβaɣwar'ðar] vt to safeguard.

salvaje [sal'βaxe] adj wild; (tribu) savage; **salvajismo** nm savagery.

salvar [sal'βar] vt (rescatar) to save, rescue; (resolver) to overcome, resolve; (cubrir distancias) to cover, travel; (hacer excepción) to except, exclude; (un barco) to salvage.

salvavidas [salβa'βiðas] adj inv: **bote/chaleco/cinturón ~** lifeboat/life jacket/life belt.

salvia ['salβja] nf sage.

salvo, a ['salβo, a] adj safe ♦ adv except (for), save; a ~ out of danger; ~ **que** unless; ~**conducto** nm safe-conduct.

san [san] adj saint; **S~ Juan** St. John.

sanar [sa'nar] vt (herida) to heal; (persona) to cure ♦ vi (persona) to get well, recover; (herida) to heal.

sanatorio [sana'torjo] nm sanatorium.

sanción [san'θjon] nf sanction; **sancionar** vt to sanction.

sandalia [san'dalja] nf sandal.

sandía [san'dia] nf watermelon.

sandwich ['sandwitʃ] (pl ~s, ~es) nm sandwich.

saneamiento [sanea'mjento] nm sanitation.

sanear [sane'ar] vt (terreno) to drain.

sangrar [san'grar] vt, vi to bleed; **sangre** nf blood.

sangría [san'gria] nf sangria, sweetened drink of red wine with fruit.

sangriento, a [san'grjento, a] adj bloody.

sanguijuela [sangi'xwela] nf (ZOOL, fig) leech.

sanguinario, a [sangi'narjo, a] adj bloodthirsty.

sanguíneo, a [san'gineo, a] adj blood cpd.

sanidad [sani'ðað] nf sanitation; (calidad de sano) health, healthiness; ~ **pública** public health.

sanitario, a [sani'tarjo, a] adj sanitary; (de la salud) health; ~**s** nmpl toilets (BRIT), washroom (US).

sano, a ['sano, a] adj healthy; (sin daños) sound; (comida) wholesome; (entero) whole, intact; ~ **y salvo** safe and sound.

Santiago [san'tjaɣo] nm: ~ **(de Chile)** Santiago.

santiamén [santja'men] nm: **en un ~** in no time at all.

santidad [santi'ðað] nf holiness, sanctity; **santificar** vt to sanctify, make holy.

santiguarse [santi'ɣwarse] vr to make the sign of the cross.

santo, a ['santo, a] adj holy; (fig) wonderful, miraculous ♦ nm/f saint ♦ nm saint's day; ~ **y seña** password.

santuario [san'twarjo] nm sanctuary, shrine.

saña ['sana] nf rage, fury.

sapo ['sapo] nm toad.

saque ['sake] nm (TENIS) service, serve; (FÚTBOL) throw-in; ~ **de esquina** corner (kick).

saquear [sake'ar] vt (MIL) to sack; (robar) to loot, plunder; (fig) to ransack; **saqueo** nm sacking; looting, plundering; ransacking.
sarampión [saram'pjon] nm measles sg.
sarcasmo [sar'kasmo] nm sarcasm; **sarcástico, a** adj sarcastic.
sardina [sar'ðina] nf sardine.
sardónico, a [sar'ðoniko, a] adj sardonic; (irónico) ironical, sarcastic.
sargento [sar'xento] nm sergeant.
sarna ['sarna] nf itch; (MED) scabies.
sarpullido [sarpu'ʎiðo] nm (MED) rash.
sartén [sar'ten] nf frying pan.
sastre ['sastre] nm tailor; **~ría** nf (arte) tailoring; (tienda) tailor's (shop).
Satanás [sata'nas] nm Satan.
satélite [sa'telite] nm satellite.
sátira ['satira] nf satire.
satisfacción [satisfak'θjon] nf satisfaction.
satisfacer [satisfa'θer] vt to satisfy; (gastos) to meet; (pérdida) to make good; **~se** vr to satisfy o.s., be satisfied; (vengarse) to take revenge; **satisfecho, a** adj satisfied; (contento) content(ed), happy; (tb: satisfecho de sí mismo) self-satisfied, smug.
saturar [satu'rar] vt to saturate.
sauce ['sauθe] nm willow; **~ llorón** weeping willow.
sauna ['sauna] nf sauna.
savia ['saβja] nf sap.
saxofón [sakso'fon] nm saxophone.
sazonado, a [saθo'naðo, a] adj (fruta) ripe; (CULIN) flavoured, seasoned.
sazonar [saθo'nar] vt to ripen; (CULIN) to flavour, season.
scotch [es'kotʃ] ® nm adhesive o sticky tape.

PALABRA CLAVE

se [se] pron **1** (reflexivo: sg: m) himself; (: f) herself; (: pl) themselves; (: cosa) itself; (: de Vd) yourself; (: de Vds) yourselves; **~ está preparando** she's preparing herself; para usos léxicos del pron ver el vb en cuestión, p.ej. **arrepentirse**
2 (con complemento indirecto) to him;

to her; to them; to it; to you; **a usted ~ lo dije ayer** I told you yesterday; **~ compró un sombrero** he bought himself a hat; **~ rompió la pierna** he broke his leg
3 (uso recíproco) each other, one another; **~ miraron (el uno al otro)** they looked at each other o one another
4 (en oraciones pasivas): **se han vendido muchos libros** a lot of books have been sold
5 (impers): **~ dice que** people say that, it is said that; **allí ~ come muy bien** the food there is very good, you can eat very well there.

SE abr (= sudeste) SE.
sé vb ver saber; ser.
sea etc vb ver ser.
sebo ['seβo] nm fat, grease.
secador [seka'ðor] nm: **~ de pelo** hairdryer.
secadora [seka'ðora] nf (ELEC) tumble dryer.
secar [se'kar] vt to dry; **~se** vr to dry (off); (río, planta) to dry up.
sección [sek'θjon] nf section.
seco, a ['seko, a] adj dry; (carácter) cold; (respuesta) sharp, curt; **habrá pan a secas** there will be just bread; **decir algo a secas** to say sth curtly; **parar en ~** to stop dead.
secretaría [sekreta'ria] nf secretariat.
secretario, a [sekre'tarjo, a] nm/f secretary.
secreto, a [se'kreto, a] adj secret; (persona) secretive ♦ nm secret; (calidad) secrecy.
secta ['sekta] nf sect; **~rio, a** adj sectarian.
sector [sek'tor] nm sector.
secuela [se'kwela] nf consequence.
secuencia [se'kwenθja] nf sequence.
secuestrar [sekwes'trar] vt to kidnap; (bienes) to seize, confiscate; **secuestro** nm kidnapping; seizure, confiscation.
secular [seku'lar] adj secular.
secundar [sekun'dar] vt to second, support.
secundario, a [sekun'darjo, a] adj

secondary.

sed [seð] *nf* thirst; **tener** ~ to be thirsty.

seda ['seða] *nf* silk.

sedal [se'ðal] *nm* fishing line.

sedante [se'ðante] *nm* sedative.

sede ['seðe] *nf* (*de gobierno*) seat; (*de compañía*) headquarters *pl*; **Santa S~** Holy See.

sediento, a [se'ðjento, a] *adj* thirsty.

sedimentar [seðimen'tar] *vt* to deposit; ~**se** *vr* to settle; **sedimento** *nm* sediment.

sedoso, a [se'ðoso, a] *adj* silky, silken.

seducción [seðuk'θjon] *nf* seduction.

seducir [seðu'θir] *vt* to seduce; (*sobornar*) to bribe; (*cautivar*) to charm, fascinate; (*atraer*) to attract; **seductor, a** *adj* seductive; charming; fascinating; attractive; (*engañoso*) deceptive, misleading ♦ *nm/f* seducer.

segadora-trilladora [seɣa'ðora triʎa'ðora] *nf* combine harvester.

seglar [se'ɣlar] *adj* secular, lay.

segregación [seɣreɣa'θjon] *nf* segregation. ~ **racial** racial segregation.

segregar [seɣre'ɣar] *vt* to segregate, separate.

seguida [se'ɣiða] *nf*: **en** ~ at once, right away.

seguido, a [se'ɣiðo, a] *adj* (*continuo*) continuous, unbroken; (*recto*) straight ♦ *adv* (*directo*) straight (on); (*después*) after; (*AM: a menudo*) often; ~**s** consecutive, successive; **5 días** ~**s** 5 days running, 5 days in a row.

seguimiento [seɣi'mjento] *nm* chase, pursuit; (*continuación*) continuation.

seguir [se'ɣir] *vt* to follow; (*venir después*) to follow on, come after; (*proseguir*) to continue; (*perseguir*) to chase, pursue ♦ *vi* (*gen*) to follow; (*continuar*) to continue, carry *o* go on; ~**se** *vr* to follow; **sigo sin comprender** I still don't understand; **sigue lloviendo** it's still raining.

según [se'ɣun] *prep* according to ♦ *adv*: ¿**irás** ~ ? — **are you going?** — it all depends ♦ *conj* as; ~ **caminamos** while we walk.

segunda [se'ɣunda] *nf* double meaning;

(*tb*: ~ *clase*) second class; (*tb*: ~ *marcha*) second (gear).

segundo, a [se'ɣundo, a] *adj* second ♦ *nm* second; **de segunda mano** second hand; **segunda enseñanza** secondary education.

seguramente [seɣura'mente] *adv* surely; (*con certeza*) for sure, with certainty.

seguridad [seɣuri'ðað] *nf* safety; (*del estado, de casa etc*) security; (*certidumbre*) certainty; (*confianza*) confidence; (*estabilidad*) stability; ~ **social** social security.

seguro, a [se'ɣuro, a] *adj* (*cierto*) sure, certain; (*fiel*) trustworthy; (*libre del peligro*) safe; (*bien defendido, firme*) secure ♦ *adv* for sure, certainly ♦ *nm* (*COM*) insurance; ~ **contra terceros/a todo riesgo** third party/comprehensive insurance; ~**s sociales** social security *sg*.

seis [seis] *num* six.

seísmo [se'ismo] *nm* tremor, earthquake.

selección [selek'θjon] *nf* selection; **seleccionar** *vt* to pick, choose, select.

selectividad [selektiβi'ðað] (*ESP*) *nf* university entrance examination.

selecto, a [se'lekto, a] *adj* select, choice; (*escogido*) selected.

selva ['selβa] *nf* (*bosque*) forest, woods *pl*; (*jungla*) jungle.

sellar [se'ʎar] *vt* (*documento oficial*) to seal; (*pasaporte, visado*) to stamp.

sello ['seʎo] *nm* stamp; (*precinto*) seal.

semáforo [se'maforo] *nm* (*AUTO*) traffic lights *pl*; (*FERRO*) signal.

semana [se'mana] *nf* week; **entre** ~ during the week; **S~ Santa** Holy Week; **semanal** *adj* weekly.

semblante [sem'blante] *nm* face; (*fig*) look.

sembrar [sem'brar] *vt* to sow; (*objetos*) to sprinkle, scatter about; (*noticias etc*) to spread.

semejante [seme'xante] *adj* (*parecido*) similar ♦ *nm* fellow man, fellow creature; ~**s** alike, similar; **nunca hizo cosa** ~ he never did any such thing;

semejanza *nf* similarity, resemblance.
semejar [seme'xar] *vi* to seem like, resemble; **~se** *vr* to look alike, be similar.
semen ['semen] *nm* semen; **~tal** *nm* stud.
semestral [semes'tral] *adj* half-yearly, bi-annual.
semicírculo [semi'θirkulo] *nm* semicircle.
semiconsciente [semikons'θjente] *adj* semiconscious.
semifinal [semifi'nal] *nf* semifinal.
semilla [se'miʎa] *nf* seed.
seminario [semi'narjo] *nm* (REL) seminary; (ESCOL) seminar.
sémola ['semola] *nf* semolina.
sempiterno, a [sempi'terno, a] *adj* everlasting.
Sena ['sena] *nm*: **el ~** the (river) Seine.
senado [se'naðo] *nm* senate; **senador, a** *nm/f* senator.
sencillez [senθi'ʎeθ] *nf* simplicity; (de persona) naturalness; **sencillo, a** *adj* simple; natural, unaffected.
senda ['senda] *nf* path, track.
sendero [sen'dero] *nm* path, track.
sendos, as ['sendos, as] *adj pl*: **les dio ~ golpes** he hit both of them.
senil [se'nil] *adj* senile.
seno ['seno] *nm* (ANAT) bosom, bust; (fig) bosom; **~s** breasts.
sensación [sensa'θjon] *nf* sensation; (sentido) sense; (sentimiento) feeling; **sensacional** *adj* sensational.
sensato, a [sen'sato, a] *adj* sensible.
sensible [sen'sible] *adj* sensitive; (apreciable) perceptible, appreciable; (pérdida) considerable; **~ro, a** *adj* sentimental.
sensitivo, a [sensi'tiβo, a] *adj* sense *cpd*.
sensorial [senso'rjal] *adj* = sensitivo.
sensual [sen'swal] *adj* sensual.
sentada [sen'taða] *nf* sitting; (protesta) sit-in.
sentado, a [sen'taðo, a] *adj* (establecido) settled; (carácter) sensible; **estar ~** to sit, be sitting (down); **dar por ~** to take for granted, assume.
sentar [sen'tar] *vt* to sit, seat; (fig) to

establish ♦ *vi* (vestido) to suit; (alimento): **~ bien/mal a** to agree/disagree with; **~se** *vr* (persona) to sit, sit down; (el tiempo) to settle (down); (los depósitos) to settle.
sentencia [sen'tenθja] *nf* (máxima) maxim, saying; (JUR) sentence; **sentenciar** *vt* to sentence.
sentido, a [sen'tiðo, a] *adj* (pérdida) regrettable; (carácter) sensitive ♦ *nm* sense; (sentimiento) feeling; (significado) sense, meaning; (dirección) direction; **mi más ~ pésame** my deepest sympathy; **~ del humor** sense of humour; **~ único** one-way (street); **tener ~** to make sense.
sentimental [sentimen'tal] *adj* sentimental; **vida ~** love life.
sentimiento [senti'mjento] *nm* (emoción) feeling, emotion; (sentido) sense; (pesar) regret, sorrow.
sentir [sen'tir] *vt* to feel; (percibir) to perceive, sense; (lamentar) to regret, be sorry for ♦ *vi* (tener la sensación) to feel; (lamentarse) to feel sorry ♦ *nm* opinion, judgement; **~se bien/mal** to feel well/ill; **lo siento** I'm sorry.
seña ['seɲa] *nf* sign; (MIL) password; **~s** *nfpl* (dirección) address *sg*; **~s personales** personal description *sg*.
señal [se'ɲal] *nf* sign; (síntoma) symptom; (FERRO, TELEC) signal; (marca) mark; (COM) deposit; **en ~ de** as a token of, as a sign of; **~ar** *vt* to mark; (indicar) to point out, indicate; (fijar) to fix, settle.
señor [se'ɲor] *nm* (hombre) man; (caballero) gentleman; (dueño) owner, master; (trato: antes de nombre propio) Mr; (: hablando directamente) sir; **muy ~ mío** Dear Sir; **el ~ alcalde/presidente** the mayor/president.
señora [se'ɲora] *nf* (dama) lady; (trato: antes de nombre propio) Mrs; (: hablando directamente) madam; (esposa) wife; **Nuestra S~** Our Lady.
señorita [seɲo'rita] *nf* (con nombre y/o apellido) Miss; (mujer joven) young lady.
señorito [seɲo'rito] *nm* young gentle-

man; (*pey*) rich kid.
señuelo [se'ɲwelo] *nm* decoy.
sepa *etc vb ver* **saber.**
separación [separa'θjon] *nf* separation; (*división*) division; (*distancia*) gap.
separar [sepa'rar] *vt* to separate; (*dividir*) to divide; ~**se** *vr* (*parte*) to come away; (*partes*) to come apart; (*persona*) to leave, go away; (*matrimonio*) to separate; **separatismo** *nm* separatism.
sepia ['sepja] *nf* cuttlefish.
septiembre [sep'tjembre] *nm* September.
séptimo, a ['septimo, a] *adj, nm* seventh.
sepultar [sepul'tar] *vt* to bury; **sepultura** *nf* (*acto*) burial; (*tumba*) grave, tomb; **sepulturero, a** *nm/f* gravedigger.
sequedad [seke'ðað] *nf* dryness; (*fig*) brusqueness, curtness.
sequía [se'kia] *nf* drought.
séquito ['sekito] *nm* (*de rey etc*) retinue; (*POL*) followers *pl*.

PALABRA CLAVE
---

ser [ser] *vi* **1** (*descripción*) to be; **es médica/muy alta** she's a doctor/very tall; **la familia es de Cuzco** his (*o* her *etc*) family is from Cuzco; **soy Ana** (*TELEC*) Ana speaking *o* here
2 (*propiedad*): **es de Joaquín** it's Joaquín's, it belongs to Joaquín
3 (*horas, fechas, números*): **es la una** it's one o'clock; **son las seis y media** it's half-past six; **es el 1 de junio** it's the first of June; **somos/son seis** there are six of us/them
4 (*en oraciones pasivas*): **ha sido descubierto ya** it's already been discovered
5 **es de esperar que ...** it is to be hoped *o* I *etc* hope that ...
6 (*locuciones con sub*): **o sea** that is to say; **sea él sea su hermana** either him or his sister
7 **a no ~ por él ...** but for him ...
8 **a no ~ que: a no ~ que tenga uno ya** unless he's got one already
♦ *nm* being; **~ humano** human being.

serenarse [sere'narse] *vr* to calm down.
sereno, a [se'reno, a] *adj* (*persona*) calm, unruffled; (*el tiempo*) fine, settled; (*ambiente*) calm, peaceful ♦ *nm* night watchman.
serial [ser'jal] *nm* serial.
serie ['serje] *nf* series; (*cadena*) sequence, succession; **fuera de ~** out of order; (*fig*) special, out of the ordinary; **fabricación en ~** mass production.
seriedad [serje'ðað] *nf* seriousness; (*formalidad*) reliability; (*de crisis*) gravity, seriousness; **serio, a** *adj* serious; reliable, dependable; grave, serious; **en serio** *adv* seriously.
sermón [ser'mon] *nm* (*REL*) sermon.
serpentear [serpente'ar] *vi* to wriggle; (*camino, río*) to wind, snake.
serpentina [serpen'tina] *nf* streamer.
serpiente [ser'pjente] *nf* snake; ~ **boa** boa constrictor; ~ **de cascabel** rattlesnake.
serranía [serra'nia] *nf* mountainous area.
serrano, a [se'rrano, a] *adj* highland *cpd*, hill ♦ *nm/f* highlander.
serrar [se'rrar] *vt* = **aserrar.**
serrín [se'rrin] *nm* = **aserrín.**
serrucho [se'rrutʃo] *nm* saw.
servicio [ser'βiθjo] *nm* service; ~**s** *nmpl* toilet(s); ~ **incluido** service charge included; ~ **militar** military service.
servidor, a [serβi'ðor, a] *nm/f* servant.
servidumbre [serβi'ðumbre] *nf* (*sujeción*) servitude; (*criados*) servants *pl*, staff.
servil [ser'βil] *adj* servile.
servilleta [serβi'ʎeta] *nf* serviette, napkin.
servir [ser'βir] *vt* to serve ♦ *vi* to serve; (*tener utilidad*) to be of use, be useful; ~**se** *vr* to serve *o* help o.s.; ~**se de algo** to make use of sth, use sth; **sírvase pasar** please come in.
sesenta [se'senta] *num* sixty.
sesgo ['sesɣo] *nm* slant; (*fig*) slant, twist.
sesión [se'sjon] *nf* (*POL*) session, sitting; (*CINE*) showing.
seso ['seso] *nm* brain; **sesudo, a** *adj*

sensible, wise.

seta ['seta] *nf* mushroom; ~ **venenosa** toadstool.

setecientos, as [sete'θjentos, as] *adj, num* seven hundred.

setenta [se'tenta] *num* seventy.

seudo... [seuðo] *prefijo* pseudo....

seudónimo [seu'ðonimo] *nm* pseudonym.

severidad [seβeri'ðað] *nf* severity; **severo, a** *adj* severe.

Sevilla [se'βiʎa] *n* Seville; **sevillano, a** *adj* of o from Seville ♦ *nm/f* native o inhabitant of Seville.

sexo ['sekso] *nm* sex.

sexto, a ['seksto, a] *adj, nm* sixth.

sexual [sek'swal] *adj* sexual; **vida** ~ sex life.

si [si] *conj* if; **me pregunto** ~ ... I wonder if o whether ....

sí [si] *adv* yes ♦ *nm* consent ♦ *pron (uso impersonal)* oneself; *(sg: m)* himself; *(: f)* herself; *(: de cosa)* itself; *(de usted)* yourself; *(pl)* themselves; *(de ustedes)* yourselves; *(recíproco)* each other; **él no quiere pero yo** ~ he doesn't want to but I do; **ella** ~ **vendrá** she will certainly come, she is sure to come; **claro que** ~ of course; **creo que** ~ I think so.

siamés, esa [sja'mes, esa] *adj, nm/f* Siamese.

SIDA ['siða] *nm abr* (= *Síndrome de Inmuno-deficiencia Adquirida*) AIDS.

siderúrgica [siðe'rurxika] *nf*: **la** ~ the iron and steel industry.

siderúrgico, a [siðe'rurxico, a] *adj* iron and steel *cpd*.

sidra ['siðra] *nf* cider.

siembra ['sjembra] *nf* sowing.

siempre ['sjempre] *adv* always; *(todo el tiempo)* all the time; ~ **que** *(cada vez)* whenever; *(dado que)* provided that; **como** ~ as usual; **para** ~ for ever.

sien [sjen] *nf* temple.

siento *etc vb ver* **sentar**; **sentir**.

sierra ['sjerra] *nf* (*TEC*) saw; *(cadena de montañas)* mountain range.

siervo, a ['sjerβo, a] *nm/f* slave.

siesta ['sjesta] *nf* siesta, nap; **echar la** ~

to have an afternoon nap o a siesta.

siete ['sjete] *num* seven.

sífilis ['sifilis] *nf* syphilis.

sifón [si'fon] *nm* syphon; **whisky con** ~ whisky and soda.

sigla ['siɣla] *nf* abbreviation; acronym.

siglo ['siɣlo] *nm* century; *(fig)* age.

significación [siɣnifika'θjon] *nf* significance.

significado [siɣnifi'kaðo] *nm* significance; *(de palabra etc)* meaning.

significar [siɣnifi'kar] *vt* to mean, signify; *(notificar)* to make known, express; **significativo, a** *adj* significant.

signo ['siɣno] *nm* sign; ~ **de admiración** o **exclamación** exclamation mark; ~ **de interrogación** question mark.

sigo *etc vb ver* **seguir**.

siguiente [si'ɣjente] *adj* next, following.

siguió *etc vb ver* **seguir**.

sílaba ['silaβa] *nf* syllable.

silbar [sil'βar] *vt, vi* to whistle; **silbato** *nm* whistle; **silbido** *nm* whistle, whistling.

silenciador [silenθja'ðor] *nm* silencer.

silenciar [silen'θjar] *vt* *(persona)* to silence; *(escándalo)* to hush up; **silencio** *nm* silence, quiet; **silencioso, a** *adj* silent, quiet.

silicio [si'liθjo] *nm* silicon.

silueta [si'lweta] *nf* silhouette; *(de edificio)* outline; *(figura)* figure.

silvestre [sil'βestre] *adj* (*BOT*) wild; *(fig)* rustic, rural.

silla ['siʎa] *nf* *(asiento)* chair; *(tb:* ~ **de montar)** saddle; ~ **de ruedas** wheelchair.

sillón [si'ʎon] *nm* armchair, easy chair.

simbólico, a [sim'boliko, a] *adj* symbolic(al).

simbolizar [simboli'θar] *vt* to symbolize.

símbolo ['simbolo] *nm* symbol.

simetría [sime'tria] *nf* symmetry.

simiente [si'mjente] *nf* seed.

similar [simi'lar] *adj* similar.

simio ['simjo] *nm* ape.

simpatía [simpa'tia] *nf* liking; *(afecto)* affection; *(amabilidad)* kindness; *(solidaridad)* mutual support, solidarity; **simpático, a** *adj* nice, pleasant; kind.

simpatizante [simpati'θante] *nm/f* sympathizer.

simpatizar [simpati'θar] *vi*: ~ **con** to get on well with.

simple ['simple] *adj* simple; (*elemental*) simple, easy; (*mero*) mere; (*puro*) pure, sheer ♦ *nm/f* simpleton; ~**za** *nf* simpleness; (*necedad*) silly thing; **simplicidad** *nf* simplicity; **simplificar** *vt* to simplify.

simular [simu'lar] *vt* to simulate.

simultáneo, a [simul'taneo, a] *adj* simultaneous.

sin [sin] *prep* without; **la ropa está ~ lavar** the clothes are unwashed; ~ **que** without; ~ **embargo** however, still.

sinagoga [sina'ɣoɣa] *nf* synagogue.

sinceridad [sinθeri'ðað] *nf* sincerity; **sincero, a** *adj* sincere.

sincronizar [sinkroni'θar] *vt* to synchronize.

sindical [sindi'kal] *adj* union *cpd*, trade-union *cpd*; ~**ista** *adj, nm/f* trade-unionist.

sindicato [sindi'kato] *nm* (*de trabajadores*) trade(s) union; (*de negociantes*) syndicate.

sinfín [sin'fin] *nm*: **un ~ de** a great many, no end of.

sinfonía [sinfo'nia] *nf* symphony.

singular [singu'lar] *adj* singular; (*fig*) outstanding, exceptional; (*pey*) peculiar, odd; ~**idad** *nf* singularity, peculiarity; ~**izar** *vt* to single out; ~**izarse** *vr* to distinguish o.s., stand out.

siniestro, a [si'njestro, a] *adj* left; (*fig*) sinister ♦ *nm* (*accidente*) accident.

sinnúmero [sin'numero] *nm* = **sinfín**.

sino ['sino] *nm* fate, destiny ♦ *conj* (*pero*) but; (*salvo*) except, save.

sinónimo, a [si'nonimo, a] *adj* synonymous ♦ *nm* synonym.

síntesis ['sintesis] *nf* synthesis; **sintético, a** *adj* synthetic.

sintetizar [sinteti'θar] *vt* to synthesize.

sintió *vb ver* **sentir**.

síntoma ['sintoma] *nm* symptom.

sinvergüenza [simber'ɣwenθa] *nm/f* rogue, scoundrel; ¡**es un ~**! he's got a

nerve!

sionismo [sjo'nismo] *nm* Zionism.

siquiera [si'kjera] *conj* even if, even though ♦ *adv* at least; **ni ~** not even.

sirena [si'rena] *nf* siren.

Siria ['sirja] *nf* Syria; **sirio, a** *adj, nm/f* Syrian.

sirviente, a [sir'βjente, a] *nm/f* servant.

sirvo *etc vb ver* **servir**.

sisear [sise'ar] *vt, vi* to hiss.

sismógrafo [sis'moɣrafo] *nm* seismograph.

sistema [sis'tema] *nm* system; (*método*) method; **sistemático, a** *adj* systematic.

sitiar [si'tjar] *vt* to besiege, lay siege to.

sitio ['sitjo] *nm* (*lugar*) place; (*espacio*) room, space; (*MIL*) siege.

situación [sitwa'θjon] *nf* situation, position; (*estatus*) position, standing.

situado, a [situ'aðo] *adj* situated, placed.

situar [si'twar] *vt* to place, put; (*edificio*) to locate, situate.

slip [slip] *nm* pants *pl*, briefs *pl*.

smoking ['smokin, es'mokin] (*pl* ~**s**) *nm* dinner jacket (*BRIT*), tuxedo (*US*).

snob [es'nob] = **esnob**.

SO *abr* (= *suroeste*) SW.

so [so] *prep* under.

sobaco [so'βako] *nm* armpit.

soberanía [soβera'nia] *nf* sovereignty; **soberano, a** *adj* sovereign; (*fig*) supreme ♦ *nm/f* sovereign.

soberbia [so'βerβja] *nf* pride; haughtiness, arrogance; magnificence.

soberbio, a [so'βerβjo, a] *adj* (*orgulloso*) proud; (*altivo*) haughty, arrogant; (*fig*) magnificent, superb.

sobornar [soβor'nar] *vt* to bribe; **soborno** *nm* bribe.

sobra ['soβra] *nf* excess, surplus; ~**s** *nfpl* left-overs, scraps; **de ~** surplus, extra; **tengo de ~** I've more than enough; ~**do, a** *adj* (*más que suficiente*) more than enough; (*superfluo*) excessive ♦ *adv* too, exceedingly; **sobrante** *adj* remaining, extra ♦ *nm* surplus, remainder.

sobrar [so'βrar] *vt* to exceed, surpass ♦ *vi* (*tener de más*) to be more than enough; (*quedar*) to remain, be left (over).

sobrasada [soβra'saða] *nf* pork sausage spread.

sobre ['soβre] *prep* (*gen*) on; (*encima*) on (top of); (*por encima de, arriba de*) over, above; (*más que*) more than; (*además*) in addition to, besides; (*alrededor de*) about ♦ *nm* envelope; ~ **todo** above all.

sobrecama [soβre'kama] *nf* bedspread.

sobrecargar [soβrekar'ɣar] *vt* (*camión*) to overload; (*COM*) to surcharge.

sobredosis [soβre'ðosis] *nf inv* overdose.

sobreentender [soβre(e)nten'der] *vt* (*adivinar*) to deduce, infer; ~**se** *vr*: **se sobreentiende que** ... it is implied that ....

sobrehumano, a [soβreu'mano, a] *adj* superhuman.

sobrellevar [soβreʎe'βar] *vt* (*fig*) to bear, endure.

sobrenatural [soβrenatu'ral] *adj* supernatural.

sobrepasar [soβrepa'sar] *vt* to exceed, surpass.

sobreponer [soβrepo'ner] *vt* (*poner encima*) to put on top; (*añadir*) to add; ~**se** *vr*: ~**se a** to overcome.

sobresaliente [soβresa'ljente] *adj* projecting; (*fig*) outstanding, excellent.

sobresalir [soβresa'lir] *vi* to project, jut out; (*fig*) to stand out, excel.

sobresaltar [soβresal'tar] *vt* (*asustar*) to scare, frighten; (*sobrecoger*) to startle; **sobresalto** *nm* (*movimiento*) start; (*susto*) scare; (*turbación*) sudden shock.

sobretodo [soβre'toðo] *nm* overcoat.

sobrevenir [soβreβe'nir] *vi* (*ocurrir*) to happen (unexpectedly); (*resultar*) to follow, ensue.

sobreviviente [soβreβi'βjente] *adj* surviving ♦ *nm/f* survivor.

sobrevivir [soβreβi'βir] *vi* to survive.

sobrevolar [soβreβo'lar] *vt* to fly over.

sobriedad [soβrje'ðað] *nf* sobriety, soberness; (*moderación*) moderation, restraint.

sobrino, a [so'βrino, a] *nm/f* nephew/niece.

sobrio, a ['soβrjo, a] *adj* (*moderado*) moderate, restrained.

socarrón, ona [soka'rron, ona] *adj* (*sarcástico*) sarcastic, ironic(al).

socavón [soka'βon] *nm* (*hoyo*) hole.

sociable [so'θjaβle] *adj* (*persona*) sociable, friendly; (*animal*) social.

social [so'θjal] *adj* social; (*COM*) company *cpd*.

socialdemócrata [soθjalde'mokrata] *nm/f* social democrat.

socialista [soθja'lista] *adj, nm/f* socialist.

socializar [soθjali'θar] *vt* to socialize.

sociedad [soθje'ðað] *nf* society; (*COM*) company; ~ **anónima** limited company; ~ **de consumo** consumer society.

socio, a ['soθjo, a] *nm/f* (*miembro*) member; (*COM*) partner.

sociología [soθjolo'xia] *nf* sociology; **sociólogo, a** *nm/f* sociologist.

socorrer [soko'rrer] *vt* to help; **socorrista** *nm/f* first aider; (*en piscina, playa*) lifeguard; **socorro** *nm* (*ayuda*) help, aid; (*MIL*) relief; ¡**socorro!** help!

soda ['soða] *nf* (*sosa*) soda; (*bebida*) soda (water).

sofá [so'fa] (*pl* ~**s**) *nm* sofa, settee; ~-**cama** *nm* studio couch; sofa bed.

sofisticación [sofistika'θjon] *nf* sophistication.

sofocar [sofo'kar] *vt* to suffocate; (*apagar*) to smother, put out; ~**se** *vr* to suffocate; (*fig*) to blush, feel embarrassed; **sofoco** *nm* suffocation; embarrassment.

soga ['soɣa] *nf* rope.

sois *vb ver* **ser**.

soja ['soxa] *nf* soya.

sojuzgar [soxuθ'ɣar] *vt* to subdue, rule despotically.

sol [sol] *nm* sun; (*luz*) sunshine, sunlight; **hace** ~ it is sunny.

solamente [sola'mente] *adv* only, just.

solapa [so'lapa] *nf* (*de chaqueta*) lapel; (*de libro*) jacket.

solar [so'lar] *adj* solar, sun *cpd*.

solaz [so'laθ] *nm* recreation, relaxation; ~**ar** *vt* (*divertir*) to amuse.

soldada [sol'daða] *nf* pay.

soldado [sol'daðo] *nm* soldier; ~ **raso** private.

soldador [solda'ðor] *nm* soldering iron; (*persona*) welder.

soldar [sol'dar] *vt* to solder, weld; (*unir*) to join, unite.

soleado, a [sole'aðo, a] *adj* sunny.

soledad [sole'ðað] *nf* solitude; (*estado infeliz*) loneliness.

solemne [so'lemne] *adj* solemn; **solemnidad** *nf* solemnity.

soler [so'ler] *vi* to be in the habit of, be accustomed to; **suele salir a las ocho** she usually goes out at 8 o'clock.

solfeo [sol'feo] *nm* solfa.

solicitar [soliθi'tar] *vt* (*permiso*) to ask for, seek; (*puesto*) to apply for; (*votos*) to canvass for; (*atención*) to attract; (*persona*) to pursue, chase after.

solícito, a [so'liθito, a] *adj* (*diligente*) diligent; (*cuidadoso*) careful; **solicitud** *nf* (*calidad*) great care; (*petición*) request; (*a un puesto*) application.

solidaridad [soliðari'ðað] *nf* solidarity; **solidario, a** *adj* (*participación*) joint, common; (*compromiso*) mutually binding.

solidez [soli'ðeθ] *nf* solidity; **sólido, a** *adj* solid.

soliloquio [soli'lokjo] *nm* soliloquy.

solista [so'lista] *nm/f* soloist.

solitario, a [soli'tarjo, a] *adj* (*persona*) lonely, solitary; (*lugar*) lonely, desolate ♦ *nm/f* (*reclusa*) recluse; (*en la sociedad*) loner ♦ *nm* solitaire.

solo, a ['solo, a] *adj* (*único*) single, sole; (*sin compañía*) alone; (*solitario*) lonely; **hay una sola dificultad** there is just one difficulty; **a solas** alone, by oneself.

sólo ['solo] *adv* only, just.

solomillo [solo'miʎo] *nm* sirloin.

soltar [sol'tar] *vt* (*dejar ir*) to let go of; (*desprender*) to unfasten, loosen; (*librar*) to release, set free; (*risa etc*) to let out.

soltero, a [sol'tero, a] *adj* single, unmarried ♦ *nm/f* bachelor/single woman; **solterón, ona** *nm/f* old bachelor/spinster.

soltura [sol'tura] *nf* looseness, slackness; (*de los miembros*) agility, ease of movement; (*en el hablar*) fluency, ease.

soluble [so'luβle] *adj* (*QUÍMICA*) soluble; (*problema*) solvable; ~ **en agua** soluble in water.

solución [solu'θjon] *nf* solution; **solucionar** *vt* (*problema*) to solve; (*asunto*) to settle, resolve.

solventar [solβen'tar] *vt* (*pagar*) to settle, pay; (*resolver*) to resolve.

sollozar [soʎo'θar] *vi* to sob; **sollozo** *nm* sob.

sombra ['sombra] *nf* shadow; (*como protección*) shade; ~**s** *nfpl* (*oscuridad*) darkness *sg*, shadows; **tener buena/mala** ~ to be lucky/unlucky.

sombrero [som'brero] *nm* hat.

sombrilla [som'briʎa] *nf* parasol, sunshade.

sombrío, a [som'brio, a] *adj* (*oscuro*) dark; (*fig*) sombre, sad; (*persona*) gloomy.

somero, a [so'mero, a] *adj* superficial.

someter [some'ter] *vt* (*país*) to conquer; (*persona*) to subject to one's will; (*informe*) to present, submit; ~**se** *vr* to give in, yield, submit; ~ **a** to subject to.

somnífero [som'nifero] *nm* sleeping pill.

somos *vb ver* **ser.**

son [son] *vb ver* **ser** ♦ *nm* sound; **en** ~ **de broma** as a joke.

sonajero [sona'xero] *nm* (baby's) rattle.

sonambulismo [sonambu'lismo] *nm* sleepwalking; **sonámbulo, a** *nm/f* sleepwalker.

sonar [so'nar] *vt* to ring ♦ *vi* to sound; (*hacer ruido*) to make a noise; (*pronunciarse*) to be sounded, be pronounced; (*ser conocido*) to sound familiar; (*campana*) to ring; (*reloj*) to strike, chime; ~**se** *vr*: ~**se (las narices)** to blow one's nose; **me suena ese nombre** that name rings a bell.

sonda ['sonda] *nf* (*NAUT*) sounding; (*TEC*) bore, drill; (*MED*) probe.

sondear [sonde'ar] *vt* to sound; to bore (into), drill; to probe, sound; (*fig*) to sound out; **sondeo** *nm* sounding; boring, drilling; (*fig*) poll, enquiry.

sónico, a ['soniko, a] *adj* sonic, sound *cpd*.

sonido [so'niðo] *nm* sound.

sonoro, a [so'noro, a] *adj* sonorous; *(resonante)* loud, resonant.

sonreír [sonre'ir] *vi* to smile; **~se** *vr* to smile; **sonriente** *adj* smiling; **sonrisa** *nf* smile.

sonrojarse [sonro'xarse] *vr* to blush, go red; **sonrojo** *nm* blush.

soñador, a [soɲa'ðor, a] *nm/f* dreamer.

soñar [so'ɲar] *vt, vi* to dream; **~ con** to dream about *o* of.

soñoliento, a [soɲo'ljento, a] *adj* sleepy, drowsy.

sopa ['sopa] *nf* soup; **sopera** *nf* soup tureen.

soplar [so'plar] *vt (polvo)* to blow away, blow off; *(inflar)* to blow up; *(vela)* to blow out ♦ *vi* to blow; **soplo** *nm* blow, puff; *(de viento)* puff, gust.

soporífero [sopo'rifero] *nm* sleeping pill.

soportable [sopor'taßle] *adj* bearable.

soportar [sopor'tar] *vt* to bear, carry; *(fig)* to bear, put up with; **soporte** *nm* support; *(fig)* pillar, support.

soprano [so'prano] *nf* soprano.

sorber [sor'ßer] *vt (chupar)* to sip; *(inhalar)* to inhale; *(tragar)* to swallow (up); *(absorber)* to soak up, absorb.

sorbete [sor'ßete] *nm* iced fruit drink.

sorbo ['sorßo] *nm (trago: grande)* gulp, swallow; *(: pequeño)* sip.

sordera [sor'ðera] *nf* deafness.

sórdido, a ['sorðiðo, a] *adj* dirty, squalid.

sordo, a ['sorðo, a] *adj (persona)* deaf ♦ *nm/f* deaf person; **~mudo, a** *adj* deaf and dumb.

soroche [so'rotʃe] *(AM) nm* mountain sickness.

sorprendente [sorpren'dente] *adj* surprising.

sorprender [sorpren'der] *vt* to surprise; **sorpresa** *nf* surprise.

sortear [sorte'ar] *vt* to draw lots for; *(rifar)* to raffle; *(dificultad)* to avoid; **sorteo** *nm (en lotería)* draw; *(rifa)* raffle.

sortija [sor'tixa] *nf* ring; *(rizo)* ringlet, curl.

sosegado, a [sose'xaðo, a] *adj* quiet, calm.

sosegar [sose'xar] *vt* to quieten, calm; *(el ánimo)* to reassure ♦ *vi* to rest; **sosiego** *nm* quiet(ness), calm(ness).

soslayo [sos'lajo]: **de ~** *adv* obliquely, sideways.

soso, a ['soso, a] *adj (CULIN)* tasteless; *(fig)* dull, uninteresting.

sospecha [sos'petʃa] *nf* suspicion; **sospechar** *vt* to suspect; **sospechoso, a** *adj* suspicious; *(testimonio, opinión)* suspect ♦ *nm/f* suspect.

sostén [sos'ten] *nm (apoyo)* support; *(sujetador)* bra; *(alimentación)* sustenance, food.

sostener [soste'ner] *vt* to support; *(mantener)* to keep up, maintain; *(alimentar)* to sustain, keep going; **~se** *vr* to support o.s.; *(seguir)* to continue, remain; **sostenido, a** *adj* continuous, sustained; *(prolongado)* prolonged.

sótano ['sotano] *nm* basement.

soviético, a [so'ßjetiko, a] *adj* Soviet; **los ~s** the Soviets.

soy *vb ver* ser.

Sr. *abr* (= *Señor*) Mr.

Sra. *abr* (= *Señora*) Mrs.

S.R.C. *abr* (= *se ruega contestación*) R.S.V.P.

Sres. *abr* (= *Señores*) Messrs.

Srta. *abr* (= *Señorita*) Miss.

Sta. *abr* (= *Santa*) St.

status ['status, e'status] *nm inv* status.

Sto. *abr* (= *Santo*) St.

su [su] *pron (de él)* his; *(de ella)* her; *(de una cosa)* its; *(de ellos, ellas)* their; *(de usted, ustedes)* your.

suave ['swaße] *adj* gentle; *(superficie)* smooth; *(trabajo)* easy; *(música, voz)* soft, sweet; **suavidad** *nf* gentleness; smoothness, softness, sweetness; **suavizar** *vt* to soften; *(quitar la aspereza)* to smooth (out).

subalimentado, a [sußalimen'taðo, a] *adj* undernourished.

subasta [su'ßasta] *nf* auction; **subastar** *vt* to auction (off).

subcampeón, ona [sußkampe'on, ona]

nm/f runner-up.

subconsciente [suβkon'sθjente] *adj, nm* subconscious.

subdesarrollado, a [suβðesarro'ʎaðo, a] *adj* underdeveloped.

subdesarrollo [suβðesa'rroʎo] *nm* underdevelopment.

subdirector, a [suβðirek'tor, a] *nm/f* assistant director.

súbdito, a ['suβðito, a] *nm/f* subject.

subdividir [suβðiβi'ðir] *vt* to subdivide.

subestimar [suβesti'mar] *vt* to underestimate, underrate.

subida [su'βiða] *nf* (*de montaña etc*) ascent, climb; (*de precio*) rise, increase; (*pendiente*) slope, hill.

subido, a [su'βiðo, a] *adj* (*color*) bright, strong; (*precio*) high.

subir [su'βir] *vt* (*objeto*) to raise, lift up; (*cuesta, calle*) to go up; (*colina, montaña*) to climb; (*precio*) to raise, put up ♦ *vi* to go up, come up; (*a un coche*) to get in; (*a un autobús, tren o avión*) to get on, board; (*precio*) to rise, go up; (*río, marea*) to rise; ~se *vr* to get up, climb.

súbito, a ['suβito, a] *adj* (*repentino*) sudden; (*imprevisto*) unexpected.

subjetivo, a [suβxe'tiβo, a] *adj* subjective.

sublevación [suβleβa'θjon] *nf* revolt, rising.

sublevar [suβle'βar[*vt* to rouse to revolt; ~se *vr* to revolt, rise.

sublime [su'βlime] *adj* sublime.

submarino, a [suβma'rino, a] *adj* underwater ♦ *nm* submarine.

subnormal [suβnor'mal] *adj* subnormal ♦ *nm/f* subnormal person.

subordinado, a [suβorði'naðo, a] *adj, nm/f* subordinate.

subrayar [suβra'jar] *vt* to underline.

subrepticio, a [suβrep'tiθjo, a] *adj* surreptitious.

subsanar [suβsa'nar] *vt* (*reparar*) to make good; (*perdonar*) to excuse; (*sobreponerse a*) to overcome.

subscribir [suβskri'βir] *vt* = suscribir.

subsidiario, a [suβsi'ðjarjo, a] *adj* subsidiary.

subsidio [suβ'siðjo] *nm* (*ayuda*) aid, financial help; (*subvención*) subsidy, grant; (*de enfermedad, paro etc*) benefit, allowance.

subsistencia [suβsis'tenθja] *nf* subsistence.

subsistir [suβsis'tir] *vi* to subsist; (*vivir*) to live; (*sobrevivir*) to survive, endure.

subterráneo, a [suβte'rraneo, a] *adj* underground, subterranean ♦ *nm* underpass, underground passage.

suburbano, a [suβur'βano, a] *adj* suburban.

suburbio [su'βurβjo] *nm* (*barrio*) slum quarter; (*afueras*) suburbs *pl*.

subvencionar [suββenθjo'nar] *vt* to subsidize.

subversión [suββer'sjon] *nf* subversion; **subversivo, a** *adj* subversive.

subyugar [suβju'var] *vt* (*país*) to subjugate, subdue; (*enemigo*) to overpower; (*voluntad*) to dominate.

succión [suk'θjon] *nf* suction.

sucedáneo, a [suθe'ðaneo, a] *adj* substitute ♦ *nm* substitute (food).

suceder [suθe'ðer] *vt, vi* to happen; (*seguir*) to succeed, follow; **lo que sucede es que ...** the fact is that ...; **sucesión** *nf* succession; (*serie*) sequence, series.

sucesivamente [suθesiβa'mente] *adv:* **y así ~** and so on.

sucesivo, a [suθe'siβo, a] *adj* successive, following; **en lo ~** in future, from now on.

suceso [su'θeso] *nm* (*hecho*) event, happening; (*incidente*) incident.

suciedad [suθje'ðað] *nf* (*estado*) dirtiness; (*mugre*) dirt, filth.

sucinto, a [su'θinto, a] *adj* (*conciso*) succinct, concise.

sucio, a ['suθjo, a] *adj* dirty.

Sucre ['sukre] *n* Sucre.

suculento, a [suku'lento, a] *adj* succulent.

sucumbir [sukum'bir] *vi* to succumb.

sucursal [sukur'sal] *nf* branch (office).

Sudáfrica [suð'afrika] *nf* South Africa.

Sudamérica [suða'merika] *nf* South America; **sudamericano, a** *adj, nm/f*

South American.

sudar [su'ðar] *vt*, *vi* to sweat.

sudeste [su'ðeste] *nm* south-east.

sudoeste [suðo'este] *nm* south-west.

sudor [su'ðor] *nm* sweat; ~**oso, a** *adj* sweaty, sweating.

Suecia ['sweθja] *nf* Sweden; **sueco, a** *adj* Swedish ♦ *nm/f* Swede.

suegro, a ['sweɣro, a] *nm/f* father-/mother-in-law.

suela ['swela] *nf* sole.

sueldo ['sweldo] *nm* pay, wage(s) (*pl*).

suele *etc vb ver* **soler.**

suelo ['swelo] *nm* (*tierra*) ground; (*de casa*) floor.

suelto, a ['swelto, a] *adj* loose; (*libre*) free; (*separado*) detached; (*ágil*) quick, agile; (*corriente*) fluent, flowing ♦ *nm* (loose) change, small change.

sueño *etc* ['sweɲo] *vb ver* **soñar** ♦ *nm* sleep; (*somnolencia*) sleepiness, drowsiness; (*lo soñado, fig*) dream; **tener** ~ to be sleepy.

suero ['swero] *nm* (*MED*) serum; (*de leche*) whey.

suerte ['swerte] *nf* (*fortuna*) luck; (*azar*) chance; (*destino*) fate, destiny; (*condición*) lot; (*género*) sort, kind; **tener** ~ to be lucky; **de otra** ~ otherwise, if not; **de** ~ **que** so that, in such a way that.

suéter ['sweter] *nm* sweater.

suficiente [sufi'θjente] *adj* enough, sufficient ♦ *nm* (*ESCOL*) pass.

sufragio [su'fraxjo] *nm* (*voto*) vote; (*derecho de voto*) suffrage.

sufrido, a [su'friðo, a] *adj* (*persona*) tough; (*paciente*) long-suffering, patient.

sufrimiento [sufri'mjento] *nm* (*dolor*) suffering.

sufrir [su'frir] *vt* (*padecer*) to suffer; (*soportar*) to bear, put up with; (*apoyar*) to hold up, support ♦ *vi* to suffer.

sugerencia [suxe'renθja] *nf* suggestion.

sugerir [suxe'rir] *vt* to suggest; (*sutilmente*) to hint.

sugestión [suxes'tjon] *nf* suggestion; (*sutil*) hint; **sugestionar** *vt* to influence.

sugestivo, a [suxes'tiβo, a] *adj* stimulating; (*fascinante*) fascinating.

suicida [sui'θiða] *adj* suicidal ♦ *nm/f* suicidal person; (*muerto*) suicide, person who has committed suicide; **suicidarse** *vr* to commit suicide, kill o.s.; **suicidio** *nm* suicide.

Suiza ['swiθa] *nf* Switzerland; **suizo, a** *adj, nm/f* Swiss.

sujeción [suxe'θjon] *nf* subjection.

sujetador [suxeta'ðor] *nm* fastener, clip; (*sostén*) bra.

sujetar [suxe'tar] *vt* (*fijar*) to fasten; (*detener*) to hold down; (*fig*) to subject, subjugate; ~**se** *vr* to subject o.s.; **sujeto, a** *adj* fastened, secure ♦ *nm* subject; (*individuo*) individual; **sujeto a** subject to.

suma ['suma] *nf* (*cantidad*) total, sum; (*de dinero*) sum; (*acto*) adding (up), addition; **en** ~ in short.

sumamente [suma'mente] *adv* extremely, exceedingly.

sumar [su'mar] *vt* to add (up); (*reunir*) to collect, gather ♦ *vi* to add up.

sumario, a [su'marjo, a] *adj* brief, concise ♦ *nm* summary.

sumergir [sumer'xir] *vt* to submerge; (*hundir*) to sink; (*bañar*) to immerse, dip.

sumidero [sumi'ðero] *nm* drain, sewer; (*TEC*) sump.

suministrar [sumini'strar] *vt* to supply, provide; **suministro** *nm* supply; (*acto*) supplying, providing.

sumir [su'mir] *vt* to sink, submerge; (*fig*) to plunge.

sumisión [sumi'sjon] *nf* (*acto*) submission; (*calidad*) submissiveness, docility; **sumiso, a** *adj* submissive, docile.

sumo, a ['sumo, a] *adj* great, extreme; (*mayor*) highest, supreme.

suntuoso, a [sun'twoso, a] *adj* sumptuous, magnificent.

supe *etc vb ver* **saber.**

super... [super] *prefijo* super..., over...; ~**bueno** *adj* great, fantastic.

súper ['super] *nm* (*gasolina*) three-star (petrol).

superar [supe'rar] vt (sobreponerse a) to overcome; (rebasar) to surpass, do better than; (pasar) to go beyond; ~se vr to excel o.s.

superávit [supe'raβit] nm inv surplus.

superficial [superfi'θjal] adj superficial; (medida) surface cpd, of the surface.

superficie [super'fiθje] nf surface; (área) area.

supérfluo, a ¶[su'pcrflwo, a] adj superfluous.

superintendente [superinten'dente] nm/f supervisor, superintendent.

superior [supe'rjor] adj (piso, clase) upper; (temperatura, número, nivel) higher; (mejor: calidad, producto) superior, better ♦ nm/f superior; ~idad nf superiority.

supermercado [supermer'kaðo] nm supermarket.

supersónico, a [super'soniko, a] adj supersonic.

superstición [supersti'θjon] nf superstition; **supersticioso, a** adj superstitious.

supervisor, a [superβi'sor, a] nm/f supervisor.

supervivencia [superβi'βenθja] nf survival.

superviviente [superβi'βjente] adj surviving.

supiera etc vb ver **saber**.

suplantar [suplan'tar] vt (persona) to supplant; (documento etc) to falsify.

suplementario, a [suplemen'tarjo, a] adj supplementary; **suplemento** nm supplement.

suplente [su'plente] adj, nm/f substitute.

supletorio, a [suple'torjo, a] adj supplementary ♦ nm supplement; **mesa supletoria** spare table.

súplica ['suplika] nf request; (JUR) petition.

suplicar [supli'kar] vt (cosa) to beg (for), plead for; (persona) to beg, plead with.

suplicio [su'pliθjo] nm torture.

suplir [su'plir] vt (compensar) to make good, make up for; (reemplazar) to replace, substitute ♦ vi: ~ a to take the place of, substitute for.

supo etc vb ver **saber**.

suponer [supo'ner] vt to suppose ♦ vi to have authority; **suposición** nf supposition.

supremacía [suprema'θia] nf supremacy.

supremo, a [su'premo, a] adj supreme.

supresión [supre'sjon] nf suppression; (de derecho) abolition; (de dificultad) removal; (de palabra etc) deletion; (de restricción) cancellation, lifting.

suprimir [supri'mir] vt to suppress; (derecho, costumbre) to abolish; (dificultad) to remove; (palabra etc) to delete; (restricción) to cancel, lift.

supuesto, a [su'pwesto, a] pp de **suponer** ♦ adj (hipotético) supposed; (falso) false ♦ nm assumption, hypothesis; ~ **que** since; **por** ~ of course.

sur [sur] nm south.

surcar [sur'kar] vt to plough; (superficie) to cut, score; **surco** nm (en metal, disco) groove; (AGR) furrow.

surgir [sur'xir] vi to arise, emerge; (dificultad) to come up, crop up.

surtido, a [sur'tiðo, a] adj mixed, assorted ♦ nm (selección) selection, assortment; (abastecimiento) supply, stock.

surtir [sur'tir] vt to supply, provide ♦ vi to spout, spurt.

susceptible [susθep'tiβle] adj susceptible; (sensible) sensitive; ~ **de** capable of.

suscitar [susθi'tar] vt to cause, provoke; (interés, sospechas) to arouse.

suscribir [suskri'βir] vt (firmar) to sign; (respaldar) to subscribe to, endorse; ~se vr to subscribe; **suscripción** nf subscription.

susodicho, a [suso'ðitʃo, a] adj abovementioned.

suspender [suspen'der] vt (objeto) to hang (up), suspend; (trabajo) to stop, suspend; (ESCOL) to fail; **suspensión** nf suspension; (fig) stoppage, suspension.

suspenso, a [sus'penso, a] adj hanging, suspended; (ESCOL) failed ♦ nm: **quedar** o **estar en** ~ to be pending.

suspicacia [suspi'kaθja] nf suspicion, mistrust; **suspicaz** adj suspicious, distrustful.

suspirar [suspi'rar] *vi* to sigh; **suspiro** *nm* sigh.

sustancia [sus'tanθja] *nf* substance.

sustentar [susten'tar] *vt* (*alimentar*) to sustain, nourish; (*objeto*) to hold up, support; (*idea, teoría*) to maintain, uphold; (*fig*) to sustain, keep going; **sustento** *nm* support; (*alimento*) sustenance, food.

sustituir [sustitu'ir] *vt* to substitute, replace; **sustituto, a** *nm/f* substitute, replacement.

susto ['susto] *nm* fright, scare.

sustraer [sustra'er] *vt* to remove, take away; (*MAT*) to subtract.

susurrar [susu'rrar] *vi* to whisper; **susurro** *nm* whisper.

sutil [su'til] *adj* (*aroma, diferencia*) subtle; (*tenue*) thin; (*inteligencia, persona*) sharp; **~eza** *nf* subtlety; thinness.

suyo, a ['sujo, a] (*con artículo o después del verbo ser*) *adj* (*de él*) his; (*de ella*) hers; (*de ellos, ellas*) theirs; (*de Ud, Uds*) yours; **un amigo ~** a friend of his (*o hers o theirs o yours*).

T

taba ['taβa] *nf* (*ANAT*) anklebone; (*juego*) jacks *sg*.

tabacalera [taβaka'lera] *nf*: **T~** *Spanish state tobacco monopoly*; *ver tb* **tabacalero.**

tabacalero, a [taβaka'lero, a] *nm/f* (*vendedor*) tobacconist.

tabaco [ta'βako] *nm* tobacco; (*fam*) cigarettes *pl*: **tabaquería** *nf* tobacconist's (*BRIT*), cigar store (*US*).

taberna [ta'βerna] *nf* bar, pub (*BRIT*); **tabernero, a** *nm/f* (*encargado*) publican; (*camarero*) barman/maid.

tabique [ta'βike] *nm* partition (wall).

tabla ['taβla] *nf* (*de madera*) plank; (*estante*) shelf; (*de vestido*) pleat; (*ARTE*) panel; **~s** *nfpl*: **estar** *o* **quedar en ~s** to draw; **~do** *nm* (*plataforma*) platform; (*TEATRO*) stage.

tablero [ta'βlero] *nm* (*de madera*) plank, board; (*de ajedrez, damas*) board; (*AUTO*) dashboard; **~ de anuncios** notice (*BRIT*) *o* bulletin (*US*) board.

tableta [ta'βleta] *nf* (*MED*) tablet; (*de chocolate*) bar.

tablilla [ta'βliʎa] *nf* small board; (*MED*) splint.

tablón [ta'βlon] *nm* (*de suelo*) plank; (*de techo*) beam; **~ de anuncios** notice board (*BRIT*), bulletin board (*US*).

tabú [ta'βu] *nm* taboo.

tabular [taβu'lar] *vt* to tabulate.

taburete [taβu'rete] *nm* stool.

tacaño, a [ta'kaɲo, a] *adj* (*avaro*) mean.

tácito, a ['taθito, a] *adj* tacit.

taciturno, a [taθi'turno, a] *adj* (*callado*) silent; (*malhumorado*) sullen.

taco ['tako] *nm* (*BILLAR*) cue; (*libro de billetes*) book; (*AM: de zapato*) heel; (*tarugo*) peg; (*palabrota*) swear word.

tacón [ta'kon] *nm* heel; **de ~ alto** high-heeled; **taconeo** *nm* (heel) stamping.

táctica ['taktika] *nf* tactics *pl*.

táctico, a ['taktiko, a] *adj* tactical.

tacto ['takto] *nm* touch; (*fig*) tact.

tacha ['tatʃa] *nf* flaw; (*TEC*) stud; **tachar** *vt* (*borrar*) to cross out; **tachar de** to accuse of.

tafetán [tafe'tan] *nm* taffeta.

tafilete [tafi'lete] *nm* morocco leather.

tahona [ta'ona] *nf* (*panadería*) bakery.

tahur, a [ta'ur, a] *nm/f* gambler; (*pey*) cheat.

taimado, a [tai'maðo, a] *adj* (*astuto*) sly.

taita ['taita] (*fam*) *nm* dad, daddy.

tajada [ta'xaða] *nf* slice.

tajante [ta'xante] *adj* sharp.

tajar [ta'xar] *vt* to cut; **tajo** *nm* (*corte*) cut; (*GEO*) cleft.

tal [tal] *adj* such; **~ vez** perhaps ♦ *pron* (*persona*) someone, such a one; (*cosa*) something, such a thing; **~ como** such as; **~ para cual** tit for tat; (*dos iguales*) two of a kind ♦ *adv*: **~ como** (*igual*) just as; **~ cual** (*como es*) just as it is; **¿qué ~?** how are things?; **¿qué**

~ **te gusta?** how do you like it? ♦ *conj:* **con ~ de que** provided that.

taladrar [tala'ðrar] *vt* to drill; **taladro** *nm* drill; (*hoyo*) drill hole.

talante [ta'lante] *nm* (*humor*) mood; (*voluntad*) will, willingness.

talar [ta'lar] *vt* to fell, cut down; (*devastar*) to devastate.

talco ['talko] *nm* (*polvos*) talcum powder.

talega [ta'leɣa] *nf* = **talego.**

talego [ta'leɣo] *nm* sack.

talento [ta'lento] *nm* talent; (*capacidad*) ability.

TALGO ['talɣo] (*ESP*) *nm abr* (= *tren articulado ligero Goicoechea-Oriol*) ≈ HST (*BRIT*).

talismán [talis'man] *nm* talisman.

talón [ta'lon] *nm* (*ANAT*) heel; (*COM*) counterfoil; (*cheque*) cheque (*BRIT*), check (*US*).

talonario [talo'narjo] *nm* (*de cheques*) chequebook (*BRIT*), checkbook (*US*); (*de billetes*) book of tickets; (*de recibos*) receipt book.

talla ['taʎa] *nf* (*estatura, fig, MED*) height, stature; (*palo*) measuring rod; (*ARTE*) carving; (*medida*) size.

tallado, a [ta'ʎaðo, a] *adj* carved ♦ *nm* carving.

tallar [ta'ʎar] *vt* (*madera*) to carve; (*metal etc*) to engrave; (*medir*) to measure.

tallarines [taʎa'rines] *nmpl* noodles.

talle ['taʎe] *nm* (*ANAT*) waist; (*fig*) appearance.

taller [ta'ʎer] *nm* (*TEC*) workshop; (*de artista*) studio.

tallo ['taʎo] *nm* (*de planta*) stem; (*de hierba*) blade; (*brote*) shoot.

tamaño, a [ta'maɲo, a] *adj* (*tan grande*) such a big; (*tan pequeño*) such a small ♦ *nm* size; **de ~ natural** full-size.

tamarindo [tama'rindo] *nm* tamarind.

tambalearse [tambale'arse] *vr* (*persona*) to stagger; (*vehículo*) to sway.

también [tam'bjen] *adv* (*igualmente*) also, too, as well; (*además*) besides.

tambor [tam'bor] *nm* drum; (*ANAT*) ear-drum; ~ **del freno** brake drum.

tamiz [ta'miθ] *nm* sieve; ~**ar** *vt* to sieve.

tampoco [tam'poko] *adv* nor, neither; **yo ~ lo compré** I didn't buy it either.

tampón [tam'pon] *nm* tampon.

tan [tan] *adv* so; ~ **es así que ...** so much so that ....

tanda ['tanda] *nf* (*gen*) series; (*turno*) shift.

tangente [tan'xente] *nf* tangent.

Tánger ['tanxer] *n* Tangier(s).

tangible [tan'xißle] *adj* tangible.

tanque ['tanke] *nm* (*cisterna, MIL*) tank; (*AUTO*) tanker.

tantear [tante'ar] *vt* (*calcular*) to reckon (up); (*medir*) to take the measure of; (*probar*) to test, try out; (*tomar la medida: persona*) to take the measurements of; (*situación*) to weigh up; (*persona: opinión*) to sound out ♦ *vi* (*DEPORTE*) to score; **tanteo** *nm* (*cálculo*) (rough) calculation; (*prueba*) test, trial; (*DEPORTE*) scoring.

tanto, a ['tanto, a] *adj* (*cantidad*) so much, as much; ~**s** so many, as many; **20 y** ~**s** 20-odd ♦ *adv* (*cantidad*) so much, as much; (*tiempo*) so long, as long ♦ *conj:* **en** ~ **que** while; **hasta** ~ **(que)** until such time as ♦ *nm* (*suma*) certain amount; (*proporción*) so much; (*punto*) point; (*gol*) goal; **un** ~ **perezoso** somewhat lazy ♦ *pron:* **cada uno paga** ~ each one pays so much; ~ **tú como yo** both you and I; ~ **como eso** it's not as bad as that; ~ **más ... cuanto que** it's all the more ... because; ~ **mejor/peor** so much the better/the worse; ~ **si viene como si va** whether he comes or whether he goes; ~ **es así que** so much so that; **por o por lo** ~ therefore; **me he vuelto ronco de o con** ~ **hablar** I have become hoarse with so much talking; **a** ~**s de agosto** on such and such a day in August.

tapa ['tapa] *nf* (*de caja, olla*) lid; (*de botella*) top; (*de libro*) cover; (*comida*) snack.

tapadera [tapa'ðera] *nf* lid, cover.

tapar [ta'par] *vt* (*cubrir*) to cover; (*en-

volver) to wrap o cover up; (*la vista*) to obstruct; (*persona, falta*) to conceal; (*AM*) to fill; ~**se** *vr* to wrap o.s. up.

taparrabo [tapa'rraβo] *nm* loincloth.

tapete [ta'pete] *nm* table cover.

tapia ['tapja] *nf* (garden) wall; **tapiar** *vt* to wall in.

tapicería [tapiθe'ria] *nf* tapestry; (*para muebles*) upholstery; (*tienda*) upholsterer's (shop).

tapiz [ta'piθ] *nm* (*alfombra*) carpet; (*tela tejida*) tapestry; ~**ar** *vt* (*muebles*) to upholster.

tapón [ta'pon] *nm* (*corcho*) stopper; (*TEC*) plug; ~ **de rosca** screw-top.

taquigrafía [takiɣra'fia] *nf* shorthand; **taquígrafo, a** *nm/f* shorthand writer, stenographer.

taquilla [ta'kiʎa] *nf* (*donde se compra*) booking office; (*suma recogida*) takings *pl*; **taquillero, a** *adj*: **función taquillera** box office success ♦ *nm/f* ticket clerk.

tara ['tara] *nf* (*defecto*) defect; (*COM*) tare.

tarántula [ta'rantula] *nf* tarantula.

tararear [tarare'ar] *vi* to hum.

tardanza [tar'ðanθa] *nf* (*demora*) delay.

tardar [tar'ðar] *vi* (*tomar tiempo*) to take a long time; (*llegar tarde*) to be late; (*demorar*) to delay; **¿tarda mucho el tren?** does the train take (very) long?; **a más ~** at the latest; **no tardes en venir** come soon.

tarde ['tarðe] *adv* late ♦ *nf* (*de día*) afternoon; (*al anochecer*) evening; **de ~ en ~** from time to time; **¡buenas ~s!** good afternoon!; **a o por la ~** in the afternoon; in the evening.

tardío, a [tar'ðio, a] *adj* (*retrasado*) late; (*lento*) slow (to arrive).

tardo, a ['tarðo, a] *adj* (*lento*) slow; (*torpe*) dull.

tarea [ta'rea] *nf* task; (*faena*) chore; (*ESCOL*) homework.

tarifa [ta'rifa] *nf* (*lista de precios*) price list; (*precio*) tariff.

tarima [ta'rima] *nf* (*plataforma*) platform.

tarjeta [tar'xeta] *nf* card; ~ **postal/de crédito/de Navidad** postcard/credit card/Christmas card.

tarro ['tarro] *nm* jar, pot.

tarta ['tarta] *nf* (*pastel*) cake; (*torta*) tart.

tartamudear [tartamuðe'ar] *vi* to stammer; **tartamudo, a** *adj* stammering ♦ *nm/f* stammerer.

tártaro, a ['tartaro, a] *adj*: **salsa tártara** tartare sauce.

tasa ['tasa] *nf* (*precio*) (fixed) price, rate; (*valoración*) valuation; (*medida, norma*) measure, standard; ~ **de cambio/interés** exchange/interest rate; ~**ción** *nf* valuation; ~**dor, a** *nm/f* valuer.

tasar [ta'sar] *vt* (*arreglar el precio*) to fix a price for; (*valorar*) to value, assess.

tasca ['taska] (*fam*) *nf* pub.

tatarabuelo, a [tatara'βwelo, a] *nm/f* great-great-grandfather/mother.

tatuaje [ta'twaxe] *nm* (*dibujo*) tattoo; (*acto*) tattooing.

tatuar [ta'twar] *vt* to tattoo.

taurino, a [tau'rino, a] *adj* bullfighting *cpd*.

Tauro ['tauro] *nm* Taurus.

tauromaquia [tauro'makja] *nf* tauromachy, (art of) bullfighting.

taxi ['taksi] *nm* taxi.

taxista [tak'sista] *nm/f* taxi driver.

taza ['taθa] *nf* cup; (*de retrete*) bowl; ~ **para café** coffee cup; **tazón** *nm* (*taza grande*) mug, large cup; (*de fuente*) basin.

te [te] *pron* (*complemento de objeto*) you; (*complemento indirecto*) (to) you; (*reflexivo*) (to) yourself; **¿~ duele mucho el brazo?** does your arm hurt a lot?; **~ equivocas** you're wrong; **¡cálma~!** calm down!

té [te] *nm* tea.

tea ['tea] *nf* torch.

teatral [tea'tral] *adj* theatre *cpd*; (*fig*) theatrical.

teatro [te'atro] *nm* theatre; (*LITERATURA*) plays *pl*, drama.

tebeo [te'βeo] *nm* comic.

tecla ['tekla] *nf* key; ~**do** *nm* keyboard; **teclear** *vi* (*MUS*) to strum; (*con los*

dedos) to tap ♦ *vt* (*INFORM*) to key in;
tecleo *nm* (*MUS: sonido*) strumming;
(*fig*) drumming.

técnica ['teknika] *nf* technique; (*arte,
oficio*) craft, *ver tb* **técnico**.

técnico, a ['tekniko, a] *adj* technical ♦
nm/f technician; (*experto*) expert.

tecnócrata [tek'nokrata] *nm/f* techno-
crat.

tecnología [teknolo'xia] *nf* technology;
tecnológico, a *adj* technological.

techo ['tetʃo] *nm* (*externo*) roof; (*interno*) ceiling; ~ **corredizo** sunroof.

tedio ['teðjo] *nm* boredom, tedium; ~**so,
a** *adj* boring, tedious.

teja ['texa] *nf* (*azulejo*) tile; (*BOT*) lime
(tree); ~**do** *nm* (tiled) roof.

tejanos [te'xanos] *nmpl* jeans.

tejemaneje [texema'nexe] *nm* (*lío*) fuss;
(*intriga*) intrigue.

tejer [te'xer] *vt* to weave; (*hacer punto*)
to knit; (*fig*) to fabricate; **tejido** *nm*
(*tela*) material, fabric; (*telaraña*) web;
(*ANAT*) tissue.

tel [tel] *abr* (= *teléfono*) tel.

teléf *abr* (= *teléfono*) tel.

tela ['tela] *nf* (*tejido*) material; (*telaraña*) web; (*en líquido*) skin; **telar** *nm*
(*máquina*) loom; **telares** *nmpl* (*fábrica*)
textile mill *sg*.

telaraña [tela'raɲa] *nf* cobweb.

tele ['tele] (*fam*) *nf* telly (*BRIT*), tube
(*US*).

tele... ['tele] *pref* tele...; ~**comunicación**
nf telecommunication; ~**control** *nm* remote control; ~**diario** *nm* television
news; ~**difusión** *nf* (television) broadcast; ~**dirigido, a** *adj* remote-
controlled.

telefax [tele'faks] *nm inv* fax; (*aparato*)
fax (machine).

teleférico [tele'feriko] *nm* (*tren*) cable-
railway; (*de esquí*) ski-lift.

telefonear [telefone'ar] *vi* to telephone.

telefónicamente [tele'fonikamente] *adv*
by (tele)phone.

telefónico, a [tele'foniko, a] *adj* telephone *cpd*.

telefonista [telefo'nista] *nm/f* telephonist.

teléfono [te'lefono] *nm* (tele)phone;
estar hablando al ~ to be on the phone;
llamar a uno por ~ to ring sb (up) *o*
phone sb (up).

telegrafía [teleɣra'fia] *nf* telegraphy.

telégrafo [te'leɣrafo] *nm* telegraph.

telegrama [tele'ɣrama] *nm* telegram.

tele: ~**impresor** *nm* teleprinter
(*BRIT*), teletype (*US*); ~**objetivo** *nm*
telephoto lens; ~**pático, a** *adj* tele-
pathic; ~**scópico, a** *adj* telescopic;
~**scopio** *nm* telescope; ~**silla** *nm* chair-
lift; ~**spectador, a** *nm/f* viewer; ~**squí**
nm ski-lift; ~**tipo** *nm* teletype.
teleteleimpresor

televidente [teleβi'ðente] *nm/f* viewer.

televisar [teleβi'sar] *vt* to televise.

televisión [teleβi'sjon] *nf* television; ~
en colores colour television.

televisor [teleβi'sor] *nm* television set.

télex ['teleks] *nm inv* telex.

telón [te'lon] *nm* curtain; ~ **de acero**
(*POL*) iron curtain; ~ **de fondo** back-
cloth, background.

tema ['tema] *nm* (*asunto*) subject, topic;
(*MUS*) theme ♦ *nf* (*obsesión*) obsession;
temático, a *adj* thematic.

temblar [tem'blar] *vi* to shake, tremble;
(*de frío*) to shiver; **tembleque** *nm*
shaking; **temblón, ona** *adj* shaking;
temblor *nm* trembling; (*de tierra*)
earthquake; **tembloroso, a** *adj*
trembling.

temer [te'mer] *vt* to fear ♦ *vi* to be
afraid; **temo que llegue tarde** I am
afraid he may be late.

temerario, a [teme'rarjo, a] *adj*
(*descuidado*) reckless; (*irreflexivo*)
hasty; **temeridad** *nf* (*imprudencia*)
rashness; (*audacia*) boldness.

temeroso, a [teme'roso, a] *adj*
(*miedoso*) fearful; (*que inspira temor*)
frightful.

temible [te'miβle] *adj* fearsome.

temor [te'mor] *nm* (*miedo*) fear; (*duda*)
suspicion.

témpano ['tempano] *nm:* ~ **de hielo**
ice-floe.

temperamento [tempera'mento] *nm*
temperament.

temperatura [tempera'tura] *nf* temperature.

tempestad [tempes'tað] *nf* storm; **tempestuoso, a** *adj* stormy.

templado, a [tem'plaðo, a] *adj* (*moderado*) moderate; (: *en el comer*) frugal; (: *en el beber*) abstemious; (*agua*) lukewarm; (*clima*) mild; (*MUS*) well-tuned; **templanza** *nf* moderation; abstemiousness; mildness.

templar [tem'plar] *vt* (*moderar*) to moderate; (*furia*) to restrain; (*calor*) to reduce; (*afinar*) to tune (up); (*acero*) to temper; (*tuerca*) to tighten up; **temple** *nm* (*ajuste*) tempering; (*afinación*) tuning; (*clima*) temperature; (*pintura*) tempera.

templete [tem'plete] *nm* bandstand.

templo ['templo] *nm* (*iglesia*) church; (*pagano etc*) temple.

temporada [tempo'raða] *nf* time, period; (*estación*) season.

temporal [tempo'ral] *adj* (*no permanente*) temporary; (*REL*) temporal ♦ *nm* storm.

tempranero, a [tempra'nero, a] *adj* (*BOT*) early; (*persona*) early-rising.

temprano, a [tem'prano, a] *adj* early; (*demasiado pronto*) too soon, too early.

ten *vb ver* **tener**.

tenaces [te'naθes] *adj pl ver* **tenaz**.

tenacidad [tenaθi'ðað] *nf* tenacity; (*dureza*) toughness; (*terquedad*) stubbornness.

tenacillas [tena'θiʎas] *nfpl* tongs; (*para el pelo*) curling tongs (*BRIT*) o iron *sg* (*US*); (*MED*) forceps.

tenaz [te'naθ] *adj* (*material*) tough; (*persona*) tenacious; (*creencia, resistencia*) stubborn.

tenaza(s) [te'naθa(s)] *nf(pl)* (*MED*) forceps; (*TEC*) pliers; (*ZOOL*) pincers.

tendedero [tende'ðero] *nm* (*para ropa*) drying place; (*cuerda*) clothes line.

tendencia [ten'denθja] *nf* tendency; (*proceso*) trend; **tener** ~ **a** to tend to, have a tendency to; **tendencioso, a** *adj* tendentious.

tender [ten'der] *vt* (*extender*) to spread out; (*colgar*) to hang out; (*vía férrea, cable*) to lay; (*estirar*) to stretch ♦ *vi*: ~ **a** to tend to, have a tendency towards; ~**se** *vr* to lie down; ~ **la cama/la mesa** (*AM*) to make the bed/lay (*BRIT*) o set (*US*) the table.

tenderete [tende'rete] *nm* (*puesto*) stall; (*exposición*) display of goods.

tendero, a [ten'dero, a] *nm/f* shopkeeper.

tendido, a [ten'diðo, a] *adj* (*acostado*) lying down, flat; (*colgado*) hanging ♦ *nm* (*TAUR*) front rows of seats; **a galope** ~ flat out.

tendón [ten'don] *nm* tendon.

tendré *etc vb ver* **tener**.

tenebroso, a [tene'βroso, a] *adj* (*oscuro*) dark; (*fig*) gloomy; (*complot*) sinister.

tenedor [tene'ðor] *nm* (*CULIN*) fork; (*poseedor*) holder; ~ **de libros** bookkeeper.

teneduría [teneðu'ria] *nf* keeping; ~ **de libros** book-keeping.

tenencia [te'nenθja] *nf* (*de casa*) tenancy; (*de oficio*) tenure; (*de propiedad*) possession.

┌─────────────────────┐
│ *PALABRA CLAVE* │
└─────────────────────┘

tener [te'ner] *vt* **1** (*poseer, gen*) to have; (*en la mano*) to hold; ¿**tienes un boli?** have you got a pen?; **va a** ~ **un niño** she's going to have a baby; ¡**ten** (*o* **tenga**)!, ¡**aquí tienes** (*o* **tiene**)! here you are!

2 (*edad, medidas*) to be; **tiene 7 años** she's 7 (years old); **tiene 15 cm de largo** it's 15 cm long; *ver* **calor, hambre** *etc*

3 (*considerar*): **lo tengo por brillante** I consider him to be brilliant; ~ **en mucho a uno** to think very highly of sb

4 (+*pp*: = *pretérito*): **tengo terminada ya la mitad del trabajo** I've done half the work already

5: ~ **que hacer algo** to have to do sth; **tengo que acabar este trabajo hoy** I have to finish this job today

6: ¿**qué tienes, estás enfermo?** what's the matter with you, are you ill?

♦ ~**se** *vr* **1**: ~**se en pie** to stand up

2: ~**se por** to think o.s.; **se tiene por muy listo** he thinks himself very clever.

tengo *etc vb ver* **tener**.

tenia ['tenja] *nf* tapeworm.

teniente [te'njente] *nm* (*rango*) lieutenant; (*ayudante*) deputy.

tenis ['tenis] *nm* tennis; ~ **de mesa** table tennis; ~**ta** *nm/f* tennis player.

tenor [te'nor] *nm* (*sentido*) meaning; (*MUS*) tenor; **a ~ de** on the lines of.

tensar [ten'sar] *vt* to tauten; (*arco*) to draw.

tensión [ten'sjon] *nf* tension; (*TEC*) stress; (*MED*): ~ **arterial** blood pressure; **tener la ~ alta** to have high blood pressure.

tenso, a ['tenso, a] *adj* tense.

tentación [tenta'θjon] *nf* temptation.

tentáculo [ten'takulo] *nm* tentacle.

tentador, a [tenta'ðor, a] *adj* tempting ♦ *nm/f* tempter/temptress.

tentar [ten'tar] *vt* (*tocar*) to touch, feel; (*seducir*) to tempt; (*atraer*) to attract; **tentativa** *nf* attempt; **tentativa de asesinato** attempted murder.

tentempié [tentem'pje] (*fam*) *nm* snack.

tenue ['tenwe] *adj* (*delgado*) thin, slender; (*neblina*) light; (*lazo, vínculo*) slight.

teñir [te'nir] *vt* to dye; (*fig*) to tinge; ~**se** *vr* to dye; ~**se el pelo** to dye one's hair.

teología [teolo'xia] *nf* theology.

teorema [teo'rema] *nm* theorem.

teoría [teo'ria] *nf* theory; **en** ~ in theory; **teóricamente** *adv* theoretically; **teórico, a** *adj* theoretic(al) ♦ *nm/f* theoretician, theorist; **teorizar** *vi* to theorize.

terapéutico, a [tera'peutiko, a] *adj* therapeutic.

terapia [te'rapja] *nf* therapy.

tercer [ter'θer] *adj ver* **tercero**.

tercermundista [terθermun'dista] *adj* Third World *cpd*.

tercero, a [ter'θero, a] *adj* (*delante de nmsg*: **tercer**) third ♦ *nm* (*JUR*) third party.

terceto [ter'θeto] *nm* trio.

terciado, a [ter'θjaðo, a] *adj* slanting.

terciar [ter'θjar] *vt* (*llevar*) to wear (across the shoulder) ♦ *vi* (*participar*) to take part; (*hacer de árbitro*) to mediate; ~**se** *vr* to come up; ~**io, a** *adj* tertiary.

tercio ['terθjo] *nm* third.

terciopelo [terθjo'pelo] *nm* velvet.

terco, a ['terko, a] *adj* obstinate.

tergiversar [terxiβer'sar] *vt* to distort.

termal [ter'mal] *adj* thermal.

termas ['termas] *nfpl* hot springs.

terminación [termina'θjon] *nf* (*final*) end; (*conclusión*) conclusion, ending.

terminal [termi'nal] *adj, nm, nf* terminal.

terminante [termi'nante] *adj* (*final*) final, definitive; (*tajante*) categorical.

terminar [termi'nar] *vt* (*completar*) to complete, finish; (*concluir*) to end ♦ *vi* (*llegar a su fin*) to end; (*parar*) to stop; (*acabar*) to finish; ~**se** *vr* to come to an end; ~ **por hacer algo** to end up (by) doing sth.

término ['termino] *nm* end, conclusion; (*parada*) terminus; (*límite*) boundary; ~ **medio** average; (*fig*) middle way; **en último** ~ (*a fin de cuentas*) in the last analysis; (*como último recurso*) as a last resort; **en** ~**s de** in terms of.

terminología [terminolo'xia] *nf* terminology.

termodinámico, a [termoði'namiko, a] *adj* thermodynamic.

termómetro [ter'mometro] *nm* thermometer.

termonuclear [termonukle'ar] *adj* thermonuclear.

termo(s) ['termo(s)] ® *nm* Thermos (flask) ®.

termostato [termo'stato] *nm* thermostat.

ternero, a [ter'nero, a] *nm/f* (*animal*) calf ♦ *nf* (*carne*) veal.

terno ['terno] (*AM*) *nm* three-piece suit.

ternura [ter'nura] *nf* (*trato*) tenderness; (*palabra*) endearment; (*cariño*) fondness.

terquedad [terke'ðað] *nf* obstinacy; (*dureza*) harshness.

terrado [te'rraðo] *nm* terrace.
terraplén [terra'plen] *nm* (*AGR*) terrace; (*cuesta*) slope.
terrateniente [terrate'njente] *nm/f* landowner.
terraza [te'rraθa] *nf* (*balcón*) balcony; (*techo*) (flat) roof; (*AGR*) terrace.
terremoto [terre'moto] *nm* earthquake.
terrenal [terre'nal] *adj* earthly.
terreno [te'rreno] *nm* (*tierra*) land; (*parcela*) plot; (*suelo*) soil; (*fig*) field; **un ~** a piece of land.
terrestre [te'rrestre] *adj* terrestrial; (*ruta*) land *cpd*.
terrible [te'rriβle] *adj* terrible, awful.
territorio [terri'torjo] *nm* territory.
terrón [te'rron] *nm* (*de azúcar*) lump; (*de tierra*) clod, lump.
terror [te'rror] *nm* terror; **~ífico, a** *adj* terrifying; **~ista** *adj*, *nm/f* terrorist.
terroso, a [te'rroso, a] *adj* earthy.
terruño [te'rruɲo] *nm* (*parcela*) plot; (*fig*) native soil.
terso, a ['terso, a] *adj* (*liso*) smooth; (*pulido*) polished; **tersura** *nf* smoothness.
tertulia [ter'tulja] *nf* (*reunión informal*) social gathering; (*grupo*) group, circle.
tesis ['tesis] *nf inv* thesis.
tesón [te'son] *nm* (*firmeza*) firmness; (*tenacidad*) tenacity.
tesorero, a [teso'rero, a] *nm/f* treasurer.
tesoro [te'soro] *nm* treasure; (*COM*, *POL*) treasury.
testaferro [testa'ferro] *nm* figurehead.
testamentaría [testamenta'ria] *nf* execution of a will.
testamentario, a [testamen'tarjo, a] *adj* testamentary ♦ *nm/f* executor/executrix.
testamento [testa'mento] *nm* will.
testar [tes'tar] *vi* to make a will.
testarudo, a [testa'ruðo, a] *adj* stubborn.
testículo [tes'tikulo] *nm* testicle.
testificar [testifi'kar] *vt* to testify; (*fig*) to attest ♦ *vi* to give evidence.
testigo [tes'tiɣo] *nm/f* witness; **~ de cargo/descargo** witness for the prosecution/defence; **~ ocular** eye witness.

testimoniar [testimo'njar] *vt* to testify to; (*fig*) to show; **testimonio** *nm* testimony.
teta ['teta] *nf* (*de biberón*) teat; (*ANAT*: *pezón*) nipple; (: *fam*) breast.
tétanos ['tetanos] *nm* tetanus.
tetera [te'tera] *nf* teapot.
tetilla [te'tiʎa] *nf* (*ANAT*) nipple; (*de biberón*) teat.
tétrico, a ['tetriko, a] *adj* gloomy, dismal.
textil [teks'til] *adj* textile; **~es** *nmpl* textiles.
texto ['teksto] *nm* text; **textual** *adj* textual.
textura [teks'tura] *nf* (*de tejido*) texture.
tez [teθ] *nf* (*cutis*) complexion; (*color*) colouring.
ti [ti] *pron* you; (*reflexivo*) yourself.
tía ['tia] *nf* (*pariente*) aunt; (*fam*) chick, bird.
tibieza [ti'βjeθa] *nf* (*temperatura*) tepidness; (*fig*) coolness; **tibio, a** *adj* lukewarm.
tiburón [tiβu'ron] *nm* shark.
tic [tik] *nm* (*ruido*) click; (*de reloj*) tick; (*MED*): **~ nervioso** nervous tic.
tictac [tik'tak] *nm* (*de reloj*) tick tock.
tiempo ['tjempo] *nm* time; (*época*, *período*) age, period; (*METEOROLOGÍA*) weather; (*LING*) tense; (*DEPORTE*) half; **a ~** in time; **a un o al mismo ~** at the same time; **al poco ~** very soon (after); **se quedó poco ~** he didn't stay very long; **hace poco ~** not long ago, **mucho ~** a long time; **de ~ en ~** from time to time; **hace buen/mal ~** the weather is fine/bad; **estar a ~ to** be in time; **hace ~** some time ago; **hacer ~** to while away the time; **motor de 2 ~s** two-stroke engine; **primer ~** first half.
tienda ['tjenda] *nf* shop, store; **~ (de campaña)** tent.
tienes *etc vb ver* **tener.**
tienta *etc* ['tjenta] *vb ver* **tentar** ♦ *nf*: **andar a ~s** to grope one's way along.
tiento ['tjento] *vb ver* **tentar** ♦ *nm* (*tacto*) touch; (*precaución*) wariness.
tierno, a ['tjerno, a] *adj* (*blando*) tender; (*fresco*) fresh; (*amable*) sweet.

tierra ['tjerra] *nf* earth; (*suelo*) soil; (*mundo*) earth, world; (*país*) country, land; ~ **adentro** inland.

tieso, a ['tjeso, a] *adj* (*rígido*) rigid; (*duro*) stiff; (*fam: orgulloso*) conceited.

tiesto ['tjesto] *nm* flowerpot.

tifoidea [tifoi'ðea] *nf* typhoid.

tifón [ti'fon] *nm* typhoon.

tifus ['tifus] *nm* typhus.

tigre ['tivre] *nm* tiger.

tijera [ti'xera] *nf* scissors *pl*; (*ZOOL*) claw; ~s *nfpl* scissors; (*para plantas*) shears.

tijereta [tixe'reta] *nf* earwig.

tijeretear [tixerete'ar] *vt* to snip.

tildar [til'dar] *vt*: ~ **de** to brand as.

tilde ['tilde] *nf* (*TIP*) tilde.

tilín [ti'lin] *nm* tinkle.

tilo ['tilo] *nm* lime tree.

timar [ti'mar] *vt* (*robar*) to steal; (*estafar*) to swindle.

timbal [tim'bal] *nm* small drum.

timbrar [tim'brar] *vt* to stamp.

timbre ['timbre] *nm* (*sello*) stamp; (*campanilla*) bell; (*tono*) timbre; (*COM*) stamp duty.

timidez [timi'ðeθ] *nf* shyness; **tímido, a** *adj* shy.

timo ['timo] *nm* swindle.

timón [ti'mon] *nm* helm, rudder; **timonel** *nm* helmsman.

tímpano ['timpano] *nm* (*ANAT*) eardrum; (*MUS*) small drum.

tina ['tina] *nf* tub; (*baño*) bath(tub); **tinaja** *nf* large jar.

tinglado [tin'glaðo] *nm* (*cobertizo*) shed; (*fig: truco*) trick; (*intriga*) intrigue.

tinieblas [ti'njeßlas] *nfpl* darkness *sg*; (*sombras*) shadows.

tino ['tino] *nm* (*habilidad*) skill; (*juicio*) insight.

tinta ['tinta] *nf* ink; (*TEC*) dye; (*ARTE*) colour.

tinte ['tinte] *nm* (*acto*) dyeing.

tintero [tin'tero] *nm* inkwell.

tintinear [tintine'ar] *vt* to tinkle.

tinto, a ['tinto, a] *adj* (*teñido*) dyed ♦ *nm* red wine.

tintorería [tintore'ria] *nf* dry cleaner's.

tintura [tin'tura] *nf* (*acto*) dyeing; (*QUÍMICA*) dye; (*farmacéutico*) tincture.

tío ['tio] *nm* (*pariente*) uncle; (*fam: individuo*) bloke (*BRIT*), guy.

tiovivo [tio'ßißo] *nm* merry-go-round.

típico, a ['tipiko, a] *adj* typical.

tiple ['tiple] *nm* soprano (voice) ♦ *nf* soprano.

tipo ['tipo] *nm* (*clase*) type, kind; (*norma*) norm; (*patrón*) pattern; (*hombre*) fellow; (*ANAT: de hombre*) build; (: *de mujer*) figure; (*IMPRENTA*) type; ~ **bancario/de descuento/de interés/de cambio** bank/discount/interest/exchange rate.

tipografía [tipovra'fia] *nf* (*tipo*) printing *cpd*; (*lugar*) printing press; **tipográfico, a** *adj* printing *cpd*; **tipógrafo, a** *nm/f* printer.

tíquet ['tiket] (*pl* ~s) *nm* ticket; (*en tienda*) cash slip.

tiquismiquis [tikis'mikis] *nm inv* fussy person ♦ *nmpl* (*querellas*) squabbling *sg*; (*escrúpulos*) silly scruples.

tira ['tira] *nf* strip; (*fig*) abundance; ~ **y afloja** give and take.

tirabuzón [tiraßu'θon] *nm* (*rizo*) curl.

tirachinas [tira'tʃinas] *nm inv* catapult.

tirada [ti'raða] *nf* (*acto*) cast, throw; (*distancia*) distance; (*serie*) series; (*TIP*) printing, edition; **de una** ~ at one go.

tiradero [tira'ðero] *nm* rubbish dump.

tirado, a [ti'raðo, a] *adj* (*barato*) dirtcheap; (*fam: fácil*) very easy.

tirador [tira'ðor] *nm* (*mango*) handle.

tiranía [tira'nia] *nf* tyranny; **tirano, a** *adj* tyrannical ♦ *nm/f* tyrant.

tirante [ti'rante] *adj* (*cuerda etc*) tight, taut; (*relaciones*) strained ♦ *nm* (*ARQ*) brace; (*TEC*) stay; (*correa*) shoulder strap; ~s *nmpl* (*de pantalón*) braces (*BRIT*), suspenders (*US*); **tirantez** *nf* tightness; (*fig*) tension.

tirar [ti'rar] *vt* to throw; (*dejar caer*) to drop; (*volcar*) to upset; (*derribar*) to knock down *o* over; (*jalar*) to pull; (*desechar*) to throw out *o* away; (*disipar*) to squander; (*imprimir*) to print; (*dar: golpe*) to deal ♦ *vi* (*disparar*) to shoot; (*jalar*) to pull; (*fig*) to draw; (*fam: andar*) to go; (*tender a, buscar realizar*) to tend to; (*DEPORTE*) to shoot; ~se *vr* to throw o.s.; (*fig*) to cheapen o.s.; ~ **abajo** to bring down, destroy; **tira más a su padre** he takes more after his father; **ir tirando** to manage; **a todo** ~ at the most.

tirita [ti'rita] *nf* (sticking) plaster (*BRIT*), bandaid (*US*).

tiritar [tiri'tar] *vi* to shiver.

tiro ['tiro] *nm* (*lanzamiento*) throw; (*disparo*) shot; (*disparar*) shooting; (*DEPORTE*) shot; (*GOLF, TENIS*) drive; (*alcance*) range; (*golpe*) blow; (*engaño*) hoax; ~ **al blanco** target practice; **caballo de** ~ cart-horse; **andar de** ~**s largos** to be all dressed up; **al** ~ (*AM*) at once.

tirón [ti'ron] *nm* (*sacudida*) pull, tug; **de un** ~ in one go, all at once.

tiroteo [tiro'teo] *nm* exchange of shots, shooting.

tísico, a ['tisiko, a] *adj* consumptive.

tisis ['tisis] *nf inv* consumption, tuberculosis.

títere ['titere] *nm* puppet.

titilar [titi'lar] *vi* (*luz, estrella*) to twinkle; (*párpado*) to flutter.

titiritero, a [titiri'tero, a] *nm/f* puppeteer.

titubeante [titußε'ante] *adj* (*inestable*) shaky, tottering; (*farfullante*) stammering; (*dudoso*) hesitant.

titubear [titußε'ar] *vi* to stagger; to stammer; (*fig*) to hesitate; **titubeo** *nm* staggering; stammering; hesitation.

titulado, a [titu'laðo, a] *adj* (*libro*) entitled; (*persona*) titled.

titular [titu'lar] *adj* titular ♦ *nm/f* occupant ♦ *nm* headline ♦ *vt* to title; ~se *vr* to be entitled; **título** *nm* title; (*de diario*) headline; (*certificado*) professional qualification; (*universitario*) (university) degree; (*fig*) right; **a título de** in the capacity of.

tiza ['tiθa] *nf* chalk.

tiznar [tiθ'nar] *vt* to blacken; (*fig*) to tarnish.

tizo ['tiθo] *nm* brand.

tizón [ti'θon] *nm* brand; (*fig*) stain.

toalla [to'aʎa] *nf* towel.

tobillo [to'βiʎo] *nm* ankle.

tobogán [toβo'γan] *nm* toboggan; (*montaña rusa*) roller-coaster; (*resbaladilla*) chute, slide.

toca ['toka] *nf* headdress.

tocadiscos [toka'ðiskos] *nm inv* record player.

tocado, a [to'kaðo, a] *adj* (*fam*) touched ♦ *nm* headdress.

tocador [toka'ðor] *nm* (*mueble*) dressing table; (*cuarto*) boudoir; (*fam*) ladies" toilet (*BRIT*) o room (*US*).

tocante [to'kante]: ~ **a** *prep* with regard to.

tocar [to'kar] *vt* to touch; (*MUS*) to play; (*topar con*) to run into, strike; (*referirse a*) to allude to; (*padecer*) to suffer ♦ *vi* (*a la puerta*) to knock (on *o* at the door); (*ser de turno*) to fall to, be the turn of; (*ser hora*) to be due; (*barco, avión*) to call at; (*atañer*) to concern; ~se *vr* (*cubrirse la cabeza*) to cover one's head; (*tener contacto*) to touch (each other); **por lo que a mí me toca** as far as I am concerned.

tocayo, a [to'kajo, a] *nm/f* namesake.

tocino [to'θino] *nm* bacon.

todavía [toða'βia] *adv* (*aun*) even; (*aún*) still, yet; ~ **mas** yet more; ~ **no** not yet.

PALABRA CLAVE

todo, a ['toðo, a] *adj* **1** (*con artículo sg*) all; **toda la carne** all the meat; **toda la noche** all night, the whole night; ~ **el libro** the whole book; **toda una botella** a whole bottle; ~ **lo contrario** quite the opposite; **está toda sucia** she's all dirty; **por** ~ **el país** throughout the whole country

2 (*con artículo pl*) all; every; ~**s los libros** all the books; **todas las noches** every night; ~**s los que quieran salir** all those who want to leave

♦ *pron* **1** everything, all; ~**s** everyone, everybody; **lo sabemos** ~ we know everything; ~**s querían más tiempo** everybody *o* everyone wanted more

time; **nos marchamos** ~**s** all of us left
2 : con ~: **con** ~ **él me sigue gustando**
even so I still like him
♦ *adv* all; **vaya** ~ **seguido** keep straight
on *o* ahead
♦ *nm*: **como un** ~ as a whole; **del** ~:
no me agrada del ~ I don't entirely like
it.

todopoderoso, a [todopoðe'roso, a] *adj*
all powerful; (*REL*) almighty.
toga ['toɣa] *nf* toga; (*ESCOL*) gown.
Tokio ['tokjo] *n* Tokyo.
toldo ['toldo] *nm* (*para el sol*) sunshade
(*BRIT*), parasol; (*tienda*) marquee.
tole ['tole] (*fam*) *nm* commotion.
tolerancia [tole'ranθja] *nf* tolerance.
tolerar [tole'rar] *vt* to tolerate; (*resistir*)
to endure.
toma ['toma] *nf* (*acto*) taking; (*MED*)
dose; ~ (**de corriente**) socket.
tomar [to'mar] *vt* to take; (*aspecto*) to
take on; (*beber*) to drink ♦ *vi* to take;
(*AM*) to drink; ~**se** *vr* to take; ~**se por**
to consider o.s. to be; ~ **a bien/a mal** to
take well/badly; ~ **en serio** to take seriously; ~ **el pelo a alguien** to pull sb's
leg; ~**la con uno** to pick a quarrel with
sb.
tomate [to'mate] *nm* tomato; ~**ra** *nf*
tomato plant.
tomavistas [toma'ßistas] *nm inv* movie
camera.
tomillo [to'miʎo] *nm* thyme.
tomo ['tomo] *nm* (*libro*) volume.
ton [ton] *abr* = **tonelada** ♦ *nm*: **sin** ~ **ni**
son without rhyme or reason.
tonada [to'naða] *nf* tune.
tonalidad [tonali'ðað] *nf* tone.
tonel [to'nel] *nm* barrel.
tonelada [tone'laða] *nf* ton; **tonelaje** *nm*
tonnage.
tonelero [tone'lero] *nm* cooper.
tónica ['tonika] *nf* (*MUS*) tonic; (*fig*) key-
note.
tónico, a ['toniko, a] *adj* tonic ♦ *nm*
(*MED*) tonic.
tonificar [tonifi'kar] *vt* to tone up.
tono ['tono] *nm* tone; **fuera de** ~ inappropriate; **darse** ~ to put on airs.

tontería [tonte'ria] *nf* (*estupidez*)
foolishness; (*cosa*) stupid thing; (*acto*)
foolish act; ~**s** *nfpl* (*disparates*)
rubbish *sg*, nonsense *sg*.
tonto, a ['tonto, a] *adj* stupid, silly ♦
nm/f fool; (*payaso*) clown.
topacio [to'paθjo] *nm* topaz.
topar [to'par] *vt* (*tropezar*) to bump
into; (*encontrar*) to find, come across;
(*ZOOL*) to butt ♦ *vi*: ~ **contra** *o* **en** to
run into; ~ **con** to run up against.
tope ['tope] *adj* maximum ♦ *nm* (*fin*)
end; (*límite*) limit; (*FERRO*) buffer;
(*AUTO*) bumper; **al** ~ end to end.
tópico, a ['topiko, a] *adj* topical ♦ *nm*
platitude.
topo ['topo] *nm* (*ZOOL*) mole; (*fig*)
blunderer.
topografía [topoɣra'fia] *nf* topography;
topógrafo, a *nm/f* topographer.
toque etc ['toke] *vb ver* **tocar** ♦ *nm*
touch; (*MUS*) beat; (*de campana*) peal;
(*fig*) crux; **dar un** ~ **a** to test; ~ **de**
queda curfew; ~**tear** *vt* to handle.
toqué *vb ver* **tocar**.
toquilla [to'kiʎa] *nf* (*pañuelo*) head-
scarf; (*chal*) shawl.
tórax ['toraks] *nm* thorax.
torbellino [torbe'ʎino] *nm* whirlwind;
(*fig*) whirl.
torcedura [torθe'ðura] *nf* twist; (*MED*)
sprain.
torcer [tor'θer] *vt* to twist; (*la esquina*)
to turn; (*MED*) to sprain ♦ *vi* (*desviar*)
to turn off; ~**se** *vr* (*ladearse*) to bend;
(*desviarse*) to go astray; (*fracasar*) to
go wrong; **torcido, a** *adj* twisted; (*fig*)
crooked ♦ *nm* curl.
tordo, a ['torðo, a] *adj* dappled ♦ *nm*
thrush.
torear [tore'ar] *vt* (*fig*: *evadir*) to avoid;
(*jugar con*) to tease ♦ *vi* to fight bulls;
toreo *nm* bullfighting; **torero, a** *nm/f*
bullfighter.
tormenta [tor'menta] *nf* storm; (*fig*:
confusión) turmoil.
tormento [tor'mento] *nm* torture; (*fig*)
anguish.
tornar [tor'nar] *vt* (*devolver*) to return,
give back; (*transformar*) to transform

♦ *vi* to go back; **~se** *vr* (*ponerse*) to become.

tornasolado, a [tornaso'laðo, a] *adj* (*brillante*) iridescent; (*reluciente*) shimmering.

torneo [tor'neo] *nm* tournament.

tornillo [tor'niʎo] *nm* screw.

torniquete [torni'kete] *nm* (*puerta*) turnstile; (*MED*) tourniquet.

torno ['torno] *nm* (*TEC*) winch; (*tambor*) drum; **en ~** (a) round, about.

toro ['toro] *nm* bull; (*fam*) he-man; **los ~s** bullfighting.

toronja [to'ronxa] *nf* grapefruit.

torpe ['torpe] *adj* (*poco hábil*) clumsy, awkward; (*necio*) dim; (*lento*) slow.

torpedo [tor'peðo] *nm* torpedo.

torpeza [tor'peθa] *nf* (*falta de agilidad*) clumsiness; (*lentitud*) slowness; (*error*) mistake.

torre ['torre] *nf* tower; (*de petróleo*) derrick.

torrefacto, a [torre'facto, a] *adj* roasted.

torrente [to'rrente] *nm* torrent.

tórrido, a ['torriðo, a] *adj* torrid.

torrija [to'rrixa] *nf* French toast.

torsión [tor'sjon] *nf* twisting.

torso ['torso] *nm* torso.

torta ['torta] *nf* cake; (*fam*) slap.

tortícolis [tor'tikolis] *nm inv* stiff neck.

tortilla [tor'tiʎa] *nf* omelette; (*AM*) maize pancake; **~ francesa/española** plain/potato omelette.

tórtola ['tortola] *nf* turtledove.

tortuga [tor'tuxa] *nf* tortoise.

tortuoso, a [tor'twoso, a] *adj* winding.

tortura [tor'tura] *nf* torture; **torturar** *vt* to torture.

tos [tos] *nf* cough; **~ ferina** whooping cough.

tosco, a ['tosko, a] *adj* coarse.

toser [to'ser] *vi* to cough.

tostado, a [tos'taðo, a] *adj* toasted; (*por el sol*) dark brown; (*piel*) tanned.

tostador [tosta'ðor] *nm* toaster.

tostar [tos'tar] *vt* to toast; (*café*) to roast; (*persona*) to tan; **~se** *vr* to get brown.

total [to'tal] *adj* total ♦ *adv* in short; (*al fin y al cabo*) when all is said and done

♦ *nm* total; **~ que** to cut (*BRIT*) o make (*US*) a long story short.

totalidad [totali'ðað] *nf* whole.

totalitario, a [totali'tarjo, a] *adj* totalitarian.

tóxico, a ['toksiko, a] *adj* toxic ♦ *nm* poison; **toxicómano, a** *nm/f* drug addict.

tozudo, a [to'θuðo, a] *adj* obstinate.

traba ['traβa] *nf* bond, tie; (*cadena*) shackle.

trabajador, a [traβaxa'ðor, a] *adj* hard-working ♦ *nm/f* worker.

trabajar [traβa'xar] *vt* to work; (*AGR*) to till; (*empeñarse en*) to work at; (*empujar: persona*) to push; (*convencer*) to persuade ♦ *vi* to work; (*esforzarse*) to strive; **trabajo** *nm* work; (*tarea*) task; (*POL*) labour; (*fig*) effort; **tomarse el trabajo de** to take the trouble to; **trabajo por turno/a destajo** shift work/piecework; **trabajoso, a** *adj* hard.

trabalenguas [traβa'lengwas] *nm inv* tongue twister.

trabar [tra'βar] *vt* (*juntar*) to join, unite; (*atar*) to tie down, fetter; (*agarrar*) to seize; (*amistad*) to strike up; **~se** *vr* to become entangled; **trabársele a uno la lengua** to be tongue-tied.

tracción [trak'θjon] *nf* traction; **~ delantera/trasera** front-wheel/rear-wheel drive.

tractor [trak'tor] *nm* tractor.

tradición [traði'θjon] *nf* tradition; **tradicional** *adj* traditional.

traducción [traðuk'θjon] *nf* translation.

traducir [traðu'θir] *vt* to translate; **traductor, a** *nm/f* translator.

traer [tra'er] *vt* to bring; (*llevar*) to carry; (*ropa*) to wear; (*incluir*) to carry; (*fig*) to cause; **~se** *vr*: **~se algo** to be up to sth.

traficar [trafi'kar] *vi* to trade.

tráfico ['trafiko] *nm* (*COM*) trade; (*AUTO*) traffic.

tragaluz [traxa'luθ] *nm* skylight.

tragaperras [traxa'perras] *nm o f inv* slot machine.

tragar [tra'xar] *vt* to swallow; (*devorar*)

to devour, bolt down; ~**se** vr to swallow.

tragedia [tra'xeðja] nf tragedy; **trágico, a** adj tragic.

trago ['trayo] nm (líquido) drink; (bocado) gulp; (fam: de bebida) swig; (desgracia) blow.

traición [trai'θjon] nf treachery; (JUR) treason; (una ~) act of treachery; **traicionar** vt to betray.

traicionero, a [traiθjo'nero, a] adj treacherous.

traidor, a [trai'ðor, a] adj treacherous ♦ nm/f traitor.

traigo etc vb ver **traer**.

traje ['traxe] vb ver **traer** ♦ nm (de hombre) suit; (de mujer) dress; (vestido típico) costume; ~ **de baño** swimsuit; ~ **de luces** bullfighter's costume.

trajera etc vb ver **traer**.

trajín [tra'xin] nm haulage; (fam: movimiento) bustle; **trajinar** vt (llevar) to carry, transport ♦ vi (moverse) to bustle about; (viajar) to travel around.

trama ['trama] nf (intriga) plot; (de tejido) weft (BRIT), woof (US); **tramar** vt to plot; (TEC) to weave.

tramitar [trami'tar] vt (asunto) to transact; (negociar) to negotiate; (manejar) to handle.

trámite ['tramite] nm (paso) step; (JUR) transaction; ~**s** nmpl (burocracia) procedure sg; (JUR) proceedings.

tramo ['tramo] nm (de tierra) plot; (de escalera) flight; (de vía) section.

tramoya [tra'moja] nf (TEATRO) piece of stage machinery; (fig) scheme; **tramoyista** nm/f scene shifter; (fig) trickster.

trampa ['trampa] nf trap; (en el suelo) trapdoor; (engaño) trick; (fam) fiddle; **trampear** vt, vi to cheat..

trampolín [trampo'lin] nm trampoline; (de piscina etc) diving board.

tramposo, a [tram'poso, a] adj crooked, cheating ♦ nm/f crook, cheat.

tranca ['tranka] nf (palo) stick; (de puerta, ventana) bar; **trancar** vt to bar.

trance ['tranθe] nm (momento difícil)

difficult moment o juncture; (estado hipnotizado) trance.

tranco ['tranko] nm stride.

tranquilidad [trankili'ðað] nf (calma) calmness, stillness; (paz) peacefulness.

tranquilizar [trankili'θar] vt (calmar) to calm (down); (asegurar) to reassure; ~**se** vr to calm down; **tranquilo, a** adj (calmado) calm; (apacible) peaceful; (mar) calm; (mente) untroubled.

transacción [transak'θjon] nf transaction.

transbordador [transβorða'ðor] nm ferry.

transbordar [transβor'ðar] vt to transfer; **transbordo** nm transfer; **hacer transbordo** to change (trains).

transcurrir [transku'rrir] vi (tiempo) to pass; (hecho) to turn out.

transcurso [trans'kurso] nm: ~ **del tiempo** lapse (of time).

transeúnte [transe'unte] adj transient ♦ nm/f passer-by.

transferencia [transfe'renθja] nf transference; (COM) transfer.

transferir [transfe'rir] vt to transfer.

transformador [transforma'ðor] nm (ELEC) transformer.

transformar [transfor'mar] vt to transform; (convertir) to convert.

tránsfuga ['transfuxa] nm/f (MIL) deserter; (POL) turncoat.

transfusión [transfu'sjon] nf transfusion.

transición [transi'θjon] nf transition.

transido, a [tran'siðo, a] adj overcome.

transigir [transi'xir] vi to compromise, make concessions.

transistor [transis'tor] nm transistor.

transitar [transi'tar] vi to go (from place to place); **tránsito** nm transit; (AUTO) traffic; **transitorio, a** adj transitory.

transmisión [transmi'sjon] nf (TEC) transmission; (transferencia) transfer; ~ **en directo/exterior** live/outside broadcast.

transmitir [transmi'tir] vt to transmit; (RADIO, TV) to broadcast.

transparencia [transpa'renθja] nf transparency; (claridad) clearness, clarity; (foto) slide.

transparentar [transparen'tar] *vt* to reveal ♦ *vi* to be transparent; **transparente** *adj* transparent; (*claro*) clear; (*ligero*) diaphanous.

transpirar [transpi'rar] *vi* to perspire; (*fig*) to transpire.

transponer [transpo'ner] *vt* to transpose; (*cambiar de sitio*) to change the place of.

transportar [transpor'tar] *vt* to transport; (*llevar*) to carry; **transporte** *nm* transport; (*COM*) haulage.

transversal [transβer'sal] *adj* transverse, cross.

tranvía [tram'bia] *nm* tram.

trapecio [tra'peθjo] *nm* trapeze; **trapecista** *nm/f* trapeze artist.

trapero, a [tra'pero, a] *nm/f* ragman.

trapicheo [trapi'tʃeo] (*fam*) *nm* scheme, fiddle.

trapo ['trapo] *nm* (*tela*) rag; (*de cocina*) cloth; **poner un ~ a** (*o* **por**) to dust.

tráquea ['trakea] *nf* windpipe.

traqueteo [trake'teo] *nm* (*golpeteo*) rattling.

tras [tras] *prep* (*detrás*) behind; (*después*) after.

trascendencia [trasθen'denθja] *nf* (*importancia*) importance; (*FILOSOFÍA*) transcendence.

trascendental [trasθenden'tal] *adj* important; (*FILOSOFÍA*) transcendental.

trascender [trasθen'der] *vi* (*noticias*) to come out; (*suceso*) to have a wide effect.

trasegar [trase'xar] *vt* (*moverse*) to move about; (*vino*) to decant.

trasero, a [tra'sero, a] *adj* back, rear ♦ *nm* (*ANAT*) bottom.

trasfondo [tras'fondo] *nm* background.

trasgredir [trasɣre'ðir] *vt* to contravene.

trashumante [trasu'mante] *adj* (*animales*) migrating.

trasladar [trasla'ðar] *vt* to move; (*persona*) to transfer; (*postergar*) to postpone; (*copiar*) to copy; **~se** *vr* (*mudarse*) to move; **traslado** *nm* move; (*mudanza*) move, removal.

traslucir [traslu'θir] *vt* to show; **~se** *vr*

to be translucent; (*fig*) to be revealed.

trasluz [tras'luθ] *nm* reflected light; **al ~** against *o* up to the light.

trasnochar [trasno'tʃar] *vi* (*acostarse tarde*) to stay up late; (*no dormir*) to have a sleepless night.

traspasar [traspa'sar] *vt* (*suj: bala etc*) to pierce, go through; (*propiedad*) to sell, transfer; (*calle*) to cross over; (*límites*) to go beyond; (*ley*) to break; **traspaso** *nm* (*venta*) transfer, sale.

traspié [tras'pje] *nm* (*tropezón*) trip; (*fig*) blunder.

trasplantar [trasplan'tar] *vt* to transplant.

traste ['traste] *nm* (*MUS*) fret; **dar al ~ con algo** to ruin sth.

trastienda [tras'tjenda] *nf* back of shop.

trasto ['trasto] (*pey*) *nm* (*cosa*) piece of junk; (*persona*) dead loss.

trastornado, a [trastor'naðo, a] *adj* (*loco*) mad, crazy.

trastornar [trastor'nar] *vt* to overturn, upset; (*fig: ideas*) to confuse; (: *nervios*) to shatter; (: *persona*) to drive crazy; **~se** *vr* (*volverse loco*) to go mad *o* crazy; **trastorno** *nm* (*acto*) overturning; (*confusión*) confusion.

tratable [tra'taβle] *adj* friendly.

tratado [tra'taðo] *nm* (*POL*) treaty; (*COM*) agreement.

tratamiento [trata'mjento] *nm* treatment.

tratar [tra'tar] *vt* (*ocuparse de*) to treat; (*manejar, TEC*) to handle; (*MED*) to treat; (*dirigirse a: persona*) to address ♦ *vi*: **~ de** (*hablar sobre*) to deal with, be about; (*intentar*) to try to; **~se** *vr* to treat each other; **~ con** (*COM*) to trade in; (*negociar*) to negotiate with; (*tener contactos*) to have dealings with; **¿de qué se trata?** what's it about?; **trato** *nm* dealings *pl*; (*relaciones*) relationship; (*comportamiento*) manner; (*COM*) agreement; (*título*) (form of) address.

trauma ['trauma] *nm* trauma.

través [tra'βes] *nm* (*fig*) reverse; **al ~** across, crossways; **a ~ de** across; (*sobre*) over; (*por*) through.

travesaño [traβe'saɲo] *nm* (*ARQ*) cross-

beam; (DEPORTE) crossbar.

travesía [traße'sia] nf (calle) cross-street; (NAUT) crossing.

travesura [traße'sura] nf (broma) prank; (ingenio) wit.

traviesa [tra'ßjesa] nf (ARQ) crossbeam.

travieso, a [tra'ßjeso, a] adj (niño) naughty.

trayecto [tra'jekto] nm (ruta) road, way; (viaje) journey; (tramo) stretch; (curso) course; ~ria nf trajectory; (fig) path.

traza ['traθa] nf (aspecto) looks pl; (señal) sign; ~do, a adj: **bien ~do** shapely, well-formed ♦ nm (ARQ) plan, design; (fig) outline.

trazar [tra'θar] vt (ARQ) to plan; (ARTE) to sketch; (fig) to trace; (plan) to follow; **trazo** nm (línea) line; (bosquejo) sketch.

trébol ['treßol] nm (BOT) clover.

trece ['treθe] num thirteen.

trecho ['tretʃo] nm (distancia) distance; (de tiempo) while; (fam) piece; **de ~ en ~** at intervals.

tregua ['treɣwa] nf (MIL) truce; (fig) lull.

treinta ['treinta] num thirty.

tremendo, a [tre'mendo, a] adj (terrible) terrible; (imponente: cosa) imposing; (fam: fabuloso) tremendous.

trémulo, a ['tremulo, a] adj quivering.

tren [tren] nm train; **~ de aterrizaje** undercarriage.

trenza ['trenθa] nf (de pelo) plait (BRIT), braid (US); **trenzar** vt (pelo) to plait, braid; **trenzarse** vr (AM) to become involved.

trepadora [trepa'ðora] nf (BOT) climber.

trepar [tre'par] vt, vi to climb.

trepidar [trepi'ðar] vi to shake, vibrate.

tres [tres] num three.

tresillo [tre'siʎo] nm three-piece suite; (MUS) triplet.

treta ['treta] nf (COM etc) gimmick; (fig) trick.

triángulo ['trjangulo] nm triangle.

tribu ['trißu] nf tribe.

tribuna [tri'ßuna] nf (plataforma) platform; (DEPORTE) (grand)stand; (fig) public speaking.

tribunal [trißu'nal] nm (JUR) court; (comisión, fig) tribunal.

tributar [trißu'tar] vt (gen) to pay; **tributo** nm (COM) tax.

tricotar [triko'tar] vi to knit.

trigal [tri'ɣal] nm wheat field.

trigo ['triɣo] nm wheat.

trigueño, a [tri'ɣeɲo, a] adj (pelo) corn-coloured; (piel) olive-skinned.

trillado, a [tri'ʎaðo, a] adj threshed; (fig) trite, hackneyed; **trilladora** nf threshing machine.

trillar [tri'ʎar] vt (AGR) to thresh.

trimestral [trimes'tral] adj quarterly; (ESCOL) termly.

trimestre [tri'mestre] nm (ESCOL) term.

trinar [tri'nar] vi (pájaros) to sing; (rabiar) to fume, be angry.

trincar [trin'kar] vt (atar) to tie up; (inmovilizar) to pinion.

trinchar [trin'tʃar] vt to carve.

trinchera [trin'tʃera] nf (fosa) trench.

trineo [tri'neo] nm sledge.

trinidad [trini'ðað] nf trio; (REL): **la T~** the Trinity.

trino ['trino] nm trill.

tripa ['tripa] nf (ANAT) intestine; (fam: tb: ~s) insides pl.

triple ['triple] adj triple.

triplicado, a [tripli'kaðo, a] adj: **por ~** in triplicate.

tripulación [tripula'θjon] nf crew.

tripulante [tripu'lante] nm/f crewman/woman.

tripular [tripu'lar] vt (barco) to man; (AUTO) to drive.

triquiñuela [triki'ɲwela] nf trick.

tris [tris] nm inv crack; **en un ~** in an instant.

triste ['triste] adj (afligido) sad; (sombrío) melancholy, gloomy; (lamentable) sorry, miserable; **~za** nf (aflicción) sadness; (melancolía) melancholy.

triturar [tritu'rar] vt (moler) to grind; (mascar) to chew.

triunfar [trjun'far] vi (tener éxito) to triumph; (ganar) to win; **triunfo** nm triumph.

trivial [tri'βjal] *adj* trivial; ~**izar** *vt* to minimize, play down.

triza ['triθa] *nf*: **hacer** ~**s** to smash to bits; (*papel*) to tear to shreds.

trizar [tri'θar] *vt* to smash to bits; (*papel*) to tear to shreds.

trocar [tro'kar] *vt* to exchange.

trocha ['trotʃa] *nf* short cut.

troche ['trotʃe]: **a** ~ **y moche** *adv* helter-skelter, pell-mell.

trofeo [tro'feo] *nm* (*premio*) trophy; (*éxito*) success.

tromba ['tromba] *nf* whirlwind.

trombón [trom'bon] *nm* trombone.

trombosis [trom'bosis] *nf inv* thrombosis.

trompa ['trompa] *nf* horn; (*trompo*) humming top; (*hocico*) snout; (*fam*): **cogerse una** ~ to get tight.

trompeta [trom'peta] *nf* trumpet; (*clarín*) bugle.

trompo ['trompo] *nm* spinning top.

trompón [trom'pon] *nm* bump.

tronar [tro'nar] *vt* (*AM*) to shoot ♦ *vi* to thunder; (*fig*) to rage.

tronco ['tronko] *nm* (*de árbol, ANAT*) trunk.

tronchar [tron'tʃar] *vt* (*árbol*) to chop down; (*fig: vida*) to cut short; (: *esperanza*) to shatter; (*persona*) to tire out; ~**se** *vr* to fall down.

tronera [tro'nera] *nf* (*MIL*) loophole; (*ARQ*) small window.

trono ['trono] *nm* throne.

tropa ['tropa] *nf* (*MIL*) troop; (*soldados*) soldiers *pl*.

tropel [tro'pel] *nm* (*muchedumbre*) crowd.

tropelía [trope'lia] *nm* outrage.

tropezar [trope'θar] *vi* to trip, stumble; (*fig*) to slip up; ~ **con** to run into; (*topar con*) to bump into; **tropezón** *nm* trip; (*fig*) blunder.

tropical [tropi'kal] *adj* tropical.

trópico [tropiko] *nm* tropic.

tropiezo [tro'pjeθo] *vb ver* **tropezar** ♦ *nm* (*error*) slip, blunder; (*desgracia*) misfortune; (*obstáculo*) snag.

trotamundos [trota'mundos] *nm inv* globetrotter.

trotar [tro'tar] *vi* to trot; **trote** *nm* trot; (*fam*) travelling; **de mucho trote** hard-wearing.

trozo ['troθo] *nm* bit, piece.

truco ['truko] *nm* (*habilidad*) knack; (*engaño*) trick.

trucha ['trutʃa] *nf* trout.

trueno ['trweno] *nm* thunder; (*estampido*) bang.

trueque *etc* ['trweke] *vb ver* **trocar** ♦ *nm* exchange; (*COM*) barter.

trufa ['trufa] *nf* (*BOT*) truffle.

truhán, ana [tru'an, ana] *nm/f* rogue.

truncar [trun'kar] *vt* (*cortar*) to truncate; (*fig: la vida etc*) to cut short; (: *el desarrollo*) to stunt.

tu [tu] *adj* your.

tú [tu] *pron* you.

tubérculo [tu'βerkulo] *nm* (*BOT*) tuber.

tuberculosis [tuβerku'losis] *nf inv* tuberculosis.

tubería [tuβe'ria] *nf* pipes *pl*; (*conducto*) pipeline.

tubo ['tuβo] *nm* tube, pipe; ~ **de ensayo** test tube; ~ **de escape** exhaust (pipe).

tuerca ['twerka] *nf* nut.

tuerto, a ['twerto, a] *adj* blind in one eye ♦ *nm/f* one-eyed person.

tuerza *etc vb ver* **torcer**.

tuétano ['twetano] *nm* marrow; (*BOT*) pith.

tufo ['tufo] *nm* vapour; (*fig: pey*) stench.

tugurio [tu'ɣurio] *nm* slum.

tul [tul] *nm* tulle.

tulipán [tuli'pan] *nm* tulip.

tullido, a [tu'ʎiðo, a] *adj* crippled.

tumba ['tumba] *nf* (*sepultura*) tomb.

tumbar [tum'bar] *vt* to knock down; ~**se** *vr* (*echarse*) to lie down; (*extenderse*) to stretch out.

tumbo ['tumbo] *nm* (*caída*) fall; (*de vehículo*) jolt.

tumbona [tum'bona] *nf* (*butaca*) easy chair; (*de playa*) deckchair (*BRIT*), beach chair (*US*).

tumido, a [tu'miðo, a] *adj* swollen.

tumor [tu'mor] *nm* tumour.

tumulto [tu'multo] *nm* turmoil.

tuna ['tuna] *nf* (*BOT*) prickly pear;

(MUS) student music group; ver tb **tuno.**

tunante [tu'nante] *nm/f* rascal.

tunda ['tunda] *nf (golpe)* beating.

túnel ['tunel] *nm* tunnel.

Túnez ['tuneθ] *nm* Tunisia; *(ciudad)* Tunis.

tuno, a ['tuno, a] *nm/f (fam)* rogue ♦ *nm member of student music group.*

tuntún [tun'tun]: **al ~** *adv* thoughtlessly.

tupido, a [tu'piðo, a] *adj (denso)* dense; *(tela)* close-woven; *(fig)* dim.

turba ['turßa] *nf* crowd.

turbación [turßa'θjon] *nf (molestia)* disturbance; *(preocupación)* worry; **turbado, a** *adj (molesto)* disturbed; *(preocupado)* worried.

turbar [tur'ßar] *vt (molestar)* to disturb; *(incomodar)* to upset; **~se** *vr* to be disturbed.

turbina [tur'ßina] *nf* turbine.

turbio, a ['turßjo, a] *adj* cloudy; *(tema etc)* confused ♦ *adv* indistinctly.

turbulencia [turßu'lenθja] *nf* turbulence; *(fig)* restlessness; **turbulento, a** *adj* turbulent; *(fig: intranquilo)* restless; *(: ruidoso)* noisy.

turco, a ['turko, a] *adj* Turkish ♦ *nm/f* Turk.

turismo [tu'rismo] *nm* tourism; *(coche)* saloon car; **turista** *nm/f* tourist; **turístico, a** *adj* tourist *cpd.*

turnar [tur'nar] *vi* to take (it in) turns; **~se** *vr* to take (it in) turns; **turno** *nm (INDUSTRIA)* shift; *(oportunidad, orden de prioridad)* opportunity; *(juegos etc)* turn.

turquesa [tur'kesa] *nf* turquoise.

Turquía [tur'kia] *nf* Turkey.

turrón [tu'rron] *nm (dulce)* nougat.

tutear [tute'ar] *vt* to address as familiar "tú"; **~se** *vr* to be on familiar terms.

tutela [tu'tela] *nf (legal)* guardianship; *(instrucción)* guidance; **tutelar** *adj* tutelary ♦ *vt* to protect.

tutor, a [tu'tor, a] *nm/f (legal)* guardian; *(ESCOL)* tutor.

tuve *etc vb ver* **tener.**

tuviera *etc vb ver* **tener.**

tuyo, a ['tujo, a] *adj* yours, of yours ♦ *pron* yours; **un amigo ~** a friend of

yours; **los ~s** *(fam)* your relations, your family.

TV ['te'ße] *nf abr (= televisión)* TV.

TVE *nf abr* = **Televisión Española.**

U

u [u] *conj* or.

ubicar [ußi'kar] *vt* to place, situate; *(: fig)* to install in a post; *(AM: encontrar)* to find; **~se** *vr* to lie, be located.

ubre ['ußre] *nf* udder.

UCD *nf abr* = **Unión del Centro Democrático.**

Ud(s) *abr* = **usted(es).**

ufanarse [ufa'narse] *vr* to boast; **~ de** to pride o.s. on; **ufano, a** *adj (arrogante)* arrogant; *(presumido)* conceited.

UGT *nf abr* = **Unión General de Trabajadores.**

ujier [u'xjer] *nm* usher; *(portero)* doorkeeper.

úlcera ['ulθera] *nf* ulcer.

ulcerar [ulθe'rar] *vt* to make sore; **~se** *vr* to ulcerate.

ulterior [ulte'rjor] *adj (más allá)* farther, further; *(subsecuente, siguiente)* subsequent.

últimamente ['ultimamente] *adv (recientemente)* lately, recently.

ultimar [ulti'mar] *vt* to finish; *(finalizar)* to finalize; *(AM: rematar)* to finish off.

último, a ['ultimo, a] *adj* last; *(más reciente)* latest, most recent; *(más bajo)* bottom; *(más alto)* top; *(fig)* final, extreme; **en las últimas** on one's last legs; **por ~** finally.

ultra ['ultra] *adj* ultra ♦ *nm/f* extreme right-winger.

ultrajar [ultra'xar] *vt (escandalizar)* to outrage; *(insultar)* to insult, abuse; **ultraje** *nm* outrage; insult.

ultramar [ultra'mar] *nm*: **de** *o* **en ~** abroad, overseas.

ultramarinos [ultrama'rinos] *nmpl* groceries; **tienda de ~** grocer's (shop).

ultranza [ul'tranθa]: **a ~** *adv (a todo trance)* at all costs; *(completo)* outright.

ultrasónico, a [ultra'soniko, a] *adj* ultra-sonic.

ultratumba [ultra'tumba] *nf*: **la vida de ~** the next life.

ulular [ulu'lar] *vi* to howl; (*búho*) to hoot.

umbral [um'bral] *nm* (*gen*) threshold.

umbrío, a [um'brio, a] *adj* shady.

umbroso, a [um'broso, a] *adj* shady.

PALABRA CLAVE
<hr>

un, una [un, 'una] *art def* a; (*antes de vocal*) an; **una mujer/naranja** a woman/an orange
♦ *adj*: **unos** (*o* **unas**): **hay unos regalos para ti** there are some presents for you; **hay unas cervezas en la nevera** there are some beers in the fridge.

---

unánime [u'nanime] *adj* unanimous;
unanimidad *nf* unanimity.

unción [un'θjon] *nf* anointing; **extrema~** extreme unction.

undécimo, a [un'deθimo, a] *adj* eleventh.

ungir [un'xir] *vt* to rub with ointment; (*REL*) to anoint.

ungüento [un'gwento] *nm* ointment; (*fig*) salve, balm.

únicamente ['unikamente] *adv* solely, only.

único, a ['uniko, a] *adj* only, sole; (*sin par*) unique.

unidad [uni'ðað] *nf* unity; (*COM, TEC etc*) unit.

unido, a [u'niðo, a] *adj* joined, linked; (*fig*) united.

unificar [unifi'kar] *vt* to unite, unify.

uniformar [unifor'mar] *vt* to make uniform, level up; (*persona*) to put into uniform.

uniforme [uni'forme] *adj* uniform, equal; (*superficie*) even ♦ *nm* uniform; **uniformidad** *nf* uniformity; (*llaneza*) levelness, evenness.

unilateral [unilate'ral] *adj* unilateral.

unión [u'njon] *nf* union; (*acto*) uniting, joining; (*calidad*) unity; (*TEC*) joint; (*fig*) closeness, togetherness; **la U~ Soviética** the Soviet Union.

unir [u'nir] *vt* (*juntar*) to join, unite; (*atar*) to tie, fasten; (*combinar*) to combine; **~se** *vr* to join together, unite; (*empresas*) to merge.

unísono [u'nisono] *nm*: **al ~** in unison.

universal [uniβer'sal] *adj* universal; (*mundial*) world *cpd*.

universidad [uniβersi'ðað] *nf* university.

universitario, a [uniβersi'tarjo, a] *adj* university *cpd* ♦ *nm/f* (*profesor*) lecturer; (*estudiante*) (university) student; (*graduado*) graduate.

universo [uni'βerso] *nm* universe.

PALABRA CLAVE
<hr>

uno, a ['uno, a] *adj* one; **es todo ~** it's all one and the same; **~s pocos** a few; **~s cien** about a hundred
♦ *pron* **1** one; **quiero ~ solo** I only want one; **~ de ellos** one of them
2 (*alguien*) somebody, someone; **conozco a ~ que se te parece** I know somebody *o* someone who looks like you; **~ mismo** oneself; **~s querían quedarse** some (people) wanted to stay
3: (los) **~s ... (los) otros ...** some ... others; each other, one another; **una y otra son muy agradables** they're both very nice
♦ *nf* one; **es la una** it's one o'clock
♦ *nm* (number) one.

---

untar [un'tar] *vt* to rub; (*engrasar*) to grease, oil; (*fig*) to bribe.

uña ['uɲa] *nf* (*ANAT*) nail; (*garra*) claw; (*casco*) hoof; (*arrancaclavos*) claw.

uranio [u'ranjo] *nm* uranium.

urbanidad [urβani'ðað] *nf* courtesy, politeness.

urbanismo [urβa'nismo] *nm* town planning.

urbanización [urβaniθa'θjon] *nf* (*barrio, colonia*) housing estate.

urbano, a [ur'βano, a] *adj* (*de ciudad*) urban; (*cortés*) courteous, polite.

urbe ['urβe] *nf* large city.

urdimbre [ur'ðimbre] *nf* (*de tejido*) warp; (*intriga*) intrigue.

urdir [ur'ðir] *vt* to warp; (*fig*) to plot, contrive.

urgencia [ur'xenθja] *nf* urgency; (*prisa*) haste, rush; (*emergencia*) emergency; **servicios de ~** emergency services; **urgente** *adj* urgent.

urgir [ur'xir] *vi* to be urgent; **me urge** I'm in a hurry for it.

urinario, a [uri'narjo, a] *adj* urinary ♦ *nm* urinal.

urna ['urna] *nf* urn; (*POL*) ballot box.

urraca [u'rraka] *nf* magpie.

URSS *nf*: **la ~** the USSR.

Uruguay [uru'ɣwai] *nm*: **el ~** Uruguay; **uruguayo, a** *adj, nm/f* Uruguayan.

usado, a [u'saðo, a] *adj* used; (*ropa etc*) worn.

usanza [u'sanθa] *nf* custom, usage.

usar [u'sar] *vt* to use; (*ropa*) to wear; (*tener costumbre*) to be in the habit of; **~se** *vr* to be used; **uso** *nm* use; wear; (*costumbre*) usage, custom; (*moda*) fashion; **al uso** in keeping with custom; **al uso de** in the style of.

usted [us'teð] *pron* (*sg*) you *sg*; (*pl*): **~es** you *pl*.

usual [u'swal] *adj* usual.

usuario, a [usu'arjo, a] *nm/f* user.

usufructo [usu'frukto] *nm* use.

usura [u'sura] *nf* usury; **usurero, a** *nm/f* usurer.

usurpar [usur'par] *vt* to usurp.

utensilio [uten'siljo] *nm* tool; (*CULIN*) utensil.

útero ['utero] *nm* uterus, womb.

útil ['util] *adj* useful ♦ *nm* tool; **utilidad** *nf* usefulness; (*COM*) profit; **utilizar** *vt* to use, utilize.

utopía [uto'pia] *nf* Utopia; **utópico, a** *adj* Utopian.

uva ['uβa] *nf* grape.

V

v *abr* (= *voltio*) V.

va *vb ver* **ir**.

vaca ['baka] *nf* (*animal*) cow; **carne de ~** beef.

vacaciones [baka'θjones] *nfpl* holidays.

vacante [ba'kante] *adj* vacant, empty ♦ *nf* vacancy.

vaciar [ba'θjar] *vt* to empty out; (*ahuecar*) to hollow out; (*moldear*) to cast ♦ *vi* (*río*): **~ (en)** to flow (into); **~se** *vr* to empty.

vaciedad [baθje'ðað] *nf* emptiness.

vacilación [baθila'θjon] *nf* hesitation.

vacilante [baθi'lante] *adj* unsteady; (*habla*) faltering; (*fig*) hesitant.

vacilar [baθi'lar] *vi* to be unsteady; (*al hablar*) to falter; (*fig*) to hesitate, waver; (*memoria*) to fail.

vacío, a [ba'θio, a] *adj* empty; (*puesto*) vacant; (*desocupado*) idle; (*vano*) vain ♦ *nm* emptiness; (*FÍSICA*) vacuum; (*un ~*) (empty) space.

vacuna [ba'kuna] *nf* vaccine; **vacunar** *vt* to vaccinate.

vacuno, a [ba'kuno, a] *adj* cow *cpd*; **ganado ~** cattle.

vacuo, a ['bakwo, a] *adj* empty.

vadear [baðe'ar] *vt* (*río*) to ford; **vado** *nm* ford.

vagabundo, a [baɣa'βundo, a] *adj* wandering; (*pey*) vagrant ♦ *nm* tramp.

vagamente [baɣa'mente] *adv* vaguely.

vagancia [ba'ɣanθja] *nf* (*pereza*) idleness, laziness.

vagar [ba'ɣar] *vi* to wander; (*no hacer nada*) to idle.

vagina [ba'xina] *nf* vagina.

vago, a ['baɣo, a] *adj* vague; (*perezoso*) lazy; (*ambulante*) wandering ♦ *nm/f* (*vagabundo*) tramp; (*flojo*) lazybones *sg*, idler.

vagón [ba'ɣon] *nm* (*FERRO*: *de pasajeros*) carriage; (: *de mercancías*) wagon.

vaguedad [baɣe'ðað] *nf* vagueness.

vaho ['bao] *nm* (*vapor*) vapour, steam; (*respiración*) breath.

vaina ['baina] *nf* sheath.

vainilla [bai'niʎa] *nf* vanilla.

vainita [bai'nita] (*AM*) *nf* green o French bean.

vais *vb ver* **ir**.

vaivén [bai'βen] *nm* to-and-fro movement; (*de tránsito*) coming and going; **vaivenes** *nmpl* (*fig*) ups and downs.

vajilla [ba'xiʎa] *nf* crockery, dishes *pl*; **lavar la ~** to do the washing-up (*BRIT*), wash the dishes (*US*).

valdré *etc vb ver* **valer**.

vale ['bale] *nm* voucher; (*recibo*) receipt; (*pagaré*) IOU.

valedero, a [bale'ðero, a] *adj* valid.

valenciano, a [balen'θjano, a] *adj* Valencian.

valentía [balen'tia] *nf* courage, bravery; (*acción*) heroic deed; **valentón, ona** *adj* blustering.

valer [ba'ler] *vt* to be worth; (*MAT*) to equal; (*costar*) to cost ♦ *vi* (*ser útil*) to be useful; (*ser válido*) to be valid; ~**se** *vr* to defend o.s.; ~**se de** to make use of, take advantage of; ~ **la pena** to be worthwhile; **¿vale?** (*ESP*) OK?

valeroso, a [bale'roso, a] *adj* brave, valiant.

valgo *etc vb ver* **valer**.

valía [ba'lia] *nf* worth, value.

validar [bali'ðar] *vt* to validate; **validez** *nf* validity; **válido, a** *adj* valid.

valiente [ba'ljente] *adj* brave, valiant ♦ *nm* hero.

valija [ba'lixa] *nf* suitcase; ~ **diplomática** diplomatic bag.

valioso, a [ba'ljoso, a] *adj* valuable; (*rico*) wealthy.

valor [ba'lor] *nm* value, worth; (*precio*) price; (*valentía*) valour, courage; (*importancia*) importance; ~**es** *nmpl* (*COM*) securities; ~**ación** *nf* valuation; ~**ar** *vt* to value.

vals [bals] *nm inv* waltz.

válvula ['balßula] *nf* valve.

valla ['baʎa] *nf* fence; (*DEPORTE*) hurdle; (*fig*) barrier; **vallar** *vt* to fence in.

valle ['baʎe] *nm* valley.

vamos *vb ver* **ir**.

vampiro, resa [bam'piro, 'resa] *nm/f* vampire.

van *vb ver* **ir**.

vanagloriarse [banaɣlo'rjarse] *vr* to boast.

vándalo, a ['bandalo, a] *nm/f* vandal; **vandalismo** *nm* vandalism.

vanguardia [ban'gwardja] *nf* vanguard; (*ARTE etc*) avant-garde.

vanidad [bani'ðað] *nf* vanity; **vanidoso, a** *adj* vain, conceited.

vano, a ['bano, a] *adj* (*irreal*) unreal, vain; (*inútil*) useless; (*persona*) vain, conceited; (*frívolo*) frivolous.

vapor [ba'por] *nm* vapour; (*vaho*) steam; **al** ~ (*CULIN*) steamed; ~**izador** *nm* atomizer; ~**izar** *vt* to vaporize; ~**oso, a** *adj* vaporous.

vaquero, a [ba'kero, a] *adj* cattle *cpd* ♦ *nm* cowboy; ~**s** *nmpl* (*pantalones*) jeans.

vara ['bara] *nf* stick; (*TEC*) rod; ~ **mágica** magic wand.

variable [ba'rjaßle] *adj, nf* variable.

variación [baria'θjon] *nf* variation.

variar [bar'jar] *vt* to vary; (*modificar*) to modify; (*cambiar de posición*) to switch around ♦ *vi* to vary.

varices [ba'riθes] *nfpl* varicose veins.

variedad [barje'ðað] *nf* variety.

varilla [ba'riʎa] *nf* stick; (*BOT*) twig; (*TEC*) rod; (*de rueda*) spoke.

vario, a ['barjo, a] *adj* varied; ~**s** various, several.

varón [ba'ron] *nm* male, man; **varonil** *adj* manly, virile.

Varsovia [bar'soßja] *n* Warsaw.

vas *vb ver* **ir**.

vasco, a ['basko, a] *adj, nm/f* Basque.

vascongado, a [baskon'gaðo, a] *adj* Basque; **las Vascongadas** the Basque Country.

vascuence [bas'kwenθe] *adj* = **vascongado**.

vaselina [base'lina] *nf* Vaseline ®.

vasija [ba'sixa] *nf* container, vessel.

vaso ['baso] *nm* glass, tumbler; (*ANAT*) vessel.

vástago ['bastaɣo] *nm* (*BOT*) shoot; (*TEC*) rod; (*fig*) offspring.

vasto, a ['basto, a] *adj* vast, huge.

Vaticano [bati'kano] *nm*: **el** ~ the Vatican.

vaticinio [bati'θinjo] *nm* prophecy.

vatio ['batjo] *nm* (*ELEC*) watt.

vaya *etc vb ver* **ir**.

Vd(s) *abr* = **usted(es)**.

ve *vb ver* **ir**; **ver**.

vecindad [beθin'dað] *nf* neighbourhood; (*habitantes*) residents *pl*.

vecindario [beθin'darjo] *nm* neighbourhood; residents *pl.*

vecino, a [be'θino, a] *adj* neighbouring ♦ *nm/f* neighbour; (*residente*) resident.

veda ['beða] *nf* prohibition.

vedado [be'ðaðo] *nm* preserve.

vedar [be'ðar] *vt* (*prohibir*) to ban, prohibit; (*impedir*) to stop, prevent.

vegetación [bexeta'θjon] *nf* vegetation.

vegetariano, a [bexeta'rjano, a] *adj, nm/f* vegetarian.

vegetal [bexe'tal] *adj, nm* vegetable.

vehemencia [be(e)'menθja] *nf* (*insistencia*) vehemence; (*pasión*) passion; (*fervor*) fervour; (*violencia*) violence; **vehemente** *adj* vehement; passionate; fervent.

vehículo [be'ikulo] *nm* vehicle; (*MED*) carrier.

veía *etc vb ver* **ver**.

veinte ['beinte] *num* twenty.

vejación [bexa'θjon] *nf* vexation; (*humillación*) humiliation.

vejar [be'xar] *vt* (*irritar*) to annoy, vex; (*humillar*) to humiliate.

vejez [be'xeθ] *nf* old age.

vejiga [be'xiɣa] *nf* (*ANAT*) bladder.

vela ['bela] *nf* (*de cera*) candle; (*NAUT*) sail; (*insomnio*) sleeplessness; (*vigilia*) vigil; (*MIL*) sentry duty; **estar a dos ~s** (*fam*) to be skint.

velado, a [be'laðo, a] *adj* veiled; (*sonido*) muffled; (*FOTO*) blurred ♦ *nf* soirée.

velador [bela'ðor] *nm* (*mesa*) pedestal table; (*AM*) lampshade.

velar [be'lar] *vt* (*vigilar*) to keep watch over ♦ *vi* to stay awake; **~ por** to watch over, look after.

veleidad [belei'ðað] *nf* (*ligereza*) fickleness; (*capricho*) whim.

velero [be'lero] *nm* (*NAUT*) sailing ship; (*AVIAT*) glider.

veleta [be'leta] *nf* weather vane.

veliz [be'lis] (*AM*) *nm* suitcase.

velo ['belo] *nm* veil.

velocidad [beloθi'ðað] *nf* speed; (*TEC*, *AUTO*) gear.

velocímetro [belo'θimetro] *nm* speedometer.

veloz [be'loθ] *adj* fast.

vello ['beʎo] *nm* down, fuzz; **vellón** *nm* fleece; **~so, a** *adj* fuzzy; **velludo, a** *adj* shaggy.

ven *vb ver* **venir**.

vena ['bena] *nf* vein.

venado [be'naðo] *nm* deer.

vencedor, a [benθe'ðor, a] *adj* victorious ♦ *nm/f* victor, winner.

vencer [ben'θer] *vt* (*dominar*) to defeat, beat; (*derrotar*) to vanquish; (*superar*, *controlar*) to overcome, master ♦ *vi* (*triunfar*) to win (through), triumph; (*plazo*) to expire; **vencido, a** *adj* (*derrotado*) defeated, beaten; (*COM*) due ♦ *adv*: **pagar vencido** to pay in arrears; **vencimiento** *nm* (*COM*) maturity.

venda ['benda] *nf* bandage; **~je** *nm* bandage, dressing; **vendar** *vt* to bandage; **vendar los ojos** to blindfold.

vendaval [benda'βal] *nm* (*viento*) gale.

vendedor, a [bende'ðor, a] *nm/f* seller.

vender [ben'der] *vt* to sell; **~ al contado/al por mayor/al por menor** to sell for cash/wholesale/retail.

vendimia [ben'dimja] *nf* grape harvest.

vendré *etc vb ver* **venir**.

veneno [be'neno] *nm* poison; (*de serpiente*) venom; **~so, a** *adj* poisonous; venomous.

venerable [bene'raβle] *adj* venerable; **venerar** *vt* (*respetar*) to revere; (*adorar*) to worship.

venéreo, a [be'nereo, a] *adj*: **enfermedad venérea** venereal disease.

venezolano, a [beneθo'lano, a] *adj* Venezuelan.

Venezuela [bene'θwela] *nf* Venezuela.

venganza [ben'ganθa] *nf* vengeance, revenge; **vengar** *vt* to avenge; **vengarse** *vr* to take revenge; **vengativo, a** *adj* (*persona*) vindictive.

vengo *etc vb ver* **venir**.

venia ['benja] *nf* (*perdón*) pardon; (*permiso*) consent.

venial [be'njal] *adj* venial.

venida [be'niða] *nf* (*llegada*) arrival; (*regreso*) return.

venidero, a [beni'ðero, a] *adj* coming, future.

venir [be'nir] *vi* to come; *(llegar)* to arrive; *(ocurrir)* to happen; *(fig)*: ~ **de** to stem from; ~ **bien/mal** to be suitable/unsuitable; **el año que viene** next year; ~**se abajo** to collapse.

venta ['benta] *nf (COM)* sale; ~ **a plazos** hire purchase; ~ **al contado/al por mayor/al por menor** *o* **al detalle** cash sale/wholesale/retail; ~ **con derecho a retorno** sale or return; **"en ~"** "for sale".

ventaja [ben'taxa] *nf* advantage; **ventajoso, a** *adj* advantageous.

ventana [ben'tana] *nf* window; **ventanilla** *nf (de taquilla)* window *(of booking office etc).*

ventilación [bentila'θjon] *nf* ventilation; *(corriente)* draught; **ventilar** *vt* to ventilate; *(para secar)* to put out to dry; *(fig)* to air, discuss.

ventisca [ben'tiska] *nf* blizzard; *(nieve amontonada)* snowdrift.

ventisquero [bentis'kero] *nm* blizzard; snowdrift.

ventoso, a [ben'toso, a] *adj* windy.

ventrílocuo, a [ben'trilokwo, a] *nm/f* ventriloquist.

ventura [ben'tura] *nf (felicidad)* happiness; *(buena suerte)* luck; *(destino)* fortune; **a la (buena) ~** at random; **venturoso, a** *adj* happy; *(afortunado)* lucky, fortunate.

veo *etc vb ver* ver.

ver [ber] *vt* to see; *(mirar)* to look at, watch; *(entender)* to understand; *(investigar)* to look into; ♦ *vi* to see; to understand; ~**se** *vr (encontrarse)* to meet; *(dejarse ~)* to be seen; *(hallarse: en un apuro)* to find o.s., be ♦ *nm* looks *pl*, appearance; **a ~** let's see; **dejarse ~** to become apparent; **no tener nada que ~ con** to have nothing to do with; **a mi modo de ~** as I see it.

vera ['bera] *nf* edge, verge; *(de río)* bank.

veracidad [beraθi'ðað] *nf* truthfulness.

veranear [berane'ar] *vi* to spend the summer; **veraneo** *nm* summer holiday; **veraniego, a** *adj* summer *cpd*.

verano [be'rano] *nm* summer.

veras ['beras] *nfpl* truth *sg*; **de ~** really, truly.

veraz [be'raθ] *adj* truthful.

verbal [ber'βal] *adj* verbal.

verbena [ber'βena] *nf (fiesta)* fair; *(baile)* open-air dance.

verbo ['berβo] *nm* verb; ~**so, a** *adj* verbose.

verdad [ber'ðað] *nf* truth; *(fiabilidad)* reliability; **de ~** real, proper; **a decir ~** to tell the truth; ~**ero, a** *adj (veraz)* true, truthful; *(fiable)* reliable; *(fig)* real.

verde ['berðe] *adj* green; *(chiste)* blue, dirty ♦ *nm* green; **viejo ~** dirty old man; ~**ar** *vi* to turn green; ~**cer** *vi* to turn green; **verdor** *nm (lo ~)* greenness; *(BOT)* verdure.

verdugo [ber'ðuɣo] *nm* executioner.

verdulero, a [berðu'lero, a] *nm/f* greengrocer.

verduras [ber'ðuras] *nfpl (CULIN)* greens.

vereda [be'reða] *nf* path; *(AM)* pavement *(BRIT)*, sidewalk *(US)*.

veredicto [bere'ðikto] *nm* verdict.

vergonzoso, a [berɣon'θoso, a] *adj* shameful; *(tímido)* timid, bashful.

vergüenza [ber'ɣwenθa] *nf* shame, sense of shame; *(timidez)* bashfulness; *(pudor)* modesty; **me da ~** I'm a-shamed.

verídico, a [be'riðiko, a] *adj* true, truthful.

verificar [berifi'kar] *vt* to check; *(corroborar)* to verify; *(llevar a cabo)* to carry out; ~**se** *vr* to occur, happen.

verja ['berxa] *nf (cancela)* iron gate; *(valla)* iron railings *pl*; *(de ventana)* grille.

vermut [ber'mut] *(pl* ~**s)** *nm* vermouth.

verosímil [bero'simil] *adj* likely, probable; *(relato)* credible.

verruga [be'rruɣa] *nf* wart.

versado, a [ber'saðo, a] *adj*: ~ **en** versed in.

versátil [ber'satil] *adj* versatile.

versión [ber'sjon] *nf* version.

verso ['berso] *nm* verse; **un ~** a line of poetry.

vértebra ['berteβra] *nf* vertebra.

verter [ber'ter] *vt* (*líquido: adrede*) to empty, pour (out); (: *sin querer*) to spill; (*basura*) to dump ♦ *vi* to flow.

vertical [berti'kal] *adj* vertical.

vértice ['bertiθe] *nm* vertex, apex.

vertiente [ber'tjente] *nf* slope; (*fig*) aspect.

vertiginoso, a [bertixi'noso, a] *adj* giddy, dizzy.

vértigo ['bertiɣo] *nm* vertigo; (*mareo*) dizziness.

vesícula [be'sikula] *nf* blister.

vespertino, a [besper'tino, a] *adj* evening *cpd*.

vestíbulo [bes'tiβulo] *nm* hall; (*de teatro*) foyer.

vestido [bes'tiðo] *pp de* **vestir**; ~ **de azul/marinero** dressed in blue/as a sailor ♦ *nm* (*ropa*) clothes *pl*, clothing; (*de mujer*) dress, frock.

vestigio [bes'tixjo] *nm* (*huella*) trace; ~**s** *nmpl* (*restos*) remains.

vestimenta [besti'menta] *nf* clothing.

vestir [bes'tir] *vt* (*poner: ropa*) to put on; (*llevar: ropa*) to wear; (*proveer de ropa a*) to clothe; (*suj: sastre*) to make clothes for ♦ *vi* to dress; (*verse bien*) to look good; ~**se** *vr* to get dressed, dress o.s.

vestuario [bes'twarjo] *nm* clothes *pl*, wardrobe; (*TEATRO: cuarto*) dressing room; (*DEPORTE*) changing room.

veta ['beta] *nf* (*vena*) vein, seam; (*en carne*) streak; (*de madera*) grain.

vetar [be'tar] *vt* to veto.

veterano, a [bete'rano, a] *adj, nm* veteran.

veterinaria [beteri'narja] *nf* veterinary science; *ver tb* **veterinario**.

veterinario, a [beteri'narjo, a] *nm/f* vet(erinary surgeon).

veto ['beto] *nm* veto.

vetusto, a [be'tusto, a] *adj* ancient.

vez [beθ] *nf* time; (*turno*) turn; **a la** ~ **que** at the same time as; **a su** ~ in its turn; **otra** ~ again; **una** ~ once; **de una** ~ in one go; **de una** ~ **para siempre** once and for all; **en** ~ **de** instead of; **a** *o* **algunas veces** sometimes; **una y otra**

~ repeatedly; **de** ~ **en cuando** from time to time; **7 veces 9** 7 times 9; **hacer las veces de** to stand in for; **tal** ~ perhaps.

vía ['bia] *nf* track, route; (*FERRO*) line; (*fig*) way; (*ANAT*) passage, tube ♦ *prep* via, by way of; **por** ~ **judicial** by legal means; **por** ~ **oficial** through official channels; **en** ~**s de** in the process of; ~ **aérea** airway; **V~ Láctea** Milky Way.

viaducto [bja'ðukto] *nm* viaduct.

viajante [bja'xante] *nm* commercial traveller.

viajar [bja'xar]· *vi* to travel; **viaje** *nm* journey; (*gira*) tour; (*NAUT*) voyage; **estar de viaje** to be on a journey; **viaje de ida y vuelta** round trip; **viaje de novios** honeymoon; **viajero, a** *adj* travelling; (*ZOOL*) migratory ♦ *nm/f* (*quien viaja*) traveller; (*pasajero*) passenger.

vial [bjal] *adj* road *cpd*, traffic *cpd*.

víbora ['biβora] *nf* viper; (*AM*) poisonous snake.

vibración [biβra'θjon] *nf* vibration; **vibrador** *nm* vibrator; **vibrante** *adj* vibrant.

vibrar [bi'βrar] *vt, vi* to vibrate.

vicario [bi'karjo] *nm* curate.

vicegerente [biθexe'rente] *nm* assistant manager.

vicepresidente [biθepresi'ðente] *nm/f* vice-president.

viceversa [biθe'βersa] *adv* vice versa.

viciado, a [bi'θjaðo, a] *adj* (*corrompido*) corrupt; (*contaminado*) foul, contaminated; **viciar** *vt* (*pervertir*) to pervert; (*JUR*) to nullify; (*estropear*) to spoil; **viciarse** *vr* to become corrupted.

vicio ['biθjo] *nm* vice; (*mala costumbre*) bad habit; ~**so, a** *adj* (*muy malo*) vicious; (*corrompido*) depraved ♦ *nm/f* depraved person.

vicisitud [biθisi'tuð] *nf* vicissitude.

víctima ['biktima] *nf* victim.

victoria [bik'torja] *nf* victory; **victorioso, a** *adj* victorious.

vicuña [bi'kuɲa] *nf* vicuna.

vid [bið] *nf* vine.

vida ['biða] *nf* (*gen*) life; (*duración*) lifetime; **de por** ~ for life; **en la/mi** ~

never; **estar con** ~ to be still alive; **ganarse la** ~ to earn one's living.

vídeo ['biðeo] *nm* video ♦ *adj inv*: **película** ~ video film.

vidriero, a [bi'ðrjero, a] *nm/f* glazier ♦ *nf* (*ventana*) stained-glass window; (*AM: de tienda*) shop window; (*puerta*) glass door.

vidrio ['biðrjo] *nm* glass; ~**so, a** *adj* glassy.

vieira ['bjeira] *nf* scallop.

viejo, a ['bjexo, a] *adj* old ♦ *nm/f* old man/woman; **hacerse** ~ to get old.

Viena ['bjena] *n* Vienna.

vienes *etc vb ver* **venir**.

vienés, esa [bje'nes, esa] *adj* Viennese.

viento ['bjento] *nm* wind; **hacer** ~ to be windy.

vientre ['bjentre] *nm* belly; (*matriz*) womb.

viernes ['bjernes] *nm inv* Friday; **V~** Santo Good Friday.

Vietnam [bjet'nam] *nm*: **el** ~ Vietnam; **vietnamita** *adj* Vietnamese.

viga ['biɣa] *nf* beam, rafter; (*de metal*) girder.

vigencia [bi'xenθja] *nf* validity; **estar en** ~ to be in force; **vigente** *adj* valid, in force; (*imperante*) prevailing.

vigésimo, a [bi'xesimo, a] *adj* twentieth.

vigía [bi'xia] *nm* look-out ♦ *nf* (*atalaya*) watchtower; (*acción*) watching.

vigilancia [bixi'lanθja] *nf*: **tener a uno bajo** ~ to keep watch on sb.

vigilar [bixi'lar] *vt* to watch over ♦ *vi* (*gen*) to be vigilant; (*hacer guardia*) to keep watch; ~ **por** to take care of.

vigilia [vi'xilja] *nf* wakefulness, being awake; (*REL*) fast.

vigor [bi'ɣor] *nm* vigour, vitality; **en** ~ in force; **entrar/poner en** ~ to come/put into effect; ~**oso, a** *adj* vigorous.

vil [bil] *adj* vile, low; ~**eza** *nf* vileness; (*acto*) base deed.

vilipendiar [bilipen'djar] *vt* to vilify, revile.

vilo ['bilo]: **en** ~ *adv* in the air, suspended; (*fig*) on tenterhooks, in suspense.

villa ['biʎa] *nf* (*casa*) villa; (*pueblo*) small town; (*municipalidad*) municipality; ~ **miseria** (*AM*) shantytown.

villancico [biʎan'θiko] *nm* (Christmas) carol.

villorrio [bi'ʎorjo] (*AM*) *nm* shantytown.

vinagre [bi'navre] *nm* vinegar; ~**ras** *nfpl* cruet *sg*.

vinagreta [bina'vreta] *nf* vinaigrette, French dressing.

vinatero, a [bina'tero, a] *adj* wine *cpd* ♦ *nm* wine merchant.

vinculación [binkula'θjon] *nf* (*lazo*) link, bond; (*acción*) linking.

vincular [binku'lar] *vt* to link, bind; **vínculo** *nm* link, bond.

vine *etc vb ver* **venir**.

vinicultura [binikul'tura] *nf* wine growing.

viniera *etc vb ver* **venir**.

vino ['bino] *vb ver* **venir** ♦ *nm* wine; ~ **blanco/tinto** white/red wine.

viña ['bina] *nf* vineyard; **viñedo** *nm* vineyard.

viola ['bjola] *nf* viola.

violación [bjola'θjon] *nf* violation; (*estupro*): ~ (**sexual**) rape.

violar [bjo'lar] *vt* to violate; (*cometer estupro*) to rape.

violencia [bjo'lenθja] *nf* (*fuerza*) violence, force; (*embarazo*) embarrassment; (*acto injusto*) unjust act; **violentar** *vt* to force; (*casa*) to break into; (*agredir*) to assault; (*violar*) to violate; **violento, a** *adj* violent; (*furioso*) furious; (*situación*) embarrassing; (*acto*) forced, unnatural.

violeta [bjo'leta] *nf* violet.

violín [bjo'lin] *nm* violin.

violón [bjo'lon] *nm* double bass.

viraje [bi'raxe] *nm* turn; (*de vehículo*) swerve; (*de carretera*) bend; (*fig*) change of direction; **virar** *vi* to change direction.

virgen ['birxen] *adj, nf* virgin.

Virgo ['birvo] *nm* Virgo.

viril [bi'ril] *adj* virile; ~**idad** *nf* virility.

virtualmente [birtwal'mente] *adv* virtually.

virtud [bir'tuð] *nf* virtue; **en** ~ **de** by

virtue of; **virtuoso, a** *adj* virtuous ♦ *nm/f* virtuoso.

viruela [bi'rwela] *nf* smallpox; **~s** *nfpl* (*granos*) pockmarks.

virulento, a [biru'lento, a] *adj* virulent.

virus ['birus] *nm inv* virus.

visa ['bisa] (*AM*) *nf* = visado.

visado [bi'saðo] *nm* visa.

viscoso, a [bis'koso, a] *adj* viscous.

visera [bi'sera] *nf* visor.

visibilidad [bisiβili'ðað] *nf* visibility; **visible** *adj* visible; (*fig*) obvious.

visillos [bi'siλos] *nmpl* lace curtains.

visión [bi'sjon] *nf* (*ANAT*) vision, (eye)sight; (*fantasía*) vision, fantasy;

visionario, a *adj* (*que prevé*) visionary; (*alucinado*) deluded ♦ *nm/f* visionary.

visita [bi'sita] *nf* call, visit; (*persona*) visitor; **hacer una ~** to pay a visit.

visitar [bisi'tar] *vt* to visit, call on.

vislumbrar [bislum'brar] *vt* to glimpse, catch a glimpse of; **vislumbre** *nf* glimpse; (*centelleo*) gleam; (*idea vaga*) glimmer.

viso ['biso] *nm* (*del metal*) glint, gleam; (*de tela*) sheen; (*aspecto*) appearance.

visón [bi'son] *nm* mink.

visor [bi'sor] *nm* (*FOTO*) viewfinder.

víspera ['bispera] *nf*: **la ~ de ...** the day before ....

vista ['bista] *nf* sight, vision; (*capacidad de ver*) (eye)sight; (*mirada*) look(s) (*pl*) ♦ *nm* customs officer; **a primera ~** at first glance; **hacer la ~ gorda** to turn a blind eye; **volver la ~ atrás** to look back; **está a la ~ que** it's obvious that; **en ~ de** in view of; **en ~ de que** in view of the fact that; **¡hasta la ~!** so long!, see you!; **con ~s a** with a view to; **~zo** *nm* glance; **dar** o **echar un ~zo a** to glance at.

visto, a ['bisto, a] *pp de* **ver** ♦ *vb ver tb* **vestir** ♦ *adj* seen; (*considerado*) considered ♦ *nm*: **~ bueno** approval; **"~ bueno"** "approved"; **por lo ~** apparently; **está ~ que** it's clear that; **está bien/mal ~** it's acceptable/unacceptable; **~ que** since, considering that.

vistoso, a [bis'toso, a] *adj* colourful.

vital [bi'tal] *adj* life *cpd*, living *cpd*; (*fig*) vital; (*persona*) lively, vivacious; **~icio, a** *adj* for life.

vitamina [bita'mina] *nf* vitamin.

viticultor, a [bitikul'tor, a] *nm/f* wine grower; **viticultura** *nf* wine growing.

vitorear [bitore'ar] *vt* to cheer, acclaim.

vítreo, a ['bitreo, a] *adj* vitreous.

vitrina [bi'trina] *nf* show case; (*AM*) shop window.

vituperio [bitu'perjo] *nm* (*condena*) condemnation; (*censura*) censure; (*insulto*) insult.

viudo, a ['bjuðo, a] *nm/f* widower/widow; **viudez** *nf* widowhood.

vivacidad [biβaθi'ðað] *nf* (*vigor*) vigour; (*vida*) liveliness.

vivaracho, a [biβa'ratʃo, a] *adj* jaunty, lively; (*ojos*) bright, twinkling.

vivaz [bi'βaθ] *adj* lively.

víveres ['biβeres] *nmpl* provisions.

vivero [bi'βero] *nm* (*para plantas*) nursery; (*para peces*) fish farm; (*fig*) hotbed.

viveza [bi'βeθa] *nf* liveliness, (*agudeza: mental*) sharpness.

vivienda [bi'βjenda] *nf* housing; (*una ~*) house; (*piso*) flat (*BRIT*), apartment (*US*).

viviente [bi'βjente] *adj* living.

vivir [bi'βir] *vt, vi* to live ♦ *nm* life, living.

vivo, a ['biβo, a] *adj* living, alive; (*fig*: *descripción*) vivid; (*persona: astuto*) smart, clever; **en ~** (*transmisión etc*) live.

vocablo [bo'kaβlo] *nm* (*palabra*) word; (*término*) term.

vocabulario [bokaβu'larjo] *nm* vocabulary.

vocación [boka'θjon] *nf* vocation; **vocacional** (*AM*) *nf* ≈ technical college.

vocal [bo'kal] *adj* vocal ♦ *nf* vowel; **~izar** *vt* to vocalize.

vocear [boθe'ar] *vt* (*para vender*) to cry; (*aclamar*) to acclaim; (*fig*) to proclaim ♦ *vi* to yell; **vocería** *nf* = **vocerío**; **vocerío** *nm* shouting.

vocero [bo'θero] *nm/f* spokesman/woman.

voces ['boθes] *pl de* **voz**.
vociferar [boθife'rar] *vt* to shout ♦ *vi* to yell.
vodka ['boðka] *nm o f* vodka.
vol *abr* = **volumen**.
volador, a [bola'ðor, a] *adj* flying.
volandas [bo'landas]: **en ~** *adv* in the air; (*fig*) swiftly.
volante [bo'lante] *adj* flying ♦ *nm* (*de coche*) steering wheel; (*de reloj*) balance.
volar [bo'lar] *vt* (*edificio*) to blow up ♦ *vi* to fly.
volátil [bo'latil] *adj* volatile.
volcán [bol'kan] *nm* volcano; ~**ico, a** *adj* volcanic.
volcar [bol'kar] *vt* to upset, overturn; (*tumbar, derribar*) to knock over; (*vaciar*) to empty out ♦ *vi* to overturn; ~**se** *vr* to tip over.
voleíbol [bolei'βol] *nm* volleyball.
volqué *etc vb ver* **volcar**.
volquete [bol'kete] *nm* (*carro*) tipcart; (*AUTO*) dumper.
voltaje [bol'taxe] *nm* voltage.
voltear [bolte'ar] *vt* to turn over; (*volcar*) to turn upside down.
voltereta [bolte'reta] *nf* somersault.
voltio ['boltjo] *nm* volt.
voluble [bo'luβle] *adj* fickle.
volumen [bo'lumen] (*pl* **volúmenes**) *nm* volume; **voluminoso, a** *adj* voluminous; (*enorme*) massive.
voluntad [bolun'taδ] *nf* will; (*resolución*) willpower; (*deseo*) desire, wish.
voluntario, a [bolun'tarjo, a] *adj* voluntary ♦ *nm/f* volunteer.
voluntarioso, a [bolunta'rjoso, a] *adj* headstrong.
voluptuoso, a [bolup'twoso, a] *adj* voluptuous.
volver [bol'βer] *vt* (*gen*) to turn; (*dar vuelta a*) to turn (over); (*voltear*) to turn round, turn upside down; (*poner al revés*) to turn inside out; (*devolver*) to return ♦ *vi* to return, go back, come back; ~**se** *vr* to turn round; ~ **la espalda** to turn one's back; ~ **triste** *etc* **a uno** to make sb sad *etc*; ~ **a hacer** to do again; ~ **en sí** to come to; ~**se**

insoportable/muy caro to get *o* become unbearable/very expensive; ~**se loco** to go mad.
vomitar [bomi'tar] *vt, vi* to vomit; **vómito** *nm* (*acto*) vomiting; (*resultado*) vomit.
voraz [bo'raθ] *adj* voracious.
vórtice ['bortiθe] *nm* whirlpool; (*de aire*) whirlwind.
vos [bos] (*AM*) *pron* you.
vosotros, as [bo'sotros, as] *pron* you; (*reflexivo*): **entre/para ~** among/for yourselves.
votación [bota'θjon] *nf* (*acto*) voting; (*voto*) vote.
votar [bo'tar] *vi* to vote; **voto** *nm* vote; (*promesa*) vow; **votos** (good) wishes.
voy *vb ver* **ir**.
voz [boθ] *nf* voice; (*grito*) shout; (*chisme*) rumour; (*LING*) word; **dar voces** to shout, yell; **a media ~** in a low voice; **a ~ en cuello** *o* **en grito** at the top of one's voice; **de viva ~** verbally; **en ~ alta** aloud; ~ **de mando** command.
vuelco ['bwelko] *vb ver* **volcar** ♦ *nm* spill, overturning.
vuelo ['bwelo] *vb ver* **volar** ♦ *nm* flight; (*encaje*) lace, frill; **coger al ~** to catch in flight; ~ **charter/regular** charter/scheduled flight.
vuelque *etc vb ver* **volcar**.
vuelta ['bwelta] *nf* (*gen*) turn; (*curva*) bend, curve; (*regreso*) return; (*revolución*) revolution; (*circuito*) lap; (*de papel, tela*) reverse; (*cambio*) change; **a la ~** on one's return; **a ~ de correo** by return of post; **dar ~s** (*suj: cabeza*) to spin; **dar ~s a una idea** to turn over an idea (in one's head); **estar de ~** to be back; **dar una ~** to go for a walk; (*en coche*) to go for a drive.
vuelto *pp de* **volver**.
vuelvo *etc vb ver* **volver**.
vuestro, a ['bwestro, a] *adj* your; **un amigo ~** a friend of yours ♦ *pron*: **el ~/la vuestra, los ~s/las vuestras** yours.
vulgar [bul'γar] *adj* (*ordinario*) vulgar; (*común*) common; ~**idad** *nf* commonness; (*acto*) vulgarity; (*expresión*)

coarse expression; **~idades** *nfpl* (*banalidades*) banalities; **~izar** *vt* to popularize.

vulgo ['bulɣo] *nm* common people.

vulnerable [bulne'raßle] *adj* vulnerable.

W

wáter ['bater] *nm* toilet.

whisky ['wiski] *nm* whisky, whiskey.

X

xenofobia [kseno'foßja] *nf* xenophobia.

xilófono [ksi'lofono] *nm* xylophone.

Y

y [i] *conj* and.

ya [ja] *adv* (*gen*) already; (*ahora*) now; (*en seguida*) at once; (*pronto*) soon ♦ *excl* all right! ♦ *conj* (*ahora que*) now that; **~ lo sé** I know; **~ que** since.

yacer [ja'θer] *vi* to lie.

yacimiento [jaθi'mjento] *nm* deposit.

yanqui ['janki] *adj, nm/f* Yankee.

yate ['jate] *nm* yacht.

yazco *etc vb ver* **yacer**.

yedra ['jeðra] *nf* ivy.

yegua ['jeɣwa] *nf* mare.

yema ['jema] *nf* (*del huevo*) yoke; (*BOT*) leaf bud; (*fig*) best part; **~ del dedo** fingertip.

yergo *etc vb ver* **erguir**.

yermo, a ['jermo, a] *adj* (*despoblado*) uninhabited; (*estéril, fig*) barren ♦ *nm* wasteland.

yerno ['jerno] *nm* son-in-law.

yerro *etc vb ver* **errar**.

yerto, a ['jerto, a] *adj* stiff.

yesca ['jeska] *nf* tinder.

yeso ['jeso] *nm* (*GEO*) gypsum; (*ARQ*) plaster.

yodo ['joðo] *nm* iodine.

yogur(t) [jo'ɣur(t)] *nm* yoghurt.

yugo ['juɣo] *nm* yoke.

Yugoslavia [juɣos'laßja] *nf* Yugoslavia.

yugular [juɣu'lar] *adj* jugular.

yunque ['junke] *nm* anvil.

yunta ['junta] *nf* yoke; **yuntero** *nm* ploughman.

yute ['jute] *nm* jute.

yuxtaponer [jukstapo'ner] *vt* to juxtapose; **yuxtaposición** *nf* juxtaposition.

Z

zafar [θa'far] *vt* (*soltar*) to untie; (*superficie*) to clear; **~se** *vr* (*escaparse*) to escape; (*TEC*) to slip off.

zafio, a ['θafjo, a] *adj* coarse.

zafiro [θa'firo] *nm* sapphire.

zaga ['θaɣa] *nf*: **a la ~** behind, in the rear.

zagal, a [θa'ɣal, a] *nm/f* boy/girl, lad/lass (*BRIT*).

zaguán [θa'ɣwan] *nm* hallway.

zaherir [θae'rir] *vt* (*criticar*) to criticize.

zahorí [θao'ri] *nm* clairvoyant.

zaino, a ['θaino, a] *adj* (*color de caballo*) chestnut.

zalamería [θalame'ria] *nf* flattery; **zalamero, a** *adj* flattering; (*relamido*) suave.

zamarra [θa'marra] *nf* (*piel*) sheepskin; (*chaqueta*) sheepskin jacket.

zambullirse [θambu'ʎirse] *vr* to dive; (*ocultarse*) to hide o.s.

zampar [θam'par] *vt* to gobble down ♦ *vi* gobble (up).

zanahoria [θana'orja] *nf* carrot.

zancada [θan'kaða] *nf* stride.

zancadilla [θanka'ðiʎa] *nf* trip; (*fig*) stratagem.

zanco ['θanko] *nm* stilt.

zancudo, a [θan'kuðo, a] *adj* long-legged ♦ *nm* (*AM*) mosquito.

zángano ['θanɣano] *nm* drone.

zanja ['θanxa] *nf* ditch; **zanjar** *vt* (*superar*) to surmount; (*resolver*) to resolve.

zapata [θa'pata] *nf* half-boot; (*MECÁNICA*) shoe.

zapatear [θapate'ar] *vi* to tap with one's feet.

zapatería [θapate'ria] *nf* (*oficio*) shoe-making; (*tienda*) shoe shop; (*fábrica*) shoe factory; **zapatero, a** *nm/f* shoemaker.

zapatilla [θapa'tiʎa] *nf* slipper.

zapato [θa'pato] *nm* shoe.

zar [θar] *nm* tsar, czar.

zarandear [θarande'ar] (*fam*) *vt* to shake vigorously.

zarpa ['θarpa] *nf* (*garra*) claw.

zarpar [θar'par] *vi* to weigh anchor.

zarza ['θarθa] *nf* (*BOT*) bramble; **zarzal** *nm* (*matorral*) bramble patch.

zarzamora [θarθa'mora] *nf* blackberry.

zarzuela [θar'θwela] *nf* Spanish light opera.

zigzag [θiɣ'θaɣ] *adj* zigzag; **zigzaguear** *vi* to zigzag.

zinc [θink] *nm* zinc.

zócalo ['θokalo] *nm* (*ARQ*) plinth, base.

zona ['θona] *nf* zone; ~ **fronteriza** border area.

zoo ['θoo] *nm* zoo.

zoología [θoolo'xia] *nf* zoology;

zoológico, a *adj* zoological ♦ *nm* (*tb*: *parque* ~) zoo; **zoólogo, a** *nm/f* zoologist.

zoom [θum] *nm* zoom lens.

zopenco, a [θo'penko, a] *nm/f* fool.

zopilote [θopi'lote] (*AM*) *nm* buzzard.

zoquete [θo'kete] *nm* (*madera*) block; (*fam*) blockhead.

zorro, a ['θorro, a] *adj* crafty ♦ *nm/f* fox/vixen.

zozobra [θo'θoβra] *nf* (*fig*) anxiety; **zozobrar** *vi* (*hundirse*) to capsize; (*fig*) to fail.

zueco ['θweko] *nm* clog.

zumbar [θum'bar] *vt* (*golpear*) to hit ♦ *vi* to buzz; **zumbido** *nm* buzzing.

zumo ['θumo] *nm* juice.

zurcir [θur'θir] *vt* (*coser*) to darn.

zurdo, a ['θurðo, a] *adj* (*mano*) left; (*persona*) left-handed.

zurrar [θu'rrar] (*fam*) *vt* to wallop.

zurrón [θu'rron] *nm* pouch.

zutano, a [θu'tano, a] *nm/f* so-and-so.

ENGLISH-SPANISH
INGLÉS-ESPAÑOL

A

A [eɪ] *n* (*MUS*) la *m*.

a [ə] *indef art* (*before vowel or silent h: an*) **1** un(a); ~ **book** un libro; **an apple** una manzana; **she's** ~ **doctor** (ella) es médica

2 (*instead of the number "one"*) un(a); ~ **year ago** hace un año; ~ **hundred/thousand** *etc* **pounds** cien/mil *etc* libras

3 (*in expressing ratios, prices etc*): 3 ~ **day/week** 3 al día/a la semana; **10 km an hour** 10 km por hora; £5 ~ **person** £5 por persona; **30p** ~ **kilo** 30p el kilo.

A.A. *n abbr* (= *Automobile Association: BRIT*) ≈ RACE *m* (*SP*); (= *Alcoholics Anonymous*) Alcohólicos Anónimos.

A.A.A. (*US*) *n abbr* (= *American Automobile Association*) ≈ RACE *m* (*SP*).

aback [ə'bæk] *adv*: **to be taken** ~ quedar desconcertado.

abandon [ə'bændən] *vt* abandonar; (*give up*) renunciar a ♦ *n* abandono; (*wild behaviour*): **with** ~ sin reparos.

abashed [ə'bæʃt] *adj* avergonzado.

abate [ə'beɪt] *vi* (*storm*) amainar; (*anger*) aplacarse; (*terror*) disminuir.

abattoir ['æbətwɑ:*] (*BRIT*) *n* matadero.

abbey ['æbɪ] *n* abadía.

abbot ['æbət] *n* abad *m*.

abbreviate [ə'bri:vɪeɪt] *vt* abreviar; **abbreviation** [-'eɪʃən] *n* (*short form*) abreviatura.

abdicate ['æbdɪkeɪt] *vt* renunciar a ♦ *vi* abdicar; **abdication** [-'keɪʃən] *n* renuncia; (*of monarch*) abdicación *f*.

abdomen ['æbdəmən] *n* abdomen *m*.

abduct [æb'dʌkt] *vt* raptar, secuestrar.

abet [ə'bet] *vt see* **aid**.

abeyance [ə'beɪəns] *n*: **in** ~ (*law*) en desuso; (*matter*) en suspenso.

abhor [əb'hɔ:*] *vt* aborrecer, abominar (de).

abide [ə'baɪd] *vt*: **I can't** ~ **it/him** no lo/le puedo ver; ~ **by** *vt fus* atenerse a.

ability [ə'bɪlɪtɪ] *n* habilidad *f*, capacidad *f*; (*talent*) talento.

abject ['æbdʒekt] *adj* (*poverty*) miserable; (*apology*) rastrero.

ablaze [ə'bleɪz] *adj* en llamas, ardiendo.

able ['eɪbl] *adj* capaz; (*skilled*) hábil; **to be** ~ **to do sth** poder hacer algo; ~-**bodied** *adj* sano; **ably** *adv* hábilmente.

abnormal [æb'nɔ:məl] *adj* anormal.

aboard [ə'bɔ:d] *adv* a bordo ♦ *prep* a bordo de.

abode [ə'bəud] *n*: **of no fixed** ~ sin domicilio fijo.

abolish [ə'bɔlɪʃ] *vt* suprimir, abolir; **abolition** [æbə'lɪʃən] *n* supresión *f*, abolición *f*.

aborigine [æbə'rɪdʒɪnɪ] *n* aborigen *m/f*.

abort [ə'bɔ:t] *vt*, *vi* abortar; ~**ion** [ə'bɔ:ʃən] *n* aborto; **to have an** ~**ion** abortar, hacerse abortar; ~**ive** *adj* malogrado.

abound [ə'baund] *vi*: **to** ~ (**in** *or* **with**) abundar (de *or* en).

about [ə'baut] *adv* **1** (*approximately*) más o menos, aproximadamente; ~ **a hundred/thousand** *etc* unos(unas) cien/mil *etc*; **it takes** ~ **10 hours** se tarda unas *or* más o menos 10 horas; **at** ~ **2 o'clock** sobre las dos; **I've just** ~ **finished** casi he terminado

2 (*referring to place*) por todas partes; **to leave things lying** ~ dejar las cosas (tiradas) por ahí; **to run** ~ correr por todas partes; **to walk** ~ pasearse, ir y venir

3: **to be** ~ **to do sth** estar a punto de

hacer algo
♦ *prep* **1** (*relating to*) de, sobre, acerca de; **a book ~ London** un libro sobre *or* acerca de Londres; **what is it ~?** ¿de qué se trata?, ¿qué pasa?; **we talked ~ it** hablamos de eso *or* ello; **what** *or* **how ~ doing this?** ¿qué tal si hacemos esto? **2** (*referring to place*) por; **to walk ~ the town** caminar por la ciudad.

above [ə'bʌv] *adv* encima, por encima, arriba ♦ *prep* encima de; (*greater than*: *in number*) más de; (: *in rank*) superior a; **mentioned ~** susodicho; **~ all** sobre todo; **~ board** *adj* legítimo.

abrasive [ə'breɪzɪv] *adj* abrasivo; (*manner*) brusco.

abreast [ə'brɛst] *adv* de frente; **to keep ~ of** (*fig*) mantenerse al corriente de.

abridge [ə'brɪdʒ] *vt* abreviar.

abroad [ə'brɔːd] *adv* (*to be*) en el extranjero; (*to go*) al extranjero.

abrupt [ə'brʌpt] *adj* (*sudden*) brusco; (*curt*) áspero.

abruptly [ə'brʌptlɪ] *adv* (*leave*) repentinamente; (*speak*) bruscamente.

abscess ['æbsɪs] *n* absceso.

abscond [əb'skɔnd] *vi* (*thief*): **to ~ with** fugarse con; (*prisoner*): **to ~ (from)** escaparse (de).

absence ['æbsəns] *n* ausencia.

absent ['æbsənt] *adj* ausente; **~ee** [-'tiː] *n* ausente *m/f*; **~-minded** *adj* distraído.

absolute ['æbsəluːt] *adj* absoluto; **~ly** [-'luːtlɪ] *adv* (*totally*) totalmente; (*certainly!*) ¡por supuesto (que sí)!

absolve [əb'zɔlv] *vt*: **to ~ sb (from)** absolver a alguien (de).

absorb [əb'zɔːb] *vt* absorber; **to be ~ed in a book** estar absorto en un libro; **~ent cotton** (*US*) *n* algodón *m* hidrófilo; **~ing** *adj* absorbente.

absorption [əb'zɔːpʃən] *n* absorción *f*.

abstain [əb'steɪn] *vi*: **to ~ (from)** abstenerse (de).

abstinence ['æbstɪnəns] *n* abstinencia.

abstract ['æbstrækt] *adj* abstracto.

abstruse [æb'struːs] *adj* oscuro.

absurd [əb'sɔːd] *adj* absurdo.

abundance [ə'bʌndəns] *n* abundancia.

abuse [*n* ə'bjuːs, *vb* ə'bjuːz] *n* (*insults*) insultos *mpl*, injurias *fpl*; (*ill-treatment*) malos tratos *mpl*; (*misuse*) abuso ♦ *vt* insultar; maltratar; abusar de; **abusive** *adj* ofensivo.

abysmal [ə'bɪzml] *adj* pésimo; (*failure*) garrafal; (*ignorance*) supino.

abyss [ə'bɪs] *n* abismo.

AC *abbr* (= *alternating current*) corriente *f* alterna.

academic [ækə'dɛmɪk] *adj* académico, universitario; (*pej*: *issue*) puramente teórico ♦ *n* estudioso/a; profesor(a) *m/f* universitario/a.

academy [ə'kædəmɪ] *n* (*learned body*) academia; (*school*) instituto, colegio; **~ of music** conservatorio.

accelerate [æk'sɛləreɪt] *vt*, *vi* acelerar; **accelerator** (*BRIT*) *n* acelerador *m*.

accent ['æksənt] *n* acento; (*fig*) énfasis *m*.

accept [ək'sɛpt] *vt* aceptar; (*responsibility*, *blame*) admitir; **~able** *adj* aceptable; **~ance** *n* aceptación *f*.

access ['æksɛs] *n* acceso; **to have ~ to** tener libre acceso a; **~ible** [-'sɛsəbl] *adj* (*place*, *person*) accesible; (*knowledge etc*) asequible.

accessory [æk'sɛsərɪ] *n* accesorio; (*LAW*): **~ to** cómplice de.

accident ['æksɪdənt] *n* accidente *m*; (*chance event*) casualidad *f*; **by ~** (*unintentionally*) sin querer; (*by chance*) por casualidad; **~al** [-'dɛntl] *adj* accidental, fortuito; **~ally** [-'dɛntəlɪ] *adv* sin querer; por casualidad; **~-prone** *adj* propenso a los accidentes.

acclaim [ə'kleɪm] *vt* aclamar, aplaudir ♦ *n* aclamación *f*, aplausos *mpl*.

acclimate [ə'klaɪmət] (*US*) *vt* = **acclimatize**.

acclimatize [ə'klaɪmətaɪz] (*BRIT*) *vt*: **to become ~d** aclimatarse.

accolade ['ækəleɪd] *n* premio.

accommodate [ə'kɔmədeɪt] *vt* (*subj*: *person*) alojar, hospedar; (: *car*, *hotel etc*) tener cabida para; (*oblige*, *help*) complacer; **accommodating** *adj* servicial, complaciente.

accommodation [əkɔmə'deɪʃən] *n* (*US*

accommodations *npl* alojamiento.
accompaniment [əˈkʌmpənɪmənt] *n* (MUS) acompañamiento.
accompany [əˈkʌmpənɪ] *vt* acompañar.
accomplice [əˈkʌmplɪs] *n* cómplice *m/f*.
accomplish [əˈkʌmplɪʃ] *vt* (finish) concluir; (achieve) lograr; ~ed *adj* experto, hábil; ~ment *n* (skill: gen pl) talento; (completion) realización *f*.
accord [əˈkɔːd] *n* acuerdo ♦ *vt* conceder; of his own ~ espontáneamente; ~ance *n*: in ~ance with de acuerdo con; ~ing: ~ing to prep según; (in accordance with) conforme a; ~ingly *adv* (appropriately) de acuerdo con esto; (as a result) en consecuencia.
accordion [əˈkɔːdɪən] *n* acordeón *m*.
accost [əˈkɔst] *vt* abordar, dirigirse a.
account [əˈkaʊnt] *n* (COMM) cuenta; (report) informe *m*; ~s *npl* (COMM) cuentas *fpl*; of no ~ de ninguna importancia; on ~ a cuenta; on no ~ bajo ningún concepto; on ~ of a causa de, por motivo de; to take into ~, take ~ of tener en cuenta; ~ for *vt fus* (explain) explicar; (represent) representar; ~able *adj*: ~able to responsable (ante).
accountancy [əˈkaʊntənsɪ] *n* contabilidad *f*.
accountant [əˈkaʊntənt] *n* contable *m/f*, contador(a) *m/f*.
account number *n* (at bank etc) número de cuenta.
accredited [əˈkrɛdɪtɪd] *adj* (agent etc) autorizado.
accrued interest [əˈkruːd-] *n* interés *m* acumulado.
accumulate [əˈkjuːmjʊleɪt] *vt* acumular ♦ *vi* acumularse.
accuracy [ˈækjʊrəsɪ] *n* (of total) exactitud *f*; (of description etc) precisión *f*.
accurate [ˈækjʊrɪt] *adj* (total) exacto; (description) preciso; (person) cuidadoso; (device) de precisión; ~ly *adv* con precisión.
accusation [ækjuːˈzeɪʃən] *n* acusación *f*.
accuse [əˈkjuːz] *vt*: to ~ sb (of sth) acusar a uno (de algo); ~d *n* (LAW) acusado/a.
accustom [əˈkʌstəm] *vt* acostumbrar;

~ed *adj*: ~ed to acostumbrado a.
ace [eɪs] *n* as *m*.
ache [eɪk] *n* dolor *m* ♦ *vi* doler; my head ~s me duele la cabeza.
achieve [əˈtʃiːv] *vt* (aim, result) alcanzar; (success) lograr, conseguir; ~ment *n* (completion) realización *f*; (success) éxito.
acid [ˈæsɪd] *adj* ácido; (taste) agrio ♦ *n* (CHEM, inf: LSD) ácido; ~ rain *n* lluvia ácida.
acknowledge [əkˈnɔlɪdʒ] *vt* (letter: also: ~ receipt of) acusar recibo de; (fact, situation, person) reconocer; ~ment *n* acuse *m* de recibo.
acne [ˈæknɪ] *n* acné *m*.
acorn [ˈeɪkɔːn] *n* bellota *f*.
acoustic [əˈkuːstɪk] *adj* acústico; ~s *n*, *npl* acústica *sg*.
acquaint [əˈkweɪnt] *vt*: to ~ sb with sth (inform) poner a uno al corriente de algo; to be ~ed with conocer; ~ance *n* (person) conocido/a; (with person, subject) conocimiento.
acquiesce [ækwɪˈɛs] *vi*: to ~ (to) consentir (en).
acquire [əˈkwaɪə*] *vt* adquirir; **acquisition** [ækwɪˈzɪʃən] *n* adquisición *f*.
acquit [əˈkwɪt] *vt* absolver, exculpar; to ~ o.s. well salir con éxito; ~tal *n* absolución *f*, exculpación *f*.
acre [ˈeɪkə*] *n* acre *m*.
acrid [ˈækrɪd] *adj* acre.
acrimonious [ækrɪˈməʊnɪəs] *adj* (remark) mordaz; (argument) reñido.
acrobat [ˈækrəbæt] *n* acróbata *m/f*.
acronym [ˈækrənɪm] *n* siglas *fpl*.
across [əˈkrɔs] *prep* (on the other side of) al otro lado de, del otro lado de; (crosswise) a través de ♦ *adv* de un lado a otro, de una parte a otra; a través, al través; (measurement): the road is 10m ~ la carretera tiene 10m de ancho; to run/swim ~ atravesar corriendo/nadando; ~ from enfrente de.
acrylic [əˈkrɪlɪk] *adj* acrílico ♦ *n* acrílica *f*.
act [ækt] *n* acto, acción *f*; (of play) acto; (in music hall etc) número; (LAW) decreto, ley *f* ♦ *vi* (behave) comportarse; (have effect: drug, chemical)

hacer efecto; (*THEATRE*) actuar; (*pretend*) fingir; (*take action*) obrar ♦ *vt* (*part*) hacer el papel de; **in the ~ of: to catch sb in the ~ of ...** pillar a uno en el momento en que ...; **to ~ as** actuar or hacer de; **~ing** *adj* suplente ♦ *n* (*activity*) actuación *f*; (*profession*) profesión *f* de actor.

action ['ækʃən] *n* acción *f*, acto; (*MIL*) acción *f*, batalla; (*LAW*) proceso, demanda; **out of ~** (*person*) fuera de combate; (*thing*) estropeado; **to take ~** tomar medidas; **~ replay** *n* (*TV*) repetición *f*.

activate ['æktɪveɪt] *vt* activar.

active ['æktɪv] *adj* activo, enérgico; (*volcano*) en actividad; **~ly** *adv* (*participate*) activamente; (*discourage, dislike*) enérgicamente; **activist** *n* activista *m/f*; **activity** [-'tɪvɪtɪ] *n* actividad *f*.

actor ['æktə*] *n* actor *m*.

actress ['æktrɪs] *n* actriz *f*.

actual ['æktjuəl] *adj* verdadero, real; (*emphatic use*) propiamente dicho; **~ly** *adv* realmente, en realidad; (*even*) incluso.

acumen ['ækjumən] *n* perspicacia.

acute [ə'kjuːt] *adj* agudo.

ad [æd] *n abbr* = **advertisement**.

A.D. *adv abbr* (= *anno Domini*) A.C.

adamant ['ædəmənt] *adj* firme, inflexible.

adapt [ə'dæpt] *vt* adaptar ♦ *vi*: **to ~ (to)** adaptarse (a), ajustarse (a); **~able** *adj* adaptable; **~er** or **~or** *n* (*ELEC*) adaptador *m*.

add [æd] *vt* añadir, agregar; (*figures: also*: **~ up**) sumar ♦ *vi*: **to ~ to** (*increase*) aumentar, acrecentar; **it doesn't ~ up** (*fig*) no tiene sentido.

adder ['ædə*] *n* víbora.

addict ['ædɪkt] *n* adicto/a; (*enthusiast*) entusiasta *m/f*; **~ed** [ə'dɪktɪd] *adj*: **to be ~ed to** ser adicto a; (*football etc*) ser fanático de; **~ion** [ə'dɪkʃən] *n* (*to drugs etc*) adicción *f*; **~ive** [ə'dɪktɪv] *adj* que causa adicción.

addition [ə'dɪʃən] *n* (*adding up*) adición *f*; (*thing added*) añadidura, añadido; **in ~** además, por añadidura; **in ~ to** ade-

más de; **~al** *adj* adicional.

additive ['ædɪtɪv] *n* aditivo.

address [ə'drɛs] *n* dirección *f*, señas *fpl*; (*speech*) discurso ♦ *vt* (*letter*) dirigir; (*speak to*) dirigirse a, dirigir la palabra a; (*problem*) tratar.

adept ['ædɛpt] *adj*: **~ at** experto or hábil en.

adequate ['ædɪkwɪt] *adj* (*satisfactory*) adecuado; (*enough*) suficiente.

adhere [əd'hɪə*] *vi*: **to ~ to** (*stick to*) pegarse a; (*fig: abide by*) observar; (*: belief etc*) ser partidario de.

adhesive [əd'hiːzɪv] *n* adhesivo; **~ tape** *n* (*BRIT*) cinta adhesiva; (*US: MED*) esparadrapo.

ad hoc [æd'hɔk] *adj* ad hoc.

adjacent [ə'dʒeɪsənt] *adj*: **~ to** contiguo a, inmediato a.

adjective ['ædʒɛktɪv] *n* adjetivo.

adjoining [ə'dʒɔɪnɪŋ] *adj* contiguo, vecino.

adjourn [ə'dʒɜːn] *vt* aplazar ♦ *vi* suspenderse.

adjudicate [ə'dʒuːdɪkeɪt] *vi* sentenciar.

adjust [ə'dʒʌst] *vt* (*change*) modificar; (*clothing*) arreglar; (*machine*) ajustar ♦ *vi*: **to ~ (to)** adaptarse (a); **~able** *adj* ajustable; **~ment** *n* adaptación *f*; (*to machine, prices*) ajuste *m*.

adjutant ['ædʒətənt] *n* ayudante *m*.

ad-lib [æd'lɪb] *vt, vi* improvisar; **ad lib** *adv* de forma improvisada.

administer [əd'mɪnɪstə*] *vt* administrar; **administration** [-'treɪʃən] *n* (*management*) administración *f*; (*government*) gobierno; **administrative** [-trətɪv] *adj* administrativo.

admiral ['ædmərəl] *n* almirante *m*; **A~ty** (*BRIT*) *n* Ministerio de Marina, Almirantazgo.

admiration [ædmə'reɪʃən] *n* admiración *f*.

admire [əd'maɪə*] *vt* admirar; **~r** *n* (*fan*) admirador(a) *m/f*.

admission [əd'mɪʃən] *n* (*to university, club*) ingreso; (*entry fee*) entrada; (*confession*) confesión *f*.

admit [əd'mɪt] *vt* (*confess*) confesar; (*permit to enter*) dejar entrar, dar entrada a; (to club, organization) admitir; (accept: defeat) reconocer; **to be ~ted to hospital** ingresar en el hospital; **~ to** vt fus confesarse culpable de; **'~tance** n entrada; **~tedly** adv es cierto or verdad que.

admonish [əd'mɔnɪʃ] vt amonestar.

ad nauseam [æd'nɔːsɪæm] adv hasta el cansancio.

ado [ə'duː] n: **without (any) more ~** sin más (ni más).

adolescent [ædəu'lɛsnt] adj, n adolescente m/f.

adopt [ə'dɔpt] vt adoptar; **~ed** adj adoptivo; **~ive** adj adoptivo; **~ion** [ə'dɔpʃən] n adopción f.

adore [ə'dɔː*] vt adorar.

Adriatic [eɪdrɪ'ætɪk] n: **the ~ (Sea)** el (Mar) Adriático.

adrift [ə'drɪft] adv a la deriva.

adult ['ædʌlt] n adulto/a ♦ adj (grown-up) adulto; (for adults) para adultos.

adultery [ə'dʌltərɪ] n adulterio.

advance [əd'vɑːns] n (progress) adelanto, progreso; (money) anticipo, préstamo; (MIL) avance m ♦ adj: **~ booking** venta anticipada; **~ notice, ~ warning** previo aviso ♦ vt (money) anticipar; (theory, idea) proponer (para la discusión) ♦ vi avanzar, adelantarse; **to make ~s (to sb)** hacer proposiciones a alguien; **in ~** por adelantado; **~d** adj avanzado; (SCOL: studies) adelantado; **~ment** n progreso; (in job) ascenso.

advantage [əd'vɑːntɪdʒ] n (also TENNIS) ventaja; **to take ~ of** (person) aprovecharse de; (opportunity) aprovechar; **~ous** [ædvən'teɪdʒəs] adj: **~ous (to)** ventajoso (para).

Advent ['ædvənt] n (REL) Adviento.

adventure [əd'vɛntʃə*] n aventura; **adventurous** [-tʃərəs] adj atrevido; aventurero.

adverb ['ædvəːb] n adverbio.

adverse ['ædvəːs] adj adverso, contrario.

adversity [əd'vəːsɪtɪ] n infortunio.

advert ['ædvəːt] (BRIT) n abbr = **advertisement.**

advertise ['ædvətaɪz] vi (in newspaper etc) anunciar, hacer publicidad; **to ~ for** (staff, accommodation etc) buscar por medio de anuncios ♦ vt anunciar; **~ment** [əd'vəːtɪsmənt] n (COMM) anuncio; **~r** n anunciante m/f; **advertising** n publicidad f, anuncios mpl; (industry) industria publicitaria.

advice [əd'vaɪs] n consejo, consejos mpl; (notification) aviso; **a piece of ~** un consejo; **to take legal ~** consultar con un abogado.

advisable [əd'vaɪzəbl] adj aconsejable, conveniente.

advise [əd'vaɪz] vt aconsejar; (inform): **to ~ sb of sth** informar a uno de algo; **to ~ sb against sth/doing sth** desaconsejar algo a uno/aconsejar a uno que no haga algo; **~dly** [əd'vaɪzɪdlɪ] adv (deliberately) deliberadamente; **~r** n = **advisor; advisor** n consejero/a; (consultant) asesor(a) m/f; **advisory** adj consultivo.

advocate ['ædvəkeɪt] vt abogar por ♦ n [-kɪt] (lawyer) abogado/a; (supporter): **~ of** defensor(a) m/f de.

Aegean [iː'dʒiːən] n: **the ~ (Sea)** el (Mar) Egeo.

aerial ['ɛərɪəl] n antena ♦ adj aéreo.

aerobics [ɛə'rəubɪks] n aerobic m.

aeroplane ['ɛərəpleɪn] (BRIT) n avión m.

aerosol ['ɛərəsɔl] n aerosol m.

aesthetic [iːs'θɛtɪk] adj estético.

afar [ə'fɑː*] adv: **from ~** desde lejos.

affair [ə'fɛə*] n asunto; (also: love ~) aventura (amorosa).

affect [ə'fɛkt] vt (influence) afectar, influir en; (afflict, concern) afectar; (move) conmover; **~ed** adj afectado.

affection [ə'fɛkʃən] n afecto, cariño; **~ate** adj afectuoso, cariñoso.

affiliated [əfɪlɪ'eɪtɪd] adj afiliado.

affinity [ə'fɪnɪtɪ] n (bond, rapport): **to feel an ~ with** sentirse identificado con; (resemblance) afinidad f.

affix [ə'fɪks] vt pegar.

afflict [ə'flɪkt] vt afligir.

affluence ['æfluəns] n opulencia, riqueza.

affluent ['æfluənt] adj (wealthy) acomodado; **the ~ society** la sociedad opulenta.

afford [ə'fɔːd] *vt* (*provide*) proporcionar; **can we ~ (to buy) it?** ¿tenemos bastante dinero para comprarlo?
affront [ə'frʌnt] *n* afrenta, ofensa.
Afghanistan [æf'gænɪstæn] *n* Afganistán *m*.
afield [ə'fiːld] *adv*: **far ~** muy lejos.
afloat [ə'fləʊt] *adv* (*floating*) a flote.
afoot [ə'fʊt] *adv*: **there is something ~** algo se está tramando.
afraid [ə'freɪd] *adj*: **to be ~ of** (*person*) tener miedo a; (*thing*) tener miedo de; **to be ~ to** tener miedo de, temer; **I am ~ that** me temo que; **I am ~ not/so** lo siento, pero no/es así.
afresh [ə'freʃ] *adv* de nuevo, otra vez.
Africa ['æfrɪkə] *n* África; **~n** *adj*, *n* africano/a *m/f*.
aft [ɑːft] *adv* (*to be*) en popa; (*to go*) a popa.
after ['ɑːftə*] *prep* (*time*) después de; (*place, order*) detrás de, tras ♦ *adv* después ♦ *conj* después (de) que; **what/who are you ~?** ¿qué/a quién busca usted?; **~ having done/he left** después de haber hecho/después de que se marchó; **to name sb ~ sb** llamar a uno por uno; **it's twenty ~ eight** (*US*) son las ocho y veinte; **to ask ~ sb** preguntar por alguien; **~ all** después de todo, al fin y al cabo; **~ you!** ¡pase usted!; **~-effects** *npl* consecuencias *fpl*, efectos *mpl*; **~math** *n* consecuencias *fpl*, resultados *mpl*; **~noon** *n* tarde *f*; **~s** (*inf*) *n* (*dessert*) postre *m*; **~-sales service** (*BRIT*) *n* servicio de asistencia pos-venta; **~-shave (lotion)** *n* aftershave *m*; **~thought** *n* ocurrencia (tardía); **~wards** (*US* **~ward**) *adv* después, más tarde.
again [ə'gen] *adv* otra vez, de nuevo; **to do sth ~** volver a hacer algo; **~ and ~** una y otra vez.
against [ə'genst] *prep* (*in opposition to*) en contra de; (*leaning on, touching*) contra, junto a.
age [eɪdʒ] *n* edad *f*; (*period*) época ♦ *vi* envejecer(se) ♦ *vt* envejecer; **she is 20 years of ~** tiene 20 años; **to come of ~** llegar a la mayoría de edad; **it's been**

~s since I saw you hace siglos que no te veo; **~d 10 de 10 años de edad; the ~d** ['eɪdʒɪd] *npl* los ancianos; **~ group** *n*: **to be in the same ~ group** tener la misma edad; **~ limit** *n* edad *f* mínima (*or* máxima).
agency ['eɪdʒənsɪ] *n* agencia.
agenda [ə'dʒendə] *n* orden *m* del día.
agent ['eɪdʒənt] *n* agente *m/f*; (*COMM: holding concession*) representante *m/f*, delegado/a; (*CHEM, fig*) agente *m*.
aggravate ['ægrəveɪt] *vt* (*situation*) agravar; (*person*) irritar.
aggregate ['ægrɪgeɪt] *n* conjunto.
aggressive [ə'gresɪv] *adj* (*belligerent*) agresivo; (*assertive*) enérgico.
aggrieved [ə'griːvd] *adj* ofendido, agraviado.
aghast [ə'gɑːst] *adj* horrorizado.
agile ['ædʒaɪl] *adj* ágil.
agitate ['ædʒɪteɪt] *vt* (*trouble*) inquietar ♦ *vi*: **to ~ for/against** hacer campaña pro *or* en favor de/en contra de; **agitator** *n* agitador(a) *m/f*.
AGM *n abbr* (= *annual general meeting*) asamblea anual.
ago [ə'gəʊ] *adv*: **2 days ~** hace 2 días; **not long ~** hace poco; **how long ~?** ¿hace cuánto tiempo?
agog [ə'gɒg] *adj* (*eager*) ansioso; (*excited*) emocionado.
agonizing ['ægənaɪzɪŋ] *adj* (*pain*) atroz; (*decision, wait*) angustioso.
agony ['ægənɪ] *n* (*pain*) dolor *m* agudo; (*distress*) angustia; **to be in ~** retorcerse de dolor.
agree [ə'griː] *vt* (*price, date*) acordar, quedar en ♦ *vi* (*have same opinion*): **to ~ (with/that)** estar de acuerdo (con/que); (*correspond*) coincidir, concordar; (*consent*) acceder; **to ~ with** (*subj: person*) estar de acuerdo con, ponerse de acuerdo con; (: *food*) sentar bien a; (*LING*) concordar con; **to ~ to sth/to do sth** consentir en algo/aceptar hacer algo; **to ~ that** (*admit*) estar de acuerdo en que; **~able** *adj* (*sensation*) agradable; (*person*) simpático; (*willing*) de acuerdo, conforme; **~d** *adj* (*time, place*) convenido; **~ment** *n*

acuerdo; (*contract*) contrato; **in ~ment** de acuerdo, conforme.

agricultural [ægrɪ'kʌltʃərəl] *adj* agrícola.

agriculture ['ægrɪkʌltʃə*] *n* agricultura.

aground [ə'graund] *adv*: **to run ~** (*NAUT*) encallar, embarrancar.

ahead [ə'hɛd] *adv* (*in front*) delante; (*into the future*): **she had no time to think** ~ no tenía tiempo de hacer planes para el futuro; **~ of** delante de; (*in advance of*) antes de; **~ of time** antes de la hora; **go right** *or* **straight ~** (*direction*) siga adelante; (*permission*) hazlo (*or* hágalo).

aid [eɪd] *n* ayuda, auxilio; (*device*) aparato ♦ *vt* ayudar, auxiliar; **in ~ of** a beneficio de; **to ~ and abet** (*LAW*) ser cómplice de.

aide [eɪd] *n* (*person, also: MIL*) ayudante *m/f*.

AIDS [eɪdz] *n abbr* (= *acquired immune deficiency syndrome*) SIDA *m*.

ailing ['eɪlɪŋ] *adj* (*person*) enfermizo; (*economy*) debilitado.

ailment ['eɪlmənt] *n* enfermedad *f*, achaque *m*.

aim [eɪm] *vt* (*gun, camera*) apuntar; (*missile, remark*) dirigir; (*blow*) asestar ♦ *vi* (*also: take ~*) apuntar ♦ *n* (*in shooting: skill*) puntería; (*objective*) propósito, meta; **to ~ at** (*with weapon*) apuntar a; (*objective*) aspirar a, pretender; **to ~ to do** tener la intención de hacer; **~less** *adj* sin propósito, sin objeto.

ain't [eɪnt] (*inf*) = **am not; aren't; isn't.**

air [ɛə*] *n* aire *m*; (*appearance*) aspecto ♦ *vt* (*room*) ventilar; (*clothes, ideas*) airear ♦ *cpd* aéreo; **to throw sth into the ~** (*ball etc*) lanzar algo al aire; **by ~** (*travel*) en avión; **to be on the ~** (*RADIO, TV*) estar en antena; **~ bed** (*BRIT*) *n* colchón *m* neumático; **~borne** *adj* (*in the air*) en el aire; **~-conditioned** *adj* climatizado; **~ conditioning** *n* aire acondicionado; **~craft** *n inv* avión *m*; **~craft carrier** *n* porta(a)viones *m inv*; **~field** *n* campo de aviación; **~ force** *n* fuerzas *fpl* aéreas, aviación *f*; **~ freshener** *n* ambientador *m*; **~gun** *n*

escopeta de aire comprimido; **~ hostess** (*BRIT*) *n* azafata; **~ letter** (*BRIT*) *n* carta aérea; **~lift** *n* puente *m* aéreo; **~line** *n* línea aérea; **~liner** *n* avión *m* de pasajeros; **~mail** *n*: **by ~mail** por avión; **~plane** (*US*) *n* avión *m*; **~port** *n* aeropuerto; **~ raid** *n* ataque *m* aéreo; **~sick** *adj*: **to be ~sick** marearse (en avión); **~space** *n* espacio aéreo; **~ terminal** *n* terminal *f*; **~tight** *adj* hermético; **~-traffic controller** *n* controlador(a) *m/f* aéreo/a; **~y** *adj* (*room*) bien ventilado; (*fig: manner*) desenfadado.

aisle [aɪl] *n* (*of church*) nave *f*; (*of theatre, supermarket*) pasillo.

ajar [ə'dʒɑ:*] *adj* entreabierto.

akin [ə'kɪn] *adj*: **~ to** parecido a.

alacrity [ə'lækrɪtɪ] *n* presteza.

alarm [ə'lɑ:m] *n* (*in shop, bank*) alarma; (*anxiety*) inquietud *f* ♦ *vt* asustar, inquietar; **~ call** *n* (*in hotel etc*) alarma; **~ clock** *n* despertador *m*.

alas [ə'læs] *adv* desgraciadamente.

albeit [ɔ:l'bi:ɪt] *conj* aunque.

album ['ælbəm] *n* álbum *m*; (*L.P.*) elepé *m*.

alcohol ['ælkəhɒl] *n* alcohol *m*; **~ic** [-'hɒlɪk] *adj*, *n* alcohólico/a *m/f*.

alcove ['ælkəuv] *n* nicho, hueco.

ale [eɪl] *n* cerveza.

alert [ə'lə:t] *adj* (*attentive*) atento; (*to danger, opportunity*) alerta ♦ *n* alerta *m*, alarma ♦ *vt* poner sobre aviso; **to be on the ~** (*also MIL*) estar alerta *or* sobre aviso.

algebra ['ældʒɪbrə] *n* álgebra.

Algeria [æl'dʒɪərɪə] *n* Argelia.

alias ['eɪlɪæs] *adv* alias, conocido por ♦ *n* (*of criminal*) apodo; (*of writer*) seudónimo.

alibi ['ælɪbaɪ] *n* coartada.

alien ['eɪlɪən] *n* (*foreigner*) extranjero/a; (*extraterrestrial*) extraterrestre *m/f* ♦ *adj*: **~ to** ajeno a; **~ate** *vt* enajenar, alejar.

alight [ə'laɪt] *adj* ardiendo; (*eyes*) brillante ♦ *vi* (*person*) apearse, bajar; (*bird*) posarse.

align [ə'laɪn] *vt* alinear.

alike [ə'laɪk] *adj* semejantes, iguales ♦

adv igualmente, del mismo modo; **to look ~** parecerse.

alimony [ˈælɪmənɪ] *n* manutención *f*.

alive [əˈlaɪv] *adj* vivo; (*lively*) alegre.

KEYWORD
---

all [ɔːl] *adj* (*sg*) todo/a; (*pl*) todos/as; **~ day** todo el día; **~ night** toda la noche; **~ men** todos los hombres; **~ five came** vinieron los cinco; **~ the books** todos los libros; **~ his life** toda su vida

♦ *pron* **1** todo; **I ate it ~, I ate ~ of it** me lo comí todo; **~ of us went** fuimos todos; **~ the boys went** fueron todos los chicos; **is that ~?** ¿eso es todo?, ¿algo más?; (*in shop*) ¿algo más?, ¿alguna cosa más?

2 (*in phrases*): **above ~** sobre todo; por encima de todo; **after ~** después de todo; **at ~: not at ~** (*in answer to question*) en absoluto; (*in answer to thanks*) ¡de nada!, ¡no hay de qué!; **I'm not at ~ tired** no estoy nada cansado/a; **anything at ~ will do** cualquier cosa viene bien; **~ in ~** a fin de cuentas

♦ *adv:* **~ alone** completamente solo/a; **it's not as hard as ~ that** no es tan difícil como lo pintas; **~ the more/the better** tanto más/mejor; **~ but** casi; **the score is 2 ~** están empatados a 2.

---

allay [əˈleɪ] *vt* (*fears*) aquietar.

all clear *n* (*after attack etc*) fin *m* de la alerta; (*fig*) luz *f* verde.

allegation [ælɪˈgeɪʃən] *n* alegato.

allege [əˈledʒ] *vt* pretender; **~dly** [əˈledʒɪdlɪ] *adv* supuestamente, según se afirma.

allegiance [əˈliːdʒəns] *n* lealtad *f*.

allergy [ˈælədʒɪ] *n* alergia.

alleviate [əˈliːvɪeɪt] *vt* aliviar.

alley [ˈælɪ] *n* callejuela.

alliance [əˈlaɪəns] *n* alianza.

allied [ˈælaɪd] *adj* aliado.

alligator [ˈælɪgeɪtə*] *n* (*ZOOL*) caimán *m*.

all-in (*BRIT*) *adj, adv* (*charge*) todo incluido; **~ wrestling** *n* lucha libre.

all-night *adj* (*café, shop*) abierto toda la noche; (*party*) que dura toda la no-

che.

allocate [ˈæləkeɪt] *vt* (*money etc*) asignar.

allot [əˈlɒt] *vt* asignar; **~ment** *n* ración *f*; (*garden*) parcela.

all-out *adj* (*effort etc*) supremo; **all out** *adv* con todas las fuerzas.

allow [əˈlau] *vt* permitir, dejar; (*a claim*) admitir; (*sum, time etc*) dar, conceder; (*concede*): **to ~ that** reconocer que; **to ~ sb to do** permitir a alguien hacer; **he is ~ed to ...** se le permite ...; **~ for** *vt fus* tener en cuenta; **~ance** *n* subvención *f*; (*welfare payment*) subsidio, pensión *f*; (*pocket money*) dinero de bolsillo; (*tax ~*) desgravación *f*; **to make ~ances for** (*person*) disculpar a; (*thing*) tener en cuenta.

alloy [ˈælɔɪ] *n* mezcla.

all: **~ right** *adv* bien; (*as answer*) ¡conforme!, ¡está bien!; **~-rounder** *n*: **he's a good ~-rounder** se le da bien todo; **~-time** *adj* (*record*) de todos los tiempos.

allude [əˈluːd] *vi*: **to ~ to** aludir a.

alluring [əˈljuərɪŋ] *adj* atractivo, tentador(a).

allusion [əˈluːʒən] *n* referencia, alusión *f*.

ally [ˈælaɪ] *n* aliado/a ♦ *vt*: **to ~ o.s. with** aliarse con.

almighty [ɔːlˈmaɪtɪ] *adj* todopoderoso; (*row etc*) imponente.

almond [ˈɑːmənd] *n* almendra.

almost [ˈɔːlməust] *adv* casi.

alms [ɑːmz] *npl* limosna.

aloft [əˈlɒft] *adv* arriba.

alone [əˈləun] *adj, adv* solo; **to leave sb ~** dejar a uno en paz; **to leave sth ~** no tocar algo, dejar algo sin tocar; **let ~ ...** y mucho menos ...

along [əˈlɒŋ] *prep* a lo largo de, por ♦ *adv*: **is he coming ~ with us?** ¿viene con nosotros?; **he was limping ~** iba cojeando; **~ with** junto con; **all ~** (*all the time*) desde el principio; **~side** *prep* al lado de ♦ *adv* al lado.

aloof [əˈluːf] *adj* reservado ♦ *adv*: **to stand ~** mantenerse apartado.

aloud [əˈlaud] *adv* en voz alta.

alphabet ['ælfəbɛt] n alfabeto.
Alps [ælps] npl: the ~ los Alpes.
already [ɔːl'rɛdɪ] adv ya.
alright ['ɔːl'raɪt] (BRIT) adv = **all right**.
Alsatian [æl'seɪʃən] n (dog) pastor m
alemán.
also ['ɔːlsəʊ] adv también, además.
altar ['ɔltə*] n altar m.
alter ['ɔltə*] vt cambiar, modificar ♦ vi
cambiar.
alteration [ɔltə'reɪʃən] n cambio; (to
clothes) arreglo; (to building) arreglos
mpl.
alternate [adj ɔl'tənɪt, vb 'ɔltə:neɪt] adj
(actions etc) alternativo; (events) alterno; (US) = **alternative** ♦ vi: to ~
(with) alternar (con); on ~ days un día
sí y otro no; **alternating current**
[-neɪtɪŋ] n corriente f alterna.
alternative [ɔl'tɔːnətɪv] adj alternativo ♦
n alternativa; ~**ly** adv: ~**ly** one could
... por otra parte se podría ....
although [ɔːl'ðəʊ] conj aunque.
altitude ['æltɪtjuːd] n altura.
alto ['æltəʊ] n (female) contralto f;
(male) alto.
altogether [ɔːltə'gɛðə*] adv completamente, del todo; (on the whole) en total, en conjunto.
altruistic [æltru'ɪstɪk] adj altruista.
aluminium [ælju'mɪnɪəm] (BRIT) n aluminio.
aluminum [ə'luːmɪnəm] (US) n =
aluminium.
always ['ɔːlweɪz] adv siempre.
am [æm] vb see **be**.
a.m. adv abbr (= ante meridiem) de la
mañana.
amalgamate [ə'mælgəmeɪt] vi amalga-
marse ♦ vt amalgamar, unir.
amass [ə'mæs] vt amontonar, acumular.
amateur ['æmətə*] n aficionado/a, amateur m/f; ~**ish** adj inexperto, superficial.
amaze [ə'meɪz] vt asombrar, pasmar; to
be ~**d** (at) quedar pasmado (de);
~**ment** n asombro, sorpresa; **amazing**
adj extraordinario; (fantastic) increíble.
Amazon ['æməzən] n (GEO) Amazonas

m.
ambassador [æm'bæsədə*] n embaja-
dor(a) m/f.
amber ['æmbə*] n ámbar m; at ~
(BRIT: AUT) en el amarillo.
ambiguity [æmbɪ'gjuɪtɪ] n ambigüedad f.
ambiguous [æm'bɪgjuəs] adj ambiguo.
ambition [æm'bɪʃən] n ambición f; **ambitious** [-ʃəs] adj ambicioso.
amble ['æmbl] vi (gen: ~ along) deambular, andar sin prisa.
ambulance ['æmbjuləns] n ambulancia.
ambush ['æmbuʃ] n emboscada ♦ vt tender una emboscada a.
amenable [ə'miːnəbl] adj: to be ~ to dejarse influir por.
amend [ə'mɛnd] vt enmendar; to make
~s dar cumplida satisfacción; ~**ment** n
enmienda.
amenities [ə'miːnɪtɪz] npl comodidades
fpl.
America [ə'mɛrɪkə] n (USA) Estados mpl
Unidos; ~**n** adj, n norteamericano/a m/
f; estadounidense m/f.
amiable ['eɪmɪəbl] adj amable, simpático.
amicable ['æmɪkəbl] adj amistoso, amigable.
amid(st) [ə'mɪd(st)] prep entre, en medio de.
amiss [ə'mɪs] adv: to take sth ~ tomar
algo a mal; there's something ~ pasa
algo.
ammonia [ə'məʊnɪə] n amoníaco.
ammunition [æmju'nɪʃən] n municiones
fpl.
amnesty ['æmnɪstɪ] n amnistía.
amok [ə'mɔk] adv: to run ~ enloquecer-
se, desbocarse.
among(st) [ə'mʌŋ(st)] prep entre, en
medio de.
amorous ['æmərəs] adj amoroso.
amorphous [ə'mɔːfəs] adj amorfo.
amount [ə'maʊnt] n (gen) cantidad f;
(of bill etc) suma, importe m ♦ vi: to ~
to sumar; (be same as) equivaler a,
significar.
amp(ère) ['æmp(ɛə*)] n amperio.
amphibious [æm'fɪbɪəs] adj anfibio.
amphitheatre ['æmfɪθɪətə*] (US amphi-

theater) n anfiteatro.

ample ['æmpl] adj (large) grande; (abundant) abundante; (enough) bastante, suficiente.

amplifier ['æmplıfaıə*] n amplificador m.

amputate ['æmpjuteıt] vt amputar.

amuck [ə'mʌk] adv = amok.

amuse [ə'mjuːz] vt divertir; (distract) distraer, entretener; ~**ment** n diversión f; (pastime) pasatiempo; (laughter) risa; ~**ment arcade** n salón m de juegos.

an [æn] indef art see **a**.

anaemia [ə'niːmıə] n (US anemia) anemia; **anaemic** [-mık] (US anemic) adj anémico; (fig) soso, insípido.

anaesthetic [ænıs'θetık] n (US anesthetic) anestesia; **anaesthetist** [æ'niːsθıtıst] (US anesthetist) n anestesista m/f.

analog(ue) ['ænələg] adj (computer, watch) analógico.

analogy [ə'nælədʒı] n analogía.

analyse ['ænəlaız] (US analyze) vt analizar; **analyses** [ə'næləsiːz] npl of **analysis**; **analysis** [ə'næləsıs] (pl **analyses**) n análisis m inv; **analyst** [-lıst] n (political ~, psycho~) analista m/f; **analytic(al)** [-'lıtık(əl)] adj analítico.

analyze ['ænəlaız] (US) vt = **analyse**.

anarchist ['ænəkıst] n anarquista m/f.

anarchy ['ænəkı] n anarquía.

anatomy [ə'nætəmı] n anatomía.

ancestor ['ænsıstə*] n antepasado.

anchor ['æŋkə*] n ancla, áncora ♦ vi (also: to drop ~) anclar ♦ vt anclar; to **weigh** ~ levar anclas.

anchovy ['æntʃəvı] n anchoa.

ancient ['eınʃənt] adj antiguo.

ancillary [æn'sılərı] adj auxiliar.

and [ænd] conj y; (before i-, hi- + consonant) e; **men** ~ **women** hombres y mujeres; **father** ~ **son** padre e hijo; **trees** ~ **grass** árboles y hierba; ~ **so on** etcétera, y así sucesivamente; **try** ~ **come** procura venir; **he talked** ~ **talked** habló sin parar; **better** ~ **better** cada vez mejor.

Andes ['ændiːz] npl: the ~ los Andes.

anemia etc [ə'niːmıə] (US) = **anaemia** etc.

anesthetic etc [ænıs'θetık] (US) = **anaesthetic** etc.

anew [ə'njuː] adv de nuevo, otra vez.

angel ['eındʒəl] n ángel m.

anger ['æŋgə*] n cólera.

angina [æn'dʒaınə] n angina (del pecho).

angle ['æŋgl] n ángulo; **from their** ~ desde su punto de vista.

angler ['æŋglə*] n pescador(a) m/f (de caña).

Anglican ['æŋglıkən] adj, n anglicano/a m/f.

angling ['æŋglıŋ] n pesca con caña.

Anglo... ['æŋgləu] prefix anglo....

angrily ['æŋgrılı] adv coléricamente, airadamente.

angry ['æŋgrı] adj enfadado, airado; (wound) inflamado; **to be** ~ **with sb/at sth** estar enfadado con alguien/por algo; **to get** ~ enfadarse, enojarse.

anguish ['æŋgwıʃ] n (physical) tormentos mpl; (mental) angustia.

angular ['æŋgjulə*] adj (shape) angular; (features) anguloso.

animal ['ænıməl] n animal m; (pej: person) bestia ♦ adj animal.

animate ['ænımıt] adj vivo; ~**d** [-meıtıd] adj animado.

animosity [ænı'mɔsıtı] n animosidad f, rencor m.

aniseed ['ænısiːd] n anís m.

ankle ['æŋkl] n tobillo m; ~ **sock** n calcetín m corto.

annex [n 'æneks, vb æ'neks] n (also: BRIT: annexe) (building) edificio anexo ♦ vt (territory) anexionar.

annihilate [ə'naıəleıt] vt aniquilar.

anniversary [ænı'vɔːsərı] n aniversario.

announce [ə'nauns] vt anunciar; ~**ment** n anuncio; (official) declaración f; ~**r** n (RADIO) locutor(a) m/f; (TV) presentador(a) m/f.

annoy [ə'nɔı] vt molestar, fastidiar; **don't get** ~**ed!** ¡no se enfade!; ~**ance** n enojo; ~**ing** adj molesto, fastidioso; (person) pesado.

annual ['ænjuəl] adj anual ♦ n (BOT) anual m; (book) anuario; ~**ly** adv anualmente, cada año.

annul [ə'nʌl] vt anular.

annum ['ænəm] n see **per**.
anomaly [ə'nɔməlɪ] n anomalía.
anonymity [ænə'nɪmɪtɪ] n (of person, place) anonimidad f.
anonymous [ə'nɔnɪməs] adj anónimo.
anorak ['ænəræk] n anorak m.
another [ə'nʌðə*] adj (one more, a different one) otro ♦ pron otro; see **one**.
answer ['ɑːnsə*] n contestación f, respuesta; (to problem) solución f ♦ vi contestar, responder ♦ vt (reply to) contestar a, responder a; (problem) resolver; (prayer) escuchar; **in** ~ **to your letter** contestando or en contestación a su carta; **to** ~ **the phone** contestar or coger el teléfono; **to** ~ **the bell** or **the door** acudir a la puerta; ~ **back** vi replicar, ser respondón/ona; ~ **for** vt fus responder de or por; ~ **to** vt fus (description) corresponder a; ~**able** adj: ~**able to sb for sth** responsable ante uno de algo; ~**ing machine** n contestador m automático.
ant [ænt] n hormiga.
antagonism [æn'tægənɪzm] n antagonismo, hostilidad f.
antagonize [æn'tægənaɪz] vt provocar la enemistad de.
Antarctic [ænt'ɑːktɪk] n: **the** ~ el Antártico.
antelope ['æntɪləup] n antílope m.
antenatal ['æntɪ'neɪtl] adj antenatal, prenatal; ~ **clinic** n clínica prenatal.
antenna [æn'tenə] (pl ~e) n antena.
antennae [æn'teniː] npl of **antenna**.
anthem ['ænθəm] n: **national** ~ himno nacional.
anthology [æn'θɔlədʒɪ] n antología.
anthropology [ænθrə'pɔlədʒɪ] n antropología.
anti... [æntɪ] prefix anti...; ~**-aircraft** [-'eəkrɑːft] adj antiaéreo; ~**biotic** [-baɪ'ɔtɪk] n antibiótico; ~**body** ['æntɪbɔdɪ] n anticuerpo.
anticipate [æn'tɪsɪpeɪt] vt prever; (expect) esperar, contar con; (look forward to) esperar con ilusión; (do first) anticiparse a, adelantarse a; **anticipation** [-'peɪʃən] n (expectation) previsión f; (eagerness) ilusión f, expectación f.

anticlimax [æntɪ'klaɪmæks] n decepción f.
anticlockwise [æntɪ'klɔkwaɪz] (BRIT) adv en dirección contraria a la de las agujas del reloj.
antics ['æntɪks] npl gracias fpl.
anticyclone [æntɪ'saɪkləun] n anticiclón m.
antidote ['æntɪdəut] n antídoto.
antifreeze ['æntɪfriːz] n anticongelante m.
antihistamine [æntɪ'hɪstəmiːn] n antihistamínico.
antipathy [æn'tɪpəθɪ] n (between people) antipatía; (to person, thing) aversión f.
antiquated ['æntɪkweɪtɪd] adj anticuado.
antique [æn'tiːk] n antigüedad f ♦ adj antiguo; ~ **dealer** n anticuario/a; ~ **shop** n tienda de antigüedades.
antiquity [æn'tɪkwɪtɪ] n antigüedad f.
anti-Semitism [æntɪ'semɪtɪzm] n antisemitismo.
antiseptic [æntɪ'septɪk] adj, n antiséptico.
antlers ['æntləz] npl cuernas fpl, cornamenta sg.
anus ['eɪnəs] n ano.
anvil ['ænvɪl] n yunque m.
anxiety [æŋ'zaɪətɪ] n inquietud f; (MED) ansiedad f; ~ **to do** deseo de hacer.
anxious ['æŋkʃəs] adj inquieto, preocupado; (worrying) preocupante; (keen): **to be** ~ **to do** tener muchas ganas de hacer.

KEYWORD
---

any ['enɪ] adj **1** (in questions etc) algún/alguna; **have you** ~ **butter/children?** ¿tienes mantequilla/hijos?; **if there are** ~ **tickets left** si quedan billetes, si queda algún billete
2 (with negative): **I haven't** ~ **money/books** no tengo dinero/libros
3 (no matter which) cualquier; ~ **excuse will do** valdrá or servirá cualquier excusa; **choose** ~ **book you like** escoge el libro que quieras; ~ **teacher you ask will tell you** cualquier profesor al que preguntes te lo dirá

4 (*in phrases*): in ~ **case** de todas formas, en cualquier caso; ~ **day now** cualquier día (de estos); at ~ **moment** en cualquier momento, de un momento a otro; at ~ **rate** en todo caso; ~ **time**: **come (at)** ~ **time** venga cuando quieras; **he might come (at)** ~ **time** podría llegar de un momento a otro
♦ *pron* **1** (*in questions etc*): **have you got** ~? ¿tienes alguno(s)/a(s)?; **can** ~ **of you sing?** ¿sabéis/saben cantar alguno de vosotros/ustedes?
2 (*with negative*): **I haven't** ~ (**of them**) no tengo ninguno
3 (*no matter which one(s)*): **take** ~ **of those books (you like)** toma cualquier libro que quieras de ésos
♦ *adv* **1** (*in questions etc*): **do you want** ~ **more soup/sandwiches?** ¿quieres más sopa/bocadillos?; **are you feeling** ~ **better?** ¿te sientes algo mejor?
2 (*with negative*): **I can't hear him** ~ **more** ya no le oigo; **don't wait** ~ **longer** no esperes más.

anybody ['ɛnɪbɔdɪ] *pron* cualquiera; (*in interrogative sentences*) alguien; (*in negative sentences*): **I don't see** ~ no veo a nadie; **if** ~ **should phone ...** si llama alguien ....

anyhow ['ɛnɪhau] *adv* (*at any rate*) de todos modos, de todas formas; (*haphazard*): **do it** ~ **you like** hazlo como quieras; **she leaves things just** ~ deja las cosas como quiera *or* de cualquier modo; **I shall go** ~ de todos modos iré.

anyone ['ɛnɪwʌn] *pron* = **anybody**.

anything ['ɛnɪθɪŋ] *pron* (*in questions etc*) algo, alguna cosa; (*with negative*) nada; **can you see** ~? ¿ves algo?; **if** ~ **happens to me ...** si algo me ocurre •...; (*no matter what*): **you can say** ~ **you like** puedes decir lo que quieras; ~ **will do** vale todo *or* cualquier cosa; **he'll eat** ~ come de todo *or* lo que sea.

anyway ['ɛnɪweɪ] *adv* (*at any rate*) de todos modos, de todas formas; **I shall go** ~ iré de todos modos; (*besides*): ~, **I couldn't come even if I wanted to** además, no podría venir aunque quisiera;

why are you phoning, ~? ¿entonces, por qué llamas?, ¿por qué llamas, pues?

anywhere ['ɛnɪwɛə*] *adv* (*in questions etc*): **can you see him** ~? ¿le ves por algún lado?; **are you going** ~? ¿vas a algún sitio?; (*with negative*): **I can't see him** ~ no le veo por ninguna parte; (*no matter where*): ~ **in the world** en cualquier parte (del mundo); **put the books down** ~ deja los libros donde quieras.

apart [ə'pɑːt] *adv* (*aside*) aparte; (*situation*): ~ (**from**) separado (de); (*movement*): **to pull** ~ separar; **10 miles** ~ separados por 10 millas; **to take** ~ desmontar; ~ **from** *prep* aparte de.

apartheid [ə'pɑːteɪt] *n* apartheid *m*.

apartment [ə'pɑːtmənt] *n* (*US*) piso (*SP*), departamento, (*AM*), apartamento; (*room*) cuarto; ~ **building** (*US*) *n* edificio de apartamentos.

apathetic [æpə'θɛtɪk] *adj* apático, indiferente.

apathy ['æpəθɪ] *n* apatía, indiferencia.

ape [eɪp] *n* mono ♦ *vt* imitar, remedar.

aperitif [ə'perɪtɪf] *n* aperitivo.

aperture ['æpətfjuə*] *n* rendija, resquicio; (*PHOT*) abertura.

apex ['eɪpɛks] *n* ápice *m*; (*fig*) cumbre *f*.

apiece [ə'piːs] *adv* cada uno.

aplomb [ə'plɔm] *n* aplomo.

apologetic [əpɔlə'dʒɛtɪk] *adj* de disculpa; (*person*) arrepentido.

apologize [ə'pɔlədʒaɪz] *vi*: **to** ~ (**for sth to sb**) disculparse (con alguien de algo).

apology [ə'pɔlədʒɪ] *n* disculpa, excusa.

apostle [ə'pɔsl] *n* apóstol *m/f*.

apostrophe [ə'pɔstrəfɪ] *n* apóstrofe *m*.

appal [ə'pɔːl] *vt* horrorizar, espantar; ~**ling** *adj* espantoso; (*awful*) pésimo.

apparatus [æpə'reɪtəs] *n* (*equipment*) equipo; (*organization*) aparato; (*in gymnasium*) aparatos *mpl*.

apparel [ə'pærl] (*US*) *n* ropa.

apparent [ə'pærənt] *adj* aparente; (*obvious*) evidente; ~**ly** *adv* por lo visto, al parecer.

appeal [ə'piːl] *vi* (*LAW*) apelar ♦ *n* (*LAW*) apelación *f*; (*request*) llamamiento; (*plea*) petición *f*; (*charm*) atractivo; **to ~ for** reclamar; **to ~ to** (*be attractive to*) atraer; **it doesn't ~ to me** no me atrae, no me llama la atención; ~**ing** *adj* (*attractive*) atractivo.

appear [əˈpɪə*] *vi* aparecer, presentarse; (*LAW*) comparecer; (*publication*) salir (a luz), publicarse; (*seem*) parecer; **to ~ on TV/in "Hamlet"** salir por la tele/hacer un papel en "Hamlet"; **it would ~ that** parecería que; ~**ance** *n* aparición *f*; (*look*) apariencia, aspecto.

appease [əˈpiːz] *vt* (*pacify*) apaciguar; (*satisfy*) satisfacer.

appendices [əˈpɛndɪsiːz] *npl of* **appendix**.

appendicitis [əpɛndɪˈsaɪtɪs] *n* apendicitis *f*.

appendix [əˈpɛndɪks] (*pl* **appendices**) *n* apéndice *m*.

appetite [ˈæpɪtaɪt] *n* apetito; (*fig*) deseo, anhelo.

appetizer [ˈæpɪtaɪzə*] *n* (*drink*) aperitivo; (*food*) tapas *fpl* (*SP*).

appetizing [ˈæpɪtaɪzɪŋ] *adj* apetitoso.

applaud [əˈplɔːd] *vt*, *vi* aplaudir.

applause [əˈplɔːz] *n* aplausos *mpl*.

apple [ˈæpl] *n* manzana; **~ tree** *n* manzano.

appliance [əˈplaɪəns] *n* aparato.

applicable [əˈplɪkəbl] *adj* (*relevant*): **to be ~ (to)** referirse (a).

applicant [ˈæplɪkənt] *n* candidato/a; solicitante *m/f*.

application [æplɪˈkeɪʃən] *n* aplicación *f*; (*for a job etc*) solicitud *f*, petición *f*; ~**form** *n* solicitud *f*.

applied [əˈplaɪd] *adj* aplicado.

apply [əˈplaɪ] *vt* (*paint etc*) poner; (*law etc: put into practice*) poner en vigor ♦ *vi*: **to ~ to** (*ask*) dirigirse a; (*be applicable*) ser aplicable a; **to ~ for** (*permit, grant, job*) solicitar; **to ~ o.s. to** aplicarse a, dedicarse a.

appoint [əˈpɔɪnt] *vt* (*to post*) nombrar; ~**ed** *adj*: **at the ~ed time** a la hora señalada; ~**ment** *n* (*with client*) cita; (*act*) nombramiento; (*post*) puesto; (*at hairdresser etc*): **to have an ~ment** tener hora; **to make an ~ment (with sb)**

citarse (con uno).

appraisal [əˈpreɪzl] *n* valoración *f*.

appreciable [əˈpriːʃəbl] *adj* sensible.

appreciate [əˈpriːʃɪeɪt] *vt* apreciar, tener en mucho; (*be grateful for*) agradecer; (*be aware of*) comprender ♦ *vi* (*COMM*) aumentar(se) en valor; **appreciation** [-ˈeɪʃən] *n* apreciación *f*; (*gratitude*) reconocimiento, agradecimiento; (*COMM*) aumento en valor.

appreciative [əˈpriːʃɪətɪv] *adj* apreciativo; (*comment*) agradecido.

apprehend [æprɪˈhɛnd] *vt* detener.

apprehension [æprɪˈhɛnʃən] *n* (*fear*) aprensión *f*; **apprehensive** [-ˈhɛnsɪv] *adj* aprensivo.

apprentice [əˈprɛntɪs] *n* aprendiz/a *m/f*; ~**ship** *n* aprendizaje *m*.

approach [əˈprəʊtʃ] *vi* acercarse ♦ *vt* acercarse a; (*ask, apply to*) dirigirse a; (*situation, problem*) abordar ♦ *n* acercamiento; (*access*) acceso; (*to problem, situation*): ~ (**to**) actitud *f* (ante); ~**able** *adj* (*person*) abordable; (*place*) accesible.

appropriate [*adj* əˈprəʊprɪɪt, *vb* əˈprəʊprɪeɪt] *adj* apropiado, conveniente ♦ *vt* (*take*) apropiarse de.

approval [əˈpruːvəl] *n* aprobación *f*, visto bueno; (*permission*) consentimiento; **on ~** (*COMM*) a prueba.

approve [əˈpruːv] *vt* aprobar; ~ **of** *vt fus* (*thing*) aprobar; (*person*): **they don't ~ of her** (ella) no les parece bien.

approximate [əˈprɒksɪmɪt] *adj* aproximado; ~**ly** *adv* aproximadamente, más o menos.

apricot [ˈeɪprɪkɒt] *n* albaricoque *m* (*SP*), damasco (*AM*).

April [ˈeɪprəl] *n* abril *m*; ~ **Fool's Day** *n* el primero de abril; ≈ día *m* de los Inocentes (*28 December*).

apron [ˈeɪprən] *n* delantal *m*.

apt [æpt] *adj* acertado, apropiado; (*likely*): ~ **to do** propenso a hacer.

aqualung [ˈækwəlʌŋ] *n* escafandra autónoma.

aquarium [əˈkwɛərɪəm] *n* acuario.

Aquarius [əˈkwɛərɪəs] *n* Acuario.

aqueduct [ˈækwɪdʌkt] *n* acueducto.

Arab ['ærəb] *adj*, *n* árabe *m/f*.
Arabian [ə'reɪbɪən] *adj* árabe.
Arabic ['ærəbɪk] *adj* árabe; (*numerals*) arábigo ♦ *n* árabe *m*.
arable ['ærəbl] *adj* cultivable.
Aragon ['ærəgən] *n* Aragón *m*.
arbitrary ['ɑːbɪtrərɪ] *adj* arbitrario.
arbitration [ɑːbɪ'treɪʃən] *n* arbitraje *m*.
arcade [ɑː'keɪd] *n* (*round a square*) soportales *mpl*; (*shopping mall*) galería comercial.
arch [ɑːtʃ] *n* arco; (*of foot*) arco del pie ♦ *vt* arquear.
archaeologist [ɑːkɪ'ɒlədʒɪst] (*US* **archeologist**) *n* arqueólogo/a.
archaeology [ɑːkɪ'ɒlədʒɪ] (*US* **archeology**) *n* arqueología.
archaic [ɑː'keɪɪk] *adj* arcaico.
archbishop [ɑːtʃ'bɪʃəp] *n* arzobispo.
arch-enemy *n* enemigo jurado.
archeology *etc* [ɑːkɪ'ɒlədʒɪ] (*US*) = **archaeology** *etc*.
archery ['ɑːtʃərɪ] *n* tiro al arco.
archipelago [ɑːkɪ'pelɪgəu] *n* archipiélago.
architect ['ɑːkɪtekt] *n* arquitecto/a; ~**ural** [-'tektʃərəl] *adj* arquitectónico; ~**ure** *n* arquitectura.
archives ['ɑːkaɪvz] *npl* archivo.
Arctic ['ɑːktɪk] *adj* ártico ♦ *n*: **the** ~ el Ártico.
ardent ['ɑːdənt] *adj* ardiente, apasionado.
arduous ['ɑːdjuəs] *adj* (*task*) arduo; (*journey*) agotador(a).
are [ɑː*] *vb see* **be**.
area ['ɛərɪə] *n* área, región *f*; (*part of place*) zona; (*MATH etc*) área, superficie *f*; (*in room: e.g. dining* ~) parte *f*; (*of knowledge, experience*) campo.
arena [ə'riːnə] *n* estadio; (*of circus*) pista.
aren't [ɑːnt] = **are not**.
Argentina [ɑːdʒən'tiːnə] *n* Argentina; **Argentinian** [-'tɪnɪən] *adj*, *n* argentino/a *m/f*.
arguably ['ɑːgjuəblɪ] *adv* posiblemente.
argue ['ɑːgjuː] *vi* (*quarrel*) discutir, pelearse; (*reason*) razonar, argumentar; **to** ~ **that** sostener que.

argument ['ɑːgjumənt] *n* discusión *f*, pelea; (*reasons*) argumento; ~**ative** [-'mentətɪv] *adj* discutidor(a).
Aries ['ɛərɪz] *n* Aries *m*.
arise [ə'raɪz] (*pt* **arose**, *pp* **arisen**) *vi* surgir, presentarse.
arisen [ə'rɪzn] *pp* of **arise**.
aristocrat ['ærɪstəkræt] *n* aristócrata *m/f*.
arithmetic [ə'rɪθmətɪk] *n* aritmética.
ark [ɑːk] *n*: **Noah's A**~ el Arca *f* de Noé.
arm [ɑːm] *n* brazo ♦ *vt* armar; ~**s** *npl* armas *fpl*; ~ **in** ~ cogidos del brazo.
armaments ['ɑːməmənts] *npl* armamento.
armchair ['ɑːmtʃɛə*] *n* sillón *m*, butaca.
armed [ɑːmd] *adj* armado; ~ **robbery** *n* robo a mano armada.
armour ['ɑːmə*] (*US* **armor**) *n* armadura; (*MIL: tanks*) blindaje *m*; ~**ed car** *n* coche (*SP*) *m* or carro (*AM*) blindado.
armpit ['ɑːmpɪt] *n* sobaco, axila.
armrest ['ɑːmrest] *n* apoyabrazos *m inv*.
army ['ɑːmɪ] *n* ejército; (*fig*) multitud *f*.
aroma [ə'rəumə] *n* aroma *m*, fragancia.
arose [ə'rəuz] *pt* of **arise**.
around [ə'raund] *adv* alrededor; (*in the area*): **there is no one else** ~ no hay nadie más por aquí ♦ *prep* alrededor de.
arouse [ə'rauz] *vt* despertar; (*anger*) provocar.
arrange [ə'reɪndʒ] *vt* arreglar, ordenar; (*organize*) organizar; **to** ~ **to do sth** quedar en hacer algo; ~**ment** *n* arreglo; (*agreement*) acuerdo; ~**ments** *npl* (*preparations*) preparativos *mpl*.
array [ə'reɪ] *n*: ~ **of** (*things*) serie *f* de; (*people*) conjunto de.
arrears [ə'rɪəz] *npl* atrasos *mpl*; **to be in** ~ **with one's rent** estar retrasado en el pago del alquiler.
arrest [ə'rest] *vt* detener; (*sb's attention*) llamar ♦ *n* detención *f*; **under** ~ detenido.
arrival [ə'raɪvəl] *n* llegada; **new** ~ recién llegado/a; (*baby*) recién nacido.
arrive [ə'raɪv] *vi* llegar; (*baby*) nacer.
arrogant ['ærəgənt] *adj* arrogante.
arrow ['ærəu] *n* flecha.
arse [ɑːs] (*BRIT: inf!*) *n* culo, trasero.

arsenal ['ɑːsɪnl] n arsenal m.
arsenic ['ɑːsnɪk] n arsénico.
arson ['ɑːsn] n incendio premeditado.
art [ɑːt] n arte m; (skill) destreza; A~s
npl (SCOL) Letras fpl.
artery ['ɑːtərɪ] n arteria.
artful ['ɑːtful] adj astuto.
art gallery n pinacoteca; (saleroom)
galería de arte.
arthritis [ɑː'θraɪtɪs] n artritis f.
artichoke ['ɑːtɪtʃəuk] n alcachofa; Jerusalem ~ aguaturma.
article ['ɑːtɪkl] n artículo; (BRIT: LAW:
training). ~s npl contrato de aprendizaje; ~ of clothing prenda de vestir.
articulate [adj ɑː'tɪkjulɪt, vb ɑː'tɪkjuleɪt]
adj claro, bien expresado ♦ vt expre-
sar; ~d lorry (BRIT) n trailer m.
artificial [ɑːtɪ'fɪʃəl] adj artificial; (affected) afectado.
artillery [ɑː'tɪlərɪ] n artillería.
artisan ['ɑːtɪzæn] n artesano.
artist ['ɑːtɪst] n artista m/f; (MUS) intérprete m/f; ~ic [ɑː'tɪstɪk] adj artístico;
~ry n arte m, habilidad f (artística).
artless ['ɑːtlɪs] adj sencillo, sin dobleces.
art school n escuela de bellas artes.

KEYWORD

as [æz] conj 1 (referring to time) cuando, mientras; a medida que; ~ the
years went by con el paso de los años;
he came in ~ I was leaving entró cuando me marchaba; ~ from tomorrow
desde or a partir de mañana
2 (in comparisons): ~ big ~ tan grande como; twice ~ big ~ el doble de
grande que; ~ much money/many
books ~ tanto dinero/tantos libros
como; ~ soon ~ en cuanto
3 (since, because) como, ya que; he
left early ~ he had to be home by 10 se
fue temprano como tenía que estar en
casa a las 10
4 (referring to manner, way): do ~ you
wish haz lo que quieras; ~ she said
como dijo; he gave it to me ~ a present
me lo dio de regalo
5 (in the capacity of): he works ~ a
barman trabaja de barman; ~ chair-

man of the company, he ... como presidente de la compañía, ...
6 (concerning): ~ for or to that por or
en lo que respecta a eso
7: ~ if or though como si; he looked ~
if he was ill parecía como si estuviera
enfermo, tenía aspecto de enfermo
see also long; such; well.

---

a.s.a.p. abbr (= as soon as possible)
cuanto antes.
asbestos [æz'bɛstəs] n asbesto, amianto.
ascend [ə'sɛnd] vt subir; (throne) ascender or subir a; ~ancy n ascendiente
m, dominio.
ascent [ə'sɛnt] n subida; (slope) cuesta,
pendiente f.
ascertain [æsə'teɪn] vt averiguar.
ascribe [ə'skraɪb] vt: to ~ sth to atribuir
algo a.
ash [æʃ] n ceniza; (tree) fresno.
ashamed [ə'ʃeɪmd] adj avergonzado,
apenado (AM); to be ~ of avergonzarse
de.
ashen ['æʃn] adj pálido.
ashore [ə'ʃɔː*] adv en tierra; (swim
etc) a tierra.
ashtray ['æʃtreɪ] n cenicero.
Ash Wednesday n miércoles m de
Ceniza.
Asia ['eɪʃə] n Asia; ~n adj, n asiático/a
m/f.
aside [ə'saɪd] adv a un lado ♦ n aparte
m.
ask [ɑːsk] vt (question) preguntar; (invite) invitar; to ~ sb sth/to do sth preguntar algo a alguien/pedir a alguien
que haga algo; to ~ sb about sth preguntar algo a alguien; to ~ (sb) a question hacer una pregunta (a alguien); to
~ sb out to dinner invitar a cenar a
uno; ~ after vt fus preguntar por; ~
for vt fus pedir; (trouble) buscar.
askance [ə'skɑːns] adv: to look ~ at sb/
sth mirar con recelo a uno/mirar algo
con recelo.
askew [ə'skjuː] adv torcido, ladeado.
asking price n precio inicial.
asleep [ə'sliːp] adj dormido; to fall ~
dormirse, quedarse dormido.

asparagus [əs'pærəgəs] n (plant) espárrago; (food) espárragos mpl.
aspect ['æspɛkt] n aspecto, apariencia; (direction in which a building etc faces) orientación f.
aspersions [əs'pəːʃənz] npl: **to cast ~ on** difamar a, calumniar a.
asphyxiation [æsfɪksɪ'eɪʃən] n asfixia.
aspirations [æspə'reɪʃənz] npl ambición f.
aspire [əs'paɪə*] vi: **to ~ to** aspirar a, ambicionar.
aspirin ['æsprɪn] n aspirina.
ass [æs] n asno, burro; (inf: idiot) imbécil m/f; (US: inf!) culo, trasero.
assailant [ə'seɪlənt] n asaltador(a) m/f, agresor(a) m/f.
assassin [ə'sæsɪn] n asesino/a; **~ate** vt asesinar; **~ation** [-'neɪʃən] n asesinato.
assault [ə'sɔːlt] n asalto; (LAW) agresión f ♦ vt asaltar, atacar; (sexually) violar.
assemble [ə'sɛmbl] vt reunir, juntar; (TECH) montar ♦ vi reunirse, juntarse.
assembly [ə'sɛmblɪ] n reunión f, asamblea; (parliament) parlamento; (construction) montaje m; **~ line** n cadena de montaje.
assent [ə'sɛnt] n asentimiento, aprobación f.
assert [ə'səːt] vt afirmar; (authority) hacer valer; **~ion** [-ʃən] n afirmación f.
assess [ə'sɛs] vt valorar, calcular; (tax, damages) fijar; (for tax) gravar; **~ment** n valoración f; (for tax) gravamen m; **~or** n asesor(a) m/f.
asset ['æsɛt] n ventaja; **~s** npl (COMM) activo; (property, funds) fondos mpl.
assign [ə'saɪn] vt: **to ~ (to)** (date) fijar (para); (task) asignar (a); (resources) destinar (a); **~ment** n tarea.
assist [ə'sɪst] vt ayudar; **~ance** n ayuda, auxilio; **~ant** n ayudante m/f; (BRIT: also: **shop ~ant**) dependiente/a m/f.
associate [adj, n ə'səʊʃiɪt, vb ə'səʊʃieɪt] adj asociado ♦ n (at work) colega m/f ♦ vt asociar; (ideas) relacionar ♦ vi: **to ~ with sb** tratar con alguien.
association [əsəʊsɪ'eɪʃən] n asociación f.
assorted [ə'sɔːtɪd] adj surtido, variado.

assortment [ə'sɔːtmənt] n (of shapes, colours) surtido; (of books) colección f; (of people) mezcla.
assume [ə'sjuːm] vt suponer; (responsibilities) asumir; (attitude) adoptar, tomar; **~d name** n nombre m falso.
assumption [ə'sʌmpʃən] n suposición f, presunción f; (of power etc) toma.
assurance [ə'ʃuərəns] n garantía, promesa; (confidence) confianza, aplomo; (insurance) seguro.
assure [ə'ʃuə*] vt asegurar.
asthma ['æsmə] n asma.
astonish [ə'stɔnɪʃ] vt asombrar, pasmar; **~ment** n asombro, sorpresa.
astound [ə'staund] vt asombrar, pasmar.
astray [ə'streɪ] adv: **to go ~** extraviarse; **to lead ~** (morally) llevar por mal camino.
astride [ə'straɪd] prep a caballo or horcajadas sobre.
astrology [æs'trɔlədʒɪ] n astrología.
astronaut ['æstrənɔːt] n astronauta m/f.
astronomy [æs'trɔnəmɪ] n astronomía.
astute [əs'tjuːt] adj astuto.
asylum [ə'saɪləm] n (refuge) asilo; (mental hospital) manicomio.

KEYWORD
---

at [æt] prep **1** (referring to position) en; (direction) a; **~ the top** en lo alto; **~ home/school** en casa/la escuela; **to look ~ sth/sb** mirar algo/a uno
2 (referring to time): **~ 4 o'clock** a las 4; **~ night** por la noche; **~ Christmas** en Navidad; **~ times** a veces
3 (referring to rates, speed etc): **~ £1 a kilo** a una libra el kilo; **two ~ a time** de dos en dos; **~ 50 km/h** a 50 km/h
4 (referring to manner): **~ a stroke** de un golpe; **~ peace** en paz
5 (referring to activity): **to be ~ work** estar trabajando; (in the office etc) estar en el trabajo; **to play ~ cowboys** jugar a los vaqueros; **to be good ~ sth** ser bueno en algo
6 (referring to cause): **shocked/surprised/annoyed ~ sth** asombrado/sorprendido/fastidiado por algo; **I went**

~ **his suggestion** fui a instancias suyas.

ate [eɪt] *pt of* eat.
atheist ['eɪθɪɪst] *n* ateo/a.
Athens ['æθɪnz] *n* Atenas.
athlete ['æθliːt] *n* atleta *m/f*.
athletic [æθ'lɛtɪk] *adj* atlético; **~s** *n* atletismo.
Atlantic [ət'læntɪk] *adj* atlántico ♦ *n*: **the ~ (Ocean)** el (Océano) Atlántico.
atlas ['ætləs] *n* atlas *m*.
atmosphere ['ætməsfɪə*] *n* atmósfera; (*of place*) ambiente *m*.
atom ['ætəm] *n* átomo; **~ic** [ə'tɔmɪk] *adj* atómico; **~(ic) bomb** *n* bomba atómica; **~izer** ['ætəmaɪzə*] *n* atomizador *m*.
atone [ə'təʊn] *vi*: **to ~ for** expiar.
atrocious [ə'trəʊʃəs] *adj* atroz.
attach [ə'tætʃ] *vt* (*fasten*) atar; (*join*) unir, sujetar; (*document, letter*) adjuntar; (*importance etc*) dar, conceder; **to be ~ed to sb/sth** (*to like*) tener cariño a alguien/algo.
attaché [ə'tæʃeɪ] *n* agregado/a; **~ case** *n* maletín *m*.
attachment [ə'tætʃmənt] *n* (*tool*) accesorio; (*love*): **~ (to)** apego (a).
attack [ə'tæk] *vt* (*MIL*) atacar; (*subj: criminal*) agredir, asaltar; (*criticize*) criticar; (*task*) emprender ♦ *n* ataque *m*, asalto; (*on sb's life*) atentado; (*fig: criticism*) crítica; (*of illness*) ataque *m*; **heart ~** infarto (de miocardio); **~er** *n* agresor(a) *m/f*, asaltante *m/f*.
attain [ə'teɪn] *vt* (*also*: **~ to**) alcanzar; (*achieve*) lograr, conseguir; **~ments** *npl* logros *mpl*.
attempt [ə'tempt] *n* tentativa, intento; (*attack*) atentado ♦ *vt* intentar; **~ed** *adj*: **~ed burglary/murder/suicide** tentativa *or* intento de robo/asesinato/suicidio.
attend [ə'tend] *vt* asistir a; (*patient*) atender; **~ to** *vt fus* ocuparse de; (*customer, patient*) atender a; **~ance** *n* asistencia, presencia; (*people present*) concurrencia; **~ant** *n* ayudante *m/f*; (*in garage etc*) encargado/a ♦ *adj* (*dangers*) concomitante.
attention [ə'tenʃən] *n* atención *f*; (*care*)

atenciones *fpl* ♦ *excl* (*MIL*) ¡firme(s)!; **for the ~ of ...** (*ADMIN*) atención ....
attentive [ə'tentɪv] *adj* atento.
attest [ə'test] *vi*: **to ~ to** demostrar; (*LAW: confirm*) dar fe de.
attic ['ætɪk] *n* desván *m*.
attitude ['ætɪtjuːd] *n* actitud *f*; (*disposition*) disposición *f*.
attorney [ə'tɜːnɪ] *n* (*lawyer*) abogado/a; **A~ General** *n* (*BRIT*) ≈ Presidente *m* del Consejo del Poder Judicial (*SP*); (*US*) ≈ ministro de justicia.
attract [ə'trækt] *vt* atraer; (*sb's attention*) llamar; **~ion** [ə'trækʃən] *n* encanto; (*gen pl: amusements*) diversiones *fpl*; (*PHYSICS*) atracción *f*; (*fig: towards sb, sth*) atractivo; **~ive** *adj* guapo; (*interesting*) atrayente.
attribute [*n* 'ætrɪbjuːt, *vb* ə'trɪbjuːt] *n* atributo ♦ *vt*: **to ~ sth to** atribuir algo a.
attrition [ə'trɪʃən] *n*: **war of ~** guerra de agotamiento.
aubergine ['əʊbəʒiːn] (*BRIT*) *n* berenjena; (*colour*) morado.
auburn ['ɔːbən] *adj* color castaño rojizo.
auction ['ɔːkʃən] *n* (*also: sale by ~*) subasta ♦ *vt* subastar; **~eer** [-'nɪə*] *n* subastador(a) *m/f*.
audacity [ɔː'dæsɪtɪ] *n* audacia, atrevimiento; (*pej*) descaro.
audible ['ɔːdɪbl] *adj* audible, que se puede oír.
audience ['ɔːdɪəns] *n* público; (*RADIO*) radioescuchas *mpl*; (*TV*) telespectadores *mpl*; (*interview*) audiencia.
audio-typist [ɔːdɪəʊ'taɪpɪst] *n* mecanógrafo/a de dictáfono.
audio-visual [ɔːdɪəʊ'vɪzjʊəl] *adj* audiovisual; **~ aid** *n* ayuda audiovisual.
audit ['ɔːdɪt] *vt* revisar, intervenir.
audition [ɔː'dɪʃən] *n* audición *f*.
auditor ['ɔːdɪtə*] *n* interventor(a) *m/f*, censor(a) *m/f* de cuentas.
augment [ɔːg'ment] *vt* aumentar.
augur ['ɔːgə*] *vi*: **it ~s well** es un buen augurio.
August ['ɔːgəst] *n* agosto.
aunt [ɑːnt] *n* tía; **~ie** *n diminutive of* aunt; **~y** *n diminutive of* **aunt**.
au pair ['əʊ'peə*] *n* (*also*: **~ girl**) au

pair *f*.

aura ['ɔːrə] *n* aura.

auspices ['ɔːspɪsɪz] *npl*: **under the ~ of** bajo los auspicios de.

auspicious [ɔːs'pɪʃəs] *adj* propicio, de buen augurio.

austerity [ɔ'stɛrətɪ] *n* austeridad *f*.

Australia [ɔs'treɪlɪə] *n* Australia; **~n** *adj*, *n* australiano/a *m/f*.

Austria ['ɒstrɪə] *n* Austria; **~n** *adj*, *n* austríaco/a *m/f*.

authentic [ɔ:'θɛntɪk] *adj* auténtico.

author ['ɔ:θə] *n* autor/a *m/f*.

authoritarian [ɔ:θɒrɪ'tɛərɪən] *adj* autoritario.

authoritative [ɔ:'θɒrɪtətɪv] *adj* autorizado; (*manner*) autoritario.

authority [ɔ:'θɒrɪtɪ] *n* autoridad *f*; (*official permission*) autorización *f*; **the authorities** *npl* las autoridades.

authorize ['ɔ:θəraɪz] *vt* autorizar.

auto ['ɔ:təʊ] (*US*) *n* coche *m* (*SP*), carro (*AM*), automóvil *m*.

autobiography [ɔ:təbaɪ'ɒgrəfɪ] *n* autobiografía.

autograph ['ɔ:təgrɑ:f] *n* autógrafo ♦ *vt* (*photo etc*) dedicar; (*programme*) firmar.

automated ['ɔ:təmeɪtɪd] *adj* automatizado.

automatic [ɔ:tə'mætɪk] *adj* automático ♦ *n* (*gun*) pistola automática; (*car*) coche *m* automático; **~ally** *adv* automáticamente.

automation [ɔ:tə'meɪʃən] *n* reconversión *f*.

automaton [ɔ:'tɒmətən] (*pl* **automata**) *n* autómata *m/f*.

automobile ['ɔ:təməbi:l] (*US*) *n* coche *m* (*SP*), carro (*AM*), automóvil *m*.

autonomy [ɔ:'tɒnəmɪ] *n* autonomía.

autopsy ['ɔ:tɒpsɪ] *n* autopsia.

autumn ['ɔ:təm] *n* otoño.

auxiliary [ɔ:g'zɪlɪərɪ] *adj*, *n* auxiliar *m/f*.

avail [ə'veɪl] *vt*: **to ~ o.s. of** aprovechar(se) de ♦ *n*: **to no ~** en vano, sin resultado.

available [ə'veɪləbl] *adj* disponible; (*unoccupied*) libre; (*person*: *unattached*) soltero y sin compromiso.

avalanche ['ævəlɑ:nʃ] *n* alud *m*, avalancha.

avant-garde ['ævɑ̃'gɑ:d] *adj* de vanguardia.

Ave. *abbr* = **avenue**.

avenge [ə'vɛndʒ] *vt* vengar.

avenue ['ævənju:] *n* avenida; (*fig*) camino.

average ['ævərɪdʒ] *n* promedio, término medio ♦ *adj* medio, de término medio; (*ordinary*) regular, corriente ♦ *vt* sacar un promedio de; **on ~** por regla general; **~ out** *vi*: **to ~ out at** salir en un promedio de.

averse [ə'vɜːs] *adj*: **to be ~ to sth/doing** sentir aversión *or* antipatía por algo/por hacer.

avert [ə'vɜːt] *vt* prevenir; (*blow*) desviar; (*one's eyes*) apartar.

aviary ['eɪvɪərɪ] *n* pajarera, avería.

avid ['ævɪd] *adj* ávido, ansioso.

avocado [ævə'kɑ:dəʊ] *n* (*also*: *BRIT*: ~ *pear*) aguacate *m* (*SP*), palta (*AM*).

avoid [ə'vɔɪd] *vt* evitar, eludir.

avuncular [ə'vʌŋkjʊlə*] *adj* paternal.

await [ə'weɪt] *vt* esperar, aguardar.

awake [ə'weɪk] (*pt* **awoke**, *pp* **awoken** *or* **awaked**) *adj* despierto ♦ *vt* despertar ♦ *vi* despertarse; **to be ~** estar despierto; **~ning** *n* el despertar.

award [ə'wɔːd] *n* premio; (*LAW*: *damages*) indemnización *f* ♦ *vt* otorgar, conceder; (*LAW*: *damages*) adjudicar.

aware [ə'weə*] *adj*: **~ (of)** consciente (de); **to become ~ of/that** (*realize*) darse cuenta de/de que; (*learn*) enterarse de/de que; **~ness** *n* conciencia; (*knowledge*) conocimiento.

awash [ə'wɒʃ] *adj*: **~ with** (*also fig*) inundado de.

away [ə'weɪ] *adv* fuera; (*movement*): **she went ~** se marchó; (*far ~*) lejos; **two kilometres ~** a dos kilómetros de distancia; **two hours ~ by car** a dos horas en coche; **the holiday was two weeks ~** faltaban dos semanas para las vacaciones; **he's ~ for a week** estará ausente una semana; **to take ~ (from)** quitar (a); (*subtract*) substraer (de); **to work/pedal ~** seguir trabajando/

pedaleando; **to fade** ~ (*colour*) desvanecerse; (*sound*) apagarse; ~ **game** n (*SPORT*) partido de fuera.

awe [ɔː] n admiración f respetuosa; ~-**inspiring** adj imponente; ~**some** adj imponente.

awful ['ɔːfəl] adj horroroso; (*quantity*): **an** ~ **lot** (**of**) cantidad (de); ~**ly** adv (*very*) terriblemente.

awhile [ə'waɪl] adv (*durante*) un rato, algún tiempo.

awkward ['ɔːkwəd] adj desmañado, torpe; (*shape*) incómodo; (*embarrassing*) delicado, difícil.

awning ['ɔːnɪŋ] n (*of tent, caravan, shop*) toldo.

awoke [ə'wəuk] pt of awake.

awoken [ə'wəukən] pp of awake.

awry [ə'raɪ] adv: **to be** ~ estar descolocado or mal puesto; **to go** ~ salir mal, fracasar.

axe [æks] (*US* ax) n hacha ♦ vt (*project*) cortar; (*jobs*) reducir.

axes ['æksiːz] npl of axis.

axis ['æksɪs] (*pl* axes) n eje m.

axle ['æksl] n eje m, árbol m.

ay(e) [aɪ] excl sí.

B

B [biː] n (*MUS*) si m.

B.A. abbr = Bachelor of Arts.

babble ['bæbl] vi barbotear; (*brook*) murmurar.

baby ['beɪbɪ] n bebé m/f; (*US: inf: darling*) mi amor; ~ **carriage** (*US*) n cochecito; ~-**sit** vi hacer de canguro; ~-**sitter** n canguro/a.

bachelor ['bætʃələ*] n soltero; **B**~ **of Arts/Science** licenciado/a en Filosofía y Letras/Ciencias.

back [bæk] n (*of person*) espalda; (*of animal*) lomo; (*of hand*) dorso; (*as opposed to front*) parte f de atrás; (*of chair*) respaldo; (*of page*) reverso; (*of book*) final m; (*of crowd*): **the ones at the** ~ los del fondo; (*FOOTBALL*) defensa m ♦ vt (*candidate: also:* ~ **up**) respaldar, apoyar; (*horse: at races*) apos-

tar a; (*car*) dar marcha atrás a or con ♦ vi (*car etc*) ir (or salir or entrar) marcha atrás ♦ adj (*payment, rent*) atrasado; (*seats, wheels*) de atrás ♦ adv (*not forward*) (hacia) atrás; (*returned*): **he's** ~ está de vuelta, ha vuelto; **he ran** ~ volvió corriendo; (*letter*): **throw the ball** ~ devuelve la pelota; **can I have it** ~? ¿me lo devuelve?; (*again*): **he called** ~ llamó de nuevo; ~ **down** vi echarse atrás; ~ **out** vi (*of promise*) volverse atrás; ~ **up** vt (*person*) apoyar, respaldar; (*. theory*) defender; (*COMPUT*) hacer una copia preventiva or de reserva; ~**bencher** (*BRIT*) n miembro del parlamento sin cargo relevante; ~**bone** n columna vertebral; ~-**cloth** n telón m de fondo; ~**date** vt (*pay rise*) dar efecto retroactivo a; (*letter*) poner fecha atrasada a; ~**drop** n = ~-**cloth**; ~**fire** vi (*AUT*) petardear; (*plans*) fallar, salir mal; ~**ground** n fondo; (*of events*) antecedentes mpl; (*basic knowledge*) bases fpl; (*experience*) conocimientos mpl, educación f; **family** ~**ground** origen m, antecedentes mpl; ~**hand** n (*TENNIS: also:* ~**hand stroke**) revés m; ~**handed** adj (*fig*) ambiguo, equívoco; ~**hander** (*BRIT*) n (*bribe*) soborno; ~**ing** n (*fig*) apoyo, respaldo; ~**lash** n reacción f; ~**log** n: ~**log of work** trabajo atrasado; ~ **number** n (*of magazine etc*) número atrasado; ~**pack** n mochila; ~ **pay** n pago atrasado; ~**side** (*inf*) n trasero, culo; ~**stage** adv entre bastidores; ~**stroke** n espalda; ~**up** adj suplementario; (*COMPUT*) de reserva ♦ n (*support*) apoyo; (*also:* ~-**up file**) copia preventiva or de reserva; ~**ward** adj (*person, country*) atrasado; ~**wards** adv hacia atrás; (*read a list*) al revés; (*fall*) de espaldas; ~**water** n (*fig*) lugar m atrasado or apartado; ~**yard** n traspatio.

bacon ['beɪkən] n tocino, beicon m.

bad [bæd] adj malo; (*mistake, accident*) grave; (*food*) podrido, pasado; **his** ~ **leg** su pierna lisiada; **to go** ~ (*food*) pasarse.

bade [bæd, beɪd] *pt of* bid.
badge [bædʒ] *n* insignia; (*policeman's*) chapa, placa.
badger ['bædʒə*] *n* tejón *m*.
badly ['bædlɪ] *adv* mal; **to reflect ~ on sb** influir negativamente en la reputación de uno; **~ wounded** gravemente herido; **he needs it ~** le hace gran falta; **to be ~ off (for money)** andar mal de dinero.
badminton ['bædmɪntən] *n* bádminton *m*.
bad-tempered *adj* de mal genio *or* carácter; (*temporarily*) de mal humor.
baffle ['bæfl] *vt* desconcertar, confundir.
bag [bæg] *n* bolsa; (*handbag*) bolso; (*satchel*) mochila; (*case*) maleta; **~s of** (*inf*) un montón de; **~gage** *n* equipaje *m*; **~gy** *adj* amplio; **~pipes** *npl* gaita.
Bahamas [bə'hɑːməz] *npl*: **the ~** las Islas Bahamas.
bail [beɪl] *n* fianza ♦ *vt* (*prisoner: gen: grant ~ to*) poner en libertad bajo fianza; (*boat: also: ~ out*) achicar; **on ~** (*prisoner*) bajo fianza; **to ~ sb out** obtener la libertad de uno bajo fianza; **~ bond** *n* garantía de fianza; *see also* bale.
bailiff ['beɪlɪf] *n* alguacil *m*.
bait [beɪt] *n* cebo ♦ *vt* poner cebo en; (*tease*) tomar el pelo a.
bake [beɪk] *vt* cocer (al horno) ♦ *vi* cocerse; **~d beans** *npl* judías *fpl* en salsa de tomate; **~r** *n* panadero; **~ry** *n* panadería; (*for cakes*) pastelería; **baking** *n* (*act*) amasar *m*; (*batch*) hornada; **baking powder** *n* levadura (en polvo).
balance ['bæləns] *n* equilibrio; (*COMM: sum*) balance *m*; (*remainder*) resto; (*scales*) balanza ♦ *vt* equilibrar; (*budget*) nivelar; (*account*) saldar; (*make equal*) equilibrar; **~ of trade/payments** balanza de comercio/pagos; **~d** *adj* (*personality, diet*) equilibrado; (*report*) objetivo; **~ sheet** *n* balance *m*.
balcony ['bælkənɪ] *n* (*open*) balcón *m*; (*closed*) galería; (*in theatre*) anfiteatro.
bald [bɔːld] *adj* calvo; (*tyre*) liso.
bale [beɪl] *n* (*AGR*) paca, fardo; (*of papers etc*) fajo; **~ out** *vi* lanzarse en pa-

racaídas.
Balearics [bælɪ'ærɪks] *npl*: **the ~** las Baleares.
baleful ['beɪlful] *adj* ceñudo, hosco.
ball [bɔːl] *n* pelota; (*football*) balón *m*; (*of wool, string*) ovillo; (*dance*) baile *m*; **to play ~** (*fig*) cooperar.
ballad ['bæləd] *n* balada, romance *m*.
ballast ['bæləst] *n* lastre *m*.
ball bearings *npl* cojinetes *mpl* de bolas.
ballerina [bælə'riːnə] *n* bailarina.
ballet ['bæleɪ] *n* ballet *m*; **~ dancer** *n* bailarín/ina *m/f*.
ballistics [bə'lɪstɪks] *n* balística.
balloon [bə'luːn] *n* globo.
ballot ['bælət] *n* votación *f*; **~ paper** *n* papeleta (para votar).
ball-point (pen) ['bɔːlpɔɪnt-] *n* bolígrafo.
ballroom ['bɔːlrum] *n* salón *m* de baile.
balm [bɑːm] *n* bálsamo.
Baltic ['bɔːltɪk] *n*: **the ~ (Sea)** el (Mar) Báltico.
balustrade ['bæləstreɪd] *n* barandilla.
ban [bæn] *n* prohibición *f*, proscripción *f* ♦ *vt* prohibir, proscribir.
banal [bə'nɑːl] *adj* banal, vulgar.
banana [bə'nɑːnə] *n* plátano (*SP*), banana (*AM*).
band [bænd] *n* grupo; (*strip*) faja, tira; (*stripe*) lista; (*MUS: jazz*) orquesta; (*: rock*) grupo; (*: MIL*) banda; **~ together** *vi* juntarse, asociarse.
bandage ['bændɪdʒ] *n* venda, vendaje *m* ♦ *vt* vendar.
Bandaid ['bændeɪd] ® (*US*) *n* tirita.
bandit ['bændɪt] *n* bandido.
bandwagon ['bændwægən] *n*: **to jump on the ~** subirse al carro.
bandy ['bændɪ] *vt* (*jokes, insults*) cambiar.
bandy-legged ['bændɪ'legd] *adj* estevado.
bang [bæŋ] *n* (*of gun, exhaust*) estallido, detonación *f*; (*of door*) portazo; (*blow*) golpe *m* ♦ *vt* (*door*) cerrar de golpe; (*one's head*) golpear ♦ *vi* estallar; (*door*) cerrar de golpe.
bangle ['bæŋgl] *n* brazalete *m*.

bangs [bæŋz] (*US*) *npl* flequillo.
banish ['bænɪʃ] *vt* desterrar.
banister(s) ['bænɪstə(z)] *n(pl)* barandilla, pasamanos *m inv*.
bank [bæŋk] *n* (*COMM*) banco; (*of river, lake*) ribera, orilla; (*of earth*) terraplén *m* ♦ *vi* (*AVIAT*) ladearse; ~ **on** *vt fus* contar con; ~ **account** *n* cuenta de banco; ~ **card** *n* tarjeta bancaria; ~**er** *n* banquero; ~**er's card** (*BRIT*) *n* = ~ **card**; **B~ holiday** (*BRIT*) *n* día *m* festivo; ~**ing** *n* banca; ~**note** *n* billete *m* de banco; ~ **rate** *n* tipo de interés bancario.
bankrupt ['bæŋkrʌpt] *adj* quebrado, insolvente; **to go** ~ hacer bancarrota; **to be** ~ estar en quiebra; ~**cy** *n* quiebra.
bank statement *n* balance *m* or detalle *m* de cuenta.
banner ['bænə*] *n* pancarta.
banns [bænz] *npl* amonestaciones *fpl*.
banquet ['bæŋkwɪt] *n* banquete *m*.
baptism ['bæptɪzəm] *n* bautismo; (*act*) bautizo.
baptize [bæp'taɪz] *vt* bautizar.
bar [bɑ:*] *n* (*pub*) bar *m*; (*counter*) mostrador *m*; (*rod*) barra; (*of window, cage*) reja; (*of soap*) pastilla; (*of chocolate*) tableta; (*fig: hindrance*) obstáculo; (*prohibition*) proscripción *f*; (*MUS*) barra ♦ *vt* (*road*) obstruir; (*person*) excluir; (*activity*) prohibir; **behind** ~**s** entre rejas; **the B~** (*LAW*) la abogacía; ~ **none** sin excepción.
barbaric [bɑ:'bærɪk] *adj* bárbaro.
barbecue ['bɑ:bɪkju:] *n* barbacoa.
barbed wire ['bɑ:bd-] *n* alambre *m* de púas.
barber ['bɑ:bə*] *n* peluquero, barbero.
bar code *n* código de barras.
bare [bɛə*] *adj* desnudo; (*trees*) sin hojas; (*necessities etc*) básico ♦ *vt* desnudar; (*teeth*) enseñar; ~**back** *adv* a pelo, sin silla; ~**faced** *adj* descarado; ~**foot** *adj*, *adv* descalzo; ~**ly** *adv* apenas.
bargain ['bɑ:gɪn] *n* pacto, negocio; (*good buy*) ganga ♦ *vi* negociar; (*haggle*) regatear; **into the** ~ además, por añadidura; ~ **for** *vt fus*: **he got more**

than he ~**ed for** le resultó peor de lo que esperaba.
barge [bɑ:dʒ] *n* barcaza; ~ **in** *vi* irrumpir; (*interrupt: conversation*) interrumpir.
bark [bɑ:k] *n* (*of tree*) corteza; (*of dog*) ladrido ♦ *vi* ladrar.
barley ['bɑ:lɪ] *n* cebada; ~ **sugar** *n* azúcar *m* cande.
barmaid ['bɑ:meɪd] *n* camarera.
barman ['bɑ:mən] *n* camarero, barman *m*.
barn [bɑ:n] *n* granero.
barometer [bə'rɒmɪtə*] *n* barómetro.
baron ['bærən] *n* barón *m*; (*press* ~ *etc*) magnate *m*; ~**ess** *n* baronesa.
barracks ['bærəks] *npl* cuartel *m*.
barrage ['bærɑ:ʒ] *n* (*MIL*) descarga, bombardeo; (*dam*) presa; (*of criticism*) lluvia, aluvión *m*.
barrel ['bærəl] *n* barril *m*; (*of gun*) cañón *m*.
barren ['bærən] *adj* estéril.
barricade [bærɪ'keɪd] *n* barricada ♦ *vt* cerrar con barricadas; **to** ~ **o.s. (in)** hacerse fuerte (en).
barrier ['bærɪə*] *n* barrera.
barring ['bɑ:rɪŋ] *prep* excepto, salvo.
barrister ['bærɪstə*] (*BRIT*) *n* abogado/a.
barrow ['bærəu] *n* (*cart*) carretilla (de mano).
bartender ['bɑ:tɛndə*] (*US*) *n* camarero, barman *m*.
barter ['bɑ:tə*] *vt*: **to** ~ **sth for sth** trocar algo por algo.
base [beɪs] *n* base *f* ♦ *vt*: **to** ~ **sth on** basar *or* fundar algo en ♦ *adj* bajo, infame.
baseball ['beɪsbɔ:l] *n* béisbol *m*.
basement ['beɪsmənt] *n* sótano.
bases¹ ['beɪsi:z] *npl of* **basis**.
bases² ['beɪsɪz] *npl of* **base**.
bash [bæʃ] (*inf*) *vt* golpear.
bashful ['bæʃful] *adj* tímido, vergonzoso.
basic ['beɪsɪk] *adj* básico; ~**ally** *adv* fundamentalmente, en el fondo; (*simply*) sencillamente; ~**s** *npl*: **the** ~**s** los fundamentos.
basil ['bæzl] *n* albahaca.
basin ['beɪsn] *n* cuenco, tazón *m*; (*GEO*)

cuenca; (also: wash~) lavabo.
basis ['beɪsɪs] (pl **bases**) n base f; **on a part-time/trial** ~ a tiempo parcial/a prueba.
bask [bɑːsk] vi: **to** ~ **in the sun** tomar el sol.
basket ['bɑːskɪt] n cesta, cesto; canasta; ~**ball** n baloncesto.
Basque [bæsk] adj, n vasco/a m/f; ~ **Country** n Euskadi m, País m Vasco.
bass [beɪs] n (MUS: instrument) contrabajo; (singer) bajo.
bassoon [bə'suːn] n fagot m.
bastard ['bɑːstəd] n bastardo; (inf!) hijo de puta (!).
bastion ['bæstɪən] n baluarte m.
bat [bæt] n (ZOOL) murciélago; (for ball games) palo; (BRIT: for table tennis) pala ♦ vt: **he didn't** ~ **an eyelid** ni pestañeó.
batch [bætʃ] n (of bread) hornada; (of letters etc) lote m.
bated ['beɪtɪd] adj: **with** ~ **breath** sin respirar.
bath [bɑːθ, pl bɑːðz] n (action) baño; (~tub) baño (SP), bañera (SP), tina (AM) ♦ vt bañar; **to have a** ~ bañarse, tomar un baño; see also **baths**.
bathe [beɪð] vi bañarse ♦ vt (wound) lavar; ~**r** n bañista m/f.
bathing ['beɪðɪŋ] n el bañarse; ~ **cap** n gorro de baño; ~ **costume** (US ~ **suit**) n traje m de baño.
bath: ~**robe** n (man's) batín m; (woman's) bata; ~**room** n (cuarto de) baño; ~**s** [bɑːðz] npl (also: swimming ~s) piscina; ~ **towel** n toalla de baño.
baton ['bætən] n (MUS) batuta; (ATHLETICS) testigo; (weapon) porra.
batter ['bætə*] vt maltratar; (subj: rain etc) azotar ♦ n masa (para rebozar); ~**ed** adj (hat, pan) estropeado.
battery ['bætərɪ] n (AUT) batería; (of torch) pila.
battle ['bætl] n batalla; (fig) lucha ♦ vi luchar; ~**ship** n acorazado.
bawdy ['bɔːdɪ] adj (joke) verde.
bawl [bɔːl] vi chillar, gritar; (child) berrear.
bay [beɪ] n (GEO) bahía; **B~ of Biscay** ≈ mar Cantábrico; **to hold sb at** ~ mantener a alguien a raya; ~ **leaf** n hoja de laurel.
bay window n ventana saledíza.
bazaar [bə'zɑː*] n bazar m; (fete) venta con fines benéficos.
B. & B. n abbr (= bed and breakfast) cama y desayuno.
BBC n abbr (= British Broadcasting Corporation) cadena de radio y televisión estatal británica.
B.C. adv abbr (= before Christ) a. de C.

KEYWORD
---

be [biː] (pt **was**, **were**, pp **been**) aux vb
1 (with present participle: forming continuous tenses): **what are you doing?** ¿qué estás haciendo?, ¿qué haces?; **they're coming tomorrow** vienen mañana; **I've been waiting for you for hours** llevo horas esperándote
2 (with pp: forming passives) ser (but often replaced by active or reflective constructions); **to** ~ **murdered** ser asesinado; **the box had been opened** habían abierto la caja; **the thief was nowhere to** ~ **seen** no se veía al ladrón por ninguna parte
3 (in tag questions): **it was fun, wasn't it?** fue divertido, ¿no? or ¿verdad?; **he's good-looking, isn't he?** es guapo, ¿no te parece?; **she's back again, is she?** entonces, ¿ha vuelto?
4 (+ to + infin): **the house is to** ~ **sold** (necessity) hay que vender la casa; (future) van a vender la casa; **he's not to open it** no tiene que abrirlo
♦ vb + complement **1** (with n or num complement, but see also **3**, **4**, **5** and impers vb below) ser; **he's a doctor** es médico; **2 and 2 are 4** 2 y 2 son 4
2 (with adj complement: expressing permanent or inherent quality) ser; (: expressing state seen as temporary or reversible) estar; **I'm English** soy inglés/esa; **she's tall/pretty** es alta/bonita; **he's young** es joven; ~ **careful/good/quiet** ten cuidado/pórtate bien/cállate; **I'm tired** estoy cansado/a; **it's dirty** está sucio/a

3 (*of health*) estar; **how are you?** ¿cómo estás?; **he's very ill** está muy enfermo; **I'm better now** ya estoy mejor
4 (*of age*) tener; **how old are you?** ¿cuántos años tienes?; **I'm sixteen (years old)** tengo dieciséis años
5 (*cost*) costar; ser; **how much was the meal?** ¿cuánto fue *or* costó la comida?; **that'll ~ £5.75, please** son £5.75, por favor; **this shirt is £17** esta camisa cuesta £17
♦ *vi* **1** (*exist, occur etc*) existir, haber; **the best singer that ever was** el mejor cantante que existió jamás; **is there a God?** ¿hay un Dios?, ¿existe Dios?; **that as it may** sea como sea; **so ~ it** así sea
2 (*referring to place*) estar; **I won't ~ here tomorrow** no estaré aquí mañana
3 (*referring to movement*): **where have you been?** ¿dónde has estado?
♦ *impers vb* **1** (*referring to time*): **it's 5 o'clock** son las 5; **it's the 28th of April** estamos a 28 de abril
2 (*referring to distance*): **it's 10 km to the village** el pueblo está a 10 km
3 (*referring to the weather*): **it's too hot/cold** hace demasiado calor/frío; **it's windy today** hace viento hoy
4 (*emphatic*): **it's me** soy yo; **it was Maria who paid the bill** fue María la que pagó la cuenta.

beach [biːtʃ] *n* playa ♦ *vt* varar.
beacon ['biːkən] *n* (*lighthouse*) faro; (*marker*) guía.
bead [biːd] *n* cuenta; (*of sweat etc*) gota.
beak [biːk] *n* pico.
beaker ['biːkə*] *n* vaso de plástico.
beam [biːm] *n* (*ARCH*) viga, travesaño; (*of light*) rayo, haz *m* de luz ♦ *vi* brillar; (*smile*) sonreír.
bean [biːn] *n* (*ARCH*) judía; **runner/broad ~** habichuela/haba; **coffee ~** grano de café; **~sprouts** *npl* brotes *mpl* de soja.
bear [beə*] (*pt* **bore**, *pp* **borne**) *n* oso ♦ *vt* (*weight etc*) llevar; (*cost*) pagar; (*responsibility*) tener; (*endure*) sopor-

tar, aguantar; (*children*) parir, tener; (*fruit*) dar ♦ *vi*: **to ~ right/left** torcer a la derecha/izquierda; **~ out** *vt* (*suspicions*) corroborar, confirmar; (*person*) dar la razón a; **~ up** *vi* (*remain cheerful*) mantenerse animado.
beard [biəd] *n* barba; **~ed** *adj* con barba, barbudo.
bearer ['beərə*] *n* portador(a) *m/f*.
bearing ['beərɪŋ] *n* porte *m*, comportamiento; (*connection*) relación *f*; **~s** *npl* (*also: ball ~s*) cojinetes *mpl* a bolas; **to take a ~** tomar marcaciones; **to find one's ~s** orientarse.
beast [biːst] *n* bestia; (*inf*) bruto, salvaje *m*; **~ly** (*inf*) *adj* horrible.
beat [biːt] (*pt* **beat**, *pp* **beaten**) *n* (*of heart*) latido; (*MUS*) ritmo, compás *m*; (*of policeman*) ronda ♦ *vt* pegar, golpear; (*eggs*) batir; (*defeat: opponent*) vencer, derrotar; (*: record*) sobrepasar ♦ *vi* (*heart*) latir; (*drum*) redoblar; (*rain, wind*) azotar; **off the ~en track** aislado; **to ~ it** (*inf*) largarse; **~ off** *vt* rechazar; **~ up** *vt* (*attack*) dar una paliza a; **~ing** *n* paliza.
beautiful ['bjuːtɪful] *adj* precioso, hermoso, bello; **~ly** *adv* maravillosamente.
beauty ['bjuːtɪ] *n* belleza; **~ salon** *n* salón *m* de belleza; **~ spot** *n* (*TOURISM*) lugar *m* pintoresco.
beaver ['biːvə*] *n* castor *m*.
became [bɪˈkeɪm] *pt* of **become**.
because [bɪˈkɔz] *conj* porque; **~ of** debido a, a causa de.
beck [bek] *n*: **to be at the ~ and call of** estar a disposición de.
beckon ['bekən] *vt* (*also: ~ to*) llamar con señas.
become [bɪˈkʌm] (*irreg: like* **come**) *vi* (*suit*) favorecer, sentar bien a ♦ *vi* (+*n*) hacerse, llegar a ser; (+*adj*) ponerse, volverse; **to ~ fat** engordar.
becoming [bɪˈkʌmɪŋ] *adj* (*behaviour*) decoroso; (*clothes*) favorecedor(a).
bed [bed] *n* cama; (*of flowers*) macizo; (*of coal, clay*) capa; (*of river*) lecho; (*of sea*) fondo; **to go to ~** acostarse; **~ and breakfast** *n* (*place*) pensión *f*;

(*terms*) cama y desayuno; **~clothes** *npl* ropa de cama; **~ding** *n* ropa de cama.

bedlam ['bɛdləm] *n* desbarajuste *m*.

bedraggled [bɪ'dræɡld] *adj* (*untidy: person*) desastrado; (*clothes, hair*) desordenado.

bed: **~ridden** *adj* postrado (en cama); **~room** *n* dormitorio; **~side** *n*: at the **~side of** a la cabecera de; **~sit(ter)** (*BRIT*) *n* estudio (*SP*), suite *m* (*AM*); **~spread** *n* cubrecama *m*, colcha; **~time** *n* hora de acostarse.

bee [bi:] *n* abeja.

beech [bi:tʃ] *n* haya.

beef [bi:f] *n* carne *f* de vaca; roast **~** rosbif *m*; **~burger** *n* hamburguesa; **B~eater** *n* *alabardero de la Torre de Londres*.

beehive ['bi:haɪv] *n* colmena.

beeline ['bi:laɪn] *n*: to make a **~ for** ir derecho a.

been [bi:n] *pp* of **be**.

beer [bɪə*] *n* cerveza.

beet [bi:t] (*US*) *n* (*also*: red **~**) remolacha.

beetle ['bi:tl] *n* escarabajo.

beetroot ['bi:tru:t] (*BRIT*) *n* remolacha.

before [bɪ'fɔ:*] *prep* (*of time*) antes de; (*of space*) delante de ♦ *conj* antes (de) que ♦ *adv* antes, anteriormente; delante, adelante; **~ going** antes de marcharse; **~ she goes** antes de que se vaya; **the week ~** la semana anterior; **I've never seen it ~** no lo he visto nunca; **~hand** *adv* de antemano, con anticipación.

beg [bɛɡ] *vi* pedir limosna ♦ *vt* pedir, rogar; (*entreat*) suplicar; to **~ sb to do sth** rogar a uno que haga algo; *see also* **pardon**.

began [bɪ'ɡæn] *pt* of **begin**.

beggar ['bɛɡə*] *n* mendigo/a.

begin [bɪ'ɡɪn] (*pt* **began**, *pp* **begun**) *vt, vi* empezar, comenzar; to **~ doing** *or* **to do sth** empezar a hacer algo; **~ner** *n* principiante *m/f*; **~ning** *n* principio, comienzo.

begun [bɪ'ɡʌn] *pp* of **begin**.

behalf [bɪ'hɑ:f] *n*: on **~ of** en nombre

de, por; (*for benefit of*) en beneficio de; **on my/his ~** por mí/él.

behave [bɪ'heɪv] *vi* (*person*) portarse, comportarse; (*well: also*: **~ o.s.**) portarse bien; **behaviour** (*US* **behavior**) *n* comportamiento, conducta.

behead [bɪ'hɛd] *vt* decapitar.

beheld [bɪ'hɛld] *pt, pp* of **behold**.

behind [bɪ'haɪnd] *prep* detrás de; (*supporting*): to be **~ sb** apoyar a alguien; (*lower in rank etc*) estar por detrás de ♦ *adv* detrás, por detrás, atrás ♦ *n* trasero; to be **~** (*schedule*) ir retrasado; **~ the scenes** (*fig*) entre bastidores.

behold [bɪ'həuld] (*irreg: like* **hold**) *vt* contemplar.

beige [beɪʒ] *adj* color beige.

being ['bi:ɪŋ] *n* ser *m*; (*existence*): **in ~** existente; **to come into ~** aparecer.

belated [bɪ'leɪtɪd] *adj* atrasado, tardío.

belch [bɛltʃ] *vi* eructar ♦ *vt* (*gen*: **~ out**: *smoke etc*) arrojar.

belfry ['bɛlfrɪ] *n* campanario.

Belgian ['bɛldʒən] *adj, n* belga *m/f*.

Belgium ['bɛldʒəm] *n* Bélgica.

belie [bɪ'laɪ] *vt* desmentir, contradecir.

belief [bɪ'li:f] *n* opinión *f*; (*faith*) fe *f*.

believe [bɪ'li:v] *vt, vi* creer; to **~ in** creer en; **~r** *n* partidario/a; (*REL*) creyente *m/f*, fiel *m/f*.

belittle [bɪ'lɪtl] *vt* quitar importancia a.

bell [bɛl] *n* campana; (*small*) campanilla; (*on door*) timbre *m*.

belligerent [bɪ'lɪdʒərənt] *adj* agresivo.

bellow ['bɛləu] *vi* bramar; (*person*) rugir.

bellows ['bɛləuz] *npl* fuelle *m*.

belly ['bɛlɪ] *n* barriga, panza.

belong [bɪ'lɒŋ] *vi*: to **~ to** pertenecer a; (*club etc*) ser socio de; **this book ~s here** este libro va aquí; **~ings** *npl* pertenencias *fpl*.

beloved [bɪ'lʌvɪd] *adj* querido/a.

below [bɪ'ləu] *prep* bajo, debajo de; (*less than*) inferior a ♦ *adv* abajo, (por) debajo; **see ~** véase más abajo.

belt [bɛlt] *n* cinturón *m*; (*TECH*) correa, cinta ♦ *vt* (*thrash*) pegar con correa; **~way** (*US*) *n* (*AUT*) carretera de circunvalación.

bemused [bɪ'mju:zd] *adj* aturdido.
bench [bɛntʃ] *n* banco; (*BRIT: POL*): **the Government/Opposition** ~**es** (los asientos de) los miembros del Gobierno/de la Oposición; **the B**~ (*LAW: judges*) magistratura.
bend [bɛnd] (*pt, pp* **bent**) *vt* doblar ♦ *vi* inclinarse ♦ *n* (*BRIT: in road, river*) curva; (*in pipe*) codo; ~ **down** *vi* inclinarse, doblarse; ~ **over** *vi* inclinarse.
beneath [bɪ'ni:θ] *prep* bajo, debajo de; (*unworthy of*) indigno de ♦ *adv* abajo, (por) debajo.
benefactor ['bɛnɪfæktə*] *n* bienhechor *m*.
beneficial [bɛnɪ'fɪʃəl] *adj* beneficioso.
benefit ['bɛnɪfɪt] *n* beneficio; (*allowance of money*) subsidio ♦ *vt* beneficiar ♦ *vi*: **he'll** ~ **from it** le sacará provecho.
benevolent [bɪ'nɛvələnt] *adj* (*person*) benévolo.
benign [bɪ'naɪn] *adj* benigno; (*smile*) afable.
bent [bɛnt] *pt, pp of* **bend** ♦ *n* inclinación *f* ♦ *adj*: **to be** ~ **on** estar empeñado en.
bequest [bɪ'kwɛst] *n* legado.
bereaved [bɪ'ri:vd] *npl*: **the** ~ los íntimos de una persona afligidos por su muerte.
beret ['bɛreɪ] *n* boina.
Berlin [bə:'lɪn] *n* Berlín.
berm [bə:m] (*US*) *n* (*AUT*) arcén *m*.
Bermuda [bə:'mju:də] *n* las Bermudas.
berry ['bɛrɪ] *n* baya.
berserk [bə'sə:k] *adj*: **to go** ~ perder los estribos.
berth [bə:θ] *n* (*bed*) litera; (*cabin*) camarote *m*; (*for ship*) amarradero ♦ *vi* atracar, amarrar.
beseech [bɪ'si:tʃ] (*pt, pp* **besought**) *vt* suplicar.
beset [bɪ'sɛt] (*pt, pp* **beset**) *vt* (*person*) acosar.
beside [bɪ'saɪd] *prep* junto a, al lado de; **to be** ~ **o.s. with anger** estar fuera de sí; **that's** ~ **the point** eso no tiene nada que ver.
besides [bɪ'saɪdz] *adv* además ♦ *prep* además de.

besiege [bɪ'si:dʒ] *vt* sitiar; (*fig*) asediar.
besought [bɪ'sɔ:t] *pt, pp of* **beseech**.
best [bɛst] *adj* (el/la) mejor ♦ *adv* (lo) mejor; **the** ~ **part of** (*quantity*) la mayor parte de; **at** ~ en el mejor de los casos; **to make the** ~ **of sth** sacar el mejor partido de algo; **to do one's** ~ hacer todo lo posible; **to the** ~ **of my knowledge** que yo sepa; **to the** ~ **of my ability** como mejor puedo; ~ **man** *n* padrino de boda.
bestow [bɪ'stəu] *vt* (*title*) otorgar.
bestseller ['bɛst'sɛlə*] *n* éxito de librería, bestseller *m*.
bet [bɛt] (*pt, pp* **bet** *or* **betted**) *n* apuesta ♦ *vt*: **to** ~ **money on** apostar dinero por; **to** ~ **sb sth** apostar algo a uno ♦ *vi* apostar.
betray [bɪ'treɪ] *vt* traicionar; (*trust*) faltar a; ~**al** *n* traición *f*.
better ['bɛtə*] *adj, adv* mejor ♦ *vt* superar ♦ *n*: **to get the** ~ **of sb** quedar por encima de alguien; **you had** ~ **do it** más vale que lo hagas; **he thought** ~ **of it** cambió de parecer; **to get** ~ (*MED*) mejorar(se); ~ **off** *adj* mejor; (*wealthier*) más acomodado.
betting ['bɛtɪŋ] *n* juego, el apostar; ~ **shop** (*BRIT*) *n* agencia de apuestas.
between [bɪ'twi:n] *prep* entre ♦ *adv* (*time*) mientras tanto; (*place*) en medio.
beverage ['bɛvərɪdʒ] *n* bebida.
beware [bɪ'wɛə*] *vi*: **to** ~ (**of**) tener cuidado (con); "~ **of the dog**" "perro peligroso".
bewildered [bɪ'wɪldəd] *adj* aturdido, perplejo.
bewitching [bɪ'wɪtʃɪŋ] *adj* hechicero, encantador(a).
beyond [bɪ'jɔnd] *prep* más allá de; (*past: understanding*) fuera de; (*after: date*) después de, más allá de; (*above*) superior a ♦ *adv* (*in space*) más allá; (*in time*) posteriormente; ~ **doubt** fuera de toda duda; ~ **repair** irreparable.
bias ['baɪəs] *n* (*prejudice*) prejuicio, pasión *f*; (*preference*) predisposición *f*; ~(**s**)**ed** *adj* parcial.
bib [bɪb] *n* babero.

Bible ['baɪbl] n Biblia.
bicarbonate of soda [baɪ'kɑːbənɪt-] n bicarbonato sódico.
bicker ['bɪkə*] vi pelearse.
bicycle ['baɪsɪkl] n bicicleta.
bid [bɪd] (pt **bade** or **bid**, pp **bidden** or **bid**) n oferta, postura; (in tender) licitación f; (attempt) tentativa, conato ♦ vi hacer una oferta ♦ vt (offer) ofrecer; **to ~ sb good day** dar a uno los buenos días; **~der** n: **the highest ~der** el mejor postor; **~ding** n (at auction) ofertas fpl.
bide [baɪd] vt: **to ~ one's time** esperar el momento adecuado.
bifocals [baɪ'fəʊklz] npl gafas fpl (SP) or anteojos mpl (AM) bifocales.
big [bɪg] adj grande; (brother, sister) mayor.
big dipper [-'dɪpə*] n montaña rusa.
bigheaded ['bɪg'hɛdɪd] adj engreído.
bigot ['bɪgət] n fanático/a, intolerante m/f; **~ed** adj fanático, intolerante; **~ry** n fanatismo, intolerancia.
big top n (at circus) carpa.
bike [baɪk] n bici f.
bikini [bɪ'kiːnɪ] n bikini m.
bile [baɪl] n bilis f.
bilingual [baɪ'lɪŋgwəl] adj bilingüe.
bill · [bɪl] n cuenta; (invoice) factura; (POL) proyecto de ley; (US: banknote) billete m; (of bird) pico; (of show) programa m; "**post no ~s**" "prohibido fijar carteles"; **to fit** or **fill the ~** (fig) cumplir con los requisitos; **~board** (US) n cartelera.
billet ['bɪlɪt] n alojamiento.
billfold ['bɪlfəʊld] (US) n cartera.
billiards ['bɪljədz] n billar m.
billion ['bɪljən] n (BRIT) billón m (millón de millones); (US) mil millones.
bin [bɪn] n (for rubbish) cubo (SP) or bote m (AM) de la basura; (container) recipiente m.
bind [baɪnd] (pt, pp **bound**) vt atar; (book) encuadernar; (oblige) obligar ♦ n (inf: nuisance) lata; **~ing** adj (contract) obligatorio.
binge [bɪndʒ] (inf) n: **to go on a ~** ir de juerga.

bingo ['bɪŋgəʊ] n bingo m.
binoculars [bɪ'nɒkjuləz] npl prismáticos mpl.
bio... [baɪə'] prefix: **~chemistry** n bioquímica; **~graphy** [baɪ'ɒgrəfɪ] n biografía; **~logical** adj biológico; **~logy** [baɪ'ɒlədʒɪ] n biología.
birch [bəːtʃ] n (tree) abedul m.
bird [bəːd] n ave f, pájaro; (BRIT: inf: girl) chica; **~'s eye view** n (aerial view) vista de pájaro; (overview) visión f de conjunto; **~ watcher** n ornitólogo/a.
Biro ['baɪrəʊ] ® n bolígrafo.
birth [bəːθ] n nacimiento; **to give ~ to** parir, dar a luz; **~ certificate** n partida de nacimiento; **~ control** n (policy) control m de natalidad; (methods) métodos mpl anticonceptivos; **~day** n cumpleaños m inv ♦ cpd (cake, card etc) de cumpleaños; **~place** n lugar m de nacimiento; **~ rate** n (tasa de) natalidad f.
biscuit ['bɪskɪt] (BRIT) n galleta, bizcocho (AM).
bisect [baɪ'sɛkt] vt bisecar.
bishop ['bɪʃəp] n obispo; (CHESS) alfil m.
bit [bɪt] pt of **bite** ♦ n trozo, pedazo, pedacito; (COMPUT) bit m, bitio; (for horse) freno, bocado; **a ~ of** un poco de; **a ~ mad** un poco loco; **~ by ~** poco a poco.
bitch [bɪtʃ] n perra; (inf!: woman) zorra (!).
bite [baɪt] (pt **bit**, pp **bitten**) vt, vi morder; (insect etc) picar ♦ n (insect ~) picadura; (mouthful) bocado; **to ~ one's nails** comerse las uñas; **let's have a ~ (to eat)** (inf) vamos a comer algo.
bitter ['bɪtə*] adj amargo; (wind) cortante, penetrante; (battle) encarnizado ♦ n (BRIT: beer) cerveza típica británica a base de lúpulos; **~ness** n lo amargo, amargura; (anger) rencor m.
bizarre [bɪ'zɑː*] adj raro, extraño.
blab [blæb] (inf) vi soplar.
black [blæk] adj negro; (tea, coffee) solo ♦ n color m negro; (person): **B~** negro/a ♦ vt (BRIT: INDUSTRY) boico-

tear; **to give sb a ~ eye** ponerle a uno el ojo morado; **~ and blue** (*bruised*) amoratado; **to be in the ~** (*bank account*) estar en números negros; **~berry** *n* zarzamora; **~bird** *n* mirlo; **~board** *n* pizarra; **~ coffee** *n* café *m* solo; **~currant** *n* grosella negra; **~en** *vt* (*fig*) desacreditar; **~ ice** *n* hielo invisible en la carretera; **~leg** (*BRIT*) *n* esquirol *m*, rompehuelgas *m inv*; **~list** *n* lista negra; **~mail** *n* chantaje *m* ♦ *vt* chantajear; **~ market** *n* mercado negro; **~out** *n* (*MIL*) oscurecimiento; (*power cut*) apagón *m*; (*TV, RADIO*) interrupción *f* de programas; (*fainting*) desvanecimiento; **B~ Sea** *n*: **the B~ Sea** el Mar Negro; **~ sheep** *n* (*fig*) oveja negra; **~smith** *n* herrero; **~ spot** *n* (*AUT*) lugar *m* peligroso; (*for unemployment etc*) punto negro.

bladder ['blædə*] *n* vejiga.

blade [bleɪd] *n* hoja; (*of propeller*) paleta; **a ~ of grass** una brizna de hierba.

blame [bleɪm] *n* culpa ♦ *vt*: **to ~ sb for sth** echar a uno la culpa de algo; **to be to ~** tener la culpa de; **~less** *adj* inocente.

bland [blænd] *adj* (*music, taste*) soso.

blank [blæŋk] *adj* en blanco; (*look*) sin expresión ♦ *n* (*of memory*): **my mind is a ~** no puedo recordar nada; (*on form*) blanco, espacio en blanco; (*cartridge*) cartucho sin bala *or* de fogueo; **~ cheque** *n* cheque *m* en blanco.

blanket ['blæŋkɪt] *n* manta (*SP*), cobija (*AM*); (*of snow*) capa; (*of fog*) manto.

blare [blɛə*] *vi* sonar estrepitosamente.

blasé ['blɑːzeɪ] *adj* hastiado.

blasphemy ['blæsfɪmɪ] *n* blasfemia.

blast [blɑːst] *n* (*of wind*) ráfaga, soplo; (*of explosive*) explosión *f* ♦ *vt* (*blow up*) volar; **~-off** *n* (*SPACE*) lanzamiento.

blatant ['bleɪtənt] *adj* descarado.

blaze [bleɪz] *n* (*fire*) fuego; (*fig*: *of colour*) despliegue *m*; (: *of glory*) esplendor *m* ♦ *vi* arder en llamas; (*fig*) brillar ♦ *vt*: **to ~ a trail** (*fig*) abrir (un) camino; **in a ~ of publicity** con gran publicidad.

blazer ['bleɪzə*] *n* chaqueta de uniforme

de colegial o de socio de club.

bleach [bliːtʃ] *n* (*also*: **household ~**) lejía ♦ *vt* blanquear; **~ed** *adj* (*hair*) teñido (de rubio); **~ers** (*US*) *npl* (*SPORT*) gradas *fpl* al sol.

bleak [bliːk] *adj* (*countryside*) desierto; (*prospect*) poco prometedor(a); (*weather*) crudo; (*smile*) triste.

bleary-eyed ['blɪərɪˈaɪd] *adj*: **to be ~** tener ojos de cansado.

bleat [bliːt] *vi* balar.

bleed [bliːd] (*pt, pp* **bled**) *vt, vi* sangrar; **my nose is ~ing** me está sangrando la nariz.

bleeper ['bliːpə*] *n* busca *m*.

blemish ['blɛmɪʃ] *n* marca, mancha; (*on reputation*) tacha.

blend [blɛnd] *n* mezcla ♦ *vt* mezclar; (*colours etc*) combinar, mezclar ♦ *vi* (*colours etc*: *also*: **~ in**) combinarse, mezclarse.

bless [bles] (*pt, pp* **blessed** *or* **blest**) *vt* bendecir; **~ you!** (*after sneeze*) ¡Jesús!; **~ing** *n* (*approval*) aprobación *f*; (*godsend*) don *m* del cielo, bendición *f*; (*advantage*) beneficio, ventaja.

blew [bluː] *pt of* **blow**.

blight [blaɪt] *vt* (*hopes etc*) frustrar, arruinar.

blimey ['blaɪmɪ] (*BRIT*: *inf*) *excl* ¡caray!

blind [blaɪnd] *adj* ciego; (*fig*): **~ (to)** ciego (a) ♦ *n* (*for window*) persiana ♦ *vt* cegar; (*dazzle*) deslumbrar; (*deceive*): **to ~ sb to ...** cegar a uno a ...; **the ~** *npl* los ciegos; **~ alley** *n* callejón *m* sin salida; **~ corner** (*BRIT*) *n* esquina escondida; **~fold** *n* venda ♦ *adv* con los ojos vendados ♦ *vt* vendar los ojos a; **~ly** *adv* a ciegas, ciegamente; **~ness** *n* ceguera; **~ spot** *n* (*AUT*) ángulo ciego.

blink [blɪŋk] *vi* parpadear, pestañear; (*light*) oscilar; **~ers** *npl* anteojeras *fpl*.

bliss [blɪs] *n* felicidad *f*.

blister ['blɪstə*] *n* ampolla ♦ *vi* (*paint*) ampollarse.

blithely ['blaɪðlɪ] *adv* alegremente.

blitz [blɪts] *n* (*MIL*) bombardeo aéreo.

blizzard ['blɪzəd] *n* ventisca.

bloated ['bləʊtɪd] *adj* hinchado; (*person*: *full*) ahíto.

blob [blɔb] n (drop) gota; (indistinct object) bulto.

bloc [blɔk] n (POL) bloque m.

block [blɔk] n bloque m; (in pipes) obstáculo; (of buildings) manzana (SP), cuadra (AM) ♦ vt obstruir, cerrar; (progress) estorbar; ~ **of flats** (BRIT) bloque m de pisos; **mental** ~ bloqueo mental; ~**ade** [-'keɪd] n bloqueo m ♦ vt bloquear; ~**age** n estorbo, obstrucción f; ~**buster** n (book) bestseller m; (film) éxito de público; ~ **letters** npl letras fpl de molde.

bloke [bləʊk] (BRIT: inf) n tipo, tío.

blond(e) [blɔnd] adj, n rubio/a m/f.

blood [blʌd] n sangre f; ~ **donor** n donante m/f de sangre; ~ **group** n grupo sanguíneo; ~**hound** n sabueso; ~ **poisoning** n envenenamiento de la sangre; ~ **pressure** n presión f sanguínea; ~**shed** n derramamiento de sangre; ~**shot** adj inyectado en sangre; ~**stream** n corriente f sanguínea; ~**test** n análisis m inv de sangre; ~**thirsty** adj sanguinario; ~ **vessel** n vaso sanguíneo; ~**y** adj sangriento; (nose etc) lleno de sangre; (BRIT: inf!): **this** ~**y...** este condenado o puñetero ... (!) ♦ adv: ~**y strong/good** (BRIT: inf!) terriblemente fuerte/bueno; ~**y-minded** (BRIT: inf) adj puñetero (!).

bloom [bluːm] n flor f ♦ vi florecer.

blossom ['blɔsəm] n flor f ♦ vi (also fig) florecer.

blot [blɔt] n borrón m; (fig) mancha ♦ vt (stain) manchar; ~ **out** vt (view) tapar.

blotchy ['blɔtʃɪ] adj (complexion) lleno de manchas.

blotting paper ['blɔtɪŋ-] n papel m secante.

blouse [blauz] n blusa.

blow [bləʊ] (pt **blew**, pp **blown**) n golpe m; (with sword) espadazo ♦ vi soplar; (dust, sand etc) volar; (fuse) fundirse ♦ vt (subj: wind) llevarse; (fuse) quemar; (instrument) tocar; **to ~ one's nose** sonarse; ~ **away** vt llevarse, arrancar; ~ **down** vt derribar; ~ **off** vt arrebatar; ~ **out** vi apagarse; ~

over vi amainar; ~ **up** vi estallar ♦ vt volar; (tyre) inflar; (PHOT) ampliar; ~**-dry** n moldeado (con secador); ~**lamp** (BRIT) n soplete m, lámpara de soldar.

blow-out n (of tyre) pinchazo.

blowtorch ['bləʊtɔːtʃ] n = blowlamp.

blue [bluː] adj azul; (depressed) deprimido; ~ **film/joke** película/chiste verde; **out of the** ~ (fig) de repente; ~**bell** n campanilla, campánula azul; ~**bottle** n moscarda, mosca azul; ~**print** n (fig) anteproyecto.

bluff [blʌf] vi tirarse un farol, farolear ♦ n farol m; **to call sb's** ~ coger a uno la palabra.

blunder ['blʌndə*] n patinazo, metedura de pata ♦ vi cometer un error, meter la pata.

blunt [blʌnt] adj (pencil) despuntado; (knife) desafilado, romo; (person) franco, directo.

blur [bləː*] n (shape): **to become a** ~ hacerse borroso ♦ vt (vision) enturbiar; (distinction) borrar.

blurb [bləːb] n comentario de sobrecubierta.

blurt out [bləːt-] vt descolgarse con, dejar escapar.

blush [blʌʃ] vi ruborizarse, ponerse colorado ♦ n rubor m.

blustering ['blʌstərɪŋ] adj (person) fanfarrón/ona.

blustery ['blʌstərɪ] adj (weather) tempestuoso, tormentoso.

boar [bɔː*] n verraco, cerdo.

board [bɔːd] n (card~) cartón m; (wooden) tabla, tablero; (on wall) tablón m; (for chess etc) tablero; (committee) junta, consejo; (in firm) mesa or junta directiva; (NAUT, AVIAT): **on** ~ a bordo ♦ vt (ship) embarcarse en; (train) subir a; **full** ~ (BRIT) pensión completa; **half** ~ (BRIT) media pensión; **to go by the** ~ (fig) ser abandonado or olvidado; ~ **up** vt (door) tapiar; ~ **and lodging** n casa y comida; ~**er** n (SCOL) interno/a; ~**ing card** (BRIT) n tarjeta de embarque; ~**ing house** n casa de huéspedes; ~**ing pass** (US) n = ~**ing card**;

~ing school n internado; ~ room n sala de juntas.

boast [bəʊst] vi: to ~ (about or of) alardear (de).

boat [bəʊt] n barco, buque m; (small) barca, bote m; ~er n (hat) canotié m; ~swain ['bəʊsn] n contramaestre m.

bob [bɔb] vi (also: ~ up and down) menearse, balancearse; ~ up vi (re)aparecer de repente.

bobby ['bɔbɪ] (BRIT: inf) n poli m.

bobsleigh ['bɔbsleɪ] n bob m.

bode [bəʊd] vi: to ~ well/ill (for) ser prometedor/poco prometedor (para).

bodily ['bɔdɪlɪ] adj corporal ♦ adv (move: person) en peso.

body ['bɔdɪ] n cuerpo; (corpse) cadáver m; (of car) caja, carrocería; (fig: group) grupo; (: organization) organismo; ~-building n culturismo; ~guard n guardaespaldas m inv; ~work n carrocería.

bog [bɔg] n pantano, ciénaga ♦ vt: to get ~ged down (fig) empantanarse, atascarse.

boggle ['bɔgl] vi: the mind ~s! ¡no puedo creerlo!

bogus ['bəʊgəs] adj falso, fraudulento.

boil [bɔɪl] vt (water) hervir; (eggs) pasar por agua, cocer ♦ vi hervir; (fig: with anger) estar furioso; (: with heat) asfixiarse ♦ n (MED) furúnculo, divieso; to come to the ~, to come to a ~ (US) comenzar a hervir; to ~ down to (fig) reducirse a; ~ over vi salirse, rebosar; (anger etc) llegar al colmo; ~ed egg n huevo cocido (SP) or pasado (AM); ~ed potatoes npl patatas fpl (SP) or papas fpl (AM) hervidas; ~er n caldera; ~er suit (BRIT) n mono; ~ing point n punto de ebullición.

boisterous ['bɔɪstərəs] adj (noisy) bullicioso; (excitable) exuberante; (crowd) tumultuoso.

bold [bəʊld] adj valiente, audaz; (pej) descarado; (colour) llamativo.

Bolivia [bə'lɪvɪə] n Bolivia; ~n adj, n boliviano/a m/f.

bollard ['bɔləd] (BRIT) n (AUT) poste m.

bolster ['bəʊlstə*] n travesero, cabezal m; ~ up vt reforzar.

bolt [bəʊlt] n (lock) cerrojo; (with nut) perno, tornillo ♦ adv: ~ upright rígido, erguido ♦ vt (door) echar el cerrojo a; (also: ~ together) sujetar con tornillos; (food) engullir ♦ vi fugarse; (horse) desbocarse.

bomb [bɔm] n bomba ♦ vt bombardear; ~ard [-'bɑːd] vt bombardear; (fig): to ~ with questions acribillar a preguntas; ~ardment [-'bɑːdmənt] n bombardeo.

bombastic [bɔm'bæstɪk] adj rimbombante; (person) farolero.

bomb: ~ disposal n desmontaje m de explosivos; ~er n (AVIAT) bombardero; ~shell n (fig) bomba.

bona fide ['bəʊnə'faɪdɪ] adj genuino, auténtico.

bond [bɔnd] n (promise) fianza; (FINANCE) bono; (link) vínculo, lazo; (COMM): in ~ en depósito bajo fianza.

bondage ['bɔndɪdʒ] n esclavitud f.

bone [bəʊn] n hueso; (of fish) espina ♦ vt deshuesar; quitar las espinas a; ~ idle adj gandul.

bonfire ['bɔnfaɪə*] n hoguera, fogata.

bonnet ['bɔnɪt] n gorra; (BRIT: of car) capó m.

bonus ['bəʊnəs] n (payment) paga extraordinaria, plus m; (fig) bendición f.

bony ['bəʊnɪ] adj (arm, face) huesudo; (MED: tissue) óseo; (meat) lleno de huesos; (fish) lleno de espinas.

boo [buː] excl ¡uh! ♦ vt abuchear, rechiflar.

booby trap ['buːbɪ-] n trampa explosiva.

book [buk] n libro; (of tickets) taco; (of stamps etc) librito ♦ vt (ticket) sacar; (seat, room) reservar; ~s npl (COMM) cuentas fpl, contabilidad f; ~case n librería, estante m para libros; ~ing office n (BRIT: RAIL) despacho de billetes (SP) or boletos (AM); (THEATRE) taquilla (SP), boletería (AM); ~keeping n contabilidad f; ~let n folleto; ~maker n corredor m de apuestas; ~seller n librero; ~shop n librería; ~store n = ~shop.

boom [buːm] n (noise) trueno, estampido; (*in prices etc*) alza rápida; (*ECON, in population*) boom *m* ♦ *vi* (*cannon*) hacer gran estruendo; retumbar; (*ECON*) estar en alza.

boon [buːn] *n* favor *m*, beneficio.

boost [buːst] *n* estímulo, empuje *m* ♦ *vt* estimular, empujar; ~**er** *n* (*MED*) reinyección *f*.

boot [buːt] *n* bota; (*BRIT: of car*) maleta, maletero ♦ *vt* (*COMPUT*) arrancar; **to** ~ (*in addition*) además, por añadidura.

booth [buːð] *n* (*at fair*) barraca; (*telephone* ~, *voting* ~) cabina.

booty [ˈbuːtɪ] *n* botín *m*.

booze [buːz] (*inf*) *n* bebida.

border [ˈbɔːdə*] *n* borde *m*, margen *m*; (*of a country*) frontera; (*for flowers*) arriate *m* ♦ *vt* (*road*) bordear; (*another country: also:* ~ *on*) lindar con; **B~s** *n*: **the B~s** *región fronteriza entre Escocia y Inglaterra*; ~ **on** *vt fus* (*insanity etc*) rayar en; ~**line** *n*: **on the** ~**line** en el límite; ~**line case** *n* caso dudoso.

bore [bɔː*] *pt of* **bear** ♦ *vt* (*hole*) hacer un agujero en; (*well*) perforar; (*person*) aburrir ♦ *n* (*person*) pelmazo, pesado; (*of gun*) calibre *m*; **to be** ~**d** estar aburrido; ~**dom** *n* aburrimiento.

boring [ˈbɔːrɪŋ] *adj* aburrido.

born [bɔːn] *adj*: **to be** ~ nacer; **I was** ~ **in 1960** nací en 1960.

borne [bɔːn] *pp of* **bear**.

borough [ˈbʌrə] *n* municipio.

borrow [ˈbɔrəu] *vt*: **to** ~ **sth** (**from sb**) tomar algo prestado (a alguien).

bosom [ˈbuzəm] *n* pecho; ~ **friend** amigo íntimo.

boss [bɔs] *n* jefe *m* ♦ *vt* (*also:* ~ *about or around*) mangonear; ~**y** *adj* mandón/ona.

bosun [ˈbəusn] *n* contramaestre *m*.

botany [ˈbɔtənɪ] *n* botánica.

botch [bɔtʃ] *vt* (*also:* ~ *up*) arruinar, estropear.

both [bəuθ] *adj, pron* ambos/as, los/las dos; ~ **of us went, we** ~ **went** fuimos los dos, ambos fuimos ♦ *adv*: ~ **A and B** tanto A como B.

bother [ˈbɔðə*] *vt* (*worry*) preocupar;

(*disturb*) molestar, fastidiar ♦ *vi* (*also:* ~ *o.s.*) molestarse ♦ *n* (*trouble*) dificultad *f*; (*nuisance*) molestia, lata; **to** ~ **doing** tomarse la molestia de hacer.

bottle [ˈbɔtl] *n* botella; (*small*) frasco; (*baby's*) biberón *m* ♦ *vt* embotellar; ~ **up** *vt* suprimir; ~**neck** *n* (*AUT*) embotellamiento; (*in supply*) obstáculo; ~**opener** *n* abrebotellas *m inv*.

bottom [ˈbɔtəm] *n* (*of box, sea*) fondo; (*buttocks*) trasero, culo; (*of page*) pie *m*; (*of list*) final *m*; (*of class*) último/a ♦ *adj* (*lowest*) más bajo; (*last*) último; ~**less** *adj* sin fondo, inacabable.

bough [bau] *n* rama.

bought [bɔːt] *pt, pp of* **buy**.

boulder [ˈbəuldə*] *n* canto rodado.

bounce [bauns] *vi* (*ball*) (*re*)botar; (*cheque*) ser rechazado ♦ *vt* hacer (re)botar ♦ *n* (*rebound*) (re)bote *m*; ~**r** (*inf*) *n* gorila *m* (*que echa a los alborotadores de un bar, club etc*).

bound [baund] *pt, pp of* **bind** ♦ *n* (*leap*) salto; (*gen pl: limit*) límite *m* ♦ *vi* (*leap*) saltar ♦ *vt* (*border*) rodear ♦ *adj*: ~ **by** rodeado de; **to be** ~ **to do sth** (*obliged*) tener el deber de hacer algo; **he's** ~ **to come** es seguro que vendrá; **out of** ~**s** prohibido el paso; ~ **for** con destino a.

boundary [ˈbaundrɪ] *n* límite *m*.

boundless [ˈbaundlɪs] *adj* ilimitado.

bouquet [ˈbukeɪ] *n* (*of flowers*) ramo.

bourgeois [ˈbuəʒwɑː] *adj* burgués/esa *m/f*.

bout [baut] *n* (*of malaria etc*) ataque *m*; (*of activity*) período; (*BOXING etc*) combate *m*, encuentro.

bow¹ [bəu] *n* (*knot*) lazo; (*weapon, MUS*) arco.

bow² [bau] *n* (*of the head*) reverencia; (*NAUT: also:* ~*s*) proa ♦ *vi* inclinarse, hacer una reverencia; (*yield*): **to** ~ **to** *or* **before** ceder ante, someterse a.

bowels [bauəlz] *npl* intestinos *mpl*, vientre *m*; (*fig*) entrañas *fpl*.

bowl [bəul] *n* tazón *m*, cuenco; (*ball*) bola ♦ *vi* (*CRICKET*) arrojar la pelota.

bow-legged [ˈbəuˈlɛgɪd] *adj* estevado.

bowler [ˈbəulə*] *n* (*CRICKET*) lanzador *m*

(de la pelota); (BRIT: also: ~ hat) hongo, bombín m.

bowling ['bəulɪŋ] n (game) bochas fpl, bolos mpl; ~ **alley** n bolera; ~ **green** n pista para bochas.

bowls [bəulz] n juego de las bochas, bolos mpl.

bow tie ['bəu-] n corbata de lazo, pajarita.

box [bɔks] n (also: cardboard ~) caja, cajón m; (THEATRE) palco ♦ vt encajonar ♦ vi (SPORT) boxear; ~**er** n (person) boxeador m; ~**ing** n (SPORT) boxeo; B~**ing Day** (BRIT) n día en que se dan los aguinaldos, 26 de diciembre; ~**ing gloves** npl guantes mpl de boxeo; ~**ing ring** n ring m, cuadrilátero; ~ **office** n taquilla (SP), boletería (AM); ~**room** n trastero.

boy [bɔɪ] n (young) niño; (older) muchacho, chico; (son) hijo.

boycott ['bɔɪkɔt] n boicot m ♦ vt boicotear.

boyfriend ['bɔɪfrɛnd] n novio.

boyish ['bɔɪɪʃ] adj juvenil; (girl) con aspecto de muchacho.

B.R. n abbr (= British Rail) ≈ RENFE f (SP).

bra [brɑ:] n sostén m, sujetador m.

brace [breɪs] n (BRIT: also: ~s: on teeth) corrector m, aparato; (tool) berbiquí m ♦ vt (knees, shoulders) tensionar; ~**s** npl (BRIT) tirantes mpl; **to ~ o.s.** (fig) prepararse.

bracelet ['breɪslɪt] n pulsera, brazalete m.

bracing ['breɪsɪŋ] adj vigorizante, tónico.

bracken ['brækən] n helecho.

bracket ['brækɪt] n (TECH) soporte m, puntal m; (group) clase f, categoría; (also: brace ~) soporte m, abrazadera; (also: round ~) paréntesis m inv; (also: square ~) corchete m ♦ vt (word etc) poner entre paréntesis.

brag [bræg] vi jactarse.

braid [breɪd] n (trimming) galón m; (of hair) trenza.

brain [breɪn] n cerebro; ~**s** npl sesos mpl; **she's got** ~**s** es muy lista; ~**child** n invento; ~**wash** vt lavar el cerebro;

~**wave** n idea luminosa; ~**y** adj muy inteligente.

braise [breɪz] vt cocer a fuego lento.

brake [breɪk] n (on vehicle) freno ♦ vi frenar; ~ **fluid** n líquido de frenos; ~ **light** n luz f de frenado.

bramble ['bræmbl] n zarza.

bran [bræn] n salvado.

branch [brɑ:ntʃ] n rama; (COMM) sucursal f; ~ **out** vi (fig) extenderse.

brand [brænd] n marca; (fig: type) tipo ♦ vt (cattle) marcar con hierro candente.

brandish ['brændɪʃ] vt blandir.

brand-new ['brænd'nju:] adj flamante, completamente nuevo.

brandy ['brændɪ] n coñac m.

brash [bræʃ] adj (forward) descarado.

brass [brɑ:s] n latón m; **the** ~ (MUS) los cobres; ~ **band** n banda de metal.

brassière ['bræsɪə*] n sostén m, sujetador m.

brat [bræt] n (pej) mocoso/a.

bravado [brə'vɑ:dəu] n fanfarronería.

brave [breɪv] adj valiente, valeroso ♦ vt (face up to) desafiar; ~**ry** n valor m, valentía.

brawl [brɔ:l] n pelea, reyerta.

brawny ['brɔ:nɪ] adj fornido, musculoso.

bray [breɪ] vi rebuznar.

brazen ['breɪzn] adj descarado, cínico ♦ vt: **to** ~ **it out** echarle cara.

brazier ['breɪzɪə*] n brasero.

Brazil [brə'zɪl] n (el) Brasil; ~**ian** adj, n brasileño/a m/f.

breach [bri:tʃ] vt abrir brecha en ♦ n (gap) brecha; (breaking): ~ **of contract** infracción f de contrato; ~ **of the peace** perturbación f del órden público.

bread [brɛd] n pan m; ~ **and butter** n pan con mantequilla; (fig) pan (de cada día); ~**bin** (US ~**box**) n panera; ~**crumbs** npl migajas fpl; (CULIN) pan rallado; ~**line** n: **on the** ~**line** en la miseria.

breadth [brɛtθ] n anchura; (fig) amplitud f.

breadwinner ['brɛdwɪnə*] n sustento m de la familia.

break [breɪk] (pt **broke**, pp **broken**) vt

romper; (*promise*) faltar a; (*law*) violar, infringir; (*record*) superar ♦ *vi* romperse, quebrarse; (*storm*) estallar; (*weather*) cambiar; (*dawn*) despuntar; (*news etc*) darse a conocer ♦ *n* (*gap*) abertura; (*fracture*) fractura; (*time*) intervalo; (: *at school*) (período de) recreo; (*chance*) oportunidad *f*; **to ~ the news to sb** comunicar la noticia a uno; **~ down** *vt* (*figures, data*) analizar, descomponer ♦ *vi* (*machine*) estropearse; (*AUT*) averiarse; (*person*) romper a llorar; (*talks*) fracasar; **~ even** *vi* cubrir los gastos; **~ free** *or* **loose** *vi* escaparse; **~ in** *vt* (*horse etc*) domar ♦ *vi* (*burglar*) forzar una entrada; (*interrupt*) interrumpir; **~ into** *vt fus* (*house*) forzar; **~ off** *vi* (*speaker*) pararse, detenerse; (*branch*) partir; **~ open** *vt* (*door etc*) abrir por la fuerza, forzar; **~ out** *vi* estallar; (*prisoner*) escaparse; **to ~ out in spots** salirle a uno granos; **~ up** *vi* (*ship*) hacerse pedazos; (*crowd, meeting*) disolverse; (*marriage*) deshacerse; (*SCOL*) terminar (el curso) ♦ *vt* (*rocks etc*) partir; (*journey*) partir; (*fight etc*) acabar con; **~age** *n* rotura; **~down** *n* (*AUT*) avería; (*in communications*) interrupción *f*; (*MED: also: nervous ~down*) colapso, crisis *f* nerviosa; (*of marriage, talks*) fracaso; (*of statistics*) análisis *m inv*; **~down van** (*BRIT*) *n* (camión *m*) grúa; **~er** *n* (ola) rompiente *f*.

breakfast ['brɛkfəst] *n* desayuno.

break: **~-in** *n* robo con allanamiento de morada; **~ing and entering** *n* (*LAW*) violación *f* de domicilio, allanamiento de morada; **~through** *n* (*also fig*) avance *m*; **~water** *n* rompeolas *m inv*.

breast [brɛst] *n* (*of woman*) pecho, seno; (*chest*) pecho; (*of bird*) pechuga; **~-feed** (*irreg: like* feed) *vt*, *vi* amamantar, criar a los pechos; **~-stroke** *n* braza (de pecho).

breath [brɛθ] *n* aliento, respiración *f*; **to take a deep ~** respirar hondo; **out of ~** sin aliento, sofocado.

Breathalyser ['brɛθəlaɪzə*] ® (*BRIT*) *n* alcoholímetro *m*.

breathe [briːð] *vt*, *vi* respirar; **~ in** *vt*, *vi* aspirar; **~ out** *vt*, *vi* espirar; **~r** *n* respiro; **breathing** *n* respiración *f*.

breath: **~less** *adj* sin aliento, jadeante; **~taking** *adj* imponente, pasmoso.

breed [briːd] (*pt, pp* **bred**) *vt* criar ♦ *vi* reproducirse, procrear ♦ *n* (*ZOOL*) raza, casta; (*type*) tipo; **~ing** *n* (*of person*) educación *f*.

breeze [briːz] *n* brisa.

breezy ['briːzɪ] *adj* de mucho viento, ventoso; (*person*) despreocupado.

brevity ['brɛvɪtɪ] *n* brevedad *f*.

brew [bruː] *vt* (*tea*) hacer; (*beer*) elaborar ♦ *vi* (*fig: trouble*) prepararse; (*storm*) amenazar; **~ery** *n* fábrica de cerveza, cervecería.

bribe [braɪb] *n* soborno ♦ *vt* sobornar, cohechar; **~ry** *n* soborno, cohecho.

bric-a-brac ['brɪkəbræk] *n inv* baratijas *fpl*.

brick [brɪk] *n* ladrillo; **~layer** *n* albañil *m*.

bridal ['braɪdl] *adj* nupcial.

bride [braɪd] *n* novia; **~groom** *n* novio; **~smaid** *n* dama de honor.

bridge [brɪdʒ] *n* puente *m*; (*NAUT*) puente *m* de mando; (*of nose*) caballete *m*; (*CARDS*) bridge *m* ♦ *vt* (*fig*): **to ~ a gap** llenar un vacío.

bridle ['braɪdl] *n* brida, freno; **~ path** *n* camino de herradura.

brief [briːf] *adj* breve, corto ♦ *n* (*LAW*) escrito; (*task*) cometido, encargo ♦ *vt* informar; **~s** *npl* (*for men*) calzoncillos *mpl*; (*for women*) bragas *fpl*; **~case** *n* cartera (*SP*), portafolio (*AM*); **~ing** *n* (*PRESS*) informe *m*; **~ly** *adv* (*glance*) fugazmente; (*say*) en pocas palabras.

brigadier [brɪgə'dɪə*] *n* general *m* de brigada.

bright [braɪt] *adj* brillante; (*room*) luminoso; (*day*) de sol; (*person: clever*) listo, inteligente; (: *lively*) alegre; (*colour*) vivo; (*future*) prometedor(a); **~en** (*also: ~en up*) *vt* (*room*) hacer más alegre; (*event*) alegrar ♦ *vi* (*weather*) despejarse; (*person*) animarse, alegrarse; (*prospects*) mejorar.

brilliance ['brɪljəns] *n* brillo, brillantez *f*;

(*of talent etc*) brillantez.

brilliant ['brɪljənt] *adj* brillante; (*inf*) fenomenal.

brim [brɪm] *n* borde *m*; (*of hat*) ala.

brine [braɪn] *n* (*CULIN*) salmuera.

bring [brɪŋ] (*pt, pp* **brought**) *vt* (*thing, person: with you*) traer; (: *to sb*) llevar, conducir; (*trouble, satisfaction*) causar; ~ **about** *vt* ocasionar, producir; ~ **back** *vt* volver a traer; (*return*) devolver; ~ **down** *vt* (*government, plane*) derribar; (*price*) rebajar; ~ **forward** *vt* adelantar; ~ **off** *vt* (*task, plan*) lograr, conseguir; ~ **out** *vt* sacar; (*book etc*) publicar; (*meaning*) subrayar; ~ **round** *vt* (*unconscious person*) hacer volver en si; ~ **up** *vt* subir; (*person*) educar, criar; (*question*) sacar a colación; (*food: vomit*) devolver, vomitar.

brink [brɪŋk] *n* borde *m*.

brisk [brɪsk] *adj* (*abrupt: tone*) brusco; (*person*) enérgico, vigoroso; (*pace*) rápido; (*trade*) activo.

bristle ['brɪsl] *n* cerda ♦ *vi*: to ~ in anger temblar de rabia.

Britain ['brɪtən] *n* (*also:* **Great** ~) Gran Bretaña.

British ['brɪtɪʃ] *adj* británico ♦ *npl*: the ~ los británicos; ~ **Isles** *npl*: the ~ Isles las Islas Británicas; ~ **Rail** *n* ≈ RENFE *f* (*SP*).

Briton ['brɪtən] *n* británico/a.

brittle ['brɪtl] *adj* quebradizo, frágil.

broach [brəutʃ] *vt* (*subject*) abordar.

broad [brɔːd] *adj* ancho; (*range*) amplio; (*smile*) abierto; (*general: outlines etc*) general; (*accent*) cerrado; in ~ daylight en pleno día; ~**cast** (*irreg: like* **cast**) *n* emisión *f* ♦ *vt* (*RADIO*) emitir; (*TV*) transmitir ♦ *vi* emitir; transmitir; ~**en** *vt* ampliar ♦ *vi* ensancharse; to ~**en** one's mind hacer más tolerante a uno; ~**ly** *adv* en general; ~**minded** *adj* tolerante, liberal.

broccoli ['brɔkəlɪ] *n* brécol *m*.

brochure ['brəufjuə*] *n* folleto.

broil [brɔɪl] *vt* (*CULIN*) asar a la parrilla.

broke [brəuk] *pt of* **break** ♦ *adj* (*inf*) pelado, sin blanca.

broken ['brəukən] *pp of* **break** ♦ *adj* roto; (*machine: also:* ~ **down**) averiado; ~ **leg** pierna rota; in ~ **English** en un inglés imperfecto; ~**-hearted** *adj* con el corazón partido.

broker ['brəukə*] *n* agente *m/f*, bolsista *m/f*; (*insurance* ~) agente de seguros.

brolly ['brɔlɪ] (*BRIT: inf*) *n* paraguas *m inv*.

bronchitis [brɔŋ'kaɪtɪs] *n* bronquitis *f*.

bronze [brɔnz] *n* bronce *m*.

brooch [brəutʃ] *n* prendedor *m*, broche *m*.

brood [bruːd] *n* camada, cría ♦ *vi* (*person*) dejarse obsesionar.

brook [bruk] *n* arroyo.

broom [brum] *n* escoba; (*BOT*) retama; ~**stick** *n* palo de escoba.

Bros. *abbr* (= *Brothers*) Hnos.

broth [brɔθ] *n* caldo.

brothel ['brɔθl] *n* burdel *m*.

brother ['brʌðə*] *n* hermano; ~**-in-law** *n* cuñado.

brought [brɔːt] *pt, pp of* **bring**.

brow [brau] *n* (*forehead*) frente *m*; (*eye*~) ceja; (*of hill*) cumbre *f*.

brown [braun] *adj* (*colour*) marrón; (*hair*) castaño; (*tanned*) bronceado, moreno ♦ *n* (*colour*) color *m* marrón or pardo ♦ *vt* (*CULIN*) dorar; ~ **bread** *n* pan integral.

brownie ['braunɪ] *n* niña exploradora; (*US: cake*) pastel de chocolate con nueces.

brown paper *n* papel *m* de estraza.

brown sugar *n* azúcar *m* terciado.

browse [brauz] *vi* (*through book*) hojear; (*in shop*) mirar.

bruise [bruːz] *n* cardenal *m* (*SP*), moretón *m* (*AM*) ♦ *vt* magullar.

brunch [brʌntʃ] *n* desayuno-almuerzo.

brunette [bruː'net] *n* morena.

brunt [brʌnt] *n*: to bear the ~ of llevar el peso de.

brush [brʌʃ] *n* cepillo; (*for painting, shaving etc*) brocha; (*artist's*) pincel *m*; (*with police etc*) roce *m* ♦ *vt* (*sweep*) barrer; (*groom*) cepillar; (*also:* ~ **against**) rozar al pasar; ~

aside vt rechazar, no hacer caso a; ~ up vt (knowledge) repasar, refrescar; ~wood n (sticks) leña.

brusque [bruːsk] adj brusco, áspero.

Brussels ['brʌslz] n Bruselas; ~ **sprout** n col f de Bruselas.

brute [bruːt] n bruto; (person) bestia ♦ adj: by ~ **force** a fuerza bruta.

B.Sc. abbr (= Bachelor of Science) licenciado en Ciencias.

bubble ['bʌbl] n burbuja ♦ vi burbujear, borbotar; ~ **bath** n espuma para el baño; ~ **gum** n chicle m de globo.

buck [bʌk] n (rabbit) conejo macho; (deer) gamo; (US: inf) dólar m ♦ vi corcovear; **to pass the** ~ (**to sb**) echar (a uno) el muerto; ~ **up** vi (cheer up) animarse, cobrar ánimo.

bucket ['bʌkɪt] n cubo, balde m.

buckle ['bʌkl] n hebilla ♦ vt abrochar con hebilla ♦ vi combarse.

bud [bʌd] n (of plant) brote m, yema; (of flower) capullo ♦ vi brotar, echar brotes.

Buddhism ['budɪzm] n Budismo.

budding ['bʌdɪŋ] adj en ciernes, en embrión.

buddy ['bʌdɪ] (US) n compañero, compinche m.

budge [bʌdʒ] vt mover; (fig) hacer ceder ♦ vi moverse, ceder.

budgerigar ['bʌdʒərɪgɑː*] n periquito.

budget ['bʌdʒɪt] n presupuesto ♦ vi: to ~ **for sth** presupuestar algo.

budgie ['bʌdʒɪ] n = **budgerigar**.

buff [bʌf] adj (colour) color de ante ♦ n (inf: enthusiast) entusiasta m/f.

buffalo ['bʌfələu] (pl ~ or ~es) n (BRIT) búfalo; (US: bison) bisonte m.

buffer ['bʌfə*] n (COMPUT) memoria intermedia; (RAIL) tope m.

buffet¹ ['bufeɪ] n (BRIT: in station) bar m, cafetería; (food) buffet m; ~ **car** (BRIT) n (RAIL) coche-comedor m.

buffet² ['bʌfɪt] vt golpear.

bug [bʌg] n (esp US: insect) bicho, sabandija; (COMPUT) error m; (germ) microbio, bacilo; (spy device) micrófono oculto ♦ vt (inf: annoy) fastidiar; (room) poner micrófono oculto en.

buggy ['bʌgɪ] n cochecito de niño.

bugle ['bjuːgl] n corneta, clarín m.

build [bɪld] (pt, pp built) n (of person) tipo ♦ vt construir, edificar; ~ **up** vt (morale, forces, production) acrecentar; (stocks) acumular; ~**er** n (contractor) contratista m/f; ~**ing** n construcción f; (structure) edificio; ~**ing society** (BRIT) n sociedad f inmobiliaria, cooperativa de construcciones.

built [bɪlt] pt, pp of **build** ♦ adj: ~-**in** (wardrobe etc) empotrado; ~-**up area** n zona urbanizada.

bulb [bʌlb] n (BOT) bulbo; (ELEC) bombilla (SP), foco (AM).

Bulgaria [bʌl'geərɪə] n Bulgaria; ~**n** adj, n búlgaro/a m/f.

bulge [bʌldʒ] n bulto, protuberancia ♦ vi bombearse, pandearse; (pocket etc): to ~ (**with**) rebosar (de).

bulk [bʌlk] n masa, mole f; **in** ~ (COMM) a granel; **the** ~ **of** la mayor parte de; ~**y** adj voluminoso, abultado.

bull [bul] n toro; (male elephant, whale) macho; (STOCK EXCHANGE) n dogo.

bulldozer ['buldəuzə*] n bulldozer m.

bullet ['bulɪt] n bala.

bulletin ['bulɪtɪn] n anuncio, parte m; (journal) boletín m.

bulletproof ['bulɪtpruːf] adj a prueba de balas.

bullfight ['bulfaɪt] n corrida de toros; ~**er** n torero; ~**ing** n los toros, el toreo.

bullion ['buljən] n oro (or plata) en barras.

bullock ['bulək] n novillo.

bullring ['bulrɪŋ] n plaza de toros.

bull's-eye n centro del blanco.

bully ['bulɪ] n valentón m, matón m ♦ vt intimidar, tiranizar.

bum [bʌm] n (inf: backside) culo; (esp US: tramp) vagabundo.

bumblebee ['bʌmblbiː] n abejorro.

bump [bʌmp] n (blow) tope m, choque m; (jolt) sacudida; (on road etc) bache m; (on head etc) chichón m ♦ vt (strike) chocar contra; ~ **into** vt fus chocar contra, tropezar con; (person) topar con; ~**er** n (AUT) parachoques m inv ♦ adj: ~**er crop/harvest** cosecha abundan-

te; ~**er cars** *npl* coches *mpl* de choque.
bumptious ['bʌmpʃəs] *adj* engreído, presuntuoso.
bumpy ['bʌmpɪ] *adj* (*road*) lleno de baches.
bun [bʌn] *n* (*BRIT: cake*) pastel *m*; (*US: bread*) bollo; (*of hair*) moño.
bunch [bʌntʃ] *n* (*of flowers*) ramo; (*of keys*) manojo; (*of bananas*) piña; (*of people*) grupo; (*pej*) pandilla; ~**es** *npl* (*in hair*) coletas *fpl*.
bundle ['bʌndl] *n* bulto, fardo; (*of sticks*) haz *m*; (*of papers*) legajo ♦ *vt* (*also: ~ up*) atar, envolver; **to ~ sth/sb into** meter algo/a alguien precipitadamente en.
bungalow ['bʌŋgələu] *n* bungalow *m*, chalé *m*.
bungle ['bʌŋgl] *vt* hacer mal.
bunion ['bʌnjən] *n* juanete *m*.
bunk [bʌŋk] *n* litera; ~ **beds** *npl* literas *fpl*.
bunker ['bʌŋkə*] *n* (*coal store*) carbonera; (*MIL*) refugio; (*GOLF*) bunker *m*.
bunny ['bʌnɪ] *n* (*also: ~ rabbit*) conejito.
bunting ['bʌntɪŋ] *n* banderitas *fpl*.
buoy [bɔɪ] *n* boya; ~ **up** *vt* (*fig*) animar; ~**ant** *adj* (*ship*) capaz de flotar; (*economy*) boyante; (*person*) optimista.
burden ['bəːdn] *n* carga ♦ *vt* cargar.
bureau [bjuə'rəu] (*pl* **bureaux**) *n* (*BRIT: writing desk*) escritorio, buró *m*; (*US: chest of drawers*) cómoda; (*office*) oficina, agencia.
bureaucracy [bjuə'rɔkrəsɪ] *n* burocracia.
bureaux [bjuə'rəuz] *npl of* **bureau**.
burglar ['bəːglə*] *n* ladrón/ona *m/f*; ~ **alarm** *n* alarma *f* antirrobo; ~**y** *n* robo con allanamiento, robo de una casa.
burial ['bɛrɪəl] *n* entierro.
burly ['bəːlɪ] *adj* fornido, membrudo.
Burma ['bəːmə] *n* Birmania.
burn [bəːn] (*pt, pp* **burned** *or* **burnt**) *vt* quemar; (*house*) incendiar ♦ *vi* quemarse, arder; incendiarse; (*sting*) escocer ♦ *n* quemadura; ~ **down** *vt* incendiar; ~**er** *n* (*on cooker etc*) quemador *m*; ~**ing** *adj* (*building etc*) en llamas; (*hot: sand etc*) abrasador(a);

(*ambition*) ardiente; **burnt** [bəːnt] *pt, pp of* **burn**.
burrow ['bʌrəu] *n* madriguera ♦ *vi* hacer una madriguera; (*rummage*) hurgar.
bursary ['bəːsərɪ] (*BRIT*) *n* beca.
burst [bəːst] (*pt, pp* **burst**) *vt* reventar; (*subj: river: banks etc*) romper ♦ *vi* reventarse; (*tyre*) pincharse ♦ *n* (*of gunfire*) ráfaga; (*also: ~ pipe*) reventón *m*; **a ~ of energy/speed/enthusiasm** una explosión de energía/un ímpetu de velocidad/un arranque de entusiasmo; **to ~ into flames** estallar en llamas, **to ~ into tears** deshacerse en lágrimas; **to ~ out laughing** soltar la carcajada; **to ~ open** abrirse de golpe; **to be ~ing with** (*subj: container*) estar lleno a rebosar de; (*person*) reventar por *or* de; ~ **into** *vt fus* (*room etc*) irrumpir en.
bury ['bɛrɪ] *vt* enterrar; (*body*) enterrar, sepultar.
bus [bʌs] *n* autobús *m*.
bush [buʃ] *n* arbusto; (*scrub land*) monte *m*; **to beat about the ~** andar(se) con rodeos; ~**y** *adj* (*thick*) espeso, poblado.
busily ['bɪzɪlɪ] *adv* afanosamente.
business ['bɪznɪs] *n* (*matter*) asunto; (*trading*) comercio, negocios *mpl*; (*firm*) empresa, casa; (*occupation*) oficio; **to be away on ~** estar en viaje de negocios; **it's my ~ to ...** me toca *or* corresponde ...; **it's none of my ~** yo no tengo nada que ver; **he means ~** habla en serio; ~**like** *adj* eficiente; ~**man** *n* hombre *m* de negocios; ~ **trip** *n* viaje *m* de negocios; ~**woman** *n* mujer *f* de negocios.
busker ['bʌskə*] (*BRIT*) *n* músico/a ambulante.
bus-stop ['bʌsstɔp] *n* parada de autobús.
bust [bʌst] *n* (*ANAT*) pecho; (*sculpture*) busto ♦ *adj* (*inf: broken*) roto, estropeado; **to go ~** quebrar.
bustle ['bʌsl] *n* bullicio, movimiento ♦ *vi* menearse, apresurarse; **bustling** *adj* (*town*) animado, bullicioso.
busy ['bɪzɪ] *adj* ocupado, atareado;

(*shop*, *street*) concurrido, animado; (*TEL*: *line*) comunicando ♦ *vt*: to ~ o.s. with ocuparse en; ~body ~ *n* entrometido/a; ~ signal (*US*) *n* (*TEL*) señal *f* de comunicando.

but [bʌt] *conj* **1** pero; **he's not very bright**, ~ **he's hard-working** no es muy inteligente, pero es trabajador
2 (*in direct contradiction*) sino; **he's not English** ~ **French** no es inglés sino francés; **he didn't sing** ~ **he shouted** no cantó sino que gritó
3 (*showing disagreement, surprise etc*): ~ **that's far too expensive!** ¡pero eso es carísimo!; ~ **it does work!** ¡(pero) sí que funciona!
♦ *prep* (*apart from, except*) menos, salvo; **we've had nothing** ~ **trouble** no hemos tenido más que problemas; **no-one** ~ **him can do it** nadie más que él puede hacerlo; **who** ~ **a lunatic would do such a thing?** ¡sólo un loco haría una cosa así!; ~ **for you/your help** si no fuera por ti/tu ayuda; **anything** ~ **that** cualquier cosa menos eso
♦ *adv* (*just, only*): **she's** ~ **a child** no es más que una niña; **had I** ~ **known** si lo hubiera sabido; **I can** ~ **try** al menos lo puedo intentar; **it's all** ~ **finished** está casi acabado.

butcher [ˈbutʃə*] *n* carnicero ♦ *vt* hacer una carnicería con; (*cattle etc*) matar; ~'s (shop)*n* carnicería.
butler [ˈbʌtlə*] *n* mayordomo.
butt [bʌt] *n* (*barrel*) tonel *m*; (*of gun*) culata; (*of cigarette*) colilla; (*BRIT*: *fig*: *target*) blanco ♦ *vt* dar cabezadas contra, top(et)ar; ~ in*vi* (*interrupt*) interrumpir.
butter [ˈbʌtə*] *n* mantequilla ♦ *vt* untar con mantequilla; ~cup *n* botón *m* de oro.
butterfly [ˈbʌtəflaɪ] *n* mariposa; (*SWIMMING*: *also*: ~ *stroke*) braza de mariposa.
buttocks [ˈbʌtəks] *npl* nalgas *fpl*.
button [ˈbʌtn] *n* botón *m*; (*US*: *badge*)

placa, chapa ♦ *vt* (*also*: ~ *up*) abotonar, abrochar ♦ *vi* abrocharse.
buttress [ˈbʌtrɪs] *n* contrafuerte *m*.
buxom [ˈbʌksəm] *adj* exuberante.
buy [baɪ] (*pt*, *pp* bought) *vt* comprar ♦ *n* compra; **to** ~ **sb sth/sth from sb** comprarle algo a alguien; **to** ~ **sb a drink** invitar a alguien a tomar algo; ~er *n* comprador(a) *m/f*.
buzz [bʌz] *n* zumbido; (*inf*: *phone call*) llamada (por teléfono) ♦ *vi* zumbar.
buzzer [ˈbʌzə*] *n* timbre *m*.
buzz word *n* palabra que está de moda.

by [baɪ] *prep* **1** (*referring to cause, agent*) por; de; **killed** ~ **lightning** muerto por un relámpago; **a painting** ~ **Picasso** un cuadro de Picasso
2 (*referring to method, manner, means*): ~ **bus/car/train** en autobús/coche/tren; **to pay** ~ **cheque** pagar con un cheque; ~ **moonlight/candlelight** a la luz de la luna/una vela; ~ **saving hard, he ...** ahorrando, ...
3 (*via, through*) por; **we came** ~ **Dover** vinimos por Dover
4 (*close to, past*): **the house** ~ **the river** la casa junto al río; **she rushed** ~ **me** pasó a mi lado como una exhalación; **I go** ~ **the post office every day** paso por delante de Correos todos los días
5 (*time: not later than*) para; (: *during*): ~ **daylight** de día; ~ **4 o'clock** para las cuatro; ~ **this time tomorrow** mañana a estas horas; ~ **the time I got here it was too late** cuando llegué ya era demasiado tarde
6 (*amount*): ~ **the metre/kilo** por metro/kilo; **paid** ~ **the hour** pagado por hora
7 (*MATH, measure*): **to divide/multiply** ~ **3** dividir/multiplicar por 3; **a room 3 metres** ~ **4** una habitación de 3 metros por 4; **it's broader** ~ **a metre** es un metro más ancho
8 (*according to*) según, de acuerdo con; **it's 3 o'clock** ~ **my watch** según mi reloj, son las tres; **it's all right** ~

me por mí, está bien
9: (all) ~ oneself *etc* todo solo; **he did it (all) ~ himself** lo hizo él solo; **he was standing (all) ~ himself in a corner** estaba de pie solo en un rincón
10: ~ the way a propósito, por cierto; **this wasn't my idea, ~ the way** pues, no fue idea mía
♦ *adv* **1** *see* **go; pass** *etc*
2: ~ and ~ finalmente; **they'll come back ~ and ~** acabarán volviendo; **~ and large** en líneas generales, en general.

bye(-bye) ['baɪ('baɪ)] *excl* adiós, hasta luego.
by(e)-law *n* ordenanza municipal.
by-election (*BRIT*) *n* elección *f* parcial.
bygone ['baɪgɒn] *adj* pasado, del pasado ♦ *n*: **let ~s be ~s** lo pasado, pasado está.
bypass ['baɪpɑːs] *n* carretera de circunvalación; (*MED*) (operación *f* de) bypass *m* ♦ *vt* evitar.
by-product *n* subproducto, derivado; (*of situation*) consecuencia.
bystander ['baɪstændə*] *n* espectador(a) *m/f*.
byte [baɪt] *n* (*COMPUT*) byte *m*, octeto.
byword ['baɪwəːd] *n*: **to be a ~ for** ser conocidísimo por.
by-your-leave *n*: **without so much as a ~** sin decir nada, sin dar ningún tipo de explicación.

C

C [siː] *n* (*MUS*) do *m*.
C. *abbr* = **centigrade**.
C.A. *abbr* = **chartered accountant**.
cab [kæb] *n* taxi *m*; (*of truck*) cabina.
cabbage ['kæbɪdʒ] *n* col *f*, berza.
cabin ['kæbɪn] *n* cabaña; (*on ship*) camarote *m*; (*on plane*) cabina; **~ cruiser** *n* yate *m* de motor.
cabinet ['kæbɪnɪt] *n* (*POL*) consejo de ministros; (*furniture*) armario; (*also: display* ~) vitrina.
cable ['keɪbl] *n* cable *m* ♦ *vt* cablegra-

fiar; **~-car** *n* teleférico; **~ television** *n* televisión *f* por cable.
cache [kæʃ] *n* (*of weapons, drugs etc*) alijo.
cackle ['kækl] *vi* lanzar risotadas; (*hen*) cacarear.
cacti ['kæktaɪ] *npl of* **cactus**.
cactus ['kæktəs] (*pl* **cacti**) cacto.
cadge [kædʒ] (*inf*) *vt* gorronear.
Caesarean [siːˈzɛərɪən] *adj*: **~ (section)** cesárea.
café ['kæfeɪ] *n* café *m*.
cafeteria [kæfɪˈtɪərɪə] *n* cafetería.
cage [keɪdʒ] *n* jaula.
cagey ['keɪdʒɪ] (*inf*) *adj* cauteloso, reservado.
cagoule [kəˈguːl] *n* chubasquero.
Cairo ['kaɪərəu] *n* el Cairo.
cajole [kəˈdʒəul] *vt* engatusar.
cake [keɪk] *n* (*CULIN: large*) tarta; (*: small*) pastel *m*; (*of soap*) pastilla; **~d** *adj*: **~d with** cubierto de.
calculate ['kælkjuleɪt] *vt* calcular; **calculating** *adj* (*scheming*) calculador(a); **calculation** [-'leɪʃən] *n* cálculo, cómputo; **calculator** *n* calculadora.
calendar ['kæləndə*] *n* calendario; **~ month/year** *n* mes *m*/año civil.
calf [kɑːf] (*pl* **calves**) *n* (*of cow*) ternero, becerro; (*of other animals*) cría; (*also: ~skin*) piel *f* de becerro; (*ANAT*) pantorrilla.
calibre ['kælɪbə*] (*US* **caliber**) *n* calibre *m*.
call [kɔːl] *vt* llamar; (*meeting*) convocar ♦ *vi* (*shout*) llamar; (*TEL*) llamar (por teléfono), telefonear (*esp AM*); (*visit: also: ~ in, ~ round*) hacer una visita ♦ *n* llamada; (*of bird*) canto; **to be ~ed** llamarse; **on ~** (*nurse, doctor etc*) de guardia; **~ back** *vi* (*return*) volver; (*TEL*) volver a llamar; **~ for** *vt fus* (*demand*) pedir, exigir; (*fetch*) venir por (*SP*), pasar por (*AM*); **~ off** *vt* (*cancel: meeting, race*) cancelar; (*: deal*) anular; (*: strike*) desconvocar; **~ on** *vt fus* (*visit*) visitar; (*turn to*) acudir a; **~ out** *vi* gritar, dar voces; **~ up** *vt* (*MIL*) llamar al servicio militar; (*TEL*) llamar; **~box** (*BRIT*) *n* cabina telefónica;

~**er** n visita; (TEL) usuario/a; ~ **girl** n prostituta; ~-**in** (US) n (programa m) coloquio (por teléfono); ~**ing** n vocación f; (occupation) profesión f; ~**ing card** (US) n tarjeta comercial or de visita.

callous ['kæləs] adj insensible, cruel.

calm [kɑːm] adj tranquilo; (sea) liso, en calma ♦ n calma, tranquilidad f ♦ vt calmar, tranquilizar; ~ **down** vi calmarse, tranquilizarse ♦ vt calmar, tranquilizar.

Calor gas ['kælə*-] ® n butano.

calorie ['kælərɪ] n caloría.

calves [kɑːvz] npl of **calf**.

camber ['kæmbə*] n (of road) combadura, comba.

Cambodia [kæm'bəʊdjə] n Camboya.

came [keɪm] pt of **come**.

camel ['kæməl] n camello.

cameo ['kæmɪəʊ] n camafeo.

camera ['kæmərə] n máquina fotográfica; (CINEMA, TV) cámara f; **in** ~ (LAW) a puerta cerrada; ~**man** n cámara m.

camouflage ['kæməflɑːʒ] n camuflaje m ♦ vt camuflar.

camp [kæmp] n campamento, camping m; (MIL) campamento; (for prisoners) campo; (fig: faction) bando ♦ vi acampar ♦ adj afectado, afeminado.

campaign [kæm'peɪn] n (MIL, POL etc) campaña ♦ vi hacer campaña.

camp: ~**bed** (BRIT) n cama de campaña; ~**er** n campista m/f; (vehicle) caravana; ~**ing** n camping m; **to go** ~**ing** hacer camping; ~**site** n camping m.

campus ['kæmpəs] n ciudad f universitaria.

can¹ [kæn] n (of oil, water) bidón m; (tin) lata, bote m ♦ vt enlatar.

KEYWORD

can² (negative **cannot, can't**; conditional and pt **could**) aux vb **1** (be able to) poder; **you** ~ **do it if you try** puedes hacerlo si lo intentas; **I** ~'**t see** you no te veo
2 (know how to) saber; **I** ~ **swim/play tennis/drive** sé nadar/jugar al tenis/conducir; ~ **you speak French?** ¿ha-

blas or sabes hablar francés?
3 (may) poder; ~ **I use your phone?** ¿me dejas or puedo usar tu teléfono?
4 (expressing disbelief, puzzlement etc): **it** ~'**t be true!** ¡no puede ser (verdad)!; **what CAN he want?** ¿qué querrá?
5 (expressing possibility, suggestion etc): **he could be in the library** podría estar en la biblioteca; **she could have been delayed** pudo haberse retrasado.

Canada ['kænədə] n (el) Canadá; **Canadian** [kə'neɪdɪən] adj, n canadiense m/f.

canal [kə'næl] n canal m.

canary [kə'nɛərɪ] n canario; **C~ Islands** npl las (Islas) Canarias.

cancel ['kænsəl] vt cancelar; (train) suprimir; (cross out) tachar, borrar; ~**lation** [-'leɪʃən] n cancelación f; supresión f.

cancer ['kænsə*] n cáncer m; **C~** (ASTROLOGY) Cáncer m.

candid ['kændɪd] adj franco, abierto.

candidate ['kændɪdeɪt] n candidato/a.

candle ['kændl] n vela; (in church) cirio; ~**light** n: **by** ~**light** a la luz de una vela; ~**stick** n (single) candelero; (low) palmatoria; (bigger, ornate) candelabro.

candour ['kændə*] (US **candor**) n franqueza.

candy ['kændɪ] n azúcar m cande; (US) caramelo; ~-**floss** (BRIT) n algodón m (azucarado).

cane [keɪn] n (BOT) caña; (stick) vara, palmeta; (for furniture) mimbre f ♦ (BRIT) vt (SCOL) castigar (con vara).

canister ['kænɪstə*] n bote m, lata; (of gas) bombona.

cannabis ['kænəbɪs] n marijuana.

canned [kænd] adj en lata, de lata.

cannibal ['kænɪbəl] n caníbal m/f.

cannon ['kænən] (pl ~ or ~s) n cañón m.

cannot ['kænɔt] = **can not**.

canny ['kænɪ] adj astuto.

canoe [kə'nuː] n canoa; (SPORT) piragua.

canon ['kænən] n (clergyman) canónigo; (standard) canon m.

can opener *n* abrelatas *m inv*.
canopy ['kænəpı] *n* dosel *m*; toldo.
can't [kænt] = **can not**.
cantankerous [kæn'tæŋkərəs] *adj* quisquillero.
canteen [kæn'ti:n] *n* (*eating place*) cantina; (*BRIT: of cutlery*) juego.
canter ['kæntə*] *vi* ir a medio galope.
canvas ['kænvəs] *n* (*material*) lona; (*painting*) lienzo; (*NAUT*) velas *fpl*.
canvass ['kænvəs] *vi* (*POL*): **to ~ for** solicitar votos por ♦ *vt* (*COMM*) sondear.
canyon ['kænjən] *n* cañón *m*.
cap [kæp] *n* (*hat*) gorra; (*of pen*) capuchón *m*; (*of bottle*) tapa, tapón *m*; (*contraceptive*) diafragma *m*; (*for toy gun*) cápsula ♦ *vt* (*outdo*) superar.
capability [keɪpə'bɪlɪtɪ] *n* capacidad *f*.
capable ['keɪpəbl] *adj* capaz.
capacity [kə'pæsɪtɪ] *n* capacidad *f*; (*position*) calidad *f*.
cape [keɪp] *n* capa; (*GEO*) cabo.
caper ['keɪpə*] *n* (*CULIN: gen*: ~s) alcaparra; (*prank*) broma.
capital ['kæpɪtl] *n* (*also*: ~ **city**) capital *f*; (*money*) capital *m*; (*also*: ~ **letter**) mayúscula; ~ **gains tax** *n* impuesto sobre las ganancias de capital; ~**ism** *n* capitalismo; ~**ist** *adj*, *n* capitalista *m/f*; ~**ize on** *vt fus* aprovechar; ~ **punishment** *n* pena de muerte.
capitulate [kə'pɪtjuleɪt] *vi* capitular, rendirse.
Capricorn ['kæprɪkɔ:n] *n* (*ASTROLOGY*) Capricornio.
capsize [kæp'saɪz] *vt* volcar, hacer zozobrar ♦ *vi* volcarse, zozobrar.
capsule ['kæpsju:l] *n* cápsula.
captain ['kæptɪn] *n* capitán *m*.
caption ['kæpʃən] *n* (*heading*) título; (*to picture*) leyenda.
captive ['kæptɪv] *adj*, *n* cautivo/a *m/f*.
capture ['kæptʃə*] *vt* prender, apresar; (*animal, COMPUT*) capturar; (*place*) tomar; (*attention*) captar, llamar ♦ *n* apresamiento; captura; toma; (*data* ~) formulación *f* de datos.
car [kɑ:*] *n* coche *m*, carro (*AM*), automóvil *m*; (*US: RAIL*) vagón *m*.
carafe [kə'ræf] *n* jarra.

carat ['kærət] *n* quilate *m*.
caravan ['kærəvæn] *n* (*BRIT*) caravana, ruló *f*; (*in desert*) caravana; ~ **site** (*BRIT*) *n* camping *m* para caravanas.
carbohydrate [kɑ:bəu'haɪdreɪt] *n* hidrato de carbono; (*food*) fécula.
carbon ['kɑ:bən] *n* carbono; ~ **copy** *n* copia al carbón; ~ **paper** *n* papel *m* carbón.
carburettor [kɑ:bju'retə*] (*US* **carburetor**) *n* carburador *m*.
carcass ['kɑ:kəs] *n* cadáver *m* (de animal).
card [kɑ:d] *n* (*material*) cartulina; (*index ~ etc*) ficha; (*playing ~*) carta, naipe *m*; (*visiting ~, greetings ~ etc*) tarjeta; ~**board** *n* cartón *m*.
cardigan ['kɑ:dɪgən] *n* rebeca.
cardinal ['kɑ:dɪnl] *adj* cardinal; (*importance, principal*) esencial ♦ *n* cardenal *m*.
card index *n* fichero.
care [kɛə*] *n* cuidado; (*worry*) inquietud *f*; (*charge*) cargo, custodia ♦ *vi*: **to ~ about** (*person, animal*) tener cariño a; (*thing, idea*) preocuparse por; ~ **of** en casa de, al cuidado de; **in sb's ~** a cargo de uno; **to take ~** to cuidarse de, tener cuidado de; **to take ~ of** cuidar; (*problem etc*) ocuparse de; **I don't ~** no me importa; **I couldn't ~ less** eso me trae sin cuidado; **~ for** *vt fus* cuidar a; (*like*) querer.
career [kə'rɪə*] *n* profesión *f*; (*in work, school*) carrera ♦ *vi* (*also*: ~ **along**) correr a toda velocidad; ~ **woman** *n* mujer *f* dedicada a su profesión.
carefree ['kɛəfri:] *adj* despreocupado.
careful ['kɛəful] *adj* cuidadoso; (*cautious*) cauteloso; (**be**) ~**!** ¡tenga cuidado!; ~**ly** *adv* con cuidado, cuidadosamente; con cautela.
careless ['kɛəlɪs] *adj* descuidado; (*heedless*) poco atento; ~**ness** *n* descuido; falta de atención.
caress [kə'rɛs] *n* caricia ♦ *vt* acariciar.
caretaker ['kɛəteɪkə*] *n* portero/a, conserje *m/f*.
car-ferry *n* transbordador *m* para coches.

cargo ['kɑːgəu] (pl ~es) n cargamento, carga.

car hire n alquiler m de automóviles.

Caribbean [kærɪ'biːən] n: **the ~ (Sea)** el (Mar) Caribe.

caring ['keərɪŋ] adj humanitario; (behaviour) afectuoso.

carnation [kɑː'neɪʃən] n clavel m.

carnival ['kɑːnɪvəl] n carnaval m; (US: funfair) parque m de atracciones.

carol ['kærəl] n: (Christmas) ~ villancico.

carp [kɑːp] n (fish) carpa; ~ **at** vt fus quejarse de.

car park (BRIT) n aparcamiento, parking m.

carpenter ['kɑːpɪntə*] n carpintero/a.

carpet ['kɑːpɪt] n alfombra; (fitted) moqueta ♦ vt alfombrar; ~ **slippers** npl zapatillas fpl; ~ **sweeper** n aparato para barrer alfombras.

carriage ['kærɪdʒ] n (BRIT: RAIL) vagón m; (horse-drawn) coche m; (of goods) transporte m; (: cost) porte m, flete m; ~ **return** n retorno del carro; ~**way** (BRIT) n (part of road) calzada.

carrier ['kærɪə*] n (transport company) transportista, empresa de transportes; (MED) portador m; ~ **bag** (BRIT) n bolsa de papel or plástico.

carrot ['kærət] n zanahoria.

carry ['kærɪ] vt (subj: person) llevar; (transport) transportar; (involve: responsibilities etc) entrañar, implicar; (MED) ser portador de ♦ vi (sound) oírse; **to get carried away** (fig) entusiasmarse; ~ **on** vi (continue) seguir (adelante), continuar ♦ vt proseguir, continuar; ~ **out** vt (orders) cumplir; (investigation) llevar a cabo, realizar; ~ **cot** (BRIT) n cuna portátil; ~-**on** (inf) n (fuss) lío.

cart [kɑːt] n carro, carreta ♦ vt (inf: transport) acarrear.

carton ['kɑːtən] n (box) caja (de cartón); (of milk etc) bote m; (of yogurt) tarrina.

cartoon [kɑː'tuːn] n (PRESS) caricatura; (comic strip) tira cómica; (film) dibujos mpl animados.

cartridge ['kɑːtrɪdʒ] n cartucho; (of pen) recambio; (of record player) cápsula.

carve [kɑːv] vt (meat) trinchar; (wood, stone) cincelar, esculpir; (initials etc) grabar; ~ **up** vt dividir, repartir; **carving** n (object) escultura; (design) talla; (art) tallado; **carving knife** n trinchante m.

car wash n lavado de coches.

case [keɪs] n (container) caja; (MED) caso; (for jewels etc) estuche m; (LAW) causa, proceso; (BRIT: also: suit~) maleta; **in ~ of** en caso de, por si; **in any ~** en todo caso; **just in ~** por si acaso.

cash [kæʃ] n dinero en efectivo, dinero contante ♦ vt cobrar, hacer efectivo; **to pay (in) ~** pagar al contado; ~ **on delivery** cóbrese al entregar; ~**book** n libro de caja; ~ **card** n tarjeta f dinero; ~**desk** (BRIT) n caja; ~ **dispenser** n cajero automático.

cashew [kæ'ʃuː] n (also: ~ nut) anacardo.

cash flow n flujo de fondos, cash-flow m.

cashier [kæ'ʃɪə*] n cajero/a.

cashmere ['kæʃmɪə*] n cachemira.

cash register n caja.

casing ['keɪsɪŋ] n revestimiento.

casino [kə'siːnəu] n casino.

cask [kɑːsk] n tonel m, barril m.

casket ['kɑːskɪt] n cofre m, estuche m; (US: coffin) ataúd m.

casserole ['kæsərəul] n (food, pot) cazuela.

cassette [kæ'set] n cassette f; ~ **player/recorder** n tocacassettes m inv, cassette m.

cast [kɑːst] (pt, pp cast) vt (throw) echar, arrojar, lanzar; (glance, eyes) dirigir; (THEATRE): **to ~ sb as Othello** dar a uno el papel de Otelo ♦ vi (FISHING) lanzar ♦ n (THEATRE) reparto; (also: plaster ~) vaciado; **to ~ one's vote** votar; **to ~ doubt on** suscitar dudas acerca de; ~ **off** vi (NAUT) desamarrar; (KNITTING) cerrar (los puntos); ~ **on** vi (KNITTING) poner los puntos.

castanets [kæstə'nɛts] npl castañuelas fpl.

castaway ['kɑːstəwəɪ] n náufrago/a.

caste [kɑːst] n casta.

caster sugar ['kɑːstə*-] (BRIT) n azúcar m extrafino.

Castile [kæs'tiːl] n Castilla; **Castilian** adj, n castellano/a m/f.

casting vote ['kɑːstɪŋ-] (BRIT) n voto decisivo.

cast iron n hierro fundido.

castle ['kɑːsl] n castillo; (CHESS) torre f.

castor ['kɑːstə*] n (wheel) ruedecilla; ~ **oil** n aceite m de ricino.

casual ['kæʒjul] adj fortuito; (irregular: work etc) eventual, temporero; (unconcerned) despreocupado; (clothes) de sport; ~**ly** adv de manera despreocupada; (dress) de sport.

casualty ['kæʒjultɪ] n víctima, herido; (dead) muerto; (MED: department)) urgencias fpl.

cat [kæt] n gato; (big ~) felino.

Catalan ['kætəlæn] adj, n catalán/ana m/f.

catalogue ['kætəlɔg] (US **catalog**) n catálogo ♦ vt catalogar.

Catalonia [kætə'ləunɪə] n Cataluña.

catalyst ['kætəlɪst] n catalizador m.

catapult ['kætəpʌlt] n tirachinas m inv.

catarrh [kə'tɑː*] n catarro.

catastrophe [kə'tæstrəfɪ] n catástrofe f.

catch [kætʃ] (pt, pp **caught**) vt coger (SP), agarrar (AM); (arrest) detener; (grasp) asir; (breath) contener; (surprise: person) sorprender; (attract: attention) captar; (hear) oír; (MED) contagiarse de, coger; (also: ~ up) alcanzar ♦ vi (fire) encenderse; (in branches etc) enredarse ♦ n (fish etc) pesca; (act of catching) cogida; (hidden problem) dificultad f; (game) pilla-pilla; (of lock) pestillo, cerradura; **to ~ fire** encenderse; **to ~ sight of** divisar; ~ **on** vi (understand) caer en la cuenta; (grow popular) hacerse popular; ~ **up** vi (fig) ponerse al día.

catching ['kætʃɪŋ] adj (MED) contagioso.

catchment area ['kætʃmənt-] (BRIT) n zona de captación.

catchphrase ['kætʃfreɪz] n lema m, eslogan m.

catchy ['kætʃɪ] adj (tune) pegadizo.

category ['kætɪgərɪ] n categoría, clase f.

cater ['keɪtə*] vi: **to ~ for** (BRIT) abastecer a; (needs) atender a; (COMM: parties etc) proveer comida a; ~**er** n abastecedor(a) m/f, proveedor(a) m/f; ~**ing** n (trade) hostelería.

caterpillar ['kætəpɪlə*] n oruga, gusano; ~ **track** n rodado de oruga.

cathedral [kə'θiːdrəl] n catedral f.

catholic ['kæθəlɪk] adj (tastes etc) amplio; **C** - adj, n (REL) católico/a m/f.

cat's-eye (BRIT) n (AUT) catafoto.

cattle ['kætl] npl ganado.

catty ['kætɪ] adj malicioso, rencoroso.

caucus ['kɔːkəs] n (POL) camarilla política; (: US: to elect candidates) comité m electoral.

caught [kɔːt] pt, pp of **catch**.

cauliflower ['kɔlɪflauə*] n coliflor f.

cause [kɔːz] n causa, motivo, razón f; (principle: also: POL) causa ♦ vt causar.

caustic ['kɔːstɪk] adj cáustico; (fig) mordaz.

caution ['kɔːʃən] n cautela, prudencia; (warning) advertencia, amonestación f ♦ vt amonestar.

cautious ['kɔːʃəs] adj cauteloso, prudente, precavido; ~**ly** adv con cautela.

cavalier [kævə'lɪə*] adj arrogante, desdeñoso.

cavalry ['kævəlrɪ] n caballería.

cave [keɪv] n cueva, caverna; ~ **in** vi (roof etc) derrumbarse, hundirse; ~**man** n cavernícola m, troglodita m.

cavity ['kævɪtɪ] n hueco, cavidad f; (in tooth) caries f inv.

cavort [kə'vɔːt] vi dar brincos.

CB n abbr (= Citizen's Band (Radio)) banda ciudadana.

CBI n abbr (= Confederation of British Industry) ≈ C.E.O.E. f (SP).

cc abbr = **cubic centimetres**; = **carbon copy**.

cease [siːs] vt, vi cesar; ~**fire** n alto m el fuego; ~**less** adj incesante.

cedar ['siːdə*] n cedro.

ceiling ['si:lɪŋ] n techo; (fig) límite m.
celebrate ['sɛlɪbreɪt] vt celebrar ♦ vi divertirse; ~d adj célebre; **celebration** [-'breɪʃən] n fiesta, celebración f.
celery ['sɛlərɪ] n apio.
celibacy ['sɛlɪbəsɪ] n celibato.
cell [sɛl] n celda; (BIOL) célula; (ELEC) elemento.
cellar ['sɛlə*] n sótano; (for wine) bodega.
'cello ['tʃɛləu] n violoncelo.
cellophane ['sɛləfeɪn] n celofán m.
Celt [kɛlt, sɛlt] adj, n celta m/f; ~ic adj celta.
cement [sə'mɛnt] n cemento; ~ mixer n hormigonera.
cemetery ['sɛmɪtrɪ] n cementerio.
censor ['sɛnsə*] n censor m ♦ vt (cut) censurar; ~ship n censura.
censure ['sɛnʃə*] vt censurar.
census ['sɛnsəs] n censo.
cent [sɛnt] n (US) (coin) centavo, céntimo; see also **per**.
centenary [sɛn'ti:nərɪ] n centenario.
center ['sɛntə*] (US) = **centre**.
centi... [sɛntɪ] prefix: ~**grade** adj centígrado; ~**litre** (US ~**liter**) n centilitro; ~**metre** (US ~**meter**) n centímetro.
centipede ['sɛntɪpi:d] n ciempiés m inv.
central ['sɛntrəl] adj central; (of house etc) céntrico; **C~ America** n Centroamérica; ~ **heating** n calefacción f central; ~**ize** vt centralizar.
centre ['sɛntə*] (US **center**) n centro; (fig) núcleo ♦ vt centrar; ~**-forward** n (SPORT) delantero centro; ~**-half** n (SPORT) medio centro.
century ['sɛntjurɪ] n siglo; **20th** ~ siglo veinte.
ceramic [sɪ'ræmɪk] adj cerámico; ~**s** n cerámica.
cereal ['si:rɪəl] n cereal m.
cerebral ['sɛrɪbrəl] adj cerebral; intelectual.
ceremony ['sɛrɪmənɪ] n ceremonia; **to stand on** ~ hacer ceremonias, estar de cumplido.
certain ['sə:tən] adj seguro; (person): **a** ~ **Mr Smith** un tal Sr Smith; (particular, some) cierto; **for** ~ a ciencia cier-

ta; ~**ly** adv (undoubtedly) ciertamente; (of course) desde luego, por supuesto; ~**ty** n certeza, certidumbre f, seguridad f; (inevitability) certeza.
certificate [sə'tɪfɪkɪt] n certificado.
certified mail ['sə:tɪfaɪd-] (US) n correo certificado.
certified public accountant (US) n contable m/f diplomado/a.
certify ['sə:tɪfaɪ] vt certificar; (award diploma to) conceder un diploma a; (declare insane) declarar loco.
cervical ['sə:vɪkl] adj cervical.
cervix ['sə:vɪks] n cuello del útero.
cesspit ['sɛspɪt] n pozo negro.
cf. abbr (= compare) cfr.
ch. abbr (= chapter) cap.
chafe [tʃeɪf] vt (rub) rozar.
chagrin ['ʃægrɪn] n (annoyance) disgusto; (disappointment) decepción f.
chain [tʃeɪn] n cadena; (of mountains) cordillera; (of events) sucesión f ♦ vt (also: ~ **up**) encadenar; ~ **reaction** n reacción f en cadena; ~**-smoke** vi fumar un cigarrillo tras otro; ~ **store** n tienda de una cadena, ≈ gran almacén.
chair [tʃeə*] n silla; (armchair) sillón m, butaca; (of university) cátedra; (of meeting etc) presidencia ♦ vt (meeting) presidir; ~**lift** n telesilla; ~**man** n presidente m.
chalet ['ʃæleɪ] n chalet m.
chalk [tʃɔ:k] n (GEO) creta; (for writing) tiza (SP), gis m (AM).
challenge ['tʃælɪndʒ] n desafío, reto ♦ vt desafiar, retar; (statement, right) poner en duda; **to** ~ **sb to do sth** retar a uno a que haga algo; **challenging** adj exigente; (tone) de desafío.
chamber ['tʃeɪmbə*] n cámara, sala; (POL) cámara; (BRIT: LAW: gen pl) despacho; ~ **of commerce** cámara de comercio; ~**maid** n camarera; ~ **music** n música de cámara.
chamois ['ʃæmwɑ:] n gamuza.
champagne [ʃæm'peɪn] n champaña m, champán m.
champion ['tʃæmpɪən] n campeón/ona m/f; (of cause) defensor(a) m/f; ~**ship** n campeonato.

chance [tʃɑ:ns] n (*opportunity*) ocasión f, oportunidad f; (*likelihood*) posibilidad f; (*risk*) riesgo ♦ vt arriesgar, probar ♦ adj fortuito, casual; **to ~ it** arriesgarse, intentarlo; **to take a ~** arriesgarse; **by ~** por casualidad.

chancellor ['tʃɑ:nsələ*] n canciller m; **C~ of the Exchequer** (*BRIT*) n Ministro de Hacienda.

chandelier [ʃændə'lɪə*] n araña (de luces).

change [tʃeɪndʒ] vt cambiar; (*replace*) cambiar, reemplazar; (*gear, clothes, job*) cambiar de; (*transform*) transformar ♦ vi cambiar(se); (*trains*) hacer transbordo; (*traffic lights*) cambiar de color; (*be transformed*): **to ~ into** transformarse en ♦ n cambio; (*alteration*) modificación f, transformación f; (*of clothes*) muda; (*coins*) suelto, sencillo; (*money returned*) vuelta; **to ~ gear** (*AUT*) cambiar de marcha; **to ~ one's mind** cambiar de opinión *or* idea; **for a ~** para variar; **~able** adj (*weather*) cambiable; **~ machine** n máquina de cambio; **~over** n (*to new system*) cambio.

changing ['tʃeɪndʒɪŋ] adj cambiante; **~ room** (*BRIT*) n vestuario.

channel ['tʃænl] n (*TV*) canal m; (*of river*) cauce m; (*groove*) conducto; (*fig: medium*) medio ♦ vt (*river etc*) encauzar; **the (English) C~** el Canal (de la Mancha); **the C~ Islands** las Islas Normandas.

chant [tʃɑ:nt] n (*of crowd*) gritos mpl; (*REL*) canto ♦ vt (*slogan, word*) repetir a gritos.

chaos ['keɪɔs] n caos m.

chap [tʃæp] (*BRIT: inf*) n (*man*) tío, tipo.

chapel ['tʃæpəl] n capilla.

chaperone ['ʃæpərəʊn] n carabina.

chaplain ['tʃæplɪn] n capellán m.

chapped [tʃæpt] adj agrietado.

chapter ['tʃæptə*] n capítulo.

char [tʃɑ:*] vt (*burn*) carbonizar, chamuscar ♦ n (*BRIT*) = **charlady**.

character ['kærɪktə*] n carácter m, naturaleza, índole f; (*moral strength, personality*) carácter; (*in novel, film*) personaje m; **~istic** [-'rɪstɪk] adj característico ♦ n característica; **~ize** vt caracterizar.

charcoal ['tʃɑ:kəʊl] n carbón m vegetal; (*ART*) carboncillo.

charge [tʃɑ:dʒ] n (*LAW*) cargo, acusación f; (*cost*) precio, coste m; (*responsibility*) cargo ♦ vt (*LAW*): **to ~ (with)** acusar (de); (*battery*) cargar; (*price*) pedir; (*customer*) cobrar ♦ vi precipitarse; (*MIL*) cargar, atacar; **~s** npl: **to reverse the ~s** (*BRIT: TEL*) revertir el cobro; **to take ~ of** hacerse cargo de, encargarse de; **to be in ~ of** estar encargado de; (*business*) mandar; **how much do you ~?** ¿cuánto cobra usted?; **to ~ an expense (up) to sb's account** cargar algo a cuenta de alguien; **~ card** n tarjeta de cuenta.

charitable ['tʃærɪtəbl] adj benéfico.

charity ['tʃærɪtɪ] n caridad f; (*organization*) sociedad f benéfica; (*money, gifts*) limosnas fpl.

charlady ['tʃɑ:leɪdɪ] (*BRIT*) n mujer f de la limpieza.

charlatan ['ʃɑ:lətən] n farsante m/f.

charm [tʃɑ:m] n encanto, atractivo; (*talisman*) hechizo; (*on bracelet*) dije m ♦ vt encantar; **~ing** adj encantador(a).

chart [tʃɑ:t] n (*diagram*) cuadro; (*graph*) gráfica; (*map*) carta de navegación ♦ vt (*course*) trazar; (*progress*) seguir; **~s** npl (*Top 40*): **the ~s** ≈ los 40 principales (*SP*).

charter ['tʃɑ:tə*] vt (*plane*) alquilar; (*ship*) fletar ♦ n (*document*) carta; (*of university, company*) estatutos mpl; **~ed accountant** (*BRIT*) n contable m/f diplomado/a; **~ flight** n vuelo chárter.

charwoman ['tʃɑ:wʊmən] n = **charlady**.

chase [tʃeɪs] vt (*pursue*) perseguir; (*also: ~ away*) ahuyentar ♦ n persecución f.

chasm ['kæzəm] n sima.

chassis ['ʃæsɪ] n chasis m.

chat [tʃæt] vi (*also: have a ~*) charlar ♦ n charla; **~ show** (*BRIT*) n programa m de entrevistas.

chatter ['tʃætə*] vi (*person*) charlar; (*teeth*) castañetear ♦ n (*of birds*) parloteo; (of people) charla, cháchara; ~box (inf) n parlanchín/ina m/f.

chatty ['tʃætɪ] adj (style) informal; (person) hablador(a).

chauffeur ['ʃəufə*] n chófer m.

chauvinist ['ʃəuvɪnɪst] n (male ~) machista m; (nationalist) chovinista m/f.

cheap [tʃiːp] adj barato; (joke) de mal gusto; (poor quality) de mala calidad ♦ adv barato; ~er adj más barato; ~ly adv barato, a bajo precio.

cheat [tʃiːt] vi hacer trampa ♦ vt: to ~ sb (out of sth) estafar (algo) a uno ♦ n (person) tramposo/a.

check [tʃɛk] vt (examine) controlar; (facts) comprobar; (halt) parar, detener; (restrain) refrenar, restringir ♦ n (inspection) control m, inspección f; (curb) freno; (US: bill) nota, cuenta; (US) = **cheque**; (pattern: gen pl) cuadro ♦ adj (also: ~ed: pattern, cloth) a cuadros; ~ **in** vi (at hotel) firmar el registro; (at airport) facturar el equipaje ♦ vt (luggage) facturar; ~ **out** vi (of hotel) marcharse; ~ **up** vi: to ~ **up on** sth comprobar algo; to ~ **up on sb** investigar a alguien; ~**ered** (US) adj = **chequered**; ~**ers** (US) n juego de damas; ~-**in** (**desk**) n mostrador m de facturación; ~**ing account** (US) n cuenta corriente; ~**mate** n jaque m mate; ~**out** n caja; ~**point** n (punto de) control m; ~**room** (US) n consigna; ~**up** n (MED) reconocimiento general.

cheek [tʃiːk] n mejilla; (impudence) descaro; **what a** ~! ¡qué cara!; ~**bone** n pómulo; ~**y** adj fresco, descarado.

cheep [tʃiːp] vi piar.

cheer [tʃɪə*] vt vitorear, aplaudir; (gladden) alegrar, animar ♦ vi dar vivas ♦ n viva m; ~**s** npl aplausos mpl; ~**s!** ¡salud!; ~ **up** vi animarse ♦ vt alegrar, animar; ~**ful** adj alegre.

cheerio [tʃɪərɪ'əu] (BRIT) excl ¡hasta luego!

cheese [tʃiːz] n queso; ~**board** n tabla de quesos.

cheetah ['tʃiːtə] n leopardo cazador.

chef [ʃɛf] n jefe/a m/f de cocina.

chemical ['kɛmɪkəl] adj químico ♦ n

producto químico.

chemist ['kɛmɪst] n (BRIT: pharmacist) farmacéutico/a; (scientist) químico/a; ~**ry** n química; ~'**s (shop)** (BRIT) n farmacia.

cheque [tʃɛk] (US **check**) n cheque m; ~**book** n talonario de cheques (SP), chequera (AM); ~ **card** n tarjeta de cheque.

chequered ['tʃɛkəd] (US **checkered**) adj (fig) accidentado.

cherish ['tʃɛrɪʃ] vt (love) querer, apreciar; (protect) cuidar; (hope etc) abrigar.

cherry ['tʃɛrɪ] n cereza; (also: ~ tree) cerezo.

chess [tʃɛs] n ajedrez m; ~**board** n tablero (de ajedrez).

chest [tʃɛst] n (ANAT) pecho; (box) cofre m, cajón m; ~ **of drawers** n cómoda.

chestnut ['tʃɛsnʌt] n castaña; ~ **(tree)** n castaño.

chew [tʃuː] vt mascar, masticar; ~**ing gum** n chicle m.

chic [ʃiːk] adj elegante.

chick [tʃɪk] n pollito, polluelo; (inf: girl) chica.

chicken ['tʃɪkɪn] n gallina, pollo; (food) pollo; (inf: coward) gallina m/f; ~ **out** (inf) vi rajarse; ~**pox** n varicela.

chicory ['tʃɪkərɪ] n (for coffee) achicoria; (salad) escarola.

chief [tʃiːf] n jefe/a m/f ♦ adj principal; ~ **executive** n director(a) m/f general; ~**ly** adv principalmente.

chiffon ['ʃɪfɔn] n gasa.

chilblain ['tʃɪlbleɪn] n sabañón m.

child [tʃaɪld] (pl **children**) n niño/a; (offspring) hijo/a; ~**birth** n parto; ~**hood** n niñez f, infancia; ~**ish** adj pueril, aniñado; ~**like** adj de niño; ~**minder** (BRIT) n niñera; ~**ren** ['tʃɪldrən] npl of **child**.

Chile ['tʃɪlɪ] n Chile m; ~**an** adj, n chileno/a m/f.

chill [tʃɪl] n frío; (MED) resfriado ♦ vt enfriar; (CULIN) congelar.

chilli ['tʃɪlɪ] (BRIT) n chile m (SP), ají m (AM).

chilly ['tʃɪlɪ] *adj* frío.
chime [tʃaɪm] *n* repique *m*; (*of clock*) campanada ♦ *vi* repicar; sonar.
chimney ['tʃɪmnɪ] *n* chimenea; ~ **sweep** *n* deshollinador *m*.
chimpanzee [tʃɪmpæn'ziː] *n* chimpancé *m*.
chin [tʃɪn] *n* mentón *m*, barbilla.
china ['tʃaɪnə] *n* porcelana; (*crockery*) loza.
China ['tʃaɪnə] *n* China; **Chinese** [tʃaɪ'niːz] *adj* chino ♦ *n inv* chino/a; (*LING*) chino.
chink [tʃɪŋk] *n* (*opening*) grieta, hendedura; (*noise*) tintineo.
chip [tʃɪp] *n* (*gen pl: CULIN: BRIT*) patata (*SP*) *or* papa (*AM*) frita; (: *US: also: potato* ~) patata *or* papa frita; (*of wood*) astilla; (*of glass, stone*) lasca; (*at poker*) ficha; (*COMPUT*) chip *m* ♦ *vt* (*cup, plate*) desconchar; ~ **in** (*inf*) *vi* interrumpir; (*contribute*) compartir los gastos.
chiropodist [kɪ'rɔpədɪst] (*BRIT*) *n* pedicuro/a, callista *m/f*.
chirp [tʃəːp] *vi* (*bird*) gorjear, piar.
chisel ['tʃɪzl] *n* (*for wood*) escoplo; (*for stone*) cincel *m*.
chit [tʃɪt] *n* nota.
chitchat ['tʃɪttʃæt] *n* chismes *mpl*, habladurías *fpl*.
chivalry ['ʃɪvəlrɪ] *n* caballerosidad *f*.
chives [tʃaɪvz] *npl* cebollinos *mpl*.
chlorine ['klɔːriːn] *n* cloro.
chock-a-block ['tʃɔkə'blɔk] *adj* atestado.
chockfull ['tʃɔk'ful] *adj* atestado.
chocolate ['tʃɔklɪt] *n* chocolate *m*; (*sweet*) bombón *m*.
choice [tʃɔɪs] *n* elección *f*, selección *f*; (*option*) opción *f*; (*preference*) preferencia ♦ *adj* escogido.
choir ['kwaɪə*] *n* coro; ~**boy** *n* niño de coro.
choke [tʃəuk] *vi* ahogarse; (*on food*) atragantarse ♦ *vt* estrangular, ahogar; (*block*): **to be** ~**d with** estar atascado de ♦ *n* (*AUT*) estárter *m*.
choose [tʃuːz] (*pt* **chose**, *pp* **chosen**) *vt* escoger, elegir; (*team*) seleccionar; **to**

~ **to do sth** optar por hacer algo.
choosy ['tʃuːzɪ] *adj* delicado.
chop [tʃɔp] *vt* (*wood*) cortar, tajar; (*CULIN: also:* ~ **up**) picar ♦ *n* (*CULIN*) chuleta; ~**s** *npl* (*jaws*) boca, labios *mpl*.
chopper ['tʃɔpə*] *n* (*helicopter*) helicóptero.
choppy ['tʃɔpɪ] *adj* (*sea*) picado, agitado.
chopsticks ['tʃɔpstɪks] *npl* palillos *mpl*.
chord [kɔːd] *n* (*MUS*) acorde *m*.
chore [tʃɔː*] *n* faena, tarea; (*routine task*) trabajo rutinario.
chortle ['tʃɔːtl] *vt* reír entre dientes.
chorus ['kɔːrəs] *n* coro; (*repeated part of song*) estribillo.
chose [tʃəuz] *pt of* **choose**.
chosen ['tʃəuzn] *pp of* **choose**.
Christ [kraɪst] *n* Cristo.
christen ['krɪsn] *vt* bautizar.
Christian ['krɪstɪən] *adj, n* cristiano/a *m/f*; ~**ity** [-'ænɪtɪ] *n* cristianismo; ~ **name** *n* nombre *m* de pila.
Christmas ['krɪsməs] *n* Navidad *f*; **Merry** ~! ¡Felices Pascuas!; ~ **card** *n* crismas *m inv*, tarjeta de Navidad; ~ **Day** *n* día *m* de Navidad; ~ **Eve** *n* Nochebuena; ~ **tree** *n* árbol *m* de Navidad.
chrome [krəum] *n* cromo.
chronic ['krɔnɪk] *adj* crónico.
chronological [krɔnə'lɔdʒɪkəl] *adj* cronológico.
chubby ['tʃʌbɪ] *adj* regordete.
chuck [tʃʌk] (*inf*) *vt* lanzar, arrojar; (*BRIT: also:* ~ **up**) abandonar; ~ **out** *vt* (*person*) echar (fuera); (*rubbish etc*) tirar.
chuckle ['tʃʌkl] *vi* reírse entre dientes.
chug [tʃʌg] *vi* resoplar; (*car, boat: also:* ~ **along**) avanzar traqueteando.
chum [tʃʌm] *n* compañero/a.
chunk [tʃʌŋk] *n* pedazo, trozo.
church [tʃəːtʃ] *n* iglesia; ~**yard** *n* cementerio.
churlish ['tʃəːlɪʃ] *adj* grosero.
churn [tʃəːn] *n* (*for butter*) mantequera; (*for milk*) lechera; ~ **out** *vt* producir en serie.
chute [ʃuːt] *n* (*also: rubbish* ~) vertedero; (*for coal etc*) rampa de caída.

chutney ['tʃʌtnɪ] n condimento a base de frutas de la India.

CIA (US) n abbr (= Central Intelligence Agency) CIA f.

CID (BRIT) n abbr (= Criminal Investigation Department) ≈ B.I.C. f (SP).

cider ['saɪdə*] n sidra.

cigar [sɪ'gɑ:*] n puro.

cigarette [sɪgə'rɛt] n cigarrillo (SP), cigarro (AM); pitillo; ~ **case** n pitillera; ~ **end** n colilla.

Cinderella [sɪndə'rɛlə] n Cenicienta.

cinders ['sɪndəz] npl cenizas fpl.

cine-camera ['sɪnɪ-] (BRIT) n cámara cinematográfica.

cine-film (BRIT) n película de cine.

cinema ['sɪnəmə] n cine m.

cinnamon ['sɪnəmən] n canela.

cipher ['saɪfə*] n cifra.

circle ['sə:kl] n círculo; (in theatre) anfiteatro ♦ vi dar vueltas ♦ vt (surround) rodear, cercar; (move round) dar la vuelta a.

circuit ['sə:kɪt] n circuito; (tour) gira; (track) pista; (lap) vuelta; ~**ous** [sə:'kjuɪtəs] adj indirecto.

circular ['sə:kjulə*] adj circular ♦ n circular f.

circulate ['sə:kjuleɪt] vi circular; (person: at party etc) hablar con los invitados ♦ vt poner en circulación; **circulation** [-'leɪʃən] n circulación f; (of newspaper) tirada.

circumcise ['sə:kəmsaɪz] vt circuncidar.

circumspect ['sə:kəmspɛkt] adj prudente.

circumstances ['sə:kəmstənsɪz] npl circunstancias fpl; (financial condition) situación f económica.

circumvent ['sə:kəmvɛnt] vt burlar.

circus ['sə:kəs] n circo.

cistern ['sɪstən] n tanque m, depósito; (in toilet) cisterna.

citizen ['sɪtɪzn] n (POL) ciudadano/a; (of city) vecino/a, habitante m/f; ~**ship** n ciudadanía.

citrus fruits ['sɪtrəs-] npl agrios mpl.

city ['sɪtɪ] n ciudad f; **the C**~ centro financiero de Londres.

civic ['sɪvɪk] adj cívico; (authorities) municipal; ~ **centre** (BRIT) n centro público.

civil ['sɪvɪl] adj civil; (polite) atento, cortés; ~ **engineer** n ingeniero de caminos (, canales y puertos); ~**ian** [sɪ'vɪlɪən] adj civil (no militar) ♦ n civil m/f, paisano/a.

civilization [sɪvɪlaɪ'zeɪʃən] n civilización f.

civilized ['sɪvɪlaɪzd] adj civilizado.

civil: ~ **law** n derecho civil; ~ **servant** n funcionario/a del Estado; **C**~ **Service** n administración f pública; ~ **war** n guerra civil.

clad [klæd] adj: ~ (**in**) vestido (de).

claim [kleɪm] vt exigir, reclamar; (rights etc) reivindicar; (assert) pretender ♦ vi (for insurance) reclamar ♦ n reclamación f; pretensión f; ~**ant** n demandante m/f.

clairvoyant [klɛə'vɔɪənt] n clarividente m/f.

clam [klæm] n almeja.

clamber ['klæmbə*] vi trepar.

clammy ['klæmɪ] adj frío y húmedo.

clamour ['klæmə*] (US **clamor**) vi: to ~ **for** clamar por, pedir a voces.

clamp [klæmp] n abrazadera, grapa ♦ vt (2 things together) cerrar fuertemente; (one thing on another) afianzar (con abrazadera); ~ **down on** vt fus (subj: government, police) reforzar la lucha contra.

clang [klæŋ] vi sonar, hacer estruendo.

clap [klæp] vi aplaudir; ~**ping** n aplausos mpl.

claret ['klærət] n clarete m.

clarify ['klærɪfaɪ] vt aclarar.

clarinet [klærɪ'nɛt] n clarinete m.

clash [klæʃ] n enfrentamiento; choque m; desacuerdo; estruendo ♦ vi (fight) enfrentarse; (beliefs) chocar; (disagree) estar en desacuerdo; (colours) desentonar; (two events) coincidir.

clasp [klɑ:sp] n (hold) apretón m; (of necklace, bag) cierre m ♦ vt apretar; abrazar.

class [klɑ:s] n clase f ♦ vt clasificar.

classic ['klæsɪk] adj, n clásico; ~**al** adj clásico.

classified ['klæsıfaıd] *adj* (*information*) reservado; ~ **advertisement** *n* anuncio por palabras.

classify ['klæsıfaı] *vt* clasificar.

classmate ['klɑ:smeıt] *n* compañero/a de clase.

classroom ['klɑ:srum] *n* aula.

clatter ['klætə*] *n* estrépito ♦ *vi* hacer ruido *or* estrépito.

clause [klɔ:z] *n* cláusula; (*LING*) oración *f*.

claw [klɔ:] *n* (*of cat*) uña; (*of bird of prey*) garra; (*of lobster*) pinza; ~ **at** *vt fus* arañar.

clay [kleı] *n* arcilla.

clean [kli:n] *adj* limpio; (*record, reputation*) bueno, intachable; (*joke*) decente ♦ *vt* limpiar; (*hands etc*) lavar; ~ **out** *vt* limpiar; ~ **up** *vt* limpiar, asear; ~-**cut** *adj* (*person*) bien parecido; ~**er** *n* (*person*) asistenta; (*substance*) producto para la limpieza; ~**er's** *n* tintorería; ~**ing** *n* limpieza; ~**liness** ['klɛnlınıs] *n* limpieza.

cleanse [klɛnz] *vt* limpiar; ~**r** *n* (*for face*) crema limpiadora.

clean-shaven *adj* sin barba, afeitado.

cleansing department (*BRIT*) *n* departamento de limpieza.

clear [klıə*] *adj* claro; (*road, way*) libre; (*conscience*) limpio, tranquilo; (*skin*) terso; (*sky*) despejado ♦ *vt* (*space*) despejar, limpiar; (*LAW: suspect*) absolver; (*obstacle*) salvar, saltar por encima de; (*cheque*) aceptar ♦ *vi* (*fog etc*) despejarse ♦ *adv*: ~ **of** a distancia de; **to ~ the table** recoger *or* levantar la mesa; ~ **up** *vt* limpiar; (*mystery*) aclarar, resolver; ~**ance** *n* (*removal*) despeje *m*; (*permission*) acreditación *f*; ~-**cut** *adj* bien definido, nítido; ~**ing** *n* (*in wood*) claro; ~**ing bank** (*BRIT*) *n* cámara de compensación; ~**ly** *adv* claramente; (*evidently*) sin duda; ~**way** (*BRIT*) *n* carretera donde no se puede parar.

cleaver ['kli:və] *n* cuchilla (de carnicero).

clef [klɛf] *n* (*MUS*) clave *f*.

cleft [klɛft] *n* (*in rock*) grieta, hendedura.

clench [klɛntʃ] *vt* apretar, cerrar.

clergy ['klə:dʒı] *n* clero; ~**man** *n* clérigo.

clerical ['klɛrıkəl] *adj* de oficina; (*REL*) clerical.

clerk [klɑ:k, (*US*) klə:rk] *n* (*BRIT*) oficinista *m/f*; (*US*) dependiente/a *m/f*, vendedor(a) *m/f*.

clever ['klɛvə*] *adj* (*intelligent*) inteligente, listo; (*skilful*) hábil; (*device, arrangement*) ingenioso.

click [klık] *vt* (*tongue*) chasquear; (*heels*) taconear.

client ['klaıənt] *n* cliente *m/f*.

cliff [klıf] *n* acantilado.

climate ['klaımıt] *n* clima *m*.

climax ['klaımæks] *n* (*of battle, career*) apogeo; (*of film, book*) punto culminante; (*sexual*) orgasmo.

climb [klaım] *vi* subir; (*plant*) trepar; (*move with effort*): **to ~ over a wall/into a car** trepar a una tapia/subir a un coche ♦ *vt* (*stairs*) subir; (*tree*) trepar a; (*mountain*) escalar ♦ *n* subida; ~-**down** *n* vuelta atrás; ~**er** *n* alpinista *m/f* (*SP*), andinista *m/f* (*AM*); ~**ing** *n* alpinismo (*SP*), andinismo (*AM*).

clinch [klıntʃ] *vt* (*deal*) cerrar; (*argument*) remachar.

cling [klıŋ] (*pt, pp* **clung**) *vi*: **to ~** agarrarse a; (*clothes*) pegarse a.

clinic ['klınık] *n* clínica; ~**al** *adj* clínico; (*fig*) frío.

clink [klıŋk] *vi* tintinar.

clip [klıp] *n* (*for hair*) horquilla; (*also: paper ~*) sujetapapeles *m inv*, clip *m*; (*TV, CINEMA*) fragmento ♦ *vt* (*cut*) cortar; (*also: ~ together*) unir; ~**pers** *npl* (*for gardening*) tijeras *fpl*; ~**ping** *n* (*newspaper*) recorte *m*.

clique [kli:k] *n* camarilla.

cloak [kləuk] *n* capa, manto ♦ *vt* (*fig*) encubrir, disimular; ~**room** *n* guardarropa; (*BRIT: WC*) lavabo (*SP*), aseos *mpl* (*SP*), baño (*AM*).

clock [klɔk] *n* reloj *m*; ~ **in** *or* **on** *vi* fichar, picar; ~ **off** *or* **out** *vi* fichar *or* picar la salida; ~**wise** *adv* en el sentido de las agujas del reloj; ~**work** *n*

aparato de relojería ♦ adj (toy) de cuerda.
clog [klɔg] n zueco, chanclo ♦ vt atascar ♦ vi (also: ~ up) atascarse.
cloister ['klɔɪstə*] n claustro.
close¹ [kləus] adj (near): ~ (to) cerca (de); (friend) íntimo; (connection) estrecho; (examination) detallado, minucioso; (weather) bochornoso; **to have a ~ shave** (fig) escaparse por un pelo ♦ adv cerca; ~ **by**, ~ **at hand** muy cerca; ~ **to** prep cerca de.
close² [kləuz] vt (shut) cerrar; (end) concluir, terminar ♦ vi (shop etc) cerrarse; (end) concluirse, terminarse ♦ n (end) fin m, final m, conclusión f; ~ **down** vi cerrarse definitivamente; ~**d** adj (shop etc) cerrado; ~**d shop** n taller m gremial.
close-knit [kləus'nɪt] adj (fig) muy unido.
closely ['kləuslɪ] adv (study) con detalle; (watch) de cerca; (resemble) estrechamente.
closet ['klɔzɪt] n armario.
close-up ['kləusʌp] n primer plano.
closure ['kləuʒə*] n cierre m.
clot [klɔt] n (gen: blood ~) coágulo; (inf: idiot) imbécil m/f ♦ vi (blood) coagularse.
cloth [klɔθ] n (material) tela, paño; (rag) trapo.
clothe [kləuð] vt vestir; ~**s** npl ropa; ~**s brush** n cepillo (para la ropa); ~**s line** n cuerda (para tender la ropa); ~**s peg** (US ~**s pin**) n pinza.
clothing ['kləuðɪŋ] n = **clothes**.
cloud [klaud] n nube f; ~**burst** n aguacero; ~**y** adj nublado, nubloso; (liquid) turbio.
clout [klaut] vt dar un tortazo a.
clove [kləuv] n clavo; ~ **of garlic** diente m de ajo.
clover ['kləuvə*] n trébol m.
clown [klaun] n payaso ♦ vi (also: ~ about, ~ around) hacer el payaso.
cloying ['klɔɪŋ] adj empalagoso.
club [klʌb] n (society) club m; (weapon) porra, cachiporra; (also: golf ~) palo ♦ vt aporrear ♦ vi: **to ~ together**

(for gift) comprar entre todos; ~**s** npl (CARDS) tréboles mpl; ~ **car** (US) n (RAIL) coche m sálon; ~**house** n local social, sobre todo en clubs deportivos.
cluck [klʌk] vi cloquear.
clue [klu:] n pista; (in crosswords) indicación f; **I haven't a ~** no tengo ni idea.
clump [klʌmp] n (of trees) grupo.
clumsy ['klʌmzɪ] adj (person) torpe, desmañado; (tool) difícil de manejar; (movement) desgarbado.
clung [klʌŋ] pt, pp of **cling**.
cluster ['klʌstə*] n grupo ♦ vi agruparse, apiñarse.
clutch [klʌtʃ] n (AUT) embrague m; (grasp): ~**es** garras fpl ♦ vt asir; agarrar.
clutter ['klʌtə*] vt atestar.
cm abbr (= centimetre) cm.
CND n abbr (= Campaign for Nuclear Disarmament) plataforma pro desarme nuclear.
Co. abbr = **county**; **company**.
c/o abbr (= care of) c/a, a/c.
coach [kəutʃ] n autocar m (SP), coche m de línea; (horse-drawn) coche m; (of train) vagón m, coche m; (SPORT) entrenador(a) m/f, instructor(a) m/f; (tutor) profesor(a) m/f particular ♦ vt (SPORT) entrenar; (student) preparar, enseñar; ~ **trip** n excursión f en autocar.
coal [kəul] n carbón m; ~ **face** n frente m de carbón; ~**field** n yacimiento de carbón.
coalition [kəuə'lɪʃən] n coalición f.
coalman ['kəulmən] n carbonero.
coal merchant n = **coalman**.
coalmine ['kəulmaɪn] n mina de carbón.
coarse [kɔːs] adj basto, burdo; (vulgar) grosero, ordinario.
coast [kəust] n costa, litoral m ♦ vi (AUT) ir en punto muerto; ~**al** adj costero, costanero; ~**guard** n guardacostas m inv; ~**line** n litoral m.
coat [kəut] n abrigo; (of animal) pelaje m, lana; (of paint) mano f, capa ♦ vt cubrir, revestir; ~ **of arms** n escudo de armas; ~ **hanger** n percha (SP), gancho (AM); ~**ing** n capa, baño.

coax [kəuks] *vt* engatusar.

cob [kɔb] *n see* **corn**.

cobbler ['kɔblə] *n* zapatero (remendón).

cobbles ['kɔblz] *npl* adoquines *mpl*.

cobblestones ['kɔblstəunz] *npl* = **cobbles**.

cobweb ['kɔbweb] *n* telaraña.

cock [kɔk] *n* (*rooster*) gallo; (*male bird*) macho ♦ *vt* (*gun*) amartillar; ~**erel** *n* gallito; ~**eyed** *adj* (*idea*) disparatado.

cockle ['kɔkl] *n* berberecho.

cockney ['kɔknɪ] *n* habitante de ciertos barrios de Londres.

cockpit ['kɔkpɪt] *n* cabina.

cockroach ['kɔkrəutʃ] *n* cucaracha.

cocktail ['kɔkteɪl] *n* coctel *m*, cóctel *m*; ~ **cabinet** *n* mueble-bar *m*; ~ **party** *n* coctel *m*, cóctel *m*.

cocoa ['kəukəu] *n* cacao; (*drink*) chocolate *m*.

coconut ['kəukənʌt] *n* coco.

cocoon [kə'ku:n] *n* (*ZOOL*) capullo.

cod [kɔd] *n* bacalao.

C.O.D. *abbr* (= *cash on delivery*) C.A.E.

code [kəud] *n* código; (*cipher*) clave *f*; (*dialling* ~) prefijo; (*post* ~) código postal.

cod-liver oil ['kɔdlɪvə*-] *n* aceite *m* de hígado de bacalao.

coercion [kəu'ə:ʃən] *n* coacción *f*.

coffee ['kɔfɪ] *n* café *m*; ~ **bar** (*BRIT*) *n* cafetería; ~ **bean** *n* grano de café; ~ **break** *n* descanso (para tomar café); ~**pot** *n* cafetera; ~ **table** *n* mesita (para servir el café).

coffin ['kɔfɪn] *n* ataúd *m*.

cog [kɔg] *n* (*wheel*) rueda dentada; (*tooth*) diente *m*.

cogent ['kəudʒənt] *adj* convincente.

cognac ['kɔnjæk] *n* coñac *m*.

coil [kɔɪl] *n* rollo; (*ELEC*) bobina, carrete *m*; (*contraceptive*) espiral *f* ♦ *vt* enrollar.

coin [kɔɪn] *n* moneda ♦ *vt* (*word*) inventar, idear; ~**age** *n* moneda; ~**box** (*BRIT*) *n* cabina telefónica.

coincide [kəuɪn'saɪd] *vi* coincidir; (*agree*) estar de acuerdo; ~**nce**

[kəu'ɪnsɪdəns] *n* casualidad *f*.

coke [kəuk] *n* (*coal*) coque *m*.

Coke [kəuk] ® *n* Coca Cola ®.

colander ['kɔləndə*] *n* colador *m*, escurridor *m*.

cold [kəuld] *adj* frío ♦ *n* frío; (*MED*) resfriado; **it's** ~ hace frío; **to be** ~ (*person*) tener frío; **to catch** ~ enfriarse; **to catch a** ~ resfriarse, acatarrarse; **in** ~ **blood** a sangre fría; ~**-shoulder** *vt* dar or volver la espalda a; ~ **sore** *n* herpes *mpl or fpl*.

coleslaw ['kəulslɔ:] *n* especie de ensalada de col.

colic ['kɔlɪk] *n* cólico.

collapse [kə'læps] *vi* hundirse, derrumbarse; (*MED*) sufrir un colapso ♦ *n* hundimiento, derrumbamiento; (*MED*) colapso; **collapsible** *adj* plegable.

collar ['kɔlə*] *n* (*of coat, shirt*) cuello; (*of dog etc*) collar; ~**bone** *n* clavícula.

collateral [kɔ'lætərəl] *n* garantía colateral.

colleague ['kɔli:g] *n* colega *m/f*.

collect [kə'lekt] *vt* (*litter, mail etc*) recoger; (*as a hobby*) coleccionar; (*BRIT: call and pick up*) recoger; (*debts, subscriptions etc*) recaudar ♦ *vi* reunirse; (*dust*) acumularse; **to call** ~ (*US: TEL*) llamar a cobro revertido; ~**ion** [kə'lekʃən] *n* colección *f*; (*of mail, for charity*) recogida.

collector [kə'lektə*] *n* coleccionista *m/f*; (*of taxes*) recaudador(a) *m/f*.

college ['kɔlɪdʒ] *n* colegio mayor; (*of agriculture, technology*) escuela universitaria.

collide [kə'laɪd] *vi* chocar.

collie ['kɔlɪ] *n* perro pastor escocés, collie *m*.

colliery ['kɔlɪərɪ] (*BRIT*) *n* mina de carbón.

collision [kə'lɪʒən] *n* choque *m*.

colloquial [kə'ləukwɪəl] *adj* familiar, coloquial.

collusion [kə'lu:ʒən] *n* confabulación *f*, connivencia.

Colombia [kə'lɔmbɪə] *n* Colombia; ~**n** *adj, n* colombiano/a.

colon ['kəulən] *n* (*sign*) dos puntos;

(*MED*) colon *m*.

colonel ['kə:nl] *n* coronel *m*.

colonial [kə'ləunɪəl] *adj* colonial.

colony ['kɔlənɪ] *n* colonia.

colour ['kʌlə*] (*US* **color**) *n* color *m* ♦ *vt* color(e)ar; (*dye*) teñir; (*fig: account*) adornar; (: *judgement*) distorsionar ♦ *vi* (*blush*) sonrojarse; ~s *npl* (*of party, club*) colores *mpl*; **in** ~ en color; ~ **in** *vt* colorear; ~ **bar** *n* segregación *f* racial; ~-**blind** *adj* daltónico; ~**ed** *adj* de color; (*photo*) en color; ~ **film** *n* película en color; ~**ful** *adj* lleno de color; (*story*) fantástico; (*person*) excéntrico; ~**ing** *n* (*complexion*) tez *f*; (*in food*) colorante *m*; ~ **scheme** *n* combinación *f* de colores; ~ **television** *n* televisión *f* en color.

colt [kəult] *n* potro.

column ['kɔləm] *n* columna; ~**ist** ['kɔləmnɪst] *n* columnista *m/f*.

coma ['kəumə] *n* coma *m*.

comb [kəum] *n* peine *m*; (*ornamental*) peineta ♦ *vt* (*hair*) peinar; (*area*) registrar a fondo.

combat ['kɔmbæt] *n* combate *m* ♦ *vt* combatir.

combination [kɔmbɪ'neɪʃən] *n* combinación *f*.

combine [*vb* kəm'baɪn, *n* 'kɔmbaɪn] *vt* combinar; (*qualities*) reunir ♦ *vi* combinarse ♦ *n* (*ECON*) cartel *m*; ~ **(harvester)** *n* cosechadora.

KEYWORD

come [kʌm] (*pt* **came**, *pp* **come**) *vi* **1** (*movement towards*) venir; **to** ~ **running** venir corriendo

2 (*arrive*) llegar; **he's** ~ **here to work** ha venido aquí para trabajar; **to** ~ **home** volver a casa

3 (*reach*): **to** ~ **to** llegar a; **the bill came to £40** la cuenta ascendía a cuarenta libras

4 (*occur*): **an idea came to me** se me ocurrió una idea

5 (*be, become*): **to** ~ **loose/undone** *etc* aflojarse/desabrocharse, desatarse *etc*; **I've** ~ **to like him** por fin ha llegado a gustarme

come about *vi* suceder, ocurrir

come across *vt fus* (*person*) topar con; (*thing*) dar con

come away *vi* (*leave*) marcharse; (*become detached*) desprenderse

come back *vi* (*return*) volver

come by *vt fus* (*acquire*) conseguir

come down *vi* (*price*) bajar; (*tree, building*) ser derribado

come forward *vi* presentarse

come from *vt fus* (*place, source*) ser de

come in *vi* (*visitor*) entrar; (*train, report*) llegar; (*fashion*) ponerse de moda; (*on deal etc*) entrar

come in for *vt fus* (*criticism etc*) recibir

come into *vt fus* (*money*) heredar; (*be involved*) tener que ver con; **to** ~ **into fashion** ponerse de moda

come off *vi* (*button*) soltarse, desprenderse; (*attempt*) salir bien

come on *vi* (*pupil*) progresar; (*work, project*) desarrollarse; (*lights*) encenderse; (*electricity*) volver; ~ **on!** ¡vamos!

come out *vi* (*fact*) salir a la luz; (*book, sun*) salir; (*stain*) quitarse

come round *vi* (*after faint, operation*) volver en sí

come to *vi* (*wake*) volver en sí

come up *vi* (*sun*) salir; (*problem*) surgir; (*event*) aproximarse; (*in conversation*) mencionarse

come up against *vt fus* (*resistance etc*) tropezar con

come up with *vt fus* (*idea*) sugerir; (*money*) conseguir

come upon *vt fus* (*find*) dar con.

---

comeback ['kʌmbæk] *n*: **to make a** ~ (*THEATRE*) volver a las tablas.

comedian [kə'mi:dɪən] *n* cómico; **comedienne** [-'ɛn] *n* cómica.

comedy ['kɔmɪdɪ] *n* comedia; (*humour*) comicidad *f*.

comet ['kɔmɪt] *n* cometa *m*.

comeuppance [kʌm'ʌpəns] *n*: **to get one's** ~ llevar su merecido.

comfort ['kʌmfət] *n* bienestar *m*; (*re-*

lief) alivio ♦ *vt* consolar; ~s *npl* (*of home etc*) comodidades *fpl*; ~**able** *adj* cómodo; (*financially*) acomodado; (*easy*) fácil; ~**ably** *adv* (*sit*) cómodamente; (*live*) holgadamente; ~ **station** (*US*) *n* servicios *mpl*.

comic ['kɔmɪk] *adj* (*also*: ~**al**) cómico ♦ *n* (*comedian*) cómico; (*BRIT*: *for children*) tebeo; (*BRIT*: *for adults*) comic *m*; ~ **strip** *n* tira cómica.

coming ['kʌmɪŋ] *n* venida, llegada ♦ *adj* que viene; ~(**s**) **and going(s)** *n*(*pl*) ir y venir *m*, ajetreo.

comma ['kɔmə] *n* coma.

command [kə'mɑːnd] *n* orden *f*, mandato; (*MIL*: *authority*) mando; (*mastery*) dominio ♦ *vt* (*troops*) mandar; (*give orders to*): **to** ~ **sb to do** mandar *or* ordenar a uno hacer; ~**eer** [kɔmən'dɪə*] *vt* requisar; ~**er** *n* (*MIL*) comandante *m/f*, jefe/a *m/f*; ~**ment** *n* (*REL*) mandamiento.

commemorate [kə'mɛmɔreɪt] *vt* conmemorar.

commence [kə'mɛns] *vt*, *vi* comenzar, empezar.

commend [kə'mɛnd] *vt* elogiar, alabar; (*recommend*) recomendar.

commensurate [kə'mɛnʃɔrɪt] *adj*: ~ **with** en proporción a, que corresponde a.

comment ['kɔmɛnt] *n* comentario ♦ *vi*: **to** ~ **on** hacer comentarios sobre; "**no** ~" (*written*) "sin comentarios"; (*spoken*) "no tengo nada que decir"; ~**ary** ['kɔmən*tərɪ] *n* comentario; ~**ator** ['kɔmənteɪtə*] *n* comentarista *m/f*.

commerce ['kɔmɔːs] *n* comercio.

commercial [kə'mɔːʃəl] *adj* comercial ♦ *n* (*TV*, *RADIO*) anuncio.

commiserate [kə'mɪzəreɪt] *vi*: **to** ~ **with** compadecerse de, condolerse de.

commission [kə'mɪʃən] *n* (*committee*, *fee*) comisión *f* ♦ *vt* (*work of art*) encargar; **out of** ~ fuera de servicio; ~**aire** [kəmɪʃə'nɛə*] (*BRIT*) *n* portero; ~**er** *n* (*POLICE*) comisario de policía.

commit [kə'mɪt] *vt* (*act*) cometer; (*resources*) dedicar; (*to sb's care*) entregar; **to** ~ **o.s. (to do)** comprometerse (a

hacer); **to** ~ **suicide** suicidarse; ~**ment** *n* compromiso; (*to ideology etc*) entrega.

committee [kə'mɪtɪ] *n* comité *m*.

commodity [kə'mɔdɪtɪ] *n* mercancía.

common ['kɔmən] *adj* común; (*pej*) ordinario ♦ *n* campo común; **the C~s** *npl* (*BRIT*) (la Cámara de) los Comunes *mpl*; **in** ~ en común; ~**er** *n* plebeyo; ~ **law** *n* ley *f* consuetudinaria; ~**ly** *adv* comúnmente; **C~ Market** *n* Mercado Común; ~**place** *adj* de lo más común; ~**room** *n* sala común; ~ **sense** *n* sentido común; **the C~wealth** *n* la Commonwealth.

commotion [kə'məuʃən] *n* tumulto, confusión *f*.

commune [*n* 'kɔmjuːn, *vb* kə'mjuːn] *n* (*group*) comuna ♦ *vi*: **to** ~ **with** comulgar *or* conversar con.

communicate [kə'mjuːnɪkeɪt] *vt* comunicar ♦ *vi*: **to** ~ (**with**) comunicarse (con); (*in writing*) estar en contacto (con).

communication [kəmjuːnɪ'keɪʃən] *n* comunicación *f*; ~ **cord** (*BRIT*) *n* timbre *m* de alarma.

communion [kə'mjuːnɪən] *n* (*also: Holy C~*) comunión *f*.

communiqué [kə'mjuːnɪkeɪ] *n* comunicado, parte *f*.

communism ['kɔmjunɪzəm] *n* comunismo; **communist** *adj*, *n* comunista *m/f*.

community [kə'mjuːnɪtɪ] *n* comunidad *f*; (*large group*) colectividad *f*; ~ **centre** *n* centro social; ~ **chest** (*US*) *n* arca comunitaria, fondo común; ~ **home** (*BRIT*) *n* correccional *m*.

commutation ticket [kɔmjuː'teɪʃən-] (*US*) *n* billete *m* de abono.

commute [kə'mjuːt] *vi* viajar a diario de la casa al trabajo ♦ *vt* conmutar; ~**r** *n* persona (que ... *see vi*).

compact [*adj* kəm'pækt, *n* 'kɔmpækt] *adj* compacto ♦ *n* (*also: powder* ~) polvera; ~ **disc** *n* compact disc *m*.

companion [kəm'pænɪən] *n* compañero/a; ~**ship** *n* compañerismo.

company ['kʌmpənɪ] *n* compañía;

(*COMM*) sociedad *f*, compañía; **to keep sb ~** acompañar a uno; **~ secretary** (*BRIT*) *n* secretario/a de compañía.

comparative [kəm'pærətɪv] *adj* relativo; (*study*) comparativo; **~ly** *adv* (*relatively*) relativamente.

compare [kəm'pɛə*] *vt*: **to ~ sth/sb with/to** comparar algo/a uno con ♦ *vi*: **to ~ (with)** compararse (con); **comparison** [-'pærɪsn] *n* comparación *f*.

compartment [kəm'pɑːtmənt] *n* (*also: RAIL*) compartim(i)ento.

compass ['kʌmpəs] *n* brújula; **~es** *npl* (*MATH*) compás *m*.

compassion [kəm'pæʃən] *n* compasión *f*; **~ate** *adj* compasivo.

compatible [kəm'pætɪbl] *adj* compatible.

compel [kəm'pɛl] *vt* obligar; **~ling** *adj* (*fig: argument*) convincente.

compensate ['kɔmpənseɪt] *vt* compensar ♦ *vi*: **to ~ for** compensar; **compensation** [-'seɪʃən] *n* (*for loss*) indemnización *f*.

compère ['kɔmpɛə*] *n* presentador *m*.

compete [kəm'piːt] *vi* (*take part*) tomar parte, concurrir; (*vie with*): **to ~ with** competir con, hacer competencia a.

competence ['kɔmpɪtəns] *n* capacidad *f*, aptitud *f*.

competent ['kɔmpɪtənt] *adj* competente, capaz.

competition [kɔmpɪ'tɪʃən] *n* (*contest*) concurso; (*rivalry*) competencia.

competitive [kəm'pɛtɪtɪv] *adj* (*ECON, SPORT*) competitivo.

competitor [kəm'pɛtɪtə*] *n* (*rival*) competidor(a) *m/f*; (*participant*) concursante *m/f*.

compile [kəm'paɪl] *vt* compilar.

complacency [kəm'pleɪsnsɪ] *n* autosatisfacción *f*.

complacent [kəm'pleɪsənt] *adj* autocomplaciente.

complain [kəm'pleɪn] *vi* quejarse; (*COMM*) reclamar; **~t** *n* queja; reclamación *f*; (*MED*) enfermedad *f*.

complement [*n* 'kɔmplɪmənt, *vb* 'kɔmplɪment] *n* complemento; (*esp of ship's crew*) dotación *f* ♦ *vt* (*enhance*) complementar; **~ary** [kɔmplɪ'mɛntərɪ]

adj complementario.

complete [kəm'pliːt] *adj* (*full*) completo; (*finished*) acabado ♦ *vt* (*fulfil*) completar; (*finish*) acabar; (*a form*) llenar; **~ly** *adv* completamente; **completion** [-'pliːʃən] *n* terminación *f*; (*of contract*) realización *f*.

complex ['kɔmplɛks] *adj*, *n* complejo.

complexion [kəm'plɛkʃən] *n* (*of face*) tez *f*, cutis *m*.

compliance [kəm'plaɪəns] *n* (*submission*) sumisión *f*; (*agreement*) conformidad *f*; **in ~ with** de acuerdo con.

complicate ['kɔmplɪkeɪt] *vt* complicar; **~d** *adj* complicado; **complication** [-'keɪʃən] *n* complicación *f*.

complicity [kəm'plɪsɪtɪ] *n* complicidad *f*.

compliment ['kɔmplɪmənt] *n* (*formal*) cumplido ♦ *vt* felicitar; **~s** *npl* (*regards*) saludos *mpl*; **to pay sb a ~** hacer cumplidos a uno; **~ary** [-'mɛntərɪ] *adj* lisonjero; (*free*) de favor.

comply [kəm'plaɪ] *vi*: **to ~ with** cumplir con.

component [kəm'pəunənt] *adj* componente ♦ *n* (*TECH*) pieza.

compose [kəm'pəuz] *vt*: **to be ~d of** componerse de; (*music etc*) componer; **to ~ o.s.** tranquilizarse; **~d** *adj* sosegado; **~r** *n* (*MUS*) compositor(a) *m/f*.

composition [kɔmpə'zɪʃən] *n* composición *f*.

compost ['kɔmpɔst] *n* abono (vegetal).

composure [kəm'pəuʒə*] *n* serenidad *f*, calma.

compound ['kɔmpaund] *n* (*CHEM*) compuesto; (*LING*) palabra compuesta; (*enclosure*) recinto ♦ *adj* compuesto; (*fracture*) complicado.

comprehend [kɔmprɪ'hɛnd] *vt* comprender; **comprehension** [-'hɛnʃən] *n* comprensión *f*.

comprehensive [kɔmprɪ'hɛnsɪv] *adj* exhaustivo; (*INSURANCE*) contra todo riesgo; **~ (school)** *n* centro estatal de enseñanza secundaria; ≈ Instituto Nacional de Bachillerato (*SP*).

compress [*vb* kəm'prɛs, *n* 'kɔmprɛs] *vt* comprimir; (*information*) condensar ♦ *n* (*MED*) compresa.

comprise [kəm'praɪz] vt (also: be ~d of) comprender, constar de; (constitute) constituir.

compromise ['kɒmprəmaɪz] n (agreement) arreglo ♦ vt comprometer ♦ vi transigir.

compulsion [kəm'pʌlʃən] n compulsión f; (force) obligación f.

compulsive [kəm'pʌlsɪv] adj compulsivo; (viewing, reading) obligado.

compulsory [kəm'pʌlsərɪ] adj obligatorio.

computer [kəm'pjuːtə*] n ordenador m, computador m, computadora; ~ize vt (data) computerizar; (system) informatizar; ~ programmer n programador(a) m/f; ~ programming n programación f; ~ science n informática.

computing [kəm'pjuːtɪŋ] n (activity, science) informática.

comrade ['kɒmrɪd] n (POL, MIL) camarada; (friend) compañero/a; ~ship n camaradería, compañerismo.

con [kɒn] vt (deceive) engañar; (cheat) estafar ♦ n estafa.

conceal [kən'siːl] vt ocultar.

conceit [kən'siːt] n presunción f; ~ed adj presumido.

conceivable [kən'siːvəbl] adj concebible.

conceive [kən'siːv] vt, vi concebir.

concentrate ['kɒnsəntreɪt] vi concentrarse ♦ vt concentrar.

concentration [kɒnsən'treɪʃən] n concentración f.

concept ['kɒnsept] n concepto.

conception [kən'sepʃən] n (idea) concepto, idea; (BIOL) concepción f.

concern [kən'sɜːn] n (matter) asunto; (COMM) empresa; (anxiety) preocupación f ♦ vt (worry) preocupar; (involve) afectar; (relate to) tener que ver con; **to be ~ed** (about) interesarse (por), preocuparse (por); ~ing prep sobre, acerca de.

concert ['kɒnsət] n concierto; ~ed [kən'sɜːtəd] adj (efforts etc) concertado; ~ hall n sala de conciertos.

concertina [kɒnsə'tiːnə] n concertina.

concerto [kən'tʃɜːtəʊ] n concierto.

concession [kən'sɛʃən] n concesión f;

tax ~ privilegio fiscal.

concise [kən'saɪs] adj conciso.

conclude [kən'kluːd] vt concluir; (treaty etc) firmar; (agreement) llegar a; (decide) llegar a la conclusión de; **conclusion** [-'kluːʒən] n conclusión f; firma; **conclusive** [-'kluːsɪv] adj decisivo, concluyente.

concoct [kən'kɒkt] vt confeccionar; (plot) tramar; ~ion [-'kɒkʃən] n mezcla.

concourse ['kɒŋkɔːs] n vestíbulo.

concrete ['kɒnkriːt] n hormigón m ♦ adj de hormigón; (fig) concreto.

concur [kən'kɜː*] vi estar de acuerdo, asentir.

concurrently [kən'kʌrntlɪ] adv al mismo tiempo.

concussion [kən'kʌʃən] n conmoción f cerebral.

condemn [kən'dem] vt condenar; (building) declarar en ruina; ~ation [kɒndem'neɪʃən] n condena.

condense [kən'dens] vi condensarse ♦ vt condensar, abreviar; ~d milk n leche f condensada.

condescending [kɒndɪ'sendɪŋ] adj condescendiente.

condition [kən'dɪʃən] n condición f, estado; (requirement) condición f ♦ vt condicionar; **on ~ that** a condición (de) que; ~al adj condicional; ~er n suavizante.

condolences [kən'dəʊlənsɪz] npl pésame m.

condom ['kɒndəm] n condón m.

condone [kən'dəʊn] vt condonar.

conducive [kən'djuːsɪv] adj: ~ to conducente a.

conduct [n 'kɒndʌkt, vb kən'dʌkt] n conducta, comportamiento ♦ vt (lead) conducir; (manage) llevar a cabo, dirigir; (MUS) dirigir; **to ~ o.s.** comportarse; ~ed tour (BRIT) n visita acompañada; ~or n (of orchestra) director m; (US: on train) revisor(a) m/f; (on bus) cobrador m; (ELEC) conductor m; ~ress n (on bus) cobradora.

cone [kəʊn] n cono; (pine ~) piña; (on road) pivote m; (for ice-cream) cucurucho.

confectioner [kən'fɛkʃənə*] n repostero/a; ~'s (shop) n confitería; ~y n dulces mpl.

confer [kən'fə:*] vt: to ~ sth on otorgar algo a ♦ vi conferenciar.

conference ['kɔnfərns] n (meeting) reunión f; (convention) congreso.

confess [kən'fɛs] vt confesar ♦ vi admitir; ~ion [-'fɛʃən] n confesión f.

confetti [kən'fɛtɪ] n confeti m.

confide [kən'faɪd] vi: to ~ in confiar en.

confidence ['kɔnfɪdns] n (also: self ~) confianza; (secret) confidencia; in ~ (speak, write) en confianza; ~ trick n timo; **confident** adj seguro de sí mismo; (certain) seguro; **confidential** [kɔnfɪ'dɛnʃəl] adj confidencial.

confine [kən'faɪn] vt (limit) limitar; (shut up) encerrar; ~d adj (space) reducido; ~ment n (prison) prisión f; ~s ['kɔnfaɪnz] npl confines mpl.

confirm [kən'fə:m] vt confirmar; ~ation [kɔnfə'meɪʃən] n confirmación f; ~ed adj empedernido.

confiscate ['kɔnfɪskeɪt] vt confiscar.

conflict [n 'kɔnflɪkt, vb kən'flɪkt] n conflicto ♦ vi (opinions) chocar; ~ing adj contradictorio.

conform [kən'fɔ:m] vi conformarse; to ~ to ajustarse a.

confound [kən'faund] vt confundir.

confront [kən'frʌnt] vt (problems) hacer frente a; (enemy, danger) enfrentarse con; ~ation [kɔnfrən'teɪʃən] n enfrentamiento.

confuse [kən'fju:z] vt (perplex) aturdir, desconcertar; (mix up) confundir; (complicate) complicar; ~d adj confuso; (person) perplejo; **confusing** adj confuso; **confusion** [-'fju:ʒən] n confusión f.

congeal [kən'dʒi:l] vi (blood) coagularse; (sauce etc) cuajarse.

congenial [kən'dʒi:nɪəl] adj agradable.

congenital [kən'dʒɛnɪtl] adj congénito.

congested [kən'dʒɛstɪd] adj congestionado.

congestion [kən'dʒɛstʃən] n congestión f.

conglomerate [kən'glɔmərət] n (COMM,

GEO) conglomerado.

congratulate [kən'grætjuleɪt] vt: to ~ sb (on) felicitar a uno (por); **congratulations** [-'leɪʃənz] npl felicitaciones fpl; ~! ¡enhorabuena!

congregate ['kɔngrɪgeɪt] vi congregarse; **congregation** [-'geɪʃən] n (of a church) feligreses mpl.

congress ['kɔngrɛs] n congreso; (US): C~ Congreso; ~man (US) n miembro del Congreso.

conifer ['kɔnɪfə*] n conífera.

conjecture [kən'dʒɛktʃə*] n conjetura.

conjugal ['kɔndʒugl] adj conyugal.

conjugate ['kɔndʒugeɪt] vt conjugar.

conjunctivitis [kəndʒʌŋktɪ'vaɪtɪs] n conjuntivitis f.

conjure ['kʌndʒə*] vi hacer juegos de manos; ~ up vt (ghost, spirit) hacer aparecer; (memories) evocar; ~r n ilusionista m/f.

conk out [kɔŋk-] (inf) vi averiarse.

con man ['kɔn-] n estafador m.

connect [kə'nɛkt] vt juntar, unir; (ELEC) conectar; (TEL: subscriber) poner; (TEL: caller) poner al habla; (fig) relacionar, asociar ♦ vi: to ~ with (train) enlazar con; to be ~ed with (associated) estar relacionado con; ~ion [-ʃən] n juntura, unión f; (ELEC) conexión f; (RAIL) enlace m; (TEL) comunicación f; (fig) relación f.

connive [kə'naɪv] vi: to ~ at hacer la vista gorda a.

connoisseur [kɔnɪ'sə*] n experto/a, entendido/a.

conquer ['kɔŋkə*] vt (territory) conquistar; (enemy, feelings) vencer; ~or n conquistador m.

conquest ['kɔŋkwɛst] n conquista.

cons [kɔnz] npl see convenience; pro.

conscience ['kɔnʃəns] n conciencia.

conscientious [kɔnʃɪ'ɛnʃəs] adj concienzudo; (objection) de conciencia.

conscious ['kɔnʃəs] adj (deliberate) deliberado; (awake, aware) consciente; ~ness n conciencia; (MED) conocimiento.

conscript ['kɔnskrɪpt] n recluta m; ~ion [kən'skrɪpʃən] n servicio militar (obligatorio).

consecrate ['kɔnsɪkreɪt] *vt* consagrar.

consensus [kən'sɛnsəs] *n* consenso.

consent [kən'sɛnt] *n* consentimiento ♦ *vi*: **to ~ (to)** consentir (en).

consequence ['kɔnsɪkwəns] *n* consecuencia; (*significance*) importancia.

consequently ['kɔnsɪkwəntlɪ] *adv* por consiguiente.

conservation [kɔnsə'veɪʃən] *n* conservación *f*.

conservative [kən'sə:vətɪv] *adj* conservador(a); (*estimate etc*) cauteloso; **C~** (*BRIT*) *adj, n* (*POL*) conservador(a) *m/f*.

conservatory [kən'sə:vətrɪ] *n* invernadero; (*MUS*) conservatorio.

conserve [kən'sə:v] *vt* conservar ♦ *n* conserva.

consider [kən'sɪdə*] *vt* considerar; (*take into account*) tener en cuenta; (*study*) estudiar, examinar; **to ~ doing sth** pensar en (la posibilidad de) hacer algo; **~able** *adj* considerable; **~ably** *adv* notablemente.

considerate [kən'sɪdərɪt] *adj* considerado; **consideration** [-'reɪʃən] *n* consideración *f*; (*factor*) factor *m*; **to give sth further consideration** estudiar algo más a fondo.

considering [kən'sɪdərɪŋ] *prep* teniendo en cuenta.

consign [kən'saɪn] *vt*: **to ~ to** (*sth unwanted*) relegar a; (*person*) destinar a; **~ment** *n* envío.

consist [kən'sɪst] *vi*: **to ~ of** consistir en.

consistency [kən'sɪstənsɪ] *n* (*of argument etc*) coherencia; consecuencia; (*thickness*) consistencia.

consistent [kən'sɪstənt] *adj* (*person*) consecuente; (*argument etc*) coherente.

consolation [kɔnsə'leɪʃən] *n* consuelo.

console¹ [kən'səul] *vt* consolar.

console² ['kɔnsəul] *n* consola.

consonant ['kɔnsənənt] *n* consonante *f*.

consortium [kən'sɔ:tɪəm] *n* consorcio.

conspicuous [kən'spɪkjuəs] *adj* (*visible*) visible.

conspiracy [kən'spɪrəsɪ] *n* conjura, complot *m*.

conspire [kən'spaɪə*] *vi* conspirar;

(*events etc*) unirse.

constable ['kʌnstəbl] (*BRIT*) *n* policía *m/f*; **chief ~** ≈ jefe *m* de policía.

constabulary [kən'stæbjulərɪ] *n* ≈ policía.

constant ['kɔnstənt] *adj* constante; **~ly** *adv* constantemente.

constipated ['kɔnstɪpeɪtəd] *adj* estreñido.

constipation [kɔnstɪ'peɪʃən] *n* estreñimiento.

constituency [kən'stɪtjuənsɪ] *n* (*POL: area*) distrito electoral; (: *electors*) electorado; **constituent** [-ənt] *n* (*POL*) elector(a) *m/f*; (*part*) componente *m*.

constitute ['kɔnstɪtju:t] *vt* constituir; (*make up: whole*) componer.

constitution [kɔnstɪ'tju:ʃən] *n* constitución *f*; **~al** *adj* constitucional.

constraint [kən'streɪnt] *n* obligación *f*; (*limit*) restricción *f*.

construct [kən'strʌkt] *vt* construir; **~ion** [-ʃən] *n* construcción *f*; **~ive** *adj* constructivo.

construe [kən'stru:] *vt* interpretar.

consul ['kɔnsl] *n* cónsul *m/f*; **~ate** ['kɔnsjulɪt] *n* consulado.

consult [kən'sʌlt] *vt* consultar; **~ant** *n* (*BRIT: MED*) especialista *m/f*; (*other specialist*) asesor(a) *m/f*; **~ation** [kɔnsəl'teɪʃən] *n* consulta; **~ing room** (*BRIT*) *n* consultorio.

consume [kən'sju:m] *vt* (*eat*) comerse; (*drink*) beberse; (*fire etc, COMM*) consumir; **~r** *n* consumidor(a) *m/f*; **~r goods** *npl* bienes *mpl* de consumo; **~rism** *n* consumismo.

consummate ['kɔnsʌmeɪt] *vt* consumar.

consumption [kən'sʌmpʃən] *n* consumo.

cont. *abbr* (= *continued*) sigue.

contact ['kɔntækt] *n* contacto; (*person*) contacto; (: *pej*) enchufe *m* ♦ *vt* ponerse en contacto con; **~ lenses** *npl* lentes *fpl* de contacto.

contagious [kən'teɪdʒəs] *adj* contagioso.

contain [kən'teɪn] *vt* contener; **to ~ o.s.** contenerse; **~er** *n* recipiente *m*; (*for shipping etc*) contenedor *m*.

contaminate [kən'tæmɪneɪt] *vt* contaminar.

cont'd *abbr* (= *continued*) sigue.

contemplate ['kɔntəmpleɪt] *vt* contemplar; (*reflect upon*) considerar.

contemporary [kən'tempərərɪ] *adj, n* contemporáneo/a *m/f*.

contempt [kən'tempt] *n* desprecio; ~ **of court** (*LAW*) desacato (a los tribunales); ~**ible** *adj* despreciable; ~**uous** *adj* desdeñoso.

contend [kən'tend] *vt* (*argue*) afirmar ♦ *vi*: **to** ~ **with/for** luchar contra/por; ~**er** *n* (*SPORT*) contendiente *m/f*.

content [*adj, vb* kən'tent, *n* 'kɔntent] *adj* (*happy*) contento; (*satisfied*) satisfecho ♦ *vt* contentar; satisfacer ♦ *n* contenido; ~**s** *npl* contenido; (**table of**) ~**s** índice *m* de materias; ~**ed** *adj* contento; satisfecho.

contention [kən'tenʃən] *n* (*assertion*) aseveración *f*; (*disagreement*) discusión *f*.

contentment [kən'tentmənt] *n* contento.

contest [*n* 'kɔntest, *vb* kən'test] *n* lucha; (*competition*) concurso ♦ *vt* (*dispute*) impugnar; (*POL*) presentarse como candidato/a en; ~**ant** [kən'testənt] *n* concursante *m/f*; (*in fight*) contendiente *m/f*.

context ['kɔntekst] *n* contexto.

continent ['kɔntɪnənt] *n* continente *m*; **the C**~ (*BRIT*) el continente europeo; ~**al** [-'nentl] *adj* continental; ~**al quilt** (*BRIT*) *n* edredón *m*.

contingency [kən'tɪndʒənsɪ] *n* contingencia.

contingent [kən'tɪndʒənt] *n* (*group*) grupo, contingente *m*.

continual [kən'tɪnjuəl] *adj* continuo; ~**ly** *adv* constantemente.

continuation [kəntɪnju'eɪʃən] *n* prolongación *f*; (*after interruption*) reanudación *f*.

continue [kən'tɪnjuː] *vi, vt* seguir, continuar.

continuous [kən'tɪnjuəs] *adj* continuo; ~ **stationery** *n* papel *m* continuo.

contort [kən'tɔːt] *vt* retorcer; ~**ion** [-'tɔːʃən] *n* (*movement*) contorsión *f*.

contour ['kɔntuə*] *n* contorno; (*also*: ~ **line**) curva de nivel.

contraband ['kɔntrəbænd] *n* contrabando.

contraception [kɔntrə'sepʃən] *n* contracepción *f*.

contraceptive [kɔntrə'septɪv] *adj, n* anticonceptivo.

contract [*n* 'kɔntrækt, *vb* kən'trækt] *n* contrato ♦ *vi* (*COMM*): **to** ~ **to do sth** comprometerse por contrato a hacer algo; (*become smaller*) contraerse, encogerse ♦ *vt* contraer; ~**ion** [kən'trækʃən] *n* contracción *f*; ~**or** *n* contratista *m/f*.

contradict [kɔntrə'dɪkt] *vt* contradecir; ~**ion** [-ʃən] *n* contradicción *f*; ~**ory** *adj* contradictorio.

contraption [kən'træpʃən] (*pej*) *n* artilugio *m*.

contrary¹ ['kɔntrərɪ] *adj* contrario ♦ *n* lo contrario; **on the** ~ al contrario; **unless you hear to the** ~ a no ser que le digan lo contrario.

contrary² [kən'treərɪ] *adj* (*perverse*) terco.

contrast [*n* 'kɔntrɑːst, *vt* kən'trɑːst] *n* contraste *m* ♦ *vt* comparar; **in** ~ **to** en contraste con; ~**ing** *adj* (*opinions*) opuesto; (*colours*) que hace contraste.

contravene [kɔntrə'viːn] *vt* infringir.

contribute [kən'trɪbjuːt] *vi* contribuir ♦ *vt*: **to** ~ **£10/an article to** contribuir con 10 libras/un artículo a; **to** ~ **to** (*charity*) donar a; (*newspaper*) escribir para; (*discussion*) intervenir en; **contribution** [kɔntrɪ'bjuːʃən] *n* (*donation*) donativo; (*BRIT: for social security*) cotización *f*; (*to debate*) intervención *f*; (*to journal*) colaboración *f*; **contributor** *n* contribuyente *m/f*; (*to newspaper*) colaborador(a) *m/f*.

contrive [kən'traɪv] *vt* (*invent*) idear ♦ *vi*: **to** ~ **to do** lograr hacer.

control [kən'trəul] *vt* controlar; (*process etc*) dirigir; (*machinery*) manejar; (*temper*) dominar; (*disease*) contener ♦ *n* control *m*; ~**s** *npl* (*of vehicle*) instrumentos *mpl* de mando; (*of radio*) controles *mpl*; (*governmental*) medidas *fpl* de control; **under** ~ bajo control; **to be in** ~ **of** tener el mando de; **the car went out of** ~ se perdió el control del coche;

~ **panel** n tablero de instrumentos; ~ **room** n sala de mando; ~ **tower** n (*AVIAT*) torre f de control.

controversial [kɔntrə'vəːʃl] adj polémico.

controversy ['kɔntrəvəːsɪ] n polémica.

conurbation [kɔnəː'beɪʃən] n urbanización f.

convalesce [kɔnvə'lɛs] vi convalecer.

convector [kən'vɛktə*] n calentador m de aire.

convene [kən'viːn] vt convocar ♦ vi reunirse.

convenience [kən'viːnɪəns] n (*easiness*) comodidad f; (*suitability*) idoneidad f; (*advantage*) ventaja; **at your** ~ cuando le sea conveniente; **all modern** ~s, **all mod cons** (*BRIT*) todo confort.

convenient [kən'viːnɪənt] adj (*useful*) útil; (*place, time*) conveniente.

convent ['kɔnvənt] n convento.

convention [kən'vɛnʃən] n convención f; (*meeting*) asamblea; (*agreement*) convenio; ~**al** adj convencional.

converge [kən'vəːdʒ] vi convergir; (*people*): **to** ~ **on** dirigirse todos a.

conversant [kən'vəːsnt] adj: **to be** ~ **with** estar al tanto de.

conversation [kɔnvə'seɪʃən] n conversación f; ~**al** adj familiar; ~**al skill** facilidad f de palabra.

converse [n 'kɔnvəːs, vb kən'vəːs] n inversa ♦ vi conversar; ~**ly** [-'vəːslɪ] adv a la inversa.

conversion [kən'vəːʃən] n conversión f.

convert [vb kən'vəːt, n 'kɔnvəːt] vt (*REL, COMM*) convertir; (*alter*): **to** ~ **sth into/to** transformar algo en/convertir algo a ♦ n converso/a; ~**ible** adj convertible ♦ n descapotable m.

convex ['kɔnvɛks] adj convexo.

convey [kən'veɪ] vt llevar; (*thanks*) comunicar; (*idea*) expresar; ~**or belt** n cinta transportadora.

convict [vb kən'vɪkt, n 'kɔnvɪkt] vt (*find guilty*) declarar culpable a ♦ n presidiario/a; ~**ion** [-ʃən] n condena; (*belief, certainty*) convicción f.

convince [kən'vɪns] vt convencer; ~**d** adj: ~**d of/that** convencido de/de que;

convincing adj convincente.

convoluted ['kɔnvəluːtɪd] adj (*argument etc*) enrevesado.

convoy ['kɔnvɔɪ] n convoy m.

convulse [kən'vʌls] vt: **to be** ~**d with laughter** desternillarse de risa; **convulsion** [-'vʌlʃən] n convulsión f.

coo [kuː] vi arrullar.

cook [kuk] vt (*stew etc*) guisar; (*meal*) preparar ♦ vi cocer; (*person*) cocinar ♦ n cocinero/a; ~ **book** n libro de cocina; ~**er** n cocina; ~**ery** n cocina; ~**ery book** (*BRIT*) n = ~ **book**; ~**ie** (*US*) n galleta; ~**ing** n cocina.

cool [kuːl] adj fresco; (*not afraid*) tranquilo; (*unfriendly*) frío ♦ vt enfriar ♦ vi enfriarse; ~**ness** n frescura; tranquilidad f; (*indifference*) falta de entusiasmo.

coop [kuːp] n gallinero ♦ vt: **to** ~ **up** (*fig*) encerrar.

cooperate [kəu'ɔpəreɪt] vi cooperar, colaborar; **cooperation** [-'reɪʃən] n cooperación f, colaboración f; **cooperative** [-rətɪv] adj (*business*) cooperativo; (*person*) servicial ♦ n cooperativa.

coordinate [vb kəu'ɔːdɪneɪt, n kəu'ɔːdɪnət] vt coordinar ♦ n (*MATH*) coordenada; ~**s** npl (*clothes*) coordinados mpl; **coordination** [-'neɪʃən] n coordinación f.

co-ownership [kəu'əunəʃɪp] n copropiedad f.

cop [kɔp] (*inf*) n poli m (*SP*), tira m (*AM*).

cope [kəup] vi: **to** ~ **with** (*problem*) hacer frente a.

copious ['kəupɪəs] adj copioso, abundante.

copper ['kɔpə*] n (*metal*) cobre m; (*BRIT: inf*) poli m; ~**s** npl (*money*) calderilla (*SP*), centavos mpl (*AM*).

coppice ['kɔpɪs] n bosquecillo.

copse [kɔps] n = **coppice**.

copulate ['kɔpjuleɪt] vi copularse.

copy ['kɔpɪ] n copia; (*of book etc*) ejemplar m ♦ vt copiar; ~**right** n derechos mpl de autor.

coral ['kɔrəl] n coral m; ~ **reef** n arrecife m (de coral).

cord [kɔːd] n cuerda; (*ELEC*) cable m;

(*fabric*) pana.
cordial ['kɔ:dɪəl] *adj* cordial ♦ *n* cordial *m*.
cordon ['kɔ:dn] *n* cordón *m*; ~ **off** *vt* acordonar.
corduroy ['kɔ:dərɔɪ] *n* pana.
core [kɔ:*] *n* centro, núcleo; (*of fruit*) corazón *m*; (*of problem*) meollo ♦ *vt* quitar el corazón de.
coriander [kɔrɪ'ændə*] *n* culantro.
cork [kɔ:k] *n* corcho; (*tree*) alcornoque *m*; ~**screw** *n* sacacorchos *m inv*.
corn [kɔ:n] *n* (*BRIT: cereal crop*) trigo; (*US: maize*) maíz *m*; (*on foot*) callo; ~ **on the cob** (*CULIN*) maíz en la mazorca (*SP*), choclo (*AM*).
corned beef ['kɔ:nd-] *n* carne *f* acecinada (en lata).
corner ['kɔ:nə*] *n* (*outside*) esquina; (*inside*) rincón *m*; (*in road*) curva; (*FOOTBALL*) córner *m*; (*BOXING*) esquina ♦ *vt* (*trap*) arrinconar; (*COMM*) acaparar ♦ *vi* (*in car*) tomar las curvas; ~**stone** *n* (*also fig*) piedra angular.
cornet ['kɔ:nɪt] *n* (*MUS*) corneta; (*BRIT: of ice-cream*) cucurucho.
cornflakes ['kɔ:nfleɪks] *npl* copos *mpl* de maíz, cornflakes *mpl*.
cornflour ['kɔ:nflauə*] (*BRIT*) *n* harina de maíz.
cornstarch ['kɔ:nstɑ:tʃ] (*US*) *n* = **cornflour**.
Cornwall ['kɔ:nwəl] *n* Cornualles *m*.
corny ['kɔ:nɪ] (*inf*) *adj* gastado.
coronary ['kɔrənərɪ] *n* (*also*: ~ *thrombosis*) infarto.
coronation [kɔrə'neɪʃən] *n* coronación *f*.
coroner ['kɔrənə*] *n* juez *m* (de instrucción).
corporal ['kɔ:pərl] *n* cabo ♦ *adj*: ~ **punishment** castigo corporal.
corporate ['kɔ:pərɪt] *adj* (*action, ownership*) colectivo; (*finance, image*) corporativo.
corporation [kɔ:pə'reɪʃən] *n* (*of town*) ayuntamiento; (*COMM*) corporación *f*.
corps [kɔ:*, *pl* kɔ:z] *n inv* cuerpo; **diplomatic** ~ cuerpo diplomático; **press** ~ gabinete *m* de prensa.
corpse [kɔ:ps] *n* cadáver *m*.

corpuscle ['kɔ:pʌsl] *n* corpúsculo.
corral [kə'rɑ:l] *n* corral *m*.
correct [kə'rɛkt] *adj* justo, exacto; (*proper*) correcto ♦ *vt* corregir; (*exam*) corregir, calificar; ~**ion** [-ʃən] *n* (*act*) corrección *f*; (*instance*) rectificación *f*.
correspond [kɔrɪs'pɔnd] *vi* (*write*): **to** ~ (**with**) escribirse (con); (*be equivalent to*): **to** ~ (**to**) corresponder (a); (*be in accordance*): **to** ~ (**with**) corresponder (con); ~**ence** *n* correspondencia; ~**ence course** *n* curso por correspondencia; ~**ent** *n* corresponsal *m/f*.
corridor ['kɔrɪdɔ:*] *n* pasillo.
corroborate [kə'rɔbəreɪt] *vt* corroborar.
corrode [kə'rəud] *vt* corroer ♦ *vi* corroerse; **corrosion** [-'rəuʒən] *n* corrosión *f*.
corrugated ['kɔrəgeɪtɪd] *adj* ondulado; ~ **iron** *n* chapa ondulada.
corrupt [kə'rʌpt] *adj* (*person*) corrupto; (*COMPUT*) corrompido ♦ *vt* corromper; (*COMPUT*) degradar; ~**ion** [-ʃən] *n* corrupción *f*.
corset ['kɔ:sɪt] *n* faja.
Corsica ['kɔ:sɪkə] *n* Córcega.
cosh [kɔʃ] (*BRIT*) *n* cachiporra.
cosmetic [kɔz'mɛtɪk] *adj*, *n* cosmético.
cosmonaut ['kɔzmənɔ:t] *n* cosmonauta *m/f*.
cosmopolitan [kɔzmə'pɔlɪtn] *adj* cosmopolita.
cosset ['kɔsɪt] *vt* mimar.
cost [kɔst] (*pt, pp* cost) *n* (*price*) precio; ~**s** *npl* (*COMM*) costes *mpl*; (*LAW*) costas *fpl* ♦ *vi* costar, valer ♦ *vt* preparar el presupuesto de; **how much does it** ~? ¿cuánto cuesta?; **to** ~ **sb time/ effort** costarle a uno tiempo/esfuerzo; **it** ~ **him his life** le costó la vida; **at all** ~**s** cueste lo que cueste.
co-star ['kəustɑ:*] *n* coprotagonista *m/f*.
Costa Rica ['kɔstə'ri:kə] *n* Costa Rica; ~**n** *adj*, *n* costarriqueño/a *m/f*.
cost-effective [kɔstɪ'fɛktɪv] *adj* rentable.
costly ['kɔstlɪ] *adj* costoso.
cost-of-living [kɔstəv'lɪvɪŋ] *adj*: ~ **allowance** plus *m* de carestía de vida; ~ **index** índice *m* del costo de vida.
cost price (*BRIT*) *n* precio de coste.

costume ['kɔstjuːm] n traje m; (BRIT: also: swimming ~) traje de baño; ~ jewellery n bisutería.

cosy ['kəuzi] (US cozy) adj (person) cómodo; (room) acogedor(a).

cot [kɔt] n (BRIT: child's) cuna; (US: campbed) cama de campaña.

cottage ['kɔtɪdʒ] n casita de campo; (rustic) barraca; ~ **cheese** n requesón m.

cotton ['kɔtn] n algodón m; (thread) hilo; ~ **on to** (inf) vt fus caer en la cuenta de; ~ **candy** (US) n algodón m (azucarado); ~ **wool** (BRIT) n algodón m (hidrófilo).

couch [kautʃ] n sofá m; (doctor's etc) diván m.

couchette [kuː'ʃet] n litera.

cough [kɔf] vi toser ♦ n tos f; ~ **drop** n pastilla para la tos.

could [kud] pt of **can**; ~**n't** = **could not**.

council ['kaunsl] n consejo; **city or town** ~ consejo municipal; ~ **estate** (BRIT) n urbanización f de viviendas municipales de alquiler; ~ **house** (BRIT) n vivienda municipal de alquiler; ~**lor** n concejal(a) m/f.

counsel ['kaunsl] n (advice) consejo; (lawyer) abogado/a ♦ vt aconsejar; ~**lor** n consejero/a; ~**or** (US) n abogado/a.

count [kaunt] vt contar; (include) incluir ♦ vi contar ♦ n cuenta; (of votes) escrutinio; (level) nivel m; (nobleman) conde m; ~ **on** vt fus contar con; ~**down** n cuenta atrás.

countenance ['kauntɪnəns] n semblante m, rostro ♦ vt (tolerate) aprobar, tolerar.

counter ['kauntə*] n (in shop) mostrador m; (in games) ficha ♦ vt contrarrestar ♦ adv: **to run** ~ **to** ser contrario a, ir en contra de; ~**act** vt contrarrestar; ~**espionage** n contraespionaje m.

counterfeit ['kauntəfɪt] n falsificación f, simulación f ♦ vt falsificar ♦ adj falso, falsificado.

counterfoil ['kauntəfɔɪl] n talón m.

countermand ['kauntəmaːnd] vt revocar, cancelar.

counterpart ['kauntəpaːt] n homólogo/a.

counter-productive [kauntəprə'dʌktɪv] adj contraproducente.

countersign ['kauntəsaɪn] vt refrendar.

countess ['kauntɪs] n condesa.

countless ['kauntlɪs] adj innumerable.

country ['kʌntrɪ] n país m; (native land) patria; (as opposed to town) campo; (region) región f, tierra; ~ **dancing** (BRIT) n baile m regional; ~ **house** n casa de campo; ~**man** n (compatriot) compatriota m; (rural) campesino, paisano; ~**side** n campo.

county ['kauntɪ] n condado.

coup [kuː] (pl ~s) n (also: ~ d'état) golpe m (de estado); (achievement) éxito.

coupé ['kuːpeɪ] n cupé m.

couple ['kʌpl] n (of things) par m; (of people) pareja; (married ~) matrimonio; **a** ~ **of** un par de.

coupon ['kuːpɔn] n cupón m; (voucher) vale m.

courage ['kʌrɪdʒ] n valor m, valentía; ~**ous** [kə'reɪdʒəs] adj valiente.

courgette [kuə'ʒet] (BRIT) n calabacín m (SP), calabacita (AM).

courier ['kurɪə*] n mensajero/a; (for tourists) guía m/f (de turismo).

course [kɔːs] n (direction) dirección f; (of river, SCOL) curso; (process) transcurso; (MED): ~ **of treatment** tratamiento; (of ship) rumbo; (part of meal) plato; (GOLF) campo; **of** ~ desde luego, naturalmente; **of** ~! ¡claro!

court [kɔːt] n (royal) corte f; (LAW) tribunal m, juzgado; (TENNIS etc) pista, cancha ♦ vt (woman) cortejar a; **to take to** ~ demandar.

courteous ['kəːtɪəs] adj cortés.

courtesan [kɔːtɪ'zæn] n cortesana.

courtesy ['kəːtəsɪ] n cortesía; (by) ~ **of** por cortesía de.

court-house ['kɔːthaus] (US) n palacio de justicia.

courtier ['kɔːtɪə*] n cortesano.

court-martial (pl **courts-martial**) n consejo de guerra.

courtroom ['kɔːtrum] n sala de justicia.

courtyard ['kɔːtjaːd] n patio.

cousin ['kʌzn] n primo/a; **first** ~ primo/a carnal, primo/a hermano/a.

cove [kəuv] n cala, ensenada.

covenant ['kʌvənənt] n pacto.

cover ['kʌvə*] vt cubrir; (feelings, mistake) ocultar; (with lid) tapar; (book etc) forrar; (distance) recorrer; (include) abarcar; (protect: also: INSURANCE) cubrir; (PRESS) investigar; (discuss) tratar ♦ n cubierta; (lid) tapa; (for chair etc) funda; (envelope) sobre m; (for book) forro; (of magazine) portada; (shelter) abrigo; (INSURANCE) cobertura; (of spy) cobertura; ~s npl (on bed) sábanas; mantas; **to take** ~ (shelter) protegerse, resguardarse; **under** ~ (indoors) bajo techo; **under** ~ **of darkness** al amparo de la oscuridad; **under separate** ~ (COMM) por separado; ~ **up** vi: **to** ~ **up for sb** encubrir a uno; ~**age** n (TV, PRESS) cobertura; ~**alls** (US) npl mono; ~ **charge** n precio del cubierto; ~**ing** n capa; ~**ing letter** (US ~ **letter**) n carta de explicación; ~ **note** n (INSURANCE) póliza provisional.

covert ['kəuvət] adj secreto, encubierto.

cover-up n encubrimiento.

covet ['kʌvɪt] vt codiciar.

cow [kau] n vaca; (inf!: woman) bruja ♦ vt intimidar.

coward ['kauəd] n cobarde m/f; ~**ice** [-ɪs] n cobardía; ~**ly** adj cobarde.

cowboy ['kaubɔɪ] n vaquero.

cower ['kauə*] vi encogerse (de miedo).

coxswain ['kɔksn] (abbr: **cox**) n timonel m/f.

coy [kɔɪ] adj tímido.

cozy ['kəuzɪ] (US) adj = **cosy**.

CPA (US) n abbr = **certified public accountant**.

crab [kræb] n cangrejo; ~ **apple** n manzana silvestre.

crack [kræk] n grieta; (noise) crujido ♦ vt agrietar, romper; (nut) cascar; (solve: problem) resolver; (: code) descifrar; (whip etc) chasquear; (knuckles) crujir; (joke) contar ♦ adj (expert) de primera; ~ **down on** vt fus adoptar fuertes medidas contra; ~ **up** vi (MED) sufrir una crisis nerviosa; ~**er**

n (biscuit) crácker m; (Christmas ~er) petardo sorpresa.

crackle ['krækl] vi crepitar.

cradle ['kreɪdl] n cuna.

craft [krɑ:ft] n (skill) arte m; (trade) oficio; (cunning) astucia; (boat: pl inv) barco; (plane: pl inv) avión m.

craftsman ['krɑ:ftsmən] n artesano; ~**ship** (quality) destreza.

crafty ['krɑ:ftɪ] adj astuto.

crag [kræg] n peñasco.

cram [kræm] vt (fill): **to** ~ **sth with** llenar algo (a reventar) de; (put): **to** ~ **sth into** meter algo a la fuerza en ♦ vi (for exams) empollar.

cramp [kræmp] n (MED) calambre m; ~**ed** adj apretado, estrecho.

cranberry ['krænbərɪ] n arándano agrio.

crane [kreɪn] n (TECH) grúa; (bird) grulla.

crank [kræŋk] n manivela; (person) chiflado; ~**shaft** n cigüeñal m.

cranny ['krænɪ] n see **nook**.

crash [kræʃ] n (noise) estrépito; (of cars etc) choque m; (of plane) accidente m de aviación; (COMM) quiebra ♦ vt (car, plane) estrellar ♦ vi (car, plane) estrellarse; (two cars) chocar; (COMM) quebrar; ~ **course** n curso acelerado; ~ **helmet** n casco (protector); ~ **landing** n aterrizaje m forzado.

crass [kræs] adj grosero, maleducado.

crate [kreɪt] n cajón m de embalaje; (for bottles) caja.

crater ['kreɪtə*] n cráter m.

cravat(e) [krə'væt] n pañuelo.

crave [kreɪv] vt, vi: **to** ~ (**for**) ansiar, anhelar.

crawl [krɔ:l] vi (drag o.s.) arrastrarse; (child) andar a gatas, gatear; (vehicle) avanzar (lentamente) ♦ n (SWIMMING) crol m.

crayfish ['kreɪfɪʃ] n inv (freshwater) cangrejo de río; (saltwater) cigala.

crayon ['kreɪən] n lápiz m de color.

craze [kreɪz] n (fashion) moda.

crazy ['kreɪzɪ] adj (person) loco; (idea) disparatado; (inf: keen): ~ **about sb/sth** loco por uno/algo; ~ **paving** (BRIT) n pavimento de baldosas irregulares.

creak [kri:k] vi (floorboard) crujir; (hinge etc) chirriar, rechinar.

cream [kri:m] n (of milk) nata, crema; (lotion) crema; (fig) flor f y nata ♦ adj (colour) color crema; ~ **cake** n pastel m de nata; ~ **cheese** n queso blanco; ~y adj cremoso; (colour) color crema.

crease [kri:s] n (fold) pliegue m; (in trousers) raya; (wrinkle) arruga ♦ vt (wrinkle) arrugar ♦ vi (wrinkle up) arrugarse.

create [kri:'eɪt] vt crear; **creation** [-ʃən] n creación f; **creative** adj creativo; **creator** n creador(a) m/f.

creature ['kri:tʃə*] n (animal) animal m, bicho; (person) criatura.

crèche [krɛʃ] n guardería (infantil).

credence ['kri:dəns] n: **to lend** or **give ~ to** creer en, dar crédito a.

credentials [krɪ'denʃlz] npl (references) referencias fpl; (identity papers) documentos mpl de identidad.

credible ['krɛdɪbl] adj creíble; (trustworthy) digno de confianza.

credit ['krɛdɪt] n crédito; (merit) honor m, mérito ♦ vt (COMM) abonar; (believe: also: **give ~ to**) creer, prestar fe a ♦ adj crediticio; ~**s** npl (CINEMA) fichas fpl técnicas; **to be in ~** (person) tener saldo a favor; **to ~ sb with** (fig) reconocer a uno el mérito de; ~ **card** n tarjeta de crédito; ~**or** n acreedor(a) m/f.

creed [kri:d] n credo.

creek [kri:k] n cala, ensenada; (US) riachuelo.

creep [kri:p] (pt, pp **crept**) vi arrastrarse; ~**er** n enredadera; ~**y** adj (frightening) horripilante.

cremate [krɪ'meɪt] vt incinerar.

crematorium [krɛmə'tɔ:rɪəm] (pl **crematoria**) n crematorio.

crêpe [kreɪp] n (fabric) crespón m; (also: ~ **rubber**) crepé m; ~ **bandage** (BRIT) n venda de crepé.

crept [krɛpt] pt, pp of **creep**.

crescent ['krɛsnt] n media luna; (street) calle f (en forma de semicírculo).

cress [krɛs] n berro.

crest [krɛst] n (of bird) cresta; (of hill) cima, cumbre f; (of coat of arms) bla-

són m; ~**fallen** adj alicaído.

crevice ['krɛvɪs] n grieta, hendedura.

crew [kru:] n (of ship etc) tripulación f; (TV, CINEMA) equipo; ~**-cut** n corte m al rape; ~**-neck** n cuello a la caja.

crib [krɪb] n cuna ♦ vt (inf) plagiar.

crick [krɪk] n (in neck) tortícolis f.

cricket ['krɪkɪt] n (insect) grillo; (game) críquet m.

crime [kraɪm] n (no pl: illegal activities) crimen m; (illegal action) delito; **criminal** ['krɪmɪnl] n criminal m/f, delincuente m/f ♦ adj criminal; (illegal) delictivo; (law) penal.

crimson ['krɪmzn] adj carmesí.

cringe [krɪndʒ] vi agacharse, encogerse.

crinkle ['krɪŋkl] vt arrugar.

cripple ['krɪpl] n lisiado/a, cojo/a ♦ vt lisiar, mutilar.

crises ['kraɪsi:z] npl of **crisis**.

crisis ['kraɪsɪs] (pl **crises**) n crisis f inv.

crisp [krɪsp] adj fresco; (vegetables etc) crujiente; (manner) seco; ~**s** (BRIT) npl patatas fpl (SP) or papas fpl (AM) fritas.

criss-cross ['krɪskrɒs] adj entrelazado.

criterion [kraɪ'tɪərɪən] (pl **criteria**) n criterio.

critic ['krɪtɪk] n crítico/a; ~**al** adj crítico; (illness) grave; ~**ally** adv (speak etc) en tono crítico; (ill) gravemente; ~**ism** ['krɪtɪsɪzm] n crítica; ~**ize** ['krɪtɪsaɪz] vt criticar.

croak [krəuk] vi (frog) croar; (raven) graznar; (person) gruñir.

crochet ['krəuʃeɪ] n ganchillo.

crockery ['krɒkərɪ] n loza, vajilla.

crocodile ['krɒkədaɪl] n cocodrilo.

crocus ['krəukəs] n croco, crocus m.

croft [krɒft] n granja pequeña.

crony ['krəunɪ] (inf: pej) n compinche m/f.

crook [kruk] n ladrón/ona m/f; (of shepherd) cayado; ~**ed** ['krukɪd] adj torcido; (dishonest) nada honrado.

crop [krɒp] n (produce) cultivo; (amount produced) cosecha; (riding ~) látigo de montar ♦ vt cortar, recortar; ~ **up** vi surgir, presentarse.

croquette [krə'kɛt] n croqueta.

cross [krɔs] n cruz f; (hybrid) cruce m ♦ vt (street etc) cruzar, atravesar ♦ adj de mal humor, enojado; ~ **out** vt tachar; ~ **over** vi cruzar; ~**bar** n travesaño; ~**country (race)** n carrera a campo traviesa, cross m; ~**-examine** vt interrogar; ~**-eyed** adj bizco; ~**fire** n fuego cruzado; ~**ing** n (sea passage) travesía; (also: pedestrian ~ing) paso para peatones; ~**ing guard** (US) n persona encargada de ayudar a los niños a cruzar la calle; ~ **purposes** npl: to be at ~ **purposes** no comprenderse uno a otro; ~**-reference** n referencia, llamada; ~**roads** n cruce m, encrucijada; ~ **section** n corte m transversal; (of population) muestra (representativa); ~**walk** (US) n paso de peatones; ~**wind** n viento de costado; ~**word** n crucigrama m.

crotch [krɔtʃ] n (ANAT, of garment) entrepierna.

crotchet ['krɔtʃɪt] n (MUS) negra.

crotchety ['krɔtʃɪtɪ] adj antipático.

crouch [krautʃ] vi agacharse, acurrucarse.

crow [krəu] n (bird) cuervo; (of cock) canto, cacareo ♦ vi (cock) cantar.

crowbar ['krəubɑ:*] n palanca.

crowd [kraud] n muchedumbre f, multitud f ♦ vt (fill) llenar ♦ vi (gather): to ~ **round** reunirse en torno a; (cram): to ~ **in** entrar en tropel; ~**ed** adj (full) atestado; (densely populated) superpoblado.

crown [kraun] n corona; (of head) coronilla; (for tooth) funda; (of hill) cumbre f ♦ vt coronar; (fig) completar, rematar; ~ **jewels** npl joyas fpl reales; ~ **prince** n príncipe m heredero.

crow's feet npl patas fpl de gallo.

crucial ['kru:ʃl] adj decisivo.

crucifix ['kru:sɪfɪks] n crucifijo; ~**ion** [-'fɪkʃən] n crucifixión f.

crude [kru:d] adj (materials) bruto; (fig: basic) tosco; (: vulgar) ordinario; ~ **(oil)** n (petróleo) crudo.

cruel ['kruəl] adj cruel; ~**ty** n crueldad f.

cruise [kru:z] n crucero ♦ vi (ship) ha-

cer un crucero; (car) ir a velocidad de crucero; ~**r** n (motorboat) yate m de motor; (warship) crucero.

crumb [krʌm] n miga, migaja.

crumble ['krʌmbl] vt desmenuzar ♦ vi (building, also fig) desmoronarse; **crumbly** adj que se desmigaja fácilmente.

crumpet ['krʌmpɪt] n ≈ bollo para tostar.

crumple ['krʌmpl] vt (paper) estrujar; (material) arrugar.

crunch [krʌntʃ] vt (with teeth) mascar; (underfoot) hacer crujir ♦ n (fig) hora or momento de la verdad; ~**y** adj crujiente.

crusade [kru:'seɪd] n cruzada.

crush [krʌʃ] n (crowd) aglomeración f; (infatuation): to have a ~ **on** sb estar loco por uno; (drink): **lemon** ~ limonada ♦ vt aplastar; (paper) estrujar; (cloth) arrugar; (fruit) exprimir; (opposition) aplastar; (hopes) destruir.

crust [krʌst] n corteza; (of snow, ice) costra.

crutch [krʌtʃ] n muleta.

crux [krʌks] n: **the** ~ **of** lo esencial de, el quid de.

cry [kraɪ] vi llorar; (shout: also: ~ **out**) gritar ♦ n (shriek) chillido; (shout) grito; ~ **off** vi echarse atrás.

cryptic ['krɪptɪk] adj enigmático, secreto.

crystal ['krɪstl] n cristal m; ~**-clear** adj claro como el agua.

cub [kʌb] n cachorro; (also: ~ **scout**) niño explorador.

Cuba ['kju:bə] n Cuba; ~**n** adj, n cubano/a m/f.

cubbyhole ['kʌbɪhəul] n cuchitril m.

cube [kju:b] n cubo ♦ vt (MATH) cubicar; **cubic** adj cúbico.

cubicle ['kju:bɪkl] n (at pool) caseta; (for bed) cubículo.

cuckoo ['kuku:] n cuco; ~ **clock** n reloj m de cucú.

cucumber ['kju:kʌmbə*] n pepino.

cuddle ['kʌdl] vt abrazar ♦ vi abrazarse.

cue [kju:] n (snooker ~) taco; (THEATRE

etc) señal *f*.

cuff [kʌf] *n* (*of sleeve*) puño; (*US: of trousers*) vuelta; (*blow*) bofetada; **off the ~** *adv* de improviso; **~links** *npl* gemelos *mpl*.

cuisine [kwɪˈziːn] *n* cocina.

cul-de-sac [ˈkʌldəsæk] *n* callejón *m* sin salida.

cull [kʌl] *vt* (*idea*) sacar ♦ *n* (*of animals*) matanza selectiva.

culminate [ˈkʌlmɪneɪt] *vi*: **to ~ in** terminar en; **culmination** [-ˈneɪʃən] *n* culminación *f*, colmo.

culottes [kuːˈlɔts] *npl* falda pantalón *f*.

culprit [ˈkʌlprɪt] *n* culpable *m/f*.

cult [kʌlt] *n* culto.

cultivate [ˈkʌltɪveɪt] *vt* (*also fig*) cultivar; **~d** *adj* culto; **cultivation** [-ˈveɪʃən] *n* cultivo.

cultural [ˈkʌltʃərəl] *adj* cultural.

culture [ˈkʌltʃə*] *n* (*also fig*) cultura; (*BIO*) cultivo; **~d** *adj* culto.

cumbersome [ˈkʌmbəsəm] *adj* de mucho bulto, voluminoso; (*process*) enrevesado.

cunning [ˈkʌnɪŋ] *n* astucia ♦ *adj* astuto.

cup [kʌp] *n* taza; (*as prize*) copa.

cupboard [ˈkʌbəd] *n* armario; (*kitchen*) alacena.

cup-tie [ˈkʌptaɪ] (*BRIT*) *n* partido de copa.

curate [ˈkjuərɪt] *n* cura *m*.

curator [kjuəˈreɪtə*] *n* director(a) *m/f*.

curb [kəːb] *vt* refrenar; (*person*) reprimir ♦ *n* freno; (*US*) bordillo.

curdle [ˈkəːdl] *vi* cuajarse.

cure [kjuə*] *vt* curar ♦ *n* cura, curación *f*; (*fig: solution*) remedio.

curfew [ˈkəːfjuː] *n* toque *m* de queda.

curio [ˈkjuərɪəu] *n* curiosidad *f*.

curiosity [kjuərɪˈɒsɪtɪ] *n* curiosidad *f*.

curious [ˈkjuərɪəs] *adj* curioso; (*person: interested*): **to be ~** sentir curiosidad.

curl [kəːl] *n* rizo ♦ *vt* (*hair*) rizar ♦ *vi* rizarse; **~ up** *vi* (*person*) hacerse un ovillo; **~er** *n* rulo; **~y** *adj* rizado.

currant [ˈkʌrnt] *n* pasa (de Corinto); (*black~, red~*) grosella.

currency [ˈkʌrnsɪ] *n* moneda; **to gain ~** (*fig*) difundirse.

current [ˈkʌrnt] *n* corriente *f* ♦ *adj* (*accepted*) corriente; (*present*) actual; **~ account** (*BRIT*) *n* cuenta corriente; **~ affairs** *npl* noticias *fpl* de actualidad; **~ly** *adv* actualmente.

curriculum [kəˈrɪkjuləm] (*pl* **~s** or **curricula**) *n* plan *m* de estudios; **~ vitae** *n* currículum *m*.

curry [ˈkʌrɪ] *n* curry *m* ♦ *vt*: **to ~ favour with** buscar favores con; **~ powder** *n* curry *m* en polvo.

curse [kəːs] *vi* soltar tacos ♦ *vt* maldecir ♦ *n* maldición *f*; (*swearword*) palabrota, taco.

cursor [ˈkəːsə*] *n* (*COMPUT*) cursor *m*.

cursory [ˈkəːsərɪ] *adj* rápido, superficial.

curt [kəːt] *adj* corto, seco.

curtail [kəːˈteɪl] *vt* (*visit etc*) acortar; (*freedom*) restringir; (*expenses etc*) reducir.

curtain [ˈkəːtn] *n* cortina; (*THEATRE*) telón *m*.

curts(e)y [ˈkəːtsɪ] *vi* hacer una reverencia.

curve [kəːv] *n* curva ♦ *vi* (*road*) hacer una curva; (*line etc*) curvarse.

cushion [ˈkuʃən] *n* cojín *m*; (*of air*) colchón *m* ♦ *vt* (*shock*) amortiguar.

custard [ˈkʌstəd] *n* natillas *fpl*.

custodian [kʌsˈtəudɪən] *n* guardián *m*.

custody [ˈkʌstədɪ] *n* custodia; **to take into ~** detener.

custom [ˈkʌstəm] *n* costumbre *f*; (*COMM*) clientela; **~ary** *adj* acostumbrado.

customer [ˈkʌstəmə*] *n* cliente *m/f*.

customized [ˈkʌstəmaɪzd] *adj* (*car etc*) hecho a encargo.

custom-made *adj* hecho a la medida.

customs [ˈkʌstəmz] *npl* aduana; **~ duty** *n* derechos *mpl* de aduana; **~ officer** *n* aduanero/a.

cut [kʌt] (*pt, pp* **cut**) *vt* cortar; (*price*) rebajar; (*text, programme*) acortar; (*reduce*) reducir ♦ *vi* cortar ♦ *n* (*of garment*) corte *m*; (*in skin*) cortadura; (*in salary etc*) rebaja; (*in spending*) reducción *f*, recorte *m*; (*slice of meat*) tajada; **to ~ a tooth** echar un diente; **~ down** *vt* (*tree*) derribar; (*reduce*) reducir; ~ **off** vt cortar; (person, place) aislar; (TEL) desconectar; ~ **out** vt (shape) recortar; (stop: activity etc) dejar; (remove) quitar; ~ **up** vt cortar (en pedazos); ~**back** n reducción f.

cute [kju:t] adj mono.

cuticle ['kju:tɪkl] n cutícula.

cutlery ['kʌtlərɪ] n cubiertos mpl.

cutlet ['kʌtlɪt] n chuleta; (nut etc cutlet) plato vegetariano hecho con nueces y verdura en forma de chuleta.

cut: ~**out** n (switch) dispositivo de seguridad, disyuntor m; (cardboard ~) recortable m; ~**-price** (US ~**-rate**) adj a precio reducido; ~**throat** n asesino/a ♦ adj feroz.

cutting ['kʌtɪŋ] adj (remark) mordaz ♦ n (BRIT: from newspaper) recorte m; (from plant) esqueje m.

CV n abbr = **curriculum vitae**.

cwt abbr = **hundredweight(s)**.

cyanide ['saɪənaɪd] n cianuro.

cycle ['saɪkl] n ciclo; (bicycle) bicicleta ♦ vi ir en bicicleta; **cycling** n ciclismo; **cyclist** n ciclista m/f.

cyclone ['saɪkləun] n ciclón m.

cygnet ['sɪgnɪt] n pollo de cisne.

cylinder ['sɪlɪndə*] n cilindro; (of gas) bombona; ~**head gasket** n junta de culata.

cymbals ['sɪmblz] npl platillos mpl.

cynic ['sɪnɪk] n cínico/a; ~**al** adj cínico; ~**ism** ['sɪnɪsɪzəm] n cinismo.

cypress ['saɪprɪs] n ciprés m.

Cypriot ['sɪprɪət] adj, n chipriota m/f.

Cyprus ['saɪprəs] n Chipre f.

cyst [sɪst] n quiste m; ~**itis** [-'taɪtɪs] n cistitis f.

czar [zɑ:*] n zar m.

Czech [tʃɛk] adj, n checo/a m/f.

Czechoslovakia [tʃɛkəslə'vækɪə] n Checoslovaquia; ~**n** adj, n checo/a m/f.

D

D [di:] n (MUS) re m.

dab [dæb] vt (eyes, wound) tocar (ligeramente); (paint, cream) poner un poco de.

dabble ['dæbl] vi: to ~ **in** ser algo aficionado a.

dad [dæd] n = **daddy**.

daddy ['dædɪ] n papá m.

daffodil ['dæfədɪl] n narciso.

daft [dɑ:ft] adj tonto.

dagger ['dægə*] n puñal m, daga.

daily ['deɪlɪ] adj diario, cotidiano ♦ adv todos los días, cada día.

dainty ['deɪntɪ] adj delicado.

dairy ['dɛərɪ] n (shop) lechería; (on farm) vaquería; ~ **farm** n granja; ~ **products** npl productos mpl lácteos; ~ **store** (US) n lechería.

dais ['deɪs] n estrado.

daisy ['deɪzɪ] n margarita; ~ **wheel** n margarita.

dale [deɪl] n valle m.

dam [dæm] n presa ♦ vt construir una presa sobre, represar.

damage ['dæmɪdʒ] n lesión f; daño; (dents etc) desperfectos mpl; (fig) perjuicio ♦ vt dañar, perjudicar; (spoil, break) estropear; ~**s** npl (LAW) daños mpl y perjuicios.

damn [dæm] vt condenar; (curse) maldecir ♦ n (inf): **I don't give a** ~ me importa un pito ♦ adj (inf: also: ~ed) maldito; ~ **(it)**! ¡maldito sea!; ~**ing** adj (evidence) irrecusable.

damp [dæmp] adj húmedo, mojado ♦ n humedad f ♦ vt (also: ~**en**: cloth, rag) mojar; (: enthusiasm) enfriar.

damson ['dæmzən] n ciruela damascena.

dance [dɑ:ns] n baile m ♦ vi bailar; ~ **hall** n salón m de baile; ~**r** n bailador(a) m/f; (professional) bailarín/ina m/f; **dancing** n baile m.

dandelion ['dændɪlaɪən] n diente m de león.

dandruff ['dændrəf] n caspa.

Dane [deɪn] n danés/esa m/f.

danger ['deɪndʒə*] n peligro; (risk) riesgo; ~! (on sign) ¡peligro de muerte!; **to be in** ~ **of** correr riesgo de; ~**ous** adj peligroso; ~**ously** adv peligrosamente.

dangle ['dæŋgl] vt colgar ♦ vi pender, colgar.

Danish ['deɪnɪʃ] *adj* danés/esa ♦ *n* (*LING*) danés *m*.

dapper ['dæpə*] *adj* pulcro, apuesto.

dare [dɛə*] *vt*: to ~ sb to do desafiar a uno a hacer ♦ *vi*: to ~ (to) do sth atreverse a hacer algo; I ~ say (*I suppose*) puede ser (que); ~**devil** *n* temerario/a, atrevido/a; **daring** *adj* atrevido, osado ♦ *n* atrevimiento, osadía.

dark [dɑːk] *adj* oscuro; (*hair, complexion*) moreno ♦ *n*: in the ~ a oscuras; to be in the ~ about (*fig*) no saber nada de; after ~ después del anochecer; ~**en** *vt* (*colour*) hacer más oscuro ♦ *vi* oscurecerse; ~ **glasses** *npl* gafas *fpl* negras (*SP*), anteojos *mpl* negros (*AM*); ~**ness** *n* oscuridad *f*; ~**room** *n* cuarto oscuro.

darling ['dɑːlɪŋ] *adj, n* querido/a *m/f*.

darn [dɑːn] *vt* zurcir.

dart [dɑːt] *n* dardo; (*in sewing*) sisa ♦ *vi* precipitarse; ~ **away/along** *vi* salir/ marchar disparado; ~**board** *n* diana; ~**s** *n* dardos *mpl*.

dash [dæʃ] *n* (*small quantity: of liquid*) gota, chorrito; (: *of solid*) pizca; (*sign*) raya ♦ *vt* (*throw*) tirar; (*hopes*) defraudar ♦ *vi* precipitarse, ir de prisa; ~ **away** *or* **off** *vi* marcharse apresuradamente.

dashboard ['dæʃbɔːd] *n* (*AUT*) salpicadero.

dashing ['dæʃɪŋ] *adj* gallardo.

data ['deɪtə] *npl* datos *mpl*; ~**base** *n* base *f* de datos; ~ **processing** *n* proceso de datos.

date [deɪt] *n* (*day*) fecha; (*with friend*) cita; (*fruit*) dátil *m* ♦ *vt* fechar; (*person*) salir con; ~ **of birth** fecha de nacimiento; to ~ *adv* hasta la fecha; ~**d** *adj* anticuado.

daub [dɔːb] *vt* embadurnar.

daughter ['dɔːtə*] *n* hija; ~-**in-law** *n* nuera, hija política.

daunting ['dɔːntɪŋ] *adj* desalentador(a).

dawdle ['dɔːdl] *vi* (*go slowly*) andar muy despacio.

dawn [dɔːn] *n* alba, amanecer *m*; (*fig*) nacimiento ♦ *vi* (*day*) amanecer; (*fig*): it ~ed on him that ... cayó en la cuenta

de que ....

day [deɪ] *n* día *m*; (*working* ~) jornada; (*hey*~) tiempos *mpl*, días *mpl*; the ~ before/after el día anterior/siguiente; the ~ after tomorrow pasado mañana; the ~ before yesterday anteayer; the following ~ el día siguiente; by ~ de día; ~**break** *n* amanecer *m*; ~**dream** *vi* soñar despierto; ~**light** *n* luz *f* (del día); ~ **return** (*BRIT*) *n* billete *m* de ida y vuelta (en un día); ~**time** *n* día *m*; ~-**to**-~ *adj* cotidiano.

daze [deɪz] *vt* (*stun*) aturdir ♦ *n*: in a ~ aturdido.

dazzle ['dæzl] *vt* deslumbrar.

DC *abbr* (= *direct current*) corriente *f* continua.

dead [dɛd] *adj* muerto; (*limb*) dormido; (*telephone*) cortado; (*battery*) agotado ♦ *adv* (*completely*) totalmente; (*exactly*) exactamente; to shoot sb ~ matar a uno a tiros; ~ tired muerto (de cansancio); to stop ~ parar en seco; the ~ *npl* los muertos; to be a ~ loss (*inf: person*) ser un inútil; ~**en** *vt* (*blow, sound*) amortiguar; (*pain etc*) aliviar; ~ **end** *n* callejón *m* sin salida; ~ **heat** *n* (*SPORT*) empate *m*; ~**line** *n* fecha (*or* hora) tope; ~**lock** *n*: to reach ~**lock** llegar a un punto muerto; ~**ly** *adj* mortal, fatal; ~**pan** *adj* sin expresión; the D~ Sea *n* el Mar Muerto.

deaf [dɛf] *adj* sordo; ~**en** *vt* ensordecer; ~**ness** *n* sordera.

deal [diːl] (*pt, pp* dealt) *n* (*agreement*) pacto, convenio; (*business* ~) trato ♦ *vt* dar; (*card*) repartir; a great ~ (of) bastante, mucho; ~ **in** *vt fus* tratar en, comerciar en; ~ **with** *vt fus* (*people*) tratar con; (*problem*) ocuparse de; (*subject*) tratar de; ~**ings** *npl* (*COMM*) transacciones *fpl*; (*relations*) relaciones *fpl*.

dealt [dɛlt] *pt, pp of* deal.

dean [diːn] *n* (*REL*) deán *m*; (*SCOL: BRIT*) decano; (: *US*) decano, rector *m*.

dear [dɪə*] *adj* querido; (*expensive*) caro ♦ *n*: my ~ mi querido/a ♦ *excl*: ~ me! ¡Dios mío!; D~ Sir/Madam (*in let-*

ter) Muy Señor Mío, Estimado Señor/ Estimada Señora; **D~ Mr/Mrs X** Estimado/a Señor(a) X; ~**ly** *adv* (*love*) mucho; (*pay*) caro.

death [deθ] *n* muerte *f*; ~ **certificate** *n* partida de defunción; ~**ly** *adj* (*white*) como un muerto; (*silence*) sepulcral; ~ **penalty** *n* pena de muerte; ~ **rate** *n* mortalidad *f*; ~ **toll** *n* número de víctimas.

debacle [deɪ'bɑːkl] *n* desastre *m*.

debar [dɪ'bɑː*] *vt*: to ~ **sb from doing** prohibir a uno hacer.

debase [dɪ'beɪs] *vt* degradar.

debatable [dɪ'beɪtəbl] *adj* discutible.

debate [dɪ'beɪt] *n* debate *m* ♦ *vt* discutir.

debauchery [dɪ'bɔːtʃərɪ] *n* libertinaje *m*.

debilitating [dɪ'bɪlɪteɪtɪŋ] *adj* (*illness etc*) debilitante.

debit ['debɪt] *n* debe *m* ♦ *vt*: to ~ **a sum to sb** *or* to **sb's account** cargar una suma en cuenta a alguien.

debris ['debriː] *n* escombros *mpl*.

debt [det] *n* deuda; to **be in** ~ tener deudas; ~**or** *n* deudor(a) *m/f*.

debunk [diː'bʌŋk] *vt* desprestigiar, desacreditar.

début ['deɪbjuː] *n* presentación *f*.

decade ['dekeɪd] *n* decenio, década.

decadence ['dekədəns] *n* decadencia.

decaffeinated [dɪ'kæfɪneɪtɪd] *adj* descafeinado.

decanter [dɪ'kæntə*] *n* garrafa.

decay [dɪ'keɪ] *n* (*of building*) desmoronamiento; (*of tooth*) caries *f inv* ♦ *vi* (*rot*) pudrirse.

deceased [dɪ'siːst] *n*: **the** ~ el/la difunto/a.

deceit [dɪ'siːt] *n* engaño; ~**ful** *adj* engañoso.

deceive [dɪ'siːv] *vt* engañar.

December [dɪ'sembə*] *n* diciembre *m*.

decent ['diːsənt] *adj* (*proper*) decente; (*person: kind*) amable, bueno.

deception [dɪ'sepʃən] *n* engaño.

deceptive [dɪ'septɪv] *adj* engañoso.

decibel ['desɪbel] *n* decibel(io) *m*.

decide [dɪ'saɪd] *vt* (*person*) decidir; (*question, argument*) resolver ♦ *vi* decidir; to ~ to **do/that** decidir hacer/que; to ~ **on sth** decidirse por algo; ~**d** *adj* (*resolute*) decidido; (*clear, definite*) indudable; ~**dly** [-dɪdlɪ] *adv* decididamente; (*emphatically*) con resolución.

deciduous [dɪ'sɪdjuəs] *adj* de hoja caduca.

decimal ['desɪməl] *adj* decimal ♦ *n* decimal *m*; ~ **point** *n* coma decimal.

decimate ['desɪmeɪt] *vt* diezmar.

decipher [dɪ'saɪfə*] *vt* descifrar.

decision [dɪ'sɪʒən] *n* decisión *f*.

decisive [dɪ'saɪsɪv] *adj* decisivo; (*person*) decidido.

deck [dek] *n* (*NAUT*) cubierta; (*of bus*) piso; (*record* ~) platina; (*of cards*) baraja; ~**chair** *n* tumbona.

declaration [deklə'reɪʃən] *n* declaración *f*.

declare [dɪ'kleə*] *vt* declarar.

decline [dɪ'klaɪn] *n* disminución *f*, descenso ♦ *vt* rehusar ♦ *vi* (*person, business*) decaer; (*strength*) disminuir.

decode [diː'kəud] *vt* descifrar.

decompose [diːkəm'pəuz] *vi* descomponerse.

décor ['deɪkɔː*] *n* decoración *f*; (*THEATRE*) decorado.

decorate ['dekəreɪt] *vt* (*adorn*): to ~ (**with**) adornar (de), decorar (de); (*paint*) pintar; (*paper*) empapelar; **decoration** [-'reɪʃən] *n* adorno; (*act*) decoración *f*; (*medal*) condecoración *f*; **decorative** ['dekərətɪv] *adj* decorativo; **decorator** *n* (*workman*) pintor *m* (decorador).

decorum [dɪ'kɔːrəm] *n* decoro.

decoy ['diːkɔɪ] *n* señuelo.

decrease [*n* 'diːkriːs, *vb* dɪ'kriːs] *n*: ~ (**in**) disminución *f* (de) ♦ *vt* disminuir, reducir ♦ *vi* reducirse.

decree [dɪ'kriː] *n* decreto; ~ **nisi** *n* sentencia provisional de divorcio.

dedicate ['dedɪkeɪt] *vt* dedicar; **dedication** [-'keɪʃən] *n* (*devotion*) dedicación *f*; (*in book*) dedicatoria.

deduce [dɪ'djuːs] *vt* deducir.

deduct [dɪ'dʌkt] *vt* restar; descontar; ~**ion** [dɪ'dʌkʃən] *n* (*amount deducted*) descuento; (*conclusion*) deducción *f*,

conclusión *f.*
deed [diːd] *n* hecho, acto; *(feat)* hazaña; *(LAW)* escritura.
deem [diːm] *vt* juzgar.
deep [diːp] *adj* profundo; *(expressing
measurements)* de profundidad; *(voice)*
bajo; *(breath)* profundo; *(colour)* intenso ♦ *adv*: **the spectators stood 20** ~ **los**
espectadores se formaron de 20 en fon-
do; **to be 4 metres** ~ tener 4 metros
de profundidad; **~en** *vt* ahondar,
profundizar ♦ *vi* aumentar, crecer;
~-freeze *n* congelador *m*; **~-fry** *vt* freír
en aceite abundante; **~ly** *adv* (*breathe*)
a pleno pulmón; *(interested, moved,
grateful)* profundamente, hondamente,
~-sea diving *n* buceo de altura;
~-seated *adj* (*beliefs*) (profundamente)
arraigado.
deer [dɪə*] *n inv* ciervo.
deface [dɪ'feɪs] *vt* (*wall, surface*) estropear, pintarrajear.
default [dɪ'fɔːlt] *n*: **by** ~ (*win*) por in-
comparecencia ♦ *adj* (*COMPUT*) por defecto.
defeat [dɪ'fiːt] *n* derrota ♦ *vt* derrotar,
vencer; **~ist** *adj, n* derrotista *m/f.*
defect [*n* 'diːfɛkt, *vb* dɪ'fɛkt] *n* defecto ♦
vi: **to** ~ **to the enemy** pasarse al enemigo; **~ive** [dɪ'fɛktɪv] *adj* defectuoso.
defence [dɪ'fɛns] (*US* **defense**) *n* defensa; **~less** *adj* indefenso.
defend [dɪ'fɛnd] *vt* defender; **~ant** *n*
acusado/a; *(in civil case)* demandado/a;
~er *n* defensor(a) *m/f*; *(SPORT)* defensa
m/f.
defense [dɪ'fɛns] (*US*) *n* = **defence.**
defensive [dɪ'fɛnsɪv] *adj* defensivo ♦ *n*:
on the ~ a la defensiva.
defer [dɪ'fəː*] *vt* aplazar; **~ence**
['dɛfərəns] *n* deferencia, respeto.
defiance [dɪ'faɪəns] *n* desafío; **in** ~ **of** en
contra de.
defiant [dɪ'faɪənt] *adj* (*challenging*) des-
afiante, retador(a).
deficiency [dɪ'fɪʃənsɪ] *n* (*lack*) falta;
(defect) defecto.
deficient [dɪ'fɪʃənt] *adj* deficiente.
deficit ['dɛfɪsɪt] *n* déficit *m.*
defile [dɪ'faɪl] *vt* manchar.

define [dɪ'faɪn] *vt* (*word etc*) definir;
(limits etc) determinar.
definite ['dɛfɪnɪt] *adj* (*fixed*) determinado; *(obvious)* claro; *(certain)* indudable; **he was** ~ **about it** no dejó lugar a
dudas (sobre ello); **~ly** *adv* desde luego, por supuesto.
definition [dɛfɪ'nɪʃən] *n* definición *f*;
(clearness) nitidez *f.*
deflate [diː'fleɪt] *vt* desinflar.
deflect [dɪ'flɛkt] *vt* desviar.
defraud [dɪ'frɔːd] *vt*: **to** ~ **sb of sth** estafar algo a uno.
defrost [diː'frɒst] *vt* descongelar; **~er**
(*US*) *n* (*demister*) eliminador *m* de
vaho.
deft [dɛft] *adj* diestro, hábil.
defunct [dɪ'fʌŋkt] *adj* difunto; *(organization etc)* ya que no existe.
defuse [diː'fjuːz] *vt* desactivar; *(situation)* calmar.
defy [dɪ'faɪ] *vt* (*resist*) oponerse a;
(challenge) desafiar; *(fig)*: **it defies description** resulta imposible describirlo.
degenerate [*vb* dɪ'dʒɛnəreɪt, *adj* dɪ'dʒɛn-
ərɪt] *vi* degenerar ♦ *adj* degenerado.
degree [dɪ'griː] *n* grado; *(SCOL)* título;
to have a ~ **in maths** tener una licenciatura en matemáticas; **by** ~**s** (*gradually*) poco a poco, por etapas; **to some**
~ hasta cierto punto.
dehydrated [diːhaɪ'dreɪtɪd] *adj* deshidra-
tado; *(milk)* en polvo.
de-ice [diː'aɪs] *vt* deshelar.
deign [deɪn] *vi*: **to** ~ **to do** dignarse hacer.
deity ['diːɪtɪ] *n* deidad *f*, divinidad *f.*
dejected [dɪ'dʒɛktɪd] *adj* abatido, desanimado.
delay [dɪ'leɪ] *vt* demorar, aplazar; *(person)* entretener; *(train)* retrasar ♦ *vi*
tardar ♦ *n* demora, retraso; **to be ~ed**
retrasarse; **without** ~ en seguida, sin
tardar.
delectable [dɪ'lɛktəbl] *adj* (*person*) en-
cantador(a); *(food)* delicioso.
delegate [*n* 'dɛlɪgɪt, *vb* 'dɛlɪgeɪt] *n*
delegado/a ♦ *vt* (*person*) delegar en;
(task) delegar.
delete [dɪ'liːt] *vt* suprimir, tachar.

deliberate [adj dɪ'lɪbərɪt, vb dɪ'lɪbəreɪt] adj (intentional) intencionado; (slow) pausado, lento ♦ vi deliberar; ~ly adv (on purpose) a propósito.

delicacy ['dɛlɪkəsɪ] n delicadeza; (choice food) manjar m.

delicate ['dɛlɪkɪt] adj delicado; (fragile) frágil.

delicatessen [dɛlɪkə'tɛsn] n ultramarinos mpl finos.

delicious [dɪ'lɪʃəs] adj delicioso.

delight [dɪ'laɪt] n (feeling) placer m, deleite m; (person, experience etc) encanto, delicia ♦ vt encantar, deleitar; **to take ~ in** deleitarse en; ~**ed** adj: ~**ed (at or with/to do)** encantado (con/de hacer); ~**ful** adj encantador(a), delicioso.

delinquent [dɪ'lɪŋkwənt] adj, n delincuente m/f.

delirious [dɪ'lɪrɪəs] adj: **to be ~** delirar, desvariar; **to be ~ with** estar loco de.

deliver [dɪ'lɪvə*] vt (distribute) repartir; (hand over) entregar; (message) comunicar; (speech) pronunciar; (MED) asistir al parto de; ~**y** n reparto; entrega; (of speaker) modo de expresarse; (MED) parto, alumbramiento; **to take ~y of** recibir.

delude [dɪ'luːd] vt engañar.

deluge ['dɛljuːdʒ] n diluvio.

delusion [dɪ'luːʒən] n ilusión f, engaño.

de luxe [də'lʌks] adj de lujo.

delve [dɛlv] vi: **to ~ into** (subject) ahondar en; (cupboard etc) hurgar en.

demand [dɪ'mɑːnd] vt (gen) exigir; (rights) reclamar ♦ n exigencia; (claim) reclamación f; (ECON) demanda; **to be in ~** ser muy solicitado; **on ~** a solicitud; ~**ing** adj (boss) exigente; (work) absorbente.

demean [dɪ'miːn] vt: **to ~ o.s.** rebajarse.

demeanour [dɪ'miːnə*] (US **demeanor**) n porte m, conducta.

demented [dɪ'mɛntɪd] adj demente.

demise [dɪ'maɪz] n (death) fallecimiento.

demister [diː'mɪstə*] n (AUT) eliminador m de vaho.

demo ['dɛməu] (inf) n abbr (= demon-

stration) manifestación f.

democracy [dɪ'mɔkrəsɪ] n democracia; **democrat** ['dɛməkræt] n demócrata m/f; **democratic** [dɛmə'krætɪk] adj democrático; (US) demócrata.

demolish [dɪ'mɔlɪʃ] vt derribar, demoler; (fig: argument) destruir; **demolition** [dɛmə'lɪʃən] n derribo, demolición f; destrucción f.

demon ['diːmən] n (evil spirit) demonio.

demonstrate ['dɛmənstreɪt] vt demostrar; (skill, appliance) mostrar ♦ vi manifestarse; **demonstration** [-'streɪʃən] n (POL) manifestación f; (proof, exhibition) demostración f; **demonstrator** n (POL) manifestante m/f; (COMM) demostrador(a) m/f; vendedor(a) m/f.

demoralize [dɪ'mɔrəlaɪz] vt desmoralizar.

demote [dɪ'məut] vt degradar.

demure [dɪ'mjuə*] adj recatado.

den [dɛn] n (of animal) guarida; (room) habitación f.

denatured alcohol [diː'neɪtʃəd-] (US) n alcohol m desnaturalizado.

denial [dɪ'naɪəl] n (refusal) negativa; (of report etc) negación f.

denim ['dɛnɪm] n tela vaquera; ~**s** npl vaqueros mpl.

Denmark ['dɛnmɑːk] n Dinamarca.

denomination [dɪnɔmɪ'neɪʃən] n valor m; (REL) confesión f.

denote [dɪ'nəut] vt indicar, significar.

denounce [dɪ'nauns] vt denunciar.

dense [dɛns] adj (crowd) denso; (thick) espeso; (: foliage etc) tupido; (inf: stupid) torpe; ~**ly** adv: ~**ly populated** con una alta densidad de población.

density ['dɛnsɪtɪ] n densidad f; **single/double-~ disk** n (COMPUT) disco de densidad sencilla/doble densidad.

dent [dɛnt] n abolladura ♦ vt (also: **make a ~ in**) abollar.

dental ['dɛntl] adj dental; ~ **surgeon** n odontólogo/a.

dentist ['dɛntɪst] n dentista m/f; ~**ry** n odontología.

dentures ['dɛntʃəz] npl dentadura (postiza).

denunciation [dɪnʌnsɪ'eɪʃən] n denuncia, denunciación f.

deny [dɪ'naɪ] vt negar; (charge) rechazar.

deodorant [diː'əudərənt] n desodorante m.

depart [dɪ'pɑːt] vi irse, marcharse; (train) salir; **to ~ from** (fig: differ from) apartarse de.

department [dɪ'pɑːtmənt] n (COMM) sección f; (SCOL) departamento; (POL) ministerio; **~ store** n gran almacén m.

departure [dɪ'pɑːtʃə*] n partida, ida; (of train) salida; (of employee) marcha; **a new ~** un nuevo rumbo; **~ lounge** n (at airport) sala de embarque.

depend [dɪ'pɛnd] vi: **to ~ on** depender de; (rely on) contar con; **it ~s** depende, según; **~ing on the result** según el resultado; **~able** adj (person) formal, serio; (watch) exacto; (car) seguro; **~ant** n dependiente m/f; **~ence** n dependencia; **~ent** adj: **to be ~ent on** depender de ♦ n = **dependant**.

depict [dɪ'pɪkt] vt (in picture) pintar; (describe) representar.

depleted [dɪ'pliːtɪd] adj reducido.

deplorable [dɪ'plɔːrəbl] adj deplorable.

deplore [dɪ'plɔː*] vt deplorar.

deploy [dɪ'plɔɪ] vt desplegar.

depopulation [diːpɔpju'leɪʃən] n despoblación f.

deport [dɪ'pɔːt] vt deportar.

deportment [dɪ'pɔːtmənt] n comportamiento; (way of walking) porte m.

depose [dɪ'pəuz] vt deponer.

deposit [dɪ'pɔzɪt] n depósito; (CHEM) sedimento; (of ore, oil) yacimiento ♦ vt (gen) depositar; **~ account** (BRIT) n cuenta de ahorros.

depot ['dɛpəu] n (storehouse) depósito; (for vehicles) parque m; (US) estación f.

depreciate [dɪ'priːʃɪeɪt] vi depreciarse, perder valor; **depreciation** [-'eɪʃən] n depreciación f.

depress [dɪ'prɛs] vt deprimir; (wages etc) hacer bajar; (press down) apretar; **~ed** adj deprimido; **~ing** adj deprimente; **~ion**[dɪ'prɛʃən] n depresión f.

deprivation [dɛprɪ'veɪʃən] n privación f.

deprive [dɪ'praɪv] vt: **to ~ sb of** privar a uno de; **~d** adj necesitado.

depth [dɛpθ] n profundidad f; (of cupboard) fondo; **to be in the ~s of despair** sentir la mayor desesperación; **to be out of one's ~** (in water) no hacer pie; (fig) sentirse totalmente perdido.

deputation [dɛpju'teɪʃən] n delegación f.

deputize ['dɛpjutaɪz] vi: **to ~ for sb** suplir a uno.

deputy ['dɛpjutɪ] adj: **~ head** subdirector(a) m/f ♦ n sustituto/a, suplente m/f; (US: POL) diputado/a; (US: also: **~ sheriff**) agente m (del sheriff).

derail [dɪ'reɪl] vt: **to be ~ed** descarrilarse; **~ment** n descarrilamiento.

deranged [dɪ'reɪndʒd] adj trastornado.

derby ['dɔːbɪ] (US) n (hat) hongo.

derelict ['dɛrɪlɪkt] adj abandonado.

deride [dɪ'raɪd] vt ridiculizar, mofarse de.

derisory [dɪ'raɪzərɪ] adj (sum) irrisorio.

derivative [dɪ'rɪvətɪv] n derivado.

derive [dɪ'raɪv] vt (benefit etc) obtener ♦ vi: **to ~ from** derivarse de.

derogatory [dɪ'rɔgətərɪ] adj despectivo.

derv [dɔːv] (BRIT) n gasoil m.

descend [dɪ'sɛnd] vt, vi descender, bajar; **to ~ from** descender de; **to ~ to** rebajarse a; **~ant** n descendiente m/f.

descent [dɪ'sɛnt] n descenso; (origin) descendencia.

describe [dɪs'kraɪb] vt describir; **description** [-'krɪpʃən] n descripción f; (sort) clase f, género.

desecrate ['dɛsɪkreɪt] vt profanar.

desert [n 'dɛzət, vb dɪ'zɔːt] n desierto ♦ vt abandonar ♦ vi (MIL) desertar; **~er** [dɪ'zɔːtə*] n desertor(a) m/f; **~ion** [dɪ'zɔːʃən] n deserción f; (LAW) abandono; **~ island** n isla desierta; **~s** [dɪ'zɔːts] npl: **to get one's just ~s** llevar su merecido.

deserve [dɪ'zɔːv] vt merecer, ser digno de; **deserving** adj (person) digno; (action, cause) meritorio.

design [dɪ'zaɪn] n (sketch) bosquejo; (layout, shape) diseño; (pattern) dibujo; (intention) intención f ♦ vt diseñar.

designate [vb 'dezigneit, adj 'dezignit] vt (appoint) nombrar; (destine) designar ♦ adj designado.

designer [di'zainə*] n diseñador(a) m/f; (fashion ~) modisto/a, diseñador(a) m/f de moda.

desirable [di'zaiərəbl] adj (proper) deseable; (attractive) atractivo.

desire [di'zaiə*] n deseo ♦ vt desear.

desk [desk] n (in office) escritorio; (for pupil) pupitre m; (in hotel, at airport) recepción f; (BRIT: in shop, restaurant) caja.

desolate ['desəlit] adj (place) desierto; (person) afligido; **desolation** [-'leifən] n (of place) desolación f; (of person) aflicción f.

despair [dis'peə*] n desesperación f ♦ vi: **to ~ of** perder la esperanza de.

despatch [dis'pætʃ] n, vt = **dispatch**.

desperate ['despərit] adj desesperado; (fugitive) peligroso; **to be ~ for sth/to do** necesitar urgentemente algo/hacer; **~ly** adv desesperadamente; (very) terriblemente, gravemente.

desperation [despə'reifən] n desesperación f; **in (sheer) ~** (absolutamente) desesperado.

despicable [dis'pikəbl] adj vil, despreciable.

despise [dis'paiz] vt despreciar.

despite [dis'pait] prep a pesar de, pese a.

despondent [dis'pondənt] adj deprimido, abatido.

dessert [di'zə:t] n postre m; **~spoon** n cuchara (de postre).

destination [desti'neifən] n destino.

destiny ['destini] n destino.

destitute ['destitju:t] adj desamparado, indigente.

destroy [dis'troi] vt destruir; (animal) sacrificar; **~er** n (NAUT) destructor m.

destruction [dis'trʌkfən] n destrucción f.

destructive [dis'trʌktiv] adj destructivo, destructor(a).

detach [di'tætʃ] vt separar; (unstick) despegar; **~able** adj de quita y pon; **~ed** adj (attitude) objetivo, imparcial;

~ed house n ≈ chalé m, ≈ chalet m; **~ment** n (aloofness) frialdad f; (MIL) destacamento.

detail ['di:teil] n detalle m; (no pl: in picture etc) detalles mpl; (trifle) pequeñez f ♦ vt detallar; (MIL) destacar; **in ~** detalladamente; **~ed** adj detallado.

detain [di'tein] vt retener; (in captivity) detener.

detect [di'tekt] vt descubrir; (MED, POLICE) identificar; (MIL, RADAR, TECH) detectar; **~ion** [di'tekfən] n descubrimiento; identificación f; **~ive** n detective m/f; **~ive story** n novela policíaca; **~or** n detector m.

détente [dei'ta:nt] n distensión f.

detention [di'tenfən] n detención f, arresto; (SCOL) castigo.

deter [di'tə:*] vt (dissuade) disuadir.

detergent [di'tə:dʒənt] n detergente m.

deteriorate [di'tiəriəreit] vi deteriorarse; **deterioration** [-'reifən] n deterioro.

determination [ditə:mi'neifən] n resolución f; (establishment) establecimiento.

determine [di'tə:min] vt determinar; **~d** adj (person) resuelto, decidido; **~d to do** resuelto a hacer.

deterrent [di'terənt] n (MIL) fuerza de disuasión.

detest [di'test] vt aborrecer.

detonate ['detəneit] vi estallar ♦ vt hacer detonar.

detour ['di:tuə*] n (gen, US: AUT) desviación f.

detract [di'trækt] vt: **to ~ from** quitar mérito a, desvirtuar.

detriment ['detrimənt] n: **to the ~ of** en perjuicio de; **~al** [detri'mentl] adj: **~al (to)** perjudicial (a).

devaluation [divælju'eifən] n devaluación f.

devalue [di:'vælju:] vt (currency) devaluar; (fig) quitar mérito a.

devastate ['devəsteit] vt devastar; (fig): **to be ~d by** quedar destrozado por; **devastating** adj devastador(a); (fig) arrollador(a).

develop [di'veləp] vt desarrollar; (PHOT) revelar; (disease) coger; (habit) adquirir; (fault) empezar a tener ♦

vi desarrollarse; (*advance*) progresar; (*facts, symptoms*) aparecer; ~**ing country** *n* país *m* en (vías de) desarrollo; ~**er** *n* promotor *m*; ~**ment** *n* desarrollo; (*advance*) progreso; (*of affair, case*) desenvolvimiento; (*of land*) urbanización *f*.

deviate ['di:vɪeɪt] *vi*: **to ~ (from)** desviarse (de); **deviation** [-'eɪʃən] *n* desviación *f*.

device [dɪ'vaɪs] *n* (*apparatus*) aparato, mecanismo.

devil ['dɛvl] *n* diablo, demonio; ~**ish** *adj* diabólico.

devious ['di:vɪəs] *adj* taimado.

devise [dɪ'vaɪz] *vt* idear, inventar.

devoid [dɪ'vɔɪd] *adj*: **~ of** desprovisto de.

devolution [di:və'lu:ʃən] *n* (*POL*) descentralización *f*.

devote [dɪ'vəut] *vt*: **to ~ sth to** dedicar algo a; ~**d** *adj* (*loyal*) leal, fiel; **to be ~d to sb** querer con devoción a alguien; **the book is ~d to politics** el libro trata de la política; ~**e** [dɛvəu'ti:] *n* entusiasta *m/f*; (*REL*) devoto/a.

devotion [dɪ'vəuʃən] *n* dedicación *f*; (*REL*) devoción *f*.

devour [dɪ'vauə*] *vt* devorar.

devout [dɪ'vaut] *adj* devoto.

dew [dju:] *n* rocío.

dexterity [dɛks'tɛrɪtɪ] *n* destreza.

diabetes [daɪə'bi:ti:z] *n* diabetes *f*; **diabetic** [-'bɛtɪk] *adj, n* diabético/a *m/f*.

diabolical [daɪə'bɔlɪkəl] (*inf*) *adj* (*weather, behaviour*) pésimo.

diagnose [daɪəg'nəuz] *vt* diagnosticar; **diagnoses** [-'nəusi:z] *npl of* **diagnosis**; **diagnosis** [-'nəusɪs] (*pl* -**ses**) *n* diagnóstico.

diagonal [daɪ'ægənl] *adj, n* diagonal *f*.

diagram ['daɪəgræm] *n* diagrama *m*, esquema *m*.

dial ['daɪəl] *n* esfera, cuadrante *m*, cara (*AM*); (*on radio etc*) selector *m*; (*of phone*) disco ♦ *vt* (*number*) marcar.

dialling ['daɪəlɪŋ]: ~ **code** (*US* **dial code**) *n* prefijo; ~ **tone** (*US* **dial tone**) *n* (*BRIT*) señal *f* or tono de marcar.

dialogue ['daɪəlɔg] (*US* **dialog**) *n* diálo-

go.

diameter [daɪ'æmɪtə*] *n* diámetro.

diamond ['daɪəmənd] *n* diamante *m*; (*shape*) rombo; ~**s** *npl* (*CARDS*) diamantes *mpl*.

diaper ['daɪəpə*] (*US*) *n* pañal *m*.

diaphragm ['daɪəfræm] *n* diafragma *m*.

diarrhoea [daɪə'ri:ə] (*US* **diarrhea**) *n* diarrea.

diary ['daɪərɪ] *n* (*daily account*) diario; (*book*) agenda.

dice [daɪs] *n inv* dados *mpl* ♦ *vt* (*CULIN*) cortar en cuadritos.

dichotomy [daɪ'kɔtəmɪ] *n* dicotomía.

Dictaphone ['dɪktəfəun] ® *n* dictáfono ®.

dictate [dɪk'teɪt] *vt* dictar; (*conditions*) imponer; **dictation** [-'teɪʃən] *n* dictado; (*giving of orders*) órdenes *fpl*.

dictator [dɪk'teɪtə*] *n* dictador *m*; ~**ship** *n* dictadura.

dictionary ['dɪkʃənrɪ] *n* diccionario.

did [dɪd] *pt of* **do**.

didn't ['dɪdənt] = **did not**.

die [daɪ] *vi* morir; (*fig: fade*) desvanecerse, desaparecer; **to be dying for sth/ to do sth** morirse por algo/de ganas de hacer algo; ~ **away** *vi* (*sound, light*) perderse; ~ **down** *vi* apagarse; (*wind*) amainar; ~ **out** *vi* desaparecer.

diehard ['daɪhɑ:d] *n* reaccionario/a.

diesel ['di:zəl] *n* vehículo con motor Diesel; ~ **engine** *n* motor *m* Diesel; ~ **(oil)** *n* gasoil *m*.

diet ['daɪət] *n* dieta; (*restricted food*) régimen *m* ♦ *vi* (*also: be on a* ~) estar a dieta, hacer régimen.

differ ['dɪfə*] *vi*: **to ~ (from)** (*be different*) ser distinto (a), diferenciarse (de); (*disagree*) discrepar (de); ~**ence** *n* diferencia; (*disagreement*) desacuerdo; ~**ent** *adj* diferente, distinto; ~**entiate** [-'rɛnʃɪeɪt] *vi*: **to ~entiate (between)** distinguir (entre); ~**ently** *adv* de otro modo, en forma distinta.

difficult ['dɪfɪkəlt] *adj* difícil; ~**y** *n* dificultad *f*.

diffident ['dɪfɪdənt] *adj* tímido.

diffuse [*adj* dɪ'fju:s, *vb* dɪ'fju:z] *adj* difuso ♦ *vt* difundir.

dig [dɪg] (*pt, pp* **dug**) *vt* (*hole, ground*) cavar ♦ *n* (*prod*) empujón *m*; (*archaeological*) excavación *f*; (*remark*) indirecta; **to ~ one's nails into** clavar las uñas en; **~ into** *vt fus* (*savings*) consumir; **~ out** *vt* (*hole*) excavar; (*fig*) sacar; **~ up** *vt* (*information*) desenterrar; (*plant*) desarraigar.

digest [*vb* daɪ'dʒɛst, *n* 'daɪdʒɛst] *vt* (*food*) digerir; (*facts*) asimilar ♦ *n* resumen *m*; **~ion** [dɪ'dʒɛstʃən] *n* digestión *f*.

digit ['dɪdʒɪt] *n* (*number*) dígito; (*finger*) dedo; **~al** *adj* digital.

dignified ['dɪgnɪfaɪd] *adj* grave, solemne.

dignity ['dɪgnɪtɪ] *n* dignidad *f*.

digress [daɪ'grɛs] *vi*: **to ~ from** apartarse de.

digs [dɪgz] (*BRIT*: *inf*) *npl* pensión *f*, alojamiento.

dike [daɪk] *n* = **dyke**.

dilapidated [dɪ'læpɪdeɪtɪd] *adj* desmoronado, ruinoso.

dilemma [daɪ'lɛmə] *n* dilema *m*.

diligent ['dɪlɪdʒənt] *adj* diligente.

dilute [daɪ'luːt] *vt* diluir.

dim [dɪm] *adj* (*light*) débil; (*outline*) indistinto; (*room*) oscuro; (*inf*: *stupid*) lerdo ♦ *vt* (*light*) bajar.

dime [daɪm] (*US*) *n* moneda de diez centavos.

dimension [dɪ'mɛnʃən] *n* dimensión *f*.

diminish [dɪ'mɪnɪʃ] *vt, vi* disminuir.

diminutive [dɪ'mɪnjutɪv] *adj* diminuto ♦ *n* (*LING*) diminutivo.

dimmers ['dɪməz] (*US*) *npl* (*AUT*: *dipped headlights*) luces *fpl* cortas; (: *parking lights*) luces *fpl* de posición.

dimple ['dɪmpl] *n* hoyuelo.

din [dɪn] *n* estruendo, estrépito.

dine [daɪn] *vi* cenar; **~r** *n* (*person*) comensal *m/f*; (*US*) restaurante *m* económico.

dinghy ['dɪŋgɪ] *n* bote *m*; (*also*: *rubber* ~) lancha (neumática).

dingy ['dɪndʒɪ] *adj* (*room*) sombrío; (*colour*) sucio.

dining car ['daɪnɪŋ-] (*BRIT*) *n* (*RAIL*) coche-comedor *m*.

dining room *n* comedor *m*.

dinner ['dɪnə*] *n* (*evening meal*) cena; (*lunch*) comida; (*public*) cena, banquete *m*; **~ jacket** *n* smoking *m*; **~ party** *n* cena; **~ time** *n* (*evening*) hora de cenar; (*midday*) hora de comer.

dinosaur ['daɪnəsɔː*] *n* dinosaurio.

dint [dɪnt] *n*: **by ~ of** a fuerza de.

diocese ['daɪəsɪs] *n* diócesis *f inv*.

dip [dɪp] *n* (*slope*) pendiente *m*; (*in sea*) baño; (*CULIN*) salsa ♦ *vt* (*in water*) mojar; (*ladle etc*) meter; (*BRIT*: *AUT*): **to ~ one's lights** poner luces de cruce ♦ *vi* (*road etc*) descender, bajar.

diphthong ['dɪfθɔŋ] *n* diptongo.

diploma [dɪ'pləumə] *n* diploma *m*.

diplomacy [dɪ'pləuməsɪ] *n* diplomacia.

diplomat ['dɪpləmæt] *n* diplomático/a; **~ic** [dɪplə'mætɪk] *adj* diplomático.

diprod ['dɪprɔd] (*US*) *n* = **dipstick**.

dipstick ['dɪpstɪk] (*BRIT*) *n* (*AUT*) varilla de nivel (del aceite).

dipswitch ['dɪpswɪtʃ] (*BRIT*) *n* (*AUT*) interruptor *m*.

dire [daɪə*] *adj* calamitoso.

direct [daɪ'rɛkt] *adj* directo; (*challenge*) claro; (*person*) franco ♦ *vt* dirigir; (*order*): **to ~ sb to do sth** mandar a uno hacer algo ♦ *adv* directo; **can you ~ me to...?** ¿puede indicarme dónde está...?; **~ debit** (*BRIT*) *n* domiciliación *f* bancaria de recibos.

direction [dɪ'rɛkʃən] *n* dirección *f*; **sense of ~** sentido de la dirección; **~s** *npl* (*instructions*) instrucciones *fpl*; **~s for use** modo de empleo.

directly [dɪ'rɛktlɪ] *adv* (*in straight line*) directamente; (*at once*) en seguida.

director [dɪ'rɛktə*] *n* director(a) *m/f*.

directory [dɪ'rɛktərɪ] *n* (*TEL*) guía (telefónica); (*COMPUT*) directorio.

dirt [dəːt] *n* suciedad *f*; (*earth*) tierra; **~-cheap** *adj* baratísimo; **~y** *adj* sucio; (*joke*) verde (*SP*), colorado (*AM*) ♦ *vt* ensuciar; (*stain*) manchar; **~y trick** *n* juego sucio.

disability [dɪsə'bɪlɪtɪ] *n* incapacidad *f*.

disabled [dɪs'eɪbld] *adj*: **to be physically ~** ser minusválido/a; **to be mentally ~** ser deficiente mental.

disadvantage [dɪsəd'vɑːntɪdʒ] *n* desven-

taja, inconveniente *m*.
disaffection [dɪsə'fekʃən] *n* descontento.
disagree [dɪsə'griː] *vi* (*differ*) discrepar;
to ~ (with) no estar de acuerdo (con);
~**able** *adj* desagradable; (*person*) antipático; ~**ment** *n* desacuerdo.
disallow [dɪsə'lau] *vt* (*goal*) anular;
(*claim*) rechazar.
disappear [dɪsə'pɪə*] *vi* desaparecer;
~**ance** *n* desaparición *f*.
disappoint [dɪsə'pɔɪnt] *vt* decepcionar,
defraudar; ~**ed** *adj* decepcionado;
~**ing** *adj* decepcionante; ~**ment** *n* decepción *f*.
disapproval [dɪsə'pruːvəl] *n* desaproba-
ción *f*.
disapprove [dɪsə'pruːv] *vi*: to ~ of ver
mal.
disarm [dɪs'ɑːm] *vt* desarmar; ~**ament**
n desarme *m*; ~**ing** *adj* (*smile etc*) que
desarma.
disarray [dɪsə'reɪ] *n*: in ~ (*army, organization*) desorganizado; (*hair, clothes*)
desarreglado.
disaster [dɪ'zɑːstə*] *n* desastre *m*.
disband [dɪs'bænd] *vt* disolver ♦ *vi* desbandarse.
disbelief [dɪsbə'liːf] *n* incredulidad *f*.
disc [dɪsk] *n* disco; (*COMPUT*) = **disk**.
discard [dɪs'kɑːd] *vt* (*old things*) tirar;
(*fig*) descartar.
discern [dɪ'sɜːn] *vt* percibir, discernir;
(*understand*) comprender; ~**ing** *adj*
perspicaz.
discharge [*vb* dɪs'tʃɑːdʒ, *n* 'dɪstʃɑːdʒ] *vt*
(*task, duty*) cumplir; (*waste*) verter;
(*patient*) dar de alta; (*employee*) despedir; (*soldier*) licenciar; (*defendant*)
poner en libertad ♦ *n* (*ELEC*) descarga;
(*MED*) supuración *f*; (*dismissal*) despedida; (*of duty*) desempeño; (*of debt*)
pago, descargo.
disciple [dɪ'saɪpl] *n* discípulo.
discipline ['dɪsɪplɪn] *n* disciplina ♦ *vt*
disciplinar; (*punish*) castigar.
disc jockey *n* pinchadiscos *m/f inv*.
disclaim [dɪs'kleɪm] *vt* negar.
disclose [dɪs'kləuz] *vt* revelar; **disclo-
sure** [-'kləuʒə*] *n* revelación *f*.
disco ['dɪskəu] *n abbr* = **discothèque**.

discoloured [dɪs'kʌləd] (*US* **discolored**)
adj descolorido.
discomfort [dɪs'kʌmfət] *n* incomodidad
f; (*unease*) inquietud *f*; (*physical*) malestar *m*.
disconcert [dɪskən'sɜːt] *vt* desconcertar.
disconnect [dɪskə'nekt] *vt* separar;
(*ELEC etc*) desconectar.
discontent [dɪskən'tent] *n* descontento;
~**ed** *adj* descontento.
discontinue [dɪskən'tɪnjuː] *vt* interrumpir; (*payments*) suspender; "~**d**"
(*COMM*) "ya no se fabrica".
discord ['dɪskɔːd] *n* discordia; (*MUS*) disonancia; ~**ant** [dɪs'kɔːdənt] *adj* discorde.
discothèque ['dɪskəutek] *n* discoteca.
discount [*n* 'dɪskaunt, *vb* dɪs'kaunt] *n* descuento ♦ *vt* descontar.
discourage [dɪs'kʌrɪdʒ] *vt* desalentar;
(*advise against*): to ~ sb **from doing**
disuadir a uno de hacer; **discouraging**
adj desalentador(a).
discover [dɪs'kʌvə*] *vt* descubrir;
(*error*) darse cuenta de; ~**y** *n* descubrimiento.
discredit [dɪs'kredɪt] *vt* desacreditar.
discreet [dɪ'skriːt] *adj* (*tactful*) discreto;
(*careful*) circunspecto, prudente.
discrepancy [dɪ'skrepənsɪ] *n* diferencia.
discretion [dɪ'skreʃən] *n* (*tact*) discreción *f*; at the ~ of a criterio de.
discriminate [dɪ'skrɪmɪneɪt] *vi*: to ~ be-
tween distinguir entre; to ~ **against** discriminar contra; **discriminating** *adj* entendido; **discrimination** [-'neɪʃən] *n* (*discernment*) perspicacia; (*bias*) discriminación *f*.
discuss [dɪ'skʌs] *vt* discutir; (*a theme*)
tratar; ~**ion** [dɪ'skʌʃən] *n* discusión *f*.
disdain [dɪs'deɪn] *n* desdén *m*.
disease [dɪ'ziːz] *n* enfermedad *f*.
disembark [dɪsɪm'bɑːk] *vt, vi* desembarcar.
disenchanted [dɪsɪn'tʃɑːntɪd] *adj*: ~
(**with**) desilusionado (con).
disengage [dɪsɪn'geɪdʒ] *vt*: to ~ **the
clutch** (*AUT*) desembragar.
disentangle [dɪsɪn'tæŋgl] *vt* soltar;
(*wire, thread*) desenredar.
disfigure [dɪs'fɪgə*] *vt* (*person*) desfigu-

rar; (*object*) afear.
disgrace [dɪs'greɪs] *n* ignominia;
(*shame*) vergüenza, escándalo ♦ *vt* deshonrar; ~**ful** *adj* vergonzoso.
disgruntled [dɪs'grʌntld] *adj* disgustado,
descontento.
disguise [dɪs'gaɪz] *n* disfraz *m* ♦ *vt* disfrazar; **in** ~ disfrazado.
disgust [dɪs'gʌst] *n* repugnancia ♦ *vt* repugnar, dar asco a; ~**ing** *adj* repugnante, asqueroso; (*behaviour etc*) vergonzoso.
dish [dɪʃ] *n* (*gen*) plato; **to do** *or* **wash
the** ~**es** fregar los platos; ~ **up** *vt* servir; ~ **out** *vt* repartir; ~**cloth** *n* estropajo.
dishearten [dɪs'hɑːtn] *vt* desalentar.
dishevelled [dɪ'ʃevəld] *adj* (*hair*) despeinado; (*appearance*) desarreglado.
dishonest [dɪs'ɒnɪst] *adj* (*person*) poco
honrado, tramposo; (*means*) fraudulento; ~**y** *n* falta de honradez.
dishonour [dɪs'ɒnə*] (*US* **dishonor**) *n*
deshonra; ~**able** *adj* deshonroso.
dishtowel ['dɪʃtauəl] (*US*) *n* estropajo.
dishwasher ['dɪʃwɒʃə*] *n* lavaplatos *m*
inv.
disillusion [dɪsɪ'luːʒən] *vt* desilusionar.
disincentive [dɪsɪn'sentɪv] *n* desincenti-
vo.
disinfect [dɪsɪn'fekt] *vt* desinfectar;
~**ant** *n* desinfectante *m*.
disintegrate [dɪs'ɪntɪgreɪt] *vi* disgregar-
se, desintegrarse.
disinterested [dɪs'ɪntrəstɪd] *adj* desinteresado.
disjointed [dɪs'dʒɔɪntɪd] *adj* inconexo.
disk [dɪsk] *n* (*esp US*) = **disc**; (*COMPUT*)
disco, disquete *m*; **single-/double-sided**
~ disco de una cara/dos caras; ~ **drive**
n disc drive *m*; ~**ette** *n* = **disk**.
dislike [dɪs'laɪk] *n* antipatía, aversión *f* ♦
vt tener antipatía a.
dislocate ['dɪsləkeɪt] *vt* dislocar.
dislodge [dɪs'lɒdʒ] *vt* sacar.
disloyal [dɪs'lɔɪəl] *adj* desleal.
dismal ['dɪzml] *adj* (*gloomy*) deprimente, triste; (*very bad*) malísimo, fatal.
dismantle [dɪs'mæntl] *vt* desmontar,
desarmar.

dismay [dɪs'meɪ] *n* consternación *f* ♦ *vt*
consternar.
dismiss [dɪs'mɪs] *vt* (*worker*) despedir;
(*pupils*) dejar marchar; (*soldiers*) dar
permiso para irse; (*idea*, *LAW*) rechazar; (*possibility*) descartar; ~**al** *n* despido.
dismount [dɪs'maunt] *vi* apearse.
disobedience [dɪsə'biːdɪəns] *n* desobediencia.
disobedient [dɪsə'biːdɪənt] *adj* desobe-
diente.
disobey [dɪsə'beɪ] *vt* desobedecer.
disorder [dɪs'ɔːdə*] *n* desorden *m*; (*riot-
ing*) disturbios *mpl*; (*MED*) trastorno;
~**ly** *adj* desordenado; (*meeting*) alborotado; (*conduct*) escandaloso.
disorientated [dɪs'ɔːrɪenteɪtəd] *adj* des-
orientado.
disown [dɪs'əun] *vt* (*action*) renegar de;
(*person*) negar cualquier tipo de relación con.
disparaging [dɪs'pærɪdʒɪŋ] *adj* despreciativo.
disparate ['dɪspərɪt] *adj* dispar.
disparity [dɪs'pærɪtɪ] *n* disparidad *f*.
dispassionate [dɪs'pæʃənɪt] *adj* (*unbiased*) imparcial.
dispatch [dɪs'pætʃ] *vt* enviar ♦ *n* (*sending*) envío; (*PRESS*) informe *m*; (*MIL*)
parte *m*.
dispel [dɪs'pel] *vt* disipar.
dispense [dɪs'pens] *vt* (*medicines*) preparar; ~ **with** *vt fus* prescindir de; ~**r**
n (*container*) distribuidor *m* automático; **dispensing chemist** (*BRIT*) *n* farmacia.
disperse [dɪs'pəːs] *vt* dispersar ♦ *vi* dispersarse.
dispirited [dɪ'spɪrɪtɪd] *adj* desanimado,
desalentado.
displace [dɪs'pleɪs] *vt* desplazar, reemplazar; ~**d person** *n* (*POL*) desplazado/
a.
display [dɪs'pleɪ] *n* (*in shop window*) escaparate *m*; (*exhibition*) exposición *f*;
(*COMPUT*) visualización *f*; (*of feeling*)
manifestación *f* ♦ *vt* exponer; manifestar; (*ostentatiously*) lucir.
displease [dɪs'pliːz] *vt* (*offend*) ofender;

(*annoy*) fastidiar; ~**d** *adj*: ~**d with** disgustado con; **displeasure** [-'plɛʒə*] *n* disgusto.

disposable [dɪs'pəuzəbl] *adj* desechable; (*income*) disponible; ~ **nappy** *n* pañal *m* desechable.

disposal [dɪs'pəuzl] *n* (*of rubbish*) destrucción *f*; **at one's** ~ a su disposición.

dispose [dɪs'pəuz] *vi*: **to** ~ **of** (*unwanted goods*) deshacerse de; (*problem etc*) resolver; ~**d** *adj*: ~**d to do** dispuesto a hacer; **to be well**~**d towards sb** estar bien dispuesto hacia uno; **disposition** [-'zɪʃən] *n* (*nature*) temperamento; (*inclination*) propensión *f*.

disproportionate [dɪsprə'pɔːʃənət] *adj* desproporcionado.

disprove [dɪs'pruːv] *vt* refutar.

dispute [dɪs'pjuːt] *n* disputa; (*also: industrial* ~) conflicto (laboral) ♦ *vt* (*argue*) disputar, discutir; (*question*) cuestionar.

disqualify [dɪs'kwɔlɪfaɪ] *vt* (*SPORT*) desclasificar; **to** ~ **sb for sth/from doing sth** incapacitar a alguien para algo/ hacer algo.

disquiet [dɪs'kwaɪət] *n* preocupación *f*, inquietud *f*.

disregard [dɪsrɪ'gɑːd] *vt* (*ignore*) no hacer caso de.

disrepair [dɪsrɪ'pɛə*] *n*: **to fall into** ~ (*building*) desmoronarse.

disreputable [dɪs'rɛpjutəbl] *adj* (*person*) de mala fama; (*behaviour*) vergonzoso.

disrespectful [dɪsrɪ'spɛktful] *adj* irrespetuoso.

disrupt [dɪs'rʌpt] *vt* (*plans*) desbaratar, trastornar; (*conversation*) interrumpir; ~**ion** [-'rʌpʃən] *n* (*disturbance*) trastorno; (*interruption*) interrupción *f*.

dissatisfaction [dɪssætɪs'fækʃən] *n* disgusto, descontento.

dissect [dɪ'sɛkt] *vt* disecar.

disseminate [dɪ'sɛmɪneɪt] *vt* divulgar, difundir.

dissent [dɪ'sɛnt] *n* disensión *f*.

dissertation [dɪsə'teɪʃən] *n* tesina.

disservice [dɪs'səːvɪs] *n*: **to do sb a** ~ perjudicar a alguien.

dissident ['dɪsɪdnt] *adj, n* disidente *m/f*.

dissimilar [dɪ'sɪmɪlə*] *adj* distinto.

dissipate ['dɪsɪpeɪt] *vt* disipar; (*waste*) desperdiciar.

dissociate [dɪ'səuʃɪeɪt] *vt* disociar.

dissolute ['dɪsəluːt] *adj* disoluto.

dissolution [dɪsə'luːʃən] *n* disolución *f*.

dissolve [dɪ'zɔlv] *vt* disolver ♦ *vi* disolverse; **to** ~ **in(to) tears** deshacerse en lágrimas.

dissuade [dɪ'sweɪd] *vt*: **to** ~ **sb (from)** disuadir a uno (de).

distance ['dɪstns] *n* distancia; **in the** ~ a lo lejos.

distant ['dɪstnt] *adj* lejano; (*manner*) reservado, frío.

distaste [dɪs'teɪst] *n* repugnancia; ~**ful** *adj* repugnante, desagradable.

distended [dɪ'stɛndɪd] *adj* (*stomach*) hinchado.

distil [dɪs'tɪl] (*US* **distill**) *vt* destilar; ~**lery** *n* destilería.

distinct [dɪs'tɪŋkt] *adj* (*different*) distinto; (*clear*) claro; (*unmistakeable*) inequívoco; **as** ~ **from** a diferencia de; ~**ion** [dɪs'tɪŋkʃən] *n* distinción *f*; (*honour*) honor *m*; (*in exam*) sobresaliente *m*; ~**ive** *adj* distintivo.

distinguish [dɪs'tɪŋgwɪʃ] *vt* distinguir; **to** ~ **o.s.** destacarse; ~**ed** *adj* (*eminent*) distinguido; ~**ing** *adj* (*feature*) distintivo.

distort [dɪs'tɔːt] *vt* distorsionar; (*shape, image*) deformar; ~**ion** [dɪs'tɔːʃən] *n* distorsión *f*; deformación *f*.

distract [dɪs'trækt] *vt* distraer; ~**ed** *adj* distraído; ~**ion** [dɪs'trækʃən] *n* distracción *f*; (*confusion*) aturdimiento.

distraught [dɪs'trɔːt] *adj* loco de inquietud.

distress [dɪs'trɛs] *n* (*anguish*) angustia, aflicción *f* ♦ *vt* afligir; ~**ing** *adj* angustioso; doloroso; ~ **signal** *n* señal *f* de socorro.

distribute [dɪs'trɪbjuːt] *vt* distribuir; (*share out*) repartir; **distribution** [-'bjuːʃən] *n* distribución *f*, reparto; **distributor** *n* (*AUT*) distribuidor *m*; (*COMM*) distribuidora.

district ['dɪstrɪkt] *n* (*of country*) zona, región *f*; (*of town*) barrio; (*ADMIN*) distrito; ~ **attorney** (*US*) *n* fiscal *m/f*; ~ **nurse** (*BRIT*) *n* enfermera que atiende a pacientes a domicilio.

distrust [dɪs'trʌst] *n* desconfianza ♦ *vt* desconfiar de.

disturb [dɪs'tɔːb] *vt* (*person: bother, interrupt*) molestar; (: *upset*) perturbar, inquietar; (*disorganize*) alterar; ~**ance** *n* (*upheaval*) perturbación *f*; (*political etc: gen pl*) disturbio; (*of mind*) trastorno; ~**ed** *adj* (*worried, upset*) preocupado, angustiado; **emotionally** ~**ed** trastornado; (*childhood*) inseguro; ~**ing** *adj* inquietante, perturbador(a).

disuse [dɪs'juːs] *n*: **to fall into** ~ caer en desuso.

disused [dɪs'juːzd] *adj* abandonado.

ditch [dɪtʃ] *n* zanja; (*irrigation* ~) acequia ♦ *vt* (*inf: partner*) deshacerse de; (: *plan, car etc*) abandonar.

dither ['dɪðə*] (*pej*) *vi* vacilar.

ditto ['dɪtəʊ] *adv* ídem, lo mismo.

divan [dɪ'væn] *n* (*also*: ~ **bed**) cama turca.

dive [daɪv] *n* (*from board*) salto; (*underwater*) buceo; (*of submarine*) sumersión *f* ♦ *vi* (*swimmer: into water*) saltar; (: *under water*) zambullirse, bucear; (*fish, submarine*) sumergirse; (*bird*) lanzarse en picado; **to** ~ **into** (*bag etc*) meter la mano en; (*place*) meterse de prisa en; ~**r** *n* (*underwater*) buzo.

diverge [daɪ'vɔːdʒ] *vi* divergir.

diverse [daɪ'vɔːs] *adj* diversos/as, varios/as.

diversion [daɪ'vɔːʃən] *n* (*BRIT: AUT*) desviación *f*; (*distraction, MIL*) diversión *f*; (*of funds*) distracción *f*.

divert [daɪ'vɔːt] *vt* (*turn aside*) desviar.

divide [dɪ'vaɪd] *vt* dividir; (*separate*) separar ♦ *vi* dividirse; (*road*) bifurcarse; ~**d highway** (*US*) *n* carretera de doble calzada.

dividend ['dɪvɪdɛnd] *n* dividendo; (*fig*): **to pay** ~**s** proporcionar beneficios.

divine [dɪ'vaɪn] *adj* (*also fig*) divino.

diving ['daɪvɪŋ] *n* (*SPORT*) salto; (*underwater*) buceo; ~ **board** *n* trampolín *m*.

divinity [dɪ'vɪnɪtɪ] *n* divinidad *f*; (*SCOL*) teología.

division [dɪ'vɪʒən] *n* división *f*; (*sharing out*) reparto; (*disagreement*) diferencias *fpl*; (*COMM*) sección *f*.

divorce [dɪ'vɔːs] *n* divorcio ♦ *vt* divorciarse de; ~**d** *adj* divorciado; ~**e** [-'siː] *n* divorciado/a.

divulge [daɪ'vʌldʒ] *vt* divulgar, revelar.

D.I.Y. (*BRIT*) *adj, n abbr* = **do-it-yourself**.

dizzy ['dɪzɪ] *adj* (*spell*) de mareo; **to feel** ~ marearse.

DJ *n abbr* = **disc jockey**.

---

do [duː] (*pt* **did**, *pp* **done**) *n* (*inf: party etc*): **we're having a little** ~ **on Saturday** damos una fiestecita el sábado; **it was rather a grand** ~ fue un acontecimiento a lo grande

♦ *aux vb* **1** (*in negative constructions: not translated*) **I don't understand** no entiendo

2 (*to form questions: not translated*) **didn't you know?** ¿no lo sabías?; **what** ~ **you think?** ¿qué opinas?

3 (*for emphasis, in polite expressions*): **people** ~ **make mistakes sometimes** sí que se cometen errores a veces; **she does seem rather late** a mí también me parece que se ha retrasado; ~ **sit down/help yourself** siéntate/sírvete por favor; ~ **take care!** ¡ten cuidado(, te pido)!

4 (*used to avoid repeating vb*): **she sings better than I** ~ canta mejor que yo; ~ **you agree? — yes, I** ~/**no, I don't** ¿estás de acuerdo? — sí (lo estoy)/no (lo estoy); **she lives in Glasgow — so** ~ **I** vive en Glasgow — yo también; **he didn't like it and neither did we** no le gustó y a nosotros tampoco; **who made this mess? — I did** ¿quién hizo esta chapuza? — yo; **he asked me to help him and I did** me pidió que le ayudara y lo hice

5 (*in question tags*): **you like him, don't you?** te gusta, ¿verdad? *or* ¿no?; **I don't know him,** ~ **I?** creo que no le conozco

♦ vt **1** (gen, carry out, perform etc): **what are you ~ing tonight?** ¿qué haces esta noche?; **what can I ~ for you?** ¿en qué puedo servirle?; **to ~ the washing-up/cooking** fregar los platos/cocinar; **~ one's teeth/hair/nails** lavarse los dientes/arreglarse el pelo/arreglarse las uñas

2 (AUT etc): **the car was ~ing 100** el coche iba a 100; **we've done 200 km already** ya hemos hecho 200 km; **he can ~ 100 in that car** puede dar los 100 en ese coche

♦ vi **1** (act, behave) hacer; **~ as I ~** haz como yo

2 (get on, fare): **he's ~ing well/badly at school** va bien/mal en la escuela; **the firm is ~ing well** la empresa anda or va bien; **how ~ you ~?** mucho gusto; (less formal) ¿qué tal?

3 (suit): **will it ~?** ¿sirve?, ¿está or va bien?

4 (be sufficient) bastar; **will £10 ~?** ¿será bastante con £10?; **that'll ~** así está bien; **that'll ~!** (in annoyance) ¡ya está bien!, ¡basta ya!; **to make ~ (with)** arreglárselas (con)

do away with vt fus (kill, disease) eliminar; (abolish: law etc) abolir; (withdraw) retirar

do up vt (laces) atar; (zip, dress, shirt) abrochar; (renovate: room, house) renovar

do with vt fus (need): **I could ~ with a drink/some help** no me vendría mal un trago/un poco de ayuda; (be connected) tener que ver con; **what has it got to ~ with you?** ¿qué tiene que ver contigo?

do without vi pasar sin; **if you're late for tea then you'll ~** without si llegas tarde para la merienda pasarás sin él ♦ vt fus pasar sin; **I can ~ without a car** puedo pasar sin coche.

dock [dɔk] n (NAUT) muelle m; (LAW) banquillo (de los acusados); **~s** npl (NAUT) muelles mpl, puerto sg ♦ vi (enter ~) atracar (la) muelle; (SPACE) acoplarse; **~er** n trabajador m portuario, estibador m; **~yard** n astillero.

doctor [ˈdɔktə*] n médico/a; (PhD etc) **doctor(a)** m/f ♦ vt (drink etc) adulterar; **D~ of Philosophy** n Doctor en Filosofía y Letras.

doctrine [ˈdɔktrɪn] n doctrina.

document [ˈdɔkjumənt] n documento; **~ary** [-ˈmentərɪ] adj documental ♦ n documental m.

dodge [dɔdʒ] n (fig) truco ♦ vt evadir; (blow) esquivar.

dodgems [ˈdɔdʒəmz] (BRIT) npl coches mpl de choque.

doe [dəu] n (deer) cierva, gama; (rabbit) coneja.

does [dʌz] vb see do; **~n't** = **~ not**.

dog [dɔg] n perro ♦ vt seguir los pasos de; (subj: bad luck) perseguir; **~ collar** n collar m de perro; (of clergyman) alzacuellos m inv; **~-eared** adj sobado.

dogged [ˈdɔgɪd] adj tenaz, obstinado.

dogsbody [ˈdɔgzbɔdɪ] (BRIT: inf) n burro de carga.

doings [ˈduɪŋz] npl (activities) actividades fpl.

do-it-yourself n bricolaje m.

doldrums [ˈdɔldrəmz] npl: **to be in the ~** (person) estar abatido; (business) estar estancado.

dole [dəul] (BRIT) n (payment) subsidio de paro; **on the ~** parado; **~ out** vt repartir.

doleful [ˈdəulful] adj triste, lúgubre.

doll [dɔl] n muñeca; (US: inf: woman) muñeca, gachí f; **~ed-up** (inf) adj arreglado.

dollar [ˈdɔlə*] n dólar m.

dolphin [ˈdɔlfɪn] n delfín m.

domain [dəˈmeɪn] n (fig) campo, competencia; (land) dominios mpl.

dome [dəum] n (ARCH) cúpula.

domestic [dəˈmestɪk] adj (animal, duty) doméstico; (flight, policy) nacional; **~ated** adj domesticado; (home-loving) casero, hogareño.

dominant [ˈdɔmɪnənt] adj dominante.

dominate [ˈdɔmɪneɪt] vt dominar.

domineering [dɔmɪˈnɪərɪŋ] adj dominante.

dominion [dəˈmɪnɪən] n dominio.

domino [ˈdɔmɪnəu] (pl ~es) n ficha de

dominó; ~es *n* (*game*) dominó.
don [dɔn] (*BRIT*) *n* profesor(a) *m/f* universitario/a.
donate [dəˈneɪt] *vt* donar; **donation** [dəˈneɪʃən] *n* donativo.
done [dʌn] *pp* of do.
donkey [ˈdɔŋkɪ] *n* burro.
donor [ˈdəunə*] *n* donante *m/f.*
don't [dəunt] = do not.
doodle [ˈduːdl] *vi* hacer dibujitos *or* garabatos.
doom [duːm] *n* (*fate*) suerte *f* ♦ *vt*: to be ~ed to failure estar condenado al fracaso; ~sday *n* día *m* del juicio final.
door [dɔ:*] *n* puerta; ~bell *n* timbre *m*; ~ handle *n* tirador *m*; (*of car*) manija; ~man *n* (*in hotel*) portero; ~mat *n* felpudo, estera; ~step *n* peldaño; ~-to-~ *adj* de puerta en puerta; ~way *n* entrada, puerta.
dope [dəup] *n* (*inf: illegal drug*) droga; (: *person*) imbécil *m/f* ♦ *vt* (*horse etc*) drogar.
dopey [ˈdəupɪ] (*inf*) *adj* (*groggy*) atontado; (*stupid*) imbécil.
dormant [ˈdɔːmənt] *adj* inactivo.
dormice [ˈdɔːmaɪs] *npl of* **dormouse**.
dormitory [ˈdɔːmɪtrɪ] *n* (*BRIT*) dormitorio; (*US*) colegio mayor.
dormouse [ˈdɔːmaus] (*pl* -mice) *n* lirón *m*.
DOS *n abbr* (= *disk operating system*) DOS *m*.
dosage [ˈdəusɪdʒ] *n* dosis *f inv*.
dose [dəus] *n* dósis *f inv*.
doss house [ˈdɔss-] (*BRIT*) *n* pensión *f* de mala muerte.
dossier [ˈdɔsɪeɪ] *n* expediente *m*, dosier *m*.
dot [dɔt] *n* punto ♦ *vi*: ~ted with salpicado de; on the ~ en punto.
dote [dəut]: to ~ on *vt fus* adorar, idolatrar.
dot-matrix printer *n* impresora matricial (*or* de matriz) de puntos.
double [ˈdʌbl] *adj* doble ♦ *adv* (*twice*): to cost ~ costar el doble ♦ *n* doble *m* ♦ *vt* doblar ♦ *vi* doblarse; on the ~, at the ~ (*BRIT*) corriendo; ~ bass *n* contrabajo; ~ bed *n* cama de matrimonio; ~

bend (*BRIT*) *n* doble curva; ~-breasted *adj* cruzado; ~cross *vt* (*trick*) engañar; (*betray*) traicionar; ~decker *n* autobús *m* de dos pisos; ~ glazing (*BRIT*) *n* doble acristalamiento; ~ room *n* habitación *f* doble; ~s (*TENNIS*) juego de dobles; doubly *adv* doblemente.
doubt [daut] *n* duda ♦ *vt* dudar; (*suspect*) dudar de; to ~ that dudar que; ~ful *adj* dudoso; (*person*): to be ~ful sth tener dudas sobre algo; ~less *adv* sin duda.
dough [dəu] *n* masa, pasta; ~nut *n* ≈ rosquilla.
douse [daus] *vt* (*drench*) mojar; (*extinguish*) apagar.
dove [dʌv] *n* paloma.
dovetail [ˈdʌvteɪl] *vi* (*fig*) encajar.
dowdy [ˈdaudɪ] *adj* (*person*) mal vestido; (*clothes*) pasado de moda.
down [daun] *n* (*feathers*) plumón *m*, flojel *m* ♦ *adv* (~*wards*) abajo, hacia abajo; (*on the ground*) por *or* en tierra ♦ *prep* abajo ♦ *vt* (*inf: drink*) beberse; ~ with X! ¡abajo X!; ~-and-out *n* vagabundo/a; ~-at-heel *adj* venido a menos; (*appearance*) desaliñado; ~cast *adj* abatido; ~fall *n* caída, ruina; ~hearted *adj* desanimado; ~hill *adv*: to go ~hill (*also fig*) ir cuesta abajo; ~ payment *n* entrada, pago al contado; ~pour *n* aguacero; ~right *adj* (*nonsense, lie*) manifiesto; (*refusal*) terminante; ~stairs *adv* (*below*) (en la casa de) abajo; (~*wards*) escaleras abajo; ~stream *adv* aguas *or* río abajo; ~-to-earth *adj* práctico; ~town *adv* en el centro de la ciudad; ~ under *adv* en Australia (*or* Nueva Zelanda); ~ward [-wəd] *adj*, *adv* hacia abajo; ~wards [-wədz] *adv* hacia abajo.
dowry [ˈdaurɪ] *n* dote *f.*
doz. *abbr* = **dozen**.
doze [dəuz] *vi* dormitar; ~ off *vi* quedarse medio dormido.
dozen [ˈdʌzn] *n* docena; a ~ books una docena de libros; ~s of cantidad de.
Dr. *abbr* = **doctor**; **drive**.
drab [dræb] *adj* gris, monótono.
draft [drɑːft] *n* (*first copy*) borrador *m*;

(*POL: of bill*) anteproyecto; (*US: call-up*) quinta ♦ *vt* (*plan*) preparar; (*write roughly*) hacer un borrador de; *see also* **draught**.

draftsman ['drɑːftsmən] (*US*) *n* = **draughtsman**.

drag [dræg] *vt* arrastrar; (*river*) dragar, rastrear ♦ *vi* (*time*) pasar despacio; (*play, film etc*) hacerse pesado ♦ *n* (*inf*) lata; (*women's clothing*): **in ~** vestido de travesti; **~ on** *vi* ser interminable.

dragon ['drægən] *n* dragón *m*.

dragonfly ['drægənflaɪ] *n* libélula.

drain [dreɪn] *n* desaguadero; (*in street*) sumidero; (*source of loss*): **to be a ~ on** consumir, agotar ♦ *vt* (*land, marshes*) desaguar; (*reservoir*) vaciar; (*vegetables*) escurrir ♦ *vi* escurrirse; **~age** *n* (*act*) desagüe *m*; (*MED, AGR*) drenaje *m*; (*sewage*) alcantarillado; **~board** ['dreɪnbɔːd] (*US*) *n* = **~ing board**; **~ing board** *n* escurridera, escurridor *m*; **~pipe** *n* tubo de desagüe.

drama ['drɑːmə] *n* (*art*) teatro; (*play*) drama *m*; (*excitement*) emoción *f*; **~tic** [drə'mætɪk] *adj* dramático; (*sudden, marked*) espectacular; **~tist** ['dræmətɪst] *n* dramaturgo/a; **~tize** ['dræmətaɪz] *vt* (*events*) dramatizar; (*adapt: for TV, cinema*) adaptar a la televisión/al cine.

drank [dræŋk] *pt of* **drink**.

drape [dreɪp] *vt* (*cloth*) colocar; (*flag*) colgar; **~s** (*US*) *npl* cortinas *fpl*.

drastic ['dræstɪk] *adj* (*measure*) severo; (*change*) radical, drástico.

draught [drɑːft] (*US* **draft**) *n* (*of air*) corriente *f* de aire; (*NAUT*) calado; **on ~** (*beer*) de barril; **~board** (*BRIT*) *n* tablero de damas; **~s** (*BRIT*) *n* (*game*) juego de damas.

draughtsman ['drɑːftsmən] (*US* **draftsman**) *n* delineante *m*.

draw [drɔː] (*pt* **drew**, *pp* **drawn**) *vt* (*picture*) dibujar; (*cart*) tirar de; (*curtain*) correr; (*take out*) sacar; (*attract*) atraer; (*money*) retirar; (*wages*) cobrar ♦ *vi* (*SPORT*) empatar ♦ *n* (*SPORT*) empate *m*; (*lottery*) sorteo; **~ near** *vi* acercarse; **~ out** *vi* (*lengthen*) alargar-

se ♦ *vt* sacar; **~ up** *vi* (*stop*) pararse ♦ *vt* (*chair*) acercar; (*document*) redactar; **~back** *n* inconveniente *m*, desventaja; **~bridge** *n* puente *m* levadizo.

drawer [drɔː*] *n* cajón *m*.

drawing ['drɔːɪŋ] *n* dibujo; **~ board** *n* tablero (de dibujante); **~ pin** (*BRIT*) *n* chincheta; **~ room** *n* salón *m*.

drawl [drɔːl] *n* habla lenta y cansina.

drawn [drɔːn] *pp of* **draw**.

dread [drɛd] *n* pavor *m*, terror *m* ♦ *vt* temer, tener miedo *or* pavor a; **~ful** *adj* horroroso.

dream [driːm] (*pt, pp* **dreamed** *or* **dreamt**) *n* sueño ♦ *vt, vi* soñar; **~er** *n* soñador(a) *m/f*; **dreamt** [drɛmt] *pt, pp of* **dream**; **~y** *adj* (*distracted*) soñador(a), distraído; (*music*) suave.

dreary ['drɪərɪ] *adj* monótono.

dredge [drɛdʒ] *vt* dragar.

dregs [drɛgz] *npl* posos *mpl*; (*of humanity*) hez *f*.

drench [drɛntʃ] *vt* empapar.

dress [drɛs] *n* vestido; (*clothing*) ropa ♦ *vt* vestir; (*wound*) vendar ♦ *vi* vestirse; **to get ~ed** vestirse; **~ up** *vi* vestirse de etiqueta; (*in fancy dress*) disfrazarse; **~ circle** (*BRIT*) *n* principal *m*; **~er** *n* (*furniture*) aparador *m*; (: *US*) cómoda (con espejo); **~ing** *n* (*MED*) vendaje *m*; (*CULIN*) aliño; **~ing gown** (*BRIT*) *n* bata; **~ing room** *n* (*THEATRE*) camarín *m*; (*SPORT*) vestuario; **~ing table** *n* tocador *m*; **~maker** *n* modista, costurera; **~ rehearsal** *n* ensayo general; **~y** (*inf*) *adj* elegante.

drew [druː] *pt of* **draw**.

dribble ['drɪbl] *vi* (*baby*) babear ♦ *vt* (*ball*) regatear.

dried [draɪd] *adj* (*fruit*) seco; (*milk*) en polvo.

drier ['draɪə*] *n* = **dryer**.

drift [drɪft] *n* (*of current etc*) flujo; (*of snow*) ventisquero; (*meaning*) significado ♦ *vi* (*boat*) ir a la deriva; (*sand, snow*) amontonarse; **~wood** *n* madera de deriva.

drill [drɪl] *n* (**~ bit**) broca; (*tool for DIY etc*) taladro; (*of dentist*) fresa; (*for mining etc*) perforadora, barrena;

(*MIL*) instrucción *f* ♦ *vt* perforar, taladrar; (*troops*) enseñar la instrucción a ♦ *vi* (*for oil*) perforar.

drink [drɪŋk] (*pt* **drank**, *pp* **drunk**) *n* bebida; (*sip*) trago ♦ *vt, vi* beber; **to have a ~** tomar algo; tomar una copa *or* un trago; **a ~ of water** un trago de agua; **~er** *n* bebedor(a) *m/f*; **~ing water** *n* agua potable.

drip [drɪp] *n* (*act*) goteo; (*one ~*) gota; (*MED*) gota a gota *m* ♦ *vi* gotear; **~-dry** *adj* (*shirt*) inarrugable; **~ping** *n* (*animal fat*) pringue *m*.

drive [draɪv] (*pt* **drove**, *pp* **driven**) *n* (*journey*) viaje *m* (en coche); (*also: ~way*) entrada; (*energy*) energía, vigor *m*; (*COMPUT: also: disk ~*) drive *m* ♦ *vt* (*car*) conducir (*SP*), manejar (*AM*); (*nail*) clavar; (*push*) empujar; (*TECH: motor*) impulsar ♦ *vi* (*AUT: at controls*) conducir; (: *travel*) pasearse en coche; **left-/right-hand ~** conducción *f* a la izquierda/derecha; **to ~ sb mad** volverle loco a uno.

drivel ['drɪvl] (*inf*) *n* tonterías *fpl*.

driven ['drɪvn] *pp* of **drive**.

driver ['draɪvə*] *n* conductor(a) *m/f* (*SP*), chofer (*AM*); (*of taxi, bus*) chofer *m*; **~'s license** (*US*) *n* carnet *m* de conducir.

driveway ['draɪvweɪ] *n* entrada.

driving ['draɪvɪŋ] *n* el conducir (*SP*), el manejar (*AM*); **~ instructor** *n* instructor(a) *m/f* de conducción *or* manejo; **~ lesson** *n* clase *f* de conducción *or* manejo; **~ licence** (*BRIT*) *n* permiso de conducir; **~ mirror** *n* retrovisor *m*; **~ school** *n* autoescuela; **~ test** *n* examen *m* de conducción *or* manejo.

drizzle ['drɪzl] *n* llovizna.

drone [drəun] *n* (*noise*) zumbido; (*bee*) zángano.

drool [druːl] *vi* babear.

droop [druːp] *vi* (*flower*) marchitarse; (*shoulders*) encorvarse; (*head*) inclinarse.

drop [drɔp] *n* (*of water*) gota; (*lessening*) baja; (*fall*) caída ♦ *vt* dejar caer; (*voice, eyes, price*) bajar; (*passenger*) dejar; (*omit*) omitir ♦ *vi* (*object*) caer;

(*wind*) amainar; **~s** *npl* (*MED*) gotas *fpl*; **~ off** *vi* (*sleep*) dormirse ♦ *vt* (*passenger*) dejar; **~ out** *vi* (*withdraw*) retirarse; **~-out** *n* marginado/a; (*SCOL*) estudiante que abandona los estudios; **~per** *n* cuentagotas *m inv*; **~pings** *npl* excremento.

drought [draut] *n* sequía.

drove [drəuv] *pt* of **drive**.

drown [draun] *vt* ahogar ♦ *vi* ahogarse.

drowsy ['drauzɪ] *adj* soñoliento; **to be ~** tener sueño.

drudgery ['drʌdʒərɪ] *n* trabajo monótono.

drug [drʌg] *n* medicamento; (*narcotic*) droga ♦ *vt* drogar; **to be on ~s** drogarse; **~ addict** *n* drogadicto/a; **~gist** (*US*) *n* farmacéutico; **~store** (*US*) *n* farmacia.

drum [drʌm] *n* tambor *m*; (*for oil, petrol*) bidón *m*; **~s** *npl* batería; **~mer** *n* tambor *m*.

drunk [drʌŋk] *pp* of **drink** ♦ *adj* borracho ♦ *n* (*also: ~ard*) borracho/a; **~en** *adj* borracho; (*laughter, party*) de borrachos.

dry [draɪ] *adj* seco; (*day*) sin lluvia; (*climate*) árido, seco ♦ *vt* secar; (*tears*) enjugarse ♦ *vi* secarse; **~ up** *vi* (*river*) secarse; **~-cleaner's** *n* tintorería; **~-cleaning** *n* lavado en seco; **~er** *n* (*for hair*) secador *m*; (*US: for clothes*) secadora; **~ness** *n* sequedad *f*; **~ rot** *n* putrefacción *f* fungoide.

DSS *n abbr* = **Department of Social Security.**

dual ['djuəl] *adj* doble; **~ carriageway** (*BRIT*) *n* carretera de doble calzada; **~ nationality** *n* doble nacionalidad *f*; **~-purpose** *adj* de doble uso.

dubbed [dʌbd] *adj* (*CINEMA*) doblado.

dubious ['djuːbɪəs] *adj* indeciso; (*reputation, company*) sospechoso.

duchess ['dʌtʃɪs] *n* duquesa.

duck [dʌk] *n* pato ♦ *vi* agacharse; **~ling** *n* patito.

duct [dʌkt] *n* conducto, canal *m*.

dud [dʌd] *n* (*object, tool*) engaño, engañifa ♦ *adj*: **~ cheque** (*BRIT*) cheque *m* sin fondos.

due [djuː] *adj (owed)*: **he is ~ £10** se le deben 10 libras; *(expected: event)*: **the meeting is ~ on Wednesday** la reunión tendrá lugar el miércoles; *(: arrival)* **the train is ~ at 8am** el tren tiene su llegada para las 8; *(proper)* debido ♦ *n*: **to give sb his** *(or* **her)** ~ ser justo con alguien ♦ *adv*: ~ **north** derecho al norte; ~**s** *npl (for club, union)* cuota; *(in harbour)* derechos *mpl*; **in ~ course** a su debido tiempo; ~ **to** debido a; **to be ~ to** deberse a.

duet [djuːˈɛt] *n* dúo.

duffel [ˈdʌfəl] *adj*: ~ **bag** *n* bolsa de lona; ~ **coat** *n* trenca, abrigo de tres cuartos.

dug [dʌɡ] *pt, pp of* **dig**.

duke [djuːk] *n* duque *m*.

dull [dʌl] *adj (light)* débil; *(stupid)* torpe; *(boring)* pesado; *(sound, pain)* sordo; *(weather, day)* gris ♦ *vt (pain, grief)* aliviar; *(mind, senses)* entorpecer.

duly [ˈdjuːlɪ] *adv* debidamente; *(on time)* a su debido tiempo.

dumb [dʌm] *adj* mudo; *(pej: stupid)* estúpido; ~**founded** [dʌmˈfaundɪd] *adj* pasmado.

dummy [ˈdʌmɪ] *n (tailor's ~)* maniquí *m*; *(mock-up)* maqueta; *(BRIT: for baby)* chupete *m* ♦ *adj* falso, postizo.

dump [dʌmp] *n (also: rubbish ~)* basurero, vertedero; *(inf: place)* cuchitril *m* ♦ *vt (put down)* dejar; *(get rid of)* deshacerse de; *(COMPUT: data)* transferir.

dumpling [ˈdʌmplɪŋ] *n bola de masa hervida*.

dumpy [ˈdʌmpɪ] *adj* regordete/a.

dunce [dʌns] *n* zopenco.

dung [dʌŋ] *n* estiércol *m*.

dungarees [dʌŋɡəˈriːz] *npl* mono.

dungeon [ˈdʌndʒən] *n* calabozo.

duo [ˈdjuːəu] *n (gen, MUS)* dúo.

dupe [djuːp] *n (victim)* víctima ♦ *vt* engañar.

duplex [ˈdjuːplɛks] *n* dúplex *m*.

duplicate [*n* ˈdjuːplɪkət, *vb* ˈdjuːplɪkeɪt] *n* duplicado ♦ *vt* duplicar; *(photocopy)* fotocopiar; *(repeat)* repetir; **in ~** por duplicado.

durable [ˈdjuərəbl] *adj* duradero.

duration [djuəˈreɪʃən] *n* duración *f*.

duress [djuəˈrɛs] *n*: **under ~** por compulsión.

during [ˈdjuərɪŋ] *prep* durante.

dusk [dʌsk] *n* crepúsculo, anochecer *m*.

dust [dʌst] *n* polvo ♦ *vt* quitar el polvo a, desempolvar; *(cake etc)*: **to ~ with** espolvorear de; ~**bin** *(BRIT)* *n* cubo de la basura *(SP)*, balde *m* *(AM)*; ~**er** *n* paño, trapo; ~**man** *(BRIT)* *n* basurero; ~**y** *adj* polvoriento.

Dutch [dʌtʃ] *adj* holandés/esa ♦ *n (LING)* holandés *m*; **the ~** *npl* los holandeses; **to go ~** *(inf)* pagar cada uno lo suyo; ~**man/woman** *n* holandés/esa *m/f*.

dutiful [ˈdjuːtɪful] *adj* obediente, sumiso.

duty [ˈdjuːtɪ] *n* deber *m*; *(tax)* derechos *mpl* de aduana; **on ~** de servicio; *(at night etc)* de guardia; **off ~** libre (de servicio); ~**-free** *adj* libre de impuestos.

duvet [ˈduːveɪ] *(BRIT)* *n* edredón *m*.

dwarf [dwɔːf] *(pl* **dwarves)** *n* enano/a ♦ *vt* empequeñecer; **dwarves** [dwɔːvz] *npl of* **dwarf**.

dwell [dwel] *(pt, pp* **dwelt)** *vi* morar; ~ **on** *vt fus* explayarse en; ~**ing** *n* vivienda.

dwindle [ˈdwɪndl] *vi* menguar, disminuir.

dye [daɪ] *n* tinte *m* ♦ *vt* teñir.

dying [ˈdaɪɪŋ] *adj* moribundo, agonizante.

dyke [daɪk] *(BRIT)* *n* dique *m*.

dynamic [daɪˈnæmɪk] *adj* dinámico.

dynamite [ˈdaɪnəmaɪt] *n* dinamita.

dynamo [ˈdaɪnəməu] *n* dínamo *f*.

dynasty [ˈdɪnəstɪ] *n* dinastía.

E

E [iː] *n (MUS)* mi *m*.

each [iːtʃ] *adj* cada *inv* ♦ *pron* cada uno; ~ **other** el uno al otro; **they hate ~ other** se odian (entre ellos *or* mutuamente); **they have 2 books ~** tienen 2 libros por persona.

eager [ˈiːɡə*] *adj (keen)* entusiasmado;

to be ~ to do sth tener muchas ganas de hacer algo, impacientarse por hacer algo; **to be ~ for** tener muchas ganas de.

eagle ['i:gl] n águila.

ear [ɪə*] n oreja; oído; (of corn) espiga; **~ache** n dolor m de oídos; **~drum** n tímpano.

earl [ɔ:l] n conde m.

earlier ['ɔ:lɪə*] adj anterior ♦ adv antes.

early ['ɔ:lɪ] adv temprano; (before time) con tiempo, con anticipación ♦ adj temprano; (settlers etc) primitivo; (death, departure) prematuro; (reply) pronto; **to have an ~ night** acostarse temprano; **in the ~ or ~ in the spring/19th century** a principios de primavera/del siglo diecinueve; **~ retirement** n jubilación f anticipada.

earmark ['ɪəmɑ:k] vt: **to ~ (for)** reservar (para), destinar (a).

earn [ɔ:n] vt (salary) percibir; (interest) devengar; (praise) merecerse.

earnest ['ɔ:nɪst] adj (wish) fervoroso; (person) serio, formal; **in ~** en serio.

earnings ['ɔ:nɪŋz] npl (personal) sueldo, ingresos fpl; (company) ganancias fpl.

ear: **~phones** npl auriculares mpl; **~ring** n pendiente m, arete m; **~shot** n: **within ~shot** al alcance del oído.

earth [ɔ:θ] n tierra; (BRIT: ELEC) cable m de toma de tierra ♦ vt (BRIT: ELEC) conectar a tierra; **~enware** n loza (de barro); **~quake** n terremoto; **~y** adj (fig: vulgar) grosero.

ease [i:z] n facilidad f; (comfort) comodidad f ♦ vt (lessen: problem) mitigar; (: pain) aliviar; (: tension) reducir; **to ~ sth in/out** meter/sacar algo con cuidado; **at ~!** (MIL) ¡descansen!; **~ off or up** vi (wind, rain) amainar; (slow down) aflojar la marcha.

easel ['i:zl] n caballete m.

easily ['i:zɪlɪ] adv fácilmente.

east [i:st] n este m ♦ adj del este, oriental; (wind) este ♦ adv al este, hacia el este; **the E~** el Oriente; (POL) los países del Este.

Easter ['i:stə*] n Pascua (de Resurrección); **~ egg** n huevo de Pascua.

easterly ['i:stəlɪ] adj (to the east) al este; (from the east) del este.

eastern ['i:stən] adj del este, oriental; (oriental) oriental; (communist) del este.

East Germany n Alemania Oriental.

eastward(s) ['i:stwəd(z)] adv hacia el este.

easy ['i:zɪ] adj fácil; (simple) sencillo; (comfortable) holgado, cómodo; (relaxed) tranquilo ♦ adv: **to take it or things ~** (not worry) tomarlo con calma; (rest) descansar; **~ chair** n sillón m; **~-going** adj acomodadizo.

eat [i:t] (pt ate, pp eaten) vt comer; **~ into** vt fus corroer; (savings) mermar; **~ away at** vt fus corroer; mermar.

eau de Cologne [əudəkə'ləun] n (agua de) Colonia.

eaves [i:vz] npl alero.

eavesdrop ['i:vzdrɔp] vi: **to ~ (on)** escuchar a escondidas.

ebb [ɛb] n reflujo ♦ vi bajar; (fig: also: ~ away) decaer.

ebony ['ɛbənɪ] n ébano.

EC n abbr (= European Community) CE f.

eccentric [ɪk'sɛntrɪk] adj, n excéntrico/a m/f.

echo ['ɛkəu] (pl ~es) n eco m ♦ vt (sound) repetir ♦ vi resonar, hacer eco.

éclair [ɪ'klɛə*] n pastelillo relleno de crema y con chocolate por encima.

eclipse [ɪ'klɪps] n eclipse m.

ecology [ɪ'kɔlədʒɪ] n ecología.

economic [i:kə'nɔmɪk] adj económico; (business etc) rentable; **~al** adj económico; **~s** n (SCOL) economía ♦ npl (of project etc) rentabilidad f.

economize [ɪ'kɔnəmaɪz] vi economizar, ahorrar.

economy [ɪ'kɔnəmɪ] n economía; **~ class** n (AVIAT) clase f económica; **~ size** n tamaño económico.

ecstasy ['ɛkstəsɪ] n éxtasis m inv; **ecstatic** [-'tætɪk] adj extático.

Ecuador ['ɛkwədɔ:r] n Ecuador m; **E~ian** adj, n ecuatoriano/a m/f.

eczema ['ɛksɪmə] n eczema m.

edge [ɛdʒ] n (of knife etc) filo; (of ob-

ject) borde *m*; (*of lake etc*) orilla ♦ *vt* (*SEWING*) ribetear; **on** ~ (*fig*) = **edgy**; **to** ~ **away from** alejarse poco a poco de; ~**ways** *adv*: **he couldn't get a word in** ~**ways** no pudo meter ni baza.

edgy ['ɛdʒɪ] *adj* nervioso, inquieto.

edible ['ɛdɪbl] *adj* comestible.

Edinburgh ['ɛdɪnbərə] *n* Edimburgo.

edit ['ɛdɪt] *vt* (*be editor of*) dirigir; (*text, report*) corregir, preparar; ~**ion** [ɪ'dɪʃən] *n* edición *f*; ~**or** *n* (*of newspaper*) director(a) *m/f*; (*of column*): **foreign/political** ~ encargado de la sección de extranjero/política; (*of book*) redactor(a) *m/f*; ~**orial** [-'tɔːrɪəl] *adj* editorial ♦ *n* editorial *m*.

educate ['ɛdjukeɪt] *vt* (*gen*) educar; (*instruct*) instruir.

education [ɛdju'keɪʃən] *n* educación *f*; (*schooling*) enseñanza; (*SCOL*) pedagogía; ~**al** *adj* (*policy etc*) educacional; (*experience*) docente; (*toy*) educativo.

EEC *n abbr* (= *European Economic Community*) CEE *f*.

eel [iːl] *n* anguila.

eerie ['ɪərɪ] *adj* misterioso.

effect [ɪ'fɛkt] *n* efecto ♦ *vt* efectuar, llevar a cabo; **to take** ~ (*law*) entrar en vigor *or* vigencia; (*drug*) surtir efecto; **in** ~ en realidad; ~**ive** *adj* eficaz; (*actual*) verdadero; ~**ively** *adv* eficazmente; (*in reality*) efectivamente; ~**iveness** *n* eficacia.

effeminate [ɪ'fɛmɪnɪt] *adj* afeminado.

efficiency [ɪ'fɪʃənsɪ] *n* eficiencia; rendimiento.

efficient [ɪ'fɪʃənt] *adj* eficiente; (*machine*) de buen rendimiento.

effigy ['ɛfɪdʒɪ] *n* efigie *f*.

effort ['ɛfət] *n* esfuerzo; ~**less** *adj* sin ningún esfuerzo; (*style*) natural.

effrontery [ɪ'frʌntərɪ] *n* descaro.

effusive [ɪ'fjuːsɪv] *adj* efusivo.

e.g. *adv abbr* (= *exempli gratia*) p. ej.

egg [ɛg] *n* huevo; **hard-boiled/soft-boiled** ~ huevo duro/pasado por agua; ~ **on** *vt* incitar; ~**cup** *n* huevera; ~ **plant** (*esp US*) *n* berenjena; ~**shell** *n* cáscara de huevo.

ego ['iːgəu] *n* ego; ~**tism** *n* egoísmo; ~**tist** *n* egoísta *m/f*.

Egypt ['iːdʒɪpt] *n* Egipto; ~**ian** [ɪ'dʒɪpʃən] *adj, n* egipcio/a *m/f*.

eiderdown ['aɪdədaun] *n* edredón *m*.

eight [eɪt] *num* ocho; ~**een** *num* diez y ocho, dieciocho; ~**h** *num* octavo; ~**y** *num* ochenta.

Eire ['ɛərə] *n* Eire *m*.

either ['aɪðə*] *adj* cualquiera de los dos; (*both, each*) cada ♦ *pron*: ~ (**of them**) cualquiera (de los dos) ♦ *adv* tampoco; **on** ~ **side** en ambos lados; **I don't like** ~ no me gusta ninguno/a de los/las dos; **no, I don't** ~ no, yo tampoco ♦ *conj*: ~ **yes or no** o sí o no.

eject [ɪ'dʒɛkt] *vt* echar, expulsar; (*tenant*) desahuciar; ~**or seat** *n* asiento proyectable.

eke [iːk]: **to** ~ **out** *vt* hacer que alcance.

elaborate [*adj* ɪ'læbərɪt, *vb* ɪ'læbəreɪt] *adj* (*complex*) complejo ♦ *vt* (*expand*) ampliar; (*refine*) refinar ♦ *vi* explicar con más detalles.

elapse [ɪ'læps] *vi* transcurrir.

elastic [ɪ'læstɪk] *n* elástico ♦ *adj* elástico; (*fig*) flexible; ~ **band** (*BRIT*) *n* gomita.

elated [ɪ'leɪtɪd] *adj*: **to be** ~ regocijarse.

elbow ['ɛlbəu] *n* codo.

elder ['ɛldə*] *adj* mayor ♦ *n* (*tree*) saúco; (*person*) mayor; ~**ly** *adj* de edad, mayor ♦ *npl*: **the** ~**ly** los mayores.

eldest ['ɛldɪst] *adj, n* el/la mayor.

elect [ɪ'lɛkt] *vt* elegir ♦ *adj*: **the president** ~ el presidente electo; **to** ~ **to do** optar por hacer; ~**ion** [ɪ'lɛkʃən] *n* elección *f*; ~**ioneering** [ɪlɛkʃə'nɪərɪŋ] *n* campaña electoral; ~**or** *n* elector(a) *m/f*; ~**oral** *adj* electoral; ~**orate** *n* electorado.

electric [ɪ'lɛktrɪk] *adj* eléctrico; ~**al** *adj* eléctrico; ~ **blanket** *n* manta eléctrica; ~ **fire** *n* estufa eléctrica.

electrician [ɪlɛk'trɪʃən] *n* electricista *m/f*.

electricity [ɪlɛk'trɪsɪtɪ] *n* electricidad *f*.

electrify [ɪ'lɛktrɪfaɪ] *vt* (*RAIL*) electrificar; (*fig: audience*) electrizar.

electron [ɪ'lɛktrɔn] *n* electrón *m*.

electronic [ɪlɛk'trɔnɪk] *adj* electrónico;

~ **mail** n correo electrónico; ~**s** n electrónica.

elegant ['ɛlɪgənt] adj elegante.

element ['ɛlɪmənt] n elemento; (of kettle etc) resistencia; ~**ary** [-'mɛntərɪ] adj elemental; (primitive) rudimentario; (school) primario.

elephant ['ɛlɪfənt] n elefante m.

elevation [ɛlɪ'veɪʃən] n elevación f; (height) altura.

elevator ['ɛlɪveɪtə*] n (US) ascensor m; (in warehouse etc) montacargas m inv.

eleven [ɪ'lɛvn] num once; ~**ses** (BRIT) npl café m de las once; ~**th** num undécimo.

elf [ɛlf] (pl **elves**) n duende m.

elicit [ɪ'lɪsɪt] vt: **to ~ (from)** sacar (de).

eligible ['ɛlɪdʒəbl] adj: **an ~ young man/woman** un buen partido; **to be ~ for sth** llenar los requisitos para algo.

eliminate [ɪ'lɪmɪneɪt] vt (eradicate) suprimir; (opponent) eliminar.

elm [ɛlm] n olmo.

elongated ['iːlɔŋgeɪtɪd] adj alargado.

elope [ɪ'ləup] vi fugarse (para casarse); ~**ment** n fuga.

eloquent ['ɛləkwənt] adj elocuente.

else [ɛls] adv: **something ~** otra cosa; **somewhere ~** en otra parte; **everywhere ~** en todas partes menos aquí; **where ~?** ¿dónde más?, ¿en qué otra parte?; **there was little ~ to do** apenas quedaba otra cosa que hacer; **nobody ~ spoke** no habló nadie más; ~**where** adv (be) en otra parte; (go) a otra parte.

elucidate [ɪ'luːsɪdeɪt] vt aclarar.

elude [ɪ'luːd] vt (subj: idea etc) escaparse a; (capture) esquivar.

elusive [ɪ'luːsɪv] adj esquivo; (quality) difícil de encontrar.

emaciated [ɪ'meɪsɪeɪtɪd] adj demacrado.

emanate ['ɛməneɪt] vi: **to ~ from** (idea) surgir de; (light, sound) despedirse.

emancipate [ɪ'mænsɪpeɪt] vt emancipar.

embankment [ɪm'bæŋkmənt] n terraplén m.

embargo [ɪm'bɑːgəu] (pl ~**es**) n prohibición f, embargo.

embark [ɪm'bɑːk] vi embarcarse ♦ vt embarcar; **to ~ on** (journey) emprender; (course of action) lanzarse a; ~**ation** [ɛmbɑː'keɪʃən] n (people) embarco; (goods) embarque m.

embarrass [ɪm'bærəs] vt avergonzar; (government etc) dejar en mal lugar; ~**ed** adj (laugh, silence) embarazoso; ~**ing** adj (situation) violento; (question) embarazoso; ~**ment** n (shame) vergüenza; (problem): **to be an ~ment for sb** poner en un aprieto a uno.

embassy ['ɛmbəsɪ] n embajada.

embedded [ɪm'bɛdɪd] adj (object) empotrado; (thorn etc) clavado.

embellish [ɪm'bɛlɪʃ] vt embellecer; (story) adornar.

embers ['ɛmbəz] npl rescoldo, ascua.

embezzle [ɪm'bɛzl] vt desfalcar, malversar.

embitter [ɪm'bɪtə*] vt (fig: sour) amargar.

embody [ɪm'bɔdɪ] vt (spirit) encarnar; (include) incorporar.

embossed [ɪm'bɔst] adj realzado.

embrace [ɪm'breɪs] vt abrazar, dar un abrazo a; (include) abarcar ♦ vi abrazarse ♦ n abrazo.

embroider [ɪm'brɔɪdə*] vt bordar; ~**y** n bordado.

embryo ['ɛmbrɪəu] n embrión m.

emerald ['ɛmərəld] n esmeralda.

emerge [ɪ'məːdʒ] vi salir; (arise) surgir.

emergency [ɪ'məːdʒənsɪ] n crisis f inv; **in an ~** en caso de urgencia; **state of ~** estado de emergencia; ~ **cord** (US) n timbre m de alarma; ~ **exit** n salida de emergencia; ~ **landing** n aterrizaje m forzoso; ~ **services** npl (fire, police, ambulance) servicios mpl de urgencia or emergencia.

emergent [ɪ'məːdʒənt] adj (nation) recién independizado; (group) recién aparecido.

emery board ['ɛmərɪ-] n lima de uñas.

emigrant ['ɛmɪgrənt] n emigrante m/f.

emigrate ['ɛmɪgreɪt] vi emigrar.

emit [ɪ'mɪt] vt emitir; (smoke) arrojar; (smell) despedir; (sound) producir.

emotion [ɪ'məuʃən] n emoción f; ~**al** adj (needs) emocional; (person) sentimental; (*scene*) conmovedor(a), emocionante; (*speech*) emocionado.

emperor ['ɛmpərə*] *n* emperador *m*.

emphases ['ɛmfəsiːz] *npl of* **emphasis**.

emphasis ['ɛmfəsis] (*pl* -ses) *n* énfasis *m inv*.

emphasize ['ɛmfəsaiz] *vt* (*word, point*) subrayar, recalcar; (*feature*) hacer resaltar.

emphatic [ɛm'fætik] *adj* (*reply*) categórico; (*person*) insistente; ~**ally** *adv* con énfasis; (*certainly*) sin ningún género de dudas.

empire ['ɛmpaiə*] *n* (*also fig*) imperio.

employ [im'plɔi] *vt* emplear; ~**ee** [-'iː] *n* empleado/a; ~**er** *n* patrón/ona *m/f*; empresario; ~**ment** *n* (*work*) trabajo; ~**ment agency** *n* agencia de colocaciones.

empower [im'pauə*] *vt*: **to ~ sb to do sth** autorizar a uno para hacer algo.

empress ['ɛmpris] *n* emperatriz *f*.

emptiness ['ɛmptinis] *n* vacío; (*of life etc*) vaciedad *f*.

empty ['ɛmpti] *adj* vacío; (*place*) desierto; (*house*) desocupado; (*threat*) vano ♦ *vt* vaciar; (*place*) dejar vacío ♦ *vi* vaciarse; (*house etc*) quedar desocupado; ~-**handed** *adj* con las manos vacías.

emulate ['ɛmjuleit] *vt* emular.

emulsion [i'mʌlʃən] *n* emulsión *f*; (*also*: ~ **paint**) pintura emulsión.

enable [i'neibl] *vt*: **to ~ sb to do sth** permitir a uno hacer algo.

enact [in'ækt] *vt* (*law*) promulgar; (*play*) representar; (*role*) hacer.

enamel [i'næməl] *n* esmalte *m*; (*also*: ~ **paint**) pintura esmaltada.

enamoured [i'næməd] *adj*: **to be ~ of** (*person*) estar enamorado de; (*activity etc*) tener gran afición a; (*idea*) aferrarse a.

encased [in'keist] *adj*: ~ **in** (*covered*) revestido de.

enchant [in'tʃɑːnt] *vt* encantar; ~**ing** *adj* encantador(a).

encircle [in'sɜːkl] *vt* rodear.

encl. *abbr* (= *enclosed*) adj.

enclose [in'kləuz] *vt* (*land*) cercar; (*let-*ter etc) adjuntar; **please find** ~**d** le mandamos adjunto.

enclosure [in'kləuʒə*] *n* cercado, recinto.

encompass [in'kʌmpəs] *vt* abarcar.

encore [ɔŋ'kɔː*] *excl* ¡otra!, ¡bis! ♦ *n* bis *m*.

encounter [in'kauntə*] *n* encuentro ♦ *vt* encontrar, encontrarse con; (*difficulty*) tropezar con.

encourage [in'kʌridʒ] *vt* alentar, animar; (*activity*) fomentar; (*growth*) estimular; ~**ment** *n* estímulo; (*of industry*) fomento.

encroach [in'krəutʃ] *vi*: **to ~ (up)on** invadir; (*rights*) usurpar; (*time*) adueñarse de.

encrusted [in'krʌstəd] *adj*: ~ **with** incrustado de.

encumber [in'kʌmbə*] *vt*: **to be ~ed with** (*baggage etc, debts*) estar cargado de.

encyclop(a)edia [ɛnsaikləu'piːdiə] *n* enciclopedia.

end [ɛnd] *n* (*gen, also aim*) fin *m*; (*of table*) extremo; (*of street*) final *m*; (*SPORT*) lado ♦ *vt* terminar, acabar; (*also*: **bring to an ~**, **put an ~ to**) acabar con ♦ *vi* terminar, acabar; **in the ~** al fin; **on ~** (*object*) de punta, de cabeza; **to stand on ~** (*hair*) erizarse; **for hours on ~** hora tras hora; ~ **up** *vi*: **to ~ up in** terminar en; (*place*) ir a parar en.

endanger [in'deindʒə*] *vt* poner en peligro.

endearing [in'diəriŋ] *adj* simpático, atractivo.

endeavour [in'dɛvə*] (*US* **endeavor**) *n* esfuerzo; (*attempt*) tentativa ♦ *vi*: **to ~ to do** esforzarse por hacer; (*try*) procurar hacer.

ending ['ɛndiŋ] *n* (*of book*) desenlace *m*; (*LING*) terminación *f*.

endive ['ɛndaiv] *n* (*chicory*) endibia; (*curly*) escarola.

endless ['ɛndlis] *adj* interminable, inacabable.

endorse [in'dɔːs] *vt* (*cheque*) endosar; (*approve*) aprobar; ~**ment** *n* (*on driv-*

ing licence) nota de inhabilitación.

endow [ɪn'dau] *vt* (*provide with money*): **to ~ (with)** dotar (de); **to be ~ed with** (*fig*) estar dotado de.

endurance [ɪn'djuərəns] *n* resistencia.

endure [ɪn'djuə*] *vt* (*bear*) aguantar, soportar ♦ *vi* (*last*) durar.

enemy ['ɛnəmɪ] *adj*, *n* enemigo/a *m/f*.

energetic [ɛnə'dʒɛtɪk] *adj* enérgico.

energy ['ɛnədʒɪ] *n* energía.

enforce [ɪn'fɔːs] *vt* (*LAW*) hacer cumplir.

engage [ɪn'geɪdʒ] *vt* (*attention*) llamar; (*interest*) ocupar; (*in conversation*) abordar; (*worker*) contratar; (*AUT*): **to ~ the clutch** embragar ♦ *vi* (*TECH*) engranar; **to ~ in** dedicarse a, ocuparse en; **~d** *adj* (*BRIT: busy, in use*) ocupado; (*betrothed*) prometido; **to get ~d** prometerse; **~d tone** (*BRIT*) *n* (*TEL*) señal *f* de comunicando; **~ment** *n* (*appointment*) compromiso, cita; (*booking*) contratación *f*; (*to marry*) compromiso; (*period*) noviazgo; **~ment ring** *n* anillo de prometida.

engaging [ɪn'geɪdʒɪŋ] *adj* atractivo.

engender [ɪn'dʒɛndə*] *vt* engendrar.

engine ['ɛndʒɪn] *n* (*AUT*) motor *m*; (*RAIL*) locomotora; **~ driver** *n* maquinista *m/f*.

engineer [ɛndʒɪ'nɪə*] *n* ingeniero; (*BRIT: for repairs*) mecánico; (*on ship, US: RAIL*) maquinista *m*; **~ing** *n* ingeniería.

England ['ɪŋglənd] *n* Inglaterra.

English ['ɪŋglɪʃ] *adj* inglés/esa ♦ *n* (*LING*) inglés *m*; **the ~** *npl* los ingleses *mpl*; **the ~ Channel** *n* (el Canal de) la Mancha; **~man/woman** *n* inglés/esa *m/f*.

engraving [ɪn'greɪvɪŋ] *n* grabado.

engrossed [ɪn'grəust] *adj*: **~ in** absorto en.

engulf [ɪn'gʌlf] *vt* (*subj: water*) sumergir, hundir; (: *fire*) prender; (: *fear*) apoderarse de.

enhance [ɪn'hɑːns] *vt* (*gen*) aumentar; (*beauty*) realzar.

enjoy [ɪn'dʒɔɪ] *vt* (*health, fortune*) disfrutar de, gozar de; (*like*) gustarle a

uno; **to ~ o.s.** divertirse; **~able** *adj* agradable; (*amusing*) divertido; **~ment** *n* (*joy*) placer *m*; (*activity*) diversión *f*.

enlarge [ɪn'lɑːdʒ] *vt* aumentar; (*broaden*) extender; (*PHOT*) ampliar ♦ *vi*: **to ~ on** (*subject*) tratar con más detalles; **~ment** *n* (*PHOT*) ampliación *f*.

enlighten [ɪn'laɪtn] *vt* (*inform*) informar; **~ed** *adj* comprensivo; **the E~ment** *n* (*HISTORY*) ≈ la Ilustración, ≈ el Siglo de las Luces.

enlist [ɪn'lɪst] *vt* alistar; (*support*) conseguir ♦ *vi* alistarse.

enmity ['ɛnmɪtɪ] *n* enemistad *f*.

enormous [ɪ'nɔːməs] *adj* enorme.

enough [ɪ'nʌf] *adj*: **~ time/books** bastante tiempo/bastantes libros ♦ *pron* bastante(s) ♦ *adv*: **big ~** bastante grande; **he has not worked ~** no ha trabajado bastante; **have you got ~?** ¿tiene usted bastante(s)?; **~ to eat** (lo) suficiente *or* (lo) bastante para comer; **~!** ¡basta ya!; **that's ~, thanks** con eso basta, gracias; **I've had ~ of him** estoy harto de él; **... which, funnily *or* oddly ~ ...** ... lo que, por extraño que parezca....

enquire [ɪn'kwaɪə*] *vt*, *vi* = **inquire**.

enrage [ɪn'reɪdʒ] *vt* enfurecer.

enrich [ɪn'rɪtʃ] *vt* enriquecer.

enrol [ɪn'rəul] *vt* (*members*) inscribir; (*SCOL*) matricular ♦ *vi* inscribirse; matricularse; **~ment** *n* inscripción *f*; matriculación *f*.

en route [ɔn'ruːt] *adv* durante el viaje.

ensue [ɪn'sjuː] *vi* seguirse; (*result*) resultar.

ensure [ɪn'ʃuə*] *vt* asegurar.

entail [ɪn'teɪl] *vt* suponer.

entangled [ɪn'tæŋgld] *adj*: **to become ~ (in)** quedarse enredado (en) *or* enmarañado (en).

enter ['ɛntə*] *vt* (*room*) entrar en; (*club*) hacerse socio de; (*army*) alistarse en; (*sb for a competition*) inscribir; (*write down*) anotar, apuntar; (*COMPUT*) meter ♦ *vi* entrar; **~ for** *vt fus* presentarse para; **~ into** *vt fus* (*discussion etc*) entablar; (*agreement*) llegar a, firmar.

enterprise ['ɛntəpraɪz] *n* empresa; (*spirit*) iniciativa; **free** ~ la libre empresa; **private** ~ la iniciativa privada; **enterprising** *adj* emprendedor(a).

entertain [ɛntə'teɪn] *vt* (*amuse*) divertir; (*invite: guest*) invitar (a casa); (*idea*) abrigar; ~**er** *n* artista *m/f*; ~**ing** *adj* divertido, entretenido; ~**ment** *n* (*amusement*) diversión *f*; (*show*) espectáculo.

enthralled [ɪn'θrɔːld] *adj* encantado.

enthusiasm [ɪn'θuːzɪæzəm] *n* entusiasmo.

enthusiast [ɪn'θuːzɪæst] *n* entusiasta *m/f*; ~**ic** [-'æstɪk] *adj* entusiasta; **to be** ~**ic about** entusiasmarse por.

entice [ɪn'taɪs] *vt* tentar.

entire [ɪn'taɪə*] *adj* entero; ~**ly** *adv* totalmente; ~**ty** [ɪn'taɪərətɪ] *n*: **in its** ~**ty** en su totalidad.

entitle [ɪn'taɪtl] *vt*: **to** ~ **sb to sth** dar a uno derecho a algo; ~**d** *adj* (*book*) titulado; **to be** ~**d to do** tener derecho a hacer.

entourage [ɔntu'rɑːʒ] *n* séquito.

entrails ['ɛntreɪlz] *npl* entrañas *fpl*.

entrance [*n* 'ɛntrəns, *vb* ɪn'trɑːns] *n* entrada ♦ *vt* encantar, hechizar; **to gain** ~ **to** (*university etc*) ingresar en; ~ **examination** *n* examen *m* de ingreso; ~ **fee** *n* cuota; ~ **ramp** (*US*) *n* (*AUT*) rampa de acceso.

entrant ['ɛntrənt] *n* (*in race, competition*) participante *m/f*; (*in examination*) candidato/a.

entreat [ɛn'triːt] *vt* rogar, suplicar.

entrenched [ɛn'trɛntʃd] *adj* inamovible.

entrepreneur [ɔntrəprə'nəː] *n* empresario.

entrust [ɪn'trʌst] *vt*: **to** ~ **sth to sb** confiar algo a uno.

entry ['ɛntrɪ] *n* entrada; (*in competition*) participación *f*; (*in register*) apunte *m*; (*in account*) partida; (*in reference book*) artículo; "**no** ~" "prohibido el paso"; (*AUT*) "dirección prohibida"; ~ **form** *n* hoja de inscripción; ~ **phone** *n* portero automático.

enunciate [ɪ'nʌnsɪeɪt] *vt* pronunciar;

(*principle etc*) enunciar.

envelop [ɪn'vɛləp] *vt* envolver.

envelope ['ɛnvələup] *n* sobre *m*.

envious ['ɛnvɪəs] *adj* envidioso; (*look*) de envidia.

environment [ɪn'vaɪərnmənt] *n* (*surroundings*) entorno; (*natural world*): **the** ~ el medio ambiente; ~**al** [-'mɛntl] *adj* ambiental; medioambiental.

envisage [ɪn'vɪzɪdʒ] *vt* prever.

envoy ['ɛnvɔɪ] *n* enviado.

envy ['ɛnvɪ] *n* envidia ♦ *vt* tener envidia a; **to** ~ **sb sth** envidiar algo a uno.

epic ['ɛpɪk] *n* épica ♦ *adj* épico.

epidemic [ɛpɪ'dɛmɪk] *n* epidemia.

epilepsy ['ɛpɪlɛpsɪ] *n* epilepsia.

episode ['ɛpɪsəud] *n* episodio.

epistle [ɪ'pɪsl] *n* epístola.

epitomize [ɪ'pɪtəmaɪz] *vt* epitomar, resumir.

equable ['ɛkwəbl] *adj* (*climate*) templado; (*character*) tranquilo, afable.

equal ['iːkwl] *adj* igual; (*treatment*) equitativo ♦ *n* igual *m/f* ♦ *vt* ser igual a; (*fig*) igualar; **to be** ~ **to** (*task*) estar a la altura de; ~**ity** [iː'kwɔlɪtɪ] *n* igualdad *f*; ~**ize** *vi* (*SPORT*) empatar; ~**ly** *adv* igualmente; (*share etc*) a partes iguales.

equate [ɪ'kweɪt] *vt*: **to** ~ **sth with** equiparar algo con; **equation** [ɪ'kweɪʒən] *n* (*MATH*) ecuación *f*.

equator [ɪ'kweɪtə*] *n* ecuador *m*.

equilibrium [iːkwɪ'lɪbrɪəm] *n* equilibrio.

equip [ɪ'kwɪp] *vt* equipar; (*person*) proveer; **to be well** ~**ped** estar bien equipado; ~**ment** *n* equipo; (*tools*) avíos *mpl*.

equitable ['ɛkwɪtəbl] *adj* equitativo.

equities ['ɛkwɪtɪz] (*BRIT*) *npl* (*COMM*) derechos *mpl* sobre *or* en el activo.

equivalent [ɪ'kwɪvəlnt] *adj*: ~ **(to)** equivalente (a) ♦ *n* equivalente *m*.

equivocal [ɪ'kwɪvəkl] *adj* (*ambiguous*) ambiguo; (*open to suspicion*) equívoco.

era ['ɪərə] *n* era, época.

eradicate [ɪ'rædɪkeɪt] *vt* erradicar.

erase [ɪ'reɪz] *vt* borrar; ~**r** *n* goma de borrar.

erect [ɪ'rɛkt] *adj* erguido ♦ *vt* erigir, levantar; (*assemble*) montar; **~ion** [-ʃən] *n* construcción *f*; (*assembly*) montaje *m*; (*PHYSIOL*) erección *f*.

ermine [ˈəːmɪn] *n* armiño.

erode [ɪˈrəud] *vt* (*GEO*) erosionar; (*metal*) corroer, desgastar; (*fig*) desgastar.

erotic [ɪˈrɔtɪk] *adj* erótico.

err [əː*] *vi* (*formal*) equivocarse.

errand [ˈɛrnd] *n* recado (*SP*), mandado (*AM*).

erratic [ɪˈrætɪk] *adj* desigual, poco uniforme.

erroneous [ɪˈrəunɪəs] *adj* erróneo.

error [ˈɛrə*] *n* error *m*, equivocación *f*.

erupt [ɪˈrʌpt] *vi* entrar en erupción; (*fig*) estallar; **~ion** [ɪˈrʌpʃən] *n* erupción *f*; (*of war*) estallido.

escalate [ˈɛskəleɪt] *vi* extenderse, intensificarse.

escalator [ˈɛskəleɪtə*] *n* escalera móvil.

escapade [ɛskəˈpeɪd] *n* travesura.

escape [ɪˈskeɪp] *n* fuga ♦ *vi* escaparse; (*flee*) huir, evadirse; (*leak*) fugarse ♦ *vt* (*responsibility etc*) evitar, eludir; (*consequences*) escapar a; (*elude*): his name ~s me no me sale su nombre; to ~ **from** (*place*) escaparse de; (*person*) escaparse a.

escort [*n* ˈɛskɔːt, *vb* ɪˈskɔːt] *n* acompañante *m/f*; (*MIL*) escolta ♦ *vt* acompañar.

Eskimo [ˈɛskɪməu] *n* esquimal *m/f*.

especially [ɪˈspɛʃlɪ] *adv* (*above all*) sobre todo; (*particularly*) en particular, especialmente.

espionage [ˈɛspɪənɑːʒ] *n* espionaje *m*.

esplanade [ɛspləˈneɪd] *n* (*by sea*) paseo marítimo.

espouse [ɪˈspauz] *vt* adherirse a.

Esquire [ɪˈskwaɪə*] (*abbr* **Esq.**) *n*: J. Brown, ~ Sr. D. J. Brown.

essay [ˈɛseɪ] *n* (*LITERATURE*) ensayo; (*SCOL*: *short*) redacción *f*; (: *long*) trabajo.

essence [ˈɛsns] *n* esencia.

essential [ɪˈsɛnʃl] *adj* (*necessary*) imprescindible; (*basic*) esencial; **~s** *npl* lo imprescindible, lo esencial; **~ly** *adv* esencialmente.

establish [ɪˈstæblɪʃ] *vt* establecer;

(*prove*) demostrar; (*relations*) entablar; (*reputation*) ganarse; **~ed** *adj* (*business*) conocido; (*practice*) arraigado; **~ment** *n* establecimiento; **the E~ment** la clase dirigente.

estate [ɪˈsteɪt] *n* (*land*) finca, hacienda; (*inheritance*) herencia; (*BRIT*: *also*: housing ~) urbanización *f*; ~ **agent** (*BRIT*) *n* agente *m/f* inmobiliario/a; ~ **car** (*BRIT*) *n* furgoneta.

esteem [ɪˈstiːm] *n*: to hold sb in high ~ estimar en mucho a uno.

esthetic [ɪsˈθɛtɪk] (*US*) *adj* = aesthetic.

estimate [*n* ˈɛstɪmət, *vb* ˈɛstɪmeɪt] *n* estimación *f*, apreciación *f*; (*assessment*) tasa, cálculo; (*COMM*) presupuesto ♦ *vt* estimar, tasar; calcular; **estimation** [-ˈmeɪʃən] *n* opinión *f*, juicio; cálculo.

estranged [ɪˈstreɪndʒd] *adj* separado.

estuary [ˈɛstjuərɪ] *n* estuario, ría.

etc *abbr* (= *et cetera*) etc.

etching [ˈɛtʃɪŋ] *n* aguafuerte *m* or *f*.

eternal [ɪˈtəːnl] *adj* eterno.

eternity [ɪˈtəːnɪtɪ] *n* eternidad *f*.

ethical [ˈɛθɪkl] *adj* ético.

ethics [ˈɛθɪks] *n* ética ♦ *npl* moralidad *f*.

Ethiopia [iːθɪˈəupɪə] *n* Etiopia.

ethnic [ˈɛθnɪk] *adj* étnico.

ethos [ˈiːθɔs] *n* genio, carácter *m*.

etiquette [ˈɛtɪkɛt] *n* etiqueta.

Eurocheque [ˈjuərəutʃɛk] *n* Eurocheque *m*.

Europe [ˈjuərəp] *n* Europa; **~an** [-ˈpiːən] *adj*, *n* europeo/a *m/f*.

evacuate [ɪˈvækjueɪt] *vt* (*people*) evacuar; (*place*) desocupar; **evacuation** [-ˈeɪʃən] *n* evacuación *f*.

evade [ɪˈveɪd] *vt* evadir, eludir.

evaluate [ɪˈvæljueɪt] *vt* evaluar.

evaporate [ɪˈvæpəreɪt] *vi* evaporarse; (*fig*) desvanecerse; **~d milk** *n* leche *f* evaporada.

evasion [ɪˈveɪʒən] *n* evasión *f*.

eve [iːv] *n*: on the ~ of en vísperas de.

even [ˈiːvn] *adj* (*level*) llano; (*smooth*) liso; (*speed, temperature*) uniforme; (*number*) par ♦ *adv* hasta, incluso; (*introducing a comparison*) aún, todavía; ~ **if**, ~ **though** aunque + *sub*; ~ **more** aun más; ~ **so** aun así; **not** ~ ni siquiera; ~ **he was there** hasta él estuvo allí; ~ **on Sundays** incluso los domingos; **to get** ~ **with sb** ajustar cuentas con uno; ~ **out** *vi* nivelarse.

evening ['iːvnɪŋ] *n* tarde *f*; (*late*) noche *f*; **in the** ~ por la tarde; ~ **class** *n* clase *f* nocturna; ~ **dress** *n* (*no pl*: *formal clothes*) traje *m* de etiqueta; (*woman's*) traje *m* de noche.

event [ɪ'vent] *n* suceso, acontecimiento; (*SPORT*) prueba; **in the** ~ **of** en caso de; ~**ful** *adj* (*life*) activo; (*day*) ajetreado.

eventual [ɪ'ventʃuəl] *adj* final; ~**ity** [-'ælɪtɪ] *n* eventualidad *f*; ~**ly** *adv* (*finally*) finalmente; (*in time*) con el tiempo.

ever ['evə*] *adv* (*at any time*) nunca, jamás; (*at all times*) siempre; (*in question*) **why** ~ **not?** ¿y por qué no?; **the best** ~ lo nunca visto; **have you** ~ **seen it?** ¿lo ha visto usted alguna vez?; **better than** ~ mejor que nunca; ~ **since** *adv* desde entonces ♦ *conj* después de que; ~**green** *n* árbol *m* de hoja perenne; ~**lasting** *adj* eterno, perpetuo.

───────────
KEYWORD
───────────

every ['evrɪ] *adj* **1** (*each*) cada; ~ **one of them** (*persons*) todos ellos/as; (*objects*) cada uno de ellos/as; ~ **shop in the town was closed** todas las tiendas de la ciudad estaban cerradas

2 (*all possible*) todo/a; **I gave you** ~ **assistance** te di toda la ayuda posible; **I have** ~ **confidence in him** tiene toda mi confianza; **we wish you** ~ **success** te deseamos toda suerte de éxitos

3 (*showing recurrence*) todo/a; ~ **day/week** todos los días/todas las semanas; ~ **other car had been broken into** habían forzado uno de cada dos coches; **she visits me** ~ **other/third day** me visita cada dos/tres días; ~ **now and then** de vez en cuando.

───────────

everybody ['evrɪbɔdɪ] *pron* = **everyone**.

everyday ['evrɪdeɪ] *adj* (*daily*) cotidiano, de todos los días; (*usual*) acostumbrado.

everyone ['evrɪwʌn] *pron* todos/as, todo

el mundo.

everything ['evrɪθɪŋ] *pron* todo; **this shop sells** ~ esta tienda vende de todo.

everywhere ['evrɪweə*] *adv*: **I've been looking for you** ~ te he estado buscando por todas partes; ~ **you go you meet ...** en todas partes encuentras ....

evict [ɪ'vɪkt] *vt* desahuciar; ~**ion** [ɪ'vɪkʃən] *n* desahucio.

evidence ['evɪdəns] *n* (*proof*) prueba; (*of witness*) testimonio; (*sign*) indicios *mpl*; **to give** ~ prestar declaración, dar testimonio.

evident ['evɪdənt] *adj* evidente, manifiesto; ~**ly** *adv* por lo visto.

evil ['iːvl] *adj* malo; (*influence*) funesto ♦ *n* mal *m*.

evocative [ɪ'vɔkətɪv] *adj* sugestivo, evocador(a).

evoke [ɪ'vəuk] *vt* evocar.

evolution [iːvə'luːʃən] *n* evolución *f*.

evolve [ɪ'vɔlv] *vt* desarrollar ♦ *vi* evolucionar, desarrollarse.

ewe [juː] *n* oveja.

ex- [eks] *prefix* ex.

exacerbate [ek'sæsəbeɪt] *vt* exacerbar.

exact [ɪg'zækt] *adj* exacto; (*person*) meticuloso ♦ *vt*: **to** ~ **sth (from)** exigir algo (de); ~**ing** *adj* exigente; (*conditions*) arduo; ~**ly** *adv* exactamente; (*indicating agreement*) exacto.

exaggerate [ɪg'zædʒəreɪt] *vt, vi* exagerar; **exaggeration** [-'reɪʃən] *n* exageración *f*.

exalted [ɪg'zɔːltɪd] *adj* eminente.

exam [ɪg'zæm] *n abbr* (*SCOL*) = **examination**.

examination [ɪgzæmɪ'neɪʃən] *n* examen *m*; (*MED*) reconocimiento.

examine [ɪg'zæmɪn] *vt* examinar; (*inspect*) inspeccionar, escudriñar; (*MED*) reconocer; ~**r** *n* examinador(a) *m/f*.

example [ɪg'zɑːmpl] *n* ejemplo; **for** ~ por ejemplo.

exasperate [ɪg'zɑːspəreɪt] *vt* exasperar, irritar; **exasperation** [-ʃən] *n* exasperación *f*, irritación *f*.

excavate ['ekskəveɪt] *vt* excavar.

exceed [ɪk'siːd] *vt* (*amount*) exceder; (*number*) pasar de; (*speed limit*) sobrepasar; (*powers*) excederse en; (*hopes*) superar; ~**ingly** *adv* sumamente, sobremanera.

excel [ɪkˈsɛl] *vi*: to ~ (at/in) sobresalir (en).

excellent [ˈɛksələnt] *adj* excelente.

except [ɪkˈsɛpt] *prep* (*also*: ~ *for*, ~*ing*) excepto, salvo ♦ *vt* exceptuar, excluir; ~ **if/when** excepto si/cuando; ~ **that** salvo que; ~**ion** [ɪkˈsɛpʃən] *n* excepción *f*; **to take** ~**ion to** ofenderse por; ~**ional** [ɪkˈsɛpʃənl] *adj* excepcional.

excerpt [ˈɛksəːpt] *n* extracto.

excess [ɪkˈsɛs] *n* exceso; ~**es** *npl* (*of cruelty etc*) atrocidades *fpl*; ~ **baggage** *n* exceso de equipaje; ~ **fare** *n* suplemento; ~**ive** *adj* excesivo.

exchange [ɪksˈtʃeɪndʒ] *n* intercambio; (*conversation*) diálogo; (*also: telephone* ~) central *f* (telefónica) ♦ *vt* : to ~ (**for**) cambiar (por); ~ **rate** *n* tipo de cambio.

exchequer [ɪksˈtʃɛkə*] (*BRIT*) *n*: **the** ~ la Hacienda del Fisco.

excise [ˈɛksaɪz] *n* impuestos *mpl* sobre el alcohol y el tabaco.

excite [ɪkˈsaɪt] *vt* (*stimulate*) estimular; (*arouse*) excitar; ~**d** *adj*: **to get** ~**d** emocionarse; ~**ment** *n* (*agitation*) excitación *f*; (*exhilaration*) emoción *f*; ~**citing** *adj* emocionante.

exclaim [ɪkˈskleɪm] *vi* exclamar; **exclamation** [ɛkskləˈmeɪʃən] *n* exclamación *f*; **exclamation mark** *n* punto de admiración.

exclude [ɪkˈskluːd] *vt* excluir; exceptuar.

exclusive [ɪkˈskluːsɪv] *adj* exclusivo; (*club, district*) selecto; ~ **of tax** excluyendo impuestos; ~**ly** *adv* únicamente.

excommunicate [ɛkskəˈmjuːnɪkeɪt] *vt* excomulgar.

excruciating [ɪkˈskruːʃɪeɪtɪŋ] *adj* (*pain*) agudísimo, atroz; (*noise, embarrassment*) horrible.

excursion [ɪkˈskəːʃən] *n* (*tourist* ~) excursión *f*.

excuse [*n* ɪkˈskjuːs, *vb* ɪkˈskjuːz] *n* disculpa, excusa; (*pretext*) pretexto ♦ *vt* (*justify*) justificar; (*forgive*) disculpar,

perdonar; **to** ~ **sb from doing sth** dispensar a uno de hacer algo; ~ **me!** (*attracting attention*) ¡por favor!; (*apologizing*) ¡perdón!; **if you will** ~ **me** con su permiso.

ex-directory [ˈɛksdɪˈrɛktərɪ] (*BRIT*) *adj* que no consta en la guía.

execute [ˈɛksɪkjuːt] *vt* (*plan*) realizar; (*order*) cumplir; (*person*) ajusticiar, ejecutar; **execution** [-ˈkjuːʃən] *n* realización *f*; cumplimiento; ejecución *f*; **executioner** [-ˈkjuːʃənə*] *n* verdugo.

executive [ɪgˈzɛkjutɪv] *n* (*person, committee*) ejecutivo; (*POL: committee*) poder *m* ejecutivo ♦ *adj* ejecutivo.

executor [ɪgˈzɛkjutə*] *n* albacea *m*, testamentario.

exemplify [ɪgˈzɛmplɪfaɪ] *vt* ejemplificar; (*illustrate*) ilustrar.

exempt [ɪgˈzɛmpt] *adj*: ~ **from** exento de ♦ *vt*: **to** ~ **sb from** eximir a uno de; ~**ion** [-ʃən] *n* exención *f*.

exercise [ˈɛksəsaɪz] *n* ejercicio ♦ *vt* (*patience*) usar de; (*right*) valerse de; (*dog*) llevar de paseo; (*mind*) preocupar ♦ *vi* (*also: to take* ~) hacer ejercicio(s); ~ **book** *n* cuaderno.

exert [ɪgˈzəːt] *vt* ejercer; **to** ~ **o.s.** esforzarse; ~**ion** [-ʃən] *n* esfuerzo.

exhale [ɛksˈheɪl] *vt* despedir ♦ *vi* exhalar.

exhaust [ɪgˈzɔːst] *n* (*AUT: also*: ~ *pipe*) escape *m*; (: *fumes*) gases *mpl* de escape ♦ *vt* agotar; ~**ed** *adj* agotado; ~**ion** [ɪgˈzɔːstʃən] *n* agotamiento; **nervous** ~**ion** postración *f* nerviosa; ~**ive** *adj* exhaustivo.

exhibit [ɪgˈzɪbɪt] *n* (*ART*) obra expuesta; (*LAW*) objeto expuesto ♦ *vt* (*show: emotions*) manifestar; (: *courage, skill*) demostrar; (*paintings*) exponer; ~**ion** [ɛksɪˈbɪʃən] *n* exposición *f*; (*of talent etc*) demostración *f*.

exhilarating [ɪgˈzɪləreɪtɪŋ] *adj* estimulante, tónico.

exile [ˈɛksaɪl] *n* exilio; (*person*) exiliado/a ♦ *vt* desterrar, exiliar.

exist [ɪgˈzɪst] *vi* existir; (*live*) vivir; ~**ence** *n* existencia; ~**ing** *adj* existente, actual.

exit ['ɛksɪt] n salida ♦ vi (THEATRE) hacer mutis; (COMPUT) salir (al sistema); ~ **ramp** (US) n (AUT) vía de acceso.
exodus ['ɛksədəs] n éxodo.
exonerate [ɪg'zɔnəreɪt] vt: to ~ from exculpar de.
exotic [ɪg'zɔtɪk] adj exótico.
expand [ɪk'spænd] vt ampliar; (number) aumentar ♦ vi (population) aumentar; (trade etc) expandirse; (gas, metal) dilatarse.
expanse [ɪk'spæns] n extensión f.
expansion [ɪk'spænʃən] n (of population) aumento; (of trade) expansión f.
expect [ɪk'spɛkt] vt esperar; (require) contar con; (suppose) suponer ♦ vi: to be ~ing (pregnant woman) estar embarazada; ~**ancy** n (anticipation) esperanza; **life** ~**ancy** esperanza de vida; ~**ant mother** n futura madre f; ~**ation** [ɛkspɛk'teɪʃən] n (hope) esperanza; (belief) expectativa.
expedience [ɪk'spi:dɪəns] n = **expediency**.
expediency [ɪk'spi:dɪənsɪ] n conveniencia.
expedient [ɪk'spi:dɪənt] adj conveniente, oportuno ♦ n recurso, expediente m.
expedition [ɛkspə'dɪʃən] n expedición f.
expel [ɪk'spɛl] vt arrojar; (from place) expulsar.
expend [ɪk'spɛnd] vt (money) gastar; (time, energy) consumir; ~**able** adj prescindible; ~**iture** n gastos mpl, desembolso; consumo.
expense [ɪk'spɛns] n gasto, gastos mpl; (high cost) costa; ~**s** npl (COMM) gastos mpl; **at the** ~ **of** a costa de; ~ **account** n cuenta de gastos.
expensive [ɪk'spɛnsɪv] adj caro, costoso.
experience [ɪk'spɪərɪəns] n experiencia ♦ vt experimentar; (suffer) sufrir; ~**d** adj experimentado.
experiment [ɪk'spɛrɪmənt] n experimento ♦ vi hacer experimentos; ~**al** [-'mɛntl] adj experimental.
expert ['ɛkspə:t] adj experto, perito ♦ n experto/a, perito/a; (specialist) especialista m/f; ~**ise** [-'ti:z] n pericia.
expire [ɪk'spaɪə*] vi caducar, vencer;

expiry n vencimiento.
explain [ɪk'spleɪn] vt explicar; **explanation** [ɛksplə'neɪʃən] n explicación f; **explanatory** [ɪk'splænətrɪ] adj explicativo; aclaratorio.
explicit [ɪk'splɪsɪt] adj explícito.
explode [ɪk'spləud] vi estallar, explotar; (population) crecer rápidamente; (with anger) reventar.
exploit [n 'ɛksplɔɪt, vb ɪk'splɔɪt] n hazaña ♦ vt explotar; ~**ation** [-'teɪʃən] n explotación f.
exploratory [ɪk'splɔrətrɪ] adj de exploración; (fig: talks) exploratorio, preliminar.
explore [ɪk'splɔ:*] vt explorar; (fig) examinar; investigar; ~**r** n explorador(a) m/f.
explosion [ɪk'spləuʒən] n (also fig) explosión f.
explosive [ɪks'pləusɪv] adj, n explosivo.
exponent [ɪk'spəunənt] n (of theory etc) partidario/a; (of skill etc) exponente m/f.
export [vb ɛk'spɔ:t, n 'ɛkspɔ:t] vt exportar ♦ n (process) exportación f; (product) producto de exportación ♦ cpd de exportación; ~**er** n exportador m.
expose [ɪk'spəuz] vt exponer; (unmask) desenmascarar; ~**d** adj expuesto.
exposure [ɪk'spəuʒə*] n exposición f; (publicity) publicidad f; (PHOT: speed) velocidad f de obturación; (: shot) fotografía; **to die from** ~ (MED) morir de frío; ~ **meter** n fotómetro.
expound [ɪk'spaund] vt exponer.
express [ɪk'sprɛs] adj (definite) expreso, explícito; (BRIT: letter etc) urgente ♦ n (train) rápido ♦ vt expresar; ~**ion** [ɪk'sprɛʃən] n expresión f; (of actor etc) sentimiento; ~**ly** adv expresamente; ~**way** (US) n (urban motorway) autopista.
exquisite [ɛk'skwɪzɪt] adj exquisito.
extend [ɪk'stɛnd] vt (visit, street) prolongar; (building) ampliar; (invitation) ofrecer ♦ vi (land) extenderse; (period of time) prolongarse.
extension [ɪk'stɛnʃən] n extensión f; (building) ampliación f; (of time) pro-

longación *f*; (*TEL*: *in private house*) línea derivada; (: *in office*) extensión *f*.

extensive [ɪk'stɛnsɪv] *adj* extenso; (*damage*) importante; (*knowledge*) amplio; ~**ly** *adv*: **he's travelled** ~**ly** **ha viajado por muchos países.**

extent [ɪk'stɛnt] *n* (*breadth*) extensión *f*; (*scope*) alcance *m*; **to some** ~ hasta cierto punto; **to the** ~ **of...** hasta el punto de...; **to such an** ~ **that...** hasta tal punto que...; **to what** ~? ¿hasta qué punto?

extenuating [ɪk'stɛnjueɪtɪŋ] *adj*: ~ **circumstances** circunstancias *fpl* atenuantes.

exterior [ɛk'stɪərɪə*] *adj* exterior, externo ♦ *n* exterior *m*.

exterminate [ɪk'stə:mɪneɪt] *vt* exterminar.

external [ɛk'stə:nl] *adj* externo.

extinct [ɪk'stɪŋkt] *adj* (*volcano*) extinguido; (*race*) extinto.

extinguish [ɪk'stɪŋgwɪʃ] *vt* extinguir, apagar; ~**er** *n* extintor *m*.

extort [ɪk'stɔ:t] *vt* obtener por fuerza; ~**ion** [ɪk'stɔ:ʃən] *n* extorsión *f*; ~**ionate** [ɪk'stɔ:ʃnət] *adj* excesivo, exorbitante.

extra ['ɛkstrə] *adj* adicional ♦ *adv* (*in addition*) de más ♦ *n* (*luxury*, *addition*) extra *m*; (*CINEMA*, *THEATRE*) extra *m/f*, comparsa *m/f*.

extra... ['ɛkstrə] *prefix* extra....

extract [*vb* ɪk'strækt, *n* 'ɛkstrækt] *vt* sacar; (*tooth*) extraer; (*money*, *promise*) obtener ♦ *n* extracto.

extracurricular [ɛkstrəkə'rɪkjulə*] *adj* extraescolar, extra-académico.

extradite ['ɛkstrədaɪt] *vt* extraditar.

extramarital [ɛkstrə'mærɪtl] *adj* extramatrimonial.

extramural [ɛkstrə'mjuərl] *adj* extraescolar.

extraordinary [ɪk'strɔ:dnrɪ] *adj* extraordinario; (*odd*) raro.

extravagance [ɪk'strævəgəns] *n* derroche *m*, despilfarro; (*thing bought*) extravagancia.

extravagant [ɪk'strævəgənt] *adj* (*lavish*: *person*) pródigo; (: *gift*) (demasiado) caro; (*wasteful*) despilfarrador(a).

extreme [ɪk'stri:m] *adj* extremo, extremado ♦ *n* extremo; ~**ly** *adv* sumamente, extremadamente.

extremity [ɪk'strɛmətɪ] *n* extremidad *f*, punta; (*of situation*) extremo.

extricate ['ɛkstrɪkeɪt] *vt*: **to** ~ **sth/sb from** librar algo/a uno de.

extrovert ['ɛkstrəvə:t] *n* extrovertido/a.

exuberant [ɪg'zju:bərnt] *adj* (*person*) eufórico; (*imagination*) exuberante.

exude [ɪg'zju:d] *vt* (*confidence*) rebosar; (*liquid*, *smell*) rezumar.

exult [ɪg'zʌlt] *vi* regocijarse.

eye [aɪ] *n* ojo ♦ *vt* mirar de soslayo, ojear; **to keep an** ~ **on** vigilar; ~**ball** *n* globo del ojo; ~**bath** *n* ojera; ~**brow** *n* ceja; ~**brow pencil** *n* lápiz *m* de cejas; ~**drops** *npl* gotas *fpl* para los ojos, colinos; ~**lash** *n* pestaña; ~**lid** *n* párpado; ~**liner** *n* lápiz *m* de ojos; ~**-opener** *n* revelación *f*, gran sorpresa; ~**shadow** *n* sombreador *m* de ojos; ~**sight** *n* vista; ~**sore** *n* monstruosidad *f*; ~ **witness** *n* testigo *m/f* presencial.

F

F [ɛf] *n* (*MUS*) fa *m*.

F. *abbr* = **Fahrenheit**.

fable ['feɪbl] *n* fábula.

fabric ['fæbrɪk] *n* tejido, tela.

fabrication [fæbrɪ'keɪʃən] *n* (*lie*) invención *f*; (*making*) fabricación *f*.

fabulous ['fæbjuləs] *adj* fabuloso.

façade [fə'sɑ:d] *n* fachada.

face [feɪs] *n* (*ANAT*) cara, rostro; (*of clock*) esfera (*SP*), cara (*AM*); (*of mountain*) cara, ladera; (*of building*) fachada ♦ *vt* (*direction*) estar de cara a; (*situation*) hacer frente a; (*facts*) aceptar; ~ **down** (*person*, *card*) boca abajo; **to lose** ~ desprestigiarse; **to make** *or* **pull a** ~ hacer muecas; **in the** ~ **of** (*difficulties etc*) ante; **on the** ~ **of it** a primera vista; ~ **to** ~ cara a cara; ~ **up to** *vt fus* hacer frente a, arrostrar; ~ **cloth** (*BRIT*) *n* manopla; ~ **cream** *n* crema (de belleza); ~ **lift** *n* estirado facial; (*of building*) renovación

f; $\sim$ **powder** n polvos mpl; $\sim$**-saving** adj para salvar las apariencias.
facetious [fə'si:ʃəs] adj gracioso.
face value n (of stamp) valor m nominal; **to take sth at** $\sim$ (fig) tomar algo en sentido literal.
facile ['fæsaɪl] adj superficial.
facilities [fə'sɪlɪtɪz] npl (buildings) instalaciones fpl; (equipment) servicios mpl; **credit** $\sim$ facilidades fpl de crédito.
facing ['feɪsɪŋ] prep frente a.
facsimile [fæk'sɪmɪlɪ] n (replica) facsímil(e) m; (machine) telefax m; (fax) fax m.
fact [fækt] n hecho; **in** $\sim$ en realidad.
factor ['fæktə*] n factor m.
factory ['fæktərɪ] n fábrica.
factual ['fæktjuəl] adj basado en los hechos.
faculty ['fækəltɪ] n facultad f; (US: teaching staff) personal m docente.
fad [fæd] n novedad f, moda.
fade [feɪd] vi desteñirse; (sound, smile) desvanecerse; (light) apagarse; (flower) marchitarse; (hope, memory) perderse.
fag [fæg] (BRIT: inf) n (cigarette) pitillo (SP), cigarro.
fail [feɪl] vt (candidate) suspender; (exam) no aprobar (SP), (AM); (subj: memory etc) fallar a ♦ vi suspender; (be unsuccessful) fracasar; (strength, brakes) fallar; (light) acabarse; **to** $\sim$ **to do sth** (neglect) dejar de hacer algo; (be unable) no poder hacer algo; **without** $\sim$ sin falta; $\sim$**ing** n falta, defecto ♦ prep a falta de; $\sim$**ure** ['feɪljə*] n fracaso; (person) fracasado/a; (mechanical etc) fallo.
faint [feɪnt] adj débil; (recollection) vago; (mark) apenas visible ♦ n desmayo ♦ vi desmayarse; **to feel** $\sim$ estar mareado, marearse.
fair [feə*] adj justo; (hair, person) rubio; (weather) bueno; (good enough) regular; (considerable) considerable ♦ adv (play) limpio ♦ n feria; (BRIT: funfair) parque m de atracciones; $\sim$**ly** adv (justly) con justicia; (quite) bastante; $\sim$**ness** n justicia, imparcialidad f; $\sim$

play n juego limpio.
fairy ['feərɪ] n hada; $\sim$ **tale** n cuento de hadas.
faith [feɪθ] n fe f; (trust) confianza; (sect) religión f; $\sim$**ful** adj (loyal: troops etc) leal; (spouse) fiel; (account) exacto; $\sim$**fully** adv fielmente; **yours** $\sim$**fully** (BRIT: in letters) le saluda atentamente.
fake [feɪk] n (painting etc) falsificación f; (person) impostor(a) m/f ♦ adj falso ♦ vt fingir; (painting etc) falsificar.
falcon ['fɔːlkən] n halcón m.
fall [fɔːl] (pt **fell**, pp **fallen**) n caída; (in price etc) descenso; (US) otoño ♦ vi caer(se); (price) bajar, descender; $\sim$**s** npl (water$\sim$) cascada, salto de agua; **to** $\sim$ **flat** (on one's face) caerse (boca abajo); (plan) fracasar; (joke, story) no hacer gracia; $\sim$ **back** vi retroceder; $\sim$ **back on** vt fus (remedy etc) recurrir a; $\sim$ **behind** vi quedarse atrás; $\sim$ **down** vi (person) caerse; (building, hopes) derrumbarse; $\sim$ **for** vt fus (trick) dejarse engañar por; (person) enamorarse de; $\sim$ **in** vi (roof) hundirse; (MIL) alinearse; $\sim$ **off** vi caerse; (diminish) disminuir; $\sim$ **out** vi (friends etc) reñir; (hair, teeth) caerse; $\sim$ **through** vi (plan, project) fracasar.
fallacy ['fæləsɪ] n error m.
fallen ['fɔːlən] pp of **fall**.
fallout ['fɔːlaut] n lluvia radioactiva; $\sim$ **shelter** n refugio antiatómico.
fallow ['fæləu] adj en barbecho.
false [fɔːls] adj falso; **under** $\sim$ **pretences** con engaños; $\sim$ **alarm** n falsa alarma; $\sim$ **teeth** (BRIT) npl dentadura postiza.
falter ['fɔːltə*] vi vacilar; (engine) fallar.
fame [feɪm] n fama.
familiar [fə'mɪlɪə*] adj conocido, familiar; (tone) de confianza; **to be** $\sim$ **with** (subject) conocer (bien).
family ['fæmɪlɪ] n familia; $\sim$ **business** n negocio familiar; $\sim$ **doctor** n médico/a de cabecera.
famine ['fæmɪn] n hambre f, hambruna.
famished ['fæmɪʃt] adj hambriento.
famous ['feɪməs] adj famoso, célebre; $\sim$**ly** adv (get on) estupendamente.

fan [fæn] n abanico; (ELEC) ventilador m; (of pop star) fan m/f; (SPORT) hincha m/f ♦ vt abanicar; (fire, quarrel) atizar; ~ **out** vi desparramarse.

fanatic [fə'nætɪk] n fanático/a.

fan belt n correa del ventilador.

fanciful ['fænsɪful] adj (design, name) fantástico.

fancy ['fænsɪ] n (whim) capricho, antojo; (imagination) imaginación f ♦ adj (luxury) lujoso, de lujo ♦ vt (feel like, want) tener ganas de; (imagine) imaginarse; (think) creer; **to take a ~ to sb** tomar cariño a uno; **he fancies her** (inf) le gusta (ella) mucho; ~ **dress** n disfraz m; ~-**dress ball** n baile m de disfraces.

fanfare ['fænfɛə*] n fanfarria (de trompeta).

fang [fæŋ] n colmillo.

fantastic [fæn'tæstɪk] adj (enormous) enorme; (strange, wonderful) fantástico.

fantasy ['fæntəzɪ] n (dream) sueño; (unreality) fantasía.

far [fɑ:*] adj (distant) lejano ♦ adv lejos; (much, greatly) mucho; ~ **away**, ~ **off** (a lo) lejos; ~ **better** mucho mejor; ~ **from** lejos de; **by** ~ con mucho; **go as ~ as the farm** vaya hasta la granja; **as ~ as I know** que yo sepa; **how ~?** ¿hasta dónde?; (fig) ¿hasta qué punto?; ~**away** adj remoto; (look) distraído.

farce [fɑ:s] n farsa; **farcical** adj absurdo.

fare [fɛə*] n (on trains, buses) precio (del billete); (in taxi: cost) tarifa; (food) comida; **half** ~ medio pasaje m; **full** ~ pasaje completo.

Far East n: **the** ~ el Extremo Oriente.

farewell [fɛə'wɛl] excl, n adiós m.

farm [fɑ:m] n granja (SP), finca (AM), estancia (AM) ♦ vt cultivar; ~**er** n granjero (SP), estanciero (AM); ~**hand** n peón m; ~**house** n granja, casa de hacienda (AM); ~**ing** n agricultura; (of crops) cultivo; (of animals) cría; ~**land** n tierra de cultivo; ~ **worker** n = ~**hand**; ~**yard** n corral m.

far-reaching [fɑ:'ri:tʃɪŋ] adj (reform, ef-

fect) de gran alcance.

fart [fɑ:t] (inf!) vi tirarse un pedo (!).

farther ['fɑ:ðə*] adv más lejos, más allá ♦ adj más lejano.

farthest ['fɑ:ðɪst] superlative of **far**.

fascinate ['fæsɪneɪt] vt fascinar; **fascination** [-'neɪʃən] n fascinación f.

fascism ['fæʃɪzəm] n fascismo.

fashion ['fæʃən] n moda; (~ industry) industria de la moda; (manner) manera ♦ vt formar; **in** ~ a la moda; **out of** ~ pasado de moda; ~**able** adj de moda; ~ **show** n desfile m de modelos.

fast [fɑ:st] adj rápido; (dye, colour) resistente; (clock): **to be** ~ estar adelantado ♦ adv rápidamente, de prisa; (stuck, held) firmemente ♦ n ayuno ♦ vi ayunar; ~ **asleep** profundamente dormido.

fasten ['fɑ:sn] vt atar, sujetar; (coat, belt) abrochar ♦ vi atarse; abrocharse; ~**er** n cierre m; (of door etc) cerrojo; ~**ing** n = ~**er**.

fast food n comida rápida, platos mpl preparados.

fastidious [fæs'tɪdɪəs] adj (fussy) quisquilloso.

fat [fæt] adj gordo; (book) grueso; (profit) grande, pingüe ♦ n grasa; (on person) carnes fpl; (lard) manteca.

fatal ['feɪtl] adj (mistake) fatal; (injury) mortal; ~**istic** [-'lɪstɪk] adj fatalista; ~**ity** [fə'tælɪtɪ] n (road death ete) víctima; ~**ly** adv fatalmente; mortalmente.

fate [feɪt] n destino; (of person) suerte f; ~**ful** adj fatídico.

father ['fɑ:ðə*] n padre m; ~-**in-law** n suegro; ~**ly** adj paternal.

fathom ['fæðəm] n braza ♦ vt (mystery) desentrañar; (understand) lograr comprender.

fatigue [fə'ti:g] n fatiga, cansancio.

fatten ['fætn] vt, vi engordar.

fatty ['fætɪ] adj (food) graso ♦ n (inf) gordito/a, gordinflón/ona m/f.

fatuous ['fætjʊəs] adj fatuo, necio.

faucet ['fɔ:sɪt] (US) n grifo (SP), llave f (AM).

fault [fɔ:lt] n (blame) culpa; (defect: in person, machine) defecto; (GEO) falla ♦

vt criticar; **it's my ~ es** culpa mía; **to find ~ with** criticar, poner peros a; **at ~ culpable**; **~y** *adj* defectuoso.

fauna ['fɔːnə] *n* fauna.

faux pas ['fəu'pɑː] *n* plancha.

favour ['feivə*] (*US* **favor**) *n* favor *m*; (*approval*) aprobación *f* ♦ *vt* (*proposition*) estar a favor de, aprobar; (*assist*) ser propicio a; **to do sb a ~** hacer un favor a uno; **to find ~ with sb** caer en gracia a uno; **in ~ of** a favor de; **~able** *adj* favorable; **~ite** [-rɪt] *adj*, *n* favorito, preferido.

fawn [fɔːn] *n* cervato ♦ *adj* (*also*: **~-coloured**) color de cervato, leonado ♦ *vi*: **to ~ (up)on** adular.

fax [fæks] *n* (*document*) fax *m*; (*machine*) telefax *m* ♦ *vt* mandar por telefax.

FBI (*US*) *n abbr* (= *Federal Bureau of Investigation*) ≈ BIC *f* (*SP*).

fear [fɪə*] *n* miedo, temor *m* ♦ *vt* tener miedo de, temer; **for ~ of** por si; **~ful** *adj* temeroso, miedoso; (*awful*) terrible; **~less** *adj* audaz.

feasible ['fiːzəbl] *adj* factible.

feast [fiːst] *n* banquete *m*; (*REL*: *also*: **~ day**) fiesta ♦ *vi* festejar.

feat [fiːt] *n* hazaña.

feather ['feðə*] *n* pluma.

feature ['fiːtʃə*] *n* característica; (*article*) artículo de fondo ♦ *vt* (*subj*: *film*) presentar ♦ *vi*: **to ~ in** tener un papel destacado en; **~s** *npl* (*of face*) facciones *fpl*; **~ film** *n* largometraje *m*.

February ['fɛbruəri] *n* febrero.

fed [fɛd] *pt*, *pp* of **feed**.

federal ['fɛdərəl] *adj* federal.

fed-up [fɛd'ʌp] *adj*: **to be ~ (with)** estar harto (de).

fee [fiː] *n* pago; (*professional*) derechos *mpl*, honorarios *mpl*; (*of club*) cuota; **school ~s** matrícula.

feeble ['fiːbl] *adj* débil; (*joke*) flojo.

feed [fiːd] (*pt*, *pp* **fed**) *n* comida; (*of animal*) pienso; (*on printer*) dispositivo de alimentación ♦ *vt* alimentar; (*BRIT*: *baby*: *breast~*) dar el pecho a; (*animal*) dar de comer a; (*data*, *information*): **to ~ into** meter en; **~ on** *vt fus* alimentarse de; **~back** *n* reacción *f*,

feedback *m*; **~ing bottle** (*BRIT*) *n* biberón *m*.

feel [fiːl] (*pt*, *pp* **felt**) *n* (*sensation*) sensación *f*; (*sense of touch*) tacto; (*impression*): **to have the ~ of** parecerse a ♦ *vt* tocar; (*pain etc*) sentir; (*think*, *believe*) creer; **to ~ hungry/cold** tener hambre/frío; **to ~ lonely/better** sentirse solo/mejor; **I don't ~ well** no me siento bien; **it ~s soft** es suave al tacto; **to ~ like** (*want*) tener ganas de; **~ about** or **around** *vi* tantear; **~er** *n* (*of insect*) antena; **to put out a ~er** or **~ers** (*fig*) sondear; **~ing** *n* (*physical*) sensación *f*; (*foreboding*) presentimiento; (*emotion*) sentimiento.

feet [fiːt] *npl* of **foot**.

feign [feɪn] *vt* fingir.

fell [fɛl] *pt* of **fall** ♦ *vt* (*tree*) talar.

fellow ['fɛləu] *n* tipo, tío (*SP*); (*comrade*) compañero; (*of learned society*) socio/a ♦ *cpd*: **~ citizen** *n* conciudadano/a; **~ countryman** *n* compatriota *m*; **~ men** *npl* semejantes *mpl*; **~ship** *n* compañerismo; (*grant*) beca.

felony ['fɛləni] *n* crimen *m*.

felt [fɛlt] *pt*, *pp* of **feel** ♦ *n* fieltro; **~-tip pen** *n* rotulador *m*.

female ['fiːmeɪl] *n* (*pej*: *woman*) mujer *f*, tía; (*ZOOL*) hembra ♦ *adj* femenino; hembra.

feminine ['fɛmɪnɪn] *adj* femenino.

feminist ['fɛmɪnɪst] *n* feminista.

fence [fɛns] *n* valla, cerca ♦ *vt* (*also*: **~ in**) cercar ♦ *vi* (*SPORT*) hacer esgrima; **fencing** *n* esgrima.

fend [fɛnd] *vi*: **to ~ for o.s.** valerse por sí mismo; **~ off** *vt* (*attack*) rechazar; (*questions*) evadir.

fender ['fɛndə*] *n* guardafuego; (*US*: *AUT*) parachoques *m inv*.

ferment [*vb* fə'mɛnt, *n* 'fəːmɛnt] *vi* fermentar ♦ *n* (*fig*) agitación *f*.

fern [fəːn] *n* helecho.

ferocious [fə'rəuʃəs] *adj* feroz; **ferocity** [-'rɔsɪtɪ] *n* ferocidad *f*.

ferret ['fɛrɪt] *n* hurón *m*; **~ out** *vt* desentrañar.

ferry ['fɛrɪ] *n* (*small*) barca (de pasaje),

balsa; (*large: also:* ~*boat*) transbordador *m* (*SP*), embarcadero (*AM*) ♦ *vt* transportar.

fertile ['fɜːtaɪl] *adj* fértil; (*BIOL*) fecundo; **fertility** [fə'tɪlɪtɪ] *n* fertilidad *f*; fecundidad *f*; **fertilize** ['fɜːtɪlaɪz] *vt* (*BIOL*) fecundar; (*AGR*) abonar; **fertilizer** *n* abono.

fervent ['fɜːvənt] *adj* ferviente, entusiasta.

fervour ['fɜːvə*] *n* fervor *m*, ardor *m*.

fester ['fɛstə*] *vi* ulcerarse.

festival ['fɛstɪvəl] *n* (*REL*) fiesta; (*ART, MUS*) festival *m*.

festive ['fɛstɪv] *adj* festivo; **the** ~ **season** (*BRIT: Christmas*) las Navidades.

festivities [fɛs'tɪvɪtɪz] *npl* fiestas *fpl*.

festoon [fɛs'tuːn] *vt*: **to** ~ **with** engalanar de.

fetch [fɛtʃ] *vt* ir a buscar; (*sell for*) venderse por.

fetching ['fɛtʃɪŋ] *adj* atractivo.

fête [feɪt] *n* fiesta.

fetish ['fɛtɪʃ] *n* obsesión *f*.

fetus ['fiːtəs] (*US*) *n* = **foetus**.

feud [fjuːd] *n* (*hostility*) enemistad *f*; (*quarrel*) disputa.

fever ['fiːvə*] *n* fiebre *f*; ~**ish** *adj* febril.

few [fjuː] *adj* (*not many*) pocos; **a** ~ *adj* unos pocos, algunos ♦ *pron* pocos; algunos; ~**er** *adj* menos; ~**est** *adj* los/las menos.

fiancé [fɪ'ãːŋseɪ] *n* novio, prometido; ~**e** *n* novia, prometida.

fiasco [fɪ'æskəu] *n* desastre *m*.

fib [fɪb] *n* mentirilla.

fibre ['faɪbə*] (*US* **fiber**) *n* fibra; ~~**-glass** *n* fibra de vidrio.

fickle ['fɪkl] *adj* inconstante.

fiction ['fɪkʃən] *n* ficción *f*; ~**al** *adj* novelesco; **fictitious** [fɪk'tɪʃəs] *adj* ficticio.

fiddle ['fɪdl] *n* (*MUS*) violín *m*; (*cheating*) trampa ♦ *vt* (*BRIT: accounts*) falsificar; ~ **with** *vt fus* juguetear con.

fidget ['fɪdʒɪt] *vi* enredar; **stop** ~**ing!** ¡estáte quieto!

field [fiːld] *n* campo; (*fig*) campo, esfera; (*SPORT*) campo, cancha (*AM*); ~ **marshal** *n* mariscal *m*; ~**work** *n* trabajo de campo.

fiend [fiːnd] *n* demonio; ~**ish** *adj* diabólico.

fierce [fɪəs] *adj* feroz; (*wind, heat*) fuerte; (*fighting, enemy*) encarnizado.

fiery ['faɪərɪ] *adj* (*burning*) ardiente; (*temperament*) apasionado.

fifteen [fɪf'tiːn] *num* quince.

fifth [fɪfθ] *num* quinto.

fifty ['fɪftɪ] *num* cincuenta; ~-~ (*deal, split*) a medias ♦ *adv* a medias, mitad por mitad.

fig [fɪg] *n* higo.

fight [faɪt] (*pt, pp* **fought**) *n* (*gen*) pelea; (*MIL*) combate *m*; (*struggle*) lucha ♦ *vt* luchar contra; (*cancer, alcoholism*) combatir; (*election*) intentar ganar; (*emotion*) resistir ♦ *vi* pelear, luchar; ~**er** *n* combatiente *m/f*; (*plane*) caza *m*; ~**ing** *n* combate *m*, pelea.

figment ['fɪgmənt] *n*: **a** ~ **of the imagination** una quimera.

figurative ['fɪgjurətɪv] *adj* (*meaning*) figurado; (*style*) figurativo.

figure ['fɪgə*] *n* (*DRAWING, GEOM*) figura, dibujo; (*number, quantity*) cifra; (*body, outline*) tipo; (*personality*) figura ♦ *vt* (*esp US*) imaginar ♦ *vi* (*appear*) figurar; ~ **out** *vt* (*work out*) resolver; ~**head** *n* (*NAUT*) mascarón *m* de proa; (*pej: leader*) figura decorativa; ~ **of speech** *n* figura retórica.

filch [fɪltʃ] (*inf*) *vt* hurtar, robar.

file [faɪl] *n* (*tool*) lima; (*dossier*) expediente *m*; (*folder*) carpeta; (*COMPUT*) fichero; (*row*) fila ♦ *vt* limar; (*LAW: claim*) presentar; (*store*) archivar; ~ **in/out** *vi* entrar/salir en fila; **filing cabinet** *n* fichero, archivador *m*.

fill [fɪl] *vt* (*space*): **to** ~ (**with**) llenar (de); (*vacancy, need*) cubrir ♦ *n*: **to eat one's** ~ llenarse; ~ **in** *vt* rellenar; ~ **up** *vt* llenar (hasta el borde) ♦ *vi* (*AUT*) poner gasolina.

fillet ['fɪlɪt] *n* filete *m*; ~ **steak** *n* filete *m* de ternera.

filling ['fɪlɪŋ] *n* (*CULIN*) relleno; (*for tooth*) empaste *m*; ~ **station** *n* estación *f* de servicio.

film [fɪlm] *n* película ♦ *vt* (*scene*) filmar ♦ *vi* rodar (una película); ~ **star** *n* astro, estrella de cine; ~**strip** *n* tira de película.

filter ['fɪltə*] *n* filtro ♦ *vt* filtrar; ~ **lane** (*BRIT*) *n* carril *m* de selección; ~**tipped** *adj* con filtro.

filth [fɪlθ] *n* suciedad *f*; ~**y** *adj* sucio; (*language*) obsceno.

fin [fɪn] *n* (*gen*) aleta.

final ['faɪnl] *adj* (*last*) final, último; (*definitive*) definitivo, terminante ♦ *n* (*BRIT: SPORT*) final *f*; ~**s** *npl* (*SCOL*) examen *m* final; (*US: SPORT*) final *f*.

finale [fɪ'nɑːlɪ] *n* final *m*.

final: ~**ist** (*SPORT*) finalista *m/f*; ~**ize** *vt* concluir, completar; ~**ly** *adv* (*lastly*) por último, finalmente; (*eventually*) por fin.

finance [faɪ'næns] *n* (*money*) fondos *mpl*; ~**s** *npl* finanzas *fpl*; (*personal* ~*s*) situación *f* económica ♦ *vt* financiar; **financial** [-'nænʃəl] *adj* financiero; **financier** *n* financiero/a.

find [faɪnd] (*pt, pp* found) *vt* encontrar, hallar; (*come upon*) descubrir ♦ *n* hallazgo; descubrimiento; **to ~ sb guilty** (*LAW*) declarar culpable a uno; ~ **out** *vt* averiguar; (*truth, secret*) descubrir; **to ~ out about** (*subject*) informarse sobre; (*by chance*) enterarse de; ~**ings** *npl* (*LAW*) veredicto, fallo; (*of report*) recomendaciones *fpl*.

fine [faɪn] *adj* excelente; (*thin*) fino ♦ *adv* (*well*) bien ♦ *n* (*LAW*) multa ♦ *vt* (*LAW*) multar; **to be ~** (*person*) estar bien; (*weather*) hacer buen tiempo; ~ **arts** *npl* bellas artes *fpl*.

finery ['faɪnərɪ] *n* adornos *mpl*.

finesse [fɪ'nɛs] *n* sutileza.

finger ['fɪŋɡə*] *n* dedo ♦ *vt* (*touch*) manosear; **little/index ~** (dedo) meñique *m*/índice *m*; ~**nail** *n* uña; ~**print** *n* huella dactilar; ~**tip** *n* yema del dedo.

finicky ['fɪnɪkɪ] *adj* delicado.

finish ['fɪnɪʃ] *n* (*end*) fin *m*; (*SPORT*) meta; (*polish etc*) acabado ♦ *vt, vi* terminar; **to ~ doing sth** acabar de hacer algo; **to ~ third** llegar el tercero; ~ **off** *vt* acabar, terminar; (*kill*) acabar con; ~ **up** *vt* acabar, terminar ♦ *vi* ir a parar, terminar; ~**ing line** *n* línea de lle-

gada *or* meta; ~**ing school** *n* academia para señoritas.

finite ['faɪnaɪt] *adj* finito; (*verb*) conjugado.

Finland ['fɪnlənd] *n* Finlandia.

Finn [fɪn] *n* finlandés/esa *m/f*; ~**ish** *adj* finlandés/esa ♦ *n* (*LING*) finlandés *m*.

fiord [fjɔːd] *n* = **fjord**.

fir [fə*] *n* abeto.

fire ['faɪə*] *n* fuego; (*in hearth*) lumbre *f*; (*accidental*) incendio; (*heater*) estufa ♦ *vt* (*gun*) disparar; (*interest*) despertar; (*inf: dismiss*) despedir ♦ *vi* (*shoot*) disparar; **on ~** ardiendo, en llamas; ~ **alarm** *n* alarma de incendios; ~**arm** *n* arma de fuego; ~ **brigade** (*US* ~ **department**) *n* (cuerpo de) bomberos *mpl*; ~ **engine** *n* coche *m* de bomberos; ~ **escape** *n* escalera de incendios; ~ **extinguisher** *n* extintor *m* (de incendios); ~**guard** *n* rejilla de protección; ~**man** *n* bombero; ~**place** *n* chimenea; ~**side** *n*: **by the ~side** al lado de la chimenea; ~ **station** *n* parque *m* de bomberos; ~**wood** *n* leña; ~**works** *npl* fuegos *mpl* artificiales.

firing squad ['faɪrɪŋ-] *n* pelotón *m* de ejecución.

firm [fəːm] *adj* firme; (*look, voice*) resuelto ♦ *n* firma, empresa; ~**ly** *adv* firmemente; resueltamente.

first [fəːst] *adj* primero ♦ *adv* (*before others*) primero; (*when listing reasons etc*) en primer lugar, primeramente ♦ *n* (*person: in race*) primero/a; (*AUT*) primera; (*BRIT: SCOL*) título de licenciado *con calificación de sobresaliente*; **at ~** al principio; ~ **of all** ante todo; ~ **aid** *n* primera ayuda, primeros auxilios *mpl*; ~**aid kit** *n* botiquín *m*; ~**class** *adj* (*excellent*) de primera (categoría); (*ticket etc*) de primera clase; ~**hand** *adj* de primera mano; **F~ Lady** (*esp US*) *n* primera dama; ~**ly** *adv* en primer lugar; ~ **name** *n* nombre *m* (de pila); ~**rate** *adj* estupendo.

fish [fɪʃ] *n inv* pez *m*; (*food*) pescado ♦ *vt, vi* pescar; **to go ~ing** ir de pesca; ~**erman** *n* pescador *m*; ~ **farm** *n* criadero de peces; ~ **fingers** (*BRIT*) *npl* croquetas *fpl* de pescado; ~ing boat *n* barca de pesca; ~ing line *n* sedal *m*; ~ing rod *n* caña (de pescar); ~monger's (shop) (*BRIT*) *n* pescadería; ~ sticks (*US*) *npl* = ~ fingers; ~y (*inf*) *adj* sospechoso.

fist [fɪst] *n* puño.

fit [fɪt] *adj* (*healthy*) en (buena) forma; (*proper*) adecuado, apropiado ♦ *vt* (*subj: clothes*) estar *or* sentar bien a; (*instal*) poner; (*equip*) proveer, dotar; (*facts*) cuadrar *or* corresponder con ♦ *vi* (*clothes*) sentar bien; (*in space, gap*) caber; (*facts*) coincidir ♦ *n* (*MED*) ataque *m*; ~ to (*ready*) a punto de; ~ for apropiado para; a ~ of anger/pride un arranque de cólera/orgullo; this dress is a good ~ este vestido me sienta bien; by ~s and starts a rachas; ~ in *vi* (*fig: person*) llevarse bien (con todos); ~ful *adj* espasmódico, intermitente; ~ment *n* módulo adosable; ~ness *n* (*MED*) salud *f*; ~ted carpet *n* moqueta, ~ted kitchen *n* cocina amueblada; ~ter *n* ajustador *m*; ~ting *adj* apropiado ♦ *n* (*of dress*) prueba; (*of piece of equipment*) instalación *f*; ~ting room *n* probador *m*; ~tings *npl* instalaciones *fpl*.

five [faɪv] *num* cinco; ~r (*inf: BRIT*) *n* billete *m* de cinco libras; (: *US*) billete *m* de cinco dólares.

fix [fɪks] *vt* (*secure*) fijar, asegurar; (*mend*) arreglar; (*prepare*) preparar ♦ *n*: to be in a ~ estar en un aprieto; ~ up (*meeting*) arreglar; to ~ sb up with sth proveer a uno de algo; ~ation [fɪk'seɪʃən] *n* obsesión *f*; ~ed [fɪkst] *adj* (*prices etc*) fijo; ~ture ['fɪkstʃə*] *n* (*SPORT*) encuentro; ~tures *npl* (*cupboards etc*) instalaciones *fpl* fijas.

fizzle out ['fɪzl-] *vi* apagarse.

fizzy ['fɪzɪ] *adj* (*drink*) gaseoso.

fjord [fjɔːd] *n* fiordo.

flabbergasted ['flæbəgɑːstɪd] *adj* pasmado, alucinado.

flabby ['flæbɪ] *adj* gordo.

flag [flæg] *n* bandera; (*stone*) losa ♦ *vi* decaer; to ~ sb down hacer señas a uno para que se pare; ~pole *n* asta de bandera; ~ship *n* buque *m* insignia; (*fig*)

bandera.

flair [flɛə*] *n* aptitud *f* especial.

flak [flæk] *n* (*MIL*) fuego antiaéreo; (*inf: criticism*) lluvia de críticas.

flake [fleɪk] *n* (*of rust, paint*) escama; (*of snow, soap powder*) copo ♦ *vi* (*also: ~ off*) desconcharse.

flamboyant [flæm'bɔɪənt] *adj* (*dress*) vistoso; (*person*) extravagante.

flame [fleɪm] *n* llama.

flamingo [flə'mɪŋgəu] *n* flamenco.

flammable ['flæməbl] *adj* inflamable.

flan [flæn] (*BRIT*) *n* tarta.

flank [flæŋk] *n* (*of animal*) ijar *m*; (*of army*) flanco ♦ *vt* flanquear.

flannel ['flænl] *n* (*BRIT: also: face ~*) manopla; (*fabric*) franela; ~s *npl* (*trousers*) pantalones *mpl* de franela.

flap [flæp] *n* (*of pocket, envelope*) solapa ♦ *vt* (*wings, arms*) agitar ♦ *vi* (*sail, flag*) ondear.

flare [flɛə*] *n* llamarada; (*MIL*) bengala; (*in skirt etc*) vuelo; ~ up *vi* encenderse; (*fig: person*) encolerizarse; (: *revolt*) estallar.

flash [flæʃ] *n* relámpago; (*also: news ~*) noticias *fpl* de última hora; (*PHOT*) flash *m* ♦ *vt* (*light, headlights*) lanzar un destello con; (*news, message*) transmitir; (*smile*) lanzar ♦ *vi* brillar; (*hazard light etc*) lanzar destellos; in a ~ en un instante; he ~ed by *or* past pasó como un rayo; ~back *n* (*CINEMA*) flashback *m*; ~bulb *n* bombilla fusible; ~ cube *n* cubo de flash; ~light *n* linterna.

flashy ['flæʃɪ] (*pej*) *adj* ostentoso.

flask [flɑːsk] *n* frasco; (*also: vacuum ~*) termo.

flat [flæt] *adj* llano; (*smooth*) liso; (*tyre*) desinflado; (*battery*) descargado; (*beer*) muerto; (*refusal etc*) rotundo; (*MUS*) desafinado; (*rate*) fijo ♦ *n* (*BRIT: apartment*) piso (*SP*), departamento (*AM*), apartamento (*AUT*) pinchazo; (*MUS*) bemol *m*; to work ~ out trabajar a toda mecha; ~ly *adv* terminantemente, de plano; ~ten *vt* (*also: ~ten out*) allanar; (*smooth out*) alisar; (*building, plants*) arrasar.

flatter ['flætə*] *vt* adular, halagar; ~ing

adj halagüeño; (*dress*) que favorece; ~**y** n adulación *f*.

flaunt [flɔːnt] *vt* ostentar, lucir.

flavour ['fleɪvə*] (*US* **flavor**) n sabor *m*, gusto ♦ *vt* sazonar, condimentar; **strawberry** ~**ed** con sabor a fresa; ~**ing** n (*in product*) aromatizante *m*.

flaw [flɔː] n defecto; ~**less** *adj* impecable.

flax [flæks] n lino; ~**en** *adj* rubio.

flea [fliː] n pulga.

fleck [flɛk] n (*mark*) mota.

flee [fliː] (*pt, pp* **fled**) *vt* huir de ♦ *vi* huir, fugarse.

fleece [fliːs] n vellón *m*; (*wool*) lana ♦ *vt* (*inf*) desplumar.

fleet [fliːt] n flota; (*of lorries etc*) escuadra.

fleeting ['fliːtɪŋ] *adj* fugaz.

Flemish ['flɛmɪʃ] *adj* flamenco.

flesh [flɛʃ] n carne *f*; (*skin*) piel *f*; (*of fruit*) pulpa; ~ **wound** n herida superficial.

flew [fluː] *pt of* **fly**.

flex [flɛks] n cordón *m* ♦ *vt* (*muscles*) tensar; ~**ibility** [-ɪ'bɪlɪtɪ] n flexibilidad *f*; ~**ible** *adj* flexible.

flick [flɪk] n capirotazo; chasquido ♦ *vt* (*with hand*) dar un capirotazo a; (*whip etc*) chasquear; (*switch*) accionar; ~ **through** *vt fus* hojear.

flicker ['flɪkə*] *vi* (*light*) parpadear; (*flame*) vacilar.

flier ['flaɪə*] n aviador(a) *m/f*.

flight [flaɪt] n vuelo; (*escape*) huida, fuga; (*also*: ~ **of steps**) tramo (de escaleras); ~ **attendant** (*US*) n camarero/azafata; ~ **deck** n (*AVIAT*) cabina de mandos; (*NAUT*) cubierta de aterrizaje.

flimsy ['flɪmzɪ] *adj* (*thin*) muy ligero; (*building*) endeble; (*excuse*) flojo.

flinch [flɪntʃ] *vi* encogerse; **to** ~ **from** retroceder ante.

fling [flɪŋ] (*pt, pp* **flung**) *vt* arrojar.

flint [flɪnt] n pedernal *m*; (*in lighter*) piedra.

flip [flɪp] *vt* dar la vuelta a; (*switch: turn on*) encender; (*: turn off*) apagar; (*coin*) echar a cara o cruz.

flippant ['flɪpənt] *adj* poco serio.

flipper ['flɪpə*] n aleta.

flirt [flɜːt] *vi* coquetear, flirtear ♦ n coqueta.

flit [flɪt] *vi* revolotear.

float [fləut] n flotador *m*; (*in procession*) carroza; (*money*) reserva ♦ *vi* flotar; (*swimmer*) hacer la plancha.

flock [flɔk] n (*of sheep*) rebaño; (*of birds*) bandada ♦ *vi*: **to** ~ **to** acudir en tropel a.

flog [flɔg] *vt* azotar.

flood [flʌd] n inundación *f*; (*of letters, imports etc*) avalancha ♦ *vt* inundar ♦ *vi* (*place*) inundarse; (*people*): **to** ~ **into** inundar; ~**ing** n inundaciones *fpl*; ~**light** n foco.

floor [flɔː*] n suelo; (*storey*) piso; (*of sea*) fondo ♦ *vt* (*subj: question*) dejar sin respuesta; (*: blow*) derribar; **ground** ~, **first** ~ (*US*) planta baja; **first** ~, **second** ~ (*US*) primer piso; ~**board** n tabla; ~ **show** n cabaret *m*.

flop [flɔp] n fracaso ♦ *vi* (*fail*) fracasar; (*fall*) derrumbarse.

floppy ['flɔpɪ] *adj* flojo ♦ n (*COMPUT: also*: ~ **disk**) floppy *m*.

flora ['flɔːrə] n flora.

floral ['flɔːrl] *adj* (*pattern*) floreado.

florid ['flɔrɪd] *adj* florido; (*complexion*) rubicundo.

florist ['flɔrɪst] n florista *m/f*; ~**'s (shop)** n florería.

flounce [flauns] n volante *m*; ~ **out** *vi* salir enfadado.

flounder ['flaundə*] *vi* (*swimmer*) patalear; (*fig: economy*) estar en dificultades ♦ n (*ZOOL*) platija.

flour ['flauə*] n harina.

flourish ['flʌrɪʃ] *vi* florecer ♦ n ademán *m*, movimiento (ostentoso); ~**ing** *adj* floreciente.

flout [flaut] *vt* burlarse de.

flow [fləu] n (*movement*) flujo; (*of traffic*) circulación *f*; (*tide*) corriente *f* ♦ *vi* (*river, blood*) fluir; (*traffic*) circular; ~ **chart** n organigrama *m*.

flower ['flauə*] n flor *f* ♦ *vi* florecer; ~ **bed** n macizo; ~**pot** n tiesto; ~**y** *adj* (*fragrance*) floral; (*pattern*) floreado;

(*speech*) florido.

flown [fləun] *pp of* **fly.**

flu [flu:] *n*: **to have ~** tener la gripe.

fluctuate ['flʌktjueit] *vi* fluctuar.

fluent ['fluːənt] *adj* (*linguist*) que habla perfectamente; (*speech*) elocuente; **he speaks ~ French, he's ~ in French** domina el francés; **~ly** *adv* con fluidez.

fluff [flʌf] *n* pelusa; **~y** *adj* de pelo suave.

fluid ['fluːɪd] *adj* (*movement*) fluido, líquido; (*situation*) inestable ♦ *n* fluido, líquido.

fluke [fluːk] (*inf*) *n* chiripa.

flung [flʌŋ] *pt, pp of* **fling.**

fluoride ['fluəraid] *n* fluoruro.

flurry ['flʌrɪ] *n* (*of snow*) temporal *m*; **~ of activity** frenesí *m* de actividad.

flush [flʌʃ] *n* rubor *m*; (*fig: of youth etc*) resplandor *m* ♦ *vt* limpiar con agua ♦ *vi* ruborizarse ♦ *adj*: **~ with** a ras de; **to ~ the toilet** hacer funcionar la cisterna; **~ out** *vt* (*game, birds*) levantar; **~ed** *adj* ruborizado.

flustered ['flʌstəd] *adj* aturdido.

flute [fluːt] *n* flauta.

flutter ['flʌtə*] *n* (*of wings*) revoloteo, aleteo; **a ~ of panic/excitement** una oleada de pánico/excitación ♦ *vi* revolotear.

flux [flʌks] *n*: **to be in a state of ~** estar continuamente cambiando.

fly [flai] (*pt* **flew**, *pp* **flown**) *n* mosca; (*on trousers*: *also: flies*) bragueta ♦ *vt* (*plane*) pilot(e)ar; (*cargo*) transportar (en avión); (*distances*) recorrer (en avión) ♦ *vi* volar; (*passengers*) ir en avión; (*escape*) evadirse; (*flag*) ondear; **~ away** *or* **off** *vi* emprender el vuelo; **~ing** *n* (*activity*) (el) volar; (*action*) vuelo ♦ *adj*: **~ing visit** visita relámpago; **with ~ing colours** con lucimiento; **~ing saucer** *n* platillo volante; **~ing start** *n*: **to get off to a ~ing start** empezar con buen pie; **~over** (*BRIT*) *n* paso a desnivel *or* superior; **~sheet** *n* (*for tent*) doble techo.

foal [fəul] *n* potro.

foam [fəum] *n* espuma ♦ *vi* hacer espuma; **~ rubber** *n* goma espuma.

fob [fɔb] *vt*: **to ~ sb off with sth** despachar a uno con algo.

focal point ['fəukl-] *n* (*fig*) centro de atención.

focus ['fəukəs] (*pl* **~es**) *n* foco; (*centre*) centro ♦ *vt* (*field glasses etc*) enfocar ♦ *vi*: **to ~ (on)** enfocar (a); (*issue etc*) centrarse en; **in/out of ~** enfocado/desenfocado.

fodder ['fɔdə*] *n* pienso.

foetus ['fiːtəs] (*US* **fetus**) *n* feto.

fog [fɔg] *n* niebla; **~gy** *adj*: **it's ~gy** hay niebla, está brumoso; **~ lamp** (*US* **~ light**) *n* (*AUT*) faro de niebla.

foil [fɔil] *vt* frustrar ♦ *n* hoja; (*kitchen* **~**) papel *m* (de) aluminio; (*complement*) complemento; (*FENCING*) florete *m*.

fold [fəuld] *n* (*bend, crease*) pliegue *m*; (*AGR*) redil *m* ♦ *vt* doblar; (*arms*) cruzar; **~ up** *vi* plegarse, doblarse; (*business*) quebrar ♦ *vt* (*map etc*) plegar; **~er** *n* (*for papers*) carpeta; **~ing** *adj* (*chair, bed*) plegable.

foliage ['fəulɪɪdʒ] *n* follaje *m*.

folk [fəuk] *npl* gente *f* ♦ *adj* popular, folklórico; **~s** *npl* (*family*) familia *sg*, parientes *mpl*; **~lore** ['fəuklɔ:*] *n* folklore *m*; **~ song** *n* canción *f* popular *or* folklórica.

follow ['fɔləu] *vt* seguir ♦ *vi* seguir; (*result*) resultar; **to ~ suit** hacer lo mismo; **~ up** *vt* (*letter, offer*) responder a; (*case*) investigar; **~er** *n* (*of person, belief*) partidario/a; **~ing** *adj* siguiente ♦ *n* afición *f*, partidarios *mpl*.

folly ['fɔlɪ] *n* locura.

fond [fɔnd] *adj* (*memory, smile etc*) cariñoso; (*hopes*) ilusorio; **to be ~ of** tener cariño a; (*pastime, food*) ser aficionado a.

fondle ['fɔndl] *vt* acariciar.

font [fɔnt] *n* pila bautismal; (*TYP*) fundición *f*.

food [fuːd] *n* comida; **~ mixer** *n* batidora; **~ poisoning** *n* intoxicación *f* alimenticia; **~ processor** *n* robot *m* de cocina; **~stuffs** *npl* comestibles *mpl*.

fool [fuːl] *n* tonto/a; (*CULIN*) puré *m* de frutas con nata ♦ *vt* engañar ♦ *vi* (*gen:*

~ *around*) bromear; ~**hardy** *adj* temerario; ~**ish** *adj* tonto; (*careless*) imprudente; ~**proof** *adj* (*plan etc*) infalible.

foot [fut] (*pl* **feet**) *n* pie *m*; (*measure*) pie *m* (= 304 *mm*); (*of animal*) pata ♦ *vt* (*bill*) pagar; **on** ~ a pie; ~**age** *n* (*CINEMA*) imágenes *fpl*; ~**ball** *n* balón *m*; (*game: BRIT*) fútbol *m*; (: *US*) fútbol *m* americano; ~**ball player** *n* (*BRIT: also*: ~**baller**) futbolista *m*; (*US*) jugador *m* de fútbol americano; ~**brake** *n* freno de pie; ~**bridge** *n* puente *m* para peatones; ~**hills** *npl* estribaciones *fpl*; ~**hold** *n* pie *m* firme; ~**ing** *n* (*fig*) posición *f*; **to lose one's** ~**ing** perder el pie; ~**lights** *npl* candilejas *fpl*; ~**man** *n* lacayo; ~**note** *n* nota (al pie de la página); ~**path** *n* sendero; ~**print** *n* huella, pisada; ~**step** *n* paso; ~**wear** *n* calzado.

KEYWORD

for [fɔː] *prep* **1** (*indicating destination, intention*) para; **the train** ~ **London** el tren con destino a *or* de Londres; **he left** ~ **Rome** marchó para Roma; **he went** ~ **the paper** fue por el periódico; **is this** ~ **me?** ¿es esto para mí?; **it's time** ~ **lunch** es la hora de comer

2 (*indicating purpose*) para; **what**('s it) ~? ¿para qué (es)?; **to pray** ~ **peace** rezar por la paz

3 (*on behalf of, representing*): **the MP** ~ **Hove** el diputado por Hove; **he works** ~ **the government/a local firm** trabaja para el gobierno/en una empresa local; **I'll ask him** ~ **you** se lo pediré por ti; **G** ~ **George** G de Gerona

4 (*because of*) por esta razón; ~ **fear of being criticized** por temor a ser criticado

5 (*with regard to*) para; **it's cold** ~ **July** hace frío para julio; **he has a gift** ~ **languages** tiene don de lenguas

6 (*in exchange for*) por; **I sold it** ~ **£5** lo vendí por £5; **to pay 50 pence** ~ **a ticket** pagar 50 peniques por un billete

7 (*in favour of*): **are you** ~ **or against us?** ¿estás con nosotros o contra nosotros?; **I'm all** ~ **it** estoy totalmente a

favor; **vote** ~ **X** vote (a) X

8 (*referring to distance*): **there are roadworks** ~ **5 km** hay obras en 5 km; **we walked** ~ **miles** caminamos kilómetros y kilómetros

9 (*referring to time*): **he was away** ~ **2 years** estuvo fuera (durante) dos años; **it hasn't rained** ~ **3 weeks** no ha llovido durante *or* en 3 semanas; **I have known her** ~ **years** la conozco desde hace años; **can you do it** ~ **tomorrow?** ¿lo podrás hacer para mañana?

10 (*with infinitive clauses*): **it is not** ~ **me to decide** la decisión no es cosa mía; **it would be best** ~ **you to leave** sería mejor que te fueras; **there is still time** ~ **you to do it** todavía te queda tiempo para hacerlo; ~ **this to be possible ...** para que esto sea posible ...

11 (*in spite of*) a pesar de; ~ **all his complaints** a pesar de sus quejas

♦ *conj* (*since, as: rather formal*) puesto que.

---

forage ['fɔrɪdʒ] *vi* (*animal*) forrajear; (*person*): **to** ~ **for** hurgar en busca de.

foray ['fɔreɪ] *n* incursión *f*.

forbad(e) [fə'bæd] *pt of* **forbid**.

forbid [fə'bɪd] (*pt* **forbad(e)**, *pp* **forbidden**) *vt* prohibir; **to** ~ **sb to do sth** prohibir a uno hacer algo; ~**ding** *adj* amenazador(a).

force [fɔːs] *n* fuerza ♦ *vt* forzar; (*push*) meter a la fuerza; **to** ~ **o.s. to do** hacer un esfuerzo por hacer; **the F**~**s** *npl* (*BRIT*) las Fuerzas Armadas; **in** ~ en vigor; ~**d** [fɔːst] *adj* forzado; ~**-feed** *vt* alimentar a la fuerza; ~**ful** *adj* enérgico.

forcibly ['fɔːsəblɪ] *adv* a la fuerza; (*speak*) enérgicamente.

ford [fɔːd] *n* vado.

fore [fɔː*] *n*: **to come to the** ~ empezar a destacar.

forearm ['fɔːrɑːm] *n* antebrazo.

foreboding [fɔː'bəudɪŋ] *n* presentimiento.

forecast ['fɔːkɑːst] *n* pronóstico ♦ *vt* (*irreg: like cast*) pronosticar.

forecourt ['fɔːkɔːt] *n* patio.

forefathers [ˈfɔːfɑːðəz] *npl* antepasados *mpl*.

forefinger [ˈfɔːfɪŋgə*] *n* (dedo) índice *m*.

forefront [ˈfɔːfrʌnt] *n*: **in the ~ of** en la vanguardia de.

forego *vt* = **forgo**.

foregone [ˈfɔːgɒn] *pp of* **forego** ♦ *adj*: **it's a ~ conclusion** es una conclusión evidente.

foreground [ˈfɔːgraund] *n* primer plano.

forehead [ˈfɔrɪd] *n* frente *f*.

foreign [ˈfɔrɪn] *adj* extranjero; (*trade*) exterior; (*object*) extraño; **~er** *n* extranjero/a; **~ exchange** *n* divisas *fpl*; **F~ Office** (*BRIT*) *n* Ministerio de Asuntos Exteriores; **F~ Secretary** (*BRIT*) *n* Ministro de Asuntos Exteriores.

foreleg [ˈfɔːleg] *n* pata delantera.

foreman [ˈfɔːmən] *n* capataz *m*; (*in construction*) maestro de obras.

foremost [ˈfɔːməust] *adj* principal ♦ *adv*: **first and ~** ante todo.

forensic [fəˈrɛnsɪk] *adj* forense.

forerunner [ˈfɔːrʌnə*] *n* precursor(a) *m/f*.

foresaw [fɔːˈsɔː] *pt of* **foresee**.

foresee [fɔːˈsiː] (*pt* **foresaw**, *pp* **foreseen**) *vt* prever; **~able** *adj* previsible.

foreshadow [fɔːˈʃædəu] *vt* prefigurar, anunciar.

foresight [ˈfɔːsaɪt] *n* previsión *f*.

forest [ˈfɔrɪst] *n* bosque *m*.

forestall [fɔːˈstɔːl] *vt* prevenir.

forestry [ˈfɔrɪstrɪ] *n* silvicultura.

foretaste [ˈfɔːteɪst] *n* muestra.

foretell [fɔːˈtɛl] (*pt*, *pp* **foretold**) *vt* predecir, pronosticar.

foretold [fɔːˈtəuld] *pt*, *pp of* **foretell**.

forever [fəˈrɛvə*] *adv* para siempre; (*endlessly*) constantemente.

forewent [fɔːˈwɛnt] *pt of* **forego**.

foreword [ˈfɔːwəːd] *n* prefacio.

forfeit [ˈfɔːfɪt] *vt* perder.

forgave [fəˈgeɪv] *pt of* **forgive**.

forge [fɔːdʒ] *n* herrería ♦ *vt* (*signature, money*) falsificar; (*metal*) forjar; **~ ahead** *vi* avanzar mucho; **~ry** *n* falsificación *f*.

forget [fəˈgɛt] (*pt* **forgot**, *pp* **forgotten**) *vt* olvidar ♦ *vi* olvidarse; **~ful** *adj* des-

pistado; **~-me-not** *n* nomeolvides *f inv*.

forgive [fəˈgɪv] (*pt* **forgave**, *pp* **forgiven**) *vt* perdonar; **to ~ sb for sth** perdonar algo a uno; **~ness** *n* perdón *m*.

forgo [fɔːˈgəu] (*pt* **forwent**, *pp* **forgone**) *vt* (*give up*) renunciar a; (*go without*) privarse de.

forgot [fəˈgɒt] *pt of* **forget**.

forgotten [fəˈgɒtn] *pp of* **forget**.

fork [fɔːk] *n* (*for eating*) tenedor *m*; (*for gardening*) horca; (*of roads*) bifurcación *f* ♦ *vi* (*road*) bifurcarse; **~ out** (*inf*) *vt* (*pay*) desembolsar; **~-lift truck** *n* máquina elevadora.

forlorn [fəˈlɔːn] *adj* (*person*) triste, melancólico; (*place*) abandonado; (*attempt, hope*) desesperado.

form [fɔːm] *n* forma; (*BRIT: SCOL*) clase *f*; (*document*) formulario ♦ *vt* formar; (*idea*) concebir; (*habit*) adquirir; **in top ~** en plena forma; **to ~ a queue** hacer cola.

formal [ˈfɔːməl] *adj* (*offer, receipt*) por escrito; (*person etc*) correcto; (*occasion, dinner*) de etiqueta; (*dress*) correcto; (*garden*) (de estilo) clásico; **~ity** [-ˈmælɪtɪ] *n* (*procedure*) trámite *m*; corrección *f*; etiqueta; **~ly** *adv* oficialmente.

format [ˈfɔːmæt] *n* formato ♦ *vt* (*COMPUT*) formatear.

formative [ˈfɔːmətɪv] *adj* (*years*) de formación; (*influence*) formativo.

former [ˈfɔːmə*] *adj* anterior; (*earlier*) antiguo; (*ex*) ex; **the ~ ... the latter ...** aquél ... éste ...; **~ly** *adv* antes.

formula [ˈfɔːmjulə] *n* fórmula.

forsake [fəˈseɪk] (*pt* **forsook**, *pp* **forsaken**) *vt* (*gen*) abandonar; (*plan*) renunciar a.

forsaken [fəˈseɪkən] *pp of* **forsake**.

fort [fɔːt] *n* fuerte *m*.

forte [ˈfɔːtɪ] *n* fuerte *m*.

forth [fɔːθ] *adv*: **back and ~** de acá para allá; **and so ~** y así sucesivamente; **~coming** *adj* próximo, venidero; (*help, information*) disponible; (*character*) comunicativo; **~right** *adj* franco; **~with** *adv* en el acto.

fortify [ˈfɔːtɪfaɪ] *vt* (*city*) fortificar; (*person) fortalecer.

fortitude ['fɔːtɪtjuːd] n fortaleza.

fortnight ['fɔːtnaɪt] (BRIT) n quince días mpl; quincena; ~**ly** adj de cada quince días, quincenal ♦ adv cada quince días, quincenalmente.

fortress ['fɔːtrɪs] n fortaleza.

fortunate ['fɔːtʃənɪt] adj afortunado; **it is ~ that ...** (es una) suerte que ...; ~**ly** adv afortunadamente.

fortune ['fɔːtʃən] n suerte f; (wealth) fortuna; ~-**teller** n adivino/a.

forty ['fɔːtɪ] num cuarenta.

forum ['fɔːrəm] n foro.

forward ['fɔːwəd] adj (movement, position) avanzado; (front) delantero; (in time) adelantado; (not shy) atrevido ♦ n (SPORT) delantero ♦ vt (letter) remitir; (career) promocionar; **to move ~** avanzar; ~(**s**) adv (hacia) adelante.

fossil ['fɔsl] n fósil m.

foster ['fɔstə*] vt (child) acoger en una familia; fomentar; ~ **child** n hijo/a adoptivo/a.

fought [fɔːt] pt, pp of **fight**.

foul [faul] adj sucio, puerco; (weather, smell etc) asqueroso; (language) grosero; (temper) malísimo ♦ n (SPORT) falta ♦ vt (dirty) ensuciar; ~ **play** n (LAW) muerte f violenta.

found [faund] pt, pp of **find** ♦ vt fundar; ~**ation** [-'deɪʃən] n (act) fundación f; (basis) base f; (also: ~**ation cream**) crema base; ~**ations** npl (of building) cimientos mpl.

founder ['faundə*] n fundador(a) m/f ♦ vi hundirse.

foundry ['faundrɪ] n fundición f.

fountain ['fauntɪn] n fuente f; ~ **pen** n pluma (estilográfica) (SP), pluma-fuente f (AM).

four [fɔː*] num cuatro; **on all ~s** a gatas; ~-**poster** (**bed**) n cama de dosel; ~**some** ['fɔːsəm] n grupo de cuatro personas; ~**teen** num catorce; ~**th** num cuarto.

fowl [faul] n ave f (de corral).

fox [fɔks] n zorro ♦ vt confundir.

foyer ['fɔɪeɪ] n vestíbulo.

fraction ['frækʃən] n fracción f.

fracture ['fræktʃə*] n fractura.

fragile ['frædʒaɪl] adj frágil.

fragment ['frægmənt] n fragmento.

fragrance ['freɪgrəns] n fragancia, perfume m.

fragrant ['freɪgrənt] adj fragante, oloroso.

frail [freɪl] adj frágil; (person) débil.

frame [freɪm] n (TECH) armazón m; (of person) cuerpo; (of picture, door etc) marco; (of spectacles: also: ~**s**) montura ♦ vt enmarcar; ~ **of mind** n estado de ánimo; ~**work** n marco.

France [frɑːns] n Francia.

franchise ['fræntʃaɪz] n (POL) derecho de votar, sufragio; (COMM) licencia, concesión f.

frank [fræŋk] adj franco ♦ vt (letter) franquear; ~**ly** adv francamente; ~**ness** n franqueza.

frantic ['fræntɪk] adj (distraught) desesperado; (hectic) frenético.

fraternity [frə'təːnɪtɪ] n (feeling) fraternidad f; (group of people) círculos mpl.

fraud [frɔːd] n fraude m; (person) impostor(a) m/f.

fraught [frɔːt] adj: ~ **with** lleno de.

fray [freɪ] n combate m, lucha ♦ vi deshilacharse; **tempers were ~ed** el ambiente se ponía tenso.

freak [friːk] n (person) fenómeno; (event) suceso anormal.

freckle ['frekl] n peca.

free [friː] adj libre; (gratis) gratuito ♦ vt (prisoner etc) poner en libertad; (jammed object) soltar; ~ (**of charge**), **for ~** gratis; ~**dom** ['friːdəm] n libertad f; ~-**for-all** n riña general; ~ **gift** n prima; ~**hold** n propiedad f vitalicia; ~ **kick** n tiro libre; ~**lance** adj independiente ♦ adv por cuenta propia; ~**ly** adv libremente; (liberally) generosamente; F~**mason** n francmasón m; F~**post** n porte m pagado; ~-**range** adj (hen, eggs) de granja; ~ **trade** n libre comercio; ~**way** (US) n autopista; ~ **will** n libre albedrío; **of one's own ~ will** por su propia voluntad.

freeze [friːz] (pt **froze**, pp **frozen**) vi (weather) helar; (liquid, pipe, person) helarse, congelarse ♦ vt helar; (food, prices, salaries) congelar ♦ n helada; (on arms, wages) congelación f; ~-dried adj liofilizado; ~r n congelador m (SP), congeladora (AM).

freezing ['fri:zɪŋ] adj helado; ~ **point** n punto de congelación; **3 degrees below** ~ tres grados bajo cero.

freight [freɪt] n (goods) carga; (money charged) flete m; ~ **train** (US) n tren m de mercancías.

French [frɛntʃ] adj francés/esa ♦ n (LING) francés m; **the** ~ npl los franceses; ~ **bean** n judía verde; ~ **fried (potatoes)** patatas fpl (SP) or papas fpl (AM) fritas; ~ **fries** (US) npl = ~ **fried (potatoes)**; ~**man/woman** n francés/esa m/f; ~ **window** n puerta de cristal.

frenzy ['frɛnzɪ] n frenesí m.

frequent [adj 'fri:kwənt, vb frɪ'kwɛnt] adj frecuente ♦ vt frecuentar; ~**ly** [-əntlɪ] adv frecuentemente, a menudo.

fresh [frɛʃ] adj fresco; (bread) tierno; (new) nuevo; ~**en** vi (wind, air) soplar más recio; ~**en up** vi (person) arreglarse, lavarse; ~**er** (BRIT: inf) n (SCOL) estudiante m/f de primer año; ~**ly** adv (made, painted etc) recién; ~**man** (US) n = ~**er**; ~**ness** n frescura; ~**water** adj (fish) de agua dulce.

fret [frɛt] vi inquietarse.

friar ['fraɪə*] n fraile m; (before name) fray m.

friction ['frɪkʃən] n fricción f.

Friday ['fraɪdɪ] n viernes m inv.

fridge [frɪdʒ] (BRIT) n nevera (SP), refrigeradora (AM).

fried [fraɪd] adj frito.

friend [frɛnd] n amigo/a; ~**ly** adj simpático; (government) amigo; (place) acogedor(a); (match) amistoso; ~**ship** f amistad f.

frieze [fri:z] n friso m.

frigate ['frɪgɪt] n fragata.

fright [fraɪt] n (terror) terror m; (scare) susto; **to take** ~ asustarse; ~**en** vt asustar; ~**ened** adj asustado; ~**ening** adj espantoso; ~**ful** adj espantoso, horrible.

frigid ['frɪdʒɪd] adj (MED) frígido, frío.

frill [frɪl] n volante m.

fringe [frɪndʒ] n (BRIT: of hair) flequillo; (on lampshade etc) flecos mpl; (of forest etc) borde m, margen m; ~ **benefits** npl beneficios mpl marginales.

frisk [frɪsk] vt cachear, registrar.

frisky ['frɪskɪ] adj juguetón/ona.

fritter ['frɪtə*] n buñuelo; ~ **away** vt desperdiciar.

frivolous ['frɪvələs] adj frívolo.

frizzy ['frɪzɪ] adj rizado.

fro [frəu] see to.

frock [frɔk] n vestido.

frog [frɔg] n rana; ~**man** n hombre-rana m.

frolic ['frɔlɪk] vi juguetear.

┌─────────────────────────┐
│ *KEYWORD* │
└─────────────────────────┘

from [frɔm] prep **1** (indicating starting place) de, desde; **where do you come** ~? ¿de dónde eres?; ~ **London to Glasgow** de Londres a Glasgow; **to escape** ~ **sth/sb** escaparse de algo/alguien
2 (indicating origin etc) de; **a letter/telephone call** ~ **my sister** una carta/llamada de mi hermana; **tell him** ~ **me that** ... dígale de mi parte que ...
3 (indicating time): ~ **one o'clock to** or **until** or **till two** de(sde) la una a or hasta las dos; ~ **January (on)** a partir de enero
4 (indicating distance) de; **the hotel is 1 km from the beach** el hotel está a 1 km de la playa
5 (indicating price, number etc) de; **prices range** ~ **£10 to £50** los precios van desde £10 a or hasta £50; **the interest rate was increased** ~ **9% to 10%** el tipo de interés fue incrementado de un 9% a un 10%
6 (indicating difference) de; **he can't tell red** ~ **green** no sabe distinguir el rojo del verde; **to be different** ~ **sb/sth** ser diferente a algo/alguien
7 (because of, on the basis of): ~ **what he says** por lo que dice; **weak** ~ **hunger** debilitado por el hambre.

front [frʌnt] n (foremost part) parte f delantera; (of house) fachada; (of *dress*) delantero; (*promenade: also: sea ~*) paseo marítimo; (*MIL, POL, METEOROLOGY*) frente *m*; (*fig: appearances*) apariencias *fpl* ♦ *adj* (*wheel, leg*) delantero; (*row, line*) primero; **in ~ (of)** delante (de); **~age** ['frʌntɪdʒ] *n* (*of building*) fachada; **~ door** *n* puerta principal; **~ier** ['frʌntɪə*] *n* frontera; **~ page** *n* primera plana; **~ room** (*BRIT*) *n* salón *m*, sala; **~-wheel drive** *n* tracción *f* delantera.

frost [frɔst] *n* helada; (*also: hoar~*) escarcha; **~bite** *n* congelación *f*; **~ed** *adj* (*glass*) deslustrado; **~y** *adj* (*weather*) de helada; (*welcome etc*) glacial.

froth [frɔθ] *n* espuma.

frown [fraun] *vi* fruncir el ceño.

froze [frəuz] *pt of* **freeze**.

frozen ['frəuzn] *pp of* **freeze**.

fruit [fru:t] *n inv* fruta; fruto; (*fig*) fruto; resultados *mpl*; **~erer** *n* frutero/a; **~erer's (shop)** *n* frutería; **~ful** *adj* provechoso; **~ion** [fru:'ɪʃən] *n*: **to come to ~ion** realizarse; **~ juice** *n* zumo (*SP*) or jugo (*AM*) de fruta; **~ machine** (*BRIT*) *n* máquina *f* tragaperras; **~ salad** *n* macedonia (*SP*) or ensalada (*AM*) de frutas.

frustrate [frʌs'treɪt] *vt* frustrar; **~d** *adj* frustrado.

fry [fraɪ] (*pt, pp* **fried**) *vt* freír; **small ~** gente *f* menuda; **~ing pan** *n* sartén *f*.

ft. *abbr* = **foot**; **feet**.

fuddy-duddy ['fʌdɪdʌdɪ] (*pej*) *n* carroza *m/f*.

fudge [fʌdʒ] *n* (*CULIN*) caramelo blando.

fuel [fjuəl] *n* (*for heating*) combustible *m*; (*coal*) carbón *m*; (*wood*) leña; (*for engine*) carburante *m*; **~ oil** *n* fuel oil *m*; **~ tank** *n* depósito (de combustible).

fugitive ['fju:dʒɪtɪv] *n* fugitivo/a.

fulfil [ful'fɪl] *vt* (*function*) cumplir con; (*condition*) satisfacer; (*wish, desire*) realizar; **~ment** *n* satisfacción *f*; (*of promise, desire*) realización *f*.

full [ful] *adj* lleno; (*fig*) pleno; (*complete*) completo; (*maximum*) máximo; (*information*) detallado; (*price*) íntegro; (*skirt*) amplio ♦ *adv*: **to know ~ well that** saber perfectamente que; **I'm ~ (up)** no puedo más; **~ employment** pleno empleo; **a ~ two hours** dos horas completas; **at ~ speed** a máxima velocidad; **in ~** (*reproduce, quote*) íntegramente; **~-length** *adj* (*novel etc*) entero; (*coat*) largo; (*portrait*) de cuerpo entero; **~ moon** *n* luna llena; **~-scale** *adj* (*attack, war*) en gran escala; (*model*) de tamaño natural; **~ stop** *n* punto; **~-time** *adj* (*work*) de tiempo completo ♦ *adv*: **to work ~-time** trabajar a tiempo completo; **~y** *adv* completamente; (*at least*) por lo menos; **~y-fledged** *adj* (*teacher, barrister*) diplomado.

fulsome ['fulsəm] (*pej*) *adj* (*praise, gratitude*) excesivo, exagerado.

fumble ['fʌmbl] *vi*: **to ~ with** manejar torpemente.

fume [fju:m] *vi* (*rage*) estar furioso; **~s** *npl* humo, gases *mpl*.

fun [fʌn] *n* (*amusement*) diversión *f*; **to have ~** divertirse; **for ~** en broma; **make ~ of** *vt fus* burlarse de.

function ['fʌŋkʃən] *n* función *f* ♦ *vi* funcionar; **~al** *adj* (*operational*) en buen estado; (*practical*) funcional.

fund [fʌnd] *n* fondo; (*reserve*) reserva; **~s** *npl* (*money*) fondos *mpl*.

fundamental [fʌndə'mentl] *adj* fundamental.

funeral ['fju:nərəl] *n* (*burial*) entierro; (*ceremony*) funerales *mpl*; **~ parlour** (*BRIT*) *n* funeraria; **~ service** *n* misa de difuntos, funeral *m*.

funfair ['fʌnfeə*] (*BRIT*) *n* parque *m* de atracciones.

fungi ['fʌŋgaɪ] *npl of* **fungus**.

fungus ['fʌŋgəs] (*pl* **fungi**) *n* hongo; (*mould*) moho.

funnel ['fʌnl] *n* embudo; (*of ship*) chimenea.

funny ['fʌnɪ] *adj* gracioso, divertido; (*strange*) curioso, raro.

fur [fə:*] *n* piel *f*; (*BRIT: in kettle etc*) sarro; **~ coat** *n* abrigo de pieles.

furious ['fjuərɪəs] *adj* furioso; (*effort*) violento.

furlong ['fə:lɔŋ] *n* octava parte de una milla, = *201.17 m*.

furlough ['fə:ləu] n (MIL) permiso.

furnace ['fə:nɪs] n horno.

furnish ['fə:nɪʃ] vt amueblar; (supply) suministrar; (information) facilitar; ~ings npl muebles mpl.

furniture ['fə:nɪtʃə*] n muebles mpl; **piece of** ~ mueble m.

furrow ['fʌrəu] n surco.

furry ['fə:rɪ] adj peludo.

further ['fə:ðə*] adj (new) nuevo, adicional ♦ adv más lejos; (more) más; (moreover) además ♦ vt promover, adelantar; ~ **education** n educación f superior; ~**more** [fə:ðə'mɔ:*] adv además.

furthest ['fə:ðɪst] superlative of **far**.

fury ['fjuərɪ] n furia.

fuse [fju:z] (US **fuze**) n fusible m; (for bomb etc) mecha ♦ vt (metal) fundir; (fig) fusionar ♦ vi fundirse; fusionarse; (BRIT: ELEC): **to** ~ **the lights** fundir los plomos; ~ **box** n caja de fusibles.

fuss [fʌs] n (excitement) conmoción f; (trouble) alboroto; **to make a** ~ armar un lío or jaleo; **to make a** ~ **of sb** mimar a uno; ~**y** adj (person) exigente; (too ornate) recargado.

futile ['fju:taɪl] adj vano.

future ['fju:tʃə*] adj futuro; (coming) venidero ♦ n futuro; (prospects) porvenir; **in** ~ de ahora en adelante.

fuze [fju:z] (US) = **fuse**.

fuzzy ['fʌzɪ] adj (PHOT) borroso; (hair) muy rizado.

G

G [dʒi:] n (MUS) sol m.

g. abbr (= gram(s)) gr.

gabble ['gæbl] vi hablar atropelladamente.

gable ['geɪbl] n aguilón m.

gadget ['gædʒɪt] n aparato.

Gaelic ['geɪlɪk] adj, n (LING) gaélico.

gaffe [gæf] n plancha.

gag [gæg] n (on mouth) mordaza; (joke) chiste m ♦ vt amordazar.

gaiety ['geɪɪtɪ] n alegría.

gaily ['geɪlɪ] adv alegremente.

gain [geɪn] n: ~ (**in**) aumento (de); (profit) ganancia ♦ vt ganar ♦ vi (watch) adelantarse; **to** ~ **from/by sth** sacar provecho de algo; **to** ~ **on sb** ganar terreno a uno; **to** ~ **3 lbs** (**in weight**) engordar 3 libras.

gait [geɪt] n (modo de) andar m.

gal. abbr = **gallon**.

gala ['gɑ:lə] n fiesta.

gale [geɪl] n (wind) vendaval m.

gallant ['gælənt] adj valiente; (towards ladies) atento; ~**ry** n valentía; galantería.

gall bladder ['gɔ:l-] n vesícula biliar.

gallery ['gælərɪ] n (also: art ~: public) pinacoteca; (: private) galería de arte; (for spectators) tribuna.

galley ['gælɪ] n (ship's kitchen) cocina.

gallon ['gælən] n galón m (BRIT = 4,546 litros, US = 3,785 litros).

gallop ['gæləp] n galope m ♦ vi galopar.

gallows ['gæləuz] n horca.

gallstone ['gɔ:lstəun] n cálculo biliario.

galore [gə'lɔ:*] adv en cantidad, en abundancia.

galvanize ['gælvənaɪz] vt: **to** ~ **sb into action** animar a uno para que haga algo.

gambit ['gæmbɪt] n (fig): (opening) ~ estrategia (inicial).

gamble ['gæmbl] n (risk) riesgo ♦ vt jugar, apostar ♦ vi (take a risk) jugárselas; (bet) apostar; **to** ~ **on** apostar a; (success etc) contar con; ~**r** n jugador(a) m/f; **gambling** n juego.

game [geɪm] n juego; (match) partido; (of cards) partida; (HUNTING) caza ♦ adj (willing): **to be** ~ **for anything** atreverse a todo; **big** ~ caza mayor; ~**keeper** n guardabosques m inv.

gammon ['gæmən] n (bacon) tocino ahumado; (ham) jamón m ahumado.

gamut ['gæmət] n gama.

gang [gæŋ] n (of criminals) pandilla; (of friends etc) grupo; (of workmen) brigada; ~ **up** vi: **to** ~ **up on sb** aliarse contra uno.

gangster ['gæŋstə*] n gángster m.

gangway ['gæŋweɪ] n (on ship) pasarela; (BRIT: in theatre, bus etc) pasillo.

gaol [dʒeɪl] (BRIT) n, vt = **jail**.

gap [gæp] n vacío, hueco (AM); (in trees, traffic) claro; (in time) intervalo; (difference): ~ (between) diferencia (entre).

gape [geɪp] vi mirar boquiabierto; (shirt etc) abrirse (completamente); **gaping** adj (completamente) abierto.

garage ['gærɑːʒ] n garaje m; (for repairs) taller m.

garbage ['gɑːbɪdʒ] (US) n basura; (inf: nonsense) tonterías fpl; ~ **can** n cubo (SP) or bote m (AM) de la basura.

garbled ['gɑːbld] adj (distorted) falsificado, amañado.

garden ['gɑːdn] n jardín m; ~**s** npl (park) parque m; ~**er** n jardinero/a; ~**ing** n jardinería.

gargle ['gɑːgl] vi hacer gárgaras, gargarear (AM).

garish ['gɛərɪʃ] adj chillón/ona.

garland ['gɑːlənd] n guirnalda.

garlic ['gɑːlɪk] n ajo.

garment ['gɑːmənt] n prenda (de vestir).

garnish ['gɑːnɪʃ] vt (CULIN) aderezar.

garrison ['gærɪsn] n guarnición f.

garrulous ['gærjuləs] adj charlatán/ana.

garter ['gɑːtə*] n (for sock) liga; (US) liguero.

gas [gæs] n gas m; (fuel) combustible m; (US: gasoline) gasolina ♦ vt asfixiar con gas; ~ **cooker** (BRIT) n cocina de gas; ~ **cylinder** n bombona de gas; ~ **fire** n estufa de gas.

gash [gæʃ] n raja; (wound) cuchillada ♦ vt rajar; acuchillar.

gasket ['gæskɪt] n (AUT) junta de culata.

gas mask n careta antigás.

gas meter n contador m de gas.

gasoline ['gæsəliːn] (US) n gasolina.

gasp [gɑːsp] n boqueada; (of shock etc) grito sofocado ♦ vi (pant) jadear; ~ **out** vt (say) decir con voz entrecortada.

gas station (US) n gasolinera.

gassy ['gæsɪ] adj gaseoso.

gastric ['gæstrɪk] adj gástrico.

gate [geɪt] n puerta; (iron ~) verja; ~**crash** (BRIT) vt colarse en; ~**way** n

(also fig) puerta.

gather ['gæðə*] vt (flowers, fruit) coger (SP), recoger; (assemble) reunir; (pick up) recoger; (SEWING) fruncir; (understand) entender ♦ vi (assemble) reunirse; **to ~ speed** ganar velocidad; ~**ing** n reunión f, asamblea.

gauche [gəuʃ] adj torpe.

gaudy ['gɔːdɪ] adj chillón/ona.

gauge [geɪdʒ] n (instrument) indicador m ♦ vt medir; (fig) juzgar.

gaunt [gɔːnt] adj (haggard) demacrado; (stark) desolado.

gauntlet ['gɔːntlɪt] n guante m; (fig): **to run the ~ of** exponerse a; **to throw down the ~** arrojar el guante.

gauze [gɔːz] n gasa.

gave [geɪv] pt of **give**.

gay [geɪ] adj (homosexual) gay; (person) alegre; (colour) vivo.

gaze [geɪz] n mirada fija ♦ vi: **to ~ at sth** mirar algo fijamente.

gazelle [gə'zɛl] n gacela.

gazetteer [gæzə'tɪə*] n diccionario geográfico.

gazumping [gə'zʌmpɪŋ] (BRIT) n la subida del precio de una casa una vez que ya ha sido apalabrado.

GB abbr = **Great Britain**.

GCE n abbr (BRIT) = General Certificate of Education.

GCSE (BRIT) n abbr (= General Certificate of Secondary Education) examen de reválida que se hace a los 16 años.

gear [gɪə*] n equipo, herramientas fpl; (TECH) engranaje m; (AUT) velocidad f, marcha ♦ vt (fig: adapt): **to ~ sth to** adaptar or ajustar algo a; **top** or **high** (US)/**low** ~ cuarta/primera velocidad; **in ~** en marcha; ~ **box** n caja de cambios; ~ **lever** n palanca de cambio; ~ **shift** (US) n = ~ **lever**.

geese [giːs] npl of **goose**.

gel [dʒel] n gel m.

gem [dʒem] n piedra preciosa.

Gemini ['dʒemɪnaɪ] n Géminis m, Gemelos mpl.

gender ['dʒendə*] n género.

gene [dʒiːn] n gen(e) m.

general ['dʒenərl] n general m ♦ adj general; **in ~** en general; **~ delivery** (*US*) *n* lista de correos; **~ election** *n* elecciones *fpl* generales; **~ization** [-aɪˈzeɪʃən] *n* generalización *f*; **~ly** *adv* generalmente, en general; **~ practitioner** *n* médico general.

generate [ˈdʒɛnəreɪt] *vt* (*ELEC*) generar; (*jobs*, *profits*) producir.

generation [dʒɛnəˈreɪʃən] *n* generación *f*.

generator [ˈdʒɛnəreɪtə*] *n* generador *m*.

generosity [dʒɛnəˈrɒsɪtɪ] *n* generosidad *f*.

generous [ˈdʒɛnərəs] *adj* generoso.

genetics [dʒɪˈnɛtɪks] *n* genética.

Geneva [dʒɪˈniːvə] *n* Ginebra.

genial [ˈdʒiːnɪəl] *adj* afable, simpático.

genitals [ˈdʒɛnɪtlz] *npl* (órganos *mpl*) genitales *mpl*.

genius [ˈdʒiːnɪəs] *n* genio.

gent [dʒɛnt] *n abbr* = **gentleman**.

genteel [dʒɛnˈtiːl] *adj* fino, elegante.

gentle [ˈdʒɛntl] *adj* apacible, dulce; (*animal*) manso; (*breeze*, *curve etc*) suave.

gentleman [ˈdʒɛntlmən] *n* señor *m*; (*well-bred man*) caballero.

gentleness [ˈdʒɛntlnɪs] *n* apacibilidad *f*, dulzura; mansedumbre *f*; suavidad *f*.

gently [ˈdʒɛntlɪ] *adv* dulcemente; suavemente.

gentry [ˈdʒɛntrɪ] *n* alta burguesía.

gents [dʒɛnts] *n* aseos *mpl* (de caballeros).

genuine [ˈdʒɛnjuɪn] *adj* auténtico; (*person*) sincero.

geography [dʒɪˈɒɡrəfɪ] *n* geografía.

geology [dʒɪˈɒlədʒɪ] *n* geología.

geometric(al) [dʒɪəˈmɛtrɪk(l)] *adj* geométrico.

geranium [dʒɪˈreɪnjəm] *n* geranio.

geriatric [dʒɛrɪˈætrɪk] *adj*, *n* geriátrico/a *m/f*.

germ [dʒəːm] *n* (*microbe*) microbio, bacteria; (*seed*, *fig*) germen *m*.

German [ˈdʒəːmən] *adj* alemán/ana ♦ *n* alemán/ana *m/f*; (*LING*) alemán *m*; **~ measles** *n* rubéola.

Germany [ˈdʒəːmənɪ] *n* Alemania.

gesture [ˈdʒɛstjə*] *n* gesto; (*symbol*) muestra.

KEYWORD

get [ɡɛt] (*pt*, *pp* **got**, *pp* **gotten** (*US*)) *vi* **1** (*become*, *be*) ponerse, volverse; **to ~ old/tired** envejecer/cansarse; **to ~ drunk** emborracharse; **to ~ dirty** ensuciarse; **to ~ married** casarse; **when do I ~ paid?** ¿cuándo me pagan *or* se me paga?; **it's ~ting late** se está haciendo tarde

2 (*go*): **to ~ to/from** llegar a/de; **to ~ home** llegar a casa

3 (*begin*) empezar a; **to ~ to know sb** (llegar a) conocer a uno; **I'm ~ting to like him** me está empezando a gustar; **let's ~ going** *or* **started** ¡vamos (a empezar)!

4 (*modal aux vb*): **you've got to do it** tienes que hacerlo

♦ *vt* **1**: **to ~ sth done** (*finish*) terminar algo; (*have done*) mandar hacer algo; **to ~ one's hair cut** cortarse el pelo; **to ~ the car going** *or* **to go** arrancar el coche; **to ~ sb to do sth** conseguir *or* hacer que alguien haga algo; **to ~ sth/sb ready** preparar algo/a alguien

2 (*obtain*: *money*, *permission*, *results*) conseguir; (*find*: *job*, *flat*) encontrar; (*fetch*: *person*, *doctor*) buscar; (*object*) ir a buscar, traer; **to ~ sth for sb** conseguir algo para alguien; **~ me Mr Jones, please** (*TEL*) póngame *or* comuníqueme (*AM*) con el Sr. Jones, por favor; **can I ~ you a drink?** ¿quieres algo de beber?

3 (*receive*: *present*, *letter*) recibir; (*acquire*: *reputation*) alcanzar; (: *prize*) ganar; **what did you ~ for your birthday?** ¿qué te regalaron por tu cumpleaños?; **how much did you ~ for the painting?** ¿cuánto sacaste por el cuadro?

4 (*catch*) coger (*SP*), agarrar (*AM*); (*hit*: *target etc*) dar en; **to ~ sb by the arm/throat** coger *or* agarrar a uno por el brazo/cuello; **~ him!** ¡cógelo! (*SP*), ¡atrápalo! (*AM*); **the bullet got him in the leg** la bala le dio en la pierna

5 (*take*, *move*) llevar; **to ~ sth to sb** hacer llegar algo a alguien; **do you**

think we'll ~ it through the door?
¿crees que lo podremos meter por la
puerta?
6 (catch, take: plane, bus etc) coger
(SP), tomar (AM); where do I ~ the
train for Birmingham? ¿dónde se coge
or se toma el tren para Birmingham?
7 (understand) entender; (hear) oír;
I've got it! ¡ya lo tengo!, ¡eureka!; I
don't ~ your meaning no te entiendo;
I'm sorry, I didn't ~ your name lo siento, no cogí tu nombre
8 (have, possess): to have got tener
get about vi salir mucho; (news) divulgarse
get along vi (agree) llevarse bien; (depart) marcharse; (manage) = get by
get at vt fus (attack) atacar; (reach)
alcanzar
get away vi marcharse; (escape) escaparse
get away with vt fus hacer impunemente
get back vi (return) volver ♦ vt recobrar
get by vi (pass) (lograr) pasar; (manage) arreglárselas
get down vi bajarse ♦ vt fus bajar ♦ vt
bajar; (depress) deprimir
get down to vt fus (work) ponerse a
get in vi entrar; (train) llegar; (arrive
home) volver a casa, regresar
get into vt fus entrar en; (vehicle) subir a; ~ into a rage enfadarse
get off vi (from train etc) bajar; (depart: person, car) marcharse ♦ vt (remove) quitar ♦ vt fus (train, bus) bajar
de
get on vi (at exam etc): how are you
~ting on? ¿cómo te va?; (agree): to ~
on (with) llevarse bien (con) ♦ vt fus
subir a
get out vi salir; (of vehicle) bajar ♦ vt
sacar
get out of vt fus salir de; (duty etc)
escaparse de
get over vt fus (illness) recobrarse de
get round vt fus rodear; (fig: person)
engatusar a
get through vi (TEL) (lograr) comuni-

carse
get through to vt fus (TEL) comunicar
con
get together vi reunirse ♦ vt reunir,
juntar
get up vi (rise) levantarse ♦ vt fus subir
get up to vt fus (reach) llegar a;
(prank) hacer.

geyser ['gi:zə*] n (water heater) calentador m de agua; (GEO) géiser m.
ghastly ['gɑːstlɪ] adj horrible.
gherkin ['gəːkɪn] n pepinillo.
ghost [gəust] n fantasma m.
giant ['dʒaɪənt] n gigante m/f ♦ adj gigantesco, gigante.
gibberish ['dʒɪbərɪʃ] n galimatías m.
gibe [dʒaɪb] n = jibe.
giblets ['dʒɪblɪts] npl menudillos mpl.
Gibraltar [dʒɪ'brɔːltə*] n Gibraltar m.
giddy ['gɪdɪ] adj mareado.
gift [gɪft] n regalo; (ability) talento;
~ed adj dotado; ~ token or voucher n
vale m canjeable por un regalo.
gigantic [dʒaɪ'gæntɪk] adj gigantesco.
giggle ['gɪgl] vi reírse tontamente.
gill [dʒɪl] n (measure) = 0.25 pints (BRIT
= 0.148l, US = 0.118l).
gills [gɪlz] npl (of fish) branquias fpl,
agallas fpl.
gilt [gɪlt] adj, n dorado; ~-edged adj
(COMM) de máxima garantía.
gimmick ['gɪmɪk] n truco.
gin [dʒɪn] n ginebra.
ginger ['dʒɪndʒə*] n jengibre m; ~ ale
= ~ beer; ~ beer (BRIT) n gaseosa de
jengibre; ~bread n pan m (or galleta)
de jengibre.
gingerly ['dʒɪndʒəlɪ] adv con cautela.
gipsy ['dʒɪpsɪ] n = gypsy.
giraffe [dʒɪ'rɑːf] n jirafa.
girder ['gəːdə*] n viga.
girdle ['gəːdl] n (corset) faja.
girl [gəːl] n (small) niña; (young woman) chica, joven f, muchacha; (daughter) hija; an English ~ una (chica) inglesa; ~friend n (of girl) amiga; (of
boy) novia; ~ish adj de niña.
giro ['dʒaɪrəu] n (BRIT: bank ~) giro

bancario; (*post office* ~) giro postal; (*state benefit*) cheque quincenal del subsidio de desempleo.

girth [gəːθ] n circunferencia; (*of saddle*) cincha.

gist [dʒɪst] n lo esencial.

give [gɪv] (*pt* **gave**, *pp* **given**) vt dar; (*deliver*) entregar; (*as gift*) regalar ♦ vi (*break*) romperse; (*stretch: fabric*) dar de sí; **to** ~ **sb sth**, ~ **sth to sb** dar algo a uno; ~ **away** vt (*give free*) regalar; (*betray*) traicionar; (*disclose*) revelar; ~ **back** vt devolver; ~ **in** vi ceder ♦ vt entregar; ~ **off** vt despedir; ~ **out** vt distribuir; ~ **up** vi rendirse, darse por vencido ♦ vt renunciar a; **to** ~ **up smoking** dejar de fumar; **to** ~ **o.s. up** entregarse; ~ **way** vi ceder; (*BRIT: AUT*) ceder el paso.

glacier ['glæsɪə*] n glaciar m.

glad [glæd] adj contento.

gladly ['glædlɪ] adv con mucho gusto.

glamorous ['glæmərəs] adj encantador(a), atractivo.

glamour ['glæmə*] n encanto, atractivo.

glance [glɑːns] n ojeada, mirada ♦ vi: **to** ~ **at** echar una ojeada a; ~ **off** vt rebotar en; **glancing** adj (*blow*) oblicuo.

gland [glænd] n glándula.

glare [gleə*] n (*of anger*) mirada feroz; (*of light*) deslumbramiento, brillo; **to be in the** ~ **of publicity** ser el foco de la atención pública ♦ vi deslumbrar; **to** ~ **at** mirar con odio a; **glaring** adj (*mistake*) manifiesto.

glass [glɑːs] n vidrio, cristal m; (*for drinking*) vaso; (: *with stem*) copa; ~**es** npl (*spectacles*) gafas fpl; ~**house** n invernadero; ~**ware** n cristalería; ~**y** adj (*eyes*) vidrioso.

glaze [gleɪz] vt (*window*) poner cristales a; (*pottery*) vidriar ♦ n vidriado.

glazier ['gleɪzɪə*] n vidriero/a.

gleam [gliːm] vi brillar.

glean [gliːn] vt (*information*) recoger.

glee [gliː] n alegría, regocijo.

glen [glɛn] n cañada.

glib [glɪb] adj de mucha labia; (*promise, response*) poco sincero.

glide [glaɪd] vi deslizarse; (*AVIAT, birds*)

planear; ~**r** n (*AVIAT*) planeador m; **gliding** n (*AVIAT*) vuelo sin motor.

glimmer ['glɪmə*] n luz f tenue; (*of interest*) muestra; (*of hope*) rayo.

glimpse [glɪmps] n vislumbre m ♦ vt vislumbrar, entrever.

glint [glɪnt] vi centellear.

glisten ['glɪsn] vi relucir, brillar.

glitter ['glɪtə*] vi relucir, brillar.

gloat [gləut] vi: **to** ~ **over** recrearse en.

global ['gləubl] adj mundial.

globe [gləub] n globo; (*model*) globo terráqueo.

gloom [gluːm] n tinieblas fpl, oscuridad f; (*sadness*) tristeza, melancolía; ~**y** adj (*dark*) oscuro; (*sad*) triste; (*pessimistic*) pesimista.

glorious ['glɔːrɪəs] adj glorioso; (*weather etc*) magnífico.

glory ['glɔːrɪ] n gloria.

gloss [glɔs] n (*shine*) brillo; (*paint*) pintura de aceite; ~ **over** vt fus disimular.

glossary ['glɔsərɪ] n glosario.

glossy ['glɔsɪ] adj lustroso; (*magazine*) de lujo.

glove [glʌv] n guante m; ~ **compartment** n (*AUT*) guantera.

glow [gləu] vi brillar.

glower ['glauə*] vi: **to** ~ **at** mirar con ceño.

glue [gluː] n goma (de pegar), cemento ♦ vt pegar.

glum [glʌm] adj (*person, tone*) melancólico.

glut [glʌt] n superabundancia.

glutton ['glʌtn] n glotón/ona m/f; **a** ~ **for work** un(a) trabajador(a) incansable.

gnarled [nɑːld] adj nudoso.

gnat [næt] n mosquito.

gnaw [nɔː] vt roer.

gnome [nəum] n gnomo.

go [gəu] (*pt* **went**, *pp* **gone**, *pl* ~**es**) vi ir; (*travel*) viajar; (*depart*) irse, marcharse; (*work*) funcionar, marchar; (*be sold*) venderse; (*time*) pasar; (*fit, suit*): **to** ~ **with** hacer juego con; (*become*) ponerse; (*break etc*) estropearse, romperse ♦ n: **to have a** ~ (**at**) probar suerte (con); **to be on the** ~ no parar;

whose ~ is it? ¿a quién le toca?; he's going to do it va a hacerlo; to ~ for a walk ir de paseo; to ~ dancing ir a bailar; how did it ~? ¿qué tal salió *or* resultó?, ¿cómo ha ido?; to ~ round the back pasar por detrás; ~ about *vi* (*rumour*) propagarse ♦ *vt fus*: how do I ~ about this? ¿cómo me las arreglo para hacer esto?; ~ ahead *vi* seguir adelante; ~ along *vi* ir ♦ *vt fus* bordear; to ~ along with (*agree*) estar de acuerdo con; ~ away *vi* irse, marcharse; ~ back *vi* volver; ~ back on *vt fus* (*promise*) faltar a; ~ by *vi* (*time*) pasar ♦ *vt fus* guiarse por; ~ down *vi* bajar; (*ship*) hundirse; (*sun*) ponerse ♦ *vt fus* bajar; ~ for *vt fus* (*fetch*) ir por; (*like*) gustar; (*attack*) atacar; ~ in *vi* entrar; ~ in for *vt fus* (*competition*) presentarse a; ~ into *vt fus* entrar en; (*investigate*) investigar; (*embark on*) dedicarse a; ~ off *vi* irse, marcharse; (*food*) pasarse; (*explode*) estallar; (*event*) realizarse ♦ *vt fus* dejar de gustar; I'm going off him/the idea ya no me gusta tanto él/la idea; ~ on *vi* (*continue*) seguir, continuar; (*happen*) pasar, ocurrir; to ~ on doing sth seguir haciendo algo; ~ out *vi* salir; (*fire, light*) apagarse; ~ over *vi* (*ship*) zozobrar ♦ *vt fus* (*check*) revisar; ~ through *vt fus* (*town etc*) atravesar; ~ up *vi, vt fus* subir; ~ without *vt fus* pasarse sin.

goad [gəud] *vt* aguijonear.

go-ahead *adj* (*person*) dinámico; (*firm*) innovador(a) ♦ *n* luz *f* verde.

goal [gəul] *n* meta; (*score*) gol *m*; ~keeper *n* portero; ~-post *n* poste *m* (de la portería).

goat [gəut] *n* cabra.

gobble [ˈgɔbl] *vt* (*also*: ~ down, ~ up) tragarse, engullir.

go-between *n* intermediario/a.

god [gɔd] *n* dios *m*; G~ *n* Dios *m*; ~child *n* ahijado/a; ~daughter *n* ahijada; ~dess *n* diosa; ~father *n* padrino; ~-forsaken *adj* dejado de la mano de Dios; ~mother *n* madrina; G~send *n* don *m* del cielo; ~son *n* ahijado.

goggles [ˈgɔglz] *npl* gafas *fpl*.

going [ˈgəuɪŋ] *n* (*conditions*) estado del terreno ♦ *adj*: the ~ rate la tarifa corriente *or* en vigor.

gold [gəuld] *n* oro ♦ *adj* de oro; ~en *adj* (*made of* ~) de oro; (~ *in colour*) dorado; ~fish *n* pez *m* de colores; ~mine *n* (*also fig*) mina de oro; ~-plated *adj* chapado en oro; ~smith *n* orfebre *m/f*.

golf [gɔlf] *n* golf *m*; ~ ball *n* (*for game*) pelota de golf; (*on typewriter*) esfera; ~ club *n* club *m* de golf; (*stick*) palo (de golf); ~ course *n* campo de golf; ~er *n* golfista *m/f*.

gone [gɔn] *pp* of go.

good [gud] *adj* bueno; (*pleasant*) agradable; (*kind*) bueno, amable; (*well-behaved*) educado ♦ *n* bien *m*, provecho; ~s *npl* (COMM) mercancías *fpl*; ~! ¡qué bien!; to be ~ at tener aptitud para; to be ~ for servir para; it's ~ for you te hace bien; would you be ~ enough to ...? ¿podría hacerme el favor de ...?, ¿sería tan amable de ...?; a ~ deal (of) mucho; a ~ many muchos; to make ~ reparar; it's no ~ complaining no vale la pena (de) quejarse; for ~ para siempre, definitivamente; ~ morning/afternoon! ¡buenos días/buenas tardes!; ~ evening! ¡buenas noches!; ~ night! ¡buenas noches!; ~bye! ¡adiós!; to say ~bye despedirse; G~ Friday *n* Viernes *m* Santo; ~-looking *adj* guapo; ~-natured *adj* amable, simpático; ~ness *n* (*of person*) bondad *f*; for ~ness sake! ¡por Dios!; ~ness gracious! ¡Dios mío!; ~s train (BRIT) *n* tren *m* de mercancías; ~will *n* buena voluntad *f*.

goose [guːs] (*pl* geese) *n* ganso, oca.

gooseberry [ˈguzbərɪ] *n* grosella espinosa; to play ~ hacer de carabina.

gooseflesh [ˈguːsflɛʃ] *n* = goose pimples.

goose pimples *npl* carne *f* de gallina.

gore [gɔː*] *vt* cornear ♦ *n* sangre *f*.

gorge [gɔːdʒ] *n* barranco ♦ *vr*: to ~ o.s. (on) atracarse (de).

gorgeous [ˈgɔːdʒəs] *adj* (*thing*) precioso; (*weather*) espléndido; (*person*) gua-

písimo.
gorilla [gə'rɪlə] n gorila m.
gorse [gɔ:s] n tojo.
gory ['gɔ:rɪ] adj sangriento.
go-slow (BRIT) n huelga de manos caídas.
gospel ['gɔspl] n evangelio.
gossip ['gɔsɪp] n (scandal) cotilleo, chismes mpl; (chat) charla; (scandalmonger) cotilla m/f, chismoso/a ♦ vi cotillear.
got [gɔt] pt, pp of get; ~**ten** (US) pp of get.
gout [gaut] n gota.
govern ['gʌvən] vt gobernar; (influence) dominar.
governess ['gʌvənɪs] n institutriz f.
government ['gʌvnmənt] n gobierno.
governor ['gʌvənə*] n gobernador(a) m/f; (of school etc) miembro del consejo; (of jail) director(a) m/f.
gown [gaun] n traje m; (of teacher, BRIT; of judge) toga.
G.P. n abbr = general practitioner.
grab [græb] vt coger (SP) or agarrar (AM), arrebatar ♦ vi: to ~ at intentar agarrar.
grace [greɪs] n gracia ♦ vt honrar; (adorn) adornar; 5 **days'** ~ un plazo de 5 días; ~**ful** adj grácil, ágil; (style, shape) elegante, gracioso; **gracious** ['greɪʃəs] adj amable.
grade [greɪd] n (quality) clase f, calidad f; (in hierarchy) grado; (SCOL: mark) nota; (US: school class) curso ♦ vt clasificar; ~ **crossing** (US) n paso a nivel; ~ **school** (US) n escuela primaria.
gradient ['greɪdɪənt] n pendiente f.
gradual ['grædjuəl] adj paulatino; ~**ly** adv paulatinamente.
graduate [n 'grædjuɪt, vb 'grædjueɪt] n (US: of high school) graduado/a; (of university) licenciado/a ♦ vi graduarse; licenciarse; **graduation** [-'eɪʃən] n (ceremony) entrega del título.
graffiti [grə'fi:tɪ] n pintadas fpl.
graft [grɑ:ft] n (AGR, MED) injerto; (BRIT: inf) trabajo duro; (bribery) corrupción f ♦ vt injertar.
grain [greɪn] n (single particle) grano;

(corn) granos mpl, cereales mpl; (of wood) fibra.
gram [græm] (US) n gramo.
grammar ['græmə*] n gramática; ~ **school** (BRIT) n ≈ instituto de segunda enseñanza, liceo (SP).
grammatical [grə'mætɪkl] adj gramatical.
gramme [græm] n = gram.
gramophone ['græməfəun] (BRIT) n tocadiscos m inv.
grand [grænd] adj magnífico, imponente; (wonderful) estupendo; (gesture etc) grandioso; ~**children** npl nietos mpl; ~**dad** (inf) n yayo, abuelito; ~**daughter** n nieta; ~**eur** ['grændjə*] n magnificencia, lo grandioso; ~**father** n abuelo; ~**ma** (inf) n yaya, abuelita; ~**mother** n abuela; ~**pa** (inf) n = ~**dad**; ~**parents** npl abuelos mpl; ~ **piano** n piano de cola; ~**son** n nieto; ~**stand** n (SPORT) tribuna.
granite ['grænɪt] n granito.
granny ['grænɪ] (inf) n abuelita, yaya.
grant [grɑ:nt] vt (concede) conceder; (admit) reconocer ♦ n (SCOL) beca; (ADMIN) subvención f; to take sth/sb for ~ed dar algo por sentado/no hacer ningún caso a uno.
granulated sugar ['grænju:leɪtɪd-] (BRIT) n azúcar m blanquilla.
granule ['grænju:l] n grano, gránulo.
grape [greɪp] n uva.
grapefruit ['greɪpfru:t] n pomelo (SP), toronja (AM).
graph [grɑ:f] n gráfica; ~**ic** adj gráfico; ~**ics** n artes fpl gráficas ♦ npl (drawings) dibujos mpl.
grapple ['græpl] vi: to ~ with sth/sb agarrar a algo/uno.
grasp [grɑ:sp] vt agarrar, asir; (understand) comprender ♦ n (grip) asimiento; (understanding) comprensión f; ~**ing** adj (mean) avaro.
grass [grɑ:s] n hierba; (lawn) césped m; ~**hopper** n saltamontes m inv; ~**roots** adj (fig) popular.
grate [greɪt] n parrilla de chimenea ♦ vi: to ~ (on) chirriar (sobre) ♦ vt (CULIN) rallar.

grateful ['greitful] *adj* agradecido.

grater ['greitə*] *n* rallador *m*.

gratifying ['grætifaiiŋ] *adj* grato.

grating ['greitiŋ] *n* (*iron bars*) reja ♦ *adj* (*noise*) áspero.

gratitude ['grætitju:d] *n* agradecimiento.

gratuity [grə'tju:iti] *n* gratificación *f*.

grave [greiv] *n* tumba ♦ *adj* serio, grave.

gravel ['grævl] *n* grava.

gravestone ['greivstəun] *n* lápida.

graveyard ['greivjɑ:d] *n* cementerio.

gravity ['græviti] *n* gravedad *f*.

gravy ['greivi] *n* salsa de carne.

gray [grei] *adj* = **grey**.

graze [greiz] *vi* pacer ♦ *vt* (*touch lightly*) rozar; (*scrape*) raspar ♦ *n* (*MED*) abrasión *f*.

grease [gri:s] *n* (*fat*) grasa; (*lubricant*) lubricante *m* ♦ *vt* engrasar; lubrificar; **~proof paper** (*BRIT*) *n* papel *m* apergaminado; **greasy** *adj* grasiento.

great [greit] *adj* grande; (*inf*) magnífico, estupendo; **G~ Britain** *n* Gran Bretaña; **~-grandfather** *n* bisabuelo; **~-grandmother** *n* bisabuela; **~ly** *adv* muy; (*with verb*) mucho; **~ness** *n* grandeza.

Greece [gri:s] *n* Grecia.

greed [gri:d] *n* (*also*: **~iness**) codicia, avaricia; (*for food*) gula; (*for power etc*) avidez *f*; **~y** *adj* avaro; (*for food*) glotón/ona.

Greek [gri:k] *adj* griego ♦ *n* griego/a; (*LING*) griego.

green [gri:n] *adj* (*also POL*) verde; (*inexperienced*) novato ♦ *n* verde *m*; (*stretch of grass*) césped *m*; (*GOLF*) green *m*; **~s** *npl* (*vegetables*) verduras *fpl*; **~ belt** *n* zona verde; **~ card** *n* (*AUT*) carta verde; (*US: work permit*) permiso de trabajo para los extranjeros en EE. UU; **~ery** *n* verdura; **~grocer** (*BRIT*) *n* verdulero/a; **~house** *n* invernadero; **~ish** *adj* verdoso.

Greenland ['gri:nlənd] *n* Groenlandia.

greet [gri:t] *vt* (*welcome*) dar la bienvenida a; (*receive: news*) recibir; **~ing** *n* (*welcome*) bienvenida; **~ing(s) card** *n* tarjeta de felicitación.

grenade [grə'neid] *n* granada.

grew [gru:] *pt* of **grow**.

grey [grei] *adj* gris; (*weather*) sombrío; **~-haired** *adj* canoso; **~hound** *n* galgo.

grid [grid] *n* reja; (*ELEC*) red *f*.

grief [gri:f] *n* dolor *m*, pena.

grievance ['gri:vəns] *n* motivo de queja, agravio.

grieve [gri:v] *vi* afligirse, acongojarse ♦ *vt* dar pena a; **to ~ for** llorar por.

grievous ['gri:vəs] *adj*: **~ bodily harm** (*LAW*) daños *mpl* corporales graves.

grill [gril] *n* (*on cooker*) parrilla; (*also: mixed ~*) parillada ♦ *vt* (*BRIT*) asar a la parrilla; (*inf: question*) interrogar.

grille [gril] *n* reja; (*AUT*) rejilla.

grim [grim] *adj* (*place*) sombrío; (*situation*) triste; (*person*) ceñudo.

grimace [gri'meis] *n* mueca ♦ *vi* hacer muecas.

grime [graim] *n* mugre *f*, suciedad *f*.

grin [grin] *n* sonrisa abierta ♦ *vi* sonreír abiertamente.

grind [graind] (*pt, pp* **ground**) *vt* (*coffee, pepper etc*) moler; (*US: meat*) picar; (*make sharp*) afilar ♦ *n* (*work*) rutina.

grip [grip] *n* (*hold*) asimiento; (*control*) control *m*, dominio; (*of tyre etc*): **to have a good/bad ~** agarrarse bien/mal; (*handle*) asidero; (*holdall*) maletín *m* ♦ *vt* agarrar; (*viewer, reader*) fascinar; **to get to ~s with** enfrentarse con; **~ping** *adj* absorbente.

grisly ['grizli] *adj* horripilante, horrible.

gristle ['grisl] *n* ternilla.

grit [grit] *n* gravilla; (*courage*) valor *m* ♦ *vt* (*road*) poner gravilla en; **to ~ one's teeth** apretar los dientes.

groan [grəun] *n* gemido; quejido ♦ *vi* gemir; quejarse.

grocer ['grəusə*] *n* tendero (de ultramarinos (*SP*)); **~ies** *npl* comestibles *mpl*; **~'s (shop)** *n* tienda de ultramarinos *or* de abarrotes (*AM*).

groggy ['grɔgi] *adj* atontado.

groin [grɔin] *n* ingle *f*.

groom [gru:m] *n* mozo/a de cuadra; (*also: bride~*) novio ♦ *vt* (*horse*) almohazar; (*fig*): **to ~ sb for** preparar a uno para; **well-~ed** de buena presencia.

groove [gruːv] n ranura, surco.
grope [grəup]: **to ~ for** vt fus buscar a tientas.
gross [grəus] adj (neglect, injustice) grave; (vulgar: behaviour) grosero; (: appearance) de mal gusto; (COMM) bruto; **~ly** adv (greatly) enormemente.
grotesque [grəˈtɛsk] adj grotesco.
grotto [ˈgrɔtəu] n gruta.
grotty [ˈgrɔtɪ] (inf) adj horrible.
ground [graund] pt, pp of **grind** ♦ n suelo, tierra; (SPORT) campo, terreno; (reason: gen pl) causa, razón f; (US: also: ~ wire) tierra ♦ vt (plane) mantener en tierra; (US: ELEC) conectar con tierra; **~s** npl (of coffee etc) poso; (gardens etc) jardines mpl, parque m; **on the ~** en el suelo; **to the ~** al suelo; **to gain/lose ~** ganar/perder terreno; **~cloth** (US) n = **~sheet**; **~ing** n (in education) conocimientos mpl básicos; **~less** adj infundado; **~sheet** (BRIT) n tela impermeable; suelo; **~ staff** n personal m de tierra; **~swell** n (of opinion) marejada; **~work** n preparación f.
group [gruːp] n grupo; (musical) conjunto ♦ vt (also: ~ together) agrupar ♦ vi (also: ~ together) agruparse.
grouse [graus] n inv (bird) urogallo ♦ vi (complain) quejarse.
grove [grəuv] n arboleda.
grovel [ˈgrɔvl] vi (fig): **to ~ before** humillarse ante.
grow [grəu] (pt grew, pp grown) vi crecer; (increase) aumentar; (expand) desarrollarse; (become) volverse; **to ~ rich/weak** enriquecerse/debilitarse ♦ vt cultivar; (hair, beard) dejar crecer; **~ up** vi crecer, hacerse hombre/mujer; **~er** n cultivador(a) m/f, productor(a) m/f; **~ing** adj creciente.
growl [graul] vi gruñir.
grown [grəun] pp of **grow**; **~-up** n adulto, mayor m/f.
growth [grəuθ] n crecimiento, desarrollo; (what has grown) brote m; (MED) tumor m.
grub [grʌb] n larva, gusano; (inf: food) comida.
grubby [ˈgrʌbɪ] adj sucio, mugriento.

grudge [grʌdʒ] n (motivo de) rencor m ♦ vt: **to ~ sb sth** dar algo a uno de mala gana; **to bear sb a ~** guardar rencor a uno.
gruelling [ˈgruəlɪŋ] adj penoso, duro.
gruesome [ˈgruːsəm] adj horrible.
gruff [grʌf] adj (voice) ronco; (manner) brusco.
grumble [ˈgrʌmbl] vi refunfuñar, quejarse.
grumpy [ˈgrʌmpɪ] adj gruñón/ona.
grunt [grʌnt] vi gruñir.
G-string [ˈdʒiːstrɪŋ] n taparrabo.
guarantee [gærənˈtiː] n garantía ♦ vt garantizar.
guard [gɑːd] n (squad) guardia; (one man) guardia m; (BRIT: RAIL) jefe m de tren; (on machine) dispositivo de seguridad; (also: fire~) rejilla de protección ♦ vt guardar; (prisoner) vigilar; **to be on one's ~** estar alerta; **~ against** vt fus (prevent) protegerse de; **~ed** (fig) cauteloso; **~ian** n guardián/ana m/f; (of minor) tutor(a) m/f; **~'s van** n (BRIT: RAIL) furgón m.
Guatemala [gwætɪˈmɑːlə] n Guatemala; **~n** adj, n guatemalteco/a m/f.
guerrilla [gəˈrɪlə] n guerrillero/a.
guess [gɛs] vi adivinar; (US) suponer ♦ vt adivinar; suponer ♦ n suposición f, conjetura; **to take** or **have a ~** tratar de adivinar; **~work** n conjeturas fpl.
guest [gɛst] n invitado/a; (in hotel) huésped(a) m/f; **~-house** n casa de huéspedes, pensión f; **~ room** n cuarto de huéspedes.
guffaw [gʌˈfɔː] vi reírse a carcajadas.
guidance [ˈgaɪdəns] n (advice) consejos mpl.
guide [gaɪd] n (person) guía m/f; (book, fig) guía ♦ vt (round museum etc) guiar; (lead) conducir; (direct) orientar; **(girl) ~** n exploradora; **~book** n guía; **~ dog** n perro m guía; **~lines** npl (advice) directrices fpl.
guild [gɪld] n gremio.
guile [gaɪl] n astucia.
guillotine [ˈgɪlətiːn] n guillotina.
guilt [gɪlt] n culpabilidad f; **~y** adj culpable.

guinea ['gɪnɪ] (*BRIT*) *n* (*old*) guinea (=
21 chelines).
guinea pig *n* cobaya; (*fig*) conejillo de
Indias.
guise [gaɪz] *n*: **in** *or* **under the ~ of** bajo
apariencia de.
guitar [gɪ'tɑː*] *n* guitarra.
gulf [gʌlf] *n* golfo; (*abyss*) abismo.
gull [gʌl] *n* gaviota.
gullet ['gʌlɪt] *n* esófago.
gullible ['gʌlɪbl] *adj* crédulo.
gully ['gʌlɪ] *n* barranco.
gulp [gʌlp] *vi* tragar saliva ♦ *vt* (*also*:
~ **down**) tragarse.
gum [gʌm] *n* (*ANAT*) encía; (*glue*)
goma, cemento; (*sweet*) caramelo de
goma; (*also: chewing-~*) chicle *m* ♦ *vt*
pegar con goma; ~**boots** (*BRIT*) *npl* botas *fpl* de goma.
gumption ['gʌmpʃən] *n* sentido común.
gun [gʌn] *n* (*small*) pistola, revólver *m*;
(*shotgun*) escopeta; (*rifle*) fusil *m*;
(*cannon*) cañón *m*; ~**boat** *n* cañonero;
~**fire** *n* disparos *mpl*; ~**man** *n* pistolero; ~**point** *n*: **at** ~**point** a mano armada; ~**powder** *n* pólvora; ~**shot** *n* esco-
petazo.
gurgle ['gəːgl] *vi* (*baby*) gorgotear; (*water*) borbotear.
guru ['guːruː] *n* gurú *m*.
gush [gʌʃ] *vi* salir a raudales; (*person*)
deshacerse en efusiones.
gusset ['gʌsɪt] *n* escudete *m*.
gust [gʌst] *n* (*of wind*) ráfaga.
gusto ['gʌstəu] *n* entusiasmo.
gut [gʌt] *n* intestino; ~**s** *npl* (*ANAT*) tripas *fpl*; (*courage*) valor *m*.
gutter ['gʌtə*] *n* (*of roof*) canalón *m*;
(*in street*) cuneta.
guy [gaɪ] *n* (*also*: ~*rope*) cuerda; (*inf:
man*) tío (*SP*), tipo; (*also: G~ Fawkes*)
monigote *m*.
guzzle ['gʌzl] *vi* tragar ♦ *vt* engullir.
gym [dʒɪm] *n* (*also: gymnasium*) gimnasio; (*also: gymnastics*) gimnasia;
~**nast** *n* gimnasta *m/f*; ~ **shoes** *npl* zapatillas *fpl* (de deporte); ~ **slip** (*BRIT*)
n túnica de colegiala.
gynaecologist [gaɪnɪ'kɔlədʒɪst] (*US*
gynecologist) *n* ginecólogo/a.

gypsy ['dʒɪpsɪ] *n* gitano/a.
gyrate [dʒaɪ'reɪt] *vi* girar.

H

haberdashery [hæbə'dæʃərɪ] (*BRIT*) *n*
mercería.
habit ['hæbɪt] *n* hábito, costumbre *f*;
(*drug ~*) adicción *f*; (*costume*) hábito.
habitat ['hæbɪtæt] *n* habitat *m*.
habitual [hə'bɪtjuəl] *adj* acostumbrado,
habitual; (*drinker, liar*) empedernido.
hack [hæk] *vt* (*cut*) cortar; (*slice*) tajar
♦ *n* (*pej: writer*) escritor(a) *m/f* a sueldo; ~**er** *n* (*COMPUT*) pirata *m/f* informá-
tico.
hackneyed ['hæknɪd] *adj* trillado.
had [hæd] *pt, pp of* **have**.
haddock ['hædək] (*pl* ~ *or* ~**s**) *n* especie de merluza.
hadn't ['hædnt] = **had not**.
haemorrhage ['hemərɪdʒ] (*US* **hemorrhage**) *n* hemorragia.
haemorrhoids ['hemərɔɪdz] (*US* **hemorrhoids**) *npl* hemorroides *fpl*.
haggard ['hægəd] *adj* ojeroso.
haggle ['hægl] *vi* regatear.
Hague [heɪg] *n*: **The ~** La Haya.
hail [heɪl] *n* granizo; (*fig*) lluvia ♦ *vt* saludar; (*taxi*) llamar a; (*acclaim*) aclamar ♦ *vi* granizar; ~**stone** *n* (piedra
de) granizo.
hair [hɛə*] *n* pelo, cabellos *mpl*; (*one ~*)
pelo, cabello; (*on legs etc*) vello; **to do
one's ~** arreglarse el pelo; **to have grey
~** tener canas *fpl*; ~**brush** *n* cepillo
(para el pelo); ~**cut** *n* corte *m* (de
pelo); ~**do** *n* peinado; ~**dresser** *n*
peluquero/a; ~**dresser's** *n* peluquería;
~**-dryer** *n* secador *m* de pelo; ~**grip** *n*
horquilla; ~**pin** *n* horquilla; ~**net** *n* re-
decilla; ~**piece** *n* postizo; ~**pin bend**
(*US* ~**pin curve**) *n* curva de horquilla;
~**raising** *adj* espeluznante; ~ **remover**
n depilatorio; ~ **spray** *n* laca; ~**style** *n*
peinado; ~**y** *adj* peludo; velludo; (*inf:
frightening*) espeluznante.
hake [heɪk] (*pl inv or* ~**s**) *n* merluza.
half [hɑːf] (*pl* **halves**) *n* mitad *f*; (*of*

beer) ≈ caña (*SP*), media pinta; (*RAIL, BUS*) billete *m* de niño ♦ *adj* medio ♦ *adv* medio, a medias; **two and a ~** dos y media; **~ a dozen** media docena; **~ a pound** media libra; **to cut sth in ~** cortar algo por la mitad; **~-caste** *n* mestizo/a; **~-hearted** *adj* indiferente, poco entusiasta; **~-hour** *n* media hora; **~-mast** *n*: **at ~-mast** (*flag*) a media asta; **~-price** *adj, adv* a mitad de precio; **~ term** (*BRIT*) *n* (*SCOL*) vacaciones *de mediados de trimestre*; **~-time** *n* descanso; **~-way** *adv* a medio camino; (*in period of time*) a mitad de.

halibut ['hælɪbət] *n inv* halibut *m*.

hall [hɔ:l] *n* (*for concerts*) sala; (*entrance way*) hall *m*; vestíbulo; **~ of residence** (*BRIT*) *n* residencia.

hallmark ['hɔ:lmɑ:k] *n* sello.

hallo [hə'ləu] *excl* = **hello**.

Hallowe'en [hæləu'i:n] *n* víspera de Todos los Santos.

hallucination [həlu:sɪ'neɪʃən] *n* alucinación *f*.

hallway ['hɔ:lweɪ] *n* vestíbulo.

halo ['heɪləu] *n* (*of saint*) halo, aureola.

halt [hɔ:lt] *n* (*stop*) alto, parada ♦ *vt* parar; interrumpir ♦ *vi* pararse.

halve [hɑ:v] *vt* partir por la mitad.

halves [hɑ:vz] *npl of* **half**.

ham [hæm] *n* jamón *m* (*cocido*).

hamburger ['hæmbə:gə*] *n* hamburguesa.

hamlet ['hæmlɪt] *n* aldea.

hammer ['hæmə*] *n* martillo ♦ *vt* (*nail*) clavar; (*force*): **to ~ an idea into sb/a message across** meter una idea en la cabeza a uno/machacar una idea ♦ *vi* dar golpes.

hammock ['hæmək] *n* hamaca.

hamper ['hæmpə*] *vt* estorbar ♦ *n* cesto.

hand [hænd] *n* mano *f*; (*of clock*) aguja; (*writing*) letra; (*worker*) obrero ♦ *vt* dar, pasar; **to give or lend sb a ~** echar una mano a uno, ayudar a uno; **at ~** a mano; **in ~** (*time*) libre; (*job etc*) entre manos; **on ~** (*person, services*) a mano, al alcance; **to ~** (*information etc*) a mano; **on the one ~ ...**, **on the other ~ ...** por una parte ... por otra

(*parte*) **~ in** *vt* entregar; **~ out** *vt* distribuir; **~ over** *vt* (*deliver*) entregar; **~bag** *n* bolso (*SP*), cartera (*AM*); **~book** *n* manual *m*; **~brake** *n* freno de mano; **~cuffs** *npl* esposas *fpl*; **~ful** *n* puñado.

handicap ['hændɪkæp] *n* minusvalía; (*disadvantage*) desventaja; (*SPORT*) handicap *m* ♦ *vt* estorbar; **mentally/ physically ~ped** deficiente *m/f* (*mental*)/minusválido/a (*físico/a*).

handicraft ['hændɪkrɑ:ft] *n* artesanía; (*object*) objeto de artesanía.

handiwork ['hændɪwɔ:k] *n* obra.

handkerchief ['hæŋkətʃɪf] *n* pañuelo.

handle ['hændl] *n* (*of door etc*) tirador *m*; (*of cup etc*) asa; (*of knife etc*) mango; (*for winding*) manivela ♦ *vt* (*touch*) tocar; (*deal with*) encargarse de; (*treat: people*) manejar; **"~ with care"** "(manéjese) con cuidado"; **to fly off the ~** perder los estribos; **~bar(s)** *n(pl)* manillar *m*.

hand-: **~luggage** *n* equipaje *m* de mano; **~made** ['hændmeɪd] *adj* hecho a mano; **~out** ['hændaut] *n* (*money etc*) limosna; (*leaflet*) folleto; **~rail** ['hændreɪl] *n* pasamanos *m inv*; **~shake** ['hændʃeɪk] *n* apretón *m* de manos.

handsome ['hænsəm] *adj* guapo; (*building*) bello; (*fig: profit*) considerable.

handwriting ['hændraɪtɪŋ] *n* letra.

handy ['hændɪ] *adj* (*close at hand*) a la mano; (*tool etc*) práctico; (*skilful*) hábil, diestro; **~man** *n* manitas *m inv*.

hang [hæŋ] (*pt, pp* hung) *vt* colgar; (*criminal: pt, pp* hanged) ahorcar ♦ *vi* (*painting, coat etc*) colgar; (*hair, drapery*) caer; **to get the ~ of sth** (*inf*) lograr dominar algo; **~ about** *or* **around** *vi* haraganear; **~ on** *vi* (*wait*) esperar; **~ up** *vi* (*TEL*) colgar ♦ *vt* colgar.

hanger ['hæŋə*] *n* percha; **~-on** *n* parásito.

hang-gliding ['-glaɪdɪŋ] *n* vuelo libre.

hangover ['hæŋəuvə*] *n* (*after drinking*) resaca.

hang-up *n* complejo.

hanker ['hæŋkə*] *vi*: **to ~ after** añorar.

hankie ['hæŋkɪ] *n abbr* = **handkerchief**.

hanky ['hæŋkɪ] n abbr = **handkerchief**.
haphazard [hæp'hæzəd] adj fortuito.
happen ['hæpən] vi suceder, ocurrir; (chance): **he ~ed to hear/see** dió la casualidad de que oyó/vió; **as it ~s** da la casualidad de que; **~ing** n suceso, acontecimiento.
happily ['hæpɪlɪ] adv (luckily) afortunadamente; (cheerfully) alegremente.
happiness ['hæpɪnɪs] n felicidad f; (cheerfulness) alegría.
happy ['hæpɪ] adj feliz; (cheerful) alegre; **to be ~ (with)** estar contento (con); **to be ~ to do** estar encantado de hacer; **~ birthday!** ¡feliz cumpleaños!; **~-go-lucky** adj despreocupado.
harass ['hærəs] vt acosar, hostigar; **~ment** n persecución f.
harbour ['hɑːbə*] (US **harbor**) n puerto ♦ vt (fugitive) dar abrigo a; (hope etc) abrigar.
hard [hɑːd] adj duro; (difficult) difícil; (work) arduo; (person) severo; (fact) innegable ♦ adv (work) mucho, duro; (think) profundamente; **to look ~ at** clavar los ojos en; **to try ~** esforzarse; **no ~ feelings!** ¡sin rencor(es)!; **to be ~ of hearing** ser duro de oído; **to be ~ done by** ser tratado injustamente; **~back** n libro en cartoné; **~ cash** n dinero contante; **~ disk** n (COMPUT) disco duro or rígido; **~en** vt endurecer; (fig) curtir ♦ vi endurecerse; curtirse; **~-headed** adj realista; **~ labour** n trabajos mpl forzados.
hardly ['hɑːdlɪ] adv apenas; **~ ever** casi nunca.
hardship ['hɑːdʃɪp] n privación f.
hard-up (inf) adj sin un duro (SP), sin plata (AM).
hardware ['hɑːdwɛə*] n ferretería; (COMPUT) hardware m; (MIL) armamento; **~ shop** n ferretería.
hard-wearing adj resistente, duradero.
hard-working adj trabajador(a).
hardy ['hɑːdɪ] adj fuerte; (plant) resistente.
hare [hɛə*] n liebre f; **~-brained** adj descabellado.
harem [hɑː'riːm] n harén m.

harm [hɑːm] n daño, mal m ♦ vt (person) hacer daño a; (health, interests) perjudicar; (thing) dañar; **out of ~'s way** a salvo; **~ful** adj dañino; **~less** adj (person) inofensivo; (joke etc) inocente.
harmony ['hɑːmənɪ] n armonía.
harness ['hɑːnɪs] n arreos mpl; (for child) arnés m; (safety ~) arneses mpl ♦ vt (horse) enjaezar; (resources) aprovechar.
harp [hɑːp] n arpa ♦ vi: **to ~ on (about)** machacar (con).
harpoon [hɑː'puːn] n arpón m.
harrowing ['hærəʊɪŋ] adj angustioso.
harsh [hɑːʃ] adj (cruel) duro, cruel; (severe) severo; (sound) áspero; (light) deslumbrador(a).
harvest ['hɑːvɪst] n (~ time) siega; (of cereals etc) cosecha; (of grapes) vendimia ♦ vt cosechar.
has [hæz] vb see **have**.
hash [hæʃ] n (CULIN) picadillo; (fig: mess) lío.
hashish ['hæʃɪʃ] n hachís m.
hasn't ['hæznt] = **has not**.
hassle ['hæsl] (inf) n lata.
haste [heɪst] n prisa; **~n** ['heɪsn] vt acelerar ♦ vi darse prisa; **hastily** adv de prisa; precipitadamente; **hasty** adj apresurado; (rash) precipitado.
hat [hæt] n sombrero.
hatch [hætʃ] n (NAUT: also: ~way) escotilla; (also: service ~) ventanilla ♦ vi (bird) salir del cascarón ♦ vt incubar; (plot) tramar; **5 eggs have ~ed** han salido 5 pollos.
hatchback ['hætʃbæk] n (AUT) tres or cinco puertas m.
hatchet ['hætʃɪt] n hacha.
hate [heɪt] vt odiar, aborrecer ♦ n odio; **~ful** adj odioso; **hatred** ['heɪtrɪd] n odio.
haughty ['hɔːtɪ] adj altanero.
haul [hɔːl] vt tirar ♦ n (of fish) redada; (of stolen goods etc) botín m; **~age** (BRIT) n transporte m; (costs) gastos mpl de transporte; **~ier** (US **~er**) n transportista m/f.
haunch [hɔːntʃ] n anca; (of meat) pierna.
haunt [hɔːnt] vt (subj: ghost) aparecer-

se en; (*obsess*) obsesionar ♦ *n* guarida.

KEYWORD
---

have [hæv] (*pt, pp* **had**) *aux vb* **1** (*gen*) haber; **to ~ arrived/eaten** haber llegado/comido; **having finished** *or* **when he had finished, he left** cuando hubo acabado, se fue
2 (*in tag questions*): **you've done it, ~n't you?** lo has hecho, ¿verdad? *or* ¿no?
3 (*in short answers and questions*): **I ~n't** no; **so I ~** pues, es verdad; **we ~n't paid — yes we ~!** no hemos pagado — ¡sí que hemos pagado!; **I've been there before, ~ you?** he estado allí antes, ¿y tú?
♦ *modal aux vb* (*be obliged*): **to ~ (got) to do sth** tener que hacer algo; **you ~n't to tell her** no hay que *or* no debes decírselo
♦ *vt* **1** (*possess*): **he has (got) blue eyes/dark hair** tiene los ojos azules/el pelo negro
2 (*referring to meals etc*): **to ~ breakfast/lunch/dinner** desayunar/comer/cenar; **to ~ a drink/a cigarette** tomar algo/fumar un cigarrillo
3 (*receive*) recibir; (*obtain*) obtener; **may I ~ your address?** ¿puedes darme tu dirección?; **you can ~ it for £5** te lo puedes quedar por £5; **I must ~ it by tomorrow** lo necesito para mañana; **to ~ a baby** tener un niño *or* bebé
4 (*maintain, allow*): **I won't ~ it/this nonsense!** ¡no lo permitiré!/¡no permitiré estas tonterías!; **we can't ~ that** no podemos permitir eso
5: to ~ sth done hacer *or* mandar hacer algo; **to ~ one's hair cut** cortarse el pelo; **to ~ sb do sth** hacer que alguien haga algo
6 (*experience, suffer*): **to ~ a cold/flu** tener un resfriado/la gripe; **she had her bag stolen/her arm broken** le robaron el bolso/se rompió un brazo; **to ~ an operation** operarse
7 (+ *noun*): **to ~ a swim/walk/bath/rest** nadar/dar un paseo/darse un baño/descansar; **let's ~ a look** vamos a ver; **to ~ a meeting/party** celebrar una reunión/una fiesta; **let me ~ a try** déjame intentarlo
have out *vt*: **to ~ it out with sb** (*settle a problem etc*) dejar las cosas en claro con alguien

---

haven ['heɪvn] *n* puerto; (*fig*) refugio.
haven't ['hævnt] = **have not**.
haversack ['hævəsæk] *n* mochila.
havoc ['hævək] *n* estragos *mpl*.
hawk [hɔːk] *n* halcón *m*.
hay [heɪ] *n* heno; **~ fever** *n* fiebre *f* del heno; **~stack** *n* almiar *m*.
haywire ['heɪwaɪə*] (*inf*) *adj*: **to go ~** (*plan*) embrollarse.
hazard ['hæzəd] *n* peligro ♦ *vt* aventurar; **~ous** *adj* peligroso; **~ warning lights** *npl* (*AUT*) señales *fpl* de emergencia.
haze [heɪz] *n* neblina.
hazelnut ['heɪzlnʌt] *n* avellana.
hazy ['heɪzɪ] *adj* brumoso; (*idea*) vago.
he [hiː] *pron* él; **~ who ...** él que ..., quien ....
head [hed] *n* cabeza; (*leader*) jefe/a *m/f*; (*of school*) director(a) *m/f* ♦ *vt* (*list*) encabezar; (*group*) capitanear; (*company*) dirigir; **~s** (*on tails*) cara (o cruz); **~ first** de cabeza; **~ over heels** (*in love*) perdidamente; **to ~ the ball** cabecear (la pelota); **~ for** *vt fus* dirigirse a; (*disaster*) ir camino de; **~ache** *n* dolor *m* de cabeza; **~dress** *n* tocado; **~ing** *n* título; **~lamp** (*BRIT*) *n* = **~light**; **~land** *n* promontorio; **~light** *n* faro; **~line** *n* titular *m*; **~long** *adv* (*fall*) de cabeza; (*rush*) precipitadamente; **~master/mistress** *n* director(a) *m/f* (de escuela); **~ office** *n* oficina central, central *f*; **~-on** *adj* (*collision*) de frente; **~phones** *npl* auriculares *mpl*; **~quarters** *npl* sede *f* central; (*MIL*) cuartel *m* general; **~-rest** *n* reposacabezas *m inv*; **~room** *n* (*in car*) altura interior; (*under bridge*) (límite *m* de) altura; **~scarf** *n* pañuelo; **~strong** *adj* testarudo; **~ waiter** *n* maître *m*; **~way** *n*: **to make ~way** (*fig*) hacer progresos; **~wind** *n* viento contrario;

~y adj (experience, period) apasionante; (wine) cabezón; (atmosphere) embriagador(a).

heal [hi:l] vt curar ♦ vi cicatrizarse.

health [hɛlθ] n salud f; **~ food** n alimentos mpl orgánicos; **the H~ Service** (BRIT) n el servicio de salud pública; ≈ el Insalud (SP); **~y** adj sano, saludable.

heap [hi:p] n montón m ♦ vt: **to ~ (up)** amontonar; **to ~ sth with** llenar algo hasta arriba de; **~s of** un montón de.

hear [hɪə*] (pt, pp **heard**) vt (also LAW) oír; (news) saber ♦ vi oír; **to ~ about** oír hablar de; **to ~ from sb** tener noticias de uno; **heard** [hɜ:d] pt, pp of **hear**; **~ing** n (sense) oído; (LAW) vista; **~ing aid** n audífono; **~say** n rumores mpl, hablillas fpl.

hearse [hɜ:s] n coche m fúnebre.

heart [hɑ:t] n corazón m; (fig) valor m; (of lettuce) cogollo; **~s** npl (CARDS) corazones mpl; **to lose/take ~** descorazonarse/cobrar ánimo; **at ~** en el fondo; **by ~** (learn, know) de memoria; **~ attack** n infarto (de miocardio); **~beat** n latido (del corazón); **~breaking** adj desgarrador(a); **~broken** adj: she was **~broken about it** esto le partió el corazón; **~burn** n acedía; **~ failure** n fallo cardíaco; **~felt** adj (deeply felt) más sentido.

hearth [hɑ:θ] n (fireplace) chimenea.

heartless [ˈhɑ:tlɪs] adj cruel.

hearty [ˈhɑ:tɪ] adj (person) campechano; (laugh) sano; (dislike, support) absoluto.

heat [hi:t] n calor m; (SPORT: also: qualifying ~) prueba eliminatoria ♦ vt calentar; **~ up** vi calentarse ♦ vt calentar; **~ed** adj caliente; (fig) acalorado; **~er** n estufa; (in car) calefacción f.

heath [hi:θ] n (BRIT) n brezal m.

heathen [ˈhi:ðn] adj, n pagano/a m/f.

heather [ˈhɛðə*] n brezo.

heating [ˈhi:tɪŋ] n calefacción f.

heatstroke [ˈhi:tstrəʊk] n insolación f.

heatwave [ˈhi:tweɪv] n ola de calor.

heave [hi:v] vt (pull) tirar; (push) empujar con esfuerzo; (lift) levantar (con esfuerzo) ♦ vi (chest) palpitar; (retch)

tener náuseas ♦ n tirón m; empujón m; **to ~ a sigh** suspirar.

heaven [ˈhɛvn] n cielo; (fig) una maravilla; **~ly** adj celestial; (fig) maravilloso.

heavily [ˈhɛvɪlɪ] adv pesadamente; (drink, smoke) con exceso; (sleep, sigh) profundamente; (depend) mucho.

heavy [ˈhɛvɪ] adj pesado; (work, blow) duro; (sea, rain, meal) fuerte; (drinker, smoker) grande; (responsibility) grave; (schedule) ocupado; (weather) bochornoso; **~ goods vehicle** n vehículo pesado; **~weight** n (SPORT) peso pesado.

Hebrew [ˈhi:bru:] adj, n (LING) hebreo.

heckle [ˈhɛkl] vt interrumpir.

hectic [ˈhɛktɪk] adj agitado.

he'd [hi:d] = he would; he had.

hedge [hɛdʒ] n seto ♦ vi contestar con evasivas; **to ~ one's bets** (fig) cubrirse.

hedgehog [ˈhɛdʒhɔg] n erizo.

heed [hi:d] vt (also: **take ~ of**) (pay attention to) hacer caso de; **~less** adj: **to be ~less (of)** no hacer caso (de).

heel [hi:l] n talón m; (of shoe) tacón m ♦ vt (shoe) poner tacón a.

hefty [ˈhɛftɪ] adj (person) fornido; (parcel, profit) gordo.

heifer [ˈhɛfə*] n novilla, ternera.

height [haɪt] n (of person) estatura; (of building) altura; (high ground) cerro; (altitude) altitud f; (fig: of season): **at the ~ of winter** en pleno invierno; (: of power etc) cúspide f; (: of stupidity etc) colmo; **~en** vt elevar; (fig) aumentar.

heir [ɛə*] n heredero; **~ess** n heredera; **~loom** n reliquia de familia.

held [hɛld] pt, pp of **hold**.

helicopter [ˈhɛlɪkɔptə*] n helicóptero.

helium [ˈhi:lɪəm] n helio.

hell [hɛl] n infierno; **~!** (inf) ¡demonios!

he'll [hi:l] = he will; he shall.

hello [həˈləʊ] excl ¡hola!; (to attract attention) ¡oiga!; (surprise) ¡caramba!

helm [hɛlm] n (NAUT) timón m.

helmet [ˈhɛlmɪt] n casco.

help [hɛlp] n ayuda; (cleaner etc) criada, asistenta ♦ vt ayudar; **~!** ¡socorro!; ~ **yourself** sírvete; he can't ~ it no es culpa suya; **~er** n ayudante m/f; **~ful** adj útil; (person) servicial; (advice) útil; **~ing** n ración f; **~less** adj (incapable) incapaz; (defenceless) indefenso.

hem [hɛm] n dobladillo ♦ vt poner or coser el dobladillo; ~ **in** vt cercar.

hemorrhage ['hɛmərɪdʒ] (US) n = **haemorrhage**.

hemorrhoids ['hɛmərɔɪdz] (US) npl = **haemorrhoids**.

hen [hɛn] n gallina; (female bird) hembra.

hence [hɛns] adv (therefore) por lo tanto; 2 years ~ de aquí a 2 años; **~forth** adv de hoy en adelante.

henchman ['hɛntʃmən] (pej) n secuaz m.

henpecked ['hɛnpɛkt] adj: ~ **husband** calzonazos m inv.

hepatitis [hɛpə'taɪtɪs] n hepatitis f.

her [hɜː*] pron (direct) la; (indirect) le; (stressed, after prep) ella ♦ adj su; see also **me, my**.

herald ['hɛrəld] n heraldo ♦ vt anunciar; **~ry** n heráldica.

herb [hɜːb] n hierba.

herd [hɜːd] n rebaño.

here [hɪə*] adv aquí; (at this point) en este punto; ~! (present) ¡presente!; ~ **is/are** aquí está/están; ~ **she is** aquí está; **~after** adv en el futuro; **~by** adv (in letter) por la presente.

heredity [hɪ'rɛdɪtɪ] n herencia.

heretic ['hɛrətɪk] n hereje m/f.

heritage ['hɛrɪtɪdʒ] n patrimonio.

hermit ['hɜːmɪt] n ermitaño/a.

hernia ['hɜːnɪə] n hernia.

hero ['hɪərəu] (pl ~**es**) n héroe m; (in book, film) protagonista m; **~ic** [hɪ'rəuɪk] adj heroico.

heroin ['hɛrəuɪn] n heroína.

heroine ['hɛrəuɪn] n heroína; (in book, film) protagonista.

heron ['hɛrən] n garza.

herring ['hɛrɪŋ] n arenque m.

hers [hɜːz] pron (el) suyo/(la) suya etc; see also **mine**.

herself [hɜː'sɛlf] pron (reflexive) se;

(emphatic) ella misma; (after prep) sí (misma); see also **oneself**.

he's [hiːz] = he is; he has.

hesitant ['hɛzɪtənt] adj vacilante.

hesitate ['hɛzɪteɪt] vi vacilar; (in speech) titubear; (be unwilling) resistirse a; **hesitation** [-'teɪʃən] n indecisión f; titubeo; dudas fpl.

heterosexual [hɛtərəu'sɛksjuəl] adj heterosexual.

hew [hjuː] vt (stone, wood) labrar.

heyday ['heɪdeɪ] n: the ~ of el apogeo de.

HGV n abbr = **heavy goods vehicle**.

hi [haɪ] excl ¡hola!; (to attract attention) ¡oiga!

hiatus [haɪ'eɪtəs] n vacío.

hibernate ['haɪbəneɪt] vi invernar.

hiccough ['hɪkʌp] = **hiccup**.

hiccup ['hɪkʌp] vi hipar; **~s** npl hipo.

hide [haɪd] (pt hid, pp hidden) n (skin) piel f ♦ vt esconder, ocultar ♦ vi: to ~ (from sb) esconderse or ocultarse (de uno); **~-and-seek** n escondite m; **~away** n escondrijo.

hideous ['hɪdɪəs] adj horrible.

hiding ['haɪdɪŋ] n (beating) paliza; **to be in ~** (concealed) estar escondido.

hierarchy ['haɪərɑːkɪ] n jerarquía.

hi-fi ['haɪfaɪ] n estéreo, hifi m ♦ adj de alta fidelidad.

high [haɪ] adj alto; (speed, number) grande; (price) elevado; (wind) fuerte; (voice) agudo ♦ adv alto, a gran altura; it is 20 m ~ tiene 20 m de altura; ~ **in the air** en las alturas; **~brow** adj intelectual; **~chair** n silla alta; **~er education** n educación f or enseñanza superior; **~-handed** adj despótico; **~-heeled** adj de tacón alto; ~ **jump** n (SPORT) salto de altura; **the H~lands** npl las tierras altas de Escocia; **~light** n (fig: of event) punto culminante; (in hair) reflejo ♦ vt subrayar; **~ly** adv (paid) muy bien; (critical, confidential) sumamente; (a lot): **to speak/think ~ly of** hablar muy bien de/tener en mucho a; **~ly strung** adj hipertenso; **~ness** n altura; **Her** or **His H~ness** Su Alteza; **~-pitched** adj agudo; **~-rise block** n torre *f* de pisos; ~ **school** *n* ≈ Instituto Nacional de Bachillerato (*SP*); ~ **season** (*BRIT*) *n* temporada alta; ~ **street** (*BRIT*) *n* calle *f* mayor; ~**way** *n* carretera; (*US*) carretera nacional; autopista; **H~way Code** (*BRIT*) *n* código de la circulación.

hijack ['haɪdʒæk] *vt* secuestrar; ~**er** *n* secuestrador(a) *m/f*.

hike [haɪk] *vi* (*go walking*) ir de excursión (a pie) ♦ *n* caminata; ~**r** *n* excursionista *m/f*.

hilarious [hɪ'lɛərɪəs] *adj* divertidísimo.

hill [hɪl] *n* colina; (*high*) montaña; (*slope*) cuesta; ~**side** *n* ladera; ~**y** *adj* montañoso.

hilt [hɪlt] *n* (*of sword*) empuñadura; **to the** ~ (*fig: support*) incondicionalmente.

him [hɪm] *pron* (*direct*) le, lo; (*indirect*) le; (*stressed, after prep*) él; *see also* **me**; ~**self** *pron* (*reflexive*) se; (*emphatic*) él mismo; (*after prep*) sí (mismo); *see also* **oneself**.

hind [haɪnd] *adj* posterior.

hinder ['hɪndə*] *vt* estorbar, impedir; **hindrance** ['hɪndrəns] *n* estorbo.

hindsight ['haɪndsaɪt] *n*: **with** ~ en retrospectiva.

Hindu ['hɪnduː] *n* hindú *m/f*.

hinge [hɪndʒ] *n* bisagra, gozne *m* ♦ *vi* (*fig*): **to** ~ **on** depender de.

hint [hɪnt] *n* indirecta; (*advice*) consejo; (*sign*) dejo ♦ *vt*: **to** ~ **that** insinuar que ♦ *vi*: **to** ~ **at** hacer alusión a.

hip [hɪp] *n* cadera.

hippopotami [hɪpəu'pɒtəmaɪ] *npl of* **hippopotamus**.

hippopotamus [hɪpə'pɒtəməs] (*pl* ~**es** *or* -**mi**) *n* hipopótamo.

hire ['haɪə*] *vt* (*BRIT: car, equipment*) alquilar; (*worker*) contratar ♦ *n* alquiler *m*; **for** ~ se alquila; (*taxi*) libre; ~ **purchase** (*BRIT*) *n* compra a plazos.

his [hɪz] *pron* (el) suyo/(la) suya *etc* ♦ *adj* su; *see also* **my, mine**.

Hispanic [hɪs'pænɪk] *adj* hispánico.

hiss [hɪs] *vi* silbar.

historian [hɪ'stɔːrɪən] *n* historiador(a) *m/f*.

historic(al) [hɪ'stɔrɪk(l)] *adj* histórico.

history ['hɪstərɪ] *n* historia.

hit [hɪt] (*pt, pp* **hit**) *vt* (*strike*) golpear, pegar; (*reach: target*) alcanzar; (*collide with: car*) chocar contra; (*fig: affect*) afectar ♦ *n* golpe *m*; (*success*) éxito; **to** ~ **it off with sb** llevarse bien con uno; ~**-and-run driver** *n* conductor(a) que atropella y huye.

hitch [hɪtʃ] *vt* (*fasten*) atar, amarrar; (*also*: ~ **up**) remangar ♦ *n* (*difficulty*) dificultad *f*; **to** ~ **a lift** hacer autostop.

hitch-hike *vi* hacer autostop; ~**r** *n* autostopista *m/f*.

hi-tech [haɪ'tɛk] *adj* de alta tecnología.

hitherto ['hɪðə'tuː] *adv* hasta ahora.

hive [haɪv] *n* colmena; ~ **off** (*inf*) *vt* (*privatize*) privatizar.

HMS *abbr* = **His (Her) Majesty's Ship**.

hoard [hɔːd] *n* (*treasure*) tesoro; (*stockpile*) provisión *f* ♦ *vt* acumular; (*goods in short supply*) acaparar; ~**ing** *n* (*for posters*) cartelera.

hoarse [hɔːs] *adj* ronco.

hoax [həuks] *n* trampa.

hob [hɒb] *n* quemador *m*.

hobble ['hɒbl] *vi* cojear.

hobby ['hɒbɪ] *n* pasatiempo, afición *f*; ~**-horse** *n* (*fig*) caballo de batalla.

hobo ['həubəu] (*US*) *n* vagabundo.

hockey ['hɒkɪ] *n* hockey *m*.

hoe [həu] *n* azadón *m*.

hog [hɒg] *n* cerdo, puerco ♦ *vt* (*fig*) acaparar; **to go the whole** ~ poner toda la carne en el asador.

hoist [hɔɪst] *n* (*crane*) grúa ♦ *vt* levantar, alzar; (*flag, sail*) izar.

hold [həuld] (*pt, pp* **held**) *vt* sostener; (*contain*) contener; (*have: power, qualification*) tener; (*keep back*) retener; (*believe*) sostener; (*consider*) considerar; (*keep in position*): **to** ~ **one's head up** mantener la cabeza alta; (*meeting*) celebrar ♦ *vi* (*withstand pressure*) resistir; (*be valid*) valer ♦ *n* (*grasp*) asimiento; (*fig*) dominio; ~ **the line!** (*TEL*) ¡no cuelgue!; **to** ~ **one's own** (*fig*) defenderse; **to catch** *or* **get (a)** ~ **of** agarrarse *or* asirse de; ~ **back** *vt* retener; (*secret*) ocultar; ~ **down** *vt* (*person*) sujetar; (*job*) mantener; ~ **off** *vt* (*enemy*) rechazar; ~ **on** *vi* agarrarse bien; (*wait*) esperar; ~ **on!** (*TEL*) ¡(espere) un momento!; ~ **on to** *vt fus* agarrarse a; (*keep*) guardar; ~ **out** *vt* ofrecer ♦ *vi* (*resist*) resistir; ~ **up** *vt* (*raise*) levantar; (*support*) apoyar; (*delay*) retrasar; (*rob*) asaltar; ~**all** (*BRIT*) *n* bolsa; ~**er** *n* (*container*) receptáculo; (*of ticket, record*) poseedor(a) *m/f*; (*of office, title etc*) titular *m/f*; ~**ing** *n* (*share*) interés *m*; (*farmland*) parcela; ~**up** *n* (*robbery*) atraco; (*delay*) retraso; (*BRIT: in traffic*) embotellamiento.

hole [həul] *n* agujero ♦ *vt* agujerear.

holiday ['hɔlɪdɪ] *n* vacaciones *fpl*; (*public* ~) (día *m* de) fiesta, día *m* feriado; **on** ~ de vacaciones; ~ **camp** *n* (*BRIT: also*: ~ **centre**) centro de vacaciones; ~**-maker** (*BRIT*) *n* turista *m/f*; ~ **resort** *n* centro turístico.

holiness ['həulɪnɪs] *n* santidad *f*.

Holland ['hɔlənd] *n* Holanda.

hollow ['hɔləu] *adj* hueco, (*claim*) vacío; (*eyes*) hundido; (*sound*) sordo ♦ *n* hueco; (*in ground*) hoyo ♦ *vt*: **to** ~ **out** excavar.

holly ['hɔlɪ] *n* acebo.

holocaust ['hɔləkɔːst] *n* holocausto.

holy ['həulɪ] *adj* santo, sagrado; (*water*) bendito.

homage ['hɔmɪdʒ] *n* homenaje *m*.

home [həum] *n* casa; (*country*) patria; (*institution*) asilo ♦ *cpd* (*domestic*) casero, de casa; (*ECON, POL*) nacional ♦ *adv* (*direction*) a casa; (*right in: nail etc*) a fondo; **at** ~ en casa; (*in country*) en el país; (*fig*) como pez en el agua; **to go/come** ~ ir/volver a casa; **make yourself at** ~ ¡estás en tu casa!; ~ **address** *n* domicilio; ~ **computer** *n* ordenador *m* doméstico; ~**land** *n* tierra natal; ~**less** *adj* sin hogar, sin casa; ~**ly** *adj* (*simple*) sencillo; ~**-made** *adj* casero; **H**~ **Office** (*BRIT*) *n* Ministerio del Interior; ~ **rule** *n* autonomía; **H**~ **Secretary** (*BRIT*) *n* Ministro del Interior; ~**sick** *adj*: **to be** ~**sick** tener morriña, sentir nostalgia; ~ **town** *n* ciudad *f* natal; ~**ward** ['həumwəd] *adj* (*journey*)

hacia casa; ~**work** *n* deberes *mpl*.

homicide ['hɔmɪsaɪd] (*US*) *n* homicidio.

homosexual [hɔməu'sɛksjuəl] *adj, n* homosexual *m/f*.

Honduran [hɔn'djuərən] *adj, n* hondureño/a *m/f*.

Honduras [hɔn'djuərəs] *n* Honduras *f*.

honest ['ɔnɪst] *adj* honrado; (*sincere*) franco, sincero; ~**ly** *adv* honradamente; francamente; ~**y** *n* honradez *f*.

honey ['hʌnɪ] *n* miel *f*; ~**comb** *n* panal *m*; ~**moon** *n* luna de miel; ~**suckle** *n* madreselva.

honk [hɔŋk] *vi* (*AUT*) tocar el pito, pitar.

honorary ['ɔnərərɪ] *adj* (*member, president*) de honor; (*title*) honorífico; ~ **degree** doctorado honoris causa.

honour, (*US* **honor**) *vt* honrar; (*commitment, promise*) cumplir con ♦ *n* honor *m*, honra; ~**able** *adj* honorable; ~**s degree** *n* (*SCOL*) título de licenciado con calificación alta.

hood [hud] *n* capucha; (*BRIT: AUT*) capota; (*US: AUT*) capó *m*; (*of cooker*) campana de humos.

hoodwink ['hudwɪŋk] (*BRIT*) *vt* timar.

hoof [huːf] (*pl* **hooves**) *n* pezuña.

hook [huk] *n* gancho; (*on dress*) corchete *m*, broche *m*; (*for fishing*) anzuelo ♦ *vt* enganchar; (*fish*) pescar.

hooligan ['huːlɪgən] *n* gamberro.

hoop [huːp] *n* aro.

hooray [huː'reɪ] *excl* = **hurray**.

hoot [huːt] (*BRIT*) *vi* (*AUT*) tocar el pito, pitar; (*siren*) sonar la sirena; (*owl*) ulular; ~**er** (*BRIT*) *n* (*AUT*) pito, claxon *m*; (*NAUT*) sirena.

hoover ['huːvə*] ® (*BRIT*) *n* aspiradora ♦ *vt* pasar la aspiradora por.

hooves [huːvz] *npl* of **hoof**.

hop [hɔp] *vi* saltar, brincar; (*on one foot*) saltar con un pie.

hope [həup] *vt, vi* esperar ♦ *n* esperanza; **I** ~ **so/not** espero que sí/no; ~**ful** *adj* (*person*) optimista; (*situation*) prometedor(a); ~**fully** *adv* con esperanza; (*one hopes*): ~**fully he will recover** esperamos que se recupere; ~**less** *adj* desesperado; (*person*): **to be** ~**less** ser un desastre.

hops [hɔps] *npl* lúpulo.
horde [hɔːd] *n* (*fig*) multitud *f*.
horizon [həˈraɪzn] *n* horizonte *m*; ~tal [hɔrɪˈzɔntl] *adj* horizontal.
hormone [ˈhɔːməʊn] *n* hormona.
horn [hɔːn] *n* cuerno; (*MUS: also: French* ~) trompa; (*AUT*) pito, claxon *m*.
hornet [ˈhɔːnɪt] *n* avispón *m*.
horny [ˈhɔːnɪ] (*inf*) *adj* cachondo.
horoscope [ˈhɔrəskəʊp] *n* horóscopo.
horrible [ˈhɔrɪbl] *adj* horrible.
horrid [ˈhɔrɪd] *adj* horrible, horroroso.
horrify [ˈhɔrɪfaɪ] *vt* horrorizar.
horror [ˈhɔrə*] *n* horror *m*; ~ **film** *n* película de horror.
hors d'œuvre [ɔːˈdəːvrə] *n* entremeses *mpl*.
horse [hɔːs] *n* caballo; **on** ~**back** a caballo; ~ **chestnut** *n* (*tree*) castaño de Indias; (*nut*) castaña de Indias; ~**man/woman** *n* jinete/a *m/f*; ~**power** *n* caballo (de fuerza); ~**-racing** *n* carreras *fpl* de caballos; ~**radish** *n* rábano picante; ~**shoe** *n* herradura.
hose [həʊz] *n* (*also:* ~**pipe**) manguera.
hosiery [ˈhəʊzɪərɪ] *n* (*in shop*) (sección *f* de) medias *fpl*.
hospitable [hɔsˈpɪtəbl] *adj* hospitalario.
hospital [ˈhɔspɪtl] *n* hospital *m*.
hospitality [hɔspɪˈtælɪtɪ] *n* hospitalidad *f*.
host [həʊst] *n* anfitrión *m*; (*TV, RADIO*) presentador *m*; (*REL*) hostia; (*large number*): **a** ~ **of** multitud de.
hostage [ˈhɔstɪdʒ] *n* rehén *m*.
hostel [ˈhɔstl] *n* hostal *m*; (**youth**) ~ *n* albergue *m* juvenil.
hostess [ˈhəʊstɪs] *n* anfitriona; (*BRIT: air* ~) azafata; (*TV, RADIO*) presentadora.
hostile [ˈhɔstaɪl] *adj* hostil.
hot [hɔt] *adj* caliente; (*weather*) caluroso, de calor; (*as opposed to warm*) muy caliente; (*spicy*) picante; (*fig*) ardiente, acalorado; **to be** ~ (*person*) tener calor; (*object*) estar caliente; (*weather*) hacer calor; ~**bed** *n* (*fig*) semillero; ~ **dog** *n* perro caliente.
hotel [həʊˈtɛl] *n* hotel *m*; ~**ier** *n* hotelero; (*manager*) director *m*.

hot: ~**headed** *adj* exaltado; ~**house** *n* invernadero; ~ **line** *n* (*POL*) teléfono rojo; ~**ly** *adv* con pasión, apasionadamente; ~**plate** *n* (*on cooker*) placa calentadora; ~**-water bottle** *n* bolsa de agua caliente.
hound [haʊnd] *vt* acosar ♦ *n* perro (de caza).
hour [ˈaʊə*] *n* hora; ~**ly** *adj* (de) cada hora.
house [*n* haus, *pl* ˈhaʊzɪz, *vb* haʊz] *n* (*gen, firm*) casa; (*POL*) cámara; (*THEATRE*) sala ♦ *vt* (*person*) alojar; (*collection*) albergar; **on the** ~ (*fig*) la casa invita; ~ **arrest** *n* arresto domiciliario; ~**boat** *n* casa flotante; ~**bound** *adj* confinado en casa; ~**breaking** *n* allanamiento de morada; ~**coat** *n* bata; ~**hold** *n* familia; (*home*) casa; ~**keeper** *n* ama de llaves; ~**keeping** *n* (*work*) trabajos *mpl* domésticos; ~**keeping (money)** *n* dinero para gastos domésticos; ~**warming party** *n* fiesta de estreno de una casa; ~**wife** *n* ama de casa; ~**work** *n* faenas *fpl* (de la casa).
housing [ˈhaʊzɪŋ] *n* (*act*) alojamiento; (*houses*) viviendas *fpl*; ~ **development** *n* urbanización *f*; ~ **estate** (*BRIT*) *n* = ~ **development**.
hovel [ˈhɔvl] *n* casucha.
hover [ˈhɔvə*] *vi* flotar (en el aire); ~**craft** *n* aerodeslizador *m*.
how [haʊ] *adv* (*in what way*) cómo; ~ **are you?** ¿cómo estás?; ~ **much milk/many people?** ¿cuánta leche/gente?; ~ **much does it cost?** ¿cuánto cuesta?; ~ **long have you been here?** ¿cuánto hace que estás aquí?; ~ **old are you?** ¿cuántos años tienes?; ~ **tall is he?** ¿cómo es de alto?; ~ **is school?** ¿cómo (te) va (en) la escuela?; ~ **was the film?** ¿qué tal la película?; ~ **lovely/awful!** ¡qué bonito/horror!
howl [haʊl] *n* aullido ♦ *vi* aullar; (*person*) dar alaridos; (*wind*) ulular.
H.P. *n abbr* = **hire purchase**.
h.p. *abbr* = **horse power**.
HQ *n abbr* = **headquarters**.
hub [hʌb] *n* (*of wheel*) cubo; (*fig*) centro.

hubbub ['hʌbʌb] *n* barahúnda.

hubcap ['hʌbkæp] *n* tapacubos *m inv*.

huddle ['hʌdl] *vi*: to ~ **together** acurrucarse.

hue [hju:] *n* color *m*, matiz *m*; ~ **and cry** *n* clamor *m*.

huff [hʌf] *n*: **in a** ~ enojado.

hug [hʌg] *vt* abrazar; *(thing)* apretar con los brazos.

huge [hju:dʒ] *adj* enorme.

hulk [hʌlk] *n* (*ship*) barco viejo; *(person, building etc)* mole *f*.

hull [hʌl] *n* (*of ship*) casco.

hullo [hə'ləu] *excl* = **hello**.

hum [hʌm] *vt* tararear, canturrear ♦ *vi* tararear, canturrear; *(insect)* zumbar.

human ['hju:mən] *adj*, *n* humano.

humane [hju:'meɪn] *adj* humano, humanitario.

humanitarian [hju:mæni'tɛərɪən] *adj* humanitario.

humanity [hju:'mænɪtɪ] *n* humanidad *f*.

humble ['hʌmbl] *adj* humilde ♦ *vt* humillar.

humbug ['hʌmbʌg] *n* tonterías *fpl*; *(BRIT: sweet)* caramelo de menta.

humdrum ['hʌmdrʌm] *adj* (*boring*) monótono, aburrido.

humid ['hju:mɪd] *adj* húmedo.

humiliate [hju:'mɪlɪeɪt] *vt* humillar.

humility [hju:'mɪlɪtɪ] *n* humildad *f*.

humor ['hju:mə*] *(US) n* = **humour**.

humorous ['hju:mərəs] *adj* gracioso, divertido.

humour ['hju:mə*] *(US* **humor**) *n* humorismo, sentido del humor; *(mood)* humor *m* ♦ *vt* (*person*) complacer.

hump [hʌmp] *n* (*in ground*) montículo; *(camel's)* giba; ~**backed** *adj*: ~**backed bridge** puente *m* (*de fuerte pendiente*).

hunch [hʌntʃ] *n* (*premonition*) presentimiento; ~**back** *n* joroba *m/f*; ~**ed** *adj* jorobado.

hundred ['hʌndrəd] *num* ciento; (*before n*) cien; ~**s of** centenares de; ~**weight** *n* (*BRIT*) = 50.8 *kg*; 112 *lb*; (*US*) = 45.3 *kg*; 100 *lb*.

hung [hʌŋ] *pt*, *pp of* **hang**.

Hungarian [hʌŋ'gɛərɪən] *adj*, *n* húngaro/a *m/f*.

Hungary ['hʌŋgərɪ] *n* Hungría.

hunger ['hʌŋgə*] *n* hambre *f* ♦ *vi*: to ~ **for** (*fig*) tener hambre de, anhelar; ~ **strike** *n* huelga de hambre.

hungry ['hʌŋgrɪ] *adj*: ~ **(for)** hambriento (de); **to be** ~ tener hambre.

hunk [hʌŋk] *n* (*of bread etc*) trozo, pedazo.

hunt [hʌnt] *vt* (*seek*) buscar; (*SPORT*) cazar ♦ *vi* (*search*): **to** ~ **(for)** buscar; (*SPORT*) cazar ♦ *n* búsqueda; caza, cacería; ~**er** *n* cazador(a) *m/f*; ~**ing** *n* caza.

hurdle ['hə:dl] *n* (*SPORT*) valla; (*fig*) obstáculo.

hurl [hə:l] *vt* lanzar, arrojar.

hurrah [hu:'rɑ:] *excl* = **hurray**.

hurray [hu'reɪ] *excl* ¡viva!

hurricane ['hʌrɪkən] *n* huracán *m*.

hurried ['hʌrɪd] *adj* (*rushed*) hecho de prisa; ~**ly** *adv* con prisa, apresuradamente.

hurry ['hʌrɪ] *n* prisa ♦ *vi* (*also:* ~ *up*) apresurarse, darse prisa ♦ *vt* (*also:* ~ *up: person*) dar prisa a; (: *work*) apresurar, hacer de prisa; **to be in a** ~ tener prisa.

hurt [hə:t] (*pt*, *pp* **hurt**) *vt* hacer daño a ♦ *vi* doler ♦ *adj* lastimado; ~**ful** *adj* (*remark etc*) hiriente.

hurtle ['hə:tl] *vi*: **to** ~ **past** pasar como un rayo; **to** ~ **down** ir a toda velocidad.

husband ['hʌzbənd] *n* marido.

hush [hʌʃ] *n* silencio ♦ *vt* hacer callar; ~! ¡chitón!, ¡cállate!; ~ **up** *vt* encubrir.

husk [hʌsk] *n* (*of wheat*) cáscara.

husky ['hʌskɪ] *adj* ronco ♦ *n* perro esquimal.

hustle ['hʌsl] *vt* (*hurry*) dar prisa a ♦ *n*: ~ **and bustle** ajetreo.

hut [hʌt] *n* cabaña; (*shed*) cobertizo.

hutch [hʌtʃ] *n* conejera.

hyacinth ['haɪəsɪnθ] *n* jacinto.

hydrant ['haɪdrənt] *n* (*also: fire* ~) boca de incendios.

hydraulic [haɪ'drɔ:lɪk] *adj* hidráulico.

hydroelectric [haɪdrəʊ'lektrɪk] *adj* hidroeléctrico.

hydrofoil ['haɪdrəfɔɪl] *n* aerodeslizador

m.
hydrogen ['haɪdrədʒən] *n* hidrógeno.
hygiene ['haɪdʒiːn] *n* higiene *f*; **hygienic** [-'dʒiːnɪk] *adj* higiénico.
hymn [hɪm] *n* himno.
hype [haɪp] (*inf*) *n* bombardeo publicitario.
hypermarket ['haɪpəmɑːkɪt] *n* hipermercado.
hyphen ['haɪfn] *n* guión *m*.
hypnotize ['hɪpnətaɪz] *vt* hipnotizar.
hypochondriac [haɪpəu'kɒndriæk] *n* hipocondríaco/a.
hypocrisy [hɪ'pɒkrɪsɪ] *n* hipocresía; **hypocrite** ['hɪpəkrɪt] *n* hipócrita *m/f*; **hypocritical** [hɪpə'krɪtɪkl] *adj* hipócrita.
hypotheses [haɪ'pɒθɪsiːz] *npl of* **hypothesis**.
hypothesis [haɪ'pɒθɪsɪs] (*pl* ~**ses**) *n* hipótesis *f inv*.
hysteria [hɪ'stɪərɪə] *n* histeria; **hysterical** [-'stɛrɪkl] *adj* histérico; (*funny*) para morirse de risa; **hysterics** [-'stɛrɪks] *npl* histeria; **to be in hysterics** (*fig*) morirse de risa.

I

I [aɪ] *pron* yo.
ice [aɪs] *n* hielo; (~ *cream*) helado ♦ *vt* (*cake*) alcorzar ♦ *vi* (*also*: ~ *over*, ~ *up*) helarse; ~**berg** *n* iceberg *m*; ~**box** *n* (*BRIT*) congelador *m*; (*US*) nevera (*SP*), refrigeradora (*AM*); ~ **cream** *n* helado; ~ **cube** *n* cubito de hielo; ~**d** *adj* (*cake*) escarchado; (*drink*) helado; ~ **hockey** *n* hockey *m* sobre hielo.
Iceland ['aɪslənd] *n* Islandia.
ice: ~ **lolly** (*BRIT*) *n* polo; ~ **rink** *n* pista de hielo; ~ **skating** *n* patinaje *m* sobre hielo.
icicle ['aɪsɪkl] *n* carámbano.
icing ['aɪsɪŋ] *n* (*CULIN*) alcorza; ~ **sugar** (*BRIT*) *n* azúcar *m* glas(eado).
icy ['aɪsɪ] *adj* helado.
I'd [aɪd] = I would; I had.
idea [aɪ'dɪə] *n* idea.
ideal [aɪ'dɪəl] *n* ideal *m* ♦ *adj* ideal; ~**ist** *n* idealista *m/f*.

identical [aɪ'dɛntɪkl] *adj* idéntico.
identification [aɪdɛntɪfɪ'keɪʃən] *n* identificación *f*; (**means of**) ~ documentos *mpl* personales.
identify [aɪ'dɛntɪfaɪ] *vt* identificar.
identikit [aɪ'dɛntɪkɪt] ® *n*: ~ (**picture**) retrato-robot *m*.
identity [aɪ'dɛntɪtɪ] *n* identidad *f*; ~ **card** *n* carnet *m* de identidad.
ideology [aɪdɪ'ɒlədʒɪ] *n* ideología.
idiom ['ɪdɪəm] *n* modismo; (*style of speaking*) lenguaje *m*; ~**atic** [-'mætɪk] *adj* idiomático.
idiosyncrasy [ɪdɪəu'sɪŋkrəsɪ] *n* idiosincrasia.
idiot ['ɪdɪət] *n* idiota *m/f*; ~**ic** [-'ɒtɪk] *adj* tonto.
idle ['aɪdl] *adj* (*inactive*) ocioso; (*lazy*) holgazán/ana; (*unemployed*) parado, desocupado; (*machinery etc*) parado; (*talk etc*) frívolo ♦ *vi* (*machine*) marchar en vacío; ~ **away** *vt*: **to** ~ **away the time** malgastar el tiempo.
idol ['aɪdl] *n* ídolo; ~**ize** *vt* idolatrar.
idyllic [ɪ'dɪlɪk] *adj* idílico.
i.e. *abbr* (= *that is*) esto es.
if [ɪf] *conj* si; ~ **necessary** si fuera necesario, si hiciese falta; ~ **I were you** yo en tu lugar; ~ **so/not** de ser así/si no; ~ **only I could!** ¡ojalá pudiera!; *see also* **as; even**.
igloo ['ɪgluː] *n* iglú *m*.
ignite [ɪg'naɪt] *vt* (*set fire to*) encender ♦ *vi* encenderse.
ignition [ɪg'nɪʃən] *n* (*AUT*: *process*) ignición *f*; (*AUT*: *mechanism*) encendido; **to switch on/off the** ~ arrancar/apagar el motor; ~ **key** *n* (*AUT*) llave *f* de contacto.
ignorance ['ɪgnərəns] *n* ignorancia.
ignorant ['ɪgnərənt] *adj* ignorante; **to be** ~ **of** ignorar.
ignore [ɪg'nɔː*] *vt* (*person, advice*) no hacer caso de; (*fact*) pasar por alto.
ill [ɪl] *adj* enfermo, malo ♦ *n* mal *m* ♦ *adv* mal; **to be taken** ~ ponerse enfermo; ~**-advised** *adj* (*decision*) imprudente; ~**-at-ease** *adj* incómodo.
I'll [aɪl] = I will; I shall.
illegal [ɪ'liːgl] *adj* ilegal.

illegible [ɪ'lɛdʒɪbl] *adj* ilegible.
illegitimate [ɪlɪ'dʒɪtɪmət]. *adj* ilegítimo.
ill-fated *adj* malogrado.
ill feeling *n* rencor *m*.
illicit [ɪ'lɪsɪt] *adj* ilícito.
illiterate [ɪ'lɪtərət] *adj* analfabeto.
ill-mannered *adj* mal educado.
illness [ɪ'lnɪs] *n* enfermedad *f*.
ill-treat *vt* maltratar.
illuminate [ɪ'luːmɪneɪt] *vt* (*room, street*) iluminar, alumbrar; **illumination** [-'neɪʃən] *n* alumbrado; **illuminations** *npl* (*decorative lights*) iluminaciones *fpl*, luces *fpl*.
illusion [ɪ'luːʒən] *n* ilusión *f*; (*trick*) truco.
illustrate [ɪ'ləstreɪt] *vt* ilustrar.
illustration [ɪlə'streɪʃən] *n* (*act of illustrating*) ilustración *f*; (*example*) ejemplo, ilustración *f*; (*in book*) lámina.
illustrious [ɪ'lʌstrɪəs] *adj* ilustre.
ill will *n* rencor *m*.
I'm [aɪm] = **I am**.
image [ɪ'mɪdʒ] *n* imagen *f*; **~ry** [-ərɪ] *n* imágenes *fpl*.
imaginary [ɪ'mædʒɪnərɪ] *adj* imaginario.
imagination [ɪmædʒɪ'neɪʃən] *n* imaginación *f*; (*inventiveness*) inventiva.
imaginative [ɪ'mædʒɪnətɪv] *adj* imaginativo.
imagine [ɪ'mædʒɪn] *vt* imaginarse.
imbalance [ɪm'bæləns] *n* desequilibrio.
imbecile [ɪ'mbəsiːl] *n* imbécil *m/f*.
imitate [ɪ'mɪteɪt] *vt* imitar; **imitation** [-'teɪʃən] *n* imitación *f*; (*copy*) copia.
immaculate [ɪ'mækjulət] *adj* inmaculado.
immaterial [ɪmə'tɪərɪəl] *adj* (*unimportant*) sin importancia.
immature [ɪmə'tjuə*] *adj* (*person*) inmaduro.
immediate [ɪ'miːdɪət] *adj* inmediato; (*pressing*) urgente, apremiante; (*nearest: family*) próximo; (: *neighbourhood*) inmediato; **~ly** *adv* (*at once*) en seguida; (*directly*) inmediatamente; **~ly next to** muy junto a.
immense [ɪ'mens] *adj* inmenso, enorme; (*importance*) enorme.
immerse [ɪ'məːs] *vt* (*submerge*) sumer-

gir; **to be ~d in** (*fig*) estar absorto en.
immersion heater [ɪ'məːʃən-] (*BRIT*) *n* calentador *m* de inmersión.
immigrant [ɪ'mɪgrənt] *n* inmigrante *m/f*.
immigration [ɪmɪ'greɪʃən] *n* inmigración *f*.
imminent [ɪ'mɪnənt] *adj* inminente.
immobile [ɪ'məubaɪl] *adj* inmóvil.
immoral [ɪ'mɔrl] *adj* inmoral.
immortal [ɪ'mɔːtl] *adj* inmortal.
immune [ɪ'mjuːn] *adj*: **~ (to)** inmune (a); **immunity** *n* (*MED, of diplomat*) inmunidad *f*.
immunize [ɪ'mjunaɪz] *vt* inmunizar.
imp [ɪmp] *n* diablillo; (*child*) pícaro.
impact [ɪ'mpækt] *n* impacto.
impair [ɪm'peə*] *vt* perjudicar.
impale [ɪm'peɪl] *vt* empalar.
impart [ɪm'paːt] *vt* comunicar; (*flavour*) proporcionar.
impartial [ɪm'paːʃl] *adj* imparcial.
impassable [ɪm'paːsəbl] *adj* (*barrier*) infranqueable; (*river, road*) intransitable.
impasse [æm'paːs] *n* punto muerto.
impassive [ɪm'pæsɪv] *adj* impasible.
impatience [ɪm'peɪʃəns] *n* impaciencia.
impatient [ɪm'peɪʃənt] *adj* impaciente; **to get *or* grow ~** impacientarse.
impeccable [ɪm'pekəbl] *adj* impecable.
impede [ɪm'piːd] *vt* estorbar.
impediment [ɪm'pedɪmənt] *n* obstáculo, estorbo; (*also: speech ~*) defecto (del habla).
impending [ɪm'pendɪŋ] *adj* inminente.
impenetrable [ɪm'penɪtrəbl] *adj* impenetrable; (*fig*) insondable.
imperative [ɪm'perətɪv] *adj* (*tone*) imperioso; (*need*) imprescindible ♦ *n* (*LING*) imperativo.
imperfect [ɪm'pəːfɪkt] *adj* (*goods etc*) defectuoso ♦ *n* (*LING: also: ~ tense*) imperfecto; **~ion** [-'fekʃən] *n* (*blemish*) desperfecto; (*fault*) defecto.
imperial [ɪm'pɪərɪəl] *adj* imperial; **~ism** *n* imperialismo.
impersonal [ɪm'pəːsənl] *adj* impersonal.
impersonate [ɪm'pəːsəneɪt] *vt* hacerse pasar por; (*THEATRE*) imitar.
impertinent [ɪm'pəːtɪnənt] *adj* imperti-

nente, insolente.
impervious [ɪm'pɜːvɪəs] *adj* impermeable; (*fig*): ~ **to** insensible a.
impetuous [ɪm'pɛtjuəs] *adj* impetuoso.
impetus ['ɪmpɪtəs] *n* ímpetu *m*; (*fig*) impulso.
impinge [ɪm'pɪndʒ]: **to** ~ **on** *vt fus* (*affect*) afectar a.
implacable [ɪm'plækəbl] *adj* implacable.
implement [*n* 'ɪmplɪmənt, *vb* 'ɪmplɪment] *n* herramienta; (*for cooking*) utensilio ♦ *vt* (*regulation*) hacer efectivo; (*plan*) realizar.
implicate ['ɪmplɪkeɪt] *vt* (*in crime etc*) involucrar; **implication** [-'keɪʃən] *n* consecuencia; (*involvement*) implicación *f*.
implicit [ɪm'plɪsɪt] *adj* implícito; (*belief, trust*) absoluto.
implore [ɪm'plɔː*] *vt* (*person*) suplicar.
imply [ɪm'plaɪ] *vt* (*involve*) suponer; (*hint*) dar a entender que.
impolite [ɪmpə'laɪt] *adj* mal educado.
import [*vb* ɪm'pɔːt, *n* 'ɪmpɔːt] *vt* importar ♦ *n* (*COMM*) importación *f*; (: *article*) producto importado; (*meaning*) significado, sentido.
importance [ɪm'pɔːtəns] *n* importancia.
important [ɪm'pɔːtənt] *adj* importante; it's not ~ no importa, no tiene importancia.
importer [ɪm'pɔːtə*] *n* importador(a) *m/f*.
impose [ɪm'pəʊz] *vt* imponer ♦ *vi*: **to** ~ **on sb** abusar de uno; **imposing** *adj* imponente, impresionante.
imposition [ɪmpə'zɪʃn] *n* (*of tax etc*) imposición *f*; **to be an** ~ **on** (*person*) molestar a.
impossible [ɪm'pɔsɪbl] *adj* imposible; (*person*) insoportable.
impostor [ɪm'pɔstə*] *n* impostor(a) *m/f*.
impotent ['ɪmpətənt] *adj* impotente.
impound [ɪm'paʊnd] *vt* embargar.
impoverished [ɪm'pɔvərɪʃt] *adj* necesitado.
impracticable [ɪm'præktɪkəbl] *adj* no factible, irrealizable.
impractical [ɪm'præktɪkl] *adj* (*person, plan*) poco práctico.
imprecise [ɪmprɪ'saɪs] *adj* impreciso.

impregnable [ɪm'prɛgnəbl] *adj* (*castle*) inexpugnable.
impregnate ['ɪmprɛgneɪt] *vt* (*saturate*) impregnar.
impresario [ɪmprə'sɑːrɪəʊ] *n* empresario teatral.
impress [ɪm'prɛs] *vt* impresionar; (*mark*) estampar; **to** ~ **sth on sb** hacer entender algo a uno.
impression [ɪm'prɛʃən] *n* impresión *f*; (*imitation*) imitación *f*; **to be under the** ~ **that** tener la impresión de que; ~**able** *adj* impresionable; ~**ist** *n* impresionista *m/f*.
impressive [ɪm'prɛsɪv] *adj* impresionante.
imprint ['ɪmprɪnt] *n* (*outline*) huella; (*PUBLISHING*) pie *m* de imprenta.
imprison [ɪm'prɪzn] *vt* encarcelar; ~**ment** *n* encarcelamiento; (*term of* ~) cárcel *f*.
improbable [ɪm'prɔbəbl] *adj* improbable, inverosímil.
impromptu [ɪm'prɔmptjuː] *adj* improvisado.
improper [ɪm'prɔpə*] *adj* (*unsuitable: conduct etc*) incorrecto; (: *activities*) deshonesto.
improve [ɪm'pruːv] *vt* mejorar; (*foreign language*) perfeccionar ♦ *vi* mejorarse; ~**ment** *n* mejoramiento; perfección *f*; progreso.
improvise ['ɪmprəvaɪz] *vt, vi* improvisar.
impudent ['ɪmpjudnt] *adj* descarado, insolente.
impulse ['ɪmpʌls] *n* impulso; **to act on** ~ obrar sin reflexión; **impulsive** [-'pʌlsɪv] *adj* irreflexivo.
impunity [ɪm'pjuːnɪtɪ] *n*: **with** ~ impunemente.
impure [ɪm'pjʊə*] *adj* (*adulterated*) adulterado; (*morally*) impuro; **impurity** *n* impureza.

KEYWORD

in [ɪn] *prep* **1** (*indicating place, position, with place names*) en; ~ **the house/ garden** en (la) casa/el jardín; ~ **here/ there** aquí/ahí *or* allí dentro; ~ **London/**

England en Londres/Inglaterra
2 (*indicating time*) en; ~ **spring** en (la)
primavera; ~ **the afternoon** por la tarde; **at 4 o'clock** ~ **the afternoon** a las 4
de la tarde; **I did it** ~ **3 hours/days** lo
hice en 3 horas/días; **I'll see you** ~ **2
weeks** *or* ~ **2 weeks' time** te veré dentro de 2 semanas
3 (*indicating manner etc*) en; ~ **a
loud/soft voice** en voz alta/baja; ~
pencil/ink a lápiz/bolígrafo; **the boy** ~
the blue shirt el chico de la camisa azul
4 (*indicating circumstances*): ~ **the
sun/shade/rain** al sol/a la sombra/bajo la
lluvia; **a change** ~ **policy** un cambio de
política
5 (*indicating mood, state*): ~ **tears** en
lágrimas, llorando; ~ **anger/despair**
enfadado/desesperado; **to live** ~ **luxury**
vivir lujosamente
6 (*with ratios, numbers*): **1** ~ **10 house-
holds, 1 household** ~ **10** una de cada 10
familias; **20 pence** ~ **the pound** 20 peniques por libra; **they lined up** ~ **twos** se
alinearon de dos en dos
7 (*referring to people, works*) en; entre; **the disease is common** ~ **children**
la enfermedad es común entre los niños; ~ **(the works of) Dickens** en (las
obras de) Dickens
8 (*indicating profession etc*): **to be** ~
teaching estar en la enseñanza
9 (*after superlative*) de; **the best pupil**
~ **the class** el/la mejor alumno/a de la
clase
10 (*with present participle*): ~ **saying
this** al decir esto
♦ *adv*: **to be** ~ (*person: at home*) estar
en casa; (*work*) estar; (*train, ship,
plane*) haber llegado; (*in fashion*) estar
de moda; **she'll be** ~ **later today** llega-
rá más tarde hoy; **to ask sb** ~ hacer
pasar a uno; **to run/limp** *etc* ~ entrar
corriendo/cojeando *etc*
♦ *npl*: **the** ~**s and outs** (*of proposal,
situation etc*) los detalles.

in. *abbr* = **inch.**
inability [ɪnəˈbɪlɪtɪ] *n*: ~ **(to do)** incapacidad *f* (de hacer).

inaccessible [ɪnəkˈsesɪbl] *adj* (*also fig*)
inaccesible.
inaccurate [ɪnˈækjurət] *adj* inexacto, incorrecto.
inactivity [ɪnækˈtɪvɪtɪ] *n* inactividad *f*.
inadequate [ɪnˈædɪkwət] *adj* (*income,
reply etc*) insuficiente; (*person*) incapaz.
inadvertently [ɪnədˈvəːtntlɪ] *adv* por
descuido.
inadvisable [ɪnədˈvaɪzəbl] *adj* poco aconsejable.
inane [ɪˈneɪn] *adj* necio, fatuo.
inanimate [ɪnˈænɪmət] *adj* inanimado.
inappropriate [ɪnəˈprəuprɪət] *adj* inadecuado; (*improper*) poco oportuno.
inarticulate [ɪnɑːˈtɪkjulət] *adj* (*person*)
incapaz de expresarse; (*speech*) mal
pronunciado.
inasmuch as [ɪnəzˈmʌtʃ-] *conj* puesto
que, ya que.
inaudible [ɪnˈɔːdɪbl] *adj* inaudible.
inaugurate [ɪˈnɔːgjureɪt] *vt* inaugurar;
inauguration [-ˈreɪʃən] *n* ceremonia de
apertura.
in-between *adj* intermedio.
inborn [ɪnˈbɔːn] *adj* (*quality*) innato.
inbred [ɪnˈbred] *adj* innato; (*family*) en-
gendrado por endogamia.
Inc. *abbr* (*US:* = *incorporated*) S.A.
incapable [ɪnˈkeɪpəbl] *adj* incapaz.
incapacitate [ɪnkəˈpæsɪteɪt] *vt*: **to** ~ **sb**
incapacitar a uno.
incapacity [ɪnkəˈpæsɪtɪ] *n* incapacidad *f*.
incarcerate [ɪnˈkɑːsəreɪt] *vt* encarcelar.
incarnation [ɪnkɑːˈneɪʃən] *n* encarnación
f.
incendiary [ɪnˈsendɪərɪ] *adj* incendiario.
incense [*n* ˈɪnsens, *vb* ɪnˈsens] *n* incienso
♦ *vt* (*anger*) indignar, encolerizar.
incentive [ɪnˈsentɪv] *n* incentivo, estímulo.
incessant [ɪnˈsesnt] *adj* incesante, continuo; ~**ly** *adv* constantemente.
incest [ˈɪnsest] *n* incesto.
inch [ɪntʃ] *n* pulgada; **to be within an** ~
of estar a dos dedos de; **he didn't give
an** ~ no dio concesión alguna; ~ **forward** *vi* avanzar palmo a palmo.
incidence [ˈɪnsɪdns] *n* (*of crime, dis-*

ease) incidencia.

incident ['ɪnsɪdnt] *n* incidente *m*.

incidental [ɪnsɪ'dentl] *adj* accesorio; ~
to relacionado con; ~**ly** [-'dentəlɪ] *adv*
(*by the way*) a propósito.

incinerator [ɪn'sɪnəreɪtə*] *n* incinerador
m.

incipient [ɪn'sɪpɪənt] *adj* incipiente.

incisive [ɪn'saɪsɪv] *adj* (*remark etc*) incisivo.

incite [ɪn'saɪt] *vt* provocar.

inclination [ɪnklɪ'neɪʃən] *n* (*tendency*)
tendencia, inclinación *f*; (*desire*) deseo;
(*disposition*) propensión *f*.

incline [*n* 'ɪnklaɪn, *vb* ɪn'klaɪn] *n* pendiente *m*, cuesta ♦ *vt* (*head*) poner de lado
♦ *vi* inclinarse; **to be** ~**d to** (*tend*) ser
propenso a.

include [ɪn'kluːd] *vt* (*incorporate*) incluir; (*in letter*) adjuntar; **including**
prep incluso, inclusive.

inclusion [ɪn'kluːʒən] *n* inclusión *f*.

inclusive [ɪn'klusɪv] *adj* inclusivo; ~ **of**
tax incluidos los impuestos.

incognito [ɪnkɒg'niːtəu] *adv* de incógnito.

incoherent [ɪnkəu'hɪərənt] *adj* incoherente.

income ['ɪŋkʌm] *n* (*earned*) ingresos
mpl; (*from property etc*) renta; (*from
investment etc*) rédito; ~ **tax** *n* impuesto sobre la renta.

incoming ['ɪnkʌmɪŋ] *adj* (*flight, government etc*) entrante.

incomparable [ɪn'kɒmpərəbl] *adj* incomparable, sin par.

incompatible [ɪnkəm'pætɪbl] *adj* incompatible.

incompetent [ɪn'kɒmpɪtənt] *adj* incompetente.

incomplete [ɪnkəm'pliːt] *adj* (*partial*:
achievement etc) incompleto; (*unfinished: painting etc*) inacabado.

incomprehensible [ɪnkɒmprɪ'hensɪbl]
adj incomprensible.

inconceivable [ɪnkən'siːvəbl] *adj* inconcebible.

incongruous [ɪn'kɒŋgruəs] *adj* (*strange*)
discordante; (*inappropriate*) incongruente.

inconsiderate [ɪnkən'sɪdərət] *adj* desconsiderado.

inconsistent [ɪnkən'sɪstnt] *adj* inconsecuente; (*contradictory*) incongruente;
~ **with** (que) no concuerda con.

inconspicuous [ɪnkən'spɪkjuəs] *adj* (*colour, building etc*) discreto; (*person*)
que llama poco la atención.

inconvenience [ɪnkən'viːnjəns] *n* incon-
venientes *mpl*; (*trouble*) molestia, incomodidad *f* ♦ *vt* incomodar.

inconvenient [ɪnkən'viːnjənt] *adj* incómodo, poco práctico; (*time, place, visit-
or*) inoportuno.

incorporate [ɪn'kɔːpəreɪt] *vt* incorporar;
(*contain*) comprender; (*add*) agregar;
~**d** *adj*: ~**d company** (*US*) ≈ sociedad *f*
anónima.

incorrect [ɪnkə'rɛkt] *adj* incorrecto.

incorrigible [ɪn'kɒrɪdʒəbl] *adj* incorregible.

incorruptible [ɪnkə'rʌptɪbl] *adj* insobor-
nable.

increase [*n* 'ɪnkriːs, *vb* ɪn'kriːs] *n* aumento ♦ *vi* aumentar; (*grow*) crecer;
(*price*) subir ♦ *vt* aumentar; (*price*)
subir; **increasing** *adj* creciente; **increa-
singly** *adv* cada vez más, más y más.

incredible [ɪn'krɛdɪbl] *adj* increíble.

incredulous [ɪn'krɛdjuləs] *adj* incrédulo.

increment ['ɪnkrɪmənt] *n* aumento, incremento.

incriminate [ɪn'krɪmɪneɪt] *vt* incriminar.

incubator ['ɪnkjubeɪtə*] *n* incubadora.

incumbent [ɪn'kʌmbənt] *n* titular *m/f* ♦
adj: **it is** ~ **on him to...** le incumbe....

incur [ɪn'kɜː*] *vt* (*expenditure*) incurrir;
(*loss*) sufrir; (*anger, disapproval*) provocar.

incurable [ɪn'kjuərəbl] *adj* incurable.

indebted [ɪn'dɛtɪd] *adj*: **to be** ~ **to sb**
estar agradecido a uno.

indecent [ɪn'diːsnt] *adj* indecente; ~ **assault** (*BRIT*) *n* atentado contra el pudor;
~ **exposure** *n* exhibicionismo.

indecisive [ɪndɪ'saɪsɪv] *adj* indeciso.

indeed [ɪn'diːd] *adv* efectivamente, en
realidad; (*in fact*) en efecto; (*furthermore*) es más; **yes** ~! ¡claro que sí!

indefinite [ɪn'dɛfɪnɪt] *adj* indefinido;

(*answer, view*) impreciso; ~**ly** *adv*
(*wait*) indefinidamente.
indelible [ɪnˈdɛlɪbl] *adj* imborrable.
indemnity [ɪnˈdɛmnɪtɪ] *n* (*insurance*) in-
demnidad *f*; (*compensation*) indemnización *f*.
independence [ɪndɪˈpɛndns] *n* independencia.
independent [ɪndɪˈpɛndənt] *adj* independiente.
indestructible [ɪndɪsˈtrʌktəbl] *adj* indestructible.
index [ˈɪndɛks] (*pl* ~**es**) *n* (*in book*) índice *m*; (: *in library etc*) catálogo; (*pl*
indices: *ratio, sign*) exponente *m*; ~
card *n* ficha; ~**ed** (*US*) *adj* = ~-**linked**;
~ **finger** *n* índice *m*; ~-**linked** (*BRIT*)
adj vinculado al índice del coste de la
vida.
India [ˈɪndɪə] *n* la India; ~**n** *adj, n*
indio/a *m/f*; **Red** ~**n** piel roja *m/f*; ~**n**
Ocean *n*: **the** ~**n Ocean** el Océano
Índico.
indicate [ˈɪndɪkeɪt] *vt* indicar; **indication**
[-ˈkeɪʃən] *n* indicio, señal *f*; **indicative**
[ɪnˈdɪkətɪv] *adj*: **to be indicative of** indicar ♦ *n* (*LING*) indicativo; **indicator** *n*
indicador *m*; (*AUT*) intermitente *m*.
indices [ˈɪndɪsiːz] *npl of* **index**.
indictment [ɪnˈdaɪtmənt] *n* acusación *f*.
indifference [ɪnˈdɪfrəns] *n* indiferencia.
indifferent [ɪnˈdɪfrənt] *adj* indiferente;
(*mediocre*) regular.
indigenous [ɪnˈdɪdʒɪnəs] *adj* indígena.
indigestion [ɪndɪˈdʒɛstʃən] *n* indigestión
f.
indignant [ɪnˈdɪgnənt] *adj*: **to be ~ at**
sth/with sb indignarse por algo/con uno.
indigo [ˈɪndɪgəu] *adj* de color añil ♦ *n*
añil *m*.
indirect [ɪndɪˈrɛkt] *adj* indirecto; ~**ly**
adv indirectamente.
indiscreet [ɪndɪsˈkriːt] *adj* indiscreto,
imprudente.
indiscriminate [ɪndɪsˈkrɪmɪnət] *adj* indis-
criminado.
indispensable [ɪndɪsˈpɛnsəbl] *adj* indispensable, imprescindible.
indisposed [ɪndɪsˈpəuzd] *adj* (*unwell*) indispuesto.

indisputable [ɪndɪsˈpjuːtəbl] *adj* incontestable.
indistinct [ɪndɪsˈtɪŋkt] *adj* (*noise, memory etc*) confuso.
individual [ɪndɪˈvɪdjuəl] *n* individuo ♦
adj individual; (*personal*) personal;
(*particular*) particular; ~**ist** *n* indivi-
dualista *m/f*; ~**ly** *adv* (*singly*) indivi-
dualmente.
indoctrinate [ɪnˈdɔktrɪneɪt] *vt* adoctrinar.
indolent [ˈɪndələnt] *adj* indolente, perezoso.
indoor [ˈɪndɔː*] *adj* (*swimming pool*)
cubierto; (*plant*) de interior; (*sport*)
bajo cubierta; ~**s** [ɪnˈdɔːz] *adv* dentro.
induce [ɪnˈdjuːs] *vt* inducir, persuadir;
(*bring about*) producir; (*birth*) provocar; ~**ment** *n* (*incentive*) incentivo;
(*pej*: *bribe*) soborno.
indulge [ɪnˈdʌldʒ] *vt* (*whim*) satisfacer;
(*person*) complacer; (*child*) mimar ♦
vi: **to ~ in** darse el gusto de; ~**nce** *n*
vicio; (*leniency*) indulgencia; ~**nt** *adj*
indulgente.
industrial [ɪnˈdʌstrɪəl] *adj* industrial; ~
action *n* huelga; ~ **estate** (*BRIT*) *n* polí-
gono (*SP*) *or* zona (*AM*) industrial; ~**ist**
n industrial *m/f*; ~**ize** *vt* industrializar;
~ **park** (*US*) *n* = ~ **estate**.
industrious [ɪnˈdʌstrɪəs] *adj* trabaja-
dor(a); (*student*) aplicado.
industry [ˈɪndəstrɪ] *n* industria; (*diligence*) aplicación *f*.
inebriated [ɪˈniːbrɪeɪtɪd] *adj* borracho.
inedible [ɪnˈɛdɪbl] *adj* incomible; (*poisonous*) no comestible.
ineffective [ɪnɪˈfɛktɪv] *adj* ineficaz, inútil.
ineffectual [ɪnɪˈfɛktjuəl] *adj* = **ineffective**.
inefficiency [ɪnɪˈfɪʃənsɪ] *n* ineficacia.
inefficient [ɪnɪˈfɪʃənt] *adj* ineficaz, ineficiente.
inept [ɪˈnɛpt] *adj* incompetente.
inequality [ɪnɪˈkwɔlɪtɪ] *n* desigualdad *f*.
inert [ɪˈnəːt] *adj* inerte, inactivo; (*immobile*) inmóvil; ~**ia** [ɪˈnəːʃə] *n* inercia;
(*laziness*) pereza.
inescapable [ɪnɪˈskeɪpəbl] *adj* ineludible.

inevitable [ɪn'ɛvɪtəbl] *adj* inevitable; **inevitably** *adv* inevitablemente.

inexcusable [ɪnɪks'kjuːzəbl] *adj* imperdonable.

inexhaustible [ɪnɪg'zɔːstɪbl] *adj* inagotable.

inexpensive [ɪnɪk'spɛnsɪv] *adj* económico.

inexperience [ɪnɪk'spɪərɪəns] *n* falta de experiencia; ~**d** *adj* inexperto.

inextricably [ɪnɪks'trɪkəblɪ] *adv* indisolublemente.

infallible [ɪn'fælɪbl] *adj* infalible.

infamous ['ɪnfəməs] *adj* infame.

infancy ['ɪnfənsɪ] *n* infancia.

infant ['ɪnfənt] *n* niño/a; (*baby*) niño pequeño, bebé *m*; ~**ile** *adj* infantil; (*pej*) aniñado; ~ **school** (*BRIT*) *n* parvulario.

infantry ['ɪnfəntrɪ] *n* infantería.

infatuated [ɪn'fætjʊeɪtɪd] *adj*: ~ **with** (*in love*) loco por.

infatuation [ɪnfætu'eɪʃən] *n* enamoramiento, pasión *f*.

infect [ɪn'fɛkt] *vt* (*wound*) infectar; (*food*) contaminar; (*person*, *animal*) contagiar; ~**ion** [ɪn'fɛkʃən] *n* infección *f*; (*fig*) contagio; ~**ious** [ɪn'fɛkʃəs] *adj* (*also fig*) contagioso.

infer [ɪn'fəː*] *vt* deducir, inferir; ~**ence** ['ɪnfərəns] *n* deducción *f*, inferencia.

inferior [ɪn'fɪərɪə*] *adj*, *n* inferior *m/f*; ~**ity** [-rɪ'ɔrətɪ] *n* inferioridad *f*; ~**ity complex** *n* complejo de inferioridad.

inferno [ɪn'fəːnəʊ] *n* (*fire*) hoguera.

infertile [ɪn'fəːtaɪl] *adj* estéril; (*person*) infecundo; **infertility** [-'tɪlɪtɪ] *n* esterilidad *f*; infecundidad *f*.

infested [ɪn'fɛstɪd] *adj*: ~ **with** plagado de.

in-fighting *n* (*fig*) lucha(s) *f*(*pl*) interna(s).

infiltrate ['ɪnfɪltreɪt] *vt* infiltrar en.

infinite ['ɪnfɪnɪt] *adj* infinito.

infinitive [ɪn'fɪnɪtɪv] *n* infinitivo.

infinity [ɪn'fɪnɪtɪ] *n* infinito; (*an* ~) infinidad *f*.

infirm [ɪn'fəːm] *adj* enfermo, débil; ~**ary** *n* hospital *m*; ~**ity** *n* debilidad *f*; (*illness*) enfermedad *f*, achaque *m*.

inflamed [ɪn'fleɪmd] *adj*: to become ~ inflamarse.

inflammable [ɪn'flæməbl] *adj* inflamable.

inflammation [ɪnflə'meɪʃən] *n* inflamación *f*.

inflatable [ɪn'fleɪtəbl] *adj* (*ball*, *boat*) inflable.

inflate [ɪn'fleɪt] *vt* (*tyre*, *price etc*) inflar; (*fig*) hinchar; **inflation** [ɪn'fleɪʃən] *n* (*ECON*) inflación *f*.

inflexible [ɪn'flɛksəbl] *adj* (*rule*) rígido; (*person*) inflexible.

inflict [ɪn'flɪkt] *vt*: to ~ **sth on sb** infligir algo en uno.

influence ['ɪnfluəns] *n* influencia ♦ *vt* influir en, influenciar; **under the** ~ **of alcohol** en estado de embriaguez; **influential** [-'ɛnʃl] *adj* influyente.

influenza [ɪnflu'ɛnzə] *n* gripe *f*.

influx ['ɪnflʌks] *n* afluencia.

inform [ɪn'fɔːm] *vt*: to ~ **sb of sth** informar a uno sobre *or* de algo ♦ *vi*: to ~ **on sb** delatar a uno.

informal [ɪn'fɔːml] *adj* (*manner*, *tone*) familiar; (*dress*, *interview*, *occasion*) informal; (*visit*, *meeting*) extraoficial; ~**ity** [-'mælɪtɪ] *n* informalidad *f*; sencillez *f*.

informant [ɪn'fɔːmənt] *n* informante *m/f*.

information [ɪnfə'meɪʃən] *n* información *f*; (*knowledge*) conocimientos *mpl*; **a piece of** ~ un dato; ~ **office** *n* información *f*.

informative [ɪn'fɔːmətɪv] *adj* informativo.

informer [ɪn'fɔːmə*] *n* (*also*: *police* ~) soplón/ona *m/f*.

infra-red [ɪnfrə'rɛd] *adj* infrarrojo.

infrastructure ['ɪnfrəstrʌktʃə*] *n* (*of system etc*) infraestructura.

infringe [ɪn'frɪndʒ] *vt* infringir, violar ♦ *vi*: to ~ **on** abusar de; ~**ment** *n* infracción *f*; (*of rights*) usurpación *f*.

infuriating [ɪn'fjʊərɪeɪtɪŋ] *adj* (*habit*, *noise*) enloquecedor(a).

ingenious [ɪn'dʒiːnjəs] *adj* ingenioso; **ingenuity** [-dʒɪ'njuːɪtɪ] *n* ingeniosidad *f*.

ingenuous [ɪn'dʒɛnjuəs] *adj* ingenuo.

ingot ['ɪŋgət] *n* lingote *m*, barra.

ingrained [ɪn'greɪnd] *adj* arraigado.

ingratiate [ɪnˈgreɪʃɪeɪt] *vt*: **to ~ o.s. with** congraciarse con.

ingredient [ɪnˈgriːdɪənt] *n* ingrediente *m*.

inhabit [ɪnˈhæbɪt] *vt* vivir en; **~ant** *n* habitante *m/f*.

inhale [ɪnˈheɪl] *vt* inhalar ♦ *vi* (*breathe in*) aspirar; (*in smoking*) tragar.

inherent [ɪnˈhɪərənt] *adj*: **~ in** *or* **to** inherente a.

inherit [ɪnˈherɪt] *vt* heredar; **~ance** *n* herencia; (*fig*) patrimonio.

inhibit [ɪnˈhɪbɪt] *vt* inhibir, impedir; **~ed** *adj* (*PSYCH*) cohibido; **~ion** [-ˈbɪʃən] *n* cohibición *f*.

inhospitable [ɪnhɔsˈpɪtəbl] *adj* (*person*) inhospitalario; (*place*) inhóspito.

inhuman [ɪnˈhjuːmən] *adj* inhumano.

iniquity [ɪˈnɪkwɪtɪ] *n* iniquidad *f*; (*injustice*) injusticia.

initial [ɪˈnɪʃl] *adj* primero ♦ *n* inicial *f* ♦ *vt* firmar con las iniciales; **~s** *npl* (*as signature*) iniciales *fpl*; (*abbreviation*) siglas *fpl*; **~ly** *adv* al principio.

initiate [ɪˈnɪʃɪeɪt] *vt* iniciar; **to ~ proceedings against sb** (*LAW*) entablar proceso contra uno; **initiation** [-ˈeɪʃən] *n* (*into secret etc*) iniciación *f*; (*beginning*) comienzo.

initiative [ɪˈnɪʃətɪv] *n* iniciativa.

inject [ɪnˈdʒɛkt] *vt* inyectar; **to ~ sb with sth** inyectar algo a uno; **~ion** [ɪnˈdʒɛkʃən] *n* inyección *f*.

injunction [ɪnˈdʒʌŋkʃən] *n* interdicto.

injure [ˈɪndʒə*] *vt* (*hurt*) herir, lastimar; (*fig: reputation etc*) perjudicar; **~d** *adj* (*person, arm*) herido, lastimado; **injury** *n* herida, lesión *f*; (*wrong*) perjuicio, daño; **injury time** *n* (*SPORT*) (tiempo de) descuento.

injustice [ɪnˈdʒʌstɪs] *n* injusticia.

ink [ɪŋk] *n* tinta.

inkling [ˈɪŋklɪŋ] *n* sospecha; (*idea*) idea.

inlaid [ˈɪnleɪd] *adj* (*with wood, gems etc*) incrustado.

inland [*adj* ˈɪnlənd, *adv* ɪnˈlænd] *adj* (*waterway, port etc*) interior ♦ *adv* tierra adentro; **I~ Revenue** (*BRIT*) *n* departamento de impuestos; ≈ Hacienda (*SP*).

in-laws *npl* suegros *mpl*.

inlet [ˈɪnlet] *n* (*GEO*) ensenada, cala; (*TECH*) admisión *f*, entrada.

inmate [ˈɪnmeɪt] *n* (*in prison*) preso/a; (*feelings*) íntimo; (*in asylum*) internado/a.

inn [ɪn] *n* posada, mesón *m*.

innate [ɪˈneɪt] *adj* innato.

inner [ˈɪnə*] *adj* (*courtyard, calm*) interior; (*feelings*) íntimo; **~ city** *n* barrios deprimidos del centro de una ciudad; **~ tube** *n* (*of tyre*) cámara (*SP*) *or* llanta (*AM*).

innings [ˈɪnɪŋz] *n* (*CRICKET*) entrada, turno.

innocence [ˈɪnəsns] *n* inocencia.

innocent [ˈɪnəsnt] *adj* inocente.

innocuous [ɪˈnɔkjuəs] *adj* inocuo.

innovation [ɪnəʊˈveɪʃən] *n* novedad *f*.

innuendo [ɪnjuˈɛndəʊ] (*pl* **~es**) *n* indirecta.

inoculation [ɪnɔkjuˈleɪʃən] *n* inoculación *f*.

inopportune [ɪnˈɔpətjuːn] *adj* inoportuno.

inordinately [ɪˈnɔːdɪnətlɪ] *adv* desmesuradamente.

in-patient *n* paciente *m/f* interno/a.

input [ˈɪnput] *n* entrada; (*of resources*) inversión *f*; (*COMPUT*) entrada de datos.

inquest [ˈɪnkwest] *n* (*coroner's*) encuesta judicial.

inquire [ɪnˈkwaɪə*] *vi* preguntar ♦ *vt*: **to ~ whether** preguntar si; **to ~ about** (*person*) preguntar por; (*fact*) informarse de; **~ into** *vt fus* investigar, indagar; **inquiry** *n* pregunta; (*investigation*) investigación *f*, pesquisa; **inquiry office** (*BRIT*) *n* oficina de información.

inquisitive [ɪnˈkwɪzɪtɪv] *adj* (*curious*) curioso.

inroads [ˈɪnrəʊdz] *npl*: **to make ~ into** mermar.

ins *abbr* = **inches**.

insane [ɪnˈseɪn] *adj* loco; (*MED*) demente.

insanity [ɪnˈsænɪtɪ] *n* demencia, locura.

insatiable [ɪnˈseɪʃəbl] *adj* insaciable.

inscription [ɪnˈskrɪpʃən] *n* inscripción *f*; (*in book*) dedicatoria.

inscrutable [ɪnˈskruːtəbl] *adj* inescrutable, insondable.

insect ['ɪnsɛkt] *n* insecto; ~**icide** [ɪn'sɛktɪsaɪd] *n* insecticida *m*.

insecure [ɪnsɪ'kjʊə*] *adj* inseguro.

insemination [ɪnsɛmɪ'neɪʃn] *n*: **artificial** ~ inseminación *f* artificial.

insensible [ɪn'sɛnsɪbl] *adj* (*unconscious*) sin conocimiento.

insensitive [ɪn'sɛnsɪtɪv] *adj* insensible.

inseparable [ɪn'sɛprəbl] *adj* inseparable.

insert [*vb* ɪn'sə:t, *n* 'ɪnsə:t] *vt* (*into sth*) introducir ♦ *n* encarte *m*; ~**ion** [ɪn'sə:ʃən] *n* inserción *f*.

in-service *adj* (*training, course*) a cargo de la empresa.

inshore [ɪn'ʃɔ:*] *adj* de bajura ♦ *adv* (*be*) cerca de la orilla; (*move*) hacia la orilla.

inside ['ɪn'saɪd] *n* interior *m* ♦ *adj* interior, interno ♦ *adv* (*be*) (por) dentro; (*go*) hacia dentro ♦ *prep* dentro de; (*of time*): ~ **10 minutes** en menos de 10 minutos; ~**s** *npl* (*inf: stomach*) tripas *fpl*; ~ **forward** *n* (*SPORT*) interior *m*; ~ **information** *n* información *f* confidencial; ~ **lane** *n* (*AUT: in Britain*) carril *m* izquierdo; (*AUT: in US, Europe etc*) carril *m* derecho; ~ **out** (*turn*) al revés; (*know*) a fondo.

insidious [ɪn'sɪdɪəs] *adj* insidioso.

insight ['ɪnsaɪt] *n* perspicacia.

insignia [ɪn'sɪgnɪə] *npl* insignias *fpl*.

insignificant [ɪnsɪg'nɪfɪknt] *adj* insignificante.

insincere [ɪnsɪn'sɪə*] *adj* poco sincero.

insinuate [ɪn'sɪnjʊeɪt] *vt* insinuar.

insipid [ɪn'sɪpɪd] *adj* soso, insulso.

insist [ɪn'sɪst] *vi* insistir; **to** ~ **on** insistir en; **to** ~ **that** insistir en que; (*claim*) exigir que; ~**ence** *n* (*determination*) empeño; ~**ent** *adj* insistente; (*noise, action*) persistente.

insole ['ɪnsəʊl] *n* plantilla.

insolent ['ɪnsələnt] *adj* insolente, descarado.

insoluble [ɪn'sɔljʊbl] *adj* insoluble.

insomnia [ɪn'sɔmnɪə] *n* insomnio.

inspect [ɪn'spɛkt] *vt* inspeccionar, examinar; (*troops*) pasar revista a; ~**ion** [ɪn'spɛkʃən] *n* inspección *f*, examen *m*; (*of troops*) revista; ~**or** *n* inspector(a)

m/f; (*BRIT: on buses, trains*) revisor(a) *m/f*.

inspiration [ɪnspə'reɪʃən] *n* inspiración *f*; **inspire** [ɪn'spaɪə*] *vt* inspirar.

instability [ɪnstə'bɪlɪtɪ] *n* inestabilidad *f*.

install [ɪn'stɔ:l] *vt* instalar; (*official*) nombrar; ~**ation** [ɪnstə'leɪʃən] *n* instalación *f*.

instalment [ɪn'stɔ:lmənt] (*US* **installment**) *n* plazo; (*of story*) entrega; (*of TV serial etc*) capítulo; **in** ~**s** (*pay, receive*) a plazos.

instance ['ɪnstəns] *n* ejemplo, caso; **for** ~ por ejemplo; **in the first** ~ en primer lugar.

instant ['ɪnstənt] *n* instante *m*, momento ♦ *adj* inmediato; (*coffee etc*) instantáneo; **instantly** *adv* en seguida.

instead [ɪn'stɛd] *adv* en cambio; ~ **of** en lugar de, en vez de.

instep ['ɪnstɛp] *n* empeine *m*.

instil [ɪn'stɪl] *vt*: **to** ~ **sth into** inculcar algo a.

instinct ['ɪnstɪŋkt] *n* instinto; ~**ive** [-'stɪŋktɪv] *adj* instintivo.

institute ['ɪnstɪtju:t] *n* instituto; (*professional body*) colegio ♦ *vt* (*begin*) iniciar, empezar; (*proceedings*) entablar; (*system, rule*) establecer.

institution [ɪnstɪ'tju:ʃən] *n* institución *f*; (*MED: home*) asilo; (: *asylum*) manicomio; (*of system etc*) establecimiento; (*of custom*) iniciación *f*.

instruct [ɪn'strʌkt] *vt*: **to** ~ **sb in sth** instruir a uno en *or* sobre algo; **to** ~ **sb to do sth** dar instrucciones a uno de hacer algo; ~**ion** [ɪn'strʌkʃən] *n* (*teaching*) instrucción *f*; ~**ions** *npl* (*orders*) órdenes *fpl*; ~**ions** (**for use**) modo de empleo; ~**ive** *adj* instructivo; ~**or** *n* instructor(a) *m/f*.

instrument ['ɪnstrəmənt] *n* instrumento; ~**al** [-'mɛntl] *adj* (*MUS*) instrumental; **to be** ~**al in** ser (el) artífice de; ~ **panel** *n* tablero (de instrumentos).

insubordination [ɪnsəbɔ:dɪ'neɪʃən] *n* insubordinación *f*.

insufferable [ɪn'sʌfrəbl] *adj* insoportable.

insufficient [ɪnsə'fɪʃənt] *adj* insuficiente.

insular ['ɪnsjʊlə*] *adj* insular; (*person*) estrecho de miras.
insulate ['ɪnsjʊleɪt] *vt* aislar; **insulating tape** *n* cinta aislante; **insulation** [-'leɪʃən] *n* aislamiento.
insulin ['ɪnsjʊlɪn] *n* insulina.
insult [*n* 'ɪnsʌlt, *vb* ɪn'sʌlt] *n* insulto ♦ *vt* insultar; ~**ing** *adj* insultante.
insurance [ɪn'ʃʊərəns] *n* seguro; **fire/life** ~ seguro contra incendios/sobre la vida; ~ **agent** *n* agente *m/f* de seguros; ~ **policy** *n* póliza (de seguros).
insure [ɪn'ʃʊə*] *vt* asegurar.
intact [ɪn'tækt] *adj* íntegro; (*unharmed*) intacto.
intake ['ɪnteɪk] *n* (*of food*) ingestión *f*; (*of air*) consumo; (*BRIT: SCOL*): **an ~ of 200 a year** 200 matriculados al año.
integral ['ɪntɪgrəl] *adj* (*whole*) íntegro; (*part*) integrante.
integrate ['ɪntɪgreɪt] *vt* integrar ♦ *vi* integrarse.
integrity [ɪn'tegrɪtɪ] *n* honradez *f*, rectitud *f*.
intellect ['ɪntəlekt] *n* intelecto; ~**ual** [-'lektjuəl] *adj*, *n* intelectual *m/f*.
intelligence [ɪn'telɪdʒəns] *n* inteligencia.
intelligent [ɪn'telɪdʒənt] *adj* inteligente.
intelligentsia [ɪntelɪ'dʒentsɪə] *n* intelectualidad *f*.
intelligible [ɪn'telɪdʒɪbl] *adj* inteligible, comprensible.
intend [ɪn'tend] *vt* (*gift etc*): **to ~ sth for** destinar algo a; **to ~ to do sth** tener intención de *or* pensar hacer algo; ~**ed** *adj* intencionado.
intense [ɪn'tens] *adj* intenso; ~**ly** *adv* (*extremely*) sumamente.
intensify [ɪn'tensɪfaɪ] *vt* intensificar; (*increase*) aumentar.
intensity [ɪn'tensɪtɪ] *n* intensidad *f*.
intensive [ɪn'tensɪv] *adj* intensivo; ~ **care unit** *n* unidad *f* de vigilancia intensiva.
intent [ɪn'tent] *n* propósito; (*LAW*) premeditación *f* ♦ *adj* (*absorbed*) absorto; (*attentive*) atento; **to all ~s and purposes** prácticamente; **to be ~ on doing sth** estar resuelto a hacer algo.
intention [ɪn'tenʃən] *n* intención *f*, propósito; ~**al** *adj* deliberado; ~**ally** *adv* a propósito.
intently [ɪn'tentlɪ] *adv* atentamente, fijamente.
inter [ɪn'tə:*] *vt* enterrar.
interact [ɪntər'ækt] *vi* influirse mutuamente; ~**ion** [-'ækʃən] *n* interacción *f*.
intercede [ɪntə'si:d] *vi*: **to ~ (with)** interceder (con).
intercept [ɪntə'sept] *vt* interceptar.
interchange ['ɪntətʃeɪndʒ] *n* intercambio; (*on motorway*) intersección *f*; ~**able** *adj* intercambiable.
intercom ['ɪntəkɒm] *n* interfono.
intercourse ['ɪntəkɔ:s] *n* (*sexual*) relaciones *fpl* sexuales.
interest ['ɪntrɪst] *n* (*also COMM*) interés *m* ♦ *vt* interesar; **to be ~ed in** interesarse por; ~**ing** *adj* interesante; ~ **rate** *n* tipo *or* tasa de interés.
interface ['ɪntəfeɪs] *n* (*COMPUT*) junción *f*.
interfere [ɪntə'fɪə*] *vi*: **to ~ in** (*quarrel, other people's business*) entrometerse en; **to ~ with** (*hinder*) estorbar; (*damage*) estropear.
interference [ɪntə'fɪərəns] *n* intromisión *f*; (*RADIO, TV*) interferencia.
interim ['ɪntərɪm] *n*: **in the ~** en el ínterin ♦ *adj* provisional.
interior [ɪn'tɪərɪə*] *n* interior *m* ♦ *adj* interior; ~ **designer** *n* interiorista *m/f*.
interjection [ɪntə'dʒekʃən] *n* interposición *f*; (*LING*) interjección *f*.
interlock [ɪntə'lɒk] *vi* entrelazarse.
interlude ['ɪntəlu:d] *n* intervalo; (*THEATRE*) intermedio.
intermarry [ɪntə'mærɪ] *vi* casarse personas de distintas razas (*or* religiones *etc*).
intermediary [ɪntə'mi:dɪərɪ] *n* intermediario/a.
intermediate [ɪntə'mi:dɪət] *adj* intermedio.
interminable [ɪn'tə:mɪnəbl] *adj* inacabable.
intermission [ɪntə'mɪʃən] *n* intermisión *f*; (*THEATRE*) descanso.
intermittent [ɪntə'mɪtnt] *adj* intermitente.

intern [vb ɪn'tə:n, n 'ɪntə:n] vt internar ♦ n (US) interno/a.

internal [ɪn'tə:nl] adj (layout, pipes, security) interior; (injury, structure, memo) internal; **~ly** adv: "not to be taken ~ly" "uso externo"; **I~ Revenue Service** (US) n departamento de impuestos; ≈ Hacienda (SP).

international [ɪntə'næʃənl] adj internacional ♦ n (BRIT: match) partido internacional.

interplay ['ɪntəpleɪ] n interacción f.

interpret [ɪn'tə:prɪt] vt interpretar; (translate) traducir; (understand) entender ♦ vi hacer de intérprete; **~ation** [-'teɪʃən] n interpretación f; traducción f; entendimiento; **~er** n intérprete m/f.

interrelated [ɪntərɪ'leɪtɪd] adj interrelacionado.

interrogate [ɪn'terəugeɪt] vt interrogar; **interrogation** [-'geɪʃən] n interrogatorio; **interrogative** [ɪntə'rɔgətɪv] adj (LING) interrogativo.

interrupt [ɪntə'rʌpt] vt, vi interrumpir; **~ion** [-'rʌpʃən] n interrupción f.

intersect [ɪntə'sekt] vi (roads) cruzarse; **~ion** [-'sekʃən] n (of roads) cruce m.

intersperse [ɪntə'spə:s] vt: **to ~ with** salpicar de.

intertwine [ɪntə'twaɪn] vt entrelazarse.

interval ['ɪntəvl] n intervalo; (BRIT: THEATRE, SPORT) descanso; (: SCOL) recreo; **at ~s** a ratos, de vez en cuando.

intervene [ɪntə'vi:n] vi intervenir; (event) interponerse; (time) transcurrir; **intervention** [-'venʃən] n intervención f.

interview ['ɪntəvju:] n entrevista ♦ vt entrevistarse con; **~er** n entrevistador(a) m/f.

intestine [ɪn'testɪn] n intestino.

intimacy ['ɪntɪməsɪ] n intimidad f.

intimate [adj 'ɪntɪmət, vb 'ɪntɪmeɪt] adj íntimo; (friendship) estrecho; (knowledge) profundo ♦ vt dar a entender.

intimidate [ɪn'tɪmɪdeɪt] vt intimidar, amedrentar.

into ['ɪntu:] prep en; (towards) a; (inside) hacia el interior de; **~ 3 pieces/French** en 3 pedazos/al francés.

intolerable [ɪn'tɔlərəbl] adj intolerable, insoportable.

intolerant [ɪn'tɔlərənt] adj: **~ (of)** intolerante (con or para).

intonation [ɪntəu'neɪʃən] n entonación f.

intoxicated [ɪn'tɔksɪkeɪtɪd] adj embriagado.

intoxication [ɪntɔksɪ'keɪʃən] n embriaguez f.

intractable [ɪn'træktəbl] adj (person) intratable; (problem) espinoso.

intransitive [ɪn'trænsɪtɪv] adj intransitivo.

intravenous [ɪntrə'vi:nəs] adj intravenoso.

in-tray n bandeja de entrada.

intricate ['ɪntrɪkət] adj (design, pattern) intrincado.

intrigue [ɪn'tri:g] n intriga ♦ vt fascinar; **intriguing** adj fascinante.

intrinsic [ɪn'trɪnsɪk] adj intrínseco.

introduce [ɪntrə'dju:s] vt introducir, meter; (speaker, TV show etc) presentar; **to ~ sb (to sb)** presentar uno (a otro); **to ~ sb to** (pastime, technique) introducir a uno a; **introduction** [-'dʌkʃən] n introducción f; (of person) presentación f; **introductory** [-'dʌktərɪ] adj introductorio; (lesson, offer) de introducción.

introvert ['ɪntrəvə:t] n introvertido/a ♦ adj (also: **~ed**) introvertido.

intrude [ɪn'tru:d] vi (person) entrometerse; **to ~ on** estorbar; **~r** n intruso/a; **intrusion** [-ʒən] n intrusión f.

intuition [ɪntju:'ɪʃən] n intuición f.

inundate ['ɪnʌndeɪt] vt: **to ~ with** inundar de.

invade [ɪn'veɪd] vt invadir.

invalid [n 'ɪnvəlɪd, adj ɪn'vælɪd] n (MED) minusválido/a ♦ adj (not valid) inválido, nulo.

invaluable [ɪn'væljuəbl] adj inestimable.

invariable [ɪn'veərɪəbl] adj invariable.

invasion [ɪn'veɪʒən] n invasión f.

invent [ɪn'vent] vt inventar; **~ion** [ɪn'venʃən] n invento; (lie) ficción f, mentira; **~ive** adj inventivo; **~or** n inventor(a) m/f.

inventory ['ɪnvəntrɪ] n inventario.

invert [ɪn'və:t] vt invertir.

invertebrate [ɪn'vɜːtɪbrət] *n* invertebra-
do.
inverted commas (*BRIT*) *npl* comillas
fpl.
invest [ɪn'vɛst] *vt* invertir ♦ *vi*: **to ~ in**
(*company etc*) invertir dinero en; (*fig*:
sth useful) comprar.
investigate [ɪn'vɛstɪgeɪt] *vt* investigar;
investigation [-'geɪʃən] *n* investigación *f*,
pesquisa; **investigator** *n* investiga-
dor(a) *m/f*.
investment [ɪn'vɛstmənt] *n* inversión *f*.
investor [ɪn'vɛstə*] *n* inversionista *m/f*.
inveterate [ɪn'vɛtərət] *adj* empedernido.
invidious [ɪn'vɪdɪəs] *adj* odioso.
invigilator [ɪn'vɪdʒɪleɪtə*] *n persona que
vigila en un examen*.
invigorating [ɪn'vɪgəreɪtɪŋ] *adj* vigorizante.
invincible [ɪn'vɪnsɪbl] *adj* invencible.
invisible [ɪn'vɪzɪbl] *adj* invisible.
invitation [ɪnvɪ'teɪʃən] *n* invitación *f*.
invite [ɪn'vaɪt] *vt* invitar; (*opinions etc*)
solicitar, pedir; **inviting** *adj* atractivo;
(*food*) apetitoso.
invoice ['ɪnvɔɪs] *n* factura ♦ *vt* facturar.
invoke [ɪn'vəuk] *vt* (*law, principle*) recurrir a.
involuntary [ɪn'vɔləntrɪ] *adj* involuntario.
involve [ɪn'vɔlv] *vt* suponer, implicar;
tener que ver con; (*concern, affect*) corresponder; **to ~ sb** (**in sth**) comprometer a uno (con algo); **~d** *adj* complicado; **to be ~d in** (*take part*) tomar parte
en; (*be engrossed*) estar muy metido
en; **~ment** *n* participación *f*; dedicación *f*.
inward ['ɪnwəd] *adj* (*movement*) interior, interno; (*thought, feeling*) íntimo;
~(s) *adv* hacia dentro.
I/O *abbr* (*COMPUT = input/output*)
entrada/salida.
iodine ['aɪəudiːn] *n* yodo.
ion ['aɪən] *n* ion *m*.
iota [aɪ'əutə] *n* jota, ápice *m*.
IOU *n abbr* (*= I owe you*) pagaré *m*.
IQ *n abbr* (*= intelligence quotient*) cociente *m* intelectual.
IRA *n abbr* (*= Irish Republican Army*)

IRA *m*.
Iran [ɪ'rɑːn] *n* Irán *m*; **~ian** [ɪ'reɪnɪən]
adj, n iraní *m/f*.
Iraq [ɪ'rɑːk] *n* Iraq; **~i** *adj, n* iraquí *m/f*.
irascible [ɪ'ræsɪbl] *adj* irascible.
irate [aɪ'reɪt] *adj* enojado, airado.
Ireland ['aɪələnd] *n* Irlanda.
iris ['aɪrɪs] (*pl* **~es**) *n* (*ANAT*) iris *m*;
(*BOT*) lirio.
Irish ['aɪrɪʃ] *adj* irlandés/esa ♦ *npl*: **the ~**
los irlandeses; **~man/woman** *n*
irlandés/esa *m/f*; **~ Sea** *n*: **the ~ Sea** el
mar de Irlanda.
irksome ['ɜːksʌm] *adj* fastidioso.
iron ['aɪən] *n* hierro; (*for clothes*) plancha ♦ *cpd* de hierro ♦ *vt* (*clothes*) planchar; **~ out** *vt* (*fig*) allanar; **I~ Curtain** *n*: **the I~ Curtain** el Telón de Acero.
ironic(al) [aɪ'rɒnɪk(l)] *adj* irónico.
ironing ['aɪənɪŋ] *n* (*activity*) planchado;
(*clothes*: *ironed*) ropa planchada; (: *to
be ironed*) ropa por planchar; **~ board**
n tabla de planchar.
ironmonger ['aɪənmʌŋgə*] (*BRIT*) *n*
ferretero/a; **~'s (shop)** *n* ferretería,
quincallería.
irony ['aɪrənɪ] *n* ironía.
irrational [ɪ'ræʃənl] *adj* irracional.
irreconcilable [ɪrɛkən'saɪləbl] *adj*
(*ideas*) incompatible; (*enemies*) irre-
conciliable.
irregular [ɪ'rɛgjulə*] *adj* irregular; (*surface*) desigual; (*action, event*) anóma-
lo; (*behaviour*) poco ortodoxo.
irrelevant [ɪ'rɛləvənt] *adj* fuera de lugar, inoportuno.
irreplaceable [ɪrɪ'pleɪsəbl] *adj* irrempla-
zable.
irrepressible [ɪrɪ'prɛsəbl] *adj* incontenible.
irresistible [ɪrɪ'zɪstɪbl] *adj* irresistible.
irresolute [ɪ'rɛzəluːt] *adj* indeciso.
irrespective [ɪrɪ'spɛktɪv]: **~ of** *prep* sin
tener en cuenta, no importa.
irresponsible [ɪrɪ'spɒnsɪbl] *adj* (*act*)
irresponsable; (*person*) poco serio.
irrigate ['ɪrɪgeɪt] *vt* regar; **irrigation**
[-'geɪʃən] *n* riego.
irritable ['ɪrɪtəbl] *adj* (*person*) de mal

humor.

irritate ['ırıteıt] *vt* fastidiar; (*MED*) picar; **irritating** *adj* fastidioso; **irritation** [-'teıʃən] *n* fastidio; irritación; picazón *f*, picor *m*.

IRS (*US*) *n abbr* = **Internal Revenue Service.**

is [ız] *vb see* be.

Islam ['ızlɑːm] *n* Islam *m*; **~ic** [ız'læmık] *adj* islámico.

island ['aılənd] *n* isla; **~er** *n* isleño/a.

isle [aıl] *n* isla.

isn't ['ıznt] = is not.

isolate ['aısəleıt] *vt* aislar; **~d** *adj* aislado; **isolation** [-'leıʃən] *n* aislamiento.

Israel ['ızreıl] *n* Israel *m*; **~i** [ız'reılı] *adj*, *n* israelí *m/f*.

issue ['ısjuː] *n* (*problem, subject, most important part*) cuestión *f*; (*outcome*) resultado; (*of banknotes etc*) emisión *f*; (*of newspaper etc*) edición *f*; (*offspring*) sucesión *f*, descendencia ♦ *vt* (*rations, equipment*) distribuir, repartir; (*orders*) dar; (*certificate, passport*) expedir; (*decree*) promulgar; (*magazine*) publicar; (*cheques*) extender; (*banknotes, stamps*) emitir; **at ~** en cuestión; **to take ~ with sb** (**over**) estar en desacuerdo con uno (sobre); **to make an ~ of sth** hacer una cuestión de algo.

isthmus ['ısməs] *n* istmo.

KEYWORD

it [ıt] *pron* **1** (*specific: subject: not generally translated*) él/ella; (: *direct object*) lo, la; (: *indirect object*) le; (*after prep*) él/ella; (*abstract concept*) ello; **~'s on the table** está en la mesa; **I can't find ~** no lo (*or* la) encuentro; **give ~ to me** dámelo (*or* dámela); **I spoke to him about ~** le hablé del asunto; **what did you learn from ~?** ¿qué aprendiste de él (*or* ella)?; **did you go to ~?** (*party, concert etc*) ¿fuiste?

2 (*impersonal*): **~'s raining** llueve, está lloviendo; **~'s 6 o'clock/the 10th of August** son las 6/es el 10 de agosto; **how far is ~?** — **~'s 10 miles/2 hours on the train** ¿a qué distancia está? — a 10 millas/2 horas en tren; **who is ~?** — **~'s me** ¿quién es? — soy yo.

Italian [ı'tæljən] *adj* italiano ♦ *n* italiano/a; (*LING*) italiano.

italics [ı'tælıks] *npl* cursiva.

Italy ['ıtəlı] *n* Italia.

itch [ıtʃ] *n* picazón *f* ♦ *vi* (*part of body*) picar; **to ~ to do sth** rabiar por hacer algo; **~y** *adj*: **my hand is ~y** me pica la mano.

it'd ['ıtd] = it would; it had.

item ['aıtəm] *n* artículo; (*on agenda*) asunto (a tratar); (*also: news ~*) noticia; **~ize** *vt* detallar.

itinerant [ı'tınərənt] *adj* ambulante.

itinerary [aı'tınərərı] *n* itinerario.

it'll ['ıtl] = it will; it shall.

its [ıts] *adj* su; sus *pl*.

it's [ıts] = it is; it has.

itself [ıt'sɛlf] *pron* (*reflexive*) sí mismo/a; (*emphatic*) él mismo/ella misma.

ITV *n abbr* (*BRIT*: = *Independent Television*) cadena de televisión comercial independiente del Estado.

I.U.D. *n abbr* (= *intra-uterine device*) DIU *m*.

I've [aıv] = I have.

ivory ['aıvərı] *n* marfil *m*; (*colour*) (color) de marfil; **~ tower** *n* torre *f* de marfil.

ivy ['aıvı] *n* (*BOT*) hiedra.

J

jab [dʒæb] *vt*: **to ~ sth into sth** clavar algo en algo ♦ *n* (*inf*) (*MED*) pinchazo.

jack [dʒæk] *n* (*AUT*) gato; (*CARDS*) sota; **~ up** *vt* (*AUT*) levantar con gato.

jackal ['dʒækɔːl] *n* (*ZOOL*) chacal *m*.

jacket ['dʒækıt] *n* chaqueta, americana, saco (*AM*); (*of book*) sobrecubierta.

jack-knife *vi* colear.

jack plug *n* (*ELEC*) enchufe *m* de clavija.

jackpot ['dʒækpɔt] *n* premio gordo.

jaded ['dʒeıdıd] *adj* (*tired*) cansado; (*fed-up*) hastiado.

jagged ['dʒægıd] *adj* dentado.

jail [dʒeɪl] *n* cárcel *f* ♦ *vt* encarcelar.

jam [dʒæm] *n* mermelada; (*also: traffic ~*) embotellamiento; (*inf: difficulty*) apuro ♦ *vt* (*passage etc*) obstruir; (*mechanism, drawer etc*) atascar; (*RADIO*) interferir ♦ *vi* atascarse, trabarse; **to ~ sth into sth** meter algo a la fuerza en algo.

Jamaica [dʒə'meɪkə] *n* Jamaica.

jangle ['dʒæŋgl] *vi* entrechocar (ruidosamente).

janitor ['dʒænɪtə*] *n* (*caretaker*) portero, conserje *m*.

January ['dʒænjuərɪ] *n* enero.

Japan [dʒə'pæn] *n* (el) Japón; **~ese** [dʒæpə'niːz] *adj* japonés/esa ♦ *n inv* japonés/esa *m/f*; (*LING*) japonés *m*.

jar [dʒɑː*] *n* tarro, bote *m* ♦ *vi* (*sound*) chirriar; (*colours*) desentonar.

jargon ['dʒɑːgən] *n* jerga.

jasmine ['dʒæzmɪn] *n* jazmín *m*.

jaundice ['dʒɔːndɪs] *n* ictericia; **~d** *adj* desilusionado, poco entusiasta.

jaunt [dʒɔːnt] *n* excursión *f*; **~y** *adj* alegre.

javelin ['dʒævlɪn] *n* jabalina.

jaw [dʒɔː] *n* mandíbula.

jay [dʒeɪ] *n* (*ZOOL*) arrendajo.

jaywalker ['dʒeɪwɔːkə*] *n* peatón/ona *m/f* imprudente.

jazz [dʒæz] *n* jazz *m*; **~ up** *vt* (*liven up*) animar, avivar.

jealous ['dʒeləs] *adj* celoso; (*envious*) envidioso; **~y** *n* celos *mpl*; envidia.

jeans [dʒiːnz] *npl* vaqueros *mpl*, tejanos *mpl*.

jeep [dʒiːp] *n* jeep *m*.

jeer [dʒɪə*] *vi*: **to ~ (at)** (*mock*) mofarse (de).

jelly ['dʒelɪ] *n* (*jam*) jalea; (*dessert etc*) gelatina; **~fish** *n inv* medusa (*SP*), aguaviva (*AM*).

jeopardy ['dʒepədɪ] *n*: **to be in ~** estar en peligro.

jerk [dʒɜːk] *n* (*jolt*) sacudida; (*wrench*) tirón *m*; (*inf*) imbécil *m/f* ♦ *vt* tirar bruscamente de ♦ *vi* (*vehicle*) traquetear.

jerkin ['dʒɜːkɪn] *n* chaleco.

jersey ['dʒɜːzɪ] *n* jersey *m*; (*fabric*) (te-

jido de) punto.

jest [dʒest] *n* broma.

Jesus ['dʒiːzəs] *n* Jesús *m*.

jet [dʒet] *n* (*of gas, liquid*) chorro; (*AVIAT*) avión *m* a reacción; **~-black** *adj* negro como el azabache; **~ engine** *n* motor *m* a reacción; **~ lag** *n* desorientación *f* después de un largo vuelo.

jettison ['dʒetɪsn] *vt* desechar.

jetty ['dʒetɪ] *n* muelle *m*, embarcadero.

Jew [dʒuː] *n* judío.

jewel ['dʒuːəl] *n* joya; (*in watch*) rubí *m*; **~ler** *n* joyero/a; **~ler's (shop)** (*US* **~ry store**) *n* joyería; **~lery** (*US* **~ry**) *n* joyas *fpl*, alhajas *fpl*.

Jewess ['dʒuːɪs] *n* judía.

Jewish ['dʒuːɪʃ] *adj* judío.

jibe [dʒaɪb] *n* mofa.

jiffy ['dʒɪfɪ] (*inf*) *n*: **in a ~** en un santiamén.

jig [dʒɪg] *n* giga.

jigsaw ['dʒɪgsɔː] *n* (*also: ~ puzzle*) rompecabezas *m inv*, puzle *m*.

jilt [dʒɪlt] *vt* dejar plantado a.

jingle ['dʒɪŋgl] *n* musiquilla ♦ *vi* tintinear.

jinx [dʒɪŋks] *n*: **there's a ~ on it** está gafado.

jitters ['dʒɪtəz] (*inf*) *npl*: **to get the ~** ponerse nervioso.

job [dʒɔb] *n* (*task*) tarea; (*post*) empleo; **it's not my ~** no me incumbe a mí; **it's a good ~ that** ... menos mal que ...; **just the ~!** ¡estupendo!; **~ centre** (*BRIT*) *n* oficina estatal de colocaciones; **~less** *adj* sin trabajo.

jockey ['dʒɔkɪ] *n* jockey *m/f* ♦ *vi*: **to ~ for position** maniobrar para conseguir una posición.

jocular ['dʒɔkjulə*] *adj* gracioso.

jog [dʒɔg] *vt* empujar (ligeramente) ♦ *vi* (*run*) hacer footing; **to ~ sb's memory** refrescar la memoria a uno; **~ along** *vi* (*fig*) ir tirando; **~ging** *n* footing *m*.

join [dʒɔɪn] *vt* (*things*) juntar, unir; (*club*) hacerse socio de; (*POL: party*) afiliarse a; (*queue*) ponerse en; (*meet: people*) reunirse con ♦ *vi* (*roads*) juntarse; (*rivers*) confluir ♦ *n* juntura; **~ in** *vi* tomar parte, participar ♦ *vt fus*

tomar parte *or* participar en; ~ **up** *vi* reunirse; (*MIL*) alistarse.
joiner ['dʒɔɪnə*] (*BRIT*) *n* carpintero/a; ~**y** *n* carpintería.
joint [dʒɔɪnt] *n* (*TECH*) junta, unión *f*; (*ANAT*) articulación *f*; (*BRIT*: *CULIN*) pieza de carne (para asar); (*inf*: *place*) tugurio; (: *of cannabis*) porro ♦ *adj* (*common*) común; (*combined*) combinado; ~ **account** (*with bank etc*) cuenta común.
joist [dʒɔɪst] *n* viga.
joke [dʒəuk] *n* chiste *m*; (*also*: *practical* ~) broma ♦ *vi* bromear; **to play a** ~ **on** gastar una broma a; ~**r** *n* (*CARDS*) comodín *m*.
jolly ['dʒɔlɪ] *adj* (*merry*) alegre; (*enjoyable*) divertido ♦ *adv* (*BRIT*: *inf*) muy, terriblemente.
jolt [dʒəult] *n* (*jerk*) sacudida; (*shock*) susto ♦ *vt* (*physically*) sacudir; (*emotionally*) asustar.
jostle ['dʒɔsl] *vt* dar empellones a, codear.
jot [dʒɔt] *n*: **not one** ~ ni jota, ni pizca; ~ **down** *vt* apuntar; ~**ter** (*BRIT*) *n* bloc *m*.
journal ['dʒə:nl] *n* (*magazine*) revista; (*diary*) periódico, diario; ~**ism** *n* periodismo; ~**ist** *n* periodista *m/f*, reportero/a.
journey ['dʒə:nɪ] *n* viaje *m*; (*distance covered*) trayecto.
jovial ['dʒəuvɪəl] *adj* risueño, jovial.
joy [dʒɔɪ] *n* alegría; ~**ful** *adj* alegre; ~**ous** *adj* alegre; ~ **ride** *n* (*illegal*) paseo en coche robado; ~ **stick** *n* (*AVIAT*) palanca de mando; (*COMPUT*) palanca de control.
J.P. *n abbr* = **Justice of the Peace**.
Jr *abbr* = **junior**.
jubilant ['dʒu:bɪlnt] *adj* jubiloso.
jubilee ['dʒu:bɪliː] *n* aniversario.
judge [dʒʌdʒ] *n* juez *m/f*; (*fig*: *expert*) perito ♦ *vt* juzgar; (*consider*) considerar; **judg(e)ment** *n* juicio.
judiciary [dʒu:'dɪʃɪərɪ] *n* poder *m* judicial.
judicious [dʒu:'dɪʃəs] *adj* juicioso.
judo ['dʒu:dəu] *n* judo.

jug [dʒʌg] *n* jarra.
juggernaut ['dʒʌgənɔːt] (*BRIT*) *n* (*huge truck*) trailer *m*.
juggle ['dʒʌgl] *vi* hacer juegos malabares; ~**r** *n* malabarista *m/f*.
Jugoslav ['juːgəuslɑːv] *etc* = **Yugoslav** *etc*.
juice [dʒuːs] *n* zumo, jugo (*esp AM*); **juicy** *adj* jugoso.
jukebox ['dʒuːkbɔks] *n* tocadiscos *m inv* tragaperras.
July [dʒuː'laɪ] *n* julio.
jumble ['dʒʌmbl] *n* revoltijo ♦ *vt* (*also*: ~ *up*) revolver; ~ **sale** (*BRIT*) *n venta de objetos usados con fines benéficos*.
jumbo (jet) ['dʒʌmbəu-] *n* jumbo.
jump [dʒʌmp] *vi* saltar, dar saltos; (*with fear, surprise*) pegar un bote; (*increase*) aumentar ♦ *vt* saltar ♦ *n* salto; aumento; **to** ~ **the queue** (*BRIT*) colarse; ~ **cables** (*US*) *npl* = **jump leads**.
jumper ['dʒʌmpə*] *n* (*BRIT*: *pullover*) suéter *m*, jersey *m*; (*US*: *dress*) mandil *m*.
jump leads (*BRIT*) *npl* cables *mpl* puente de batería.
jumpy ['dʒʌmpɪ] (*inf*) *adj* nervioso.
Jun. *abbr* = **junior**.
junction ['dʒʌŋkʃən] *n* (*BRIT*: *of roads*) cruce *m*; (*RAIL*) empalme *m*.
juncture ['dʒʌŋktʃə*] *n*: **at this** ~ en este momento, en esta coyuntura.
June [dʒuːn] *n* junio.
jungle ['dʒʌŋgl] *n* selva, jungla.
junior ['dʒuːnɪə*] *adj* (*in age*) menor, más joven; (*brother/sister etc*): **7 years her** ~ siete años menor que ella; (*position*) subalterno ♦ *n* menor *m/f*, joven *m/f*; ~ **school** (*BRIT*) *n* escuela primaria.
junk [dʒʌŋk] *n* (*cheap goods*) baratijas *fpl*; (*rubbish*) basura; ~ **food** *n* alimentos preparados y envasados de escaso valor nutritivo.
junkie ['dʒʌŋkɪ] (*inf*) *n* drogadicto/a, yonqui *m/f*.
junk shop *n* tienda de objetos usados.
Junr *abbr* = **junior**.
jurisdiction [dʒuərɪs'dɪkʃən] *n* jurisdicción *f*.

juror [ˈdʒuərə*] n jurado.

jury [ˈdʒuərɪ] n jurado.

just [dʒʌst] adj justo ♦ adv (exactly) exactamente; (only) sólo, solamente; he's ~ done it/left acaba de hacerlo/irse; ~ right perfecto; ~ two o'clock las dos en punto; she's ~ as clever as you (ella) es tan lista como tú; ~ as well that ... menos mal que ...; ~ as he was leaving en el momento en que se marchaba; ~ before/enough justo antes/lo suficiente; ~ here aquí mismo; he ~ missed ha fallado por poco; ~ listen to this escucha esto un momento.

justice [ˈdʒʌstɪs] n justicia; (US: judge) juez m; to do ~ to (fig) hacer justicia a; J~ of the Peace n juez m de paz.

justify [ˈdʒʌstɪfaɪ] vt justificar; (text) alinear.

jut [dʒʌt] vi (also: ~ out) sobresalir.

juvenile [ˈdʒuːvənaɪl] adj (court) de menores; (humour, mentality) infantil ♦ n menor m de edad.

juxtapose [ˈdʒʌkstəpəuz] vt yuxtaponer.

K

K abbr (= one thousand) mil; (= kilobyte) kilobyte m, kiloocteto.

kaleidoscope [kəˈlaɪdəskəup] n calidoscopio.

kangaroo [kæŋgəˈruː] n canguro.

karate [kəˈrɑːtɪ] n karate m.

kebab [kəˈbæb] n pincho moruno.

keel [kiːl] n quilla; on an even ~ (fig) en equilibrio.

keen [kiːn] adj (interest, desire) grande, vivo; (eye, intelligence) agudo; (competition) reñido; (edge) afilado; (eager) entusiasta; to be ~ to do or on doing sth tener muchas ganas de hacer algo; to be ~ on sth/sb interesarse por algo/uno.

keep [kiːp] (pt, pp kept) vt (preserve, store) guardar; (hold back) quedarse con; (maintain) mantener; (detain) detener; (shop) ser propietario de; (feed: family etc) mantener; (promise) cumplir; (chickens, bees etc) criar; (ac-counts) llevar; (diary) escribir; (prevent): to ~ sb from doing sth impedir a uno hacer algo ♦ vi (food) conservarse; (remain) seguir, continuar ♦ n (of castle) torreón m; (food etc) comida, subsistencia; (inf): for ~s para siempre; to ~ doing sth seguir haciendo algo; to ~ sb happy tener a uno contento; to ~ a place tidy mantener un lugar limpio; to ~ sth to o.s. guardar algo para sí mismo; to ~ sth (back) from sb ocultar algo a uno; to ~ time (clock) mantener la hora exacta; ~ on vi: to ~ on doing seguir or continuar haciendo; to ~ on (about sth) no parar de hablar (de algo); ~ out vi (stay out) permanecer fuera; "~ out" "prohibida la entrada"; ~ up vt mantener, conservar ♦ vi no retrasarse; to ~ up with (pace) ir al paso de; (level) mantenerse a la altura de; ~er n guardián/ana m/f; ~-fit n gimnasia (para mantenerse en forma); ~ing n (care) cuidado; in ~ing with de acuerdo con; ~sake n recuerdo.

kennel [ˈkɛnl] n perrera; ~s npl residencia canina.

Kenya [ˈkɛnjə] n Kenia.

kept [kɛpt] pt, pp of keep.

kerb [kəːb] (BRIT) n bordillo.

kernel [ˈkəːnl] n (nut) almendra; (fig) meollo.

ketchup [ˈkɛtʃəp] n salsa de tomate, catsup m.

kettle [ˈkɛtl] n hervidor m de agua; ~drum n (MUS) timbal m.

key [kiː] n llave f; (MUS) tono; (of piano, typewriter) tecla ♦ adj (issue etc) clave inv ♦ vt (also: ~ in) teclear; ~board n teclado; ~ed up adj (person) nervioso; ~hole n ojo (de la cerradura); ~note n (MUS) tónica; (of speech) punto principal or clave; ~ring n llavero.

khaki [ˈkɑːkɪ] n caqui.

kick [kɪk] vt dar una patada or un puntapié a; (inf: habit) quitarse de ♦ vi (horse) dar coces ♦ n patada, puntapié m; (of animal) coz f; (thrill): he does it for ~s lo hace por pura diversión; ~ off vi (SPORT) hacer el saque inicial.

kid [kɪd] n (inf: child) chiquillo/a; (animal) cabrito; (leather) cabritilla ♦ vi (inf) bromear.

kidnap ['kɪdnæp] vt secuestrar; ~per n secuestrador(a) m/f; ~ping n secuestro.

kidney ['kɪdnɪ] n riñón m.

kill [kɪl] vt matar; (murder) asesinar ♦ n matanza; to ~ time matar el tiempo; ~er n asesino/a; ~ing n (one) asesinato; (several) matanza; to make a ~ing (fig) hacer su agosto; ~joy (BRIT) n aguafiestas m/f inv.

kiln [kɪln] n horno.

kilo ['kiːləu] n kilo; ~byte n (COMPUT) kilobyte m, kiloocteto; ~gram(me) ['kɪləugræm] n kilo, kilogramo; ~metre ['kɪləmiːtə*] (US ~meter) n kilómetro; ~watt ['kɪləuwɔt] n kilovatio.

kilt [kɪlt] n falda escocesa.

kin [kɪn] n see kith; next.

kind [kaɪnd] adj amable, atento ♦ n clase f, especie f; (species) género; in ~ (COMM) en especie; a ~ of una especie de; to be two of a ~ ser tal para cual.

kindergarten ['kɪndəgɑːtn] n jardín m de la infancia.

kind-hearted adj bondadoso, de buen corazón.

kindle ['kɪndl] vt encender; (arouse) despertar.

kindly ['kaɪndlɪ] adj bondadoso; cariñoso ♦ adv bondadosamente, amablemente; will you ~ ... sea usted tan amable de ....

kindness ['kaɪndnɪs] n (quality) bondad f, amabilidad f; (act) favor m.

kindred ['kɪndrɪd] n familia ♦ adj: ~ spirits almas fpl gemelas.

kinetic [kɪ'netɪk] adj cinético.

king [kɪŋ] n rey m; ~dom n reino; ~fisher n martín m pescador; ~-size adj de tamaño extra.

kinky ['kɪŋkɪ] adj (pej: person, behaviour) extraño; (: sexually) perverso.

kiosk ['kiːɔsk] n quiosco; (BRIT: TEL) cabina.

kipper ['kɪpə*] n arenque m ahumado.

kiss [kɪs] n beso ♦ vt besar; to ~ (each other) besarse; ~ of life n respiración f boca a boca.

kit [kɪt] n (equipment) equipo; (tools etc) (caja de) herramientas fpl; (assembly ~) juego de armar.

kitchen ['kɪtʃɪn] n cocina; ~ sink n fregadero.

kite [kaɪt] n (toy) cometa.

kith [kɪθ] n: ~ and kin parientes mpl y allegados.

kitten ['kɪtn] n gatito/a.

kitty ['kɪtɪ] n (pool of money) fondo común.

kleptomaniac [klɛptəu'meɪnɪæk] n cleptómano/a.

km abbr (= kilometre) km.

knack [næk] n: to have the ~ of doing sth tener el don de hacer algo.

knapsack ['næpsæk] n mochila.

knead [niːd] vt amasar.

knee [niː] n rodilla; ~cap n rótula.

kneel [niːl] (pt, pp knelt) vi (also: ~ down) arrodillarse.

knell [nɛl] n toque m de difuntos.

knelt [nɛlt] pt, pp of kneel.

knew [njuː] pt of know.

knickers ['nɪkəz] (BRIT) npl bragas fpl.

knife [naɪf] (pl knives) n cuchillo ♦ vt acuchillar.

knight [naɪt] n caballero; (CHESS) caballo; ~hood (BRIT) n (title): to receive a ~hood recibir el título de Sir.

knit [nɪt] vt tejer, tricotar ♦ vi hacer punto, tricotar; (bones) soldarse; to ~ one's brows fruncir el ceño; ~ting n labor f de punto; ~ting machine n máquina de tricotar; ~ting needle n aguja de hacer punto; ~wear n prendas fpl de punto.

knives [naɪvz] npl of knife.

knob [nɔb] n (of door) tirador m; (of stick) puño; (on radio, TV) botón m.

knock [nɔk] vt (strike) golpear; (bump into) chocar contra; (inf) criticar ♦ vi (at door etc): to ~ at/on llamar a ♦ n golpe m; (on door) llamada; ~ down vt atropellar; ~ off (inf) vi (finish) salir del trabajo ♦ vt (from price) descontar; (inf: steal) birlar; ~ out vt dejar sin sentido; (BOXING) poner fuera de combate, dejar K.O.; (in competition) eliminar; ~ **over** vt (object) tirar; (person) atropellar; ~**er** n (on door) aldabón m; ~**out** n (BOXING) K.O. m, knockout m ♦ cpd (competition etc) eliminatorio.

knot [nɔt] n nudo ♦ vt anudar; ~**ty** adj (fig) complicado.

know [nəu] (pt **knew**, pp **known**) vt (facts) saber; (be acquainted with) conocer; (recognize) reconocer, conocer; **to ~ how to swim** saber nadar; **to ~ about** or **of sb/sth** saber de uno/algo; ~**-all** n sabelotodo m/f; ~**-how** n conocimientos mpl; ~**ing** adj (look) de complicidad; ~**ingly** adv (purposely) adrede; (smile, look) con complicidad.

knowledge ['nɔlɪdʒ] n conocimiento; (learning) saber m, conocimientos mpl; ~**able** adj entendido.

known [nəun] pp of **know**.

knuckle ['nʌkl] n nudillo.

K.O. n abbr = **knockout**.

Koran [kɔ'rɑːn] n Corán m.

Korea [kɔ'rɪə] n Corea.

kosher ['kəuʃə*] adj autorizado por la ley judía.

L

L (BRIT) abbr = **learner driver**.

l. abbr (= litre) l.

lab [læb] n abbr = **laboratory**.

label ['leɪbl] n etiqueta ♦ vt poner etiqueta a.

labor etc ['leɪbə*] (US) = **labour**.

laboratory [lə'bɔrətəri] n laboratorio.

laborious [lə'bɔːriəs] adj penoso.

labour ['leɪbə*] (US **labor**) n (hard work) trabajo; (~ force) mano f de obra; (MED): **to be in ~** estar de parto ♦ vi: **to ~ (at sth)** trabajar (en algo) ♦ vt: **to ~ a point** insistir en un punto; **L~, the L~ party** (BRIT) el partido laborista, los laboristas mpl; ~**ed** adj (breathing) fatigoso; ~**er** n peón m; **farm ~er** peón m; (day ~er) jornalero.

labyrinth ['læbɪrɪnθ] n laberinto.

lace [leɪs] n encaje m; (of shoe etc) cordón m ♦ vt (shoes: also: ~ **up**) atarse

(los zapatos).

lack [læk] n (absence) falta ♦ vt faltarle a uno, carecer de; **through** or **for ~ of** por falta de; **to be ~ing** faltar, no haber; **to be ~ing in sth** faltarle a uno algo.

lackadaisical [lækə'deɪzɪkl] adj: **he's very ~** vive en otro mundo.

lacquer ['lækə*] n laca.

lad [læd] n muchacho, chico.

ladder ['lædə*] n escalera (de mano); (BRIT: in tights) carrera.

laden ['leɪdn] adj: ~ (**with**) cargado (de).

ladle ['leɪdl] n cucharón m.

lady ['leɪdɪ] n señora; (dignified, graceful) dama; "**ladies and gentlemen ...**" "señoras y caballeros ..."; **young ~** señorita; **the ladies' (room)** los servicios de señoras; ~**bird** (US ~**bug**) n mariquita; ~**like** adj fino; **L~ship** n: **your L~ship** su Señoría.

lag [læg] n retraso ♦ vi (also: ~ **behind**) retrasarse, quedarse atrás ♦ vt (pipes) revestir.

lager ['lɑːgə*] n cerveza (rubia).

lagoon [lə'guːn] n laguna.

laid [leɪd] pt, pp of **lay**; ~ **back** (inf) adj relajado; ~ **up** adj: **to be ~ up (with)** tener que guardar cama (a causa de).

lain [leɪn] pp of **lie**.

lair [lɛə*] n guarida.

lake [leɪk] n lago.

lamb [læm] n cordero; (meat) (carne f de) cordero; ~ **chop** n chuleta de cordero; ~**swool** n lana de cordero.

lame [leɪm] adj cojo; (excuse) poco convincente.

lament [lə'ment] n quejo ♦ vt lamentarse de.

laminated ['læmɪneɪtɪd] adj (metal) laminado; (wood) contrachapado; (surface) plastificado.

lamp [læmp] n lámpara.

lampoon [læm'puːn] vt satirizar.

lamp: ~**post** (BRIT) n (poste m de) farol m; ~**shade** n pantalla.

lance [lɑːns] n lanza ♦ vt (MED) abrir con lanceta.

land [lænd] n tierra; (country) país m;

(*piece of* ~) terreno; (*estate*) tierras *fpl*, finca ♦ *vi* (*from ship*) desembarcar; (*AVIAT*) aterrizar; (*fig: fall*) caer, terminar ♦ *vt* (*passengers, goods*) desembarcar; **to ~ sb with sth** (*inf*) hacer cargar a uno con algo; ~ **up** *vi*: **to ~ up in/at** ir a parar a/en; ~**ing** *n* aterrizaje *m*; (*of staircase*) rellano; ~**ing gear** *n* (*AVIAT*) tren *m* de aterrizaje; ~**ing strip** *n* pista de aterrizaje; ~**lady** *n* (*of rented house, pub etc*) dueña; ~**lord** *n* propietario; (*of pub etc*) patrón *m*; ~**mark** *n* lugar *m* conocido; **to be a** ~**mark** (*fig*) marcar un hito histórico; ~**owner** *n* terrateniente *m/f*.
landscape ['lænskeɪp] *n* paisaje *m*; ~ **gardener** *n* arquitecto de jardines.
landslide ['lændslaɪd] *n* (*GEO*) corrimiento de tierras; (*fig: POL*) victoria arrolladora.
lane [leɪn] *n* (*in country*) camino; (*AUT*) carril *m*; (*in race*) calle *f*.
language ['læŋgwɪdʒ] *n* lenguaje *m*; (*national tongue*) idioma *m*, lengua; **bad** ~ palabrotas *fpl*; ~ **laboratory** *n* laboratorio de idiomas.
languid ['læŋgwɪd] *adj* lánguido.
languish ['læŋgwɪʃ] *vi* languidecer.
lank [læŋk] *adj* (*hair*) lacio.
lanky ['læŋkɪ] *adj* larguirucho.
lantern ['læntn] *n* linterna, farol *m*.
lap [læp] *n* (*of track*) vuelta; (*of body*) regazo; **to sit on sb's** ~ sentarse en las rodillas de uno ♦ *vt* (*also:* ~ **up**) beber a lengüetadas ♦ *vi* (*waves*) chapotear; ~ **up** *vt* (*fig*) tragarse.
lapel [lə'pɛl] *n* solapa.
Lapland ['læplænd] *n* Laponia.
lapse [læps] *n* fallo; (*moral*) desliz *m*; (*of time*) intervalo ♦ *vi* (*expire*) caducar; (*time*) pasar, transcurrir; **to ~ into bad habits** caer en malos hábitos.
larceny ['lɑːsənɪ] *n* latrocinio.
larch [lɑːtʃ] *n* alerce *m*.
lard [lɑːd] *n* manteca (de cerdo).
larder ['lɑːdə*] *n* despensa.
large [lɑːdʒ] *adj* grande; **at** ~ (*free*) en libertad; (*generally*) en general; ~**ly** *adv* (*mostly*) en su mayor parte; (*introducing reason*) en gran parte; ~**-scale**

adj (*map*) en gran escala; (*fig*) importante.
largesse [lɑː'ʒɛs] *n* generosidad *f*.
lark [lɑːk] *n* (*bird*) alondra; (*joke*) broma; ~ **about** *vi* bromear, hacer el tonto.
laryngitis [lærɪn'dʒaɪtɪs] *n* laringitis *f*.
larynx ['lærɪŋks] *n* laringe *f*.
laser ['leɪzə*] *n* láser *m*; ~ **printer** *n* impresora (por) láser.
lash [læʃ] *n* latigazo; (*also: eye*~) pestaña ♦ *vt* azotar; (*tie*): **to ~ to/together** atar a/atar; ~ **out** *vi*: **to ~ out (at sb)** (*hit*) arremeter (contra uno); **to ~ out against sb** lanzar invectivas contra uno.
lass [læs] (*BRIT*) *n* chica.
lasso [læ'suː] *n* lazo.
last [lɑːst] *adj* último; (*end: of series etc*) final ♦ *adv* (*most recently*) la última vez; (*finally*) por último ♦ *vi* durar; (*continue*) continuar, seguir; ~ **night** anoche; ~ **week** la semana pasada; **at** ~ por fin; ~ **but one** penúltimo; ~**-ditch** *adj* (*attempt*) último, desesperado; ~**ing** *adj* duradero; ~**ly** *adv* por último, finalmente; ~**-minute** *adj* de última hora.
latch [lætʃ] *n* pestillo.
late [leɪt] *adj* (*far on: in time, process etc*) al final de; (*not on time*) tarde, atrasado; (*dead*) fallecido ♦ *adv* tarde; (*behind time, schedule*) con retraso; **of** ~ últimamente; ~ **at night** a última hora de la noche; **in** ~ **May** hacia fines de mayo; **the** ~ **Mr X** el difunto Sr X; ~**comer** *n* recién llegado/a; ~**ly** *adv* últimamente.
later ['leɪtə*] *adj* (*date etc*) posterior; (*version etc*) más reciente ♦ *adv* más tarde, después.
lateral ['lætərl] *adj* lateral.
latest ['leɪtɪst] *adj* último; **at the** ~ a más tardar.
lathe [leɪð] *n* torno.
lather ['lɑːðə*] *n* espuma (de jabón) ♦ *vt* enjabonar.
Latin ['lætɪn] *n* latín *m* ♦ *adj* latino; ~ **America** *n* América latina; ~**-American** *adj, n* latinoamericano/a.
latitude ['lætɪtjuːd] *n* latitud *f*; (*fig*) li-

bertad f.

latrine [lə'triːn] n letrina.

latter ['lætə*] adj último; (of two) segundo ♦ n: the ~ el último, éste; ~ly adv últimamente.

lattice ['lætɪs] n enrejado.

laudable ['lɔːdəbl] adj loable.

laugh [lɑːf] n risa ♦ vi reír(se); (to do sth) for a ~ (hacer algo) en broma; ~ at vt fus reírse de; ~ off vt tomar algo a risa; ~able adj ridículo; ~ing stock n: the ~ing stock of el hazmerreír de; ~ter n risa.

launch [lɔːntʃ] n lanzamiento; (boat) lancha ♦ vt (ship) botar; (rocket etc) lanzar; (fig) comenzar; ~(ing) pad n plataforma de lanzamiento; ~ into vt fus lanzarse a.

launder ['lɔːndə*] vt lavar.

launderette [lɔːn'drɛt] (BRIT) n lavandería (automática).

laundromat ['lɔːndrəmæt] (US) n = launderette.

laundry ['lɔːndrɪ] n (dirty) ropa sucia; (clean) colada; (room) lavadero.

laureate ['lɔːrɪət] adj see poet.

lavatory ['lævətərɪ] n wáter m.

lavender ['lævəndə*] n lavanda.

lavish ['lævɪʃ] adj (amount) abundante; (person): ~ with pródigo en ♦ vt: to ~ sth on sb colmar a uno de algo.

law [lɔː] n ley f; (SCOL) derecho; (a rule) regla; (professions connected with ~) jurisprudencia; ~-abiding adj respetuoso de la ley; ~ and order n orden m público; ~ court n tribunal m (de justicia); ~ful adj legítimo, lícito; ~less adj (action) criminal.

lawn [lɔːn] n césped m; ~mower n cortacésped m; ~ tennis n tenis m sobre hierba.

law school (US) n (SCOL) facultad f de derecho.

lawsuit ['lɔːsuːt] n pleito.

lawyer ['lɔːjə*] n abogado/a; (for sales, wills etc) notario/a.

lax [læks] adj laxo.

laxative ['læksətɪv] n laxante m.

lay [leɪ] (pt, pp laid) pt of lie ♦ adj laico; (not expert) lego ♦ vt (place) colo-

car; (eggs, table) poner; (cable) tender; (carpet) extender; ~ aside or by vt dejar a un lado; ~ down vt (pen etc) dejar; (rules etc) establecer; to ~ down the law (pej) imponer las normas; ~ off vt (workers) despedir; ~ on vt (meal, facilities) proveer; ~ out vt (spread out) disponer, exponer; ~about (inf) n vago/a; ~-by n (BRIT: AUT) área de aparcamiento.

layer ['leɪə*] n capa.

layman ['leɪmən] n lego.

layout ['leɪaut] n (design) plan m, trazado; (PRESS) composición f.

laze [leɪz] vi (also: ~ about) holgazanear.

laziness ['leɪzɪnɪs] n pereza.

lazy ['leɪzɪ] adj perezoso, vago; (movement) lento.

lb. abbr = pound (weight).

lead¹ [liːd] n (pt, pp led) n (front position) delantera; (clue) pista; (ELEC) cable m; (for dog) correa; (THEATRE) papel m principal ♦ vt (walk etc in front of) ir a la cabeza de; (guide): to ~ sb somewhere conducir a uno a algún sitio; (be leader of) dirigir; (start, guide: activity) protagonizar ♦ vi (road, pipe etc) conducir a; (SPORT) ir primero; to be in the ~ (SPORT) llevar la delantera; (fig) ir a la cabeza; to ~ the way (also fig) llevar la delantera; ~ away vt llevar; ~ back vt (person, route) llevar de vuelta; ~ on vt (tease) engañar; ~ to vt fus producir, provocar; ~ up to vt fus (events) conducir a; (in conversation) preparar el terreno para.

lead² [lɛd] n (metal) plomo; (in pencil) mina.

leader ['liːdə*] n jefe/a m/f, líder m; (SPORT) líder m; ~ship n dirección f; (position) mando; (quality) iniciativa.

leading ['liːdɪŋ] adj (main) principal; (first) primero; (front) delantero; ~ lady n (THEATRE) primera actriz f; ~ light n (person) figura central; ~ man n (THEATRE) primer galán m.

lead singer n cantante m/f.

leaf [liːf] (pl leaves) n hoja ♦ vi: to ~

through hojear; **to turn over a new ~** reformarse.
leaflet ['liːflɪt] n folleto.
league [liːg] n sociedad f; (FOOTBALL) liga; **to be in ~ with** haberse confabulado con.
leak [liːk] n (of liquid, gas) escape m, fuga; (in pipe) agujero; (in roof) gotera; (in security) filtración f ♦ vi (shoes, ship) hacer agua; (pipe) tener (un) escape; (roof) gotear; (liquid, gas) escaparse, fugarse, (fig) divulgarse ♦ vt (fig) filtrar.
lean [liːn] (pt, pp **leaned** or **leant**) adj (thin) flaco; (meat) magro ♦ vt: **to ~ sth on sth** apoyar algo en algo ♦ vi (slope) inclinarse; **to ~ against** apoyarse contra; **to ~ on** apoyarse en; **~ back/forward** vi inclinarse hacia atrás/adelante; **~ out** vi asomarse; **~ over** vi inclinarse; **~ing** n: **~ing (towards)** inclinación f (hacia); **leant** [lɛnt] pt, pp of **lean**.
leap [liːp] (pt, pp **leaped** or **leapt**) n salto ♦ vi saltar; **~frog** n pídola; **leapt** [lɛpt] pt, pp of **leap**; **~ year** n año bisiesto.
learn [ləːn] (pt, pp **learned** or **learnt**) vt aprender ♦ vi 'aprender; **to ~ about sth** enterarse de algo; **to ~ to do sth** aprender a hacer algo; **~ed** ['ləːnɪd] adj erudito; **~er** n (BRIT: also: **~er driver**) principiante m/f; **~ing** n el saber m, conocimientos mpl; **learnt** [ləːnt] pt, pp of **learn**.
lease [liːs] n arriendo ♦ vt arrendar.
leash [liːʃ] n correa.
least [liːst] adj: **the ~** (slightest) el menor, el más pequeño; (smallest amount of) mínimo ♦ adv (+vb) menos; (+adj): **the ~ expensive** el/la menos costoso/a; **the ~ possible effort** el menor esfuerzo posible; **at ~** por lo menos, al menos; **you could at ~ have written** por lo menos podías haber escrito; **not in the ~** en absoluto.
leather ['lɛðə*] n cuero.
leave [liːv] (pt, pp **left**) vt dejar; (go away from) abandonar; (place etc: permanently) salir de ♦ vi irse; (train

etc) salir ♦ n permiso; **to ~ sth to sb** (money etc) legar algo a uno; (responsibility etc) encargar a uno de algo; **to be left** quedar, sobrar; **there's some milk left over** sobra or queda algo de leche; **on ~** de permiso; **~ behind** vt (on purpose) dejar; (accidentally) dejarse; **~ out** vt omitir; **~ of absence** n permiso de ausentarse.
leaves [liːvz] npl of **leaf**.
Lebanon ['lɛbənən] n: **the ~** el Líbano.
lecherous ['lɛtʃərəs] (pej) adj lascivo.
lecture ['lɛktʃə*] n conferencia; (SCOL) clase f ♦ vi dar una clase ♦ vt (scold): **to ~ sb on** or **about sth** echar una reprimenda a uno por algo; **to give a ~ on** dar una conferencia sobre; **~r** n conferenciante m/f; (BRIT: at university) profesor(a) m/f.
led [lɛd] pt, pp of **lead**.
ledge [lɛdʒ] n repisa; (of window) alféizar m; (of mountain) saliente m.
ledger ['lɛdʒə*] n libro mayor.
lee [liː] n sotavento.
leech [liːtʃ] n sanguijuela.
leek [liːk] n puerro.
leer [lɪə*] vi: **to ~ at sb** mirar de manera lasciva a uno.
leeway ['liːweɪ] n (fig): **to have some ~** tener cierta libertad de acción.
left [lɛft] pt, pp of **leave** ♦ adj izquierdo; (remaining): **there are 2 ~** quedan dos ♦ n izquierda ♦ adv a la izquierda; **on** or **to the ~** a la izquierda; **the L~** (POL) la izquierda; **~-handed** adj zurdo; **the ~-hand side** n la izquierda; **~-luggage (office)** (BRIT) n consigna; **~-overs** npl sobras fpl; **~-wing** adj (POL) de izquierdas, izquierdista.
leg [lɛg] n pierna; (of animal, chair) pata; (trouser ~) pernera; (CULIN: of lamb) pierna; (of chicken) pata; (of journey) etapa.
legacy ['lɛgəsɪ] n herencia.
legal ['liːgl] adj (permitted by law) lícito; (of law) legal; **~ holiday** (US) n fiesta oficial; **~ize** vt legalizar; **~ly** adv legalmente; **~ tender** n moneda de curso legal.
legend ['lɛdʒənd] n (also fig: person) le-

yenda.

legislation [lɛdʒɪs'leɪʃən] n legislación f.

legislature ['lɛdʒɪslətʃə*] n cuerpo legislativo.

legitimate [lɪ'dʒɪtɪmət] adj legítimo.

leg-room n espacio para las piernas.

leisure ['lɛʒə*] n ocio, tiempo libre; **at ~** con tranquilidad; **~ centre** n centro de recreo; **~ly** adj sin prisa; lento.

lemon ['lɛmən] n limón m; **~ade** [-'neɪd] n (fizzy) gaseosa; **~ tea** n té m con limón.

lend [lɛnd] (pt, pp lent) vt: **to ~ sth to sb** prestar algo a alguien; **~ing library** n biblioteca de préstamo.

length [lɛŋθ] n (size) largo, longitud f; (distance): **the ~** of todo lo largo de; (of swimming pool, cloth) largo; (of wood, string) trozo; (amount of time) duración f; **at ~** (at last) por fin, finalmente; (lengthily) largamente; **~en** vt alargar ♦ vi alargarse; **~ways** adv a lo largo; **~y** adj largo, extenso.

lenient ['liːnɪənt] adj indulgente.

lens [lɛnz] n (of spectacles) lente f; (of camera) objetivo.

lent [lɛnt] pt, pp lend.

Lent [lɛnt] n Cuaresma.

lentil ['lɛntl] n lenteja.

Leo ['liːəu] n Leo.

leotard ['liːətɑːd] n mallas fpl.

leprosy ['lɛprəsɪ] n lepra.

lesbian ['lɛzbɪən] n lesbiana.

less [lɛs] adj (in size, degree etc) menor; (in quality) menos ♦ pron, adv menos ♦ prep: **~ tax/10% discount** menos impuestos/el 10 por ciento de descuento; **~ than half** menos de la mitad; **~ than ever** menos que nunca; **~ and ~** cada vez menos; **the ~ he works...** cuanto menos trabaja....

lessen ['lɛsn] vi disminuir, reducirse ♦ vt disminuir, reducir.

lesser ['lɛsə*] adj menor; **to a ~ extent** en menor grado.

lesson ['lɛsn] n clase f; (warning) lección f.

lest [lɛst] conj para que.

let [lɛt] (pt, pp let) vt (allow) dejar, permitir; (BRIT: lease) alquilar; **to ~ sb do**

sth dejar que uno haga algo; **to ~ sb know sth** comunicar algo a uno; **~'s go** ¡vamos!; **~ him come** que venga; **"to ~"** "se alquila"; **~ down** vt (tyre) desinflar; (disappoint) defraudar; **~ go** vi, vt soltar; **~ in** vt dejar entrar; (visitor etc) hacer pasar; **~ off** vt (culprit) dejar escapar; (gun) disparar; (bomb) accionar; (firework) hacer estallar; **~ on** (inf) vt divulgar; **~ out** vt dejar salir; (sound) soltar; **~ up** vi amainar, disminuir.

lethal ['liːθl] adj (weapon) mortífero; (poison, wound) mortal.

lethargic [lə'θɑːdʒɪk] adj letárgico.

letter ['lɛtə*] n (of alphabet) letra; (correspondence) carta; **~ bomb** n cartabomba; **~box** (BRIT) n buzón m; **~ing** n letras fpl.

lettuce ['lɛtɪs] n lechuga.

let-up n disminución f.

leukaemia [luː'kiːmɪə] (US **leukemia**) n leucemia.

level ['lɛvl] adj (flat) llano ♦ adv: **to draw ~ with** llegar a la altura de ♦ n nivel m; (height) altura ♦ vt nivelar; allanar; (destroy: building) derribar; (: forest) arrasar; **to be ~ with** estar a nivel de; **"A" ~s** (BRIT) npl ≈ exámenes mpl de bachillerato superior, B.U.P.; **"O" ~s** (BRIT) npl ≈ exámenes mpl de octavo de básica; **on the ~** (fig: honest) serio; **~ off** or **out** vi (prices etc) estabilizarse; **~ crossing** (BRIT) n paso a nivel; **~-headed** adj sensato.

lever ['liːvə*] n (also fig) palanca ♦ vt: **to ~ up** levantar con palanca; **~age** n (using bar etc) apalancamiento; (fig: influence) influencia.

levity ['lɛvɪtɪ] n frivolidad f.

levy ['lɛvɪ] n impuesto ♦ vt exigir, recaudar.

lewd [luːd] adj lascivo; (joke) obsceno, colorado (AM).

liability [laɪə'bɪlətɪ] n (pej: person, thing) estorbo, lastre m; (JUR: responsibility) responsabilidad f; **liabilities** npl (COMM) pasivo.

liable ['laɪəbl] adj (subject): **~ to** sujeto a; (responsible): **~ for** responsable de;

(*likely*): ~ **to do** propenso a hacer.

liaise [lɪ'eɪz] *vi*: **to ~ with** enlazar con.

liaison [liː'eɪzɔn] *n* (*coordination*) enlace *m*; (*affair*) relaciones *fpl* amorosas.

liar ['laɪə*] *n* mentiroso/a.

libel ['laɪbl] *n* calumnia ♦ *vt* calumniar.

liberal ['lɪbərl] *adj* liberal; (*offer, amount etc*) generoso.

liberate ['lɪbəreɪt] *vt* (*people: from poverty etc*) librar; (*prisoner*) libertar; (*country*) liberar.

liberty ['lɪbətɪ] *n* libertad *f*; (*criminal*): **to be at ~** estar en libertad; **to be at ~ to do** estar libre para hacer; **to take the ~ of doing sth** tomarse la libertad de hacer algo.

Libra ['liːbrə] *n* Libra.

librarian [laɪ'brɛərɪən] *n* bibliotecario/a.

library ['laɪbrərɪ] *n* biblioteca.

libretto [lɪ'brɛtəu] *n* libreto.

Libya ['lɪbɪə] *n* Libia; **~n** *adj, n* libio/a *m/f*.

lice [laɪs] *npl of* **louse**.

licence ['laɪsns] (*US* **license**) *n* licencia; (*permit*) permiso; (*also: driving ~, (US) driver's ~*) carnet *m* de conducir (*SP*), permiso (*AM*).

license ['laɪsns] *n* (*US*) = **licence** ♦ *vt* autorizar, dar permiso a; **~d** *adj* (*for alcohol*) autorizado para vender bebidas alcohólicas; (*car*) matriculado; **~ plate** (*US*) *n* placa (de matrícula).

lichen ['laɪkən] *n* líquen *m*.

lick [lɪk] *vt* lamer; (*inf: defeat*) dar una paliza a; **to ~ one's lips** relamerse.

licorice ['lɪkərɪs] (*US*) *n* = **liquorice**.

lid [lɪd] *n* (*of box, case*) tapa; (*of pan*) tapadera.

lido ['laɪdəu] *n* (*BRIT*) piscina.

lie [laɪ] (*pt* **lay**, *pp* **lain**) *vi* (*rest*) estar echado, estar acostado; (*of object: be situated*) estar, encontrarse; (*tell lies*: *pt, pp* **lied**) mentir ♦ *n* mentira; **to ~ low** (*fig*) mantenerse a escondidas; **~ about** *or* **around** *vi* (*things*) estar tirado; (*BRIT: people*) estar tumbado; **~-down** (*BRIT*) *n*: **to have a ~-down** echarse (una siesta); **~-in** (*BRIT*) *n*: **to have a ~-in** quedarse en la cama.

lieu [luː]: **in ~ of** *prep* en lugar de.

lieutenant [lɛf'tɛnənt, (*US*) luː'tɛnənt] *n* (*MIL*) teniente *m*.

life [laɪf] (*pl* **lives**) *n* vida; **to come to ~** animarse; **~ assurance** (*BRIT*) *n* seguro de vida; **~belt** (*BRIT*) *n* cinturón *m* salvavidas; **~boat** *n* lancha de socorro; **~guard** *n* vigilante *m/f*, socorrista *m/f*; **~ imprisonment** *n* cadena perpetua; **~ insurance** *n* = **~ assurance**; **~ jacket** *n* chaleco salvavidas; **~less** *adj* sin vida; (*dull*) soso; **~like** *adj* (*model etc*) que parece vivo; (*realistic*) realista; **~line** *n* (*fig*) cordón *m* umbilical; **~long** *adj* de toda la vida; **~ preserver** (*US*) *n* = **~belt**; **~ sentence** *n* cadena perpetua; **~-size** *adj* de tamaño natural; **~ span** *n* vida; **~style** *n* estilo de vida; **~ support system** *n* (*MED*) sistema *m* de respiración asistida; **~time** *n* (*of person*) vida; (*of thing*) período de vida.

lift [lɪft] *vt* levantar; (*end: ban, rule*) levantar, suprimir ♦ *vi* (*fog*) disiparse ♦ *n* (*BRIT: machine*) ascensor *m*; **to give sb a ~** (*BRIT*) llevar a uno en el coche; **~-off** *n* despegue *m*.

light [laɪt] (*pt, pp* **lighted** *or* **lit**) *n* luz *f*; (*lamp*) luz *f*, lámpara; (*AUT*) faro; (*for cigarette etc*): **have you got a ~?** ¿tienes fuego? ♦ *vt* (*candle, cigarette, fire*) encender (*SP*), prender (*AM*); (*room*) alumbrar ♦ *adj* (*colour*) claro; (*not heavy, also fig*) ligero; (*room*) con mucha luz; (*gentle, graceful*) ágil; **~s** *npl* (*traffic ~s*) semáforos *mpl*; **to come to ~** salir a luz; **in the ~ of** (*new evidence etc*) a la luz de; **~ up** *vi* (*smoke*) encender un cigarrillo; (*face*) iluminarse ♦ *vt* (*illuminate*) iluminar, alumbrar; (*set fire to*) encender; **~ bulb** *n* bombilla (*SP*), foco (*AM*); **~en** *vt* (*make less heavy*) aligerar; **~er** *n* (*also: cigarette ~er*) encendedor *m*, mechero; **~-headed** *adj* (*dizzy*) mareado; (*excited*) exaltado; **~-hearted** *adj* (*person*) alegre; (*remark etc*) divertido; **~house** *n* faro; **~ing** *n* (*system*) alumbrado; **~ly** *adv* ligeramente; (*not seriously*) con poca seriedad; **to get off ~ly** ser castigado con poca severidad; **~ness** *n* (*in weight*) ligereza.

lightning ['laɪtnɪŋ] n relámpago, rayo; ~ **conductor** (US = **rod**) n pararrayos m inv.

light: ~ **pen** n lápiz m óptico; ~**weight** adj (suit) ligero ♦ n (BOXING) peso ligero; ~ **year** n año luz.

like [laɪk] vt gustarle a uno ♦ prep como ♦ adj parecido, semejante ♦ n: and the ~ y otros por el estilo; his ~s and dislikes sus gustos y aversiones; I would ~, I'd ~ me gustaría; (for purchase) quisiera; would you ~ a coffee? ¿te apetece un café?; I ~ swimming me gusta nadar; she ~s apples le gustan las manzanas; to be or look ~ sb/sth parecerse a alguien/algo; what does it look/taste/sound ~? ¿cómo es/a qué sabe/cómo suena?; that's just ~ him es muy de él, es característico de él; do it ~ this hazlo así; it is nothing ~ ... no tiene parecido alguno con ...; ~**able** adj simpático, agradable.

likelihood ['laɪklɪhud] n probabilidad f.

likely ['laɪklɪ] adj probable; he's ~ to leave es probable que se vaya; not ~! ¡ni hablar!

likeness ['laɪknɪs] n semejanza, parecido; that's a good ~ se parece mucho.

likewise ['laɪkwaɪz] adv igualmente; to do ~ hacer lo mismo.

liking ['laɪkɪŋ] n: ~ (for) (person) cariño (a); (thing) afición (a); to be to sb's ~ ser del gusto de uno.

lilac ['laɪlək] n (tree) lilo; (flower) lila.

lily ['lɪlɪ] n lirio, azucena; ~ of the valley n lirio de los valles.

limb [lɪm] n miembro.

limber ['lɪmbə*]: to ~ up vi (SPORT) hacer ejercicios de calentamiento.

limbo ['lɪmbəʊ] n: to be in ~ (fig) quedar a la expectativa.

lime [laɪm] n (tree) limero; (fruit) lima; (GEO) cal f.

limelight ['laɪmlaɪt] n: to be in the ~ (fig) ser el centro de atención.

limerick ['lɪmərɪk] n especie de poema humorístico.

limestone ['laɪmstəʊn] n piedra caliza.

limit ['lɪmɪt] n límite m ♦ vt limitar; **limitation** n limitación f; (weak point)

punto flaco; (restriction) restricción f; ~**ed** adj limitado; to be ~ed to limitarse a; ~**ed (liability) company** (BRIT) n sociedad f anónima.

limousine ['lɪməziːn] n limusina.

limp [lɪmp] n: to have a ~ tener cojera ♦ vi cojear ♦ adj flojo; (material) flácido.

limpet ['lɪmpɪt] n lapa.

line [laɪn] n línea; (rope) cuerda; (for fishing) sedal m; (wire) hilo; (row, series) fila, hilera; (of writing) renglón m, línea; (of song) verso; (on face) arruga; (RAIL) vía ♦ vt (road etc) llenar; (SEWING) forrar; to ~ the streets llenar las aceras; in ~ with alineado con; (according to) de acuerdo con; ~ up vi hacer cola ♦ vt alinear; (prepare) preparar; organizar.

linear ['lɪnɪə*] adj lineal.

lined [laɪnd] adj (face) arrugado; (paper) rayado.

linen ['lɪnɪn] n ropa blanca; (cloth) lino.

liner ['laɪnə*] n vapor m de línea, transatlántico; (for bin) bolsa (de basura).

linesman ['laɪnzmən] n (SPORT) juez m de línea.

line-up n (US: queue) cola; (SPORT) alineación f.

linger ['lɪŋgə*] vi retrasarse, tardar en marcharse; (smell, tradition) persistir.

lingerie ['lænʒəriː] n lencería.

lingo ['lɪŋgəʊ] (pl ~es) (inf) n jerga.

linguist ['lɪŋgwɪst] n lingüista m/f; ~**ic** adj lingüístico; ~**ics** n lingüística.

lining ['laɪnɪŋ] n forro; (ANAT) (membrana) mucosa.

link [lɪŋk] n (of a chain) eslabón m; (relationship) relación f, vínculo ♦ vt vincular, unir; (associate): to ~ with or to relacionar con; ~**s** npl (GOLF) campo de golf; ~ **up** vt acoplar ♦ vi unirse.

lino ['laɪnəʊ] n = **linoleum**.

linoleum [lɪ'nəʊlɪəm] n linóleo.

lion ['laɪən] n león m; ~**ess** n leona.

lip [lɪp] n labio; ~**read** vi leer los labios; ~ **salve** n crema protectora para labios; ~ **service** n: to pay ~ service to sth (pej) prometer algo de boquilla; ~**stick** n lápiz m de labios, carmín m.

liqueur [lɪˈkjuə*] n licor m.
liquid [ˈlɪkwɪd] adj, n líquido.
liquidize [ˈlɪkwɪdaɪz] vt (CULIN) licuar.
liquidizer [ˈlɪkwɪdaɪzə*] n licuadora.
liquor [ˈlɪkə*] n licor m, bebidas fpl alcohólicas.
liquorice [ˈlɪkərɪs] (BRIT) n regaliz m.
liquor store (US) n bodega, tienda de vinos y bebidas alcohólicas.
Lisbon [ˈlɪzbən] n Lisboa.
lisp [lɪsp] n ceceo ♦ vi cecear.
list [lɪst] n lista ♦ vt (mention) enumerar; (put on a list) poner en una lista; ~ed building (BRIT) n monumento declarado de interés histórico-artístico.
listen [ˈlɪsn] vi escuchar, oír; to ~ to sb/sth escuchar a uno/algo; ~er n oyente m/f; (RADIO) radioyente m/f.
listless [ˈlɪstlɪs] adj apático, indiferente.
lit [lɪt] pt, pp of **light**.
litany [ˈlɪtənɪ] n letanía.
liter [ˈliːtə*] (US) n = **litre**.
literacy [ˈlɪtərəsɪ] n capacidad f de leer y escribir.
literal [ˈlɪtərl] adj literal.
literary [ˈlɪtərərɪ] adj literario.
literate [ˈlɪtərət] adj que sabe leer y escribir; (educated) culto.
literature [ˈlɪtərɪtʃə*] n literatura; (brochures etc) folletos mpl.
lithe [laɪð] adj ágil.
litigation [lɪtɪˈgeɪʃən] n litigio.
litre [ˈliːtə*] (US **liter**) n litro.
litter [ˈlɪtə*] n (rubbish) basura; (young animals) camada, cría; ~ bin (BRIT) n papelera; ~ed adj: ~ed with (scattered) lleno de.
little [ˈlɪtl] adj (small) pequeño; (not much) poco ♦ adv poco; a ~ un poco (de); ~ house/bird casita/pajarito; a ~ bit un poquito; ~ by ~ poco a poco; ~ finger n dedo meñique.
live [vi lɪv, adj laɪv] vi vivir ♦ adj (animal) vivo; (wire) conectado; (broadcast) en directo; (shell) cargado; ~ down vt hacer olvidar; ~ on vt fus (food, salary) vivir de; ~ together vi vivir juntos; ~ up to vt fus (fulfil) cumplir con.
livelihood [ˈlaɪvlɪhud] n sustento.

lively [ˈlaɪvlɪ] adj vivo; (interesting: place, book etc) animado.
liven up [ˈlaɪvn-] vt animar ♦ vi animarse.
liver [ˈlɪvə*] n hígado.
livery [ˈlɪvərɪ] n librea.
lives [laɪvz] npl of **life**.
livestock [ˈlaɪvstɔk] n ganado.
livid [ˈlɪvɪd] adj lívido; (furious) furioso.
living [ˈlɪvɪŋ] adj (alive) vivo ♦ n: to earn or make a ~ ganarse la vida; ~ conditions npl condiciones fpl de vida; ~ room n sala (de estar); ~ standards npl nivel m de vida; ~ wage n jornal m suficiente para vivir.
lizard [ˈlɪzəd] n lagarto; (small) lagartija.
load [ləud] n carga; (weight) peso ♦ vt (COMPUT) cargar; (also: ~ up): to ~ (with) cargar (con or de); a ~ of rubbish (inf) tonterías fpl; a ~ of, ~s of (fig) (gran) cantidad de, montones de; ~ed adj (vehicle): to be ~ed with estar cargado de; (question) intencionado; (inf: rich) forrado (de dinero).
loaf [ləuf] (pl **loaves**) n (barra de) pan m.
loan [ləun] n préstamo ♦ vt prestar; on ~ prestado.
loath [ləuθ] adj: to be ~ to do sth estar poco dispuesto a hacer algo.
loathe [ləuð] vt aborrecer; (person) odiar; **loathing** n aversión f; odio.
loaves [ləuvz] npl of **loaf**.
lobby [ˈlɔbɪ] n vestíbulo, sala de espera; (POL: pressure group) grupo de presión ♦ vt presionar.
lobe [ləub] n lóbulo.
lobster [ˈlɔbstə*] n langosta.
local [ˈləukl] adj local ♦ n (pub) bar m; the ~s npl los vecinos, los del lugar; ~ anaesthetic n (MED) anestesia local; ~ authority n municipio, ayuntamiento (SP); ~ call n (TEL) llamada local; ~ government n gobierno municipal; ~ity [-ˈkælɪtɪ] n localidad f; ~ly [-kəlɪ] adv en la vecindad; por aquí.
locate [ləuˈkeɪt] vt (find) localizar; (situate): to be ~d in estar situado en.
location [ləuˈkeɪʃən] n situación f; on ~

(*CINEMA*) en exteriores.
loch [lɔx] *n* lago.
lock [lɔk] *n* (*of door, box*) cerradura; (*of canal*) esclusa; (*of hair*) mechón *m* ♦ *vt* (*with key*) cerrar (con llave) ♦ *vi* (*door etc*) cerrarse (con llave); (*wheels*) trabarse; ~ **in** *vt* encerrar; ~ **out** *vt* (*person*) cerrar la puerta a; ~ **up** *vt* (*criminal*) meter en la cárcel; (*mental patient*) encerrar; (*house*) cerrar (con llave) ♦ *vi* echar la llave.
locker [ˈlɔkə*] *n* casillero.
locket [ˈlɔkɪt] *n* medallón *m*.
locksmith [ˈlɔksmɪθ] *n* cerrajero/a.
lockup [ˈlɔkʌp] *n* (*jail, cell*) cárcel *f*.
locomotive [ləukəˈməutɪv] *n* locomotora.
locum [ˈləukəm] *n* (*MED*) (médico/a) interino/a.
locust [ˈləukəst] *n* langosta.
lodge [lɔdʒ] *n* casita (del guarda) ♦ *vi* (*person*): **to** ~ (**with**) alojarse (en casa de); (*bullet, bone*) incrustarse ♦ *vt* (*complaint*) presentar; ~**r** *n* huésped(a) *m/f*.
lodgings [ˈlɔdʒɪŋz] *npl* alojamiento.
loft [lɔft] *n* desván *m*.
lofty [ˈlɔftɪ] *adj* (*noble*) sublime; (*haughty*) altanero.
log [lɔg] *n* (*of wood*) leño, tronco; (*written account*) diario ♦ *vt* anotar.
logbook [ˈlɔgbuk] *n* (*NAUT*) diario de a bordo; (*AVIAT*) libro de vuelo; (*of car*) documentación *f* (del coche (*SP*) *or* carro (*AM*)).
loggerheads [ˈlɔgəhɛdz] *npl*: **to be at** ~ (**with**) estar en desacuerdo (con).
logic [ˈlɔdʒɪk] *n* lógica; ~**al** *adj*. lógico.
logo [ˈləugəu] *n* logotipo.
loin [lɔɪn] *n* (*CULIN*) lomo, solomillo.
loiter [ˈlɔɪtə*] *vi* (*linger*) entretenerse.
loll [lɔl] *vi* (*also*: ~ **about**) repantigarse.
lollipop [ˈlɔlɪpɔp] *n* chupa-chup *m* ®, pirulí *m*; ~ **lady/man** (*BRIT*) *n persona encargada de ayudar a los niños a cruzar la calle.*
London [ˈlʌndən] *n* Londres; ~**er** *n* londinense *m/f*.
lone [ləun] *adj* solitario.
loneliness [ˈləunlɪnɪs] *n* soledad *f*; aislamiento.

lonely [ˈləunlɪ] *adj* (*situation*) solitario; (*person*) solo; (*place*) aislado.
long [lɔŋ] *adj* largo ♦ *adv* mucho tiempo, largamente ♦ *vi*: **to** ~ **for sth** anhelar algo; **so** *or* **as** ~ **as** mientras, con tal que; **don't be** ~! ¡no tardes!, ¡vuelve pronto!; **how** ~ **is the street?** ¿cuánto tiene la calle de largo?; **how** ~ **is the lesson?** ¿cuánto dura la clase?; **6 metres** ~ que mide 6 metros, de 6 metros de largo; **6 months** ~ que dura 6 meses, de 6 meses de duración; **all night** ~ toda la noche; **he no** ~**er comes** ya no viene; ~ **before** mucho antes; **before** ~ (+*future*) dentro de poco; (+*past*) poco tiempo después; **at** ~ **last** al fin, por fin; ~**-distance** *adj* (*race*) de larga distancia; (*call*) interurbano; ~**-haired** *adj* de pelo largo; ~**hand** *n* escritura sin abreviaturas; ~**ing** *n* anhelo, ansia; (*nostalgia*) nostalgia ♦ *adj* anhelante.
longitude [ˈlɔŋgɪtjuːd] *n* longitud *f*.
long: ~ **jump** *n* salto de longitud; ~**-life** *adj* (*batteries*) de larga duración; (*milk*) uperizado; ~**-lost** *adj* desaparecido hace mucho tiempo; ~**-playing record** *n* elepé *m*, disco de larga duración; ~**-range** *adj* (*plan*) de gran alcance; (*missile*) de largo alcance; ~**-sighted** (*BRIT*) *adj* présbita; ~**-standing** *adj* de mucho tiempo; ~**-suffering** *adj* sufrido; ~**-term** *adj* a largo plazo; ~ **wave** *n* onda larga; ~**-winded** *adj* prolijo.
loo [luː] (*BRIT*: *inf*) *n* váter *m*.
look [luk] *vi* mirar; (*seem*) parecer; (*building etc*): **to** ~ **south/on to the sea** dar al sur/al mar ♦ *n* (*gen*): **to have a** ~ mirar; (*glance*) mirada; (*appearance*) aire *m*, aspecto; ~**s** *npl* (*good* ~*s*) belleza; ~ (**here**)! (*expressing annoyance etc*) ¡oye!; ~! (*expressing surprise*) ¡mira!; ~ **after** *vt fus* (*care for*) cuidar a; (*deal with*) encargarse de; ~ **at** *vt fus* mirar; (*read quickly*) echar un vistazo a; ~ **back** *vi* mirar hacia atrás; ~ **down on** *vt fus* (*fig*) despreciar, mirar con desprecio; ~ **for** *vt fus* buscar; ~ **forward to** *vt fus* es-

perar con ilusión; (*in letters*): **we ~ forward to hearing from you** quedamos a la espera de sus gratas noticias; **~ into** *vt* investigar; **~ on** *vi* mirar (como espectador); **~ out** *vi* (*beware*): **to ~ out (for)** tener cuidado (de); **~ out for** *vt fus* (*seek*) buscar; (*await*) esperar; **~ round** *vi* volver la cabeza; **~ through** *vt fus* (*examine*) examinar; **~ to** *vt fus* (*rely on*) contar con; **~ up** *vi* mirar hacia arriba; (*improve*) mejorar ♦ *vt* (*word*) buscar; **~ up to** *vt fus* admirar; **~-out** *n* (*tower etc*) puesto de observación; (*person*) vigía *m/f*; **to be on the ~-out for sth** estar al acecho de algo.

loom [luːm] *vi*: **~ (up)** (*threaten*) surgir, amenazar; (*event: approach*) aproximarse.

loony ['luːnɪ] (*inf*) *n, adj* loco/a *m/f*.

loop [luːp] *n* lazo ♦ *vt*: **to ~ sth round sth** pasar algo alrededor de algo; **~hole** *n* escapatoria.

loose [luːs] *adj* suelto; (*clothes*) ancho; (*morals, discipline*) relajado; **to be on the ~** estar en libertad; **to be at a ~ end** *or* **at ~ ends** (*US*) no saber qué hacer; **~ change** *n* cambio; **~ chippings** *npl* (*on road*) gravilla suelta; **~ly** *adv* libremente, aproximadamente; **~n** *vt* aflojar.

loot [luːt] *n* botín *m* ♦ *vt* saquear.

lop off [lɔp-] *vt* (*branches*) podar.

lop-sided *adj* torcido.

lord [lɔːd] *n* señor *m*; **L~ Smith** Lord Smith; **the L~** el Señor; **my ~** (*to bishop*) Ilustrísima; (*to noble etc*) Señor; **good L~!** ¡Dios mío!; **the (House of) L~s** (*BRIT*) la Cámara de los Lores; **~ship** *n*: **your L~ship** su Señoría.

lore [lɔː*] *n* tradiciones *fpl*.

lorry ['lɔrɪ] (*BRIT*) *n* camión *m*; **~ driver** *n* camionero/a.

lose [luːz] (*pt, pp* lost) *vt* perder ♦ *vi* perder, ser vencido; **to ~** (*time*) (*clock*) atrasarse; **~r** *n* perdedor(a) *m/f*.

loss [lɔs] *n* pérdida; **heavy ~es** (*MIL*) grandes pérdidas; **to be at a ~** no saber qué hacer; **to make a ~** sufrir pérdidas.

lost [lɔst] *pt, pp of* lose ♦ *adj* perdido; **~ property** (*US* **~ and found**) *n* objetos *mpl* perdidos.

lot [lɔt] *n* (*group: of things*) grupo; (*at auctions*) lote *m*; **the ~** el todo, todos; **a ~** (*large number: of books etc*) muchos; (*a great deal*) mucho, bastante; **a ~ of, ~s of** mucho(s) (*pl*); **I read a ~** leo bastante; **to draw ~s (for sth)** echar suertes (para decidir algo).

lotion ['ləʊʃən] *n* loción *f*.

lottery ['lɔtərɪ] *n* lotería.

loud [laʊd] *adj* (*voice, sound*) fuerte; (*laugh, shout*) estrepitoso; (*condemnation etc*) enérgico; (*gaudy*) chillón/ona ♦ *adv* (*speak etc*) fuerte; **out ~** en voz alta; **~hailer** (*BRIT*) *n* megáfono; **~ly** *adv* (*noisily*) fuerte; (*aloud*) en voz alta; **~speaker** *n* altavoz *m*.

lounge [laʊndʒ] *n* salón *m*, sala (de estar); (*at airport etc*) sala; (*BRIT: also:* **~-bar**) salón-bar *m* ♦ *vi* (*also: ~ about or around*) reposar, holgazanear; **~ suit** (*BRIT*) *n* traje *m* de calle.

louse [laʊs] (*pl* lice) *n* piojo.

lousy ['laʊzɪ] (*inf*) *adj* (*bad quality*) malísimo, asqueroso; (*ill*) fatal.

lout [laʊt] *n* gamberro/a.

lovable ['lʌvəbl] *adj* amable, simpático.

love [lʌv] *n* (*romantic, sexual*) amor *m*; (*kind, caring*) cariño ♦ *vt* amar, querer; (*thing, activity*) encantarle a uno; **"~ from Anne"** (*on letter*) "un abrazo (de) Anne"; **to ~ to do** encantarle a uno hacer; **to be/fall in ~ with** estar enamorado/enamorarse de; **to make ~** hacer el amor; **for the ~ of** por amor de; **"15 ~"** (*TENNIS*) "15 a cero"; **I ~ paella** me encanta la paella; **~ affair** *n* aventura sentimental; **~ letter** *n* carta de amor; **~ life** *n* vida sentimental.

lovely ['lʌvlɪ] *adj* (*delightful*) encantador(a); (*beautiful*) precioso.

lover ['lʌvə*] *n* amante *m/f*; (*person in love*) enamorado; (*amateur*): **a ~ of** un(a) aficionado/a *or* un(a) amante de.

loving ['lʌvɪŋ] *adj* amoroso, cariñoso; (*action*) tierno.

low [ləʊ] *adj, ad* bajo ♦ *n* (*METEOROLOGY*) área de baja presión; **to be ~**

on (*supplies etc*) andar mal de; **to feel** ~ sentirse deprimido; **to turn (down)** ~ bajar; ~-**alcohol** *adj* de bajo contenido en alcohol; ~-**cut** *adj* (*dress*) escotado.

lower ['ləuə*] *adj* más bajo; (*less important*) menos importante ♦ *vt* bajar; (*reduce*) reducir ♦ *vr*: **to** ~ **o.s. to** (*fig*) rebajarse a.

low: ~-**fat** *adj* (*milk, yoghurt*) desnatado; (*diet*) bajo en calorías; ~**lands** *npl* (*GEO*) tierras *fpl* bajas; ~**ly** *adj* humilde, inferior.

loyal ['lɔɪəl] *adj* leal; ~**ty** *n* lealtad *f*.

lozenge ['lɔzɪndʒ] *n* (*MED*) pastilla.

L.P. *n abbr* (= *long-playing record*) elepé *m*.

L-plates ['ɛl-] (*BRIT*) *npl* placas *fpl* de aprendiz de conductor.

Ltd *abbr* (= *limited company*) S.A.

lubricate ['luːbrɪkeɪt] *vt* lubricar, engrasar.

lucid ['luːsɪd] *adj* lúcido.

luck [lʌk] *n* suerte *f*; **bad** ~ mala suerte; **good** ~! ¡que tengas suerte!, ¡suerte!; **bad** *or* **hard** *or* **tough** ~! ¡qué pena!; ~**ily** *adv* afortunadamente; ~**y** *adj* afortunado; (*at cards etc*) con suerte; (*object*) que trae suerte.

ludicrous ['luːdɪkrəs] *adj* absurdo.

lug [lʌg] *vt* (*drag*) arrastrar.

luggage ['lʌgɪdʒ] *n* equipaje *m*; ~ **rack** *n* (*on car*) baca, portaequipajes *m inv*.

lukewarm ['luːkwɔːm] *adj* tibio.

lull [lʌl] *n* tregua ♦ *vt*: **to** ~ **sb to sleep** arrullar a uno; **to** ~ **sb into a false sense of security** dar a alguien una falsa sensación de seguridad.

lullaby ['lʌləbaɪ] *n* nana.

lumbago [lʌm'beɪgəu] *n* lumbago.

lumber ['lʌmbə*] *n* (*junk*) trastos *mpl* viejos; (*wood*) maderos *mpl*; ~ *vt*: **to be** ~**ed with** tener que cargar con algo; ~**jack** *n* maderero.

luminous ['luːmɪnəs] *adj* luminoso.

lump [lʌmp] *n* terrón *m*; (*fragment*) trozo; (*swelling*) bulto ♦ *vt* (*also*: ~ *together*) juntar; ~ **sum** *n* suma global; ~**y** *adj* (*sauce*) lleno de grumos; (*mattress*) lleno de bultos.

lunar ['luːnə*] *adj* lunar.

lunatic ['luːnətɪk] *adj* loco.

lunch [lʌntʃ] *n* almuerzo, comida ♦ *vi* almorzar.

luncheon ['lʌntʃən] *n* almuerzo; ~ **meat** *n* tipo de fiambre; ~ **voucher** (*BRIT*) *n* vale *m* de comida.

lunch time *n* hora de comer.

lung [lʌŋ] *n* pulmón *m*.

lunge [lʌndʒ] *vi* (*also*: ~ *forward*) abalanzarse; **to** ~ **at** arremeter contra.

lurch [ləːtʃ] *vi* dar sacudidas ♦ *n* sacudida; **to leave sb in the** ~ dejar a uno plantado.

lure [luə*] *n* (*attraction*) atracción *f* ♦ *vt* tentar.

lurid ['luərɪd] *adj* (*colour*) chillón/ona; (*account*) espeluznante.

lurk [ləːk] *vi* (*person, animal*) estar al acecho; (*fig*) acechar.

luscious ['lʌʃəs] *adj* (*attractive*: *person, thing*) precioso; (*food*) delicioso.

lush [lʌʃ] *adj* exuberante.

lust [lʌst] *n* lujuria; (*greed*) codicia; ~ **after** *or* **for** *vt fus* codiciar.

lustre ['lʌstə*] (*US* **luster**) *n* lustre *m*, brillo.

lusty ['lʌstɪ] *adj* robusto, fuerte.

Luxembourg ['lʌksəmbəːg] *n* Luxemburgo.

luxuriant [lʌg'zjuərɪənt] *adj* exuberante.

luxurious [lʌg'zjuərɪəs] *adj* lujoso.

luxury ['lʌkʃərɪ] *n* lujo ♦ *cpd* de lujo.

lying ['laɪɪŋ] *n* mentiras *fpl* ♦ *adj* mentiroso.

lyrical ['lɪrɪkl] *adj* lírico.

lyrics ['lɪrɪks] *npl* (*of song*) letra.

M

m. *abbr* = **metre**; **mile**; **million**.

M.A. *abbr* = **Master of Arts**.

mac [mæk] (*BRIT*) *n* impermeable *m*.

macaroni [mækə'rəunɪ] *n* macarrones *mpl*.

machine [mə'ʃiːn] *n* máquina ♦ *vt* (*dress etc*) coser a máquina; (*TECH*) hacer a máquina; ~ **gun** *n* ametralladora; ~ **language** *n* (*COMPUT*) lenguaje *m* máquina; ~**ry** *n* maquinaria; (*fig*) mecanismo.

macho ['mætʃəu] *adj* machista.

mackerel ['mækrl] *n inv* caballa.

mackintosh ['mækɪntɔʃ] (*BRIT*) *n* impermeable *m*.

mad [mæd] *adj* loco; (*idea*) disparatado; (*angry*) furioso; (*keen*): **to be ~ about sth** volverle loco a uno algo.

madam ['mædəm] *n* señora.

madden ['mædn] *vt* volver loco.

made [meɪd] *pt, pp of* **make**.

Madeira [mə'dɪərə] *n* (*GEO*) Madera; (*wine*) vino de Madera.

made-to-measure (*BRIT*) *adj* hecho a la medida.

madly ['mædlɪ] *adv* locamente.

madman ['mædmən] *n* loco.

madness ['mædnɪs] *n* locura.

Madrid [mə'drɪd] *n* Madrid.

Mafia ['mæfɪə] *n* Mafia.

magazine [mægə'ziːn] *n* revista; (*RADIO*, *TV*) programa *m* magazina.

maggot ['mægət] *n* gusano.

magic ['mædʒɪk] *n* magia ♦ *adj* mágico; **~ian** [mə'dʒɪʃən] *n* mago/a; (*conjurer*) prestidigitador(a) *m/f*.

magistrate ['mædʒɪstreɪt] *n* juez *m/f* (*municipal*).

magnet ['mægnɪt] *n* imán *m*; **~ic** [-'nɛtɪk] *adj* magnético; (*personality*) atrayente; **~ic tape** *n* cinta magnética.

magnificent [mæg'nɪfɪsnt] *adj* magnífico.

magnify ['mægnɪfaɪ] *vt* (*object*) ampliar; (*sound*) aumentar; **~ing glass** *n* lupa.

magpie ['mægpaɪ] *n* urraca.

mahogany [mə'hɔgənɪ] *n* caoba.

maid [meɪd] *n* criada; **old ~** (*pej*) solterona.

maiden ['meɪdn] *n* doncella ♦ *adj* (*aunt etc*) solterona; (*speech, voyage*) inaugural; **~ name** *n* nombre *m* de soltera.

mail [meɪl] *n* correo; (*letters*) cartas *fpl* ♦ *vt* echar al correo; **~box** (*US*) *n* buzón *m*; **~ing list** *n* lista de direcciones; **~-order** *n* pedido postal.

maim [meɪm] *vt* mutilar, lisiar.

main [meɪn] *adj* principal, mayor ♦ *n* (*pipe*) cañería maestra; (*US*) red *f* eléctrica; **the ~s** *npl* (*BRIT: ELEC*) la red

eléctrica; **in the ~** en general; **~frame** *n* (*COMPUT*) ordenador *m* central; **~land** *n* tierra firme; **~ly** *adv* principalmente; **~ road** *n* carretera; **~stay** *n* (*fig*) pilar *m*; **~stream** *n* corriente *f* principal.

maintain [meɪn'teɪn] *vt* mantener; **maintenance** ['meɪntənəns] *n* mantenimiento; (*LAW*) manutención *f*.

maize [meɪz] (*BRIT*) *n* maíz *m* (*SP*), choclo (*AM*).

majestic [mə'dʒɛstɪk] *adj* majestuoso.

majesty ['mædʒɪstɪ] *n* majestad *f*; (*title*): **Your M~** Su Majestad.

major ['meɪdʒə*] *n* (*MIL*) comandante *m* ♦ *adj* principal; (*MUS*) mayor.

Majorca [mə'jɔːkə] *n* Mallorca.

majority [mə'dʒɔrɪtɪ] *n* mayoría.

make [meɪk] (*pt, pp* **made**) *vt* hacer; (*manufacture*) fabricar; (*mistake*) cometer; (*speech*) pronunciar; (*cause to be*): **to ~ sb sad** poner triste a alguien; (*force*): **to ~ sb do sth** obligar a alguien a hacer algo; (*earn*) ganar; (*equal*): **2 and 2 ~ 4** 2 y 2 son 4 ♦ *n* marca; **to ~ the bed** hacer la cama; **to ~ a fool of sb** poner a alguien en ridículo; **to ~ a profit/loss** obtener ganancias/sufrir pérdidas; **to ~ it** (*arrive*) llegar; (*achieve sth*) tener éxito; **what time do you ~ it?** ¿qué hora tienes?; **to ~ do with** contentarse con; **~ for** *vt fus* (*place*) dirigirse a; **~ out** *vt* (*decipher*) descifrar; (*understand*) entender; (*see*) distinguir; (*cheque*) extender; **~ up** *vt* (*invent*) inventar; (*prepare*) hacer; (*constitute*) constituir ♦ *vi* reconciliarse; (*with cosmetics*) maquillarse; **~ up for** *vt fus* compensar; **~-believe** *n* ficción *f*, invención *f*; **~r** *n* fabricante *m/f*; (*of film, programme*) autor(a) *m/f*; **~shift** *adj* improvisado; **~-up** *n* maquillaje *m*; **~-up remover** *n* desmaquillador *m*.

making ['meɪkɪŋ] *n* (*fig*): **in the ~** en vías de formación; **to have the ~s of** (*person*) tener madera de.

malaise [mæ'leɪz] *n* malestar *m*.

Malaya [mə'leɪə] *n* Malaya, Malaca.

Malaysia [mə'leɪzɪə] *n* Malasia.

male [meɪl] n (BIOL) macho ♦ adj (sex, attitude) masculino; (child etc) varón.
malfunction [mæl'fʌŋkʃən] n mal funcionamiento.
malice [mælɪs] n malicia; **malicious** [mə'lɪʃəs] adj malicioso; rencoroso.
malign [mə'laɪn] vt difamar, calumniar.
malignant [mə'lɪɡnənt] adj (MED) maligno.
mall [mɔːl] (US) n (also: shopping ~) centro comercial.
mallet [mælɪt] n mazo.
malnutrition [mælnjuː'trɪʃən] n desnutrición f.
malpractice [mæl'præktɪs] n negligencia profesional.
malt [mɔːlt] n malta; (whisky) whisky m de malta.
Malta [mɔːltə] n Malta; **Maltese** adj, n inv maltés/esa m/f.
maltreat [mæl'triːt] vt maltratar.
mammal [mæml] n mamífero.
mammoth [mæməθ] n mamut m ♦ adj gigantesco.
man [mæn] (pl men) n hombre m; (~kind) el hombre ♦ vt (NAUT) tripular; (MIL) guarnecer; (operate: machine) manejar; **an old ~** un viejo; **~ and wife** marido y mujer.
manage [mænɪdʒ] vi arreglárselas, ir tirando ♦ vt (be in charge of) dirigir; (control: person) manejar; (: ship) gobernar; **~able** adj manejable; **~ment** n dirección f; **~r** n director(a) m/f; (of pop star) mánayer m/f; (SPORT) entrenador(a) m/f; **~ress** n directora; entrenadora; **~rial** [-ə'dʒɪərɪəl] adj directivo; **managing director** n director(a) m/f general.
mandarin [mændərɪn] n (also: ~ orange) mandarina; (person) mandarín m.
mandate [mændeɪt] n mandato.
mandatory [mændətərɪ] adj obligatorio.
mane [meɪn] n (of horse) crin f; (of lion) melena.
maneuver [mə'nuːvə*] (US) = **manoeuvre**.
manfully [mænfəlɪ] adv valientemente.
mangle [mæŋɡl] vt mutilar, destrozar.

mangy [meɪndʒɪ] adj (animal) sarnoso.
manhandle [mænhændl] vt maltratar.
manhole [mænhəʊl] n agujero de acceso.
manhood [mænhʊd] n edad f viril; (state) virilidad f.
man-hour n hora-hombre f.
manhunt [mænhʌnt] n (POLICE) búsqueda y captura.
mania [meɪnɪə] n manía; **~c** [meɪnɪæk] n maníaco/a; (fig) maniático.
manic [mænɪk] adj frenético; **~-depressive** n maníaco/a depresivo/a.
manicure [mænɪkjʊə*] n manicura.
manifest [mænɪfest] vt manifestar, mostrar ♦ adj manifiesto.
manifesto [mænɪ'festəʊ] n manifiesto.
manipulate [mə'nɪpjuleɪt] vt manipular.
mankind [mæn'kaɪnd] n humanidad f, género humano.
manly [mænlɪ] adj varonil.
man-made adj artificial.
manner [mænə*] n manera, modo; (behaviour) conducta, manera de ser; (type) all ~ **of things** toda clase de cosas; **~s** npl (behaviour) modales mpl; **bad ~s** mala educación; **~ism** n peculiaridad f de lenguaje (or de comportamiento).
manoeuvre [mə'nuːvə*] (US **maneuver**) vt, vi maniobrar ♦ n maniobra.
manor [mænə*] n (also: ~ house) casa solariega.
manpower [mænpaʊə*] n mano f de obra.
mansion [mænʃən] n palacio, casa grande.
manslaughter [mænslɔːtə*] n homicidio no premeditado.
mantelpiece [mæntlpiːs] n repisa, chimenea.
manual [mænjʊəl] adj manual ♦ n manual m.
manufacture [mænju'fæktʃə*] vt fabricar ♦ n fabricación f; **~r** n fabricante m/f.
manure [mə'njuə*] n estiércol m.
manuscript [mænjuskrɪpt] n manuscrito.
many [menɪ] adj, pron muchos/as; **a great ~** muchísimos, un buen número

map 155 **mass**

de; ~ **a time** muchas veces.
map [mæp] *n* mapa *m*; **to ~ out** *vt* proyectar.
maple ['meɪpl] *n* arce *m* (*SP*), maple *m* (*AM*).
mar [mɑ:*] *vt* estropear.
marathon ['mærəθən] *n* maratón *m*.
marauder [mə'rɔːdə*] *n* merodeador(a) *m/f*.
marble ['mɑːbl] *n* mármol *m*; (*toy*) canica.
March [mɑːtʃ] *n* marzo.
march [mɑːtʃ] *vi* (*MIL*) marchar; (*demonstrators*) manifestarse ♦ *n* marcha; (*demonstration*) manifestación *f*.
mare [meə*] *n* yegua.
margarine [mɑːdʒə'riːn] *n* margarina.
margin ['mɑːdʒɪn] *n* margen *m*; (*COMM*: *profit ~*) margen *m* de beneficios; ~**al** *adj* marginal; ~**al seat** *n* (*POL*) escaño electoral difícil de asegurar.
marigold ['mærɪgəʊld] *n* caléndula.
marijuana [mærɪ'wɑːnə] *n* marijuana.
marina [mə'riːnə] *n* puerto deportivo.
marinate ['mærɪneɪt] *vt* marinar.
marine [mə'riːn] *adj* marino ♦ *n* soldado de marina.
marital ['mærɪtl] *adj* matrimonial; ~ **status** estado civil.
maritime ['mærɪtaɪm] *adj* marítimo.
marjoram ['mɑːdʒərəm] *n* mejorana.
mark [mɑːk] *n* marca, señal *f*; (*in snow, mud etc*) huella; (*stain*) mancha; (*BRIT*: *SCOL*) nota; (*currency*) marco ♦ *vt* marcar; manchar; (*damage*: *furniture*) rayar; (*indicate*: *place etc*) señalar; (*BRIT*: *SCOL*) calificar, corregir; **to ~ time** marcar el paso; (*fig*) marcar(se) un ritmo; ~**ed** *adj* (*obvious*) marcado, acusado; ~**er** *n* (*sign*) marcador *m*; (*bookmark*) señal *f* (de libro).
market ['mɑːkɪt] *n* mercado ♦ *vt* (*COMM*) comercializar; ~ **garden** (*BRIT*) *n* huerto; ~**ing** *n* márketing *m*; ~**place** *n* mercado; ~ **research** *n* análisis *m inv* de mercados.
marksman ['mɑːksmən] *n* tirador *m*.
marmalade ['mɑːməleɪd] *n* mermelada de naranja.
maroon [mə'ruːn] *vt*: **to be ~ed** quedar

aislado; (*fig*) quedar abandonado.
marquee [mɑː'kiː] *n* entoldado.
marquess ['mɑːkwɪs] *n* marqués *m*.
marquis ['mɑːkwɪs] *n* = **marquess.**
marriage ['mærɪdʒ] *n* (*relationship, institution*) matrimonio; (*wedding*) boda; (*act*) casamiento; ~ **bureau** *n* agencia matrimonial; ~ **certificate** *n* partida de casamiento.
married ['mærɪd] *adj* casado; (*life, love*) conyugal.
marrow ['mærəʊ] *n* médula; (*vegetable*) calabacín *m*.
marry ['mærɪ] *vt* casarse con; (*subj*: *father, priest etc*) casar ♦ *vi* (*also*: *get married*) casarse.
Mars [mɑːz] *n* Marte *m*.
marsh [mɑːʃ] *n* pantano; (*salt ~*) marisma.
marshal ['mɑːʃl] *n* (*MIL*) mariscal *m*; (*at sports meeting etc*) oficial *m*; (*US*: *of police, fire department*) jefe/a *m/f* ♦ *vt* (*thoughts etc*) ordenar; (*soldiers*) formar.
marshy ['mɑːʃɪ] *adj* pantanoso.
martial ['mɑːʃl] *adj* marcial; ~ **law** *n* ley *f* marcial.
martyr ['mɑːtə*] *n* mártir *m/f*; ~**dom** *n* martirio.
marvel ['mɑːvl] *n* maravilla, prodigio ♦ *vi*: **to ~ (at)** maravillarse (de); ~**lous** (*US* ~**ous**) *adj* maravilloso.
Marxist ['mɑːksɪst] *adj, n* marxista *m/f*.
marzipan ['mɑːzɪpæn] *n* mazapán *m*.
mascara [mæs'kɑːrə] *n* rimel *m*.
masculine ['mæskjʊlɪn] *adj* masculino.
mash [mæʃ] *vt* machacar; ~**ed potatoes** *npl* puré *m* de patatas (*SP*) or papas (*AM*).
mask [mɑːsk] *n* máscara ♦ *vt* (*cover*): **to ~ one's face** ocultarse la cara; (*hide*: *feelings*) esconder.
masochist ['mæsəkɪst] *n* masoquista *m/f*.
mason ['meɪsn] *n* (*also*: *stone~*) albañil *m*; (*also*: *free~*) masón *m*; ~**ry** *n* (*in building*) mampostería.
masquerade [mæskə'reɪd] *vi*: **to ~ as** disfrazarse de, hacerse pasar por.
mass [mæs] *n* (*people*) muchedumbre *f*;

(of air, liquid etc) masa; (of detail, hair etc) gran cantidad f; (REL) misa ♦ cpd masivo ♦ vi reunirse; concentrarse; **the ~es** npl las masas; **~es of** (inf) montones de.

massacre ['mæsəkə*] n masacre f.

massage ['mæsɑ:ʒ] n masaje m ♦ vt dar masaje en.

masseur [mæ'sə:*] n masajista m.

masseuse [mæ'sə:z] n masajista f.

massive ['mæsɪv] adj enorme; (support, changes) masivo.

mass media npl medios mpl de comunicación.

mass-production n fabricación f en serie.

mast [mɑ:st] n (NAUT) mástil m; (RADIO etc) torre f.

master ['mɑ:stə*] n (of servant) amo; (of situation) dueño, maestro; (in primary school) maestro; (in secondary school) profesor m; (title for boys): **M~ X** Señorito X ♦ vt dominar; **M~ of Arts/Science** n licenciatura superior en Letras/Ciencias; **~ key** n llave f maestra; **~ly** adj magistral; **~mind** n inteligencia superior ♦ vt dirigir, planear; **~piece** n obra maestra; **~y** n maestría.

masturbate ['mæstəbeɪt] vi masturbarse.

mat [mæt] n estera; (also: door~) felpudo; (also: table ~) salvamanteles m inv, posavasos m inv ♦ adj = matt.

match [mætʃ] n cerilla, fósforo; (game) partido; (equal) igual m/f ♦ vt (go well with) hacer juego con; (equal) igualar; (correspond to) corresponderse con; (pair: also: ~ up) casar con ♦ vi hacer juego; **to be a good ~** hacer juego; **~box** n caja de cerillas; **~ing** adj que hace juego.

mate [meɪt] n (work~) colega m/f; (inf: friend) amigo/a; (animal) macho m/ hembra f; (in merchant navy) segundo de a bordo ♦ vi acoplarse, aparearse ♦ vt aparear.

material [mə'tɪərɪəl] n (substance) materia; (information) material m; (cloth) tela, tejido ♦ adj material; (important) esencial; **~s** npl materiales mpl;**~istic** [-'lɪstɪk] adj materialista;**~ize** vi materializarse.

maternal [mə'tə:nl] adj maternal.

maternity [mə'tə:nɪti] n maternidad f; **~ dress** n vestido premamá.

math [mæθ] (US) n = **mathematics**.

mathematical [mæθə'mætɪkl] adj matemático.

mathematician [mæθəmə'tɪʃən] n matemático/a.

mathematics [mæθə'mætɪks] n matemáticas fpl.

maths [mæθs] (BRIT) n = **mathematics**.

matinée ['mætɪneɪ] n sesión f de tarde.

mating ['meɪtɪŋ] n apareamiento.

matrices ['meɪtrɪsiːz] npl of **matrix**.

matriculation [mətrɪkju'leɪʃən] n (formalización f de) matrícula.

matrimony ['mætrɪmənɪ] n matrimonio.

matrix ['meɪtrɪks] (pl **matrices**) n matriz f.

matron ['meɪtrən] n enfermera f jefe; (in school) ama de llaves.

mat(t) [mæt] adj mate.

matted ['mætɪd] adj enmarañado.

matter ['mætə*] n cuestión f, asunto; (PHYSICS) sustancia, materia; (reading ~) material m; (MED: pus) pus m ♦ vi importar; **~s** npl (affairs) asuntos mpl, temas mpl; **it doesn't ~** no importa; **what's the ~?** ¿qué pasa?; **no ~ what** pase lo que pase; **as a ~ of course** por rutina; **as a ~ of fact** de hecho; **~-of-fact** adj prosaico, práctico.

mattress ['mætrɪs] n colchón m.

mature [mə'tjuə*] adj maduro ♦ vi madurar; **maturity** n madurez f.

maul [mɔ:l] vt magullar.

mauve [məuv] adj de color malva (SP) or guinda (AM).

maverick ['mævərɪk] n hombre/mujer m/f poco ortodoxo/a.

maxim ['mæksɪm] n máxima.

maximum ['mæksɪməm] (pl **maxima**) adj máximo ♦ n máximo.

May [meɪ] n mayo.

may [meɪ] (conditional: **might**) vi (indicating possibility): **he ~ come** puede que venga; (be allowed to): **~ I**

smoke? ¿puedo fumar?; (wishes): ~ God bless you! ¡que Dios le bendiga!; you ~ as well go bien puedes irte.

maybe ['meɪbiː] adv quizá(s).

May Day n el primero de Mayo.

mayhem ['meɪhɛm] n caos m total.

mayonnaise [meɪə'neɪz] n mayonesa.

mayor [mɛə*] n alcalde m; ~ess n alcaldesa.

maze [meɪz] n laberinto.

M.D. abbr = Doctor of Medicine.

me [miː] pron (direct) me; (stressed, after pron) mí; **can you hear** ~? ¿me oyes?; **he heard me**! me oyó a mí; **it's** ~ soy yo; **give them to** ~ dámelos/las; **with/without** ~ conmigo/sin mí.

meadow ['mɛdəu] n prado, pradera.

meagre ['miːgə*] (US **meager**) adj escaso, pobre.

meal [miːl] n comida; (flour) harina; ~**time** n hora de comer.

mean [miːn] (pt, pp **meant**) adj (with money) tacaño; (unkind) mezquino, malo; (shabby) humilde; (average) medio ♦ vt (signify) querer decir, significar; (refer to) referirse a; (intend): **to** ~ **to do sth** pensar or pretender hacer algo ♦ n medio, término medio; ~**s** npl (way) medio, manera; (money) recursos mpl, medios mpl; **by** ~**s of** mediante, por medio de; **by all** ~**s!** ¡naturalmente!, ¡claro que sí!; **do you** ~ **it?** ¿lo dices en serio?; **what do you** ~? ¿qué quiere decir?; **to be meant for sb/sth** ser para uno/algo.

meander [mɪ'ændə*] vi (river) serpentear.

meaning ['miːnɪŋ] n significado, sentido; (purpose) sentido, propósito; ~**ful** adj significativo; ~**less** adj sin sentido.

meanness ['miːnnɪs] n (with money) tacañería; (unkindness) maldad f, mezquindad f; (shabbiness) humildad f.

meant [mɛnt] pt, pp of **mean**.

meantime ['miːntaɪm] adv (also: **in the** ~) mientras tanto.

meanwhile ['miːnwaɪl] adv = **meantime**.

measles ['miːzlz] n sarampión m.

measly ['miːzlɪ] (inf) adj miserable.

measure ['mɛʒə*] vt, vi medir ♦ n medida; (ruler) regla; ~**d** adj (tone, step) comedido; ~**ments** npl medidas fpl.

meat [miːt] n carne f; **cold** ~ fiambre m; ~**ball** n albóndiga; ~ **pie** n pastel m de carne.

Mecca ['mɛkə] n La Meca.

mechanic [mɪ'kænɪk] n mecánico/a; ~**s** n mecánica ♦ npl mecanismo; ~**al** adj mecánico.

mechanism ['mɛkənɪzəm] n mecanismo.

medal ['mɛdl] n medalla; ~**lion** [mɪ'dælɪən] n medallón m; ~**list** (US ~**ist**) n (SPORT) medallista m/f.

meddle ['mɛdl] vi: **to** ~ entrometerse en; **to** ~ **with sth** manosear algo.

media ['miːdɪə] npl medios mpl de comunicación ♦ npl of **medium**.

mediaeval [mɛdɪ'iːvl] adj = **medieval**.

mediate ['miːdɪeɪt] vi mediar; **mediator** n intermediario/a, mediador(a) m/f.

Medicaid ['mɛdɪkeɪd] (US) n programa de ayuda médica para los pobres.

medical ['mɛdɪkl] adj médico ♦ n reconocimiento médico.

Medicare ['mɛdɪkɛə*] (US) n programa de ayuda médica para los ancianos.

medicated ['mɛdɪkeɪtɪd] adj medicinal.

medication [mɛdɪ'keɪʃən] n medicación f.

medicine ['mɛdsɪn] n medicina; (drug) medicamento.

medieval [mɛdɪ'iːvl] adj medieval.

mediocre [miːdɪ'əukə*] adj mediocre.

meditate ['mɛdɪteɪt] vi meditar.

Mediterranean [mɛdɪtə'reɪnɪən] adj mediterráneo; **the** ~ (**Sea**) el (Mar) Mediterráneo.

medium ['miːdɪəm] (pl **media**) adj mediano, regular ♦ n (means) medio; (pl **mediums**: person) médium m/f; ~ **wave** n onda media.

medley ['mɛdlɪ] n mezcla; (MUS) popurrí m.

meek [miːk] adj manso, sumiso.

meet [miːt] (pt, pp **met**) vt encontrar; (accidentally) encontrarse con, tropezar con; (by arrangement) reunirse con; (for the first time) conocer; (go and fetch) ir a buscar; (opponent) enfrentarse con; (obligations) cumplir; (encounter: problem) hacer frente a; (need) satisfacer ♦ vi encontrarse; (in session) reunirse; (join: objects) unirse; (for the first time) conocerse; ~ with vt fus (difficulty) tropezar con; to ~ with success tener éxito; ~ing n encuentro; (arranged) cita, compromiso; (business ~) reunión f; (POL) mítin m.

megabyte ['mɛgəbaɪt] n (COMPUT) megabyte m, megaocteto.

megaphone ['mɛgəfəun] n megáfono.

melancholy ['mɛlənkəlɪ] n melancolía ♦ adj melancólico.

mellow ['mɛləu] adj (wine) añejo; (sound, colour) suave ♦ vi (person) ablandar.

melody ['mɛlədɪ] n melodía.

melon ['mɛlən] n melón m.

melt [mɛlt] vi (metal) fundirse; (snow) derretirse ♦ vt fundir; ~down n (in nuclear reactor) fusión f de un reactor (nuclear); ~ing pot n (fig) crisol m.

member ['mɛmbə*] n (gen, ANAT) miembro; (of club) socio/a; M~ of Parliament (BRIT) diputado/a; M~ of the European Parliament (BRIT) eurodiputado/a; ~ship n (members) número de miembros; (state) filiación f; ~ship card n carnet m de socio.

memento [mə'mɛntəu] n recuerdo.

memo ['mɛməu] n apunte m, nota.

memoirs ['mɛmwɑːz] npl memorias fpl.

memorandum [mɛmə'rændəm] (pl memoranda) n apunte m, nota; (official note) acta.

memorial [mɪ'mɔːrɪəl] n monumento conmemorativo ♦ adj conmemorativo.

memorize ['mɛmərɑɪz] vt aprender de memoria.

memory ['mɛmərɪ] n (also: COMPUT) memoria; (instance) recuerdo; (of dead person): in ~ of a la memoria de.

men [mɛn] npl of man.

menace ['mɛnəs] n amenaza ♦ vt amenazar; **menacing** adj amenazador(a).

mend [mɛnd] vt reparar, arreglar; (darn) zurcir ♦ vi reponerse ♦ n arreglo, reparación f; zurcido ♦ n: to be on the ~ ir mejorando; to ~ one's ways

enmendarse; ~ing n reparación f; (clothes) ropa por remendar.

menial ['miːnɪəl] (often pej) adj bajo.

meningitis [mɛnɪn'dʒaɪtɪs] n meningitis f.

menopause ['mɛnəupɔːz] n menopausia.

menstruation [mɛnstru'eɪʃən] n menstruación f.

mental ['mɛntl] adj mental; ~ity [-'tælɪtɪ] n mentalidad f.

mention ['mɛnʃən] n mención f ♦ vt mencionar; (speak of) hablar de; don't ~ it! ¡de nada!

menu ['mɛnjuː] n (set ~) menú m; (printed) carta; (COMPUT) menú m.

MEP n abbr = Member of the European Parliament.

mercenary ['məːsɪnərɪ] adj, n mercenario/a.

merchandise ['məːtʃəndaɪz] n mercancías fpl.

merchant ['məːtʃənt] n comerciante m/f; ~ bank (BRIT) n banco comercial; ~ navy (US ~ marine) n marina mercante.

merciful ['məːsɪful] adj compasivo; (fortunate) afortunado.

merciless ['məːsɪlɪs] adj despiadado.

mercury ['məːkjurɪ] n mercurio.

mercy ['məːsɪ] n compasión f; (REL) misericordia; **at the** ~ of a la merced de.

mere [mɪə*] adj simple, mero; ~ly adv simplemente, sólo.

merge [məːdʒ] vt (join) unir ♦ vi unirse; (COMM) fusionarse; (colours etc) fundirse; ~r n (COMM) fusión f.

meringue [mə'ræŋ] n merengue m.

merit ['mɛrɪt] n mérito ♦ vt merecer.

mermaid ['məːmeɪd] n sirena.

merry ['mɛrɪ] adj alegre; M~ Christmas! ¡Felices Pascuas!; ~-go-round n tiovivo.

mesh [mɛʃ] n malla.

mesmerize ['mɛzmərɑɪz] vt hipnotizar.

mess [mɛs] n (muddle: of situation) confusión f; (: of room) revoltijo; (dirt) porquería; (MIL) comedor m; ~ about or around (inf) vi perder el tiempo; (pass the time) entretenerse; ~ about or around with (inf) vt fus divertirse con; ~ **up** *vt* (*spoil*) estropear; (*dirty*) ensuciar.

message ['mɛsɪdʒ] *n* recado, mensaje *m*.

messenger ['mɛsɪndʒə*] *n* mensajero/a.

Messrs *abbr* (*on letters*: = *Messieurs*) Sres.

messy ['mɛsɪ] *adj* (*dirty*) sucio; (*untidy*) desordenado.

met [mɛt] *pt, pp of* **meet**.

metabolism [mɛ'tæbəlɪzəm] *n* metabolismo.

metal ['mɛtl] *n* metal *m*; ~**lic** [-'tælɪk] *adj* metálico.

metaphor ['mɛtəfə*] *n* metáfora.

mete [miːt]: **to ~ out** *vt* (*punishment*) imponer.

meteor ['miːtɪə*] *n* meteoro; ~**ite** [-aɪt] *n* meteorito.

meteorology [miːtɪə'rɔlədʒɪ] *n* meteorología.

meter ['miːtə*] *n* (*instrument*) contador *m*; (*US: unit*) = **metre** ♦ *vt* (*US: POST*) franquear.

method ['mɛθəd] *n* método.

Methodist ['mɛθədɪst] *adj, n* metodista *m/f.*

meths [mɛθs] (*BRIT*) *n* = **methylated spirit**.

methylated spirit ['mɛθɪleɪtɪd-] (*BRIT*) *n* alcohol *m* metilado *or* desnaturalizado.

metre ['miːtə*] (*US* **meter**) *n* metro.

metric ['mɛtrɪk] *adj* métrico.

metropolis [mɪ'trɔpəlɪs] *n* metrópoli *f.*

metropolitan [mɛtrə'pɔlɪtən] *adj* metropolitano; **the M~ Police** (*BRIT*) *n* la policía londinense.

mettle ['mɛtl] *n*: **to be on one's ~** estar dispuesto a mostrar todo lo que uno vale.

mew [mjuː] *vi* (*cat*) maullar.

mews [mjuːz] *n*: ~ **flat** (*BRIT*) piso acondicionado en antiguos establos o cocheras.

Mexican ['mɛksɪkən] *adj, n* mejicano/a *m/f,* mexicano/a *m/f.*

Mexico ['mɛksɪkəʊ] *n* Méjico (*SP*), México (*AM*); ~ **City** *n* Ciudad *f* de Méjico *or* México.

miaow [miː'aʊ] *vi* maullar.

mice [maɪs] *npl of* **mouse**.

micro... [maɪkrəʊ] *prefix* micro...; ~**chip** *n* microplaqueta; ~**(computer)** *n* microordenador *m*; ~**phone** *n* micrófono; ~**processor** *n* microprocesador *m*; ~**scope** *n* microscopio; ~**wave** *n* (*also*: ~*wave oven*) horno microondas.

mid [mɪd] *adj*: **in ~ May** a mediados de mayo; **in ~ afternoon** a media tarde; **in ~ air** en el aire; ~**day** *n* mediodía *m.*

middle ['mɪdl] *n* centro; (*half-way point*) medio; (*waist*) cintura ♦ *adj* de en medio; (*course, way*) intermedio; **in the ~ of the night** en plena noche; ~**-aged** *adj* de mediana edad; **the M~ Ages** *npl* la Edad Media; ~**-class** *adj* de clase media; **the ~ class(es)** *n*(*pl*) la clase media; **M~ East** *n* Oriente *m* Medio; ~**man** *n* intermediario; ~**name** *n* segundo nombre; ~**-of-the-road** *adj* moderado; ~**weight** *n* (*BOXING*) peso medio.

middling ['mɪdlɪŋ] *adj* mediano.

midge [mɪdʒ] *n* mosquito.

midget ['mɪdʒɪt] *n* enano/a.

Midlands ['mɪdləndz] *npl*: **the ~** la región central de Inglaterra.

midnight ['mɪdnaɪt] *n* medianoche *f.*

midriff ['mɪdrɪf] *n* diafragma *m.*

midst [mɪdst] *n*: **in the ~ of** (*crowd*) en medio de; (*situation, action*) en mitad de.

midsummer [mɪd'sʌmə*] *n*: **in ~** en pleno verano.

midway [mɪd'weɪ] *adj, adv*: ~ **(between)** a medio camino (entre); ~ **through** a la mitad (de).

midweek [mɪd'wiːk] *adv* entre semana.

midwife ['mɪdwaɪf] (*pl* **midwives**) *n* comadrona, partera.

midwinter [mɪd'wɪntə*] *n*: **in ~** en pleno invierno.

might [maɪt] *vb see* **may** ♦ *n* fuerza, poder *m*; ~**y** *adj* fuerte, poderoso.

migraine ['miːgreɪn] *n* jaqueca.

migrant ['maɪgrənt] *n adj* (*bird*) migratorio; (*worker*) emigrante.

migrate [maɪ'greɪt] *vi* emigrar.

mike [maɪk] *n abbr* (= *microphone*) micro.

mild [maɪld] *adj* (*person*) apacible; (*climate*) templado; (*slight*) ligero; (*taste*) suave; (*illness*) leve.

mildew ['mɪldjuː] *n* moho.

mildly ['maɪldlɪ] *adv* ligeramente; suavemente; **to put it ~** para no decir más.

mile [maɪl] *n* milla; **~age** *n* número de millas, ≈ kilometraje *m*; **~ometer** *n* ≈ cuentakilómetros *m inv*; **~stone** *n* mojón *m*.

milieu ['miːljəː] *n* (medio) ambiente *m*.

militant ['mɪlɪtnt] *adj, n* militante *m/f*.

military ['mɪlɪtərɪ] *adj* militar.

militate ['mɪlɪteɪt] *vi*: **to ~ against** ir en contra de, perjudicar.

militia [mɪ'lɪʃə] *n* milicia.

milk [mɪlk] *n* leche *f* ♦ *vt* (*cow*) ordeñar; (*fig*) chupar; **~ chocolate** *n* chocolate *m* con leche; **~man** *n* lechero; **~shake** *n* batido, malteada (*AM*); **~y** *adj* lechoso; **M~y Way** *n* Vía Láctea.

mill [mɪl] *n* (*windmill etc*) molino; (*coffee ~*) molinillo; (*factory*) fábrica ♦ *vt* moler ♦ *vi* (*also*: **~ about**) arremolinarse.

millennium [mɪ'lɛnɪəm] (*pl* **~s** *or* **millennia**) *n* milenio, milenario.

miller ['mɪlə*] *n* molinero.

milli... ['mɪlɪ] *prefix*: **~gram(me)** *n* miligramo; **~metre** (*US* **~meter**) *n* milímetro.

millinery ['mɪlɪnrɪ] *n* sombrerería.

million ['mɪljən] *n* millón *m*; **a ~ times** un millón de veces; **~aire** *n* millonario/a.

milometer [maɪ'lɔmɪtə*] (*BRIT*) *n* = mileometer.

mime [maɪm] *n* mímica; (*actor*) mimo/a ♦ *vt* remedar ♦ *vi* actuar de mimo.

mimic ['mɪmɪk] *n* imitador(a) *m/f* ♦ *adj* mímico ♦ *vt* remedar, imitar.

min. *abbr* = **minute(s)**; **minimum**.

minaret [mɪnə'rɛt] *n* alminar *m*.

mince [mɪns] *vt* picar ♦ *vi* (*in walking*) andar con pasos menudos ♦ *n* (*BRIT: CULIN*) carne *f* picada; **~meat** *n* conserva de fruta picada; (*US: meat*) carne *f* picada; **~ pie** *n* empanadilla *rellena de fruta picada*; **~r** *n* picadora de carne.

mind [maɪnd] *n* mente *f*; (*intellect*) intelecto; (*contrasted with matter*) espíritu ♦ *vt* (*attend to, look after*) ocuparse de, cuidar; (*be careful of*) tener cuidado con; (*object to*): **I don't ~ the noise** no me molesta el ruido; **it is on my ~** me preocupa; **to bear sth in ~** tomar *or* tener algo en cuenta; **to make up one's ~** decidirse; **I don't ~** me es igual; **~ you,** ... te advierto que ...; **never ~!** ¡es igual!, ¡no importa!; (*don't worry*) ¡no te preocupes!; **"~ the step"** "cuidado con el escalón"; **~er** *n* guardaespaldas *m inv*; (*child ~er*) ≈ niñera; **~ful** *adj*: **~ful of** consciente de; **~less** *adj* (*crime*) sin motivo; (*work*) de autómata.

mine¹ [maɪn] *pron* el mío/la mía *etc*; **a friend of ~** un(a) amigo/a mío/mía ♦ *adj*: **this book is ~** este libro es mío.

mine² [maɪn] *n* mina ♦ *vt* (*coal*) extraer; (*bomb: beach etc*) minar; **~field** *n* campo de minas; **~r** *n* minero/a.

mineral ['mɪnərəl] *adj* mineral ♦ *n* mineral *m*; **~s** *npl* (*BRIT: soft drinks*) refrescos *mpl*; **~ water** *n* agua mineral.

mingle ['mɪŋgl] *vi*: **to ~ with** mezclarse con.

miniature ['mɪnətʃə*] *adj* (en) miniatura ♦ *n* miniatura.

minibus ['mɪnɪbʌs] *n* microbús *m*.

minim ['mɪnɪm] *n* (*MUS*) blanca.

minimal ['mɪnɪml] *adj* mínimo.

minimize ['mɪnɪmaɪz] *vt* minimizar; (*play down*) empequeñecer.

minimum ['mɪnɪməm] (*pl* **minima**) *n*, *adj* mínimo.

mining ['maɪnɪŋ] *n* explotación *f* minera.

miniskirt ['mɪnɪskəːt] *n* minifalda.

minister ['mɪnɪstə*] *n* (*BRIT: POL*) ministro/a (*SP*), secretario/a (*AM*); (*REL*) pastor *m* ♦ *vi*: **to ~** atender a.

ministry ['mɪnɪstrɪ] *n* (*BRIT: POL*) ministerio (*SP*), secretaria (*AM*); (*REL*) sacerdocio.

mink [mɪŋk] *n* visón *m*.

minnow ['mɪnəu] *n* pececillo (*de agua dulce*).

minor ['maɪnə*] *adj* (*repairs, injuries*) leve; (*poet, planet*) menor; (*MUS*) menor ♦ *n* (*LAW*) menor *m* de edad.

Minorca [mɪˈnɔːkə] n Menorca.

minority [maɪˈnɔrɪtɪ] n minoría.

mint [mɪnt] n (plant) menta, hierbabuena; (sweet) caramelo de menta ♦ vt (coins) acuñar; **the (Royal) M~**, **the (US) M~** la Casa de la Moneda; **in ~ condition** en perfecto estado.

minus [ˈmaɪnəs] n (also: ~ sign) signo de menos ♦ prep menos; **12 ~ 6 equals 6** 12 menos 6 son 6; **~ 24°C** menos 24 grados.

minute [n ˈmɪnɪt, adj maɪˈnjuːt] n minuto; (fig) momento; ~**s** npl (of meeting) actas fpl ♦ adj diminuto; (search) minucioso; **at the last ~** a la última hora.

miracle [ˈmɪrəkl] n milagro.

mirage [ˈmɪrɑːʒ] n espejismo.

mirror [ˈmɪrə*] n espejo; (in car) retrovisor m.

mirth [mɜːθ] n alegría.

misadventure [mɪsədˈvɛntʃə*] n desgracia.

misapprehension [mɪsæprɪˈhɛnʃən] n equivocación f.

misappropriate [mɪsəˈprəuprɪeɪt] vt malversar.

misbehave [mɪsbɪˈheɪv] vi portarse mal.

miscalculate [mɪsˈkælkjuleɪt] vt calcular mal.

miscarriage [ˈmɪskærɪdʒ] n (MED) aborto; ~ **of justice** error m judicial.

miscellaneous [mɪsɪˈleɪnɪəs] adj varios/as, diversos/as.

mischance [mɪsˈtʃɑːns] n desgracia.

mischief [ˈmɪstʃɪf] n travesuras fpl, diabluras fpl; (maliciousness) malicia; **mischievous** [-ʃɪvəs] adj travieso.

misconception [mɪskənˈsɛpʃən] n idea equivocada; equivocación f.

misconduct [mɪsˈkɔndʌkt] n mala conducta; **professional ~** falta profesional.

misdemeanour [mɪsdɪˈmiːnə*] (US **misdemeanor**) n delito, ofensa.

miser [ˈmaɪzə*] n avaro/a.

miserable [ˈmɪzərəbl] adj (unhappy) triste, desgraciado; (unpleasant, contemptible) miserable.

miserly [ˈmaɪzəlɪ] adj avariento, tacaño.

misery [ˈmɪzərɪ] n tristeza; (wretchedness) miseria, desdicha.

misfire [mɪsˈfaɪə*] vi fallar.

misfit [ˈmɪsfɪt] n inadaptado/a.

misfortune [mɪsˈfɔːtʃən] n desgracia.

misgiving [mɪsˈgɪvɪŋ] n (apprehension) presentimiento; **to have ~s about sth** tener dudas acerca de algo.

misguided [mɪsˈgaɪdɪd] adj equivocado.

mishandle [mɪsˈhændl] vt (mismanage) manejar mal.

mishap [ˈmɪshæp] n desgracia, contratiempo.

misinform [mɪsɪnˈfɔːm] vt informar mal.

misinterpret [mɪsɪnˈtɜːprɪt] vt interpretar mal.

misjudge [mɪsˈdʒʌdʒ] vt juzgar mal.

mislay [mɪsˈleɪ] (irreg) vt extraviar, perder.

mislead [mɪsˈliːd] (irreg) vt llevar a conclusiones erróneas; ~**ing** adj engañoso.

mismanage [mɪsˈmænɪdʒ] vt administrar mal.

misnomer [mɪsˈnəumə*] n término inapropiado or equivocado.

misogynist [mɪˈsɔdʒɪnɪst] n misógino.

misplace [mɪsˈpleɪs] vt extraviar.

misprint [ˈmɪsprɪnt] n errata, error m de imprenta.

Miss [mɪs] n Señorita.

miss [mɪs] vt (train etc) perder; (fail to hit: target) errar; (regret the absence of): **I ~ him** (yo) le echo de menos or a faltar; (fail to see): **you can't ~ it** no tiene pérdida ♦ vi fallar ♦ n (shot) tiro fallido or perdido; ~ **out** (BRIT) vt omitir.

misshapen [mɪsˈʃeɪpən] adj deforme.

missile [ˈmɪsaɪl] n (AVIAT) mísil m; (object thrown) proyectil m.

missing [ˈmɪsɪŋ] adj (pupil) ausente; (thing) perdido; (MIL): ~ **in action** desaparecido en combate.

mission [ˈmɪʃən] n misión f; (official representation) delegación f; ~**ary** n misionero/a.

misspent [ˈmɪsˈspɛnt] adj: **his ~ youth** su juventud disipada.

mist [mɪst] n (light) neblina; (heavy) niebla; (at sea) bruma ♦ vi (eyes: also: ~ over, ~ up) llenarse de lágri-

mistake

162

Monday

mas; (*BRIT*: windows: *also*: ~ over, ~ up) empañarse.

mistake [mɪsˈteɪk] (*vt*: *irreg*) *n* error *m* ♦ *vt* entender mal; **by** ~ por equivocación; **to make a** ~ equivocarse; **to** ~ **A for B** confundir A con B; **mistaken** *pp of* mistake ♦ *adj* equivocado; **to be mistaken** equivocarse, engañarse.

mister [ˈmɪstə*] (*inf*) *n* señor *m*; *see* **Mr.**

mistletoe [ˈmɪsltəu] *n* muérdago.

mistook [mɪsˈtuk] *pt of* **mistake.**

mistress [ˈmɪstrɪs] *n* (*lover*) amante *f*; (*of house*) señora (de la casa); (*BRIT*: *in primary school*) maestra; (*in secondary school*) profesora; (*of situation*) dueña.

mistrust [mɪsˈtrʌst] *vt* desconfiar de.

misty [ˈmɪstɪ] *adj* (*day*) de niebla; (*glasses etc*) empañado.

misunderstand [mɪsʌndəˈstænd] (*irreg*) *vt*, *vi* entender mal; ~**ing** *n* malentendido.

misuse [*n* mɪsˈjuːs, *vb* mɪsˈjuːz] *n* mal uso; (*of power*) abuso; (*of funds*) malversación *f* ♦ *vt* abusar de; malversar.

mitt(en) [ˈmɪt(n)] *n* manopla.

mix [mɪks] *vt* mezclar; (*combine*) unir ♦ *vi* mezclarse; (*people*) llevarse bien ♦ *n* mezcla; ~ **up** *vt* mezclar; (*confuse*) confundir; ~**ed** *adj* mixto; (*feelings etc*) encontrado; ~**ed-up** *adj* (*confused*) confuso, revuelto; ~**er** *n* (*for food*) licuadora; (*for drinks*) coctelera; (*person*): **he's a good** ~**er** tiene don de gentes; ~**ture** *n* mezcla; (*also*: *cough* ~) jarabe *m*; ~**-up** *n* confusión *f*.

mm *abbr* (= *millimetre*) mm.

moan [məun] *n* gemido ♦ *vi* gemir; (*inf*: *complain*): **to** ~ (**about**) quejarse (de).

moat [məut] *n* foso.

mob [mɔb] *n* multitud *f* ♦ *vt* acosar.

mobile [ˈməubaɪl] *adj* móvil ♦ *n* móvil *m*; ~ **home** *n* caravana.

mock [mɔk] *vt* (*ridicule*) ridiculizar; (*laugh at*) burlarse de ♦ *adj* fingido; ~ **exam** *examen preparatorio antes de los exámenes oficiales*; ~**ery** *n* burla; ~**-up** *n* maqueta.

mod [mɔd] *adj see* **convenience.**

mode [məud] *n* modo.

model [ˈmɔdl] *n* modelo; (*fashion* ~, *artist's* ~) modelo *m/f* ♦ *adj* modelo ♦ *vt* (*with clay etc*) modelar (*copy*): **to** ~ **o.s. on** tomar como modelo a ♦ *vi* ser modelo; ~ **railway** *n* ferrocarril *m* de juguete; **to** ~ **clothes** pasar modelos, ser modelo.

modem [ˈməudəm] *n* modem *m*.

moderate [*adj* ˈmɔdərət, *vb* ˈmɔdəreɪt] *adj* moderado/a ♦ *vi* moderarse, calmarse ♦ *vt* moderar.

modern [ˈmɔdən] *adj* moderno; ~**ize** *vt* modernizar.

modest [ˈmɔdɪst] *adj* modesto; (*small*) módico; ~**y** *n* modestia.

modicum [ˈmɔdɪkəm] *n*: **a** ~ **of** un mínimo de.

modify [ˈmɔdɪfaɪ] *vt* modificar.

mogul [ˈməugəl] *n* (*fig*) magnate *m*.

mohair [ˈməuhɛə*] *n* mohair *m*.

moist [mɔɪst] *adj* húmedo; ~**en** [ˈmɔɪsn] *vt* humedecer; ~**ure** [ˈmɔɪstʃə*] *n* humedad *f*; ~**urizer** [ˈmɔɪstʃəraɪzə*] *n* crema hidratante.

molar [ˈməulə*] *n* muela.

mold [məuld] (*US*) *n*, *vt* = **mould.**

mole [məul] *n* (*animal*, *spy*) topo; (*spot*) lunar *m*.

molecule [ˈmɔlɪkjuːl] *n* molécula.

molest [məuˈlɛst] *vt* importunar; (*assault sexually*) abusar sexualmente de.

mollycoddle [ˈmɔlɪkɔdl] *vt* mimar.

molt [məult] (*US*) *vi* = **moult.**

molten [ˈməultən] *adj* fundido; (*lava*) líquido.

mom [mɔm] (*US*) *n* = **mum.**

moment [ˈməumənt] *n* momento; **at the** ~ de momento, por ahora; ~**ary** *adj* momentáneo; ~**ous** [-ˈmɛntəs] *adj* trascendental, importante.

momentum [məuˈmɛntəm] *n* momento; (*fig*) ímpetu *m*; **to gather** ~ cobrar velocidad; (*fig*) ganar fuerza.

mommy [ˈmɔmɪ] (*US*) *n* = **mummy.**

Monaco [ˈmɔnəkəu] *n* Mónaco.

monarch [ˈmɔnək] *n* monarca *m/f*; ~**y** *n* monarquía.

monastery [ˈmɔnəstərɪ] *n* monasterio.

Monday [ˈmʌndɪ] *n* lunes *m inv*.

monetary ['mʌnɪtərɪ] *adj* monetario.
money ['mʌnɪ] *n* dinero; *(currency)* moneda; **to make ~** ganar dinero; **~ order** *n* giro; **~-spinner** *(inf)* *n*: **to be a ~-spinner** dar mucho dinero.
mongol ['mɔŋgəl] *adj, n (MED)* mongólico/a.
mongrel ['mʌŋgrəl] *n (dog)* perro mestizo.
monitor ['mɔnɪtə*] *n (SCOL)* monitor *m*; *(also: television ~)* receptor *m* de control; *(of computer)* monitor *m* ♦ *vt* controlar.
monk [mʌŋk] *n* monje *m*.
monkey ['mʌŋkɪ] *n* mono; **~ nut** *(BRIT)* *n* cacahuete *m (SP)*, maní *m (AM)*; **~ wrench** *n* llave *f* inglesa.
mono ['mɔnəu] *adj (recording)* mono.
monopoly [mə'nɔpəlɪ] *n* monopolio.
monotone ['mɔnətəun] *n* voz *f (or* tono*)* monocorde.
monotonous [mə'nɔtənəs] *adj* monótono.
monsoon [mɔn'suːn] *n* monzón *m*.
monster ['mɔnstə*] *n* monstruo.
monstrosity [mɔns'trɔsɪtɪ] *n* monstruosidad *f*.
monstrous ['mɔnstrəs] *adj (huge)* enorme; *(atrocious, ugly)* monstruoso.
month [mʌnθ] *n* mes *m*; **~ly** *adj* mensual ♦ *adv* mensualmente.
monument ['mɔnjumənt] *n* monumento; **~al** [-'mɛntl] *adj* monumental.
moo [muː] *vi* mugir.
mood [muːd] *n* humor *m*; *(of crowd, group)* clima *m*; **to be in a good/bad ~** estar de buen/mal humor; **~y** *adj (changeable)* de humor variable; *(sullen)* malhumorado.
moon [muːn] *n* luna; **~light** *n* luz *f* de la luna; **~lighting** *n* pluriempleo; **~lit** *adj*: **a ~lit night** una noche de luna.
Moor [muə*] *n* moro/a.
moor [muə*] *n* páramo ♦ *vt (ship)* amarrar ♦ *vi* echar las amarras.
Moorish ['muərɪʃ] *adj* moro; *(architecture)* árabe, morisco.
moorland ['muələnd] *n* páramo, brezal *m*.
moose [muːs] *n inv* alce *m*.

mop [mɔp] *n* fregona; *(of hair)* greña, melena ♦ *vt* fregar; **~ up** *vt* limpiar.
mope [məup] *vi* estar *or* andar deprimido.
moped ['məuped] *n* ciclomotor *m*.
moral ['mɔrl] *adj* moral ♦ *n* moraleja; **~s** *npl* moralidad *f*, moral *f*.
morale [mɔ'rɑːl] *n* moral *f*.
morality [mə'rælɪtɪ] *n* moralidad *f*.
morass [mə'ræs] *n* pantano.
morbid ['mɔːbɪd] *adj (interest)* morboso.

KEYWORD

more [mɔː*] *adj* **1** *(greater in number etc)* más; **~ people/work than before** más gente/trabajo que antes
2 *(additional)* más; **do you want (some) ~ tea?** ¿quieres más té?; **is there any ~ wine?** ¿queda vino?; **it'll take a few ~ weeks** tardará unas semanas más; **it's 2 kms ~ to the house** faltan 2 kms para la casa; **~ time/letters than we expected** más tiempo del que/ más cartas de las que esperábamos
♦ *pron (greater amount, additional amount)* más; **~ than 10** más de 10; **it cost ~ than the other one/than we expected** costó más que el otro/más de lo que esperábamos; **is there any ~?** ¿hay más?; **many/much ~** muchos(as)/ mucho(a) más
♦ *adv* más; **~ dangerous/easily (than)** más peligroso/fácilmente (que); **~ and ~ expensive** cada vez más caro; **~ or less** más o menos; **~ than ever** más que nunca

---

moreover [mɔː'rəuvə*] *adv* además, por otra parte.
morgue [mɔːg] *n* depósito de cadáveres.
Mormon ['mɔːmən] *n* mormón/ona *m/f*.
morning ['mɔːnɪŋ] *n* mañana; *(early ~)* madrugada ♦ *cpd* matutino, de la mañana; **in the ~** por la mañana; **7 o'clock in the ~** las 7 de la mañana; **~ sickness** *n* náuseas *fpl* matutinas.
Morocco [mə'rɔkəu] *n* Marruecos *m*.
moron ['mɔːrɔn] *(inf)* *n* imbécil *m/f*.
morose [mə'rəus] *adj* hosco, malhumo-

rado.

morphine ['mɔːfiːn] n morfina.

Morse [mɔːs] n (also: ~ code) (código) Morse.

morsel ['mɔːsl] n (of food) bocado.

mortal ['mɔːtl] adj, n mortal m.

mortar ['mɔːtə*] n argamasa; (implement) mortero.

mortgage ['mɔːgɪdʒ] n hipoteca ♦ vt hipotecar; ~ **company** (US) n ≈ banco hipotecario.

mortify ['mɔːtɪfaɪ] vt mortificar, humillar.

mortuary ['mɔːtjuərɪ] n depósito de cadáveres.

Moscow ['mɔskəu] n Moscú.

Moslem ['mɔzləm] adj, n = **Muslim**.

mosque [mɔsk] n mezquita.

mosquito [mɔs'kiːtəu] (pl ~es) n mosquito (SP), zancudo (AM).

moss [mɔs] n musgo.

most [məust] adj la mayor parte de, la mayoría de ♦ pron la mayor parte, la mayoría ♦ adv el más; (very) muy; **the** ~ (also: +adj) el más; ~ **of them** la mayor parte de ellos; **I saw the** ~ yo vi el que más; **at the (very)** ~ a lo sumo, todo lo más; **to make the** ~ **of** aprovechar (al máximo); **a** ~ **interesting book** un libro interesantísimo.

mostly ['məustlɪ] adv en su mayor parte, principalmente.

MOT (BRIT) n abbr (= Ministry of Transport): **the** ~ (test) inspección (anual) obligatoria de coches y camiones.

motel [məu'tɛl] n motel m.

moth [mɔθ] n mariposa nocturna; (clothes ~) polilla; ~**ball** n bola de naftalina.

mother ['mʌðə*] n madre f ♦ adj materno ♦ vt (care for) cuidar (como una madre); ~**hood** n maternidad f; ~**-in-law** n suegra; ~**ly** adj maternal; ~**-of-pearl** n nácar m; ~**-to-be** n futura madre f; ~ **tongue** n lengua materna.

motif [məu'tiːf] n motivo.

motion ['məuʃən] n movimiento; (gesture) ademán m, señal f; (at meeting) moción f ♦ vt, vi: **to** ~ (**to**) sb **to do sth**

hacer señas a uno para que haga algo; ~**less** adj inmóvil; ~ **picture** n película.

motivated ['məutɪveɪtɪd] adj motivado.

motive ['məutɪv] n motivo.

motley ['mɔtlɪ] adj variado.

motor ['məutə*] n motor m; (BRIT: inf: vehicle) coche m (SP), carro (AM), automóvil m ♦ adj motor (f: motora or motriz); ~**bike** n moto f; ~**boat** n lancha motora; ~**car** (BRIT) n coche m, carro, automóvil m; ~**cycle** n motocicleta; ~**cycle racing** n motociclismo; ~**cyclist** n motociclista m/f; ~**ing** (BRIT) n automovilismo; ~**ist** n conductor(a) m/f, automovilista m/f; ~ **racing** (BRIT) n carreras fpl de coches, automovilismo; ~ **vehicle** n automóvil m; ~**way** (BRIT) n autopista.

mottled ['mɔtld] adj abigarrado, multicolor.

motto ['mɔtəu] (pl ~es) n lema m; (watchword) consigna.

mould [məuld] (US **mold**) n molde m; (mildew) moho ♦ vt moldear; (fig) formar; ~**y** adj enmohecido.

moult [məult] (US **molt**) vi mudar la piel (or las plumas).

mound [maund] n montón m, montículo.

mount [maunt] n monte m ♦ vt montar, subir a; (jewel) engarzar; (picture) enmarcar; (exhibition etc) organizar ♦ vi (increase) aumentar; ~ **up** vi aumentar.

mountain ['mauntɪn] n montaña ♦ cpd de montaña; ~**eer** [-'nɪə*] n montañero/a (SP), andinista m/f (AM); ~**eering** [-'nɪərɪŋ] n montañismo, andinismo; ~**ous** adj montañoso; ~ **rescue team** n equipo de rescate de montaña; ~**side** n ladera de la montaña.

mourn [mɔːn] vt llorar, lamentar ♦ vi: **to** ~ **for** llorar la muerte de; ~**er** n doliente m/f; dolorido/a; ~**ful** adj triste, lúgubre; ~**ing** n luto; **in** ~**ing** de luto.

mouse [maus] (pl **mice**) n (ZOOL, COMPUT) ratón m; ~**trap** n ratonera.

mousse [muːs] n (CULIN) crema batida; (for hair) espuma (moldeadora).

moustache [məs'tɑːʃ] (US **mustache**) n

bigote *m*.

mousy ['mausɪ] *adj* (*hair*) pardusco.

mouth [mauθ, *pl* mauðz] *n* boca; (*of river*) desembocadura; ~**ful** *n* bocado; ~ **organ** *n* armónica; ~**piece** *n* (*of musical instrument*) boquilla; (*spokesman*) portavoz *m/f*; ~**wash** *n* enjuague *m*; ~**-watering** *adj* apetitoso.

movable ['muːvəbl] *adj* movible.

move [muːv] *n* (*movement*) movimiento; (*in game*) jugada; (: *turn to play*) turno; (*change: of house*) mudanza; (: *of job*) cambio de trabajo ♦ *vt* mover; (*emotionally*) conmover; (*POL: resolution etc*) proponer ♦ *vi* moverse; (*traffic*) circular; (*also*: ~ *house*) trasladarse, mudarse; **to** ~ **sb to do sth** mover a uno a hacer algo; **to get a** ~ **on** darse prisa; ~ **about** *or* **around** *vi* moverse; (*travel*) viajar; ~ **along** *vi* avanzar, adelantarse; ~ **away** *vi* alejarse; ~ **back** *vi* retroceder; ~ **forward** *vi* avanzar; ~ **in** *vi* (*to a house*) instalarse; (*police, soldiers*) intervenir; ~ **on** *vi* ponerse en camino; ~ **out** *vi* (*of house*) mudarse; ~ **over** *vi* apartarse, hacer sitio; ~ **up** *vi* (*employee*) ser ascendido.

moveable ['muːvəbl] *adj* = movable.

movement ['muːvmənt] *n* movimiento.

movie ['muːvɪ] *n* película; **to go to the** ~**s** ir al cine; ~ **camera** *n* cámara cinematográfica.

moving ['muːvɪŋ] *adj* (*emotional*) conmovedor(a); (*that moves*) móvil.

mow [məu] (*pt* mowed, *pp* mowed *or* mown) *vt* (*grass, corn*) cortar, segar; ~ **down** *vt* (*shoot*) acribillar; ~**er** *n* (*also*: *lawn*~*er*) cortacéspedes *m inv*, segadora.

MP *n abbr* = Member of Parliament.

m.p.h. *abbr* = *miles per hour* (60 *m.p.h.* = 96 *k.p.h.*).

Mr ['mɪstə*] (*US* Mr.) *n*: ~ **Smith** (el) Sr. Smith.

Mrs ['mɪsɪz] (*US* Mrs.) *n*: ~ **Smith** (la) Sra. Smith.

Ms [mɪz] (*US* Ms.) *n* (= *Miss or Mrs*): ~ **Smith** (la) Sr(t)a. Smith.

M.Sc. *abbr* = Master of Science.

much [mʌtʃ] *adj* mucho ♦ *adv* mucho; (*before pp*) muy ♦ *n or pron* mucho; **how** ~ **is it?** ¿cuánto es?, ¿cuánto cuesta?; **too** ~ demasiado; **it's not** ~ no es mucho; **as** ~ **as** tanto como; **however** ~ **he tries** por mucho que se esfuerce.

muck [mʌk] *n* suciedad *f*; ~ **about** *or* **around** (*inf*) *vi* perder el tiempo; (*enjoy o.s.*) entretenerse; ~ **up** (*inf*) *vt* arruinar, estropear.

mucus ['mjuːkəs] *n* moco.

mud [mʌd] *n* barro, lodo.

muddle ['mʌdl] *n* desorden *m*, confusión *f*; (*mix-up*) embrollo, lío ♦ *vt* (*also*: ~ *up*) embrollar, confundir; ~ **through** *vi* salir del paso.

muddy ['mʌdɪ] *adj* fangoso, cubierto de lodo.

mudguard ['mʌdgɑːd] *n* guardabarros *m inv*.

muffin ['mʌfɪn] *n* panecillo dulce.

muffle ['mʌfl] *vt* (*sound*) amortiguar; (*against cold*) embozar; ~**d** *adj* (*noise etc*) amortiguado, apagado; ~**r** (*US*) *n* (*AUT*) silenciador *m*.

mug [mʌg] *n* taza grande (*sin platillo*); (*for beer*) jarra; (*inf: face*) jeta; (: *fool*) bobo ♦ *vt* (*assault*) asaltar; ~**ging** *n* asalto.

muggy ['mʌgɪ] *adj* bochornoso.

mule [mjuːl] *n* mula.

mull over [mʌl-] *vt* meditar sobre.

multi... [mʌltɪ] *prefix* multi....

multi-level [mʌltɪ'levl] (*US*) *adj* = multistorey.

multiple ['mʌltɪpl] *adj* múltiple ♦ *n* múltiplo; ~ **sclerosis** *n* esclerosis *f* múltiple.

multiplication [mʌltɪplɪ'keɪʃən] *n* multiplicación *f*.

multiply ['mʌltɪplaɪ] *vt* multiplicar ♦ *vi* multiplicarse.

multistorey [mʌltɪ'stɔːrɪ] (*BRIT*) *adj* de muchos pisos.

multitude ['mʌltɪtjuːd] *n* multitud *f*.

mum [mʌm] (*BRIT: inf*) *n* mamá ♦ *adj*: **to keep** ~ mantener la boca cerrada.

mumble ['mʌmbl] *vt, vi* hablar entre dientes, refunfuñar.

mummy ['mʌmɪ] *n* (*BRIT: mother*) mamá; (*embalmed*) momia.

mumps [mʌmps] *n* paperas *fpl*.

munch [mʌntʃ] *vt, vi* mascar.

mundane [mʌn'deɪn] *adj* trivial.

municipal [mju:'nɪsɪpl] *adj* municipal.

munitions [mju:'nɪʃənz] *npl* munición *f*.

mural ['mjuərl] *n* mural *m*.

murder ['mə:də*] *n* asesinato; (*in law*) homicidio ♦ *vt* asesinar, matar; ~**er/ ess** *n* asesino/a; ~**ous** *adj* homicida.

murky ['mə:kɪ] *adj* (*water*) turbio; (*street, night*) lóbrego.

murmur ['mə:mə*] *n* murmullo ♦ *vt, vi* murmurar.

muscle ['mʌsl] *n* músculo; (*fig: strength*) garra, fuerza; ~ **in** *vi* entrometerse; **muscular** ['mʌskjulə*] *adj* muscular; (*person*) musculoso.

muse [mju:z] *vi* meditar ♦ *n* musa.

museum [mju:'zɪəm] *n* museo.

mushroom ['mʌʃrum] *n* seta, hongo; (*CULIN*) champiñón *m* ♦ *vi* crecer de la noche a la mañana.

music ['mju:zɪk] *n* música; ~**al** *adj* musical; (*sound*) melodioso; (*person*) con talento musical ♦ *n* (*show*) comedia musical; ~**al instrument** *n* instrumento musical; ~ **hall** *n* teatro de variedades; ~**ian** [-'zɪʃən] *n* músico/a.

musk [mʌsk] *n* almizcle *m*.

Muslim ['mʌzlɪm] *adj, n* musulmán/ana *m/f*.

muslin ['mʌzlɪn] *n* muselina.

mussel ['mʌsl] *n* mejillón *m*.

must [mʌst] *aux vb* (*obligation*): **I** ~ **do it** debo hacerlo, tengo que hacerlo; (*probability*): **he** ~ **be there by now** ya debe (de) estar allí ♦ *n*: **it's a** ~ es imprescindible.

mustache ['mʌstæʃ] (*US*) *n* = **moustache**.

mustard ['mʌstəd] *n* mostaza.

muster ['mʌstə*] *vt* juntar, reunir.

mustn't ['mʌsnt] = **must not**.

musty ['mʌstɪ] *adj* mohoso, que huele a humedad.

mute [mju:t] *adj, n* mudo/a.

muted ['mju:tɪd] *adj* callado; (*colour*) apagado.

mutilate ['mju:tɪleɪt] *vt* (*person*) muti-

lar; (*thing*) destrozar.

mutiny ['mju:tɪnɪ] *n* motín *m* ♦ *vi* amotinarse.

mutter ['mʌtə*] *vt, vi* murmurar.

mutton ['mʌtn] *n* carne *f* de cordero.

mutual ['mju:tʃuəl] *adj* mutuo; (*interest*) común; ~**ly** *adv* mutuamente.

muzzle ['mʌzl] *n* hocico; (*for dog*) bozal *m*; (*of gun*) boca ♦ *vt* (*dog*) poner un bozal a.

my [maɪ] *adj* mi(s); ~ **house/brother/ sisters** mi casa/mi hermano/mis hermanas; **I've washed** ~ **hair/cut** ~ **finger** me he lavado el pelo/cortado un dedo; **is this** ~ **pen or yours?** ¿es este bolígrafo mío o tuyo?

myopic [maɪ'ɔpɪk] *adj* miope.

myself [maɪ'sɛlf] *pron* (*reflexive*) me; (*emphatic*) yo mismo; (*after prep*) mí (mismo); *see also* **oneself**.

mysterious [mɪs'tɪərɪəs] *adj* misterioso.

mystery ['mɪstərɪ] *n* misterio.

mystify ['mɪstɪfaɪ] *vt* (*perplex*) dejar perplejo.

mystique [mɪs'ti:k] *n* misterio (profesional *etc*).

myth [mɪθ] *n* mito.

N

n/a *abbr* (= *not applicable*) no interesa.

nag [næg] *vt* (*scold*) regañar; ~**ging** *adj* (*doubt*) persistente; (*pain*) continuo.

nail [neɪl] *n* (*human*) uña; (*metal*) clavo ♦ *vt* clavar; **to** ~ **sth to sth** clavar algo en algo; **to** ~ **sb down to doing sth** comprometer a uno a que haga algo; ~**brush** *n* cepillo para las uñas; ~**file** *n* lima para las uñas; ~ **polish** *n* esmalte *m or* laca para las uñas; ~ **polish remover** *n* quitaesmalte *m*; ~ **scissors** *npl* tijeras *fpl* para las uñas; ~ **varnish** (*BRIT*) *n* = ~ **polish**.

naïve [naɪ'i:v] *adj* ingenuo.

naked ['neɪkɪd] *adj* (*nude*) desnudo; (*flame*) expuesto al aire.

name [neɪm] *n* nombre *m*; (*surname*) apellido; (*reputation*) fama, renombre *m* ♦ *vt* (*child*) poner nombre a; (*crimi-*

nal) identificar; (*price, date etc*) fijar;
what's your ~? ¿cómo se llama?; **by ~**
de nombre; **in the ~ of** en nombre de;
to give one's ~ and address dar sus señas; **~less** *adj* (*unknown*) desconocido;
(*anonymous*) anónimo, sin nombre; **~ly**
adv a saber; **~sake** *n* tocayo/a.
nanny ['nænɪ] *n* niñera.
nap [næp] *n* (*sleep*) sueñecito, siesta; **to
be caught ~ping** estar desprevenido.
nape [neɪp] *n*: **~ of the neck** nuca, cogote *m*.
napkin ['næpkɪn] *n* (*also: table ~*) servilleta.
nappy ['næpɪ] (*BRIT*) *n* pañal *m*; **~ rash**
n prurito.
narcotic [nɑ:'kɒtɪk] *adj*, *n* narcótico.
narrative ['nærətɪv] *n* narrativa.
narrow ['nærəʊ] *adj* estrecho, angosto;
(*fig: majority etc*) corto; (: *ideas etc*)
estrecho ♦ *vi* (*road*) estrecharse;
(*diminish*) reducirse; **to have a ~ escape** escaparse por los pelos; **to ~ sth
down** reducir algo; **~ly** *adv* (*miss*) por
poco; **~-minded** *adj* de miras estrechas.
nasty ['nɑ:stɪ] *adj* (*remark*) feo; (*person*) antipático; (*revolting*: *taste,
smell*) asqueroso; (*wound, disease etc*)
peligroso, grave.
nation ['neɪʃən] *n* nación *f*.
national ['næʃənl] *adj*, *n* nacional *m/f*;
~ dress *n* vestido nacional; **N~ Health
Service** (*BRIT*) *n* servicio nacional de
salud pública; ≈ Insalud *m* (*SP*); **N~
Insurance** (*BRIT*) *n* seguro social nacional; **~ism** *n* nacionalismo; **~ist** *adj*, *n*
nacionalista *m/f*; **~ity** [-'nælɪtɪ] *n* nacionalidad *f*; **~ize** *vt* nacionalizar; **~ly**
adv (*nationwide*) en escala nacional;
(*as a nation*) nacionalmente, como nación.
nationwide ['neɪʃənwaɪd] *adj* en escala
or a nivel nacional.
native ['neɪtɪv] *n* (*local inhabitant*) natural *m/f*, nacional *m/f*; (*of tribe etc*) indígena *m/f*, nativo/a ♦ *adj* (*indigenous*)
indígena; (*country*) natal; (*innate*) natural, innato; **a ~ of Russia** un(a) natural *m/f* de Rusia; **a ~ speaker of**

French un hablante nativo de francés;
~ language *n* lengua materna.
Nativity [nə'tɪvɪtɪ] *n*: **the ~** Navidad *f*.
NATO ['neɪtəʊ] *n abbr* (= *North Atlantic
Treaty Organization*) OTAN *f*.
natural ['nætʃrəl] *adj* natural; **~ize** *vt*:
to become ~ized (*person*) naturalizarse; (*plant*) aclimatarse; **~ly** *adv*
(*speak, act*) naturalmente; (*of course*)
desde luego, por supuesto.
nature ['neɪtʃə*] *n* (*also*: *N~*) naturaleza; (*group, sort*) género, clase *f*; (*character*) carácter *m*, genio; **by ~** por *or*
de naturaleza.
naught [nɔ:t] *n* = **nought**.
naughty ['nɔ:tɪ] *adj* (*child*) travieso.
nausea ['nɔ:sɪə] *n* náuseas *fpl*; **~te**
[-sɪeɪt] *vt* dar náuseas a; (*fig*) dar asco
a.
nautical ['nɔ:tɪkl] *adj* náutico, marítimo; (*mile*) marino.
naval ['neɪvl] *adj* naval, de marina; **~
officer** *n* oficial *m/f* de marina.
nave [neɪv] *n* nave *f*.
navel ['neɪvl] *n* ombligo.
navigate ['nævɪgeɪt] *vt* gobernar ♦ *vi* navegar; (*AUT*) ir de copiloto; **navigation**
[-'geɪʃən] *n* (*action*) navegación *f*;
(*science*) náutica; **navigator** *n* navega-
dor(a) *m/f*, navegante *m/f*; (*AUT*) copiloto *m/f*.
navvy ['nævɪ] (*BRIT*) *n* peón *m* camine-
ro.
navy ['neɪvɪ] *n* marina de guerra;
(*ships*) armada, flota; **~(-blue)** *adj* azul
marino.
Nazi ['nɑ:tsɪ] *n* nazi *m/f*.
NB *abbr* (= *nota bene*) nótese.
near [nɪə*] *adj* (*place, relation*) cercano; (*time*) próximo ♦ *adv* cerca ♦ *prep*
(*also*: **~ to**: *space*) cerca de, junto a;
(: *time*) cerca de ♦ *vt* acercarse a,
aproximarse a; **~by** [nɪə'baɪ] *adj* cercano, próximo ♦ *adv* cerca; **~ly** *adv* casi,
por poco; **I ~ly fell** por poco me caigo;
~ miss *n* tiro cercano; **~side** *n* (*AUT*:
in Britain) lado izquierdo; (: *in US, Europe etc*) lado derecho; **~-sighted** *adj*
miope, corto de vista.
neat [ni:t] *adj* (*place*) ordenado, bien

cuidado; (*person*) pulcro; (*plan*) ingenioso; (*spirits*) solo; **~ly** *adv* (*tidily*) con esmero; (*skilfully*) ingeniosamente.

necessarily ['nesɪsrɪlɪ] *adv* necesariamente.

necessary ['nesɪsrɪ] *adj* necesario, preciso.

necessitate [nɪ'sesɪteɪt] *vt* hacer necesario.

necessity [nɪ'sesɪtɪ] *n* necesidad *f*; necessities *npl* artículos *mpl* de primera necesidad.

neck [nek] *n* (*of person, garment, bottle*) cuello; (*of animal*) pescuezo ♦ *vi* (*inf*) besuquearse; **~ and ~** parejos.

necklace ['neklɪs] *n* collar *m*.

neckline ['neklaɪn] *n* escote *m*.

necktie ['nektaɪ] *n* corbata.

née [neɪ] *adj*: **~ Scott** de soltera Scott.

need [niːd] *n* (*lack*) escasez *f*, falta; (*necessity*) necesidad *f* ♦ *vt* (*require*) necesitar; **I ~ to do it** tengo que *or* debo hacerlo; **you don't ~ to go** no hace falta que (te) vayas.

needle ['niːdl] *n* aguja ♦ *vt* (*fig: inf*) picar, fastidiar.

needless ['niːdlɪs] *adj* innecesario; **~ to say** huelga decir que.

needlework ['niːdlwəːk] *n* (*activity*) costura, labor *f* de aguja.

needn't ['niːdnt] = need not.

needy ['niːdɪ] *adj* necesitado.

negative ['negətɪv] *n* (*PHOT*) negativo; (*LING*) negación *f* ♦ *adj* negativo.

neglect [nɪ'glekt] *vt* (*one's duty*) faltar a, no cumplir con; (*child*) descuidar, desatender ♦ *n* (*of house, garden etc*) abandono; (*of child*) desatención *f*; (*of duty*) incumplimiento.

negligee ['neglɪʒeɪ] *n* (*nightgown*) salto de cama.

negligence ['neglɪdʒəns] *n* negligencia, descuido.

negligible ['neglɪdʒɪbl] *adj* insignificante, despreciable.

negotiate [nɪ'gəʊʃɪeɪt] *vt* (*treaty, loan*) negociar; (*obstacle*) franquear; (*bend in road*) tomar ♦ *vi*: **to ~ (with)** negociar (con); **negotiation** [-'eɪʃən] *n* negociación *f*, gestión *f*.

Negress ['niːgrɪs] *n* negra.

Negro ['niːgrəʊ] *adj*, *n* negro.

neigh [neɪ] *vi* relinchar.

neighbour ['neɪbə*] (*US* **neighbor**) *n* vecino/a; **~hood** *n* (*place*) vecindad *f*, barrio; (*people*) vecindario; **~ing** *adj* vecino; **~ly** *adj* (*person*) amable; (*attitude*) de buen vecino.

neither ['naɪðə*] *adj* ni ♦ *conj*: **I didn't move and ~ did John** no me he movido, ni Juan tampoco ♦ *pron* ninguno; **~ is true** ninguno/a de los/las dos es cierto/a ♦ *adv*: **~ good nor bad** ni bueno ni malo.

neon ['niːɔn] *n* neón *m*; **~ light** *n* lámpara de neón.

nephew ['nevjuː] *n* sobrino.

nerve [nəːv] *n* (*ANAT*) nervio; (*courage*) valor *m*; (*impudence*) descaro, frescura; **a fit of ~s** un ataque de nervios; **~-racking** *adj* desquiciante.

nervous ['nəːvəs] *adj* (*anxious, ANAT*) nervioso; (*timid*) tímido, miedoso; **~ breakdown** *n* crisis *f* nerviosa.

nest [nest] *n* (*of bird*) nido; (*wasp's ~*) avispero ♦ *vi* anidar; **~ egg** *n* (*fig*) ahorros *mpl*.

nestle ['nesl] *vi*: **to ~ down** acurrucarse.

net [net] *n* (*gen*) red *f*; (*fabric*) tul *m* ♦ *adj* (*COMM*) neto, líquido ♦ *vt* coger (*SP*) *or* agarrar (*AM*) con red; (*SPORT*) marcar; **~ball** *n* básquet *m*; **~ curtains** *npl* visillos *mpl*.

Netherlands ['neðələndz] *npl*: **the ~** los Países Bajos.

nett [net] *adj* = net.

netting ['netɪŋ] *n* red *f*, redes *fpl*.

nettle ['netl] *n* ortiga.

network ['netwəːk] *n* red *f*.

neurotic [njuə'rɔtɪk] *adj*, *n* neurótico/a *m/f*.

neuter ['njuːtə*] *adj* (*LING*) neutro ♦ *vt* castrar, capar.

neutral ['njuːtrəl] *adj* (*person*) neutral; (*colour etc, ELEC*) neutro ♦ *n* (*AUT*) punto muerto; **~ize** *vt* neutralizar.

never ['nevə*] *adv* nunca, jamás; **I ~ went** no fui nunca; **~ in my life** jamás en la vida; *see also* **mind**; **~-ending** *adj* interminable, sin fin; **~theless**

[nɛvəðə'lɛs] *adv* sin embargo, no obstante.

new [njuː] *adj* nuevo; (*brand new*) a estrenar; (*recent*) reciente; ~**born** *adj* recién nacido; ~**comer** ['njuːkʌmə*] *n* recién venido/a *or* llegado/a; ~**fangled** (*pej*) *adj* modernísimo; ~**found** *adj* (*friend*) nuevo; (*enthusiasm*) recién adquirido; ~**ly** *adv* nuevamente, recién; ~**ly-weds** *npl* recién casados *mpl*.

news [njuːz] *n* noticias *fpl*; **a piece of ~** una noticia; **the ~** (*RADIO, TV*) las noticias *fpl*; ~ **agency** *n* agencia de noticias; ~**agent** (*BRIT*) *n* vendedor(a) *m/f* de periódicos; ~**caster** *n* presentador(a) *m/f*, locutor(a) *m/f*; ~ **dealer** (*US*) *n* = ~**agent**; ~ **flash** *n* noticia de última hora; ~**letter** *n* hoja informativa, boletín *m*; ~**paper** *n* periódico, diario; ~**print** *n* papel *m* de periódico; ~**reader** *n* = ~**caster**; ~**reel** *n* noticiario; ~ **stand** *n* quiosco *or* puesto de periódicos.

newt [njuːt] *n* tritón *m*.

New Year *n* Año Nuevo; ~**'s Day** *n* Día *m* de Año Nuevo; ~**'s Eve** *n* Nochevieja.

New York ['njuː'jɔːk] *n* Nueva York.

New Zealand [njuː'ziːlənd] *n* Nueva Zelanda; ~**er** *n* neozelandés/esa *m/f*.

next [nɛkst] *adj* (*house, room*) vecino; (*bus stop, meeting*) próximo; (*following: page etc*) siguiente ♦ *adv* después; **the ~ day** el día siguiente; ~ **time** la próxima vez; ~ **year** el año próximo *or* que viene; ~ **to** junto a, al lado de; ~ **to nothing** casi nada; ~ **please!** ¡el siguiente! ~ **door** *adv* en la casa de al lado ♦ *adj* vecino, de al lado; ~**of-kin** *n* pariente *m* más cercano.

NHS *n abbr* = **National Health Service**.

nib [nɪb] *n* plumilla.

nibble ['nɪbl] *vt* mordisquear, mordiscar.

Nicaragua [nɪkə'ræɡjuə] *n* Nicaragua; ~**n** *adj*, *n* nicaragüense *m/f*.

nice [naɪs] *adj* (*likeable*) simpático; (*kind*) amable; (*pleasant*) agradable; (*attractive*) bonito, mono, lindo (*AM*); ~**ly** *adv* amablemente; bien.

nick [nɪk] *n* (*wound*) rasguño; (*cut, indentation*) mella, muesca ♦ *vt* (*inf*) birlar, robar; **in the ~ of time** justo a tiempo.

nickel ['nɪkl] *n* níquel *m*; (*US*) *moneda de 5 centavos*.

nickname ['nɪkneɪm] *n* apodo, mote *m* ♦ *vt* apodar.

nicotine ['nɪkətiːn] *n* nicotina.

niece [niːs] *n* sobrina.

Nigeria [naɪ'dʒɪərɪə] *n* Nigeria; ~**n** *adj*, *n* nigeriano/a *m/f*.

nigger ['nɪɡə*] (*inf!*) *n* (*highly offensive*) negro/a.

niggling ['nɪɡlɪŋ] *adj* (*trifling*) nimio, insignificante; (*annoying*) molesto.

night [naɪt] *n* noche *f*; (*evening*) tarde *f*; **the ~ before last** anteanoche; **at ~,** **by ~** de noche, por la noche; ~**cap** *n* (*drink*) *bebida que se toma antes de acostarse*; ~ **club** *n* cabaret *m*; ~**dress** (*BRIT*) *n* camisón *m*; ~**fall** *n* anochecer *m*; ~**gown** *n* = ~**dress**; ~**ie** ['naɪtɪ] *n* = ~**dress**.

nightingale ['naɪtɪŋɡeɪl] *n* ruiseñor *m*.

nightlife ['naɪtlaɪf] *n* vida nocturna.

nightly ['naɪtlɪ] *adj* de todas las noches ♦ *adv* todas las noches, cada noche.

nightmare ['naɪtmɛə*] *n* pesadilla.

night: ~ **porter** *n* portero de noche; ~ **school** *n* clase(s) *f(pl)* nocturna(s); ~ **shift** *n* turno nocturno *or* de noche; ~**time** *n* noche *f*; ~ **watchman** *n* vigilante *m* nocturno.

nil [nɪl] (*BRIT*) *n* (*SPORT*) cero, nada.

Nile [naɪl] *n*: **the ~** el Nilo.

nimble ['nɪmbl] *adj* (*agile*) ágil, ligero; (*skilful*) diestro.

nine [naɪn] *num* nueve; ~**teen** *num* diecinueve, diez y nueve; ~**ty** *num* noventa.

ninth [naɪnθ] *adj* noveno.

nip [nɪp] *vt* (*pinch*) pellizcar; (*bite*) morder.

nipple ['nɪpl] *n* (*ANAT*) pezón *m*.

nitrogen ['naɪtrədʒən] *n* nitrógeno.

KEYWORD
---

no [nəʊ] (*pl* ~**es**) *adv* (*opposite of "yes"*) no; **are you coming? — — ~ (I'm**

not) ¿vienes? — no; **would you like
some more?** — ~ **thank you** ¿quieres
más? — no gracias
♦ *adj* (*not any*): **I have ~ money/time/
books** no tengo dinero/tiempo/libros; **~
other man would have done it** ningún
otro lo hubiera hecho; "~ **entry**" "prohibido el paso"; "~ **smoking**" "prohibido fumar"
♦ *n* no *m*.

nobility [nou'bɪlɪtɪ] *n* nobleza.
noble ['noubl] *adj* noble.
nobody ['noubədɪ] *pron* nadie.
nod [nod] *vi* saludar con la cabeza; (*in
agreement*) decir que sí con la cabeza;
(*doze*) dar cabezadas ♦ *vt*: **to ~ one's
head** inclinar la cabeza ♦ *n* inclinación *f*
de cabeza; ~ **off** *vi* dar cabezadas.
noise [nɔɪz] *n* ruido; (*din*) escándalo,
estrépito; **noisy** *adj* ruidoso; (*child*) escandaloso.
nominate ['nomɪneɪt] *vt* (*propose*) proponer; (*appoint*) nombrar; **nomination**
[-'neɪʃən] *n* propuesta; nombramiento.
nominee [nomɪ'niː] *n* candidato/a.
non... [non] *prefix* no, des..., in...; ~**-
alcoholic** *adj* no alcohólico; ~**-aligned**
adj no alineado.
nonchalant ['nonʃələnt] *adj* indiferente.
non-committal ['nonkə'mɪtl] *adj* evasivo.
nondescript ['nondɪskrɪpt] *adj* soso.
none [nʌn] *pron* ninguno/a ♦ *adv* de ninguna manera; ~ **of you** ninguno de vosotros; **I've ~ left** no me queda
ninguno/a; **he's ~ the worse for it** no le
ha hecho ningún mal.
nonentity [no'nentɪtɪ] *n* cero a la izquierda, nulidad *f*.
nonetheless [nʌnðə'lɛs] *adv* sin embargo, no obstante.
non-existent *adj* inexistente.
non-fiction *n* literatura no novelesca.
nonplussed [non'plʌst] *adj* perplejo.
nonsense ['nonsəns] *n* tonterías *fpl*, disparates *fpl*; ~! ¡qué tonterías!
non: ~**-smoker** *n* no fumador(a) *m/f*;
~**-stick** *adj* (*pan, surface*) antiadheren-
te; ~**-stop** *adj* continuo; (*RAIL*) directo

♦ *adv* sin parar.
noodles ['nuːdlz] *npl* tallarines *mpl*.
nook [nuk] *n*: ~**s and crannies** escondri-
jos *mpl*.
noon [nuːn] *n* mediodía *m*.
no-one *pron* = **nobody**.
noose [nuːs] *n* (*hangman's*) dogal *m*.
nor [nɔː*] *conj* = **neither** ♦ *adv* see
neither.
norm [nɔːm] *n* norma.
normal ['nɔːml] *adj* normal; ~**ly** *adv*
normalmente.
north [nɔːθ] *n* norte *m* ♦ *adj* del norte,
norteño ♦ *adv* al *or* hacia el norte; **N~
America** *n* América del Norte; ~**-east** *n*
nor(d)este *m*; ~**erly** ['nɔːðəlɪ] *adj*
(*point, direction*) norteño; ~**ern**
['nɔːðən] *adj* norteño del norte; **N~ern
Ireland** *n* Irlanda del Norte; **N~ Pole** *n*
Polo Norte; **N~ Sea** *n* Mar *m* del Norte; ~**ward(s)** ['nɔːθwəd(z)] *adv* hacia el
norte; ~**-west** *n* nor(d)oeste *m*.
Norway ['nɔːweɪ] *n* Noruega; **Norwegian** [-'wiːdʒən] *adj* noruego/a ♦ *n*
noruego/a; (*LING*) noruego.
nose [nəuz] *n* (*ANAT*) nariz *f*; (*ZOOL*)
hocico; (*sense of smell*) olfato ♦ *vi*: **to
~ about** curiosear; ~**bleed** *n* hemorragia nasal; ~**-dive** *n* (*of plane*: *deliberate*) picado vertical; (: *involuntary*)
caída en picado; ~**y** (*inf*) *adj* curioso,
fisgón/ona.
nostalgia [nos'tældʒɪə] *n* nostalgia.
nostril ['nostrɪl] *n* ventana de la nariz.
nosy ['nəuzɪ] (*inf*) *adj* = **nosey.**
not [not] *adv* no; ~ **that ...** no es que ...;
it's too late, isn't it? es demasiado tarde, ¿verdad *or* no?; ~ **yet/now** todavía/
ahora no; **why ~?** ¿por qué no?; *see
also* **all**; **only.**
notably ['nəutəblɪ] *adv* especialmente.
notary ['nəutərɪ] *n* notario/a.
notch [notʃ] *n* muesca, corte *m*.
note [nəut] *n* (*MUS, record, letter*) nota;
(*banknote*) billete *m*; (*tone*) tono ♦ *vt*
(*observe*) notar, observar; (*write
down*) apuntar, anotar; ~**book** *n* libreta, cuaderno; ~**d** ['nəutɪd] *adj* célebre,
conocido; ~**pad** *n* bloc *m*; ~**paper** *n*
papel *m* para cartas.

nothing ['nʌθɪŋ] n nada; (*zero*) cero; **he does** ~ no hace nada; ~ **new** nada nuevo; ~ **much** no mucho; **for** ~ (*free*) gratis, sin pago; (*in vain*) en balde.

notice ['nəutɪs] n (*announcement*) anuncio; (*warning*) aviso; (*dismissal*) despido; (*resignation*) dimisión f; (*period of time*) plazo ♦ vt (*observe*) notar, observar; **to bring sth to sb's** ~ (*attention*) llamar la atención de uno sobre algo; **to take** ~ **of** tomar nota de, prestar atención a; **at short** ~ con poca anticipación; **until further** ~ hasta nuevo aviso; **to hand in one's** ~ dimitir; **~able** adj evidente, obvio; ~ **board** (*BRIT*) n tablón m de anuncios.

notify ['nəutɪfaɪ] vt: **to** ~ **sb** (**of sth**) comunicar (algo) a uno.

notion ['nəuʃən] n idea; (*opinion*) opinión f.

notorious [nəu'tɔːrɪəs] adj notorio.

notwithstanding [nɔtwɪθ'stændɪŋ] adv no obstante, sin embargo ♦ prep a pesar de.

nougat ['nuːgaː] n turrón m.

nought [nɔːt] n cero.

noun [naun] n nombre m, sustantivo.

nourish ['nʌrɪʃ] vt nutrir; (*fig*) alimentar; **~ing** adj nutritivo; **~ment** n alimento, sustento.

novel ['nɔvl] n novela ♦ adj (*new*) nuevo, original; (*unexpected*) insólito; **~ist** n novelista m/f; **~ty** n novedad f.

November [nəu'vɛmbə*] n noviembre m.

novice ['nɔvɪs] n principiante m/f, novato/a; (*REL*) novicio/a.

now [nau] adv (*at the present time*) ahora; (*these days*) actualmente, hoy día ♦ conj: ~ (**that**) ya que, ahora que; **right** ~ ahora mismo; **by** ~ ya; **just** ~ ahora mismo; ~ **and then,** ~ **and again** de vez en cuando; **from** ~ **on** de ahora en adelante; **~adays** ['nauədeɪz] adv hoy (en) día, actualmente.

nowhere ['nəuwɛə*] adv (*direction*) a ninguna parte; (*location*) en ninguna parte.

nozzle ['nɔzl] n boquilla.

nuance ['njuːɑːns] n matiz m.

nuclear ['njuːklɪə*] adj nuclear.

nuclei ['njuːklɪaɪ] npl of **nucleus**.

nucleus ['njuːklɪəs] (*pl* **nuclei**) n núcleo.

nude [njuːd] adj, n desnudo/a m/f; **in the** ~ desnudo.

nudge [nʌdʒ] vt dar un codazo a.

nudist ['njuːdɪst] n nudista m/f.

nudity ['njuːdɪtɪ] n desnudez f.

nuisance ['njuːsns] n molestia, fastidio; (*person*) pesado, latoso; **what a** ~! ¡qué lata!

nuke [njuːk] (*inf*) n bomba atómica ♦ vt atacar con arma nuclear.

null [nʌl] adj: ~ **and void** nulo y sin efecto.

numb [nʌm] adj: ~ **with cold/fear** entumecido por el frío/paralizado de miedo.

number ['nʌmbə*] n número; (*quantity*) cantidad f ♦ vt (*pages etc*) numerar, poner número a; (*amount to*) sumar, ascender a; **to be** ~**ed among** figurar entre; **a** ~ **of** varios, algunos; **they were ten in** ~ eran diez; ~ **plate** (*BRIT*) n matrícula, placa.

numeral ['njuːmərəl] n número, cifra.

numerate ['njuːmərɪt] adj competente en la aritmética.

numerous ['njuːmərəs] adj numeroso.

nun [nʌn] n monja, religiosa.

nurse [nəːs] n enfermero/a; (*also*: ~**maid**) niñera ♦ vt (*patient*) cuidar, atender.

nursery ['nəːsərɪ] n (*institution*) guardería infantil; (*room*) cuarto de los niños; (*for plants*) criadero, semillero; ~ **rhyme** n canción f infantil; ~ **school** n parvulario, escuela de párvulos; ~ **slope** (*BRIT*) n (*SKI*) cuesta para principiantes.

nursing ['nəːsɪŋ] n (*profession*) profesión f de enfermera; (*care*) asistencia, cuidado; ~ **home** n clínica de reposo; ~ **mother** n madre f lactante.

nurture ['nəːtʃə*] vt (*child, plant*) alimentar, nutrir.

nut [nʌt] n (*TECH*) tuerca; (*BOT*) nuez f; **~crackers** npl cascanueces m inv.

nutmeg ['nʌtmɛg] n nuez f moscada.

nutritious [njuː'trɪʃəs] adj nutritivo, alimenticio.

nuts [nʌts] (*inf*) *adj* loco.
nutshell ['nʌtʃel] *n* cáscara de nuez; **in a ~** en resumidas cuentas.
nylon ['naɪlɒn] *n* nilón *m* ♦ *adj* de nilón.

O

oak [əuk] *n* roble *m* ♦ *adj* de roble.
O.A.P. (*BRIT*) *n abbr* = **old-age pensioner**.
oar [ɔː*] *n* remo.
oases [əu'eɪsiːz] *npl of* **oasis**.
oasis [əu'eɪsɪs] (*pl* **oases**) *n* oasis *m inv*.
oath [əuθ] *n* juramento; (*swear word*) palabrota; **on** (*BRIT*) *or* **under** ~ bajo juramento.
oatmeal ['əutmiːl] *n* harina de avena.
oats [əuts] *n* avena.
obedience [ə'biːdɪəns] *n* obediencia.
obedient [ə'biːdɪənt] *adj* obediente.
obey [ə'beɪ] *vt* obedecer; (*instructions, regulations*) cumplir.
obituary [ə'bɪtjuərɪ] *n* necrología.
object [*n* 'ɒbdʒɪkt, *vb* əb'dʒekt] *n* objeto; (*purpose*) objeto, propósito; (*LING*) complemento ♦ *vi*: **to ~ to** estar en contra de; (*proposal*) oponerse a; **to ~ that** objetar que; **expense is no ~** no importa cuánto cuesta; **I ~!** ¡yo protesto!; **~ion** [əb'dʒekʃən] *n* protesta; **I have no ~ion to ...** no tengo inconveniente en que ...; **~ionable** [əb'dʒekʃənəbl] *adj* desagradable; (*conduct*) censurable; **~ive** *adj, n* objetivo.
obligation [ɒblɪ'geɪʃən] *n* obligación *f*; (*debt*) deber *m*; **without ~** sin compromiso.
oblige [ə'blaɪdʒ] *vt* (*do a favour for*) complacer, hacer un favor a; **to ~ sb to do sth** forzar *or* obligar a uno a hacer algo; **to be ~d to sb for sth** estarle agradecido a uno por algo; **obliging** *adj* servicial, atento.
oblique [ə'bliːk] *adj* oblicuo; (*allusion*) indirecto.
obliterate [ə'blɪtəreɪt] *vt* borrar.
oblivion [ə'blɪvɪən] *n* olvido; **oblivious** [-ɪəs] *adj*: **oblivious of** inconsciente de.
oblong ['ɒblɒŋ] *adj* rectangular ♦ *n* rectángulo.

obnoxious [əb'nɒkʃəs] *adj* odioso, detestable; (*smell*) nauseabundo.
oboe ['əubəu] *n* oboe *m*.
obscene [əb'siːn] *adj* obsceno.
obscure [əb'skjuə*] *adj* oscuro ♦ *vt* oscurecer; (*hide: sun*) esconder.
obsequious [əb'siːkwɪəs] *adj* servil.
observance [əb'zəːvns] *n* observancia, cumplimiento.
observant [əb'zəːvnt] *adj* observador(a).
observation [ɒbzə'veɪʃən] *n* observación *f*; (*MED*) examen *m*.
observe [əb'zəːv] *vt* observar; (*rule*) cumplir; **~r** *n* observador(a) *m/f*.
obsess [əb'ses] *vt* obsesionar; **~ive** *adj* obsesivo; obsesionante.
obsolete ['ɒbsəliːt] *adj*: **to be ~** estar en desuso.
obstacle ['ɒbstəkl] *n* obstáculo; (*nuisance*) estorbo; **~ race** *n* carrera de obstáculos.
obstetrics [ɒb'stetrɪks] *n* obstetricia.
obstinate ['ɒbstɪnɪt] *adj* terco, porfiado; (*determined*) obstinado.
obstruct [əb'strʌkt] *vt* obstruir; (*hinder*) estorbar, obstaculizar; **~ion** [əb-'strʌkʃən] *n* (*action*) obstrucción *f*; (*object*) estorbo, obstáculo.
obtain [əb'teɪn] *vt* obtener; (*achieve*) conseguir; **~able** *adj* asequible.
obvious ['ɒbvɪəs] *adj* obvio, evidente; **~ly** *adv* evidentemente, naturalmente; **~ly not** por supuesto que no.
occasion [ə'keɪʒən] *n* oportunidad *f*, ocasión *f*; (*event*) acontecimiento; **~al** *adj* poco frecuente, ocasional; **~ally** *adv* de vez en cuando.
occult [ə'kʌlt] *n*: **the ~** lo sobrenatural, lo oculto.
occupant ['ɒkjupənt] *n* (*of house*) inquilino/a; (*of car*) ocupante *m/f*.
occupation [ɒkju'peɪʃən] *n* ocupación *f*; (*job*) trabajo; (*pastime*) ocupaciones *fpl*; **~al hazard** *n* riesgo profesional.
occupier ['ɒkjupaɪə*] *n* inquilino/a.
occupy ['ɒkjupaɪ] *vt* (*seat, post, time*) ocupar; (*house*) habitar; **to ~ o.s. in doing** pasar el tiempo haciendo.

occur [ə'kə:*] vi pasar, suceder; **to ~ to sb** ocurrírsele a uno; **~rence** [ə'kʌrəns] n acontecimiento; (existence) existencia.

ocean ['əuʃən] n océano; **~-going** adj de alta mar.

ochre ['əukə*] (US **ocher**) n ocre m.

o'clock [ə'klɔk] adv: **it is** 5 ~ son las 5.

OCR n abbr = **optical character recognition/reader.**

octave ['ɔktɪv] n octava.

October [ɔk'təubə*] n octubre m.

octopus ['ɔktəpəs] n pulpo.

odd [ɔd] adj extraño, raro; (number) impar; (sock, shoe etc) suelto; 60~ 60 y pico; **at ~ times** de vez en cuando; **to be the ~ one out** estar de más; **~ity** n rareza; (person) excéntrico; **~-job** (COMM) retales mpl; **~s** npl (in betting) puntos mpl de ventaja; **it makes no ~s** da lo mismo; **at ~s** reñidos/as; **~s-and-ends** npl minucias fpl.

ode [əud] n oda.

odometer [ə'dɔmɪtə*] (US) n cuentakilómetros m inv.

odour ['əudə*] (US **odor**) n olor m; (unpleasant) hedor m.

KEYWORD

of [ɔv, əv] prep **1** (gen) de; **a friend ~ ours** un amigo nuestro; **a boy ~ 10** un chico de 10 años; **that was kind ~ you** eso fue muy amable por or de tu parte **2** (expressing quantity, amount, dates etc) de; **a kilo ~ flour** un kilo de harina; **there were 3 ~ them** había tres; **3 ~ us** went tres de nosotros fuimos; **the 5th ~ July** el 5 de julio **3** (from, out of) de; **made ~ wood** (hecho) de madera.

---

off [ɔf] adj, adv (engine) desconectado; (light) apagado; (tap) cerrado; (BRIT: food: bad) pasado, malo; (: milk) cortado; (cancelled) cancelado ♦ prep de; **to be ~** (to leave) irse, marcharse; **to be ~ sick** estar enfermo or de baja; **a**

day ~ un día libre or sin trabajar; **to have an ~ day** tener un día malo; **he had his coat ~** se había quitado el abrigo; 10% ~ (COMM) (con el) 10% de descuento; **5 km ~ (the road)** a 5 km (de la carretera); **~ the coast** frente a la costa; **I'm ~ meat** (no longer eat/like it) paso de la carne; **on the ~ chance** por si acaso; **~ and on** de vez en cuando.

offal ['ɔfl] (BRIT) n (CULIN) menudencias fpl.

off-colour (BRIT) adj (ill) indispuesto.

offence [ə'fɛns] (US **offense**) n (crime) delito; **to take ~ at** ofenderse por.

offend [ə'fɛnd] vt (person) ofender; **~er** n delincuente m/f.

offensive [ə'fɛnsɪv] adj ofensivo, (smell etc) repugnante ♦ n (MIL) ofensiva.

offer ['ɔfə*] n oferta, ofrecimiento; (proposal) propuesta ♦ vt ofrecer; (opportunity) facilitar; **"on ~"** (COMM) "en oferta"; **~ing** n ofrenda.

offhand [ɔf'hænd] adj informal ♦ adv de improviso.

office ['ɔfɪs] n (place) oficina; (room) despacho; (position) carga, oficio; **doctor's ~** (US) consultorio; **to take ~** entrar en funciones; **~ automation** n ofimática, buromática; **~ block** (US **~ building**) n bloque m de oficinas; **~ hours** npl horas fpl de oficina; (US: MED) horas fpl de consulta.

officer ['ɔfɪsə*] n (MIL etc) oficial m/f; (also: **police ~**) agente m/f de policía; (of organization) director(a) m/f.

office worker n oficinista m/f.

official [ə'fɪʃl] adj oficial, autorizado ♦ n funcionario, oficial m; **~dom** n burocracia.

offing ['ɔfɪŋ] n: **in the ~** (fig) en perspectiva.

off: **~-licence** (BRIT) n (shop) bodega, tienda de vinos y bebidas alcohólicas; **~-line** adj, adv (COMPUT) fuera de línea; **~-peak** adj (electricity) de banda económica; (ticket) billete de precio reducido por viajar fuera de las horas punta; **~-putting** (BRIT) adj (person) asqueroso; (remark) desalentador(a);

~-**season** *adj, adv* fuera de temporada.

offset ['ɔfsɛt] (*irreg*) *vt* contrarrestar, compensar.

offshoot ['ɔfʃuːt] *n* (*fig*) ramificación *f*.

offshore [ɔf'ʃɔː*] *adj* (*breeze, island*) costera; (*fishing*) de bajura.

offside ['ɔf'saɪd] *adj* (*SPORT*) fuera de juego; (*AUT: in Britain*) del lado derecho; (: *in US, Europe etc*) del lado izquierdo.

offspring ['ɔfsprɪŋ] *n inv* descendencia.

off: ~**stage** *adv* entre bastidores; ~-**the-peg** (*US* ~-**the-rack**) *adv* confeccionado; ~-**white** *adj* blanco grisáceo.

often ['ɔfn] *adv* a menudo, con frecuencia; **how** ~ **do you go?** ¿cada cuánto vas?

ogle ['ɔugl] *vt* comerse con los ojos a.

oh [əu] *excl* ¡ah!

oil [ɔɪl] *n* aceite *m*; (*petroleum*) petróleo; (*for heating*) aceite *m* combustible ♦ *vt* engrasar; ~ **can** *n* lata de aceite; ~**field** *n* campo petrolífero; ~ **filter** *n* (*AUT*) filtro de aceite; ~ **painting** *n* pintura al óleo; ~ **rig** *n* torre *f* de perforación; ~**skins** *npl* impermeables *mpl* de hule, chubasquero; ~ **tanker** *n* petrolero; (*truck*) camión *m* cisterna; ~ **well** *n* pozo (de petróleo); ~**y** *adj* aceitoso; (*food*) grasiento.

ointment ['ɔɪntmənt] *n* ungüento.

O.K. ['əu'keɪ] = **okay**.

okay ['əu'keɪ] *excl* O.K., ¡está bien!, ¡vale! (*SP*) ♦ *adj* bien ♦ *vt* dar el visto bueno a.

old [əuld] *adj* viejo; (*former*) antiguo; **how** ~ **are you?** ¿cuántos años tienes?, ¿qué edad tienes?; **he's 10 years** ~ tiene 10 años; ~**er brother** hermano mayor; ~ **age** *n* vejez *f*; ~-**age pensioner** (*BRIT*) *n* jubilado/a; ~-**fashioned** *adj* anticuado, pasado de moda.

olive ['ɔlɪv] *n* (*fruit*) aceituna; (*tree*) olivo ♦ *adj* (*also*: ~-**green**) verde oliva; ~ **oil** *n* aceite *m* de oliva.

Olympic [əu'lɪmpɪk] *adj* olímpico; **the** ~ **Games** *npl* las Olimpiadas; **the** ~**s** *npl* las Olimpiadas.

omelet(te) ['ɔmlɪt] *n* tortilla (*SP*), tortilla de huevo (*AM*).

omen ['əumən] *n* presagio.

ominous ['ɔmɪnəs] *adj* de mal agüero, amenazador(a).

omit [əu'mɪt] *vt* omitir.

KEYWORD
---

on [ɔn] *prep* **1** (*indicating position*) en; sobre; ~ **the wall** en la pared; **it's** ~ **the table** está sobre *or* en la mesa; ~ **the left** a la izquierda

2 (*indicating means, method, condition etc*): ~ **foot** a pie; ~ **the train/plane** (*go*) en tren/avión; (*be*) en el tren/avión; ~ **the radio/television/telephone** por *or* en la radio/televisión/al teléfono; **to be** ~ **drugs** drogarse; (*MED*) estar a tratamiento; **to be** ~ **holiday/business** estar de vacaciones/en viaje de negocios

3 (*referring to time*): ~ **Friday** el viernes; ~ **Fridays** los viernes; ~ **June 20th** el 20 de junio; **a week** ~ **Friday** del viernes en una semana; ~ **arrival** al llegar; ~ **seeing this** al ver esto

4 (*about, concerning*) sobre, acerca de; **a book** ~ **physics** un libro de *or* sobre física

♦ *adv* **1** (*referring to dress*): **to have one's coat** ~ tener *or* llevar el abrigo puesto; **she put her gloves** ~ se puso los guantes

2 (*referring to covering*): "**screw the lid** ~ **tightly**" "cerrar bien la tapa"

3 (*further, continuously*): **to walk** *etc* ~ seguir caminando *etc*

♦ *adj* **1** (*functioning, in operation: machine, radio, TV, light*) encendido/a (*SP*), prendido/a (*AM*); (: *tap*) abierto/a; (: *brakes*) echado/a, puesto/a; **is the meeting still** ~? (*in progress*) ¿todavía continúa la reunión?; (*not cancelled*) ¿va a haber reunión al fin?; **there's a good film** ~ **at the cinema** ponen una buena película en el cine

2: that's not ~! (*inf: not possible*) ¡eso ni hablar!; (: *not acceptable*) ¡eso no se hace!

---

once [wʌns] *adv* una vez; (*formerly*) antiguamente ♦ *conj* una vez que; ~ **he**

had left/it was done una vez que se había marchado/se hizo; **at** ~ en seguida, inmediatamente; (*simultaneously*) a la vez; ~ **a week** una vez por semana; ~ **more** otra vez; ~ **and for all** de una vez por todas; ~ **upon a time** érase una vez.

oncoming ['ɔnkʌmɪŋ] *adj* (*traffic*) que viene de frente.

KEYWORD

one [wʌn] *num* un(o)/una; ~ **hundred and fifty** ciento cincuenta; ~ **by** ~ uno a uno

♦ *adj* **1** (*sole*) único; **the** ~ **book which** el único libro que; **the** ~ **man who** el único que

2 (*same*) mismo/a; **they came in the** ~ **car** vinieron en un solo coche

♦ *pron* **1**: **this** ~ éste/ésta; **that** ~ ése/ésa; (*more remote*) aquél/aquella; **I've already got (a red)** ~ ya tengo uno/a (rojo/a); ~ **by** ~ uno/a por uno/a

2: ~ **another** os (*SP*), se (+*el uno al otro, unos a otros etc*); **do you two ever see** ~ **another?** ¿vosotros dos os veis alguna vez? (*SP*), ¿se ven ustedes dos alguna vez?; **they didn't dare look at** ~ **another** los chicos no se atrevieron a mirarse (el uno al otro); **they all kissed** ~ **another** se besaron unos a otros

3 (*impers*): **never knows** nunca se sabe; **to cut** ~'**s finger** cortarse el dedo; ~ **needs to eat** hay que comer.

one: ~-**day excursion** (*US*) *n* billete *m* de ida y vuelta en un día; ~-**man** *adj* (*business*) individual; ~-**man band** *n* hombre-orquesta *m*; ~-**off** (*BRIT: inf*) *n* (*event*) acontecimiento único.

oneself [wʌn'sɛlf] *pron* (*reflexive*) se; (*after prep*) sí; (*emphatic*) uno/a mismo/a; **to hurt** ~ hacerse daño; **to keep sth for** ~ guardarse algo; **to talk to** ~ hablar solo.

one: ~-**sided** *adj* (*argument*) parcial; ~-**to**-~ *adj* (*relationship*) de dos; ~-**upmanship** *n* arte *m* de aventajar a los demás; ~-**way** *adj* (*street*) de sentido único. •

ongoing ['ɔngəʊɪŋ] *adj* continuo.

onion ['ʌnjən] *n* cebolla.

on-line *adj, adv* (*COMPUT*) en línea.

onlooker ['ɔnlʊkə*] *n* espectador(a) *m/f*.

only ['əʊnlɪ] *adv* solamente, sólo ♦ *adj* único, solo ♦ *conj* solamente que, pero; **an** ~ **child** un hijo único; **not** ~ **... but also ...** no sólo ... sino también ....

onset ['ɔnsɛt] *n* comienzo.

onshore ['ɔnʃɔ:*] *adj* (*wind*) que sopla del mar hacia la tierra.

onslaught ['ɔnslɔ:t] *n* ataque *m*, embestida.

onto ['ɔntu] *prep* = **on to**.

onus ['əʊnəs] *n* responsabilidad *f*.

onward(s) ['ɔnwəd(z)] *adv* (*move*) (hacia) adelante; **from that time** ~ desde entonces en adelante.

onyx ['ɔnɪks] *n* ónice *m*.

ooze [u:z] *vi* rezumar.

opaque [əʊ'peɪk] *adj* opaco.

OPEC ['əʊpek] *n abbr* (= *Organization of Petroleum-Exporting Countries*) OPEP *f*.

open ['əʊpn] *adj* abierto; (*car*) descubierto; (*road, view*) despejado; (*meeting*) público; (*admiration*) manifiesto ♦ *vt* abrir ♦ *vi* abrirse; (*book etc: commence*) comenzar; **in the** ~ (**air**) al aire libre; ~ **on to** *vt fus* (*subj: room, door*) dar a; ~ **up** *vt* abrir; (*blocked road*) despejar ♦ *vi* abrirse, empezar; ~**ing** *n* abertura; (*start*) comienzo; (*opportunity*) oportunidad *f*; ~**ly** *adv* abiertamente; ~-**minded** *adj* imparcial; ~-**necked** *adj* (*shirt*) desabrochado; sin corbata; ~-**plan** *adj*: ~-**plan office** gran oficina sin particiones.

opera ['ɔpərə] *n* ópera; ~ **house** *n* teatro de la ópera.

operate ['ɔpəreɪt] *vt* (*machine*) hacer funcionar; (*company*) dirigir ♦ *vi* funcionar; **to** ~ **on sb** (*MED*) operar a uno.

operatic [ɔpə'rætɪk] *adj* de ópera.

operating table ['ɔpəreɪtɪŋ-] *n* mesa de operaciones.

operating theatre *n* sala de operaciones.

operation [ɔpə'reɪʃən] *n* operación *f*; (*of machine*) funcionamiento; **to be in** ~

estar funcionando *or* en funcionamiento; **to have an ~** (*MED*) ser operado; **~al** *adj* operacional, en buen estado.
operative ['ɔpərətɪv] *adj* en vigor.
operator ['ɔpəreɪtə*] *n* (*of machine*) maquinista *m/f*, operario/a; (*TEL*) operador(a) *m/f*, telefonista *m/f*.
ophthalmic [ɔf'θælmɪk] *adj* oftálmico.
opinion [ə'pɪnɪən] *n* opinión *f*; **in my ~** en mi opinión, a mi juicio; **~ated** *adj* testarudo; **~ poll** *n* encuesta, sondeo.
opponent [ə'pəunənt] *n* adversario/a, contrincante *m/f*.
opportunist [ɔpə'tjuːnɪst] *n* oportunista *m/f*.
opportunity [ɔpə'tjuːnɪtɪ] *n* oportunidad *f*; **to take the ~ of doing** aprovechar la ocasión para hacer.
oppose [ə'pəuz] *vt* oponerse a; **to be ~d to sth** oponerse a algo; **as ~d to** a diferencia de; **opposing** *adj* opuesto, contrario.
opposite ['ɔpəzɪt] *adj* opuesto, contrario a; (*house etc*) de enfrente ♦ *adv* en frente ♦ *prep* en frente de, frente a ♦ *n* lo contrario.
opposition [ɔpə'zɪʃən] *n* oposición *f*.
oppress [ə'prɛs] *vt* oprimir; **~sion** [ə'prɛʃən] *n* opresión *f*; **~ive** *adj* opresivo; (*weather*) agobiante.
opt [ɔpt] *vi*: **to ~ for** optar por; **to ~ to do** optar por hacer; **~ out** *vi*: **to ~ out of** optar por no hacer.
optical ['ɔptɪkl] *adj* óptico.
optician [ɔp'tɪʃən] *n* óptico *m/f*.
optimist ['ɔptɪmɪst] *n* optimista *m/f*; **~ic** [-'mɪstɪk] *adj* optimista.
optimum ['ɔptɪməm] *adj* óptimo.
option ['ɔpʃən] *n* opción *f*; **~al** *adj* facultativo, discrecional.
or [ɔː*] *conj* o; (*before o, ho*) u; (*with negative*): **he hasn't seen ~ heard anything** no ha visto ni oído nada; **~ else** si no.
oracle ['ɔrəkl] *n* oráculo.
oral ['ɔːrəl] *adj* oral ♦ *n* examen *m* oral.
orange ['ɔrɪndʒ] *n* (*fruit*) naranja ♦ *adj* color naranja.
orator ['ɔrətə*] *n* orador(a) *m/f*.
orbit ['ɔːbɪt] *n* órbita ♦ *vt, vi* orbitar.

orchard ['ɔːtʃəd] *n* huerto.
orchestra ['ɔːkɪstrə] *n* orquesta; (*US: seating*) platea.
orchid ['ɔːkɪd] *n* orquídea.
ordain [ɔː'deɪn] *vt* (*REL*) ordenar, decretar.
ordeal [ɔː'diːl] *n* experiencia horrorosa.
order ['ɔːdə*] *n* orden *m*; (*command*) orden *f*; (*good ~*) buen estado; (*COMM*) pedido ♦ *vt* (*also: put in ~*) arreglar, poner en orden; (*COMM*) pedir; (*command*) mandar, ordenar; **in ~** en orden; (*of document*) en regla; **in (working) ~** en funcionamiento; **in ~ to do/ that** para hacer/que; **on ~** (*COMM*) pedido; **to be out of ~** estar desordenado; (*not working*) no funcionar; **to ~ sb to do sth** mandar a uno hacer algo; **~ form** *n* hoja de pedido; **~ly** *n* (*MIL*) ordenanza *m*; (*MED*) enfermero/a (auxiliar) ♦ *adj* ordenado.
ordinary ['ɔːdnrɪ] *adj* corriente, normal; (*pej*) común y corriente; **out of the ~** fuera de lo común.
Ordnance Survey ['ɔːdnəns-] (*BRIT*) *n* servicio oficial de topografía.
ore [ɔː*] *n* mineral *m*.
organ ['ɔːgən] *n* órgano; **~ic** [ɔː'gænɪk] *adj* orgánico; **~ism** *n* organismo.
organization [ɔːgənaɪ'zeɪʃən] *n* organización *f*.
organize ['ɔːgənaɪz] *vt* organizar; **~r** *n* organizador(a) *m/f*.
orgasm ['ɔːgæzəm] *n* orgasmo.
orgy ['ɔːdʒɪ] *n* orgía.
Orient ['ɔːrɪənt] *n* Oriente *m*; **oriental** [-'ɛntl] *adj* oriental.
orientate ['ɔːrɪənteɪt] *vt*: **to ~ o.s.** orientarse.
origin ['ɔrɪdʒɪn] *n* origen *m*.
original [ə'rɪdʒɪnl] *adj* original; (*first*) primero; (*earlier*) primitivo ♦ *n* original *m*; **~ity** [-'nælɪtɪ] *n* originalidad *f*; **~ly** *adv* al principio.
originate [ə'rɪdʒɪneɪt] *vi*: **to ~ from, to ~ in** surgir de, tener su origen en.
Orkneys ['ɔːknɪz] *npl*: **the ~** (*also: the Orkney Islands*) las Orcadas.
ornament ['ɔːnəmənt] *n* adorno; (*trinket*) chuchería; **~al** [-'mɛntl] *adj* decora-

tivo, de adorno.

ornate [ɔːˈneɪt] *adj* muy ornado, vistoso.

orphan [ˈɔːfn] *n* huérfano/a; **~age** *n* orfanato.

orthodox [ˈɔːθədɔks] *adj* ortodoxo; **~y** *n* ortodoxia.

orthopaedic [ɔːθəˈpiːdɪk] (*US* **orthopedic**) *adj* ortopédico.

oscillate [ˈɔsɪleɪt] *vi* oscilar; (*person*) vacilar.

ostensibly [ɔsˈtɛnsɪblɪ] *adv* aparentemente.

ostentatious [ɔstɛnˈteɪʃəs] *adj* ostentoso.

osteopath [ˈɔstɪəpæθ] *n* osteópata *m/f*.

ostracize [ˈɔstrəsaɪz] *vt* hacer el vacío a.

ostrich [ˈɔstrɪtʃ] *n* avestruz *m*.

other [ˈʌðə*] *adj* otro ♦ *pron*: the ~ (one) el/la otro/a ♦ *adv*: ~ than aparte de; ~s (~ people) otros; the ~ day el otro día; **~wise** *adv* de otra manera ♦ *conj* (*if not*) si no.

otter [ˈɔtə*] *n* nutria.

ouch [autʃ] *excl* ¡ay!

ought [ɔːt] (*pt* ought) *aux vb*: I ~ to do it debería hacerlo; this ~ to have been corrected esto debiera haberse corregido; he ~ to win (*probability*) debe or debiera ganar.

ounce [auns] *n* onza (*28.35g*).

our [ˈauə*] *adj* nuestro; *see also* my; **~s** *pron* (el) nuestro/(la) nuestra *etc*; *see also* mine; **~selves** *pron pl* (*reflexive, after prep*) nosotros; (*emphatic*) nosotros mismos; *see also* oneself.

oust [aust] *vt* desalojar.

out [aut] *adv* fuera, afuera; (*not at home*) fuera (de casa); (*light, fire*) apagado; ~ there allí (fuera); he's ~ (*absent*) no está, ha salido; to be ~ in one's calculations equivocarse (en sus cálculos); to run ~ salir corriendo; ~ loud en alta voz; ~ of (*outside*) fuera de; (*because of: anger etc*) por; ~ of petrol sin gasolina; "~ of order" "no funciona".

out-and-out *adj* (*liar, thief etc*) redomado, empedernido.

outback [ˈautbæk] *n* interior *m*.

outboard [ˈautbɔːd] *adj*: ~ motor (motor *m*) fuera borda *m*.

outbreak [ˈautbreɪk] *n* (*of war*) comienzo; (*of disease*) epidemia; (*of violence etc*) ola.

outburst [ˈautbəːst] *n* explosión *f*, arranque *m*.

outcast [ˈautkɑːst] *n* paria *m/f*.

outcome [ˈautkʌm] *n* resultado.

outcrop [ˈautkrɔp] *n* (*of rock*) afloramiento.

outcry [ˈautkraɪ] *n* protestas *fpl*.

outdated [autˈdeɪtɪd] *adj* anticuado, fuera de moda.

outdo [autˈduː] (*irreg*) *vt* superar.

outdoor [autˈdɔː*] *adj* exterior, de aire libre; (*clothes*) de calle; **~s** *adv* al aire libre.

outer [ˈautə*] *adj* exterior, externo; ~ **space** *n* espacio exterior.

outfit [ˈautfɪt] *n* (*clothes*) conjunto.

outgoing [ˈautgəuɪŋ] *adj* (*character*) extrovertido; (*retiring: president etc*) saliente; **~s** (*BRIT*) *npl* gastos *mpl*.

outgrow [autˈgrəu] (*irreg*) *vt*: he has ~n his clothes su ropa le queda pequeña ya.

outhouse [ˈauthaus] *n* dependencia.

outing [ˈautɪŋ] *n* excursión *f*, paseo.

outlandish [autˈlændɪʃ] *adj* estrafalario.

outlaw [ˈautlɔː] *n* proscrito ♦ *vt* proscribir.

outlay [ˈautleɪ] *n* inversión *f*.

outlet [ˈautlɛt] *n* salida; (*of pipe*) desagüe *m*; (*US: ELEC*) toma de corriente; (*also: retail ~*) punto de venta.

outline [ˈautlaɪn] *n* (*shape*) contorno, perfil *m*; (*sketch, plan*) esbozo ♦ *vt* (*plan etc*) esbozar; in ~ (*fig*) a grandes rasgos.

outlive [autˈlɪv] *vt* sobrevivir a.

outlook [ˈautluk] *n* (*fig: prospects*) perspectivas *fpl*; (: *for weather*) pronóstico.

outlying [ˈautlaɪɪŋ] *adj* remoto, aislado.

outmoded [autˈməudɪd] *adj* anticuado, pasado de moda.

outnumber [autˈnʌmbə*] *vt* superar en número.

out-of-date *adj* (*passport*) caducado; (*clothes*) pasado de moda.

out-of-the-way *adj* apartado.

outpatient [ˈautpeɪʃənt] n paciente m/f externo/a.
outpost [ˈautpəust] n puesto avanzado.
output [ˈautput] n (volumen m de) producción f, rendimiento; (COMPUT) salida.
outrage [ˈautreɪdʒ] n escándalo; (atrocity) atrocidad f ♦ vt ultrajar; ~**ous** [-ˈreɪdʒəs] adj monstruoso.
outright [adv autˈraɪt, adj ˈautraɪt] adv (ask, deny) francamente; (refuse) rotundamente; (win) de manera absoluta; (be killed) en el acto ♦ adj franco; rotundo.
outset [ˈautset] n principio.
outside [autˈsaɪd] n exterior m ♦ adj exterior, externo ♦ adv fuera ♦ prep fuera de; (beyond) más allá de; **at the ~** (fig) a lo sumo; ~ **lane** n (AUT: in Britain) carril m de la derecha; (: in US, Europe etc) carril m de la izquierda; ~-**left/right** n (FOOTBALL) extremo izquierdo/derecho; ~ **line** n (TEL) línea (exterior); ~**r** n (stranger) extraño, forastero.
outsize [ˈautsaɪz] adj (clothes) de talla grande.
outskirts [ˈautskɜːts] npl alrededores mpl, afueras fpl.
outspoken [autˈspəukən] adj muy franco.
outstanding [autˈstændɪŋ] adj excepcional, destacado; (remaining) pendiente.
outstay [autˈsteɪ] vt: to ~ **one's welcome** quedarse más de la cuenta.
outstretched [autˈstretʃt] adj (hand) extendido.
outstrip [autˈstrɪp] vt (competitors, demand) dejar atrás, aventajar.
out-tray n bandeja de salida.
outward [ˈautwəd] adj externo; (journey) de ida; ~**ly** adv por fuera.
outweigh [autˈweɪ] vt pesar más que.
outwit [autˈwɪt] vt ser más listo que.
oval [ˈəuvl] adj ovalado ♦ n óvalo.
ovary [ˈəuvərɪ] n ovario.
oven [ˈʌvn] n horno; ~**proof** adj resistente al horno.
over [ˈəuvə*] adv encima, por encima ♦ adj (or adv) (finished) terminado; (sur-

plus) de sobra ♦ prep (por) encima de; (above) sobre; (on the other side of) al otro lado de; (more than) más de; (during) durante; ~ **here** (por) aquí; ~ **there** (por) allí or allá; **all** ~ (everywhere) por todas partes; ~ **and ~ (again)** una y otra vez; ~ **and above** además de; **to ask sb** ~ invitar a uno a casa; **to bend** ~ inclinarse.
overall [adj, n ˈəuvərɔːl, adv əuvərˈɔːl] adj (length etc) total; (study) de conjunto ♦ adv en conjunto ♦ n (BRIT) guardapolvo; ~**s** npl mono (SP), overol m (AM).
overawe [əuvərˈɔː] vt: `to be ~d (by)` quedar impresionado (con).
overbalance [əuvəˈbæləns] vi perder el equilibrio.
overbearing [əuvəˈbeərɪŋ] adj autoritario, imperioso.
overboard [ˈəuvəbɔːd] adv (NAUT) por la borda.
overbook [əuvəˈbuk] vt sobrereservar.
overcast [ˈəuvəkɑːst] adj encapotado.
overcharge [əuvəˈtʃɑːdʒ] vt: to ~ **sb** cobrar un precio excesivo a uno.
overcoat [ˈəuvəkəut] n abrigo, sobretodo.
overcome [əuvəˈkʌm] (irreg) vt vencer; (difficulty) superar.
overcrowded [əuvəˈkraudɪd] adj atestado de gente; (city, country) superpoblado.
overdo [əuvəˈduː] (irreg) vt exagerar; (overcook) cocer demasiado; **to ~ it** (work etc) pasarse.
overdose [ˈəuvədəus] n sobredosis f inv.
overdraft [ˈəuvədrɑːft] n saldo deudor.
overdrawn [əuvəˈdrɔːn] adj (account) en descubierto.
overdue [əuvəˈdjuː] adj retrasado.
overestimate [əuvərˈestɪmeɪt] vt sobreestimar.
overflow [vb əuvəˈfləu, n ˈəuvəfləu] vi desbordarse ♦ n (also: ~ **pipe**) (cañería de) desagüe m.
overgrown [əuvəˈgrəun] adj (garden) invadido por la vegetación.
overhaul [vb əuvəˈhɔːl, n ˈəuvəhɔːl] vt revisar, repasar ♦ n revisión f.
overhead [adv əuvəˈhed, adj ˈəuvəhed]

adv por arriba *or* encima ♦ *adj* (*cable*) aéreo ♦ *n* (*US*) = ~s; ~s *npl* (*expenses*) gastos *mpl* generales.

overhear [əuvə'hıə*] (*irreg*) *vt* oír por casualidad.

overheat [əuvə'hi:t] *vi* (*engine*) recalentarse.

overjoyed [əuvə'dʒɔıd] *adj* encantado, lleno de alegría.

overkill ['əuvəkıl] *n* excesos *mpl*.

overland ['əuvəlænd] *adj, adv* por tierra.

overlap [əuvə'læp] *vi* traslaparse.

overleaf [əuvə'li:f] *adv* al dorso.

overload [əuvə'ləud] *vt* sobrecargar.

overlook [əuvə'luk] *vt* (*have view of*) dar a, tener vistas a; (*miss: by mistake*) pasar por alto; (*excuse*) perdonar.

overnight [əuvə'naıt] *adv* durante la noche; (*fig*) de la noche a la mañana ♦ *adj* de noche; **to stay ~** pasar la noche.

overpass ['əuvəpɑːs] (*US*) *n* paso superior.

overpower [əuvə'pauə*] *vt* dominar; (*fig*) embargar; ~**ing** *adj* (*heat*) agobiante; (*smell*) penetrante.

overrate [əuvə'reıt] *vt* sobreestimar.

override [əuvə'raıd] (*irreg*) *vt* no hacer caso de; **overriding** *adj* predominante.

overrule [əuvə'ru:l] *vt* (*decision*) anular; (*claim*) denegar.

overrun [əuvə'rʌn] (*irreg*) *vt* (*country*) invadir; (*time limit*) rebasar, exceder.

overseas [əuvə'si:z] *adv* (*abroad: live*) en el extranjero; (*: travel*) al extranjero ♦ *adj* (*trade*) exterior; (*visitor*) extranjero.

overshadow [əuvə'ʃædəu] *vt*: **to be ~ed by** estar a la sombra de.

overshoot [əuvə'ʃu:t] (*irreg*) *vt* excederse.

oversight ['əuvəsaıt] *n* descuido.

oversleep [əuvə'sli:p] (*irreg*) *vi* quedarse dormido.

overstate [əuvə'steıt] *vt* exagerar.

overstep [əuvə'step] *vt*: **to ~ the mark** pasarse de la raya.

overt [əu'vɜːt] *adj* abierto.

overtake [əuvə'teık] (*irreg*) *vt* sobrepasar; (*BRIT: AUT*) adelantar.

overthrow [əuvə'θrəu] (*irreg*) *vt* (*government*) derrocar.

overtime ['əuvətaım] *n* horas *fpl* extraordinarias.

overtone ['əuvətəun] *n* (*fig*) tono.

overture ['əuvətʃuə*] *n* (*MUS*) obertura; (*fig*) preludio.

overturn [əuvə'tɜːn] *vt* volcar; (*fig: plan*) desbaratar; (*: government*) derrocar ♦ *vi* volcar.

overweight [əuvə'weıt] *adj* demasiado gordo *or* pesado.

overwhelm [əuvə'welm] *vt* aplastar; (*subj: emotion*) sobrecoger; ~**ing** *adj* (*victory, defeat*) arrollador(a); (*feeling*) irresistible.

overwork [əuvə'wɜːk] *n* trabajo excesivo ♦ *vi* trabajar demasiado.

overwrought [əuvə'rɔːt] *adj* sobreexcitado.

owe [əu] *vt*: **to ~ sb sth, to ~ sth to sb** deber algo a uno; **owing to** *prep* debido a, por causa de.

owl [aul] *n* búho, lechuza.

own [əun] *vt* tener, poseer ♦ *adj* propio; **a room of my ~** una habitación propia; **to get one's ~ back** tomar revancha; **on one's ~** solo, a solas; **~ up** *vi* confesar; ~**er** *n* dueño/a; ~**ership** *n* posesión *f*.

ox [ɔks] (*pl* ~**en**) *n* buey *m*.

oxtail ['ɔksteıl] *n*: **~ soup** sopa de rabo de buey.

oxygen ['ɔksıdʒən] *n* oxígeno; **~ mask/ tent** *n* máscara/tienda de oxígeno.

oyster ['ɔıstə*] *n* ostra.

oz. *abbr* = **ounce**(s).

ozone ['əuzəun] *n*: **~ layer** capa de ozono, capa ozónica.

P

p [piː] *abbr* = **penny; pence**.

P.A. *n abbr* = **personal assistant; public address system**.

p.a. *abbr* = **per annum**.

pa [pɑː] (*inf*) *n* papá *m*.

pace [peıs] *n* paso ♦ *vi*: **to ~ up and down** pasearse de un lado a otro; **to keep ~ with** llevar el mismo paso que;

~**maker** n (MED) regulador m cardíaco, marcapasos m inv; (SPORT: also: ~setter) liebre f.

Pacific [pə'sɪfɪk] n: the P~ (Ocean) el (Océano) Pacífico.

pacify ['pæsɪfaɪ] vt apaciguar.

pack [pæk] n (packet) paquete m; (of hounds) jauría; (of people) manada, bando; (of cards) baraja; (bundle) fardo; (US: of cigarettes) paquete m; (back ~) mochila ♦ vt (fill) llenar; (in suitcase etc) meter, poner; (cram) llenar, atestar; to ~ (one's bags) hacerse la maleta; to ~ sb off despachar a uno; ~ it in! (inf) ¡déjalo!

package ['pækɪdʒ] n paquete m; (bulky) bulto; (also: ~ deal) acuerdo global; ~ **holiday** n vacaciones fpl organizadas; ~ **tour** n viaje m organizado.

packed lunch n almuerzo frío.

packet ['pækɪt] n paquete m.

packing ['pækɪŋ] n embalaje m; ~ **case** n cajón m de embalaje.

pact [pækt] n pacto.

pad [pæd] n (of paper) bloc m; (cushion) cojinete m; (inf: home) casa ♦ vt rellenar; ~**ding** n (material) relleno.

paddle ['pædl] n (oar) canalete m; (US: for table tennis) paleta ♦ vt impulsar con canalete ♦ vi (with feet) chapotear; ~ **steamer** n vapor m de ruedas; **paddling pool** (BRIT) n estanque m de juegos.

paddock ['pædək] n corral m.

paddy field ['pædɪ-] n arrozal m.

padlock ['pædlɔk] n candado.

paediatrics [pi:dɪ'ætrɪks] (US **pediatrics**) n pediatría.

pagan ['peɪgən] adj, n pagano/a m/f.

page [peɪdʒ] n (of book) página; (of newspaper) plana; (also: ~ boy) paje m ♦ vt (in hotel etc) llamar por altavoz a.

pageant ['pædʒənt] n (procession) desfile m; (show) espectáculo m; ~**ry** n pompa.

paid [peɪd] pt, pp of **pay** ♦ adj (work) remunerado; (holiday) pagado; (official etc) a sueldo; to put ~ to (BRIT) acabar con.

pail [peɪl] n cubo, balde m.

pain [peɪn] n dolor m; to be in ~ sufrir; to take ~s to do sth tomarse grandes molestias en hacer algo; ~**ed** adj (expression) afligido; ~**ful** adj doloroso; (difficult) penoso; (disagreeable) desagradable; ~**fully** adv (fig: very) terriblemente; ~**killer** n analgésico; ~**less** adj que no causa dolor; ~**staking** ['peɪnzteɪkɪŋ] adj (person) concienzudo, esmerado.

paint [peɪnt] n pintura ♦ vt pintar; to ~ the door blue pintar la puerta de azul; ~**brush** n (artist's) pincel m; (decorator's) brocha; ~**er** n pintor(a) m/f; ~**ing** n pintura; ~**work** n pintura.

pair [pɛə*] n (of shoes, gloves etc) par m; (of people) pareja; a ~ of scissors unas tijeras; a ~ of trousers unos pantalones, un pantalón.

pajamas [pə'dʒɑ:məz] (US) npl pijama m.

Pakistan [pɑ:kɪ'stɑ:n] n Paquistán m; ~**i** adj, n paquistaní m/f.

pal [pæl] (inf) n compinche m/f, compañero/a.

palace ['pæləs] n palacio.

palatable ['pælɪtəbl] adj sabroso.

palate ['pælɪt] n paladar m.

palatial [pə'leɪʃəl] adj suntuoso, espléndido.

palaver [pə'lɑ:və*] (inf) n (fuss) lío.

pale [peɪl] adj (gen) pálido; (colour) claro ♦ n: to be beyond the ~ pasarse de la raya.

Palestine ['pælɪstaɪn] n Palestina; **Palestinian** [-'tɪnɪən] adj, n palestino/a m/f.

palette ['pælɪt] n paleta.

palings ['peɪlɪŋz] npl (fence) valla.

pall [pɔːl] n (of smoke) capa (de humo) ♦ vi perder el sabor.

pallet ['pælɪt] n (for goods) pallet m.

pallid ['pælɪd] adj pálido.

pallor ['pælə*] n palidez f.

palm [pɑːm] n (ANAT) palma; (also: ~ tree) palmera, palma ♦ vt: to ~ sth off on sb (inf) encajar algo a uno; **P~ Sunday** n Domingo de Ramos.

palpable ['pælpəbl] adj palpable.

paltry ['pɔːltrɪ] adj irrisorio.

pamper ['pæmpə*] *vt* mimar.

pamphlet ['pæmflət] *n* folleto.

pan [pæn] *n* (*also: sauce~*) cacerola, cazuela, olla; (: *also: frying ~*) sartén *f*.

panache [pə'næʃ] *n*: **with ~** con estilo.

Panama ['pænəmɑ:] *n* Panamá *m*; **the ~ Canal** el Canal de Panamá.

pancake ['pænkeɪk] *n* crepe *f*.

panda ['pændə] *n* panda *m*; **~ car** (*BRIT*) *n* coche *m* Z (*SP*).

pandemonium [pændɪ'məunɪəm] *n* jaleo.

pander ['pændə*] *vi*: **to ~ to** complacer a.

pane [peɪn] *n* cristal *m*.

panel ['pænl] *n* (*of wood etc*) panel *m*; (*RADIO*, *TV*) panel *m* de invitados; **~ling** (*US* **~ing**) *n* paneles *mpl*.

pang [pæŋ] *n*: **a ~ of regret** (una punzada de) remordimiento; **hunger ~s** dolores *mpl* del hambre.

panic ['pænɪk] *n* (terror *m*) pánico ♦ *vi* dejarse llevar por el pánico; **~ky** *adj* (*person*) asustadizo; **~-stricken** *adj* preso de pánico.

pansy ['pænzɪ] *n* (*BOT*) pensamiento; (*inf: pej*) maricón *m*.

pant [pænt] *vi* jadear.

panther ['pænθə*] *n* pantera *f*.

panties ['pæntɪz] *npl* bragas *fpl*, pantis *mpl*.

pantihose ['pæntɪhəuz] (*US*) *n* pantimedias *fpl*.

pantomime ['pæntəmaɪm] (*BRIT*) *n* revista musical representada en Navidad, basada en cuentos de hadas.

pantry ['pæntrɪ] *n* despensa.

pants [pænts] *n* (*BRIT: underwear: woman's*) bragas *fpl*; (: *man's*) calzoncillos *mpl*; (*US: trousers*) pantalones *mpl*.

papal ['peɪpəl] *adj* papal.

paper ['peɪpə*] *n* papel *m*; (*also: news~*) periódico, diario; (*academic essay*) ensayo; (*exam*) examen *m* ♦ *adj* de papel ♦ *vt* empapelar (*SP*), tapizar (*AM*); **~s** *npl* (*also: identity ~s*) papeles *mpl*, documentos *mpl*; **~back** *n* libro en rústica; **~ bag** *n* bolsa de papel; **~ clip** *n* clip *m*; **~ hankie** *n* pañuelo de papel; **~weight** *n* pisapapeles *m inv*;

~work *n* trabajo administrativo.

papier-mâché ['pæpɪeɪ'mæʃeɪ] *n* cartón *m* piedra.

paprika ['pæprɪkə] *n* pimentón *m*.

par [pɑ:*] *n* par *f*; (*GOLF*) par *m*; **to be on a ~ with** estar a la par con.

parable ['pærəbl] *n* parábola.

parachute ['pærəʃu:t] *n* paracaídas *m inv*.

parade [pə'reɪd] *n* desfile *m* ♦ *vt* (*show off*) hacer alarde de ♦ *vi* desfilar; (*MIL*) pasar revista.

paradise ['pærədaɪs] *n* paraíso.

paradox ['pærədɔks] *n* paradoja; **~ically** [-'dɔksɪklɪ] *adv* paradójicamente.

paraffin ['pærəfɪn] (*BRIT*) *n* (*also: ~ oil*) parafina.

paragon ['pærəgən] *n* modelo.

paragraph ['pærəgrɑ:f] *n* párrafo.

Paraguay ['pærəgwaɪ] *n* Paraguay *m*.

parallel ['pærəlɛl] *adj* en paralelo; (*fig*) semejante ♦ *n* (*line*) paralela; (*fig*, *GEO*) paralelo.

paralyse ['pærəlaɪz] *vt* paralizar.

paralysis [pə'rælɪsɪs] *n* parálisis *f inv*.

paralyze ['pærəlaɪz] (*US*) *vt* = **paralyse**.

paramount ['pærəmaunt] *adj*: **of ~ importance** de suma importancia.

paranoid ['pærənɔɪd] *adj* (*person*, *feeling*) paranoico.

paraphernalia [pærəfə'neɪlɪə] *n* (*gear*) avíos *mpl*.

paraphrase ['pærəfreɪz] *vt* parafrasear.

parasite ['pærəsaɪt] *n* parásito/a.

parasol ['pærəsɔl] *n* sombrilla, quitasol *m*.

paratrooper ['pærətru:pə*] *n* paracaidista *m/f*.

parcel ['pɑ:sl] *n* paquete *m* ♦ *vt* (*also: ~ up*) empaquetar, embalar.

parch [pɑ:tʃ] *vt* secar, resecar; **~ed** *adj* (*person*) muerto de sed.

parchment ['pɑ:tʃmənt] *n* pergamino.

pardon ['pɑ:dn] *n* (*LAW*) indulto ♦ *vt* perdonar; **~ me!, I beg your ~!** (*I'm sorry!*) ¡perdone usted!; (**I beg your**) **~?, ~ me?** (*what did you say?*) ¿cómo?

parent ['pɛərənt] *n* (*mother*) madre *f*; (*father*) padre *m*; **~s** *npl* padres *mpl*; **~al** [pə'rɛntl] *adj* paternal/maternal.

parentheses [pə'rɛnθɪsiːz] *npl of* **parenthesis**.
parenthesis [pə'rɛnθɪsɪs] (*pl* **parentheses**) *n* paréntesis *m inv*.
Paris ['pærɪs] *n* París.
parish ['pærɪʃ] *n* parroquia.
Parisian [pə'rɪzɪən] *adj, n* parisiense *m/f*.
parity ['pærɪtɪ] *n* paridad *f*, igualdad *f*.
park [pɑːk] *n* parque *m* ♦ *vt* aparcar, estacionar ♦ *vi* aparcar, estacionarse.
parka ['pɑːkə] *n* anorak *m*.
parking ['pɑːkɪŋ] *n* aparcamiento, estacionamiento; **"no ~"** "prohibido estacionarse"; **~ lot** (*US*) *n* parking *m*; **~ meter** *n* parquímetro; **~ ticket** *n* multa de aparcamiento.
parlance ['pɑːləns] *n* lenguaje *m*.
parliament ['pɑːləmənt] *n* parlamento; (*Spanish*) Cortes *fpl*; **~ary** [-'mɛntərɪ] *adj* parlamentario.
parlour ['pɑːlə*] (*US* **parlor**) *n* sala de recibo, salón *m*, living (*AM*).
parochial [pə'rəukɪəl] (*pej*) *adj* de miras estrechas.
parody ['pærədɪ] *n* parodia.
parole [pə'rəul] *n*: **on ~** libre bajo palabra.
parquet ['pɑːkeɪ] *n*: **~ floor(ing)** parquet *m*.
parrot ['pærət] *n* loro, papagayo.
parry ['pærɪ] *vt* parar.
parsimonious [pɑːsɪ'məunɪəs] *adj* tacaño.
parsley ['pɑːslɪ] *n* perejil *m*.
parsnip ['pɑːsnɪp] *n* chirivía.
parson ['pɑːsn] *n* cura *m*.
part [pɑːt] *n* (*gen, MUS*) parte *f*; (*bit*) trozo; (*of machine*) pieza; (*THEATRE etc*) papel *m*; (*of serial*) entrega; (*US: in hair*) raya ♦ *adv* = **partly** ♦ *vt* separar ♦ *vi* (*people*) separarse; (*crowd*) apartarse; **to take ~ in** tomar parte *or* participar en; **to take sth in good ~** tomar algo en buena parte; **to take sb's ~** defender a uno; **for my ~** por mi parte; **for the most ~** en su mayor parte; **to ~ one's hair** hacerse la raya; **~ with** *vt fus* ceder, entregar; (*money*) pagar; **~ exchange** (*BRIT*) *n*: **in ~ exchange** como parte del pago.

partial ['pɑːʃl] *adj* parcial; **to be ~ to** ser aficionado a.
participant [pɑː'tɪsɪpənt] *n* (*in competition*) concursante *m/f*; (*in campaign etc*) participante *m/f*.
participate [pɑː'tɪsɪpeɪt] *vi*: **to ~ in** participar en; **participation** [-'peɪʃən] *n* participación *f*.
participle ['pɑːtɪsɪpl] *n* participio.
particle ['pɑːtɪkl] *n* partícula; (*of dust*) grano.
particular [pə'tɪkjulə*] *adj* (*special*) particular; (*concrete*) concreto; (*given*) determinado; (*fussy*) quisquilloso; (*demanding*) exigente; **~s** *npl* (*information*) datos *mpl*; (*details*) pormenores *mpl*; **in ~** en particular; **~ly** *adv* (*in particular*) sobre todo; (*difficult, good etc*) especialmente.
parting ['pɑːtɪŋ] *n* (*act of*) separación *f*; (*farewell*) despedida; (*BRIT: in hair*) raya ♦ *adj* de despedida.
partisan [pɑːtɪ'zæn] *adj* partidista ♦ *n* partidario/a.
partition [pɑː'tɪʃən] *n* (*POL*) división *f*; (*wall*) tabique *m*.
partly ['pɑːtlɪ] *adv* en parte.
partner ['pɑːtnə*] *n* (*COMM*) socio/a; (*SPORT, at dance*) pareja; (*spouse*) cónyuge *m/f*; (*boy/girlfriend etc*) compañero/a; **~ship** *n* asociación *f*; (*COMM*) sociedad *f*.
partridge ['pɑːtrɪdʒ] *n* perdiz *f*.
part-time *adj, adv* a tiempo parcial.
party ['pɑːtɪ] *n* (*POL*) partido; (*celebration*) fiesta; (*group*) grupo; (*LAW*) parte *f* interesada ♦ *cpd* (*POL*) de partido; **~ dress** *n* vestido de fiesta; **~ line** *n* (*TEL*) línea compartida.
pass [pɑːs] *vt* (*time, object*) pasar; (*place*) pasar por; (*overtake*) rebasar; (*exam*) aprobar; (*approve*) aprobar ♦ *vi* pasar; (*SCOL*) aprobar, ser aprobado ♦ *n* (*permit*) permiso; (*membership card*) carnet *m*; (*in mountains*) puerto, desfiladero; (*SPORT*) pase *m*; (*SCOL: also: ~ mark*): **to get a ~ in** aprobar en; **to ~ sth through sth** pasar algo por algo; **to make a ~ at sb** (*inf*) hacer proposiciones a uno; **~ away** *vi* falle-

cer; ~ **by** *vi* pasar ♦ *vt* (*ignore*) pasar por alto; ~ **for** *vt fus* pasar por; ~ **on** *vt* transmitir; ~ **out** *vi* desmayarse; ~ **up** *vt* (*opportunity*) renunciar a; ~**able** *adj* (*road*) transitable; (*tolerable*) pasable.

passage ['pæsɪdʒ] *n* (*also*: ~**way**) pasillo; (*act of passing*) tránsito; (*fare, in book*) pasaje *m*; (*by boat*) travesía; (*ANAT*) tubo.

passbook ['pɑːsbuk] *n* libreta de banco.

passenger ['pæsɪndʒə*] *n* pasajero/a, viajero/a.

passer-by [pɑːsə'baɪ] *n* transeúnte *m/f*.

passing ['pɑːsɪŋ] *adj* (*gen*) in ~ de paso; ~ **place** *n* (*AUT*) apartadero.

passion ['pæʃən] *n* pasión *f*; ~**ate** *adj* apasionado.

passive ['pæsɪv] *adj* (*gen, also* LING) pasivo.

Passover ['pɑːsəuvə*] *n* Pascua (de los judíos).

passport ['pɑːspɔːt] *n* pasaporte *m*; ~ **control** *n* control *m* de pasaporte.

password ['pɑːswəːd] *n* contraseña.

past [pɑːst] *prep* (*in front of*) por delante de; (*further than*) más allá de; (*later than*) después de ♦ *adj* pasado; (*president etc*) antiguo ♦ *n* (*time*) pasado; (*of person*) antecedentes *mpl*; **he's** ~ **forty** tiene más de cuarenta años; **ten/ quarter** ~ **eight** las ocho y diez/cuarto; **for the** ~ **few/3 days** durante los últimos días/últimos 3 días; **to run** ~ **sb** pasar a uno corriendo.

pasta ['pæstə] *n* pasta.

paste [peɪst] *n* pasta; (*glue*) engrudo ♦ *vt* pegar.

pastel ['pæstl] *adj* pastel.

pasteurized ['pæstəraɪzd] *adj* pasteurizado.

pastille ['pæstl] *n* pastilla.

pastime ['pɑːstaɪm] *n* pasatiempo.

pastry ['peɪstrɪ] *n* (*dough*) pasta; (*cake*) pastel *m*.

pasture ['pɑːstʃə*] *n* pasto.

pasty¹ ['pæstɪ] *n* empanada.

pasty² ['peɪstɪ] *adj* (*complexion*) pálido.

pat [pæt] *vt* dar una palmadita a; (*dog etc*) acariciar.

patch [pætʃ] *n* (*of material, eye* ~) parche *m*; (*mended part*) remiendo; (*of land*) terreno ♦ *vt* remendar; (**to go through**) **a bad** ~ (pasar por) una mala racha; ~ **up** *vt* reparar; (*quarrel*) hacer las paces en; ~**work** *n* labor *m* de retazos; ~**y** *adj* desigual.

pâté ['pæteɪ] *n* paté *m*.

patent ['peɪtnt] *n* patente *f* ♦ *vt* patentar ♦ *adj* patente, evidente; ~ **leather** *n* charol *m*.

paternal [pə'tɔːnl] *adj* paternal; (*relation*) paterno.

paternity [pə'tɔːnɪtɪ] *n* paternidad *f*.

path [pɑːθ] *n* camino, sendero; (*trail, track*) pista; (*of missile*) trayectoria.

pathetic [pə'θetɪk] *adj* patético, lastimoso; (*very bad*) malísimo.

pathological [pæθə'lɔdʒɪkəl] *adj* patológico.

pathology [pə'θɔlədʒɪ] *n* patología.

pathos ['peɪθɔs] *n* patetismo.

pathway ['pɑːθweɪ] *n* sendero, vereda.

patience ['peɪʃns] *n* paciencia; (*BRIT: CARDS*) solitario.

patient ['peɪʃnt] *n* paciente *m/f* ♦ *adj* paciente, sufrido.

patio ['pætɪəu] *n* patio.

patriot ['peɪtrɪət] *n* patriota *m/f*; ~**ic** [pætrɪ'ɔtɪk] *adj* patriótico.

patrol [pə'trəul] *n* patrulla ♦ *vt* patrullar por; ~ **car** *n* coche *m* patrulla; ~**man** (*US*) *n* policía *m*.

patron ['peɪtrən] *n* (*in shop*) cliente *m/f*; (*of charity*) patrocinador(a) *m/f*; ~ **of the arts** mecenas *m*; ~**age** ['pætrənɪdʒ] *n* patrocinio; ~**ize** ['pætrənaɪz] *vt* (*shop*) ser cliente de; (*artist etc*) proteger; (*look down on*) condescender con; ~ **saint** *n* santo/a patrón/ona *m/f*.

patter ['pætə*] *n* golpeteo; (*sales talk*) labia ♦ *vi* (*rain*) tamborilear.

pattern ['pætən] *n* (*SEWING*) patrón *m*; (*design*) dibujo.

paunch [pɔːntʃ] *n* panza, barriga.

pauper ['pɔːpə*] *n* pobre *m/f*.

pause [pɔːz] *n* pausa ♦ *vi* hacer una pausa.

pave [peɪv] *vt* pavimentar; **to** ~ **the way for** preparar el terreno para.

pavement ['peɪvmənt] (*BRIT*) n acera (*SP*), vereda (*AM*).
pavilion [pə'vɪlɪən] n (*SPORT*) caseta.
paving ['peɪvɪŋ] n pavimento, enlosado; ~ **stone** n losa.
paw [pɔː] n pata.
pawn [pɔːn] n (*CHESS*) peón m; (*fig*) instrumento ♦ vt empeñar; ~ **broker** n prestamista m/f; ~**shop** n monte m de piedad.
pay [peɪ] (*pt, pp* **paid**) n (*wage etc*) sueldo, salario ♦ vt pagar ♦ vi (*be profitable*) rendir; to ~ **attention** (to) prestar atención (a); **to ~ sb a visit** hacer una visita a uno; **to ~ one's respects to sb** presentar sus respetos a uno; ~ **back** vt (*money*) reembolsar; (*person*) pagar; ~ **for** vt *fus* pagar; ~ **in** vt ingresar; ~ **off** vt saldar ♦ vi (*scheme, decision*) dar resultado; ~ **up** vt pagar (de mala gana); ~**able** *adj*: ~able to pagadero a; ~ **day** n día m de paga; ~**ee** n portador(a) m/f; ~ **envelope** (*US*) n = ~ **packet**; ~**ment** n pago; monthly ~**ment** mensualidad f; ~ **packet** (*BRIT*) n sobre m (de paga); ~**phone** n teléfono público; ~**roll** n nómina; ~ **slip** n recibo de sueldo.
PC n *abbr* = **personal computer**; (*BRIT*) = **police constable**.
p.c. *abbr* = **per cent**.
pea [piː] n guisante m (*SP*), chícharo (*AM*), arveja (*AM*).
peace [piːs] n paz f; (*calm*) paz f, tranquilidad f; ~**ful** *adj* (*gentle*) pacífico; (*calm*) tranquilo, sosegado.
peach [piːtʃ] n melocotón m (*SP*), durazno (*AM*).
peacock ['piːkɔk] n pavo real.
peak [piːk] n (*of mountain*) cumbre f, cima; (*of cap*) visera; (*fig*) cumbre f; ~ **hours** npl = ~ **period**; ~ **period** n horas fpl punta.
peal [piːl] n (*of bells*) repique m; ~ **of** laughter carcajada.
peanut ['piːnʌt] n cacahuete m (*SP*), maní m (*AM*); ~ **butter** manteca de cacahuete or maní.
pear [pɛə*] n pera.
pearl [pəːl] n perla.

peasant ['pɛznt] n campesino/a.
peat [piːt] n turba.
pebble ['pɛbl] n guijarro.
peck [pɛk] vt (*also*: ~ at) picotear ♦ n picotazo; (*kiss*) besito; ~**ing order** n orden m de jerarquía; ~**ish** (*BRIT*: *inf*) *adj*: **I feel** ~**ish** tengo ganas de picar algo.
peculiar [pɪ'kjuːlɪə*] *adj* (*odd*) extraño, raro; (*typical*) propio, característico; ~ **to** propio de; ~**ity** [pɪkjuːlɪ'ærɪtɪ] n peculiaridad f, característica.
pedal ['pɛdl] n pedal m ♦ vi pedalear.
pedantic [pɪ'dæntɪk] *adj* pedante.
peddler ['pɛdlə*] n: **drugs** ~ traficante m/f; camello.
pedestrian [pɪ'dɛstrɪən] n peatón/ona m/f ♦ *adj* pedestre; ~ **crossing** (*BRIT*) n paso de peatones.
pediatrics [piːdɪ'ætrɪks] (*US*) n = **paediatrics**.
pedigree ['pɛdɪgriː] n genealogía; (*of animal*) raza, pedigrí m ♦ *cpd* (*animal*) de raza, de casta.
pee [piː] (*inf*) vi mear.
peek [piːk] vi mirar a hurtadillas.
peel [piːl] n piel f; (*of orange, lemon*) cáscara; (: *removed*) peladuras fpl ♦ vt pelar ♦ vi (*paint etc*) desconcharse; (*wallpaper*) despegarse, desprenderse; (*skin*) pelar.
peep [piːp] n (*BRIT*: *look*) mirada furtiva; (*sound*) pío ♦ vi (*BRIT*: *look*) mirar furtivamente; ~ **out** vi salir (un poco); ~**hole** n mirilla.
peer [pɪə*] vi: to ~ **at** esudriñar ♦ n (*noble*) par m; (*equal*) igual m; (*contemporary*) contemporáneo/a; ~**age** n nobleza.
peeved [piːvd] *adj* enojado.
peg [pɛg] n (*for coat etc*) gancho, colgadero; (*BRIT*: *also*: **clothes** ~) pinza.
Pekingese [piːkɪ'niːz] n (*dog*) pequinés/esa m/f.
pelican ['pɛlɪkən] n pelícano; ~ **crossing** (*BRIT*) n (*AUT*) paso de peatones señalizado.
pellet ['pɛlɪt] n bolita; (*bullet*) perdigón m.
pelt [pɛlt] vt: **to ~ sb with sth** arrojarle

algo a uno ♦ *vi* (*rain*) llover a cántaros: (*inf: run*) correr ♦ *n* pellejo.

pen [pɛn] *n* (*fountain* ~) pluma; (*ballpoint* ~) bolígrafo; (*for sheep*) redil *m*.

penal ['piːnl] *adj* penal; ~**ize** *vt* castigar.

penalty ['pɛnltɪ] *n* (*gen*) pena; (*fine*) multa; ~ (**kick**) *n* (*FOOTBALL*) penalty *m*; (*RUGBY*) golpe *m* de castigo.

penance ['pɛnəns] *n* penitencia.

pence [pɛns] *npl cf* **penny**.

pencil ['pɛnsl] *n* lápiz *m*, lapicero (*AM*); ~ **case** *n* estuche *m*; ~ **sharpener** *n* sacapuntas *m inv*.

pendant ['pɛndnt] *n* pendiente *m*.

pending ['pɛndɪŋ] *prep* antes de ♦ *adj* pendiente.

pendulum ['pɛndjuləm] *n* péndulo.

penetrate ['pɛnɪtreɪt] *vt* penetrar; **penetrating** *adj* penetrante.

penfriend ['pɛnfrɛnd] (*BRIT*) *n* amigo/a por carta.

penguin ['pɛŋgwɪn] *n* pingüino.

penicillin [pɛnɪ'sɪlɪn] *n* penicilina.

peninsula [pə'nɪnsjulə] *n* península.

penis ['piːnɪs] *n* pene *m*.

penitent ['pɛnɪtnt] *adj* arrepentido.

penitentiary [pɛnɪ'tɛnʃərɪ] (*US*) *n* cárcel *f*, presidio.

penknife ['pɛnnaɪf] *n* navaja.

pen name *n* seudónimo.

penniless ['pɛnɪlɪs] *adj* sin dinero.

penny ['pɛnɪ] (*pl* **pennies** *or* (*BRIT*) **pence**) *n* penique *m*; (*US*) centavo.

penpal ['pɛnpæl] *n* amigo/a por carta.

pension ['pɛnʃən] *n* (*state benefit*) jubilación *f*; ~**er** (*BRIT*) *n* jubilado/a; ~**fund** *n* caja *or* fondo de pensiones.

pensive ['pɛnsɪv] *adj* pensativo; (*withdrawn*) preocupado.

pentagon ['pɛntəgən] *n*: **the P~** (*US: POL*) el Pentágono.

Pentecost ['pɛntɪkɔst] *n* Pentecostés *m*.

penthouse ['pɛnthaus] *n* ático de lujo.

pent-up ['pɛntʌp] *adj* reprimido.

people ['piːpl] *npl* gente *f*; (*citizens*) pueblo, ciudadanos *mpl*; (*POL*): **the ~** el pueblo ♦ *n* (*nation, race*) pueblo, nación *f*; **several ~ came** vinieron varias personas; ~ **say that** ... dice la gente

que ....

pep [pɛp] (*inf*) *n* energía; ~ **up** *vt* animar.

pepper ['pɛpə*] *n* (*spice*) pimienta; (*vegetable*) pimiento ♦ *vt*: **to ~ with** (*fig*) salpicar de; ~**mint** *n* (*sweet*) pastilla de menta.

peptalk ['pɛptɔːk] *n*: **to give sb a ~** darle a uno una inyección de ánimo.

per [pəː*] *prep* por; ~ **day/person** por día/persona; ~ **annum** al año; ~ **capita** *adj, adv* per capita.

perceive [pə'siːv] *vt* percibir; (*realize*) darse cuenta de.

per cent *n* por ciento.

percentage [pə'sɛntɪdʒ] *n* porcentaje *m*.

perception [pə'sɛpʃən] *n* percepción *f*; (*insight*) perspicacia; (*opinion etc*) opinión *f*; **perceptive** [-'sɛptɪv] *adj* perspicaz.

perch [pəːtʃ] *n* (*fish*) perca; (*for bird*) percha ♦ *vi*: **to ~** (**on**) (*bird*) posarse (en); (*person*) encaramarse (en).

percolator ['pəːkəleɪtə*] *n* (*also: coffee* ~) cafetera de filtro.

peremptory [pə'rɛmptərɪ] *adj* perentorio; (*person*) autoritario.

perennial [pə'rɛnɪəl] *adj* perenne.

perfect [*adj, n* 'pəːfɪkt, *vb* pə'fɛkt] *adj* perfecto ♦ *n* (*also:* ~ **tense**) perfecto ♦ *vt* perfeccionar; ~**ly** ['pəːfɪktlɪ] *adv* perfectamente.

perforate ['pəːfəreɪt] *vt* perforar.

perform [pə'fɔːm] *vt* (*carry out*) realizar, llevar a cabo; (*THEATRE*) representar; (*piece of music*) interpretar ♦ *vi* (*well, badly*) funcionar; ~**ance** *n* (*of a play*) representación *f*; (*of actor, athlete etc*) actuación *f*; (*of car, engine, company*) rendimiento; (*of economy*) resultados *mpl*; ~**er** *n* (*actor*) actor *m*, actriz *f*.

perfume ['pəːfjuːm] *n* perfume *m*.

perfunctory [pə'fʌŋktərɪ] *adj* superficial.

perhaps [pə'hæps] *adv* quizá(s), tal vez.

peril ['pɛrɪl] *n* peligro, riesgo.

perimeter [pə'rɪmɪtə*] *n* perímetro.

period ['pɪərɪəd] *n* período; (*SCOL*) clase *f*; (*full stop*) punto; (*MED*) regla ♦ *adj* (*costume, furniture*) de época; ~**ic(al)**

[-'ɔdɪk(l)] *adj* periódico; ~**ical** [-'ɔdɪkl] *n* periódico; ~**ically** [-'ɔdɪklɪ] *adv* de vez en cuando, cada cierto tiempo.

peripheral [pə'rɪfərəl] *adj* periférico ♦ *n* (*COMPUT*) periférico, unidad *f* periférica.

perish ['perɪʃ] *vi* perecer; (*decay*) echarse a perder; ~**able** *adj* perecedero.

perjury ['pɜːdʒərɪ] *n* (*LAW*) perjurio.

perk [pɜːk] *n* extra *m*; ~ **up** *vi* (*cheer up*) animarse; ~**y** *adj* alegre, despabilado.

perm [pɜːm] *n* permanente *f*.

permanent ['pɜːmənənt] *adj* permanente.

permeate ['pɜːmɪeɪt] *vi* penetrar, trascender ♦ *vt* penetrar, trascender a.

permissible [pə'mɪsɪbl] *adj* permisible, lícito.

permission [pə'mɪʃən] *n* permiso.

permissive [pə'mɪsɪv] *adj* permisivo.

permit [*n* 'pɜːmɪt, *vt* pə'mɪt] *n* permiso, licencia ♦ *vt* permitir.

pernicious [pɜː'nɪʃəs] *adj* nocivo; (*MED*) pernicioso.

perpetrate ['pɜːpɪtreɪt] *vt* cometer.

perpetual [pə'petjuəl] *adj* perpetuo.

perpetuate [pə'petjueɪt] *vt* perpetuar.

perplex [pə'pleks] *vt* dejar perplejo.

persecute ['pɜːsɪkjuːt] *vt* perseguir.

perseverance [pɜːsɪ'vɪərəns] *n* perseverancia.

persevere [pɜːsɪ'vɪə*] *vi* persistir.

Persian ['pɜːʃən] *adj*, *n* persa *m/f*; **the** (~) **Gulf** *n* el Golfo Pérsico.

persist [pə'sɪst] *vi*: **to** ~ (**in doing sth**) persistir (en hacer algo); ~**ence** *n* empeño; ~**ent** *adj* persistente; (*determined*) porfiado.

person ['pɜːsn] *n* persona; **in** ~ en persona; ~**al** *adj* personal; individual; (*visit*) en persona; ~**al assistant** *n* ayudante *m/f* personal; ~**al call** *n* (*TEL*) llamada persona a persona; ~**al column** *n* anuncios *mpl* personales; ~**al computer** *n* ordenador *m* personal; ~**ality** [-'nælɪtɪ] *n* personalidad *f*; ~**ally** *adv* personalmente; (*in person*) en persona; **to take sth** ~**ally** tomarse algo a mal; ~**al**

organizer *n* agenda; ~**ify** [-'sɔnɪfaɪ] *vt* encarnar.

personnel [pɜːsə'nel] *n* personal *m*.

perspective [pə'spektɪv] *n* perspectiva.

Perspex ['pɜːspeks] ® *n* plexiglás *m*.

perspiration [pɜːspɪ'reɪʃən] *n* transpiración *f*.

persuade [pə'sweɪd] *vt*: **to** ~ **sb to do sth** persuadir a uno para que haga algo.

pertaining [pɜː'teɪnɪŋ]: ~ **to** *prep* relacionado con.

pertinent ['pɜːtɪnənt] *adj* pertinente, a propósito.

Peru [pə'ruː] *n* el Perú.

peruse [pə'ruːz] *vt* leer con detención, examinar.

Peruvian [pə'ruːvɪən] *adj*, *n* peruano/a *m/f*.

pervade [pə'veɪd] *vt* impregnar, infundirse en.

perverse [pə'vɜːs] *adj* perverso; (*wayward*) travieso.

pervert [*n* 'pɜːvɜːt, *vb* pə'vɜːt] *n* pervertido/a ♦ *vt* pervertir; (*truth, sb's words*) tergiversar.

pessimist ['pesɪmɪst] *n* pesimista *m/f*; ~**ic** [-'mɪstɪk] *adj* pesimista.

pest [pest] *n* (*insect*) insecto nocivo; (*fig*) lata, molestia.

pester ['pestə*] *vt* molestar, acosar.

pesticide ['pestɪsaɪd] *n* pesticida *m*.

pet [pet] *n* animal *m* doméstico ♦ *cpd* favorito ♦ *vt* acariciar ♦ *vi* (*inf*) besuquearse; **teacher's** ~ favorito/a (del profesor); ~ **hate** manía.

petal ['petl] *n* pétalo.

peter ['piːtə*]: **to** ~ **out** *vi* agotarse, acabarse.

petite [pə'tiːt] *adj* chiquita.

petition [pə'tɪʃən] *n* petición *f*.

petrified ['petrɪfaɪd] *adj* horrorizado.

petrol ['petrəl] (*BRIT*) *n* gasolina; **two/ four-star** ~ gasolina normal/súper; ~ **can** *n* bidón *m* de gasolina.

petroleum [pə'trəʊlɪəm] *n* petróleo.

petrol: ~ **pump** (*BRIT*) *n* (*in garage*) surtidor *m* de gasolina; ~ **station** (*BRIT*) *n* gasolinera; ~ **tank** (*BRIT*) *n* depósito (de gasolina).

petticoat ['petɪkəʊt] *n* enaguas *fpl*.

petty ['pɛtɪ] *adj* (*mean*) mezquino; (*unimportant*) insignificante; ~ **cash** *n* dinero para gastos menores; ~ **officer** *n* contramaestre *m*.

petulant ['pɛtjulənt] *adj* malhumorado.

pew [pjuː] *n* banco.

pewter ['pjuːtə*] *n* peltre *m*.

phantom ['fæntəm] *n* fantasma *m*.

pharmacist ['fɑːməsɪst] *n* farmacéutico/a.

pharmacy ['fɑːməsɪ] *n* farmacia.

phase [feɪz] *n* fase *f* ♦ *vt*: **to ~ sth in/out** introducir/retirar algo por etapas.

Ph.D. *abbr* = **Doctor of Philosophy**.

pheasant ['fɛznt] *n* faisán *m*.

phenomenon [fə'nɔmɪnən] (*pl* **phenomena**) *n* fenómeno.

philanthropist [fɪ'lænθrəpɪst] *n* filántropo/a.

Philippines ['fɪlɪpiːnz] *npl*: **the ~** las Filipinas.

philosopher [fɪ'lɔsəfə*] *n* filósofo/a.

philosophy [fɪ'lɔsəfɪ] *n* filosofía.

phlegm [flɛm] *n* flema; ~**atic** [flɛg-'mætɪk] *adj* flemático.

phobia ['fəubjə] *n* fobia.

phone [fəun] *n* teléfono ♦ *vt* telefonear, llamar por teléfono; **to be on the ~** tener teléfono; (*be calling*) estar hablando por teléfono; ~ **back** *vt, vi* volver a llamar; ~ **up** *vt, vi* llamar por teléfono; ~ **book** *n* guía telefónica; ~ **box** (*BRIT*) *n* = ~ **booth**; ~ **booth** *n* cabina telefónica; ~ **call** *n* llamada (telefónica); ~**-in** (*BRIT*) *n* (*RADIO*, *TV*) programa *m* de participación (telefónica).

phonetics [fə'nɛtɪks] *n* fonética.

phoney ['fəunɪ] *adj* falso.

phonograph ['fəunəgræf] (*US*) *n* fonógrafo, tocadiscos *m inv*.

photo ['fəutəu] *n* foto *f*.

photo... ['fəutəu] *prefix*: ~**copier** *n* fotocopiadora; ~**copy** *n* fotocopia ♦ *vt* fotocopiar.

photograph ['fəutəgrɑːf] *n* fotografía ♦ *vt* fotografiar; ~**er** [fə'tɔgrəfə*] *n* fotógrafo; ~**y** [fə'tɔgrəfɪ] *n* fotografía.

phrase [freɪz] *n* frase *f* ♦ *vt* expresar; ~ **book** *n* libro de frases.

physical ['fɪzɪkl] *adj* físico; ~ **education** *n* educación *f* física; ~**ly** *adv* físicamente.

physician [fɪ'zɪʃən] *n* médico/a.

physicist ['fɪzɪsɪst] *n* físico/a.

physics ['fɪzɪks] *n* física.

physiotherapy [fɪzɪəu'θɛrəpɪ] *n* fisioterapia.

physique [fɪ'ziːk] *n* físico.

pianist ['piːənɪst] *n* pianista *m/f*.

piano [pɪ'ænəu] *n* piano.

piccolo ['pɪkələu] *n* (*MUS*) flautín *m*.

pick [pɪk] *n* (*tool: also:* ~-*axe*) pico, piqueta ♦ *vt* (*select*) elegir, escoger; (*gather*) coger (*SP*), recoger; (*remove, take out*) sacar, quitar; (*lock*) abrir con ganzúa; **take your ~** escoja lo que quiera; **the ~ of** lo mejor de; **to ~ one's nose/teeth** hurgarse las narices/limpiarse los dientes; **to ~ a quarrel with sb** meterse con alguien; ~ **at** *vt fus*: **to ~ at one's food** comer con poco apetito; ~ **on** *vt fus* (*person*) meterse con; ~ **out** *vt* escoger; (*distinguish*) identificar; ~ **up** *vi* (*improve: sales*) ir mejor; (*: patient*) reponerse; (*: FINANCE*) recobrarse ♦ *vt* recoger; (*learn*) aprender; (*POLICE: arrest*) detener; (*person: for sex*) ligar; (*RADIO*) captar; **to ~ up speed** acelerarse; **to ~ o.s. up** levantarse.

picket ['pɪkɪt] *n* piquete *m* ♦ *vt* piquetear.

pickle ['pɪkl] *n* (*also:* ~s: *as condiment*) escabeche *m*; (*fig: mess*) apuro ♦ *vt* encurtir.

pickpocket ['pɪkpɔkɪt] *n* carterista *m/f*.

pickup ['pɪkʌp] *n* (*small truck*) furgoneta.

picnic ['pɪknɪk] *n* merienda ♦ *vi* ir de merienda.

picture ['pɪktʃə*] *n* cuadro; (*painting*) pintura; (*photograph*) fotografía; (*TV*) imagen *f*; (*film*) película; (*fig: description*) descripción *f*; (*: situation*) situación *f* ♦ *vt* (*imagine*) imaginar; ~**s** *npl*: **the ~s** (*BRIT*) el cine; ~ **book** *n* libro de dibujos.

picturesque [pɪktʃə'rɛsk] *adj* pintoresco.

pie [paɪ] *n* pastel *m*; (*open*) tarta; (*small: of meat*) empanada.

piece [piːs] n pedazo, trozo; (of cake) trozo; (item): a ~ of clothing/furniture/ advice una prenda (de vestir)/un mueble/un consejo ♦ vt: to ~ together juntar; (TECH) armar; to take to ~s desmontar; ~meal adv poco a poco; ~work n trabajo a destajo.

pie chart n gráfico de sectores or tarta.

pier [pɪə*] n muelle m, embarcadero.

pierce [pɪəs] vt perforar.

piercing ['pɪəsɪŋ] adj penetrante.

piety ['paɪətɪ] n piedad f.

pig [pɪg] n cerdo (SP), puerco (SP), chancho (AM); (pej: unkind person) asqueroso; (: greedy person) glotón/ona m/f.

pigeon ['pɪdʒən] n paloma; (as food) pichón m; ~hole n casilla.

piggy bank ['pɪgɪ-] n hucha (en forma de cerdito).

pigheaded ['pɪg'hɛdɪd] adj terco, testarudo.

piglet ['pɪglɪt] n cochinillo.

pigskin ['pɪgskɪn] n piel f de cerdo.

pigsty ['pɪgstaɪ] n pocilga.

pigtail ['pɪgteɪl] n (girl's) trenza; (Chinese, TAUR) coleta.

pike [paɪk] n (fish) lucio.

pilchard ['pɪltʃəd] n sardina.

pile [paɪl] n montón m; (of carpet, cloth) pelo ♦ vt (also: ~ up) amontonar; (fig) acumular ♦ vi (also: ~ up) amontonarse; acumularse; ~ into vt fus (car) meterse en.

piles [paɪlz] npl (MED) almorranas fpl, hemorroides mpl.

pile-up n (AUT) accidente m múltiple.

pilfering ['pɪlfərɪŋ] n ratería.

pilgrim ['pɪlgrɪm] n peregrino/a; ~age n peregrinación f, romería.

pill [pɪl] n píldora; the ~ la píldora.

pillage ['pɪlɪdʒ] vt pillar, saquear.

pillar ['pɪlə*] n pilar m; ~ box (BRIT) n buzón m.

pillion ['pɪljən] n (of motorcycle) asiento trasero.

pillory ['pɪlərɪ] vt poner en la picota, criticar con dureza.

pillow ['pɪləu] n almohada; ~case n funda.

pilot ['paɪlət] n piloto ♦ cpd (scheme

etc) piloto ♦ vt pilotar; ~ light n piloto.

pimp [pɪmp] n chulo (SP), cafiche m (AM).

pimple ['pɪmpl] n grano.

pin [pɪn] n alfiler m ♦ vt prender (con alfiler); ~s and needles hormigueo; to ~ sb down (fig) hacer que uno concrete; to ~ sth on sb (fig) colgarle a uno el sambenito de algo.

pinafore ['pɪnəfɔː*] n delantal m; ~ dress (BRIT) n mandil m.

pinball ['pɪnbɔːl] n mesa americana.

pincers ['pɪnsəz] npl pinzas fpl, tenazas fpl.

pinch [pɪntʃ] n (of salt etc) pizca ♦ vt pellizcar; (inf: steal) birlar; at a ~ en caso de apuro.

pincushion ['pɪnkuʃən] n acerico.

pine [paɪn] n (also: ~ tree, wood) pino ♦ vi: to ~ for suspirar por; ~ away vi morirse de pena.

pineapple ['paɪnæpl] n piña, ananás m.

ping [pɪŋ] n (noise) sonido agudo; ~-pong ® n pingpong m ®.

pink [pɪŋk] adj rosado, (color de) rosa ♦ n (colour) rosa; (BOT) clavel m, clavellina.

pinnacle ['pɪnəkl] n cumbre f.

pinpoint ['pɪnpɔɪnt] vt precisar.

pint [paɪnt] n pinta (BRIT = 568cc; US = 473cc); (BRIT: inf: of beer) pinta de cerveza, ≈ jarra (SP).

pin-up n fotografía erótica.

pioneer [paɪə'nɪə*] n pionero/a.

pious ['paɪəs] adj piadoso, devoto.

pip [pɪp] n (seed) pepita; the ~s (BRIT) la señal.

pipe [paɪp] n tubo, caño; (for smoking) pipa ♦ vt conducir en cañerías; ~s npl (gen) cañería; (also: bag~s) gaita; ~ down (inf) vi callarse; ~ cleaner n limpiapipas m inv; ~ dream n sueño imposible; ~line n (for oil) oleoducto; (for gas) gasoducto; ~r n gaitero/a.

piping ['paɪpɪŋ] adv: to be ~ hot estar que quema.

piquant ['piːkənt] adj picante; (fig) agudo.

pique [piːk] n pique m, resentimiento.

pirate ['paɪərət] n pirata m/f ♦ vt (cas-

sette, book) piratear; ~ **radio** *(BRIT)* *n* emisora pirata.

pirouette [pɪruˈɛt] *n* pirueta.

Pisces [ˈpaɪsiːz] *n* Piscis *m*.

piss [pɪs] *(inf!)* *vi* mear; ~**ed** *(inf!)* *adj* *(drunk)* borracho.

pistol [ˈpɪstl] *n* pistola.

piston [ˈpɪstən] *n* pistón *m*, émbolo.

pit [pɪt] *n* hoyo; *(also: coal ~)* mina; *(in garage)* foso de inspección; *(also: orchestra ~)* platea ♦ *vt*: **to ~ one's wits against sb** medir fuerzas con uno; ~**s** *npl* *(AUT)* box *m*.

pitch [pɪtʃ] *n* *(MUS)* tono; *(BRIT: SPORT)* campo, terreno; *(fig)* punto; *(tar)* brea ♦ *vt (throw)* arrojar, lanzar ♦ *vi (fall)* caer(se); **to ~ a tent** montar una tienda (de campaña); ~-**black** *adj* negro como boca de lobo; ~**ed battle** *n* batalla campal.

pitchfork [ˈpɪtʃfɔːk] *n* horca.

piteous [ˈpɪtɪəs] *adj* lastimoso.

pitfall [ˈpɪtfɔːl] *n* riesgo.

pith [pɪθ] *n* *(of orange)* médula.

pithy [ˈpɪθɪ] *adj (fig)* jugoso.

pitiful [ˈpɪtɪful] *adj (touching)* lastimoso, conmovedor(a).

pitiless [ˈpɪtɪlɪs] *adj* despiadado.

pittance [ˈpɪtns] *n* miseria.

pity [ˈpɪtɪ] *n* compasión *f*, piedad *f* ♦ *vt* compadecer(se de); **what a ~!** ¡qué pena!

pivot [ˈpɪvət] *n* eje *m*.

pizza [ˈpiːtsə] *n* pizza.

placard [ˈplækɑːd] *n* letrero; *(in march etc)* pancarta.

placate [pləˈkeɪt] *vt* apaciguar.

place [pleɪs] *n* lugar *m*, sitio; *(seat)* plaza, asiento; *(post)* puesto; *(home)*: **at/to his ~** en/a su casa; *(role: in society etc)* papel *m* ♦ *vt (object)* poner, colocar; *(identify)* reconocer; **to take ~** tener lugar; **to be ~d** *(in race, exam)* colocarse; **out of ~** *(not suitable)* fuera de lugar; **in the first ~** en primer lugar; **to change ~s with sb** cambiarse de sitio con uno; ~ **of birth** *n* lugar *m* de nacimiento.

placid [ˈplæsɪd] *adj* apacible.

plagiarism [ˈpleɪdʒɪərɪzəm] *n* plagio.

plague [pleɪg] *n* plaga; *(MED)* peste *f* ♦ *vt (fig)* acosar, atormentar.

plaice [pleɪs] *n inv* platija.

plaid [plæd] *n (material)* tartán *m*.

plain [pleɪn] *adj (unpatterned)* liso; *(clear)* claro, evidente; *(simple)* sencillo; *(not handsome)* poco atractivo ♦ *adv* claramente ♦ *n* llano, llanura; ~ **chocolate** *n* chocolate *m* amargo; ~-**clothes** *adj (police)* vestido de paisano; ~**ly** *adv* claramente.

plaintiff [ˈpleɪntɪf] *n* demandante *m/f*.

plaintive [ˈpleɪntɪv] *adj* lastimero.

plait [plæt] *n* trenza.

plan [plæn] *n (drawing)* plano; *(scheme)* plan *m*, proyecto ♦ *vt* proyectar, planificar ♦ *vi* hacer proyectos; **to ~ to do** pensar hacer.

plane [pleɪn] *n (AVIAT)* avión *m*; *(MATH, fig)* plano; *(also: ~ tree)* plátano; *(tool)* cepillo.

planet [ˈplænɪt] *n* planeta *m*.

plank [plæŋk] *n* tabla.

planner [ˈplænə*] *n* planificador(a) *m/f*.

planning [ˈplænɪŋ] *n* planificación *f*; **family ~** planificación familiar; ~ **permission** *n* permiso para realizar obras.

plant [plɑːnt] *n* planta; *(machinery)* maquinaria; *(factory)* fábrica ♦ *vt* plantar; *(field)* sembrar; *(bomb)* colocar.

plaque [plæk] *n* placa.

plaster [ˈplɑːstə*] *n (for walls)* yeso; *(also: ~ of Paris)* yeso mate; *(BRIT: also: sticking ~)* tirita *(SP)*, esparadrapo, curita *(AM)* ♦ *vt* enyesar; *(cover)*: **to ~ with** llenar or cubrir de; ~**ed** *(inf)* *adj* borracho; ~**er** *n* yesero.

plastic [ˈplæstɪk] *n* plástico ♦ *adj* de plástico; ~ **bag** *n* bolsa de plástico.

plasticine [ˈplæstɪsiːn] ® *(BRIT)* *n* plastilina ®.

plastic surgery *n* cirujía plástica.

plate [pleɪt] *n (dish)* plato; *(metal, in book)* lámina; *(dental ~)* placa de dentadura postiza.

plateau [ˈplætəu] *(pl* ~**s** *or* ~**x)** *n* meseta, altiplanicie *f*.

plateaux [ˈplætəuz] *npl of* **plateau**.

plate glass *n* vidrio cilindrado.

platform [ˈplætfɔːm] *n (RAIL)* andén *m*;

(*stage*, *BRIT*: *on bus*) plataforma; (*at meeting*) tribuna; (*POL*) programa *m* (electoral).

platinum ['plætɪnəm] *adj*, *n* platino.

platitude ['plætɪtjuːd] *n* lugar *m* común, tópico.

platoon [plə'tuːn] *n* pelotón *m*.

platter ['plætə*] *n* fuente *f*.

plausible ['plɔːzɪbl] *adj* verosímil; (*person*) convincente.

play [pleɪ] *n* (*THEATRE*) obra, comedia ♦ *vt* (*game*) jugar; (*compete against*) jugar contra; (*instrument*) tocar; (*part: in play etc*) hacer el papel de; (*tape, record*) poner ♦ *vi* jugar; (*band*) tocar; (*tape, record*) sonar; **to ~ safe** ir a lo seguro; **~ down** *vt* quitar importancia a; **~ up** *vi* (*cause trouble to*) dar guerra; **~boy** *n* playboy *m*; **~er** *n* jugador(a) *m/f*; (*THEATRE*) actor/actriz *m/f*; (*MUS*) músico/a; **~ful** *adj* juguetón/ona; **~ground** *n* (*in school*) patio de recreo; (*in park*) parque *m* infantil; **~group** *n* jardín *m* de niños; **~ing card** *n* naipe *m*, carta; **~ing field** *n* campo de deportes; **~mate** *n* compañero/a de juego; **~-off** *n* (*SPORT*) (partido de) desempate *m*; **~pen** *n* corral *m*; **~thing** *n* juguete *m*; **~time** *n* (*SCOL*) recreo; **~wright** *n* dramaturgo/a.

plc *abbr* (= *public limited company*) ≈ S.A.

plea [pliː] *n* súplica, petición *f*; (*LAW*) alegato, defensa.

plead [pliːd] *vt* (*LAW*): **to ~ sb's case** defender a uno; (*give as excuse*) poner como pretexto ♦ *vi* (*LAW*) declararse; (*beg*): **to ~ with sb** suplicar *or* rogar a uno.

pleasant ['plɛznt] *adj* agradable; **~ries** *npl* cortesías *fpl*.

please [pliːz] *excl* ¡por favor! ♦ *vt* (*give pleasure to*) dar gusto a, agradar ♦ *vi* (*think fit*): **do as you ~** haz lo que quieras; **~ yourself!** (*inf*) ¡haz lo que te da la gana!, ¡como quieras!; **~d** *adj* (*happy*) alegre, contento; **~d** (**with**) satisfecho (de); **~d to meet you** ¡encantado!, ¡tanto gusto!; **pleasing** *adj* agradable, grato.

pleasure ['plɛʒə*] *n* placer *m*, gusto; "it's a ~" "el gusto es mío"; **~ boat** *n* barco de recreo.

pleat [pliːt] *n* pliegue *m*.

pledge [plɛdʒ] *n* (*promise*) promesa, voto ♦ *vt* prometer.

plentiful ['plɛntɪful] *adj* copioso, abundante.

plenty ['plɛntɪ] *n*: **~ of** mucho(s)/a(s).

pliable ['plaɪəbl] *adj* flexible.

pliant ['plaɪənt] *adj* = **pliable**.

pliers ['plaɪəz] *npl* alicates *mpl*, tenazas *fpl*.

plight [plaɪt] *n* situación *f* difícil.

plimsolls ['plɪmsɔlz] (*BRIT*) *npl* zapatos *mpl* de tenis.

plinth [plɪnθ] *n* plinto.

plod [plɔd] *vi* caminar con paso pesado; (*fig*) trabajar laboriosamente.

plonk [plɔŋk] (*inf*) *n* (*BRIT*: *wine*) vino peleón ♦ *vt*: **to ~ sth down** dejar caer algo.

plot [plɔt] *n* (*scheme*) complot *m*, conjura; (*of story*, *play*) argumento; (*of land*) terreno, lote *m* (*AM*) ♦ *vt* (*mark out*) trazar; (*conspire*) tramar, urdir ♦ *vi* conspirar; **~ter** *n* (*instrument*) trazador *m* de gráficos.

plough [plau] (*US* **plow**) *n* arado ♦ *vt* (*earth*) arar; **to ~ money into** invertir dinero en; **~ through** *vt fus* (*crowd*) abrirse paso por la fuerza por; **~man's lunch** (*BRIT*) *n* almuerzo de pub a base de pan, queso y encurtidos.

ploy [plɔɪ] *n* truco, estratagema.

pluck [plʌk] *vt* (*fruit*) coger (*SP*), recoger (*AM*); (*musical instrument*) puntear; (*bird*) desplumar; (*eyebrows*) depilar ♦ *n* valor *m*, ánimo; **to ~ up courage** hacer de tripas corazón.

plug [plʌg] *n* tapón *m*; (*ELEC*) enchufe *m*, clavija; (*AUT*: *also*: **spark(ing)** ~) bujía ♦ *vt* (*hole*) tapar; (*inf*: *advertise*) dar publicidad a; **~ in** *vt* (*ELEC*) enchufar.

plum [plʌm] *n* (*fruit*) ciruela ♦ *cpd*: **~ job** (*inf*) puesto (de trabajo) muy codiciado.

plumb [plʌm] *vt*: **to ~ the depths of** alcanzar los mayores extremos de.

plumber ['plʌmə*] n fontanero/a (SP), plomero/a (AM).

plumbing ['plʌmɪŋ] n (trade) fontanería, plomería; (piping) cañería.

plume [pluːm] n pluma; (on helmet etc) penacho.

plummet ['plʌmɪt] vi: to ~ (down) caer a plomo.

plump [plʌmp] adj rechoncho, rollizo ♦ vi: to ~ for (inf: choose) optar por; ~ up vt mullir.

plunder ['plʌndə*] n pillaje m; (loot) botín m ♦ vt pillar, saquear.

plunge [plʌndʒ] n zambullida ♦ vt sumergir, hundir ♦ vi (fall) caer; (dive) saltar; (person) arrojarse; to take the ~ lanzarse; ~r n (for drain) desatascador m; **plunging** adj: **plunging neckline** escote m pronunciado.

pluperfect [pluːˈpəːfɪkt] n pluscuamperfecto.

plural ['pluərl] adj plural ♦ n plural m.

plus [plʌs] n (also: ~ sign) signo más ♦ prep más, y, además de; **ten/twenty** ~ más de diez/veinte.

plush [plʌʃ] adj lujoso.

plutonium [pluːˈtəunɪəm] n plutonio.

ply [plaɪ] vt (a trade) ejercer ♦ vi (ship) ir y venir ♦ n (of wool, rope) cabo; to ~ sb with drink insistir en ofrecer a uno muchas copas; ~**wood** n madera contrachapada.

P.M. n abbr = **Prime Minister**.

p.m. adv abbr (= post meridiem) de la tarde or noche.

pneumatic [njuːˈmætɪk] adj neumático; ~ **drill** n martillo neumático.

pneumonia [njuːˈməunɪə] n pulmonía.

poach [pəutʃ] vt (cook) escalfar; (steal) cazar (or pescar) en vedado ♦ vi cazar (or pescar) en vedado; ~**ed** adj escalfado; ~**er** n cazador(a) m/f furtivo/a.

P.O. Box n abbr = **Post Office Box**.

pocket ['pɒkɪt] n bolsillo; (fig: small area) bolsa ♦ vt meter en el bolsillo; (steal) embolsar; **to be out of** ~ (BRIT) salir perdiendo; ~**book** n (US) n cartera; ~ **calculator** n calculadora de bolsillo; ~ **knife** n navaja; ~ **money** n asignación f.

pod [pɒd] n vaina.

podgy ['pɒdʒɪ] adj gordinflón/ona.

podiatrist [pɒˈdiːətrɪst] (US) n pedicuro/a.

poem ['pəuɪm] n poema m.

poet ['pəuɪt] n poeta m/f; ~**ic** [-ˈɛtɪk] adj poético; ~ **laureate** n poeta m laureado; ~**ry** n poesía.

poignant ['pɔɪnjənt] adj conmovedor(a).

point [pɔɪnt] n punto; (tip) punta; (purpose) fin m, propósito; (use) utilidad f; (significant part) lo significativo; (moment) momento; (ELEC) toma (de corriente); (also: decimal ~): **2 ~ 3** (2.3) dos coma tres (2,3) ♦ vt señalar; (gun etc): **to ~ sth at sb** apuntar algo a uno ♦ vi: **to ~ at** señalar; ~**s** npl (AUT) contactos mpl; (RAIL) agujas fpl; **to be on the ~ of doing sth** estar a punto de hacer algo; **to make a ~ of** poner empeño en; **to get/miss the ~** comprender/no comprender; **to come to the ~** ir al meollo; **there's no ~ (in doing)** no tiene sentido (hacer); ~ **out** vt señalar; ~ **to** vt fus (fig) indicar, señalar; ~**-blank** adv (say, refuse) sin más hablar; (also: **at** ~**-blank range**) a quemarropa; ~**ed** adj (shape) puntiagudo, afilado; (remark) intencionado; ~**edly** adv intencionadamente; ~**er** n (needle) aguja, indicador m; ~**less** adj sin sentido; ~ **of view** n punto de vista.

poise [pɔɪz] n aplomo, elegancia.

poison ['pɔɪzn] n veneno ♦ vt envenenar; ~**ing** n envenenamiento; ~**ous** adj venenoso; (fumes etc) tóxico.

poke [pəuk] vt (jab with finger, stick etc) empujar; (put): **to ~ sth in(to)** introducir algo en; ~ **about** vi fisgonear.

poker ['pəukə*] n atizador m; (CARDS) póker m; ~**-faced** adj de cara impasible.

poky ['pəukɪ] adj estrecho.

Poland ['pəulənd] n Polonia.

polar ['pəulə*] adj polar; ~ **bear** n oso polar.

Pole [pəul] n polaco/a.

pole [pəul] n palo; (fixed) poste m; (GEO) polo; ~ **bean** (US) n ≈ judía verde; ~ **vault** n salto con pértiga.

police [pə'liːs] *n* policía ♦ *vt* vigilar; ~ **car** *n* coche-patrulla *m*; ~**man** *n* policía *m*, guardia *m*; ~ **state** *n* estado policial; ~ **station** *n* comisaría; ~**woman** *n* mujer *f* policía.
policy ['pɒlɪsɪ] *n* política; (*also: insurance* ~) póliza.
polio ['pəulɪəu] *n* polio *f*.
Polish ['pəulɪʃ] *adj* polaco ♦ *n* (*LING*) polaco.
polish ['pɒlɪʃ] *n* (*for shoes*) betún *m*; (*for floor*) cera (de lustrar); (*shine*) brillo, lustre *m*; (*fig: refinement*) educación *f* ♦ *vt* (*shoes*) limpiar; (*make shiny*) pulir, sacar brillo a; ~ **off** *vt* (*work*) terminar; (*food*) despachar; ~**ed** *adj* (*fig: person*) elegante.
polite [pə'laɪt] *adj* cortés, atento; ~**ness** *n* cortesía.
political [pə'lɪtɪkl] *adj* político.
politician [pɒlɪ'tɪʃən] *n* político/a.
politics ['pɒlɪtɪks] *n* política.
poll [pəul] *n* (*election*) votación *f*; (*also: opinion* ~) sondeo, encuesta ♦ *vt* encuestar; (*votes*) obtener.
pollen ['pɒlən] *n* polen *m*.
pollinate ['pɒlɪneɪt] *vt* polinizar.
polling day ['pəulɪŋ-] *n* día *m* de elecciones.
polling station *n* centro electoral.
pollute [pə'luːt] *vt* contaminar.
pollution [pə'luːʃən] *n* polución *f*, contaminación *f* del medio ambiente.
polo ['pəuləu] *n* (*sport*) polo; ~-**necked** *adj* de cuello vuelto.
polyester [pɒlɪ'estə*] *n* poliéster *m*.
polystyrene [pɒlɪ'staɪriːn] *n* poliestireno.
polytechnic [pɒlɪ'teknɪk] *n* politécnico.
polythene ['pɒlɪθiːn] (*BRIT*) *n* politeno.
pomegranate ['pɒmɪgrænɪt] *n* granada.
pomp [pɒmp] *n* pompa.
pompom ['pɒmpɒm] *n* borla, pompón *m*.
pompous ['pɒmpəs] *adj* pomposo.
pond [pɒnd] *n* (*natural*) charca; (*artificial*) estanque *m*.
ponder ['pɒndə*] *vt* meditar.
ponderous ['pɒndərəs] *adj* pesado.
pong [pɒŋ] (*BRIT: inf*) *n* hedor *m*.
pontoon [pɒn'tuːn] *n* pontón *m*.

pony ['pəunɪ] *n* poney *m*, jaca, potro (*AM*); ~**tail** *n* cola de caballo; ~ **trekking** (*BRIT*) *n* excursión *f* a caballo.
poodle ['puːdl] *n* caniche *m*.
pool [puːl] *n* (*natural*) charca; (*also: swimming* ~) piscina (*SP*), alberca (*AM*); (*fig: of light etc*) charco; (*SPORT*) chapolín *m* ♦ *vt* juntar; ~**s** *npl* (*football* ~**s**) quinielas *fpl*; **typing** ~ servicio de mecanografía.
poor [puə*] *adj* pobre; (*bad*) de mala calidad ♦ *npl*: **the** ~ los pobres; ~**ly** *adj* mal, enfermo ♦ *adv* mal.
pop [pɒp] *n* (*sound*) ruido seco; (*MUS*) (música) pop *m*; (*inf: father*) papá *m*; (*drink*) gaseosa ♦ *vt* (*put quickly*) meter (de prisa) ♦ *vi* reventar; (*cork*) saltar; ~ **in/out** *vi* entrar/salir un momento; ~ **up** *vi* aparecer inesperadamente; ~**corn** *n* palomitas *fpl*.
pope [pəup] *n* papa *m*.
poplar ['pɒplə*] *n* álamo.
poplin ['pɒplɪn] *n* popelina.
popper ['pɒpə*] (*BRIT*) *n* automático.
poppy ['pɒpɪ] *n* amapola.
popsicle ['pɒpsɪkl] (*US*) *n* polo.
pop star *n* estrella del pop.
populace ['pɒpjuləs] *n* pueblo, plebe *f*.
popular ['pɒpjulə*] *adj* popular; ~**ize** *vt* popularizar; (*disseminate*) vulgarizar.
population [pɒpju'leɪʃən] *n* población *f*.
porcelain ['pɔːslɪn] *n* porcelana.
porch [pɔːtʃ] *n* pórtico, entrada; (*US*) veranda.
porcupine ['pɔːkjupaɪn] *n* puerco *m* espín.
pore [pɔː*] *n* poro ♦ *vi*: **to** ~ **over** engolfarse en.
pork [pɔːk] *n* carne *f* de cerdo (*SP*) or chancho (*AM*).
pornography [pɔː'nɒgrəfɪ] *n* pornografía.
porpoise ['pɔːpəs] *n* marsopa.
porridge ['pɒrɪdʒ] *n* gachas *fpl* de avena.
port [pɔːt] *n* puerto; (*NAUT: left side*) babor *m*; (*wine*) vino de Oporto; ~ **of call** puerto de escala.
portable ['pɔːtəbl] *adj* portátil.
porter ['pɔːtə*] *n* (*for luggage*) maleté-

ro; (*doorkeeper*) portero/a, conserje *m/f*.
portfolio [pɔːt'fəuliəu] *n* cartera.
porthole ['pɔːthəul] *n* portilla.
portion ['pɔːʃən] *n* porción *f*; (*of food*) ración *f*.
portly ['pɔːtlɪ] *adj* corpulento.
portrait ['pɔːtreɪt] *n* retrato.
portray [pɔː'treɪ] *vt* retratar; (*subj: actor*) representar; ~**al** *n* retrato; representación *f*.
Portugal ['pɔːtjugl] *n* Portugal *m*.
Portuguese [pɔːtju'giːz] *adj* portugués/esa ♦ *n inv* portugués/esa *m/f*; (*LING*) portugués *m*.
pose [pəuz] *n* postura, actitud *f* ♦ *vi* (*pretend*): to ~ as hacerse pasar por ♦ *vt* (*question*) plantear; to ~ for posar para.
posh [pɔʃ] (*inf*) *adj* elegante, de lujo.
position [pə'zɪʃən] *n* posición *f*; (*job*) puesto; (*situation*) situación *f* ♦ *vt* colocar.
positive ['pɔzɪtɪv] *adj* positivo; (*certain*) seguro; (*definite*) definitivo.
possess [pə'zes] *vt* poseer; ~**ion** [pə'zeʃən] *n* posesión *f*; ~**ions** *npl* (*belongings*) pertenencias *fpl*.
possibility [pɔsɪ'bɪlɪtɪ] *n* posibilidad *f*.
possible ['pɔsɪbl] *adj* posible; **as big as** ~ lo más grande posible; **possibly** *adv* posiblemente; **I cannot possibly come** me es imposible venir.
post [pəust] *n* (*BRIT: system*) correos *mpl*; (*BRIT: letters, delivery*) correo; (*job, situation*) puesto; (*pole*) poste *m* ♦ *vt* (*BRIT: send by post*) echar al correo; (*BRIT: appoint*): to ~ to enviar a; ~**age** *n* porte *m*, franqueo; ~**age stamp** *n* sello de correos; ~**al** *adj* postal, de correos; ~**al order** *n* giro postal; ~**box** (*BRIT*) *n* buzón *m*; ~**card** *n* tarjeta postal; ~**code** (*BRIT*) *n* código postal.
postdate [pəust'deɪt] *vt* (*cheque*) poner fecha adelantada a.
poster ['pəustə*] *n* cartel *m*.
poste restante [pəust'restɔ̃t] (*BRIT*) *n* lista de correos.
postgraduate ['pəust'grædjuət] *n* posgra-

duado/a.
posthumous ['pɔstjuməs] *adj* póstumo.
postman ['pəustmən] *n* cartero.
postmark ['pəustmɑːk] *n* matasellos *m inv*.
post-mortem [-'mɔːtəm] *n* autopsia.
post office *n* (*building*) (oficina de) correos *m*; (*organization*): the P~ O~ Administración *f* General de Correos; P~ O~ **Box** *n* apartado postal (*SP*), casilla de correos (*AM*).
postpone [pəs'pəun] *vt* aplazar.
postscript ['pəustskrɪpt] *n* posdata.
posture ['pɔstʃə*] *n* postura, actitud *f*.
postwar [pəust'wɔː*] *adj* de la posguerra.
posy ['pəuzɪ] *n* ramillete *m* (de flores).
pot [pɔt] *n* (*for cooking*) olla; (*tea~*) tetera; (*coffee~*) cafetera; (*for flowers*) maceta; (*for jam*) tarro, pote *m*; (*inf: marijuana*) chocolate *m* ♦ *vt* (*plant*) poner en tiesto; to go to ~ (*inf*) irse al traste.
potato [pə'teɪtəu] (*pl* ~**es**) *n* patata (*SP*), papa (*AM*); ~ **peeler** *n* pelapatatas *m inv*.
potent ['pəutnt] *adj* potente, poderoso; (*drink*) fuerte.
potential [pə'tenʃl] *adj* potencial, posible ♦ *n* potencial *m*; ~**ly** *adv* en potencia.
pothole ['pɔthəul] *n* (*in road*) bache *m*; (*BRIT: underground*) gruta; **potholing** (*BRIT*) *n*: to go potholing dedicarse a la espeleología.
potion ['pəuʃən] *n* poción *f*, pócima.
potluck [pɔt'lʌk] *n*: to take ~ tomar lo que haya.
potted ['pɔtɪd] *adj* (*food*) en conserva; (*plant*) en tiesto *or* maceta; (*shortened*) resumido.
potter ['pɔtə*] *n* alfarero/a ♦ *vi*: to ~ around, ~ about (*BRIT*) hacer trabajitos; ~**y** *n* cerámica; (*factory*) alfarería.
potty ['pɔtɪ] *adj* (*inf: mad*) chiflado ♦ *n* orinal *m* de niño.
pouch [pautʃ] *n* (*ZOOL*) bolsa; (*for tobacco*) petaca.
poultry ['pəultrɪ] *n* aves *fpl* de corral;

(*meat*) pollo.

pounce [pauns] *vi*: to ~ on precipitarse sobre.

pound [paund] *n* libra (*weight* = 453g or 16oz; *money* = 100 pence) ♦ *vt* (*beat*) golpear; (*crush*) machacar ♦ *vi* (*heart*) latir; ~ **sterling** *n* libra esterlina.

pour [pɔː*] *vt* echar; (*tea etc*) servir ♦ *vi* correr, fluir; to ~ **sb a drink** servirle a uno una copa; ~ **away** *or* **off** *vt* vaciar, verter; ~ **in** *vi* (*people*) entrar en tropel; ~ **out** *vi* salir en tropel ♦ *vt* (*drink*) echar, servir; (*fig*): to ~ **out** one's feelings desahogarse; ~**ing** *adj*: ~**ing rain** lluvia torrencial.

pout [paut] *vi* hacer pucheros.

poverty ['pɔvətɪ] *n* pobreza, miseria; ~**-stricken** *adj* necesitado.

powder ['paudə*] *n* polvo; (*face* ~) polvos *mpl* ♦ *vt* polvorear; to ~ **one's face** empolvarse la cara; ~ **compact** *n* polvera; ~**ed milk** *n* leche *f* en polvo; ~ **puff** *n* borla; ~ **room** *n* aseos *mpl*.

power ['pauə*] *n* poder *m*; (*strength*) fuerza; (*nation, TECH*) potencia; (*drive*) empuje *m*; (*ELEC*) fuerza, energía ♦ *vt* impulsar; **to be in** ~ (*POL*) estar en el poder; ~ **cut** (*BRIT*) *n* apagón *m*; ~**ed** *adj*: ~**ed by** impulsado por; ~ **failure** *n* = ~ **cut**; ~**ful** *adj* poderoso; (*engine*) potente; (*speech etc*) convincente; ~**less** *adj*: ~**less (to do)** incapaz (de hacer); ~ **point** (*BRIT*) *n* enchufe *m*; ~ **station** *n* central *f* eléctrica.

p.p. *abbr* (= *per procurationem*): ~ **J. Smith** p.p. (por poder de) J. Smith; (= *pages*) págs.

PR *n abbr* = **public relations**.

practicable ['præktɪkəbl] *adj* factible.

practical ['præktɪkl] *adj* práctico; ~**ity** [-'kælɪtɪ] *n* factibilidad *f*; ~ **joke** *n* broma pesada; ~**ly** *adv* (*almost*) casi.

practice ['præktɪs] *n* (*habit*) costumbre *f*; (*exercise*) práctica, ejercicio; (*training*) adiestramiento; (*MED: of profession*) práctica, ejercicio; (*MED, LAW: business*) consulta ♦ *vt, vi* (*US*) = **practise**; **in** ~ (*in reality*) en la práctica; **out of** ~ desentrenado.

practise ['præktɪs] (*US* **practice**) *vt*

(*carry out*) practicar; (*profession*) ejercer; (*train at*) practicar ♦ *vi* ejercer; (*train*) practicar; **practising** *adj* (*Christian etc*) practicante; (*lawyer*) en ejercicio.

practitioner [præk'tɪʃənə*] *n* (*MED*) médico/a.

prairie ['preərɪ] *n* pampa.

praise [preɪz] *n* alabanza(s) *f(pl)*, elogio(s) *m(pl)* ♦ *vt* alabar, elogiar; ~**worthy** *adj* loable.

pram [præm] (*BRIT*) *n* cochecito de niño.

prance [prɑːns] *vi* (*person*) contonearse.

prank [præŋk] *n* travesura.

prawn [prɔːn] *n* gamba.

pray [preɪ] *vi* rezar.

prayer [preə*] *n* oración *f*, rezo; (*entreaty*) ruego, súplica.

preach [priːtʃ] *vi* (*also fig*) predicar; ~**er** *n* predicador(a) *m/f*.

preamble [prɪ'æmbl] *n* preámbulo.

precaution [prɪ'kɔːʃən] *n* precaución *f*.

precede [prɪ'siːd] *vt, vi* preceder.

precedence ['presɪdəns] *n* precedencia; (*priority*) prioridad *f*.

precedent ['presɪdənt] *n* precedente *m*.

preceding [prɪ'siːdɪŋ] *adj* anterior.

precinct ['priːsɪŋkt] *n* recinto; ~**s** *npl* contornos *mpl*; **pedestrian** ~ (*BRIT*) zona peatonal; **shopping** ~ (*BRIT*) centro comercial.

precious ['preʃəs] *adj* precioso.

precipice ['presɪpɪs] *n* precipicio.

precipitate [prɪ'sɪpɪteɪt] *vt* precipitar.

precise [prɪ'saɪs] *adj* preciso, exacto; ~**ly** *adv* precisamente, exactamente.

preclude [prɪ'kluːd] *vt* excluir.

precocious [prɪ'kəuʃəs] *adj* precoz.

preconceived [priːkən'siːvd] *adj* preconcebido.

precondition [priːkən'dɪʃən] *n* condición *f* previa.

predator ['predətə*] *n* animal *m* de rapiña, depredador *m*.

predecessor ['priːdɪsesə*] *n* antecesor(a) *m/f*.

predicament [prɪ'dɪkəmənt] *n* apuro.

predict [prɪ'dɪkt] *vt* pronosticar; ~**able** *adj* previsible; ~**ion** [-'dɪkʃən] *n* predicción *f*.

predominantly [prɪ'dɒmɪnəntlɪ] *adv* en su mayoría.

predominate [prɪ'dɒmɪneɪt] *vi* predominar.

pre-empt [priː'ɛmt] *vt* adelantarse a.

preen [priːn] *vt*: **to ~ itself** (*bird*) limpiarse (las plumas); **to ~ o.s.** pavonearse.

prefab ['priːfæb] *n* casa prefabricada.

preface ['prɛfəs] *n* prefacio.

prefect ['priːfɛkt] (*BRIT*) *n* (*in school*) monitor(a) *m/f*.

prefer [prɪ'fəː*] *vt* preferir; **to ~ doing** *or* **to do** preferir hacer; **~able** ['prɛfrəbl] *adj* preferible; **~ably** ['prɛfrəblɪ] *adv* de preferencia; **~ence** ['prɛfrəns] *n* preferencia; (*priority*) prioridad *f*; **~ential** [prɛfə'rɛnʃəl] *adj* preferente.

prefix ['priːfɪks] *n* prefijo.

pregnancy ['prɛgnənsɪ] *n* (*of woman*) embarazo; (*of animal*) preñez *f*.

pregnant ['prɛgnənt] *adj* (*woman*) embarazada; (*animal*) preñada.

prehistoric ['priːhɪs'tɒrɪk] *adj* prehistórico.

prejudice ['prɛdʒudɪs] *n* prejuicio; **~d** *adj* (*person*) predispuesto.

preliminary [prɪ'lɪmɪnərɪ] *adj* preliminar.

prelude ['prɛljuːd] *n* preludio.

premarital ['priː'mærɪtl] *adj* premarital.

premature ['prɛmətʃuə*] *adj* prematuro.

premier ['prɛmɪə*] *adj* primero, principal ♦ *n* (*POL*) primer(a) ministro/a.

première [prɛmɪ'ɛə*] *n* estreno.

premise ['prɛmɪs] *n* premisa; **~s** *npl* (*of business etc*) local *m*; **on the ~s** en el lugar mismo.

premium ['priːmɪəm] *n* premio; (*insurance*) prima; **to be at a ~** ser muy solicitado; **~ bond** (*BRIT*) *n* bono del estado que participa en una lotería nacional.

premonition [prɛmə'nɪʃən] *n* presentimiento.

preoccupied [priː'ɔkjupaɪd] *adj* ensimismado.

prep [prɛp] *n* (*SCOL*: *study*) deberes *mpl*.

prepaid [priː'peɪd] *adj* porte pagado.

preparation [prɛpə'reɪʃən] *n* preparación *f*; **~s** *npl* preparativos *mpl*.

preparatory [prɪ'pærətərɪ] *adj* preparatorio, preliminar; **~ school** *n* escuela preparatoria.

prepare [prɪ'pɛə*] *vt* preparar, disponer; (*CULIN*) preparar ♦ *vi*: **to ~ for** (*action*) prepararse *or* disponerse para; (*event*) hacer preparativos para; **~d to** dispuesto a; **~d for** listo para.

preponderance [prɪ'pɒndərns] *n* predominio.

preposition [prɛpə'zɪʃən] *n* preposición *f*.

preposterous [prɪ'pɒstərəs] *adj* absurdo, ridículo.

prep school *n* = **preparatory school**.

prerequisite [priː'rɛkwɪzɪt] *n* requisito.

prerogative [prɪ'rɒgətɪv] *n* prerrogativa.

Presbyterian [prɛzbɪ'tɪərɪən] *adj*, *n* presbiteriano/a *m/f*.

preschool ['priː'skuːl] *adj* preescolar.

prescribe [prɪ'skraɪb] *vt* (*MED*) recetar.

prescription [prɪ'skrɪpʃən] *n* (*MED*) receta.

presence ['prɛzns] *n* presencia; **in sb's ~** en presencia de uno; **~ of mind** aplomo.

present [*adj, n* 'prɛznt, *vb* prɪ'zɛnt] *adj* (*in attendance*) presente; (*current*) actual ♦ *n* (*gift*) regalo; (*actuality*): **the ~** la actualidad, el presente ♦ *vt* (*introduce, describe*) presentar; (*expound*) exponer; (*give*) presentar, dar, ofrecer; (*THEATRE*) representar; **to give sb a ~** regalar algo a uno; **at ~** actualmente; **~able** [prɪ'zɛntəbl] *adj*: **to make o.s. ~able** arreglarse; **~ation** [-'teɪʃən] *n* presentación *f*; (*of report etc*) exposición *f*; (*formal ceremony*) entrega de un regalo; **~-day** *adj* actual; **~er** [prɪ'zɛntə*] *n* (*RADIO, TV*) locutor(a) *m/f*; **~ly** *adv* (*soon*) dentro de poco; (*now*) ahora.

preservation [prɛzə'veɪʃən] *n* conservación *f*.

preservative [prɪ'zəːvətɪv] *n* conservante *m*.

preserve [prɪ'zəːv] *vt* (*keep safe*) preservar, proteger; (*maintain*) mantener;

(*food*) conservar ♦ *n* (*for game*) coto, vedado; (*often pl: jam*) conserva, confitura.

preside [prɪ'zaɪd] *vi*: to ~ **over** presidir.

president ['prezɪdənt] *n* presidente *m/f*; ~**ial** [-'denʃl] *adj* presidencial.

press [pres] *n* (*newspapers*): **the P**~ la prensa; (*printer's*) imprenta; (*of button*) pulsación *f* ♦ *vt* empujar; (*button etc*) apretar; (*clothes: iron*) planchar; (*put pressure on: person*) presionar; (*insist*): to ~ **sth on sb** insistir en que uno acepte algo ♦ *vi* (*squeeze*) apretar; (*pressurize*): to ~ **for** presionar por; **we are** ~**ed** for time/money estamos apurados de tiempo/dinero; ~ **on** *vi* avanzar; (*hurry*) apretar el paso; ~ **agency** *n* agencia de prensa; ~ **conference** *n* rueda de prensa; ~**ing** *adj* apremiante; ~ **stud** (*BRIT*) *n* botón *m* de presión; ~**up** (*BRIT*) *n* plancha.

pressure ['preʃə*] *n* presión *f*; to put ~ **on sb** presionar a uno; ~ **cooker** *n* olla a presión; ~ **gauge** *n* manómetro; ~ **group** *n* grupo de presión; **pressurized** *adj* (*container*) a presión.

prestige [pres'tiːʒ] *n* prestigio.

presumably [prɪ'zjuːməblɪ] *adv* es de suponer que, cabe presumir que.

presume [prɪ'zjuːm] *vt*: to ~ (**that**) presumir (que), suponer (que).

presumption [prɪ'zʌmpʃən] *n* suposición *f*.

presumptuous [prɪ'zʌmptjuəs] *adj* presumido.

presuppose [priːsə'pəuz] *vt* presuponer.

pretence [prɪ'tens] (*US* **pretense**) *n* fingimiento; **under false** ~**s** con engaños.

pretend [prɪ'tend] *vt, vi* (*feign*) fingir.

pretense [prɪ'tens] (*US*) *n* = **pretence**.

pretentious [prɪ'tenʃəs] *adj* presumido; (*ostentatious*) ostentoso, aparatoso.

pretext ['priːtekst] *n* pretexto.

pretty ['prɪtɪ] *adj* bonito (*SP*), lindo (*AM*) ♦ *adv* bastante.

prevail [prɪ'veɪl] *vi* (*gain mastery*) prevalecer; (*be current*) predominar; ~**ing** *adj* (*dominant*) predominante.

prevalent ['prevələnt] *adj* (*widespread*) extendido.

prevent [prɪ'vent] *vt*: to ~ **sb from doing sth** impedir a uno hacer algo; to ~ **sth from happening** evitar que ocurra algo; ~**ative** *adj* = **preventive**; ~**ive** *adj* preventivo.

preview ['priːvjuː] *n* (*of film*) preestreno.

previous ['priːvɪəs] *adj* previo, anterior; ~**ly** *adv* antes.

prewar [priː'wɔː*] *adj* de antes de la guerra.

prey [preɪ] *n* presa ♦ *vi*: to ~ **on** (*feed on*) alimentarse de; **it was** ~**ing on his mind** le preocupaba, le obsesionaba.

price [praɪs] *n* precio ♦ *vt* (*goods*) fijar el precio de; ~**less** *adj* que no tiene precio; ~ **list** *n* tarifa.

prick [prɪk] *n* (*sting*) picadura ♦ *vt* pinchar; (*hurt*) picar; to ~ **up one's ears** aguzar el oído.

prickle ['prɪkl] *n* (*sensation*) picor *m*; (*BOT*) espina; **prickly** *adj* espinoso; (*fig: person*) enojadizo; **prickly heat** *n* sarpullido causado por exceso de calor.

pride [praɪd] *n* orgullo; (*pej*) soberbia ♦ *vt*: to ~ **o.s.** enorgullecerse de.

priest [priːst] *n* sacerdote *m*; ~**ess** *n* sacerdotisa; ~**hood** *n* sacerdocio.

prig [prɪg] *n* gazmoño/a.

prim [prɪm] *adj* (*demure*) remilgado; (*prudish*) gazmoño.

primarily ['praɪmərɪlɪ] *adv* ante todo.

primary ['praɪmərɪ] *adj* (*first in importance*) principal ♦ *n* (*US: POL*) (elección *f*) primaria; ~ **school** (*BRIT*) *n* escuela primaria.

primate ['praɪmeɪt] *n* (*ZOOL*) primate *m*.

prime [praɪm] *adj* primero, principal; (*excellent*) selecto, de primera clase ♦ *n*: **in the** ~ **of life** en la flor de la vida ♦ *vt* (*wood, fig*) preparar; ~ **example** *n* ejemplo típico; **P**~ **Minister** *n* primer(a) ministro/a.

primeval [praɪ'miːvəl] *adj* primitivo.

primitive ['prɪmɪtɪv] *adj* primitivo; (*crude*) rudimentario.

primrose ['prɪmrəuz] *n* primavera, prímula.

primus (stove) ['praɪməs-] ® (*BRIT*) *n* hornillo de camping.

prince [prɪns] *n* príncipe *m*.

princess [prɪnˈses] *n* princesa.

principal [ˈprɪnsɪpl] *adj* principal, mayor ♦ *n* director(a) *m/f*; **~ity** [-ˈpælɪtɪ] *n* principado.

principle [ˈprɪnsɪpl] *n* principio; **in ~** en principio; **on ~** por principio.

print [prɪnt] *n* (*foot~*) huella; (*finger~*) huella dactilar; (*letters*) letra de molde; (*fabric*) estampado; (*ART*) grabado; (*PHOT*) impresión *f* ♦ *vt* imprimir; (*cloth*) estampar; (*write in capitals*) escribir en letras de molde; **out of ~** agotado; **~ed matter** *n* impresos *mpl*; **~er** *n* (*person*) impresor(a) *m/f*; (*machine*) impresora; **~ing** *n* (*art*) imprenta; (*act*) impresión *f*; **~out** *n* (*COMPUT*) impresión *f*.

prior [ˈpraɪə*] *adj* anterior, previo; (*more important*) más importante; **~ to** antes de.

priority [praɪˈɔrɪtɪ] *n* prioridad *f*; **to have ~ (over)** tener prioridad (sobre).

prise [praɪz] *vt*: **to ~ open** abrir con palanca.

prison [ˈprɪzn] *n* cárcel *f*, prisión *f* ♦ *cpd* carcelario; **~er** *n* (*in prison*) preso/a; (*captured person*) prisionero; **~er-of-war** *n* prisionero de guerra.

pristine [ˈprɪstiːn] *adj* inmaculado.

privacy [ˈprɪvəsɪ] *n* intimidad *f*.

private [ˈpraɪvɪt] *adj* (*personal*) particular; (*property, industry, discussion etc*) privado; (*person*) reservado; (*place*) tranquilo ♦ *n* soldado raso; **"~"** (*on envelope*) "confidencial"; (*on door*) "prohibido el paso"; **in ~** en privado; **~ enterprise** *n* empresa privada; **~ eye** *n* detective *m/f* privado/a; **~ property** *n* propiedad *f* privada; **~ school** *n* colegio particular.

privet [ˈprɪvɪt] *n* alheña.

privilege [ˈprɪvɪlɪdʒ] *n* privilegio; (*prerogative*) prerrogativa.

privy [ˈprɪvɪ] *adj*: **to be ~ to** estar enterado de.

prize [praɪz] *n* premio ♦ *adj* de primera clase ♦ *vt* apreciar, estimar; **~-giving** *n* distribución *f* de premios; **~winner** *n* premiado/a.

pro [prəu] *n* (*SPORT*) profesional *m/f* ♦ *prep* a favor de; **the ~s and cons** los pros y los contras.

probability [prɔbəˈbɪlɪtɪ] *n* probabilidad *f*; **in all ~** con toda probabilidad.

probable [ˈprɔbəbl] *adj* probable.

probably [ˈprɔbəblɪ] *adv* probablemente.

probation [prəˈbeɪʃən] *n*: **on ~** (*employee*) a prueba; (*LAW*) en libertad condicional.

probe [prəub] *n* (*MED, SPACE*) sonda; (*enquiry*) encuesta, investigación *f* ♦ *vt* sondar; (*investigate*) investigar.

problem [ˈprɔbləm] *n* problema *m*.

procedure [prəˈsiːdʒə*] *n* procedimiento; (*bureaucratic*) trámites *mpl*.

proceed [prəˈsiːd] *vi* (*do afterwards*): **to ~ to do sth** proceder a hacer algo; (*continue*): **to ~ (with)** continuar *or* seguir (con); **~ings** *npl* acto(s) (*pl*); (*LAW*) proceso; **~s** [ˈprəusiːdz] *npl* (*money*) ganancias *fpl*, ingresos *mpl*.

process [ˈprəuses] *n* proceso ♦ *vt* tratar, elaborar; **~ing** *n* tratamiento, elaboración *f*; (*PHOT*) revelado.

procession [prəˈseʃən] *n* desfile *m*; **funeral ~** cortejo fúnebre.

proclaim [prəˈkleɪm] *vt* (*announce*) anunciar; **proclamation** [prɔkləˈmeɪʃən] *n* proclamación *f*; (*written*) proclama.

procrastinate [prəuˈkræstɪneɪt] *vi* demorarse.

procure [prəˈkjuə*] *vt* conseguir.

prod [prɔd] *vt* empujar ♦ *n* empujón *m*.

prodigal [ˈprɔdɪgl] *adj* pródigo.

prodigy [ˈprɔdɪdʒɪ] *n* prodigio.

produce [*n* ˈprɔdjuːs, *vt* prəˈdjuːs] *n* (*AGR*) productos *mpl* agrícolas ♦ *vt* producir; (*play, film, programme*) presentar; **~r** *n* productor(a) *m/f*; (*of film, programme*) director(a) *m/f*; ((*of record*) productor(a) *m/f*.

product [ˈprɔdʌkt] *n* producto.

production [prəˈdʌkʃən] *n* producción *f*; (*THEATRE*) presentación *f*; **~ line** *n* línea de producción.

productive [prəˈdʌktɪv] *adj* productivo; **productivity** [prɔdʌkˈtɪvɪtɪ] *n* productividad *f*.

profane [prəˈfeɪn] *adj* profano.

profession [prəˈfɛʃən] *n* profesión *f*; ~**al** *adj* profesional ♦ *n* profesional *m/f*; (*skilled person*) perito.

professor [prəˈfɛsə*] *n* (*BRIT*) catedrático/a; (*US, Canada*) profesor(a) *m/f*.

proficiency [prəˈfɪʃənsi] *n* capacidad *f*, habilidad *f*.

proficient [prəˈfɪʃənt] *adj* experto, hábil.

profile [ˈprəufaɪl] *n* perfil *m*.

profit [ˈprɔfɪt] *n* (*COMM*) ganancia ♦ *vi*: **to ~ by** *or* **from** aprovechar *or* sacar provecho de; ~**ability** [-əˈbɪlɪtɪ] *n* rentabilidad *f*; ~**able** *adj* (*ECON*) rentable.

profound [prəˈfaund] *adj* profundo.

profusely [prəˈfjuːslɪ] *adv* profusamente.

profusion [prəˈfjuːʒən] *n* profusión *f*, abundancia.

programme [ˈprəugræm] (*US* **program**) *n* programa *m* ♦ *vt* programar; ~**r** (*US* **programer**) *n* programador(a) *m/f*; **programming** (*US* **programing**) *n* programación *f*.

progress [*n* ˈprəugrɛs, *vi* prəˈgrɛs] *n* progreso; (*development*) desarrollo ♦ *vi* progresar, avanzar; **in** ~ en curso; ~**ive** [-ˈgrɛsɪv] *adj* progresivo; (*person*) progresista.

prohibit [prəˈhɪbɪt] *vt* prohibir; **to ~ sb from doing sth** prohibir a uno hacer algo; ~**ion** [-ˈbɪʃn] *n* prohibición *f*; (*US*): **P~ion** Ley *f* Seca.

project [*n* ˈprɔdʒɛkt, *vb* prəˈdʒɛkt] *n* proyecto ♦ *vt* proyectar ♦ *vi* (*stick out*) salir, sobresalir.

projectile [prəˈdʒɛktaɪl] *n* proyectil *m*.

projection [prəˈdʒɛkʃən] *n* proyección *f*; (*overhang*) saliente *m*.

projector [prəˈdʒɛktə*] *n* proyector *m*.

proletarian [prəulɪˈtɛərɪən] *n* proletario/a.

proletariat [prəulɪˈtɛərɪət] *n* proletariado.

prologue [ˈprəulɔg] *n* prólogo.

prolong [prəˈlɔŋ] *vt* prolongar, extender.

prom [prɔm] *n abbr* = **promenade**; (*US*: *ball*) baile *m* de gala.

promenade [prɔməˈnaːd] *n* (*by sea*) paseo marítimo; ~ **concert** (*BRIT*) *n* concierto (en que parte del público permanece de pie).

prominence [ˈprɔmɪnəns] *n* importancia.

prominent [ˈprɔmɪnənt] *adj* (*standing out*) saliente; (*important*) eminente, importante.

promiscuous [prəˈmɪskjuəs] *adj* (*sexually*) promiscuo.

promise [ˈprɔmɪs] *n* promesa ♦ *vt, vi* prometer; **promising** *adj* prometedor(a).

promote [prəˈməut] *vt* (*employee*) ascender; (*product, pop star*) hacer propaganda por; (*ideas*) fomentar; ~**r** (*of event*) promotor(a) *m/f*; (*of cause etc*) impulsor(a) *m/f*; **promotion** [-ˈməuʃən] *n* (*advertising campaign*) campaña de promoción *f*; (*in rank*) ascenso.

prompt [prɔmpt] *adj* rápido ♦ *adv*: **at 6 o'clock** ~ a las seis en punto ♦ *n* (*COMPUT*) aviso ♦ *vt* (*urge*) mover, incitar; (*when talking*) instar; (*THEATRE*) apuntar; **to ~ sb to do sth** instar a uno a hacer algo; ~**ly** *adv* rápidamente; (*exactly*) puntualmente.

prone [prəun] *adj* (*lying*) postrado; ~ **to** propenso a.

prong [prɔŋ] *n* diente *m*, punta.

pronoun [ˈprəunaun] *n* pronombre *m*.

pronounce [prəˈnauns] *vt* pronunciar; ~**d** *adj* (*marked*) marcado.

pronunciation [prənʌnsɪˈeɪʃən] *n* pronunciación *f*.

proof [pruːf] *n* prueba ♦ *adj*: ~ **against** a prueba de.

prop [prɔp] *n* apoyo; (*fig*) sostén *m* ♦ *vt* (*also*: ~ **up**) apoyar; (*lean*): **to ~ sth against** apoyar algo contra.

propaganda [prɔpəˈgændə] *n* propaganda.

propagate [ˈprɔpəgeɪt] *vt* (*idea, information*) difundir.

propel [prəˈpɛl] *vt* impulsar, propulsar; ~**ler** *n* hélice *f*.

propensity [prəˈpɛnsɪtɪ] *n* propensión *f*.

proper [ˈprɔpə*] *adj* (*suited, right*) propio; (*exact*) justo; (*seemly*) correcto, decente; (*authentic*) verdadero; (*referring to place*): **the village** ~ el pueblo mismo; ~**ly** *adv* (*adequately*) correcta-

mente; (*decently*) decentemente; ~
noun n nombre m propio.
property ['prɒpətɪ] n propiedad f; (*personal*) bienes mpl muebles; ~ **owner** n
dueño/a de propiedades.
prophecy ['prɒfɪsɪ] n profecía.
prophesy ['prɒfɪsaɪ] vt (*fig*) predecir.
prophet ['prɒfɪt] n profeta m.
proportion [prə'pɔːʃən] n proporción f;
(*share*) parte f; ~**al** adj: ~**al** (**to**) en
proporción (con); ~**al representation** n
representación f proporcional; ~**ate**
adj: ~**ate** (**to**) en proporción (con).
proposal [prə'pəuzl] n (*offer of marriage*) oferta de matrimonio; (*plan*) proyecto.
propose [prə'pəuz] vt proponer ♦ vi declararse; **to** ~ **to do** tener intención de
hacer.
proposition [prɒpə'zɪʃən] n propuesta.
proprietor [prə'praɪətə*] n propietario/a,
dueño/a.
propriety [prə'praɪətɪ] n decoro.
pro rata [-'rɑːtə] adv a prorrateo.
prose [prəuz] n prosa.
prosecute ['prɒsɪkjuːt] vt (*LAW*) procesar; **prosecution** [-'kjuːʃən] n proceso,
causa; (*accusing side*) acusación f;
prosecutor n acusador(a) m/f; (*also:
public prosecutor*) fiscal m.
prospect [n 'prɒspɛkt, vb prə'spɛkt] n
(*possibility*) posibilidad f; (*outlook*)
perspectiva ♦ vi: **to** ~ **for** buscar; ~**s**
npl (*for work etc*) perspectivas fpl;
~**ing** n prospección f; ~**ive** [prə'spɛktɪv]
adj futuro.
prospectus [prə'spɛktəs] n prospecto.
prosper ['prɒspə*] vi prosperar; ~**ity**
[-'spɛrɪtɪ] n prosperidad f; ~**ous** adj
próspero.
prostitute ['prɒstɪtjuːt] n prostituta;
(*male*) hombre que se dedica a la prostitución.
prostrate ['prɒstreɪt] adj postrado.
protagonist [prə'tægənɪst] n protagonista m/f.
protect [prə'tɛkt] vt proteger; ~**ion**
[-'tɛkʃən] n protección f; ~**ive** adj protector(a).
protégé ['prəutɛʒeɪ] n protegido/a.

protein ['prəutiːn] n proteína.
protest [n 'prəutɛst, vb prə'tɛst] n protesta ♦ vi: **to** ~ **about** or **at/against** protestar de/contra ♦ vt (*insist*): **to** ~ (**that**)
insistir en (que).
Protestant ['prɒtɪstənt] adj, n protestante m/f.
protester [prə'tɛstə*] n manifestante m/
f.
protracted [prə'træktɪd] adj prolongado.
protrude [prə'truːd] vi salir, sobresalir.
proud [praud] adj orgulloso; (*pej*) soberbio, altanero.
prove [pruːv] vt probar; (*show*) demostrar ♦ vi: **to** ~ (**to be**) correct resultar
correcto; **to** ~ **o.s.** probar su valía.
proverb ['prɒvəːb] n refrán m.
provide [prə'vaɪd] vt proporcionar, dar;
to ~ **sb with sth** proveer a uno de algo;
~**d** (**that**) conj con tal de que, a condición de que; ~ **for** vt fus (*person*) mantener a; (*problem etc*) tener en cuenta.
providing [prə'vaɪdɪŋ] conj: ~ (**that**) a
condición de que, con tal de que.
province ['prɒvɪns] n provincia; (*fig*) esfera; **provincial** [prə'vɪnʃəl] adj provincial; (*pej*) provinciano.
provision [prə'vɪʒən] n (*supplying*) suministro, abastecimiento; (*of contract
etc*) disposición f; ~**s** npl (*food*) comestibles mpl; ~**al** adj provisional.
proviso [prə'vaɪzəu] n condición f, estipulación f.
provocative [prə'vɒkətɪv] adj provocativo.
provoke [prə'vəuk] vt (*cause*) provocar,
incitar; (*anger*) enojar.
prow [prau] n proa.
prowess ['prauɪs] n destreza.
prowl [praul] vi (*also:* ~ **about,** ~
around) merodear ♦ n: **on the** ~ de merodeo; ~**er** n merodeador(a) m/f.
proxy ['prɒksɪ] n: **by** ~ por poderes.
prude [pruːd] n remilgado/a.
prudence ['pruːdns] n prudencia.
prudent ['pruːdənt] adj prudente.
prune [pruːn] n ciruela pasa ♦ vt podar.
pry [praɪ] vi: **to** ~ (**into**) entrometerse
(en).
PS n abbr (= *postscript*) P.D.

psalm [sɑ:m] *n* salmo.
pseudo- [sju:dəu] *prefix* seudo-;
  pseudonym *n* seudónimo.
psyche ['saɪkɪ] *n* psique *f*.
psychiatric [saɪkɪ'ætrɪk] *adj* psiquiátrico.
psychiatrist [saɪ'kaɪətrɪst] *n* psiquiatra *m/f*.
psychiatry [saɪ'kaɪətrɪ] *n* psiquiatría.
psychic ['saɪkɪk] *adj* (*also*: ~**al**) psíquico.
psychoanalyse [saɪkəu'ænəlaɪz] *vt* psicoanalizar; **psychoanalysis** [-ə'nælɪsɪs] *n* psicoanálisis *m inv*.
psychological [saɪkə'lɔdʒɪkl] *adj* psicológico.
psychologist [saɪ'kɔlədʒɪst] *n* psicólogo/a.
psychology [saɪ'kɔlədʒɪ] *n* psicología.
PTO *abbr* (= *please turn over*) sigue.
pub [pʌb] *n abbr* (= *public house*) 'pub *m*, taberna.
puberty ['pju:bətɪ] *n* pubertad *f*.
pubic ['pju:bɪk] *adj* púbico.
public ['pʌblɪk] *adj* público ♦ *n*: **the** ~ el público; **in** ~ en público; **to make** ~ hacer público; ~ **address system** *n* megafonía.
publican ['pʌblɪkən] *n* tabernero/a.
publication [pʌblɪ'keɪʃən] *n* publicación *f*.
public: ~ **company** *n* sociedad *f* anónima; ~ **convenience** (*BRIT*) *n* aseos *mpl* públicos (*SP*), sanitarios *mpl* (*AM*); ~ **holiday** *n* día de fiesta (*SP*), (día) feriado (*AM*); ~ **house** (*BRIT*) *n* bar *m*, pub *m*.
publicity [pʌb'lɪsɪtɪ] *n* publicidad *f*.
publicize ['pʌblɪsaɪz] *vt* publicitar.
publicly ['pʌblɪklɪ] *adv* públicamente, en público.
public: ~ **opinion** *n* opinión *f* pública; ~ **relations** *n* relaciones *fpl* públicas; ~ **school** *n* (*BRIT*) escuela privada; (*US*) instituto; ~ **-spirited** *adj* que tiene sentido del deber ciudadano; ~ **transport** *n* transporte *m* público.
publish ['pʌblɪʃ] *vt* publicar; ~**er** *n* (*person*) editor/a *m/f*; (*firm*) editorial *f*; ~**ing** *n* (*industry*) industria del libro.
puce [pju:s] *adj* de color pardo rojizo.

pucker ['pʌkə*] *vt* (*pleat*) arrugar; (*brow etc*) fruncir.
pudding ['pudɪŋ] *n* pudín *m*; (*BRIT*: *dessert*) postre *m*; **black** ~ morcilla.
puddle ['pʌdl] *n* charco.
puff [pʌf] *n* soplo; (*of smoke*, *air*) bocanada; (*of breathing*) resoplido ♦ *vt*: **to** ~ **one's pipe** chupar la pipa ♦ *vi* (*pant*) jadear; ~ **out** *vt* hinchar; ~**ed** (*inf*) *adj* (*out of breath*) sin aliento; ~ **pastry** *n* hojaldre *m*; ~**y** *adj* hinchado.
pull [pul] *n* (*tug*): **to give sth a** ~ dar un tirón a algo ♦ *vt* tirar de; (*press*: *trigger*) apretar; (*haul*) tirar, arrastrar; (*close*: *curtain*) echar ♦ *vi* tirar; **to** ~ **to pieces** hacer pedazos; **to not** ~ **one's punches** no andarse con bromas; **to** ~ **one's weight** hacer su parte; **to** ~ **o.s. together** sobreponerse; **to** ~ **sb's leg** tomar el pelo a uno; ~ **apart** *vt* (*break*) romper; ~ **down** *vt* (*building*) derribar; ~ **in** *vi* (*car etc*) parar (junto a la acera); (*train*) llegar a la estación; ~ **off** *vt* (*deal etc*) cerrar; ~ **out** *vi* (*car*, *train etc*) salir ♦ *vt* sacar, arrancar; ~ **over** *vi* (*AUT*) hacerse a un lado; ~ **through** *vi* (*MED*) reponerse; ~ **up** *vi* (*stop*) parar ♦ *vt* (*raise*) levantar; (*uproot*) arrancar, desarraigar.
pulley ['pulɪ] *n* polea.
pullover ['puləuvə*] *n* jersey *m*, suéter *m*.
pulp [pʌlp] *n* (*of fruit*) pulpa.
pulpit ['pulpɪt] *n* púlpito.
pulsate [pʌl'seɪt] *vi* pulsar, latir.
pulse [pʌls] *n* (*ANAT*) pulso; (*rhythm*) pulsación *f*; (*BOT*) legumbre *f*.
pummel ['pʌml] *vt* aporrear.
pump [pʌmp] *n* bomba; (*shoe*) zapatilla ♦ *vt* sacar con una bomba; ~ **up** *vt* inflar.
pumpkin ['pʌmpkɪn] *n* calabaza.
pun [pʌn] *n* juego de palabras.
punch [pʌntʃ] *n* (*blow*) golpe *m*, puñetazo; (*tool*) punzón *m*; (*drink*) ponche *m* ♦ *vt* (*hit*): **to** ~ **sb/sth** dar un puñetazo *or* golpear a uno/algo; ~**line** *n* palabras que rematan un chiste; ~**-up** (*BRIT*: *inf*) *n* riña.
punctual ['pʌŋktjuəl] *adj* puntual.

punctuation [pʌŋktju'eɪʃən] n puntuación f.
puncture ['pʌŋktʃə*] (BRIT) n pinchazo ♦ vt pinchar.
pundit ['pʌndɪt] n experto/a.
pungent ['pʌndʒənt] adj acre.
punish ['pʌnɪʃ] vt castigar; ~ment n castigo.
punk [pʌŋk] n (also: ~ rocker) punki m/f; (also: ~ rock) música punk; (US: inf: hoodlum) rufián m.
punt [pʌnt] n (boat) batea.
punter ['pʌntə*] (BRIT) n (gambler) jugador(a) m/f; (: inf) cliente m/f.
puny ['pju:nɪ] adj débil.
pup [pʌp] n cachorro.
pupil ['pju:pl] n alumno/a; (of eye) pupila.
puppet ['pʌpɪt] n títere m.
puppy ['pʌpɪ] n cachorro, perrito.
purchase ['pə:tʃɪs] n compra ♦ vt comprar; ~r n comprador(a) m/f.
pure [pjuə*] adj puro.
purée ['pjuəreɪ] n puré m.
purely ['pjuəlɪ] adv puramente.
purge [pə:dʒ] n (MED, POL) purga ♦ vt purgar.
purify ['pjuərɪfaɪ] vt purificar, depurar.
puritan ['pjuərɪtən] n puritano/a.
purity ['pjuərɪtɪ] n pureza.
purple ['pə:pl] adj purpúreo; morado.
purport [pə:'pɔ:t] vi: to ~ to be/do dar a entender que es/hace.
purpose ['pə:pəs] n propósito; on ~ a propósito, adrede; ~ful adj resuelto, determinado.
purr [pə:*] vi ronronear.
purse [pə:s] n monedero; (US) bolsa (SP), cartera (AM) ♦ vt fruncir.
purser ['pə:sə*] n (NAUT) comisario/a.
pursue [pə'sju:] vt seguir; ~r n perseguidor(a) m/f.
pursuit [pə'sju:t] n (chase) caza; (occupation) actividad f.
push [puʃ] n empuje m, empujón m; (of button) presión f; (drive) empuje m ♦ vt empujar; (button) apretar; (promote) promover ♦ vi empujar; (demand): to ~ for luchar por; ~ aside vt apartar con la mano; ~ off (inf) vi largarse; ~

on vi seguir adelante; ~ through vi (crowd) abrirse paso a empujones ♦ vt (measure) despachar; ~ up vt (total, prices) hacer subir; ~chair (BRIT) n sillita de ruedas; ~er n (drug ~er) traficante m/f de drogas; ~over (inf) n: it's a ~over está tirado; ~-up (US) n plancha; ~y (pej) adj agresivo.
puss [pus] (inf) n minino.
pussy(-cat) ['pusɪ-] (inf) n = **puss.**
put [put] (pt, pp put) vt (place) poner, colocar; (~ into) meter; (say) expresar; (a question) hacer; (estimate) estimar; ~ about or around vt (rumour) diseminar; ~ across vt (ideas etc) comunicar; ~ away vt (store) guardar; ~ back vt (replace) devolver a su lugar; (postpone) aplazar; ~ by vt (money) guardar; ~ down vt (on ground) poner en el suelo; (animal) sacrificar; (in writing) apuntar; (revolt etc) sofocar; (attribute): to ~ sth down to atribuir algo a; ~ forward vt (ideas) presentar, proponer; ~ in vt (complaint) presentar; (time) dedicar; ~ off vt (postpone) aplazar; (discourage) desanimar; ~ on vt ponerse; (light etc) encender; (play etc) presentar; (gain): to ~ on weight engordar; (brake) echar; (record, kettle etc) poner; (assume) adoptar; ~ out vt (fire, light) apagar; (rubbish etc) sacar; (cat etc) echar; (one's hand) alargar; (inf: person): to be ~ out alterarse; ~ through vt (TEL) poner; (plan etc) hacer aprobar; ~ up vt (raise) levantar, alzar; (hang) colgar; (build) construir; (increase) aumentar; (accommodate) alojar; ~ up with vt fus aguantar.
putrid ['pju:trɪd] adj podrido.
putt [pʌt] n putt m, golpe m corto; ~ing green n green m; minigolf m.
putty ['pʌtɪ] n masilla.
put-up: ~ **job** (BRIT) n amaño.
puzzle ['pʌzl] n rompecabezas m inv; (also: crossword ~) crucigrama m; (mystery) misterio ♦ vt dejar perplejo, confundir ♦ vi: to ~ over sth devanarse los sesos con algo; **puzzling** adj misterioso, extraño.

pyjamas [pɪ'dʒɑːməz] (*BRIT*) *npl* pijama *m*.

pylon ['paɪlən] *n* torre *f* de conducción eléctrica.

pyramid ['pɪrəmɪd] *n* pirámide *f*.

Pyrenees [pɪrə'niːz] *npl*: **the ~** los Pirineos.

python ['paɪθən] *n* pitón *m*.

Q

quack [kwæk] *n* graznido; (*pej: doctor*) curandero/a.

quad [kwɒd] *n abbr* = **quadrangle**; **quadruplet**.

quadrangle ['kwɒdræŋgl] *n* patio.

quadruple [kwɒ'druːpl] *vt, vi* cuadruplicar.

quadruplets [kwɒ'druːplɪts] *npl* cuatrillizos/as.

quagmire ['kwægmaɪə*] *n* lodazal *m*, cenegal *m*.

quail [kweɪl] *n* codorniz *f* ♦ *vi*: **to ~ at** *or* **before** amedrentarse ante.

quaint [kweɪnt] *adj* extraño; (*picturesque*) pintoresco.

quake [kweɪk] *vi* temblar ♦ *n abbr* = **earthquake**.

Quaker ['kweɪkə*] *n* cuáquero/a.

qualification [kwɒlɪfɪ'keɪʃən] *n* (*ability*) capacidad *f*; (*often pl: diploma etc*) título; (*reservation*) salvedad *f*.

qualified ['kwɒlɪfaɪd] *adj* capacitado; (*professionally*) titulado; (*limited*) limitado.

qualify ['kwɒlɪfaɪ] *vt* (*make competent*) capacitar; (*modify*) modificar ♦ *vi* (*in competition*): **to ~ (for)** calificarse (para); (*pass examination(s)*): **to ~ (as)** calificarse (de), graduarse (en); (*be eligible*): **to ~ (for)** reunir los requisitos (para).

quality ['kwɒlɪtɪ] *n* calidad *f*; (*of person*) cualidad *f*.

qualm [kwɑːm] *n* escrúpulo.

quandary ['kwɒndrɪ] *n*: **to be in a ~** tener dudas.

quantity ['kwɒntɪtɪ] *n* cantidad *f*; **in ~** en grandes cantidades; **~ surveyor** *n*

aparejador(a) *m/f*.

quarantine ['kwɒrntiːn] *n* cuarentena.

quarrel ['kwɒrl] *n* riña, pelea ♦ *vi* reñir, pelearse; **~some** *adj* pendenciero.

quarry ['kwɒrɪ] *n* cantera; (*animal*) presa.

quart [kwɔːt] *n* ≈ litro.

quarter ['kwɔːtə*] *n* cuarto, cuarta parte *f*; (*US: coin*) *moneda de 25 centavos*; (*of year*) trimestre *m*; (*district*) barrio ♦ *vt* dividir en cuartos; (*MIL: lodge*) alojar; **~s** *npl* (*barracks*) cuartel *m*; (*living ~s*) alojamiento; **a ~ of an hour** un cuarto de hora; **~ final** *n* cuarto de final; **~ly** *adj* trimestral ♦ *adv* cada 3 meses, trimestralmente.

quartet(te) [kwɔː'tɛt] *n* cuarteto.

quartz [kwɔːts] *n* cuarzo.

quash [kwɒʃ] *vt* (*verdict*) anular.

quasi- ['kweɪzaɪ] *prefix* cuasi.

quaver ['kweɪvə*] (*BRIT*) *n* (*MUS*) corchea ♦ *vi* temblar.

quay [kiː] *n* (*also:* **~side**) muelle *m*.

queasy ['kwiːzɪ] *adj*: **to feel ~** tener náuseas.

queen [kwiːn] *n* reina; (*CARDS etc*) dama; **~ mother** *n* reina madre.

queer [kwɪə*] *adj* raro, extraño ♦ *n* (*inf: highly offensive*) maricón *m*.

quell [kwɛl] *vt* (*feeling*) calmar; (*rebellion etc*) sofocar.

quench [kwɛntʃ] *vt*: **to ~ one's thirst** apagar la sed.

querulous ['kwɛruləs] *adj* quejumbroso.

query ['kwɪərɪ] *n* (*question*) pregunta ♦ *vt* dudar de.

quest [kwɛst] *n* busca, búsqueda.

question ['kwɛstʃən] *n* pregunta; (*doubt*) duda; (*matter*) asunto, cuestión *f* ♦ *vt* (*doubt*) dudar de; (*interrogate*) interrogar, hacer preguntas a; **beyond ~** fuera de toda duda; **out of the ~** imposible; ni hablar; **~able** *adj* dudoso; **~ mark** *n* punto de interrogación; **~naire** [-'nɛə*] *n* cuestionario.

queue [kjuː] (*BRIT*) *n* cola ♦ *vi* (*also:* **~ up**) hacer cola.

quibble ['kwɪbl] *vi* sutilizar.

quick [kwɪk] *adj* rápido; (*agile*) ágil; (*mind*) listo ♦ *n*: **cut to the ~** (*fig*) heri-

do en lo vivo; **be** ~! ¡date prisa!; **~en**
vt apresurar ♦ *vi* apresurarse, darse
prisa; **~ly** *adv* rápidamente, de prisa;
~sand *n* arenas *fpl* movedizas; **~-
witted** *adj* perspicaz.

quid [kwɪd] (*BRIT: inf*) *n inv* libra.

quiet ['kwaɪət] *adj* (*voice, music etc*)
bajo; (*person, place*) tranquilo; (*ceremony*) íntimo ♦ *n* silencio; (*calm*) tranquilidad *f* ♦ *vt, vi* (*US*) = **~en**; **~en**
(*also: ~en down*) *vi* calmarse; (*grow
silent*) callarse ♦ *vt* càlmar; hacer callar; **~ly** *adv* tranquilamente; (*silently*)
silenciosamente; **~ness** *n* silencio;
tranquilidad *f*.

quilt [kwɪlt] *n* edredón *m*.

quin [kwɪn] *n abbr* = **quintuplet**.

quinine [kwɪˈniːn] *n* quinina.

quintet(te) [kwɪnˈtet] *n* quinteto.

quintuplets [kwɪnˈtjuːplɪts] *npl* quinti-
llizos/as.

quip [kwɪp] *n* pulla.

quirk [kwəːk] *n* peculiaridad *f*; (*accident*) capricho.

quit [kwɪt] (*pt, pp* **quit** *or* **quitted**) *vt* dejar, abandonar; (*premises*) desocupar ♦
vi (*give up*) renunciar; (*resign*) dimitir.

quite [kwaɪt] *adv* (*rather*) bastante; (*entirely*) completamente; **that's not ~ big
enough** no acaba de ser lo bastante
grande; **~ a few of them** un buen número de ellos; **~ (so)!** ¡así es!, ¡exactamente!

quits [kwɪts] *adj*: **~ (with)** en paz
(con); **let's call it ~** dejémoslo en tablas.

quiver ['kwɪvə*] *vi* estremecerse

quiz [kwɪz] *n* concurso ♦ *vt* interrogar;
~zical *adj* burlón(ona).

quota ['kwəutə] *n* cuota.

quotation [kwəuˈteɪʃən] *n* cita; (*estimate*) presupuesto; **~ marks** *npl* comillas *fpl*.

quote [kwəut] *n* cita; (*estimate*) presupuesto ♦ *vt* citar; (*price*) cotizar ♦ *vi*:
to ~ from citar de; **~s** *npl* (*inverted
commas*) comillas *fpl*.

quotient ['kwəuʃənt] *n* cociente *m*.

R

rabbi ['ræbaɪ] *n* rabino.

rabbit ['ræbɪt] *n* conejo; **~ hutch** *n* conejera.

rabble ['ræbl] (*pej*) *n* chusma, popula-
cho.

rabies ['reɪbiːz] *n* rabia.

RAC (*BRIT*) *n abbr* = **Royal Automobile
Club**.

raccoon [rəˈkuːn] *n* mapache *m*.

race [reɪs] *n* carrera; (*species*) raza ♦ *vt*
(*horse*) hacer correr; (*engine*) acelerar
♦ *vi* (*compete*) competir; (*run*) correr;
(*pulse*) latir a ritmo acelerado; **~ car**
(*US*) *n* = **racing car**; **~ car driver** (*US*)
n = **racing driver**; **~course** *n* hipódromo; **~horse** *n* caballo de carreras;
~track *n* pista; (*for cars*) autódromo.

racial ['reɪʃl] *adj* racial.

racing ['reɪsɪŋ] *n* carreras *fpl*; **~ car**
(*BRIT*) *n* coche *m* de carreras; **~ driver**
(*BRIT*) *n* corredor(a) *m/f* de coches.

racism ['reɪsɪzəm] *n* racismo; **racist**
[-sɪst] *adj, n* racista *m/f*.

rack [ræk] *n* (*also: luggage ~*) rejilla;
(*shelf*) estante *m*; (*also: roof ~*) baca,
portaequipajes *m inv*; (*dish ~*) escurreplatos *m inv*; (*clothes ~*) percha ♦ *vt*
atormentar; **to ~ one's brains** devanarse los sesos.

racket ['rækɪt] *n* (*for tennis*) raqueta;
(*noise*) ruido, estrépito; (*swindle*) estafa, timo.

racoon [rəˈkuːn] *n* = **raccoon**.

racquet ['rækɪt] *n* raqueta.

racy ['reɪsɪ] *adj* picante, salado.

radar ['reɪdɑː*] *n* radar *m*.

radiance ['reɪdɪəns] *n* brillantez *f*, resplandor *m*.

radiant ['reɪdɪənt] *adj* radiante (de felicidad).

radiate ['reɪdɪeɪt] *vt* (*heat*) radiar;
(*emotion*) irradiar ♦ *vi* (*lines*) extenderse.

radiation [reɪdɪˈeɪʃən] *n* radiación *f*.

radiator ['reɪdɪeɪtə*] *n* radiador *m*.

radical ['rædɪkl] *adj* radical.

radii ['reɪdɪaɪ] *npl of* **radius.**

radio ['reɪdɪəu] *n* radio *f*; **on the** ~ por radio.

radio... [reɪdɪəu] *prefix*: ~**active** *adj* radioactivo; **radiography** [-'ɔgrəfɪ] *n* radiografía; **radiology** [-'ɔlədʒɪ] *n* radiología; **radio station** *n* emisora; **radiotherapy** ['-θerəpɪ] *n* radioterapia.

radish ['rædɪʃ] *n* rábano.

radius ['reɪdɪəs] (*pl* **radii**) *n* radio.

RAF *n abbr* = **Royal Air Force.**

raffle ['ræfl] *n* rifa, sorteo.

raft [rɑːft] *n* balsa; (*also: life* ~) balsa salvavidas.

rafter ['rɑːftə*] *n* viga.

rag [ræg] *n* (*piece of cloth*) trapo; (*torn cloth*) harapo; (*pej: newspaper*) periodicucho; (*for charity*) *actividades estudiantiles benéficas*; ~**s** *npl* (*torn clothes*) harapos *mpl*; ~**-and-bone man** (*BRIT*) *n* = ~**man**; ~ **doll** *n* muñeca de trapo.

rage [reɪdʒ] *n* rabia, furor *m* ♦ *vi* (*person*) rabiar, estar furioso; (*storm*) bramar; **it's all the** ~ (*very fashionable*) está muy de moda.

ragged ['rægɪd] *adj* (*edge*) desigual, mellado; (*appearance*) andrajoso, harapiento.

ragman ['rægmæn] *n* trapero.

raid [reɪd] *n* (*MIL*) incursión *f*; (*criminal*) asalto; (*by police*) redada ♦ *vt* invadir, atacar; asaltar.

rail [reɪl] *n* (*on stair*) barandilla, pasamanos *m inv*; (*on bridge, balcony*) pretil *m*; (*of ship*) barandilla; (*also: towel* ~) toallero; ~**s** *npl* (*RAIL*) vía; **by** ~ por ferrocarril; ~**ing(s)** *n(pl)* vallado; ~**road** (*US*) *n* = ~**way**; ~**way** (*BRIT*) *n* ferrocarril *m*, vía férrea; ~**way line** (*BRIT*) *n* línea (de ferrocarril); ~**wayman** (*BRIT*) *n* ferroviario; ~**way station** (*BRIT*) *n* estación *f* de ferrocarril.

rain [reɪn] *n* lluvia ♦ *vi* llover; **in the** ~ bajo la lluvia; **it's** ~**ing** llueve, está lloviendo; ~**bow** *n* arco iris; ~**coat** *n* impermeable *m*; ~**drop** *n* gota de lluvia; ~**fall** *n* lluvia; ~**y** *adj* lluvioso.

raise [reɪz] *n* aumento ♦ *vt* levantar; (*increase*) aumentar; (*improve: mo-*

rale) subir; (: *standards*) mejorar; (*doubts*) suscitar; (*a question*) plantear; (*cattle, family*) criar; (*crop*) cultivar; (*army*) reclutar; (*loan*) obtener; **to** ~ **one's voice** alzar la voz.

raisin ['reɪzn] *n* pasa de Corinto.

rake [reɪk] *n* (*tool*) rastrillo; (*person*) libertino ♦ *vt* (*garden*) rastrillar; (*with machine gun*) barrer.

rally ['rælɪ] *n* (*POL etc*) reunión *f*, mitin *m*; (*AUT*) rallye *m*; (*TENNIS*) peloteo ♦ *vt* reunir ♦ *vi* recuperarse; ~ **round** *vt fus* (*fig*) dar apoyo a.

RAM [ræm] *n abbr* (= *random access memory*) RAM *f*.

ram [ræm] *n* carnero; (*also: battering* ~) ariete *m* ♦ *vt* (*crash into*) dar contra, chocar con; (*push: fist etc*) empujar con fuerza.

ramble ['ræmbl] *n* caminata, excursión *f* en el campo ♦ *vi* (*pej: also:* ~ **on**) divagar; ~**r** *n* excursionista *m/f*; (*BOT*) trepadora; **rambling** *adj* (*speech*) inconexo; (*house*) laberíntico; (*BOT*) trepador(a).

ramp [ræmp] *n* rampa; **on/off** ~ (*US: AUT*) vía de acceso/salida.

rampage [ræm'peɪdʒ] *n*: **to be on the** ~ desmandarse ♦ *vi*: **they went rampaging through the town** recorrieron la ciudad armando alboroto.

rampant ['ræmpənt] *adj* (*disease etc*): **to be** ~ estar extendiéndose mucho.

rampart ['ræmpɑːt] *n* (*fortification*) baluarte *m*.

ramshackle ['ræmʃækl] *adj* destartalado.

ran [ræn] *pt of* **run.**

ranch [rɑːntʃ] *n* hacienda, estancia; ~**er** *n* ganadero.

rancid ['rænsɪd] *adj* rancio.

rancour ['ræŋkə*] (*US* **rancor**) *n* rencor *m*.

random ['rændəm] *adj* fortuito, sin orden; (*COMPUT, MATH*) aleatorio ♦ *n*: **at** ~ al azar.

randy ['rændɪ] (*BRIT: inf*) *adj* cachondo.

rang [ræŋ] *pt of* **ring.**

range [reɪndʒ] *n* (*of mountains*) cadena de montañas, cordillera; (*of missile*) alcance *m*; (*of voice*) registro; (*series*) serie *f*; (*of products*) surtido; (*MIL: also: shooting ~*) campo de tiro; (*also: kitchen ~*) fogón *m* ♦ *vt* (*place*) colocar; (*arrange*) arreglar ♦ *vi*: to ~ over (*extend*) extenderse por; to ~ from ... to ... oscilar entre ... y ....

ranger [reindʒə*] *n* guardabosques *m inv.*

rank [ræŋk] *n* (*row*) fila; (*MIL*) rango; (*status*) categoría; (*BRIT: also: taxi ~*) parada de taxis ♦ *vi*: to ~ among figurar entre ♦ *adj* fétido, rancio; the ~ and file (*fig*) la base.

rankle [ræŋkl] *vi* doler.

ransack [rænsæk] *vt* (*search*) registrar; (*plunder*) saquear.

ransom [rænsəm] *n* rescate *m*; to hold to ~ (*fig*) hacer chantaje a.

rant [rænt] *vi* divagar, desvariar.

rap [ræp] *vt* golpear, dar un golpecito en.

rape [reip] *n* violación *f*; (*BOT*) colza ♦ *vt* violar; ~ (seed) oil *n* aceite *m* de colza.

rapid [ræpid] *adj* rápido; ~ity [rə'piditi] *n* rapidez *f*; ~ly *adv* rápidamente; ~s *npl* (*GEO*) rápidos *mpl.*

rapist [reipist] *n* violador *m.*

rapport [ræ'pɔ:*] *n* simpatía.

rapture [ræptʃə*] *n* éxtasis *m*; **rapturous** *adj* extático.

rare [rɛə*] *adj* raro, poco común; (*CULIN: steak*) poco hecho.

rarely [rɛəli] *adv* pocas veces.

raring [rɛəriŋ] *adj*: to be ~ to go (*inf*) tener muchas ganas de empezar.

rarity [rɛəriti] *n* rareza, escasez *f.*

rascal [rɑ:skl] *n* pillo, pícaro.

rash [ræʃ] *adj* imprudente, precipitado ♦ *n* (*MED*) sarpullido, erupción *f* (cutánea); (*of events*) serie *f.*

rasher [ræʃə*] *n* lonja.

raspberry [rɑ:zbəri] *n* frambuesa.

rasping [rɑ:spiŋ] *adj*: a ~ noise un ruido áspero.

rat [ræt] *n* rata.

rate [reit] *n* (*ratio*) razón *f*; (*price*) precio; (: *of hotel etc*) tarifa; (*of interest*) tipo; (*speed*) velocidad *f* ♦ *vt* (*value*) tasar; (*estimate*) estimar; ~s *npl* (*BRIT: property tax*) impuesto municipal; (*fees*) tarifa; to ~ sth/sb as considerar algo/a uno como; ~able value (*BRIT*) *n* valor *m* impuesto; ~payer (*BRIT*) *n* contribuyente *m/f.*

rather [rɑ:ðə*] *adv*: it's ~ expensive es algo caro; (*too much*) es demasiado caro; (*to some extent*) más bien; there's ~ a lot hay bastante; I would *or* I'd ~ go preferiría ir; or ~ mejor dicho.

ratify [rætifai] *vt* ratificar.

rating [reitiŋ] *n* tasación *f*; (*score*) índice *m*; (*BRIT: NAUT: sailor*) marinero; (*of ship*) clase *f*; ~s *npl* (*RADIO, TV*) niveles *mpl* de audiencia.

ratio [reiʃiəu] *n* razón *f*; in the ~ of 100 to 1 a razón de 100 a 1.

ration [ræʃən] *n* ración *f* ♦ *vt* racionar; ~s *npl* víveres *mpl.*

rational [ræʃənl] *adj* (*solution, reasoning*) lógico, razonable; (*person*) cuerdo, sensato; ~e [-'nɑ:l] *n* razón *f* fundamental; ~ize *vt* justificar.

rationing [ræʃniŋ] *n* racionamiento.

rat race *n* lucha incesante por la supervivencia.

rattle [rætl] *n* golpeteo; (*of train etc*) traqueteo; (*for baby*) sonaja, sonajero ♦ *vi* castañetear; (*car, bus*): to ~ along traquetear ♦ *vt* hacer sonar agitando; ~snake *n* serpiente *f* de cascabel.

raucous [rɔ:kəs] *adj* estridente, ronco.

ravage [rævidʒ] *vt* hacer estragos en, destrozar; ~s *npl* estragos *mpl.*

rave [reiv] *vi* (*in anger*) encolerizarse; (*with enthusiasm*) entusiasmarse; (*MED*) delirar, desvariar.

raven [reivən] *n* cuervo.

ravenous [rævənəs] *adj* hambriento.

ravine [rə'vi:n] *n* barranco.

raving [reiviŋ] *adj*: ~ lunatic loco/a de atar.

ravishing [ræviʃiŋ] *adj* encantador(a).

raw [rɔ:] *adj* crudo; (*not processed*) bruto; (*sore*) vivo; (*inexperienced*) novato, inexperto; ~ deal (*inf*) n injusticia; ~ material *n* materia prima.

ray [rei] *n* rayo; ~ of hope (rayo de) esperanza.

rayon ['reɪɔn] n rayón m.

raze [reɪz] vt arrasar.

razor ['reɪzə*] n (open) navaja; (safety ~) máquina de afeitar; (electric ~) máquina (eléctrica) de afeitar; ~ **blade** n hoja de afeitar.

Rd abbr = road.

re [ri:] prep con referencia a.

reach [ri:tʃ] n alcance m; (of river etc) extensión f entre dos recodos ♦ vt alcanzar, llegar a; (achieve) lograr ♦ vi extenderse; **within ~** al alcance (de la mano); **out of ~** fuera del alcance; **~ out** vt: (hand) tender ♦ vi: **to ~ out for** sth alargar or tender la mano para tomar algo.

react [ri:'ækt] vi reaccionar; **~ion** [-'ækʃən] n reacción f.

reactor [ri:'æktə*] n (also: nuclear ~) reactor m (nuclear).

read [ri:d, pt, pp red] (pt, pp read) vi leer ♦ vt leer; (understand) entender; (study) estudiar; **~ out** vt leer en alta voz; **~able** adj (willingly) legible; (book) leíble; **~er** n lector(a) m/f; (book) libro de lecturas; (BRIT: at university) profesor(a) m/f adjunto/a; **~ership** n (of paper etc) (número de) lectores mpl.

readily ['redɪlɪ] adv (willingly) de buena gana; (easily) fácilmente; (quickly) en seguida.

readiness ['redɪnɪs] n buena voluntad f; (preparedness) preparación f; **in ~** (prepared) listo, preparado.

reading ['ri:dɪŋ] n lectura f; (on instrument) indicación f.

readjust [ri:ə'dʒʌst] vt reajustar ♦ vi (adapt): **to ~ (to)** reajustarse (a).

ready ['redɪ] adj listo, preparado; (willing) dispuesto; (available) disponible ♦ adv: **~-cooked** listo para comer ♦ n: **at the ~** (MIL) listo para tirar; **to get ~** vi prepararse ♦ vt preparar; **~-made** adj confeccionado; **~ money** n dinero contante; **~ reckoner** n libro de cálculos hechos; **~-to-wear** adj confeccionado.

real [rɪəl] adj verdadero, auténtico; **in ~ terms** en términos reales; **~ estate** n

bienes mpl raíces; **~istic** [-'lɪstɪk] adj realista.

reality [ri:'ælɪtɪ] n realidad f.

realization [rɪəlaɪ'zeɪʃən] n comprensión f; (fulfilment, COMM) realización f.

realize ['rɪəlaɪz] vt (understand) darse cuenta de; (fulfil, COMM: asset) realizar.

really ['rɪəlɪ] adv realmente; (for emphasis) verdaderamente; (actually): **what ~ happened** lo que pasó en realidad; **~?** ¿de veras?; **~!** (annoyance) ¡vamos!, ¡por favor!

realm [relm] n reino; (fig) esfera.

realtor ['rɪəltɔ:*] (US) n corredor(a) m/f de bienes raíces.

reap [ri:p] vt segar; (fig) cosechar, recoger.

reappear [ri:ə'pɪə*] vi reaparecer.

rear [rɪə*] adj trasero ♦ n parte f trasera ♦ vt (cattle, family) criar ♦ vi (also: ~ up) (animal) encabritarse; **~guard** n retaguardia.

rearmament [ri:'ɑ:məmənt] n rearme m.

rearrange [ri:ə'reɪndʒ] vt ordenar or arreglar de nuevo.

rear-view: **~ mirror** n (AUT) (espejo) retrovisor m.

reason ['ri:zn] n razón f ♦ vi: **to ~ with sb** tratar de que uno entre en razón; **it stands to ~ that** es lógico que; **~able** adj razonable; (sensible) sensato; **~ably** adv razonablemente; **~ed** adj (argument) razonado; **~ing** n razonamiento, argumentos mpl.

reassurance [ri:ə'ʃuərəns] n consuelo.

reassure [ri:ə'ʃuə*] vt tranquilizar, alentar; **to ~ sb that** tranquilizar a uno asegurando que; **reassuring** adj alentador(a).

rebate ['ri:beɪt] n (on tax etc) desgravación f.

rebel [n 'rebl, vi ri'bel] n rebelde m/f ♦ vi rebelarse, sublevarse; **~lion** [rɪ'beljən] n rebelión f, sublevación f; **~lious** [rɪ'beljəs] adj rebelde; (child) revoltoso.

rebirth ['ri:bə:θ] n renacimiento.

rebound [vi ri'baund, n 'ri:baund] vi (ball) rebotar ♦ n rebote m; **on the ~**

(*also fig*) de rebote.

rebuff [rɪ'bʌf] *n* desaire *m*, rechazo.

rebuild [ri:'bɪld] (*irreg*) *vt* reconstruir.

rebuke [rɪ'bju:k] *n* reprimenda ♦ *vt* reprender.

rebut [rɪ'bʌt] *vt* rebatir.

recalcitrant [rɪ'kælsɪtrənt] *adj* reacio.

recall [rɪ'kɔ:l] *vt* (*remember*) recordar; (*ambassador etc*) retirar ♦ *n* recuerdo; retirada.

recant [rɪ'kænt] *vi* retractarse.

recap ['ri:kæp] *vt, vi* recapitular.

recapitulate [ri:kə'pɪtjuleɪt] *vt, vi* = **recap.**

recapture [ri:'kæptʃə*] *vt* recobrar.

rec'd *abbr* (= *received*) rbdo.

recede [rɪ'si:d] *vi* (*memory*) ir borrándose; (*hair*) retroceder; **receding** *adj* (*forehead, chin*) huidizo; (*hair*): **to have a receding hairline** tener entradas.

receipt [rɪ'si:t] *n* (*document*) recibo; (*for parcel etc*) acuse *m* de recibo; (*act of receiving*) recepción *f*; **~s** *npl* (*COMM*) ingresos *mpl*.

receive [rɪ'si:v] *vt* recibir; (*guest*) acoger; (*wound*) sufrir; **~r** *n* (*TEL*) auricular *m*; (*RADIO*) receptor *m*; (*of stolen goods*) perista *m/f*; (*COMM*) administrador *m* jurídico.

recent ['ri:snt] *adj* reciente; **~ly** *adv* recientemente; **~ly arrived** recién llegado.

receptacle [rɪ'septɪkl] *n* receptáculo.

reception [rɪ'sepʃən] *n* recepción *f*; (*welcome*) acogida; **~ desk** *n* recepción *f*; **~ist** *n* recepcionista *m/f*.

recess [rɪ'ses] *n* (*in room*) hueco; (*for bed*) nicho; (*secret place*) escondrijo; (*POL etc: holiday*) clausura; **~ion** [-'seʃən] *n* recesión *f*.

recharge [ri:'tʃɑːdʒ] *vt* (*battery*) recargar.

recipe ['resɪpɪ] *n* receta; (*for disaster, success*) fórmula.

recipient [rɪ'sɪpɪənt] *n* recibidor(a) *m/f*; (*of letter*) destinatario/a.

recital [rɪ'saɪtl] *n* recital *m*.

recite [rɪ'saɪt] *vt* (*poem*) recitar.

reckless ['rekləs] *adj* temerario, imprudente; (*driving, driver*) peligroso; **~ly**

adv imprudentemente; de modo peligroso.

reckon ['rekən] *vt* calcular; (*consider*) considerar; (*think*): **I ~ that ...** me parece que ...; **~ on** *vt fus* contar con; **~ing** *n* cálculo.

reclaim [rɪ'kleɪm] *vt* (*land, waste*) recuperar; (*land: from sea*) rescatar; (*demand back*) reclamar.

reclamation [reklə'meɪʃən] *n* (*of land*) acondicionamiento de tierras.

recline [rɪ'klaɪn] *vi* reclinarse; **reclining** *adj* (*seat*) reclinable.

recluse [rɪ'klu:s] *n* recluso/a.

recognition [rekəg'nɪʃən] *n* reconocimiento; **transformed beyond ~** irreconocible.

recognizable ['rekəgnaɪzəbl] *adj*: **~ (by)** reconocible (por).

recognize ['rekəgnaɪz] *vt*: **to ~ (by/as)** reconocer (por/como).

recoil [*vi* rɪ'kɔɪl, *n* 'ri:kɔɪl] *vi* (*person*): **to ~ from doing sth** retraerse de hacer algo ♦ *n* (*of gun*) retroceso.

recollect [rekə'lekt] *vt* recordar, acordarse de; **~ion** [-'lekʃən] *n* recuerdo.

recommend [rekə'mend] *vt* recomendar.

recompense ['rekəmpens] *n* recompensa.

reconcile ['rekənsaɪl] *vt* (*two people*) reconciliar; (*two facts*) compaginar; **to ~ o.s. to sth** conformarse a algo.

recondition [ri:kən'dɪʃən] *vt* (*machine*) reacondicionar.

reconnaissance [rɪ'kɔnɪsns] *n* (*MIL*) reconocimiento.

reconnoitre [rekə'nɔɪtə*] (*US* **reconnoiter**) *vt, vi* (*MIL*) reconocer.

reconsider [ri:kən'sɪdə*] *vt* repensar.

reconstruct [ri:kən'strʌkt] *vt* reconstruir.

record [*n* 'rekɔːd, *vt* rɪ'kɔːd] *n* (*MUS*) disco; (*of meeting etc*) acta; (*register*) registro, partida; (*file*) archivo; (*also: criminal ~*) antecedentes *mpl*; (*written*) expediente *m*; (*SPORT, COMPUT*) récord *m* ♦ *vt* registrar; (*MUS: song etc*) grabar; **in ~ time** en un tiempo récord; **off the ~** *adj* no oficial ♦ *adv* confidencialmente; ~ **card** n (in file) ficha; ~**ed delivery** (BRIT) n (POST) entrega con acuse de recibo; ~**er** n (MUS) flauta de pico; ~ **holder** n (SPORT) actual poseedor(a) m/f del récord; ~**ing** n (MUS) grabación f; ~ **player** n tocadiscos m inv.

recount [rɪ'kaunt] vt contar.

re-count [n 'riːkaunt, vb riː'kaunt] n (POL: of votes) segundo escrutinio ♦ vt volver a contar.

recoup [rɪ'kuːp] vt: **to ~ one's losses** recuperar las pérdidas.

recourse [rɪ'kɔːs] n: **to have ~ to** recurrir a.

recover [rɪ'kʌvə*] vt recuperar ♦ vi (from illness, shock) recuperarse; ~**y** n recuperación f.

recreation [rɛkrɪ'eɪʃən] n recreo; ~**al** adj de recreo.

recruit [rɪ'kruːt] n recluta m/f ♦ vt reclutar; (staff) contratar (personal); ~**ment** n reclutamiento.

rectangle ['rɛktæŋgl] n rectángulo; **rectangular** [-'tæŋgjulə*] adj rectangular.

rectify ['rɛktɪfaɪ] vt rectificar.

rector ['rɛktə*] n (REL) párroco; ~**y** n casa del párroco.

recuperate [rɪ'kuːpəreɪt] vi reponerse, restablecerse.

recur [rɪ'kɜː*] vi repetirse; (pain, illness) producirse de nuevo; ~**rence** [rɪ'kʌrens] n repetición f; ~**rent** [rɪ'kʌrent] adj repetido.

red [rɛd] n rojo ♦ adj rojo; (hair) pelirrojo; (wine) tinto; **to be in the ~** (account) estar en números rojos; (business) tener un saldo negativo; **to give sb the ~ carpet treatment** recibir a uno con todos los honores; **R~ Cross** n Cruz f Roja; ~**currant** n grosella roja; ~**den** vt enrojecer ♦ vi enrojecerse; ~**dish** adj rojizo.

redeem [rɪ'diːm] vt redimir; (promises) cumplir; (sth in pawn) desempeñar; (fig, also REL) rescatar; ~**ing** adj: ~**ing feature** rasgo bueno or favorable.

redeploy [riːdɪ'plɔɪ] vt (resources) reorganizar.

red: ~**-haired** adj pelirrojo; ~**-handed**

adj: **to be caught ~-handed** cogerse (SP) or pillarse (AM) con las manos en la masa; ~**head** n pelirrojo/a; ~ **herring** n (fig) pista falsa; ~**-hot** adj candente.

redirect [riːdaɪ'rɛkt] vt (mail) reexpedir.

red light n: **to go through a ~** (AUT) pasar la luz roja; **red-light district** n barrio chino.

redo [riː'duː] (irreg) vt rehacer.

redolent ['rɛdələnt] adj: ~ **of** (smell) con fragancia a; **to be ~ of** (fig) recordar.

redouble [riː'dʌbl] vt: **to ~ one's efforts** intensificar los esfuerzos.

redress [rɪ'drɛs] n reparación f ♦ vt reparar.

Red Sea n: **the ~** el mar Rojo.

redskin ['rɛdskɪn] n piel roja m/f.

red tape n (fig) trámites mpl.

reduce [rɪ'djuːs] vt reducir; **to ~ sb to tears** hacer llorar a uno; **to be ~d to begging** no quedarle a uno otro remedio que pedir limosna; "**~ speed now**" (AUT) "reduzca la velocidad"; **at a ~d price** (of goods) (a precio) rebajado; **reduction** [rɪ'dʌkʃən] n reducción f; (of price) rebaja; (discount) descuento; (smaller-scale copy) copia reducida.

redundancy [rɪ'dʌndənsɪ] n (dismissal) despido; (unemployment) desempleo.

redundant [rɪ'dʌndnt] adj (BRIT: worker) parado, sin trabajo; (detail, object) superfluo; **to be made ~** quedar(se) sin trabajo.

reed [riːd] n (BOT) junco, caña; (MUS) lengüeta.

reef [riːf] n (at sea) arrecife m.

reek [riːk] vi: **to ~** (of) apestar (a).

reel [riːl] n carrete m, bobina; (of film) rollo; (dance) baile m escocés ♦ vt (also: ~ up) devanar; (also: ~ in) sacar ♦ vi (sway) tambalear(se).

ref [rɛf] (inf) n abbr = referee.

refectory [rɪ'fɛktərɪ] n comedor m.

refer [rɪ'fɜː*] vt (send: patient) referir; (: matter) remitir ♦ vi: **to ~ to** (allude to) referirse a, aludir a; (apply to) relacionarse con; (consult) consultar.

referee [rɛfə'riː] n árbitro; (BRIT: for job

application): **to be a ~ for** sb proporcionar referencias a uno ♦ *vt* (*match*) arbitrar en.

reference ['rɛfrəns] *n* referencia; (*for job application: letter*) carta de recomendación; **with ~ to** (*COMM: in letter*) me remito a; **~ book** *n* libro de consulta; **~ number** *n* número de referencia.

refill [*vt* riː'fɪl, *n* 'riːfɪl] *vt* rellenar ♦ *n* repuesto, recambio.

refine [rɪ'faɪn] *vt* refinar; **~d** *adj* (*person*) fino; **~ment** *n* cultura, educación *f*; (*of system*) refinamiento.

reflect [rɪ'flɛkt] *vt* reflejar ♦ *vi* (*think*) reflexionar, pensar; **it ~s badly/well on him** le perjudica/le hace honor; **~ion** [-'flɛkʃən] *n* (*act*) reflexión *f*; (*image*) reflejo; (*criticism*) crítica; **on ~ion** pensándolo bien; **~or** *n* (*AUT*) captafaros *m inv*; (*of light, heat*) reflector *m*.

reflex ['riːflɛks] *adj, n* reflejo; **~ive** [rɪ'flɛksɪv] *adj* (*LING*) reflexivo.

reform [rɪ'fɔːm] *n* reforma ♦ *vt* reformar; **the R~ation** [rɛfə'meɪʃən] *n* la Reforma; **~atory** (*US*) *n* reformatorio.

refrain [rɪ'freɪn] *vi:* **to ~ from doing** abstenerse de hacer ♦ *n* estribillo.

refresh [rɪ'frɛʃ] *vt* refrescar; **~er course** (*BRIT*) *n* curso de repaso; **~ing** *adj* refrescante; **~ments** *npl* refrescos *mpl*.

refrigerator [rɪ'frɪdʒəreɪtə*] *n* nevera (*SP*), refrigeradora (*AM*).

refuel [riː'fjuəl] *vi* repostar (combustible).

refuge ['rɛfjuːdʒ] *n* refugio, asilo; **to take ~ in** refugiarse en.

refugee [rɛfju'dʒiː] *n* refugiado/a.

refund [*n* 'riːfʌnd, *vb* rɪ'fʌnd] *n* reembolso ♦ *vt* devolver, reembolsar.

refurbish [riː'fəːbɪʃ] *vt* restaurar, renovar.

refusal [rɪ'fjuːzəl] *n* negativa; **to have first ~** tener la primera opción a.

refuse [*n* 'rɛfjuːs, *vb* rɪ'fjuːz] *n* basura ♦ *vt* rechazar; (*invitation*) declinar; (*permission*) denegar ♦ *vi:* **to ~ to do sth** negarse a hacer algo; (*horse*) rehusar; **~ collection** *n* recolección *f* de basuras.

regain [rɪ'geɪn] *vt* recobrar, recuperar.

regal ['riːgl] *adj* regio, real.

regalia [rɪ'geɪlɪə] *n* insignias *fpl*.

regard [rɪ'gɑːd] *n* mirada; (*esteem*) respeto; (*attention*) consideración *f* ♦ *vt* (*consider*) considerar; **to give one's ~s to** saludar de su parte a; **"with kindest ~s"** "con muchos recuerdos"; **~ing, as ~s, with ~ to** con respecto a, en cuanto a; **~less** *adv* a pesar de todo; **~less of** sin reparar en.

régime [reɪ'ʒiːm] *n* régimen *m*.

regiment ['rɛdʒɪmənt] *n* regimiento; **~al** [-'mɛntl] *adj* militar.

region ['riːdʒən] *n* región *f*; **in the ~ of** (*fig*) alrededor de; **~al** *adj* regional.

register ['rɛdʒɪstə*] *n* registro ♦ *vt* registrar; (*birth*) declarar; (*car*) matricular; (*letter*) certificar; (*subj: instrument*) marcar, indicar ♦ *vi* (*at hotel*) registrarse; (*as student*) matricularse; (*make impression*) producir impresión; **~ed** *adj* (*letter, parcel*) certificado; **~ed trademark** *n* marca registrada.

registrar ['rɛdʒɪstrɑː*] *n* secretario/a (del registro civil).

registration [rɛdʒɪs'treɪʃən] *n* (*act*) declaración *f*; (*AUT: also: ~ number*) matrícula.

registry ['rɛdʒɪstrɪ] *n* registro; **~ office** (*BRIT*) *n* registro civil; **to get married in a ~ office** casarse por lo civil.

regret [rɪ'grɛt] *n* sentimiento, pesar *m* ♦ *vt* sentir, lamentar; **~fully** *adv* con pesar; **~table** *adj* lamentable.

regular ['rɛgjulə*] *adj* regular; (*soldier*) profesional; (*usual*) habitual; (: *doctor*) de cabecera ♦ *n* (*client etc*) cliente/a *m/f* habitual; **~ity** [-'lærɪtɪ] *n* regularidad *f*; **~ly** *adv* con regularidad; (*often*) repetidas veces.

regulate ['rɛgjuleɪt] *vt* controlar; **regulation** [-'leɪʃən] *n* (*rule*) regla, reglamento.

rehearsal [rɪ'həːsəl] *n* ensayo.

rehearse [rɪ'həːs] *vt* ensayar.

reign [reɪn] *n* reinado; (*fig*) predominio ♦ *vi* reinar; (*fig*) imperar.

reimburse [riːɪm'bəːs] *vt* reembolsar.

rein [reɪn] *n* (*for horse*) rienda.

reindeer ['reɪndɪə*] *n inv* reno.

reinforce [riːɪnˈfɔːs] *vt* reforzar; ~d **concrete** *n* hormigón *m* armado; ~**ment** *n* (*action*) refuerzo; ~**ments** *npl* (*MIL*) refuerzos *mpl*.

reinstate [riːɪnˈsteɪt] *vt* reintegrar; (*tax, law*) reinstaurar.

reiterate [riːˈɪtəreɪt] *vt* reiterar, repetir.

reject [*n* ˈriːdʒɛkt, *vb* rɪˈdʒɛkt] *n* (*thing*) desecho ♦ *vt* rechazar; (*suggestion*) descartar; (*coin*) expulsar; ~**ion** [rɪˈdʒɛkʃən] *n* rechazo.

rejoice [rɪˈdʒɔɪs] *vi*: **to ~ at** *or* **over** regocijarse *or* alegrarse de.

rejuvenate [rɪˈdʒuːvəneɪt] *vt* rejuvenecer.

relapse [rɪˈlæps] *n* recaída.

relate [rɪˈleɪt] *vt* (*tell*) contar, relatar; (*connect*) relacionar ♦ *vi* relacionarse; ~**d** *adj* afín; (*person*) emparentado; ~**d to** (*subject*) relacionado con; **relating to** referente a.

relation [rɪˈleɪʃən] *n* (*person*) familiar *m/f*, pariente/a *m/f*; (*link*) relación *f*; ~**s** *npl* (*relatives*) familiares *mpl*; ~**ship** *n* relación *f*; (*personal*) relaciones *fpl*; (*also:* **family** ~**ship**) parentesco.

relative [ˈrɛlətɪv] *n* pariente/a *m/f*, familiar *m/f* ♦ *adj* relativo; ~**ly** *adv* (*comparatively*) relativamente.

relax [rɪˈlæks] *vi* descansar; (*unwind*) relajarse ♦ *vt* (*one's grip*) soltar, aflojar; (*control*) relajar; (*mind, person*) descansar; ~**ation** [riːlækˈseɪʃən] *n* descanso; (*of rule, control*) relajamiento; (*entertainment*) diversión *f*; ~**ed** *adj* relajado; (*tranquil*) tranquilo; ~**ing** *adj* relajante.

relay [ˈriːleɪ] *n* (*race*) carrera de relevos ♦ *vt* (*RADIO, TV*) retransmitir.

release [rɪˈliːs] *n* (*liberation*) liberación *f*; (*from prison*) puesta en libertad; (*of gas etc*) escape *m*; (*of film etc*) estreno; (*of record*) lanzamiento ♦ *vt* (*prisoner*) poner en libertad; (*gas*) despedir, arrojar; (*from wreckage*) soltar; (*catch, spring etc*) desenganchar; (*film*) estrenar; (*book*) publicar; (*news*) difundir.

relegate [ˈrɛləgeɪt] *vt* relegar; (*BRIT: SPORT*): **to be ~d to** bajar a.

relent [rɪˈlɛnt] *vi* ablandarse; ~**less** *adj* implacable.

relevant [ˈrɛləvənt] *adj* (*fact*) pertinente; ~ **to** relacionado con.

reliability [rɪlaɪəˈbɪlɪtɪ] *n* fiabilidad *f*; seguridad *f*; veracidad *f*.

reliable [rɪˈlaɪəbl] *adj* (*person, firm*) de confianza, de fiar; (*method, machine*) seguro; (*source*) fidedigno; **reliably** *adv*: **to be reliably informed that ...** saber de fuente fidedigna que ....

reliance [rɪˈlaɪəns] *n*: ~ (**on**) dependencia (de).

relic [ˈrɛlɪk] *n* (*REL*) reliquia; (*of the past*) vestigio.

relief [rɪˈliːf] *n* (*from pain, anxiety*) alivio; (*help, supplies*) socorro, ayuda; (*ART, GEO*) relieve *m*.

relieve [rɪˈliːv] *vt* (*pain*) aliviar; (*bring help to*) ayudar, socorrer; (*take over from*) sustituir; (: *guard*) relevar; **to ~ sb of sth** quitar algo a uno; **to ~ o.s.** hacer sus necesidades.

religion [rɪˈlɪdʒən] *n* religión *f*; **religious** *adj* religioso.

relinquish [rɪˈlɪŋkwɪʃ] *vt* abandonar; (*plan, habit*) renunciar a.

relish [ˈrɛlɪʃ] *n* (*CULIN*) salsa; (*enjoyment*) entusiasmo ♦ *vt* (*food etc*) saborear; (*enjoy*): **to ~ sth** hacerle mucha ilusión a uno algo.

relocate [riːləʊˈkeɪt] *vt* cambiar de lugar, mudar ♦ *vi* mudarse.

reluctance [rɪˈlʌktəns] *n* renuencia; **reluctant** *adj* renuente; **reluctantly** *adv* de mala gana.

rely on [rɪˈlaɪ-] *vt fus* depender de; (*trust*) contar con.

remain [rɪˈmeɪn] *vi* (*survive*) quedar; (*be left*) sobrar; (*continue*) quedar(se), permanecer; ~**der** *n* resto; ~**ing** *adj* que queda(n); (*surviving*) restante(s); ~**s** *npl* restos *mpl*.

remand [rɪˈmɑːnd] *n*: **on ~** detenido (bajo custodia) ♦ *vt*: **to be ~ed in custody** quedar detenido bajo custodia; ~ **home** (*BRIT*) *n* reformatorio.

remark [rɪˈmɑːk] *n* comentario ♦ *vt* comentar; ~**able** *adj* (*outstanding*) extraordinario.

remarry [riː'mærɪ] *vi* volver a casarse.
remedial [rɪ'miːdɪəl] *adj* de recuperación.
remedy ['remədɪ] *n* remedio ♦ *vt* remediar, curar.
remember [rɪ'membə*] *vt* recordar, acordarse de; (*bear in mind*) tener presente; (*send greetings to*): ~ **me to him** dale recuerdos de mi parte;. **remembrance** *n* recuerdo.
remind [rɪ'maɪnd] *vt*: **to ~ sb to do sth** recordar a uno que haga algo; **to ~ sb of sth** (*of fact*) recordar algo a uno; **she ~s me of her mother** me recuerda a su madre; **~er** *n* notificación *f*; (*memento*) recuerdo.
reminisce [remɪ'nɪs] *vi* recordar (viejas historias); **~nt** *adj*: **to be ~nt of sth** recordar algo.
remiss [rɪ'mɪs] *adj* descuidado; **it was ~ of him** fue un descuido de su parte.
remission [rɪ'mɪʃən] *n* remisión *f*; (*of prison sentence*) disminución *f* de pena; (*REL*) perdón *m*.
remit [rɪ'mɪt] *vt* (*send: money*) remitir, enviar; **~tance** *n* remesa, envío.
remnant ['remnənt] *n* resto; (*of cloth*) retal *m*; **~s** *npl* (*COMM*) restos *mpl* de serie.
remorse [rɪ'mɔːs] *n* remordimientos *mpl*; **~ful** *adj* arrepentido; **~less** *adj* (*fig*) implacable, inexorable.
remote [rɪ'məut] *adj* (*distant*) lejano; (*person*) distante; **~ control** *n* telecontrol *m*; **~ly** *adv* remotamente; (*slightly*) levemente.
remould ['riːməuld] (*BRIT*) *n* (*tyre*) neumático *or* llanta (*AM*) recauchutado/a.
removable [rɪ'muːvəbl] *adj* (*detachable*) separable.
removal [rɪ'muːvəl] *n* (*taking away*) el quitar; (*BRIT: from house*) mudanza; (*from office: dismissal*) destitución *f*; (*MED*) extirpación *f*; **~ van** (*BRIT*) *n* camión *m* de mudanzas.
remove [rɪ'muːv] *vt* quitar; (*employee*) destituir; (*name: from list*) tachar, borrar; (*doubt*) disipar; (*abuse*) suprimir, acabar con; (*MED*) extirpar; **~rs** (*BRIT*) *npl* (*company*) agencia de mu-

danzas.
Renaissance [rɪ'neɪsɔns] *n*: **the ~** el Renacimiento.
render ['rendə*] *vt* (*thanks*) dar; (*aid*) proporcionar, prestar; (*make*): **to ~ sth useless** hacer algo inútil; **~ing** *n* (*MUS etc*) interpretación *f*.
rendez-vous ['rɔndɪvuː] *n* cita.
renegade ['renɪgeɪd] *n* renegado/a.
renew [rɪ'njuː] *vt* renovar; (*resume*) reanudar; (*loan etc*) prorrogar; **~al** *n* reanudación *f*; prórroga.
renounce [rɪ'nauns] *vt* renunciar a; (*right, inheritance*) renunciar.
renovate ['renəveɪt] *vt* renovar.
renown [rɪ'naun] *n* renombre *m*; **~ed** *adj* renombrado.
rent [rent] *n* (*for house*) arriendo, renta ♦ *vt* alquilar; **~al** *n* (*for television, car*) alquiler *m*.
renunciation [rɪnʌnsɪ'eɪʃən] *n* renuncia.
rep [rep] *n abbr* = **representative**; **repertory**.
repair [rɪ'peə*] *n* reparación *f*, compostura ♦ *vt* reparar, componer; (*shoes*) remendar; **in good/bad ~** en buen/mal estado; **~ kit** *n* caja de herramientas.
repatriate [riːpætrɪ'eɪt] *vt* repatriar.
repay [riː'peɪ] (*irreg*) *vt* (*money*) devolver, reembolsar; (*person*) pagar; (*debt*) liquidar; (*sb's efforts*) corresponder a; **~ment** *n* reembolso, devolución *f*; (*sum of money*) recompensa.
repeal [rɪ'piːl] *n* revocación *f* ♦ *vt* revocar.
repeat [rɪ'piːt] *n* (*RADIO, TV*) reposición *f* ♦ *vt* repetir ♦ *vi* repetirse; **~edly** *adv* repetidas veces.
repel [rɪ'pel] *vt* (*drive away*) rechazar; (*disgust*) repugnar; **~lent** *adj* repugnante ♦ *n*: **insect ~lent** crema (*or* loción *f*) anti-insectos.
repent [rɪ'pent] *vi*: **to ~ (of)** arrepentirse (de); **~ance** *n* arrepentimiento.
repercussions [riːpə'kʌʃənz] *npl* consecuencias *fpl*.
repertoire ['repətwɑː*] *n* repertorio.
repertory ['repətərɪ] *n* (*also*: **~ theatre**) teatro de repertorio.

repetition [rɛpɪ'tɪʃən] n repetición f.
repetitive [rɪ'pɛtɪtɪv] adj repetitivo.
replace [rɪ'pleɪs] vt (put back) devolver a su sitio; (take the place of) reemplazar, sustituir; ~ment n (act) reposición f; (thing) recambio; (person) suplente m/f.
replay ['riːpleɪ] n (SPORT) desempate m; (of tape, film) repetición f.
replenish [rɪ'plɛnɪʃ] vt rellenar; (stock etc) reponer.
replete [rɪ'pliːt] adj repleto, lleno.
replica ['rɛplɪkə] n copia, reproducción f (exacta).
reply [rɪ'plaɪ] n respuesta, contestación f ♦ vi contestar, responder; ~ **coupon** n cupón-respuesta m.
report [rɪ'pɔːt] n informe m; (PRESS etc) reportaje m; (BRIT: also: school ~) boletín m escolar; (of gun) estallido ♦ vt informar de; (PRESS etc) hacer un reportaje sobre; (notify: accident, culprit) denunciar ♦ vi (make a report) presentar un informe; (present o.s.): to ~ (to sb) presentarse (ante uno); ~ **card** n (US, Scottish) cartilla escolar; ~**edly** adv según se dice; ~**er** n periodista m/f.
repose [rɪ'pəuz] n: in ~ (face, mouth) en reposo.
reprehensible [rɛprɪ'hɛnsɪbl] adj reprensible, censurable.
represent [rɛprɪ'zɛnt] vt representar; (COMM) ser agente de; (describe): to ~ **sth as** describir algo como; ~**ation** [-'teɪʃən] n representación f; ~**ations** npl (protest) quejas fpl; ~**ative** n representante m/f; (US: POL) diputado/a m/f ♦ adj representativo.
repress [rɪ'prɛs] vt reprimir; ~**ion** [-'prɛʃən] n represión f.
reprieve [rɪ'priːv] n (LAW) indulto; (fig) alivio.
reprimand ['rɛprɪmɑːnd] n reprimenda ♦ vt reprender.
reprint ['riːprɪnt] n reimpresión f ♦ vt reimprimir.
reprisals [rɪ'praɪzlz] npl represalias fpl.
reproach [rɪ'prəutʃ] n reproche m ♦ vt: to ~ **sb for sth** reprochar algo a uno;

~**ful** adj de reproche, de acusación.
reproduce [riːprə'djuːs] vt reproducir ♦ vi reproducirse; **reproduction** [-'dʌkʃən] n reproducción f.
reproof [rɪ'pruːf] n reproche m.
reprove [rɪ'pruːv] vt: to ~ **sb for sth** reprochar algo a uno.
reptile ['rɛptaɪl] n reptil m.
republic [rɪ'pʌblɪk] n república; ~**an** adj, n republicano/a m/f.
repudiate [rɪ'pjuːdɪeɪt] vt rechazar; (violence etc) repudiar.
repulse [rɪ'pʌls] vt rechazar; **repulsive** adj repulsivo.
reputable ['rɛpjutəbl] adj (make etc) de renombre.
reputation [rɛpju'teɪʃən] n reputación f.
reputed [rɪ'pjuːtɪd] adj supuesto; ~**ly** adv según dicen or se dice.
request [rɪ'kwɛst] n petición f; (formal) solicitud f ♦ vt: to ~ **sth of** or **from sb** solicitar algo a uno; ~ **stop** (BRIT) n parada discrecional.
require [rɪ'kwaɪə*] vt (need: subj: person) necesitar, tener necesidad de; (: thing, situation) exigir; (want) pedir; to ~ **sb to do sth** pedir a uno que haga algo; ~**ment** n requisito; (need) necesidad f.
requisite ['rɛkwɪzɪt] n requisito ♦ adj necesario.
requisition [rɛkwɪ'zɪʃən] n: ~ (**for**) solicitud f (de) ♦ vt (MIL) requisar.
resale ['riːseɪl] n reventa.
rescind [rɪ'sɪnd] vt (law) abrogar; (contract, order etc) anular.
rescue ['rɛskjuː] n rescate m ♦ vt rescatar; ~ **party** n expedición f de salvamento; ~**r** n salvador(a) m/f.
research [rɪ'sɜːtʃ] n investigaciones fpl ♦ vt investigar; ~**er** n investigador(a) m/f.
resemblance [rɪ'zɛmbləns] n parecido.
resemble [rɪ'zɛmbl] vt parecerse a.
resent [rɪ'zɛnt] vt tomar a mal; ~**ful** adj resentido; ~**ment** n resentimiento.
reservation [rɛzə'veɪʃən] n reserva.
reserve [rɪ'zɜːv] n reserva; (SPORT) suplente m/f ♦ vt (seats etc) reservar; ~**s** npl (MIL) reserva; in ~ de reserva; ~**d**

adj reservado.

reservoir ['rɛzəvwɑ:*] *n* embalse *m*.

reshuffle [ri:'ʃʌfl] *n*: **Cabinet ~** (*POL*) remodelación *f* del gabinete.

reside [rɪ'zaɪd] *vi* residir, vivir.

residence ['rɛzɪdəns] *n* (*formal: home*) domicilio; (*length of stay*) permanencia; **~ permit** (*BRIT*) *n* permiso de permanencia.

resident ['rɛzɪdənt] *n* (*of area*) vecino/a; (*in hotel*) huésped(a) *m/f* ♦ *adj* (*population*) permanente; (*doctor*) residente; **~ial** [-'dɛnʃəl] *adj* residencial.

residue ['rɛzɪdju:] *n* resto.

resign [rɪ'zaɪn] *vt* renunciar a ♦ *vi* dimitir; **to ~ o.s. to** (*situation*) resignarse a; **~ation** [rɛzɪg'neɪʃən] *n* dimisión *f*; (*state of mind*) resignación *f*; **~ed** *adj* resignado.

resilience [rɪ'zɪlɪəns] *n* elasticidad *f*; resistencia.

resilient [rɪ'zɪlɪənt] *adj* (*material*) elástico; (*person*) resistente.

resin ['rɛzɪn] *n* resina.

resist [rɪ'zɪst] *vt* resistir, oponerse a; **~ance** *n* resistencia.

resolute ['rɛzəlu:t] *adj* resuelto; (*refusal*) tajante.

resolution [rɛzə'lu:ʃən] *n* (*gen*) resolución *f*.

resolve [rɪ'zɒlv] *n* resolución *f* ♦ *vt* resolver ♦ *vi*: **to ~ to do** resolver hacer; **~d** *adj* resuelto.

resort [rɪ'zɔ:t] *n* (*town*) centro turístico; (*recourse*) recurso ♦ *vi*: **to ~ to** recurrir a; **in the last ~** como último recurso.

resound [rɪ'zaund] *vi*: **to ~ (with)** resonar (con); **~ing** *adj* sonoro; (*fig*) clamoroso.

resource [rɪ'sɔ:s] *n* recurso; **~s** *npl* recursos *mpl*; **~ful** *adj* despabilado, ingenioso.

respect [rɪs'pɛkt] *n* respeto ♦ *vt* respetar; **~s** *npl* recuerdos *mpl*, saludos *mpl*; **with ~ to** con respecto a; **in this ~** en cuanto a eso; **~able** *adj* respetable; (*large: amount*) apreciable; (*passable*) tolerable; **~ful** *adj* respetuoso.

respective [rɪs'pɛktɪv] *adj* respectivo;

~ly *adv* respectivamente.

respite ['rɛspaɪt] *n* respiro.

resplendent [rɪs'plɛndənt] *adj* resplandeciente.

respond [rɪs'pɒnd] *vi* responder; (*react*) reaccionar; **response** [-'pɒns] *n* respuesta; reacción *f*.

responsibility [rɪspɒnsɪ'bɪlɪti] *n* responsabilidad *f*.

responsible [rɪs'pɒnsɪbl] *adj* (*character*) serio, formal; (*job*) de confianza; (*liable*): **~ (for)** responsable (de).

responsive [rɪs'pɒnsɪv] *adj* sensible.

rest [rɛst] *n* descanso, reposo; (*MUS, pause*) pausa, silencio; (*support*) apoyo; (*remainder*) resto ♦ *vi* descansar; (*be supported*): **to ~ on** descansar sobre ♦ *vt* (*lean*): **to ~ sth on/against** apoyar algo en *or* sobre/contra; **the ~ of them** (*people, objects*) los demás; **it ~s with him to ...** depende de él el que ....

restaurant ['rɛstərɒŋ] *n* restaurante *m*; **~ car** (*BRIT*) *n* (*RAIL*) coche-comedor *m*.

restful ['rɛstful] *adj* descansado, tranquilo.

rest home *n* residencia para jubilados.

restitution [rɛstɪ'tju:ʃən] *n*: **to make ~ to sb for sth** indemnizar a uno por algo.

restive ['rɛstɪv] *adj* inquieto; (*horse*) rebelón(ona).

restless ['rɛstlɪs] *adj* inquieto.

restoration [rɛstə'reɪʃən] *n* restauración *f*; devolución *f*.

restore [rɪ'stɔ:*] *vt* (*building*) restaurar; (*sth stolen*) devolver; (*health*) restablecer; (*to power*) volver a poner a.

restrain [rɪs'treɪn] *vt* (*feeling*) contener, refrenar; (*person*): **to ~ (from doing)** disuadir (de hacer); **~ed** *adj* reservado; **~t** *n* (*restriction*) restricción *f*; (*moderation*) moderación *f*; (*of manner*) reserva.

restrict [rɪs'trɪkt] *vt* restringir, limitar; **~ion** [-kʃən] *n* restricción *f*, limitación *f*; **~ive** *adj* restrictivo.

rest room (*US*) *n* aseos *mpl*.

result [rɪ'zʌlt] *n* resultado ♦ *vi*: **to ~ in** terminar en, tener por resultado; **as a ~ of** a consecuencia de.

resume [rɪ'zjuːm] *vt* reanudar ♦ *vi* comenzar de nuevo.

résumé ['reɪzjuːmeɪ] *n* resumen *m*; (*US*) currículum *m*.

resumption [rɪ'zʌmpʃən] *n* reanudación *f*.

resurgence [rɪ'səːdʒəns] *n* resurgimiento.

resurrection [rezə'rekʃən] *n* resurrección *f*.

resuscitate [rɪ'sʌsɪteɪt] *vt* (*MED*) resucitar.

retail ['riːteɪl] *adj, adv* al por menor; ~**er** *n* detallista *m/f* ~ **price** *n* precio de venta al público.

retain [rɪ'teɪn] *vt* (*keep*) retener, conservar; ~**er** *n* (*fee*) anticipo.

retaliate [rɪ'tælɪeɪt] *vi*: to ~ (*against*) tomar represalias (contra); **retaliation** [-'eɪʃən] *n* represalias *fpl*.

retarded [rɪ'tɑːdɪd] *adj* retrasado.

retch [retʃ] *vi* dársele a uno arcadas.

retentive [rɪ'tentɪv] *adj* (*memory*) retentivo.

reticent ['retɪsnt] *adj* reservado.

retire [rɪ'taɪə*] *vi* (*give up work*) jubilarse; (*withdraw*) retirarse; (*go to bed*) acostarse; ~**d** *adj* (*person*) jubilado; ~**ment** *n* (*giving up work*: *state*) retiro; (*: act*) jubilación *f*; **retiring** *adj* (*leaving*) saliente; (*shy*) retraído.

retort [rɪ'tɔːt] *vi* contestar.

retrace [riː'treɪs] *vt*: to ~ one's steps volver sobre sus pasos, desandar lo andado.

retract [rɪ'trækt] *vt* (*statement*) retirar; (*claws*) retraer; (*undercarriage, aerial*) replegar.

retrain [riː'treɪn] *vt* reciclar; ~**ing** *n* readaptación *f* profesional.

retread ['riːtred] *n* neumático (*SP*) or llanta (*AM*) recauchutado/a.

retreat [rɪ'triːt] *n* (*place*) retiro; (*MIL*) retirada ♦ *vi* retirarse.

retribution [retrɪ'bjuːʃən] *n* desquite *m*.

retrieval [rɪ'triːvəl] *n* recuperación *f*.

retrieve [rɪ'triːv] *vt* recobrar; (*situation, honour*) salvar; (*COMPUT*) recuperar; (*error*) reparar; ~**r** *n* perro cobrador.

retrograde ['retrəgreɪd] *adj* retrógrado.

retrospect ['retrəspekt] *n*: in ~ retrospectivamente; ~**ive** [-'spektɪv] *adj* retrospectivo; (*law*) retroactivo.

return [rɪ'təːn] *n* (*going or coming back*) vuelta, regreso; (*of sth stolen etc*) devolución *f*; (*FINANCE: from land, shares*) ganancia, ingresos *mpl* ♦ *cpd* (*journey*) de regreso; (*BRIT: ticket*) de ida y vuelta; (*match*) de vuelta ♦ *vi* (*person etc*: *come or go back*) volver, regresar; (*symptoms etc*) reaparecer; (*regain*): to ~ to recuperar ♦ *vt* devolver; (*favour, love etc*) corresponder a; (*verdict*) pronunciar; (*POL: candidate*) elegir; ~**s** *npl* (*COMM*) ingresos *mpl*; in ~ (**for**) a cambio (de); by ~ **of** post a vuelta de correo; **many happy** ~**s** (**of the day**)! ¡feliz cumpleaños!

reunion [riː'juːnɪən] *n* (*of family*) reunión *f*; (*of two people, school*) reencuentro.

reunite [riːjuː'naɪt] *vt* reunir; (*reconcile*) reconciliar.

rev [rev] (*AUT*) *n abbr* (= *revolution*) revolución *f* ♦ *vt* (*also*: ~ **up**) acelerar.

revamp [riː'væmp] *vt* (*company etc*) reorganizar.

reveal [rɪ'viːl] *vt* revelar; ~**ing** *adj* revelador(a).

reveille [rɪ'vælɪ] *n* (*MIL*) diana.

revel ['revl] *vi*: to ~ in sth/in doing sth gozar de algo/con hacer algo.

revelry ['revlrɪ] *n* jarana, juerga.

revenge [rɪ'vendʒ] *n* venganza; to take ~ on vengarse de.

revenue ['revənjuː] *n* ingresos *mpl*, rentas *fpl*.

reverberate [rɪ'vəːbəreɪt] *vi* (*sound*) resonar, retumbar; (*fig: shock*) repercutir; **reverberation** [-'reɪʃən] *n* retumbo, eco; repercusión *f*.

revere [rɪ'vɪə*] *vt* venerar; ~**nce** ['revərəns] *n* reverencia.

Reverend ['revərənd] *adj* (*in titles*): the ~ John Smith (*Anglican*) el Reverendo John Smith; (*Catholic*) el Padre John Smith; (*Protestant*) el Pastor John Smith.

reversal [rɪ'vəːsl] *n* (*of order*) inversión *f*; (*of direction, policy*) cambio; (*of de-*

cision) revocación f.

reverse [rɪ'vɜːs] n (*opposite*) contrario; (*back: of cloth*) revés m; (: *of coin*) reverso; (: *of paper*) dorso; (*AUT: also:* ~ *gear*) marcha atrás; (*setback*) revés m ♦ adj (*order*) inverso; (*direction*) contrario; (*process*) opuesto ♦ vt (*decision, AUT*) dar marcha atrás a; (*position, function*) invertir ♦ vi (*BRIT: AUT*) dar marcha atrás; ~-**charge call** (*BRIT*) n llamada a cobro revertido; **reversing lights** (*BRIT*) npl (*AUT*) luces fpl de retroceso.

revert [rɪ'vɜːt] vi: **to ~ to** volver a.

review [rɪ'vjuː] n (*magazine, MIL*) revista; (*of book, film*) reseña; (*US: examination*) repaso, examen m ♦ vt repasar, examinar; (*MIL*) pasar revista a; (*book, film*) reseñar; ~**er** n crítico/a.

revile [rɪ'vaɪl] vt injuriar, vilipendiar.

revise [rɪ'vaɪz] vt (*manuscript*) corregir; (*opinion*) modificar; (*price, procedure*) revisar ♦ vi (*study*) repasar; **revision** [rɪ'vɪʒən] n corrección f; modificación f; (*for exam*) repaso.

revitalize [riː'vaɪtəlaɪz] vt revivificar.

revival [rɪ'vaɪvəl] n (*recovery*) reanimación f; (*of interest*) renacimiento f; (*THEATRE*) reestreno; (*of faith*) despertar m.

revive [rɪ'vaɪv] vt resucitar; (*custom*) restablecer; (*hope*) despertar; (*play*) reestrenar ♦ vi (*person*) volver en sí; (*business*) reactivarse.

revolt [rɪ'vəʊlt] n rebelión f ♦ vi rebelarse, sublevarse ♦ vt dar asco a, repugnar; ~**ing** adj asqueroso, repugnante.

revolution [revə'luːʃən] n revolución f; ~**ary** adj, n revolucionario/a m/f; ~**ize** vt revolucionar.

revolve [rɪ'vɒlv] vi dar vueltas, girar; (*life, discussion*): **to ~ (a)round** girar en torno a.

revolver [rɪ'vɒlvə*] n revólver m.

revolving [rɪ'vɒlvɪŋ] adj (*chair, door etc*) giratorio.

revue [rɪ'vjuː] n (*THEATRE*) revista.

revulsion [rɪ'vʌlʃən] n asco, repugnancia.

reward [rɪ'wɔːd] n premio, recompensa ♦ vt: **to ~ (for)** recompensar or premiar (por); ~**ing** adj (*fig*) valioso.

rewind [riː'waɪnd] (*irreg*) rebobinar.

rewire [riː'waɪə*] vt (*house*) renovar la instalación eléctrica de.

rewrite [riː'raɪt] (*irreg*) vt reescribir.

rhapsody ['ræpsədɪ] n (*MUS*) rapsodia.

rhetorical [rɪ'tɒrɪkl] adj retórico.

rheumatism ['ruːmətɪzəm] n reumatismo, reúma m.

Rhine [raɪn] n: **the ~** el (río) Rin.

rhinoceros [raɪ'nɒsərəs] n rinoceronte m.

rhododendron [rəʊdə'dendrn] n rododendro.

Rhone [rəʊn] n: **the ~** el (río) Ródano.

rhubarb ['ruːbɑːb] n ruibarbo.

rhyme [raɪm] n rima; (*verse*) poesía.

rhythm ['rɪðm] n ritmo.

rib [rɪb] n (*ANAT*) costilla ♦ vt (*mock*) tomar el pelo a.

ribbon ['rɪbən] n cinta; **in ~s** (*torn*) hecho trizas.

rice [raɪs] n arroz m; ~ **pudding** n arroz m con leche.

rich [rɪtʃ] adj rico; (*soil*) fértil; (*food*) pesado; (: *sweet*) empalagoso; (*abundant*): ~ **in** (*minerals etc*) rico en; **the ~** npl los ricos; ~**es** npl riqueza; ~**ly** adv ricamente; (*deserved, earned*) bien.

rickets ['rɪkɪts] n raquitismo.

rickety ['rɪkɪtɪ] adj tambaleante.

rickshaw ['rɪkʃɔː] n carro de culí.

ricochet ['rɪkəʃeɪ] vi rebotar.

rid [rɪd] (*pt, pp* **rid**) vt: **to ~ sb of sth** librar a uno de algo; **to get ~ of** deshacerse or desembarazarse de.

ridden ['rɪdn] pp of **ride**.

riddle ['rɪdl] n (*puzzle*) acertijo; (*mystery*) enigma m, misterio ♦ vt: **to be ~d with** ser lleno or plagado de.

ride [raɪd] (*pt* **rode**, *pp* **ridden**) n paseo; (*distance covered*) viaje m, recorrido ♦ vi (*as sport*) montar; (*go somewhere: on horse, bicycle*) dar un paseo, pasearse; (*travel: on bicycle, motorcycle, bus*) viajar ♦ vt (*a horse*) montar a; (*a bicycle, motorcycle*) andar en; (*distance*) recorrer; **to take sb for a ~** (*fig*) engañar a uno; **to ~ at anchor** (*NAUT*) estar fondeado; **~r** *n* (*on horse*) jinete/a *m/f*; (*on bicycle*) ciclista *m/f*; (*on motorcycle*) motociclista *m/f*.

ridge [rɪdʒ] *n* (*of hill*) cresta; (*of roof*) caballete *m*; (*wrinkle*) arruga.

ridicule ['rɪdɪkjuːl] *n* irrisión *f*, burla ♦ *vt* poner en ridículo, burlarse de; **ridiculous** [-'dɪkjuləs] *adj* ridículo.

riding ['raɪdɪŋ] *n* equitación *f*; **I like ~** me gusta montar a caballo; **~ school** *n* escuela de equitación.

rife [raɪf] *adj*: **to be ~** ser muy común; **to be ~ with** abundar en.

riffraff ['rɪfræf] *n* gentuza.

rifle ['raɪfl] *n* rifle *m*, fusil *m* ♦ *vt* saquear; **~ through** *vt* (*papers*) registrar; **~ range** *n* campo de tiro; (*at fair*) tiro al blanco.

rift [rɪft] *n* (*in clouds*) claro; (*fig: disagreement*) desavenencia.

rig [rɪg] *n* (*also*: **oil ~**: *at sea*) plataforma petrolera ♦ *vt* (*election etc*) amañar; **~ out** (*BRIT*) *vt* disfrazar; **~ up** *vt* improvisar; **~ging** *n* (*NAUT*) aparejo.

right [raɪt] *adj* (*correct*) correcto, exacto; (*suitable*) indicado, debido; (*proper*) apropiado; (*just*) justo; (*morally good*) bueno; (*not left*) derecho ♦ *n* bueno; (*title, claim*) derecho; (*not left*) derecha ♦ *adv* bien, correctamente; (*not left*) a la derecha; (*exactly*): **~ now** ahora mismo ♦ *vt* enderezar; (*correct*) corregir ♦ *excl* ¡bueno!, ¡está bien!; **to be ~** (*person*) tener razón; (*answer*) ser correcto; (*of clock*): **is that the ~ time?** ¿es esa la hora buena?; **by ~s** en justicia; **on the ~** a la derecha; **to be in the ~** tener razón; **~ away** en seguida; **~ in the middle** exactamente en el centro; **~ angle** *n* ángulo recto; **~eous** ['raɪtʃəs] *adj* justado, honrado; (*anger*) justificado; **~ful** *adj* legítimo; **~-handed** *adj* diestro; **~-hand man** *n* brazo derecho; **~-hand side** *n* derecha; **~ly** *adv* correctamente, debidamente; (*with reason*) con razón; **~ of way** *n* (*on path etc*) derecho de paso; (*AUT*) prioridad *f*; **~-wing** *adj* (*POL*) derechis-

ta.

rigid ['rɪdʒɪd] *adj* rígido; (*person, ideas*) inflexible.

rigmarole ['rɪgmərəul] *n* galimatías *m inv.*

rigorous ['rɪgərəs] *adj* riguroso.

rigour ['rɪgə°] (*US* **rigor**) *n* rigor *m*, severidad *f*.

rile [raɪl] *vt* irritar.

rim [rɪm] *n* borde *m*; (*of spectacles*) aro; (*of wheel*) llanta.

rind [raɪnd] *n* (*of bacon*) corteza; (*of lemon etc*) cáscara; (*of cheese*) costra.

ring [rɪŋ] (*pt* **rang**, *pp* **rung**) *n* (*of metal*) aro; (*on finger*) anillo; (*of people*) corro; (*of objects*) círculo; (*gang*) banda; (*for boxing*) cuadrilátero; (*of circus*) pista; (*bull ~*) ruedo, plaza; (*sound of bell*) toque *m* ♦ *vi* (*on telephone*) llamar por teléfono; (*bell*) repicar; (*doorbell, phone*) sonar; (*also*: **~ out**) sonar; (*ears*) zumbar ♦ *vt* (*BRIT: TEL*) llamar, telefonear; (*bell etc*) hacer sonar; (*doorbell*) tocar; **to give sb a ~** (*BRIT: TEL*) llamar or telefonear a alguien; **~ back** (*BRIT: TEL*) *vt, vi* (*TEL*) devolver la llamada; **~ off** (*BRIT*) *vi* (*TEL*) colgar, cortar la comunicación; **~ up** (*BRIT*) *vt* (*TEL*) llamar, telefonear; **~ing** *n* (*of bell*) repique *m*; (*of phone*) el sonar; (*in ears*) zumbido; **~ing tone** *n* (*TEL*) tono de llamada; **~leader** *n* (*of gang*) cabecilla *m*.

ringlets ['rɪŋlɪts] *npl* rizos *mpl*, bucles *mpl*.

ring road (*BRIT*) *n* carretera periférica or de circunvalación.

rink [rɪŋk] *n* (*also*: **ice ~**) pista de hielo.

rinse [rɪns] *n* aclarado; (*dye*) tinte *m* ♦ *vt* aclarar; (*mouth*) enjuagar.

riot ['raɪət] *n* motín *m*, disturbio ♦ *vi* amotinarse; **to run ~** desmandarse; **~ous** *adj* alborotado; (*party*) bullicioso.

rip [rɪp] *n* rasgón *m*, rasgadura ♦ *vt* rasgar, desgarrar ♦ *vi* rasgarse, desgarrarse; **~cord** *n* cabo de desgarre.

ripe [raɪp] *adj* maduro; **~n** *vt* madurar; (*cheese*) curar ♦ *vi* madurar.

ripple ['rɪpl] *n* onda, rizo; (*sound*) murmullo ♦ vi rizarse.

rise [raɪz] (pt **rose**, pp **risen**) n (slope)
cuesta, pendiente f; (hill) altura; (BRIT:
in wages) aumento; (in prices, temperature) subida; (fig: to power etc) ascenso ♦ vi subir; (waters) crecer; (sun,
moon) salir; (person: from bed etc) levantarse; (also: ~ **up**: rebel) sublevarse; (in rank) ascender; **to give ~ to** dar
lugar or origen a; **to ~ to the occasion**
ponerse a la altura de las circunstancias; **risen** ['rɪzn] pp of **rise**; **rising**
adj (increasing: number) creciente;
(: prices) en aumento or alza; (tide)
creciente; (sun, moon) naciente.

risk [rɪsk] n riesgo, peligro ♦ vt arriesgar; (run the ~ of) exponerse a; **to
take** or **run the ~** of doing correr el
riesgo de hacer; **at ~** en peligro; **at
one's own ~** bajo su propia responsabilidad; ~**y** adj arriesgado, peligroso.

risqué ['riːskeɪ] adj verde.

rissole ['rɪsəul] n croqueta.

rite [raɪt] n rito; **last ~s** exequias fpl.

ritual ['rɪtjuəl] adj ritual ♦ n ritual m,
rito.

rival ['raɪvl] n rival m/f; (in business)
competidor(a) m/f ♦ adj rival, opuesto
♦ vt competir con; ~**ry** n competencia.

river ['rɪvə*] n río ♦ cpd (port) de río;
(traffic) fluvial; **up/down ~** río arriba/
abajo; ~**bank** n orilla (del río); ~**bed**
n lecho, cauce m.

rivet ['rɪvɪt] n roblón m, remache m ♦ vt
(fig) captar.

Riviera [rɪvɪ'ɛərə] n: **the (French) ~** la
Costa Azul (francesa).

road [rəud] n camino; (motorway etc)
carretera; (in town) calle f ♦ cpd (accident) de tráfico; **major/minor ~** carretera principal/secundaria; ~**block** n barricada; ~**hog** n loco/a del volante; ~
map n mapa m de carreteras; ~ **safety** n seguridad f vial; ~**side** n borde m
(del camino); ~**sign** n señal f de tráfico; ~ **user** n usuario/a de la vía pública; ~**way** n calzada; ~**works** npl
obras fpl; ~**worthy** adj (car) en buen
estado para circular.

roam [rəum] vi vagar.

roar [rɔː*] n rugido; (of vehicle, storm)
estruendo; (of laughter) carcajada ♦ vi
rugir; hacer estruendo; **to ~ with
laughter** reírse a carcajadas; **to do a
~ing trade** hacer buen negocio.

roast [rəust] n carne f asada, asado ♦ vt
asar; (coffee) tostar; ~ **beef** n rosbif
m.

rob [rɔb] vt robar; **to ~ sb of sth** robar
algo a uno; (fig: deprive) quitar algo a
uno; ~**ber** n ladrón/ona m/f; ~**bery** n
robo.

robe [rəub] n (for ceremony etc) toga;
(also: bath ~, US) albornoz m.

robin ['rɔbɪn] n petirrojo.

robot ['rəubɔt] n robot m.

robust [rəu'bʌst] adj robusto, fuerte.

rock [rɔk] n roca; (boulder) peña, peñasco; (US: small stone) piedrecita;
(BRIT: sweet) ≈ pirulí ♦ vt (swing
gently: cradle) balancear, mecer;
(: child) arrullar; (shake) sacudir ♦ vi
mecerse, balancearse; sacudirse; **on
the ~s** (drink) con hielo; (marriage
etc) en ruinas; ~ **and roll** n rocanrol
m; ~**-bottom** n (fig) punto más bajo;
~**ery** n cuadro alpino.

rocket ['rɔkɪt] n cohete m.

rocking ['rɔkɪŋ]: ~ **chair** n mecedora;
~ **horse** n caballo de balancín.

rocky ['rɔkɪ] adj rocoso; (table, marriage etc) poco estable.

rod [rɔd] n vara, varilla; (also: fishing
~) caña.

rode [rəud] pt of **ride**.

rodent ['rəudnt] n roedor m.

roe [rəu] n (species: also: ~ deer) cor-
zo; (of fish): **hard/soft ~** hueva/lecha.

rogue [rəug] n pícaro, pillo.

role [rəul] n papel m.

roll [rəul] n rollo; (of bank notes) fajo;
(also: bread ~) panecillo; (register,
list) lista, nómina; (sound: of drums
etc) redoble m ♦ vt hacer rodar; (also:
~ **up**: string) enrollar; (: sleeves) arremangar; (cigarette) liar; (also: ~ **out**:
pastry) aplanar; (flatten: road, lawn)
apisonar ♦ vi rodar; (drum) redoblar;
(ship) balancearse; ~ **about** or **around**
vi (person) revolcarse; (object) rodar

(por); ~ **by** vi (time) pasar; ~ **in** vi (mail, cash) entrar a raudales; ~ **over** vi dar una vuelta; ~ **up** vi (inf: arrive) aparecer ♦ vt (carpet) arrollar; ~ **call** n: **to take a** ~ **call** pasar lista; ~**er** n rodillo; (wheel) rueda; (for road) apisonadora; (for hair) rulo; ~**er coaster** n montaña rusa; ~**er skates** npl patines mpl de rueda.

rolling ['rəʊlɪŋ] adj (landscape) ondulado; ~ **pin** n rodillo (de cocina); ~ **stock** n (RAIL) material m rodante.

ROM [rɔm] n abbr (COMPUT: = read only memory) ROM f.

Roman ['rəʊmən] adj romano/a; ~ **Catholic** adj, n católico/a m/f (romano/a).

romance [rə'mæns] n (love affair) amor m; (charm) lo romántico; (novel) novela de amor.

Romania [ruː'meɪnɪə] n = **Rumania**.

Roman numeral n número romano.

romantic [rə'mæntɪk] adj romántico.

Rome [rəʊm] n Roma.

romp [rɔmp] n retozo, juego ♦ vi (also: ~ **about**) jugar, brincar.

rompers ['rɔmpəz] npl pelele m.

roof [ruːf] (pl ~s) n (gen) techo; (of house) techo, tejado ♦ vt techar, poner techo a; **the** ~ **of the mouth** el paladar; ~**ing** n techumbre f; ~ **rack** n (AUT) baca, portaequipajes m inv.

rook [rʊk] n (bird) graja; (CHESS) torre f.

room [ruːm] n cuarto, habitación f, pieza (esp AM); (also: bed~) dormitorio; (in school etc) sala; (space, scope) sitio, cabida; ~**s** npl (lodging) alojamiento; "~**s to let**", "~**s for rent**" (US) "se alquilan cuartos"; **single/double** ~ habitación individual/doble or para dos personas; ~**ing house** n (US) n pensión f; ~**mate** n compañero/a de cuarto; ~ **service** n servicio de habitaciones; ~**y** adj espacioso; (garment) amplio.

roost [ruːst] vi pasar la noche.

rooster ['ruːstə*] n gallo.

root [ruːt] n raíz f ♦ vi arraigarse; ~ **about** vi (fig) buscar y rebuscar; ~ **for** vt fus (support) apoyar a; ~ **out** vt

desarraigar.

rope [rəʊp] n cuerda; (NAUT) cable m ♦ vt (tie) atar or amarrar con (una) cuerda; (climbers: also: ~ **together**) encordarse; (an area: also: ~ **off**) acordonar; **to know the** ~**s** (fig) conocer los trucos (del oficio); ~ **in** vt (fig): **to** ~ **sb in** persuadir a uno a tomar parte; ~ **ladder** n escala de cuerda.

rosary ['rəʊzərɪ] n rosario.

rose [rəʊz] pt of **rise** ♦ n rosa; (shrub) rosal m; (on watering can) roseta.

rosé ['rəʊzeɪ] n vino rosado.

rosebud ['rəʊzbʌd] n capullo de rosa.

rosebush ['rəʊzbʊʃ] n rosal m.

rosemary ['rəʊzmərɪ] n romero.

rosette [rəʊ'zet] n escarapela.

roster ['rɔstə*] n: **duty** ~ lista de deberes.

rostrum ['rɔstrəm] n tribuna.

rosy ['rəʊzɪ] adj rosado, sonrosado; **a** ~ **future** un futuro prometedor.

rot [rɔt] n podredumbre f; (fig: pej) tonterías fpl ♦ vt pudrir ♦ vi pudrirse.

rota ['rəʊtə] n (sistema m de) turnos mpl.

rotary ['rəʊtərɪ] adj rotativo.

rotate [rəʊ'teɪt] vt (revolve) hacer girar, dar vueltas a; (jobs) alternar ♦ vi girar, dar vueltas; **rotating** adj rotativo; **rotation** [-'teɪʃən] n rotación f.

rote [rəʊt] n: **by** ~ maquinalmente, de memoria.

rotten ['rɔtn] adj podrido; (dishonest) corrompido; (inf: bad) pocho; **to feel** ~ (ill) sentirse fatal.

rotund [rəʊ'tʌnd] adj regordete.

rouble ['ruːbl] (US **ruble**) n rublo.

rouge [ruːʒ] n colorete m.

rough [rʌf] adj (skin, surface) áspero; (terrain) quebrado; (road) desigual; (voice) bronco; (person, manner) tosco, grosero; (weather) borrascoso; (treatment) brutal; (sea) picado; (town, area) peligroso; (cloth) basto; (plan) preliminar; (guess) aproximado ♦ n (GOLF): **in the** ~ en las hierbas altas; **to** ~ **it** vivir sin comodidades; **to sleep** ~ (BRIT) pasar la noche al raso; ~**age** n fibra(s) f(pl); ~**-and-ready** adj improvisado; ~**cast** n mezcla gruesa; ~ **copy** n borrador m; ~ **draft** n = ~ **copy**; ~**en** vt (a surface) poner áspero; ~**ly** adv (handle) torpemente; (make) toscamente; (speak) groseramente; (approximately) aproximadamente; ~**ness** n (of surface) aspereza; (of person) rudeza.

roulette [ruː'lɛt] n ruleta.

Roumania [ruː'meɪnɪə] n = **Rumania**.

round [raund] adj redondo ♦ n círculo; (BRIT: of toast) rebanada; (of policeman) ronda; (of milkman) recorrido; (of doctor) visitas fpl; (game: of cards, in competition) partida; (of ammunition) cartucho; (BOXING) asalto; (of talks) ronda ♦ vt (corner) doblar ♦ prep alrededor de ♦ prep (surrounding): ~ **his neck/the table** en su cuello/alrededor de la mesa; (in a circular movement): **to move** ~ **the room/sail** ~ **the world** dar una vuelta a la habitación/circunnavegar el mundo; (in various directions): **to move** ~ **a room/house** moverse por toda la habitación/casa; (approximately) alrededor de ♦ adv: **all** ~ por todos lados; **the long way** ~ por el camino menos directo; **all the year** ~ durante todo el año; **it's just** ~ **the corner** (fig) está a la vuelta de la esquina; ~ **the clock** adv las 24 horas; **to go** ~ **to sb's (house)** ir a casa de uno; **to go** ~ **the back** pasar por atrás; **to go** ~ **a house** visitar una casa; **enough to go** ~ bastante (para todos); **a** ~ **of applause** una salva de aplausos; **a** ~ **of drinks/sandwiches** una ronda de bebidas/bocadillos; ~ **off** vt (speech etc) acabar, poner término a; ~ **up** vt (cattle) acorralar; (people) reunir; (price) redondear; ~**about** (BRIT) n (AUT) isleta; (at fair) tiovivo ♦ adj (route, means) indirecto; ~**ers** n (game) juego similar al béisbol; ~**ly** adv (fig) rotundamente; ~**-shouldered** adj cargado de espaldas; ~ **trip** n viaje m de ida y vuelta; ~**up** n rodeo; (of criminals) redada; (of news) resumen m.

rouse [rauz] vt (wake up) despertar; (stir up) suscitar; **rousing** adj (cheer, welcome) caluroso.

rout [raut] n (MIL) derrota ♦ vt derrotar.

route [ruːt] n ruta, camino; (of bus) recorrido; (of shipping) derrota; ~ **map** (BRIT) n (for journey) mapa m de carreteras.

routine [ruː'tiːn] adj rutinario ♦ n rutina; (THEATRE) número.

rove [rəuv] vt vagar or errar por.

row¹ [rəu] n (line) fila, hilera; (KNITTING) pasada ♦ vi (in boat) remar ♦ vt conducir remando; **4 days in a** ~ 4 días seguidos.

row² [rau] n (racket) escándalo; (dispute) bronca, pelea; (scolding) regaño ♦ vi pelear(se).

rowboat ['rəubəut] (US) n bote m de remos.

rowdy ['raudɪ] adj (person: noisy) ruidoso; (occasion) alborotado.

rowing ['rəuɪŋ] n remo; ~ **boat** (BRIT) n bote m de remos.

royal ['rɔɪəl] adj real; **R~ Air Force** n Fuerzas fpl Aéreas Británicas; ~**ty** n (~ persons) familia real; (payment to author) derechos mpl de autor.

rpm abbr (= revs per minute) r.p.m.

R.S.V.P. abbr (= répondez s'il vous plaît) SRC.

Rt.Hon. abbr (BRIT: = Right Honourable) título honorífico de diputado.

rub [rʌb] vt frotar; (scrub) restregar ♦ n: **to give sth a** ~ frotar algo; **to** ~ **sb up** or ~ **sb** (US) **the wrong way** entrarle uno por mal ojo; ~ **off** vi borrarse; ~ **off on** vt fus influir en; ~ **out** vt borrar.

rubber ['rʌbə*] n caucho, goma; (BRIT: eraser) goma de borrar; ~ **band** n goma, gomita; ~ **plant** n ficus m; ~**y** adj elástico; (meat) gomoso.

rubbish ['rʌbɪʃ] n basura; (waste) desperdicios mpl; (fig: pej) tonterías fpl; (junk) pacotilla; ~ **bin** (BRIT) n cubo (SP) or bote m (AM) de la basura; ~ **dump** n vertedero, basurero.

rubble ['rʌbl] n escombros mpl.

ruble ['ruːbl] (US) n = **rouble**.

ruby ['ruːbɪ] n rubí m.

rucksack ['rʌksæk] n mochila.
rudder ['rʌdə*] n timón m.
ruddy ['rʌdɪ] adj (face) rubicundo; (inf: damned) condenado.
rude [ru:d] adj (impolite: person) mal educado; (: word, manners) grosero; (crude) crudo; (indecent) indecente; ~ness n descortesía.
rueful ['ru:ful] adj arrepentido.
ruffian ['rʌfɪən] n matón m, criminal m.
ruffle ['rʌfl] vt (hair) despeinar; (clothes) arrugar; **to get** ~**d** (fig: person) alterarse.
rug [rʌg] n alfombra; (BRIT: blanket) manta.
rugby ['rʌgbɪ] n (also: ~ football) rugby m.
rugged ['rʌgɪd] adj (landscape) accidentado; (features) robusto.
rugger ['rʌgə*] (BRIT: inf) n rugby m.
ruin ['ruːɪn] n ruina ♦ vt arruinar; (spoil) estropear; ~**s** npl ruinas fpl, restos mpl; ~**ous** adj desastroso.
rule [ruːl] n (norm) norma, costumbre f; (regulation, ruler) regla; (government) dominio ♦ vt (country, person) gobernar ♦ vi gobernar; (LAW) fallar; **as a** ~ por regla general; ~ **out** vt excluir; ~**d** adj (paper) rayado; ~**r** n (sovereign) soberano; (for measuring) regla; **ruling** adj (party) gobernante; (class) dirigente n (LAW) fallo, decisión f.
rum [rʌm] n ron m.
Rumania [ruːˈmeɪnɪə] n Rumanía; ~**n** adj rumano/a ♦ n rumano/a m/f; (LING) rumano.
rumble ['rʌmbl] n (noise) ruido sordo ♦ vi retumbar, hacer un ruido sordo; (stomach, pipe) sonar.
rummage ['rʌmɪdʒ] vi (search) hurgar.
rumour ['ruːmə*] (US **rumor**) n rumor m ♦ vt: **it is** ~**ed that** ... se rumorea que ....
rump [rʌmp] n (of animal) ancas fpl, grupa; ~ **steak** n filete m de lomo.
rumpus ['rʌmpəs] n lío, jaleo.
run [rʌn] (pt **ran**, pp **run**) n (fast pace): **at a** ~ corriendo; (SPORT, in tights) carrera; (outing) paseo, excursión f; (dis-

tance travelled) trayecto; (series) serie f; (THEATRE) temporada; (SKI) pista ♦ vt correr; (operate: business) dirigir; (: competition, course) organizar; (: hotel, house) administrar, llevar; (COMPUT) ejecutar; (pass: hand) pasar; (PRESS: feature) publicar ♦ vi correr; (work: machine) funcionar, marchar; (bus, train: operate) circular, ir; (: travel) ir; (continue: play) seguir; (: contract) ser válido; (flow: river) fluir; (colours, washing) desteñirse; (in election) ser candidato; **there was a** ~ **on** (meat, tickets) hubo mucha demanda de; **in the long** ~ a la larga; **on the** ~ en fuga; **I'll** ~ **you** to the station te llevaré a la estación (en coche); **to** ~ **a risk** correr un riesgo; **to** ~ **a bath** llenar la bañera; ~ **about** or **around** vi (children) correr por todos lados; ~ **across** vt fus (find) dar or topar con; ~ **away** vi huir; ~ **down** vt (production) ir reduciendo; (factory) ir restringiendo la producción en; (subj: car) atropellar; (criticize) criticar; **to be** ~ **down** (person: tired) estar debilitado; ~ **in** (BRIT) vt (car) rodar; ~ **into** vt fus (meet: person, trouble) tropezar con; (collide with) chocar con; ~ **off** vt (water) dejar correr; (copies) sacar ♦ vi huir corriendo; ~ **out** vi (person) salir corriendo; (liquid) irse; (lease) caducar, vencer; (money etc) acabarse; ~ **out of** vt fus quedar sin; ~ **over** vt (AUT) atropellar ♦ vt fus (revise) repasar; ~ **through** vt fus (instructions) repasar; ~ **up** vt (debt) contraer; **to** ~ **up against** (difficulties) tropezar con; ~**away** adj (horse) desbocado; (truck) sin frenos; (child) escapado de casa.
rung [rʌŋ] pp of **ring** ♦ n (of ladder) escalón m, peldaño.
runner ['rʌnə*] n (in race: person) corredor(a) m/f; (: horse) caballo; (on sledge) patín m; ~ **bean** (BRIT) n ≈ judía verde; ~-**up** n subcampeón/ona m/f.
running ['rʌnɪŋ] n (sport) atletismo; (business) administración f ♦ adj (water, costs) corriente; (commentary)

continuo; **to be in/out of the ~ for sth** tener/no tener posibilidades de ganar algo; **6 days ~** 6 días seguidos; **~ commentary** n (*TV, RADIO*) comentario en directo; (*on guided tour etc*) comentario detallado; **~ costs** npl gastos mpl corrientes.

runny ['rʌnɪ] adj fluido; (*nose, eyes*) gastante.

run-of-the-mill adj común y corriente.

runt [rʌnt] n (*also pej*) redrojo, enano.

run-up n: **~ to** (*election etc*) período previo a.

runway ['rʌnweɪ] n (*AVIAT*) pista de aterrizaje.

rupee [ru:'pi:] n rupia.

rupture ['rʌptʃə*] n (*MED*) hernia.

rural ['ruərl] adj rural.

ruse [ru:z] n ardid m.

rush [rʌʃ] n ímpetu m; (*hurry*) prisa; (*COMM*) demanda repentina; (*current*) corriente f fuerte; (*of feeling*) torrente; (*BOT*) junco ♦ vt apresurar; (*work*) hacer de prisa ♦ vi correr, precipitarse; **~ hour** n horas fpl punta.

rusk [rʌsk] n bizcocho tostado.

Russia ['rʌʃə] n Rusia; **~n** adj ruso/a ♦ n ruso/a m/f; (*LING*) ruso.

rust [rʌst] n herrumbre f, moho ♦ vi oxidarse.

rustic ['rʌstɪk] adj rústico.

rustle ['rʌsl] vi susurrar ♦ vt (*paper*) hacer crujir; (*US: cattle*) hurtar, robar.

rustproof ['rʌstpru:f] adj inoxidable.

rusty ['rʌstɪ] adj oxidado.

rut [rʌt] n surco; (*ZOOL*) celo; **to be in a ~** ser esclavo de la rutina.

ruthless ['ru:θlɪs] adj despiadado.

rye [raɪ] n centeno; **~ bread** n pan de centeno.

S

Sabbath ['sæbəθ] n domingo; (*Jewish*) sábado.

sabotage ['sæbətɑ:ʒ] n sabotaje m ♦ vt sabotear.

saccharin(e) ['sækərɪn] n sacarina.

sachet ['sæʃeɪ] n sobrecito.

sack [sæk] n (*bag*) saco, costal m ♦ vt (*dismiss*) despedir; (*plunder*) saquear; **to get the ~** ser despedido; **~ing** n despido; (*material*) arpillera.

sacred ['seɪkrɪd] adj sagrado, santo.

sacrifice ['sækrɪfaɪs] n sacrificio ♦ vt sacrificar.

sacrilege ['sækrɪlɪdʒ] n sacrilegio.

sacrosanct ['sækrəusæŋkt] adj sacrosanto.

sad [sæd] adj (*unhappy*) triste; (*deplorable*) lamentable.

saddle ['sædl] n silla (de montar); (*of cycle*) sillín m ♦ vt (*horse*) ensillar; **to be ~d with sth** (*inf*) quedar cargado con algo; **~bag** n alforja.

sadistic [sə'dɪstɪk] adj sádico.

sadly ['sædlɪ] adv lamentablemente; **to be ~ lacking in** estar por desgracia carente de.

sadness ['sædnɪs] n tristeza.

s.a.e. abbr (= *stamped addressed envelope*) sobre con las propias señas de uno y con sello.

safari [sə'fɑ:rɪ] n safari m.

safe [seɪf] adj (*out of danger*) fuera de peligro; (*not dangerous, sure*) seguro; (*unharmed*) ileso ♦ n caja de caudales, caja fuerte; **~ and sound** sano y salvo; **(just) to be on the ~ side** para mayor seguridad; **~-conduct** n salvoconducto; **~-deposit** n (*vault*) cámara acorazada; (*box*) caja de seguridad; **~guard** n protección f, garantía ♦ vt proteger, defender; **~keeping** n custodia; **~ly** adv seguramente, con seguridad; **to arrive ~ly** llegar bien.

safety ['seɪftɪ] n seguridad f; **~ belt** n cinturón m (de seguridad); **~ pin** n imperdible m (*SP*), seguro (*AM*); **~ valve** n válvula de seguridad.

saffron ['sæfrən] n azafrán m.

sag [sæg] vi aflojarse.

sage [seɪdʒ] n (*herb*) salvia; (*man*) sabio.

Sagittarius [sædʒɪ'tɛərɪəs] n Sagitario.

Sahara [sə'hɑ:rə] n: **the ~ (Desert)** el (desierto del) Sáhara.

said [sed] pt, pp of **say**.

sail [seɪl] n (*on boat*) vela; (*trip*): **to go**

for a ~ dar un paseo en barco ♦ *vt* (*boat*) gobernar ♦ *vi* (*travel: ship*) navegar; (*SPORT*) hacer vela; (*begin voyage*) salir; **they** ~**ed into Copenhagen** arribaron a Copenhague; ~ **through** *vt fus* (*exam*) aprobar sin ningún problema; ~**boat** (*US*) *n* velero, barco de vela; ~**ing** *n* (*SPORT*) vela; **to go** ~**ing** hacer vela; ~**ing boat** *n* barco de vela; ~**ing ship** *n* velero; ~**or** *n* marinero, marino.

saint [seɪnt] *n* santo; ~**ly** *adj* santo.

sake [seɪk] *n*: **for the** ~ **of** por.

salad ['sæləd] *n* ensalada; ~ **bowl** *n* ensaladera; ~ **cream** (*BRIT*) *n* (especie *f* de) mayonesa; ~ **dressing** *n* aliño.

salary ['sæləɾɪ] *n* sueldo.

sale [seɪl] *n* venta; (*at reduced prices*) liquidación *f*, saldo; (*auction*) subasta; ~**s** *npl* (*total amount sold*) ventas *fpl*, facturación *f*; "**for** ~" "se vende"; **on** ~ en venta; **on** ~ **or return** (*goods*) venta por reposición; ~**room** *n* sala de subastas; ~**s assistant** (*US* ~**s clerk**) *n* dependiente/a *m/f*; **salesman/woman** *n* (*in shop*) dependiente/a *m/f*; (*representative*) viajante *m/f*.

salient ['seɪlɪənt] *adj* sobresaliente.

saliva [sə'laɪvə] *n* saliva.

sallow ['sæləu] *adj* cetrino.

salmon ['sæmən] *n inv* salmón *m*.

salon ['sælɔn] *n* (*hairdressing* ~) peluquería; (*beauty* ~) salón *m* de belleza.

saloon [sə'luːn] *n* (*US*) bar *m*, taberna; (*BRIT: AUT*) (coche *m* de) turismo; (*ship's lounge*) cámara, salón *m*.

salt [sɔlt] *n* sal *f* ♦ *vt* salar; (*put* ~ *on*) poner sal en; ~ **away** (*inf*) *vt* (*money*) ahorrar; ~ **cellar** *n* salero; ~**water** *adj* de agua salada; ~**y** *adj* salado.

salutary ['sæljutəɾɪ] *adj* saludable.

salute [sə'luːt] *n* saludo; (*of guns*) salva ♦ *vt* saludar.

salvage ['sælvɪdʒ] *n* (*saving*) salvamento, recuperación *f*; (*things saved*) objetos *mpl* salvados ♦ *vt* salvar.

salvation [sæl'veɪʃən] *n* salvación *f*; **S**~ **Army** *n* Ejército de Salvación.

salvo ['sælvəu] *n* (*MIL*) salva.

same [seɪm] *adj* mismo ♦ *pron*: **the** ~

el/la mismo/a, los/las mismos/as; **the** ~ **book as** el mismo libro que; **at the** ~ **time** (*at the* ~ *moment*) al mismo tiempo; (*yet*) sin embargo; **all** *or* **just the** ~ sin embargo, aun así; **to do the** ~ (as **sb**) hacer lo mismo (que uno); **the** ~ **to you!** ¡igualmente!

sample ['sɑːmpl] *n* muestra ♦ *vt* (*food*) probar; (*wine*) catar.

sanatorium [sænə'tɔːɾɪəm] (*pl* **sanatoria**) (*BRIT*) *n* sanatorio.

sanctimonious [sæŋktɪ'məunɪəs] *adj* mojigato.

sanction ['sæŋkʃən] *n* aprobación *f* ♦ *vt* sancionar; aprobar; ~**s** *npl* (*POL*) sanciones *fpl*.

sanctity ['sæŋktɪtɪ] *n* santidad *f*; (*inviolability*) inviolabilidad *f*.

sanctuary ['sæŋktjuəɾɪ] *n* santuario; (*refuge*) asilo, refugio; (*for wildlife*) reserva.

sand [sænd] *n* arena; (*beach*) playa ♦ *vt* (*also:* ~ *down*) lijar.

sandal ['sændl] *n* sandalia.

sand: ~**box** (*US*) *n* = ~**pit**; ~**castle** *n* castillo de arena; ~ **dune** *n* duna; ~**paper** *n* papel *m* de lija; ~**pit** *n* (*for children*) cajón *m* de arena; ~**stone** *n* piedra arenisca.

sandwich ['sændwɪtʃ] *n* bocadillo (*SP*), sandwich *m*, emparedado (*AM*) ♦ *vt* intercalar; ~**ed between** apretujado entre; **cheese/ham** ~ sandwich de queso/jamón; ~ **course** (*BRIT*) *n* curso de medio tiempo.

sandy ['sændɪ] *adj* arenoso; (*colour*) rojizo.

sane [seɪn] *adj* cuerdo; (*sensible*) sensato.

sang [sæŋ] *pt of* **sing**.

sanitarium [sænɪ'tɛəɾɪəm] (*US*) *n* = **sanatorium**.

sanitary ['sænɪtəɾɪ] *adj* sanitario; (*clean*) higiénico; ~ **towel** (*US* ~ **napkin**) *n* paño higiénico, compresa.

sanitation [sænɪ'teɪʃən] *n* (*in house*) servicios *mpl* higiénicos; (*in town*) servicio de desinfección; ~ **department** (*US*) *n* departamento de limpieza y recogida de basuras.

sanity ['sænɪtɪ] n cordura; (of judgment) sensatez f.

sank [sæŋk] pt of sink.

Santa Claus [sæntə'klɔːz] n San Nicolás, Papá Noel.

sap [sæp] n (of plants) savia ♦ vt (strength) minar, agotar.

sapling ['sæplɪŋ] n árbol nuevo or joven.

sapphire ['sæfaɪə*] n zafiro.

sarcasm ['sɑːkæzm] n sarcasmo.

sardine [sɑː'diːn] n sardina.

Sardinia [sɑː'dɪnɪə] n Cerdeña.

sash [sæʃ] n faja.

sat [sæt] pt, pp of sit.

Satan ['seɪtn] n Satanás m.

satchel ['sætʃl] n (child's) cartera (SP), mochila (AM).

satellite ['sætəlaɪt] n satélite m; ~ dish n antena de televisión por satélite.

satin ['sætɪn] n raso ♦ adj de raso.

satire ['sætaɪə*] n sátira.

satisfaction [sætɪs'fækʃən] n satisfacción f.

satisfactory [sætɪs'fæktərɪ] adj satisfactorio.

satisfy ['sætɪsfaɪ] vt satisfacer; (convince) convencer; ~ing adj satisfactorio.

saturate ['sætʃəreɪt] vt: to ~ (with) empapar or saturar (de).

Saturday ['sætədɪ] n sábado.

sauce [sɔːs] n salsa; (sweet) crema; jarabe m; ~pan n cacerola, olla.

saucer ['sɔːsə*] n platillo.

saucy ['sɔːsɪ] adj fresco, descarado.

Saudi ['saudɪ]: ~ **Arabia** n Arabia Saudí or Saudita; ~ **(Arabian)** adj, n saudí m/f, saudita m/f.

sauna ['sɔːnə] n sauna.

saunter ['sɔːntə*] vi: to ~ in/out entrar/salir sin prisa.

sausage ['sɔsɪdʒ] n salchicha; ~ **roll** n empanadita de salchicha.

sauté ['səuteɪ] adj salteado.

savage ['sævɪdʒ] adj (cruel, fierce) feroz, furioso; (primitive) salvaje ♦ n salvaje m/f ♦ vt (attack) embestir; ~ry n salvajismo, salvajería.

save [seɪv] vt (rescue) salvar, rescatar; (money, time) ahorrar; (put by, keep: seat) guardar; (COMPUT) salvar (y guardar); (avoid: trouble) evitar; (SPORT) parar ♦ vi (also: ~ up) ahorrar ♦ n (SPORT) parada ♦ prep salvo, excepto.

saving ['seɪvɪŋ] n (on price etc) economía ♦ adj: the ~ **grace of** el único mérito de; ~s npl ahorros mpl; ~s **account** n cuenta de ahorros; ~s **bank** n caja de ahorros.

saviour ['seɪvjə*] (US savior) n salvador(a) m/f.

savour ['seɪvə*] (US savor) vt saborear; ~y adj sabroso; (dish: not sweet) salado.

saw [sɔː] (pt sawed, pp sawed or sawn) pt of see ♦ n (tool) sierra ♦ vt serrar; ~dust n (a)serrín m; ~mill n aserradero; ~-off shotgun n escopeta de cañones recortados.

saxophone ['sæksəfəun] n saxófono.

say [seɪ] (pt, pp said) n: to have one's ~ expresar su opinión; to have a or some ~ in sth tener voz or tener que ver en algo ♦ vt decir; to ~ yes/no decir que sí/no; could you ~ that again? ¿podría repetir eso?; that is to ~ es decir; that goes without ~ing ni que decir tiene; ~ing n dicho, refrán m.

scab [skæb] n costra; (pej) esquirol m.

scaffold ['skæfəuld] n cadalso; ~ing n andamio, andamiaje m.

scald [skɔːld] n escaldadura ♦ vt escaldar.

scale [skeɪl] n (gen, MUS) escala; (of fish) escama; (of salaries, fees etc) escalafón m ♦ vt (mountain) escalar; (tree) trepar; ~s npl (for weighing: small) balanza; (: large) báscula; on a large ~ en gran escala; ~ of charges tarifa, lista de precios; ~ down vt reducir a escala.

scallop ['skɔləp] n (ZOOL) venera; (SEWING) festón m.

scalp [skælp] n cabellera ♦ vt escalpar.

scalpel ['skælpl] n bisturí m.

scamper ['skæmpə*] vi: to ~ away or off irse corriendo.

scampi ['skæmpɪ] npl gambas fpl.

scan [skæn] vt (examine) escudriñar; (glance at quickly) dar un vistazo a;

(*TV, RADAR*) explorar, registrar ♦ *n* (*MED*): **to have a** ~ pasar por el escáner.

scandal ['skændl] *n* escándalo; (*gossip*) chismes *mpl*.

Scandinavia [skændɪ'neɪvɪə] *n* Escandinavia; ~**n** *adj, n* escandinavo/a *m/f*.

scant [skænt] *adj* escaso; ~**y** *adj* (*meal*) insuficiente; (*clothes*) ligero.

scapegoat ['skeɪpgəut] *n* cabeza de turco, chivo expiatorio.

scar [skɑ:] *n* cicatriz *f*; (*fig*) señal *f* ♦ *vt* dejar señales en.

scarce [skɛəs] *adj* escaso; **to make o.s.** ~ (*inf*) esfumarse; ~**ly** *adv* apenas; **scarcity** *n* escasez *f*.

scare [skɛə*] *n* susto, sobresalto; (*panic*) pánico ♦ *vt* asustar, espantar; **to** ~ **sb stiff** dar a uno un susto de muerte; **bomb** ~ amenaza de bomba; ~ **off** *or* **away** *vt* ahuyentar; ~**crow** *n* espantapájaros *m inv*; ~**d** *adj*: **to be** ~**d** estar asustado.

scarf [skɑ:f] (*pl* ~**s** *or* **scarves**) *n* (*long*) bufanda; (*square*) pañuelo.

scarlet ['skɑ:lɪt] *adj* escarlata; ~ **fever** *n* escarlatina.

scarves [skɑ:vz] *npl of* **scarf**.

scary ['skɛərɪ] (*inf*) *adj* espeluznante.

scathing ['skeɪðɪŋ] *adj* mordaz.

scatter ['skætə*] *vt* (*spread*) esparcir, desparramar; (*put to flight*) dispersar ♦ *vi* desparramarse; dispersarse; ~**brained** *adj* ligero de cascos.

scavenger ['skævəndʒə*] *n* (*person*) basurero/a.

scenario [sɪ'nɑ:rɪəu] *n* (*THEATRE*) argumento; (*CINEMA*) guión *m*; (*fig*) escenario.

scene [si:n] *n* (*THEATRE, fig etc*) escena; (*of crime etc*) escenario; (*view*) panorama *m*; (*fuss*) escándalo; ~**ry** *n* (*THEATRE*) decorado; (*landscape*) paisaje *m*; **scenic** *adj* pintoresco.

scent [sɛnt] *n* perfume *m*, olor *m*; (*fig: track*) rastro, pista.

sceptic ['skɛptɪk] (*US* **skeptic**) *n* escéptico/a; ~**al** *adj* escéptico; ~**ism** ['skɛptɪsɪzm] *n* escepticismo.

sceptre ['sɛptə*] (*US* **scepter**) *n* cetro.

schedule ['ʃɛdju:l, (*US*) 'skɛdju:l] *n* (*timetable*) horario; (*of events*) programa *m*; (*list*) lista ♦ *vt* (*visit*) fijar la hora de; **to arrive on** ~ llegar a la hora debida; **to be ahead of/behind** ~ estar adelantado/en retraso; ~**d flight** *n* vuelo regular.

schematic [skɪ'mætɪk] *adj* (*diagram etc*) esquemático.

scheme [ski:m] *n* (*plan*) plan *m*, proyecto; (*plot*) intriga; (*arrangement*) disposición *f*; (*pension* ~ *etc*) sistema *m* ♦ *vi* (*intrigue*) intrigar; **scheming** *adj* intrigante ♦ *n* intrigas *fpl*.

schism ['skɪzəm] *n* cisma *m*.

schizophrenic [skɪtzə'frɛnɪk] *adj* esquizofrénico.

scholar ['skɔlə*] *n* (*pupil*) alumno/a; (*learned person*) sabio/a, erudito/a; ~**ly** *adj* erudito; ~**ship** *n* erudición *f*; (*grant*) beca.

school [sku:l] *n* escuela, colegio; (*in university*) facultad *f* ♦ *cpd* escolar; ~ **age** *n* edad *f* escolar; ~**book** *n* libro de texto; ~**boy** *n* alumno; ~ **children** *npl* alumnos *mpl*; ~**days** *npl* años *mpl* del colegio; ~**girl** *n* alumna; ~**ing** *n* enseñanza; ~**master/mistress** *n* (*primary*) maestro/a; (*secondary*) profesor/a *m/f*; ~**teacher** *n* (*primary*) maestro/a; (*secondary*) profesor(a) *m/f*.

schooner ['sku:nə*] *n* (*ship*) goleta.

sciatica [saɪ'ætɪkə] *n* ciática.

science ['saɪəns] *n* ciencia; ~ **fiction** *n* ciencia-ficción *f*; **scientific** [-'tɪfɪk] *adj* científico; **scientist** *n* científico/a.

scintillating ['sɪntɪleɪtɪŋ] *adj* brillante, ingenioso.

scissors ['sɪzəz] *npl* tijeras *fpl*; **a pair of** ~ unas tijeras.

scoff [skɔf] *vt* (*BRIT: inf: eat*) engullir ♦ *vi*: **to** ~ (**at**) (*mock*) mofarse (de).

scold [skəuld] *vt* regañar.

scone [skɔn] *n* pastel de pan.

scoop [sku:p] *n* (*for flour etc*) pala; (*PRESS*) exclusiva; ~ **out** *vt* excavar; ~ **up** *vt* recoger.

scooter ['sku:tə*] *n* moto *f*; (*toy*) patinete *m*.

scope [skəup] *n* (*of plan*) ámbito; (*of*

person) competencia; *(opportunity)* libertad *f* (de acción).

scorch [skɔːtʃ] *vt (clothes)* chamuscar; *(earth, grass)* quemar, secar.

score [skɔː*] *n (points etc)* puntuación *f*; *(MUS)* partitura; *(twenty)* veintena ♦ *vt (goal, point)* ganar; *(mark)* rayar; *(achieve: success)* conseguir ♦ *vi* marcar un tanto; *(FOOTBALL)* marcar (un) gol; *(keep score)* llevar el tanteo; ~**s of** *(very many)* decenas de; **on that** ~ en lo que se refiere a eso; **to** ~ **6 out of 10** obtener una puntuación de 6 sobre 10; ~ **out** *vt* tachar; ~ **over** *vt fus* obtener una victoria sobre; ~**board** *n* marcador *m*.

scorn [skɔːn] *n* desprecio ♦ *vt* despreciar; ~**ful** *adj* desdeñoso, despreciativo.

Scorpio ['skɔːpɪəu] *n* Escorpión *m*.

scorpion ['skɔːpɪən] *n* alacrán *m*.

Scot [skɔt] *n* escocés/esa *m/f*.

scotch [skɔtʃ] *vt (rumour)* desmentir; *(plan)* abandonar; **S**~ *n* whisky *m* escocés.

scot-free *adv*: **to get off** ~ *(unpunished)* salir impune.

Scotland ['skɔtlənd] *n* Escocia.

Scots [skɔts] *adj* escocés/esa; ~**man/ woman** *n* escocés/esa *m/f*; **Scottish** ['skɔtɪʃ] *adj* escocés/esa.

scoundrel ['skaundrl] *n* canalla *m/f*, sinvergüenza *m/f*.

scour ['skauə*] *vt (search)* recorrer, registrar.

scourge [skɜːdʒ] *n* azote *m*.

scout [skaut] *n (MIL, also: boy* ~) explorador *m*; **girl** ~ *(US)* niña exploradora; ~ **around** *vi* reconocer el terreno.

scowl [skaul] *vi* fruncir el ceño; **to** ~ **at sb** mirar con ceño a uno.

scrabble ['skræbl] *vi (claw)*: **to** ~ **(at)** arañar; *(also: to* ~ *around: search)* revolver todo buscando ♦ *n*: **S**~ ® Scrabble *m* ®.

scraggy ['skrægɪ] *adj* descarnado.

scram [skræm] *(inf) vi* largarse.

scramble ['skræmbl] *n (climb)* subida (difícil); *(struggle)* pelea ♦ *vi*: **to** ~ **through/out** abrirse paso/salir con dificultad; **to** ~ **for** pelear por; ~**d eggs**

npl huevos *mpl* revueltos.

scrap [skræp] *n (bit)* pedacito; *(fig)* pizca; *(fight)* riña, bronca; *(also:* ~ *iron)* chatarra, hierro viejo ♦ *vt (discard)* desechar, descartar ♦ *vi* reñir, armar (una) bronca; ~**s** *npl (waste)* sobras *fpl*, desperdicios *mpl*; ~**book** *n* álbum *m* de recortes; ~ **dealer** *n* chatarrero/a.

scrape [skreɪp] *n*: **to get into a** ~ meterse en un lío ♦ *vt* raspar; *(skin etc)* rasguñar; *(*~ *against)* rozar ♦ *vi*: **to** ~ **through** *(exam)* aprobar por los pelos; ~ **together** *vt (money)* arañar, juntar.

scrap: ~ **heap** *n (fig)*: **to be on the** ~ **heap** estar acabado; ~ **merchant** *(BRIT) n* chatarrero/a; ~ **paper** *n* pedazos *mpl* de papel; ~**py** *adj (work)* imperfecto.

scratch [skrætʃ] *n* rasguño; *(from claw)* arañazo ♦ *cpd*: ~ **team** equipo improvisado ♦ *vt (paint, car)* rayar; *(with claw, nail)* rasguñar, arañar; *(rub: nose etc)* rascarse ♦ *vi* rascarse; **to start from** ~ partir de cero; **to be up to** ~ cumplir con los requisitos.

scrawl [skrɔːl] *n* garabatos *mpl* ♦ *vi* hacer garabatos.

scrawny ['skrɔːnɪ] *adj* flaco.

scream [skriːm] *n* chillido ♦ *vi* chillar.

scree [skriː] *n* cono de desmoronamiento.

screech [skriːtʃ] *vi* chirriar.

screen [skriːn] *n (CINEMA, TV)* pantalla; *(movable barrier)* biombo ♦ *vt (conceal)* tapar; *(from the wind etc)* proteger; *(film)* proyectar; *(candidates etc)* investigar a; ~**ing** *n (MED)* investigación *f* médica; ~**play** *n* guión *m*.

screw [skruː] *n* tornillo ♦ *vt (also:* ~ *in)* atornillar; ~ **up** *vt (paper etc)* arrugar; **to** ~ **up one's eyes** arrugar el entrecejo; ~**driver** *n* destornillador *m*.

scribble ['skrɪbl] *n* garabatos *mpl* ♦ *vt, vi* garabatear.

script [skrɪpt] *n (CINEMA etc)* guión *m*; *(writing)* escritura, letra.

scripture(s) ['skrɪptʃə*(z)] *n (pl)* Sagrada Escritura.

scroll [skrəul] *n* rollo.

scrounge [skraundʒ] *(inf) vt*: **to** ~ **sth**

off or **from sb** obtener algo de uno de gorra ♦ *n*: **on the** ~ de gorra; ~**r** *n* gorrón/ona *m/f*.

scrub [skrʌb] *n* (*land*) maleza ♦ *vt* fregar, restregar; (*inf: reject*) cancelar, anular.

scruff [skrʌf] *n*: **by the** ~ **of the neck** por el pescuezo.

scruffy ['skrʌfɪ] *adj* desaliñado, piojoso.

scrum(mage) ['skrʌm(mɪdʒ)] *n* (*RUGBY*) melée *f*.

scruple ['skruːpl] *n* (*gen pl*) escrúpulo.

scrutinize ['skruːtɪnaɪz] *vt* escudriñar; (*votes*) escrutar.

scrutiny ['skruːtɪnɪ] *n* escrutinio, examen *m*.

scuff [skʌf] *vt* (*shoes, floor*) rayar.

scuffle ['skʌfl] *n* refriega.

sculptor ['skʌlptə*] *n* escultor(a) *m/f*.

sculpture ['skʌlptʃə*] *n* escultura.

scum [skʌm] *n* (*on liquid*) espuma; (*pej: people*) escoria.

scupper ['skʌpə*] (*BRIT: inf*) *vt* (*plans*) dar al traste con.

scurrilous ['skʌrɪləs] *adj* difamatorio, calumnioso.

scurry ['skʌrɪ] *vi* correr; **to** ~ **off** escabullirse.

scuttle ['skʌtl] *n* (*also: coal* ~) cubo, carbonera ♦ *vt* (*ship*) barrenar ♦ *vi* (*scamper*): **to** ~ **away**, ~ **off** escabullirse.

scythe [saɪð] *n* guadaña.

SDP (*BRIT*) *n abbr* = **Social Democratic Party**.

sea [siː] *n* mar *m* ♦ *cpd* de mar, marítimo; **by** ~ (*travel*) en barco; **on the** ~ (*boat*) en el mar; (*town*) junto al mar; **to be all at** ~ (*fig*) estar despistado; **out to** ~, **at** ~ en alta mar; ~**board** *n* litoral *m*; ~**food** *n* mariscos *mpl*; ~ **front** *n* paseo marítimo; ~**-going** *adj* de altura; ~**gull** *n* gaviota.

seal [siːl] *n* (*animal*) foca; (*stamp*) sello ♦ *vt* (*close*) cerrar; ~ **off** *vt* (*area*) acordonar.

sea level *n* nivel *m* del mar.

sea lion *n* león *m* marino.

seam [siːm] *n* costura; (*of metal*) juntura; (*of coal*) veta, filón *m*.

seaman ['siːmən] *n* marinero.

seamy ['siːmɪ] *adj* sórdido.

seance ['seɪɒns] *n* sesión *f* de espiritismo.

seaplane ['siːpleɪn] *n* hidroavión *m*.

seaport ['siːpɔːt] *n* puerto de mar.

search [sɜːtʃ] *n* (*for person, thing*) busca, búsqueda; (*COMPUT*) búsqueda; (*inspection: of sb's home*) registro ♦ *vt* (*look in*) buscar en; (*examine*) examinar; (*person, place*) registrar ♦ *vi*: **to** ~ **for** buscar; **in** ~ **of** en busca de; ~ **through** *vt fus* registrar; ~**ing** *adj* penetrante; ~**light** *n* reflector *m*; ~ **party** *n* pelotón *m* de salvamento; ~ **warrant** *n* mandamiento (judicial).

sea: ~**shore** *n* playa, orilla del mar; ~**sick** *adj* mareado; ~**side** *n* playa, orilla del mar; ~**side resort** *n* centro turístico costero.

season ['siːzn] *n* (*of year*) estación *f*; (*sporting etc*) temporada; (*of films etc*) ciclo ♦ *vt* (*food*) sazonar; **in/out of** ~ en sazón/fuera de temporada; ~**al** *adj* estacional; ~**ed** *adj* (*fig*) experimentado; ~**ing** *n* condimento, aderezo; ~ **ticket** *n* abono.

seat [siːt] *n* (*in bus, train*) asiento; (*chair*) silla; (*PARLIAMENT*) escaño; (*buttocks*) culo, trasero; (*of trousers*) culera ♦ *vt* sentar; (*have room for*) tener cabida para; **to be** ~**ed** sentarse; ~ **belt** *n* cinturón *m* de seguridad.

sea: ~ **water** *n* agua del mar; ~**weed** *n* alga marina; ~**worthy** *adj* en condiciones de navegar.

sec. *abbr* = **second(s)**.

secluded [sɪ'kluːdɪd] *adj* retirado.

seclusion [sɪ'kluːʒən] *n* reclusión *f*.

second ['sɛkənd] *adj* segundo ♦ *adv* en segundo lugar ♦ *n* segundo; (*AUT: also:* ~ **gear**) segunda; (*COMM*) artículo con algún desperfecto; (*BRIT: SCOL: degree*) título de licenciado con calificación de notable ♦ *vt* (*motion*) apoyar; (*BRIT: worker*) transferir; ~**ary** *adj* secundario; ~**ary school** *n* escuela secundaria; ~**-class** *adj* de segunda clase ♦ *adv* (*RAIL*) en segunda; ~**hand** *adj* de segunda mano, usado; ~ **hand** *n* (*on* *clock*) segundero; ~**ly** *adv* en segundo lugar; ~**ment** [sɪ'kɔndmənt] (*BRIT*) *n* traslado temporal; ~**-rate** *adj* de segunda categoría; ~ **thoughts** *npl*: **to have** ~ **thoughts** cambiar de opinión; **on** ~ **thoughts** *or* **thought** (*US*) pensándolo bien.

secrecy ['si:krəsɪ] *n* secreto.

secret ['si:krɪt] *adj*, *n* secreto; **in** ~ en secreto.

secretarial [sɛkrɪ'tɛərɪəl] *adj* de secretario; (*course, staff*) de secretariado.

secretariat [sɛkrɪ'tɛərɪət] *n* secretaría.

secretary ['sɛkrətərɪ] *n* secretario/a; **S~ of State (for)** (*BRIT*: *POL*) Ministro (de).

secretion [sɪ'kri:ʃən] *n* secreción *f*.

secretive ['si:krətɪv] *adj* reservado, sigiloso.

secretly ['si:krɪtlɪ] *adv* en secreto.

sect [sɛkt] *n* secta; ~**arian** [-'tɛərɪən] *adj* sectario.

section ['sɛkʃən] *n* sección *f*; (*part*) parte *f*; (*of document*) artículo; (*of opinion*) sector *m*; (*cross-*~) corte *m* transversal.

sector ['sɛktə°] *n* sector *m*.

secular ['sɛkjulə°] *adj* secular, seglar.

secure [sɪ'kjuə°] *adj* seguro; (*firmly fixed*) firme, fijo ♦ *vt* (*fix*) asegurar, afianzar; (*get*) conseguir.

security [sɪ'kjuərɪtɪ] *n* seguridad *f*; (*for loan*) fianza; (: *object*) prenda.

sedan [sɪ'dæn] (*US*) *n* (*AUT*) sedán *m*.

sedate [sɪ'deɪt] *adj* tranquilo; ♦ *vt* tratar con sedantes.

sedation [sɪ'deɪʃən] *n* (*MED*) sedación *f*.

sedative ['sɛdɪtɪv] *n* sedante *m*, sedativo.

seduce [sɪ'dju:s] *vt* seducir; **seduction** [-'dʌkʃən] *n* seducción *f*; **seductive** [-'dʌktɪv] *adj* seductor(a).

see [si:] (*pt* **saw**, *pp* **seen**) *vt* ver; (*accompany*): **to** ~ **sb to the door** acompañar a uno a la puerta; (*understand*) ver, comprender ♦ *vi* ver ♦ *n* (arz)obispado; **to** ~ **that** (*ensure*) asegurar que; ~ **you soon!** ¡hasta pronto!; ~ **about** *vt fus* atender a, encargarse de; ~ **off** *vt* despedir; ~ **through** *vt fus* (*fig*) calar ♦ *vt* (*plan*) llevar a

cabo; ~ **to** *vt fus* atender a, encargarse de.

seed [si:d] *n* semilla; (*in fruit*) pepita; (*fig*: *gen pl*) germen *m*; (*TENNIS*) preseleccionado/a; **to go to** ~ (*plant*) granar; (*fig*) descuidarse; ~**ling** *n* planta de semillero; ~**y** *adj* (*shabby*) desaseado, raído.

seeing ['si:ɪŋ] *conj*: ~ (**that**) visto que, en vista de que.

seek [si:k] (*pt*, *pp* **sought**) *vt* buscar; (*post*) solicitar.

seem [si:m] *vi* parecer; **there seems to be ...** parece que hay ...; ~**ingly** *adv* aparentemente, según parece.

seen [si:n] *pp* de **see**.

seep [si:p] *vi* filtrarse.

seesaw ['si:sɔ:] *n* subibaja.

seethe [si:ð] *vi* hervir; **to** ~ **with anger** estar furioso.

see-through *adj* transparente.

segment ['sɛgmənt] *n* (*part*) sección *f*; (*of orange*) gajo.

segregate ['sɛgrɪgeɪt] *vt* segregar.

seismic ['saɪzmɪk] *adj* sísmico.

seize [si:z] *vt* (*grasp*) agarrar, asir; (*take possession of*) secuestrar; (: *territory*) apoderarse de; (*opportunity*) aprovecharse de; ~ (**up)on** *vt fus* aprovechar; ~ **up** *vi* (*TECH*) agarrotarse.

seizure ['si:ʒə°] *n* (*MED*) ataque *m*; (*LAW, of power*) incautación *f*.

seldom ['sɛldəm] *adv* rara vez.

select [sɪ'lɛkt] *adj* selecto, escogido ♦ *vt* escoger, elegir; (*SPORT*) seleccionar; ~**ion** [-'lɛkʃən] *n* selección *f*, elección *f*; (*COMM*) surtido.

self [sɛlf] (*pl* **selves**) *n* uno mismo; **the** ~ el yo ♦ *prefix* auto...; ~**-assured** *adj* seguro de sí mismo; ~**-catering** (*BRIT*) *adj* (=*flat etc*) con cocina; ~**-centred** (*US* ~**-centered**) *adj* egocéntrico; ~**-coloured** (*US* ~**-colored**) *adj* (*of one colour*) de un color; ~**-confidence** *n* confianza en sí mismo; ~**-conscious** *adj* cohibido; ~**-contained** (*BRIT*) *adj* (*flat*) con entrada particular; ~**-control** *n* autodominio; ~**-defence** (*US* ~**-defense**) *n* defensa propia; ~**-discipline** *n* autodisciplina; ~**-employed** *adj* que trabaja por cuenta propia; ~**-evident** *adj* patente; ~**-governing** *adj* autónomo; ~**-indulgent** *adj* autocomplaciente; ~**-interest** *n* egoísmo; ~**ish** *adj* egoísta; ~**ishness** *n* egoísmo; ~**less** *adj* desinteresado; ~**-made** *adj*: ~**-made man** hombre *m* que se ha hecho a sí mismo; ~**-pity** *n* lástima de sí mismo; ~**-portrait** *n* autorretrato; ~**-possessed** *adj* sereno, dueño de sí mismo; ~**-preservation** *n* propia conservación *f*; ~**-respect** *n* amor *m* propio; ~**-righteous** *adj* santurrón/ona; ~**-sacrifice** *n* abnegación *f*; ~**-satisfied** *adj* satisfecho de sí mismo; ~**-service** *adj* de autoservicio; ~**-sufficient** *adj* autosuficiente; ~**-taught** *adj* autodidacta.

sell [sɛl] (*pt, pp* **sold**) *vt* vender ♦ *vi* venderse; **to ~ at** *or* **for £10** venderse a 10 libras; ~ **off** *vt* liquidar; ~ **out** *vi*: **to ~ out of tickets/milk** vender todas las entradas/toda la leche; ~**-by date** *n* fecha de caducidad; ~**er** *n* vendedor(a) *m/f*; ~**ing price** *n* precio de venta.

sellotape ['sɛləʊteɪp] ® (*BRIT*) *n* cinta adhesiva, celo (*SP*), scotch *m* (*AM*).

selves [sɛlvz] *npl of* **self**.

semaphore ['sɛməfɔ:*] *n* semáforo.

semblance ['sɛmbləns] *n* apariencia.

semen ['si:mən] *n* semen *m*.

semester [sɪ'mɛstə*] (*US*) *n* semestre *m*.

semi... [sɛmɪ] *prefix* semi..., medio...; ~**circle** *n* semicírculo; ~**colon** *n* punto y coma; ~**conductor** *n* semiconductor *m*; ~**detached (house)** *n* (casa) semiseparada; ~**-final** *n* semi-final *m*.

seminar ['sɛmɪnɑ:*] *n* seminario.

seminary ['sɛmɪnərɪ] *n* (*REL*) seminario.

semiskilled ['sɛmɪskɪld] *adj* (*work, worker*) semi-cualificado.

senate ['sɛnɪt] *n* senado; **senator** *n* senador(a) *m/f*.

send [sɛnd] (*pt, pp* **sent**) *vt* mandar, enviar; (*signal*) transmitir; ~ **away** *vt* despachar; ~ **away for** *vt fus* pedir; ~ **back** *vt* devolver; ~ **for** *vt fus* mandar traer; ~ **off** *vt* (*goods*) despachar; (*BRIT*: *SPORT*: *player*) expulsar; ~ **out** *vt* (*invitation*) mandar; (*signal*) emitir;

~ **up** *vt* (*person, price*) hacer subir; (*BRIT*: *parody*) parodiar; ~**er** *n* remitente *m/f*; ~**-off** *n*: **a good ~-off** una buena despedida.

senior ['si:nɪə*] *adj* (*older*) mayor, más viejo; (: *on staff*) de más antigüedad; (*of higher rank*) superior; ~ **citizen** *n* persona de la tercera edad; ~**ity** [-'ɔrɪtɪ] *n* antigüedad *f*.

sensation [sɛn'seɪʃən] *n* sensación *f*; ~**al** *adj* sensacional.

sense [sɛns] *n* (*faculty, meaning*) sentido; (*feeling*) sensación *f*; (*good ~*) sentido común, juicio ♦ *vt* sentir, percibir; **it makes ~** tiene sentido; ~**less** *adj* estúpido, insensato; (*unconscious*) sin conocimiento; ~ **of humour** *n* sentido del humor.

sensible ['sɛnsɪbl] *adj* sensato; (*reasonable*) razonable, lógico.

sensitive ['sɛnsɪtɪv] *adj* sensible; (*touchy*) susceptible.

sensual ['sɛnsjʊəl] *adj* sensual.

sensuous ['sɛnsjʊəs] *adj* sensual.

sent [sɛnt] *pt, pp of* **send**.

sentence ['sɛntns] *n* (*LING*) oración *f*; (*LAW*) sentencia, fallo ♦ *vt*: **to ~ sb to death/to 5 years (in prison)** condenar a uno a muerte/a 5 años de cárcel.

sentiment ['sɛntɪmənt] *n* sentimiento; (*opinion*) opinión *f*; ~**al** [-'mɛntl] *adj* sentimental.

sentry ['sɛntrɪ] *n* centinela *m*.

separate [*adj* 'sɛprɪt, *vb* 'sɛpəreɪt] *adj* separado; (*distinct*) distinto ♦ *vt* separar; (*part*) dividir ♦ *vi* separarse; ~**s** *npl* (*clothes*) coordinados *mpl*; ~**ly** *adv* por separado; **separation** [-'reɪʃən] *n* separación *f*.

September [sɛp'tɛmbə*] *n* se(p)tiembre *m*.

septic ['sɛptɪk] *adj* séptico; ~ **tank** *n* fosa séptica.

sequel ['si:kwl] *n* consecuencia, resultado; (*of story*) continuación *f*.

sequence ['si:kwəns] *n* sucesión *f*, serie *f*; (*CINEMA*) secuencia.

sequin ['si:kwɪn] *n* lentejuela.

serene [sɪ'ri:n] *adj* sereno, tranquilo.

sergeant ['sɑ:dʒənt] *n* sargento.

serial ['sɪərɪəl] n (TV) telenovela, serie f televisiva; (BOOK) serie f; ~**ize** vt emitir como serial; ~ **number** n número de serie.

series ['sɪəriːs] n inv serie f.

serious ['sɪərɪəs] adj serio; (grave) grave; ~**ly** adv en serio; (ill, wounded etc) gravemente; ~**ness** n seriedad f; gravedad f.

sermon ['sɜːmən] n sermón m.

serrated [sɪ'reɪtɪd] adj serrado, dentellado.

serum ['sɪərəm] n suero.

servant ['sɜːvənt] n servidor(a) m/f; (house ~) criado/a.

serve [sɜːv] vt servir; (customer) atender; (subj: train) pasar por; (apprenticeship) hacer; (prison term) cumplir ♦ vi (at table) servir; (TENNIS) sacar; to ~ as/for/to do servir de/para/para hacer ♦ n (TENNIS) saque m; it ~s him right se lo tiene merecido; ~ out vt (food) servir; ~ up vt = ~ out.

service ['sɜːvɪs] n servicio; (REL) misa; (AUT) mantenimiento; (dishes etc) juego ♦ vt (car, washing machine) revisar; (: repair) reparar; the S~s npl las fuerzas armadas; to be of ~ to sb ser útil a uno; ~**able** adj servible, utilizable; ~ **area** n (on motorway) area de servicio; ~ **charge** (BRIT) n servicio; ~**man** n militar m; ~ **station** n estación f de servicio.

serviette [sɜːvɪ'et] (BRIT) n servilleta.

session ['seʃən] n sesión f; to be in ~ estar en sesión.

set [set] (pt, pp set) n juego; (RADIO) aparato; (TV) televisor m; (of utensils) batería; (of cutlery) cubierto; (of books) colección f; (TENNIS) set m; (group of people) grupo; (CINEMA) plató m; (THEATRE) decorado ♦ adj (fixed) fijo; (ready) listo ♦ vt (place) poner, colocar; (fix) fijar; (adjust) ajustar, arreglar; (decide: rules etc) establecer, decidir ♦ vi (sun) ponerse; (jam, jelly) cuajarse; (concrete) fraguar; (bone) componerse; to be ~ on doing sth estar empeñado en hacer algo; to ~ to music po-

ner música a; to ~ on fire incendiar, poner fuego a; to ~ free poner en libertad; to ~ sth going poner algo en marcha; to ~ sail zarpar, hacerse a la vela; ~ **about** vt fus ponerse a; ~ **aside** vt poner aparte, dejar de lado; (money, time) reservar; ~ **back** vt (cost): to ~ sb back £5 costar a uno cinco libras; (: in time): to ~ back (by) retrasar (por); ~ **off** vi partir ♦ vt (bomb) hacer estallar; (events) poner en marcha; (show up well) hacer resaltar; ~ **out** vi partir ♦ vt (arrange) disponer; (state) exponer; to ~ **out** to do sth proponerse hacer algo; ~ **up** vt establecer; ~**back** n revés m, contratiempo; ~ **menu** n menú m.

settee [se'tiː] n sofá m.

setting ['setɪŋ] n (scenery) marco; (position) disposición f; (of sun) puesta; (of jewel) engaste m, montadura.

settle ['setl] vt (argument) resolver; (accounts) ajustar, liquidar; (MED: calm) calmar, sosegar ♦ vi (dust etc) depositarse; (weather) serenarse; (also: ~ down) instalarse; tranquilizarse; to ~ for sth convenir en aceptar algo; to ~ on sth decidirse por algo; ~ **in** vi instalarse; ~ **up** vi: to ~ **up** with sb ajustar cuentas con uno; ~**ment** n (payment) liquidación f; (agreement) acuerdo, convenio; (village etc) pueblo; ~**r** n colono/a, colonizador(a) m/f.

setup ['setʌp] n sistema m; (situation) situación f.

seven ['sevn] num siete; ~**teen** num diez y siete, diecisiete; ~**th** num séptimo; ~**ty** num setenta.

sever ['sevə*] vt cortar; (relations) romper.

several ['sevərl] adj, pron varios/as m/fpl, algunos/as mpl/fpl; ~ **of us** varios de nosotros.

severance ['sevərəns] n (of relations) ruptura; ~ **pay** n indemnización f por despido.

severe [sɪ'vɪə*] adj severo; (serious) grave; (hard) duro; (pain) intenso; **severity** [sɪ'verɪtɪ] n severidad f; gravedad f; intensidad f.

sew [səu] (*pt* **sewed**, *pp* **sewn**) *vt*, *vi* coser; ~ **up** *vt* coser, zurcir.
sewage ['su:ɪdʒ] *n* aguas *fpl* residuales.
sewer ['su:ə*] *n* alcantarilla, cloaca.
sewing ['səuɪŋ] *n* costura; ~ **machine** *n* máquina de coser.
sewn [səun] *pp of* **sew**.
sex [sɛks] *n* sexo; (*lovemaking*): **to have** ~ hacer el amor; ~**ist** *adj*, *n* sexista *m/f*; **sexual** ['sɛksjuəl] *adj* sexual; **sexy** *adj* sexy.
shabby ['ʃæbɪ] *adj* (*person*) desharrapado; (*clothes*) raído, gastado; (*behaviour*) ruin *inv*.
shack [ʃæk] *n* choza, chabola.
shackles ['ʃæklz] *npl* grillos *mpl*, grilletes *mpl*.
shade [ʃeɪd] *n* sombra; (*for lamp*) pantalla; (*for eyes*) visera; (*of colour*) matiz *m*, tonalidad *f*; (*small quantity*): **a** ~ (**too big/more**) un poquitín (grande/más) ♦ *vt* dar sombra a; (*eyes*) proteger del sol; **in the** ~ en la sombra.
shadow ['ʃædəu] *n* sombra ♦ *vt* (*follow*) seguir y vigilar; ~ **cabinet** (*BRIT*) *n* (*POL*) *gabinete paralelo formado por el partido de oposición*; ~**y** *adj* oscuro; (*dim*) indistinto.
shady ['ʃeɪdɪ] *adj* sombreado; (*fig: dishonest*) sospechoso; (: *deal*) turbio.
shaft [ʃɑːft] *n* (*of arrow*, *spear*) astil *m*; (*AUT*, *TECH*) eje *m*, árbol *m*; (*of mine*) pozo; (*of lift*) hueco, caja; (*of light*) rayo.
shaggy ['ʃægɪ] *adj* peludo.
shake [ʃeɪk] (*pt* **shook**, *pp* **shaken**) *vt* sacudir; (*building*) hacer temblar; (*bottle*, *cocktail*) agitar ♦ *vi* (*tremble*) temblar; **to** ~ **one's head** (*in refusal*) negar con la cabeza; (*in dismay*) mover or menear la cabeza, incrédulo; **to** ~ **hands with sb** estrechar la mano a uno; ~ **off** *vt* sacudirse; (*fig*) deshacerse de; ~ **up** *vt* agitar; (*fig*) reorganizar; **shaky** *adj* (*hand*, *voice*) trémulo; (*building*) inestable.
shall [ʃæl] *aux vb*: ~ **I help you?** ¿quieres que te ayude?; **I'll buy three,** ~ **I?** compro tres, ¿no te parece?
shallow ['ʃæləu] *adj* poco profundo;

(*fig*) superficial.
sham [ʃæm] *n* fraude *m*, engaño ♦ *vt* fingir, simular.
shambles ['ʃæmblz] *n* confusión *f*.
shame [ʃeɪm] *n* vergüenza ♦ *vt* avergonzar; **it is a** ~ **that/to do** es una lástima que/hacer; **what a** ~! ¡qué lástima!; ~**faced** *adj* avergonzado; ~**ful** *adj* vergonzoso; ~**less** *adj* desvergonzado.
shampoo [ʃæm'pu:] *n* champú *m* ♦ *vt* lavar con champú; ~ **and set** *n* lavado y marcado.
shamrock ['ʃæmrɔk] *n* trébol *m* (*emblema nacional irlandés*).
shandy ['ʃændɪ] *n* *mezcla de cerveza con gaseosa*.
shan't [ʃɑːnt] = **shall not**.
shanty town ['ʃæntɪ-] *n* barrio de chabolas.
shape [ʃeɪp] *n* forma ♦ *vt* formar, dar forma a; (*sb's ideas*) formar; (*sb's life*) determinar; **to take** ~ tomar forma; ~ **up** *vi* (*events*) desarrollarse; (*person*) formarse; ~**-d** *suffix*: **heart**~**d** en forma de corazón; ~**less** *adj* informe, sin forma definida; ~**ly** *adj* (*body etc*) esbelto.
share [ʃɛə*] *n* (*part*) parte *f*, porción *f*; (*contribution*) cuota; (*COMM*) acción *f* ♦ *vt* dividir; (*have in common*) compartir; **to** ~ **out** (*among or between*) repartir (*entre*); ~**holder** (*BRIT*) *n* accionista *m/f*.
shark [ʃɑːk] *n* tiburón *m*.
sharp [ʃɑːp] *adj* (*blade*, *nose*) afilado; (*point*) puntiagudo; (*outline*) definido; (*pain*) intenso; (*MUS*) desafinado; (*contrast*) marcado; (*voice*) agudo; (*person: quick-witted*) astuto; (: *dishonest*) poco escrupuloso ♦ *n* (*MUS*) sostenido ♦ *adv*: **at 2 o'clock** ~ a las 2 en punto; ~**en** *vt* afilar; (*pencil*) sacar punta a; (*fig*) agudizar; ~**ener** *n* (*also*: **pencil** ~**ener**) sacapuntas *m inv*; ~**-eyed** *adj* de vista aguda; ~**ly** *adv* (*turn*, *stop*) bruscamente; (*stand out*, *contrast*) claramente; (*criticize*, *retort*) severamente.
shatter ['ʃætə*] *vt* hacer añicos *or* pedazos; (*fig: ruin*) destruir, acabar con ♦

vi hacerse añicos.

shave [ʃeɪv] *vt* afeitar, rasurar ♦ *vi* afeitarse, rasurarse ♦ *n*: **to have a ~** afeitarse; **~r** *n* (*also: electric ~r*) máquina de afeitar (eléctrica).

shaving [ʃeɪvɪŋ] *n* (*action*) el afeitarse, rasurado; **~s** *npl* (*of wood etc*) virutas *fpl*; **~ brush** *n* brocha (de afeitar); **~ cream** *n* crema de afeitar; **~ foam** *n* espuma de afeitar.

shawl [ʃɔːl] *n* chal *m*.

she [ʃiː] *pron* ella; **~-cat** *n* gata.

sheaf [ʃiːf] (*pl* **sheaves**) *n* (*of corn*) gavilla; (*of papers*) fajo.

shear [ʃɪə*] (*pt* **sheared**, *pp* **sheared** *or* **shorn**) *vt* esquilar, trasquilar; **~s** *npl* (*for hedge*) tijeras *fpl* de jardín; **~ off** *vi* romperse.

sheath [ʃiːθ] *n* vaina; (*contraceptive*) preservativo.

sheaves [ʃiːvz] *npl* of **sheaf**.

shed [ʃed] (*pt, pp* **shed**) *n* cobertizo ♦ *vt* (*skin*) mudar; (*tears, blood*) derramar; (*load*) derramar; (*workers*) despedir.

she'd [ʃiːd] = **she had**; **she would**.

sheen [ʃiːn] *n* brillo, lustre *m*.

sheep [ʃiːp] *n inv* oveja; **~dog** *n* perro pastor; **~ish** *adj* tímido, vergonzoso; **~skin** *n* piel *f* de carnero.

sheer [ʃɪə*] *adj* (*utter*) puro, completo; (*steep*) escarpado; (*material*) diáfano ♦ *adv* verticalmente.

sheet [ʃiːt] *n* (*on bed*) sábana; (*of paper*) hoja; (*of glass, metal*) lámina; (*of ice*) capa.

sheik(h) [ʃeɪk] *n* jeque *m*.

shelf [ʃelf] (*pl* **shelves**) *n* estante *m*.

shell [ʃel] *n* (*on beach*) concha; (*of egg, nut etc*) cáscara; (*explosive*) proyectil *m*, obús *m*; (*of building*) armazón *f* ♦ *vt* (*peas*) desenvainar; (*MIL*) bombardear.

she'll [ʃiːl] = **she will**; **she shall**.

shellfish [ʃelfɪʃ] *n inv* crustáceo; (*as food*) mariscos *mpl*.

shelter [ʃeltə*] *n* abrigo, refugio ♦ *vt* (*aid*) amparar, proteger; (*give lodging to*) abrigar ♦ *vi* abrigarse, refugiarse; **~ed** *adj* (*life*) protegido; (*spot*) abrigado; **~ed housing** *n* viviendas vigiladas

para ancianos y minusválidos.

shelve [ʃelv] *vt* (*fig*) aplazar; **~s** *npl* of **shelf**.

shepherd [ʃepəd] *n* pastor *m* ♦ *vt* (*guide*) guiar, conducir; **~'s pie** (*BRIT*) *n* pastel de carne y patatas.

sherry [ʃeri] *n* jerez *m*.

she's [ʃiːz] = **she is**; **she has**.

Shetland [ʃetlənd] *n* (*also: the ~s, the ~ Isles*) las Islas de Zetlandia.

shield [ʃiːld] *n* escudo; (*protection*) blindaje *m* ♦ *vt*: **to ~ (from)** proteger (de).

shift [ʃɪft] *n* (*change*) cambio; (*at work*) turno ♦ *vt* trasladar; (*remove*) quitar ♦ *vi* moverse; **~less** *adj* (*person*) perezoso; **~ work** *n* trabajo a turnos; **~y** *adj* tramposo; (*eyes*) furtivo.

shilling [ʃɪlɪŋ] (*BRIT*) *n* chelín *m*.

shilly-shally [ʃɪlɪʃælɪ] *vi* titubear, vacilar.

shimmer [ʃɪmə*] *n* reflejo trémulo.

shin [ʃɪn] *n* espinilla.

shine [ʃaɪn] (*pt, pp* **shone**) *n* brillo, lustre *m* ♦ *vi* brillar, relucir ♦ *vt* (*shoes*) lustrar, sacar brillo a; **to ~ a torch on sth** dirigir una linterna hacia algo.

shingle [ʃɪŋgl] *n* (*on beach*) guijarros *mpl*; **~s** *n* (*MED*) herpes *mpl or fpl*.

shiny [ʃaɪnɪ] *adj* brillante, lustroso.

ship [ʃɪp] *n* buque *m*, barco ♦ *vt* (*goods*) embarcar; (*send*) transportar *or* enviar por vía marítima; **~building** *n* construcción *f* de buques; **~ment** *n* (*goods*) envío; **~per** *n* exportador(a) *m/f*; **~ping** *n* (*act*) embarque *m*; (*traffic*) buques *mpl*; **~shape** *adj* en buen orden; **~wreck** *n* naufragio ♦ *vt*: **to be ~wrecked** naufragar; **~yard** *n* astillero.

shire [ʃaɪə*] (*BRIT*) *n* condado.

shirk [ʃəːk] *vt* (*obligations*) faltar a.

shirt [ʃəːt] *n* camisa; **in (one's) ~ sleeves** en mangas de camisa.

shit [ʃɪt] (*inf!*) *excl* ¡mierda! (!)

shiver [ʃɪvə*] *n* escalofrío ♦ *vi* temblar, estremecerse; (*with cold*) tiritar.

shoal [ʃəul] *n* (*of fish*) banco; (*fig: also: ~s*) tropel *m*.

shock [ʃɔk] *n* (*impact*) choque *m*; (*ELEC*) descarga (eléctrica); (*emotional*) conmoción *f*; (*start*) sobresalto, sus-

to; (MED) postración f nerviosa ♦ vt dar
un susto a; (offend) escandalizar; ~
absorber n amortiguador m; ~**ing** adj
(awful) espantoso; (outrageous) escandaloso.
shod [ʃɔd] pt, pp of **shoe**.
shoddy [ˈʃɔdɪ] adj de pacotilla.
shoe [ʃuː] (pt, pp **shod**) n zapato; (for
horse) herradura ♦ vt (horse) herrar;
~**brush** n cepillo para zapatos; ~**lace** n
cordón m; ~ **polish** n betún m; ~**shop**
n zapatería; ~**string** n (fig): on a
~**string** con muy poco dinero.
shone [ʃɔn] pt, pp of **shine**.
shoo [ʃuː] excl ¡fuera!
shook [ʃuk] pt of **shake**.
shoot [ʃuːt] (pt, pp **shot**) n (on branch,
seedling) retoño, vástago ♦ vt disparar;
(kill) matar a tiros; (wound) pegar un
tiro; (execute) fusilar; (film) rodar,
filmar ♦ vi (FOOTBALL) chutar; ~
down vt (plane) derribar; ~ **in/out** vi
entrar corriendo/salir disparado; ~ **up**
vi (prices) dispararse; ~**ing** n (shots)
tiros mpl; (HUNTING) caza con escopeta; ~**ing star** n estrella fugaz.
shop [ʃɔp] n tienda; (workshop) taller
m ♦ vi (also: go ~**ping**) ir de compras;
~ **assistant** (BRIT) n dependiente/a m/f;
~ **floor** (BRIT) n (fig) taller m, fábrica;
~**keeper** n tendero/a; ~**lifting** n meche-
ría; ~**per** n comprador(a) m/f; ~**ping**
n (goods) compras fpl; ~**ping bag** n
bolsa (de compras); ~**ping centre** (US
~**ping center**) n centro comercial; ~-
soiled adj usado; ~ **steward** (BRIT) n
(INDUSTRY) enlace m sindical; ~ **window** n escaparate m (SP), vidriera
(AM).
shore [ʃɔː*] n orilla ♦ vt: to ~ (up) reforzar; on ~ en tierra.
shorn [ʃɔːn] pp of **shear**.
short [ʃɔːt] adj corto; (in time) breve,
de corta duración; (person) bajo;
(curt) brusco, seco; (insufficient) insuficiente; to be ~ of sth estar falto de
algo; in ~ en pocas palabras; ~ of
doing ... fuera de hacer ...; it is ~ for
es la forma abreviada de; to cut ~
(speech, visit) interrumpir, terminar

inesperadamente; **everything** ~ **of** ...
todo menos ...; **to fall** ~ **of** no alcanzar;
to run ~ **of** quedarle a uno poco; **to stop**
~ parar en seco; **to stop** ~ **of** detenerse
antes de; ~**age** n: **a** ~**age of** una falta
de; ~**bread** n especie de mantecada;
~**change** vt no dar el cambio completo
a; ~**circuit** n cortocircuito; ~**coming** n
defecto, deficiencia; ~**(crust) pastry**
(BRIT) n pasta quebradiza; ~**cut** n atajo; ~**en** vt acortar; (visit) interrumpir;
~**fall** n déficit m; ~**hand** (BRIT) n taquigrafía; ~**hand typist** (BRIT) n
taquimecanógrafo/a; ~ **list** (BRIT) n
(for job) lista de candidatos escogidos;
~**lived** adj efímero; ~**ly** adv en breve,
dentro de poco; ~**sighted** (BRIT) adj
miope; (fig) imprudente; ~**staffed**
adj: **to be** ~**staffed** estar falto de personal; ~ **story** n cuento; ~**tempered**
adj enojadizo; ~**term** adj (effect) a
corto plazo; ~**wave** n (RADIO) onda
corta.
shot [ʃɔt] pt, pp of **shoot** ♦ n (sound)
tiro, disparo; (try) tentativa; (injection) inyección f; (PHOT) toma, fotografía; **to be a good/poor** ~ (person) tener
buena/mala puntería; **like a** ~ (without
any delay) como un rayo; ~**gun** n escopeta.
should [ʃud] aux vb: **I** ~ **go now** debo
irme ahora; **he** ~ **be there now** debe de
haber llegado (ya); **I** ~ **go if I were
you** yo en tu lugar me iría; **I** ~ **like to**
me gustaría.
shoulder [ˈʃəuldə*] n hombro ♦ vt (fig)
cargar con; ~ **bag** n cartera de bando-
lera; ~ **blade** n omóplato; ~ **strap** n tirante m.
shouldn't [ˈʃudnt] = **should not**.
shout [ʃaut] n grito ♦ vt gritar ♦ vi gritar, dar voces; ~ **down** vt acallar a
gritos; ~**ing** n griterío.
shove [ʃʌv] n empujón m ♦ vt empujar;
(inf: put): **to** ~ **sth in** meter algo a empellones; ~ **off** (inf) vi largarse.
shovel [ˈʃʌvl] n pala; (mechanical) excavadora ♦ vt mover con pala.
show [ʃəu] (pt **showed**, pp **shown**) n (of
emotion) demostración f; (semblance)

apariencia; (*exhibition*) exposición *f*; (*THEATRE*) función *f*, espectáculo; (*TV*) show *m* ♦ *vt* mostrar, enseñar; (*courage etc*) mostrar, manifestar; (*exhibit*) exponer; (*film*) proyectar ♦ *vi* mostrarse; (*appear*) aparecer; **for** ~ para impresionar; **on** ~ (*exhibits etc*) expuesto; ~ **in** *vt* (*person*) hacer pasar; ~ **off** (*pej*) *vi* presumir ♦ *vt* (*display*) lucir; ~ **out** *vt*: **to** ~ **sb out** acompañar a uno a la puerta; ~ **up** *vi* (*stand out*) destacar; (*inf*: *turn up*) aparecer ♦ *vt* (*unmask*) desenmascarar; ~ **business** *n* mundo del espectáculo; ~**down** *n* enfrentamiento (final).

shower ['ʃauə*] *n* (*rain*) chaparrón *m*, chubasco; (*of stones etc*) lluvia; (*for bathing*) ducha (*SP*), regadera (*AM*) ♦ *vi* llover ♦ *vt* (*fig*): **to** ~ **sb with sth** colmar a uno de algo; **to have a** ~ ducharse; ~**proof** *adj* impermeable.

showing ['ʃəuɪŋ] *n* (*of film*) proyección *f*.

show jumping *n* hípica.

shown [ʃəun] *pp* of **show**.

show: ~-**off** (*inf*) *n* (*person*) presumido/a; ~**piece** *n* (*of exhibition etc*) objeto cumbre; ~**room** *n* sala de muestras.

shrank [ʃræŋk] *pt* of **shrink**.

shrapnel ['ʃræpnl] *n* metralla.

shred [ʃred] *n* (*gen pl*) triza, jirón *m* ♦ *vt* hacer trizas; (*CULIN*) desmenuzar; ~**der** *n* (*vegetable* ~**der**) picadora; (*document* ~**der**) trituradora (de papel).

shrewd [ʃruːd] *adj* astuto.

shriek [ʃriːk] *n* chillido ♦ *vi* chillar.

shrill [ʃrɪl] *adj* agudo, estridente.

shrimp [ʃrɪmp] *n* camarón *m*.

shrine [ʃraɪn] *n* santuario, sepulcro.

shrink [ʃrɪŋk] (*pt* **shrank**, *pp* **shrunk**) *vi* encogerse; (*be reduced*) reducirse; (*also*: ~ *away*) retroceder ♦ *vt* encoger ♦ *n* (*inf*: *pej*) loquero/a; **to** ~ **from** (*doing*) **sth** no atreverse a hacer algo; ~**age** *n* encogimiento; reducción *f*; ~**wrap** *vt* embalar con película de plástico.

shrivel ['ʃrɪvl] (*also*: ~ *up*) *vt* (*dry*) secar ♦ *vi* secarse.

shroud [ʃraud] *n* sudario ♦ *vt*: ~**ed in mystery** envuelto en el misterio.

Shrove Tuesday ['ʃrəuv-] *n* martes *m* de carnaval.

shrub [ʃrʌb] *n* arbusto; ~**bery** *n* arbustos *mpl*.

shrug [ʃrʌg] *n* encogimiento de hombros ♦ *vt*, *vi*: **to** ~ (**one's shoulders**) encogerse de hombros; ~ **off** *vt* negar importancia a.

shrunk [ʃrʌŋk] *pp* of **shrink**.

shudder ['ʃʌdə*] *n* estremecimiento, escalofrío ♦ *vi* estremecerse.

shuffle ['ʃʌfl] *vt* (*cards*) barajar ♦ *vi*: ~ (**one's feet**) arrastrar los pies.

shun [ʃʌn] *vt* rehuir, esquivar.

shunt [ʃʌnt] *vt* (*train*) maniobrar; (*object*) empujar.

shut [ʃʌt] (*pt*, *pp* **shut**) *vt* cerrar ♦ *vi* cerrarse; ~ **down** *vt*, *vi* cerrar; ~ **off** *vt* (*supply etc*) cortar; ~ **up** *vi* (*inf*: *keep quiet*) callarse ♦ *vt* (*close*) cerrar; (*silence*) hacer callar; ~**ter** *n* contraventana; (*PHOT*) obturador *m*.

shuttle ['ʃʌtl] *n* lanzadera; (*also*: ~ *service*) servicio rápido y continuo entre dos puntos: (: *AER*) puente *m* aéreo.

shuttlecock ['ʃʌtlkɔk] *n* volante *m*.

shy [ʃaɪ] *adj* tímido; ~**ness** *n* timidez *f*.

sibling ['sɪblɪŋ] *n* hermano/a.

Sicily ['sɪsɪlɪ] *n* Sicilia.

sick [sɪk] *adj* (*ill*) enfermo; (*nauseated*) mareado; (*humour*) negro; (*vomiting*): **to be** ~ (*BRIT*) vomitar; **to feel** ~ tener náuseas; **to be** ~ **of** (*fig*) estar harto de; ~ **bay** *n* enfermería; ~**en** *vt* dar asco a; ~**ening** *adj* (*fig*) asqueroso.

sickle ['sɪkl] *n* hoz *f*.

sick: ~ **leave** *n* baja por enfermedad; ~**ly** *adj* enfermizo; (*smell*) nauseabundo; ~**ness** *n* enfermedad *f*, mal *m*; (*vomiting*) náuseas *fpl*; ~ **pay** *n* subsidio de enfermedad.

side [saɪd] *n* (*gen*) lado; (*of body*) costado; (*of lake*) orilla; (*of hill*) ladera; (*team*) equipo; ♦ *adj* (*door, entrance*) lateral ♦ *vi*: **to** ~ **with sb** tomar el partido de uno; **by the** ~ **of** al lado de; ~ **by** ~ juntos/as; **from** ~ **to** ~ de un lado para otro; **from all** ~**s** de todos lados;

to take ~s (with) tomar partido (con);
~board n aparador m; **~boards** (BRIT)
npl = **sideburns**; **~burns** npl patillas
fpl; **~ drum** n tambor m; **~ effect** n
efecto secundario; **~light** n (AUT) luz f
lateral; **~line** n (SPORT) línea de banda; (fig) empleo suplementario; **~long**
adj de soslayo; **~saddle** adv a mujerie-
gas, a la inglesa; **~ show** n (stall) caseta; **~step** vt (fig) esquivar; **~ street**
n calle f lateral; **~track** vt (fig) desviar
(de su propósito); **~walk** (US) n acera;
~ways adv de lado.
siding ['saɪdɪŋ] n (RAIL) apartadero, vía
muerta.
sidle ['saɪdl] vi: **to ~ up (to)** acercarse
furtivamente (a).
siege [siːdʒ] n cerco, sitio.
sieve [sɪv] n colador m ♦ vt cribar.
sift [sɪft] vt cribar; (fig: information) escudriñar.
sigh [saɪ] n suspiro ♦ vi suspirar.
sight [saɪt] n (faculty) vista; (spectacle)
espectáculo; (on gun) mira, alza ♦ vt
divisar; **in ~** a la vista; **out of ~** fuera
de (la) vista; **on ~** (shoot) sin previo
aviso; **~seeing** n excursionismo, turismo; **to go ~seeing** hacer turismo.
sign [saɪn] n (with hand) señal f, seña;
(trace) huella, rastro; (notice) letrero;
(written) signo ♦ vt firmar; (SPORT)
fichar; **to ~ sth over to sb** firmar el
traspaso de algo a uno; **~ on** vi (MIL)
alistarse; (BRIT: as unemployed) registrarse como desempleado; (for course)
inscribirse ♦ vt (MIL) alistar; (employee) contratar; **~ up** vi (MIL) alistarse;
(for course) inscribirse ♦ vt (player)
fichar.
signal ['sɪgnl] n señal f ♦ vi señalizar ♦
vt (person) hacer señas a; (message)
comunicar por señales; **~man** n (RAIL)
guardavía m.
signature ['sɪgnətʃə*] n firma; **~ tune** n
sintonía de apertura de un programa.
signet ring ['sɪgnət-] n anillo de sello.
significance [sɪg'nɪfɪkəns] n (importance) trascendencia.
significant [sɪg'nɪfɪkənt] adj significativo; (important) trascendente.

signify ['sɪgnɪfaɪ] vt significar.
sign language n lenguaje m para sor-
domudos.
signpost ['saɪnpəʊst] n indicador m.
silence ['saɪlns] n silencio ♦ vt acallar;
(guns) reducir al silencio; **~r** n (on
gun, BRIT: AUT) silenciador m.
silent ['saɪlnt] adj silencioso; (not speaking) callado; (film) mudo; **to remain ~**
guardar silencio; **~ partner** n (COMM)
socio/a comanditario/a.
silhouette [sɪluːˈet] n silueta.
silicon chip ['sɪlɪkən-] n plaqueta de silicio.
silk [sɪlk] n seda ♦ adj de seda; **~y** adj
sedoso.
silly ['sɪlɪ] adj (person) tonto; (idea) absurdo.
silo ['saɪləʊ] n silo.
silt [sɪlt] n sedimento.
silver ['sɪlvə*] n plata; (money) moneda
suelta ♦ adj de plata; (colour) plateado; **~ paper** (BRIT) n papel m de plata;
~-plated adj plateado; **~smith** n
platero/a; **~ware** n plata; **~y** adj argentino.
similar ['sɪmɪlə*] adj: **~ (to)** parecido or
semejante (a); **~ity** [-'lærɪtɪ] n semejanza; **~ly** adv del mismo modo.
simile ['sɪmɪlɪ] n símil m.
simmer ['sɪmə*] vi hervir a fuego lento.
simpering ['sɪmpərɪŋ] adj (foolish)
bobo.
simple ['sɪmpl] adj (easy) sencillo;
(foolish, COMM: interest) simple; **simplicity** [-'plɪsɪtɪ] n sencillez f; **simplify**
['sɪmplɪfaɪ] vt simplificar.
simply ['sɪmplɪ] adv (live, talk) sencillamente; (just, merely) sólo.
simulate ['sɪmjuːleɪt] vt fingir, simular;
~d adj simulado; (fur) de imitación.
simultaneous [sɪməl'teɪnɪəs] adj simultáneo; **~ly** adv simultáneamente.
sin [sɪn] n pecado ♦ vi pecar.
since [sɪns] adv desde entonces, después
♦ prep desde ♦ conj (time) desde que;
(because) ya que, puesto que; **~ then,
ever ~** desde entonces.
sincere [sɪn'sɪə*] adj sincero; **~ly** adv:
yours ~ly (in letters) le saluda atenta-

mente; **sincerity** [-'sɛrɪtɪ] n sinceridad f.

sinew ['sɪnjuː] n tendón m.

sinful ['sɪnful] adj (thought) pecaminoso; (person) pecador(a).

sing [sɪŋ] (pt **sang**, pp **sung**) vt, vi cantar.

Singapore [sɪŋə'pɔː*] n Singapur m.

singe [sɪndʒ] vt chamuscar.

singer ['sɪŋə*] n cantante m/f.

singing ['sɪŋɪŋ] n canto.

single ['sɪŋgl] adj único, solo; (unmarried) soltero; (not double) simple, sencillo ♦ n (BRIT: also: ~ **ticket**) billete m sencillo; (record) sencillo, single m; ~**s** npl (TENNIS) individual m; ~ **bed** cama individual; ~ **out** vt (choose) escoger; ~-**breasted** adj recto; ~ **file** n: **in** ~ **file** en fila de uno; ~-**handed** adv sin ayuda; ~-**minded** adj resuelto, firme; ~ **room** n cuarto individual.

singly ['sɪŋglɪ] adv uno por uno.

singular ['sɪŋgjulə*] adj (odd) raro, extraño; (outstanding) excepcional; (LING) singular ♦ n (LING) singular m.

sinister ['sɪnɪstə*] adj siniestro.

sink [sɪŋk] (pt **sank**, pp **sunk**) n fregadero ♦ vt (ship) hundir, echar a pique; (foundations) excavar ♦ vi (gen) hundirse; **to** ~ **sth into** hundir algo en; ~ **in** vi (fig) penetrar, calar.

sinner ['sɪnə*] n pecador(a) m/f.

sinus ['saɪnəs] n (ANAT) seno.

sip [sɪp] n sorbo ♦ vt sorber, beber a sorbitos.

siphon ['saɪfən] n sifón m; ~ **off** vt desviar.

sir [sə*] n señor m; S~ **John Smith** Sir John Smith; **yes** ~ sí, señor.

siren ['saɪərn] n sirena.

sirloin ['səːlɔɪn] n (also: ~ **steak**) solomillo.

sissy ['sɪsɪ] (inf) n marica m.

sister ['sɪstə*] n hermana; (BRIT: nurse) enfermera jefe; ~-**in-law** n cuñada.

sit [sɪt] (pt, pp **sat**) vi sentarse; (be sitting) estar sentado; (assembly) reunirse; (for painter) posar ♦ vt (exam) presentarse a; ~ **down** vi sentarse; ~ **in on** vt fus asistir a; ~ **up** vi incorporarse; (not go to bed) velar.

sitcom ['sɪtkɔm] n abbr (= situation comedy) comedia de situación.

site [saɪt] n sitio; (also: building ~) solar m ♦ vt situar.

sit-in n (demonstration) sentada.

sitting ['sɪtɪŋ] n (of assembly etc) sesión f; (in canteen) turno; ~ **room** n sala de estar.

situated ['sɪtjueɪtɪd] adj situado.

situation [sɪtju'eɪʃən] n situación f; "~**s vacant**" (BRIT) "ofrecen trabajo".

six [sɪks] num seis; ~**teen** num diez y seis, dieciséis; ~**th** num sexto; ~**ty** num sesenta.

size [saɪz] n tamaño; (extent) extensión f; (of clothing) talla; (of shoes) número; ~ **up** vt formarse una idea de; ~**able** adj importante, considerable.

sizzle ['sɪzl] vi crepitar.

skate [skeɪt] n patín m; (fish: pl inv) raya ♦ vi patinar; ~**board** n monopatín m; ~**r** n patinador(a) m/f; **skating** n patinaje m; **skating rink** n pista de patinaje.

skeleton ['skɛlɪtn] n esqueleto; (TECH) armazón f; (outline) esquema m; ~ **staff** n personal m reducido.

skeptic etc ['skɛptɪk] (US) = **sceptic**.

sketch [skɛtʃ] n (drawing) dibujo; (outline) esbozo, bosquejo; (THEATRE) sketch m ♦ vt dibujar; (plan etc: also: ~ **out**) esbozar; ~ **book** n libro de dibujos; ~**y** adj incompleto.

skewer ['skjuːə*] n broqueta.

ski [skiː] n esquí m ♦ vi esquiar; ~ **boot** n bota de esquí.

skid [skɪd] n patinazo ♦ vi patinar.

ski: ~**er** n esquiador(a) m/f; ~**ing** n esquí m; ~ **jump** n salto con esquís.

skilful ['skɪlful] (BRIT) adj diestro, experto.

ski lift n telesilla m, telesquí m.

skill [skɪl] n destreza, pericia; técnica; ~**ed** adj hábil, diestro; (worker) cualificado; ~**full** (US) adj = **skilful**.

skim [skɪm] vt (milk) desnatar; (glide over) rozar, rasar ♦ vi: **to** ~ **through** (book) hojear; ~**med milk** n leche f desnatada.

skimp [skɪmp] vt (also: ~ **on**: work)

chapucear; (*cloth etc*) escatimar; ~**y** *adj* escaso; (*skirt*) muy corto.

skin [skɪn] *n* piel *f*; (*complexion*) cutis *m* ♦ *vt* (*fruit etc*) pelar; (*animal*) despellejar; ~**-deep** *adj* superficial; ~ **diving** *n* buceo; ~**ny** *adj* flaco; ~**tight** *adj* (*dress etc*) muy ajustado.

skip [skɪp] *n* brinco, salto; (*BRIT: container*) contenedor *m* ♦ *vi* brincar; (*with rope*) saltar a la comba ♦ *vt* saltarse.

ski pants *npl* pantalones *mpl* de esquí.

ski pole *n* bastón *m* de esquiar.

skipper ['skɪpə*] *n* (*NAUT*, *SPORT*) capitán *m*.

skipping rope ['skɪpɪŋ-] (*BRIT*) *n* comba.

skirmish ['skə:mɪʃ] *n* escaramuza.

skirt [skə:t] *n* falda (*SP*), pollera (*AM*) ♦ *vt* (*go round*) ladear; ~**ing board** (*BRIT*) *n* rodapié *m*.

ski slope *n* pista de esquí.

ski suit *n* traje *m* de esquiar.

skit [skɪt] *n* sátira, parodia.

skittle ['skɪtl] *n* bolo; ~**s** *n* (*game*) boliche *m*.

skive [skaɪv] (*BRIT: inf*) *vi* gandulear.

skulk [skʌlk] *vi* esconderse.

skull [skʌl] *n* calavera; (*ANAT*) cráneo.

skunk [skʌŋk] *n* mofeta.

sky [skaɪ] *n* cielo; ~**light** *n* tragaluz *m*, claraboya; ~**scraper** *n* rascacielos *m inv*.

slab [slæb] *n* (*stone*) bloque *m*; (*flat*) losa; (*of cake*) trozo.

slack [slæk] *adj* (*loose*) flojo; (*slow*) de poca actividad; (*careless*) descuidado; ~**s** *npl* pantalones *mpl*; ~**en** (*also*: ~**en off*) *vi* aflojarse ♦ *vt* aflojar; (*speed*) disminuir.

slag heap ['slæg-] *n* escorial *m*, escombrera.

slag off (*BRIT: inf*) *vt* poner como un trapo.

slain [sleɪn] *pp of* slay.

slam [slæm] *vt* (*throw*) arrojar (violentamente); (*criticize*) criticar duramente ♦ *vi* (*door*) cerrarse de golpe; **to ~ the door** dar un portazo.

slander ['slɑ:ndə*] *n* calumnia, difamación *f*.

slang [slæŋ] *n* argot *m*; (*jargon*) jerga.

slant [slɑ:nt] *n* sesgo, inclinación *f*; (*fig*) interpretación *f*; ~**ed** *adj* (*fig*) parcial; ~**ing** *adj* inclinado; (*eyes*) rasgado.

slap [slæp] *n* palmada; (*in face*) bofetada ♦ *vt* dar una palmada *or* bofetada a; (*paint etc*): **to ~ sth on sth** embadurnar algo con algo ♦ *adv* (*directly*) exactamente, directamente; ~**dash** *adj* descuidado; ~**stick** *n* comedia de golpe y porrazo; ~**-up** *adj*: **a ~-up meal** (*BRIT*) un banquetazo, una comilona.

slash [slæʃ] *vt* acuchillar; (*fig: prices*) fulminar.

slat [slæt] *n* tablilla, listón *m*.

slate [sleɪt] *n* pizarra ♦ *vt* (*fig: criticize*) criticar duramente.

slaughter ['slɔ:tə*] *n* (*of animals*) matanza; (*of people*) carnicería ♦ *vt* matar; ~**house** *n* matadero.

Slav [slɑ:v] *adj* eslavo.

slave [sleɪv] *n* esclavo/a ♦ *vi* (*also*: ~ *away*) sudar tinta; ~**ry** *n* esclavitud *f*.

slay [sleɪ] (*pt* slew, *pp* slain) *vt* matar.

sleazy ['sli:zɪ] *adj* de mala fama.

sledge [sledʒ] *n* trineo; ~**hammer** *n* mazo.

sleek [sli:k] *adj* (*shiny*) lustroso; (*car etc*) elegante.

sleep [sli:p] (*pt, pp* slept) *n* sueño ♦ *vi* dormir; **to go to ~** quedarse dormido; ~ **around** *vi* acostarse con cualquiera; ~ **in** *vi* (*oversleep*) quedarse dormido; ~**er** *n* (*person*) durmiente *m/f*; (*BRIT: RAIL: on track*) traviesa; (*: train*) coche-cama *m*; ~**ing bag** *n* saco de dormir; ~**ing car** *n* coche-cama *m*; ~**ing partner** (*BRIT*) *n* (*COMM*) socio comanditario; ~**ing pill** *n* somnífero; ~**less** *adj*: **a ~less night** una noche en blanco; ~**walker** *n* sonámbulo/a; ~**y** *adj* soñoliento; (*place*) soporífero.

sleet [sli:t] *n* aguanieve *f*.

sleeve [sli:v] *n* manga; (*TECH*) manguito; (*of record*) portada; ~**less** *adj* sin mangas.

sleigh [sleɪ] *n* trineo.

sleight [slaɪt] *n*: ~ **of hand** escamoteo.

slender ['slendə*] *adj* delgado; (*means*) escaso.

slept [slɛpt] *pt, pp of* **sleep**.

slew [sluː] *pt of* **slay** ♦ *vi* (BRIT: *veer*) torcerse.

slice [slaɪs] *n* (*of meat*) tajada; (*of bread*) rebanada; (*of lemon*) rodaja; (*utensil*) pala ♦ *vt* cortar (en tajos); rebanar.

slick [slɪk] *adj* (*skilful*) hábil, diestro; (*clever*) astuto ♦ *n* (*also:* oil ~) marea negra.

slide [slaɪd] (*pt, pp* slid) *n* (*movement*) descenso, desprendimiento; (*in playground*) tobogán *m*; (PHOT) diapositiva; (BRIT: *also:* hair ~) pasador *m* ♦ *vt* correr, deslizar ♦ *vi* (*slip*) resbalarse; (*glide*) deslizarse; ~ **rule** *n* regla de cálculo; **sliding** *adj* (*door*) corredizo; **sliding scale** *n* escala móvil.

slight [slaɪt] *adj* (*slim*) delgado; (*frail*) delicado; (*pain etc*) leve; (*trivial*) insignificante; (*small*) pequeño ♦ *n* desaire *m* ♦ *vt* (*insult*) ofender, desairar; **not in the** ~**est** en absoluto; ~**ly** *adv* ligeramente, un poco.

slim [slɪm] *adj* delgado, esbelto; (*fig: chance*) remoto ♦ *vi* adelgazar.

slime [slaɪm] *n* limo, cieno; **slimy** *adj* cenagoso.

slimming ['slɪmɪŋ] *n* adelgazamiento.

sling [slɪŋ] (*pt, pp* slung) *n* (MED) cabestrillo; (*weapon*) honda ♦ *vt* tirar, arrojar.

slip [slɪp] *n* (*slide*) resbalón *m*; (*mistake*) descuido; (*underskirt*) combinación *f*; (*of paper*) papelito ♦ *vt* (*slide*) deslizar ♦ *vi* deslizarse; (*stumble*) resbalar(se); (*decline*) decaer; (*move smoothly*): **to ~ into/out of** (*room etc*) introducirse en/salirse de; **to give sb the ~** eludir a uno; **a ~ of the tongue** un lapsus; **to ~ sth on/off** ponerse/quitarse algo; ~ **away** *vi* escabullirse; ~ **in** *vt* meter ♦ *vi* meterse; ~ **out** *vi* (*go out*) salir (un momento); ~ **up** *vi* (*make mistake*) equivocarse; meter la pata; ~**ped disc** *n* vértebra dislocada.

slipper ['slɪpə*] *n* zapatilla, pantufla.

slippery ['slɪpərɪ] *adj* resbaladizo.

slip: ~ **road** (BRIT) *n* carretera de acceso; ~**shod** *adj* descuidado; ~**-up** *n*

(*error*) desliz *m*; ~**way** *n* grada, gradas *fpl*.

slit [slɪt] (*pt, pp* slit) *n* raja; (*cut*) corte *m* ♦ *vt* rajar; cortar.

slither ['slɪðə*] *vi* deslizarse.

sliver ['slɪvə*] *n* (*of glass, wood*) astilla; (*of cheese etc*) raja.

slob [slɔb] (*inf*) *n* abandonado/a.

slog [slɔg] (BRIT) *vi* sudar tinta; **it was a ~** costó trabajo (hacerlo).

slogan ['sləʊgən] *n* eslogan *m*, lema *m*.

slop [slɔp] *vi* (*also:* ~ **over**) derramarse, desbordarse ♦ *vt* derramar, verter.

slope [sləʊp] *n* (*up*) cuesta, pendiente *f*; (*down*) declive *m*; (*side of mountain*) falda, vertiente *m* ♦ *vi*: **to ~ down** estar en declive; **to ~ up** inclinarse; **sloping** *adj* en pendiente; en declive; (*writing*) inclinado.

sloppy ['slɔpɪ] *adj* (*work*) descuidado; (*appearance*) desaliñado.

slot [slɔt] *n* ranura ♦ *vt*: **to ~ into** encajar en.

sloth [sləʊθ] *n* (*laziness*) pereza.

slot machine *n* (BRIT: *vending machine*) distribuidor *m* automático; (*for gambling*) tragaperras *m inv*.

slouch [slaʊtʃ] *vi* andar *etc* con los hombros caídos.

slovenly ['slʌvənlɪ] *adj* desaliñado, desaseado; (*careless*) descuidado.

slow [sləʊ] *adj* lento; (*not clever*) lerdo; (*watch*): **to be ~** atrasar ♦ *adv* lentamente, despacio ♦ *vt, vi* (*also:* ~ **down**, ~ **up**) retardar; "~" (*road sign*) "disminuir velocidad"; ~**down** (US) *n* huelga de manos caídas; ~**ly** *adv* lentamente, despacio; ~ **motion** *n*: **in ~ motion** a cámara lenta.

sludge [slʌdʒ] *n* lodo, fango.

slue [sluː] (US) *vi* = **slew**.

slug [slʌg] *n* babosa; (*bullet*) posta; ~**gish** *adj* lento; (*person*) perezoso.

sluice [sluːs] *n* (*gate*) esclusa; (*channel*) canal *m*.

slum [slʌm] *n* casucha.

slump [slʌmp] *n* (*economic*) depresión *f* ♦ *vi* hundirse; (*prices*) caer en picado.

slung [slʌŋ] *pt, pp of* **sling**.

slur [sləː*] *n*: **to cast a ~ on** insultar ♦

vt (*speech*) pronunciar mal.

slush [slʌʃ] *n* nieve *f* a medio derretir; ~ **fund** *n* caja negra (*fondos para sobornar*).

slut [slʌt] *n* putana.

sly [slaɪ] *adj* astuto; (*smile*) taimado.

smack [smæk] *n* bofetada ♦ *vt* dar con la mano a; (*child, on face*) abofetear ♦ *vi*: **to ~ of** saber a, oler a.

small [smɔːl] *adj* pequeño; ~ **ads** (*BRIT*) *npl* anuncios *mpl* por palabras; ~ **change** *n* suelto, cambio; ~ **fry** *npl* gente *f* del montón; ~**holder** (*BRIT*) *n* granjero/a, parcelero/a; ~ **hours** *npl*: **in the ~ hours** a las altas horas (de la noche); ~**pox** *n* viruela; ~ **talk** *n* cháchara.

smart [smɑːt] *adj* elegante; (*clever*) listo, inteligente; (*quick*) rápido, vivo ♦ *vi* escocer, picar; ~**en up** *vi* arreglarse ♦ *vt* arreglar.

smash [smæʃ] *n* (*also:* ~-*up*) choque *m*; (*MUS*) exitazo ♦ *vt* (*break*) hacer pedazos; (*car etc*) estrellar; (*SPORT: record*) batir ♦ *vi* hacerse pedazos; (*against wall etc*) estrellarse; ~**ing** (*inf*) *adj* estupendo.

smattering ['smætərɪŋ] *n*: **a ~ of** algo de.

smear [smɪə*] *n* mancha; (*MED*) frotis *m inv* ♦ *vt* untar; ~ **campaign** *n* campaña de desprestigio.

smell [smɛl] (*pt, pp* **smelt** *or* **smelled**) *n* olor *m*; (*sense*) olfato ♦ *vt, vi* oler; ~**y** *adj* maloliente.

smile [smaɪl] *n* sonrisa ♦ *vi* sonreír.

smirk [smə:k] *n* sonrisa falsa *or* afectada.

smith [smɪθ] *n* herrero; ~**y** ['smɪðɪ] *n* herrería.

smock [smɔk] *n* blusa; (*children's*) mandilón *m*; (*US: overall*) guardapolvo.

smog [smɔg] *n* esmog *m*.

smoke [sməuk] *n* humo ♦ *vi* fumar; (*chimney*) echar humo ♦ *vt* (*cigarettes*) fumar; ~**d** *adj* (*bacon, glass*) ahumado; ~**r** *n* fumador(a) *m/f*; (*RAIL*) coche *m* fumador; ~ **screen** *n* cortina de humo; ~ **shop** (*US*) *n* estanco (*SP*), tabaquería (*AM*); **smoking** *n*: "no smok-

ing" "prohibido fumar"; **smoky** *adj* (*room*) lleno de humo; (*taste*) ahumado.

smolder ['sməuldə*] (*US*) *vi* = **smoulder**.

smooth [smu:ð] *adj* liso; (*sea*) tranquilo; (*flavour, movement*) suave; (*sauce*) fino; (*person: pej*) meloso ♦ *vt* (*also:* ~ *out*) alisar; (*creases, difficulties*) allanar.

smother ['smʌðə*] *vt* sofocar; (*repress*) contener.

smoulder ['sməuldə*] (*US* **smolder**) *vi* arder sin llama.

smudge [smʌdʒ] *n* mancha ♦ *vt* manchar.

smug [smʌg] *adj* presumido; orondo.

smuggle ['smʌgl] *vt* pasar de contrabando; ~**r** *n* contrabandista *m/f*; **smuggling** *n* contrabando.

smutty ['smʌtɪ] *adj* (*fig*) verde, obsceno.

snack [snæk] *n* bocado; ~ **bar** *n* cafetería.

snag [snæg] *n* problema *m*.

snail [sneɪl] *n* caracol *m*.

snake [sneɪk] *n* serpiente *f*.

snap [snæp] *n* (*sound*) chasquido; (*photograph*) foto *f* ♦ *adj* (*decision*) instantáneo ♦ *vt* (*break*) quebrar; (*fingers*) castañetear ♦ *vi* quebrarse; (*fig: speak sharply*) contestar bruscamente; **to ~ shut** cerrarse de golpe; ~ **at** *vt fus* (*subj: dog*) intentar morder; ~ **off** *vi* partirse; ~ **up** *vt* agarrar; ~ **fastener** (*US*) *n* botón *m* de presión; ~**py** (*inf*) *adj* (*answer*) instantáneo; (*slogan*) conciso; **make it ~py!** (*hurry up*) ¡date prisa!; ~**shot** *n* foto *f* (*instantánea*).

snare [snɛə*] *n* trampa.

snarl [snɑːl] *vi* gruñir.

snatch [snætʃ] *n* (*small piece*) fragmento ♦ *vt* (~ *away*) arrebatar; (*fig*) agarrar; **to ~ some sleep** encontrar tiempo para dormir.

sneak [sni:k] (*pt* (*US*) **snuck**) *vi*: **to ~ in/out** entrar/salir a hurtadillas ♦ *n* (*fam*) soplón/ona *m/f*; **to ~ up on sb** aparecérsele de improviso a uno; ~**ers** *npl zapatos mpl* de lona; ~**y** *adj* furtivo.

sneer [snɪə*] *vi* reír con sarcasmo;

(*mock*): **to ~ at** burlarse de.

sneeze [sniːz] *vi* estornudar.

sniff [snɪf] *vi* sollozar ♦ *vt* husmear, oler; (*drugs*) esnifar.

snigger ['snɪgə*] *n* *vi* reírse con disimulo.

snip [snɪp] *n* tijeretazo; (*BRIT: inf: bargain*) ganga ♦ *vt* tijeretear.

sniper ['snaɪpə*] *n* francotirador(a) *m/f*.

snippet ['snɪpɪt] *n* retazo.

snivelling ['snɪvlɪŋ] *adj* llorón/ona.

snob [snɔb] *n* *m/f*; ~**bery** *n* (e)snobismo; ~**bish** *adj* (e)snob.

snooker ['snuːkə*] *n* especie de billar.

snoop [snuːp] *vi*: **to ~ about** fisgonear.

snooty ['snuːtɪ] *adj* (e)snob.

snooze [snuːz] *n* siesta ♦ *vi* echar una siesta.

snore [snɔː*] *n* ronquido ♦ *vi* roncar.

snorkel ['snɔːkl] *n* (tubo) respirador *m*.

snort [snɔːt] *n* bufido ♦ *vi* bufar.

snout [snaut] *n* hocico, morro.

snow [snəu] *n* nieve *f* ♦ *vi* nevar; ~**ball** *n* bola de nieve ♦ *vi* (*fig*) agrandirse, ampliarse; ~**bound** *adj* bloqueado por la nieve; ~**drift** *n* ventisquero; ~**drop** *n* campanilla; ~**fall** *n* nevada; ~**flake** *n* copo de nieve; ~**man** *n* figura de nieve; ~**plough** (*US* ~**plow**) *n* quitanieves *m inv*; ~**shoe** *n* raqueta (de nieve); ~**storm** *n* nevada, nevasca.

snub [snʌb] *vt* (*person*) desairar ♦ *n* desaire *m*, repulsa; ~**nosed** *adj* chato.

snuff [snʌf] *n* rapé *m*.

snug [snʌg] *adj* (*cosy*) cómodo; (*fitted*) ajustado.

snuggle ['snʌgl] *vi*: **to ~ up to sb** arrimarse a uno.

KEYWORD

so [səu] *adv* **1** (*thus, likewise*) así, de este modo; **if ~** de ser así; **I like swimming — ~ do I** a mí me gusta nadar — a mí también; **I've got work to do — ~ has Paul** tengo trabajo que hacer — Paul también; **it's 5 o'clock — ~ it is!** son las cinco — ¡pues es verdad!; **I hope/think ~** espero/creo que sí; **~ far** hasta ahora; (*in past*) hasta este momento

2 (*in comparisons etc: to such a degree*) tan; **~ quickly (that)** tan rápido (que); **~ big (that)** tan grande (que); **she's not ~ clever as her brother** no es tan lista como su hermano; **we were ~ worried** estábamos preocupadísimos

3: **~ much** *adj, adv* tanto; **~ many** tantos/as

4 (*phrases*): **10 or ~** unos 10, 10 o así; **~ long!** (*inf: goodbye*) ¡hasta luego!

♦ *conj* **1** (*expressing purpose*): **~ as to** do para hacer; **~ (that)** para que + *sub*

2 (*expressing result*) así que; **~ you see, I could have gone** así que ya ves, (yo) podría haber ido.

---

soak [səuk] *vt* (*drench*) empapar; (*steep in water*) remojar ♦ *vi* remojarse, estar a remojo; **~ in** *vi* penetrar; **~ up** *vt* absorber.

soap [səup] *n* jabón *m*; ~**flakes** *npl* escamas *fpl* de jabón; **~ opera** *n* telenovela; **~ powder** *n* jabón *m* en polvo; ~**y** *adj* jabonoso.

soar [sɔː*] *vi* (*on wings*) remontarse; (*rocket, prices*) dispararse; (*building etc*) elevarse.

sob [sɔb] *n* sollozo ♦ *vi* sollozar.

sober ['səubə*] *adj* (*serious*) serio; (*not drunk*) sobrio; (*colour, style*) discreto; **~ up** *vt* quitar la borrachera.

so-called *adj* así llamado.

soccer ['sɔkə*] *n* fútbol *m*.

social ['səuʃl] *adj* social ♦ *n* velada, fiesta; **~ club** *n* club *m*; ~**ism** *n* socialismo; ~**ist** *adj, n* socialista *m/f*; ~**ize** *vi*: **to ~ize (with)** alternar (con); ~**ly** *adv* socialmente; **~ security** *n* seguridad *f* social; **~ work** *n* asistencia social; **~ worker** *n* asistente/a *m/f* social.

society [sə'saɪətɪ] *n* sociedad *f*; (*club*) asociación *f*; (*also: high ~*) alta sociedad.

sociologist [səusɪ'ɔlədʒɪst] *n* sociólogo/a.

sociology [səusɪ'ɔlədʒɪ] *n* sociología.

sock [sɔk] *n* calcetín *m* (*SP*), media (*AM*).

socket ['sɔkɪt] *n* cavidad *f*; (*BRIT: ELEC*) enchufe *m*.

sod [sɔd] *n* (*of earth*) césped *m*; (*BRIT:*

inf!) cabrón/ona *m/f* (*!*).

soda ['səudə] *n* (*CHEM*) sosa; (*also: ~ water*) soda; (*US: also: ~ pop*) gaseosa.

sodden ['sɔdn] *adj* empapado.

sodium ['səudɪəm] *n* sodio.

sofa ['səufə] *n* sofá *m*.

soft [sɔft] *adj* (*lenient, not hard*) blando; (*gentle, not tight*) suave; ~ **drink** *n* bebida no alcohólica; ~**en** ['sɔfn] *vt* ablandar; suavizar; (*effect*) amortiguar ♦ *vi* ablandarse; suavizarse; ~**ly** *adv* suavemente; (*gently*) delicadamente, con delicadeza; ~**ness** *n* blandura; suavidad *f*; ~ **spot** *n*: **to have a ~ spot for sb** tener debilidad por uno; ~**ware** *n* (*COMPUT*) software *m*.

soggy ['sɔgɪ] *adj* empapado.

soil [sɔɪl] *n* (*earth*) tierra, suelo ♦ *vt* ensuciar; ~**ed** *adj* sucio.

solace ['sɔlɪs] *n* consuelo.

sold [səuld] *pt, pp* of **sell**; ~ **out** *adj* (*COMM*) agotado.

solder ['səuldə*] *vt* soldar ♦ *n* soldadura.

soldier ['səuldʒə*] *n* soldado; (*army man*) militar *m*.

sole [səul] *n* (*of foot*) planta; (*of shoe*) suela; (*fish: pl inv*) lenguado ♦ *adj* único.

solemn ['sɔləm] *adj* solemne.

sole trader *n* (*COMM*) comerciante *m* exclusivo.

solicit [sə'lɪsɪt] *vt* (*request*) solicitar ♦ *vi* (*prostitute*) importunar.

solicitor [sə'lɪsɪtə*] (*BRIT*) *n* (*for wills etc*) ≈ notario/a; (*in court*) ≈ abogado/a.

solid ['sɔlɪd] *adj* sólido; (*gold etc*) macizo ♦ *n* sólido; ~**s** *npl* (*food*) alimentos *mpl* sólidos.

solidarity [sɔlɪ'dærɪtɪ] *n* solidaridad *f*.

solitaire [sɔlɪ'tɛə*] *n* (*game, gem*) solitario.

solitary ['sɔlɪtərɪ] *adj* solitario, solo; ~ **confinement** *n* incomunicación *f*.

solitude ['sɔlɪtjuːd] *n* soledad *f*.

solo ['səuləu] *n* solo ♦ *adv* (*fly*) en solitario; ~**ist** *n* solista *m/f*.

soluble ['sɔljubl] *adj* soluble.

solution [sə'luːʃən] *n* solución *f*.

solve [sɔlv] *vt* resolver, solucionar.

solvent ['sɔlvənt] *adj* (*COMM*) solvente ♦ *n* (*CHEM*) solvente *m*.

sombre ['sɔmbə*] (*US* **somber**) *adj* sombrío.

KEYWORD
---

some [sʌm] *adj* **1** (*a certain amount or number of*): ~ **tea/water/biscuits** té/agua/(unas) galletas; **there's ~ milk in the fridge** hay leche en el frigo; **there were ~ people outside** había algunas personas fuera; **I've got ~ money, but not much** tengo algo de dinero, pero no mucho

2 (*certain: in contrasts*) algunos/as; ~ **people say that ...** hay quien dice que ...; ~ **films were excellent, but most were mediocre** hubo películas excelentes, pero la mayoría fueron mediocres

3 (*unspecified*): ~ **woman was asking for you** una mujer estuvo preguntando por ti; **he was asking for ~ book** (*or other*) pedía un libro; ~ **day** algún día; ~ **day next week** un día de la semana que viene

♦ *pron* **1** (*a certain number*): **I've got ~** (*books etc*) tengo algunos/as

2 (*a certain amount*) algo; **I've got ~** (*money, milk*) tengo algo; **could I have ~ of that cheese?** ¿me puede dar un poco de ese queso?; **I've read ~ of the book** he leído parte del libro

♦ *adv*: ~ **10 people** unas 10 personas, una decena de personas

---

somebody ['sʌmbədɪ] *pron* = **someone**.

somehow ['sʌmhau] *adv* de alguna manera; (*for some reason*) por una u otra razón.

someone ['sʌmwʌn] *pron* alguien.

someplace ['sʌmpleɪs] (*US*) *adv* = **somewhere**.

somersault ['sʌməsɔːlt] *n* (*deliberate*) salto mortal; (*accidental*) vuelco ♦ *vi* dar un salto mortal; dar vuelcos.

something ['sʌmθɪŋ] *pron* algo; **would you like ~ to eat/drink?** ¿te gustaría cenar/tomar algo?

sometime ['sʌmtaɪm] *adv* (*in future*) algún día, en algún momento; (*in past*):

~ **last month** durante el mes pasado.
sometimes ['sʌmtaɪmz] *adv* a veces.
somewhat ['sʌmwɒt] *adv* algo.
somewhere ['sʌmweə*] *adv* (*be*) en alguna parte; (*go*) a alguna parte; ~ **else** (*be*) en otra parte; (*go*) a otra parte.
son [sʌn] *n* hijo.
song [sɒŋ] *n* canción *f*.
sonic ['sɒnɪk] *adj* sónico.
son-in-law *n* yerno.
sonnet ['sɒnɪt] *n* soneto.
sonny ['sʌnɪ] (*inf*) *n* hijo.
soon [su:n] *adv* pronto, dentro de poco; ~ **afterwards** poco después; *see also* as; ~**er** *adv* (*time*) antes, más temprano; (*preference*): **I would** ~**er do that** preferiría hacer eso; ~**er or later** tarde o temprano.
soot [sut] *n* hollín *m*.
soothe [su:ð] *vt* tranquilizar; (*pain*) aliviar.
sophisticated [sə'fɪstɪkeɪtɪd] *adj* sofisticado.
sophomore ['sɒfəmɔ:*] (*US*) *n* estudiante *m/f* de segundo año.
sopping ['sɒpɪŋ] *adj*: ~ (**wet**) empapado.
soppy ['sɒpɪ] (*pej*) *adj* tonto.
soprano [sə'prɑ:nəu] *n* soprano *f*.
sorcerer ['sɔ:sərə*] *n* hechicero.
sore [sɔ:*] *adj* (*painful*) doloroso, que duele ♦ *n* llaga; ~**ly** *adv*: **I am** ~**ly tempted to** estoy muy tentado a.
sorrow ['sɒrəu] *n* pena, dolor *m*; ~**s** *npl* pesares *mpl*; ~**ful** *adj* triste.
sorry ['sɒrɪ] *adj* (*regretful*) arrepentido; (*condition, excuse*) lastimoso; ~! ¡perdón!, ¡perdone!; ~? ¿cómo?; **to feel** ~ **for sb** tener lástima a uno; **I feel** ~ **for him** me da lástima.
sort [sɔ:t] *n* clase *f*, género, tipo ♦ *vt* (*also*: ~ **out**: *papers*) clasificar; (: *problems*) arreglar, solucionar; ~**ing office** *n* sala de batalla.
SOS *n abbr* (= *save our souls*) SOS *m*.
so-so *adv* regular, así así.
soufflé ['su:fleɪ] *n* suflé *m*.
sought [sɔ:t] *pt, pp* **of seek**.
soul [səul] *n* alma; ~**-destroying** *adj* (*work*) deprimente; ~**ful** *adj* lleno de

sentimiento.
sound [saund] *n* (*noise*) sonido, ruido; (*volume: on TV etc*) volumen *m*; (*GEO*) estrecho ♦ *adj* (*healthy*) sano; (*safe, not damaged*) en buen estado; (*reliable: person*) digno de confianza; (*sensible*) sensato, razonable; (*secure: investment*) seguro ♦ *adv*: ~ **asleep** profundamente dormido ♦ *vt* (*alarm*) sonar ♦ *vi* sonar, resonar; (*fig: seem*) parecer; **to** ~ **like** sonar a; ~ **out** *vt* sondear; ~ **barrier** *n* barrera del sonido; ~ **effects** *npl* efectos *mpl* sonoros; ~**ly** *adv* (*sleep*) profundamente; (*defeated*) completamente; ~**proof** *adj* insonorizado; ~**track** *n* (*of film*) banda sonora.
soup [su:p] *n* (*thick*) sopa; (*thin*) caldo; **in the** ~ (*fig*) en apuros; ~ **plate** *n* plato sopero; ~**spoon** *n* cuchara sopera.
sour ['sauə*] *adj* agrio; (*milk*) cortado; **it's** ~ **grapes** (*fig*) están verdes.
source [sɔ:s] *n* fuente *f*.
south [sauθ] *n* sur *m* ♦ *adj* del sur, sureño ♦ *adv* al sur, hacia el sur; **S~ Africa** *n* África del Sur; **S~ African** *adj*, *n* sudafricano/a *m/f*; **S~ America** *n* América del Sur, Sudamérica; **S~ American** *adj*, *n* sudamericano/a *m/f*; ~**-east** *n* sudeste *m*; ~**erly** ['sʌðəlɪ] *adj* sur; (*from the* ~) del sur; ~**ern** ['sʌðən] *adj* del sur, meridional; **S~ Pole** *n* Polo Sur; ~**ward(s)** *adv* hacia el sur; ~**-west** *n* suroeste *m*.
souvenir [su:və'nɪə*] *n* recuerdo.
sovereign ['sɒvrɪn] *adj*, *n* soberano/a *m/f*; ~**ty** *n* soberanía.
soviet ['səuvɪət] *adj* soviético; **the S~ Union** la Unión Soviética.
sow[1] [səu] (*pt* **sowed**, *pp* **sown**) ♦ *vt* sembrar.
sow[2] [sau] *n* cerda (*SP*), puerca (*SP*), chancha (*AM*).
soy [sɔɪ] (*US*) *n* = **soya**.
soya ['sɔɪə] (*BRIT*) *n* soja; ~ **bean** *n* haba de soja; ~ **sauce** *n* salsa de soja.
spa [spɑ:] *n* balneario.
space [speɪs] *n* espacio; (*room*) sitio ♦ *cpd* espacial ♦ *vt* (*also*: ~ **out**) espaciar; ~**craft** *n* nave *f* espacial; ~**man/woman** *n* astronauta *m/f*, cosmonauta

m/f; ~**ship** *n* = ~**craft**; **spacing** *n* espaciado.
spacious ['speɪʃəs] *adj* amplio.
spade [speɪd] *n* (*tool*) pala, laya; ~**s** *npl* (*CARDS: British*) picas *fpl*; (: *Spanish*) espadas *fpl*.
spaghetti [spə'gɛtɪ] *n* espaguetis *mpl*, fideos *mpl*.
Spain [speɪn] *n* España.
span [spæn] *n* (*of bird, plane*) envergadura; (*of arch*) luz *f*; (*in time*) lapso ♦ *vt* extenderse sobre, cruzar; (*fig*) abarcar.
Spaniard ['spænjəd] *n* español(a) *m/f*.
spaniel ['spænjəl] *n* perro de aguas.
Spanish ['spænɪʃ] *adj* español(a) ♦ *n* (*LING*) español *m*, castellano; **the** ~ *npl* los españoles.
spank [spæŋk] *vt* zurrar.
spanner ['spænə*] (*BRIT*) *n* llave *f* (inglesa).
spar [spɑ:*] *n* palo, verga ♦ *vi* (*BOXING*) entrenarse.
spare [spɛə*] *adj* de reserva; (*surplus*) sobrante, de más ♦ *n* = ~ **part** ♦ *vt* (*do without*) pasarse sin; (*refrain from hurting*) perdonar; **to** ~ (*surplus*) sobrante, de sobra; ~ **part** *n* pieza de repuesto; ~ **time** *n* tiempo libre; ~ **wheel** *n* (*AUT*) rueda de recambio.
sparing ['spɛərɪŋ] *adj*: **to be** ~ **with** ser parco en; ~**ly** *adv* con moderación.
spark [spɑ:k] *n* chispa; (*fig*) chispazo; ~(**ing**) **plug** *n* bujía.
sparkle ['spɑ:kl] *n* centelleo, destello ♦ *vi* (*shine*) relucir, brillar; **sparkling** *adj* (*eyes, conversation*) brillante; (*wine*) espumoso.
sparrow ['spærəu] *n* gorrión *m*.
sparse [spɑ:s] *adj* esparcido, escaso.
spartan ['spɑ:tən] *adj* (*fig*) espartano.
spasm ['spæzəm] *n* (*MED*) espasmo.
spastic ['spæstɪk] *n* espástico/a.
spat [spæt] *pt, pp* de **spit**.
spate [speɪt] *n* (*fig*): **a** ~ **of** un torrente de.
spatter ['spætə*] *vt*: **to** ~ **with** salpicar de.
spawn [spɔ:n] *vi* desovar, frezar ♦ *n* huevas *fpl*.

speak [spi:k] (*pt* **spoke**, *pp* **spoken**) *vt* (*language*) hablar; (*truth*) decir ♦ *vi* hablar; (*make a speech*) intervenir; **to** ~ **to sb/of** *or* **about sth** hablar con uno/de *or* sobre algo; ~ **up!** ¡habla fuerte!; ~**er** *n* (*in public*) orador(a) *m/f*; (*also*: **loud**~**er**) altavoz *m*; (*for stereo etc*) bafle *m*; (*POL*): **the S~er** (*BRIT*) **el Presidente de la Cámara de los Comunes**; (*US*) **el Presidente del Congreso**.
spear [spɪə*] *n* lanza ♦ *vt* alancear; ~**head** *vt* (*attack etc*) encabezar.
spec [spɛk] (*inf*) *n*: **on** ~ como especulación.
special ['spɛʃl] *adj* especial; (*edition etc*) extraordinario; (*delivery*) urgente; ~**ist** *n* especialista *m/f*; ~**ity** [spɛʃɪ'ælɪtɪ] (*BRIT*) *n* especialidad *f*; ~**ize** *vi*: **to** ~**ize** (**in**) especializarse (en); ~**ly** *adv* sobre todo, en particular; ~**ty** (*US*) *n* = ~**ity**.
species ['spi:ʃi:z] *n inv* especie *f*.
specific [spə'sɪfɪk] *adj* específico; ~**ally** *adv* específicamente.
specify ['spɛsɪfaɪ] *vt, vi* especificar, precisar.
specimen ['spɛsɪmən] *n* ejemplar *m*; (*MED: of urine*) espécimen *m* (: *of blood*) muestra.
speck [spɛk] *n* grano, mota.
speckled ['spɛkld] *adj* moteado.
specs [spɛks] (*inf*) *npl* gafas *fpl* (*SP*), anteojos *mpl*.
spectacle ['spɛktəkl] *n* espectáculo; ~**s** *npl* (*BRIT: glasses*) gafas *fpl* (*SP*), anteojos *mpl*; **spectacular** [-'tækjulə*] *adj* espectacular; (*success*) impresionante.
spectator [spɛk'teɪtə*] *n* espectador(a) *m/f*.
spectre ['spɛktə*] (*US* **specter**) *n* espectro, fantasma *m*.
spectrum ['spɛktrəm] (*pl* **spectra**) *n* espectro.
speculate ['spɛkjuleɪt] *vi*: **to** ~ (**on**) especular (en).
speculation [spɛkju'leɪʃən] *n* especulación *f*.
speech [spi:tʃ] *n* (*faculty*) habla; (*formal talk*) discurso; (*spoken language*) lenguaje *m*; ~**less** *adj* mudo, estupefac-

to; ~ **therapist** n especialista que corrige defectos de pronunciación en los niños.

speed [spi:d] n velocidad f; (haste) prisa; (promptness) rapidez f; **at full** or **top** ~ a máxima velocidad; ~ **up** vi acelerarse ♦ vt acelerar; ~**boat** n lancha motora; ~**ily** adv rápido, rápidamente; ~**ing** n (AUT) exceso de velocidad; ~ **limit** n límite m de velocidad, velocidad f máxima; ~**ometer** [spi'dɔmitə°] n velocímetro; ~**way** n (sport) pista de carrera; ~**y** adj (fast) veloz, rápido; (prompt) pronto.

spell [spel] (pt, pp **spelt** (BRIT) or **spelled**) n (also: magic ~) encanto, hechizo; (period of time) rato, período ♦ vt deletrear; (fig) anunciar, presagiar; **to cast a ~ on sb** hechizar a uno; **he can't ~** pone faltas de ortografía; ~**bound** adj embelesado, hechizado; ~**ing** n ortografía.

spend [spend] (pt, pp **spent**) vt (money) gastar; (time) pasar; (life) dedicar; ~**thrift** n derrochador(a) m/f, pródigo/a.

sperm [spə:m] n esperma.

spew [spju:] vt vomitar, arrojar.

sphere [sfiə°] n esfera.

sphinx [sfɪŋks] n esfinge f.

spice [spais] n especia ♦ vt condimentar.

spick-and-span ['spɪkən'spæn] adj aseado, (bien) arreglado.

spicy ['spaisi] adj picante.

spider ['spaidə°] n araña.

spike [spaik] n (point) punta; (BOT) espiga.

spill [spil] (pt, pp **spilt** or **spilled**) vt derramar, verter ♦ vi derramarse; **to ~ over** desbordarse.

spin [spin] (pt, pp **spun**) n (AVIAT) barrena; (trip in car) paseo (en coche); (on ball) efecto ♦ vt (wool etc) hilar; (ball etc) hacer girar ♦ vi girar, dar vueltas; ~ **out** vt alargar, prolongar.

spinach ['spɪnɪtʃ] n espinaca; (as food) espinacas fpl.

spinal ['spainl] adj espinal; ~ **cord** n columna vertebral.

spindly ['spindli] adj (leg) zanquivano.

spin-dryer (BRIT) n secador m centrífugo.

spine [spain] n espinazo, columna vertebral; (thorn) espina; ~**less** adj (fig) débil, pusilánime.

spinning ['spɪnɪŋ] n hilandería; ~ **top** n peonza; ~ **wheel** n torno de hilar.

spin-off n derivado, producto secundario.

spinster ['spinstə°] n soltera.

spiral ['spaiərl] n espiral f ♦ vi (fig: prices) subir desorbitadamente; ~ **staircase** n escalera de caracol.

spire ['spaiə°] n aguja, chapitel m.

spirit ['spirit] n (soul) alma f; (ghost) fantasma m; (courage) valor m, ánimo; ~**s** npl (drink) licor(es) m(pl); **in good ~s** alegre, de buen ánimo; ~**ed** adj enérgico, vigoroso; ~ **level** n nivel m de aire.

spiritual ['spiritjuəl] adj espiritual ♦ n espiritual m.

spit [spit] (pt, pp **spat**) n (for roasting) asador m, espetón m; (saliva) saliva ♦ vi escupir; (sound) chisporrotear; (rain) lloviznar.

spite [spait] n rencor m, ojeriza ♦ vt causar pena a, mortificar; **in ~ of** a pesar de, pese a; ~**ful** adj rencoroso, malévolo.

spittle ['spitl] n saliva, baba.

splash [splæʃ] n (sound) chapoteo; (of colour) mancha ♦ vt salpicar ♦ vi (also: ~ about) chapotear.

spleen [spli:n] n (ANAT) bazo.

splendid ['splendid] adj espléndido.

splint [splint] n tablilla.

splinter ['splintə°] n (of wood etc) astilla; (in finger) espigón m ♦ vi astillarse, hacer astillas.

split [split] (pt, pp **split**) n hendedura, raja; (fig) división f; (POL) escisión f ♦ vt partir, rajar; (party) dividir; (share) repartir ♦ vi dividirse, escindirse; ~ **up** vi (couple) separarse; (meeting) acabarse.

splutter ['splʌtə°] vi chisporrotear; (person) balbucear.

spoil [spɔil] (pt, pp **spoilt** or **spoiled**) vt (damage) dañar; (mar) estropear; (child) mimar, consentir; ~**s** npl despojo, botín *m*; ~**sport** *n* aguafiestas *m inv*.

spoke [spəuk] *pt of* speak ♦ *n* rayo, radio.

spoken ['spəukn] *pp of* speak.

spokesman ['spəuksmən] *n* portavoz *m*; **spokeswoman** ['spəukswumən] *n* portavoz *f*.

sponge [spʌndʒ] *n* esponja; (*also*: ~ *cake*) bizcocho ♦ *vt* (*wash*) lavar con esponja ♦ *vi*: **to** ~ **off** *or* **on sb** vivir a costa de uno; ~ **bag** (*BRIT*) *n* esponjera.

sponsor ['spɔnsə*] *n* patrocinador(a) *m/f* ♦ *vt* (*applicant, proposal etc*) proponer; ~**ship** *n* patrocinio.

spontaneous [spɔn'teɪnɪəs] *adj* espontáneo.

spooky ['spuːkɪ] (*inf*) *adj* espeluznante, horripilante.

spool [spuːl] *n* carrete *m*.

spoon [spuːn] *n* cuchara; ~**feed** *vt* dar de comer con cuchara a; (*fig*) tratar como un niño a; ~**ful** *n* cucharada.

sport [spɔːt] *n* deporte *m*; (*person*): **to be a good** ~ ser muy majo ♦ *vt* (*wear*) lucir, ostentar; ~**ing** *adj* deportivo; (*generous*) caballeroso; **to give sb a** ~**ing chance** darle a uno una (buena) oportunidad; ~ **jacket** (*US*) *n* = ~**s jacket**; ~**s car** *n* coche *m* deportivo; ~**s jacket** (*BRIT*) *n* chaqueta deportiva; ~**sman** *n* deportista *m*; ~**smanship** *n* deportividad *f*; ~**swear** *n* trajes *mpl* de deporte *or* sport; ~**swoman** *n* deportista; ~**y** *adj* deportista.

spot [spɔt] *n* sitio, lugar *m*; (*dot*: *on pattern*) punto, mancha; (*pimple*) grano; (*RADIO*) cuña publicitaria; (*TV*) espacio publicitario; (*small amount*): **a** ~ **of** un poquito de ♦ *vt* (*notice*) notar, observar; **on the** ~ allí mismo; ~ **check** *n* reconocimiento rápido; ~**less** *adj* perfectamente limpio; ~**light** *n* foco, reflector *m*; (*AUT*) faro auxiliar; ~**ted** *adj* (*pattern*) de puntos; ~**ty** *adj* (*face*) con granos.

spouse [spauz] *n* cónyuge *m/f*.

spout [spaut] *n* (*of jug*) pico; (*of pipe*) caño ♦ *vi* salir en chorro.

sprain [spreɪn] *n* torcedura ♦ *vt*: **to** ~ **one's ankle/wrist** torcerse el tobillo/la muñeca.

sprang [spræŋ] *pt of* spring.

sprawl [sprɔːl] *vi* tumbarse.

spray [spreɪ] *n* rociada; (*of sea*) espuma; (*container*) atomizador *m*; (*for paint etc*) pistola rociadora; (*of flowers*) ramita ♦ *vt* rociar; (*crops*) regar.

spread [spred] (*pt, pp* spread) *n* extensión *f*; (*for bread etc*) pasta para untar; (*inf: food*) comilona ♦ *vt* extender; (*butter*) untar; (*wings, sails*) desplegar; (*work, wealth*) repartir; (*scatter*) esparcir ♦ *vi* (*also*: ~ *out*: *stain*) extenderse; (*news*) diseminarse; ~ **out** *vi* (*move apart*) separarse; ~**eagled** *adj* a pata tendida; ~**sheet** *n* (*COMPUT*) hoja electrónica *or* de cálculo.

spree [spriː] *n*: **to go on a** ~ ir de juerga.

sprightly ['spraɪtlɪ] *adj* vivo, enérgico.

spring [sprɪŋ] (*pt* sprang, *pp* sprung) *n* (*season*) primavera; (*leap*) salto, brinco; (*coiled metal*) resorte *m*; (*of water*) fuente *f*, manantial *m* ♦ *vi* saltar, brincar; ~ **up** *vi* (*thing*: *appear*) aparecer; (*problem*) surgir; ~**board** *n* trampolín *m*; ~**clean(ing)** *n* limpieza general; ~**time** *n* primavera.

sprinkle ['sprɪŋkl] *vt* (*pour*: *liquid*) rociar; (: *salt, sugar*) espolvorear; **to** ~ **water** *etc* **on**, ~ **with water** *etc* rociar *or* salpicar de agua *etc*; ~**r** (*for lawn*) rociadera; (*to put out fire*) aparato de rociadura automática.

sprint [sprɪnt] *n* esprint *m* ♦ *vi* esprintar.

sprout [spraut] *vi* brotar, retoñar; **(Brussels)** ~**s** *npl* coles *fpl* de Bruselas.

spruce [spruːs] *n inv* (*BOT*) pícea ♦ *adj* aseado, pulcro.

sprung [sprʌŋ] *pp of* spring.

spry [spraɪ] *adj* ágil, activo.

spun [spʌn] *pt, pp of* spin.

spur [spəː*] *n* espuela; (*fig*) estímulo, aguijón *m* ♦ *vt* (*also*: ~ *on*) estimular, incitar; **on the** ~ **of the moment** de improviso.

spurious ['spjuərɪəs] *adj* falso.

spurn [spə:n] *vt* desdeñar, rechazar.

spurt [spə:t] *n* chorro; *(of energy)* arrebato ♦ *vi* chorrear.

spy [spaɪ] *n* espía *m/f* ♦ *vi*: **to ~ on** espiar a ♦ *vt (see)* divisar, lograr ver; **~ing** *n* espionaje *m*.

sq. *abbr* = **square**.

squabble ['skwɔbl] *vi* reñir, pelear.

squad [skwɔd] *n (MIL)* pelotón *m*; *(POLICE)* brigada; *(SPORT)* equipo.

squadron ['skwɔdrn] *n (MIL)* escuadrón *m*; *(AVIAT, NAUT)* escuadra.

squalid ['skwɔlɪd] *adj* vil; *(fig: sordid)* sórdido.

squall [skwɔ:l] *n (storm)* chubasco; *(wind)* ráfaga.

squalor ['skwɔlə*] *n* miseria.

squander ['skwɔndə*] *vt (money)* derrochar, despilfarrar; *(chances)* desperdiciar.

square [skweə*] *n* cuadro; *(in town)* plaza; *(inf: person)* carca *m/f* ♦ *adj* cuadrado; *(inf: ideas, tastes)* trasnochado ♦ *vt (arrange)* arreglar; *(MATH)* cuadrar; *(reconcile)* compaginar; **all ~** igual(es); **to have a ~ meal** comer caliente; **2 metres ~** 2 metros en cuadro; **2 ~ metres** 2 metros cuadrados; **~ly** *adv* de lleno.

squash [skwɔʃ] *n (BRIT: drink)*: **lemon/orange ~** zumo *(SP)* or jugo *(AM)* de limón/naranja; *(US: BOT)* calabacín *m*; *(SPORT)* squash *m*, frontenis *m* ♦ *vt* aplastar.

squat [skwɔt] *adj* achaparrado ♦ *vi (also: ~ down)* agacharse, sentarse en cuclillas; **~ter** *n* persona que ocupa ilegalmente una casa.

squawk [skwɔ:k] *vi* graznar.

squeak [skwi:k] *vi (hinge)* chirriar, rechinar; *(mouse)* chillar.

squeal [skwi:l] *vi* chillar, dar gritos agudos.

squeamish ['skwi:mɪʃ] *adj* delicado, remilgado.

squeeze [skwi:z] *n* presión *f*; *(of hand)* apretón *m*; *(COMM)* restricción *f* ♦ *vt (hand, arm)* apretar; **~ out** *vt* exprimir.

squelch [skweltʃ] *vi* chapotear.

squid [skwɪd] *n inv* calamar *m*; *(CULIN)* calamares *mpl*.

squiggle ['skwɪgl] *n* garabato.

squint [skwɪnt] *vi* bizquear, ser bizco ♦ *n (MED)* estrabismo.

squire ['skwaɪə*] *(BRIT)* *n* terrateniente *m*.

squirm ['skwə:m] *vi* retorcerse, revolverse.

squirrel ['skwɪrəl] *n* ardilla.

squirt [skwə:t] *vi* salir a chorros ♦ *vt* chiscar.

Sr *abbr* = **senior**.

St *abbr* = **saint**; **street**.

stab [stæb] *n (with knife)* puñalada; *(of pain)* pinchazo; *(inf: try)*: **to have a ~ at (doing) sth** intentar (hacer) algo ♦ *vt* apuñalar.

stable ['steɪbl] *adj* estable ♦ *n* cuadra, caballeriza.

stack [stæk] *n* montón *m*, pila ♦ *vt* amontonar, apilar.

stadium ['steɪdɪəm] *n* estadio.

staff [sta:f] *n (work force)* personal *m*, plantilla; *(BRIT: SCOL)* cuerpo docente ♦ *vt* proveer de personal.

stag [stæg] *n* ciervo, venado.

stage [steɪdʒ] *n* escena; *(point)* etapa; *(platform)* plataforma; *(profession)*: **the ~** el teatro ♦ *vt (play)* poner en escena, representar; *(organize)* montar, organizar; **in ~s** por etapas; **~coach** *n* diligencia; **~ manager** *n* director(a) *m/f* de escena.

stagger ['stægə*] *vi* tambalearse ♦ *vt (amaze)* asombrar; *(hours, holidays)* escalonar; **~ing** *adj* asombroso.

stagnant ['stægnənt] *adj* estancado.

stagnate [stæg'neɪt] *vi* estancarse.

stag party *n* despedida de soltero.

staid [steɪd] *adj* serio, formal.

stain [steɪn] *n* mancha; *(colouring)* tintura ♦ *vt* manchar; *(wood)* teñir; **~ed glass window** *n* vidriera de colores; **~less steel** *n* acero inoxidable; **~ remover** *n* quitamanchas *m inv*.

stair [steə*] *n (step)* peldaño, escalón *m*; **~s** *npl* escaleras *fpl*; **~case** *n* = **~way**; **~way** *n* escalera.

stake [steɪk] *n* estaca, poste *m*; *(COMM)*

interés *m*; (*BETTING*) apuesta ♦ *vt*
(*money*) apostar; (*life*) arriesgar;
(*reputation*) poner en juego; (*claim*)
presentar una reclamación; **to be at ~**
estar en juego.
stale [steɪl] *adj* (*bread*) duro; (*food*) pasado; (*smell*) rancio; (*beer*) agrio.
stalemate ['steɪlmeɪt] *n* tablas *fpl* (por
ahogado); (*fig*) estancamiento.
stalk [stɔ:k] *n* tallo, caña ♦ *vt* acechar,
cazar al acecho; **~ off** *vi* irse airado.
stall [stɔ:l] *n* (*in market*) puesto; (*in
stable*) casilla (de establo) ♦ *vt* (*AUT*)
calar; (*fig*) dar largas a ♦ *vi* (*AUT*) calarse; (*fig*) andarse con rodeos; **~s** *npl*
(*BRIT*: *in cinema, theatre*) butacas *fpl*.
stallion ['stælɪən] *n* semental *m*.
stalwart ['stɔ:lwət] *n* leal.
stamina ['stæmɪnə] *n* resistencia.
stammer ['stæmə*] *n* tartamudeo ♦ *vi*
tartamudear.
stamp [stæmp] *n* sello (*SP*), estampilla
(*AM*); (*mark, also fig*) marca, huella;
(*on document*) timbre *m* ♦ *vi* (*also: ~
one's foot*) patear ♦ *vt* (*mark*) marcar;
(*letter*) poner sellos or estampillas en;
(*with rubber ~*) sellar; **~ album** *n* álbum *m* para sellos or estampillas; **~
collecting** *n* filatelia.
stampede [stæm'pi:d] *n* estampida.
stance [stæns] *n* postura.
stand [stænd] (*pt, pp* **stood**) *n* (*position*)
posición *f*, postura; (*for taxis*) parada;
(*hall ~*) perchero; (*music ~*) atril *m*;
(*SPORT*) tribuna; (*at exhibition*) stand
m ♦ *vi* (*be*) estar, encontrarse; (*be on
foot*) estar de pie; (*rise*) levantarse;
(*remain*) quedar en pie; (*in election*)
presentar candidatura ♦ *vt* (*place*) poner, colocar; (*withstand*) aguantar, soportar; (*invite to*) invitar; **to make a ~**
(*fig*) mantener una postura firme; **to ~
for parliament** (*BRIT*) presentar
(como candidato) a las elecciones; **~
by** *vi* (*be ready*) estar listo ♦ *vt fus*
(*opinion*) aferrarse a; (*person*) apoyar;
~ down *vi* (*withdraw*) ceder el puesto;
~ for *vt fus* (*signify*) significar; (*tolerate*) aguantar, permitir; **~ in for** *vt
fus* suplir a; **~ out** *vi* destacarse; **~ up**

vi levantarse, ponerse de pie; **~ up for**
vt fus defender; **~ up to** *vt fus* hacer
frente a.
standard ['stændəd] *n* patrón *m*, norma;
(*level*) nivel *m*; (*flag*) estandarte *m* ♦
adj (*size etc*) normal, corriente; (*text*)
básico; **~s** *npl* (*morals*) valores *mpl*
morales; **~ize** *vt* normalizar; **~ lamp**
(*BRIT*) *n* lámpara de pie; **~ of living** *n*
nivel *m* de vida.
stand-by ['stændbaɪ] *n* (*reserve*) recurso
seguro; **to be on ~** estar sobre aviso; **~
ticket** *n* (*AVIAT*) (billete *m*) standby *m*.
stand-in ['stændɪn] *n* suplente *m/f*.
standing ['stændɪŋ] *adj* (*on foot*) de pie,
en pie; (*permanent*) permanente ♦ *n*
reputación *f*; **of many years' ~** que lleva muchos años; **~ joke** *n* broma permanente; **~ order** (*BRIT*) *n* (*at bank*)
orden *f* de pago permanente; **~ room** *n*
sitio para estar de pie.
stand: **~-offish** *adj* reservado, poco
afable; **~point** *n* punto de vista; **~still**
n: **at a ~still** (*industry, traffic*) paralizado; (*car*) parado; **to come to a ~still**
quedar paralizado; pararse.
stank [stæŋk] *pt of* **stink**.
staple ['steɪpl] *n* (*for papers*) grapa ♦
adj (*food etc*) básico ♦ *vt* grapar; **~r** *n*
grapadora.
star [stɑ:*] *n* estrella; (*celebrity*) estrella, astro ♦ *vt* (*THEATRE, CINEMA*) ser
el/la protagonista de; **the ~s** *npl* (*AS-
TROLOGY*) el horóscopo.
starboard ['stɑ:bəd] *n* estribor *m*.
starch [stɑ:tʃ] *n* almidón *m*.
stardom ['stɑ:dəm] *n* estrellato.
stare [steə*] *n* mirada fija ♦ *vi*: **~ at**
mirar fijo.
starfish ['stɑ:fɪʃ] *n* estrella de mar.
stark [stɑ:k] *adj* (*bleak*) severo, escueto
♦ *adv*: **~ naked** en cueros.
starling ['stɑ:lɪŋ] *n* estornino.
starry ['stɑ:rɪ] *adj* estrellado; **~-eyed**
adj (*innocent*) inocentón/ona, ingenuo.
start [stɑ:t] *n* principio, comienzo; (*departure*) salida; (*sudden movement*)
salto, sobresalto; (*advantage*) ventaja ♦
vt empezar, comenzar; (*cause*) causar;
(*found*) fundar; (*engine*) poner en mar-

cha ♦ *vi* comenzar, empezar; *(with fright)* asustarse, sobresaltarse; *(train etc)* salir; **to ~ doing** *or* **to do sth** empezar a hacer algo; **~ off** *vi* empezar, comenzar; *(leave)* salir, ponerse en camino; **~ up** *vi* comenzar; *(car)* ponerse en marcha ♦ *vt* comenzar; poner en marcha; **~er** *n* *(AUT)* botón *m* de arranque; *(SPORT: official)* juez *m/f* de salida; *(BRIT: CULIN)* entrada; **~ing point** *n* punto de partida.

startle ['stɑːtl] *vt* asustar, sobrecoger; **startling** *adj* alarmante.

starvation [stɑː'veɪʃən] *n* hambre *f*.

starve [stɑːv] *vi* tener mucha hambre; *(to death)* morir de hambre ♦ *vt* hacer pasar hambre.

state [steɪt] *n* estado ♦ *vt* *(say, declare)* afirmar; **the S~s** los Estados Unidos; **to be in a ~** estar agitado; **~ly** *adj* majestuoso, imponente; **~ment** *n* afirmación *f*; **~sman** *n* estadista *m*.

static ['stætɪk] *n* *(RADIO)* parásitos *mpl* ♦ *adj* estático; **~ electricity** *n* estática.

station ['steɪʃən] *n* *(gen)* estación *f*; *(RADIO)* emisora; *(rank)* posición *f* social ♦ *vt* colocar, situar; *(MIL)* apostar.

stationary ['steɪʃnərɪ] *adj* estacionario, fijo.

stationer ['steɪʃənə*] *n* papelero/a; **~'s (shop)** *(BRIT)* papelería; **~y** [-nərɪ] *n* papel *m* de escribir, artículos *mpl* de escritorio.

station master *n* *(RAIL)* jefe *m* de estación.

station wagon *(US)* *n* ranchera.

statistic [stə'tɪstɪk] *n* estadística; **~al** *adj* estadístico; **~s** *n* *(science)* estadística.

statue ['stætjuː] *n* estatua.

status ['steɪtəs] *n* estado; *(reputation)* estatus *m*; **~ symbol** *n* símbolo de prestigio.

statute ['stætjuːt] *n* estatuto, ley *f*; **statutory** *adj* estatutario.

staunch [stɔːntʃ] *adj* leal, incondicional.

stave [steɪv] *vt*: **to ~ off** *(attack)* rechazar; *(threat)* evitar.

stay [steɪ] *n* estancia ♦ *vi* quedar(se); *(as guest)* hospedarse; **to ~ put** seguir en el mismo sitio; **to ~ the night/5 days** pasar la noche/estar 5 días; **~ behind** *vi* quedar atrás; **~ in** *vi* quedarse en casa; **~ on** *vi* quedarse; **~ out** *vi* *(of house)* no volver a casa; *(on strike)* permanecer en huelga; **~ up** *vi* *(at night)* velar, no acostarse; **~ing power** *n* aguante *m*.

stead [sted] *n*: **in sb's ~** en lugar de uno; **to stand sb in good ~** ser muy útil a uno.

steadfast ['stedfɑːst] *adj* firme, resuelto.

steadily ['stedɪlɪ] *adv* constantemente; *(firmly)* firmemente; *(work, walk)* sin parar; *(gaze)* fijamente.

steady ['stedɪ] *adj* *(firm)* firme; *(regular)* regular; *(person, character)* sensato, juicioso; *(boyfriend)* formal; *(look, voice)* tranquilo ♦ *vt* *(stabilize)* estabilizar; *(nerves)* calmar.

steak [steɪk] *n* *(gen)* filete *m*; *(beef)* bistec *m*.

steal [stiːl] *(pt stole, pp stolen)* *vt* robar ♦ *vi* robar; *(move secretly)* andar a hurtadillas.

stealth [stelθ] *n*: **by ~** a escondidas, sigilosamente; **~y** *adj* cauteloso, sigiloso.

steam [stiːm] *n* vapor *m*; *(mist)* vaho, humo ♦ *vt* *(CULIN)* cocer al vapor ♦ *vi* echar vapor; **~ engine** *n* máquina de vapor; **~er** *n* (buque *m* de) vapor *m*; **~roller** *n* apisonadora; **~ship** *n* = **~er**; **~y** *adj* *(room)* lleno de vapor; *(window)* empañado; *(heat, atmosphere)* bochornoso.

steel [stiːl] *n* acero ♦ *adj* de acero; **~works** *n* acería.

steep [stiːp] *adj* escarpado, abrupto; *(stair)* empinado; *(price)* exorbitante, excesivo ♦ *vt* empapar, remojar.

steeple ['stiːpl] *n* aguja; **~chase** *n* carrera de obstáculos.

steer [stɪə*] *vt* *(car)* conducir *(SP)*, manejar *(AM)*; *(person)* dirigir ♦ *vi* conducir, manejar; **~ing** *n* *(AUT)* dirección *f*; **~ing wheel** *n* volante *m*.

stem [stem] *n* *(of plant)* tallo; *(of glass)* pie *m* ♦ *vt* detener; *(blood)* restañar; **~ from** *vt fus* ser consecuencia de.

stench [stentʃ] *n* hedor *m*.

stencil ['stɛnsl] n (pattern) plantilla ♦ vt hacer un cliché de.

stenographer [stɛ'nɔgrəfə*] (US) n taquígrafo/a.

step [stɛp] n paso; (on stair) peldaño, escalón m ♦ vi: to ~ forward/back dar un paso adelante/hacia atrás; ~s npl (BRIT) = ~ladder; in/out of ~ (with) acorde/en disonancia (con); ~ down vi (fig) retirarse; ~ on vt fus pisar; ~ up vt (increase) aumentar; ~brother n hermanastro; ~daughter n hijastra; ~father n padrastro; ~ladder n escalera doble or de tijera; ~mother n madrastra; ~ping stone n pasadera; ~sister n hermanastra; ~son n hijastro.

stereo ['stɛrɪəu] n estéreo ♦ adj (also: ~phonic) estéreo, estereofónico.

sterile ['stɛraɪl] adj estéril; **sterilize** ['stɛrɪlaɪz] vt esterilizar.

sterling ['stə:lɪŋ] adj (silver) de ley ♦ n (ECON) (libras fpl) esterlinas fpl; one pound ~ una libra esterlina.

stern [stə:n] adj severo, austero ♦ n (NAUT) popa.

stethoscope ['stɛθəskəup] n estetoscopio.

stew [stju:] n cocido (SP), estofado (SP), guisado (AM) ♦ vt estofar, guisar; (fruit) cocer.

steward ['stju:əd] n camarero; ~ess n (esp on plane) azafata.

stick [stɪk] (pt, pp stuck) n palo; (of dynamite) barreno; (as weapon) porra; (walking ~) bastón m ♦ vt (glue) pegar; (inf: put) meter; (: tolerate) aguantar, soportar; (thrust): to ~ sth into clavar or hincar algo en ♦ vi pegarse; (be unmoveable) quedarse parado; (in mind) quedarse grabado; ~ out vi sobresalir; ~ up vi sobresalir; ~ up for vt fus defender; ~er n (label) etiqueta engomada; (with slogan) pegatina; ~ing plaster n esparadrapo.

stickler ['stɪklə*] n: to be a ~ for insistir mucho en.

stick-up (inf) n asalto, atraco.

sticky ['stɪkɪ] adj pegajoso; (label) engomado; (fig) difícil.

stiff [stɪf] adj rígido, tieso; (hard) duro; (manner) estirado; (difficult) difícil; (person) inflexible; (price) exorbitante ♦ adv: **scared/bored** ~ muerto de miedo/aburrimiento; ~en vi (muscles etc) agarrotarse; ~ neck n tortícolis m inv; ~ness n rigidez f, tiesura.

stifle ['staɪfl] vt ahogar, sofocar; **stifling** adj (heat) sofocante, bochornoso.

stigma ['stɪgmə] n (fig) estigma m.

stile [staɪl] n portillo, portilla.

stiletto [stɪ'lɛtəu] (BRIT) n (also: ~ heel) tacón m de aguja.

still [stɪl] adj inmóvil, quieto ♦ adv todavía; (even) aun; (nonetheless) sin embargo, aun así; ~born adj nacido muerto; ~ life n naturaleza muerta.

stilt [stɪlt] n zanco; (pile) pilar m, soporte m.

stilted ['stɪltɪd] adj afectado.

stimulate ['stɪmjuleɪt] vt estimular.

stimuli ['stɪmjulaɪ] npl of **stimulus**.

stimulus ['stɪmjuləs] (pl **stimuli**) n estímulo, incentivo.

sting [stɪŋ] (pt, pp **stung**) n picadura; (pain) escozor m, picazón f; (organ) aguijón m ♦ vt, vi picar.

stingy ['stɪndʒɪ] adj tacaño.

stink [stɪŋk] (pt **stank**, pp **stunk**) n hedor m, tufo ♦ vi heder, apestar; ~ing adj hediondo, fétido; (fig: inf) horrible.

stint [stɪnt] n tarea, trabajo ♦ vi: to ~ on escatimar.

stir [stə:*] n (fig: agitation) conmoción f ♦ vt (tea etc) remover; (fig: emotions) provocar ♦ vi moverse; ~ up vt (trouble) fomentar.

stirrup ['stɪrəp] n estribo.

stitch [stɪtʃ] n (SEWING) puntada; (KNITTING) punto; (MED) punto (de sutura); (pain) punzada ♦ vt coser; (MED) suturar.

stoat [stəut] n armiño.

stock [stɔk] n (COMM: reserves) existencias fpl, stock m; (: selection) surtido; (AGR) ganado, ganadería; (CULIN) caldo; (descent) raza, estirpe f; (FINANCE) capital m ♦ adj (fig: reply etc) clásico ♦ vt (have in ~) tener existencias de; ~s and shares acciones y valores; in ~

en existencia *or* almacén; **out of** ~ agotado; **to take** ~ **of** (*fig*) asesorar, examinar; ~ **up with** *vt fus* abastecerse de.

stockbroker ['stɔkbrəukə*] *n* agente *m/f or* corredor(a) *m/f* de bolsa.

stock cube (*BRIT*) *n* pastilla de caldo.

stock exchange *n* bolsa.

stocking ['stɔkɪŋ] *n* media.

stock: ~**ist** (*BRIT*) *n* distribuidor(a) *m/ f*; ~ **market** *n* bolsa (de valores); ~ **phrase** *n* cliché *m*; ~**pile** *n* reserva ♦ *vt* acumular, almacenar; ~**taking** (*BRIT*) *n* (*COMM*) inventario.

stocky ['stɔkɪ] *adj* (*strong*) robusto; (*short*) achaparrado.

stodgy ['stɔdʒɪ] *adj* indigesto, pesado.

stoke [stəuk] *vt* atizar.

stole [stəul] *pt of* **steal** ♦ *n* estola.

stolen ['stəuln] *pp of* **steal**.

stolid ['stɔlɪd] *adj* imperturbable, impasible.

stomach ['stʌmək] *n* (*ANAT*) estómago; (*belly*) vientre *m* ♦ *vt* tragar, aguantar; ~**ache** *n* dolor *m* de estómago.

stone [stəun] *n* piedra; (*in fruit*) hueso; (*BRIT: weight*) = *6.348kg; 14 libras* ♦ *adj* de piedra ♦ *vt* apedrear; (*fruit*) deshuesar; ~-**cold** *adj* helado; ~-**deaf** *adj* sordo como una tapia; ~**work** *n* (*art*) cantería; **stony** *adj* pedregoso; (*fig*) frío.

stood [stud] *pt, pp of* **stand**.

stool [stu:l] *n* taburete *m*.

stoop [stu:p] *vi* (*also*: ~ *down*) doblarse, agacharse; (*also: have a* ~) ser cargado de espaldas.

stop [stɔp] *n* parada; (*in punctuation*) punto ♦ *vt* parar, detener; (*break off*) suspender; (*block: pay*) suspender; (: *cheque*) invalidar; (*also: put a* ~ *to*) poner término a ♦ *vi* pararse, detenerse; (*end*) acabarse; **to** ~ **doing sth** dejar de hacer algo; ~ **dead** *vi* pararse en seco; ~ **off** *vi* interrumpir el viaje; ~ **up** *vt* (*hole*) tapar; ~**gap** *n* (*person*) interino/a; (*thing*) recurso provisional; ~**over** *n* parada; (*AVIAT*) escala.

stoppage ['stɔpɪdʒ] *n* (*strike*) paro; (*blockage*) obstrucción *f*.

stopper ['stɔpə*] *n* tapón *m*.

stop press *n* noticias *fpl* de última hora.

stopwatch ['stɔpwɔtʃ] *n* cronómetro.

storage ['stɔːrɪdʒ] *n* almacenaje *m*; ~ **heater** *n* acumulador *m*.

store [stɔː*] *n* (*stock*) provisión *f*; (*depot*: *BRIT: large shop*) almacén *m*; (*US*) tienda; (*reserve*) reserva, repuesto ♦ *vt* almacenar; ~**s** *npl* víveres *mpl*; **in** ~ (*fig*): **to be in** ~ **for sb** esperarle a uno; ~ **up** *vt* acumular; ~**room** *n* despensa.

storey ['stɔːrɪ] (*US* **story**) *n* piso.

stork [stɔːk] *n* cigüeña.

storm [stɔːm] *n* tormenta; (*fig: of applause*) salva; (: *of criticism*) nube *f* ♦ *vi* (*fig*) rabiar ♦ *vt* tomar por asalto; ~**y** *adj* tempestuoso.

story ['stɔːrɪ] *n* historia; (*lie*) mentira; (*US*) = **storey**; ~**book** *n* libro de cuentos.

stout [staut] *adj* (*strong*) sólido; (*fat*) gordo, corpulento; (*resolute*) resuelto ♦ *n* cerveza negra.

stove [stəuv] *n* (*for cooking*) cocina; (*for heating*) estufa.

stow [stəu] *vt* (*also*: ~ *away*) meter, poner; (*NAUT*) estibar; ~**away** *n* polizón/ona *m/f*.

straddle ['strædl] *vt* montar a horcajadas; (*fig*) abarcar.

straggle ['strægl] *vi* (*houses etc*) extenderse; (*lag behind*) rezagarse; **straggly** *adj* (*hair*) desordenado.

straight [streɪt] *adj* recto, derecho; (*frank*) franco, directo; (*simple*) sencillo ♦ *adv* derecho, directamente; (*drink*) sin mezcla; **to put** *or* **get sth** ~ dejar algo en claro; ~ **away**, ~ **off** en seguida; ~**en** *vt* (*also*: ~*en out*) enderezar, poner derecho; ~-**faced** *adj* serio; ~**forward** *adj* (*simple*) sencillo; (*honest*) honrado, franco.

strain [streɪn] *n* tensión *f*; (*TECH*) presión *f*; (*MED*) torcedura; (*breed*) tipo, variedad *f* ♦ *vt* (*back etc*) torcerse; (*resources*) agotar; (*stretch*) estirar; (*food, tea*) colar; ~**s** *npl* (*MUS*) son *m*; ~**ed** *adj* (*muscle*) torcido; (*laugh*) forzado; (*relations*) tenso; ~**er** *n* colador *m.*

strait [streɪt] *n* (*GEO*) estrecho; **to be in dire ~s** pasar grandes apuros; **~-jacket** *n* camisa de fuerza; **~-laced** *adj* mojigato, gazmoño.

strand [strænd] *n* (*of thread*) hebra; (*of hair*) trenza; (*of rope*) ramal *m*; **~ed** *adj* (*holidaymakers*) colgado.

strange [streɪndʒ] *adj* (*not known*) desconocido; (*odd*) extraño, raro; **~ly** *adv* de un modo raro; *see also* **enough**; **~r** *n* desconocido/a; (*from another area*) forastero/a.

strangle [ˈstræŋgl] *vt* estrangular; **~hold** *n* (*fig*) dominio completo.

strap [stræp] *n* correa; (*of slip, dress*) tirante *m*.

strapping [ˈstræpɪŋ] *adj* robusto, fornido.

stratagem [ˈstrætɪdʒəm] *n* estratagema.

strategic [strəˈtiːdʒɪk] *adj* estratégico.

strategy [ˈstrætɪdʒɪ] *n* estrategia.

straw [strɔː] *n* paja; (*drinking ~*) caña, pajita; **that's the last ~!** ¡eso es el colmo!

strawberry [ˈstrɔːbərɪ] *n* fresa (*SP*), frutilla (*AM*).

stray [streɪ] *adj* (*animal*) extraviado; (*bullet*) perdido; (*scattered*) disperso ♦ *vi* extraviarse, perderse; (*thoughts*) vagar.

streak [striːk] *n* raya; (*in hair*) raya ♦ *vt* rayar ♦ *vi*: **to ~ past** pasar como un rayo.

stream [striːm] *n* riachuelo, arroyo; (*of people, vehicles*) riada, caravana; (*of smoke, insults etc*) chorro ♦ *vt* (*SCOL*) dividir en grupos por habilidad ♦ *vi* correr, fluir; **to ~ in/out** (*people*) entrar/salir en tropel.

streamer [ˈstriːmə*] *n* serpentina.

streamlined [ˈstriːmlaɪnd] *adj* aerodinámico.

street [striːt] *n* calle *f*; **~car** (*US*) *n* tranvía *m*; **~ lamp** *n* farol *m*; **~ plan** *n* plano; **~wise** (*inf*) *adj* que tiene mucha calle.

strength [streŋθ] *n* fuerza; (*of girder, knot etc*) resistencia; (*fig: power*) poder *m*; **~en** *vt* fortalecer, reforzar.

strenuous [ˈstrɛnjuəs] *adj* (*energetic, determined*) enérgico.

stress [strɛs] *n* presión *f*; (*mental strain*) estrés *m*; (*accent*) acento ♦ *vt* subrayar, recalcar; (*syllable*) acentuar.

stretch [stretʃ] *n* (*of sand etc*) trecho ♦ *vi* estirarse; (*extend*): **to ~ to** *or* **as far as** extenderse hasta ♦ *vt* extender, estirar; (*make demands of*) exigir el máximo esfuerzo a; **to ~ to** *or* **as far as** extenderse hasta; **~ out** *vi* tenderse ♦ *vt* (*arm etc*) extender; (*spread*) estirar.

stretcher [ˈstretʃə*] *n* camilla.

strewn [struːn] *adj*: **~ with** cubierto *or* sembrado de.

stricken [ˈstrɪkən] *adj* (*person*) herido; (*city, industry etc*) condenado; **~ with** (*disease*) afectado por.

strict [strɪkt] *adj* severo; (*exact*) estricto; **~ly** *adv* severamente; estrictamente.

stride [straɪd] (*pt* **strode**, *pp* **stridden**) *n* zancada, tranco ♦ *vi* dar zancadas, andar a trancos.

strident [ˈstraɪdnt] *adj* estridente.

strife [straɪf] *n* lucha.

strike [straɪk] (*pt, pp* **struck**) *n* huelga; (*of oil etc*) descubrimiento; (*attack*) ataque *m* ♦ *vt* golpear, pegar; (*oil etc*) descubrir; (*bargain, deal*) cerrar ♦ *vi* declarar la huelga; (*attack*) atacar; (*clock*) dar la hora; **on ~** (*workers*) en huelga; **to ~ a match** encender un fósforo; **~ down** *vt* derribar; **~ up** *vt* (*MUS*) empezar a tocar; (*conversation*) entablar; (*friendship*) trabar; **~r** *n* huelguista *m/f*; (*SPORT*) delantero; **striking** *adj* llamativo.

string [strɪŋ] (*pt, pp* **strung**) *n* (*gen*) cuerda; (*row*) hilera ♦ *vt*: **to ~ together** ensartar; **to ~ out** extenderse; **the ~s** *npl* (*MUS*) los instrumentos de cuerda; **to pull ~s** (*fig*) mover palancas; **~ bean** *n* judía verde, habichuela; **~(ed) instrument** *n* (*MUS*) instrumento de cuerda.

stringent [ˈstrɪndʒənt] *adj* riguroso, severo.

strip [strɪp] *n* tira; (*of land*) franja; (*of metal*) cinta, lámina ♦ *vt* desnudar;

(paint) quitar; (also: ~ down: machine) desmontar ♦ vi desnudarse; ~ cartoon n tira cómica (SP), historieta (AM).

stripe [straip] n raya; (MIL) galón m; ~d adj a rayas, rayado.

strip lighting n alumbrado fluorescente.

stripper ['stripə*] n artista m/f de striptease.

strive [straiv] (pt strove, pp striven) vi: to ~ for sth/to do sth luchar por conseguir/hacer algo; **striven** ['strivn] pp of strive.

strode [strəud] pt of stride.

stroke [strəuk] n (blow) golpe m; (SWIMMING) brazada; (MED) apoplejía; (of paintbrush) toque m ♦ vt acariciar; at a ~ de un solo golpe.

stroll [strəul] n paseo, vuelta ♦ vi dar un paseo or una vuelta; ~er (US) n (for child) sillita de ruedas.

strong [strɔŋ] adj fuerte; they are 50 ~ son 50; ~hold n fortaleza; (fig) baluarte m; ~ly adv fuertemente, con fuerza; (believe) firmemente; ~room n cámara acorazada.

strove [strəuv] pt of strive.

struck [strʌk] pt, pp of strike.

structure ['strʌktʃə*] n estructura; (building) construcción f.

struggle ['strʌgl] n lucha ♦ vi luchar.

strum [strʌm] vt (guitar) rasguear.

strung [strʌŋ] pt, pp of string.

strut [strʌt] n puntal m ♦ vi pavonearse.

stub [stʌb] n (of ticket etc) talón m; (of cigarette) colilla; to ~ one's toe on sth dar con el dedo (del pie) contra algo; ~ out vt apagar.

stubble ['stʌbl] n rastrojo; (on chin) barba (incipiente).

stubborn ['stʌbən] adj terco, testarudo.

stuck [stʌk] pt, pp of stick ♦ adj (jammed) atascado; ~-up adj engreído, presumido.

stud [stʌd] n (shirt ~) corchete m; (of boot) taco; (earring) pendiente m (de bolita); (also: ~ farm) caballeriza; (also: ~ horse) caballo semental ♦ vt (fig): ~ded with salpicado de.

student ['stju:dənt] n estudiante m/f ♦ adj estudiantil; ~ driver (US) n aprendiz(a) m/f.

studio ['stju:diəu] n estudio; (artist's) taller m; ~ flat (US ~ apartment) n estudio.

studious ['stju:diəs] adj estudioso; (studied) calculado; ~ly adv (carefully) con esmero.

study ['stʌdi] n estudio ♦ vt estudiar; (examine) examinar, investigar ♦ vi estudiar.

stuff [stʌf] n materia; (substance) material m, sustancia; (things) cosas fpl ♦ vt llenar; (CULIN) rellenar; (animals) disecar; (inf: push) meter; ~ing n relleno; ~y adj (room) mal ventilado; (person) de miras estrechas.

stumble ['stʌmbl] vi tropezar, dar un traspié; to ~ across, ~ on (fig) tropezar con; **stumbling block** n tropiezo, obstáculo.

stump [stʌmp] n (of tree) tocón m; (of limb) muñón m ♦ vt: to be ~ed for an answer no saber qué contestar.

stun [stʌn] vt dejar sin sentido.

stung [stʌŋ] pt, pp of sting.

stunk [stʌŋk] pp of stink.

stunning ['stʌnɪŋ] adj (fig: news) pasmoso; (: outfit etc) sensacional.

stunt [stʌnt] n (in film) escena peligrosa; (publicity ~) truco publicitario; ~ed adj enano, achaparrado; ~man n doble m.

stupefy ['stju:pɪfaɪ] vt dejar estupefacto.

stupendous [stju:'pɛndəs] adj estupendo, asombroso.

stupid ['stju:pɪd] adj estúpido, tonto; ~ity [-'pɪdɪti] n estupidez f.

sturdy ['stə:di] adj robusto, fuerte.

stutter ['stʌtə*] n tartamudeo ♦ vi tartamudear.

sty [stai] n (for pigs) pocilga.

stye [stai] n (MED) orzuelo.

style [stail] n estilo; **stylish** adj elegante, a la moda.

stylus ['stailəs] n aguja.

suave [swa:v] adj cortés.

sub... [sʌb] prefix sub...; ~conscious adj subconsciente; ~contract vt subcontratar; ~**divide** *vt* subdividir.

subdue [səb'djuː] *vt* sojuzgar; *(passions)* dominar; ~**d** *adj (light)* tenue; *(person)* sumiso, manso.

subject [*n* 'sʌbdʒɪkt, *vb* səb'dʒɛkt] *n* súbdito; *(SCOL)* asignatura; *(matter)* tema *m*; *(GRAMMAR)* sujeto ♦ *vt*: to ~ sb to sth someter a uno a algo; to be ~ to *(law)* estar sujeto a; *(subj: person)* ser propenso a; ~**ive** [-'dʒɛktɪv] *adj* subjetivo; ~ **matter** *n (content)* contenido.

subjunctive [səb'dʒʌŋktɪv] *adj, n* subjuntivo.

sublet [sʌb'lɛt] *vt* subarrendar.

submachine gun ['sʌbmə'ʃiːn-] *n* metralleta.

submarine [sʌbmə'riːn] *n* submarino.

submerge [səb'məːdʒ] *vt* sumergir ♦ *vi* sumergirse.

submissive [səb'mɪsɪv] *adj* sumiso.

submit [səb'mɪt] *vt* someter ♦ *vi*: to ~ to sth someterse a algo.

subnormal [sʌb'nɔːməl] *adj* anormal.

subordinate [sə'bɔːdɪnət] *adj, n* subordinado/a *m/f*.

subpoena [səb'piːnə] *n (LAW)* citación *f*.

subscribe [səb'skraɪb] *vi* suscribir; to ~ to *(opinion, fund)* suscribir, aprobar; *(newspaper)* suscribirse a; ~**r** *n (to periodical)* subscriptor(a) *m/f*; *(to telephone)* abonado/a.

subscription [səb'skrɪpʃən] *n* abono; *(to magazine)* subscripción *f*.

subsequent ['sʌbsɪkwənt] *adj* subsiguiente, posterior; ~**ly** *adv* posteriormente, más tarde.

subside [səb'saɪd] *vi* hundirse; *(flood)* bajar; *(wind)* amainar; ~**nce** [-'saɪdns] *n* hundimiento; *(in road)* socavón *m*.

subsidiary [səb'sɪdɪərɪ] *adj* secundario ♦ *n (also: ~ company)* sucursal *f*, filial *f*.

subsidize ['sʌbsɪdaɪz] *vt* subvencionar.

subsidy ['sʌbsɪdɪ] *n* subvención *f*.

subsistence [səb'sɪstəns] *n* subsistencia; ~ **allowance** *n* salario mínimo.

substance ['sʌbstəns] *n* sustancia.

substantial [səb'stænʃl] *adj* sustancial, sustancioso; *(fig)* importante.

substantiate [səb'stænʃɪeɪt] *vt* comprobar.

substitute ['sʌbstɪtjuːt] *n (person)* suplente *m/f*; *(thing)* sustituto ♦ *vt*: to ~ A for B sustituir A por B, reemplazar B por A.

subtitle ['sʌbtaɪtl] *n* subtítulo.

subtle ['sʌtl] *adj* sutil; ~**ty** *n* sutileza.

subtotal [sʌb'təʊtl] *n* total *m* parcial.

subtract [səb'trækt] *vt* restar, sustraer; ~**ion** [-'trækʃən] *n* resta, sustracción *f*.

suburb ['sʌbəːb] *n* barrio residencial; the ~**s** las afueras (de la ciudad); ~**an** [sə'bəːbən] *adj* suburbano; *(train etc)* de cercanías; ~**ia** [sə'bəːbɪə] *n* barrios *mpl* residenciales.

subway ['sʌbweɪ] *n (BRIT)* paso subterráneo *or* inferior; *(US)* metro.

succeed [sək'siːd] *vi (person)* tener éxito; *(plan)* salir bien ♦ *vt* suceder a; to ~ in doing lograr hacer; ~**ing** *adj (following)* sucesivo.

success [sək'sɛs] *n* éxito; ~**ful** *adj* exitoso; *(business)* próspero; to be ~**ful (in doing)** lograr (hacer); ~**fully** *adv* con éxito.

succession [sək'sɛʃən] *n* sucesión *f*, serie *f*.

successive [sək'sɛsɪv] *adj* sucesivo, consecutivo.

succinct [sək'sɪŋkt] *adj* sucinto.

succumb [sə'kʌm] *vi*: to ~ to sucumbir a; *(illness)* ser víctima de.

such [sʌtʃ] *adj* tal, semejante; *(of that kind)*: ~ **a book** tal libro; *(so much)*: ~ **courage** tanto valor ♦ *adv* tan; ~ **a long trip** un viaje tan largo; ~ **a lot of** tanto(s)/a(s); ~ **as** *(like)* tal como; as ~ como tal; ~**-and-~** *adj* tal o cual.

suck [sʌk] *vt* chupar; *(bottle)* sorber; *(breast)* mamar; ~**er** *n (ZOOL)* ventosa; *(inf)* bobo, primo.

suction ['sʌkʃən] *n* succión *f*.

Sudan [su'dæn] *n* Sudán *m*.

sudden ['sʌdn] *adj (rapid)* repentino, súbito; *(unexpected)* imprevisto; all of a ~ de repente; ~**ly** *adv* de repente.

suds [sʌdz] *npl* espuma de jabón.

sue [suː] *vt* demandar.

suede [sweɪd] *n* ante *m (SP)*, gamuza *(AM)*.

suet ['suɪt] *n* sebo.

Suez ['suːɪz] n: **the ~ Canal** el Canal de Suez.

suffer ['sʌfə*] vt sufrir, padecer; (tolerate) aguantar, soportar ♦ vi sufrir; **to ~ from** (illness etc) padecer; **~er** n víctima; (MED) enfermo/a; **~ing** n sufrimiento.

suffice [sə'faɪs] vi bastar, ser suficiente.

sufficient [sə'fɪʃənt] adj suficiente, bastante; **~ly** ad suficientemente, bastante.

suffix ['sʌfɪks] n sufijo.

suffocate ['sʌfəkeɪt] vi ahogarse, asfixiarse; **suffocation** [-'keɪʃən] n asfixia.

suffrage ['sʌfrɪdʒ] n sufragio.

suffused [sə'fjuːzd] adj: **~ with** bañado de.

sugar ['ʃugə*] n azúcar m ♦ vt echar azúcar a, azucarar; **~ beet** n remolacha; **~ cane** n caña de azúcar.

suggest [sə'dʒɛst] vt sugerir; **~ion** [-'dʒɛstʃən] n sugerencia; **~ive** (pej) adj indecente.

suicide ['suɪsaɪd] n suicidio; (person) suicida m/f; see also **commit**.

suit [suːt] n (man's) traje m; (woman's) conjunto; (LAW) pleito; (CARDS) palo ♦ vt convenir; (clothes) sentar a, ir bien a; (adapt): **to ~ sth to** adaptar or ajustar algo a; **well ~ed** (well matched: couple) hecho el uno para el otro; **~able** adj conveniente; (apt) indicado; **~ably** adv convenientemente; (impressed) apropiadamente.

suitcase ['suːtkeɪs] n maleta (SP), valija (AM).

suite [swiːt] n (of rooms, MUS) suite f; (furniture): **bedroom/dining room ~** (juego de) dormitorio/comedor.

suitor ['suːtə*] n pretendiente m.

sulfur ['sʌlfə*] (US) n = **sulphur**.

sulk [sʌlk] vi estar de mal humor; **~y** adj malhumorado.

sullen ['sʌlən] adj hosco, malhumorado.

sulphur ['sʌlfə*] (US **sulfur**) n azufre m.

sultana [sʌl'tɑːnə] n (fruit) pasa de Esmirna.

sultry ['sʌltrɪ] adj (weather) bochornoso.

sum [sʌm] n suma; (total) total m; **~ up** vt resumir ♦ vi hacer un resumen.

summarize ['sʌməraɪz] vt resumir.

summary ['sʌmərɪ] n resumen m ♦ adj (justice) sumario.

summer ['sʌmə*] n verano ♦ cpd de verano; **in ~** en verano; **~ holidays** npl vacaciones fpl de verano; **~house** n (in garden) cenador m, glorieta; **~time** n (season) verano; **~ time** n (by clock) hora de verano.

summit ['sʌmɪt] n cima, cumbre f; (also: **~ conference**, **~ meeting**) (conferencia) cumbre f.

summon ['sʌmən] vt (person) llamar; (meeting) convocar; (LAW) citar; **~ up** vt (courage) armarse de; **~s** n llamamiento, llamada ♦ vt (LAW) citar.

sump [sʌmp] (BRIT) n (AUT) cárter m.

sumptuous ['sʌmptjuəs] adj suntuoso.

sun [sʌn] n sol m.

sunbathe ['sʌnbeɪð] vi tomar el sol.

sunburn ['sʌnbəːn] n (painful) quemadura; (tan) bronceado.

Sunday ['sʌndɪ] n domingo; **~ school** n catequesis f dominical.

sundial ['sʌndaɪəl] n reloj m de sol.

sundown ['sʌndaun] n anochecer m.

sundry ['sʌndrɪ] adj varios/as, diversos/as; **all and ~** todos sin excepción; **sundries** npl géneros mpl diversos.

sunflower ['sʌnflauə*] n girasol m.

sung [sʌŋ] pp of **sing**.

sunglasses ['sʌnglɑːsɪz] npl gafas fpl (SP) or anteojos mpl de sol.

sunk [sʌŋk] pp of **sink**.

sun: ~light n luz f del sol; **~lit** adj iluminado por el sol; **~ny** adj soleado; (day) de sol; (fig) alegre; **~rise** n salida del sol; **~ roof** n (AUT) techo corredizo; **~set** n puesta del sol; **~shade** n (over table) sombrilla; **~shine** n sol m; **~stroke** n insolación f; **~tan** n bronceado; **~tan oil** n aceite m bronceador.

super ['suːpə*] (inf) adj genial.

superannuation [suːpərænjuˈeɪʃən] n cuota de jubilación.

superb [suːˈpəːb] adj magnífico, espléndido.

supercilious [suːpəˈsɪlɪəs] adj altanero.

superfluous [suˈpəːfluəs] adj superfluo, de sobra.

superhuman [su:pə'hju:mən] *adj* sobrehumano.

superimpose ['su:pərɪm'pəuz] *vt* sobreponer.

superintendent [su:pərɪn'tɛndənt] *n* director(a) *m/f*; (*POLICE*) subjefe/a *m/f*.

superior [su'pɪərɪə*] *adj* superior; (*smug*) desdeñoso ♦ *n* superior *m*; ~**ity** [-'ɔrɪtɪ] *n* superioridad *f*.

superlative [su'pɜ:lətɪv] *n* superlativo.

superman ['su:pəmæn] *n* superhombre *m*.

supermarket ['su:pəmɑːkɪt] *n* supermercado.

supernatural [su:pə'nætʃərəl] *adj* sobrenatural ♦ *n*: **the** ~ lo sobrenatural.

superpower ['su:pəpauə*] *n* (*POL*) superpotencia.

supersede [su:pə'si:d] *vt* suplantar.

supersonic ['su:pə'sɔnɪk] *adj* supersónico.

superstar ['su:pəstɑ:*] *n* gran estrella.

superstitious [su:pə'stɪʃəs] *adj* supersticioso.

supertanker ['su:pətæŋkə*] *n* superpetrolero.

supervise ['su:pəvaɪz] *vt* supervisar; **supervision** [-'vɪʒən] *n* supervisión *f*; **supervisor** *n* supervisor(a) *m/f*.

supper ['sʌpə*] *n* cena.

supplant [sə'plɑ:nt] *vt* suplantar.

supple ['sʌpl] *adj* flexible.

supplement [*n* 'sʌplɪmənt, *vb* sʌplɪ'mɛnt] *n* suplemento ♦ *vt* suplir; ~**ary** [-'mɛntərɪ] *adj* suplementario; ~**ary benefit** (*BRIT*) *n* subsidio suplementario de la seguridad social.

supplier [sə'plaɪə*] *n* (*COMM*) distribuidor(a) *m/f*.

supply [sə'plaɪ] *vt* (*provide*) suministrar; (*equip*): **to** ~ (**with**) proveer (de) ♦ *n* provisión *f*; (*gas, water etc*) suministro; **supplies** *npl* (*food*) víveres *mpl*; (*MIL*) pertrechos *mpl*; ~ **teacher** *n* profesor(a) *m/f* suplente.

support [sə'pɔːt] *n* apoyo; (*TECH*) soporte *m* ♦ *vt* apoyar; (*financially*) mantener; (*uphold, TECH*) sostener; ~**er** *n* (*POL etc*) partidario/a; (*SPORT*) aficionado/a.

suppose [sə'pəuz] *vt* suponer; (*imagine*) imaginarse; (*duty*): **to be** ~**d to do** sth deber hacer algo; ~**dly** [sə'pəuzɪdlɪ] *adv* según cabe suponer; **supposing** *conj* en caso de que.

suppress [sə'prɛs] *vt* suprimir; (*yawn*) ahogar.

supreme [su'pri:m] *adj* supremo.

surcharge ['sɜ:tʃɑːdʒ] *n* sobretasa, recargo.

sure [ʃuə*] *adj* seguro; (*definite, convinced*) cierto; **to make** ~ **of** sth/that asegurarse de algo/asegurar que; ~! (*of course*) ¡claro!, ¡por supuesto!; ~ **enough** efectivamente; ~-**footed** *adj* ágil y seguro; ~**ly** *adv* (*certainly*) seguramente.

surety ['ʃuərətɪ] *n* fianza.

surf [sɜ:f] *n* olas *fpl*.

surface ['sɜ:fɪs] *n* superficie *f* ♦ *vt* (*road*) revestir ♦ *vi* (*also fig*) salir a la superficie; ~ **mail** *n* vía terrestre.

surfboard ['sɜ:fbɔːd] *n* tabla (de surf).

surfeit ['sɜ:fɪt] *n*: **a** ~ **of** un exceso de.

surfing ['sɜ:fɪŋ] *n* surf *m*.

surge [sɜ:dʒ] *n* oleada, oleaje *m* ♦ *vi* (*wave*) romper; (*people*) avanzar en tropel.

surgeon ['sɜ:dʒən] *n* cirujano/a.

surgery ['sɜ:dʒərɪ] *n* cirugía; (*BRIT: room*) consultorio; ~ **hours** (*BRIT*) *npl* horas *fpl* de consulta.

surgical ['sɜ:dʒɪkl] *adj* quirúrgico; ~ **spirit** (*BRIT*) *n* alcohol *m* de 90°.

surly ['sɜ:lɪ] *adj* hosco, malhumorado.

surmount [sɜ:'maunt] *vt* superar, vencer.

surname ['sɜ:neɪm] *n* apellido.

surpass [sɜ:'pɑːs] *vt* superar, exceder.

surplus ['sɜ:pləs] *n* excedente *m*; (*COMM*) superávit *m* ♦ *adj* excedente, sobrante.

surprise [sə'praɪz] *n* sorpresa ♦ *vt* sorprender; **surprising** *adj* sorprendente; **surprisingly** *adv*: **was surprisingly easy** me *etc* sorprendió lo fácil que fue.

surrender [sə'rɛndə*] *n* rendición *f*, entrega ♦ *vi* rendirse, entregarse.

surreptitious [sʌrəp'tɪʃəs] *adj* subrepticio.

surrogate ['sʌrəgɪt] n sucedáneo; ~ **mother** n madre f portadora.

surround [sə'raund] vt rodear, circundar; (MIL etc) cercar; ~**ing** adj circundante; ~**ings** npl alrededores mpl, cercanías fpl.

surveillance [səː'veɪləns] n vigilancia.

survey [n 'səːveɪ, vb səː'veɪ] n inspección f, reconocimiento; (inquiry) encuesta ♦ vt examinar, inspeccionar; (look at) mirar, contemplar; ~**or** n agrimensor(a) m/f.

survival [sə'vaɪvl] n supervivencia.

survive [sə'vaɪv] vi sobrevivir; (custom etc) perdurar ♦ vt sobrevivir a; **survivor** n superviviente m/f.

susceptible [sə'septəbl] adj: ~ (**to**) (disease) susceptible (a); (flattery) sensible (a).

suspect [adj, n 'sʌspekt, vb səs'pekt] adj, n sospechoso/a m/f ♦ vt (person) sospechar de; (think) sospechar.

suspend [səs'pend] vt suspender; ~**ed sentence** n (LAW) libertad f condicional; ~**er belt** n portaligas m inv; ~**ers** npl (BRIT) ligas fpl; (US) tirantes mpl.

suspense [səs'pens] n incertidumbre f, duda; (in film etc) suspense m; **to keep sb in** ~ mantener a uno en suspense.

suspension [səs'penʃən] n (gen, AUT) suspensión f; (of driving licence) privación f; ~ **bridge** n puente m colgante.

suspicion [səs'pɪʃən] n sospecha; (distrust) recelo; **suspicious** [-ʃəs] adj receloso; (causing ~) sospechoso.

sustain [səs'teɪn] vt sostener, apoyar; (suffer) sufrir, padecer; ~**ed** adj (effort) sostenido.

sustenance ['sʌstɪnəns] n sustento.

swab [swɔb] n (MED) algodón m.

swagger ['swægə*] vi pavonearse.

swallow ['swɔləu] n (bird) golondrina ♦ vt tragar; (fig, pride) tragarse. ~ **up** vt (savings etc) consumir.

swam [swæm] pt of swim.

swamp [swɔmp] n pantano, ciénaga ♦ vt (with water etc) inundar; (fig) abrumar, agobiar; ~**y** adj pantanoso.

swan [swɔn] n cisne m.

swap [swɔp] n canje m, intercambio ♦

vt: **to** ~ (**for**) cambiar (por).

swarm [swɔːm] n (of bees) enjambre m; (fig) multitud f ♦ vi (bees) formar un enjambre; (people) pulular; **to be** ~**ing with** ser un hervidero de.

swarthy ['swɔːðɪ] adj moreno.

swastika ['swɔstɪkə] n esvástica.

swat [swɔt] vt aplastar.

sway [sweɪ] vi mecerse, balancearse ♦ vt (influence) mover, influir en.

swear [swɛə*] (pt **swore**, pp **sworn**) vi (curse) maldecir; (promise) jurar ♦ vt jurar; ~**word** n taco, palabrota.

sweat [swɛt] n sudor m ♦ vi sudar.

sweater ['swɛtə*] n suéter m.

sweatshirt ['swɛtʃəːt] n suéter m.

sweaty ['swɛtɪ] adj sudoroso.

Swede [swiːd] n sueco/a.

swede [swiːd] (BRIT) n nabo.

Sweden ['swiːdn] n Suecia.

Swedish ['swiːdɪʃ] adj sueco ♦ n (LING) sueco.

sweep [swiːp] (pt, pp **swept**) n (act) barrido; (also: **chimney** ~) deshollinador(a) m/f ♦ vt barrer; (with arm) empujar; (subj: current) arrastrar ♦ vi barrer; (arm etc) moverse rápidamente; (wind) soplar con violencia; ~ **away** vt barrer; ~ **past** vi pasar majestuosamente; ~ **up** vi barrer; ~**ing** adj (gesture) dramático; (generalized: statement) generalizado.

sweet [swiːt] n (candy) dulce m, caramelo; (BRIT: pudding) postre m ♦ adj dulce; (fig: kind) dulce, amable; (: attractive) mono; ~**corn** n maíz m; ~**en** vt (add sugar to) poner azúcar a; (person) endulzar; ~**heart** n novio/a; ~**ness** n dulzura; ~ **pea** n guisante m de olor.

swell [swel] (pt **swelled**, pp **swollen** or **swelled**) n (of sea) marejada, oleaje m ♦ adj (US: inf: excellent) estupendo, fenomenal ♦ vt hinchar, inflar ♦ vi (also: ~ **up**) hincharse; (numbers) aumentar; (sound, feeling) ir aumentando; ~**ing** n (MED) hinchazón f.

sweltering ['swɛltərɪŋ] adj sofocante, de mucho calor.

swept [swɛpt] pt, pp of sweep.

swerve [swəːv] vi desviarse bruscamente.

swift [swɪft] n (bird) vencejo ♦ adj rápido, veloz; ~**ly** adv rápidamente.

swig [swɪg] (inf) n (drink) trago.

swill [swɪl] vt (also: ~ out, ~ down) lavar, limpiar con agua.

swim [swɪm] (pt swam, pp swum) n: to go for a ~ ir a nadar or a bañarse ♦ vi nadar; (head, room) dar vueltas ♦ vt nadar; (the Channel etc) cruzar a nado; ~**mer** n nadador(a) m/f; ~**ming** n natación f; ~**ming cap** n gorro de baño; ~**ming costume** (BRIT) n bañador m, traje m de baño; ~**ming pool** n piscina (SP), alberca (AM); ~**ming trunks** n bañador m (de hombre); ~**suit** n = ~ming costume.

swindle ['swɪndl] n estafa ♦ vt estafar.

swine [swaɪn] (inf!) n canalla (!).

swing [swɪŋ] (pt, pp swung) n (in playground) columpio; (movement) balanceo, vaivén m; (change of direction) viraje m; (rhythm) ritmo ♦ vt balancear; (also: ~ round) voltear, girar ♦ vi balancearse, columpiarse; (also: ~ round) dar media vuelta; to be in full ~ estar en plena marcha; ~ **bridge** n puente m giratorio; ~ **door** (US ~**ing door**) n puerta giratoria.

swingeing ['swɪndʒɪŋ] (BRIT) adj (blow) abrumador(a); (cuts) atroz.

swipe [swaɪp] vt (hit) golpear fuerte; (inf: steal) guindar.

swirl [swəːl] vi arremolinarse.

swish [swɪʃ] vi chasquear.

Swiss [swɪs] adj, n inv suizo/a m/f.

switch [swɪtʃ] n (for light etc) interruptor m; (change) cambio ♦ vt (change) cambiar de; ~ **off** vt apagar; (engine) parar; ~ **on** vt encender (SP), prender (AM); (engine, machine) arrancar; ~**board** n (TEL) centralita (de teléfonos) (SP), conmutador m (AM).

Switzerland ['swɪtsələnd] n Suiza.

swivel ['swɪvl] vi (also: ~ round) girar.

swollen ['swəulən] pp of swell.

swoon [swuːn] vi desmayarse.

swoop [swuːp] n (by police etc) redada ♦ vi (also: ~ down) calarse.

swop [swɔp] = swap.

sword [sɔːd] n espada; ~**fish** n pez m espada.

swore [swɔː*] pt of swear.

sworn [swɔːn] pp of swear ♦ adj (statement) bajo juramento; (enemy) implacable.

swot [swɔt] (BRIT) vt, vi empollar.

swum [swʌm] pp of swim.

swung [swʌŋ] pt, pp of swing.

sycamore ['sɪkəmɔː*] n sicomoro.

syllable ['sɪləbl] n sílaba.

syllabus ['sɪləbəs] n programa m de estudios.

symbol ['sɪmbl] n símbolo.

symmetry ['sɪmɪtrɪ] n simetría.

sympathetic [sɪmpə'θetɪk] adj (understanding) comprensivo; (likeable) simpático; (showing support): ~ **to(wards)** bien dispuesto hacia.

sympathize ['sɪmpəθaɪz] vi: to ~ **with** (person) compadecerse de; (feelings) comprender; (cause) apoyar; ~**r** n (POL) simpatizante m/f.

sympathy ['sɪmpəθɪ] n (pity) compasión f; **sympathies** npl (tendencies) tendencias fpl; **with our deepest** ~ nuestro más sentido pésame; **in** ~ en solidaridad.

symphony ['sɪmfənɪ] n sinfonía.

symposium [sɪm'pəuzɪəm] n simposio.

symptom ['sɪmptəm] n síntoma m, indicio.

synagogue ['sɪnəgɔg] n sinagoga.

syndicate ['sɪndɪkɪt] n (gen) sindicato; (of newspapers) agencia (de noticias).

syndrome ['sɪndrəum] n síndrome m.

synonym ['sɪnənɪm] n sinónimo.

synopses [sɪ'nɔpsiːz] npl of synopsis.

synopsis [sɪ'nɔpsɪs] (pl synopses) n sinopsis f inv.

syntax ['sɪntæks] n sintaxis f inv.

syntheses ['sɪnθəsiːz] npl of synthesis.

synthesis ['sɪnθəsɪs] (pl syntheses) n síntesis f inv.

synthetic [sɪn'θetɪk] adj sintético.

syphilis ['sɪfɪlɪs] n sífilis f.

syphon ['saɪfən] n = siphon.

Syria ['sɪrɪə] n Siria; ~**n** adj, n sirio/a.

syringe [sɪ'rɪndʒ] n jeringa.

syrup ['sɪrəp] n jarabe m; (also: golden ~) almíbar m.
system ['sɪstəm] n sistema m; (ANAT) organismo; ~**atic** [-'mætɪk] adj sistemático, metódico; ~ **disk** n (COMPUT) disco del sistema; ~**s analyst** n analista m/f de sistemas.

T

ta [tɑː] (BRIT: inf) excl ¡gracias!
tab [tæb] n lengüeta; (label) etiqueta; to keep ~s on (fig) vigilar.
tabby ['tæbɪ] n (also: ~ cat) gato atigrado.
table ['teɪbl] n mesa; (of statistics etc) cuadro, tabla ♦ vt (BRIT: motion etc) presentar; to lay or set the ~ poner la mesa; ~**cloth** n mantel m; ~ **of contents** n índice m de materias; ~ **d'hôte** [tɑːbl'dəut] adj del menú; ~ **lamp** n lámpara de mesa; ~**mat** n (for plate) posaplatos m inv; (for hot dish) salvamantel m; ~**spoon** n cuchara de servir; (also: ~spoonful: as measurement) cucharada.
tablet ['tæblɪt] n (MED) pastilla, comprimido; (of stone) lápida.
table tennis n ping-pong m, tenis m de mesa.
table wine n vino de mesa.
tabloid ['tæblɔɪd] n periódico popular sensacionalista.
tabulate ['tæbjuleɪt] vt disponer en tablas.
tack [tæk] n (nail) tachuela; (fig) hilván ♦ vt (nail) clavar con tachuelas; (stitch) hilvanar ♦ vi virar.
tackle ['tækl] n (fishing ~) aparejo (de pescar); (for lifting) aparejo ♦ vt (difficulty) enfrentarse con; (challenge: person) hacer frente a; (grapple with) agarrar, (FOOTBALL) cargar; (RUGBY) placar.
tacky ['tækɪ] adj pegajoso; (pej) cutre.
tact [tækt] n tacto, discreción f; ~**ful** adj discreto, diplomático.
tactics ['tæktɪks] n, npl táctica.
tactless ['tæktlɪs] adj indiscreto.

tadpole ['tædpəul] n renacuajo.
taffy ['tæfɪ] (US) n toffee m.
tag [tæg] n (label) etiqueta; ~ **along** vi ir (or venir) también.
tail [teɪl] n cola; (of shirt, coat) faldón m ♦ vt (follow) vigilar a; ~**s** npl (formal suit) levita; ~ **away** vi (in size, quality etc) ir disminuyendo; ~ **off** vi = ~ away; ~**back** (BRIT) n (AUT) cola; ~ **end** n cola, parte f final; ~**gate** n (AUT) puerta trasera.
tailor ['teɪlə*] n sastre m; ~**ing** n (cut) corte m; (craft) sastrería; ~**-made** adj (also fig) hecho a la medida.
tailwind ['teɪlwɪnd] n viento de cola.
tainted ['teɪntɪd] adj (food) pasado; (water, air) contaminado; (fig) manchado.
take [teɪk] (pt took, pp taken) vt tomar; (grab) coger (SP), agarrar (AM); (gain: prize) ganar; (require: effort, courage) exigir; (tolerate: pain etc) aguantar; (hold: passengers etc) tener cabida para; (accompany, bring, carry) llevar; (exam) presentarse a; to ~ sth from (drawer etc) sacar algo de; (person) quitar algo a; I ~ it that ... supongo que ...; ~ **after** vt fus parecerse a; ~ **apart** vt desmontar; ~ **away** vt (remove) quitar; (carry off) llevar; (MATH) restar; ~ **back** vt (return) devolver; (one's words) retractarse de; ~ **down** vt (building) derribar; (letter etc) apuntar; ~ **in** vt (deceive) engañar; (understand) entender; (include) abarcar; (lodger) acoger, recibir; ~ **off** vi (AVIAT) despegar ♦ vt (remove) quitar; ~ **on** vt (work) aceptar; (employee) contratar; (opponent) desafiar; ~ **out** vt sacar; ~ **over** vt (business) tomar posesión de; (country) tomar el poder ♦ vi: to ~ over from sb reemplazar a uno; ~ **to** vt fus (person) coger cariño a, encariñarse con; (activity) aficionarse a; ~ **up** vt (a dress) acortar; (occupy: time, space) ocupar; (engage in: hobby etc) dedicarse a; (accept): to ~ sb up on aceptar; ~**away** (BRIT) adj (food) para llevar ♦ n tienda (or restaurante m) de comida para lle-

var; ~**off** *n* (*AVIAT*) despegue *m*; ~**over** *n* (*COMM*) absorción *f*; ~**out** (*US*) *n* = ~**away**.

takings ['teɪkɪŋz] *npl* (*COMM*) ingresos *mpl*.

talc [tælk] *n* (*also*: ~*um powder*) (polvos de) talco.

tale [teɪl] *n* (*story*) cuento; (*account*) relación *f*; **to tell** ~**s** (*fig*) chivarse.

talent ['tælnt] *n* talento; ~**ed** *adj* de talento.

talk [tɔ:k] *n* charla; (*conversation*) conversación *f*; (*gossip*) habladurías *fpl*, chismes *mpl* ♦ *vi* hablar; ~**s** *npl* (*POL etc*) conversaciones *fpl*; **to ~ about** hablar de; **to ~ sb into doing sth** convencer a uno para que haga algo; **to ~ sb out of doing sth** disuadir a uno de que haga algo; **to ~ shop** hablar del trabajo; ~ **over** *vt* discutir; ~**ative** *adj* hablador(a); ~ **show** *n* programa *m* de entrevistas.

tall [tɔ:l] *adj* alto; (*object*) grande; **to be 6 feet ~** (*person*) ≈ medir 1 metro 80.

tally ['tælɪ] *n* cuenta ♦ *vi*: **to ~ (with)** corresponder (con).

talon ['tælən] *n* garra.

tambourine [tæmbə'ri:n] *n* pandereta.

tame [teɪm] *adj* domesticado; (*fig*) mediocre.

tamper ['tæmpə*] *vi*: **to ~ with** tocar, andar con.

tampon ['tæmpən] *n* tampón *m*.

tan [tæn] *n* (*also*: *sun*~) bronceado ♦ *vi* ponerse moreno ♦ *adj* (*colour*) marrón.

tang [tæŋ] *n* sabor *m* fuerte.

tangent ['tændʒənt] *n* (*MATH*) tangente *f*; **to go off at a ~** (*fig*) salirse por la tangente.

tangerine [tændʒə'ri:n] *n* mandarina.

tangle ['tæŋgl] *n* enredo; **to get in(to) a ~** enredarse.

tank [tæŋk] *n* (*water* ~) depósito, tanque *m*; (*for fish*) acuario; (*MIL*) tanque *m*.

tanker ['tæŋkə*] *n* (*ship*) buque *m* cisterna; (*truck*) camión *m* cisterna.

tanned [tænd] *adj* (*skin*) moreno.

tantalizing ['tæntəlaɪzɪŋ] *adj* tentador(a)

tantamount ['tæntəmaunt] *adj*: ~ **to** equivalente a.

tantrum ['tæntrəm] *n* rabieta.

tap [tæp] *n* (*BRIT*: *on sink etc*) grifo (*SP*), canilla (*AM*); (*gas* ~) llave *f*; (*gentle blow*) golpecito ♦ *vt* (*hit gently*) dar golpecitos en; (*resources*) utilizar, explotar; (*telephone*) intervenir; **on** ~ (*fig*: *resources*) a mano; ~-**dancing** *n* claqué *m*.

tape [teɪp] *n* (*also*: *magnetic* ~) cinta magnética; (*cassette*) cassette *f*, cinta; (*sticky* ~) cinta adhesiva; (*for tying*) cinta ♦ *vt* (*record*) grabar (en cinta); (*stick with* ~) pegar con cinta adhesiva; ~ **deck** *n* grabadora; ~ **measure** *n* cinta métrica, metro.

taper ['teɪpə*] *n* cirio ♦ *vi* afilarse.

tape recorder *n* grabadora.

tapestry ['tæpɪstrɪ] *n* (*object*) tapiz *m*; (*art*) tapicería.

tar [tɑ:] *n* alquitrán *m*, brea.

target ['tɑ:gɪt] *n* (*gen*) blanco.

tariff ['tærɪf] *n* (*on goods*) arancel *m*; (*BRIT*: *in hotels etc*) tarifa.

tarmac ['tɑ:mæk] *n* (*BRIT*: *on road*) asfaltado; (*AVIAT*) pista (de aterrizaje).

tarnish ['tɑ:nɪʃ] *vt* deslustrar.

tarpaulin [tɑ:'pɔ:lɪn] *n* lona impermeabilizada.

tarragon ['tærəgən] *n* estragón *m*.

tart [tɑ:t] *n* (*CULIN*) tarta; (*BRIT*: *inf*: *prostitute*) puta ♦ *adj* agrio, ácido; ~ **up** (*BRIT*: *inf*) *vt* (*building*) remozar; **to ~ o.s. up** acicalarse.

tartan ['tɑ:tn] *n* tejido escocés *m*.

tartar ['tɑ:tə*] *n* (*on teeth*) sarro; ~(**e**) **sauce** *n* salsa tártara.

task [tɑ:sk] *n* tarea; **to take to** ~ reprender; ~ **force** *n* (*MIL*, *POLICE*) grupo de operaciones.

taste [teɪst] *n* (*sense*) gusto; (*flavour*) sabor *m*; (*also*: *after*~) sabor *m*, dejo; (*sample*) muestra ♦ ~ **a ~!** ¡prueba un poquito!; (*fig*) muestra, idea ♦ *vt* (*also fig*) probar ♦ *vi*: **to ~ of** *or* **like** (*fish, garlic etc*) saber a; **you can ~ the garlic (in it)** se nota el sabor a ajo; **in good/bad ~** de buen/mal gusto; ~**ful** *adj* de buen gusto; ~**less** *adj* (*food*) soso; (*remark* *etc*) de mal gusto; **tasty** *adj* sabroso, rico.

tatters ['tætəz] *npl*: **in ~** hecho jirones.

tattoo [tə'tu:] *n* tatuaje *m*; (*spectacle*) espectáculo militar ♦ *vt* tatuar.

tatty ['tætɪ] (*BRIT*: *inf*) *adj* cochambroso.

taught [tɔ:t] *pt*, *pp of* **teach**.

taunt [tɔ:nt] *n* burla ♦ *vt* burlarse de.

Taurus ['tɔ:rəs] *n* Tauro.

taut [tɔ:t] *adj* tirante, tenso.

tax [tæks] *n* impuesto ♦ *vt* gravar (con un impuesto); (*fig*: *memory*) poner a prueba (: *patience*) agotar; **~able** *adj* (*income*) gravable; **~ation** [-'seɪʃən] *n* impuestos *mpl*; **~ avoidance** *n* evasión *f* de impuestos; **~ disc** (*BRIT*) *n* (*AUT*) pegatina del impuesto de circulación; **~ evasion** *n* evasión *f* fiscal; **~-free** *adj* libre de impuestos.

taxi ['tæksɪ] *n* taxi *m* ♦ *vi* (*AVIAT*) rodar por la pista; **~ driver** *n* taxista *m/f*; **~ rank** (*BRIT*) *n* = **~ stand**; **~ stand** *n* parada de taxis.

tax: **~ payer** *n* contribuyente *m/f*; **~ relief** *n* desgravación *f* fiscal; **~ return** *n* declaración *f* de ingresos.

TB *n abbr* = **tuberculosis**.

tea [ti:] *n* té *m*; (*BRIT*: *meal*) ≈ merienda (*SP*); cena; **high ~** (*BRIT*) merienda-cena (*SP*); **~ bag** *n* bolsita de té; **~ break** (*BRIT*) *n* descanso para el té.

teach [ti:tʃ] (*pt*, *pp* **taught**) *vt*: **to ~ sb sth**, **~ sth to sb** enseñar algo a uno ♦ *vi* (*be a teacher*) ser profesor(a), enseñar; **~er** *n* (*in secondary school*) profesor(a) *m/f*; (*in primary school*) maestro/a, profesor(a) de EGB; **~ing** *n* enseñanza.

tea cosy *n* cubretetera *m*.

teacup ['ti:kʌp] *n* taza para el té.

teak [ti:k] *n* (madera de) teca.

team [ti:m] *n* equipo; (*of horses*) tiro; **~work** *n* trabajo en equipo.

teapot ['ti:pɔt] *n* tetera.

tear[1] [tɪə*] *n* lágrima; **in ~s** llorando.

tear[2] [tɛə*] (*pt* **tore**, *pp* **torn**) *n* rasgón *m*, desgarrón *m* ♦ *vt* romper, rasgar ♦ *vi* rasgarse; **~ along** *vi* (*rush*) precipitarse; **~ up** *vt* (*sheet of paper etc*) romper.

tearful ['tɪəfəl] *adj* lloroso.

tear gas *n* gas *m* lacrimógeno.

tearoom ['ti:ru:m] *n* salón *m* de té.

tease [ti:z] *vt* tomar el pelo a.

tea: **~ set** *n* servicio de té; **~spoon** *n* cucharita; (*also*: **~spoonful**: *as measurement*) cucharadita.

teat [ti:t] *n* (*of bottle*) tetina.

teatime ['ti:taɪm] *n* hora del té.

tea towel (*BRIT*) *n* paño de cocina.

technical ['tɛknɪkl] *adj* técnico; **~ college** (*BRIT*) *n* ≈ escuela de artes y oficios (*SP*); **~ity** [-'kælɪtɪ] *n* (*point of law*) formalismo; (*detail*) detalle *m* técnico; **~ly** *adv* en teoría; (*regarding technique*) técnicamente.

technician [tɛk'nɪʃn] *n* técnico/a.

technique [tɛk'ni:k] *n* técnica.

technology [tɛk'nɒlədʒɪ] *n* tecnología.

teddy (bear) ['tɛdɪ-] *n* osito de felpa.

tedious ['ti:dɪəs] *adj* pesado, aburrido.

teem [ti:m] *vi*: **to ~ with** rebosar de; **it is ~ing (with rain)** llueve a cántaros.

teenage ['ti:neɪdʒ] *adj* (*fashions etc*) juvenil; (*children*) quinceañero; **~r** *n* quinceañero/a.

teens [ti:nz] *npl*: **to be in one's ~** ser adolescente.

tee-shirt ['ti:ʃə:t] *n* = **T-shirt**.

teeter ['ti:tə*] *vi* balancearse; (*fig*): **to ~ on the edge of ...** estar al borde de ....

teeth [ti:θ] *npl of* **tooth**.

teethe [ti:ð] *vi* echar los dientes.

teething ['ti:ðɪŋ]: **~ ring** *n* mordedor *m*; **~ troubles** *npl* (*fig*) dificultades *fpl* iniciales.

teetotal ['ti:'təutl] *adj* abstemio.

telegram ['tɛlɪgræm] *n* telegrama *m*.

telegraph ['tɛlɪgra:f] *n* telégrafo; **~ pole** *n* poste *m* telegráfico.

telepathy [tə'lɛpəθɪ] *n* telepatía.

telephone ['tɛlɪfəun] *n* teléfono ♦ *vt* llamar por teléfono, telefonear; (*message*) dar por teléfono; **to be on the ~** (*talking*) hablar por teléfono; (*possessing ~*) tener teléfono; **~ booth** *n* cabina telefónica; **~ box** (*BRIT*) *n* = **~ booth**; **~ call** *n* llamada (telefónica); **~ directory** *n* guía (telefónica); **~ number** *n* número de teléfono; **telephonist** [təˈlɛfənɪst] (*BRIT*) *n* telefonista *m/f*.

telescope [ˈtɛlɪskəup] *n* telescopio.

television [ˈtɛlɪvɪʒən] *n* televisión *f*; **on ~** en la televisión; **~ set** *n* televisor *m*.

telex [ˈtɛlɛks] *n* télex *m* ♦ *vt* enviar un télex a.

tell [tɛl] (*pt, pp* **told**) *vt* decir; (*relate: story*) contar; (*distinguish*): **to ~ sth from** distinguir algo de ♦ *vi* (*talk*): **to ~ (of)** contar; (*have effect*) tener efecto; **to ~ sb to do sth** mandar a uno hacer algo; **~ off** *vt*: **to ~ sb off** regañar a uno; **~er** *n* (*in bank*) cajero/a; **~ing** *adj* (*remark, detail*) revelador(a); **~tale** *adj* (*sign*) indicador(a).

telly [ˈtɛlɪ] (*BRIT*: *inf*) *n abbr* (= *television*) tele *f*.

temp [tɛmp] *n abbr* (*BRIT*: = *temporary*) temporero/a.

temper [ˈtɛmpə*] *n* (*nature*) carácter *m*; (*mood*) humor *m*; (*bad ~*) (mal) genio; (*fit of anger*) acceso de ira ♦ *vt* (*moderate*) moderar; **to be in a ~** estar furioso; **to lose one's ~** enfadarse, enojarse.

temperament [ˈtɛmprəmənt] *n* (*nature*) temperamento.

temperate [ˈtɛmprət] *adj* (*climate etc*) templado.

temperature [ˈtɛmprətʃə*] *n* temperatura; **to have** *or* **run a ~** tener fiebre.

tempi [ˈtɛmpɪ] *npl of* **tempo**.

temple [ˈtɛmpl] *n* (*building*) templo; (*ANAT*) sien *f*.

tempo [ˈtɛmpəu] (*pl* **tempos** *or* **tempi**) *n* (*MUS*) tempo, tiempo; (*fig*) ritmo.

temporarily [ˈtɛmpərərɪlɪ] *adv* temporalmente.

temporary [ˈtɛmpərərɪ] *adj* provisional; (*passing*) transitorio; (*worker*) temporero; (*job*) temporal.

tempt [tɛmpt] *vt* tentar; **to ~ sb into doing sth** tentar *or* inducir a uno a hacer algo; **~ation** [-ˈteɪʃən] *n* tentación *f*; **~ing** *adj* tentador(a); (*food*) apetitoso/a.

ten [tɛn] *num* diez.

tenacity [təˈnæsɪtɪ] *n* tenacidad *f*.

tenancy [ˈtɛnənsɪ] *n* arrendamiento, al-

quiler *m*.

tenant [ˈtɛnənt] *n* inquilino/a.

tend [tɛnd] *vt* cuidar ♦ *vi*: **to ~ to do sth** tener tendencia a hacer algo.

tendency [ˈtɛndənsɪ] *n* tendencia.

tender [ˈtɛndə*] *adj* (*person, care*) tierno, cariñoso; (*meat*) tierno; (*sore*) sensible ♦ *n* (*COMM*: *offer*) oferta; (*money*): **legal ~** moneda de curso legal ♦ *vt* ofrecer; **~ness** *n* ternura; (*of meat*) blandura.

tenement [ˈtɛnəmənt] *n* casa de pisos (*SP*).

tenet [ˈtɛnət] *n* principio.

tennis [ˈtɛnɪs] *n* tenis *m*; **~ ball** *n* pelota de tenis; **~ court** *n* cancha de tenis; **~ player** *n* tenista *m/f*; **~ racket** *n* raqueta de tenis.

tenor [ˈtɛnə*] *n* (*MUS*) tenor *m*.

tenpin bowling [ˈtɛnpɪn-] *n* (juego de los) bolos.

tense [tɛns] *adj* (*person*) nervioso; (*moment, atmosphere*) tenso; (*muscle*) tenso, en tensión ♦ *n* (*LING*) tiempo.

tension [ˈtɛnʃən] *n* tensión *f*.

tent [tɛnt] *n* tienda (de campaña) (*SP*), carpa (*AM*).

tentative [ˈtɛntətɪv] *adj* (*person, smile*) indeciso; (*conclusion, plans*) provisional.

tenterhooks [ˈtɛntəhuks] *npl*: **on ~** sobre ascuas.

tenth [tɛnθ] *num* décimo.

tent peg *n* clavija, estaca.

tent pole *n* mástil *m*.

tenuous [ˈtɛnjuəs] *adj* tenue.

tenure [ˈtɛnjuə*] *n* (*of land etc*) tenencia; (*of office*) ejercicio.

tepid [ˈtɛpɪd] *adj* tibio.

term [tə:m] *n* (*word*) término; (*period*) período; (*SCOL*) trimestre *m* ♦ *vt* llamar; **~s** *npl* (*conditions*, *COMM*) condiciones *fpl*; **in the short/long ~** a corto/largo plazo; **to be on good ~s with sb** llevarse bien con uno; **to come to ~s with** (*problem*) aceptar.

terminal [ˈtə:mɪnl] *adj* (*disease*) mortal; (*patient*) terminal ♦ *n* (*ELEC*) borne *m*; (*COMPUT*) terminal *m*; (*also: air ~*) terminal *f*; (*BRIT: also: coach ~*) (esta-

ción *f*) terminal *f*.
terminate ['tɜːmɪneɪt] *vt* terminar.
terminus ['tɜːmɪnəs] (*pl* **termini**) *n* término, (estación *f*) terminal *f*.
terrace ['tɛrəs] *n* terraza; (*BRIT: row of houses*) hilera de casas adosadas; the ~s (*BRIT: SPORT*) las gradas *fpl*; ~d *adj* (*garden*) en terrazas; (*house*) adosado.
terrain [tɛ'reɪn] *n* terreno.
terrible ['tɛrɪbl] *adj* terrible, horrible; (*inf*) atroz; **terribly** *adv* terriblemente; (*very badly*) malísimamente.
terrier ['tɛrɪə*] *n* terrier *m*.
terrific [tə'rɪfɪk] *adj* (*very great*) tremendo; (*wonderful*) fantástico, fenomenal.
terrify ['tɛrɪfaɪ] *vt* aterrorizar.
territory ['tɛrɪtərɪ] *n* (*also fig*) territorio.
terror ['tɛrə*] *n* terror *m*; ~**ism** *n* terrorismo; ~**ist** *n* terrorista *m/f*.
terse [tɜːs] *adj* brusco, lacónico.
test [tɛst] *n* (*gen, CHEM*) prueba; (*MED*) examen *m*; (*SCOL*) examen *m*, test *m*; (*also: driving* ~) examen *m* de conducir ♦ *vt* probar, poner a prueba; (*MED, SCOL*) examinar.
testament ['tɛstəmənt] *n* testamento; the **Old/New T~** el Antiguo/Nuevo Testamento.
testicle ['tɛstɪkl] *n* testículo.
testify ['tɛstɪfaɪ] *vi* (*LAW*) prestar declaración; **to** ~ **to** sth atestiguar algo.
testimony ['tɛstɪmənɪ] *n* (*LAW*) testimonio.
test: ~ **match** *n* (*CRICKET, RUGBY*) partido internacional; ~ **pilot** *n* piloto/mujer piloto *m/f* de pruebas; ~ **tube** *n* probeta.
tetanus ['tɛtənəs] *n* tétano.
tether ['tɛðə*] *vt* atar (con una cuerda) ♦ *n*: **to be at the end of one's** ~ no aguantar más.
text [tɛkst] *n* texto; ~**book** *n* libro de texto.
textiles ['tɛkstaɪlz] *npl* textiles *mpl*; (*textile industry*) industria textil.
texture ['tɛkstʃə*] *n* textura.
Thailand ['taɪlænd] *n* Tailandia.
Thames [tɛmz] *n*: the ~ el (río) Támesis.

than [ðæn] *conj* (*in comparisons*): **more** ~ **10/once** más de 10/una vez; **I have more/less** ~ **you/Paul** tengo más/menos que tú/Paul; **she is older** ~ **you think** es mayor de lo que piensas.
thank [θæŋk] *vt* dar las gracias a, agradecer; ~ **you (very much)** muchas gracias; ~**God!** ¡gracias a Dios!; ~**s** *npl* gracias *fpl* ♦ *excl* (*also: many* ~**s,** ~**s a lot*) ¡gracias!; ~**s to** *prep* gracias a; ~**ful** *adj*: ~**ful (for)** agradecido (por); ~**less** *adj* ingrato; **T~sgiving (Day)** *n* día *m* de Acción de Gracias.

KEYWORD

that [ðæt] (*pl* **those**) *adj* (*demonstrative*) ese/a, *pl* esos/as; (*more remote*) aquel/aquella, *pl* aquellos/as; **leave those books on the table** deja esos libros sobre la mesa; ~ **one** ése/ésa; (*more remote*) aquél/aquélla; ~ **over there** ése/ésa de ahí; aquél/aquélla de allí

♦ *pron* **1** (*demonstrative*) ése/a, *pl* ésos/as; (*neuter*) eso; (*more remote*) aquél/aquélla, *pl* aquéllos/as; (*neuter*) aquello; **what's** ~? ¿qué es eso (*or* aquello)?; **who's** ~? ¿quién es ése/a (*or* aquél/aquélla)?; **is** ~ **you?** ¿eres tú?; **will you eat all** ~? ¿vas a comer todo eso?; ~**'s my house** ésa es mi casa; ~**'s what he said** eso es lo que dijo; ~ **is (to say)** es decir

2 (*relative: subject, object*) que; (*with preposition*) (el/la) que *etc*, el/la cual *etc*; **the book** (~) **I read** el libro que leí; **the books** ~ **are in the library** los libros que están en la biblioteca; **all** (~) **I have** todo lo que tengo; **the box** (~) **I put it in** la caja en la que *or* donde lo puse; **the people** (~) **I spoke to** la gente con la que hablé

3 (*relative: of time*) que; **the day** (~) **he came** el día (en) que vino

♦ *conj* que; **he thought** ~ **I was ill** creyó que yo estaba enfermo

♦ *adv* (*demonstrative*): **I can't work** ~ **much** no puedo trabajar tanto; **I didn't realise it was** ~ **bad** no creí que fuera tan malo; ~ **high** así de alto.

thatched [θætʃt] adj (roof) de paja; (cottage) con tejado de paja.
thaw [θɔ:] n deshielo ♦ vi (ice) derretirse; (food) descongelarse ♦ vt (food) descongelar.

KEYWORD

the [δi:, δə] def art **1** (gen) el, f la, pl los, fpl las (NB = el immediately before f n beginning with stressed (h)a; a+el = al; de+el = del); ~ **boy/girl** el chico/la chica; ~ **books/flowers** los libros/las flores; **to** ~ **postman/from** ~ **drawer** al cartero/del cajón; **I haven't** ~ **time/money** no tengo tiempo/dinero
2 (+ adj to form n) los; lo; ~ **rich and** ~ **poor** los ricos y los pobres; **to attempt** ~ **impossible** intentar lo imposible
3 (in titles): **Elizabeth** ~ **First** Isabel primera; **Peter** ~ **Great** Pedro el Grande
4 (in comparisons): ~ **more he works** ~ **more he earns** cuanto más trabaja más gana.

theatre ['θɪətə*] (US **theater**) n teatro; (also: lecture ~) aula; (MED: also: operating ~) quirófano; ~-**goer** n aficionado/a al teatro.
theatrical [θɪ'ætrɪkl] adj teatral.
theft [θeft] n robo.
their [δeə*] adj su; ~**s** pron (el) suyo/(la) suya etc; see also **my**; **mine**.
them [δem, δəm] pron (direct) los/las; (indirect) les; (stressed, after prep) ellos/ellas; see also **me**.
theme [θi:m] n tema m; ~ **park** n parque de atracciones (en torno a un tema central); ~ **song** n tema m (musical).
themselves [δəm'selvz] pl pron (subject) ellos mismos/ellas mismas; (complement) se; (after prep) sí (mismos/as); see also **oneself**.
then [δen] adv (at that time) entonces; (next) después; (later) luego, después; (and also) además ♦ conj (therefore) en ese caso, entonces ♦ adj: **the** ~ **president** el entonces presidente; **by** ~ para entonces; **from** ~ **on** desde entonces.

theology [θɪ'ɔlədʒɪ] n teología.
theorem ['θɪərəm] n teorema m.
theoretical [θɪə'retɪkl] adj teórico.
theory ['θɪərɪ] n teoría.
therapist ['θerəpɪst] n terapeuta m/f.
therapy [θerəpɪ] n terapia.

KEYWORD

there [δeə*] adv **1**: ~ **is**, ~ **are** hay; ~ **is no-one here/no bread left** no hay nadie aquí/no queda pan; ~ **has been an accident** ha habido un accidente
2 (referring to place) ahí; (distant) allí; **it's** ~ está ahí; **put it in/on/up/down** ~ ponlo ahí dentro/encima/arriba/abajo; **I want that book** ~ quiero ese libro de ahí; ~ **he is!** ¡ahí está!
3: ~, ~ (esp to child) ea, ea.

there: ~**abouts** adv por ahí; ~**after** adv después; ~**by** adv así, de ese modo; ~**fore** adv por lo tanto; ~'**s** = there is; there has.
thermal ['θə:ml] adj termal; (paper) térmico.
thermometer [θə'mɔmɪtə*] n termómetro.
Thermos ['θə:məs] ® n (also: ~ flask) termo.
thermostat ['θə:məustæt] n termostato.
thesaurus [θɪ'sɔ:rəs] n tesoro.
these [δi:z] pl adj estos/as ♦ pl pron éstos/as.
theses ['θi:si:z] npl of thesis.
thesis ['θi:sɪs] (pl **theses**) n tesis f inv.
they [δeɪ] pl pron ellos/ellas; (stressed) ellos (mismos)/ellas (mismas); ~ **say that...** (it is said that) se dice que...; ~'**d** = they had; they would; ~'**ll** = they shall; they will; ~'**re** = they are; ~'**ve** = they have.
thick [θɪk] adj (in consistency) espeso; (in size) grueso; (stupid) torpe ♦ n: **in the** ~ **of the battle** en lo más reñido de la batalla; **it's 20 cm** ~ tiene 20 cm de espesor; ~**en** vi espesarse ♦ vt (sauce etc) espesar; ~**ness** n espesor m; grueso; ~**set** adj fornido; ~**skinned** adj (fig) insensible.

thief [θiːf] (pl **thieves**) n ladrón/ona m/f.
thieves [θiːvz] npl of **thief**.
thigh [θaɪ] n muslo.
thimble ['θɪmbl] n dedal m.
thin [θɪn] adj (person, animal) flaco; (in size) delgado; (in consistency) poco espeso; (hair, crowd) escaso ♦ vt: to ~ (down) diluir.
thing [θɪŋ] n cosa; (object) objeto, artículo; (matter) asunto; (mania): to have a ~ about sb/sth estar obsesionado con uno/algo; ~s npl (belongings) efectos mpl (personales); the best ~ would be to ... lo mejor sería ...; how are ~s? ¿qué tal?
think [θɪŋk] (pt, pp **thought**) vi pensar ♦ vt pensar, creer; what did you ~ of them? ¿qué te parecieron?; to ~ about sth/sb pensar en algo/uno; I'll ~ about it lo pensaré; to ~ of doing sth pensar en hacer algo; I ~ so/not creo que sí/no; to ~ well of sb tener buen concepto de uno; ~ over vt reflexionar sobre, meditar; ~ up vt (plan etc) idear; ~ tank n gabinete m de estrategia.
thinly ['θɪnlɪ] adv (cut) fino; (spread) ligeramente.
third [θəːd] adj (before n) tercer(a); (following n) tercero/a ♦ n tercero/a; (fraction) tercio; (BRIT: SCOL: degree) título de licenciado con calificación de aprobado; ~ly adv en tercer lugar; ~ party insurance (BRIT) n seguro contra terceros; ~-rate adj (de calidad) mediocre; T~ World n Tercer Mundo.
thirst [θəːst] n sed f; ~y adj (person, animal) sediento; (work) que da sed; to be ~y tener sed.
thirteen [θəː'tiːn] num trece.
thirty ['θəːtɪ] num treinta.

this [ðɪs] (pl **these**) adj (demonstrative) este/a; pl estos/as; (neuter) esto; ~ man/woman este hombre/esta mujer; these children/flowers estos chicos/estas flores; ~ one (here) éste/a, esto (de aquí)
♦ pron (demonstrative) éste/a; pl éstos/as; (neuter) esto; who is ~? ¿quién es

éste/ésta?; what is ~? ¿qué es esto?; ~ is where I live aquí vivo; ~ is what he said esto es lo que dijo; ~ is Mr Brown (in introductions) le presento al Sr. Brown; (photo) éste es el Sr. Brown; (on telephone) habla el Sr. Brown
♦ adv (demonstrative): ~ high/long etc así de alto/largo etc; ~ far hasta aquí.

thistle ['θɪsl] n cardo.
thong [θɒŋ] n correa.
thorn [θɔːn] n espina.
thorough ['θʌrə] adj (search) minucioso; (wash) a fondo; (knowledge, research) profundo; (person) meticuloso; ~bred adj (horse) de pura sangre; ~fare n calle f; "no ~fare" "prohibido el paso"; ~ly adv (search) minuciosamente; (study) profundamente; (wash) a fondo; (utterly: bad, wet etc) completamente, totalmente.
those [ðəʊz] pl adj esos/esas; (more remote) aquellos/as.
though [ðəʊ] conj aunque ♦ adv sin embargo.
thought [θɔːt] pt, pp of **think** ♦ n pensamiento; (opinion) opinión f; ~ful adj pensativo; (serious) serio; (considerate) atento; ~less adj desconsiderado.
thousand ['θaʊzənd] num mil; two ~ dos mil; ~s of miles de; ~th num milésimo.
thrash [θræʃ] vt azotar; (defeat) derrotar; ~ about or around vi debatirse; ~ out vt discutir a fondo.
thread [θred] n hilo; (of screw) rosca ♦ vt (needle) enhebrar; ~bare adj raído.
threat [θret] n amenaza; ~en vi amenazar ♦ vt: to ~en sb with/to do amenazar a uno con/con hacer.
three [θriː] num tres; ~-dimensional adj tridimensional; ~-piece suit n traje m de tres piezas; ~-piece suite n tresillo; ~-ply adj (wool) de tres cabos.
thresh [θreʃ] vt (AGR) trillar.
threshold ['θreʃhəʊld] n umbral m.
threw [θruː] pt of **throw**.
thrifty ['θrɪftɪ] adj económico.
thrill [θrɪl] n (excitement) emoción f; (shudder) estremecimiento ♦ vt emocio-

nar; **to be ~ed** (*with gift etc*) estar encantado; **~er** *n* novela (*or* obra *or* película) de suspense; **~ing** *adj* emocionante.

thrive [θraɪv] (*pt* **thrived** *or* **throve**, *pp*
thrived *or* **thriven**) *vi* (*grow*) crecer;
(*do well*): **to ~ on sth** sentarle muy
bien a uno algo; **thriven** ['θrɪvn] *pp of*
thrive; **thriving** *adj* próspero.

throat [θrəut] *n* garganta; **to have a
sore ~** tener dolor de garganta.

throb [θrɔb] *n* (*of heart*) latido; (*of
wound*) punzada; (*of engine*) vibración
f ♦ *vi* latir; dar punzadas; vibrar.

throes [θrəuz] *npl*: **in the ~ of** en medio
de.

throne [θrəun] *n* trono.

throng [θrɔŋ] *n* multitud *f*, muchedumbre *f* ♦ *vt* agolparse en.

throttle ['θrɔtl] *n* (*AUT*) acelerador *m* ♦
vt estrangular.

through [θru:] *prep* por, a través de;
(*time*) durante; (*by means of*) por medio de, mediante; (*owing to*) gracias a
♦ *adj* (*ticket, train*) directo ♦ *adv* completamente, de parte a parte; de principio a fin; **to put sb ~ to sb** (*TEL*) poner
or pasar a uno con uno; **to be ~** (*TEL*)
tener comunicación; (*have finished*) haber terminado; **"no ~ road"** (*BRIT*)
"calle sin salida"; **~out** *prep* (*place*)
por todas partes de, por todo; (*time*)
durante todo ♦ *adv* por *or* en todas partes.

throve [θrəuv] *pt of* thrive.

throw [θrəu] (*pt* **threw**, *pp* **thrown**) *n*
tiro; (*SPORT*) lanzamiento ♦ *vt* tirar,
echar; (*SPORT*) lanzar; (*rider*) derribar; (*fig*) desconcertar; **to ~ a party**
dar una fiesta; **~ away** *vt* tirar; (*money*) derrochar; **~ off** *vt* deshacerse de;
~ out *vt* tirar; (*person*) echar; expulsar; **~ up** *vi* vomitar; **~away** *adj* para
tirar, desechable; (*remark*) hecho de
paso; **~-in** *n* (*SPORT*) saque *m*.

thru [θru:] (*US*) = **through**.

thrush [θrʌʃ] *n* zorzal *m*, tordo.

thrust [θrʌst] (*pt, pp* **thrust**) *n* (*TECH*)
empuje *m* ♦ *vt* empujar (con fuerza).

thud [θʌd] *n* golpe *m* sordo.

thug [θʌg] *n* gamberro/a.

thumb [θʌm] *n* (*ANAT*) pulgar *m*; **to ~ a
lift** hacer autostop; **~ through** *vt fus*
(*book*) hojear; **~tack** (*US*) *n* chincheta
(*SP*).

thump [θʌmp] *n* golpe *m*; (*sound*) ruido
seco *or* sordo ♦ *vt* golpear ♦ *vi* (*heart
etc*) palpitar.

thunder ['θʌndə*] *n* trueno ♦ *vi* tronar;
(*train etc*): **to ~ past** pasar como un
trueno; **~bolt** *n* rayo; **~clap** *n* trueno;
~storm *n* tormenta; **~y** *adj* tormentoso.

Thursday ['θə:zdɪ] *n* jueves *m inv*.

thus [ðʌs] *adv* así, de este modo.

thwart [θwɔ:t] *vt* frustrar.

thyme [taɪm] *n* tomillo.

thyroid ['θaɪrɔɪd] *n* (*also*: **~ gland**) tiroi-
des *m inv*.

tic [tɪk] *n* tic *m*.

tick [tɪk] *n* (*sound*: *of clock*) tictac *m*;
(*mark*) palomita; (*ZOOL*) garrapata;
(*BRIT*: *inf*): **in a ~** en un instante ♦ *vi*
hacer tictac ♦ *vt* marcar; **~ off** *vt* marcar; (*person*) reñir; **~ over** *vi* (*engine*)
girar en marcha lenta; (*fig*) ir tirando.

ticket ['tɪkɪt] *n* billete *m* (*SP*), tíquet *m*,
boleto (*AM*); (*for cinema etc*) entrada
(*SP*), boleto (*AM*); (*in shop*: *on goods*)
etiqueta; (*for raffle*) papeleta; (*for library*) tarjeta; (*parking ~*) multa por
estacionamiento ilegal; **~ collector** *n*
revisor(a) *m/f*; **~ office** *n* (*THEATRE*)
taquilla (*SP*), boletería (*AM*); (*RAIL*)
despacho de billetes (*SP*) *or* boletos
(*AM*).

tickle ['tɪkl] *vt* hacer cosquillas a ♦ *vi*
hacer cosquillas; **ticklish** *adj* (*person*)
cosquilloso; (*problem*) delicado.

tidal ['taɪdl] *adj* de marea; **~ wave** *n*
maremoto.

tidbit ['tɪdbɪt] (*US*) *n* = **titbit**.

tiddlywinks ['tɪdlɪwɪŋks] *n* juego infantil
con fichas de plástico.

tide [taɪd] *n* marea; (*fig*: *of events etc*)
curso, marcha; **~ over** *vt* (*help out*)
ayudar a salir del apuro.

tidy ['taɪdɪ] *adj* (*room etc*) ordenado;
(*dress, work*) limpio; (*person*) (bien)
arreglado ♦ *vt* (*also*: **~ up**) poner en

orden.

tie [taɪ] n (string etc) atadura; (BRIT: also: neck~) corbata; (fig: link) vínculo, lazo; (SPORT etc: draw) empate m ♦ vt atar ♦ vi (SPORT etc) empatar; **to ~ in a bow** atar con un lazo; **to ~ a knot in sth** hacer un nudo en algo; **~ down** vt (fig: person: restrict) atar; (: to price, date etc) obligar a; **~ up** vt (parcel) envolver; (dog, person) atar; (arrangements) concluir; **to be ~d up** (busy) estar ocupado.

tier [tɪə*] n grada; (of cake) piso.

tiger ['taɪgə*] n tigre m.

tight [taɪt] adj (rope) tirante; (money) escaso; (clothes) ajustado; (bend) cerrado; (shoes, schedule) apretado; (budget) ajustado; (security) estricto; (inf: drunk) borracho ♦ adv (squeeze) muy fuerte; (shut) bien; **~s** (BRIT) npl panti mpl; **~en** vt (rope) estirar; (screw, grip) apretar; (security) reforzar ♦ vi estirarse; apretarse; **~-fisted** adj tacaño; **~ly** adv (grasp) muy fuerte; **~rope** n cuerda floja.

tile [taɪl] n (on roof) teja; (on floor) baldosa; (on wall) azulejo; **~d** adj de tejas; embaldosado; (wall) alicatado.

till [tɪl] n caja (registradora) ♦ vt (land) cultivar ♦ prep, conj = **until**.

tilt [tɪlt] vt inclinar ♦ vi inclinarse.

timber ['tɪmbə*] n (material) madera; (trees) árboles mpl.

time [taɪm] n tiempo; (epoch: often pl) época; (by clock) hora; (moment) momento; (occasion) vez f; (MUS) compás m ♦ vt calcular or medir el tiempo de; (race) cronometrar; (remark, visit etc) elegir el momento para; **a long ~** mucho tiempo; **4 at a ~** de 4 en 4; **4 a la vez**; **for the ~ being** de momento, por ahora; **from ~ to ~** de vez en cuando; **at ~s** a veces; **in ~** (soon enough) a tiempo; (after some time) con el tiempo; (MUS) al compás; **in a week's ~** dentro de una semana; **in no ~** en un abrir y cerrar de ojos; **any ~** cuando sea; **on ~** a la hora; **5 ~s 5** 5 por 5; **what ~ is it?** ¿qué hora es?; **to have a good ~** pasarlo bien, divertirse; **~**

bomb n bomba de efecto retardado; **~ lag** n desfase m; **~less** adj eterno; **~ limit** n plazo; **~ly** adj oportuno; **~ off** n tiempo libre; **~r** n (in kitchen etc) programador m horario; **~ scale** (BRIT) n escala de tiempo; **~ share** n apartamento (or casa) a tiempo compartido; **~ switch** (BRIT) n interruptor m (horario); **~table** n horario; **~ zone** n huso horario.

timid ['tɪmɪd] adj tímido.

timing ['taɪmɪŋ] n (SPORT) cronometraje m; **the ~ of his resignation** el momento que eligió para dimitir.

timpani ['tɪmpənɪ] npl tímpanos mpl.

tin [tɪn] n estaño; (also: ~ plate) hojalata; (BRIT: can) lata; **~foil** n papel m de estaño.

tinge [tɪndʒ] n matiz m ♦ vt: **~d with** teñido de.

tingle ['tɪŋgl] vi (person): **to ~ (with)** estremecerse (de); (hands etc) hormiguear.

tinker ['tɪŋkə*]: **~ with** vt fus jugar con, tocar.

tinned [tɪnd] (BRIT) adj (food) en lata, en conserva.

tin opener [-əʊpnə*] (BRIT) n abrelatas m inv.

tinsel ['tɪnsl] n (guirnalda de) espumillón m.

tint [tɪnt] n matiz m; (for hair) tinte m; **~ed** adj (hair) teñido; (glass, spectacles) ahumado.

tiny ['taɪnɪ] adj minúsculo, pequeñito.

tip [tɪp] n (end) punta; (gratuity) propina; (BRIT: for rubbish) vertedero; (advice) consejo ♦ vt (waiter) dar una propina a; (tilt) inclinar; (empty: also: ~ out) vaciar, echar; (overturn: also: ~ over) volcar; **~-off** n (hint) advertencia; **~ped** (BRIT) adj (cigarette) con filtro.

Tipp-Ex ['tɪpɛks] ® n Tipp-Ex ® m.

tipsy ['tɪpsɪ] (inf) adj alegre, mareado.

tiptoe ['tɪptəʊ] n: **on ~** de puntillas.

tiptop ['tɪp'tɒp] adj: **in ~ condition** en perfectas condiciones.

tire ['taɪə*] n (US) = **tyre** ♦ vt cansar ♦ vi (gen) cansarse; (become bored) aburrirse; ~d adj cansado; to be ~d of sth estar harto de algo; ~less adj incansable; ~some adj aburrido; tiring adj cansado.

tissue ['tɪʃuː] n tejido; (paper handkerchief) pañuelo de papel, kleenex ® m; ~ paper n papel m de seda.

tit [tɪt] n (bird) herrerillo común; to give ~ for tat dar ojo por ojo.

titbit ['tɪtbɪt] (US tidbit) n (food) golosina; (news) noticia sabrosa.

titillate ['tɪtɪleɪt] vt estimular, excitar.

title ['taɪtl] n título; ~ deed n (LAW) título de propiedad; ~ role n papel m principal.

titter ['tɪtə*] vi reírse entre dientes.

TM abbr = trademark.

KEYWORD

to [tuː, tə] prep 1 (direction) a; to go ~ France/London/school/the station ir a Francia/Londres/al colegio/a la estación; to go ~ Claude's/the doctor's ir a casa de Claude/al médico; the road ~ Edinburgh la carretera de Edimburgo

2 (as far as) hasta, a; from here ~ London de aquí a or hasta Londres; to count ~ 10 contar hasta 10; from 40 ~ 50 people entre 40 y 50 personas

3 (with expressions of time): a quarter/twenty ~ 5 las 5 menos cuarto/veinte

4 (for, of): the key ~ the front door la llave de la puerta principal; she is secretary ~ the director es la secretaria del director; a letter ~ his wife una carta a or para su mujer

5 (expressing indirect object) a; to give sth ~ sb darle algo a alguien; to talk ~ sb hablar con alguien; to be a danger ~ sb ser un peligro para alguien; to carry out repairs ~ sth hacer reparaciones en algo

6 (in relation to): 3 goals ~ 2 3 goles a 2; 30 miles ~ the gallon ≈ 9,4 litros a los cien (kms)

7 (purpose, result): to come ~ sb's aid venir en auxilio or ayuda de alguien; to sentence sb ~ death condenar a uno a muerte; ~ my great surprise con gran

sorpresa mía

♦ with vb 1 (simple infin): ~ go/eat ir/comer

2 (following another vb): to want/try/start ~ do querer/intentar/empezar a hacer; see also relevant vb

3 (with vb omitted): I don't want ~ no quiero

4 (purpose, result) para; I did it ~ help you lo hice para ayudarte; he came ~ see you vino a verte

5 (equivalent to relative clause): I have things ~ do tengo cosas que hacer; the main thing is ~ try lo principal es intentarlo

6 (after adj etc): ready ~ go listo para irse; too old ~ ... demasiado viejo (como) para ...

♦ adv: pull/push the door ~ tirar de/empujar la puerta

---

toad [təud] n sapo; ~stool n hongo venenoso.

toast [təust] n (CULIN) tostada; (drink, speech) brindis m ♦ vt (CULIN) tostar; (drink to) brindar por; ~er n tostador m.

tobacco [tə'bækəu] n tabaco; ~nist n estanquero/a (SP), tabaquero/a (AM); ~nist's (shop) (BRIT) n estanco (SP), tabaquería (AM).

toboggan [tə'bɔgən] n tobogán m.

today [tə'deɪ] adv, n (also fig) hoy m.

toddler ['tɔdlə*] n niño/a (que empieza a andar).

to-do n (fuss) lío.

toe [təu] n dedo (del pie); (of shoe) punta; to ~ the line (fig) conformarse; ~nail n uña del pie.

toffee ['tɔfɪ] n toffee m; ~ apple (BRIT) n manzana acaramelada.

together [tə'gɛðə*] adv juntos; (at same time) al mismo tiempo, a la vez; ~ with junto con.

toil [tɔɪl] n trabajo duro, labor f ♦ vi trabajar duramente.

toilet ['tɔɪlət] n retrete m; (BRIT: room) servicios mpl (SP), wáter m (SP), sanitario (AM) ♦ cpd (soap etc) de aseo; ~ paper n papel m higiénico; ~ries npl artículos *mpl* de tocador; ~ **roll** *n* rollo de papel higiénico; ~ **water** *n* (agua de) colonia.

token ['təukən] *n* (*sign*) señal *f*, muestra; (*souvenir*) recuerdo; (*disc*) ficha ♦ *adj* (*strike, payment etc*) simbólico; **book/record/gift** ~ (*BRIT*) vale *m* para comprar libros/discos/vale-regalo.

Tokyo ['təukjəu] *n* Tokio, Tokío.

told [təuld] *pt, pp* of **tell**.

tolerable ['tɔlərəbl] *adj* (*bearable*) soportable; (*fairly good*) pasable.

tolerance ['tɔlərns] *n* (*also: TECH*) tolerancia.

tolerant ['tɔlərnt] *adj*: ~ **of** tolerante con.

tolerate ['tɔləreɪt] *vt* tolerar.

toll [təul] *n* (*of casualties*) número de víctimas; (*tax, charge*) peaje *m* ♦ *vi* (*bell*) doblar.

tomato [tə'mɑːtəu] (*pl* ~**es**) *n* tomate *m*.

tomb [tuːm] *n* tumba.

tomboy ['tɔmbɔɪ] *n* marimacho.

tombstone ['tuːmstəun] *n* lápida.

tomcat ['tɔmkæt] *n* gato (macho).

tomorrow [tə'mɔrəu] *adv, n* (*also: fig*) mañana; **the day after** ~ pasado mañana; ~ **morning** mañana por la mañana.

ton [tʌn] *n* tonelada (*BRIT = 1016 kg; US = 907 kg*); (*metric* ~) tonelada métrica; ~**s of** (*inf*) montones de.

tone [təun] *n* tono ♦ *vi* (*also:* ~ **in**) armonizar; ~ **down** *vt* (*criticism*) suavizar; (*colour*) atenuar; ~ **up** *vt* (*muscles*) tonificar; ~**-deaf** *adj* con mal oído.

tongs [tɔŋz] *npl* (*for coal*) tenazas *fpl*; (*curling* ~) tenacillas *fpl*.

tongue [tʌŋ] *n* lengua; ~ **in cheek** irónicamente; ~**-tied** *adj* (*fig*) mudo; ~**twister** *n* trabalenguas *m inv*.

tonic ['tɔnɪk] *n* (*MED, also fig*) tónico; (*also:* ~ *water*) (agua) tónica.

tonight [tə'naɪt] *adv, n* esta noche; esta tarde.

tonnage ['tʌnɪdʒ] *n* (*NAUT*) tonelaje *m*.

tonsil ['tɔnsl] *n* amígdala; ~**litis** [-'laɪtɪs] *n* amigdalitis *f*.

too [tuː] *adv* (*excessively*) demasiado;

(*also*) también; ~ **much** demasiado; ~ **many** demasiados/as.

took [tuk] *pt* of **take**.

tool [tuːl] *n* herramienta; ~ **box** *n* caja de herramientas.

toot [tuːt] *n* pitido ♦ *vi* tocar el pito.

tooth [tuːθ] (*pl* **teeth**) *n* (*ANAT, TECH*) diente *m*; (*molar*) muela; ~**ache** *n* dolor *m* de muelas; ~**brush** *n* cepillo de dientes; ~**paste** *n* pasta de dientes; ~**pick** *n* palillo.

top [tɔp] *n* (*of mountain*) cumbre *f*, cima; (*of tree*) copa; (*of head*) coronilla; (*of ladder, page*) lo alto; (*of table*) superficie *f*; (*of cupboard*) parte *f* de arriba; (*lid: of box*) tapa; (: *of bottle, jar*) tapón *m*; (*of list etc*) cabeza; (*toy*) peonza; (*garment*) blusa; camiseta ♦ *adj* de arriba; (*in rank*) principal, primero; (*best*) mejor ♦ *vt* (*exceed*) exceder; (*be first in*) encabezar; **on** ~ **of** (*above*) sobre, encima de; (*in addition to*) además de; **from** ~ **to bottom** de pies a cabeza; ~ **off** (*US*) *vt* = ~ **up**; ~ **up** *vt* llenar; ~ **floor** *n* último piso; ~ **hat** *n* sombrero de copa; ~**-heavy** *adj* (*object*) mal equilibrado.

topic ['tɔpɪk] *n* tema *m*; ~**al** *adj* actual.

top: ~**less** *adj* (*bather, bikini*) topless *inv*; ~**-level** *adj* (*talks*) al más alto nivel; ~**most** *adj* más alto.

topple ['tɔpl] *vt* derribar ♦ *vi* caerse.

top-secret *adj* de alto secreto.

topsy-turvy ['tɔpsɪ'təːvɪ] *adj* al revés ♦ *adv* patas arriba.

torch [tɔːtʃ] *n* antorcha; (*BRIT: electric*) linterna.

tore [tɔː*] *pt* of **tear**.

torment [*n* 'tɔːment, *vt* tɔː'ment] *n* tormento ♦ *vt* atormentar; (*fig: annoy*) fastidiar.

torn [tɔːn] *pp* of **tear**.

torrent ['tɔrnt] *n* torrente *m*.

torrid ['tɔrɪd] *adj* (*fig*) apasionado.

tortoise ['tɔːtəs] *n* tortuga; ~**shell** ['tɔːtəʃel] *adj* de carey.

torture ['tɔːtʃə*] *n* tortura ♦ *vt* torturar; (*fig*) atormentar.

Tory ['tɔːrɪ] (*BRIT*) *adj, n* (*POL*) conservador(a) *m/f*.

toss [tɔs] *vt* tirar, echar; (*one's head*) sacudir; **to ~ a coin** echar a cara o cruz; **to ~ up for sth** jugar a cara o cruz algo; **to ~ and turn** (*in bed*) dar vueltas.

tot [tɔt] *n* (*BRIT: drink*) copita; (*child*) nene/a *m/f*.

total ['təutl] *adj* total, entero; (*emphatic: failure etc*) completo, total ♦ *n* total *m*, suma ♦ *vt* (*add up*) sumar; (*amount to*) ascender a.

totalitarian [təutælɪ'tɛərɪən] *adj* totalitario.

totally ['təutəlɪ] *adv* totalmente.

totter ['tɔtə*] *vi* tambalearse.

touch [tʌtʃ] *n* tacto; (*contact*) contacto ♦ *vt* tocar; (*emotionally*) conmover; **a ~ of** (*fig*) un poquito de; **to get in ~ with sb** ponerse en contacto con uno; **to lose ~** (*friends*) perder contacto; **~ on** *vt fus* (*topic*) aludir (brevemente) a; **~ up** *vt* (*paint*) retocar; **~-and-go** *adj* arriesgado; **~down** *n* aterrizaje *m*; (*on sea*) amerizaje *m*; (*US: FOOTBALL*) ensayo; **~ed** *adj* (*moved*) conmovido; **~ing** *adj* (*moving*) conmovedor(a); **~line** *n* (*SPORT*) línea de banda; **~y** *adj* (*person*) quisquilloso.

tough [tʌf] *adj* (*material*) resistente; (*meat*) duro; (*problem etc*) difícil; (*policy, stance*) inflexible; (*person*) fuerte; **~en** *vt* endurecer.

toupée ['tuːpeɪ] *n* peluca.

tour [tuə*] *n* viaje *m*, vuelta; (*also: package ~*) viaje *m* todo comprendido; (*of town, museum*) visita; (*by band etc*) gira ♦ *vt* recorrer, visitar.

tourism ['tuərɪzm] *n* turismo.

tourist ['tuərɪst] *n* turista *m/f* ♦ *cpd* turístico; **~ office** *n* oficina de turismo.

tournament ['tuənəmənt] *n* torneo.

tousled ['tauzld] *adj* (*hair*) despeinado.

tout [taut] *vi*: **to ~ for business** solicitar clientes ♦ *n* (*also: ticket ~*) revendedor(a) *m/f*.

tow [təu] *vt* remolcar; "**on** *or* **in** (*US*) **~**" (*AUT*) "a remolque".

toward(s) [tə'wɔːd(z)] *prep* hacia; (*attitude*) respecto a, con; (*purpose*) para.

towel ['tauəl] *n* toalla; **~ling** *n* (*fabric*) felpa; **~ rail** (*US ~* **rack**) *n* toallero.

tower ['tauə*] *n* torre *f*; **~ block** (*BRIT*) *n* torre *f* (de pisos); **~ing** *adj* muy alto, imponente.

town [taun] *n* ciudad *f*; **to go to ~** ir a la ciudad; (*fig*) echar la casa por la ventana; **~ centre** *n* centro de la ciudad; **~ council** *n* ayuntamiento, consejo municipal; **~ hall** *n* ayuntamiento; **~ plan** *n* plano de la ciudad; **~ planning** *n* urbanismo.

towrope ['təurəup] *n* cable *m* de remolque.

tow truck *n* camión *m* grúa.

toy [tɔɪ] *n* juguete *m*; **~ with** *vt fus* jugar con; (*idea*) acariciar; **~shop** *n* juguetería.

trace [treɪs] *n* rastro ♦ *vt* (*draw*) trazar, delinear; (*locate*) encontrar; (*follow*) seguir la pista de; **tracing paper** *n* papel *m* de calco.

track [træk] *n* (*mark*) huella, pista; (*path: gen*) camino, senda; (: *of bullet etc*) trayectoria; (: *of suspect, animal*) pista, rastro; (*RAIL*) vía; (*SPORT*) pista; (*on tape, record*) canción *f* ♦ *vt* seguir la pista de; **to keep ~ of** mantenerse al tanto de, seguir; **~ down** *vt* (*prey*) seguir el rastro de; (*sth lost*) encontrar; **~suit** *n* chandal *m*.

tract [trækt] *n* (*GEO*) región *f*; (*pamphlet*) folleto.

traction ['trækʃən] *n* (*power*) tracción *f*; **in ~** (*MED*) en tracción.

tractor ['træktə*] *n* tractor *m*.

trade [treɪd] *n* comercio; (*skill, job*) oficio ♦ *vi* negociar, comerciar ♦ *vt* (*exchange*): **to ~ sth** (**for sth**) cambiar algo (por algo); **~ in** *vt* (*old car etc*) ofrecer como parte del pago; **~ fair** *n* feria comercial; **~mark** *n* marca de fábrica; **~ name** *n* marca registrada; **~r** *n* comerciante *m/f*; **~sman** *n* (*shopkeeper*) tendero; **~ union** *n* sindicato; **~ unionist** *n* sindicalista *m/f*.

tradition [trə'dɪʃən] *n* tradición *f*; **~al** *adj* tradicional.

traffic ['træfɪk] *n* (*gen, AUT*) tráfico, circulación *f*, tránsito (*AM*) ♦ *vi*: **to ~ in** (*pej: liquor, drugs*) traficar en; **~ cir-**

cle (*US*) *n* isleta; ~ **jam** *n* embotellamiento; ~ **lights** *npl* semáforo; ~ **warden** *n* guardia *m/f* de tráfico.

tragedy ['trædʒədɪ] *n* tragedia.

tragic ['trædʒɪk] *adj* trágico.

trail [treɪl] *n* (*tracks*) rastro, pista; (*path*) camino, sendero; (*dust, smoke*) estela ♦ *vt* (*drag*) arrastrar; (*follow*) seguir la pista de ♦ *vi* arrastrar; (*in contest etc*) ir perdiendo; ~ **behind** *vi* quedar a la zaga; ~**er** *n* (*AUT*) remolque *m*; (*caravan*) caravana; (*CINEMA*) trailer *m*, avance *m*; ~**er truck** (*US*) *n* trailer *m*.

train [treɪn] *n* tren *m*; (*of dress*) cola; (*series*) serie *f* ♦ *vt* (*educate, teach skills to*) formar; (*sportsman*) entrenar; (*dog*) adiestrar; (*point: gun etc*): **to** ~ **on** apuntar a ♦ *vi* (*SPORT*) entrenarse; (*learn a skill*): **to** ~ **as a teacher** *etc* estudiar para profesor *etc*; **one's** ~ **of thought** el razonamiento de uno; ~**ed** *adj* (*worker*) cualificado; (*animal*) amaestrado; ~**ee** [treɪ'niː] *n* aprendiz(a) *m/f*; (*dog*) ~**er** *n* (*SPORT: coach*) entrenador(a) *m/f*; (*: shoe*): ~**ers** zapatillas *fpl* (de deporte); (*of animals*) domador(a) *m/f*; ~**ing** *n* formación *f*; entrenamiento; **to be in** ~**ing** (*SPORT*) estar entrenando; ~**ing college** *n* (*gen*) colegio de formación profesional; (*for teachers*) escuela de formación del profesorado; ~**ing shoes** *npl* zapatillas *fpl* (de deporte).

traipse [treɪps] *vi* andar penosamente.

trait [treɪt] *n* rasgo.

traitor ['treɪtə*] *n* traidor(a) *m/f*.

tram [træm] (*BRIT*) *n* (*also:* ~**car**) tranvía *m*.

tramp [træmp] *n* (*person*) vagabundo/a; (*inf: pej: woman*) puta ♦ *vi* andar con pasos pesados.

trample ['træmpl] *vt*: **to** ~ (**underfoot**) pisotear.

trampoline ['træmpəliːn] *n* trampolín *m*.

tranquil ['træŋkwɪl] *adj* tranquilo; ~**lizer** *n* (*MED*) tranquilizante *m*.

transact [træn'zækt] *vt* (*business*) despachar; ~**ion** [-'zækʃən] *n* transacción *f*, operación *f*.

transcend [træn'sɛnd] *vt* rebasar.

transcript ['trænskrɪpt] *n* copia.

transfer [*n* 'trænsfə:*, *vb* træns'fə:*] *n* (*of employees*) traslado; (*of money, power*) transferencia; (*SPORT*) traspaso; (*picture, design*) calcomanía ♦ *vt* trasladar; transferir; **to** ~ **the charges** (*BRIT: TEL*) llamar a cobro revertido.

transform [træns'fɔːm] *vt* transformar.

transfusion [træns'fjuːʒən] *n* transfusión *f*.

transient ['trænzɪənt] *adj* transitorio.

transistor [træn'zɪstə*] *n* (*ELEC*) transistor *m*; ~ **radio** *n* transistor *m*.

transit ['trænzɪt] *n*: **in** ~ en tránsito.

transitional [træn'zɪʃənl] *adj* de transición.

transitive ['trænzɪtɪv] *adj* (*LING*) transitivo.

transit lounge *n* sala de tránsito.

translate [trænz'leɪt] *vt* traducir; **translation** [-'leɪʃən] *n* traducción *f*; **translator** *n* traductor(a) *m/f*.

transmit [trænz'mɪt] *vt* transmitir; ~**ter** *n* transmisor *m*.

transparency [træns'pɛərnsɪ] *n* transparencia; (*BRIT: PHOT*) diapositiva.

transparent [træns'pærnt] *adj* transparente.

transpire [træns'paɪə*] *vi* (*turn out*) resultar; (*happen*) ocurrir, suceder; **it** ~**d that ...** se supo que ....

transplant ['trænsplɑːnt] *n* (*MED*) transplante *m*.

transport [*n* 'trænspɔːt, *vt* træns'pɔːt] *n* transporte *m*; (*car*) coche (*SP*), carro (*AM*), automóvil *m* ♦ *vt* transportar; ~**ation** [-'teɪʃən] *n* transporte *m*; ~ **café** (*BRIT*) *n* bar-restaurant *m* de carretera.

transvestite [trænz'vɛstaɪt] *n* travestí *m/f*.

trap [træp] *n* (*snare, trick*) trampa; (*carriage*) cabriolé *m* ♦ *vt* coger (*SP*) or agarrar (*AM*) en una trampa; (*trick*) engañar; (*confine*) atrapar; ~ **door** *n* escotilla.

trapeze [trə'piːz] *n* trapecio.

trappings ['træpɪŋz] *npl* adornos *mpl*.

trash [træʃ] *n* (*rubbish*) basura; (*pej*): **the book/film is** ~ el libro/la película no

vale nada; (*nonsense*) tonterías *fpl*; ~
can (*US*) *n* cubo (*SP*) *or* balde *m* (*AM*)
de la basura.

travel ['trævl] *n* el viajar ♦ *vi* viajar ♦ *vt*
(*distance*) recorrer; ~s *npl* (*journeys*)
viajes *mpl*; ~ **agent** *n* agente *m/f* de
viajes; ~**ler** (*US* ~**er**) *n* viajero/a;
~**ler's cheque** (*US* ~**er's check**) *n* cheque *m* de viajero; ~**ling** (*US* ~**ing**) *n* los
viajes, el viajar; ~ **sickness** *n* mareo.

travesty ['trævəsti] *n* parodia.

trawler ['trɔːlə*] *n* pesquero de arrastre.

tray [treɪ] *n* bandeja; (*on desk*) cajón
m.

treacherous ['tretʃərəs] *adj* traidor,
traicionero; (*dangerous*) peligroso.

treacle ['triːkl] (*BRIT*) *n* melaza.

tread [tred] (*pt* **trod**, *pp* **trodden**) *n*
(*step*) paso, pisada; (*sound*) ruido de
pasos; (*of stair*) escalón *m*; (*of tyre*)
banda de rodadura ♦ *vi* pisar; ~ **on** *vt*
fus pisar.

treason ['triːzn] *n* traición *f*.

treasure ['treʒə*] *n* (*also fig*) tesoro ♦ *vt*
(*value: object, friendship*) apreciar;
(: *memory*) guardar.

treasurer ['treʒərə*] *n* tesorero/a.

treasury ['treʒərɪ] *n*: **the T~** el Ministerio de Hacienda.

treat [triːt] *n* (*present*) regalo ♦ *vt* tratar; **to ~ sb to sth** invitar a uno a algo.

treatment ['triːtmənt] *n* tratamiento.

treaty ['triːtɪ] *n* tratado.

treble ['trebl] *adj* triple ♦ *vt* triplicar ♦
vi triplicarse; ~ **clef** *n* (*MUS*) clave *f* de
sol.

tree [triː] *n* árbol *m*; ~ **trunk** tronco (de
árbol).

trek [trek] *n* (*long journey*) viaje *m* largo y difícil; (*tiring walk*) caminata.

trellis ['trelɪs] *n* enrejado.

tremble ['trembl] *vi* temblar.

tremendous [trɪ'mendəs] *adj* tremendo,
enorme; (*excellent*) estupendo.

tremor ['tremə*] *n* temblor *m*; (*also*:
earth ~) temblor *m* de tierra.

trench [trentʃ] *n* zanja.

trend [trend] *n* (*tendency*) tendencia;
(*of events*) curso; (*fashion*) moda; ~**y**
adj de moda.

trepidation [trepɪ'deɪʃən] *n* inquietud *f*.

trespass ['trespəs] *vi*: **to ~ on** entrar sin
permiso en; "**no ~ing**" "prohibido el
paso".

trestle ['tresl] *n* caballete *m*.

trial ['traɪəl] *n* (*LAW*) juicio, proceso;
(*test: of machine etc*) prueba; ~**s** *npl*
(*hardships*) dificultades *fpl*; **by ~ and
error** a fuerza de probar.

triangle ['traɪæŋgl] *n* (*MATH, MUS*) triángulo.

tribe [traɪb] *n* tribu *f*.

tribulations [trɪbju'leɪʃənz] *npl* dificultades *fpl*, sufrimientos.

tribunal [traɪ'bjuːnl] *n* tribunal *m*.

tributary ['trɪbjuːtərɪ] *n* (*river*) afluente
m.

tribute ['trɪbjuːt] *n* homenaje *m*, tributo;
to pay ~ to rendir homenaje a.

trice [traɪs] *n*: **in a ~** en un santiamén.

trick [trɪk] *n* (*skill, knack*) tino, truco;
(*conjuring ~*) truco; (*joke*) broma;
(*CARDS*) baza ♦ *vt* engañar; **to play a ~
on sb** gastar una broma a uno; **that
should do the ~** a ver si funciona así;
~**ery** *n* engaño.

trickle ['trɪkl] *n* (*of water etc*) goteo ♦ *vi*
gotear.

tricky ['trɪkɪ] *adj* difícil; delicado.

tricycle ['traɪsɪkl] *n* triciclo.

trifle ['traɪfl] *n* bagatela; (*CULIN*) dulce
de bizcocho borracho, gelatina, fruta y
natillas ♦ *adv*: **a ~ long** un poquito largo; **trifling** *adj* insignificante.

trigger ['trɪgə*] *n* (*of gun*) gatillo; ~ **off**
vt desencadenar.

trill [trɪl] *vi* trinar, gorjear.

trim [trɪm] *adj* (*house, garden*) en buen
estado; (*person, figure*) esbelto ♦ *n*
(*haircut etc*) recorte *m*; (*on car*) guarnición *f* ♦ *vt* (*neaten*) arreglar; (*cut*)
recortar; (*decorate*) adornar; (*NAUT: a
sail*) orientar; ~**mings** *npl* (*CULIN*)
guarnición *f*.

trinket ['trɪŋkɪt] *n* chuchería.

trip [trɪp] *n* viaje *m*; (*excursion*) excursión *f*; (*stumble*) traspié *m* ♦ *vi* (*stumble*) tropezar; (*go lightly*) andar a paso
ligero; **on a ~** de viaje; ~ **up** *vi* tropezar, caerse ♦ *vt* hacer tropezar *or* caer.

tripe [traɪp] n (CULIN) callos mpl; (pej: rubbish) tonterías fpl.

triple ['trɪpl] adj triple.

triplets ['trɪplɪts] npl trillizos/as mpl/fpl.

triplicate ['trɪplɪkət] n: **in ~** por triplicado.

trite [traɪt] adj trillado.

triumph ['traɪʌmf] n triunfo ♦ vi: **to ~ (over)** vencer; **~ant** [traɪˈʌmfənt] adj (team etc) vencedor(a); (wave, return) triunfal.

trivia ['trɪvɪə] npl trivialidades fpl.

trivial ['trɪvɪəl] adj insignificante; (commonplace) banal.

trod [trɒd] pt of **tread**.

trodden ['trɒdn] pp of **tread**.

trolley ['trɒlɪ] n carrito; (also: ~ **bus**) trolebús m.

trombone [trɒmˈbəʊn] n trombón m.

troop [truːp] n grupo, banda; **~s** npl (MIL) tropas fpl; **~ in/out** vi entrar/ salir en tropel; **~ing the colour** n (ceremony) presentación f de la bandera.

trophy ['trəʊfɪ] n trofeo.

tropical ['trɒpɪkl] adj tropical.

trot [trɒt] n trote m ♦ vi trotar; **on the ~** (BRIT: fig) seguidos/as.

trouble ['trʌbl] n problema m, dificultad f; (worry) preocupación f; (bother, effort) molestia, esfuerzo; (unrest) inquietud f; (MED): **stomach etc ~** problemas mpl gástricos etc ♦ vt (disturb) molestar; (worry) preocupar, inquietar ♦ vi: **to ~ to do sth** molestarse en hacer algo; **~s** npl (POL etc) conflictos mpl; (personal) problemas mpl; **to be in ~** estar en un apuro; **it's no ~!** ¡no es molestia (ninguna)!; **what's the ~?** (with broken TV etc) ¿cuál es el problema?; (doctor to patient) ¿qué pasa?; **~d** adj (person) preocupado; (country, epoch, life) agitado; **~maker** n agitador(a) m/f; (child) alborotador m; **~shooter** n (in conflict) conciliador(a) m/f; **~some** adj molesto.

trough [trɒf] n (also: drinking ~) abrevadero; (also: feeding ~) comedero; (depression) depresión f.

troupe [truːp] n grupo.

trousers ['traʊzəz] npl pantalones mpl;

short ~ pantalones mpl cortos.

trousseau ['truːsəʊ] (pl ~x or ~s) n ajuar m.

trout [traʊt] n inv trucha.

trowel ['traʊəl] n (of gardener) palita; (of builder) paleta.

truant ['truːənt] n: **to play ~** (BRIT) hacer novillos.

truce [truːs] n tregua.

truck [trʌk] n (lorry) camión m; (RAIL) vagón m; **~ driver** n camionero; **~ farm** (US) n huerto.

trudge [trʌdʒ] vi (also: ~ **along**) caminar penosamente.

true [truː] adj verdadero; (accurate) exacto; (genuine) auténtico; (faithful) fiel; **to come ~** realizarse.

truffle ['trʌfl] n trufa.

truly ['truːlɪ] adv (really) realmente; (truthfully) verdaderamente; (faithfully): **yours ~** (in letter) le saluda atentamente.

trump [trʌmp] n triunfo; **~ed-up** adj inventado.

trumpet ['trʌmpɪt] n trompeta.

truncheon ['trʌntʃən] n porra.

trundle ['trʌndl] vt (pushchair etc) empujar; hacer rodar ♦ vi: **to ~ along** ir sin prisas.

trunk [trʌŋk] n (of tree, person) tronco; (of elephant) trompa; (case) baúl m; (US: AUT) maletero; **~s** npl (also: swimming ~s) bañador m (de hombre).

truss [trʌs] n (MED) braguero; **~ (up)** vt atar.

trust [trʌst] n confianza; (responsibility) responsabilidad f; (LAW) fideicomiso ♦ vt (rely on) tener confianza en; (hope) esperar; (entrust): **to ~ sth to sb** confiar algo a uno; **to take sth on ~** aceptar algo a ojos cerrados; **~ed** adj de confianza; **~ee** [trʌsˈtiː] n (LAW) fideicomisario; (of school) administrador m; **~ful** adj confiado; **~ing** adj confiado; **~worthy** adj digno de confianza.

truth [truːθ, pl truːðz] n verdad f; **~ful** adj veraz.

try [traɪ] n tentativa, intento; (RUGBY) ensayo ♦ vt (attempt) intentar; (test: also: ~ **out**) probar, someter a prueba;

(*LAW*) juzgar, procesar; (*strain: patience*) hacer perder ♦ *vi* probar; to have a ~ probar suerte; to ~ to do sth intentar hacer algo; ~ again! ¡vuelve a probar!; ~ harder! ¡esfuérzate más!; well, I tried al menos lo intenté; ~ on *vt* (*clothes*) probarse; ~ing *adj* (*experience*) cansado; (*person*) pesado.

tsar [zɑː*] *n* zar *m*.

T-shirt ['tiːʃəːt] *n* camiseta.

T-square *n* regla en T.

tub [tʌb] *n* cubo (*SP*), balde *m* (*AM*); (*bath*) tina, bañera.

tuba ['tjuːbə] *n* tuba.

tubby ['tʌbɪ] *adj* regordete.

tube [tjuːb] *n* tubo; (*BRIT: underground*) metro; (*for tyre*) cámara de aire.

tuberculosis [tjubəːkjuˈləʊsɪs] *n* tuberculosis *f inv*.

tube station (*BRIT*) *n* estación *f* de metro.

tubular ['tjuːbjʊlə*] *adj* tubular.

TUC (*BRIT*) *n abbr* (= *Trades Union Congress*) *federación nacional de sindicatos*.

tuck [tʌk] *vt* (*put*) poner; ~ away *vt* (*money*) guardar; (*building*): to be ~ed away esconderse, ocultarse; ~ in *vt* meter dentro; (*child*) arropar ♦ *vi* (*eat*) comer con apetito; ~ up *vt* (*child*) arropar; ~ shop *n* (*SCOL*) tienda; ≈ bar *m* (del colegio) (*SP*).

Tuesday ['tjuːzdɪ] *n* martes *m inv*.

tuft [tʌft] *n* mechón *m*; (*of grass etc*) manojo.

tug [tʌg] *n* (*ship*) remolcador *m* ♦ *vt* tirar de; ~-of-war *n* lucha de tiro de cuerda; (*fig*) tira y afloja *m*.

tuition [tjuːˈɪʃən] *n* (*BRIT*) enseñanza; (: *private* ~) clases *fpl* particulares; (*US: school fees*) matrícula.

tulip ['tjuːlɪp] *n* tulipán *m*.

tumble ['tʌmbl] *n* (*fall*) caída ♦ *vi* caer; to ~ to sth (*inf*) caer en la cuenta de algo; ~down *adj* destartalado; ~ dryer (*BRIT*) *n* secadora.

tumbler ['tʌmblə*] *n* (*glass*) vaso.

tummy ['tʌmɪ] (*inf*) *n* barriga, tripa.

tumour ['tjuːmə*] (*US* **tumor**) *n* tumor *m*.

tuna ['tjuːnə] *n inv* (*also*: ~ *fish*) atún *m*.

tune [tjuːn] *n* melodía ♦ *vt* (*MUS*) afinar; (*RADIO, TV, AUT*) sintonizar; to be in/out of ~ (*instrument*) estar afinado/desafinado; (*singer*) cantar afinadamente/desafinar; to be in/out of ~ with (*fig*) estar de acuerdo/en desacuerdo con; ~ in *vi*: to ~ in (to) (*RADIO, TV*) sintonizar (con); ~ up *vi* (*musician*) afinar (su instrumento); ~ful *adj* melodioso; ~r *n*: piano ~r afinador(a) *m/f* de pianos.

tunic ['tjuːnɪk] *n* túnica.

Tunisia [tjuːˈnɪzɪə] *n* Túnez *m*.

tunnel ['tʌnl] *n* túnel *m*; (*in mine*) galería ♦ *vi* construir un túnel/una galería.

turban ['təːbən] *n* turbante *m*.

turbine ['təːbaɪn] *n* turbina.

turbulent ['təːbjʊlənt] *adj* turbulento.

tureen [təˈriːn] *n* sopera.

turf [təːf] *n* césped *m*; (*clod*) tepe *m* ♦ *vt* cubrir con césped; ~ out (*inf*) *vt* echar a la calle.

turgid ['təːdʒɪd] *adj* (*prose*) pesado.

Turk [təːk] *n* turco/a.

Turkey ['təːkɪ] *n* Turquía.

turkey ['təːkɪ] *n* pavo.

Turkish ['təːkɪʃ] *adj, n* turco.

turmoil ['təːmɔɪl] *n* desorden *m*, alboroto; in ~ revuelto.

turn [təːn] *n* turno; (*in road*) curva; (*of mind, events*) rumbo; (*THEATRE*) número; (*MED*) ataque *m* ♦ *vt* girar, volver; (*collar, steak*) dar la vuelta a; (*page*) pasar; (*change*): to ~ sth into convertir algo en ♦ *vi* volver; (*person: look back*) volverse; (*reverse direction*) dar la vuelta; (*milk*) cortarse; (*become*): to ~ nasty/forty ponerse feo/cumplir los cuarenta; a good ~ un favor; it gave me quite a ~ me dio un susto; "no left ~" (*AUT*) "prohibido girar a la izquierda"; it's your ~ te toca a ti; in ~ por turnos; to take ~s (at) turnarse (en); ~ away *vi* apartar la vista ♦ *vi* rechazar; ~ back *vi* volverse atrás ♦ *vt* hacer retroceder; (*clock*) retrasar; ~ down *vt* (*refuse*) rechazar; (*reduce*) bajar; (*fold*) doblar; ~ in *vi* (*inf: go to*) *bed*) acostarse ♦ *vt* (*fold*) doblar hacia dentro; ~ **off** *vi* (*from road*) desviarse ♦ *vt* (*light, radio etc*) apagar; (*tap*) cerrar; (*engine*) parar; ~ **on** *vt* (*light, radio etc*) encender (*SP*), prender (*AM*); (*tap*) abrir; (*engine*) poner en marcha; ~ **out** *vt* (*light, gas*) apagar; (*produce*) producir ♦ *vi* (*voters*) concurrir; **to** ~ **out to be** ... resultar ser ...; ~ **over** *vi* (*person*) volverse ♦ *vt* (*object*) dar la vuelta a; (*page*) volver; ~ **round** *vi* volverse; (*rotate*) girar; ~ **up** *vi* (*person*) llegar, presentarse; (*lost object*) aparecer ♦ *vt* (*gen*) subir; ~**ing** *n* (*in road*) vuelta; ~**ing point** *n* (*fig*) momento decisivo.

turnip ['tə:nɪp] *n* nabo.

turnout ['tə:naut] *n* concurrencia.

turnover ['tə:nəuvə*] *n* (*COMM: amount of money*) volumen *m* de ventas; (*: of goods*) movimiento.

turnpike ['tə:npaɪk] (*US*) *n* autopista de peaje.

turnstile ['tə:nstaɪl] *n* torniquete *m*.

turntable ['tə:nteɪbl] *n* plato.

turn-up (*BRIT*) *n* (*on trousers*) vuelta.

turpentine ['tə:pəntaɪn] *n* (*also: turps*) trementina.

turquoise ['tə:kwɔɪz] *n* (*stone*) turquesa ♦ *adj* color túrquesa.

turret ['tʌrɪt] *n* torreón *m*.

turtle ['tə:tl] *n* galápago; ~**neck (sweater)** *n* jersey *m* de cuello vuelto.

tusk [tʌsk] *n* colmillo.

tussle ['tʌsl] *n* pelea.

tutor ['tju:tə*] *n* profesor(a) *m/f*; ~**ial** [-'tɔ:rɪəl] *n* (*SCOL*) seminario.

tuxedo [tʌk'si:dəu] (*US*) *n* smóking *m*, esmoquin *m*.

TV [ti:'vi:] *n abbr* (= *television*) tele *f*.

twang [twæŋ] *n* (*of instrument*) punteado; (*of voice*) timbre *m* nasal.

tweezers ['twi:zəz] *npl* pinzas *fpl* (de depilar).

twelfth [twelfθ] *num* duodécimo.

twelve [twelv] *num* doce; **at** ~ **o'clock** (*midday*) a mediodía; (*midnight*) a medianoche.

twentieth ['twentɪθ] *adj* vigésimo.

twenty ['twentɪ] *num* veinte.

twice [twaɪs] *adv* dos veces; ~ **as much** dos veces más.

twiddle ['twɪdl] *vt* juguetear con ♦ *vi*: **to** ~ (**with**) **sth** dar vueltas a algo; **to** ~ **one's thumbs** (*fig*) estar mano sobre mano.

twig [twɪg] *n* ramita ♦ *vi* (*inf*) caer en la cuenta.

twilight ['twaɪlaɪt] *n* crepúsculo.

twin [twɪn] *adj, n* gemelo/a *m/f* ♦ *vt* hermanar; ~**-bedded room** *n* habitación *f* doble.

twine [twaɪn] *n* bramante *m* ♦ *vi* (*plant*) enroscarse.

twinge [twɪndʒ] *n* (*of pain*) punzada; (*of conscience*) remordimiento.

twinkle ['twɪŋkl] *vi* centellear; (*eyes*) brillar.

twirl [twə:l] *vt* dar vueltas a ♦ *vi* dar vueltas.

twist [twɪst] *n* (*action*) torsión *f*; (*in road, coil*) vuelta; (*in wire, flex*) doblez *f*; (*in story*) giro ♦ *vt* torcer; (*weave*) trenzar; (*roll around*) enrollar; (*fig*) deformar ♦ *vi* serpentear.

twit [twɪt] (*inf*) *n* tonto.

twitch [twɪtʃ] *n* (*pull*) tirón *m*; (*nervous*) tic *m* ♦ *vi* crisparse.

two [tu:] *num* dos; **to put** ~ **and** ~ **together** (*fig*) atar cabos; ~**-door** *adj* (*AUT*) de dos puertas; ~**-faced** *adj* (*pej: person*) falso; ~**fold** *adv*: **to increase** ~**fold** doblarse; ~**-piece (suit)** *n* traje *m* de dos piezas; ~**-piece (swimsuit)** *n* dos piezas *m inv*, bikini *m*; ~**some** *n* (*people*) pareja; ~**-way** *adj*: ~**-way traffic** circulación *f* de dos sentidos.

tycoon [taɪ'ku:n] *n*: (*business*) ~ magnate *m*.

type [taɪp] *n* (*category*) tipo, género; (*model*) tipo; (*TYP*) tipo, letra ♦ *vt* (*letter etc*) escribir a máquina; ~**-cast** *adj* (*actor*) encasillado; ~**-face** *n* letra; ~**script** *n* texto mecanografiado; ~**-writer** *n* máquina de escribir; ~**-written** *adj* mecanografiado.

typhoid ['taɪfɔɪd] *n* tifoidea.

typical ['tɪpɪkl] *adj* típico.

typing ['taɪpɪŋ] *n* mecanografía.

typist ['taɪpɪst] n mecanógrafo/a.
tyranny ['tɪrənɪ] n tiranía.
tyrant ['taɪərnt] n tirano/a.
tyre ['taɪə*] (US tire) n neumático (SP), llanta (AM); ~ **pressure** n presión f de los neumáticos.
tzar [zɑː*] n = tsar.

U

U-bend ['juːbend] n (AUT, in pipe) recodo.
udder ['ʌdə*] n ubre f.
UFO ['juːfəu] n abbr = (unidentified flying object) OVNI m.
ugh [əːh] excl ¡uf!
ugly ['ʌglɪ] adj feo; (dangerous) peligroso.
UK n abbr = United Kingdom.
ulcer ['ʌlsə*] n úlcera; (mouth ~) llaga.
Ulster ['ʌlstə*] n Ulster m.
ulterior [ʌl'tɪərɪə*] adj: ~ **motive** segundas intenciones fpl.
ultimate ['ʌltɪmət] adj último, final; (greatest) máximo; ~**ly** adv (in the end) por último, al final; (fundamentally) a or en fin de cuentas.
umbilical cord [ʌm'bɪlɪkl-] n cordón m umbilical.
umbrella [ʌm'brelə] n paraguas m inv; (for sun) sombrilla.
umpire ['ʌmpaɪə*] n árbitro.
umpteen [ʌmp'tiːn] adj enésimos/as; ~**th** adj: for the ~**th time** por enésima vez.
UN n abbr (= United Nations) NN. UU.
unable [ʌn'eɪbl] adj: to be ~ to do sth no poder hacer algo.
unaccompanied [ʌnə'kʌmpənɪd] adj no acompañado; (song) sin acompañamiento.
unaccountably [ʌnə'kauntəblɪ] adv inexplicablemente.
unaccustomed [ʌnə'kʌstəmd] adj: to be ~ to no estar acostumbrado a.
unanimous [juː'nænɪməs] adj unánime.
unarmed [ʌn'ɑːmd] adj (defenceless) inerme; (without weapon) desarmado.
unashamed [ʌnə'ʃeɪmd] adj descarado.

unassuming [ʌnə'sjuːmɪŋ] adj modesto, sin pretensiones.
unattached [ʌnə'tætʃt] adj (person) soltero y sin compromiso; (part etc) suelto.
unattended [ʌnə'tendɪd] adj desatendido.
unattractive [ʌnə'træktɪv] adj poco atractivo.
unauthorized [ʌn'ɔːθəraɪzd] adj no autorizado.
unavoidable [ʌnə'vɔɪdəbl] adj inevitable.
unaware [ʌnə'wɛə*] adj: to be ~ of ignorar; ~**s** adv de improviso.
unbalanced [ʌn'bælənst] adj (report) poco objetivo; (mentally) trastornado.
unbearable [ʌn'bɛərəbl] adj insoportable.
unbeatable [ʌn'biːtəbl] adj (team) invencible; (price) inmejorable; (quality) insuperable.
unbelievable [ʌnbɪ'liːvəbl] adj increíble.
unbend [ʌn'bend] (irreg) vi (relax) relajarse ♦ vt (wire) enderezar.
unbiased [ʌn'baɪəst] adj imparcial.
unborn [ʌn'bɔːn] adj que va a nacer.
unbroken [ʌn'brəukən] adj (seal) intacto; (series) continuo; (record) no batido; (spirit) indómito.
unbutton [ʌn'bʌtn] vt desabrochar.
uncalled-for [ʌn'kɔːldfɔː*] adj gratuito, inmerecido.
uncanny [ʌn'kænɪ] adj extraño.
unceremonious ['ʌnsɛrɪ'məunɪəs] adj (abrupt, rude) brusco, hosco.
uncertain [ʌn'səːtn] adj incierto; (indecisive) indeciso.
unchanged [ʌn'tʃeɪndʒd] adj igual, sin cambios.
unchecked [ʌn'tʃekt] adv sin estorbo, sin restricción.
uncivilized [ʌn'sɪvɪlaɪzd] adj inculto; (fig: behaviour etc) bárbaro; (hour) inoportuno.
uncle ['ʌŋkl] n tío.
uncomfortable [ʌn'kʌmfətəbl] adj incómodo; (uneasy) inquieto.
uncommon [ʌn'kɔmən] adj poco común, raro.

uncompromising [ʌn'kɒmprəmaɪzɪŋ] *adj* intransigente.

unconcerned [ʌnkən'sɜːnd] *adj* indiferente, despreocupado.

unconditional [ʌnkən'dɪʃənl] *adj* incondicional.

unconscious [ʌn'kɒnʃəs] *adj* sin sentido; (*unaware*): **to be ~ of** no darse cuenta de ♦ *n*: **the ~** el inconsciente.

uncontrollable [ʌnkən'trəuləbl] *adj* (*child etc*) incontrolable; (*temper*) indomable; (*laughter*) incontenible.

unconventional [ʌnkən'vɛnʃənl] *adj* poco convencional.

uncouth [ʌn'kuːθ] *adj* grosero, inculto.

uncover [ʌn'kʌvə*] *vt* descubrir; (*take lid off*) destapar.

undecided [ʌndɪ'saɪdɪd] *adj* (*character*) indeciso; (*question*) no resuelto.

undeniable [ʌndɪ'naɪəbl] *adj* innegable.

under ['ʌndə*] *prep* debajo de; (*less than*) menos de; (*according to*) según, de acuerdo con; (*sb's leadership*) bajo ♦ *adv* debajo, abajo; **~ there** allí abajo; **~ repair** en reparación.

under... ['ʌndə*] *prefix* sub; **~-age** *adj* menor de edad; (*drinking etc*) de los menores de edad; **~carriage** (*BRIT*) *n* (*AVIAT*) tren *m* de aterrizaje; **~charge** *vt* cobrar menos de la cuenta; **~clothes** *npl* ropa interior (*SP*) or íntima (*AM*); **~coat** *n* (*paint*) primera mano; **~cover** *adj* clandestino; **~current** *n* (*fig*) corriente *f* oculta; **~cut** *vt irreg* vender más barato que; **~developed** *adj* subdesarrollado; **~dog** *n* desvalido/a; **~done** *adj* (*CULIN*) poco hecho; **~estimate** *vt* subestimar; **~exposed** *adj* (*PHOT*) subexpuesto; **~fed** *adj* subalimentado; **~foot** *adv* con los pies; **~go** *vt irreg* sufrir; (*treatment*) recibir; **~graduate** *n* estudiante *m/f*; **~ground** *n* (*BRIT: railway*) metro; (*POL*) movimiento clandestino ♦ *adj* (*car park*) subterráneo ♦ *adv* (*work*) en la clandestinidad; **~growth** *n* maleza; **~hand(ed)** *adj* (*fig*) socarrón; **~lie** *vt irreg* (*fig*) ser la razón fundamental de; **~line** *vt* subrayar; **~ling** ['ʌndəlɪŋ] (*pej*) *n* subalterno/a; **~mine** *vt* socavar, mi-

nar; **~neath** [ʌndə'niːθ] *adv* debajo ♦ *prep* debajo de, bajo; **~paid** *adj* mal pagado; **~pants** *npl* calzoncillos *mpl*; **~pass** (*BRIT*) *n* paso subterráneo; **~privileged** *adj* desposeído; **~rate** *vt* menospreciar, subestimar; **~shirt** (*US*) *n* camiseta; **~shorts** (*US*) *npl* calzoncillos *mpl*; **~side** *n* parte *f* inferior; **~skirt** (*BRIT*) *n* enaguas *fpl*.

understand [ʌndə'stænd] (*irreg*) *vt, vi* entender, comprender; (*assume*) tener entendido; **~able** *adj* comprensible; **~ing** *adj* comprensivo ♦ *n* comprensión *f*, entendimiento; (*agreement*) acuerdo.

understatement ['ʌndəsteɪtmənt] *n* modestia (excesiva); **that's an ~!** ¡eso es decir poco!

understood [ʌndə'stud] *pt, pp of* **understand** ♦ *adj* (*agreed*) acordado; (*implied*): **it is ~ that** se sobreentiende que.

understudy ['ʌndəstʌdɪ] *n* suplente *m/f*.

undertake [ʌndə'teɪk] (*irreg*) *vt* emprender; **to ~ to do sth** comprometerse a hacer algo.

undertaker ['ʌndəteɪkə*] *n* director(a) *m/f* de pompas fúnebres.

undertaking ['ʌndəteɪkɪŋ] *n* empresa; (*promise*) promesa.

undertone ['ʌndətəun] *n*: **in an ~** en voz baja.

underwater [ʌndə'wɔːtə*] *adv* bajo el agua ♦ *adj* submarino.

underwear ['ʌndəwɛə*] *n* ropa interior (*SP*) or íntima (*AM*).

underworld ['ʌndəwɜːld] *n* (*of crime*) hampa, inframundo.

underwriter ['ʌndəraɪtə*] *n* (*INSURANCE*) asegurador(a) *m/f*.

undesirable [ʌndɪ'zaɪrəbl] *adj* (*person*) indeseable; (*thing*) poco aconsejable.

undies ['ʌndɪz] (*inf*) *npl* ropa interior (*SP*) or íntima (*AM*).

undisputed [ʌndɪs'pjuːtɪd] *adj* indiscutible.

undo [ʌn'duː] (*irreg*) *vt* (*laces*) desatar; (*button etc*) desabrochar; (*spoil*) deshacer; **~ing** *n* ruina, perdición *f*.

undoubted [ʌn'dautɪd] *adj* indudable.

undress [ʌn'drɛs] *vi* desnudarse.

undulating ['ʌndjuleɪtɪŋ] *adj* ondulante.

unduly [ʌn'djuːlɪ] *adv* excesivamente, demasiado.

unearth [ʌn'ɜːθ] *vt* desenterrar.

unearthly [ʌn'ɜːθlɪ] *adj* (*hour*) inverosímil.

uneasy [ʌn'iːzɪ] *adj* intranquilo, preocupado; (*feeling*) desagradable; (*peace*) inseguro.

uneducated [ʌn'ɛdjukeɪtɪd] *adj* ignorante, inculto.

unemployed [ʌnɪm'plɔɪd] *adj* parado, sin trabajo ♦ *npl*: **the ~** los parados.

unemployment [ʌnɪm'plɔɪmənt] *n* paro, desempleo.

unending [ʌn'ɛndɪŋ] *adj* interminable.

unerring [ʌn'ɜːrɪŋ] *adj* infalible.

uneven [ʌn'iːvn] *adj* desigual; (*road etc*) lleno de baches.

unexpected [ʌnɪk'spɛktɪd] *adj* inesperado; **~ly** *adv* inesperadamente.

unfailing [ʌn'feɪlɪŋ] *adj* (*support*) indefectible; (*energy*) inagotable.

unfair [ʌn'fɛə*] *adj*: **~** (**to sb**) injusto (con uno).

unfaithful [ʌn'feɪθful] *adj* infiel.

unfamiliar [ʌnfə'mɪlɪə*] *adj* extraño, desconocido; **to be ~ with** desconocer.

unfashionable [ʌn'fæʃnəbl] *adj* pasado *or* fuera de moda.

unfasten [ʌn'fɑːsn] *vt* (*knot*) desatar; (*dress*) desabrochar; (*open*) abrir.

unfavourable [ʌn'feɪvərəbl] (*US* **unfavorable**) *adj* desfavorable.

unfeeling [ʌn'fiːlɪŋ] *adj* insensible.

unfinished [ʌn'fɪnɪʃt] *adj* inacabado, sin terminar.

unfit [ʌn'fɪt] *adj* bajo de forma; (*incompetent*): **~** (**for**) incapaz (de); **~ for work** no apto para trabajar.

unfold [ʌn'fəuld] *vt* desdoblar ♦ *vi* abrirse.

unforeseen ['ʌnfɔː'siːn] *adj* imprevisto.

unforgettable [ʌnfə'gɛtəbl] *adj* inolvidable.

unforgivable [ʌnfə'gɪvəbl] *adj* imperdonable.

unfortunate [ʌn'fɔːtʃnət] *adj* desgraciado; (*event, remark*) inoportuno; **~ly** *adv* desgraciadamente.

unfounded [ʌn'faundɪd] *adj* infundado.

unfriendly [ʌn'frɛndlɪ] *adj* antipático; (*behaviour, remark*) hostil, poco amigable.

ungainly [ʌn'geɪnlɪ] *adj* desgarbado.

ungodly [ʌn'gɔdlɪ] *adj*: **at an ~ hour** a una hora inverosímil.

ungrateful [ʌn'greɪtful] *adj* ingrato.

unhappiness [ʌn'hæpɪnɪs] *n* tristeza, desdicha.

unhappy [ʌn'hæpɪ] *adj* (*sad*) triste; (*unfortunate*) desgraciado; (*childhood*) infeliz; **~ about/with** (*arrangements etc*) poco contento con, descontento de.

unharmed [ʌn'hɑːmd] *adj* ileso.

unhealthy [ʌn'hɛlθɪ] *adj* (*place*) malsano; (*person*) enfermizo; (*fig: interest*) morboso.

unheard-of *adj* inaudito, sin precedente.

unhurt [ʌn'hɜːt] *adj* ileso.

unidentified [ʌnaɪ'dɛntɪfaɪd] *adj* no identificado, sin identificar; *see also* **UFO.**

uniform ['juːnɪfɔːm] *n* uniforme *m* ♦ *adj* uniforme.

unify ['juːnɪfaɪ] *vt* unificar, unir.

uninhabited [ʌnɪn'hæbɪtɪd] *adj* desierto.

unintentional [ʌnɪn'tɛnʃənəl] *adj* involuntario.

union ['juːnjən] *n* unión *f*; (*also: trade ~*) sindicato ♦ *cpd* sindical; **U~ Jack** *n* bandera del Reino Unido.

unique [juː'niːk] *adj* único.

unison ['juːnɪsn] *n*: **in ~** (*speak, reply, sing*) al unísono.

unit ['juːnɪt] *n* unidad *f*; (*section: of furniture etc*) elemento; (*team*) grupo; **kitchen ~** módulo de cocina.

unite [juː'naɪt] *vt* unir ♦ *vi* unirse; **~d** *adj* unido; (*effort*) conjunto; **U~d Kingdom** *n* Reino Unido; **U~d Nations (Organization)** *n* Naciones *fpl* Unidas; **U~d States (of America)** *n* Estados *mpl* Unidos.

unit trust (*BRIT*) *n* bono fiduciario.

unity ['juːnɪtɪ] *n* unidad *f*.

universe ['juːnɪvɜːs] *n* universo.

university [juːnɪ'vɜːsɪtɪ] *n* universidad *f*.

unjust [ʌn'dʒʌst] *adj* injusto.

unkempt [ʌn'kɛmpt] *adj* (*appearance*)

descuidado; (*hair*) despeinado.

unkind [ʌn'kaɪnd] *adj* poco amable; (*behaviour*, *comment*) cruel.

unknown [ʌn'nəun] *adj* desconocido.

unlawful [ʌn'lɔːful] *adj* ilegal, ilícito.

unleash [ʌn'liːʃ] *vt* desatar.

unless [ʌn'lɛs] *conj* a menos que; ~ he comes a menos que venga; ~ otherwise stated salvo indicación contraria.

unlike [ʌn'laɪk] *adj* (*not alike*) distinto de *or* a; (*not like*) poco propio de ♦ *prep* a diferencia de.

unlikely [ʌn'laɪklɪ] *adj* improbable; (*unexpected*) inverosímil.

unlimited [ʌn'lɪmɪtɪd] *adj* ilimitado.

unlisted [ʌn'lɪstɪd] (*US*) *adj* (*TEL*) que no consta en la guía.

unload [ʌn'ləud] *vt* descargar.

unlock [ʌn'lɔk] *vt* abrir (con llave).

unlucky [ʌn'lʌkɪ] *adj* desgraciado; (*object*, *number*) que da mala suerte; to be ~ tener mala suerte.

unmarried [ʌn'mærɪd] *adj* soltero.

unmask [ʌn'mɑːsk] *vt* desenmascarar.

unmistakable [ʌnmɪs'teɪkəbl] *adj* inconfundible.

unnatural [ʌn'nætʃrəl] *adj* (*gen*) antinatural; (*manner*) afectado; (*habit*) perverso.

unnecessary [ʌn'nɛsəsərɪ] *adj* innecesario, inútil.

unnoticed [ʌn'nəutɪst] *adj*: to go *or* pass ~ pasar desapercibido.

UNO ['juːnəu] *n abbr* (= *United Nations Organization*) ONU *f*.

unobtainable [ʌnəb'teɪnəbl] *adj* inconseguible; (*TEL*) inexistente.

unobtrusive [ʌnəb'truːsɪv] *adj* discreto.

unofficial [ʌnə'fɪʃl] *adj* no oficial; (*news*) sin confirmar.

unorthodox [ʌn'ɔːθədɔks] *adj* poco ortodoxo; (*REL*) heterodoxo.

unpack [ʌn'pæk] *vi* deshacer las maletas ♦ *vt* deshacer.

unpalatable [ʌn'pælətəbl] *adj* incomible; (*truth*) desagradable.

unparalleled [ʌn'pærəlɛld] *adj* (*unequalled*) incomparable.

unpleasant [ʌn'plɛznt] *adj* (*disagreeable*) desagradable; (*person*, *manner*) antipático.

unplug [ʌn'plʌg] *vt* desenchufar, desconectar.

unpopular [ʌn'pɔpjulə*] *adj* impopular, poco popular.

unprecedented [ʌn'prɛsɪdəntɪd] *adj* sin precedentes.

unpredictable [ʌnprɪ'dɪktəbl] *adj* imprevisible.

unprofessional [ʌnprə'fɛʃənl] *adj* (*attitude*, *conduct*) poco ético.

unqualified [ʌn'kwɔlɪfaɪd] *adj* sin título, no cualificado; (*success*) total.

unquestionably [ʌn'kwɛstʃənəblɪ] *adv* indiscutiblemente.

unravel [ʌn'rævl] *vt* desenmarañar; (*mystery*) desentrañar.

unreal [ʌn'rɪəl] *adj* irreal; (*extraordinary*) increíble.

unrealistic [ʌnrɪə'lɪstɪk] *adj* poco realista.

unreasonable [ʌn'riːznəbl] *adj* irrazonable; (*demand*) excesivo.

unrelated [ʌnrɪ'leɪtɪd] *adj* sin relación; (*family*) no emparentado.

unrelenting [ʌnrɪ'lɛntɪŋ] *adj* inexorable.

unreliable [ʌnrɪ'laɪəbl] *adj* (*person*) informal; (*machine*) poco fiable.

unremitting [ʌnrɪ'mɪtɪŋ] *adj* constante.

unreservedly [ʌnrɪ'zɜːvɪdlɪ] *adv* sin reserva.

unrest [ʌn'rɛst] *n* inquietud *f*, malestar *m*; (*POL*) disturbios *mpl*.

unroll [ʌn'rəul] *vt* desenrollar.

unruly [ʌn'ruːlɪ] *adj* indisciplinado.

unsafe [ʌn'seɪf] *adj* peligroso.

unsaid [ʌn'sɛd] *adj*: to leave sth ~ dejar algo sin decir.

unsatisfactory ['ʌnsætɪs'fæktərɪ] *adj* poco satisfactorio.

unsavoury [ʌn'seɪvərɪ] (*US* **unsavory**) *adj* (*fig*) repugnante.

unscathed [ʌn'skeɪðd] *adj* ileso.

unscrew [ʌn'skruː] *vt* destornillar.

unscrupulous [ʌn'skruːpjuləs] *adj* sin escrúpulos.

unsettled [ʌn'sɛtld] *adj* inquieto, intranquilo; (*weather*) variable.

unshaven [ʌn'ʃeɪvn] *adj* sin afeitar.

unsightly [ʌn'saɪtlɪ] *adj* feo.

unskilled [ʌn'skɪld] *adj* (*work*) no especializado; (*worker*) no cualificado.
unspeakable [ʌn'spiːkəbl] *adj* indecible; (*awful*) incalificable.
unstable [ʌn'steɪbl] *adj* inestable.
unsteady [ʌn'stɛdɪ] *adj* inestable.
unstuck [ʌn'stʌk] *adj*: **to come ~** despegarse; (*fig*) fracasar.
unsuccessful [ʌnsək'sɛsful] *adj* (*attempt*) infructuoso; (*writer, proposal*) sin éxito; **to be ~** (*in attempting sth*) no tener éxito, fracasar; **~ly** *adv* en vano, sin éxito.
unsuitable [ʌn'suːtəbl] *adj* inapropiado; (*time*) inoportuno.
unsure [ʌn'ʃuə*] *adj* inseguro, poco seguro.
unsuspecting ['ʌnsəs'pɛktɪŋ] *adj* desprevehido.
unsympathetic [ʌnsɪmpə'θɛtɪk] *adj* poco comprensivo; (*unlikeable*) antipático.
untapped [ʌn'tæpt] *adj* (*resources*) sin explotar.
unthinkable [ʌn'θɪŋkəbl] *adj* inconcebible, impensable.
untidy [ʌn'taɪdɪ] *adj* (*room*) desordenado; (*appearance*) desaliñado.
untie [ʌn'taɪ] *vt* desatar.
until [ən'tɪl] *prep* hasta ◆ *conj* hasta que; **~ he comes** hasta que venga; **~ now** hasta ahora; **~ then** hasta entonces.
untimely [ʌn'taɪmlɪ] *adj* inoportuno; (*death*) prematuro.
untold [ʌn'təʊld] *adj* (*story*) nunca contado; (*suffering*) indecible; (*wealth*) incalculable.
untoward [ʌntə'wɔːd] *adj* adverso.
unused [ʌn'juːzd] *adj* sin usar.
unusual [ʌn'juːʒuəl] *adj* insólito, poco común; (*exceptional*) inusitado.
unveil [ʌn'veɪl] *vt* (*statue*) descubrir.
unwanted [ʌn'wɒntɪd] *adj* (*clothing*) viejo; (*pregnancy*) no deseado.
unwavering [ʌn'weɪvərɪŋ] *adj* (*faith*) inquebrantable; (*gaze*) fijo.
unwelcome [ʌn'wɛlkəm] *adj* inoportuno; (*news*) desagradable.
unwell [ʌn'wɛl] *adj*: **to be/feel ~** estar indispuesto/sentirse mal.

unwieldy [ʌn'wiːldɪ] *adj* difícil de manejar.
unwilling [ʌn'wɪlɪŋ] *adj*: **to be ~ to do sth** estar poco dispuesto a hacer algo; **~ly** *adv* de mala gana.
unwind [ʌn'waɪnd] (*irg: like* **wind**) *vt* desenvolver ◆ *vi* (*relax*) relajarse.
unwise [ʌn'waɪz] *adj* imprudente.
unwitting [ʌn'wɪtɪŋ] *adj* inconsciente.
unworkable [ʌn'wəːkəbl] *adj* (*plan*) impracticable.
unworthy [ʌn'wəːðɪ] *adj* indigno.
unwrap [ʌn'ræp] *vt* desenvolver.
unwritten [ʌn'rɪtn] *adj* (*agreement*) tácito; (*rules, law*) no escrito.

KEYWORD
---

up [ʌp] *prep*: **to go/be ~ sth** subir/estar subido en algo; **he went ~ the stairs/the hill** subió las escaleras/la colina; **we walked/climbed ~ the hill** subimos la colina; **they live further ~ the street** viven más arriba en la calle; **go ~ that road and turn left** sigue por esa calle y gira a la izquierda
◆ *adv* **1** (*upwards, higher*) más arriba; **~ in the mountains** en lo alto (de la montaña); **put it a bit higher ~** ponlo un poco más arriba *or* alto; **~ there** ahí *or* allí arriba; **~ above** en lo alto, por encima, arriba
2: **to be ~** (*out of bed*) estar levantado; (*prices, level*) haber subido
3: **~ to** (*as far as*) hasta; **~ to now** hasta ahora *or* la fecha
4: **to be ~ to** (*depending on*): **it's ~ to you** depende de ti; **he's not ~ to it** (*job, task etc*) no es capaz de hacerlo; **his work is not ~ to the required standard** su trabajo no da la talla; (*inf: be doing*): **what is he ~ to?** ¿que estará tramando?
◆ *n*: **~s and downs** altibajos *mpl*.

---

upbringing ['ʌpbrɪŋɪŋ] *n* educación *f*.
update [ʌp'deɪt] *vt* poner al día.
upgrade [ʌp'greɪd] *vt* (*house*) modernizar; (*employee*) ascender.
upheaval [ʌp'hiːvl] *n* trastornos *mpl*; (*POL*) agitación *f*.

uphill [ʌp'hɪl] *adj* cuesta arriba; *(fig: task)* penoso, difícil ♦ *adv*: **to go ~** ir cuesta arriba.

uphold [ʌp'həuld] *(irreg) vt* defender.

upholstery [ʌp'həulstərɪ] *n* tapicería.

upkeep ['ʌpkiːp] *n* mantenimiento.

upon [ə'pɔn] *prep* sobre.

upper ['ʌpə*] *adj* superior, de arriba ♦ *n (of shoe: also:* ~s) empeine *m*; ~ **class** *adj* de clase alta; ~ **hand** *n*: **to have the ~ hand** tener la sartén por el mango; ~**most** *adj* el más alto; **what was ~most in my mind** lo que me preocupaba más.

upright ['ʌpraɪt] *adj* derecho; *(vertical)* vertical; *(fig)* honrado.

uprising ['ʌpraɪzɪŋ] *n* sublevación *f*.

uproar ['ʌprɔː*] *n* escándalo.

uproot [ʌp'ruːt] *vt (also fig)* desarraigar.

upset [*n* 'ʌpset, *vb, adj* ʌp'set] *n (to plan etc)* revés *m*, contratiempo; *(MED)* trastorno ♦ *(irreg) vt (glass etc)* volcar; *(plan)* alterar; *(person)* molestar, disgustar ♦ *adj* molesto, disgustado; *(stomach)* revuelto.

upshot ['ʌpʃɔt] *n* resultado.

upside-down *adv* al revés; **to turn a place ~** *(fig)* revolverlo todo.

upstairs [ʌp'steəz] *adv* arriba ♦ *adj (room)* de arriba ♦ *n* el piso superior.

upstart ['ʌpstɑːt] *n* advenedizo/a.

upstream [ʌp'striːm] *adv* río arriba.

uptake ['ʌpteɪk] *n*: **to be quick/slow on the ~** ser muy listo/torpe.

uptight [ʌp'taɪt] *adj* tenso, nervioso.

up-to-date *adj* al día.

upturn ['ʌptəːn] *n (in luck)* mejora; *(COMM: in market)* resurgimiento económico.

upward ['ʌpwəd] *adj* ascendente; ~**(s)** *adv* hacia arriba; *(more than)*: ~**(s) of** más de.

urban ['əːbən] *adj* urbano.

urchin ['əːtʃɪn] *n* pilluelo, golfillo.

urge [əːdʒ] *n (desire)* deseo ♦ *vt*: **to ~ sb to do sth** animar a uno a hacer algo.

urgent ['əːdʒənt] *adj* urgente; *(voice)* perentorio.

urinate ['juərɪneɪt] *vi* orinar.

urine ['juərɪn] *n* orina, orines *mpl*.

urn [əːn] *n* urna; *(also: tea ~)* cacharro metálico grande para hacer té.

Uruguay ['juerəgwaɪ] *n* (el) Uruguay; ~**an** *adj, n* uruguayo/a *m/f*.

US *n abbr* (= *United States*) EE. UU.

us [ʌs] *pron* nos; *(after prep)* nosotros/as; *see also* **me**.

USA *n abbr* (= *United States (of America)*) EE. UU.

usage ['juːzɪdʒ] *n (LING)* uso.

use [*n* juːs, *vb* juːz] *n* uso, empleo; *(usefulness)* utilidad *f* ♦ *vt* usar, emplear; **she ~d to do it** (ella) solía *or* acostumbraba hacerlo; **in ~** en uso; **out of ~** en desuso; **to be of ~** servir; **it's no ~** *(pointless)* es inútil; *(not useful)* no sirve; **to be ~d to** estar acostumbrado a, acostumbrar; ~ **up** *vt (food)* consumir; *(money)* gastar; ~**d** *adj (car)* usado; ~**ful** *adj* útil; ~**fulness** *n* utilidad *f*; ~**less** *adj (unusable)* inservible; *(pointless)* inútil; *(person)* inepto; ~**r** *n* usuario/a; ~**r-friendly** *adj (computer)* amistoso.

usher ['ʌʃə*] *n (at wedding)* ujier *m*; ~**ette** [-'ret] *n (in cinema)* acomodadora.

USSR *n*: **the ~** la URSS.

usual ['juːʒuəl] *adj* normal, corriente; **as ~** como de costumbre; ~**ly** *adv* normalmente.

utensil [juː'tensl] *n* utensilio; **kitchen ~s** batería de cocina.

uterus ['juːtərəs] *n* útero.

utility [juː'tɪlɪtɪ] *n* utilidad *f*; *(public ~)* (empresa de) servicio público; ~ **room** *n* ofis *m*.

utilize ['juːtɪlaɪz] *vt* utilizar.

utmost ['ʌtməust] *adj* mayor ♦ *n*: **to do one's ~** hacer todo lo posible.

utter ['ʌtə*] *adj* total, completo ♦ *vt* pronunciar, proferir; ~**ance** *n* palabras *fpl*, declaración *f*; ~**ly** *adv* completamente, totalmente.

U-turn ['juː'təːn] *n* viraje *m* en redondo.

V

v. *abbr* = **verse; versus;** (= *volt*) **v;** (= *vide*) **véase.**

vacancy ['veɪkənsɪ] *n* (*BRIT: job*) vacante *f*; (*room*) habitación *f* libre.

vacant ['veɪkənt] *adj* desocupado, libre; (*expression*) distraído; ~ **lot** (*US*) *n* solar *m*.

vacate [və'keɪt] *vt* (*house, room*) desocupar; (*job*) dejar (vacante).

vacation [və'keɪʃən] *n* vacaciones *fpl*.

vaccinate ['væksɪneɪt] *vt* vacunar.

vaccine ['væksiːn] *n* vacuna.

vacuum ['vækjʊm] *n* vacío; ~ **cleaner** *n* aspiradora; ~-**packed** *adj* empaquetado al vacío.

vagina [və'dʒaɪnə] *n* vagina.

vagrant ['veɪgrnt] *n* vagabundo/a.

vague [veɪg] *adj* vago; (*blurred: memory*) borroso; (*ambiguous*) impreciso; (*person: absent-minded*) distraído; (: *evasive*): **to be** ~ no decir las cosas claramente; ~**ly** *adv* vagamente; distraídamente; con evasivas.

vain [veɪn] *adj* (*conceited*) presumido; (*useless*) vano, inútil; **in** ~ en vano.

valentine ['væləntaɪn] *n* (*also*: ~ **card**) tarjeta del Día de los Enamorados.

valet ['væleɪ] *n* ayuda *m* de cámara.

valid ['vælɪd] *adj* válido; (*ticket*) valedero; (*law*) vigente.

valley ['vælɪ] *n* valle *m*.

valour ['vælə*] (*US* **valor**) *n* valor *m*, valentía.

valuable ['væljuəbl] *adj* (*jewel*) de valor; (*time*) valioso; ~**s** *npl* objetos *mpl* de valor.

valuation [vælju'eɪʃən] *n* tasación *f*, valuación *f*; (*judgement of quality*) valoración *f*.

value ['væljuː] *n* valor *m*; (*importance*) importancia ♦ *vt* (*fix price of*) tasar, valorar; (*esteem*) apreciar; ~**s** *npl* (*principles*) principios *mpl*; ~ **added tax** (*BRIT*) *n* impuesto sobre el valor añadido; ~**d** *adj* (*appreciated*) apreciado.

valve [vælv] *n* válvula.

van [væn] *n* (*AUT*) furgoneta (*SP*), camioneta (*AM*).

vandal ['vændl] *n* vándalo/a; ~**ism** *n* vandalismo; ~**ize** *vt* dañar, destruir.

vanilla [və'nɪlə] *n* vainilla.

vanish ['vænɪʃ] *vi* desaparecer.

vanity ['vænɪtɪ] *n* vanidad *f*.

vantage point ['vɑːntɪdʒ-] *n* (*for views*) punto panorámico.

vapour ['veɪpə*] (*US* **vapor**) *n* vapor *m*; (*on breath, window*) vaho.

variable ['vɛərɪəbl] *adj* variable.

variance ['vɛərɪəns] *n*: **to be at** ~ (**with**) estar en desacuerdo (con).

variation [vɛərɪ'eɪʃən] *n* variación *f*.

varicose ['værɪkəʊs] *adj*: ~ **veins** varices *fpl*.

varied ['vɛərɪd] *adj* variado.

variety [və'raɪətɪ] *n* (*diversity*) diversidad *f*; (*type*) variedad *f*; ~ **show** *n* espectáculo de variedades.

various ['vɛərɪəs] *adj* (*several: people*) varios/as; (*reasons*) diversos/as.

varnish ['vɑːnɪʃ] *n* barniz *m*; (*nail* ~) esmalte *m* ♦ *vt* barnizar; (*nails*) pintar (con esmalte).

vary ['vɛərɪ] *vt* variar; (*change*) cambiar ♦ *vi* variar.

vase [vɑːz] *n* florero.

Vaseline ['væsɪliːn] ® *n* Vaselina ®.

vast [vɑːst] *adj* enorme.

VAT [væt] (*BRIT*) *n abbr* (= *Value Added Tax*) IVA *m*.

vat [væt] *n* tina, tinaja.

Vatican ['vætɪkən] *n*: **the** ~ el Vaticano.

vault [vɔːlt] *n* (*of roof*) bóveda; (*tomb*) panteón *m*; (*in bank*) cámara acorazada ♦ *vt* (*also*: ~ **over**) saltar (por encima de).

vaunted ['vɔːntɪd] *adj*: **much** ~ cacareado, alardeado.

VCR *n abbr* = **video cassette recorder.**

VD *n abbr* = **venereal disease.**

VDU *n abbr* (= *visual display unit*) UPV *f*.

veal [viːl] *n* ternera.

veer [vɪə*] *vi* (*vehicle*) virar; (*wind*) girar.

vegetable ['vedʒtəbl] *n* (*BOT*) vegetal

m; (*edible plant*) legumbre *f*, hortaliza
♦ *adj* vegetal; ~s *npl* (*cooked*) verduras *fpl*.
vegetarian [vedʒɪ'teərɪən] *adj*, *n*
vegetariano/a *m/f*.
vehement ['viːɪmənt] *adj* vehemente,
apasionado.
vehicle ['viːɪkl] *n* vehículo; (*fig*) medio.
veil [veɪl] *n* velo ♦ *vt* velar; ~**ed** *adj*
(*fig*) velado.
vein [veɪn] *n* vena; (*of ore etc*) veta.
velocity [vɪ'lɔsɪtɪ] *n* velocidad *f*.
velvet ['velvɪt] *n* terciopelo.
vending machine ['vendɪŋ-] *n* distribuidor *m* automático.
vendor ['vendə*] *n* vendedor(a) *m/f*.
veneer [və'nɪə*] *n* chapa, enchapado;
(*fig*) barniz *m*.
venereal disease [vɪ'nɪərɪəl-] *n* enfermedad *f* venérea.
Venetian blind [vɪ'niːʃən-] *n* persiana.
Venezuela [venɪ'zweɪlə] *n* Venezuela;
~**n** *adj*, *n* venezolano/a *m/f*.
vengeance ['vendʒəns] *n* venganza;
with a ~ (*fig*) con creces.
venison ['venɪsn] *n* carne *f* de venado.
venom ['venəm] *n* veneno; (*bitterness*)
odio; ~**ous** *adj* venenoso; lleno de odio.
vent [vent] *n* (*in jacket*) respiradero;
(*in wall*) rejilla (de ventilación) ♦ *vt*
(*fig: feelings*) desahogar.
ventilator ['ventɪleɪtə*] *n* ventilador *m*.
venture ['ventʃə*] *n* empresa ♦ *vt* (*opinion*) ofrecer ♦ *vi* arriesgarse, lanzarse;
business ~ empresa comercial.
venue ['venjuː] *n* lugar *m*.
veranda(h) [və'rændə] *n* terraza.
verb [vəːb] *n* verbo; ~**al** *adj* verbal.
verbatim [vəː'beɪtɪm] *adj*, *adv* palabra
por palabra.
verbose [vəː'bəus] *adj* prolijo.
verdict ['vəːdɪkt] *n* veredicto, fallo; (*fig*)
opinión *f*, juicio.
verge [vəːdʒ] (*BRIT*) *n* borde *m*; "**soft
~s**" (*AUT*) "arcén *m* no asfaltado"; **to
be on the ~ of doing sth** estar a punto
de hacer algo; ~ **on** *vt fus* rayar en.
verify ['verɪfaɪ] *vt* comprobar, verificar.
veritable ['verɪtəbl] *adj* verdadero, auténtico.

vermin ['vəːmɪn] *npl* (*animals*) alimañas
fpl; (*insects*, *fig*) parásitos *mpl*.
vermouth ['vəːməθ] *n* vermut *m*.
vernacular [və'nækjulə*] *n* lengua vernácula.
versatile ['vəːsətaɪl] *adj* (*person*) polifacético; (*machine*, *tool etc*) versátil.
verse [vəːs] *n* poesía; (*stanza*) estrofa;
(*in bible*) versículo.
versed [vəːst] *adj*: (**well-**)~ **in** versado
en.
version ['vəːʃən] *n* versión *f*.
versus ['vəːsəs] *prep* contra.
vertebra ['vəːtɪbrə] (*pl* ~**e**) *n* vértebra.
vertical ['vəːtɪkl] *adj* vertical.
verve [vəːv] *n* brío.
very ['verɪ] *adv* muy ♦ *adj*: **the ~ book
which** el mismo libro que; **the ~ last** el
último de todos; **at the ~ least** al menos; ~ **much** muchísimo.
vessel ['vesl] *n* (*ship*) barco; (*container*) vasija; *see* **blood**.
vest [vest] *n* (*BRIT*) camiseta; (*US*:
waistcoat) chaleco; ~**ed interests** *npl*
(*COMM*) intereses *mpl* creados.
vestige ['vestɪdʒ] *n* vestigio, rastro.
vet [vet] *vt* (*candidate*) investigar ♦ *n*
abbr (*BRIT*) = **veterinary surgeon**.
veteran ['vetərn] *n* veterano.
veterinary surgeon ['vetrɪnərɪ] (*US* **veterinarian**) *n* veterinario/a *m/f*.
veto ['viːtəu] (*pl* ~**es**) *n* veto ♦ *vt* prohibir, poner el veto a.
vex [veks] *vt* fastidiar; ~**ed** *adj* (*question*) controvertido.
VHF *abbr* (= *very high frequency*) muy
alta frecuencia.
via ['vaɪə] *prep* por, por medio de.
vibrant ['vaɪbrənt] *adj* (*lively*) animado;
(*bright*) vivo; (*voice*) vibrante.
vibrate [vaɪ'breɪt] *vi* vibrar.
vicar ['vɪkə*] *n* párroco (de la Iglesia
Anglicana); ~**age** *n* parroquia.
vice [vaɪs] *n* (*evil*) vicio; (*TECH*) torno
de banco.
vice- [vaɪs] *prefix* vice-; ~**-chairman** *n*
vicepresidente *m*.
vice squad *n* brigada antivicio.
vice versa ['vaɪsɪ'vəːsə] *adv* viceversa.
vicinity [vɪ'sɪnɪtɪ] *n*: **in the ~ (of)** cerca

no (a).
vicious ['vɪʃəs] *adj* (*attack*) violento;
(*words*) cruel; (*horse, dog*) resabido;
~ **circle** *n* círculo vicioso.
victim ['vɪktɪm] *n* víctima; ~**ize** *vt* tomar represalias contra.
victor ['vɪktə*] *n* vencedor(a) *m/f*.
victorious [vɪk'tɔːrɪəs] *adj* (*team*) vence-
dor(a).
victory ['vɪktərɪ] *n* victoria.
video ['vɪdɪəu] *cpd* video ♦ *n* (~ *film*) vi-
deofilm *m*; (*also*: ~ *cassette*) videoca-
ssette *f*; (*also*: ~ *cassette recorder*)
magnetoscopio; ~ **tape** *n* cinta de vídeo.
vie [vaɪ] *vi*: to ~ (*with sb for sth*) competir (con uno por algo).
Vienna [vɪ'ɛnə] *n* Viena.
Vietnam [vjɛt'næm] *n* Vietnam *m*; ~**ese**
[-nə'miːz] *n inv, adj* vietnamita *m/f*.
view [vjuː] *n* vista; (*outlook*) perspectiva; (*opinion*) opinión *f*, criterio ♦ *vt*
(*look at*) mirar; (*fig*) considerar; **on** ~
(*in museum etc*) expuesto; **in full** ~
(**of**) en plena vista (de); **in** ~ **of the
weather/the fact that** en vista del
tiempo/del hecho de que; **in my** ~ en
mi opinión; ~**er** *n* espectador(a) *m/f*;
(*TV*) telespectador(a) *m/f*; ~**finder** *n* visor *m* de imagen; ~**point** *n* (*attitude*)
punto de vista; (*place*) mirador *m*.
vigil ['vɪdʒɪl] *n* vigilia..
vigour ['vɪgə*] (*US* **vigor**) *n* energía, vigor *m*.
vile [vaɪl] *adj* vil, infame; (*smell*) asqueroso; (*temper*) endemoniado.
villa ['vɪlə] *n* (*country house*) casa de
campo; (*suburban house*) chalet *m*.
village ['vɪlɪdʒ] *n* aldea; ~**r** *n* aldeano/a.
villain ['vɪlən] *n* (*scoundrel*) malvado/a;
(*in novel*) malo; (*BRIT: criminal*) maleante *m/f*.
vindicate ['vɪndɪkeɪt] *vt* vindicar, justificar.
vindictive [vɪn'dɪktɪv] *adj* vengativo.
vine [vaɪn] *n* vid *f*.
vinegar ['vɪnɪgə*] *n* vinagre *m*.
vineyard ['vɪnjɑːd] *n* viña, viñedo.
vintage ['vɪntɪdʒ] *n* (*year*) vendimia, cosecha ♦ *cpd* de época; ~ **wine** *n* vino

añejo.
vinyl ['vaɪnl] *n* vinilo.
viola [vɪ'əulə] *n* (*MUS*) viola.
violate ['vaɪəleɪt] *vt* violar.
violence ['vaɪələns] *n* violencia.
violent ['vaɪələnt] *adj* violento; (*intense*)
intenso.
violet ['vaɪələt] *adj* violado, violeta ♦ *n*
(*plant*) violeta.
violin [vaɪə'lɪn] *n* violín *m*; ~**ist** *n* violi-
nista *m/f*.
VIP *n abbr* (= *very important person*)
VIP *m*.
virgin ['vɜːdʒɪn] *n* virgen *f*.
Virgo ['vɜːgəu] *n* Virgo.
virtually ['vɜːtjuəlɪ] *adv* prácticamente.
virtue ['vɜːtjuː] *n* virtud *f*; (*advantage*)
ventaja; **by** ~ **of** en virtud de.
virtuous ['vɜːtjuəs] *adj* virtuoso.
virus ['vaɪərəs] *n* virus *m*.
visa ['viːzə] *n* visado (*SP*), visa (*AM*).
vis-à-vis [viːzə'viː] *prep* con respecto a.
visible ['vɪzəbl] *adj* visible.
vision ['vɪʒən] *n* (*sight*) vista; (*foresight, in dream*) visión *f*.
visit ['vɪzɪt] *n* visita ♦ *vt* (*person: US:
also*: ~ *with*) visitar, hacer una visita
a; (*place*) ir a, (ir a) conocer; ~**ing
hours** *npl* (*in hospital etc*) horas *fpl* de
visita; ~**or** *n* (*in museum*) visitante *m/
f*; (*invited to house*) visita; (*tourist*) turista *m/f*.
visor ['vaɪzə*] *n* visera.
vista ['vɪstə] *n* vista, panorama *m*.
visual ['vɪzjuəl] *adj* visual; ~ **aid** *n* medio visual; ~ **display unit** *n* unidad *f* de
presentación visual; ~**ize** *vt* imaginarse.
vital ['vaɪtl] *adj* (*essential*) esencial, imprescindible; (*dynamic*) dinámico; (*organ*) vital; ~**ly** *adv*: ~**ly important** de
primera importancia; ~ **statistics** *npl*
(*fig*) medidas *fpl* vitales.
vitamin ['vɪtəmɪn] *n* vitamina.
vivacious [vɪ'veɪʃəs] *adj* vivaz, alegre.
vivid ['vɪvɪd] *adj* (*account*) gráfico;
(*light*) intenso; (*imagination, memory*)
vivo; ~**ly** *adv* gráficamente; (*remember*) como si fuera hoy.
V-neck ['viːnɛk] *n* cuello de pico.

vocabulary [vəu'kæbjulərɪ] *n* vocabulario.

vocal ['vəukl] *adj* vocal; (*articulate*) elocuente; ~ **chords** *npl* cuerdas *fpl* vocales.

vocation [vəu'keɪʃən] *n* vocación *f*; ~**al** *adj* profesional.

vodka ['vɔdkə] *n* vodka *m*.

vogue [vəug] *n*: **in** ~ en boga, de moda.

voice [vɔɪs] *n* voz *f* ♦ *vt* expresar.

void [vɔɪd] *n* vacío; (*hole*) hueco ♦ *adj* (*invalid*) nulo, inválido; (*empty*): ~ **of** carente *or* desprovisto de.

volatile ['vɔlətaɪl] *adj* (*situation*) inestable; (*person*) voluble; (*liquid*) volátil.

volcano [vɔl'keɪnəu] (*pl* ~**es**) *n* volcán *m*.

volition [və'lɪʃən] *n*: **of one's own** ~ de su propia voluntad.

volley ['vɔlɪ] *n* (*of gunfire*) descarga; (*of stones etc*) lluvia; (*fig*) torrente *m*; (*TENNIS etc*) volea; ~**ball** *n* vol(e)ibol *m*.

volt [vəult] *n* voltio; ~**age** *n* voltaje *m*.

voluble ['vɔljubl] *adj* locuaz, hablador(a).

volume ['vɔljuːm] *n* (*gen*) volumen *m*; (*book*) tomo *m*.

voluminous [və'luːmɪnəs] *adj* (*clothes*) amplio; (*notes*) prolijo.

voluntary ['vɔləntərɪ] *adj* voluntario.

volunteer [vɔlən'tɪə*] *n* voluntario/a ♦ *vt* (*information*) ofrecer ♦ *vi* ofrecerse (de voluntario); **to** ~ **to do** ofrecerse a hacer.

vomit ['vɔmɪt] *n* vómito ♦ *vt*, *vi* vomitar.

vote [vəut] *n* voto; (*votes cast*) votación *f*; (*right to* ~) derecho de votar; (*franchise*) sufragio ♦ *vt* (*chairman*) elegir; (*propose*): **to** ~ **that** proponer que ♦ *vi* votar, ir a votar; ~ **of thanks** voto de gracias; ~**r** *n* votante *m/f*; **voting** *n* votación *f*.

vouch [vautʃ]: **to** ~ **for** *vt fus* garantizar, responder de.

voucher ['vautʃə*] *n* (*for meal, petrol*) vale *m*.

vow [vau] *n* voto ♦ *vt*: **to** ~ **to do/that** jurar hacer/que.

vowel ['vauəl] *n* vocal *f*.

voyage ['vɔɪɪdʒ] *n* viaje *m*.

V-sign (*BRIT*) *n* ≈ corte *m* de mangas.

vulgar ['vʌlgə*] *adj* (*rude*) ordinario, grosero; (*in bad taste*) de mal gusto; ~**ity** [-'gærɪtɪ] *n* groseria; mal gusto.

vulnerable ['vʌlnərəbl] *adj* vulnerable.

vulture ['vʌltʃə*] *n* buitre *m*.

W

wad [wɔd] *n* bolita; (*of banknotes etc*) fajo.

waddle ['wɔdl] *vi* anadear.

wade [weɪd] *vi*: **to** ~ **through** (*water*) vadear; (*fig*: *book*) leer con dificultad; **wading pool** (*US*) *n* piscina para niños.

wafer ['weɪfə*] *n* galleta, barquillo.

waffle ['wɔfl] *n* (*CULIN*) gofre *m* ♦ *vi* dar el rollo.

waft [wɔft] *vt* llevar por el aire ♦ *vi* flotar.

wag [wæg] *vt* menear, agitar ♦ *vi* moverse, menearse.

wage [weɪdʒ] *n* (*also*: ~**s**) sueldo, salario ♦ *vt*: **to** ~ **war** hacer la guerra; ~ **earner** *n* asalariado/a; ~ **packet** *n* sobre *m* de paga.

wager ['weɪdʒə*] *n* apuesta.

waggle ['wægl] *vt* menear, mover.

wag(g)on ['wægən] *n* (*horse-drawn*) carro; (*BRIT*: *RAIL*) vagón *m*.

wail [weɪl] *n* gemido ♦ *vi* gemir.

waist [weɪst] *n* cintura, talle *m*; ~**coat** (*BRIT*) *n* chaleco; ~**line** *n* talle *m*.

wait [weɪt] *n* (*interval*) pausa ♦ *vi* esperar; **to lie in** ~ **for** acechar a; **I can't** ~ **to** (*fig*) estoy deseando; **to** ~ **for** esperar (a); ~ **behind** *vi* quedarse; ~ **on** *vt fus* servir a; ~**er** *n* camarero; ~**ing** *n*: "**no** ~**ing**" (*BRIT*: *AUT*) "prohibido estacionarse"; ~**ing list** *n* lista de espera; ~**ing room** *n* sala de espera; ~**ress** *n* camarera.

waive [weɪv] *vt* suspender.

wake [weɪk] (*pt* **woke** *or* **waked**, *pp* **woken** *or* **waked**) *vt* (*also*: ~ **up**) despertar ♦ *vi* (*also*: ~ **up**) despertarse ♦ *n* (*for dead person*) vela, velatorio;

(*NAUT*) estela; **waken** *vt*, *vi* = **wake**.

Wales [weɪlz] *n* País *m* de Gales; **the Prince of** ~ el príncipe de Gales.

walk [wɔːk] *n* (*stroll*) paseo; (*hike*) excursión *f* a pie, caminata; (*gait*) paso, andar *m*; (*in park etc*) paseo, alameda ♦ *vi* andar, caminar; (*for pleasure, exercise*) pasear ♦ *vt* (*distance*) recorrer a pie, andar; (*dog*) pasear; **10 minutes'** ~ **from here** a 10 minutos de aquí andando; **people from all** ~**s of life** gente de todas las esferas; ~ **out** *vi* (*audience*) salir; (*workers*) declararse en huelga; ~ **out on** (*inf*) *vt fus* abandonar; ~**er** *n* (*person*) paseante *m/f*, caminante *m/f*; ~**ie-talkie** ['wɔːkɪ'tɔːkɪ] *n* walkie-talkie *m*; ~**ing** *n* el andar; ~**ing shoes** *npl* zapatos *mpl* para andar; ~**ing stick** *n* bastón *m*; ~**out** *n* huelga; ~**over** (*inf*) *n*: **it was a** ~**over** fue pan comido; ~**way** *n* paseo.

wall [wɔːl] *n* pared *f*; (*exterior*) muro; (*city* ~ *etc*) muralla; ~**ed** *adj* amurallado; (*garden*) con tapia.

wallet ['wɔlɪt] *n* cartera (*SP*), billetera (*AM*).

wallflower ['wɔːlflauə*] *n* alhelí *m*; **to 'be a** ~ (*fig*) comer pavo.

wallop ['wɔləp] (*inf*) *vt* zurrar.

wallow ['wɔləu] *vi* revolcarse.

wallpaper ['wɔːlpeɪpə*] *n* papel *m* pintado ♦ *vt* empapelar.

wally ['wɔlɪ] (*BRIT*: *inf*) *n* gilipollas *m inv*.

walnut ['wɔːlnʌt] *n* nuez *f*; (*tree*) nogal *m*.

walrus ['wɔːlrəs] (*pl* ~ *or* ~**es**) *n* morsa.

waltz [wɔːlts] *n* vals *m* ♦ *vi* bailar el vals.

wan [wɔn] *adj* pálido.

wand [wɔnd] *n* (*also*: *magic* ~) varita (mágica).

wander ['wɔndə*] *vi* (*person*) vagar; deambular; (*thoughts*) divagar ♦ *vt* recorrer, vagar por.

wane [weɪn] *vi* menguar.

wangle ['wæŋgl] (*BRIT*: *inf*) *vt* agenciarse.

want [wɔnt] *vt* querer, desear; (*need*) necesitar ♦ *n*: **for** ~ **of** por falta de; ~**s**

npl (*needs*) necesidades *fpl*; **to** ~ **to do** querer hacer; **to** ~ **sb to do sth** querer que uno haga algo; ~**ed** *adj* (*criminal*) buscado; "~**ed**" (*in advertisements*) "se busca"; ~**ing** *adj*: **to be found** ~**ing** no estar a la altura de las circunstancias.

wanton ['wɔntn] *adj* (*playful*) juguetón/ona; (*licentious*) lascivo.

war [wɔː*] *n* guerra; **to make** ~ **(on)** (*also fig*) declarar la guerra (a).

ward [wɔːd] *n* (*in hospital*) sala; (*POL*) distrito electoral; (*LAW*: *child*: *also*: ~ *of court*) pupilo/a; ~ **off** *vt* (*blow*) desviar, parar; (*attack*) rechazar.

warden ['wɔːdn] *n* (*BRIT*: *of institution*) director(a) *m/f*; (*of park, game reserve*) guardián/ana *m/f*; (*BRIT*: *also*: *traffic* ~) guardia *m/f*.

warder ['wɔːdə*] (*BRIT*) *n* guardián/ana *m/f*, carcelero/a.

wardrobe ['wɔːdrəub] *n* armario, guardarropa, ropero (*esp LAm*).

warehouse ['wɛəhaus] *n* almacén *m*, depósito.

wares [wɛəz] *npl* mercancías *fpl*.

warfare ['wɔːfɛə*] *n* guerra.

warhead ['wɔːhɛd] *n* cabeza armada.

warily ['wɛərɪlɪ] *adv* con cautela, cautelosamente.

warlike ['wɔːlaɪk] *adj* guerrero; (*appearance*) belicoso.

warm [wɔːm] *adj* caliente; (*thanks*) efusivo; (*clothes etc*) abrigado; (*welcome, day*) caluroso; **it's** ~ hace calor; **I'm** ~ tengo calor; ~ **up** *vi* (*room*) calentarse; (*person*) entrar en calor; (*athlete*) hacer ejercicios de calentamiento ♦ *vt* calentar; ~**-hearted** *adj* afectuoso; ~**ly** *adv* afectuosamente; ~**th** *n* calor *m*.

warn [wɔːn] *vt* avisar, advertir; ~**ing** *n* aviso, advertencia; ~**ing light** *n* luz *f* de advertencia; ~**ing triangle** *n* (*AUT*) triángulo señalizador.

warp [wɔːp] *vi* (*wood*) combarse ♦ *vt* combar; (*mind*) pervertir.

warrant ['wɔrnt] *n* autorización *f*; (*LAW*: *to arrest*) orden *f* de detención; (*: to search*) mandamiento de registro.

warranty ['wɔrəntɪ] *n* garantía.

warren ['wɒrən] *n* (*of rabbits*) madriguera; (*fig*) laberinto.

warrior ['wɒrɪə*] *n* guerrero/a.

Warsaw ['wɔːsɔː] *n* Varsovia.

warship ['wɔːʃɪp] *n* buque *m* o barco *m* de guerra.

wart [wɔːt] *n* verruga.

wartime ['wɔːtaɪm] *n*: **in ~** en tiempos de guerra, en la guerra.

wary ['weərɪ] *adj* cauteloso.

was [wɒz] *pt of* be.

wash [wɒʃ] *vt* lavar ♦ *vi* lavarse; (*sea etc*): **to ~ against/over sth** llegar hasta/cubrir algo ♦ *n* (*clothes etc*) lavado; (*of ship*) estela; **to have a ~** lavarse; **~ away** *vt* (*stain*) quitar lavando; (*subj: river etc*) llevarse; **~ off** *vi* quitarse (al lavar); **~ up** *vi* (*BRIT*) fregar los platos; (*US*) lavarse; **~able** *adj* lavable; **~basin** (*US* **~bowl**) *n* lavabo; **~ cloth** (*US*) *n* manopla; **~er** *n* (*TECH*) arandela; **~ing** (*dirty*) ropa sucia; (*clean*) colada; **~ing machine** *n* lavadora; **~ing powder** (*BRIT*) *n* detergente *m* (en polvo); **~ing-up** *n* fregado, platos *mpl* (para fregar); **~ing-up liquid** *n* líquido lavavajillas; **~-out** (*inf*) *n* fracaso; **~room** (*US*) *n* servicios *mpl*.

wasn't ['wɒznt] = **was not**.

wasp [wɒsp] *n* avispa.

wastage ['weɪstɪdʒ] *n* desgaste *m*; (*loss*) pérdida.

waste [weɪst] *n* derroche *m*, despilfarro; (*of time*) pérdida; (*food*) sobras *fpl*; (*rubbish*) basura, desperdicios *mpl* ♦ *adj* (*material*) de desecho; (*left over*) sobrante; (*land*) baldío, descampado ♦ *vt* malgastar, derrochar; (*time*) perder; (*opportunity*) desperdiciar; **~s** *npl* (*area of land*) tierras *fpl* baldías; **to lay ~** devastar, arrasar; **~ away** *vi* consumirse; **~ disposal unit** (*BRIT*) *n* triturador *m* de basura; **~ful** *adj* derrochador(a); (*process*) antieconómico; **~ ground** (*BRIT*) *n* terreno baldío; **~paper basket** *n* papelera; **~ pipe** *n* tubo de desagüe.

watch [wɒtʃ] *n* (*also: wrist ~*) reloj *m*; (*MIL: group of guards*) centinela *m*; (*act*) vigilancia; (*NAUT: spell of duty*) guardia ♦ *vt* (*look at*) mirar, observar; (: *match, programme*) ver; (*spy on, guard*) vigilar; (*be careful of*) cuidarse de, tener cuidado de ♦ *vi* ver, mirar; (*keep guard*) montar guardia; **~ out** *vi* cuidarse, tener cuidado; **~dog** *n* perro guardián; (*fig*) persona u organismo encargado de asegurarse de que las empresas actúan dentro de la legalidad; **~ful** *adj* vigilante, sobre aviso; **~maker** *n* relojero/a; **~man** *n see* **night**; **~ strap** *n* pulsera (de reloj).

water ['wɔːtə*] *n* agua ♦ *vt* (*plant*) regar ♦ *vi* (*eyes*) llorar; (*mouth*) hacerse la boca agua; **~ down** *vt* (*milk etc*) aguar; (*fig: story*) dulcificar, diluir; **~ closet** *n* wáter *m*; **~colour** *n* acuarela; **~cress** *n* berro; **~fall** *n* cascada, salto de agua; **~ heater** *n* calentador *m* de agua; **~ing can** *n* regadera; **~ lily** *n* nenúfar *m*; **~line** *n* (*NAUT*) línea de flotación; **~logged** *adj* (*ground*) inundado; **~ main** *n* cañería del agua; **~melon** *n* sandía; **~proof** *adj* impermeable; **~shed** *n* (*GEO*) cuenca; (*fig*) momento crítico; **~-skiing** *n* esquí *m* acuático; **~tight** *adj* hermético; **~way** *n* vía fluvial *or* navegable; **~works** *n* central *f* depuradora; **~y** *adj* (*coffee etc*) aguado; (*eyes*) lloroso.

watt [wɒt] *n* vatio.

wave [weɪv] *n* (*of hand*) señal *f* con la mano; (*on water*) ola; (*RADIO, in hair*) onda; (*fig*) oleada ♦ *vi* agitar la mano; (*flag etc*) ondear ♦ *vt* (*handkerchief, gun*) agitar; **~length** *n* longitud *f* de onda.

waver ['weɪvə*] *vi* (*voice, love etc*) flaquear; (*person*) vacilar.

wavy ['weɪvɪ] *adj* ondulado.

wax [wæks] *n* cera ♦ *vt* encerar ♦ *vi* (*moon*) crecer; **~ paper** (*US*) *n* papel *m* apergaminado; **~works** *n* museo de cera ♦ *npl* figuras *fpl* de cera.

way [weɪ] *n* camino; (*distance*) trayecto, recorrido; (*direction*) dirección *f*, sentido; (*manner*) modo, manera; (*habit*) costumbre *f*; **which ~? — this ~** ¿por dónde?, ¿en qué dirección? — por aquí; **on the ~** (*en route*) en (el) cami-

no; **to be on one's ~** estar en camino;
to be in the ~ bloquear el camino; (*fig*)
estorbar; **to go out of one's ~ to do sth**
desvivirse por hacer algo; **under ~** en
marcha; **to lose one's ~** extraviarse; **in
a ~** en cierto modo *or* sentido; **no ~!**
(*inf*) ¡de eso nada!; **by the ~** ... a propósito ...; **"~ in"** (*BRIT*) "entrada"; **"~
out"** (*BRIT*) "salida"; **the ~ back** el camino de vuelta; **"give ~"** (*BRIT: AUT*)
"ceda el paso".

waylay [weɪˈleɪ] (*irreg*) *vt* salir al paso
a.

wayward [ˈweɪwəd] *adj* díscolo.

W.C. *n* (*BRIT*) wáter *m*.

we [wiː] *pl pron* nosotros/as.

weak [wiːk] *adj* débil, flojo; (*tea etc*)
claro; **~en** *vi* debilitarse; (*give way*)
ceder ♦ *vt* debilitar; **~ling** *n* debilucho/
a; (*morally*) persona de poco carácter;
~ness *n* debilidad *f*; (*fault*) punto débil; **to have a ~ness for** tener debilidad
por.

wealth [welθ] *n* riqueza; (*of details*)
abundancia; **~y** *adj* rico.

wean [wiːn] *vt* destetar.

weapon [ˈwepən] *n* arma.

wear [wɛəʳ] (*pt* **wore**, *pp* **worn**) *n* (*use*)
uso; (*deterioration through use*) desgas-
te *m*; (*clothing*): **sports/baby~** ropa de
deportes/de niños; **evening ~** ropa de
etiqueta ♦ *vt* (*clothes*) llevar; (*shoes*)
calzar; (*damage: through use*) gastar,
usar ♦ *vi* (*last*) durar; (*rub through
etc*) desgastarse; **~ away** *vt* gastar ♦
vi desgastarse; **~ down** *vt* gastar;
(*strength*) agotar; **~ off** *vi* (*pain etc*)
pasar, desaparecer; **~ out** *vt* desgastar; (*person, strength*) agotar; **~ and
tear** *n* desgaste *m*.

weary [ˈwɪərɪ] *adj* cansado; (*dispirited*)
abatido ♦ *vi*: **to ~ of** cansarse de.

weasel [ˈwiːzl] *n* (*ZOOL*) comadreja.

weather [ˈwɛðəʳ] *n* tiempo ♦ *vt* (*storm,
crisis*) hacer frente a; **under the ~** (*fig:
ill*) indispuesto, pachucho; **~-beaten**
adj (*skin*) curtido; (*building*) deteriora-
do por la intemperie; **~cock** *n* veleta;
~ forecast *n* boletín *m* meteorológico;
~man (*inf*) *n* hombre *m* del tiempo; **~**

vane *n* = **~cock**.

weave [wiːv] (*pt* **wove**, *pp* **woven**) *vt*
(*cloth*) tejer; (*fig*) entretejer; **~r** *n* te-
jedor(a) *m/f*; **weaving** *n* tejeduría.

web [wɛb] *n* (*of spider*) telaraña; (*on
duck's foot*) membrana; (*network*) red
f.

wed [wɛd] (*pt, pp* **wedded**) *vt* casar ♦ *vi*
casarse.

we'd [wiːd] = **we had**; **we would**.

wedding [ˈwɛdɪŋ] *n* boda, casamiento;
silver/golden ~ (**anniversary**) bodas *fpl*
de plata/de oro; **~ day** *n* día *m* de la
boda; **~ dress** *n* traje *m* de novia; **~
present** *n* regalo de boda; **~ ring** *n*
alianza.

wedge [wɛdʒ] *n* (*of wood etc*) cuña; (*of
cake*) trozo ♦ *vt* acuñar; (*push*) apretar.

Wednesday [ˈwɛnzdɪ] *n* miércoles *m
inv*.

wee [wiː] (*Scottish*) *adj* pequeñito.

weed [wiːd] *n* mala hierba, maleza ♦ *vt*
escardar, desherbar; **~killer** *n* herbicida *m*; **~y** *adj* (*person*) mequetréfico.

week [wiːk] *n* semana; **a ~ today/on
Friday** de hoy/del viernes en ocho días;
~day *n* día *m* laborable; **~end** *n* fin *m*
de semana; **~ly** *adv* semanalmente,
cada semana ♦ *adj* semanal ♦ *n* sema-
nario.

weep [wiːp] (*pt, pp* **wept**) *vi, vt* llorar;
~ing willow *n* sauce *m* llorón.

weigh [weɪ] *vt, vi* pesar; **to ~ anchor**
levar anclas; **~ down** *vt* sobrecargar;
(*fig: with worry*) agobiar; **~ up** *vt* so-
pesar.

weight [weɪt] *n* peso; (*metal ~*) pesa;
to lose/put on ~ adelgazar/engordar;
~ing *n* (*allowance*): (**London**) **~ing** *dietas* (*por residir en Londres*); **~lifter** *n*
levantador *m* de pesas; **~y** *adj* pesado;
(*matters*) de relevancia *or* peso.

weir [wɪəʳ] *n* presa.

weird [wɪəd] *adj* raro, extraño.

welcome [ˈwɛlkəm] *adj* bienvenido ♦ *n*
bienvenida ♦ *vt* dar la bienvenida a;
(*be glad of*) alegrarse de; **thank you —
you're ~** gracias — de nada.

weld [wɛld] *n* soldadura ♦ *vt* soldar.

welfare ['wɛlfɛə*] n bienestar m; (social aid) asistencia social; ~ **state** n estado del bienestar; ~ **work** n asistencia social.

well [wɛl] n fuente f, pozo ♦ adv bien ♦ adj: to be ~ estar bien (de salud) ♦ excl ¡vaya!, ¡bueno!; as ~ también; as ~ as además de; ~ done! ¡bien hecho!; get ~ soon! ¡que te mejores pronto!; to do ~ (business) ir bien; (person) tener éxito; ~ up vi (tears) saltar.

we'll [wi:l] = we will; we shall.

well: ~-**behaved** adj bueno; ~-**being** n bienestar m; ~-**built** adj (person) fornido; ~-**deserved** adj merecido; ~-**dressed** adj bien vestido; ~-**groomed** adj de buena presencia; ~-**heeled** (inf) adj (wealthy) rico.

wellingtons ['wɛlɪŋtənz] npl (also: wellington boots) botas fpl de goma.

well: ~-**known** adj (person) conocido; ~-**mannered** adj educado; ~-**meaning** adj bienintencionado; ~-**off** adj acomodado; ~-**read** adj leído; ~-**to-do** adj acomodado; ~-**wisher** n admirador(a) m/f.

Welsh [wɛlʃ] adj galés/esa ♦ n (LING) galés m; **the** ~ npl los galeses; ~**man** n galés m; ~ **rarebit** n pan m con queso tostado; ~**woman** n galesa.

went [wɛnt] pt of go.

wept [wɛpt] pt, pp of weep.

were [wə:*] pt of be.

we're [wɪə*] = we are.

weren't [wə:nt] = were not.

west [wɛst] n oeste m ♦ adj occidental, del oeste ♦ adv al or hacia el oeste; **the W~** n el Oeste, el Occidente; **W~ Country** (BRIT) n: **the W~ Country** el suroeste de Inglaterra; ~**erly** adj occidental; (wind) del oeste; ~**ern** adj occidental ♦ n (CINEMA) película del oeste; **W~ Germany** n Alemania Occidental; **W~ Indian** adj, n antillano/a m/f; **W~ Indies** npl Antillas fpl; ~**ward(s)** adv hacia el oeste.

wet [wɛt] adj (damp) húmedo; (~ through) mojado; (rainy) lluvioso ♦ (BRIT) n (POL) conservador(a) m/f moderado/a; to get ~ mojarse; "~

paint" "recién pintado"; ~ **blanket** n: to be a ~ **blanket** (fig) ser un/una aguafiestas; ~**suit** n traje m térmico.

we've [wi:v] = we have.

whack [wæk] vt dar un buen golpe a.

whale [weɪl] n (ZOOL) ballena.

wharf [wɔ:f] n muelle m; **wharves** [wɔ:vz] npl of wharf.

KEYWORD
---

what [wɔt] adj **1** (in direct/indirect questions) qué; ~ **size is he?** ¿qué talla usa?; ~ **colour/shape is it?** ¿de qué color/forma es?

2 (in exclamations): ~ **a mess!** ¡qué desastre!; ~ **a fool I am!** ¡qué tonto soy!

♦ pron **1** (interrogative) qué; ~ **are you doing?** ¿qué haces or estás haciendo?; ~ **is happening?** ¿qué pasa or está pasando?; ~ **is it called?** ¿cómo se llama?; ~ **about me?** ¿y yo qué?; ~ **about doing ...?** ¿qué tal si hacemos ...?

2 (relative) lo que; **I saw ~ you did/was on the table** vi lo que hiciste/había en la mesa

♦ excl (disbelieving) ¡cómo!; ~, **no coffee!** ¡que no hay café!

---

whatever [wɔt'ɛvə*] adj: ~ **book you choose** cualquier libro que elijas ♦ pron: **do ~ is necessary** haga lo que sea necesario; ~ **happens** pase lo que pase; **no reason ~ or whatsoever** ninguna razón sea la que sea; **nothing ~** nada en absoluto.

whatsoever [wɔtsəu'ɛvə*] adj = whatever.

wheat [wi:t] n trigo.

wheedle ['wi:dl] vt: to ~ **sb into doing sth** engatusar a uno para que haga algo; to ~ **sth out of sb** sonsacar algo a uno.

wheel [wi:l] n rueda; (AUT: also: steering ~) volante m; (NAUT) timón m ♦ vt (pram etc) empujar ♦ vi (also: ~ round) dar la vuelta, girar; ~**barrow** n carretilla; ~**chair** n silla de ruedas; ~ **clamp** n (AUT) cepo.

wheeze [wi:z] vi resollar.

KEYWORD

when [wɛn] *adv* cuando; ~ **did it happen?** ¿cuándo ocurrió?; **I know ~ it happened** sé cuándo ocurrió
♦ *conj* **1** (*at, during, after the time that*) cuando; **be careful ~ you cross the road** ten cuidado al cruzar la calle; **that was ~ I needed you** fue entonces que te necesité
2 (*on, at which*): **on the day ~ I met him** el día en que le conocí
3 (*whereas*) cuando.

whenever [wɛn'ɛvə⁰] *conj* cuando; (*every time that*) cada vez que ♦ *adv* cuando sea.

where [wɛə⁰] *adv* dónde ♦ *conj* donde; **this is ~** aquí es donde; ~**abouts** *adv* dónde ♦ *n*: **nobody knows his ~abouts** nadie conoce su paradero; ~**as** *conj* visto que, mientras; ~**by** *pron* por lo cual; ~**upon** *conj* con lo cual, después de lo cual; ~**ver** [-'ɛvə⁰] *conj* dondequiera que; (*interrogative*) dónde; ~**withal** *n* recursos *mpl*.

whet [wɛt] *vt* estimular.

whether ['wɛðə⁰] *conj* si; **I don't know ~ to accept or not** no sé si aceptar o no; ~ **you go or not** vayas o no vayas.

KEYWORD

which [wɪtʃ] *adj* **1** (*interrogative: direct, indirect*) qué; ~ **picture(s) do you want?** ¿qué cuadro(s) quieres?; ~ **one?** ¿cuál?
2 **in ~ case** en cuyo caso; **we got there at 8 pm, by ~ time the cinema was full** llegamos allí a las 8, cuando el cine estaba lleno
♦ *pron* **1** (*interrogative*) cual; **I don't mind ~** el/la que sea
2 (*relative: replacing noun*) que; (: *replacing clause*) lo que; (: *after preposition*) (el/la) que *etc*, el/la cual *etc*; **the apple ~ you ate/~ is on the table** la manzana que comiste/que está en la mesa; **the chair on ~ you are sitting** la silla en la que estás sentado; **he said he knew, ~ is true/I feared** dijo que lo sabía, lo cual *or* lo que es cierto/me temía.

whichever [wɪtʃ'ɛvə⁰] *adj*: **take ~ book you prefer** coja (*SP*) el libro que prefiera; ~ **book you take** cualquier libro que coja.

whiff [wɪf] *n* vaharada.

while [waɪl] *n* rato, momento ♦ *conj* mientras; (*although*) aunque; **for a ~** durante algún tiempo; ~ **away** *vt* pasar.

whim [wɪm] *n* capricho.

whimper ['wɪmpə⁰] *n* sollozo ♦ *vi* lloriquear.

whimsical ['wɪmzɪkl] *adj* (*person*) caprichoso; (*look*) juguetón/ona.

whine [waɪn] *n* (*of pain*) gemido; (*of engine*) zumbido; (*of siren*) aullido ♦ *vi* gemir; zumbar; (*fig: complain*) gimotear.

whip [wɪp] *n* látigo; (*POL: person*) encargado de la disciplina partidaria en el parlamento ♦ *vt* azotar; (*CULIN*) batir; (*move quickly*): **to ~ sth out/off** sacar/quitar algo de un tirón; ~**ped cream** *n* nata *or* crema montada; ~**-round** (*BRIT*) *n* colecta.

whirl [wəːl] *vt* hacer girar, dar vueltas a ♦ *vi* girar, dar vueltas; (*leaves, water etc*) arremolinarse; ~**pool** *n* remolino; ~**wind** *n* torbellino.

whirr [wəː⁰] *vi* zumbar.

whisk [wɪsk] *n* (*CULIN*) batidor *m* ♦ *vt* (*CULIN*) batir; **to ~ sb away** *or* **off** llevar volando a uno.

whiskers ['wɪskəz] *npl* (*of animal*) bigotes *mpl*; (*of man*) patillas *fpl*.

whiskey ['wɪskɪ] (*US, Ireland*) *n* = **whisky**.

whisky ['wɪskɪ] *n* whisky *m*.

whisper ['wɪspə⁰] *n* susurro ♦ *vi, vt* susurrar.

whist [wɪst] (*BRIT*) *n* juego de naipes.

whistle ['wɪsl] *n* (*sound*) silbido; (*object*) silbato ♦ *vi* silbar.

white [waɪt] *adj* blanco; (*pale*) pálido ♦ *n* blanco; (*of egg*) clara; ~ **coffee** (*BRIT*) *n* café *m* con leche; ~**-collar worker** *n* oficinista *m/f*; ~ **elephant** *n* (*fig*) maula; ~ **lie** *n* mentirilla; ~**ness** *n* blancura; ~ **noise** *n* sonido blanco; ~ **paper** *n* (*POL*) libro rojo; ~**wash** *n* (*paint*) jalbegue *m*, cal *f* ♦ *vt* (*also fig*) blanquear.

whiting ['waɪtɪŋ] *n inv* (*fish*) pescadilla.

Whitsun ['wɪtsn] *n* pentecostés *m*.

whittle ['wɪtl] *vt*: to ~ **away**, ~ **down** ir reduciendo.

whizz [wɪz] *vi*: to ~ **past** *or* **by** pasar a toda velocidad; ~ **kid** (*inf*) *n* prodigio.

who [hu:] *pron* **1** (*interrogative*) quién; ~ **is it?**, ~'**s there?** ¿quién es?; ~ **are you looking for?** ¿a quién buscas?; **I told her** ~ **I was** le dije quién era yo
2 (*relative*) que; **the man/woman** ~ **spoke to me** el hombre/la mujer que habló conmigo; **those** ~ **can swim** los que saben *or* sepan nadar.

whodun(n)it [hu:'dʌnɪt] (*inf*) *n* novela policíaca.

whoever [hu:'evə*] *pron*: ~ **finds it** cualquiera *or* quienquiera que lo encuentre; **ask** ~ **you like** pregunta a quien quieras; ~ **he marries** no importa con quién se case.

whole [həʊl] *adj* (*entire*) todo, entero; (*not broken*) intacto ♦ *n* todo; (*all*): **the** ~ **of the town** toda la ciudad, la ciudad entera ♦ *n* (*total*) total *m*; (*sum*) conjunto; **on the** ~, **as a** ~ en general; ~ **food(s)** *n(pl)* alimento(s) *m(pl)* integral(es); ~**hearted** *adj* sincero, cordial; ~**meal** *adj* integral; ~**sale** *n* venta al por mayor ♦ *adj* al por mayor; (*fig: destruction*) sistemático; ~**saler** *n* mayorista *m/f*; ~**some** *adj* sano; ~**wheat** *adj* = ~**meal**; **wholly** *adv* totalmente, enteramente.

whom [hu:m] *pron* **1** (*interrogative*): ~ **did you see?** ¿a quién viste?; **to** ~ **did you give it?** ¿a quién se lo diste?; **tell me from** ~ **you received it** dígame de quién lo recibí
2 (*relative*) que; **to** ~ a quien(es); **of** ~

de quien(es), del/de la que *etc*; **the man** ~ **I saw/to** ~ **I wrote** el hombre que vi/a quien escribí; **the lady about/with** ~ **I was talking** la señora de (la) que/con quien *or* (la) que hablaba.

whooping cough ['hu:pɪŋ-] *n* tos *f* ferina.

whore [hɔ:*] (*inf: pej*) *n* puta.

whose [hu:z] *adj* **1** (*possessive: interrogative*): ~ **book is this?**, ~ **is this book?** ¿de quién es este libro?; ~ **pencil have you taken?** ¿de quién es el lápiz que has cogido?; ~ **daughter are you?** ¿de quién eres hija?
2 (*possessive: relative*) cuyo/a, *pl* cuyos/as; **the man** ~ **son you rescued** el hombre cuyo hijo rescataste; **those** ~ **passports I have** aquellas personas cuyos pasaportes tengo; **the woman** ~ **car was stolen** la mujer a quien le robaron el coche
♦ *pron* de quién; ~ **is this?** ¿de quién es esto?; **I know** ~ **it is** sé de quién es.

why [waɪ] *adv* por qué; ~ **not?** ¿por qué no?; ~ **not do it now?** ¿por qué no lo haces (*or* hacemos *etc*) ahora?
♦ *conj*: **I wonder** ~ **he said that** me pregunto por qué dijo eso; **that's not** ~ **I'm here** no es por eso (por lo) que estoy aquí; **the reason** ~ la razón por la que
♦ *excl* (*expressing surprise, shock, annoyance*): ~, **it's you!** ¡hombre, eres tú!; ~, **that's impossible** ¡pero sí eso es imposible!

wicked ['wɪkɪd] *adj* malvado, cruel.

wickerwork ['wɪkəwɜːk] *n* artículos *mpl* de mimbre ♦ *adj* de mimbre.

wicket ['wɪkɪt] *n* (*CRICKET: stumps*) palos *mpl*; (: *grass area*) terreno de juego.

wide [waɪd] *adj* ancho; (*area, knowledge*) vasto, grande; (*choice*) amplio ♦

adv: **to open** ~ abrir de par en par; **to shoot** ~ errar el tiro; ~**-angle lens** *n* objetivo de gran angular; ~**-awake** *adj* bien despierto; ~**ly** *adv* (*travelled*) mucho; (*spaced*) muy; **it is** ~**ly believed/known that...** mucha gente piensa/sabe que...; ~**n** *vt* ensanchar; (*experience*) ampliar ♦ *vi* ensancharse; ~ **open** *adj* abierto de par en par; ~**spread** *adj* extendido, general.

widow ['wɪdəu] *n* viuda; ~**ed** *adj* viudo; ~**er** *n* viudo.

width [wɪdθ] *n* anchura; (*of cloth*) ancho.

wield [wiːld] *vt* (*sword*) blandir; (*power*) ejercer.

wife [waɪf] (*pl* **wives**) *n* mujer *f*, esposa.

wig [wɪg] *n* peluca.

wiggle ['wɪgl] *vt* menear.

wild [waɪld] *adj* (*animal*) salvaje; (*plant*) silvestre; (*person*) furioso, violento; (*idea*) descabellado; (*rough: sea*) bravo; (*: land*) agreste; (*: weather*) muy revuelto; ~**s** *npl* regiones *fpl* salvajes, tierras *fpl* vírgenes; ~**erness** ['wɪldənɪs] *n* desierto; ~**-goose chase** *n* (*fig*) búsqueda inútil; ~**life** *n* fauna; ~**ly** *adv* (*behave*) locamente; (*lash out*) a diestro y siniestro; (*guess*) a lo loco; (*happy*) a más no poder.

wilful ['wɪlful] (*US* **willful**) *adj* (*action*) deliberado; (*obstinate*) testarudo.

KEYWORD
---

will [wɪl] *aux vb* **1** (*forming future tense*): **I** ~ **finish it tomorrow** lo terminaré *or* voy a terminar mañana; **I** ~ **have finished it by tomorrow** lo habré terminado para mañana; ~ **you do it?** — **yes I** ~/**no I won't** ¿lo harás? — sí/no **2** (*in conjectures, predictions*): **he** ~ *or* **he'll be there by now** ya habrá *or* debe (de) haber llegado; **that** ~ **be the postman** será *or* debe ser el cartero **3** (*in commands, requests, offers*): ~ **you be quiet!** ¿quieres callarte?; ~ **you help me?** ¿quieres ayudarme?; ~ **you have a cup of tea?** ¿te apetece un té?; **I won't put up with it!** ¡no lo soporto!

♦ *vt* (*pt, pp* **willed**): **to** ~ **sb to do sth** desear que alguien haga algo; **he** ~**ed himself to go on** con gran fuerza de voluntad, continuó
♦ *n* voluntad *f*; (*testament*) testamento.

---

willful ['wɪlful] (*US*) *adj* = **wilful**.

willing ['wɪlɪŋ] *adj* (*with goodwill*) de buena voluntad; (*enthusiastic*) entusiasta; **he's** ~ **to do it** está dispuesto a hacerlo; ~**ly** *adv* con mucho gusto; ~**ness** *n* buena voluntad.

willow ['wɪləu] *n* sauce *m*.

willpower ['wɪlpauə*] *n* fuerza de voluntad.

willy-nilly [wɪlɪ'nɪlɪ] *adv* quiérase o no.

wilt [wɪlt] *vi* marchitarse.

wily ['waɪlɪ] *adj* astuto.

win [wɪn] (*pt, pp* **won**) *n* victoria, triunfo ♦ *vt* ganar; (*obtain*) conseguir, lograr ♦ *vi* ganar; ~ **over** *vt* convencer a; ~ **round** (*BRIT*) *vt* = ~ **over**.

wince ['wɪns] *vi* encogerse.

winch [wɪntʃ] *n* torno.

wind¹ [wɪnd] *n* viento; (*MED*) gases *mpl* ♦ *vt* (*take breath away from*) dejar sin aliento a.

wind² [waɪnd] (*pt, pp* **wound**) *vt* enrollar; (*wrap*) envolver; (*clock, toy*) dar cuerda a ♦ *vi* (*road, river*) serpentear; ~ **up** *vt* (*clock*) dar cuerda a; (*debate, meeting*) concluir, terminar.

windfall ['wɪndfɔːl] *n* golpe *m* de suerte.

winding ['waɪndɪŋ] *adj* (*road*) tortuoso; (*staircase*) de caracol.

wind instrument [wɪnd-] *n* (*MUS*) instrumento de viento.

windmill ['wɪndmɪl] *n* molino de viento.

window ['wɪndəu] *n* ventana; (*in car, train*) ventanilla; (*in shop etc*) escaparate *m* (*SP*), vitrina (*AM*); ~ **box** *n* jardinera de ventana; ~ **cleaner** *n* (*person*) limpiador *m* de cristales; ~ **ledge** *n* alféizar *m*, repisa; ~ **pane** *n* cristal *m*; ~**-shopping** *n*: **to go** ~**-shopping** ir de escaparates; ~**sill** *n* alféizar *m*, repisa.

windpipe ['wɪndpaɪp] *n* tráquea.

windscreen ['wɪndskriːn] *n* (*US* **windshield**) *n* parabrisas *m inv*; ~ **washer** *n* lavaparabrisas *m inv*; ~ **wiper** *n* limpiaparabrisas *m inv.*

windswept ['wɪndswept] *adj* azotado por el viento.

windy ['wɪndɪ] *adj* de mucho viento; it's ~ hace viento.

wine [waɪn] *n* vino; ~ **bar** *n* enoteca; ~ **cellar** *n* bodega; ~ **glass** *n* copa (para vino); ~ **list** *n* lista de vinos; ~ **merchant** *n* vinatero; ~ **waiter** *n* escanciador *m.*

wing [wɪŋ] *n* ala; (*AUT*) aleta; ~s *npl* (*THEATRE*) bastidores *mpl*; ~**er** *n* (*SPORT*) extremo.

wink [wɪŋk] *n* guiño, pestañeo ♦ *vi* guiñar, pestañear.

winner ['wɪnə*] *n* ganador(a) *m/f.*

winning ['wɪnɪŋ] *adj* (*team*) ganador(a); (*goal*) decisivo; (*smile*) encantador(a); ~**s** *npl* ganancias *fpl.*

winter ['wɪntə*] *n* invierno ♦ *vi* invernar.

wintry ['wɪntrɪ] *adj* invernal.

wipe [waɪp] *n*: **to give sth a** ~ pasar un trapo sobre algo ♦ *vt* limpiar; (*tape*) borrar; ~ **off** *vt* limpiar con un trapo; (*remove*) quitar; ~ **out** *vt* (*debt*) liquidar; (*memory*) borrar; (*destroy*) destruir; ~ **up** *vt* limpiar.

wire ['waɪə*] *n* alambre *m*; (*ELEC*) cable *m* (eléctrico); (*TEL*) telegrama *m* ♦ *vt* (*house*) poner la instalación eléctrica en; (*also*: ~ **up**) conectar; (*person*: *telegram*) telegrafiar.

wireless ['waɪəlɪs] (*BRIT*) *n* radio *f.*

wiring ['waɪərɪŋ] *n* instalación *f* eléctrica.

wiry ['waɪərɪ] *adj* (*person*) enjuto y fuerte; (*hair*) crespo.

wisdom ['wɪzdəm] *n* sabiduría, saber *m*; (*good sense*) cordura; ~ **tooth** *n* muela del juicio.

wise [waɪz] *adj* sabio; (*sensible*) juicioso.

...wise [waɪz] *suffix*: **time**~ en cuanto a *or* respecto al tiempo.

wisecrack ['waɪzkræk] *n* broma.

wish [wɪʃ] *n* deseo ♦ *vt* querer; **best** ~**es** (*on birthday etc*) felicidades *fpl*; **with best** ~**es** (*in letter*) saludos *mpl*, recuerdos *mpl*; **to** ~ **sb goodbye** despedir-

se de uno; **he** ~**ed me well** me deseó mucha suerte; **to** ~ **to do/sb to do sth** querer hacer/que alguien haga algo; **to** ~ **for** desear; ~**ful** *adj*: it's ~**ful thinking** eso sería soñar.

wishy-washy ['wɪʃɪwɔʃɪ] (*inf*) *adj* (*colour*, *ideas*) desvaído.

wisp [wɪsp] *n* mechón *m*; (*of smoke*) voluta.

wistful ['wɪstful] *adj* pensativo.

wit [wɪt] *n* ingenio, gracia; *also*: ~**s**) inteligencia; (*person*) chistoso/a.

witch [wɪtʃ] *n* bruja; ~**craft** *n* brujería; ~**-hunt** *n* (*fig*) caza de brujas.

KEYWORD
---

with [wɪð, wɪθ] *prep* **1** (*accompanying, in the company of*) con (*con*+*mí, ti, sí* = *conmigo, contigo, consigo*); **I was** ~ **him** estaba con él; **we stayed** ~ **friends** nos hospedamos en casa de unos amigos; **I'm (not)** ~ **you** (*understand*) (no) te entiendo; **to be** ~ **it** (*inf: person*: *up-to-date*) estar al tanto; (: *alert*) ser despabilado

2 (*descriptive, indicating manner etc*) con; de; **a room** ~ **a view** una habitación con vistas; **the man** ~ **the grey hat/blue eyes** el hombre del sombrero gris/de los ojos azules; **red** ~ **anger** rojo de ira; **to shake** ~ **fear** temblar de miedo; **to fill sth** ~ **water** llenar algo de agua.

withdraw [wɪθ'drɔ:] (*irreg*) *vt* retirar, sacar ♦ *vi* retirarse; **to** ~ **money (from the bank)** retirar fondos (del banco); ~**al** *n* retirada; (*of money*) reintegro; ~**al symptoms** *npl* (*MED*) síndrome *m* de abstinencia; ~**n** *adj* (*person*) reservado, introvertido.

wither ['wɪðə*] *vi* marchitarse.

withhold [wɪθ'həuld] (*irreg*) *vt* (*money*) retener; (*decision*) aplazar; (*permission*) negar; (*information*) ocultar.

within [wɪð'ɪn] *prep* dentro de ♦ *adv* dentro; ~ **reach (of)** al alcance (de); ~ **sight (of)** a la vista (de); ~ **the week** antes de acabar la semana; ~ **a mile (of)** a menos de una milla (de).

without [wɪð'aut] *prep* sin; **to go ~ sth** pasar sin algo.

withstand [wɪθ'stænd] (*irreg*) *vt* resistir a.

witness ['wɪtnɪs] *n* testigo *m/f* ♦ *vt* (*event*) presenciar; (*document*) atestiguar la veracidad de; **to bear ~ to** (*fig*) ser testimonio de; **~ box** *n* tribuna de los testigos; **~ stand** (*US*) *n* = **~ box**.

witty ['wɪtɪ] *adj* ingenioso.

wives [waɪvz] *npl of* **wife**.

wizard ['wɪzəd] *n* hechicero.

wk *abbr* = **week**.

wobble ['wɔbl] *vi* temblar; (*chair*) cojear.

woe [wəu] *n* desgracia.

woke [wəuk] *pt of* **wake**.

woken ['wəukən] *pp of* **wake**.

wolf [wulf] *n* lobo; **wolves** [wulvz] *npl of* **wolf**.

woman ['wumən] (*pl* **women**) *n* mujer *f*; **~ doctor** *n* médica; **women's lib** (*inf: pej*) *n* liberación *f* de la mujer; **~ly** *adj* femenino.

womb [wu:m] *n* matriz *f*, útero.

women ['wɪmɪn] *npl of* **woman**.

won [wʌn] *pt, pp of* **win**.

wonder ['wʌndə*] *n* maravilla, prodigio; (*feeling*) asombro ♦ *vi*: **to ~ whether/why** preguntarse si/por qué; **to ~ at** asombrarse de; **to ~ about** pensar sobre *or* en; **it's no ~ (that)** no es de extrañarse (que + *subjun*); **~ful** *adj* maravilloso; **~fully** *adv* maravillosamente, estupendamente.

won't [wəunt] = **will not**.

woo [wu:] *vt* (*woman*) cortejar.

wood [wud] *n* (*timber*) madera; (*forest*) bosque *m*; **~ carving** *n* (*act*) tallado en madera; (*object*) talla en madera; **~ed** *adj* arbolado; **~en** *adj* de madera; (*fig*) inexpresivo; **~pecker** *n* pájaro carpintero; **~wind** *n* (*MUS*) instrumentos *mpl* de viento de madera; **~work** *n* carpintería; **~worm** *n* carcoma.

wool [wul] *n* lana; **to pull the ~ over sb's eyes** (*fig*) engatusar a uno; **~en**, (*US*) *adj* = **~len**; **~len** *adj* de lana; **~lens** *npl* géneros *mpl* de lana; **~ly** *adj*

lanudo, de lana; (*fig: ideas*) confuso; **~y** (*US*) *adj* = **~ly**.

word [wə:d] *n* palabra; (*news*) noticia; (*promise*) palabra (de honor) ♦ *vt* redactar; **in other ~s** en otras palabras; **to break/keep one's ~** faltar a la palabra/cumplir la promesa; **to have ~s with sb** reñir con uno; **~ing** *n* redacción *f*; **~ processing** *n* proceso de textos; **~ processor** *n* procesador *m* de textos..

wore [wɔ:*] *pt of* **wear**.

work [wə:k] *n* trabajo; (*job*) empleo, trabajo; (*ART, LITERATURE*) obra ♦ *vi* trabajar; (*mechanism*) funcionar, marchar; (*medicine*) ser eficaz, surtir efecto ♦ *vt* (*shape*) trabajar; (*stone etc*) tallar; (*mine etc*) explotar; (*machine*) manejar, hacer funcionar; **to be out of ~** estar parado, no tener trabajo; **~s** *n* (*BRIT: factory*) fábrica ♦ *npl* (*of clock, machine*) mecanismo; **to ~ loose** (*part*) desprenderse; (*knot*) aflojarse; **~ on** *vt fus* trabajar en, dedicarse a; (*principle*) basarse en; **~ out** *vi* (*plans etc*) salir bien, funcionar ♦ *vt* (*problem*) resolver; (*plan*) elaborar; **it ~s out at £100** suma 100 libras; **~ up** *vt*: **to get ~ed up** excitarse; **~able** *adj* (*solution*) práctico, factible; **~aholic** *n* trabajador(a) obsesivo/a *m/f*; **~er** *n* trabajador(a) *m/f*, obrero/a; **~force** *n* mano *f* de obra; **~ing class** *n* clase *f* obrera; **~ing-class** *adj* obrero; **~ing order** *n*: **in ~ing order** en funcionamiento; **~man** *n* obrero; **~manship** *n* habilidad *f*, trabajo; **~sheet** *n* hoja de trabajo; **~shop** *n* taller *m*; **~ station** *n* puesto *or* estación *f* de trabajo; **~-to-rule** (*BRIT*) *n* huelga de celo.

world [wə:ld] *n* mundo ♦ *cpd* (*champion*) del mundo; (*power, war*) mundial; **to think the ~ of sb** (*fig*) tener un concepto muy alto de uno; **~ly** *adj* mundano; **~-wide** *adj* mundial, universal.

worm [wə:m] *n* (*also: earth~*) lombriz *f*.

worn [wɔ:n] *pp of* **wear** ♦ *adj* usado; **~-out** *adj* (*object*) gastado; (*person*)

rendido, agotado.
worried ['wʌrɪd] *adj* preocupado.
worry ['wʌrɪ] *n* preocupación *f* ♦ *vt* preocupar, inquietar ♦ *vi* preocuparse; ~**ing** *adj* inquietante.
worse [wɜːs] *adj, adv* peor ♦ *n* lo peor; **a change for the** ~ un empeoramiento; ~**n** *vt, vi* empeorar; ~ **off** *adj* (*financially*): **to be** ~ **off** tener menos dinero; (*fig*): **you'll be** ~ **off** this way de esta forma estarás peor que nunca.
worship ['wɜːʃɪp] *n* adoración *f* ♦ *vt* adorar; **Your W~** (*BRIT*: *to mayor*) señor alcalde; (: *to judge*) señor juez.
worst [wɜːst] *adj, adv* peor ♦ *n* lo peor; **at** ~ en lo peor de los casos.
worth [wɜːθ] *n* valor *m* ♦ *adj*: **to be** ~ valer; **it's** ~ **it** vale *or* merece la pena; **to be** ~ **one's while** (**to do**) merecer la pena (hacer); ~**less** *adj* sin valor; (*useless*) inútil; ~**while** *adj* (*activity*) que merece la pena; (*cause*) loable.
worthy ['wɜːðɪ] *adj* respetable; (*motive*) honesto; ~ **of** digno de.

KEYWORD
---

would [wud] *aux vb* **1** (*conditional tense*): **if you asked him he** ~ **do it** si se lo pidieras, lo haría; **if you had asked him he** ~ **have done it** si se lo hubieras pedido, lo habría *or* hubiera hecho
2 (*in offers, invitations, requests*): ~ **you like a biscuit?** ¿quieres una galleta?; (*formal*) ¿querría una galleta?; ~ **you ask him to come in?** ¿quiere hacerle pasar?; ~ **you open the window please?** ¿quiere *or* podría abrir la ventana, por favor?
3 (*in indirect speech*): **I said I** ~ **do it** dije que lo haría
4 (*emphatic*): **it** WOULD **have to snow today!** ¡tenía que nevar precisamente hoy!
5 (*insistence*): **she** ~**n't behave** no quiso comportarse bien
6 (*conjecture*): **it** ~ **have been midnight** sería medianoche; **it** ~ **seem so** parece ser que sí
7 (*indicating habit*): **he** ~ **go there on** Mondays iba allí los lunes.

would-be (*pej*) *adj* presunto.
wouldn't ['wudnt] = **would not.**
wound¹ [wuːnd] *n* herida ♦ *vt* herir.
wound² [waund] *pt, pp* of **wind.**
wove [wəuv] *pt* of **weave.**
woven ['wəuvən] *pp* of **weave.**
wrangle ['ræŋgl] *n* riña.
wrap [ræp] *n* (*stole*) chal *m*; (*cape*) capa ♦ *vt* (*also*: ~ **up**) envolver; ~**per** *n* (*on chocolate*) papel *m*; (*BRIT*: *of book*) sobrecubierta; ~**ping paper** *n* papel *m* de envolver; (*fancy*) papel de regalo.
wrath [rɔθ] *n* cólera.
wreak [riːk] *vt*: **to** ~ **havoc** (**on**) hacer estragos (en); **to** ~ **vengeance** (**on**) vengarse (de).
wreath [riːθ, *pl* riːðz] *n* (*funeral* ~) corona.
wreck [rɛk] *n* (*ship*: *destruction*) naufragio; (: *remains*) restos *mpl* del barco; (*pej*: *person*) ruina ♦ *vt* (*car etc*) destrozar; (*chances*) arruinar; ~**age** *n* restos *mpl*; (*of building*) escombros *mpl.*
wren [rɛn] *n* (ZOOL) reyezuelo.
wrench [rɛntʃ] *n* (TECH) llave *f* inglesa; (*tug*) tirón *m*; (*fig*) dolor *m* ♦ *vt* arrancar; **to** ~ **sth from sb** arrebatar algo violentamente a uno.
wrestle ['rɛsl] *vi*: **to** ~ (**with sb**) luchar (con *or* contra uno); ~**r** *n* luchador(a) *m/f* (de lucha libre); **wrestling** *n* lucha libre.
wretched ['rɛtʃɪd] *adj* miserable.
wriggle ['rɪgl] *vi* (*also*: ~ **about**) menearse, retorcerse.
wring [rɪŋ] (*pt, pp* **wrung**) *vt* retorcer; (*wet clothes*) escurrir; (*fig*): **to** ~ **sth out of sb** sacar algo por la fuerza a uno.
wrinkle ['rɪŋkl] *n* arruga ♦ *vt* arrugar ♦ *vi* arrugarse.
wrist [rɪst] *n* muñeca; ~ **watch** *n* reloj *m* de pulsera.
writ [rɪt] *n* mandato judicial.
write [raɪt] (*pt* **wrote**, *pp* **written**) *vt* escribir; (*cheque*) extender ♦ *vi* escribir; ~ **down** *vt* escribir; (*note*) apuntar; ~

off *vt* (*debt*) borrar (como incobrable); (*fig*) desechar por inútil; ~ **out** *vt* escribir; ~ **up** *vt* redactar; ~**-off** *n* siniestro total; ~**r** *n* escritor(a) *m/f*.
writhe [raɪð] *vi* retorcerse.
writing ['raɪtɪŋ] *n* escritura; (*hand-*~) letra; (*of author*) obras *fpl*; **in** ~ por escrito; ~ **paper** *n* papel *m* de escribir.
written ['rɪtn] *pp* of **write**.
wrong [rɒŋ] *adj* (*wicked*) malo; (*unfair*) injusto; (*incorrect*) equivocado, incorrecto; (*not suitable*) inoportuno, inconveniente; (*reverse*) del revés ♦ *adv* equivocadamente ♦ *n* injusticia ♦ *vt* ser injusto con; **you are** ~ no tienes razón; **to do it ha-ces mal en hacerlo; you are** ~ **about that, you've got it** ~ en eso estás equivocado; **to be in the** ~ no tener razón, tener la culpa; **what's** ~? ¿qué pasa?; **to go** ~ (*person*) equivocarse; (*plan*) salir mal; (*machine*) estropearse; ~**ful** *adj* injusto; ~**ly** *adv* mal, incorrectamente; (*by mistake*) por error.
wrote [raut] *pt* of **write**.
wrought [rɔːt] *adj*: ~ **iron** hierro forjado.
wrung [rʌŋ] *pt, pp* of **wring**.
wry [raɪ] *adj* irónico.
wt. *abbr* = **weight**.

X

Xmas ['ɛksməs] *n abbr* = **Christmas**.
X-ray [ɛks'reɪ] *n* radiografía ♦ *vt* radiografiar, sacar radiografías de.
xylophone ['zaɪləfəun] *n* xilófono.

Y

yacht [jɒt] *n* yate *m*; ~**ing** *n* (*sport*) balandrismo; ~**sman/woman** *n* balandrista *m/f*.
Yank [jæŋk] (*pej*) *n* yanqui *m/f*.
Yankee ['jæŋkɪ] (*pej*) *n* = **Yank**.
yap [jæp] *vi* (*dog*) aullar.
yard [jɑːd] *n* patio; (*measure*) yarda; ~**stick** *n* (*fig*) criterio, norma.
yarn [jɑːn] *n* hilo; (*tale*) cuento, histo-

ria.
yawn [jɔːn] *n* bostezo ♦ *vi* bostezar; ~**ing** *adj* (*gap*) muy abierto.
yd(s). *abbr* = **yard(s)**.
yeah [jɛə] (*inf*) *adv* sí.
year [jɪə*] *n* año; **to be 8** ~**s old** tener 8 años; **an eight-**~**-old child** un niño de ocho años (de edad); ~**ly** *adj* anual ♦ *adv* anualmente, cada año.
yearn [jəːn] *vi*: **to** ~ **for sth** añorar algo, suspirar por algo; ~**ing** *n* ansia, añoranza.
yeast [jiːst] *n* levadura.
yell [jɛl] *n* grito, alarido ♦ *vi* gritar.
yellow ['jɛləu] *adj* amarillo.
yelp [jɛlp] *n* aullido ♦ *vi* aullar.
yeoman ['jəumən] *n*: **Y**~ **of the Guard** alabardero de la Casa Real.
yes [jɛs] *adv* sí ♦ *n* sí *m*; **to say/answer** ~ decir/contestar que sí.
yesterday ['jɛstədɪ] *adv* ayer ♦ *n* ayer *m*; ~ **morning/evening** ayer por la mañana/tarde; **all day** ~ todo el día de ayer.
yet [jɛt] *adv* ya; (*negative*) todavía ♦ *conj* sin embargo, a pesar de todo; **it is not finished** ~ todavía no está acabado; **the best** ~ el/la mejor hasta ahora; **as** ~ hasta ahora, todavía.
yew [juː] *n* tejo.
yield [jiːld] *n* (*AGR*) cosecha; (*COMM*) rendimiento ♦ *vt* ceder; (*results*) producir, dar; (*profit*) rendir ♦ *vi* rendirse, ceder; (*US: AUT*) ceder el paso.
YMCA *n abbr* (= *Young Men's Christian Association*) Asociación *f* de Jóvenes Cristianos.
yog(h)ourt ['jəugət] *n* yogur *m*.
yog(h)urt ['jəugət] *n* = **yog(h)ourt**.
yoke [jəuk] *n* yugo.
yolk [jəuk] *n* yema (de huevo).
yonder ['jɒndə*] *adv* allá (a lo lejos).

KEYWORD

you [juː] *pron* **1** (*subject: familiar*) tú, *pl* vosotros/as (*SP*), ustedes (*AM*); (*polite*) usted, *pl* ustedes; ~ **are very kind** eres/es muy amable; ~ **French enjoy your food** a vosotros (*or* ustedes) los franceses os (*or* les) gusta la comi-

da; ~ **and I will go** iremos tú y yo
2 (*object: direct: familiar*) te, *pl* os
(*SP*), les (*AM*); (*polite*) le, *pl* les, *f* la, *pl*
las; **I know ~** te/le *etc* conozco
3 (*object: indirect: familiar*) te, *pl* os
(*SP*), les (*AM*); (*polite*) le, *pl* les; **I gave
the letter to ~ yesterday** te/os *etc* di la
carta ayer
4 (*stressed*): **I told** you **to do it** te dije a
ti que lo hicieras, es a ti a quien dije
que lo hicieras; *see also* 3, 5
5 (*after prep: NB: con+ ti = contigo:
familiar*) ti, *pl* vosotros/as (*SP*), ustedes
(*AM*); (: *polite*) usted, *pl* ustedes; **it's
for ~** es para ti/vosotros *etc*.
6 (*comparisons: familiar*) tú, *pl* voso-
tros/as (*SP*), ustedes (*AM*); (: *polite*) usted, *pl* ustedes; **she's younger than ~** es
más joven que tú/vosotros *etc*
7 (*impersonal: one*): **fresh air does ~
good** el aire puro (te) hace bien; **~
never know** nunca se sabe; **~ can't do
that!** ¡eso no se hace!

you'd [juːd] = **you had; you would.**
you'll [juːl] = **you will; you shall.**
young [jʌŋ] *adj* joven ♦ *npl* (*of animal*)
cría; (*people*): **the ~** los jóvenes, la juventud; **~er** *adj* (*brother etc*) menor;
~ster *n* joven *m/f*.
your [jɔː*] *adj* tu; (*pl*) vuestro; (*formal*) su; *see also* **my.**
you're [juə*] = **you are.**
yours [jɔːz] *pron* tuyo; (*pl*) vuestro;
(*formal*) suyo; *see also* **faithfully;
mine; sincerely.**
yourself [jɔːˈself] *pron* tú mismo (*complement*) te; (*after prep*) tí (mismo);
(*formal*) usted mismo; (: *complement*)
se; (: *after prep*) sí (mismo); **yourselves** *pl pron* vosotros mismos; (*after
prep*) vosotros (mismos); (*formal*) ustedes (mismos); (: *complement*) se; (:
after prep) sí mismos; *see also* **oneself.**

youth [juːθ, *pl* juːðz] *n* juventud *f*;
(*young man*) joven *m*; **~ club** *n* club *m*
juvenil; **~ful** *adj* juvenil; **~ hostel** *n*
albergue *m* de juventud.
you've [juːv] = **you have.**
Yugoslav [ˈjuːgəuslɑːv] *adj*, *n*
yugo(e)slavo/a *m/f*.
Yugoslavia [juːgəuˈslɑːvɪə] *n* Yugoslavia.
yuppie [ˈjʌpɪ] (*inf*) *adj*, *n* yupi *m/f*,
yupy *m/f*.
YWCA *n abbr* (= *Young Women's
Christian Association*) Asociación *f* de
Jóvenes Cristianas.

Z

zany [ˈzeɪnɪ] *adj* estrafalario.
zap [zæp] *vt* (*COMPUT*) borrar.
zeal [ziːl] *n* celo, entusiasmo; **~ous**
[ˈzɛləs] *adj* celoso, entusiasta.
zebra [ˈziːbrə] *n* cebra; **~ crossing**
(*BRIT*) *n* paso de peatones.
zenith [ˈzenɪθ] *n* cénit *m*.
zero [ˈzɪərəu] *n* cero.
zest [zest] *n* ánimo, vivacidad *f*; (*of
orange*) piel *f*.
zigzag [ˈzɪgzæg] *n* zigzag *m* ♦ *vi* zigzaguear, hacer eses.
zinc [zɪŋk] *n* cinc *m*, zinc *m*.
zip [zɪp] *n* (*also:* ~ **fastener**, (*US*) **~per**)
cremallera (*SP*), cierre *m* (*AM*) ♦ *vt*
(*also:* ~ **up**) cerrar la cremallera de;
~ code (*US*) *n* código postal.
zodiac [ˈzəudɪæk] *n* zodíaco.
zone [zəun] *n* zona.
zoo [zuː] *n* (jardín *m*) zoo *m*.
zoologist [zuˈɔlədʒɪst] *n* zoólogo/a.
zoology [zuːˈɔlədʒɪ] *n* zoología.
zoom [zuːm] *vi*: **to ~ past** pasar zum-
bando; **~ lens** *n* zoom *m*.
zucchini [zuːˈkiːnɪ] (*US*) *n(pl)* calaba-
cín(ines) *m(pl)*.

USING YOUR COLLINS POCKET DICTIONARY

Introduction

We are delighted that you have decided to invest in this Collins Pocket Dictionary! Whether you intend to use it in school, at home, on holiday or at work, we are sure that you will find it very useful.

The purpose of this supplement is to help you become aware of the wealth of vocabulary and grammatical information your dictionary contains, to explain how this information is presented and also to point out some of the traps one can fall into when using a Spanish-English English-Spanish dictionary.

In the pages which follow you will find explanations and wordgames (not too difficult!) designed to give you practice in exploring the dictionary's contents and in retrieving information for a variety of purposes. Answers are provided at the end. If you spend a little time on these pages you should be able to use your dictionary more efficiently and effectively. Have fun!

Contents

HOW INFORMATION IS PRESENTED IN YOUR DICTIONARY

A great deal of information is packed into your Collins Pocket Dictionary using colour, various typefaces, sizes of type, symbols, abbreviations and brackets. The purpose of this section is to acquaint you with the conventions used in presenting information.

Headwords

A headword is the word you look up in a dictionary. Headwords are listed in alphabetical order throughout the dictionary. They are printed in colour so that they stand out clearly from all the other words on the dictionary page.

Note that at the top of each page two headwords appear. These tell you which is the first and last word dealt with on the page in question. They are there to help you scan through the dictionary more quickly.

The Spanish alphabet consists of 29 letters: the same 26 letters as the English alphabet, in the same order, plus 'ch', 'll' and 'ñ', which come after letters 'c', 'l' and 'n' respectively. You will need to remember that words containing these letters will be listed slightly differently from what you would expect according to English alphabetical order: thus 'echar' does not come immediately after 'eccema', but follows the last word beginning with 'ec-' in the list, namely 'ecuestre'.

Where two Spanish words are distinguished only by an accent, the accented form follows the unaccented, e.g. 'de', 'dé'.

A dictionary entry

An entry is made up of a headword and all the information about that headword. Entries will be short or long depending on how frequently a word is used in either English or Spanish and how many meanings it has. Inevitably, the fuller the dictionary entry the more care is needed in sifting through it to find the information you require.

Meanings

The translations of a headword are given in ordinary type. Where there is more than one meaning or usage, a semi-colon separates one from the other.

298

completo, a [kom'pleto, a] *adj* complete; (*perfecto*) perfect; (*lleno*) full ♦ *nm* full complement.

complicado, a [kompli'kaðo, a] *adj* complicated; **estar ~ en** to be mixed up in.

complicar [kompli'kar] *vt* to complicate.

cómplice ['kompliθe] *nm/f* accomplice.

luggage rack.

portal [por'tal] *nm* (*entrada*) vestibule,

put gently ♦ *vi* to sit, pose; **~se** *vr* to settle; (*pájaro*) to perch; (*avión*) to

nevar [ne'ßar] *vi* to snow.

cuenta *etc* ['kwenta] *vb ver* **contar** ♦ *nf* (*cálculo*) count, counting; (*en café, restaurante*) bill; (*COM*) account; (*de collar*) bead; (*fig*) account; **a fin de ~s** in the end; **caer en la ~** to catch on; **darse ~ de** to realize; **tener en ~** to bear in mind; **echar ~s** to take stock; **~ corriente/de ahorros** current/savings account; **~kilómetros** *nm inv* ≈ milometer; (*de velocidad*) speedometer.

titubear [tituße'ar] *vi* to stagger; to stammer; (*fig*) to hesitate; **titubeo** *nm* staggering; stammering; hesitation.

In addition, you will often find other words appearing in *italics* in brackets before the translations. These either give some notion of the contexts in which the headword might appear (as with 'agudo' opposite — 'una voz aguda', 'un dolor agudo', etc.) or else they provide synonyms (as with 'meter' opposite — 'colocar', 'introducir', etc.).

Phonetic spellings

The phonetic spelling of each headword — i.e. its pronunciation — is given in square brackets immediately after it. The phonetic transcription of Spanish and English vowels and consonants is given on pages vi to ix at the front of your dictionary.

Additional information about headwords

Information about the usage or form of certain headwords is given in brackets between the phonetics and the translation or translations. Have a look at the entries for 'COU', 'cuenca', 'diente' and 'burócrata' opposite.

This information is usually given in abbreviated form. A helpful list of abbreviations is given on pages iv and v at the front of your dictionary.

You should be particularly careful with colloquial words or phrases. Words labelled (*fam*) would not normally be used in formal speech, while those labelled (*fam!*) would be considered offensive.

Careful consideration of such style labels will help indicate the degree of formality and appropriateness of a word and could help you avoid many an embarrassing situation when using Spanish!

Expressions in which the headword appears

An entry will often feature certain common expressions in which the headword appears. These expressions are in **bold** type, but in black as opposed to colour. A swung dash (~) is used instead of repeating a headword in an entry. 'Tono' and 'mano' opposite illustrate this point.

Related words

In the Pocket Dictionary words related to certain headwords are sometimes given at the end of an entry, as with 'ambición' and 'accept' opposite. These are easily picked out as they are also in colour. To help you find these words, they are placed in alphabetical order after the headword to which they belong: cf. 'accept, general' opposite.

agudo, a [a'ɣuðo, a] *adj* sharp; *(voz)* high-pitched, piercing; *(dolor, enfermedad)* acute.

embrollar [embro'ʎar] *vt (el asunto)* to confuse, complicate; *(persona)* to involve, embroil; **~se** *vr (confundirse)* to get into a muddle o mess.

COU [kou] *(ESP) nm abr (= Curso de Orientación Universitaria) 1 year course leading to final school leaving certificate and university entrance examinations.*
cuenca ['kwenka] *nf (ANAT)* eye socket; *(GEO)* bowl, deep valley.

menudo, a [me'nuðo, a] *adj (pequeño)* small, tiny; *(sin importancia)* petty, insignificant; ¡**~ negocio!** *(fam)* some deal!; **a ~** often, frequently.

tono ['tono] *nm* tone; **fuera de ~** inappropriate; **darse ~** to put on airs.

ambición [ambi'θjon] *nf* ambition; **ambicionar** *vt* to aspire to; **ambicioso, a** *adj* ambitious.
accept [ək'sept] *vt* aceptar; *(responsibility, blame)* admitir; **~able** *adj* aceptable; **~ance** *n* aceptación *f*.

meter [me'ter] *vt (colocar)* to put, place; *(introducir)* to put in, insert; *(involucrar)* to involve; *(causar)* to make, cause; **~se** *vr*: **~se en** to go into, enter; *(fig)* to interfere in, meddle in; **~se a** to start; **~se a escritor** to become a writer; **~se con uno** to provoke sb, pick a quarrel with sb.

repoblación [repoβla'θjon] *nf* repopulation; *(de río)* restocking; **~ forestal** reafforestation.

diente ['djente] *nm (ANAT, TEC)* tooth; *(ZOOL)* fang; *(: de elefante)* tusk; *(de ajo)* clove; **hablar entre ~s** to mutter, mumble.
burócrata [bu'rokrata] *nm/f* civil servant; *(pey)* bureaucrat.

bocazas [bo'kaθas] *(fam) nm inv* bigmouth.
cabrón [ka'βron] *nm* cuckold; *(fam!)* bastard (!).

mano ['mano] *nf* hand; *(ZOOL)* foot, paw; *(de pintura)* coat; *(serie)* lot, series; **a ~** by hand; **a ~ derecha/izquierda** on the right(-hand side)/left(-hand side); **de primera ~** (at) first hand; **de segunda ~** (at) second hand; **robo a ~ armada** armed robbery; **~ de obra** labour, manpower; **estrechar la ~ a uno** to shake sb's hand.

general [xene'ral] *adj* general ♦ *nm* general; **por lo** *o* **en ~** in general; **G~itat** *nf* Catalan parliament; **~izar** *vt* to generalize; **~izarse** *vr* to become generalized, spread; **~mente** *adv* generally.

301

'Key' words

Your Collins Pocket Dictionary gives special status to certain Spanish and English words which can be looked on as 'key' words in each language. These are words which have many different usages. 'Poder', 'menos' and 'se' opposite are typical examples in Spanish. You are likely to become familiar with them in your day-to-day language studies.

There will be occasions, however, when you want to check on a particular usage. Your dictionary can be very helpful here. Note how with 'poder', for example, different parts of speech and different usages are clearly indicated by a combination of lozenges - ◆ - and numbers. In addition, further guides to usage are given in the language of the user who needs them. These are bracketed and in italics.

poder [po'ðer] *vi* **1** (*capacidad*) can, be able to; **no puedo hacerlo** I can't do it, I'm unable to do it

2 (*permiso*) can, may, be allowed to; **¿se puede?** may I (*o* we)?; **puedes irte ahora** you may go now; **no se puede fumar en este hospital** smoking is not allowed in this hospital

3 (*posibilidad*) may, might, could; **puede llegar mañana** he may *o* might arrive tomorrow; **pudiste haberte hecho daño** you might *o* could have hurt yourself; **¡podías habérmelo dicho antes!** you might have told me before!

4: puede ser: puede ser perhaps; **puede ser que lo sepa Tomás** Tomás may *o* might know

5: ¡no puedo más! I've had enough!; **no pude menos que dejarlo** I couldn't help but leave it; **es tonto a más no ~** he's as stupid as they come

6: ~ **con: no puedo con este crío** this kid's too much for me
♦ *nm* power; ~ **adquisitivo** purchasing power; **detentar** *o* **ocupar** *o* **estar en el** ~ to be in power.

se [se] *pron* **1** (*reflexivo: sg: m*) himself; (*: f*) herself; (*: pl*) themselves; (*: cosa*) itself; (*: de Vd*) yourself; (*: de Vds*) yourselves; ~ **está preparando** she's preparing herself; *para usos léxicos del pron ver el vb en cuestión, p.ej.* **arrepentirse**

2 (*con complemento indirecto*) to him; to her; to them; to it; to you; **a usted** ~ **lo dije ayer** I told you yesterday; ~ **compró un sombrero** he bought himself a hat; ~ **rompió la pierna** he broke his leg

3 (*uso recíproco*) each other, one another; ~ **miraron (el uno al otro)** they looked at each other *o* one another

4 (*en oraciones pasivas*): **se han vendido muchos libros** a lot of books have been sold

5 (*impers*): ~ **dice que** people say that, it is said that; **allí** ~ **come muy bien** the food there is very good, you can eat very well there.

menos [menos] *adj* **1:** ~ **(que, de)** (*compar: cantidad*) less (than); (*: número*) fewer (than); **con** ~ **entusiasmo** with less enthusiasm; ~ **gente** fewer people; *ver tb* **cada**

2 (*superl*): **es el que** ~ **culpa tiene** he is the least to blame
♦ *adv* **1** (*compar*): ~ **(que, de)** less (than); **me gusta** ~ **que el otro** I like it less than the other one

2 (*superl*): **es el** ~ **listo (de su clase)** he's the least bright in his class; **de todas ellas es la que** ~ **me agrada** out of all of them she's the one I like least; **(por) lo** ~ at (the very) least

3 (*locuciones*): **no quiero verle y** ~ **visitarle** I don't want to see him let alone visit him; **tenemos 7 de** ~ we're seven short
♦ *prep* except; (*cifras*) minus; **todos** ~ **él** everyone except (for) him; **5** ~ **2** 5 minus 2

WORDGAME 1

HEADWORDS

Study the following sentences. In each sentence a wrong word spelt very similarly to the correct word has deliberately been put in and the sentence doesn't make sense. This word is shaded each time. Write out each sentence again, putting in the <u>correct</u> word which you will find in your dictionary near the wrong word.

> Example: Aparcar aquí no es delirio.
>
> ['Delirio' (= delirium) is the wrong word and should be replaced by 'delito' (= offence)]

1. El mecánico se negó a arrebatarme el coche.

2. El baúl estaba cubierto de pólvora.

3. Es muy caro reventar las fotos en esa tienda.

4. Les gusta mucho dar pasillos a caballo.

5. Para ayunar a su madre pone la mesa todos los días.

6. La ballesta es el animal más grande del mundo.

7. Mientras esquiábamos nos cayó una nevera tremenda.

8. No me gustó el último capitolio del libro.

9. Tuvimos un pinchito y hubo que parar el coche.

10. Hay que cerrar la puerta con candidato.

WORDGAME 2

DICTIONARY ENTRIES

Complete the crossword below by looking up the English words in the list and finding the correct Spanish translations. There is a slight catch, however! All the English words can be translated several ways into Spanish, but only one translation will fit correctly into each part of the crossword. So look carefully through the entries in the English-Spanish section of your dictionary.

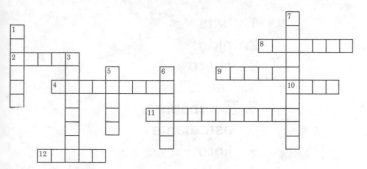

1. HORN

2. THROW

3. REMEMBER

4. PERFORMANCE

5. SPEECH

6. WHOLE

7. AMUSE

8. OLD

9. BELL

10. MATERIAL

11. ENDING

12. PART

WORDGAME 3

FINDING MEANINGS

In this list there are eight pairs of words that have some sort of connection with each other. For example, **'curso'** (= 'course') and **'estudiante'** (= 'student') are linked. Find the other pairs by looking up the words in your dictionary.

1. bata
2. nido
3. cuero
4. zapatillas
5. campanario
6. estudiante
7. libro
8. bolso
9. pasarela
10. aleta
11. curso
12. estante
13. urraca
14. barco
15. veleta
16. tiburón

WORDGAME 4

SYNONYMS

Complete the crossword by supplying SYNONYMS of the words below. You will sometimes find the synonym you are looking for in italics and bracketed at the entries for the words listed below. Sometimes you will have to turn to the English-Spanish section for help.

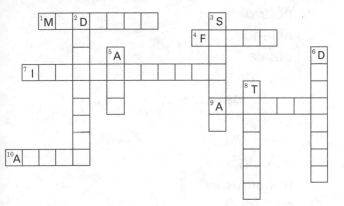

1. maneras
2. desilusión
3. exceder
4. incendio
5. cariño

6. vencer
7. inacabable
8. éxito
9. complacer
10. aeroplano

WORDGAME 5

SPELLING

You will often use your dictionary to check spellings. The person who has compiled this list of ten Spanish words has made <u>three</u> spelling mistakes. Find the three words which have been misspelt and write them out correctly.

1. pájaro
2. acienda
3. oleaje
4. gigante
5. avalorios
6. peregil
7. ahora
8. velocidad
9. quinientos
10. abridor

WORDGAME 6

ANTONYMS

Complete the crossword by supplying ANTONYMS (i.e. opposites) in Spanish of the words below. Use your dictionary to help.

1. feo
2. abrir
3. ligero
4. riqueza
5. salir
6. engordar
7. inquieto
8. poner
9. todo
10. oscuro

WORDGAME 7

PHONETIC SPELLINGS

The phonetic transcriptions of twenty Spanish words are given below. If you
study pages vi to ix at the front of your dictionary you should be able to work
out what the words are.

1. 'aɣwa

2. θju'ðað

3. alreðe'ðor

4. mu'tʃatʃo

5. 'bjento

6. 'niɲo

7. bol'βer

8. 'kaʎe

9. θiɣ'θaɣ

10. 'xenjo

11. 'gwarða

12. 'tʃoke

13. em'bjar

14. ka'βaʎo

15. aβo'ɣaðo

16. korre'xir

17. ko'mjenθo

18. 'eʎos

19. xer'sei

20. i'ɣwal

WORDGAME 8

EXPRESSIONS IN WHICH THE HEADWORD APPEARS

If you look up the headword 'mismo' in the Spanish-English section of your dictionary you will find that the word can have many meanings. Study the entry carefully and translate the following sentences into English.

1. Ahora mismo se lo llevo.

2. A mí me da lo mismo.

3. Lo mismo que tú estudias francés yo estudio español.

4. En ese mismo momento llegó la policía.

5. Acudió el mismo Presidente.

6. Todos los domingos se ponía el mismo traje.

7. Lo hice yo mismo.

8. Era un hipócrita, y por lo mismo despreciado por todos.

9. Tenemos que empezar hoy mismo.

10. Lo vi aquí mismo.

WORDGAME 9

RELATED WORDS

Fill in the blanks in the pairs of sentences below. The missing words are
related to the headwords on the left. Choose the correct 'relative' each time.
You will find it in your dictionary near the headword provided.

HEADWORD	RELATED WORDS
estudiante	1. Realiza sus _____ en la Universidad.
	2. Hay que _____ bien el texto.
pertenecer	3. Estos son los terrenos _____ al Ayuntamiento.
	4. Recogió todas sus _____ y se fue.
empleo	5. Es _____ de banco.
	6. Voy a _____ todos los medios a mi alcance.
atractivo	7. Esa perspectiva no me _____ nada.
	8. Aquella mujer ejercía una gran _____ sobre él.
terminante	9. Al _____ de la reunión todos se fueron a tomar café.
	10. No le dejaron _____ lo que estaba diciendo.
falsedad	11. Lo que estás diciendo es completamente _____.
	12. Se dedicaban a _____ billetes de banco.

312

WORDGAME 10

'KEY' WORDS

Study carefully the entry **'hacer'** in your dictionary and find translations for the following:

1. it's cold

2. I made them come

3. to study Economics

4. this will make it more difficult

5. to do the cooking

6. they became friends

7. I've been going for a month

8. to turn a deaf ear

9. if it's alright with you

10. to get hold of something

THE DICTIONARY AND GRAMMAR

While it is true that a dictionary can never be a substitute for a detailed grammar reference book, it nevertheless provides a great deal of grammatical information. If you know how to extract this information you will be able to use Spanish more accurately both in speech and in writing.

The Collins Pocket Dictionary presents grammatical information as follows.

Parts of speech

Parts of speech are given in italics immediately after the phonetic spellings of headwords. Abbreviated forms are used. Abbreviations can be checked on pages iv and v.

Changes in parts of speech within an entry — for example, from adjective to adverb to noun, or from noun to intransitive verb to transitive verb — are indicated by means of lozenges - ♦ - as with the Spanish 'derecho' and the English 'act' opposite.

Genders of Spanish nouns

The gender of each noun in the Spanish-English section of the dictionary is indicated in the following way:

    nm = nombre masculino

    nf = nombre femenino

You will occasionally see *nm/f* beside an entry. This indicates that a noun — 'habitante', for example — can be either masculine or feminine.

Feminine forms of nouns are shown, as with 'ministro' opposite.

It is most important that you know the correct gender of a Spanish noun, since it is going to determine the form of both adjectives and past participles. If you are in any doubt as to the gender of a noun, it is always best to check it in your dictionary.

estría [es'tria] *nf* groove.

tenue ['tenwe] *adj* (*delgado*) thin, slender; (*neblina*) light; (*lazo, vínculo*) slight.

porque ['porke] *conj* (*a causa de*) because; (*ya que*) since; (*con el fin de*) so that, in order that.

---

criterio [kri'terjo] *nm* criterion; (*juicio*) judgement.

manguera [man'gera] *nf* (*de riego*) hose; (*tubo*) pipe.

habitante [aßi'tante] *nmf* inhabitant.

ministro, a [mi'nistro, a] *nm/f* minister.

derecho, a [de'retʃo, a] *adj* right, right-hand ♦ *nm* (*privilegio*) right; (*lado*) right(-hand) side; (*leyes*) law ♦ *adv* straight, directly; ~s *nmpl* (*de aduana*) duty *sg*; (*de autor*) royalties; **tener ~ a** to have a right to.

act [ækt] *n* acto, acción *f*; (*of play*) acto; (*in music hall etc*) número; (*LAW*) decreto, ley *f* ♦ *vi* (*behave*) comportarse; (*have effect: drug, chemical*) hacer efecto; (*THEATRE*) actuar; (*pretend*) fingir; (*take action*) obrar ♦ *vt* (*part*) hacer el papel de; **in the ~ of:** to **catch sb in the ~ of ...** pillar a uno en el momento en que ...; **to ~ as** actuar *or* hacer de; **~ing** *adj* suplente ♦ *n* (*activity*) actuación *f*; (*profession*) profesión *f* de actor.

Adjectives

Adjectives are given in both their masculine and feminine forms, where these are different. The usual rule is to drop the 'o' of the masculine form and add an 'a' to make an adjective feminine, as with 'negro' opposite.

Some adjectives have identical masculine and feminine forms. Where this occurs, there is no 'a' beside the basic masculine form.

Adverbs

The normal 'rule' for forming adverbs in Spanish is to add '-mente' to the feminine form of the adjective. Thus:

$$\text{seguro} > \text{segura} > \text{seguramente}$$

The '-mente' ending is often the equivalent of the English '-ly':

> seguramente — surely
> lentamente — slowly

In your dictionary Spanish adverbs are not generally given, since the English translation can usually be derived from the relevant translation of the adjective headword. Usually the translation can be formed by adding '-ly' to the relevant adjective translation: e.g.

> fiel — faithful
> fielmente — faithfully

In cases where the basic translations for the adverb cannot be derived from those for the adjective, the adverb is likely to be listed as a headword in alphabetical order. This means it may not be immediately adjacent to the adjective headword: see 'actual' and 'actualmente' opposite.

Information about verbs

A major problem facing language learners is that the form of a verb will change according to the subject and/or the tense being used. A typical Spanish verb can take many different forms — too many to list in a dictionary entry.

negro, a ['neɣro, a] *adj* black; *(suerte)* awful ♦ *nm* black ♦ *nm/f* Negro/ Negress, Black; **negrura** *nf* blackness.

valiente [ba'ljente] *adj* brave, valiant ♦ *nm* hero.

seguramente [seɣura'mente] *adv* surely; *(con certeza)* for sure, with certainty.

actual [ak'twal] *adj* present(-day), current; **~idad** *nf* present; **~idades** *nfpl* *(noticias)* news *sg*; **en la ~idad** at present; *(hoy día)* nowadays.
actualizar [aktwali'θar] *vt* to update, modernize.
actualmente [aktwal'mente] *adv* at present; *(hoy día)* nowadays.

Yet, although verbs are listed in your dictionary in their infinitive forms only, this does not mean that the dictionary is of limited value when it comes to handling the verb system of the Spanish language. On the contrary, it contains much valuable information.

First of all, your dictionary will help you with the meanings of unfamiliar verbs. If you came across the word 'decidió' in a text and looked it up in your dictionary you wouldn't find it. What you must do is assume that it is part of a verb and look for the infinitive form. Thus you will deduce that 'decidió' is a form of the verb 'decidir'. You now have the basic meaning of the word you are concerned with — something to do with the English verb 'decide' — and this should be enough to help you understand the text you are reading.

It is usually an easy task to make the connection between the form of a verb and the infinitive. For example, 'decidieran', 'decidirá', 'decidimos' and 'decidido' are all recognisable as parts of the infinitive 'decidir'. However, sometimes it is less obvious — for example, 'pueda', 'podrán' and 'pude' are all parts of 'poder'. The only real solution to this problem is to learn the various forms of the main Spanish regular and irregular verbs.

And this is the second source of help offered by your dictionary as far as verbs are concerned. The verb tables on page x of the Collins Pocket Dictionary provide a summary of some of the main forms of the main tenses of regular and irregular verbs. Consider the verb 'poder' below where the following information is given:

1	pudiendo	— Present Participle
2	puede	— Imperative
3	puedo, puedes, puede, pueden	— Present Tense forms
4	pude, pudiste, pudo, pudimos, pudisteis, pudieron	— Preterite forms
5	podré *etc*	— 1st Person Singular of the Future Tense
6	pueda, puedas, pueda, puedan	— Present Subjunctive forms
7	pudiera *etc*	— 1st Person Singular of the Imperfect Subjunctive

The regular '-ar', '-er', and '-ir' verbs — 'hablar', 'comer' and 'vivir' — are presented in greater detail. The main tenses and the different endings are given in full. This information can be transferred and applied to all verbs in the list. In addition, the main parts of the most common irregular verbs are listed in the body of the dictionary.

HABLAR

1 hablando
2 habla, hablad
3 hablo, hablas, habla, hablamos, habláis, hablan
4 hablé, hablaste, habló, hablamos, hablasteis, hablaron
5 hablaré, hablarás, hablará, hablaremos, hablaréis, hablarán
6 hable, hables, hable, hablemos, habléis, hablen
7 hablara, hablaras, hablara, habláramos, hablarais, hablaran
8 hablado
9 hablaba, hablabas, hablaba, hablábamos, hablabais, hablaban

In order to make maximum use of the information contained in these pages, a good working knowledge of the various rules affecting Spanish verbs is required. You will acquire this in the course of your Spanish studies and your Collins dictionary will serve as a useful reminder. If you happen to forget how to form the second person singular form of the Future Tense of 'poder' (i.e. how to translate 'you will be able to'), there will be no need to panic — your dictionary contains the information!

WORDGAME 11

PARTS OF SPEECH

In each sentence below a word has been shaded. Put a tick in the appropriate box to indicate the underlined part of speech each time.

SENTENCE	Noun	Adj	Adv	Verb
1. Es estudiante de derecho.				
2. No hables tan alto.				
3. No tiene mucho dinero en su haber.				
4. Es un escrito muy largo.				
5. Vaya todo seguido.				
6. Es un dicho muy frecuente.				
7. Llegamos a casa muy tarde.				
8. Le gusta mucho andar por el campo.				
9. Lo hacemos por tu bien.				
10. A mi parecer es una buena película.				

WORDGAME 12

MEANING CHANGING WITH GENDER

Some Spanish nouns change meaning according to their gender, i.e. according to whether they are masculine or feminine. Look at the pairs of sentences below and fill in the blanks with either 'un', 'una', 'el' or 'la'. Use your dictionary to help.

1. No podía comprender _____ cólera de su padre.
   _____ cólera hace estragos en las regiones tropicales.

2. Perdí _____ pendiente en su casa.
   El coche no podía subir por _____ pendiente.

3. Los niños jugaban con _____ cometa.
   Dicen que en abril caerá _____ cometa.

4. Vimos _____ policía dentro de su coche.
   _____ policía ha descubierto una red de traficantes de droga.

5. Hay que cambiar _____ orden de los números.
   En cuanto recibió _____ orden su puso en camino.

6. ¿Ha llegado _____ parte de la policía?
   _____ parte de atrás de la casa es muy sombría.

7. Pasó dos días en _____ coma profundo.
   Tienes que poner _____ coma ahí.

8. Los soldados están todavía en _____ frente.
   El pelo le cubría _____ frente.

WORDGAME 13

ADVERBS

Translate the following Spanish adverbs into English (generally by adding **-ly** to the adjective).

1. recientemente

2. lamentablemente

3. constantemente

4. mensualmente

5. pesadamente

6. inconscientemente

7. inmediatamente

8. ampliamente

9. tenazmente

10. brillantemente

WORDGAME 14

VERB TENSES

Use your dictionary to help you fill in the blanks in the table below. (Remember the important pages at the front of your dictionary.)

INFINITIVE	PRESENT SUBJUNCTIVE	PRETERITE	FUTURE
tener		yo	
hacer			yo
poder			yo
decir		yo	
agradecer	yo		
saber			yo
reír	yo		
querer		yo	
caber	yo		
ir	yo		
salir			yo
ser		yo	

WORDGAME 15

IRREGULAR VERBS

Use your dictionary to find the <u>first person</u> present indicative of these verbs.

INFINITIVE	PRESENT INDICATIVE
conocer	
saber	
estar	
ofrecer	
poder	
ser	
poner	
divertir	
traer	
decir	
preferir	
negar	
dar	
instruir	

WORDGAME 16

IDENTIFYING INFINITIVES

In the sentences below you will see various Spanish verbs shaded. Use your dictionary to help you find the **infinitive** form of each verb.

1. Cuando era pequeño dormía en la misma habitación que mi hermano.

2. Mis amigos vienen conmigo.

3. No cupieron todos los libros en el estante.

4. ¿Es que no veías lo que pasaba?

5. El sábado saldremos todos juntos.

6. Ya hemos visto la casa.

7. ¿Quieres que lo ponga aquí?

8. Le dije que viniera a las ocho.

9. Nos han escrito tres cartas ya.

10. No sabían qué hacer.

11. Tuvimos que salir temprano.

12. En cuanto supe lo de su padre la llamé por teléfono.

13. ¿Por qué no trajiste el dinero?

14. Prefiero quedarme en casa.

15. Quiero que conozcas a mi padre.

MORE ABOUT MEANING

In this section we will consider some of the problems associated with using a bilingual dictionary.

Overdependence on your dictionary

That the dictionary is an invaluable tool for the language learner is beyond dispute. Nevertheless, it is possible to become overdependent on your dictionary, turning to it in an almost automatic fashion every time you come up against a new word or phrase in a Spanish text. Tackling an unfamiliar text in this way will turn reading in Spanish into an extremely tedious activity. It is possible to argue that if you stop to look up every new word you may actually be *hindering* your ability to read in Spanish — you are so concerned with the individual words that you pay no attention to the text as a whole and to the context which gives them meaning. It is therefore important to develop appropriate reading skills — using clues such as titles, headlines, illustrations, etc, understanding relations within a sentence, etc to predict or infer what a text is about.

A detailed study of the development of reading skills is not within the scope of this supplement; we are concerned with knowing how to use a dictionary, which is only one of several important skills involved in reading. Nevertheless, it may be instructive to look at one example. You see the following text in a Spanish newspaper and are interested in working out what it is about.

Contextual clues here include the heading in large type, which indicates that this is some sort of announcement, and the names. The verb 'recibir' is very much like the English 'receive' and you will also know 'form' words such as 'una', 'y' and so forth from your general studies in Spanish, as well as essential vocabulary such as 'niña', 'hijos', 'nombre'. Given that this

Natalicios

La señora de García Rodríguez (don Alfonso), de soltera Laura Montes de la Torre, ha dado a luz una niña, cuarta de sus hijos, que recibirá el nombre de Beatriz y tendrá como padrinos a doña Mercedes Sánchez Serrano y don Felipe Gómez Morales.

extract appeared in a newspaper, you will probably have worked out by now that this is an announcement placed in the 'Personal Column.'

So you have used contextual and word-formation clues to get you to the point where you have understood that this notice has been placed in the personal column because something has happened to señora de García Rodríguez and that somebody is going to be given the name of 'Beatriz'. And you have reached this point *without* opening your dictionary once. Common sense and your knowledge of newspaper contents in this country will suggest that this must be an announcement of someone's birth or death. Thus 'dar a luz' ('to give birth') and 'padrinos' ('godparents') become the only words that you need to look up in order to confirm that this is indeed a birth announcement.

When learning Spanish we are helped considerably by the fact that many Spanish and English words look and sound alike and have exactly the same meaning. Such words are called 'COGNATES'. Many words which look similar in Spanish and English come from a common Latin root. Other words are the same or nearly the same in both languages because the Spanish language has borrowed a word from English or vice versa. The dictionary will often not be necessary where cognates are concerned — provided you know the English word that the Spanish word resembles!

Words with more than one meaning

The need to examine with care *all* the information contained in a dictionary entry must be stressed. This is particularly important with the many Spanish words which have more than one meaning. For example, the Spanish 'destino' can mean 'destiny' as well as 'destination'. How you translated the word would depend on the context in which you found it.

Similarly, if you were trying to translate a phrase such as 'sigo sin saber', you would have to look through the whole entry for 'seguir' to get the right translation. If you restricted your search to the first line of the entry and saw that the first meaning given is 'to follow', you might be tempted to assume that the phrase meant 'I follow without knowing'. But if you examined the entry closely you would see that 'seguir sin . . .' means 'to still do . . . or 'to still be . . .'. So 'sigo sin saber' means 'I still don't know'.

The same need for care applies when you are using the English-Spanish section of your dictionary to translate a word from English into Spanish. Watch out in particular for the lozenges indicating changes in parts of speech.

The noun 'sink' is 'fregadero', while the verb is 'hundir'. If you don't watch what you are doing, you could end up with ridiculous non-Spanish e.g. 'Dejó los platos en el hundir'!

Phrasal verbs

Another potential source of difficulty is English phrasal verbs. These consist of a common verb ('make', 'get', etc.) plus an adverb and/or a preposition to give English expressions such as 'to make out', 'to get on', etc. Entries for such verbs tend to be fairly full, so close examination of the contents is required. Note how these verbs appear in colour within the entry.

Falsos amigos

sink [sɪŋk] (*pt* **sank**, *pp* **sunk**) *n* fregadero ♦ *vt* (*ship*) hundir, echar a pique; (*foundations*) excavar ♦ *vi* (*gen*) hundirse; **to ~ sth into** hundir algo en; **~ in** *vi* (*fig*) penetrar, calar.

make [meɪk] (*pt, pp* **made**) *vt* hacer; (*manufacture*) fabricar; (*mistake*) cometer; (*speech*) pronunciar; (*cause to be*): **to ~ sb sad** poner triste a alguien; (*force*): **to ~ sb do sth** obligar a alguien a hacer algo; (*earn*) ganar; (*equal*): **2 and 2 ~ 4** 2 y 2 son 4 ♦ *n* marca; **to ~ the bed** hacer la cama; **to ~ a fool of** sb poner a alguien en ridículo; **to ~ a profit/loss** obtener ganancias/sufrir pérdidas; **to ~ it** (*arrive*) llegar; (*achieve sth*) tener éxito; **what time do you ~ it?** ¿qué hora tienes?; **to ~ do with** contentarse con; **~ for** *vt fus* (*place*) dirigirse a; **~ out** *vt* (*decipher*) descifrar; (*understand*) entender; (*see*) distinguir; (*cheque*) extender; **~ up** *vt* (*invent*) inventar; (*prepare*) hacer; (*constitute*) constituir ♦ *vi* reconciliarse; (*with cosmetics*) maquillarse; **~ up for** *vt fus* compensar;

We noted above that many Spanish and English words have similar forms *and* meanings. There are, however, many Spanish words which *look* like English words but have a completely *different* meaning. For example, 'la carpeta' means 'the folder': 'sensible' means 'sensitive'. This can easily lead to serious mistranslations.

Sometimes the meaning of the Spanish word is quite close to the English. For example, 'la moneda' means 'coin' rather than 'money'; 'simpático' means 'nice' rather than 'sympathetic'. But some Spanish words which look similar to English words have two meanings, one the same as the English, the other completely different! 'El plato' can mean 'course' (in a meal) as well as 'plate'; 'la cámara' can mean 'camera', but also 'chamber'.

Such words are often referred to as FALSOS AMIGOS ('false friends'). You will have to look at the context in which they appear to arrive at the correct meaning. If they seem to fit in with the sense of the passage as a whole, you will probably not need to look them up. If they don't make sense, however, you may well be dealing with 'falsos amigos'.

WORDGAME 17

WORDS IN CONTEXT

Study the sentences below. Translations of the shaded words are given at the bottom. Match the number of the sentence and the letter of the translation correctly each time.

1. Tendremos que atarlo con una cuerda.
2. La cuerda del reloj se ha roto.
3. Iremos al cine para entretener a los niños.
4. No me entretengas, que llegaré tarde.
5. Le dieron una patada en la espinilla.
6. Tenía una espinilla enorme en la nariz.
7. Siempre le da mucho sueño después de comer.
8. Anoche me desperté sobresaltada por un mal sueño.
9. El niño tocaba todo lo que veía.
10. Su padre tocaba muy bien la guitarra.
11. Tuvo un acceso de tos.
12. Todas las vías de acceso estaban cerradas.
13. Me gustaría estudiar la carrera de Derecho.
14. Todos querían participar en la carrera.
15. He quebrado el plato sin darme cuenta.
16. No sabían que esa empresa había quebrado.

a. touched	i. rope
b. shin(bone)	j. hold up
c. entertain	k. entry
d. spring	l. race
e. fit	m. gone bankrupt
f. course	n. played
g. sleepiness	o. dream
h. blackhead	p. broken

WORDGAME 18

WORDS WITH MORE THAN ONE MEANING

Look at the advertisements below. The words which are shaded can have more than one meaning. Use your dictionary to help you work out the correct translation in the context.

1

El Pescador
RESTAURANTE

Mariscos de viveros propios

Teléfono 406 12 80 – MADRID 6

P | FÁCIL
APARCAMIENTO

2

Restaurante
LOS CEREZOS

ALTA COCINA REGIONAL

Para amantes de lo tradicional

RESERVAS: 574 34 11/12

3

INTERLANGUE
ANUNCIA CURSO MASTER DE
INGLÉS JURÍDICO PARA
PROFESIONALES DEL DERECHO
Inicio: 20 de octubre

4

¡¡¡BUTACAS PIEL A MEDIDA!!!

APROVECHE GRANDES REBAJAS EN OCTUBRE

¡En fábrica, más calidad y menor precio!

Horario continuado de 9,30 a 20,30 –
incluso sábados

5

GRANDES ALMACENES "EL CONDOR"
IMPORTANTES REBAJAS DE FIN DE TEMPORADA

6

Guía **TELEVISION**

JUEVES, 19
19.00. – Partido adelantado de la
JORNADA DE LIGA de PRIMERA DIVISION:
Atlético de Madrid – Barcelona (TV-2)

7

Bar-restaurante "La Ballena"

platos combinados desde 300 ptas.
helados, postres nuestra especialidad

8

ULTIMAS VIVIENDAS
de 2 y 3 dormitorios con
plaza de garaje opcional
Lunes a Viernes mañanas de 11 a 13,30.
Tardes de 16,30 a 19,30.

9

Calle de
ISABEL LA CATOLICA
N.ºs 50 – 56

PISOS EXTERIORES
DE 80 m^2

FINANCIACION A 11 AÑOS
13 Y 13,5% CON LA CAJA DE BARCELONA

WORDGAME 19

FALSE FRIENDS

Look at the advertisements below. The words which are shaded resemble
English words but have different meanings here. Find a correct translation
for each word in the context.

1

LA MAYOR COLECCION DE
ALFOMBRAS
PERSAS Y
ORIENTALES
*¡¡¡VENTA DE LIQUIDACION
POR CAMBIO DE DOMICILIO!!!*

2

Teatro Nacional:
"El Alcalde de Zalamea"
Localidades en venta a partir de mañana

3

PRODUCTOS BENGOLEA
¡NO RECURRA A
LA COMPETENCIA!
Visite nuestro local en Castellana 500

4

OFERTA ESPECIAL
cubiertos de acero inoxidable de
primerísima calidad en planta baja

5

**INTERSEGUR
SEGUROS**

ASEGURE HOY SU
JUBILACIÓN DE MAÑANA

6

HOSTAL DEL REY
Habitaciones con baño
Muy céntrico
Tel. 315 48 67

7

PENSION "LA GAVIOTA"
camas, comidas, a dos minutos de la
playa, habitaciones muy cómodas a
un precio incomparable.

8

**VENDO
LOCAL**

Ortega y Gasset
piso interior
10.750.000 pesetas

Teléfono 593 87 60

9

**SEGUROS
"NON PLUS ULTRA"**
Desea comunicarle su nueva
dirección a partir del 1°
de enero:

**DIAGONAL 348
BARCELONA 07008**

Tel. 260 7000/1/2

333

HAVE FUN WITH YOUR DICTIONARY

Here are some word games for you to try. You will find your dictionary helpful as you attempt the activities.

WORDGAME 20

In the boxes below the letters of eight Spanish words have been replaced by numbers. A number represents the same letter each time (though an accent may be required sometimes).

Try to crack the code and find the eight words. If you need help, use your dictionary.

Here is a clue: all the words you are looking for have something to do with TRANSPORT.

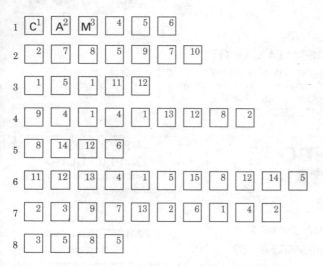

1. | C¹ | A² | M³ | 4 | 5 | 6 |

2. | 2 | 7 | 8 | 5 | 9 | 7 | 10 |

3. | 1 | 5 | 1 | 11 | 12 |

4. | 9 | 4 | 1 | 4 | 1 | 13 | 12 | 8 | 2 |

5. | 8 | 14 | 12 | 6 |

6. | 11 | 12 | 13 | 4 | 1 | 5 | 15 | 8 | 12 | 14 | 5 |

7. | 2 | 3 | 9 | 7 | 13 | 2 | 6 | 1 | 4 | 2 |

8. | 3 | 5 | 8 | 5 |

WORDGAME 21

If you 'behead' certain Spanish words, i.e. take away their first letter, you are left with another Spanish word. For example, if you behead **'aplomo'** (= 'self-assurance'), you get **'plomo'** (= 'lead'), and **'bala'** (= 'bullet') gives **'ala'** (= 'wing').

The following words have their heads chopped off, i.e. the first letter has been removed. Use your dictionary to help you form a new Spanish word by adding one letter to the start of each word below. Write down the new Spanish word and its meaning.

1. bajo (= low)
2. oler (= to smell)
3. año (= year)
4. oro (= gold)
5. reparar (= to repair)
6. ama (= owner)
7. rendido (= worn-out)
8. cuerdo (= sane)
9. ave (= bird)
10. batir (= to beat)
11. resto (= rest)
12. precio (= price)
13. cera (= wax)
14. hora (= hour)
15. pinar (= pine forest)

WORDGAME 22

PALABRAS CRUZADAS

Complete this crossword by looking up the words listed below in the English-Spanish section of your dictionary. Remember to read through the entry carefully to find the word that will fit.

DOWN

1. to identify
2. to go out
3. regrettable
4. to love
5. streamlined
6. heating
9. expensive
14. to oblige
15. tricks
16. now

ACROSS

3. to bark
4. wing
7. lie
8. above
10. to work out
11. to lighten
12. to need
13. usual
17. cornet
18. to stink
19. radius

WORDGAME 23

There are twelve Spanish words hidden in the grid below. Each word is made up of five letters but has been split into two parts.

Find the Spanish words. Each group of letters can only be used once.

Use your dictionary to help you.

bla	lir	bu	ma	que	go
gor	co	ver	vi	asi	jor
cal	me	ha	jo	lar	so
jo	jía	lo	vol	sa	eno

WORDGAME 24

Here is a list of Spanish words for things you will find in the kitchen. Unfortunately, they have all been jumbled up. Try to work out what each word is and put the word in the boxes on the right. You will see that there are seven shaded boxes below. With the seven letters in the shaded boxes make up <u>another</u> Spanish word for an object you can find in the kitchen.

1 azta   ¿Quieres una ____ de café?

2 eanevr   ¡Mete la mantequilla en la ____ !

3 asme   ¡La comida está en la ____!

4 zoac   Su madre está calentando la leche en el ____

5 roegcanldo ¡No saques el helado del ____ todavía!

6 uclclohi   ¿Dónde has puesto el ____ del queso?

7 rgoif   ¿Puedes cerrar ya el ____ del agua caliente?

The word you are looking for is:

338

WORDGAME 25

PALABRAS CRUZADAS

Take the four letters given each time and put them in the four empty boxes in the centre of each grid. Arrange them in such a way that you form four six-letter words. Use your dictionary to check the words.

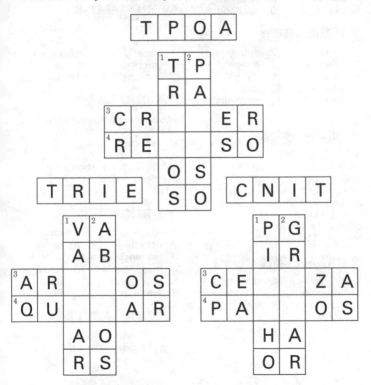

ANSWERS

WORDGAME 1

1	arreglarme	6	ballena
2	polvo	7	nevada
3	revelar	8	capítulo
4	paseos	9	pinchazo
5	ayudar	10	candado

WORDGAME 2

1	cuerno	7	entretener
2	echar	8	antiguo
3	recordar	9	timbre
4	actuación	10	tela
5	habla	11	terminación
6	entero	12	parte

WORDGAME 3

bata + zapatillas
nido + urraca
cuero + bolso
campanario + veleta
estudiante + curso
libro + estante
pasarela + barco
aleta + tiburón

WORDGAME 4

1	modales	6	derrotar
2	decepción	7	interminable
3	superar	8	triunfo
4	fuego	9	agradar
5	amor	10	avión

WORDGAME 5

2	hacienda
5	abalorios
6	perejil

WORDGAME 6

1	bonito	6	adelgazar
2	cerrar	7	tranquilo
3	pesado	8	quitar
4	pobreza	9	nada
5	entrar	10	claro

WORDGAME 7

agua, ciudad, alrededor,
muchacho, viento, niño,
volver, calle, zigzag,
genio, guarda, choque,
enviar, caballo, abogado,
corregir, comienzo, ellos,
jersé, igual

WORDGAME 9

1	estudios	7	atrae
2	estudiar	8	atracción
3	pertenecientes	9	término
4	pertenencias	10	terminar
5	empleado	11	falso
6	emplear	12	falsificar

WORDGAME 11

1 n	2 adv	3 n	4 n	5 adv
6 n	7 adv	8 v	9 n	10 n

WORDGAME 12

1 la; El	5 el; la
2 el; la	6 el; La
3 una; un	7 un; una
4 un; La	8 el; la

WORDGAME 14

tuve	ría
haré	quise
podré	quepa
dije	vaya
agradezca	saldré
sabré	fui

WORDGAME 15

conozco	divierto
sé	traigo
estoy	digo
ofrezco	prefiero
puedo	niego
soy	doy
pongo	instruyo

WORDGAME 16

1 dormir	9 escribir
2 venir	10 saber
3 caber	11 tener
4 ver	12 saber
5 salir	13 traer
6 ver	14 preferir
7 poner	15 conocer
8 venir	

WORDGAME 17

1 i	5 b	9 a	13 f
2 d	6 h	10 n	14 l
3 c	7 g	11 e	15 p
4 j	8 o	12 k	16 m

WORDGAME 18

1 fish farm
2 cuisine
3 law
4 leather
5 significant
6 league
7 set main course
8 space
9 savings bank

WORDGAME 19

1 clearance sale;
  home (Here: address)
2 tickets
3 competition
4 cutlery
5 retirement
6 small hotel; rooms
7 guest house
8 premises
9 address

WORDGAME 20

1 camión		5 tren	
2 autobús		6 helicóptero	
3 coche		7 ambulancia	
4 bicicleta		8 moto	

WORDGAME 21

1	abajo	9	nave
2	doler	10	abatir
3	baño	11	presto
4	coro	12	aprecio
5	preparar	13	acera
6	cama	14	ahora
7	prendido	15	opinar
8	acuerdo		

WORDGAME 22

ACROSS:
3 ladrar
4 ala
7 mentira
8 encima
10 elaborar
11 aligerar
12 necesitar
13 corriente
17 cucurucho
18 apestar
19 radio

DOWN:
1 identificar
2 salir
3 lamentable
4 amar
5 aerodinámico
6 calefacción
9 caro
14 obligar
15 trucos
16 ahora

WORDGAME 23

enojo	cojo
queso	calma
salir	asilo
volver	largo
vigor	mejor
bujía	habla

WORDGAME 24

1	taza	5	congelador
2	nevera	6	cuchillo
3	mesa	7	grifo
4	cazo		

Missing word — ARMARIO

WORDGAME 25

1)	1 trapos		2	patoso
	3 cráter		4	reposo
2)	1 variar		2	abetos
	3 arreos		4	quitar
3)	1 pincho		2	gritar
	3 ceniza		4	pactos